WORLD POLITICS
SINCE 1945

WORLD POLITICS SINCE 1945

Ninth Edition

PETER CALVOCORESSI

PEARSON
Longman

Harlow, England • London • New York • Boston • San Francisco • Toronto
Sydney • Tokyo • Singapore • Hong Kong • Seoul • Taipei • New Delhi
Cape Town • Madrid • Mexico City • Amsterdam • Munich • Paris • Milan

Pearson Education Limited
Edinburgh Gate
Harlow
Essex CM20 2JE
England

and Associated Companies throughout the world

Visit us on the World Wide Web at:
www.pearsoned.co.uk

First published 1968
Second edition 1971
Third edition 1977
Fourth edition 1982
Fifth edition 1987
Sixth edition 1991
Seventh edition 1996
Eighth edition 2001
Ninth edition 2009

ISBN 978-1-4058-9938-3

British Library Cataloguing-in-Publication Data
A catalogue record for this book is available from the British Library

Library of Congress Cataloging-in-Publication Data
Calvocoressi, Peter,
    World politics since 1945 / Peter Calvocoressi, – 9th ed.
        p. cm.
    Rev. ed. of: World politics, 1945–2000.
    Includes bibliographical references and index.
    ISBN 978-1-4058-9938-3 (pbk.)
    1. World politics – 1945–1989.   2. World politics – 1989–
I. Calvocoressi, Peter. World politics, 1945–2000.   II. Title.
D843.C25 2008
909.82—dc22

                                        2008033901

10 9 8 7 6 5 4 3 2 1
12 11 10 09 08

Typeset in 10.5/13.5pt Minion by 35
Printed by Ashford Colour Press Ltd., Gosport

The publisher's policy is to use paper manufactured from sustainable forests.

Contents

List of maps

Acknowledgements

We are grateful to the following for permission to reproduce copyright material:

Figure 30.4 'Antarctica' in *An Atlas of World Affairs*, 10th edition, Routledge (Andrew Boyd, 1998).

In some instances we have been unable to trace the owners of copyright material, and we would appreciate any information that would enable us to do so.

Introduction

The Second World War was a huge man-made catastrophe. When it ended two issues towered over all others: recovery and a new political order. Their respective symbols were American aid (chiefly the Marshall Plan) and the United Nations. The main business of the UN was to prevent wars, especially big wars and very specifically nuclear war, but the UN and its affiliated bodies were also designed to promote prosperity, relieve poverty and bolster justice. Coincidentally the political map of the world was transformed by the demolition of European empires outside Europe. The main aim of this book is to provide material to help to assess how far this programme of unparalleled ambition has been achieved over the short span of two generations.

PART ONE

The Cold War

CHAPTER 1

The Cold War

Beginnings

The Cold War of the two postwar superpowers was not an episode like other wars of modern times. The term 'cold war' was invented to describe a state of affairs. The principal ingredient in this state of affairs was the mutual hostility and fears of the protagonists. These emotions were rooted in their several historical and political differences and were powerfully stimulated by myths which at times turned hostility into hatred. The Cold War dominated world affairs for a generation and more.

President Franklin D. Roosevelt had believed, or perhaps only hoped, that he could persuade Joseph Stalin not to create a separate Soviet sphere of influence over eastern Europe but to co-operate instead with the United States in creating a global economic order based on free trade and beneficial to all involved, not least the USSR. Wartime Lend-Lease to the USSR had been a first step; the postwar Marshall Plan was to be a somewhat forlorn last hope, for even after Roosevelt's death in April 1945 there were some in Washington who preferred a policy of resuscitating western Europe without military confrontation with the USSR. But to most Americans the USSR seemed dedicated to the conquest of Europe and the world for itself and for communism and was capable of achieving, or at least initiating, this destructive and evil course by armed force abetted by subversion. On this view the necessary riposte by the United States was military confrontation in alliance with Europeans and others and on the assumption that Soviet hostility was ineradicable. Seen from Moscow, the western world was inspired by capitalist values which demanded the destruction of the USSR and the extirpation of communism by any means available, but above all by force or the threat of irresistible force. Both these appreciations were absurd. When the Second World War ended the USSR was incapable of further military exertion, while the communist parties beyond its immediate sphere were unable to achieve anything of significance. The western powers, while profoundly mistrustful of the USSR and hostile to its system and beliefs, had no intention of attacking it and were not even prepared to disturb the dominance of central and eastern Europe secured by its armies in the last years of the war. Each side armed itself to win a war which it expected the other to begin but for which it had no stomach.

The focus of the Cold War was Germany, where confrontation over Berlin in 1948–49 came close to armed conflict but ended in victory for the western side without a military engagement. This controlled trial of strength stabilized Europe, which became the world's most stable area for several decades, but hostilities were almost simultaneously carried into Asia, beginning with the triumph of communism in China and war in Korea. These events led in turn to an acceleration of the independence and rearmament of West Germany within a new Euro-American alliance and to a succession of conflicts in Asia, of which the Vietnam War was the most devastating. At no point did the protagonists directly engage each other but both sought to extend their influence and win territorial advantage in adjacent parts of the world, notably the Middle East and – after its decolonization – Africa. None of these excursions was decisive and for nearly half a century the chief outward expression of the Cold War was not advances or retreats but the accumulation and refinement of the means by which the two sides tried to intimidate each other: that is to say, their arms race. The slackening of the Cold War resulted from the combined effect of the huge cost of these armaments and the gradual waning of the myths which underlay it.

In the summer of 1945 it was known both in Washington and Moscow that Japan was ready to acknowledge defeat and abandon the war which it had begun by the attack on Pearl Harbor in 1941. In July the Americans experimentally exploded the first nuclear weapon in the history of mankind and in August they dropped two bombs on Hiroshima and Nagasaki. Japan surrendered forthwith and this clinching of the imminent American victory deprived the Russians of all but a token share in the postwar settlement in the Far East.

In the European theatre conflict remained for a short time veiled. The organs and habits of wartime collaboration were to be adapted to the problems of peace, not discarded. The Russian spring offensive of 1944 had set the USSR on the way to military dominance and political authority in Europe unequalled since Alexander I had ridden into Paris in 1814 with plans for a concert of victors which would order the affairs of Europe and keep them ordered. The nature of mid-twentieth-century great power control was a matter for debate – how far the powers were collectively to order the whole world, how far each was to dominate a sector. The Russians and the British, with the reluctant assent of President Franklin D. Roosevelt (and the dissent of his secretary of state, Cordell Hull), discussed the practical aspects of an immediate division of responsibilities, and in October 1944, at a conference in Moscow which the president was unable to attend owing to the American election campaign, these dispositions were expressed in numerical terms. About western Europe no questions arose because western control was uncontested. Poland was not included because, in parts effectively, in parts imminently, it was under Stalin's military control. Elsewhere the realities were expressed by Winston Churchill as percentages. The Russian degree of influence in Romania was described as 90 per cent, in Bulgaria and Hungary as 80, in Yugoslavia 50, in Greece 10. In practice these figures, although expressed as a bargain, described a situation: 90 and 10 were polite ways of saying 100 and 0, and the diagnosis in the two extreme cases of Romania and Greece was confirmed when the British took control in Greece without Russian protest and the USSR installed a pro-communist regime in Romania with only perfunctory American or British protest. Bulgaria and Hungary went the same way as Romania for military reasons. Yugoslavia appeared to fall within the Russian sphere but soon fell out of it. Europe became divided into two segments appertaining to the two principal victors, the United States and the USSR. These two powers continued for a while to talk in terms of alliance, and they were specifically pledged to collaborate in the governance of the German and Austrian territories which they and their allies had conquered.

The position of the USSR in these years was one of great weakness. For the USSR the war had been a huge economic disaster accompanied by loss of life so grievous that its full extent was not disclosed. The Russian state was a land power which had expanded generation by generation within a zone which evoked a persistent German threat. In the Soviet phase of history Russian external politics were further characterized by a diplomacy which led to isolation and so, in 1941, to the threshold of military defeat. The USSR had been saved by its extraordinary geographical and spiritual resources and by the concurrent war in the west in which the Germans were already engaged before they attacked the USSR and which became graver for them when, shortly afterwards, Hitler gratuitously declared war on the United States of America. For Stalin, however, the anti-fascist alliance of 1941–45 can hardly have appeared to be more than a marriage of convenience and limited span; nor did it look any different when seen from the western end, at any rate by governments, if not in the popular view. With the war over, the purpose of the alliance had been achieved, and there was little in the mentalities and traditions of the allies to encourage the idea that it might be converted into an entente: on the contrary, the diplomatic history of all parties up to 1941 and their respective attitudes to international political, social and economic problems suggest exactly the reverse.

The elimination, permanent or temporary, of the German threat coincided with the explosion of the first American nuclear bombs. For the first time in the history of the world one state had become more powerful than all other states put together. The USSR, no less than the most trivial state, was at the mercy of the Americans should they be willing to do to Moscow and Leningrad what they had done to Hiroshima and Nagasaki. There were reasons for supposing that they were not so willing, but no government in the Kremlin could responsibly proceed upon this assumption. Stalin's only prudent course in this bitterly disappointing situation was to combine the maximum strengthening of the USSR with a nice assessment of the safe level of provocation of the United States, and to subordinate everything, including postwar reconstruction, to catching up with the Americans in military technology. He possessed a large army, he had occupied large areas of eastern and central Europe, and he had natural allies and servants in communists in various parts of the world.

At home his tasks were immense: they included the safeguarding of the USSR against a repetition of the catastrophe of 1941–45, and the resurrection of the USSR from the catastrophe which had cost 25 million or perhaps even 40 million lives, the destruction or displacement of a large part of its industry and the distortion of its industrial pattern to the detriment of all except war production, and the devastation and depopulation of its cultivated land so that food production was almost halved. To a man with Stalin's past and temperament the tasks of restitution included the reassertion of party rule and communist orthodoxy and the reduction therefore of the prominence of the army and other national institutions and the reshackling of all modes of thinking outside the prescribed doctrinal run. In matters of national security, in economic affairs and in the life of the spirit the outlook was grim. At home artists and intellectuals were regimented, victorious marshals were slighted and the officer class persistently if quietly purged, while the first postwar five-year plan prescribed strenuous tasks for heavy industry and offered little comfort to a war-weary populace.

Externally, Stalin made it clear that the protective acquisitions of 1939–40 were not for disgorging (the three Baltic states, the eastern half of Poland which the Russians called Western Ukraine and Western Byelorussia, Bessarabia and northern Bukovina, and the territory exacted from Finland after the winter war); elsewhere in eastern and central Europe all states must have governments well disposed to the USSR, a vague formula which seemed to mean governments which could be relied upon never again to give facilities to a German aggressor and which came, after 1947 or thereabouts, to mean governments reliably hostile to the United States in the Cold War. Such governments must be installed and maintained by whatever means might be necessary. During the wartime conferences between Stalin, Roosevelt and Churchill parts of the USSR were still occupied by German forces, and during the war and its psychological aftermath (a period of indefinable duration) Stalin was no doubt obsessed with his German problem. The Cold War first substituted the Americans for the Germans as the main enemy but then, after the rearmament of Western Germany, combined the two threats as a new American–German one. These developments, to which Stalin himself contributed by his actions in eastern and central Europe, may nevertheless have been a disappointment to him if, as seems possible, he had entertained at one time a very different prospect of Russo-American relations.

To Stalin during the war the Americans were personified by Franklin D. Roosevelt, who made no secret of his desire to get on well with the USSR or of his distrust of British and other western imperialisms. Moreover, Roosevelt wanted a Russian alliance against Japan and did not seem at all likely to do the one thing which Stalin would have feared; namely, to keep troops permanently in Europe and make the United States a European power. On the contrary, Roosevelt was not much interested in postwar Europe and showed, for example, little of Churchill's concern about what was going to happen in Poland and Greece. Whereas Russo-British relations came near to breaking-point over Poland, Russo-American relations did not; and Stalin, whether out of genuine lack of interest or calculated diplomacy, avoided serious disagreement with Roosevelt over problems of world organization (such as the representation of Soviet republics in the UN) in which Roosevelt was seriously interested. On the basis that the United States would be remote from Europe and in some degree friendly towards the USSR, Stalin was prepared to moderate his support for European communists in order not to alarm the United States. He did not foresee that by abandoning Greece to Britain he was preparing the way for the transfer of Greece to the United States within three years. His failure to help the Greek communists may have been principally a result of a calculation that they were not worth helping, but he may also have reflected that helping them would alarm and irritate Americans in Roosevelt's entourage. He was continuing a line of policy applied in Yugoslavia during the war when he restrained the Yugoslav communists' desire to plan and prosecute their social revolution while the war was still in progress, and urged them to co-operate with other parties, even monarchists. Again he persuaded the Italian communists to be less anti-monarchical than the non communist Action Party; it was the communist leader Palmiro Togliatti who proposed, after the fall of Mussolini, that the future of the Italian monarchy should remain in abeyance until the war was finished. By that time, however, Roosevelt was dead and whatever Stalin's policies towards the United States may have been, they could no longer be based on his relations with Roosevelt and his estimate of Roosevelt's intentions. Even if Roosevelt had survived, his policies might have been radically altered – as were those of Harry S. Truman, who succeeded Roosevelt in April 1945 – by the successful explosion of two nuclear bombs and by the evolution of Stalin's policies in Europe.

For Stalin, confronted in August 1945 with the evidence from Hiroshima and Nagasaki, the outstanding fact was that the USSR possessed no strategic air force which could deliver a direct attack on the United States. The best that Stalin could do was to pose a threat to western Europe which might deter the Americans from attacking the USSR. The Russian armies were not demobilized or withdrawn from the areas which they had occupied in the last campaigns of the war and which included the capital cities of Budapest, Prague, Vienna and Berlin. Thus Stalin created a glacis in advance of his vulnerable heartlands and at the same time scared the exhausted and tremulous Europeans and their American protectors into asking themselves whether the Russian advance had really been halted by the German surrender or might be resumed until Paris and Milan, Brest and Bordeaux were added to the Russian bag. But by keeping a huge army in being and reducing most of central and eastern Europe to vassalage while Russian money and brains were producing the Russian bomb, Stalin accentuated the American hostility which he had cause to fear.

Nuclear parity was an inescapable objective for the Kremlin, but there was in theory an alternative, which some Americans tried to bring within the scope of practical politics. This was to sublimate or internationalize atomic energy and so remove it from inter-state politics. One of the first actions of the United Nations was to create in 1946

1.1 The Cold War division of Europe

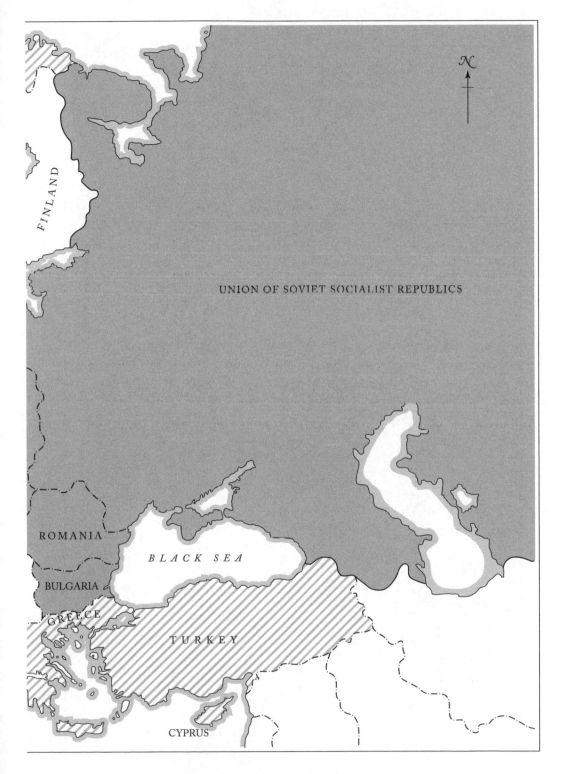

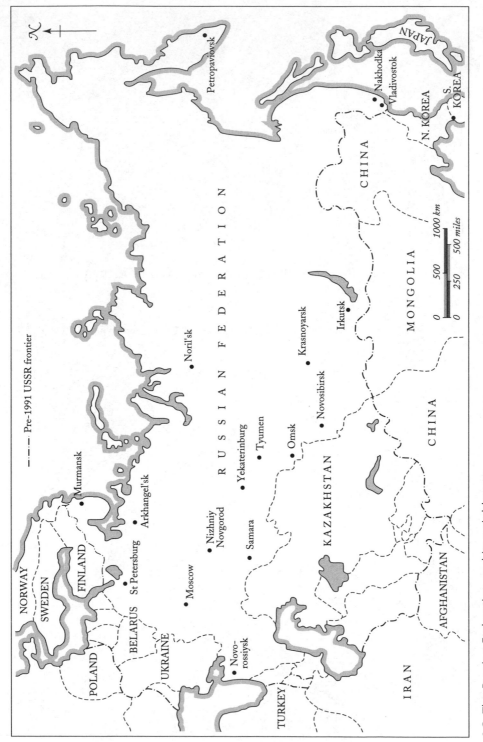

1.2 The Russian Federation and its neighbours

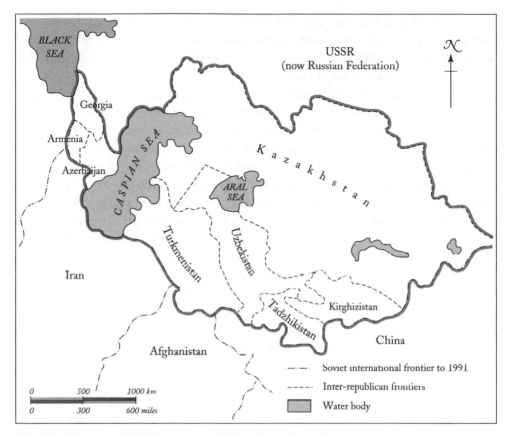

1.3 The five central Asian states and the Caucasus

an Atomic Energy Commission. At the first meeting of this commission Bernard M. Baruch presented on behalf of the United States a plan for an international Atomic Development Authority which would have exclusive control and ownership in all potential war-making nuclear activities. The Russians presented a different plan. The two plans were irreconcilable and in 1948 the Atomic Energy Commission decided to adjourn indefinitely. The Russian rejection of the Baruch Plan was an additional factor in persuading Truman that the USSR was no longer an ally but a dangerous adversary.

American policy-makers had more freedom of choice than their Russian counterparts. The nuclear bomb was a weapon which had been used to bring the war with Japan to an end and also a political weapon with which to shackle Russian power. The war left the United States a major power in Europe with considerable military forces in Europe and nuclear weapons in the background. Endowed with mighty technical superiority, the Americans might strike or threaten, or wait and see. To strike – to start a preventive war – was in practice impossible because they were unable to summon up the will to do so. A preventive war is a war undertaken to remove a threat by a people which feels threatened, and the Americans did not feel threatened by Russian weaponry: a preventive war was an abstract intellectual concept. (For the Russians it was substantive but also suicidal.) The Americans therefore pursued policies which combined threats with waiting to see.

All weapons have political implications and the biggest weapons have the biggest implications. A weapon which is too frightful to use – or turns out to be, in military terms, useless except in the most exceptional circumstances – has the most implications, since its possessors will want to put it to political use in order to compensate for the anomalous limitations on its military usefulness. Truman's position was automatically different from Roosevelt's as soon as Hiroshima had been destroyed. The question was not whether he was to make political use of the new weapon, but to what political end he should use it. The context in which this question first arose was not Asian but European, for it was in Europe that the principal political issues lay. The United States disliked the idea of spheres of influence, and in particular the prospect of exclusive Russian control over half Europe as the Russians broke pledges to install democratic governments in countries liberated from German rule. In addition the climate of opinion was changing. Truman was a very different man from Roosevelt and conscious of the differences: an American of some eminence but in no sense a world figure, a man respected for the qualities which go with directness rather than subtlety, a man in whom political courage would have to take the place of political sophistication, a man typically American in his attachment to a few basic principles where Roosevelt had generally preferred the modes of thought of the pragmatist. Truman, in the last resort, played politics by precept and not by ear, and where Roosevelt had been concerned with the problem of relations between two great powers, Truman was more influenced by the conflict between communism and an even vaguer entity called anti-communism. Again, so far as these generalizations are pardonable, Truman was the more representative American of the late 1940s and more inclined to regard the meeting of Americans and Russians in the middle of Europe as a confrontation of systems and civilizations rather than of states. Reports of indiscipline and barbarities by Russian troops, often described as Asian or mongoloid, increased this propensity.

The United States had some cause to hope that the implications of Hiroshima for Europe were not lost on the Russians. Elections in Hungary in 1945 gave the communists only a minor share in the government of the capital and the state. Elections in Bulgaria were postponed on American insistence and against Russian wishes. In Romania the United States aligned itself with the anti-communists and the king against the prime minister, Petru Groza, whom (although not a communist) the Russians had installed when they entered the country in 1944. But the crucial testing ground was Poland, where coalition government, under a socialist prime minister, was maintained until 1947 but gradually transformed in that and the following year – the years which saw the extinction of any hope of preventing the partition of Europe into spheres of influence and the formalization of the Cold War.

American policy veered away from the attempt to maximize American influence throughout Europe in favour of giving the USSR to understand that further territorial advances in Europe were forbidden. This prohibition was to be enforced by a series of open political arrangements, backed by military dispositions. The overwhelming power of the United States would be used obstructively but not destructively. In so far as the USSR presented a material menace, it would be contained by physical barriers; in so far as it presented an ideological menace, it would be countered by democratic example, money and the seeds of decay which westerners discerned in the communist system (as Marxists did in capitalism). American policy was also constructive and reconstructive. The UN Relief and Reconstruction Agency (UNRRA) was financed mainly by American money; its help was enormous, especially to the USSR and Yugoslavia. In March 1947 the United States took over Britain's traditional and now too costly role of keeping the Russians out of the eastern Mediterranean: Truman took Greece and Turkey under the American wing and promised material aid to states threatened by communism. Three months later the United States inaugurated the Marshall Plan to avert an economic collapse of Europe which could, it was feared, leave the whole continent helplessly exposed to Russian power and communist lures. The offer of American economic aid was made to the whole of Europe, including the USSR, but Moscow refused for itself and for its satellites. For a second time – the Baruch Plan being the first – the Russians rejected a generous overture from Washington rather than accept collaboration which would have enabled Americans and others to move around in the USSR and observe its true plight. Separate development of western and eastern Europe was affirmed. Europe was still a battlefield – not, as Europeans mostly saw it – a zone where yet another war had just ended. The coup which substituted communist for coalition rule in Prague the next year sharpened the image of the battlefield, for although there was no fighting except locally and sporadically, everybody concurred in describing the situation as a war. Then, in Germany the struggle for the only important piece of Europe in dispute between the two camps produced a challenge which seemed bound to lead to shooting.

The division of Germany

At the end of the Second World War the United States, the USSR and Britain were in apparent agreement on two propositions about Germany, both of which they failed to maintain. The first of these was that Germany should be kept under constraint, and the second was that it should remain a single unit. The former depended on the latter, which ran counter to the (largely unconscious) assumptions of the moment that, first, Europe had fallen into two parts and, secondly, that the western allies and the Russians should each control the conquered bits in their half. There had been talk and even general agreement of joint allied control over all of Europe but the reality from the conquest of Sicily in 1943 onward was otherwise. Within a decade Germany became divided into two separate states, for reasons which included the inability of the victors to agree on the German problem, the intrinsic importance of Germany itself, and external circumstances, of which the Korean War was the most important. So Germany too was partitioned, like Europe as a whole, as a consequence of Russo-American rivalry in the conference chamber and on the ground in Europe and beyond. The bipolarity of postwar power politics led inevitably to delineation and demarcation – even, in a celebrated and late episode, to the building of a wall, a tactic reminiscent of such antique devices as the attempt to bar the Golden Horn to ships or the isthmus of Corinth to armies.

The principal victors were initially agreed that Germany should be disarmed and denazified, divided administratively into zones of occupation but treated economically as a single unit which would pay for imported necessities out of current production. Dismemberment, which had been discussed and may have lingered on in some French minds, was tacitly abandoned without being officially repudiated, and the territorial amputations suffered by Germany were the loss of east Prussia to the USSR and of all other territories beyond the Oder and Western Neisse rivers, which were left under Polish administration pending the final delimitation of the German state by the peace conference that never took place. Churchill opposed the designation of the Western as opposed to the Eastern Neisse as the western limit of Poland's sphere (the Western Neisse flows northward into the Oder at a point where the upstream line of the Oder turns sharply eastward) but he felt unable to persist in a seemingly anti-Polish attitude. The Potsdam decision on Germany's frontiers, although expressed in provisional terms, was in reality a victory for the Russians. Germany lost nearly one-quarter of its pre-1938 territory.

The victors were divided in their views on the economic policy of the occupation and on the future structure of the German state. The general principles of economic unity and the balancing of imports and production, adopted at Potsdam, were traversed by the problem of reparations which had been inconclusively discussed at Yalta and then shelved at Potsdam. It was agreed at Yalta that the sum of $20 billion should be taken as a basis for further discussions, half of this sum being claimed by the USSR for itself and Poland. At Potsdam the Russians, whose need for reparations in kind or cash was intense, secured agreement for removals from their zone of occupation to meet Russian and Polish reparation claims but nothing was settled about the extent of these claims. The western allies were likewise to be entitled to dismantle and remove property in their zones but this arrangement was bound to make nonsense of the principle of economic unity since the various zones were economically dissimilar both in manufacture and agricultural production. It also made nonsense of the principle of paying for imports out of current production, since it permitted the occupiers to destroy the sources of production. Germany could be looted or milked, but it could not for long be both looted and milked. The western allies soon found that dismantling left them with an obligation to provide their zones with imported goods which had to be paid for by their own taxpayers since German production was unable to foot the bill.

Moreover, Russian dismantling and removals on a vast scale, coupled with severe shortages in the USSR itself, placed upon the western occupiers and their taxpayers the additional burden of supplying the Russian zone with essential foods and goods. Although the Americans might have been willing to help the Russians directly with equipment for reconstruction, they resented the round-about way in which the Russians helped themselves to German equipment at eventual American expense, while for their part the Russians were happy to take from Germany what their *amour propre* prevented them from accepting from the Americans.

This conflict was accompanied by related disagreements about the political structure of Germany and its political attachments. The British were pragmatically predisposed in favour of a unitary rather than a federal structure, for economic rather than political reasons. The main Russian concern was strategic: to maintain their position in eastern Germany. This was the essential minimum to which they subsequently adhered unfalteringly. It was strengthened, in November 1945, by the first significant political event in the reviving postwar Europe – the elections in Austria in which the communists were decisively defeated. If, compatibly with the aim of holding fast to eastern Germany, Russian power could be extended to the whole of Germany, so much the better; but this wider aim can never have seemed more than problematical after the first few disordered months of peace. So long, however, as it remained a possibility, the Russians favoured a strong central government for Germany in the hope that it would be captured by the Socialist Unity Party (SED – an attempt to create a left-wing party under communist control and prevent the operation of a distinct socialist party). They only abandoned this sub-policy after it became evident that a united Germany would no more be a communist Germany in the 1940s than it had been after 1918. They thereupon switched not to a federal solution for Germany as a whole but to a two-Germanies policy.

The supporters of federation, meaning a federation with a weak central government, were the French. Incapable themselves of imposing any control over Germany and dubious of their allies' capacity to do so for long, the French wanted a weak German state, disarmed and disabled by internal political fragmentation. They also wanted coal for their own reconstruction plans and the Saar. Their changes in policy came in stages: first, Georges Bidault, when foreign minister, reluctantly acknowledged the hostility between the USSR and the western allies, threw France's lot in with the latter and accepted the establishment of a new western German state, including the French zone; next, Robert Schuman sought, in a wider European context, to win German friendship rather than insure against German hostility, and René Pleven, in the same context, accepted a modified rearmament of Germany; finally, de Gaulle, developing Schuman's policy of reconciliation, concluded with Schuman's old colleague, Konrad Adenauer, a bilateral Franco-German alliance.

In the three years after the Potsdam conference the occupiers, having failed to produce a coherent German policy, drifted away from the notion of Germany as

something to be constrained to the notion of Germany as something to be acquired –
from a basically collaborative to a basically competitive position. Two conferences of
foreign ministers in 1947, at Moscow in March and at London in November, failed to
elaborate the peace treaty which was supposed to emerge. In the same year, which was
also the year of the Truman Doctrine and the Marshall Plan, the American and British
zones were fused and endowed with an economic council of 54 members. In the next
year the Americans and the British moved determinedly towards turning their joint
zone into a solvent and autonomous parliamentary democracy. The economic council
was doubled in size and given a second chamber; a plan was produced for the internationalization of the Ruhr in order to counter the fears of those who found it difficult
to stomach the reappearance of a sovereign German state; the Americans and British
devalued the mark in their zones, a long-discussed and necessary reform which the
Russians had obstructed by appealing to the principle of economic unity; and a constituent assembly met in Bonn. These steps were supplemented in April 1949 when the
French zone was joined with the Anglo-American. The western occupiers invigorated
this joint zone (and embryonic state) with American financial aid and a reform of its
currency; and they prepared to extend the new mark to their sectors of Berlin. At this
point the Russians decided to challenge the whole western policy of separate development of a western German state. They chose Berlin, where their position was special.

Berlin had been excluded from the zonal system and placed under a separate, joint
allied authority. The city was divided into four sectors but these sectors did not have
the administrative autonomy of the zones. However, the Russian position in Berlin was
distinct for two reasons. It was the Russians who first entered the city, occupying it
a few days before the German surrender and setting about the business of clearing
rubble, organizing rations, installing new local authorities and establishing a police
force before the arrival of American or British units; and, secondly, the drawing of the
zonal boundaries left Berlin an enclave within the Russian zone and 260 km beyond
the nearest point under British control. Subsequently, there was much debate about the
lack of foresight and political sense of the western allies in allowing the Russians to
reach Berlin first and in accepting the virtual isolation of the city without even securing clearly and formally defined rights of access to it. Although something must be
allowed for the temper and exigencies of wartime collaboration, there can be little
doubt that the Americans and the British would have driven a different bargain if they
had realized that they were, in effect, handing Berlin over to the Russians subject only
to the right to be imprisoned within it.

Berlin was the central point of a Russian attempt to gain control of Germany which,
having started with auspicious expedition, quickly ran into trouble. The socialists
refused to submerge themselves in a single party with the communists and promoted
instead an anti-Russian coalition which, in elections in October 1946, thwarted the
Russian design to place the city's administration in communist hands. In 1947 Ernst
Reuter, an ex-communist socialist, was elected mayor in a symbolic contest in which

the non-Russian occupiers were clearly, if still discreetly, aligned with Reuter against the Russians and the communists. The independent political life of the city had revived before the Russians had been able to impose a throttling substitute so that, while the Russian strategic position remained strong, the Russian political position had not thrived and the western occupiers found themselves indebted to the anti-Russian activities of Berliners. In return for this uncovenanted aid the western occupiers felt committed to the maintenance of the independence of Berlin from the Russian zone and its successor, the East German state or German Democratic Republic.

The steps taken by the western occupiers in 1947–48 to establish a West German state threatened the Russian ambition to keep Germany whole and turn it communist. They also foreshadowed the revival of an independent German power in world politics, armed and hostile to the USSR. The Russians decided to make a major issue of these developments and to resort to force to stop them. They cut the road, rail and water routes by which the western occupiers communicated with Berlin and stopped food, electricity, gas and other necessities from being supplied regularly to the western sectors from the east. The legal right to use the routes uninterruptedly was vague – and also irrelevant in what was clearly a trial of strength. The western occupiers, having considered and rejected the possibility of asserting their rights by sending an armed convoy to force its way along the road from the British zone to the boundary of the city, decided instead to pierce the Russian siege by air, thus placing the Russians in the position of having to fire a first shot. They also imposed a counter-blockade on the Russian zone, and the Americans moved part of their long-range bomber force to airfields in England. Between July 1948 and May 1949 the American and British air forces carried over 1.5 million tons of food, fuel and other goods into Berlin (the highest load in one day exceeded 12,000 tons), thus ensuring the needs of the entire civilian population of the blockaded sectors as well as their western guardians. This doubly extraordinary feat – extraordinary for what it did and extraordinary for doing it without leading to open hostilities – defeated the Russians, who abandoned the blockade in May after 318 days in return for a promise of one more conference on Germany, which was held in Paris but achieved nothing.

The western victory over Berlin was followed by the transformation of the western zone of Germany into a sovereign state and an armed member of the Euro-American alliance against the USSR. The German Federal Republic came into being on 20 September 1949 with its capital in Bonn and Dr Konrad Adenauer as its chancellor. Adenauer thereby tacitly agreed to postpone German reunification by joining the western camp. An occupation statute and a series of agreements (the Petersburg agreements) defined the relations between the new state and the western powers and imposed certain restrictions on its sovereignty, but these detailed provisions were of no importance compared with the transcendent fact that the greater part of Germany had been removed from the joint control of its conquerors and attached to a new anti-communist western alliance. Exactly a year after the inauguration of the Federal

Republic its rearmament became a live issue: as a result of the outbreak of war in Korea in June 1950 the Americans persuaded themselves and, with more difficulty, their British and French allies and Adenauer (who was initially opposed) that the Federal Republic should contribute to the armament of the west.

NATO and the Soviet empire to the Cuban crisis

The western alliance which was created to wage the Cold War came into existence on 4 April 1949, during the blockade of Berlin. Two years earlier such an alliance would have seemed impossible because of the strength of the communist parties of France and Italy, but during 1947 communists were excluded from the government of these two countries and the belief that they were ungovernable without communist participation was proved false. The North Atlantic Treaty Organization (NATO) was an association of 12 states which declared that an armed attack on any one of them in Europe or North America would be regarded as an attack on them all, and that each would, in such an event, go to the help of the ally attacked by taking such action, including the use of force, as it deemed necessary. The area covered by the treaty was defined as the territories of any signatory in Europe or North America, Algeria and islands, vessels or aircraft of any signatory in the Atlantic north of the tropic of Cancer; the treaty would also be brought into operation by an attack on the occupation forces of any signatory in Europe. Greece and Turkey joined the alliance in 1952 and the German Federal Republic in 1955. The creation of NATO was an affirmation of the dissolution of the wartime alliance. It was based on fear of Russian aggression, compounded by revulsion against the nature of Russian domination in eastern Europe, frustration turning to hostility in German affairs, the exposure of western Europe as a result of war damage and demobilization, and the failure to internationalize the control of atomic energy.

In 1945 the American war-making capacity had been supreme even without nuclear weapons, but in the next years a new pattern was created by American demobilization. While American supremacy was guaranteed by the nuclear bomb, the Russians, by not demobilizing, established superiority in mobilized land power in Europe. Thus, all future attempts to disarm were bedevilled by the impossibility of comparing like with like; the defence of western Europe became dependent on nuclear power and nuclear strategy and ultimately the collective defence of western Europe provoked dissension about inter-allied control over nuclear weapons. Whereas in 1945 there had been some qualms and, on the Russian side, some hopes of an American retreat from Europe, four years later the United States was formally committed to a dominant role in European affairs for the next 20 years. Realizing too late what had been brought about, Stalin proposed in 1948 the withdrawal of all foreign troops from Germany, but his offer was regarded as a mere device to make the Americans take a long journey from which they would not return, while the Russians remained within striking distance of Germany.

So long as Germany was debatable ground the United States would remain on it. Hence western Germany's eventual place in NATO alongside its recent enemies.

The Cold War was a short episode in the history of Europe but it assumed at the time an air of permanence owing to the metaphors of frigidity and rigour in which it was discussed. Its two principal features were apparent in 1946 in the speeches by Churchill at Fulton, Missouri, in February in Truman's presence and by Truman's secretary of state, James F. Byrnes, at Stuttgart in September. These speeches showed that the tripartite wartime alliance was being replaced by a new pattern of two against one and that the United States, so far from turning its back on Europe (and in spite of the reduction of American forces in Europe from 2.5 million men to fewer than half a million at the date of the Fulton speech), regarded Europe as an essential American sphere of influence. Although Truman had to accept virtual exclusion from central and eastern Europe, he secured by the Truman Doctrine of March 1947 a foothold in the Balkans and the Middle East at the time when he was preparing to consolidate anti-communist and anti-Russian positions in western Europe by a combination of economic aid and military alliance — embodied in the Marshall Plan and the North Atlantic Treaty. These were the beginnings of the policy of containment, designed to curb Russian power and change the Russian mood, but little more than a year after the signing of the North Atlantic Treaty this essentially European policy was complicated by a distant event, the outbreak of war in Korea, which became a drain on the forces available for containment in Europe and converted containment from a European to a more nearly global policy.

The Korean War also embittered the atmosphere. In the United States it was treated as evidence to fortify the myth of a masterly communist conspiracy to conquer the world. Senator Joseph McCarthy, alleging that this conspiracy extended into the United States government itself and other centres of influence, conducted a repellent smear campaign in which he and his associates intimidated important segments of the public service by denouncing as communists (or homosexuals) anybody who did not subscribe to their extreme views of how loyal Americans ought to think: a number of Americans were driven into exile and some to suicide, and the formulation and conduct of American external policies were corrupted and demoralized before McCarthyism was anaesthetized by a few bold individuals, by its own excesses and by the residual good sense of the American people – without much help from their more supine elected leaders. This atmospheric pressure affected the American election campaign of 1952 in which the Republicans, in their bid to recapture the presidency for the first time since 1932, adopted General Dwight D. Eisenhower as their candidate. The principal Republican spokesman on foreign affairs was John Foster Dulles, soon to be secretary of state.

McCarthyism apart, there were grounds for questioning the Democrats' foreign policies. The United States was engaged in a grievous war; the USSR was not; containment seemed to mean peace for the Russians who, although prevented from expanding, remained unconstrained in their treatment of their satellites, whose fate bore uneasily on the American conscience. In his election speeches Dulles gave the impression that the Republicans would come to the aid of the enslaved people of eastern Europe and somehow liberate them from Russian domination. This was Dulles' contribution, aimed at Americans with eastern European roots, to making a Republican president electable and after the Republican victory it was rapidly forgotten. Instead Dulles proceeded with the policy of containment, filling the gap between NATO and the American position in Japan by fostering SEATO (the South East Asia Treaty Organization) and the Baghdad Pact (pp. 328, 395). He also tried to escape from the frustrations of containment, which he had criticized for being a series of responses to Russian initiatives, by evolving a strategy of massive retaliation to be applied at times and places of American choosing. But when in Indo-China in 1954 the United States had the choice between massive retaliation and acquiescence in an ally's defeat, it chose the latter and so acknowledged that massive retaliation contained a large element of bluff.

In Europe the United States, having successfully annexed western Germany to NATO, accepted as a corollary the impossibility of dislodging the Russians from eastern Germany, which was turned into a satellite communist adjunct of the Russian empire in Europe. After passing through similar stages – an economic council, a parliament, a constitution, the election of a president (Wilhelm Pieck) and prime minister (Otto Grotewohl) – the eastern zone became in March 1954 a separate state under the name of the German Democratic Republic. The integration of western Germany into the western camp involved the end of the occupation and the negotiation of agreements which would both ally the Federal Republic with other western states and allow the latter some control over German rearmament. The three principal western powers offered to terminate their occupation of the Federal Republic if it would join a European Defence Community in which national forces would be subject to international control, and in May 1952 a convention was signed at Bonn ending the occupation and a European Defence Treaty was signed the next day. Elections in 1953 gave Adenauer's Christian Democratic Union and its Bavarian counterpart, the Christian Social Union, a two-to-one victory and in 1954 the Federal Republic ratified the European Defence Treaty. The French parliament, however, refused to ratify a treaty which restored German military might without a countervailing British commitment, whereupon Britain jettisoned part of its traditional aversion to meaningful peacetime associations and promoted the Western European Union (WEU) created by the Treaty of Paris in 1954 and comprising Britain, France and the Benelux countries (which had been associated by treaty since 1948) together with Italy and the Federal Republic. The end of the occupation of West Germany was confirmed and the Federal Republic joined NATO. With the ratification of these agreements in May 1955 the Federal Republic became an almost fully fledged member of the western alliance. It forswore the manufacture of nuclear, bacteriological and chemical weapons and accepted a form of inspection over industrial concerns. In return it got a reiterated pledge on reunification, the recognition of the government in Bonn as the government of the whole of Germany, and the privilege of contributing 12 divisions to NATO's forces.

In March 1953 Stalin died. Churchill thought he saw an opportunity to arrest the collision course of the two alliances. In keeping with his own predilections in international diplomacy he proposed a personal meeting of heads of government, but the temper of the times was inimical, the Americans (and many in Britain) were cool, the West Germans suspicious, and Churchill himself soon afterwards suffered a stroke. Riots in eastern Germany in June encouraged those in the west who preferred to wait for the USSR to get into deeper trouble, while in the USSR Stalin's death was followed by an interlude of three years. But neither in those years nor for a generation after did any Russian leader make any radical attempt to change the system which Stalin had inherited from Lenin. Nikita Khrushchev attacked Stalin as an individual and an icon; Leonid Brezhnev adhered to the system for fear of something worse; Yuri Andropov, who was alert, and Konstantin Chernenko, who was not, accepted the inadvisability of doing otherwise. Only after 1989 did Mikhail Gorbachev embark on reform and Boris Yeltsin lead a revolution.

Stalin's death followed very closely the election of Eisenhower to the presidency of the United States. Eisenhower was a president who had seen more of the world and its affairs than his immediate predecessor or any of his successors in the twentieth century. By standing for that office he fended off a victory for the potentially isolationist or McCarthyite section of the Republican Party and, in partnership with his secretary of state John Foster Dulles, marginally but decisively adjusted Truman's more combative nuclear style. He continued Truman's policy of aid to anti-communist allies and developed the politics of arms control which became after many tedious years a major element in the dismantling of the Cold War. He eschewed the personal style which characterized Nixon and Reagan in their different ways and was of so retiring a nature that he was accused of indolence, but he may be judged in longer retrospect the most significant president of the United States in the relatively peaceable half of the twentieth century.

In the year before Stalin's death the Communist Party of the Soviet Union had held its nineteenth congress after an unconstitutional delay of 13 years, probably occasioned by the party leaders' need for time after the war to set many houses in order. Although nobody knew how nearly Stalin's death was approaching, the succession was uppermost in all minds. By his handling of the congress's business Stalin indicated a preference for G. M. Malenkov who, having outlived A. A. Zhdanov, looked like outpointing his most serious rival N. S. Khrushchev. Zhdanov's death in 1948 had been followed in 1949 by a purge of his associates; the older men had been regressing for some years and the two most eminent among them, Molotov and Mikoyan, had lost their ministerial posts (though not their other positions) in 1949; the police chief Lavrenti Beria, too, seemed somewhat less favoured and less powerful in the early 1950s, despite his control over a police force of 1.5 million men and a militia of

300,000. Then in January 1953 in a mounting frenzy of anti-Semitism nine doctors, seven of them Jews, were accused of complicity in the death of Zhdanov. This so-called doctors' plot, which was declared to be baseless after Stalin's death, combined anti-Semitism with an attack on Zhdanov's enemies, and it was no secret that Zhdanov's principal enemy was the man who had most markedly profited by his death, Malenkov. When, therefore, Stalin died Malenkov's position was less promising than it had seemed a year earlier, but it was still strong enough to ensure his succession to the top posts in both government and party. This initial victory was secured in alliance with Beria but it did not last long. Malenkov and Beria may have had some similar ideas, notably in helping the consumer industries at the expense of heavy and armaments industries, but Beria was an exceptionally unpopular and dangerous man, personally and *ex officio*, and for Malenkov the support of the country's chief policeman was off-set by the hostility of the armed services, which disliked both Beria's private army and Malenkov's economic policy: Beria was killed within a few months of Stalin's death.

Soon after the end of the war Stalin, who did not see himself as a Bonaparte and did not want any Bonapartes around, had set about putting the army and its leaders safely back in a position of subordination to the civil power, but in the struggle for power after his death the army was inevitably a major counter and Khrushchev, who had military friends from his days as a commissar on the Stalingrad front, decided to use it. At first he did not have to. The devolution of Stalin's entire position on any one man was more than any of the principal civilian leaders, except Malenkov himself and possibly Beria, was prepared to tolerate. Power was almost immediately divided. Malenkov was forced to choose between being head of the government and head of the party. He chose the former and ceded the latter post to Khrushchev. The antagonism of the two men was thus institutionalized. Two teams of five faced each other. Malenkov and four others formed the top layer of government while Khrushchev and four others constituted the party secretariat. This position lasted until 1955 when Khrushchev defeated Malenkov, partly by reviving rumours of Malenkov's complicity in Zhdanov's death and the subsequent purge and by accusing Malenkov of having conspired with Beria to establish personal instead of collective rule on Stalin's death and partly by manu-facturing a war scare which created the alliance between himself and the army. In February 1955 Khrushchev secured the removal of Malenkov and his substitution at the head of the government by Bulganin, who was destined to stay there as long as Khrushchev felt it inopportune to claim the post for himself. Bulganin was succeeded at the ministry of defence by Marshal G. K. Zhukhov. Other changes were made at top ministerial level where there seemed to be a shift from political veterans to technical experts, although the chopping and changing of these years more probably reflected uncertainties and inconsistencies in economic planning.

Khrushchev's personal pre-eminence lasted from 1957 to 1964 but was never as secure as it seemed to outsiders. It was won in spite of mistakes which were not forgotten, notably his failure when put in charge of agriculture by Stalin. His policy of exploiting virgin lands in Kazakhstan was radical and sound but disastrously applied in the short run. His political acumen and agility enabled him to survive this setback and, for some years thereafter, the disfavour and machinations of his colleagues who, after forcing Malenkov into the shadows, discovered that Khrushchev was at least as keen on personal authority and impatient with the committee system. But when the elder statesmen in the party tried in 1957 to remove him, he outwitted them and strengthened his own position until he forfeited it through waywardness.

In external affairs Khrushchev's term consisted of a short and emollient prelude when he was manoeuvring against domestic rivals and a longer period which displayed his erratic, if agreeable and extrovert, temperament. This latter period included major events: risings in Poland and Hungary, the launching of the first sputnik, the building of the Berlin wall, irremediable quarrels with China and his attempt to install nuclear missiles in Cuba.

In the uncertain years immediately after Stalin's death Russian foreign policy was cautious. The German and Austrian problems were brought to the conference table, as were also Korea, where an armistice had been signed in July 1953, and Indo China. Bulganin and Khrushchev made their peace with Tito, surrendered Porkkala in Finland and Port Arthur, put forward new disarmament proposals, visited India, Burma, Afghanistan (the first non-communist recipient of Russian aid) and Britain, and repaired in July 1955 to a meeting at Geneva with the American president and the British and French prime ministers. This meeting was a demonstration in favour of relaxing the Cold War. It produced some euphoric notions – a non-aggression treaty between NATO and the Warsaw Pact, proposed by the USSR; a free-inspection zone, proposed by Eden; and an open-skies survey, proposed by Eisenhower. An ancillary conference of foreign ministers, designed to give point and precision to the Geneva atmosphere, was a failure and this first attempt to thaw the Cold War was brought to nought by the Polish and Hungarian revolts of 1956. But the leaders had met and had set an example of decent manners and the pursuit of tolerance. In the late 1950s the Russian armed forces were cut from 5.8 to 3.6 million. A further cut of 1.2 million, announced in 1960, was postponed, presumably as a result of military pressure which became more potent after the failure of the summit conference in Paris in 1960.

In relation to Germany Stalin's successors toyed with schemes for reunification, evacuation and neutralization, but in the knowledge that the Americans were committed to two propositions unacceptable to the USSR: reunification by means of free elections and not by sticking the two Germanies together (which the Russians wanted and which entailed treating the Federal Republic and the much smaller and undemocratically constituted Democratic Republic as equals), and freedom for the reunified state to make alliances (namely, to join NATO). At a conference in Berlin at the beginning of 1954 Eden and Molotov produced plans which demonstrated the impossibility of reaching agreement. Eden proposed reunification in five stages: free elections, a constituent assembly, a constitution, an all-German government and a peace treaty.

Molotov seemed ready to agree to elections on certain conditions but also wanted a 50-year European security treaty (with, it was later explained, the United States as a party) with a ban on joining other alliances; that is to say, he dropped the earlier Russian method of reunification in a bid to secure the dissolution of NATO. When this plan failed the USSR even suggested that it join NATO. In 1955 Bulganin and Khrushchev agreed to the evacuation and neutralization of Austria, and by the State Treaty of that year Austria recovered its full sovereignty within its January 1938 borders, subject only to two prohibitions: no *Anschluss* with Germany and no alliance with either side in the Cold War. (Since by the Warsaw Treaty of the same year the USSR acquired the right to station troops in Hungary and Romania, it lost nothing strategically by renouncing its postwar rights in occupied Austria and the concomitant rights of access through adjacent territories.) But Bulganin and Khrushchev secured no comparable arrangement for Germany, even though they recognized the Federal Republic and exchanged ambassadors with it. The attempt to stop the rearmament of the Federal Republic as a part of the anti-Russian alliance had failed. In the same year the Russians created a counterpart to NATO by the Warsaw Treaty and in 1956 the German Democratic Republic became a member of it.

In the same year the congress of the Communist Party of the Soviet Union, assembled for its twentieth session, was astonished to hear, first from Mikoyan and then from Khrushchev, wide-ranging and vehement denunciations of Stalin and Stalinism reaching back to what Lenin's wife had said more than 30 years earlier and to the murder of Kirov in 1934. This repudiation of the past, which did not long remain secret and included a specific undertaking to revise the USSR's relations with its satellite neighbours, contributed to risings in Poland and Hungary. In Poznan in Poland there were strikes for better wages and a conflict within the Polish Communist Party between the faction of Boleslaw Bierut, who had died earlier in the year, and the more nationalist faction led by Wladyslaw Gomulka, who had recently been released from a prison to which he had been consigned in 1949. Khrushchev, Bulganin and other Russian leaders went suddenly to Warsaw and vehemently invaded discussions in the central committee of the Polish party. They were, however, unable to prevent the victory of the Gomulka faction. Gomulka was appointed first secretary and the Russians, discovering that they must choose between allowing Gomulka to take over the government and using force to prevent it, chose the former course and accepted changes which included the dismissal of the defence minister, the Russian Marshal Konstanty Rokossovsky.

In Hungary the nature of the disturbances and their outcome were different. In July the established rulers Matyas Rakosi and Erno Gerö went to Moscow to urge reforms in order to forestall trouble. In October demonstrators demanded better wages and liberty. Hungarian police and Russian troops failed to prevent these demonstrations from turning into an anti-communist revolution. Imre Nagy, who had been prime minister from Stalin's death to 1955, was reinstated. Mikoyan and Suslov arrived from Moscow to direct operations and decided to back Janos Kádár, the reasonably well-regarded first secretary of the Communist Party who represented a compromise between the Rakosi/Gerö team and Nagy, but the revolution gained strength and after withdrawing their troops from Budapest for tactical reasons the Russians resorted to full-scale military measures. Faced with this turn of events, Kádár sided with the Russians, while Nagy named a new coalition government, promised free elections, proposed to take Hungary out of the Warsaw Pact and appealed to the outside world for help. With the western powers enmeshed at Suez and the USSR vetoing UN action, the revolution was extinguished in the first week of November. The reality of Russian power was underlined by the fact that the American administration not only took no action but never looked as though it might.

These events were a setback both for Khrushchev and for the policy of east–west *rapprochement*. Both, however, recovered. In June 1957 Khrushchev was attacked by Malenkov in the presidium of the Communist Party and defeated on a vote, but he resiliently summoned a meeting of the central committee which expelled Malenkov from the presidium and, for good measure, disgraced the veterans Voroshilov and Kaganovich and virtually exiled even Molotov, the oldest of old bolsheviks and the man who had been second only to Stalin among the civilians who had directed the war against the Germans. In October Zhukhov too was removed and replaced by Marshal Rodion Malinovsky. This year saw the triumph of Khrushchev over his adversaries and over the doctrine of collective leadership. In March 1958 he became prime minister as well as first secretary and he remained predominant until his unexpected fall in 1964. He reaped the benefit, in external affairs, of the dramatic appearance in 1957 of the first intercontinental ballistic missile and the first earth satellite (sputnik). From a platform thus fortified, and observing the alarm in the United States at the thought that the American technological lead had been eliminated, Khrushchev adopted peaceful coexistence as a general description of his intentions. Peaceful coexistence was a benevolent and reassuring (but not new) political slogan of vague import and useful variability. By it Khrushchev reverted to the belief that communism, while remaining unshakeably hostile to capitalism, would prevail over it without war. (The reassertion of this doctrine was intended, among other things, to enlist the sympathies of the emerging Third World.)

Khrushchev's problems in central Europe in 1956 and at home in 1957 were followed by critical developments in Germany and in Sino-Soviet relations. Throughout 1958 exchanges about and between the two Germanies had been clouding the atmosphere and the Poles were urging the USSR to find a way of preventing the Federal Republic from becoming a nuclear power and from making mischief in central Europe in association with NATO. Khrushchev was anxious to secure wider international recognition for the German Democratic Republic in order to stabilize the map of Europe and his own frontiers and facilitate the reduction of the USSR's costly military commitments abroad. He chose to begin with threats and when these did not work reverted to blandishments. He threatened to transfer the USSR's authority in Berlin to the German Democratic Republic unless a solution of the German problems were found within six months, but when the western occupiers contented themselves with controverting the USSR's right to act as it proposed, he toned down his ultimatum and then let it die. The failure of this gambit, coupled with Khrushchev's growing conviction that the United States did not intend to attack the USSR, and with the presentation to the twenty-first congress of the Communist Party in January 1959 of a seven-year economic plan which depended on switching funds from guns to butter, led to the second serious attempt to thaw the Cold War. After a visit to Moscow by Vice-President Richard Nixon, Khrushchev visited the United States, conferred privately with Eisenhower at Camp David, presented a plan for general and complete disarmament in four years to the General Assembly of the UN, and announced the second major cut in Russian military manpower. The centrepiece of the détente of 1959–60 was to have been a second summit conference in May 1960 but it was ruined by the shooting down of an American reconnaissance aircraft over Russian territory on 1 May. Reconnaissance flights by U-2 aircraft flying at great heights between bases in Norway and Pakistan provided the United States with valuable information at no political risk so long as the aircraft were not intercepted and their missions not made public by either side. The American president either did not know about the flights or had not thought of cancelling them in the pre-conference weeks, and the Russian government either had not thought of telling its defences to stop trying to shoot them down in this delicate period or – a plausible alternative view – had ordered them to do so. False statements in Washington about the aircraft's mission only compounded the American discomfiture because they were quickly exposed by the Russians, who had captured the pilot alive and with his spy kit.

After the consequent failure of the Paris conference Khrushchev repeated, in Warsaw and Moscow, his belief in the policy of *rapprochement*, but for the time being practical progress had been halted by the U-2 as surely as it had been halted in 1956 by the Hungarian revolution and it was arguable that Khrushchev had deliberately engineered this stop on his own policies in response to pressures from military and pro-Chinese lobbies. His *rapprochement* with the United States affronted the Chinese, who did not share his view about American aggressive intentions, resented and feared Russo-American confabulations, and refused to be mollified when he went to Beijing on his return from the United States. These views found some echo in the Kremlin. Further, Khrushchev's defence policy of relying on nuclear missiles and cutting non-nuclear forces was too bold for some of his colleagues. Although a Rocket Force Command was established under Marshal Nedelin (later succeeded by Marshal Moskalenko), the second cut was cancelled and at the twenty-second congress in October 1961 Malinovsky stated that he did not see eye to eye with Khrushchev. (This tussle was resumed in 1963–64 when cuts were again proposed and again opposed. Khrushchev was forced to promise that the cuts would be reasonable but this persistence was probably one of the causes of his downfall.) Finally, Khrushchev had discovered that his attempt to secure recognition of the German Democratic Republic by raising the Berlin question could be turned against him by the Americans, who proceeded to couple a settlement in Berlin with a general Russian withdrawal in Europe for which neither Khrushchev himself nor the ruling group in Moscow as a whole was ready.

After the dismal experiences of the 1950s the next decade opened with mixed signals. The Russo-Chinese quarrel had become public property (p. 126) and was held to be an incentive to Russo-American accords. In Washington the Eisenhower era was succeeded by the short presidency of John F. Kennedy, whose youth and intellect seemed to promise that the 1960s would be different from the 1950s and less grim. A ceasefire was arranged in Laos, but in an encounter with Khrushchev in Vienna Kennedy made no great mark and may even have left Khrushchev with the impression that the omens were propitious for an anti-American stroke. At any rate Khrushchev gave permission for a new essay in Berlin.

The government of the German Democratic Republic was threatened with collapse. Its citizens were escaping from it at the rate of 1,000 a day, which was economically and psychologically ruinous. Its boss Walter Ulbricht had to act urgently in order to maintain his regime, while Khrushchev was probably persuaded that if he did not support Ulbricht the crisis in the German Democratic Republic would lead to a war in Germany. He accordingly gave his consent to the erection of a wall between the eastern and western sectors in Berlin so that the eastern should become a part of the German Democratic Republic and the western might be made too uncomfortable for continued western occupation. In the night of 12 13 August the wall was built and the flow of refugees virtually stopped. Kennedy had told Khrushchev a few weeks earlier in Vienna that the United States remained committed to the use of all necessary forces to defend the status and freedom of Berlin. The building of the wall was a provocative act which the United States accepted and which may have influenced Khrushchev's estimate of how far it was safe to provoke the United States: in the next year in Cuba he himself was to venture much further than the East Germans.

Kennedy inherited from his predecessor a Cuban problem which was initially a chapter in the relations between the United States and Latin America. Its origins are described in Part Seven of this book. Kennedy was more riled by Castro than the more judicious Eisenhower had been and in April 1961 he aided an attempt by refugees to invade Cuba and overthrow Castro. It was immediately and totally unsuccessful. At some point thereafter Khrushchev, who was already giving Castro financial and diplomatic aid, decided on an audacious throw. Instead of merely helping Castro to remain in power, he decided to convert Cuba into a Russian base directly threatening the United States with Russian nuclear missiles. Surface-to-air missiles were despatched in the summer of 1962, followed by MiG 21 fighters, Il. 28 jet nuclear bombers and ground-to-ground (that is, offensive) missiles, of which 42 out of a projected 64 arrived early in October. This array included short-range Frog missiles designed to protect Soviet SS 4s and 5s against air attack or invasion and under the command of Soviet commanders authorized to fire them on their own initiative. The Americans became aware of this build-up but not of the missile sites or any missiles until 14 October when air reconnaissance unequivocally showed a launching pad and at least one missile. By that date Kennedy had publicly warned the USSR against creating an offensive Russian capability in Cuba and Khrushchev had stated positively that it was not doing so. After that date Kennedy knew that Khrushchev's assurances were mendacious and he was under considerable pressure from his chiefs of staff to deliver air strikes and invade Cuba. The president himself and his principal civilian advisers – notably Robert McNamara, defense secretary, and Robert Kennedy, attorney general – shrank from this step and adopted instead the device of proclaiming an embargo: within 800 miles of Cuba westward bound vessels might be stopped and searched. He explained this strategy to the American people by television and to his allies by special emissaries, and his ambassador at the UN Adlai Stevenson, displayed to the Security Council photographic proof of the threat which had prompted it. With the proclamation of the embargo on 22 October and its implementation two days later a critical point was reached between clash and compromise. On 24 October Khrushchev sent an ambiguously mollifying message which suggested that he was having second thoughts. The Americans intercepted a harmless vessel flying the Panamanian flag and allowed it to proceed and – at the suggestion of the British ambassador in Washington Lord Harlech – Kennedy reduced the 800-mile limit to 500 miles. The United States appeared to have stopped any reinforcement of the Russian weapons on Cuba but not necessarily to have secured their removal. In a further message on 26 October Khrushchev signalled a climb-down but it was accompanied by repeated assurances that the Russian operation had included no offensive weapons (and was completed) and it sought an American undertaking not to invade Cuba. This bargaining was stiffened by a yet further message the next day in which Khrushchev asked for a *quid pro quo* in the form of the removal of American missiles from Turkey whose usefulness had been suspect even to Eisenhower, who installed them. In this dilemma Kennedy chose to reply to the message of the 26th, ignoring that of the 27th, while in talks with the Soviet ambassador in Washington, Robert Kennedy effected an informal agreement to remove the American missile sites in Turkey. On this basis Khrushchev agreed to ship all Russian missiles back to the USSR. They were removed by the end of the year and American missiles were withdrawn from Turkey four months later.

Throughout these negotiations the UN secretary-general U Thant played a role as crucial as it was unobtrusive. The critical issue was whether Soviet vessels approaching Cuba would stop before reaching the point at which the American president had publicly committed himself to forcing them to do so. U Thant was the first to urge Khrushchev to order his ships not to cross the American interception line and Khrushchev promptly gave U Thant this undertaking. Khrushchev also agreed, in response to U Thant, to remove Russian missiles and bombers under UN supervision. U Thant flew to Havana, where he found Castro much less accommodating, partly because he feared

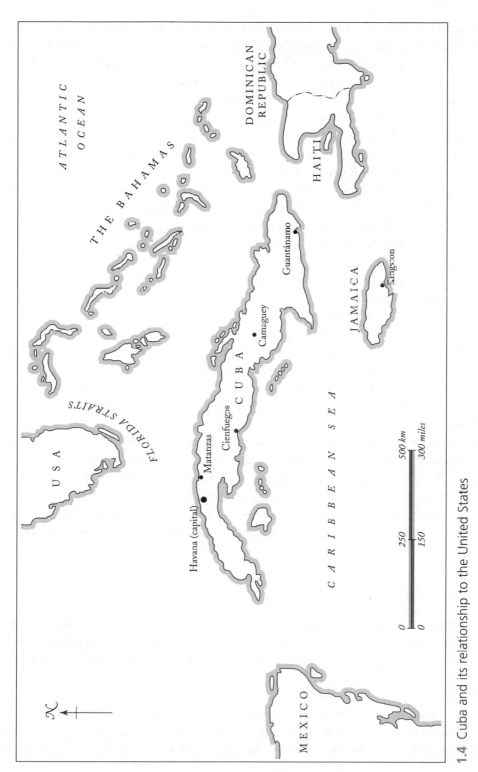

1.4 Cuba and its relationship to the United States

an American invasion but no less because Khrushchev had omitted to inform him of what he had agreed with U Thant. Castro had already announced that he would broadcast that day and he could not be dissuaded from doing so for more than one day, but in response to U Thant's pleas he toned down his speech, particularly an inflammatory condemnation of Moscow for accepting without recourse to him the presence in Cuba of a UN supervisory mission. U Thant later praised the statesmanship and diplomacy of Kennedy and Khrushchev but theirs were not greater than his. Strategically, the crisis ended as a victory for sense and cool management. In political terms it was an American victory: the Russian vessels and missiles went back. And to this victory there was an important corollary. For domestic reasons the American government had magnified the Russian nuclear threat to the point of representing the USSR as the leader in the nuclear arms race, an alarming judgement which was not true and never had been. Khrushchev's retreat enabled Kennedy and his successors to rid themselves of this pretence.

The clash off Cuba, like the conflict over Berlin 16 years earlier, brought the superpowers face to face and once more no shot was fired. Khrushchev's attempt to leap into equality with the United States was doubly insane, first, because the United States was bound to go to extremes to prevent nuclear weapons being installed on Cuba and, secondly, because the USSR was already well on the way to deploying submarine and other weapons which would threaten American cities without being placed on Cuba or anywhere on the American continent. Khrushchev was peaceably ousted by his own colleagues. The United States became deeply drawn into Vietnam after the Bay of Tonkin incident in August. From the mid-1960s the Cold War relapsed into static posturing, marginally shaken by peripheral adventures (Ethiopia, Afghanistan) and maintained by the arms race. It was also, on the American side, imbued with a new certainty. The nuclear bomb was not the only technological invention of the first importance. From the 1950s intelligence was transformed by striking developments in aerial surveillance, first by aircraft and later from satellites in space, which dispelled ignorance, defused paranoia and armed the United States with factual knowledge as well as brute force.

The arms race

In 1946 the United States had propounded the Baruch Plan for an international Atomic Development Authority which would control and own war-making nuclear activities and have the right to inspect all other nuclear activities. Upon the inauguration of effective international control, the United States would stop making nuclear weapons and destroy its existing stocks or transfer them to an international body. But the United States could not destroy its advanced technological knowledge and it would therefore retain a huge advantage over the USSR which, by accepting the American plan, would inhibit its own advances in nuclear physics. A. A. Gromyko proposed

instead a treaty banning the use of nuclear weapons, requiring the immediate destruction of existing stocks (which were exclusively American) and creating an international
control commission which would be subordinate to the Security Council and so to the
veto; inspection would be limited to those plants offered for inspection by the state in
which they were situated. The United States insisted that there could be no destruction
of stocks until effective international machinery had been established and was not
satisfied with the very limited range of the inspection proposed by Gromyko.

The USSR accepted the principle of international control but rejected international
ownership. It conceded that an international body might proceed in some matters by
majority vote and without a veto, but it insisted that any proposed enforcement action
must be subject to a veto. In the Russian view an international convention should be
reinforced by domestic legislation in each of the states signing the treaty but not by any
transfer of sovereign powers to an international organ empowered to carry out inspections and to observe whether the convention was being honoured. Inspection was not
entirely ruled out by the USSR but was to be limited to the inspection of proclaimed
nuclear establishments, excluding any search for clandestine activities. These attitudes
reflected the strategic realities of the moment. So did contemporary controversy over
the reduction of non-nuclear weapons, the United States wishing to link disarmament
of this kind with an agreement on nuclear weapons, while the USSR urged a proportionate reduction of forces (by one-third) which would alter the level of armaments
without disturbing the relative strengths of states in these types of armament.

In 1949, the year of the conclusion of the North Atlantic Treaty, the USSR exploded
its first nuclear weapon and in the next year it abandoned the UN Disarmament Commission (created in 1948 by fusing the Atomic Energy and Conventional Armaments
Committees). In 1952–53 the United States and the USSR exploded their first thermonuclear or hydrogen bombs within nine months of each other. Both rapidly developed
their means of delivery and in 1961 both put a man into space – the Russian Yuri
Gagarin leading the American John Glenn by six months. American stocks were at all
times much greater than Russian stocks and American superiority was enhanced in the
early 1960s as Polaris and Minuteman missiles came into service. Unfounded American
fears of a missile gap in the USSR's favour had the effect of spurring the United States
into extending what was a gap in its own favour.

The Baruch Plan was tacitly dropped. The USSR continued to oppose anything
which could be construed as international intervention in its affairs. The United States,
Britain and France proposed in 1952 quantitative limits for the armed manpower of all
states, and two years later Britain and France produced a new graduated plan designed
to reconcile the differing American and Russian priorities in a step-by-step disarmament process. The USSR countered with a programme which began with a reduction
in conventional forces and then in nuclear stocks and led to the elimination of bases
on foreign soil, a cut-off in nuclear weapons production and a conference on a test ban
treaty. The USSR also accepted quantitative manpower ceilings, thereby embarrassing

the United States whose worldwide commitments demanded larger forces than those envisaged. The United States proposed in return higher ceilings (which would nevertheless have required some reduction in American forces) and an 'open skies' inspection licence, whereby each side would keep the other under permanent observation from aircraft or satellites in orbit round the globe, but continued to press for an international control organ – even if subject to a veto – and rejected the idea of a ban on the use of nuclear weapons and destruction of existing stocks. In the American view the time for prohibiting the use of nuclear weapons had gone. The attempt, initiated by the Baruch Plan, to insulate the science of war from the latest advances in physics had to be abandoned.

The pretence that these disarmament plans were serving any practical purpose wore thin and palliatives were sought in schemes for disengagement, demilitarization and other forms of arms control. Disengagement – that is, putting a distance between opposing war machines by a mutual retreat from advanced positions – was attractive for a variety of reasons: it might minimize the risk of unpremeditated clashes, it might prove to be a successful experiment in local disarmament which could be repeated on a larger scale, and it might lessen political tensions in the centre of Europe and so lead towards a solution of the German problem. In 1955 Anthony Eden proposed limitations on forces in Germany and (unnamed) neighbouring states together with a system of inspection and verification controlled by a reunited German state and its four previous occupiers. Eden also proposed a European experiment in demilitarization, beginning with a zone along Germany's eastern borders, and added a few days later as an experiment in arms control a plan for mixed inspection teams on both sides of the division between eastern and western Europe. These ideas were not well received by the Americans or the West Germans, whom Eden failed to consult in advance and who objected to the implied recognition of the German Democratic Republic. Russian proposals presented by Gromyko in 1956 and 1957 for a zone of limitation and inspection were rejected on the same grounds. Similar plans were advanced by the leader of the British parliamentary opposition, Hugh Gaitskell. He proposed a gradual thinning out of foreign forces in the two Germanies, Poland, Czechoslovakia and Hungary and a ban on nuclear weapons throughout the same zone; the two Germanies would be reunited, the Federal Republic would withdraw from NATO and the three eastern states from the Warsaw military alliance. Finally, in 1957 the Polish foreign minister Adam Rapacki, with Russian backing, proposed at the UN General Assembly a ban on the manufacture and presence of nuclear weapons in both Germanies. He promised that Poland would follow suit, and the Czechoslovak government promised to do so too. The Rapacki plan dealt only with nuclear weapons in a specified area and did not overtly attack the surrounding political issues – the reunification of Germany, the freedom of Germany to join alliances, the presence of considerable American and Russian forces in central European states, the balance of American and Russian power in Europe, which would be unsettled by the removal of American nuclear forces without a corresponding withdrawal of Russian non-nuclear forces. It was rejected by the United States in 1958. Disengagement was thereupon dropped from the political agenda. It had been defeated by the entirely opposite trend of arming the two Germanies as separate contributions to the strength of the forward positions of the two rival blocs, by western fears of the USSR's large non-nuclear forces, by the NATO policy of putting nuclear weapons into forward positions, and by distrust of methods of inspection and verification. The fortification of the alliances had priority over the dismantling of them.

There was, however, some mutual inclination to restrict nuclear tests. The development of varieties of nuclear weapons, large and small, substantiated the need for tests, and these tests produced worldwide alarm about the effects of radioactive fall-out, especially after American tests in the Pacific in 1954 which killed some Japanese fishermen, poisoned vast numbers of fish and infected an area of 18,000 sq. km. In 1957 there was a cessation of nuclear tests by tacit agreement – partly a consequence of the conclusion of series of American and Russian tests at this time – and some preliminary examination of the possibility of a more formal and permanent ban. But there was a serious gap between what was acceptable to the United States and what to the USSR: on the constitution of a control organ and the voting within it, on the manning of control posts by observers of foreign nationality, and on the number of on-site inspections to be carried out in any year in a specified area. On all these matters the gaps between the protagonists were narrowed during discussions in 1958–60 but insufficiently to produce agreement before the destruction of the American U-2 aircraft over the USSR in May 1960 and the abandonment of the summit conference of that month temporarily ruffled the Russo-American *rapprochement*.

Less fruitfully, although with every appearance of seriousness, both superpowers sponsored unreal plans for general and complete disarmament and spent much time talking about them. The Russian proposals focused on such favourite objectives as the withdrawal of foreign troops and bases rather than on the less spectacular topics of control and verification with which American and British negotiators were more particularly concerned. The Russian plan, presented by Khrushchev to the UN General Assembly in 1959, was followed in 1960 by two American statements and a ten-nation disarmament conference at Geneva, which was short-lived but also the occasion for a joint Russo-American initiative in the shape of a series of recommendations elaborated by John J. McCloy and V. Zorin. No conference was held in 1961. The Americans and Russians agreed a set of principles but failed to agree on a statement about controls submitted by the Americans; both sides produced draft treaties on general and complete disarmament in time for the autumn session of the General Assembly.

The high-water mark of these negotiations was the McCloy–Zorin recommendations. These consisted of a set of principles to govern continuing disarmament negotiations, beginning with the acceptance of general and complete disarmament as an ultimate goal. This document was in effect an agreed statement of what had to be agreed. It clarified the issues but did not resolve them. It predicted the need to establish reliable procedures for the peaceful settlement of disputes and the maintenance of peace; the retention by each state of adequate non-nuclear forces for the preservation of law and order; the disbanding of superfluous forces and the elimination of all nuclear, chemical and bacteriological weapons, all means of delivering weapons of mass destruction, all military training institutions and all military budgets; an agreed sequence of stages in the disarmament process, subject to verification at the conclusion of each stage; balanced measures to ensure that neither side secured a temporary advantage as disarmament proceeded; and strict and effective international control of the process and thereafter through an International Disarmament Organization within the UN. This visionary package required agreement on the order in which different operations would be carried out, agreement on the equivalence of different types of armament, and agreement on the nature and modes of operation of an inspectorate. Agreement on these and other points required a degree of trust which no political leader felt or could have evinced without incurring plausible charges of gambling with national security. The Russians, for example, accepted at one stage the principle of inspection, but it transpired that what was to be inspected was weapons destroyed and not weapons surviving; they were reluctant to disclose what was left through fear of having it attacked and destroyed. Ingenious schemes for circumventing this difficulty, such as Professor Louis Sohn's proposal to divide national territory into zones and give inspectors the right to search only a limited number of zones at defined intervals, did not suffice to overcome nationalist conservatism.

The crucial feature of the revived disarmament discussion was the problem of inspection and verification (an element which had not obtruded in earlier negotiations such as those which preceded the Washington Treaty of 1922, though it had engaged the attention of the disarmament conference of 1932, which proposed a Permanent Disarmament Commission with powers of inspection but no powers of enforcement). The evolution of nuclear weapons had enormously increased the dangers of allowing a party to a disarmament agreement to cheat and conceal; he might by doing so gain the mastery of the world. But concealment was also regarded as one of the conditions of survival. To any power inspectors were potential spies who were licensed to discover and might then reveal how the inspected territory could be denuded of its defences at a blow. The impulses of politicians who took up disarmament for one reason or another were therefore continually countered by more cautious questionings which prevented the conclusion of any except partial agreements.

Partial agreements were, however, made on the cessation of nuclear tests in the atmosphere and on the neutralization of the Antarctic continent. Tests were resumed by the Russians unilaterally in September 1961, chiefly because they had proceeded to a point at which they had something new to test, whereupon the Americans and British offered to conclude a treaty banning atmospheric tests without any provision for inspection. But the Russians were not to be deterred from their new series of tests and shortly afterwards the Americans resumed testing too. At the end of the year the Russians proposed a treaty banning all tests, subterranean as well as atmospheric, without inspection; this proposal was immediately rejected, and the three powers reported to the UN their failure to agree and the abandonment of their attempts to do so.

Alarmed by this breakdown, the UN resolved to convene another disarmament conference, this time with 18 members, including eight neutrals, an innovation inasmuch as neutrals had not previously participated in test ban discussions but only in discussions on general and complete disarmament. The French, who were developing a nuclear armoury of their own and therefore had no wish to ban tests, took no part in the proceedings, but the neutrals (Brazil, Burma, Egypt, Ethiopia, India, Mexico, Nigeria, Sweden) proved persistent in devising compromises and keeping the discussions going. The debate on inspection was resumed between the nuclear powers and was narrowed down to a question of numbers, the western powers ultimately refusing to go below seven a year and the Russians refusing to concede more than two or three. In the early part of 1963 the failure of the talks was generally expected but was avoided and then converted into success largely by the unobtrusive pertinacity of the British prime minister Harold Macmillan. Khrushchev hinted publicly that a partial ban might be agreed and in July the United States, Britain and Russia agreed in Moscow the terms of a treaty banning nuclear tests in the atmosphere, in outer space and underwater for an unlimited period but subject to the right of any party to withdraw from its undertakings if its supreme interests were jeopardized by extraordinary events connected with the subject matter of the treaty. Many other states adhered to the treaty. They did not include China or France.

The conclusion of this treaty raised the question of what to try next. It gave a fillip to the partial approach and therefore to the search for parts ripe for tackling. Lyndon B. Johnson, who had become president in the United States upon the assassination of Kennedy in November 1963, listed some topics early in the next year. They included an anti-proliferation programme to include a total ban on nuclear tests, a ban on the transfer of nuclear materials to non-nuclear states and inspection of peaceful nuclear activities; a chain of observer posts to guard against surprise attack; a verified freeze on missiles; a verified cessation of the production of fissile material; and a ban on the use of force to alter boundaries or otherwise transfer territory from one state's control to another. Proposals from other quarters included a bomber bonfire (applying to B47s and Tu-16s) and percentage cuts in military budgets. In Poland Gomulka recast and revived the Rapacki plan by proposing, in December 1963, a nuclear freeze in Europe, which, however, the Americans disliked, partly because they attached little value to controls over the location of weapons unaccompanied by controls over their production, and partly out of deference to the suspicions of their German allies.

These plans bore no immediate fruit for three reasons. First, the achievement of the test ban treaty was as much as the leaders on either side could for the time being digest and make palatable in their own countries. More might become possible, but not too soon. Secondly, discussions within NATO about joint control over nuclear dispositions and nuclear weapons roused eastern fears of a nuclear Germany. The United States was caught between the desire for a continuing dialogue with the USSR and the desire to accord to its most effective continental ally the status and authority in allied councils which its contributions to the alliance warranted. (To the Russians the proposed NATO multilateral force (MLF – see p. 167) was a form of proliferation of nuclear weapons, although the Americans had devised it as an anti-proliferation policy to satisfy the Federal Republic and France with something less than independent nuclear forces.) And, thirdly, the increasing American involvement in Vietnam put an additional strain on Russo-American relations. The American attempt to buttress an independent and non-communist South Vietnamese state entailed war against the Vietcong, which ranked in communist terminology as a national liberation movement, and war against the communist state of North Vietnam, and something like war against the vastly more important communist state of China. For the Russians to fail to support President Ho Chi Minh of North Vietnam would be a betrayal of communist solidarity, dangerous at any time to Russian standing in the communist world and doubly dangerous at a time when Russian pre-eminence and doctrinal purity were being assailed by the Chinese. Further, for the Russians to fail to support the Vietcong was again doubly dangerous, for if the Vietcong lost, communists would blame the Russians, whereas if the Vietcong won without Russian help, Chinese influence might rout Russian influence in Asia. When by 1965 the Americans had become unconcealed principals in the war and not merely adjutants of the South Vietnamese, the scale and the nature of the fighting were changed and the Americans had to face worldwide protests against the ensuing horrors. The Russians joined in the outcry. Although, therefore, the evolution of nuclear strategies and the resurgence of China and the passage of time were combining to put an end to the bipolar Cold War, the principal adversaries were prevented by crisis in Asia and by habit from acknowledging the fact and acting on it: only de Gaulle did both.

Nevertheless, whether by understanding or as a result of blinder forces, a significant degree of stability and tolerance had evolved on the biggest question of the time: whether the Cold War would engender a nuclear war. In the nuclear age peace could be preserved so long as each side relied on the threat of retaliation to keep the other side from attacking first. But one side might conclude that the only way to avert an attack was to pre-empt it. Using the modern version of the pre-nuclear blitzkrieg, it would therefore adopt a counter-force strategy and build up, advertise and possibly use its power to destroy the enemy's war-making capacity at a single blow. In order to neutralize this strategy it was necessary to protect aircraft and missile sites so effectively as to make it unlikely that they could all be destroyed by a first-strike surprise attack. Their protection by anti-aircraft and fighter defences had been rendered obsolete by the enormous increase in the destructive power of each single bomb and by the vastly increased speed and accuracy of missiles. Two new and extremely expensive forms of defence were developed: missiles were placed in dispersed, hardened sites and, in the case of Polaris, under the sea in submarines; and an early warning system gave the defence enough time to get aircraft into the air and save them from being destroyed on the ground. Before the appearance of the intercontinental missile an early warning of two to three hours was achieved by the Americans, and when this was rendered inadequate it was improved to half an hour, at which point a part of the bomber force was kept always in the air and a part at 15 minutes' readiness on the ground. These measures to ensure the survival of an effective part of the retaliatory force, bombers and missiles, caused both antagonists to concentrate on second-strike strategies. It was essential to the success of this attitude that each side should be seen by the other to have adopted it, and it was a consoling feature of the later years of the Cold War that each side succeeded (with the help of the fact that a first-strike force differed in size and composition from a retaliatory force) in transmitting to the other tacit messages to this effect. The probability of a surprise attack diminished.

Nuclear forces could, however, be used in reply to a non-nuclear attack. The use of nuclear weapons was not ruled out by the reticence and deterrence of the two principal nuclear powers in relation to each other. Both could and did threaten to use them offensively in other contexts. In January 1954 Eisenhower and Dulles spoke on separate occasions of massive and instant retaliation. The last phase of the French war in Vietnam had begun and the Americans were faced with a choice between helping the French by a nuclear strike or letting them be finally beaten. The Americans tried to make political use of their nuclear armoury while knowing that they would not use it militarily; in a display of brinkmanship Dulles used tough language in order to scare the Russians and the Chinese and prevent them moving into the battle area – and perhaps in order to scare the British too and so get them to restrain him from a course from which he wanted to be diverted in any case. In 1956 Khrushchev, faced simultaneously with a war in the Middle East and a revolution in Hungary, made vague threats of using nuclear weapons in unspecified places in order to terrify the British and French governments and peoples and gain credit in the Arab world, and after the U-2 episode in 1960 he threatened smaller nations with nuclear attack if they facilitated American reconnaissance activities. But in the event both sides reserved their nuclear armaments for each other and became increasingly concerned not merely to keep nuclear weapons out of use but also to keep them out of other nations' hands. Yet one of the more sinister consequences of the Cold War was the postponement, throughout the 1950s and into the 1960s, of the realization of this common interest until after two other powers, France and China, had become nuclear powers and a number of others had acquired the capability and, in the absence of an international control system, the will to follow suit. During the Cold War the two protagonists had developed an increasing sobriety in relation to one another, even a sort of fearful intimacy. There was, however, no reason to suppose that other possessors of nuclear weapons would acquire sobriety with might, or – if, for example, they were Israel, Egypt or Iraq – would develop this intimate understanding of the permitted limits of nuclear politics; nor was there reason to suppose that the two giant powers would find it as easy to control the conflicts of others as to control their own.

These two problems – how to prevent a nuclear war between nuclear powers and how to prevent more states graduating to the nuclear elite – were aspects of the wider problem of arms control which superseded more traditional approaches to disarmament during the 1960s. Arms control, the regulation as opposed to the elimination of the use of weapons of war, was not new. It had been applied to naval weapons by, for example, the Rush–Bagot Treaty of 1817 which barred navies from the Great Lakes, and by the Washington treaties of 1922 and 1930 which sought to limit the naval power of one state in proportion to that of another. Interest in similar schemes was revived in the 1960s by scepticism about general disarmament, and academic discussion of arms control was taken up by politicians in Washington and Moscow who were feeling the need to communicate with one another (as in the Cuba missile crisis or the Middle East crises of the decade). The idea that major powers had more in common than the need to avoid mutual annihilation was further fortified by their common interest in their own superiority. Neither of them wanted to see nuclear weapons in other states' armouries and in 1968 they, together with Britain, concluded a Nuclear Non-Proliferation Treaty to which they invited all other states to adhere. The object of this treaty was to freeze the existing nuclear hierarchy, keeping France and China in the grade of second-rate nuclear powers and every other state permanently excluded from acquiring nuclear weapons. France and China predictably refused to sign at this point. From non-nuclear states there were sounds of discontent. Before subscribing to such an act of abnegation they objected that they should not be asked to forgo modern weapons without a better prospect of escaping embroilment in a nuclear war and they urged the nuclear powers to balance their enthusiasm for non-proliferation by a more serious attempt to control their own arms race.

The treaty came into force in 1970 and review conferences were held quinquennially. Hopes for a more comprehensive ban were vain so long as the principal nuclear powers continued to develop and test new weapons. Progress was limited to an agreement between the superpowers, concluded in 1974 but not ratified until 1990, limiting the scale of underground tests, and a further agreement of 1976, also ratified in 1990. South Africa adhered to the NPT in 1991 and destroyed nuclear devices constructed by the old regime. Brazil and Argentina renounced the production of long-range nuclear weapons. North and South Korea agreed in 1992 to make the Korean peninsula a nuclear-free zone but this did not prevent North Korea from firing long-range missiles over South Korea and Japan (see p. 152). China resumed tests in 1993. The 1968 treaty was renewed indefinitely by 178 states in 1995 but not without criticism of nuclear states, notably France and Britain, for their minimal compliance with their treaty obligations. In the same year Jacques Chirac resumed French tests in the Pacific shortly after his election as president. In 1998 India and Pakistan carried out nuclear tests (see p. 450). At this date only two countries, Israel and Cuba, had not acceded to the NPT. This treaty was supplemented in 1996 by a Comprehensive Test Ban Treaty to extend the ban to underground tests, introduce new restrictions on the manufacture of fissile materials and extend the scope of disclosure of trade in such materials. This treaty identified 44 states whose signature and ratification were needed to bring it into force and provided that a fresh conference be held if the treaty were not in force in three months of its conclusion. When this period expired in 1999 all the necessary signatures had been obtained except those of India, Pakistan and North Korea but Russia and China had failed to ratify and the United States Senate rejected the treaty by 51 votes to 48 without serious debate. (Disarmament and arms control were not limited to nuclear weapons. A Biological Weapons Convention of 1972 extended the ban (1925) on the use of such weapons to their manufacture. A Chemical Weapons Convention, concluded in 1993 after nearly 20 years' discussion and brought into force in 1997, did the same for these weapons.)

Alarm at the spread of nuclear weapons was accompanied by alarm at the development of weapons technology. The MIRV (multiple independent re-entry vehicle), whose separately controlled multiple warheads greatly increased the threat from each missile; and ABM (anti-ballistic missile) systems, which could counter a first strike and so destroy the deterrent stability which rested upon the presumptive efficacy of first strike, were enormously increasing the cost of the arms race. At the same time the deadliness of new missiles capable of landing within a few dozen yards of a target, combined with new defences which could destroy incoming missiles only at the cost of removing the deterrent factor which was designed to prevent their discharge in the first place, inclined the superpowers to talk about the control of the use and development, as well as the proliferation, of nuclear weapons. Strategic arms limitation talks (SALT) were begun in 1969.

Strategic arms are long-range weapons which can reach targets in another territory from bases or launching sites in one's own territory or on the high seas. They include missiles or bombs carried by long-range aircraft as well as missiles launched from static or mobile land sites or submarines. The category of strategic arms is complex and it is further complicated by the fact that a single missile with many warheads, each of which can be independently directed to a different target, is far from being the equivalent of a missile with a single warhead that can hit one target only. There are furthermore two incompatible ways of calculating the effectiveness of a nation's strategic armoury. On the one hand it may be assessed by the number of enemy targets theoretically vulnerable, an assessment which involves counting the number of independently targeted warheads deployed; or it may be assessed by the weight of explosive which can be delivered by all available launchers and aircraft on a single occasion. Finally, the category of strategic arms is not a closed one since there is argument about whether to include nuclear weapons of shorter range which are nevertheless brought within range of the enemy by being based on intermediate territory or capable of being sent there at short notice.

Given these complexities, it is remarkable that, by an exercise of political will over technical intractabilities, two agreements were signed in May 1972 (and two minor agreements in the previous year). In lengthy negotiations in 1970 at Vienna and Helsinki the Americans proposed a total ban on mobile land sites, a special limitation on particularly potent weapons and an overall numerical limit on the sum of the land and sea sites and bombers which either country might possess. Next year the two countries reached agreement on a seabed treaty banning the placing of nuclear weapons on the ocean floor and updated their agreement of 1963 for a hotline between Washington and Moscow by adapting to the new means of communication by satellites. The United States then proposed a standstill on the deployment of intercontinental land-based missiles and all submarine-based missiles. Concurrently, the negotiators tackled the defensive as distinct from the offensive aspects of strategic nuclear war by trying to set limits to the deployment of ABM systems, but the familiar problem of distinguishing a defensive from an offensive weapon bedevilled progress since it was impossible to say that every missile or launcher in an ABM system could never be used except for defensive purposes.

Notwithstanding these conundrums, an ABM treaty and an interim agreement on offensive missiles were concluded in 1972. The USSR had at this point an incomplete ABM system around Moscow and the United States was planning two systems for the protection of its intercontinental launching sites. The treaty, of indefinite duration although subject to quinquennial review, permitted each party to deploy two systems, one for the defence of its capital and the other for the defence of some part of its intercontinental missiles, the centres of the two systems to be not less than 1,300 km apart and the radius of each no more than 150 km; each system might contain 100 launchers, all of them static and capable of firing one warhead only. The agreement on offensive missiles was barer. It was of limited duration, would expire in 1977 and did no more than impose a freeze on new construction subject to a proviso permitting the substitution of more modern for obsolescent equipment on land and in submarines. The United States and the USSR also agreed to begin a second round of SALT talks.

SALT 2 was to be concerned with what had been omitted from the 1972 agreements. This was much. The United States maintained its plea, rejected by the USSR, to ban mobile land-based launchers totally. The Russians had tried but failed to include in the interim agreement specific provisions about long-range bomber aircraft which were still a significant part of the American armoury, although not of the Russian: the Americans had over 500 such aircraft and the Russians, who wanted each aircraft to count as one launcher, had 140. There had been no agreement about shorter-range aircraft based outside the United States: the Americans had about 1,300 such aircraft, capable of carrying nuclear weapons, 500 of them in Europe. Above all there was the problem of MIRVs. The USSR had, so far as was known, no operational MIRVs, although it had more intercontinental missiles than the United States. The United States, however, had begun deploying MIRVs on land (Minuteman 3) in 1970 and at sea (Poseidon) in 1971. By 1972 the USSR was believed to have 2,090 strategic missiles capable of hitting that number of targets, whereas the United States had 1,710 capable of reaching 3,550 targets and, within a few years as re-equipment with MIRVs proceeded, over 7,000 targets. The Russians were expected to begin deploying MIRVs in 1975, at which point the effectiveness of the Russian force in terms of targets reachable would begin to multiply while the American force, already largely re-equipped, would be static. So in order to retain their superiority and match the expanding number of warheads sprouting from Russian launchers, the Americans would have to increase the number of their launchers above the total frozen by the interim agreement. If they did not do this after 1977 the Russians would, it was assumed, have almost twice as many American targets in their sights by 1980 as the Americans had Russian. The Americans therefore were primarily concerned to set limits to the land-based missile capacity of each side. The Russians countered by proposing the elimination of American forward bases (aircraft bases in Europe and submarine bases in Spain and Scotland), a limitation on the number of aircraft carriers to be permitted in European waters (the Russians had no carriers of the conventional type but only carriers with helicopters or vertical take-off aircraft), and the relegation of nuclear-armed submarines to parts of the ocean from which they could not hit enemy territory. Progress in SALT 2 was in consequence laborious and negligible until Nixon visited Moscow in mid-1974, when the impasse was shifted by three minor accords: a modification of the ABM treaty, an agreement to ban underground weapons tests of 150 kilotons and over from March 1976, and agreement that a new SALT treaty would extend to 1985. This last agreement was reflected in November when Gerald Ford, who had stepped into the presidency when Nixon resigned in August, met Brezhnev at Vladivostok in an attempt to prevent the steam going out of Russo-American détente in general and SALT in particular. Ford and Brezhnev agreed that the talks should continue on the basis that each side might have up to 2,400 strategic launchers of all kinds (a somewhat high ceiling) of which no more than 1,320 might be fitted with MIRVs. The attempt to transpose this core into a formal agreement took years. The political will was there, fortified by the wish of both leaders to reach agreement before, in Brezhnev's case, the twenty-fifth congress of the Communist Party of the Soviet Union in February 1976 and, in Ford's, the presidential campaign which would take up most of that year. But the complexities and technicalities, themselves in constant flux, overpowered the negotiators. Discussions broke down in 1977 but a new president, Jimmy Carter, tabled fresh proposals and put a stop to the development of the neutron warhead and the long-range B-1 bomber. In 1979 a SALT 2 treaty was signed.

It was to run to 1985 when a third treaty was to continue the process. At its core was the restriction of nuclear delivery systems to 2,400 on each side, declining to 2,250 in 1985. Within this overall limitation there were interlocking sub-limitations in more precisely defined categories: MIRV'd systems together with aircraft-carrying cruise missiles; land-based and sea-based MIRV'd missiles; and land-based MIRV'd missiles alone. Missiles over a certain size, of which the United States had none and the USSR had 308, were banned. So too were air-launched missiles delivered otherwise than from aircraft. Limits were set on the number of warheads per missile and the number of cruise missiles per aircraft. Any launcher which fired a MIRV'd missile remained, for the purpose of the treaty, a MIRV'd launcher whatever weapons might be fixed to it. Restrictions, albeit modest, were placed on the modernization of weapons; they affected neither submarine delivery systems nor land-based intercontinental ballistic missiles and so permitted the deployment of the American Trident 1 and 2 and the MX mobile missile system, and their rough Russian equivalents. The parties to the treaty undertook to give notification of certain tests and stocks. A non-circumvention clause aimed to prevent either side from using a third party to get round its treaty obligations; this clause alarmed European members of NATO, who feared that the United States might interpret it as a prohibition on the transfer of new technology. A protocol to the treaty pointed the way towards further restrictions on the deployment, although not on the testing, of new weapons: for example, cruise missiles (other than cruise missiles delivered from aircraft) with an extended range. In the United States the Senate Foreign Relations Committee recommended ratification of the treaty but public protest and expert disquiet (which concentrated on what the treaty did not secure) and the Russian invasion of Afghanistan killed it. Non-ratification was a prominent feature in Ronald Reagan's bid for the presidency in 1980.

The political atmosphere had become uncongenial to such agreements. The late 1970s were a time of increasing mistrust. On the American side the Russo-Cuban intervention in Angola in 1975 began a series of Russian moves – Ethiopia, Vietnam and Afghanistan were widely separated theatres of menacing Russian activity – which hardened American distrust and sharpened the American concern for rearmament rather than arms control. At this time too, official American estimates of the size of the Russian defence budget were drastically increased. The passage of the warship *Kiev* from the Black Sea to the Mediterranean, an incident which would hardly have ruffled the waters a few years earlier, led to charges that the USSR had broken the Montreux Convention of 1936 (on the assumption, which was contested, that the *Kiev* was an aircraft carrier within the meaning of that instrument). In 1979 a more serious scare was caused, and deliberately publicized, by the discovery of a Russian brigade in Cuba. President Carter had stopped American intelligence flights over Cuba as a conciliatory gesture, but these were resumed when Cuba was suspected of having a hand in revolution in Nicaragua. What they revealed was a Russian training unit which had been in Cuba for some years, but the temper of the times converted it into a new threat to the United States.

On the Russian side entente between the United States and China, and Deng Xiaoping's attempt to turn it into a triple alliance with Japan, aggravated Moscow's enduring fears of encirclement, which became more acute as the USSR became increasingly dependent on American grains to feed its beasts and so its peoples. The USSR alleged, and perhaps believed, that its troubles in Afghanistan and Poland were accentuated by American undercover interference. Its ageing leadership (procedures for an orderly succession had never been evolved) was plagued at home by an economy which failed to secure basic amenities and was consigning perhaps 20 per cent of GNP to armaments and defence.

Concurrent with this worsening of the political climate were technical advances which were altering the nature of the arms race. The nuclear deterrent had been a crude and inflexible weapon, whose effectiveness depended on its crudeness and inflexibility. It was aimed at cities and their inhabitants. On the American side there were until the late 1970s only two courses that an American president could take in an emergency. He could order an attack on all the targets on which his weapons were trained; or he could order the destruction of all these targets except Moscow. He had no third choice, and because he had none his armoury posed a most fearful threat to the USSR. It was an effective deterrent – so long as it was possible to believe that the president would use it.

But during the 1970s this credibility began to wear thin. Would a president nerve himself to order so vast a massacre within the minutes available to him for a decision? The very question undermined the strategy of deterrence. It also revived American fears that the USSR would be tempted to revert to a first-strike strategy. At the same time the refinement of targeting techniques enabled strategists to think once more in terms of waging war instead of deterring it. The aggressor might attack a single pinpointed military target, such as a missile site or a command headquarters or a bunker containing a head of state; each side might then exchange attacks on such single targets and carry on a war for weeks or months. Surviving a war, even winning a war – concepts which had seemed nonsense in the early nuclear age – became possibilities.

A special element in the contest between the superpowers, making that contest global, was the growth of Russian naval power in the 1970s. If a great power is a power that can act in any quarter of the globe – and that is as good a definition as any – then sea power is crucial. The United States was without question a great naval power capable of sailing all the world's oceans and of commanding passage through all but the most private waterways. The USSR was not such a power but was determined to become one. Because it was aiming to be what it was not, its efforts roused considerable alarm. The world was not used to seeing Russian fleets in many oceans, but the universalization of Russian power required this to happen. On land the USSR had advanced little since 1945. Its hold on eastern Europe, although sometimes troubled, remained undisputed and with it the power to pose a threat to western Europe whose credibility was a constant conundrum. It had established in the 1950s its rights to be considered a power in the Middle East, although in the 1970s the limits of this power were exposed by its eviction from Egypt and by its negative role in the diplomacy that followed the war of 1973. Its sallies into the Congo in 1960 and the Caribbean in 1962 were failures, its role in the wars in South-east Asia marginal, the poor performances of communists in Portugal and Greece in 1974 disappointing, the illness and absences of Brezhnev and the uncertainty of the succession a source of hesitations. Its economy and the quality of life of its peoples remained vulnerable to the vagaries of the weather and of an unwieldy bureaucratic system, both of which could perpetrate massive shocks. For all its vast armed strength the USSR was in one vital respect a power of a different kind from the United States, a power still confined whereas American power roamed free. The seaways, and the under-seaways, offered one escape from this inferiority.

By the mid-1970s the Russian navy surpassed the American in the number of its submarines but was inferior in every other respect. American naval manpower, including marines, was 733,000 against 500,000 Russian equivalents. The United States had 15 aircraft carriers, the USSR had none other than helicopter carriers; of cruisers and destroyers with nuclear weapons the United States had 110 and the USSR 79. But the USSR had 265 submarines against 75, albeit that in nuclear-powered submarines the balance was more even at 75 Russian to 64 American. Such figures ignore a great deal, and a closer comparison of the two navies would have to take account of the age of vessels, their armaments, each nation's reserves, research expenditure and other indicators of comparative effectiveness. Political effectiveness moreover is not the same as military effectiveness. What would happen if the two navies engaged each other in combat was a nearly academic question, but the effect of the appearance of a Russian flotilla of any size in, for example, the Mediterranean was not. This fleet varied between 25 and 60 surface and submarine vessels, sometimes larger in numbers and sometimes smaller than the US Sixth Fleet but without air cover, smaller than the French, much smaller than the Italian and trivial beside the combined forces of NATO in this theatre. It was none the less a portent. It had its effect on the conduct of relations between the USSR and Algeria and Libya, two strategically placed anti-western but not pro-Russian states. It reminded western governments that their fears, acute in the late 1940s, of Russian bases in Yugoslavia and Albania might yet one day be realized, with incalculable consequences for Mediterranean politics. A foretaste of these consequences was provided by the prime minister of Malta Dom Mintoff, whose search for money for his impoverished island led him to demand from Britain greatly increased fees for the use of Malta's harbour, with more than a hint that if Britain did not care to use it at the going price the Russians would. As a result Mintoff secured in 1972 a rental of £14 million a year for seven years, of which Britain's NATO partners were to provide £8.74 million, and additional lump sums of £2.5 million from Italy and £7 million from other members of NATO.

The election of Ronald Reagan to the presidency of the United States in 1980 owed a great deal to the feeling that the United States ought to be making better use of its power instead of striking deals with an adversary that was getting stronger and was not to be trusted. Reagan was not the choice of the nation's political leaders. He was the choice, in the first place, of a group of reactionary conservatives with enough money to buy for him the candidature of the Republican Party and, secondly, of the people at large who liked his personality and simplicity and responded to his forthright reduction of public issues to contests between good and evil in which it behoved the good to exert themselves with more faith than calculation. Reagan retained his popularity and won re-election in 1984 by a landslide. He had powerful support in western Europe, which likewise moved to the right in the early 1980s. In Britain Thatcher's electoral victory in 1979 brought to power a prime minister who was temperamentally in favour of tough talking and acting (and was also committed to monetarist economic policies which she believed to be the same as his); her success at the polls was repeated in 1983, when the Labour Party's espousal of unilateral disarmament was a major element in a disastrous campaign, and again in 1987. In West Germany conservatives triumphed when Helmut Kohl ended 13 years of socialist rule in 1982 and began a stint which lasted until 1998. Left-wing parties lost power in Norway and Belgium (1981) and the Netherlands (1982) and although France elected a socialist president in 1981, François Mitterrand proved to be more explicit than his predecessor in his support for the deployment of cruise and Pershing II missiles in Europe, even though he was also critical of American policies in Africa and Central America and went so far as to give encouragement to Reagan's enemies in Nicaragua. Until the unforeseen advent of Gorbachev in 1985 the western alliance was at least superficially united behind the tough attitudes expressed by Reagan, and disarmament at all levels from the SALT process to non-nuclear forces appeared to be stalled.

But there were currents of a different kind. The shift to the right in Europe cleared the ground on the left for criticism of American policies more trenchant than left-wing parties were wont to express when in government. Reagan's bellicosity towards the USSR, however congenial in the United States, found fewer echoes among Europeans who, much as they disliked and distrusted the USSR, were convinced of the need for a *modus vivendi* with it and did not believe that the threats and abuse to which the president seemed naturally drawn were a sensible way forward. They consorted ill with his affirmation of a two-track policy – strength plus negotiation – and made his readiness to negotiate look shallow and insincere, particularly after his unbridled speech at Orlando, Florida, in March 1985 when he stigmatized the USSR as an evil empire destined for the dustbin of history. His apparent belief that the USSR could be forced to disarm by an escalation of American armaments – a bigger Trident programme, the resurrection of the discarded B-1 bomber, MX missiles, all of which were approved by Congress and, in the case of MX, later expanded – dismayed many among his allies as both dangerous and silly, his 'Star Wars' programme doubly so. In the background were laser beams, chemical weapons and other alternatives to nuclear weapons.

When General Jaruzelski imposed martial law in Poland and imprisoned many of his political opponents Reagan, treating Jaruzelski as a mere Kremlin puppet, imposed sanctions on the USSR as well as Poland and did so without consulting his European allies, who regarded these moves as ineffective and economically hurtful to themselves. He, in his turn, regarded them as soft on the USSR and their proposals for a mere freeze on Polish borrowing as ludicrously feeble. A more serious conflict arose when Reagan moved to obstruct the building of a pipeline for conveying gas from the USSR to Europe – a project of significance for western Europe as well as the USSR but regarded in the United States as malign strengthening of the USSR, which would double its exports of gas by the end of the century and so earn much-needed foreign currency. In using events in Poland to impose sanctions against the USSR Reagan threatened those European businesses which were participating in the construction of the pipeline and had subsidiaries or operations in the United States. This threat to extend the effects of sanctions to European firms was resented as impertinent and illegal. A compromise was reached at Versailles in June 1982 but it immediately broke down, whereupon Reagan – against the advice of his secretary of state Alexander Haig, who resigned – imposed sanctions, which the Europeans ignored. By the end of that year the affair had fizzled out, governments on both sides of the Atlantic being concerned to secure the planned deployment of cruise and Pershing without too much fuss. For the same reason – the solidarity of the alliance – disagreements over other matters were kept down to the muttering level (over American partiality for South Africa and the consequent stalling of negotiations on Namibia, over American policies in the Middle East and Central America), and even the American invasion without notice of a member of the Commonwealth, Grenada, was handled by Thatcher with decorous restraint in public.

A second problem was more technical. It had been convenient to keep discussions on nuclear and non-nuclear weapons separate, and to divide nuclear weapons into distinct categories – long-range, intermediate and battlefield. But this way of handling the broad field of disarmament was proving unreal. At the core of SALT was the attempt to set limits to the delivery systems which either side might possess. The fixing of numbers was a matter for haggling. More difficult was the definition of the systems which the treaty should cover. The weapons on either side were not precisely comparable, nor was it any longer easy to agree which were strategic and which not. The Americans wanted the treaty to include the Russian Backfire bomber, which, with its in-air refuelling service, was arguably a strategic weapon capable of hitting American cities; and also those categories of mobile missile (such as the SS-16) which, although classified as intermediate, were easily convertible into an SS-20 strategic missile. The Russians were as much concerned about NATO's intermediate-range weapons in Europe as with the ultimate deterrent based in the United States. The USSR was deploying SS-20s targeted on European cities at the rate of about one a week and striving to delay the renovation of NATO's counter-weapons in the European theatre. Thus the limitation of strategic arms – the province of the bilateral SALT talks – could no longer be divorced from the development and deployment of theatre weapons, which involved all the NATO allies and not merely the United States. The regulation of intermediate weapons (INF) became therefore interlocked with the SALT process, now renamed START.

Throughout the 1970s NATO's nuclear capacity in Europe had lain largely in its aircraft delivering air-to-ground missiles – the British Vulcan and the American F-111 – but in the face of the deployment of the SS-20 NATO resolved in 1979 to deploy new intermediate weapons (464 cruise missiles, non-ballistic, low-flying and very accurate, and 108 Pershing II ballistic missiles) in five European countries, thereby reducing by a factor of five the time needed for a retaliatory strike against targets in the USSR. This decision, urged on the Americans by the Europeans and particularly by West Germany, was to some extent a miscalculation. The SS-20, which began to replace the SS-4 and SS-5 from 1976, was a mobile launcher with three warheads and a range of 5,000 km: the SS-4 and SS-5, in service from 1959 and 1961 respectively, had single warheads with ranges of 2,000 and 4,000 km. Together with the TU-26 (Backfire) aircraft the SS-20 greatly strengthened the Russian position in Europe. The European members of NATO wanted a similar weapon within the theatre in order to square up to the SS-20, reassert the credibility of NATO's strategy in Europe and reknit the Euro-American linkage which, Europeans feared, was becoming frayed. But European leaders underestimated the opposition of their electorates to this proliferation of nuclear weapons and the USSR was able to play on this dissension in the hope of getting NATO's 1979 resolve reversed. In 1981 NATO, in order to placate the critics in its midst, adopted the 'zero option' for INF – that is to say, their total elimination – in the conviction that the USSR would reject it, which it immediately did. The manoeuvring continued with an offer by Moscow to withdraw SS-20s in return for the abandonment of the cruise/Pershing II deployment and a later offer to destroy considerable numbers of them for the same consideration. The key to the manoeuvring was in Bonn and it ended when the Bundestag confirmed the acceptance of West Germany's quota of Pershing IIs. Their arrival at the end of 1983 marked the failure of the Russian attempt to stop the programme. Moscow strengthened its nuclear forces in East Germany and Czechoslovakia and broke off all negotiations, including the START talks on strategic weapons as well as the INF negotiations.

At this point the USSR was confronted with a fresh development which it was even more anxious to obstruct than the deployment of cruise and Pershing II. This was Reagan's Strategic Defence Initiative (SDI), unveiled in 1982. The SDI emphasized the distinction between offensive and defensive nuclear weapons. It consisted of startling new proposals for defence against nuclear attack which, if practicable, would destroy nuclear missiles after they had been fired and so provide invulnerability against a first strike. The president proposed to spend $26 billion on research over an initial five years. This stupendous cost and the implications for the American economy and budget (which the president had promised to reduce) added to the air of fantasy implicit in SDI's nickname of Star Wars. There were also more sober doubts. Many experts thought the proposals intrinsically unworkable or even absurd. They were untestable to any precise degree except in war. They were open to the objection that, by the time they were developed, counter-measures would also have been developed. They seemed to entail contravention or denunciation of the ABM treaty of 1972 or a request to amend it which would give the USSR a chance, by refusing, to provoke fresh friction in the relations between the United States and its European allies. (Washington began at this time to claim, correctly, that the ABM treaty had already been broken by the USSR.) Most important: SDI aimed to replace deterrence by defence and so was bound to undermine the deterrence which, however crude and unappealing, had helped to keep the peace between the superpowers for a long generation. In western Europe governments were unwilling to be too openly critical, partly because they did not want to add to discord within NATO but also because Reagan invited them to share in the research and they sensed, mistakenly, that there was a great deal of money to be made by accepting.

The disarmament scene was transformed by a change in leadership in Moscow and a change of heart in Washington. Gorbachev was a new broom who needed above all to cut costs in order to save the USSR from catastrophe and Reagan, whether coincidentally or not, decided to exchange the role of Great Scourge for that of Great Peacemaker. In 1985 the two leaders met in Geneva. Nothing of great consequence was agreed but they met and – as when Napoleon and Alexander met on their raft at Tilsit – there was a kind of humanity about the mere event which cheered onlookers and was deemed to be a part of statecraft. More potent was the stark fact that the USSR was incapable of financing the Cold War and the United States too was heading towards insolvency. As both superpowers took account of the depreciation of their super-status in the world, they were forced to acknowledge the need to disarm.

The position on disarmament when Gorbachev came to power was as follows. The reduction of non-nuclear forces in Europe had been under discussion in Vienna since 1974 between all the members (22) of NATO and the Warsaw Pact. These discussions were designated MBFR (Mutual and Balanced Force Reductions). Proposals for thinning out conventional forces in central Europe were first made by NATO in 1969 and 1970, and in 1973 NATO proposed a 15 per cent cut by both sides in the central sector to be followed by a reduction to 700,000, which proportionately would be a bigger cut by the Warsaw alliance than by NATO. The Warsaw Pact responded by proposing initial cuts of 20,000 by both sides, followed by a 5 per cent reduction and then a 10 per cent reduction. This scheme, more proportional than numerical, reflected the Warsaw Pact's advantage in numbers, which it designed to keep. NATO, on the other hand, favoured a mainly numerical approach leading to a parity in numbers which it did not possess. After these opening gambits nothing much happened and nobody seemed to be in a hurry that it should, until 1979 when Brezhnev – possibly in order to sow doubts among the NATO allies about the wisdom of NATO's programme for modernizing its theatre weapons – announced the impending withdrawal of 1,000 tanks and 20,000 men from East Germany. The talks continued, however, to be bedevilled by inadequate and suspect statistics and by the problem of verification. They were wound up in 1989 after nearly 500 sessions and were submerged in a new Vienna colloquy in which all European states were involved and the subject matter was extended to the entire area from the Atlantic to the Urals. This successor conference was dubbed CFE (Conventional Forces in Europe). An even larger group of 35 states – 33 in Europe plus the United States and Canada – deriving from the Helsinki Final Act in 1975 and its review conference, had since 1983 been discussing security and co-operation in Europe (Conference on Security and Cooperation in Europe [CSCE]) and it convoked in 1986 in Stockholm a Conference on Confidence- and Security-Building Measures and Disarmament in Europe (CDE). Whereas the function of the MBFR/CFE negotiations was to reduce the size of the armed forces of NATO and the Warsaw Pact in central Europe and beyond, the CDE was concerned with the movements of these forces and the framing of rules to obviate surprise attack (and the fear of surprise attack) through such measures as advance notification of movements involving more than a given number of men or tanks. A CFE Convention of 1990 was affirmed and elaborated in 1997.

In the nuclear field both strategic and intermediate weapons were under discussion, the former wholly, the latter primarily, in the province of the superpowers. At their first meeting, at Geneva, Reagan and Gorbachev had declared themselves in favour of halving their long-range or strategic nuclear weaponry and finding an interim agreement on INF. Gorbachev had inherited his predecessors' failure to prevent the deployment of new NATO INF in Europe. He was anxious to use his bargaining position over strategic weapons to halt Reagan's SDI. After Geneva he tried to accelerate the disarmament process with a surprising proposal for the elimination of all nuclear weapons of all categories by the year 2000. The United States responded with a mixed package which repeated the Geneva target on strategic weapons and coupled it with the removal of all INF from Europe in three years and the continuing attempt to remove the imbalances in the two sides' conventional forces. Gorbachev declared himself flexible on INF and willing to accept a reduced cut in strategic weapons – 30 per cent instead of 50 per cent – and he also modified his tactics on SDI by implying that some research might be permissible provided the United States undertook to observe strictly the ABM treaty for the next 15 to 20 years. He thereby set the development of SDI firmly within the existing ABM regime and argued for a precise term during which it might not be amended. The United States, while maintaining the proposal to reduce strategic weapons by half, proposed that the ABM treaty be guaranteed for seven and a half years on condition that SDI weapons might be deployed from 1992 (they could not in fact be ready for deployment before that date) and that after 1992 SDI technology would be shared with the USSR. The essence of the American position was to secure freedom of action after a given period during which the constraints in the ABM treaty would be observed. This was the position when Reagan and Gorbachev met again at Reykjavik in Iceland.

They wished, without saying so, to end the arms race. Gorbachev wished in addition to improve relations with Western Europe ahead of abandoning the rest of it. His overt aim was to affirm the goodwill established at Geneva; to stop SDI; affirm the strict letter of the ABM treaty for a fixed term and, if possible, strengthen its provisions on testing by getting the United States to agree that while laboratory tests might be permissible, tests in space were not; remove all INF from Europe; and negotiate the reduction of strategic weapons by 50 per cent or at least 30 per cent. He was prepared to limit INF in Asia to 100, and to discuss – and meanwhile freeze – short-range weapons (less than 500 km). He rejected Reagan's offer to share SDI technology. On his side Reagan wanted all INF to be eliminated in Asia as well as Europe. He was not prepared to yield anything on SDI. Surprise at the progress marked by these exchanges was turned to astonishment by a new proposal which appeared to be approved by both leaders, although some doubt was later cast on Reagan's endorsement of it. This proposal was for the complete elimination of nuclear weapons of all kinds in ten years, this process to be geared to the elimination of 50 per cent of strategic weapons in the first five years and the remaining 50 per cent in the next five. The confused euphoria emanating from Reykjavik was dampened when it became apparent that without concessions on SDI Gorbachev would sign nothing. He had failed in his main aim.

He returned to the attack in 1987 by repeating his Reykjavik offer on INF (zero in Europe, 100 in Asia) but without linking it to agreement on SDI, to which the United States replied by agreeing on condition that the USSR's surviving INF should be out of range of western Europe and Japan. This *rapprochement* brought up the question of short-range weapons, which had been skirted at Reykjavik, and Gorbachev sprang another surprise by proposing their total elimination (the 'third zero'). He also agreed to forgo the 100 INF in Asia. The outcome was an INF treaty concluded in Washington at the end of the year, and in force from June 1988, for the destruction of all INF weapons by 1991, the USSR being thereby required to destroy more than twice as many missiles and launchers as NATO.

A START I compact was completed after a ten-year gestation when it was signed by Presidents Bush and Gorbachev in 1991. It was followed two years later by START II, signed by Bush and Yeltsin to come into force provided START I did so. By START II the United States and Russia were to reduce their stocks of land-based strategic nuclear weapons from 12,600/11,000 to 3,500/3,000, sea-based weapons to 1,750 each and eliminate all MIRV'd weapons – all over ten years. Some variations, entailing concessions by the United States, were agreed to take account of particular Russian objections. The implementation of these agreements was complicated when the one party to them split into numerous states, four of which – Russia, Ukraine, Belarus and Kazakhstan – possessed on their territory weapons within the scope of the agreements. The last three of these states separately undertook to implement the agreements, to clear their territory of all relevant weapons within seven years and also to adhere to the Non-Proliferation Treaty. (Ukraine prevaricated but fell into line: see p. 70.) Between the signature of the two treaties, both superpowers took unilateral decisions which further reduced their strategic and non-strategic armouries. START II was ratified by the US Senate in 1996 but the Russian parliament withheld its assent in the hope (initially) of securing favourable modifications and embarrassing Yeltsin. In order to circumvent this obstacle, the American and Russian governments inaugurated a START III which, by an agreement between the two presidents at Helsinki in 1997, was to come into operation only after the implementation of START II, which was extended from 2003 to 2007. START III was to reduce still further the nuclear armouries of the two states and provided also, and for the first time, for the destruction of warheads as well as the means of their delivery – an innovation which must entail peculiarly rigorous verification procedures.

The arms race of the superpowers had been an economic catastrophe sustained by the psychology of the Cold War. The abatement of the Cold War created new problems for both sides: for the Russian side, how to preserve the semblance of superpower status; on the western side, what to do about NATO. NATO had owed its effectiveness to its huge – mainly American – power and this power had masked doubts about the credibility of its successive strategies. In its first, formative years NATO had adopted, at Lisbon in 1952, a programme to create forces, including German units, capable of fighting a prolonged non-nuclear war, but these forces never came into existence and NATO was refashioned as a link in a chain or ladder whose credibility depended on the existence in the chain of nuclear weapons of rising malignity. This doctrine of flexible response went through a number of phases. The invention of short-range nuclear weapons enabled NATO to plan for smaller forces with more ferocious weapons but once again the targets (set in 1957) were not reached. NATO's role was, however, set as that of a delaying agency. Whether with non-nuclear weapons or short-range nuclear weapons or intermediate nuclear weapons NATO would resist an attack and cause the attacker to think again before carrying on with his operations. Although this vision of a future conflict was not demonstrably ridiculous, it was difficult to see a war developing in this way and NATO's military function was therefore always ambiguous. It relied on the assumption that the aggressor's first step or steps would be taken without much thought but that the same thoughtless aggressor would quickly be made to think better. But whatever the practicalities were likely to be, the theory demanded a graduated response which, given NATO's make-up, was a graduated nuclear response. When Reagan was persuaded at Reykjavik to approve zero options for both INF and strategic weapons he was removing the steps in the ladder – and at the same time dismantling the American strategic nuclear umbrella which Europeans had learnt to regard as the ultimate guarantee of their security. The European dilemma was intensified when Gorbachev proposed to apply the zero option to short-range or battlefield nuclear weapons also. The response could no longer be flexible and a Russian attack would start with considerable advantages, offset only by the counter-fear of an all-out American riposte with what might be left of the strategic missile force.

The Reagan–Gorbachev exchanges of 1986–87 and the ensuing START agreements checked the arms race but did not give Gorbachev what he needed in the long term. This phase of the Cold War ended without any settlement or even discussion of the opponents' relations in their principal field of battle: Europe. That issue was only fleetingly and obliquely addressed when the United States, rather than making peace or at least constructing a working relationship with the evolving new Russia, gave priority to bundling Moscow's ex-satellites into NATO. Gorbachev's failure to do better probably contributed to his own downfall and to the incoherent, although at times brave, politics of Yeltsin, so bequeathing to Putin an isolated and disintegrating state, its remaining strengths much overrated (as in 1945) but adequate if he could master local proconsuls and oligarchs, defeat separatism in the Caucasus and reassure the Russian peoples with the right amount of bravado.

The perplexities of the United States

The 1980s were the decade in which the superpowers ceased to be regarded as so far above and beyond all other states as to constitute a distinct species. This was preeminently true of the USSR, which no longer looked like a match for the United States, was no longer able to dominate central or eastern Europe, was in acute economic decline and was threatened with disintegration. The depreciation of the United States, although of a very different order, was hardly less startling, given its unchallenged superiority over the past generation and its continuing massive resources and massive industrial and agricultural output.

The decline in American power and prestige was self-inflicted, a consequence of mistakes and misjudgements in economic management and external policies. Fumbling in foreign affairs was most unhappily displayed in Central America, where Reagan failed in his declared intention to pacify the small republic of El Salvador and make it safe for a decent right-wing democracy. In Panama the United States subsidized a known drug dealer and, when his crimes became too blatant, failed to unseat him by bribery and resorted to a military invasion on a flimsy pretext. In Nicaragua Reagan failed to overthrow the Sandinista regime in spite of waging an expensive vicarious war and resorting to clear breaches of international law, for which the United States was censured by the International Court of Justice; the government of President Daniel Ortega was later defeated not by arms but by the economic sanctions which led Nicaraguans to vote against Ortega in elections of surprising democratic rectitude. (For these matters see Chapter 28.) These failures against weak neighbours in the American continent itself betokened an inadequate grasp on the uses of power. The United States was the world's greatest military and industrial power and yet unable to operate efficiently as a regional power.

In the Middle East the United States, confronted with the loss of its ally, the shah of Iran, and the seizure of hostages from the American embassy by the new regime, became mired in contradictions and subterfuge: the moral imperative to rescue the hostages clashed with the publicly reiterated determination not to let terrorism pay. During the elections of 1980 the release of the hostages was obstructed – to Carter's detriment and Reagan's benefit. It was then effected by secret negotiations involving the supply of arms to Iran via Israel from 1980 to 1986 when public scandal put an end to it. High prices were exacted for the arms and the money was used to arm the Nicaraguan Contras by devious means by which the conspirators – who included President Reagan and Vice-President Bush – deceived the Congress and people: a combination of the illicit and hypocritical which the president and his advisers sought to justify on vaguely ideological grounds.

The second and associated venture arose from the determination to go on arming and funding the Contra opposition to the Nicaraguan government covertly and in defiance of the Boland amendment whereby in 1984 Congress had resolved against providing further military aid. The approach to Iran, pursued in collaboration with Israeli and other arms dealers, involved supplying Iran with weapons with which to wage its war with Iraq; no arms would go directly to Iran from the United States but from stocks in Israel which the United States would then replenish. Senior American officials travelled in secret to Teheran with a consignment of parts for missile launchers. But both sides were expecting more than they could reasonably hope to get at that date. Iran raised its demands not only for weaponry but also for political concessions such as an Israeli withdrawal from southern Lebanon and the Golan Heights and the release of prisoners held in Kuwait on charges of terrorism in Lebanon. One American hostage was released in exchange for more spare parts, a second for yet more weapons. There were many clandestine meetings and much mutual deception by overstatement. The proceedings became public knowledge. Reagan dismissed his national security adviser, Admiral John Poindexter, and his principal subordinate in these matters, Colonel Oliver North, who managed to destroy much documentation before quitting his office. Reagan's first public statements were untrue, and although he knew that the Boland amendment was being bypassed in numerous ways his positive knowledge of the Iran–Contra operations remained unproved throughout the remainder of his presidency. In later testimony he more than a hundred times pleaded an inability to remember crucial matters, so that it was not clear whether he had not been told or had not understood or whether neither of these evasions was valid. His reputation for straightforwardness, competence and application to business did not recover. The importance of the Iran–Contra affair was not that it weakened the United States militarily but that it caught the attention of the world and raised questions about the dependability of the United States in world affairs. The smell of scandal was the more harmful since it came not much more than a decade after the astonishing behaviour of Richard Nixon, who had been forced in 1974 by the exposure of his chicanery and mendacity to resign the presidency and transfer it to a congressman of mediocre capacity, Gerald Ford, in exchange for exemption from impeachment.

For the Euro-American alliance these American shortcomings were troubling since the position of the United States in the alliance was uniquely important: no anti-Russian alliance without the United States was conceivable so long as the Cold War prevailed. The alliance had always suffered strains, although these were usually re-paired by the crassness of Russian policies in Europe and beyond. The most serious rift in the 1960s was the Franco-American acerbity which half-removed France from the alliance, but soon after the departure of de Gaulle French units again took part in NATO's naval exercises in the Mediterranean (1970). The 1970s were nevertheless often uneasy. NATO was no longer a preponderantly American host with European facilities: in European theatres and waters the European allies were providing 75 per cent of the air forces, 80 per cent of naval forces and 90 per cent of land forces. The American contribution was symbolic and financially crucial, so that Americans were moved to argue that Europe could not have this costly American military umbrella and at the same time obstruct American policies in other directions. The war in Vietnam had been fiercely criticized in Europe, but the war in the Middle East in 1973 raised ill will to governmental level. The United States was angered by European refusals to per-mit the use of airfields for the air lift to Israel and by their hurried truckling to Arab threats of an oil boycott. Europeans retorted by pointing out that they depended on the Middle East for 80 per cent of their oil, the United States for 5 per cent, and by chid-ing Washington for making policy on the Middle East without consulting its allies and then expecting them to assist it. Europeans were further estranged when Washington appeared to be toying with schemes for assuring the flow of oil by force of arms and they were reluctant to attend a consumers' conference proposed by the United States as a way of putting pressure on Arab producers. For similar reasons France refused to join an Energy Authority created within the OECD or to take part in a consumers' oil-sharing agreement. Europeans preferred a conference between consumers and pro-ducers, negotiation rather than confrontation.

At this point the alliance was virtually in abeyance and matters were not improved by the Turkish invasion of Cyprus in 1974. Greece, blaming the United States for not taking a firmer stand against Turkey's excessive exploitation of the Greek dictatorship's inept interference in Cyprus, withdrew from active participation in NATO operations – a protest caused by events in Cyprus but also grounded in a more pervasive anti-Americanism which had grown with American benevolence towards the dictators throughout 1967–74. This Greek hostility was not offset by any countervailing Turkish sentiment, since the US Congress, taking the Greek side, voted in December 1974 to cut off aid to Turkey, whereupon the Turkish government took control of 24 American military installations in Turkey, concluded a treaty of friendship with the USSR and accepted a large Russian loan.

At the diametrically opposite corner of NATO's territory two other members were engaged in a different conflict which also had implications for NATO installations. In 1972 the Icelandic parliament resolved to extend fishing limits to 50 miles. This act, which particularly affected Britain and West Germany, was a unilateral alteration of treaty dispositions of 1961. At the same time the Althing rejected in advance recourse to the International Court of Justice (which, however, ruled in August 1972 that British and West German vessels had the right to fish to a 12-mile limit). West Germany and Iceland compromised the resulting dispute in 1975 but with Britain, whose interests were more severely affected, Iceland's action led to armed clashes as Britain provided its fishing vessels with naval protection against the armed Icelandic coastguards trying to drive them away or destroy their gear. A two-year agreement was reached at the end of 1973, limiting the areas in which British vessels might fish and the type of vessel that might be used. This was a way of limiting the catch. Iceland, however, also declared that in 1975 it would extend its exclusive fishing rights to 200 miles. The dispute remained legally unresolved but the tensions were reduced in 1976 by a considerable British abandonment of reasonably well-founded rights. For Iceland the episode was an unyielding assertion of vital economic claims assisted by the advantages of operating in home waters; the real embarrassment of the British as a whole (as opposed to the fishing community); the likelihood that the current conference on the law of the sea would in any case recommend substantial extensions of normally accepted fishing limits; and the NATO connection, which could be used to bring pressure on Britain by the United States, which did not wish to see NATO's strategic installations in the northern sector imperilled by Icelandic action like that of Greece or Turkey.

In the midst of these aggravating conflicts and policy disputes Nixon upbraided his allies for ganging up on the United States. His national security adviser and secretary of state Henry Kissinger, no less irritated but more constructive, proposed in 1973 a new Atlantic Charter to define the common aims of the United States, western Europe and Japan (added because of the economic conflicts which the United States had with both Europeans and Japanese). The United States, Kissinger said, was prepared to defend western Europe and continued to approve European unity, but it objected to Europeans concerting, among themselves and without consulting Washington, policies objectionable to the United States – which was pretty much what Europeans were objecting to in reverse. The 1970s closed with the Russian invasion of Afghanistan, which evoked in Washington proposals for action which many Europeans regarded as futile, while in relation to the Middle East, European leaders, sceptical about the Camp David accords, set themselves to devise a European policy which, although expressed as a sequel to Camp David, was more precisely an alternative to an American policy which had, in their eyes, failed.

Then there was the question of paying for the alliance. For years the United States had borne a heavily disproportionate share of the costs and had regarded this burden as both inevitable and just so long as Europe was prostrate after the Second World War, but Europe recovered (with massive American aid) while the United States began to feel the unfamiliar pains of economic overstrain. The Europeans had to acknowledge the unfairness of the economic burden-sharing but when in 1977 NATO resolved that all members should increase their defence spending by 3 per cent a year in real terms many of the Europeans failed to live up to their promises. In this context the question of leadership was an added irritant. There could be only one leader – the president of the United States. But respect for the presidency was calamitously impaired when Lyndon Johnson decided not to run for a further term because he felt that he had failed. Every president after Johnson contributed, sometimes powerfully, to the decline in the standing of the presidency among Europeans and so boosted the latent anti-Americanism which lay not far beneath the surface of European opinion. Yet this anti-Americanism was not so much a foundation for an alternative policy as an emotional luxury.

To this pattern the Helsinki conference of 1972–75 on Security and Cooperation in Europe (CSCE), attended by 35 states, including the United States and Canada (which were accepted as rightful and essential members of the European polity) was the most comprehensive conference assembled in Europe since the war and it turned itself into a permanent institution, which presented a challenge to the prevailing bipolarity fashioned by the superpowers.

The instigator of the Helsinki conference was the USSR. The west concurred after insisting on the inclusion of the United States and Canada. The Russian purpose was to secure endorsement of the post-Hitlerian frontiers in Europe which no peace conference had ratified; and, secondly, to discuss security in terms of military bases and troop levels. The western approach to the conference was at first a mixture of boredom and cynicism, but towards the end it decided to use the occasion to exact conditions from the USSR. The west and the neutrals combined to reject a Russian proposal to declare Europe's frontiers immutable; the conference declared only that they should not be altered by force. Further, the west and the neutrals insisted on a wider interpretation of security, embracing not only military dispositions but also mutual understanding. Consequently, the Helsinki Final Act contained declarations – not legally binding but nevertheless formal and normative – concerning governmental and non-governmental contacts for economic, social and technical co-operation and what was called co-operation in humanitarian fields. This phrase opened the door to discussion about human rights and breaches thereof. A Russian attempt to limit the ambit of these declarations to discussions between systems, as opposed to states, was defeated. Had it been accepted, the Final Act would have permitted abstract debate about the relative merits and vices of the capitalist and communist systems but not criticism of the policies and practices of particular states. The USSR, which had initiated the Helsinki conference, was outmanoeuvred and came to regret that it had ever set this particular ball rolling.

The Helsinki conference provided for periodic reviews of the implementation of its undertakings. The first review took place in Belgrade in 1977 in a climate of considerable animosity. It achieved nothing except agreement to meet again. This next meeting began in Madrid in 1980 after protracted Russian attempts to abort it. The west made great play with the Russian invasion of Afghanistan and the plight of dissidents in the USSR. France proposed yet another conference on disarmament in Europe and Brezhnev spoke warmly of confidence-building measures which he was willing to extend to all Europe up to the Urals. There was nothing new in any of these proposals, which evinced only a determination to keep talking and to find something to say. But Helsinki's greater effect was outside these review conferences, for the Helsinki process coincided with a ferment in central Europe, amounting in Poland to a political revolution. The Helsinki declarations and the Helsinki watch committees set up in many countries (including the USSR) to monitor the behaviour of the signatories, contributed to this turbulence of hopes, unquantifiably but far from insignificantly, and after 1989 the CSCE became the pan-European forum which was felt to be needed after the demolition of Russian and communist power in central and eastern Europe and the consequent confusion over the continuing purposes and usefulness of NATO. In 1990 the CSCE participants established a standing headquarters as a step away from armed bipolarity and towards a new, if dimly perceived, order in which confrontation between Europeans would be relegated, if not to the dustbin, at any rate to the pages of history. The CSCE was bidding to become the regional organization for Europe in terms of article 52 of the UN Charter with the United States and Canada as part of Europe in this context. In 1994, by which date it had 53 members, the CSCE was renamed OSCE (O for Organization).

But the OSCE was not – or not yet – a secure foothold for the United States in Europe. Not only was it untried; it had no armed forces. NATO and the North Atlantic Treaty remained the practical and legal instruments for American participation in European affairs. On the other hand, although Russia was an acceptable member of the OSCE, it was NATO's obvious enemy and it was strongly opposed to the extension of NATO to European states on its borders. These states, however, wanted to join NATO as soon as possible (as too did a number of the new Caucasian and Central Asian states): there were some 20 states knocking on NATO's door. Among NATO's existing European members Germany was keenest on extending it to states between Germany and Russia. In 1993 Volker Ruhe, the German minister of defence, publicly advocated an association of Poland, Hungary and the Czech and Slovak Republics with NATO (and WEU). More generally, existing members wanted to preserve the alliance as a symbol of American concern about Europe and involvement in its affairs and a warning that a revival of Russian power could not be permanently discounted. The United States devised a plan under the title of Partnership for Peace for associating former communist enemies with NATO, largely in order to delay the question of full membership: they were to be admitted to a queue in an ante-room. Yeltsin claimed (1992) membership if any other were admitted; announced (1993) in Warsaw that he had no objection to Polish membership but, back in Moscow a few weeks later, formally informed the United States and other leading NATO states that there must be no eastward extension of their alliance; declared (1995) his readiness to join the Partnership and his opposition to NATO exercises in conjunction with the new proposed partners (this was a year of pre-election nationalism in Russia); protested unavailingly against American insistence that military operations in Bosnia should be under NATO's command; accepted (1997) an undertaking by NATO not to place nuclear weapons in the territory of new members (NATO did not need to do so). Yeltsin had little real choice. He settled for what he could get, which was an agreement providing for consultation within NATO without any hand in operations or policies. A similar position was offered to Ukraine.

The United States had choices and was divided in its own higher councils over how to choose. It chose to pursue the expansion of NATO at the expense, if necessary, of friction with Russia – and to do so in stages, which pleased the favoured few and disgruntled the rest. By common consent within the alliance, Poland, Hungary and the Czech Republic were placed at the head of the queue. Other candidates for the first batch – Slovenia, sponsored by Italy, Romania by France and Estonia by Sweden – were blocked by the United States with the support of Britain. Negotiations with the favoured three were begun in 1997.

This course had uncomfortable implications. It gave new members guarantees under the North Atlantic Treaty which the old members could with difficulty be expected to honour. When the treaty was signed in 1949 its authors envisaged aggression by the USSR in Europe, its European members were united in seeking a formal American guarantee to take military action against it and the United States perceived it to be in its interests to do so. Fifty years later, with the USSR dissolved and none of its successor states presenting a menace of that nature or magnitude, the threat to the peace in Europe arose from disputes within central or eastern Europe and it was not evidently in the American interest to commit the United States to military action in the event of conflict of that kind or likely that it would (as witness American reluctance to become involved in the wars in Yugoslavia). By accepting the obligations of article 1 of the North Atlantic Treaty in the post-Soviet context the United States took the grievous step of exposing its integrity to disbelief. But NATO was an established organization with a record of efficiency, which the OCSE was not; without being redirected and expanded NATO was likely to wither; the raucous Russian nationalism of Zhirinovski and his like reminded Americans that enduring American–Russian friendship might be as visionary in the 1990s as it had been in the days of Roosevelt and Stalin. NATO must stay and – see Chapter 7 – be used more aggressively than ever before.

In economic affairs Reagan inherited a perplexity of problems and made them worse. American supremacy in the world was before all else economic and its fame throughout the century had derived from the incomparable performance of American capitalism in times of adversity as well as times of ease. One of the main elements in the post-1945 international order was the economic system devised in 1944 at Bretton Woods and comprising the World Bank and the International Monetary Fund (IMF). This system presupposed the ascendancy of the US dollar and enshrined the importance of stable exchange rates with the dollar itself pegged to – or determining – the price of gold (at $35 an ounce). In 1945 the strength of the American economy and therefore of the dollar were axiomatic and within the Bretton Woods span of years the United States exported capital on a huge scale, partly in pursuit of foreign policies which demanded massive expenditure on forces overseas and ultimately in waging war in Vietnam, and partly in capital disbursements by corporations investing in and buying up foreign enterprises. At the same time the United States began, intermittently from 1959, to run deficits on its foreign trade and to seek to finance all these operations with no – or, after 1968, only minor – contributions from American citizens in the shape of higher taxes. The consequent growth in the 1960s of piles of Eurodollars (dollars outside the United States) added both to the uncertainties about the continuing strength of the dollar and to the difficulties of managing the American currency and to the very existence of the ruling world economic order. In the 1970s American industrial growth slid behind the Japanese, German and French and even the Italian, while sharp rises in the price of oil in 1973 and 1979 – coinciding with the conversion of the United States into a net importer of oil and clashing with a habit of cheap energy – compounded the discomfiture of the dollar and the collapse of the system.

The soaring price of oil was a function of, first, the transfer of Middle East oil to Middle Eastern ownership and political manipulation and, secondly, war and revolution in the Middle East. OPEC, the cartel of mainly Middle Eastern producers and exporters created in 1961, did little to alter prices in its first ten years but prices were edging upwards in the early 1970s and increased tenfold during that decade, which included the war of 1973 and the overthrow of the shah's regime in Iran in 1979. These increases were checked by the creation of an Industrial Energy Agency and then reversed when new exploration and production by major oil companies outside the Middle East reminded the OPEC producers of the laws of supply and demand. But during the 1970s and early 1980s governments did not foresee this outcome. They were more harassed by the collapse of the Bretton Woods monetary system, particularly the devaluation of the dollar by one-third in terms of gold – a consequence of the Vietnam War and Washington's financing of it by borrowing – and an end to exchange stability. In the ensuing Reagan–Bush decade, the world's economically leading states – the Group of Five, from 1986 Seven, and, with Russia from 1997, Eight – tried to form an interim system. The chief function or hope of the Group was to regulate jointly economic processes which each had previously regulated separately, so long as it had sovereignty in reality as well as in name. The Group was trying to find a place between two non-existent worlds: that of the sovereign state and that of an international powerhouse. Its leadership was originally European (Franco–German with Valéry Giscard d'Estaing and Helmut Schmidt), then American. The Plaza (1985) and Louvre (1987) agreements were an attempt by central banks to manage the devaluation of the dollar by financial measures which were unsuccessful because they were unaccompanied by similarly co-ordinated fiscal measures by governments. The very large sums expended by the banks were largely spent in vain. At the end of 1987 crashing prices on Wall Street advertised the extent of the malady and of public and private fears that the administration had lost control of budget and trade balances. Growth, which had averaged about 3 per cent a year from 1945 to the beginning of Reagan's presidency, was almost zero. Domestic saving and investment were at their lowest recorded levels and unemployment wavered between 10 and 7.5 per cent over the 12 years of Republican rule. The Group of Seven sidestepped the predominantly American anxieties over the overvalued yen, Japan's almost unimaginable trade surpluses, hyperinflation in Russia and other menacing consequences of the collapse of communist rule in half of Europe and the disintegration of the Soviet Union.

In this context Reagan's policies of deficit financing (not confined to the United States) and tackling inflation by cutting output and jobs contributed to the decline of the United States' unique position in the world. His determination to boost American pride and self-confidence to his own cheery level was accompanied by an equal determination to reduce taxes. Since his way to pride was papered with unprecedentedly costly expenditure on weapons of war, his term of office was marked by massive borrowing and the neglect of social services. His promise on entering the White House to balance the budget was even rasher than such promises usually are. He seemed to believe that the gap between spending and revenue would evaporate because lower taxes, in association with monetarist controls, would produce higher profits and so higher tax yields to bridge the gap. But low taxes and tight money did not lay these golden eggs. Deficits grew both absolutely and as a percentage of GNP. After 1982 monetary constraints were relaxed and interest rates lowered, growth continued but so too did the gap, and the only salvation lay in pulling in foreign money to finance current government spending and domestic investment: budget deficits of tens of millions of dollars were half financed by Japanese and other foreign investors who might change their minds unless tempted by higher and higher interest rates. The dollar was allowed to rise but rose so strongly that its exchange value ceased to be credible and it fell even more spectacularly than it had risen.

When Reagan left office in 1989 the United States had swung in less than a decade from being the world's biggest creditor to being its biggest debtor. Its external debt, which exceeded $660 billion, had risen by 25 per cent in a single year. External deficits reached $12 billion a month and interest on external debts was costing $50 billion a year. Export business was crippled and foreign assets were being sold. Within the United States capital resources shrank by $500 billion as shares in corporations were extinguished or replaced by debt (particularly through the invention of junk bonds). Half the population was worse off in real terms than it had been in 1980. Personal savings had fallen below 15 per cent (half the Japanese rate); higher education in technology and science was threatened with decline; the economic infrastructure was in decay and so were inner cities, where housing and infant mortality approximated to the black spots of the Third World and crime and drugs were alarmingly prevalent. Corruption in the public sector was widespread up to the level of the cabinet. These ills were remediable but they required a stark reversal of attitudes and a robust exercise of political will. Given the strength of manufacturing industry, budget deficits could be handled by modest increases in taxation; social decay could be tackled by abandoning

Reagan's view that government must be minimized – itself an abdication of responsibility. For the time being, however, the United States seemed to be no longer the sole front-runner in a world in which Japan and the European Community were the thrusting societies. The confidence which Reagan had given Americans through military might and talk was being jeopardized by economic and social malfunction and mediocre leadership. Reagan armed the United States against the USSR but disarmed it against Japan, an equally aggressive adversary although one whose weapons were not military.

Budgetary and external deficits, whatever their narrowly economic significance, sapped domestic and foreign confidence and destroyed the standing of the dollar as a world currency on its own or as a currency of last resort. In this political and psychological climate the dollar had a predisposition to sink against the major currencies and particularly against the yen, which had an even greater predisposition to rise for a special reason: that the Japanese were saving twice as much per head as were the Americans and were not using their savings to buy American or other foreign goods. Although Japanese spending habits were to a large extent cultural, Americans believed them to be controlled – more comprehensively than was probably the case – by the covert protectionism of Japanese governments using bureaucratic obstructionism and deviousness to make life for foreign exporters impossible.

The Bush administration began with a general weakness and a rare rebuff. For good or ill it was not Reaganite but sub-Reaganism presided over by a vice-president who had not been able to emerge from the vice-presidential shadows either at home or abroad. The rebuff was the refusal of the Senate to approve the new president's nominee as secretary of defense. Further, in the months preceding mid-term elections in 1990 the president became damagingly embroiled with both parties in Congress over ways of reducing the deficits which he had inherited from his predecessor. External affairs were more congenial to Bush than domestic and he filled the office of president at the climax of the country's greatest postwar triumph – the liberation of central and eastern Europe from communist rule and the elimination of the world's second superpower. He scored resounding successes in the war against Iraq in 1991 and proclaimed the advent of a new world order. But what was new – a broad American-led coalition in the Middle East – did not last and Bush's exertions and proclamations were not enough to win him a second term in the face of domestic discontents, financial and social (drugs and crime, abortion, ethics in government). In 1992 the Democrats regained the White House with Bill Clinton as president.

Clinton took office after winning 43 per cent of the popular vote. He was intelligent, articulate and forthright in speech but was only sporadically and inconsistently attuned to external affairs and handicapped as an international leader by constitutional and political restraints on his powers. His first concern was to win congressional and popular approval for a budget which would combine hard measures for reducing a frightening federal deficit running at $2–300 billion: but he won in the Senate by no more than the casting vote of his vice-president. This precarious beginning was accompanied by a number of ill-judged appointments to high offices and the revival of scandalous allegations against his private life and his earlier business affairs. It was followed by the defeat of a modest but over-complex plan for nationwide health care irrespective of age, which foundered. These setbacks seemed to put a stop to his appetite for domestic reforms and he became a largely negative president even before his second term, when the Congress sought his impeachment for public crimes and personal misdemeanours – a rare distinction which, since it was too obviously spiced by party vengeance, discredited his enemies as much as himself. He was favoured – and to some extent justly credited with – a turn in the economic tide. During his first term the political effects were slight because middle-class incomes continued to decline and the mid-term elections dealt the Democrats one of their severest blows of the century, including the loss for the first time in 40 years of a majority in the House of Representatives as well as the Senate. Two years later, however, he was re-elected as inflation and unemployment fell to their lowest levels for a generation, interest and mortgage rates were falling, growth was at a steady 4 per cent a year and budget deficits were turning into large surpluses.

In external affairs the American mood was perplexed. At first sight this was strange since the United States had only recently marked the dissolution of the Soviet Union, an unambiguous victory in a global contest. But world communism had provided a compass in world affairs and its disappearance made much of American foreign policy directionless. This aphasia roughly coincided with the removal of the second main assumption about the position of the United States in the world: that in the international economy the United States not only outstripped every other national economy but also knew how to direct a world economy. From one angle the end of the Cold War was a victory for capitalism over communism, leaving capitalism without a rival. But capitalism was triumphant without being in good health and the dexterity of the United States in a world capitalist system was ambiguous. Throughout the postwar period there had been a concealed flaw or trap in the American position. A resolute refusal to revert to isolationism and to combat communism worldwide had entailed foreign operations and disbursements on an unscheduled scale, which could be financed only by a commensurate expansion in foreign earnings: hence American insistence on the dismantling of imperialist protection and on free trade generally on the best terms that the dollar could command. In these matters the United States largely got its way but the scale kept on growing so that the problem did not go away. The United States found it difficult to pay its way in the world. Domestically, the economy was improving in the 1990s but there was also a feeling that the administration lacked the political courage to make the best of the improvements – a failing in will in the Congress as well as the presidency. Commercial disputes with Japan were handled with erratic inconsistency, meetings of the Group of Seven became little more than group photographs attached to platitudinous communiqués. Yet the United States remained uniquely favoured. Its economy excelled, being in sheer volume more productive than any other and being underpinned by an educational system which (however bad in parts) included the best universities and research institutes in the world: this educational excellence made the economy innovative as well as massive. And it still had a unique currency. No other currency vied with the dollar as a magnet for foreign investors or bolthole seekers. The Japanese yen did not deflect foreign money away from the dollar in the postwar period, least of all in the 1990s, and no single European currency had the range or base to do so. If after its inauguration in 1999 the Euro suffered no disaster it could in time become an alternative attraction to the dollar, assuming that the United States continued to run large deficits on external account, but for the foreseeable future the dollar, although regularly described as overvalued, was irreplaceable.

Militarily the United States was in a class of its own. Its destructive power was overwhelming but there were perplexities here too. It was easier for a superpower to possess vast military forces than to use them. Successive administrations recoiled, under the continuing impact of failure in Vietnam, from engaging in wars with ground forces. Even in Iraq in 1991 and 1998, where American national interests and personal obsessions were added to Iraqi breaches of international law on aggressive war and human rights, the United States wished to rely on air power, which could more easily be switched on and off (see pp. 395–404).

The world's assessment of the strengths of the United States was clouded by misconceptions – four in particular. Although the American president was commonly described as the most powerful man in the world, his power was, by the constitution, shared with the representatives of the people so that the president had within his own democracy less power than many heads of government in other democracies, let alone open or covert autocracies. Second, the long-standing growth of the central bureaucracy was turning the Congress from the partnership with the executive presupposed by the constitution into a more entrenched opposition to the president, from whichever party he might come. A third common misconception about the American political system concerned the route to the presidency. A president of the United States did not normally sit in cabinet before presiding over one and, although as well versed in politics as any statesman anywhere, he lacked the experience of government which a European president or prime minister acquired over a lifetime in a variety of departmental offices before reaching the topmost. Finally, Europeans particularly thought of the United States as a state like European states but bigger and richer. But this was to miss a significant historical point. The United States had developed over two centuries in a wide zone where there were no other states. It lacked the kind of statecraft which Europeans imbibed from life in a multiplicity of states hostile to one another, dependent on alliances with one another and rarely out of sight or out of mind of their neighbours. The basic instinct of the United States in international affairs was to go it alone. European history was marked by the disasters of doing so.

The Cold War had provided the United States with a clear purpose and allies. American foreign policy was mesmerized by the Cold War which, for the United States, all but turned world affairs into a single-issue drama. The end of the Cold War eliminated that purpose, weakened the nearly automatic support of other countries for American policies, and resuscitated the UN Security Council, where the veto (without which the United States would never have joined the UN) threatened to become an obstacle to American actions – notably in relation to Iraq but potentially anywhere in the world. A partial correction might be found in extending NATO's sphere of action by amending or removing the territorial limits set by the North Atlantic Treaty, but here too the United States faced opposition to turning the alliance into an arm of global American policies. Furthermore: at the century's close, as at its midway point, the United States was a country of unmatched economic productivity and superdominant military might but unsure of matching the latter by the former. The crucial element in this equation lay in an open worldwide trading system. When the Second World War ended the United States faced overseas markets closed by the British Commonwealth and other colonial empires and by the newly inflated and would-be autarkic Soviet empire. Demolishing empires was an ideological and material imperative and in this the United States was largely successful. But the Cold War and its attendant military commitments put continuing pressures on the American economy to earn by foreign commerce the surpluses needed to meet the accumulating demands of American foreign policies, and even when the Cold War was over the Gulf War of 1991 together with the balance sheets of the Reagan and Bush presidencies advertised the fact that the crucial issue of 2000 was the same as that of 1945. There was nothing, not even communism, that scared the American people more than persistent deficits in the national accounts but they could not be sure of the skills and the luck needed to meet these economic dangers.

Americans were as strongly imbued as any people with respect for legality and morality. What perplexed many foreigners – and Americans – was the very emphasis which politicians and other leaders in the United States put on rules and ethics, suggesting that American foreign policies were not, in the last resort, fashioned by the elliptical and essentially amoral concept of the national interest – which, however, they were. Briefly, in the Cold War, the presidencies of Nixon and Ford, whose foreign policies were shaped by Kissinger, abandoned – if tacitly and temporarily – the ideological cladding of these policies. By piloting Nixon to Beijing while disapproving of West Germany's Ostpolitik, Kissinger repositioned American foreign policy in a balance-of-power mode which the American people traditionally condemned as immoral. Americans embraced with enthusiasm Reagan's reversion to ideological stances and rhetoric. Yet Cold War ideology was itself cynically amoral in that it promoted alliances with ideological friends, some of whom were villains. The result – an ideology which was more fig leaf than principle – was doubly uncomfortable. Americans craved for a more defensible combination of the national interest with ethical guidelines. There were two possible approaches. The first was to insist on the distinction between democrats and non-democrats and to favour only, or principally, the democrats: American and international aid should be made conditional on democratic credentials or at least promises. But the criterion of democracy – a multiparty parliamentary constitution – was fallible. Autocrats had little difficulty in permitting opposition parties to exist while ensuring that they did not win elections and such autocrats could even strengthen their position by holding elections and claiming a democratic mandate. A second way to sanitize power politics was to go beyond constitutions to actual behaviour and refuse the hand of friendship to any regime guilty of gross breaches of human rights. This might be more satisfying but it was also more hazardous. It entailed unpalatable admissions of past errors in, for example, Latin America and – more embarrassing – unacceptable constraints on future policy towards, for example, China. In practice it meant being disagreeable to lesser miscreants but condoning the shortcomings of the powerful: back to *Realpolitik* with the minimum of ethical restraints and the question whether or not to avow that this was the case, a conclusion more painful for the United States than for most countries. It was an American sage who most uncompromisingly expressed this bleak dilemma: Good men must not obey the laws too well.

The disintegration of the USSR

The problems of the second superpower were very different from those of the United States. Its economic problems were of a different order of hopelessness, its society more corrupt, cruel and inefficient, its very existence as a state in question. The end of the Cold War was no ordinary capitulation. If in one sense a military defeat caused by the economic impossibility of continuing the war, the failure was also one which permeated the political and social system, atrophied the nerve and spirit, and created a sense of doom.

After Krushchev's dismissal in 1964 Leonid Brezhnev had emerged as his successor and remained at the head of affairs until he died in 1982 after a long but – in domestic matters – stagnant term and a slow personal decline. He had three successors in three years: Yuri Andropov, who died in 1984, Konstantin Chernenko, who died in 1985 and Mikhail Gorbachev, with whom the long-awaited next generation at last reached the top. By this time the USSR no longer even looked like a match for the United States. Its empire in central and eastern Europe was unsustainable and the Union itself was threatened with disintegration on all sides of its Slav core. It was not without material resources but, mismanaged and under-equipped (except in certain heavy industries), they sufficed neither to feed its people nor to provide an acceptable standard of living, nor to make the USSR a world power. Gorbachev – intelligent, courageous and politically agile – embarked upon a course of economic and political reforms under the twin banners of *glasnost* and *perestroika*: *glasnost* meaning openness and in particular an end to the pervasive falsification of economic performance;

perestroika meaning the restructuring of the economy in the broadest sense of that word. He insisted that *perestroika* was not to be achieved without *glasnost* and that *glasnost* entailed not only inroads on censorship and habits of subservience but also reform of the entire political system, including the abolition of the Communist Party's monopoly of power and its control over the institutions of the state and the machinery of the economy. *Glasnost*, however unpalatable to some, was easy to understand. *Perestroika*, though, was a more ambiguous concept since it betokened change without specifying the pace of change or defining the new system into which the old system was to be changed. First steps included greater independence for co-operatives and for the managers of state enterprises, and the introduction of regulation by market forces to some extent. Even if it were agreed (which it was not) that there was a wrong system and a right one, there would still be difficulties in getting from the one to the other. How far, for example, should prices be allowed to find their own levels, if that meant that they would soar, putting goods out of reach of purchasers and leaving producers without a market? Should the prices of some things – food, for example – be controlled and, if so, by whom and on what principles and for how long? The government was caught between conflicting needs to let prices rip and to moderate their inevitable rise. While there was all but universal agreement on the need for a new economic order, there was no agreement on what it was to be: Lenin's New Economic Policy (which promoted small retailers and businesses in the hope of attracting foreign capital and skills), or the state of affairs before the NEP, or a new mixture of private capitalism and free trading and state socialism, or a plunge into something hardly distinguishable from western capitalism. The development of *perestroika* was therefore tentative and shapeless. It was contested in varying degrees; was obstructed by the thousands of people whose posts were likely to be put at risk by it; and was further complicated by the state of the economy, which continued to go generally backward and was as fit for surgery as a patient with a weak heart. The economy suffered blows from the slump in the price of oil (to some extent engineered by the United States and its Middle East allies), the disaster to the nuclear reactor at Chernobyl in 1986 and an exceptionally grim earthquake in Armenia in 1988.

A first basic law for economic reform in 1987 began the process of decentralization, deregulation of prices, and financial rewards for enterprises but gave industry little freedom to shop around for its supplies and made little alteration to the discredited system of central targeting. These partial measures were extended a year later, although still in a tentative and experimental mode and limited to special zones and undertakings below a prescribed size. They were hampered by the lack of trained managers and by the inertia or opposition of the *nomenklatura*, the privileged and ossified administrators who, having survived the Brezhnev years, were in no mood to lose their jobs and perks in the aftermath.

Gorbachev's political aims did not include diminished executive authority at the centre. The road to power in the USSR might be made freer but the power at the end of the road was to be no less comprehensive. As with the development of *perestroika* in industry and commerce, so with the accompanying political reforms, Gorbachev was not so much a strategic thinker as a nimble tactician who remained in control of the processes which he inaugurated by quick perception and quick moves which kept him ahead – if only just ahead – of events. At an extraordinary party conference in 1988 he promised to convoke a Congress of People's Deputies of 2,250 members, some chosen by special groups of which the Communist Party was one, but the greater number (1,500) in territorial constituencies where the voters were promised a choice of candidates. All candidates were required to issue election manifestos. In elections which followed in the next year there was no contest in 384 constituencies, while in 271 no candidate got half the votes cast. The Congress elected a smaller Supreme Soviet of 750 members, which met when the Congress dispersed. At the same time, and by something like a coup, Gorbachev secured the disappearance of hundreds of party regulars likely to obstruct his plans, purged the Central Committee of the Communist Party and had himself elected president of the USSR in the place of Andrei Gromyko, who obligingly resigned. His powers as president were to be considerable but not absolute. The Supreme Court might declare his acts to be unconstitutional; two-thirds of the Supreme Soviet might override a presidential veto of new laws. He was obliged to accord prominence at the centre to the republics by instituting a Council of the Federation consisting of himself and all the presidents of the 15 republics, and by abolishing the Council of Ministers – stronghold of centripetalism – and replacing it by a less prestigious and less powerful cabinet of experts. The resignation at the end of 1990 of his foreign minister Eduard Shevardnadze – a close colleague, successful minister and known advocate of liberal reforms – weakened Gorbachev and reinforced suspicions that he was being forced to veer to the conservative side and might even be becoming a captive of military leaders fearful of losing essential defence installations in dissident republics. (The armed forces were, with the KGB, the principal outward and visible sign of centralized power as opposed to the centrifugal ambitions of Baltic and other dissidents or the champions of greater autonomy in the Russian Republic (RSFSR) and the Ukraine.) Gorbachev's weakened position was exposed when, seeking approval for his nominee for the new post of vice-president of the Union – for which Shevardnadze had seemed destined – his candidate was rejected by the Congress of People's Deputies and only subsequently approved after a second, strictly unconstitutional, vote.

None of these shifts and changes produced an economic policy. As the economy crumbled, two competing strategies imposed themselves: to move fast or very fast. To the bolder or more desperate spirits the situation required a dash for change, damning the consequences and hoping for the best. The protagonists of this strategy produced a 500-day plan for installing a mixed economy in four stages. The first comprised selling government and Communist Party properties and enterprises, dissolving all state and collective farms, giving occupiers their plots or apartments, and cutting the budget by 5 million roubles in three months (including sharp cuts in the costs of defence and the KGB). The prime aim of this stage was to get hoarded money – money hoarded because there was nothing on which to spend it – into circulation and to do so before prices were freed and massive inflation let loose. In the second stage prices would be gradually freed and interest rates raised, but the prices of basic foods would remain controlled. In the third and longest stage (days 250–400) half the manufacturing and service enterprises would be sold and a stock exchange and other exchanges would be established. Finally, all these measures would be accelerated and 90 per cent of retail business would be put up for sale. This programme was opposed by, among others, the prime minister Nicolai Ryzhkov, on the grounds that the time limits were too rigid and unreal; that more palliatives were needed for the poorer classes, pensioners and students; and that the bureaucratic machinery for doing so much so quickly did not exist, with the result that there would be more chaos than reform. The objectors argued also that the economic disruption which they foresaw would add to the anarchic forces which were threatening to dissolve the Union. Gorbachev, who seemed to favour first one side and then the other and who did not want to lose his prime minister, tried to force the discordant groups to find a compromise. He failed. The Supreme Soviet preferred to give him emergency powers, shuffling off to the presidency the task of finding an answer and imposing it by decree. The outcome was a new plan, duly endorsed by the Supreme Soviet but so vague as to leave the future not only hazardously obscure but apparently beyond the control of the government. There were rival schemes but no coherent policy.

The political and economic transformation of the USSR was bedevilled by the simultaneous upsurge of dissidence, amounting in places to separatism. Of the USSR's 15 republics (see Maps 1.2 and 1.3, pp. 10–11) only three were preponderantly Slav: the Russian (which included Siberia), the Ukraine and White Russia (Byelorussia). Ethnic Slavs accounted for not much more than half the population, and the solidarity of the Ukraine with other Slavs could not be taken for granted since the Ukraine had a history of oscillating between subjection to Moscow (or Warsaw or Vilna) and bouts of asserting its independence up to and into the twentieth century. The remaining 12 republics – three Baltic republics, Moldavia, three in the Caucasus and five in central Asia – all had grievances and disruptive separatist aspirations.

Of the *Baltic republics* Latvia and Estonia – representatives of medieval Livonia – had historical and other links primarily with Finland, Sweden and Germany, while Lithuania, the largest of the three, was linked primarily with Poland and Russia. Russians numbered about a third of the inhabitants of Latvia and Estonia but only one in ten in Lithuania. All three countries had been overrun by Stalin's armies in 1944–45 and incorporated in the USSR. Many Lithuanians had fled westward, others – perhaps a quarter of a million – were deported or killed and Poles and Russians came to number a fifth of the population, Poles in the south and Russians mostly in Klaipeda (former Memel). Lithuania's Sanjudis movement came into being in 1988 under the leadership of the romantic nationalist and musicologist Vytautis Landsbergis and, as in Czechoslovakia and Hungary, evolved into a political party: its aim was independence. Economically, Lithuania's chief features were, on the one hand, an exportable agricultural surplus and, on the other, all but total dependence on the USSR for oil and gas. The economy as a whole suffered from the malformation, stultification and corruption which characterized the USSR. In 1990 elections were held for the republic's Supreme Soviet. Candidates approved by Sanjudis won a majority, which immediately declared Lithuania independent, repeating the similar declaration of 1918. To Gorbachev this was a challenge which had to be resisted because of its repercussions not only in the other Baltic republics but in all parts of the USSR. He was prepared to give the republics greater freedom in a relaxed USSR, to give them the constitutional right to secede, but he was not prepared to accept a unilateral act which could destroy the Union before he had had time to reform it. In addition, the Baltic republics formed part of an overall defensive system which neither Gorbachev nor his military chiefs could afford to dismantle in a hurry. Gorbachev sent troops into Lithuania and imposed an economic blockade which forced Lithuania's new leaders to moderate, if not their aims, at least their timetable – but not before they had found allies in the heart of the Union, in Moscow itself, where Gorbachev's principal Russian antagonist, Boris Yeltsin, had won control of the vast Russian republic (RSFSR). All three Baltic republics declared independence in 1991 but the joys of independence were tempered by material hardship as economic links with the USSR and trading preferences were broken, inflation soared and industrial and agricultural output were crippled: in Lithuania, for example, they were halved in three years. None of the three joined the Commonwealth of Independent States (CIS) – Gorbachev's Soviet Union Mark II. All left the rouble zone in 1992. They all fared better than other parts of the USSR in fending off hyperinflation and creating economies independent of Russia but Lithuania reverted to left-wing government in 1992–96 and Estonia in 1995. Latvia by contrast sprang a surprise by very nearly giving first place in 1995 to a party of the extreme right led by an immigrant from Germany who could speak no Latvian. Unlike Lithuania, Latvia and Estonia restricted citizenship to inhabitants with forebears resident before 1940, changed in Latvia's case to 1991 in order to facilitate its bid for entry into the European Union. All three states wanted to join the EU, to which Russia had little objection, provided they did not also join NATO.

Ukraine, after Russia the largest, most populous and most productive of the Soviet republics, occupying a strategic position between Russia and the Black Sea, peopled by 100 ethnic groups of which besides Ukrainians the most prominent were Great Russians (22 per cent) and Poles, declared itself an independent state and nuclear-free zone in 1990, a declaration subsequently affirmed by referendum. A focus of revolt against the centralizing thrust of tsarist Russia in the eighteenth and nineteenth centuries, it had sustained a precarious independence between 1917 and 1920 but was then invaded by a resuscitated Poland (which captured Kiev) before being absorbed into the Soviet Union. The western part of the post-Second World War republic was added to it only in 1939. The nationalist Rukh (or Movement), revived in 1989, won 110 seats in that year in the Supreme Soviet of the Ukraine. A Ukrainian Orthodox Church, seceding from the Russian Orthodox Church and opposed to Roman Catholics and to the mainly Polish Uniates, came into existence in 1990. Communist leaders, including Leonid Kravchuk, transformed themselves into nationalists and won enough support for Kravchuk to win the presidency in 1991.

Kravchuk was a leading proponent of the CIS. If for Gorbachev this was a means to salvage as much unity as possible from the Soviet disintegration, for Kravchuk it was a means to minimize the interdependence of the former Soviet republics. He argued that the Soviet Black Sea fleet, a force of some 300 ageing vessels and a relatively small part of the Soviet navy, should not be assigned to Russia, although he was prepared to partition it with Russia. The fleet's bases were in the Crimea, which in 1992 asserted its independence from both Russia and Ukraine – but abandoned this claim in return for substantial devolution of powers as an autonomous republic within Ukraine. Russia and Ukraine made and unmade a series of agreements on the fleet and the use of the naval base at Sebastopol: to control the fleet jointly, to divide it equally, to transfer all of it to Russia for cash. After holding out for much-needed cash, Ukraine adhered in 1993 to the Russo-American START I treaty of 1991 and undertook to despatch half of its nuclear weapons to Russia for destruction, a promise later enlarged to the surrender of all these weapons by 1999. Ukraine also obtained promises of cheap fuel from Russia and guarantees of its territorial integrity from Russia, the United States and France.

The *Crimea*, annexed by tsarist Russia in 1783, had a substantial Tatar population which was deported *en masse* during the Second World War on charges of collaboration with the Germans. Absolved of these accusations after the war, they were allowed back but many remained in exile from their ancestral lands. In 1954 the Crimea was transferred from the RSFSR to the Ukrainian Soviet Republic but neither then nor after that change did the Tatars recover their prewar autonomy. By the early 1990s they constituted 10 per cent of the population. Ukrainians numbered 25 per cent, Russians 62 per cent. The Russian language was all but universal. With the break-up of the Soviet Union the Crimea became an autonomous republic within the Ukraine. A presidential election in 1994, sanctioned by the government in Kiev in the false expectation of a victory by its favoured candidate, was won by Yuri Meshkov, who advocated reunion with Russia. His success was an embarrassment for Moscow which, by a tripartite treaty with the United States and Ukraine, had simultaneously guaranteed the territorial integrity of the latter in return for the surrender of all its nuclear weapons. But Meshkov proved incompetent as well as awkward and Ukraine stripped him of his powers and then abolished his post without provoking any protest from Moscow.

Elections in the Crimea were followed by elections in the Ukraine itself where a plethora of parties, and candidates belonging to no party, emphasized the divisions between Ukrainians and Russians and the Ukrainians' difficulties in asserting their separate national identity without abandoning to Russia the eastern half of the state and the whole Crimea. In yet further elections for the Ukrainian presidency Kravchuk lost to Leonid Kuchma, who was the clear choice of the eastern part of the state, an advocate of renewed close links with Russia and the beneficiary of general discontent with the economy. Kuchma's economic strategies had mixed yields. Inflation was reduced, the level of real wages maintained, reserves built up and interest on debts to Russia paid. But land reform stagnated, subsidies to (unsaleable) state industries and farms continued and, after a bout of retrenchment, deficits soared. Kuchma failed to curb gargantuan corruption and racketeering which vitiated his reforms, severely reduced foreign investment and loans, and turned his prime minister Pavel Lazarenko into a dangerous enemy. He was nevertheless re-elected in 1999 in spite of a decade of post-communism which halved the economy without convincing many Ukrainians that this was a way to better things.

Politically Ukraine was about equally split between advocates of close links with Russia (led by Viktor Yushchenko, president 2004) and an opposition seeking opportunities and security from the west (led by Viktor Yanukovych) with a third party more inclined to the former but not always so (led by Yulia Tymoschenko). Economically the overriding factor was Ukraine's dependence on Russia for oil and gas. Culturally the eastern half of the country belonged to the Orthodox community of churches, the westerners were mostly Uniates in communion with Rome.

North-west of Ukraine the Belorussian Republic of the USSR became the state of *Belarus* – overwhelmingly Russian but with small and scattered Polish minorities, its independence threatened less by ethnic divisions than by its nature as an artificial creation of the Soviet regime. In a referendum in 1995 its people voted emphatically for a form of reunion with Russia which President Alexander Lukashenko, stressing Slav unity, and Boris Yeltsin, seeking a shield against an expanded NATO, concluded in 1999. Lukashenko, an ambitious authoritarian, secured in 1996 an unconstitutional extension of his presidential term.

West of Belarus the Moldavian Soviet Republic (before 1940 an autonomous republic of the Ukraine and immemorially part of one of Europe's most mixed zones) became independent *Moldova*, with a mixed population of Romanians, Ukrainians, Russians, Gagauz Turks and others. The Romanian element accrued when Bessarabia was ceded to the USSR by Romania in 1940.

All three Caucasian republics became independent in 1991–92. *Georgia*, an ethnic and religious maze which had lost its independence when its last king gave it to the Russian Tsar in 1800 (in much the same way as the last Medici Duke of Tuscany had bequeathed his duchy to the Habsburg emperor), was governed by Russian proconsuls until 1917, when it received its independence with some help from British troops. It was reconquered a few years later by the Soviet Union. It declared independence once more in 1989. An earlier upheaval in 1972 (which brought Eduard Shevardnadze to power there) was a foretaste of anti-Russian demonstrations in the late 1980s, which were suppressed with considerable, probably unnecessary, force. It prompted speculation that army officers hostile to Gorbachev had deliberately inflamed the situation at a moment when Gorbachev was out of the USSR. From independence in 1991 Georgia collapsed into anarchy as its president Zviad Gamsakhourdia, a fervent nationalist, annulled the powers and privileges of its Ossetian, Abkhaz and other minorities. The Abkhaz – Turks but Christian in the north-west corner of the country (once the land of Medea and the Golden Fleece) – constituted 17 per cent of the population and had been incorporated into the republic only in 1930. They took to arms and worsted Gamsakhourdia, who was forced to flee into neighbouring Chechnya (he committed suicide in 1994). Shevardnadze, a conciliator rather than a battler, was invited to return from Moscow as president. He grudgingly joined the CIS in order to get Russian help and conceded to Russia the right to keep forces in Georgia – whose Black Sea ports and lines of communication (notably for oil) were strategically important to Russia. Abkhazia was virtually independent from 1993 and virtually quiescent for five years, but it was not the central government's only headache. The Ajars (Muslims) in the south-west with their port of Bakumi, South Ossetians in the north, Mingrellians between Tiflis and Abkhazia, Armenians in the south – all threatened Georgia's integrity, were partially patrolled by Russian forces and taxed the ingenuity of UNOMIG (UN Observer Mission in Georgia). In 2003 Shevardnadze was supplanted by Mikhail Saakashvili who exchanged residence in the United States for a role in the Caucusus and annoyed Moscow by talking of Georgian membership in NATO. He was re-elected in 2008.

In neighbouring *Armenia*, landlocked, mostly Christian, and *Azerbaijan*, mostly Muslim and Turkish, fighting between the two antedated independence by a number of years. At the core of their conflict was the region of Nagorno-Karabakh, which had been created in 1921 as a region of Azerbaijan but in which Armenians outnumbered Azeris by two to one. First Armenians, then Azeris and then again Armenians had the better of it. Both blamed Moscow for their troubles. When in 1991 Armenians seized Azeri areas and put Azeris to flight, these appealed for help to Turkey, their co-religionists and kinsmen with a pronounced history of oppressing Armenians in Turkey. But the Azerbaijani army overthrew the post-communist and pro-Turkish President Abulfaz Elchibey and restored the former KGB chief Gaidar Aliyev. He turned his attention to exploiting Azerbaijan's oil in partnership with foreign companies and planning pipelines in negotiations with foreign states anxious for access, transit dues and political advantages. The Armenian president Levon Ter-Petrosian was forced by scandal to resign in 1998, succeeded by his prime minister Robert Kocharian. In all these states the anti-Soviet nationalism which created them was modified within a decade by a sense that independence without special links with Russia might be sterile. Consciously or not, they hankered after something like Gorbachev's still-born CIS.

The northern part of the Caucasus had been apportioned not into Soviet republics but into regions of the Russian Soviet Republic, so that upon the dissolution of the USSR they did not become independent states. However, in 1998 the two largest areas – Dagestan and Chechnya – formed a joint Congress which demanded independence. Dagestan was a poor agglomeration of 3 million people and some 30 distinct languages and mutually distrustful groups. It was heavily dependent on Russia for funds (which either failed to arrive or were embezzled when they did) but also valuable to Russia because any oil pipeline from the Caspian must pass through Dagestan and Chechnya if it were to reach the wider world through Russian territory and the Black Sea. The United States preferred a (longer) route through Georgia and Turkey to the Mediterranean, by-passing Russia, and in 1999 in Istanbul and in Clinton's presence two agreements were signed which excluded Russia – the one between Turkey, Georgia, Azerbaijan and Kazakhstan for oil from central Asia to the Mediterranean and the other for natural gas from Turkmenistan to Turkey. (For the part played by Chechnya see pp. 77–82 and for the five Asian republics pp. 499–500.)

The progressive disintegration of the USSR was one of Gorbachev's failures. He had hoped to retain a form of unity but the spirit of the times was against him. The CIS was little more than a transitional device rushed through towards the end of his term in office to secure at least free trade between the former Socialist republics and find a new way to deal with nuclear weapons in diverse new states. His second major failure was the devaluation and demotion (in many places the virtual disappearance) of the Communist Party of the Soviet Union, through which he had hoped to exercise power in default of any other political base. Gorbachev's great achievements had been his boldness in abandoning the Soviet empire in Europe and his initiatives in the mutual disarmament of the Cold War. But he had also wished to preserve the Soviet Union in some modified form and to preserve a reformed Communist Party. In both of these aims he prevaricated and so opened the way for a more single-minded leader – Boris Yeltsin, a Russian nationalist with little concern for the Union and no use for the Communist Party, which in Russia he dissolved. Gorbachev had divested the Communist Party of its monopoly of power, carried first instalments of privatization of land and industry, and made the first moves towards a market economy. But although a convinced reformer and modernizer he was no democrat. He did not believe that reform in the USSR could be effective otherwise than through a benevolent autocracy. He secured extended powers for the Soviet president; reassumed the post of general secretary of the Communist Party which he had earlier relinquished; created new advisory bodies which, whether by confusion or design, were too numerous to be coherent; and seemed by the first half of 1990 to be veering towards the conservatives. But his economic policy was confused and the economic situation catastrophic. No believer in market economics, he allowed a dozen economic reform plans to follow one another without being put into operation and he failed to press any sustained programme to reform food production.

The difficulties were huge: no foreign exchange, a budget deficit equal to one-third of GDP, nearly all industries losing money, the dead hand of state monopolies still in place, little foreign aid, much but poor foreign advice. After the defeat in March 1991 of his proposals for a new Soviet Union of sovereign republics by popular vote in six of them (the three Baltic republics, Moldova, Georgia and Armenia) a new Soviet constitution with restricted powers for the central government was published, in response to which a group of military, KGB and civilian reactionaries staged a coup against him when he was away in the Crimea. The coup collapsed after three weeks. The conspirators were incompetent but not aimless. They had lost faith in Gorbachev, whom they held responsible for allowing the Soviet Union to disintegrate by reacting feebly to disturbances in the Caucasus and Asian and Baltic Republics and allowing Russia and other core republics to filch too much power from the Union. Their aim was to usurp Gorbachev's authority or force him into subservience to themselves. They accelerated his fall but also the rise of Yeltsin and Russia and therefore the decentralization which they deplored. Before the year ended Gorbachev was eliminated, resigning the presidency of the Soviet Union which (created in 1923 six years after the bolshevik revolution) had ceased to exist.

The history of Europe in the twentieth century offers no more startling contrast than that between the brevity and the achievements of Gorbachev's rule. He confronted the most daunting problems from the impossible continuance of the Cold War to the internal impossibilities of the Soviet Union and empire. He was limited not only by the constraints of his situation but also by the isolation inseparable from an autocratic temperament and his failure to seek the support of close or competent advisers. But above all Gorbachev failed because he was trying to reform the unreformable. Soviet communism relied essentially on central planning by planners who had no theories or institutions with which to perform the economic functions which a market system supplied. The Soviet system lasted as long as it did because it embodied a tyranny which enabled its rulers to exact from its peoples the sacrifices demanded by a hopeless system. Its collapse condemned the system without, however, vindicating any alternative. It left capitalism triumphant but – as Karl Marx had discerned – deeply unsatisfying. Gorbachev's successors and their subjects were left not only in a mess; they were trapped between a rock and a hard place.

Yeltsin's power base was not the USSR but Russia. He had acted with courage during the anti-Gorbachev coup, risking his life in confronting the plotters and increasing his personal popularity in Russia, which had been growing since 1990. In that year the Congress of People's Deputies elected under Gorbachev's reforms of 1988 (and containing an overwhelming majority of professed communists) was replaced by a Russian parliament which chose Yeltsin as its president. A few weeks before the coup of 1991 he was elected president of the Russian Republic by direct popular vote: he got 57 per cent of the vote, a narrow majority but much more than any other candidate. This victory turned out to be the high point of his career. By it he stamped his personality on the Russian scene but he failed thereafter to display any mastery over either of the two major problems on that scene: economic policy and nationalities. Economic reform he half supported, barely commended to the public, which suffered from it without understanding the case for it, and allowed to be subverted by the institutions of the state itself (including the central bank). His similar ambiguity over the rights of nationalities led to the bungling of the Chechnyan revolt, which did him as much harm as any other episode in his years as president.

Yeltsin was given special powers to formulate and implement economic reforms. These, propounded by Yegor Gaidar, Anatoly Chubais, Gennady Bubulis and other adventurous advisers, comprised severe cuts in government spending, the privatization of state enterprises of all kinds for which purchasers could be found, the dismantling of much of the central bureaucracy and a pitiless face to lame ducks. But this programme proved not only painful but far more protracted than anticipated and was hamstrung by the independent central bank, which was outside the executive's control and continued to print money to rescue or simply to please flagging undertakings and their managers. Inflation soared into four figures, production collapsed and the reformers appeared to be benefiting nobody except a handful of enterprising delinquents expert at finding rich pickings in the prevailing confusion. Former allies of Yeltsin, among them Vice-President Alexander Rutskoi, former air force general and hero of the war in Afghanistan, recoiled, judging that Yeltsin, under the influence of the reformers, was trying to do in 5 years what should be spread over 20. Critics formed the Civic Union, which became a principal group in the Congress and joined forces with the ex-communists, who were even more hostile to Yeltsin than they had been to Gorbachev. Yeltsin was forced to withdraw his nomination of Gaidar as prime minister and appointed instead (1992) Victor Chernomyrdin, who was expected to be an amenable mediator between Yeltsin and the Congress chairman Ruslan Khasbulatov, another former ally of Yeltsin turned adversary.

Opposition to Yeltsin was not confined to his economic policies and advisers. His strength of character offended as many people as it attracted. His assertiveness verged on the authoritarian. Although he could be stout in defence of a broad principle or belief, he gave an uncertain lead over policies, either because he was naturally devious or because he was out of his depth. There was in the Congress a hard core of Yeltsin loyalists but a comparable number of opponents with a middle group – probably the largest but also the least coherent – which accepted the need for substantial reform but saw with alarm and dismay the suffering involved and wanted less decontrol of prices (especially of necessities), less privatization and above all less speed. This group, however, offered no convincing alternative programme and was influential mainly in preventing the anti-Yeltsin groups from mustering the two-thirds required to impeach or displace him. Given that the constitution forbade the president to dissolve the Congress before the end of its term in 1995 there was stalemate.

Yeltsin continued to command popular approval, which was reaffirmed in 1993. He had no adversary of equal stature or eminence, neither Rutskoi nor Khasbulatov having much popular appeal; and he had at least adequate support in the armed forces, perhaps two-thirds among senior officers and more lower down the line. On the other hand, he had created no political party of which he could be described as the leader; he was powerful but isolated; he was less determined than, for example, Walesa in Poland; and his conflict with the Congress distracted him from tackling a frightening economic slide. Prices continued to soar, in one year the rouble lost nine-tenths of its value against the dollar, foreign aid was hard to come by and over the years 1989–93 output nearly halved. In 1993 Yeltsin recalled Gaidar, suspended Rutskoi and, in a move that was almost certainly illegal, dissolved the Congress. The battle between Yeltsin and his enemies became violent, Yeltsin ordered the bombardment of the parliament buildings and put Rutskoi and Khasbulatov in prison.

The election of a new Congress was contested by three main forces: reformers, communists/conservatives and nationalists. Yeltsin himself adopted an aloofness which was not easily distinguishable from indecisiveness. He neither formed a party of his own nor clearly supported any other and so stationed himself autocratically outside party battle. Half the new Congress was elected by proportional representation of lists, half by personal contests in constituencies. The reformers, who took the name Russia's Choice and counted Gaidar as their most prominent leader, debated among themselves instead of presenting a united front to the electorate and came only second (15 per cent of the vote) in the first section but won more constituencies than any other party. The nationalists were led by Vladimir Zhirinovski, who had come third in the presidential election of 1991 and campaigned on a demagogic mixture of xenophobia and populism – from the restoration of Russian power and territory (including Alaska) to cheap vodka. His main appeal, which seemed to be irrespective of age, was to people who were fearful of impending chaos and national humiliation. The communists took 12 per cent of the vote in the first section and came third in the second. Together these three groups won half – but only half – the seats in each section. Although Yeltsin prevailed over his adversaries his position was not firm. He wanted a strong centralized Russian state with an effective economic base and himself in charge. But his personal fitness was undermined by severe heart illness and intemperate drinking; he vacillated over economic policies; and he became enmeshed in a war in the Caucasus which he humiliatingly lost. He did not seem likely to be re-elected president in 1996.

For Yeltsin, as for Gorbachev, grasping the economic nettle was a step too far. Russia's central economic problem was the demolition of an incompetent and corrupt command economy and the substitution of a new system with, in particular, capitalist institutions and a stable currency. This conversion required very large foreign subsidies or credits, a wide measure of agreement in the Russian political world and a minimal level of administrative and fiscal integrity. Some of all this came about but the net balance over a decade fell far short of what was needed, so that by the late 1990s the government inspired no confidence at home or abroad. In the first years of the post-communist revolution foreigners had two main motives for giving Russia prompt aid but neither was related to the immediate future. The first was that Soviet Russia had been a fearsome power and the second was that the new Russia contained resources which would one day yield substantial profits. A subsidiary motive was the sheer uncertainty about what Russia might or could do if it were to become anarchic. In the event, the 1990s were the years when Russia failed in western eyes to qualify for significant aid and the west failed to provide whatever might have enabled a Russian government to do better.

Under the direction of Gaidar and Chubais in 1992–94 half the industrial workforce and two-thirds of industrial businesses – over 100,000 distinct enterprises – were privatized, albeit by transferring them mainly to their managers at knockdown prices (half the shares were allotted to managers and workers and a further 30 per cent were auctioned except in the oil, gas and defence industries) but output continued to fall. In agriculture almost all collective farms were converted into limited companies but distribution remained inefficient or became chaotic. Only the service sectors of the economy registered promising advances. Foreign investment languished, the rouble spiralled downward and inflation, after falling from astronomic figures to 25 per cent, began to rise again. The budget, burdened with continuing subsidies to bankrupt businesses and farms, failed to meet the 7.7 per cent of GDP set by the IMF as a precondition for its loans ($6.5 billion in 1995, $10.2 billion in 1996). Gaidar and Chubais were turned out.

Economic failings engendered crime, extortion and corruption. Wages in the public services, including the armed forces, were frequently unpaid and government drifted into cronydom. Yeltsin's inconsistencies recalled the false start of Russia's last reformer-autocrat, Tsar Alexander II, a century and a half earlier. Yet more damaging was the mismanagement of a crisis in Chechnya in the Caucasus, which turned into a particularly grisly war.

Russia was even less a nation state than most European countries. It was an ethnic and administrative federation which contained 21 republics and 10 autonomous districts, all of which elected their own presidents from 1991; 52 regions and 6 territories which elected their own governors from 1997; and about 50 internal border disputes. The calamitous economic and confused political situation fed disintegration, forcing ethnic, local or merely makeshift groups to take authority into their own hands. In 1992 Yeltsin secured the agreement of all but two of the republics (Chechen and Tatar) for a Russian federation in which they and the cities of Moscow and (renamed) St Petersburg would have extensive powers over their own affairs, but the Chechens were

already in a state of defiance. They had been kicking against the pricks of Russian domination for two centuries; there was a serious uprising in 1929; and during the Second
World War they were deported from their homelands *en masse* – 250,000 people, of
whom four in five died and the survivors remained in exile until after Stalin died. They
were reputedly Russia's foremost arms and drugs dealers, with an established position
in Moscow's underworld. In 1991 Dzokar Dudayev, a Soviet general who had seen
service in Afghanistan but was adventitiously on leave in his native Chechnya, was propelled into the leadership of a group which proclaimed independence with Dudayev
as president. After an unsuccessful attempt to reinstate the regional government by
force Yeltsin withdrew Russian troops and imposed an economic embargo, which was
ineffective. He was alarmed about the possibility of revolts in other ethnic regions and
about the flow of Caspian oil, which reached the Russian port of Novorossisk via the
Chechnyan capital Grozny, site of Russia's second largest refinery. For their part,
Dudayev and his supporters feared that Russian troops sent to Georgia to help
Shevardnadze against Gamsakhouria (who alone recognized Chechnyan independence) would be turned against Chechnya. Yeltsin toyed with a number of Dudayev's
local antagonists – about whom he would have bothered less had he been better
informed – but not with the most serious of them, Ruslan Khasbulatov, who had been
one of his fiercest enemies in the recent clash between him and the parliament in
Moscow. Sporadic fighting continued on the borders of Chechnya until 1994, when
Yeltsin resolved to extinguish the Dudayev regime by full military action. Bungled but
ferocious, this venture was reported to have cost in a few weeks more lives than the
Russians lost in ten years in Afghanistan. The Chechens retaliated by raids into Russia
and seized 1,500 hostages. Russian attempts to rescue them cost more lives, the
destruction of an entire hospital and an agreement by which the Chechens were
allowed to retreat to their homelands by bus, taking some of their hostages with them.
The war was greatly unpopular in Russia; raised awkward questions about military
mismanagement and Yeltsin's relations with his army chiefs; raised even more awkward questions about Russia's control of the whole of the Caucasus, a region the size
of France, which included 50 languages as well as varying brands of Christianity and
Islam; compromised Russia's chances of receiving foreign aid – private, national and
international; and endangered Yeltsin's prospects of being re-elected president. When,
therefore, Dudayev was killed (probably assassinated) Yeltsin took the opportunity to
fly to Chechnya with peace proposals and after his re-election he despatched his outspoken and dangerously popular rival General Alexander Lebed to finalize a deal with
Dudayev's successor Aslan Maskhadov. Yeltsin then got rid of Lebed and himself concluded an agreement which gave Chechnya – renamed the Republic of Ichkeria – independence in all but name but postponed to 2002. This was a way to sidestep disaster
but it settled neither the Chechnyan question nor the wider issue of anti-Russian
nationalism in the Caucasus. From Moscow's point of view, Maskhadov proved a
failure: he failed to win control over much of Chechnya. Other Chechens, such as

Shamil Basayev and Habib 'Khattab', opposed his deal with Moscow and sought support from malcontents in neighbouring Dagestan – a much larger and ethnically less homogeneous country than Chechnya. Dagestanis generally distrusted Chechnyans and were less addicted to lawlessness but they shared Chechnya's hostility to Russian rule and its Sunni Muslim faith. In Dagestan a small minority had been attracted to Wahhabism, the puritan strand in Sunni Islam which was endemic in Saudi Arabia. Wahhabis advocated strict clerical government by the rules of the Sharia but in Dagestan they were not popular and were outlawed in 1997 on the grounds that they were tools of foreign forces. Caucasian Wahhabism was, however, strengthened when it spread to the more militant Chechens and Khattab, who had spent part of his youth in Saudi Arabia, sought financial aid from that country and possibly also from the Wahhabi Saudi exile Osama bin Laden in Afghanistan (whence the Caucasian Wahhabis were sometimes called Afghanis). In 1999 attacks on civilian buildings in Moscow and other Russian cities provoked Yeltsin into renewing the war against Chechnya.

In elections at the end of 1995 the communists led by Gennadi Zyuganov were the most successful party, with Zhirinovski's ultra-nationalists in second place: most of the 40 or so parties failed to attain the 5 per cent threshold required for a place in the parliament, while the reformers were cripplingly divided between Gaidar's followers and those of Grigori Yavlinski (the leading reformer of the Gorbachev years). These results galvanized Yeltsin into active manoeuvres to retain the presidency in the next year against the communists on the one hand and Lebed, who had emerged as the new man of destiny. When Lebed came third in the first round Yeltsin bought him off with high posts and responsibilities in government and triumphed once more. He then dismissed Lebed. He gave his government a reformist touch by restoring Chubais to favour together with the youthful provincial politician Boris Nemtsov, but after a year he demoted Chubais (largely on account of a private financial transaction which was at least dubious) and in 1998 he dismissed his prime minister Victor Chernomyrdin and his cabinet on grounds of insufficient dynamism and appointed one of its least-known members, Grigori Kirilenko, prime minister. Twice rejected by the parliament, Kirilenko's appointment was approved only at the third asking when, the voting being secret, party leaders could maintain their opposition to it while enough members voted in favour in order to avoid the automatic dissolution of their parliament. This was victory for nobody. Yeltsin's parliamentary opponents did more to spite than defeat him. They fought shy of currents of popular discontent (striking coal miners, for example) and allowed him a free hand in foreign affairs. By reaching frontier agreements with Lithuania and Latvia, China and (if tentatively) Japan, Yeltsin was able to retain some of his reputation as a man of action. He appeared regularly at important international conferences and cultivated the support of his staunchest foreign ally, Helmut Kohl. With the United States and NATO, however, he achieved only the minimum – an undertaking by NATO not to deploy nuclear weapons on the territories of new members.

Backing for Yeltsin among foreigners – particularly among those who fancied that he might be some sort of democrat – was muted by his catalogue of mistakes, misfortunes and mismanagement and by a realization of the true scale of the effective financial help required. Foreign lenders became warier and as early as 1991 the Group of Seven cut back its offers. Western aid – in the lead were the German government and banks and the European Bank for Reconstruction and Development created in 1989 – was conditioned by three aims or expectations: that Russia should become a national instead of an imperial state, a democracy and a market economy with a predominance of private property. Russian interference in Georgia and Tajikistan was overlooked but the assault on the Chechens caused greater disquiet. Yeltsin's bombardment of the parliament was overlooked because Yeltsin seemed a more reliable ruler than any likely successor, but not without uneasiness over the present and future roles of military leaders to whom Yeltsin appeared increasingly indebted. The third, economic condition was the most perplexing, not least because it directly involved the supply of cash credits in very large amounts. To the political need to promote stability and democracy in Russia through economic aid was added the prospect, ultimately, of profits from a country with considerable natural resources and an evident need for western technology and advice. Donors were divided over the pace at which the old economy should be replaced. They tended to favour a fast track with sharp shocks to shorten the painful process, even at the price of rising unemployment and privation amounting in places to starvation. Some, however – notably the UN Economic Commission for Europe – opposed the more desperate remedies advocated by the IMF, the World Bank and western governments and experts, not only because of their severity but also on the grounds that a short sharp transformation required institutions, skills and habits which could not be conjured out of very thin air. The transfer of assets, initially blocked by practical and legal problems (shortage of private capital, non-existence of appropriate assignees), gained momentum but was accompanied by profiteering, corruption and conspicuous consumption by a few and widespread distress and disillusion among the many. The initial goodwill of foreigners was muted. Although inflation was reduced to 15 per cent during the term of the discarded Chernomyrdin the economy was without direction and in 1998 it descended from recession to catastrophe. Russia defaulted on its pre-1992 (Soviet) debts. It was able neither to collect taxes nor stem corruption; with internal and foreign debt out of control (the latter equalled about 75 per cent of GDP); with a debt service expected to rise to $15 billion a year by 2000 and interest rates up to 50 per cent, even at one point 150 per cent; with falling oil, gold and commodity prices ravaging the comparatively healthy trade balances: the rouble was devalued in August by 30 per cent, debt servicing was suspended for three months, banks failed, foreign credits were cut off, foreign capital was withdrawn at the rate of 10 per cent a month and the nascent stock market saw 85 per cent of the value of its traded shares disappear. Despairingly, the IMF provided in 1999 new credits of $4.5 billion over 18 months to enable the government to meet its immediate obligations and the Paris Club of creditors reduced interest payments for 1999 and 2000 from $8 billion to $600 million a year. The dismissal of Kirilenko, following that of Chubais, advertised the end of anything in the nature of a reform programme. The collapsed communist system remained without a functioning economic alternative as proto-capitalist hustlers dug for gold in the rubble and the rest of the population faced ruin and starvation.

When he installed Kirilenko in place of Chernomyrdin Yeltsin had displayed his dominance but when he reversed that appointment he did so because he was forced to. He no longer dared risk a dissolution of the parliament and was obliged to accept a curtailment of presidential powers and agree not to run for re-election in 2000. This was a coup, executed not by the army but by the Russian equivalent of big business. But it was not accepted by politicians, who tried to exact a larger transfer of power to the parliament by repeatedly rejecting Yeltsin's renomination of Chernomyrdin in place of Kirilenko. The conflict between Yeltsin and the politicians was also one between politicians and tycoons while the army – which had lost much of its technical equipment, the allegiance of its unpaid rank and file and its solidarity – remained in the background. Yevgeny Primakov, a competent politician without as yet a political power base, was accepted as prime minister but after eight months he too was summarily dismissed, ostensibly for economic incompetence but more probably because he had begun to make a name for himself and was probing corruption in areas which Yeltsin preferred to leave in the dark. Primakov's successor Sergei Stepanshin had an even shorter term, replaced after three months by Vladimir Putin, whom Yeltsin also named as his favoured candidate for the presidency in 2000. Political incoherence was increased by the failure of the communists to profit from Yeltsin's decline. The old Soviet Communist Party had sought to distance itself from its past by transforming itself in 1990 into the Russian Communist Party and by espousing a Russian nationalism less ridiculous than Zhirinovski's and less obviously self-seeking than Lebed's but it suffered splits and defections. The appointment of Putin accelerated the formation of a new block comprising city and provincial notables with Primakov as its presidential candidate; it displayed a more anti-western tilt than either Gorbachev or Yeltsin, opposing the expansion of NATO and its use in Yugoslavia, promising to end neglect of the Russian armed forces and the feebleness and muddle which had all but lost Chechnya to the Russian state in 1994–96, and adopting the popular view that free market economics had been a catastrophe and the western concern for human rights was a sham. They were, in effect, saying that although the Cold War had been lost those who had handled the aftermath had made matters worse.

The renewal of the war against Chechnya in 1999 was, in its own terms, a success and popular: the determination with which it was conducted outweighed in Russia its brutality and miseries. It turned 200,000 Chechens – nearly half the population – into refugees and killed countless innocent civilians but Russians accepted the stereotype of the terrorist Chechen bandit as a threat to civilized living and to the integrity of the

Russian state. Putin gained more than Yeltsin, who had already been forced to abandon whatever hopes he had of a further term of office. Putin became an alternative to Primakov as the next Russian president (Putin was the younger by 20 years) and in parliamentary elections at the end of 1999 a Putin alliance outscored the Primakov alliance. The communists, still the largest party, gained votes but lost seats; Yavlinski's economic reformers and Zhirinovski's ultra-nationalists barely struggled into the parliament with 6 per cent of the vote each; the rest of some two dozen groups failed to win any seats. On the last day of the year Yeltsin transformed the political scene by resigning his office and nominating Putin as acting president pending an election which constitutionally would have to be held in March instead of June 2000. Like Richard Nixon, Yeltsin exchanged his office for immunity from prosecution for crimes against the state.

Putin's first task, therefore, was the restoration of Russian authority in Chechnya. Hardly less urgent was the restoration of the authority of central government against provincial bosses and organized crime, over-mighty plutocrats and organized crime – the modern counterparts to the Cossack revolts of the seventeenth and eighteenth centuries which had tried to defeat the consolidation and expansion of the Muscovite state. Russia remained the embodiment in Europe of the somewhat old fashioned nation state and Putin was its champion. Appropriately, therefore, when his term as president approached its end, he manoeuvred himself without difficulty into the post of prime minister whence he might, if he so wished, return to the presidency after the time prescribed by the constitution. But Putin's legacy included – besides a degree of stability, some economic bright spots (mainly sales of oil and gas) and himself as a semi-permanent tsar – neglect in areas such as corruption, a collapsing pensions system, education, housing and equality before the law.

The Second World War and the Cold War combined to thrust upon the USSR the status of a superpower. The shredding of the Soviet empire, followed by the disintegration of the USSR itself, left Russia in no great position in the world nor any clear position in Europe. Viewed from the west, the scene to the east was one of weakness tending towards anarchy. Yet Russia remained a state of some consequence. During the years of its conversion into a superpower and back again the other principal European states – Germany and France – had changed the nature of European politics by a Franco-German alliance and the shaping of a European Union in the conviction that the old European states system would most likely lead to more war. This endeavour lacked an essential element so long as Russia was excluded or its position ambiguous. Russia's position in the 1990s was similar to that of France in 1815 or Germany in 1919 and 1945 – a power defeated but still in being, which its peers might either seek to subjugate or to incorporate into whatever system they were intent on creating. Continental Europeans preferred the latter (that is, Vienna 1815 rather than Versailles 1919); the Americans wavered between extending half an olive branch with credits attached and, on the other hand, giving priority and favours to intermediate states created in *Mitteleuropa* after 1919 by the magic of self-determination, reborn by the outcome of the Cold War and fundamentally hostile to Russia. The west in general, having backed Yeltsin as a democrat hopeful *faute de mieux*, was wrong-footed when he was worsted by the parliament in the name of democracy, but without any apparent democratic or economic programme.

The last decade of the century witnessed the end of Soviet rule in central and eastern Europe, the disintegration of the Soviet Union and unexpectedly violent conflicts in south-east Europe as the Yugoslav federation too broke up and Serbia embarked on attempts to annex much of Bosnia and evict from Kosovo (a province of Serbia) that nine-tenths of its inhabitants who were Albanian Muslims. These Balkan upheavals coincided with, first, a still embryonic stage in the evolution of the European Union, particularly in the matter of joint military forces and their purposes; secondly, plans for the gradual extension of NATO over much or all of the former Soviet empire outside the Soviet Union; and, thirdly, hesitations over the place of Russia in Europe. On the one hand, Russia was viewed, particularly by many Americans, as a failed superpower whose pretensions and susceptibilities could be ignored for some time to come; on the other hand – and particularly by many Europeans – as a state which had played a major role in European affairs ever since Catherine the Great and Frederick of Prussia had partitioned Poland and Alexander I had defeated Napoleon and ridden into Paris.

The limits of superpower

For most of the second half of the twentieth century and much of the world the Cold War dictated the pattern of world politics. The Cold War was an enormously costly and destructive conflict, notwithstanding that it took comparatively few lives. It was a power struggle of a familiar kind between mutually distrustful antagonists with envenoming ideological additives, but it had also two distinguishing features, both of them profoundly misleading. The protagonists, for whom the new category of superpower was invented, were opposed in a pattern which was neither a duel between exclusive autocracies such as Chinese or Roman or Mogul empires nor a mutable constellation of several powers like the European states system which it superseded. The superpowers were two and supposedly roughly equal. But in truth they never were equal. The United States was superior to the USSR in material resources, in education and invention, and in governmental skills and principles; and the disparity was made manifest when the Cold War wrecked the Soviet communist economy without doing comparable damage to American capitalism.

The second special feature of the Cold War was the existence of nuclear weapons which were deemed to be specific to superpowers – their badge – and cast a hellish shadow over the prospect of hot war. In the event they spread to other states in many parts of the world, so that by the end of the century they appeared less dangerous in the hands of superpowers than in regional conflicts. Although potentially devastating, they were inefficient weapons of war, barely credible political weapons, and not used after the Second World War. They made war supremely irrational, conferred more power on fanatics than on sanely calculating statesmen and distracted attention from the undiminished incidence and mounting toll of non-nuclear wars.

The emotions embodied in the Cold War enabled the United States to construct an alliance – the NATO alliance – which endured for as long as the Cold War itself, longer than most alliances in modern history. The power of the alliance rested in and was exercised by the United States, but NATO testified to the determination of a dozen other states to give the Cold War priority in the formation of their own policies. At the point where the Cold War ended the United States created a new alliance (against Iraq) which lasted less than a year. This contrast, while not one of strictly analogous situations, nevertheless marked a tidal change. Bismarck was wont to categorize allies as *bündnisfähig* or the reverse. He had in mind minor parties in an alliance, but the distinction could as well be applied to the central figure, and the Gulf War of 1991 demonstrated among other things that the United States had ceased to be a virtually unchallengeable and necessary ringmaster in world affairs. Although indubitably a dominant power, it no longer commanded the same kind of leadership, no longer possessed a simple touchstone whereby to test and tune its foreign policies and might no longer choose to act in concert rather than alone. These confusions tempered the relief and jubilation properly attendant on the defeat and disintegration of the Soviet empire.

One problem to emerge with unexpected harshness was the relationship between the United States and the United Nations, between a world power and a worldwide organization. The UN, created by an international act on American soil in 1945, represented a stage in the development of inter-state co-operation for a variety of purposes, of which the chief was the prevention of wars between states. Its Charter proscribed recourse to war by a member state except in self-defence and transferred to the UN – acting on findings of the Security Council – the right to make war. In addition to this radically novel enactment, the Charter laid on UN members the obligation to uphold certain standards of behaviour within states, such as the protection of minorities and the observance of human and political rights. But herein lay, if not a contradiction, at least an ambiguity, since the UN was an association of states pledged to the mutual recognition of the sovereign independence of each and explicitly forbidden to intervene in the domestic affairs of others (unless the Security Council found a state guilty of a threat to peace, a breach of the peace or an act of aggression). This fundamental, although qualified, immunity of the state from intervention severely restricted the capacity of the UN to discharge its obligation to uphold human rights since, on the one hand, it frequently could not do so without forcible intervention and, on the other, such intervention was no less frequently blocked by a veto – or threat of a veto – in the Security Council. Disunity in the Security Council might also work the other way round when a powerful member, determined on action, was opposed by a majority in the Council; that member would then be forced to choose between abandoning its purpose or proceeding in defiance of the law. The operations against Iraq after the war of 1991 and against Serbia in 1999 were undertaken in breach of the law of the Charter, but not without good cause. The consequences included a diminution of the UN's effectiveness and prestige and a blow to the aim of strengthening the rule of law in international affairs.

The UN's agenda has been more crowded than that of its predecessor, the League of Nations, especially from the 1960s when the waves of decolonization turned the UN into a truly worldwide body. Where the UN has differed little from the League is in having many functions but little power. The founders of these bodies designed them as ancillary instruments for the regulation of (mainly) inter-state affairs. They had no intention of creating a superior or rival focus of power above the state. Yet the founders of the UN wished to make it stronger than the League, which by the time of its demise was widely regarded as a feeble failure. The UN Charter purported to give the UN authority and powers which, however, it failed to exercise over the next decades, partly because they were aborted by the Cold War, but more seriously because they were in advance of realities and mentalities. The Cold War destroyed the projected Military Staffs Committee and plans for embryonic UN armed forces. The stronger UN members simply did not believe in or attempt to accustom themselves to limitations on their freedom of manoeuvre – they signed the Charter without meaning everything which they themselves had put in it. So there were at the core of the international system tensions between the UN and its more powerful members and with the end of the Cold War the United States, uniquely powerful, found itself in a fateful position. It might in any particular crisis act on its own (with or without allies) in pursuit of its national interests and its sense of what world order and justice required; or it might abide strictly by the law of the Charter in order to reinstate the UN at the centre of world affairs and assert the overriding importance of the rule of law. The end of the Cold War did not, as widely expected, automatically liberate and enhance the UN after a period of temporary occlusion; it created a new situation inherently inimical to the role given to it in 1945. Created as an ancillary of law and order, it appeared from the American point of view to be on occasions an impediment to these *desiderata*.

The crises over Iraq and Kosovo demonstrated an American readiness to give law a less than absolute place in the regulation of world affairs. So too did use of NATO in Yugoslavia contrary to the terms of the North Atlantic Treaty and in breach of the UN Charter and the 2003 invasion of Iraq and the bombing of Iraq in the late 1990s without the explicit authority of the Security Council. The United States found it difficult to map a course between leadership and high-handedness. Yet the American action could not be censured out of hand. Law is not the whole of politics. The rule of law, a valid and urgent goal, remains just that, and so long as it is more goal than reality there is a 'meanwhile' during which particular crises will be handled with a mixture of expediency, improvisation and impatience. Police forces all over the world which fail to catch criminals within the rules break the rules and then claim to have got the right result, even if at some cost to principle. What is not so easily excusable is to flout the law and fail to get the results. In postwar Iraq American policies failed for years to unseat Saddam Hussein and caused more suffering to innocents than to miscreants: international rules were broken without benefit to anyone. Then came Kosovo. The removal of all Albanians from Kosovo – 90 per cent of the population of 2 million – was the proclaimed aim of Serb leaders including Milosevic from 1980. The extremes of brutality with which it was carried out ten years later were latent in this criminal determination but were probably sharpened, first, by the discovery that the KLA had become more than a tiresome guerrilla faction and, secondly, by NATO's resort to war to prevent it. This war was an illicit war with a just cause. Its aims were to protect the Albanians of Kosovo and force Milosevic to accept the terms presented at Rambouillet for the future of that province. It was fought, on American insistence, with air power only and with aircraft flying above 15,000 feet. Many in Europe were sceptical of the efficacy of air power alone, particularly over the terrain in question, but the EU possessed no unified military institutions or forces independent of the United States and so no independent voice. The war lasted ten weeks. It failed to prevent the slaughter or eviction of the Kosovo Albanians and it gravely threatened the stability of the neighbouring Macedonian and Albanian republics, but it forced Milosevic to surrender. The NATO forces suffered not a single casualty; and the dead were Albanian or Serbian. Whether these results were achieved by air power alone or by air power bolstered by a growing prospect of action by ground forces too was a question with no clear answer. Like Saddam Hussein, Milosevic survived air warfare but probably would not have survived a ground attack.

The war had a number of political consequences. It strengthened the arguments in favour of international intervention (by the UN) in the affairs of a sovereign state on humanitarian grounds and it also strengthened the trend towards the creation of unified EU military institutions and capabilities independent of, although not necessarily divorced from, the United States. These were arguments which were likely to continue for decades in the coming century. Kosovo was an example of how arguments may be advanced by events. More urgently, the war raised questions about the position of Russia in European affairs. For Russians, civilians and military alike, the main issue was the expansion of NATO towards the frontiers of Russia and its use in action in south-east Europe – all of which amounted in Russian eyes to an American policy of threatening and humiliating Russia in Cold War mode. Taking its stand on the letter of the law, Russia, although willing to concur with Security Council measures directed against Serbia, was adamantly opposed to operations by NATO and to Russian participation in an international peacekeeping force under NATO command and control. When Milosevic surrendered and Serb forces began to evacuate Kosovo, Russian units in Bosnia were despatched through Serbia into Kosovo, where they reached Pristina airport ahead of NATO's advance guard. By this gesture Russia sought to emphasize that it could not be left out of account, but the Russian *démarche*, besides being disconcertingly unexpected, revealed splits and an absence of authority in the Yeltsin regime. The immediate consequences were slight. Russia showed that it could make trouble but not that it could much influence events.

The last decade of the century did not end the Cold War cleanly. It blew away some Cold War perceptions and so helped to chart a new political geography which had been taking shape in the shadows of the Cold War. Essential elements in the accepted formulation of world politics suddenly seemed to be false. The first was the very concept of bipolarity. The resurrection of Japan after 1945 and the later resurrection of China made bipolarity look quaint. Such was the strength of the Cold War matrix that Japan had been regarded as an adjunct of the United States, and China of the USSR. As a power struggle, the Cold War had the appearance of a traditionally territorial contest but its ideological wrappings gave it a scope with no territorial bounds. From the American point of view it extended to China and all parts of the world supposedly open to Chinese influence. But the reintroduction of China into world affairs had the opposite effect, for it caused the first major breach in the bipolar mirage (Yugoslavia provided the first but lesser breach). Recovering in mid-century the sovereign independence which it had let slip over 300 years to a Manchurian dynasty and then to Japanese and (if marginally) European invaders, China, a once and future giant, suffered the calamities of Mao's rule but was always at least as nationalist as communist and – as President Nixon's surprising appearance in Beijing in 1972 showed – was marking its resurrection not as an actor in a solid communist array in a Manichaean epic but as a power among others in a multiple states system. Not many years later, the century's last American president demonstrated his belief that China, together with Japan, South-east Asia and the Pacific's rims were as strategically and above all as economically important to the United States as its entrenched interests in Europe and the Middle East. Clearly, however, the American position in this vast sphere could not be hegemonic in the sense that it had been in the Cold War pattern nor as amenable to the demonologies which had been so handy in the Cold War. If there was to be a New World Order it would arise not, as President Bush (senior) proclaimed, out of the defeat of Iraq in the war of 1991 but for a variety of causes, chief among them the resurgence of China and the economic weight of eastern Asia and the Pacific: and in that New Order the United States, sole surviving superpower of the Old Order, would be less, not more, dominant than the collapse of the Soviet power at first seemed to forecast. At the same moment as it became unique the United States was shown – not least to itself – to be well short of omnipotent.

A second shift at the base of world politics concerned the state itself. The state remained the essential building block of the international system, there were more states than ever before and they were more diverse culturally as well as politically. The main source of this multiplication – decolonization in Asia and Africa – produced new states which cherished their independence but discovered that, economically, it was a sham. This discrepancy was experienced in other parts of the world too. States had been wont to make and unmake alliances which were in most cases avowedly temporary but this political mutability, at odds with long-term economic planning, was, if not superseded, supplemented by the construction of blocks designed to persist indefinitely, even permanently, and to operate for some purposes as single entities. The main impulses behind these associations were the demands and opportunities of international trade and transnational investment. They were groups of states, geographically contiguous, culturally akin, with common interests and the feeling that none of them might by itself count for much in the not too distant future. Prototypes included ASEAN and a variety of experiments in Latin America and in west and southern Africa. They were a vote of no confidence by states in themselves, therefore hesitant and guarded, but even the mightiest flirted with such ventures, including the United States with pan-American or Pacific groupings.

The leading entrepreneurs in this genre were the founders and later adherents of what became the European Union. This was the outstanding political innovation of the century, an audacious experiment attempting in Europe as a whole what the Swiss cantons had achieved centuries earlier: the subordination of political, economic and religious distinctions in a new powerbase, new cultural identity and new common institutions. When at mid-century Europe was knocked off the top perch in the world it retained enviable special advantages. It was a special case: small, recognizable, culturally coherent, long endowed with good education, technically advanced, comparatively rich, better administered and organized than most parts of the world. The promoters of a united Europe had two broad aims. They sought a way to prevent a third great war against the hegemonic ambitions of the German state and jointly to maximize Europe's economic strengths and technical and political inventiveness. The principal obstacle to these aims was the divisive nationalism grounded in the adversarial, if inspiriting, competitiveness of the separate 'nation' states into which the continent had been progressively divided from the late Middle Ages onwards. A lesser obstacle – in some sense a paradoxical advantage in the first stages – was the alienation from western Europe of *Mitteleuropa* and the Balkans under communist rule. By the end of the century a European Union was in being but how it would develop the relationship between its members and its whole remained unsettled and unsettling. It put practice before constitution. The light at the end of the tunnel was to be clearly visible only half way through: no journey for faint hearts. The prospect was not the extinction of the European state but its demotion, imprecisely delineated.

World affairs are conducted within constraints which are not, or are barely, amenable to human control. This is not the place for an extended examination of these supernal forces but two may be mentioned: population growth and globalization.

The number of people in the world had been doubling and redoubling at shorter and shorter intervals. It reached 6 billion at the end of the twentieth century, having doubled in less than 50 years – in 1800 it was 1 billion. This sort of growth was not necessarily a disaster. Growth had been in the past checked and even reversed and it was not impossible to bring the supply of food into line with the needs of larger populations. But growing numbers allied with growing mobility created political problems besides economic and humanitarian ones. The borders between states become regularly pierced not only by refugees from brutality but also by migrants in search of a basic or a better livelihood. States and their citizens resent and resist these movements which, as they nevertheless become easier, become also a source of disorders and disasters as murderous as wars. This disturbing demographic fluidity could be magnified by changes in climate: at the end of the twentieth century global warming and consequent flooding were causing migrations and hostilities in north-east India and Bangladesh.

Secondly, globalization: this is a term coined to describe a revolution of Copernican magnitude. This revolution stems from the impact of technology on space and time as experienced by human beings; it affects what men and women know and think about one another, how they do business with one another and what institutions they need to regulate their affairs. It is not a new process but it has reached a critical phase. What was begun by the electric telegraph and the internal combustion engine assumed a new significance, different not in degree but in kind, when modern technology enabled people and ideas and knowledge, materials and money to move from one place to another with astonishing speed, in unprecedented volume and by means which lie outside the control of political authorities and established economic institutions and partially outside the world itself. Grounded in technical invention, it is irreversible. One of its impulses is towards anarchy, for it calls in question the capacities of organizations which are territorially delimited, including the state whose reach it transcends. In economic matters it undermines the activities of free markets by laying them open to the operations of anarchic rogues, individual or corporate. It extends, again anarchically, the opportunities for the demagogic manipulation of opinion, whether by self-serving politicians or intolerant fundamentalists. But by the same token it prefigures new democratic forces by bringing more and more individuals into contact with public affairs and with one another, which could be its most revolutionary product.

In the shorter term globalization may be seen not so much as a destructive force but a limiting one. It does not destroy the state, yet just as the city state disappeared centuries ago but cities did not, so the sovereign state will disappear but states will not. Markets in goods or funds will not disappear but the notion that the freer the market the more efficient and benign it is will seem as simplistic and tawdry as it did to Keynes half a century ago. As the globe shrinks in human terms it becomes more complex and contradictory, demanding more efficient co-operation in the restraint of armed conflict, the protection of human rights and the management of resources and production.

One dimension of power is distance. Good communications, physical or technical, extend power. Rome's roads were a major item in Roman imperialism and in the spread of Christianity, their neglect and decay a cause of the swift dissolution of Charlemagne's empire. In modern times information technology sharpens the attractions of economic warfare as an alternative to crude military might but also disturbs settled political patterns by allowing information and transactions to reach to the ends of the planet and so to escape the control of political power and law. Globalization creates hostility in so far as it serves the interests of an unacceptably small proportion of mankind. It creates protest movements, directed mainly against the state, sometimes striving to stop the unstoppable, sometimes violent, sometimes turning a blind eye to the benefits among the changes that protest seeks to arrest; but many also acting in the spirit of Pascal when he pointed out that the heart has reasons which reason overlooks. These people were profoundly moved when, for example, they learned that a quarter of the world's population was existing on $1 a day or less. The conjunction of abject poverty with spectacular enrichment gave the Third World and its sympathizers moral strength but the Third World was itself split. Some sought salvation through co-operation with international organizations even though these were dominated by rich states with priorities of their own; more radical campaigners denounced the existing world order even though they had little prospect of changing it by attacking it.

There was, however, another aspect of a development which seemed at first sight to be the current version of the old conflict of rich vs. poor. The main target of the anti-global protesters was the old bogey big business and its capacities or intentions but business found itself in an anomalous position partly brought about by globalization. The very successes of its commercial and financial expansion propelled it beyond the confines and control of the state at a time when dominant political patterns remained national rather than international. Big business was becoming a law unto itself, insufficiently regulated or accountable – a maverick in a new world. It had few friends.

Finally, politics by protest or demonstration posed a threat to democratic government. Parliamentary democracy is a compromise. It is not what was described by Aristotle or indeed what was practised in classical Athens which covered about 1,000 square miles and had a political population (i.e. excluding women, minors, foreigners and slaves) of about 80,000 at its classical peak. It was never realistically possible for the citizen farmers beyond the city walls to walk or ride into the city week after week to debate and vote. Hence the invention for the modern state of parliamentary democracy in which the millions of citizens delegate government to an elected parliament for a limited (fixed or unfixed) number of years. This is a fragile arrangement since one essential of democracy is the right to protest. But if the protest threatens to derogate from the power or prestige of a parliament – if frequent recourse to a referendum is used to bypass or supplant the parliamentary process – then the only practicable form of democracy, which is as valuable as it is rare, is maimed along with peace, prosperity and justice.

Related reading: part one

The USA

Adams, Henry: *The Education of Henry Adams* (1907)
Kennan, George F.: *American Diplomacy 1900–1952* (1957)
Lasch, Christopher: *The Agony of the American Left* (1970)

Russia

Brown, Archie: *Seven Years that Changed the World* (2007)
Malia, Martin: *The Soviet Tragedy – A History of Socialism in Russia 1917–1990* (1994)
Service, Robert: *A History of Twentieth Century Russia* (1997)
Tolstoi, Leo: *Hadji Murat* (1912) [Chechens]

General

Aron, Raymond: *Memoirs – Forty Years of Political Reflection* (1990)
Halle, Louis J. *The Cold War as History* (1991)
Mitrany, David: *Marx against the Peasants* (1951)

PART TWO

The Far East

CHAPTER 2

Japan

In 1945 Japan was prostrate, its military power annihilated and its national symbol, the emperor, nullified. Many of its cities had been devastated, some 10–15 million were unemployed, and it was occupied and ruled by the United States. Within a generation Japan regained the status of a great power, not by replacing its armouries but by rebuilding its industries, regaining its foreign trade and reconstituting its reserves of cash and currencies; it was the one power in the world that could be referred to as a great power but had no nuclear capacity and it was evidently more powerful than some powers – Britain, France, India – which had made nuclear explosions.

Furthermore, Japan in this period lacked not only the military trappings with which states are wont to make their mark in the world; it was also conspicuously short of primary resources. It had no – or virtually no – oil, uranium, aluminium or nickel; very little coal, iron ore, copper or natural gas; only half its requirements of lead and zinc. These shortages were made all the more acute by the great expansion of industry, an expansion which was both essential to Japan's recovery and exacerbated its dependence on foreign materials. This need to secure primary products, whether by participating in exploration or by establishing commercial-political control in the places where they lay, became a major imperative of Japanese foreign policy.

The American share in the defeat of Japan had been so overwhelming that the United States could reduce postwar allied co-operation in the occupation to a not very polite figment. Two bodies were created: the Allied Council for Japan, located in Tokyo and consisting of the United States, the USSR, China and a representative of Britain and the Pacific members of the Commonwealth; and the Far Eastern Commission, located in Washington, with 11 members. But in fact Japan was ruled by the supreme commander, who was General MacArthur and whose ways of treating associates, subjects and problems were akin to those of the shoguns. Retribution took the form of disarmament, demilitarization and trials of war criminals. Then came a new constitution, administrative and social reforms, and attempts to alter the industrial and cultural patterns of the country on the basis, however, of the retention of imperial rule and the emperor himself (who lived on until 1989). The MacArthur regime was a strict paternal autocracy but also radical. The Japanese were commanded to become democratic.

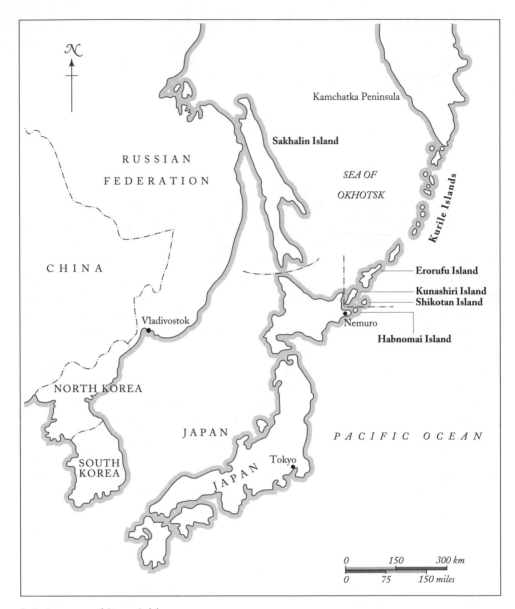

N

Kamchatka Peninsula

Sakhalin Island

RUSSIAN

FEDERATION

SEA OF

OKHOTSK

Kurile Islands

CHINA

Erorufu Island

Kunashiri Island
Shikotan Island

Vladivostok

Nemuro

Habnomai Island

NORTH KOREA

JAPAN

PACIFIC   OCEAN

SOUTH
KOREA

JAPAN

Tokyo

| 0 | 150 | 300 km |
| 0 | 75 | 150 miles |

2.1 Japan and its neighbours

The emperor was cut down to human size, over 200,000 (mostly military) persons were barred from public life, the prime minister and all his colleagues were to be civilians, the great financial conglomerates or *zaibatsus* were to be broken up, land reform was imposed on paper and carried out in practice.

None of this stood in the way of revival when the opportunity came, and much of it was helpful. The purge eliminated a number of able men but it cleared the way to the top for many more who, without it, would not have got there so quickly: some European bureaucracies and businesses would have benefited from such a purge. The elimination of big, often absentee, landowners facilitated the modernization and re-equipment of agriculture, established a rich rural sector alongside the reviving industrial and commercial sectors, and gave Japan the efficient food production which was vital for so densely populated a country. A new abortion law halved the birthrate over a period of five years and stabilized the population. As in Germany, the Americans were quickly converted from exacting reparations to repairing the Japanese economy, first in the general Cold War context of anti-communism and then more specifically and vigorously by the Korean War: in the course of 1948–51 the United States dispensed to Japan post-war relief equal to twice the war reparations exacted from it. War in Asia – the Korean War and later the wars in Vietnam – gave Japan the boost which transformed its fortunes in an astonishingly short time. Like the United States in the Second World War, Japan became an arsenal of war and a war-fuelled economy with the advantage of not being itself a belligerent. It constructed a powerful economy on the basis of low-interest loans for industry, subsidies for public services, high levels of saving, the revival of the prewar *zaibatsu* and a form of guided capitalism in which the state regulated priorities and the allocation of resources without seeking managerial control of operations. At the outset MacArthur's autocratic rule permitted no interference by strikes or unions to the process of making goods and money and, together with the discipline and determination of the Japanese people, shaped a harsh capitalist culture which sent the weak to the wall but encouraged that adventurousness and vision which had characterized the nineteenth-century English merchant and industrialist before he was turned into a conservative twentieth-century financier. Finally, it was a condition of Japan's success that its new leaders should co-operate closely with the Americans who ruled in Tokyo and Washington. When MacArthur left Tokyo in 1951, dismissed by Truman, he did so as a friend and hero and after a personal farewell visit by the emperor.

Japan's first postwar prime minister, Shigeru Yoshida, was already 70 when he was installed in 1948 in the office which he held for six years. He understood the constraints and had no inhibitions about tackling Japan's alarming postwar inflation by the most familiar deflationary devices, killing off weak businesses and adding to the unemployed. His overall purpose was to restore Japan's power in the world but not the power of the military in Japan. He struck lucky. With the Korean War prosperity bloomed and the United States was happy to turn Japan from defeated enemy to principal ally. It organized a peace treaty which was signed in 1952 by the two countries and 40 others – the USSR, China, India and Burma being among the absentees. By the Treaty of Portsmouth Japan renounced Korea, which it had ruled since 1910; Taiwan and the Pescadores, which had been Japanese for over half a century; the islands in the Pacific which had been administered under mandate since the end of the First World War, after being seized from Germany; all its rights and claims in China and Antarctica; and southern Sakhalin and the Kuriles. The status of these last territories remained ambiguous because the USSR, which had occupied them in 1945, was not a party to the treaty. They were formed in 1947 into a district or *oblast* of the Russian Soviet Federal Socialist Republic: the island of Sakhalin, stretching northward from Japan's northern tip, runs offshore of the RSFSR for nearly 970 km; the Kurile archipelago, comprising 30 comparatively large volcanic islands and as many smaller ones, runs north-east from Japan to the Kamchatka peninsula. The Ryuku islands (including Okinawa) and the Bonins, which had been annexed by Japan at the end of the nineteenth century and were occupied by the United States during and after the Second World War, were gradually recovered by Japan in 1968–72, subject to the continuing presence of American troops and military installations.

Japan's territorial losses were considerable but it was not required to pay any war reparations and it suffered nothing like the bisection of Germany. On the same day as the signing of the peace treaty Japan and the United States signed a security treaty followed by an administrative agreement which gave the latter the right to station forces throughout Japan for purposes defined as the maintenance of international peace and security in the Far East, the defence of Japan against external aggression and the suppression of rebellion or disorders instigated by an outside power. No such rights were to be accorded to any other state except with American consent. The American occupation came formally to an end in April 1952. What had begun as a crusade to make Japan safe for democracy in the western style was superseded by the recruitment of Japan to the anti-communist side in the Cold War and, less obviously but not without considerable popular discontent, fettered Japan's renewed sovereignty.

Although Japan's constitution forbade the creation of armed forces this ban had been circumvented in 1950 by the creation of a National Police Reserve and Self Defence Forces which looked and lived very like an army. These forces gradually expanded to the comparatively modest figure of 250,000. Defence expenditure was kept below 1 per cent of GNP (which was, however, rising steeply) and around 6–7 per cent of government expenditure, again a modest figure. By the 1970s there were the beginnings of a debate about whether Japan should go nuclear: its weight in the world pointed in that direction but there were political as well as constitutional obstacles. Japan signed the Partial Test Ban Treaty – an act of supererogation if the constitution were to be taken at its face value – and public opinion in the land of Hiroshima and Nagasaki was ultra-sensitive to the exercise of the nuclear option. An incident in 1954 dramatized these feelings. A Japanese fishing vessel, the *Fukuryu Maru* or *Fortunate Dragon*, a few miles outside an area closed to fishing on account of American nuclear tests on the island of Bikini, was caught in the fall-out of an H-bomb. Before this terrifying fact was realized the *Fukuryu Maru* had returned to port and sold part of its catch. Panic followed. One member of the crew died. Later the United States paid $2 million by way of damages or conscience money for this terrible accident. It also had to pay a political price as Japanese opinion gathered hostility to the United States and to Yoshida as the symbol of the Japanese–American alliance.

This episode coincided with the conclusion in 1954 of new defence, financial and commercial agreements between the United States and Japan, which included a Mutual Defence Agreement providing for mutual assistance against communism and reorganization of Japan's pseudo-military forces. Yoshida, however, was weakened by scandals, charges of undue subservience to Washington and rifts in his own party and was replaced at the end of the year by an old rival Ichiro Hatoyama, whose foreign minister Mamoru Shigemitsu expressed the intention to restore normal relations with the USSR and China. But Hatoyama did not last long and was succeeded by Nobusuke Kishi, another of the Liberal Democratic Party's numerous but not harmonious chiefs. Kishi preferred to pursue the policy of restoring relations with Japan's former enemies in South-east Asia rather than the Hatoyama–Shigemitsu approach to the USSR and China which, in view of Japan's continuing attachment to the United States, was still too hot a potato. Kishi also negotiated in 1960 a revised version of the Security Treaty of 1951, but the new treaty – and especially a clause making it last for ten years – was unpopular. The government was accused of involving Japan in the Cold War by allowing American nuclear weapons to be held on Japanese territory. There were disorderly scenes in the Japanese parliament and outside it, and although the new treaty was ratified a projected visit by Eisenhower had to be cancelled and Kishi resigned before the end of the year.

The 1960s were the years when Japan impressed itself on the rest of the world by annual growth rates of 10 per cent or more; when the alternation of boom and slump which had characterized the 1950s seemed to have gone for good; when the new shape of Japanese industry with its emphasis on heavy goods and chemicals in place of textiles became apparent; when Japan's investment and performance in the most advanced technology captivated the world; and when its admission to the ranks of the OECD publicly designated it as one of the world's economic heavyweights. In 1962 Japan concluded with China a five-year commercial agreement on a barter basis. The vastness of China and its population mesmerized some Japanese industrialists but the government remained inhibited by Washington's hostility to China, the present gains in trade with China were small and Japan's trade with Taiwan was substantially larger: the 1962 agreement was no more than a gesture towards a vague future. More concretely, Japan embarked on a policy of economic co-operation in South-east Asia and the Pacific rimlands. Already in the 1950s Japan had paved the way with agreements for the payment of reparations to Burma (1956), the Philippines (1956) and Indonesia (1958), and in 1967 the prime minister Eisaku Sato undertook a tour of South-east Asian capitals, preceded and followed by visits to South Korea, Australia and New Zealand. He was the first Japanese prime minister to visit these last two countries. Japan's course was not easy. Besides being a former imperialist aggressor with an unforgotten reputation for peculiar cruelty, Japan was a rapidly developing country in a largely underdeveloped region. Sato lavished loans for development and, in the case of Vietnam, for postwar reconstruction, while by supporting ventures such as the Asian Development Bank and the Agricultural Fund for South-east Asia he hoped to stress Japan's pacific amiability in contrast not only to its past but also to the militaristic policies of the United States evinced by the SEATO alliance and the war in Vietnam. Japan was at pains to supply its poorer neighbours with high-grade capital and consumer goods rather than drain them of their natural resources in the classical colonial mode. Further afield, in Australia, Japan became the leading purveyor of investment funds, exceeding the sum of British, American and German funds; Australia was by the mid-1960s importing more goods from Japan than from Britain and selling more of its mineral and agricultural products (including wool) to Japan than to any other country. In its smaller way New Zealand was turning in the same direction. Even Canada, another Pacific state, although more firmly fixed in the North American economy, considerably increased its trade with Japan and its loans to and investment in the South-east Asian sector of what was becoming a vast Asian–Pacific economic zone dominated by Japan. The achievements of the 1960s were crowned by the spectacular Expo 70 in Tokyo.

But shortly after Expo 70 Japan suffered two serious setbacks. Its industrial recovery and commercial expansion had depended on a strong dollar (which made Japanese exports to its largest market exceptionally profitable) and cheap oil. In 1971 Nixon devalued the dollar and in 1973 war in the Middle East created an economic crisis in Japan. Japan relied entirely on imported oil, 85 per cent of which came from the Middle East. The war so reduced supply that Japanese stocks fell to a few days' consumption and when the flow was resumed as a result of urgent, even grovelling, diplomacy the price had quadrupled. Ruthless economies cut consumption by half but many businesses went under, unemployment rose sharply and the employed had to accept strict wage restraint. A second oil shock occurred with the fall of the shah in Iran in 1979 but in the interval Japan, uniquely among industrialized countries, had regained its economic health by abandoning old and moribund industries without compunction, by experimenting in automation and robots, by massive investment of government money at cheap rates, and by extensive retraining of the workforce, again with government funds. In the next decade the same combination of industrialists, experts and government seized for Japan the world's leading place in electronics. In the same period the United States was applying its knowledge and its funds in going to the moon and creating huge, but largely useless, armaments.

Japan's prosperity made it a voracious consumer of the world's products: one estimate in the 1970s had it that by 1981 Japan would need one-tenth of the world's total exports and in oil more than one-tenth of the world's total production. But Japan had no sure way of securing its needs. Britain in the nineteenth century and then the United States had had a similar problem and had solved it by a variety of means which go under the name of imperialism. The essence of imperialism from this viewpoint was not the domination of an area for glory's sake but domination in order to secure materials, whether by taking them, or by ensuring that the producers go on producing them and not something else, or by encouraging a bigger output. The means included investment and so partial or total ownership of minerals, crops or manufacturing enterprises. Japan had plenty of money to invest but there were difficulties about investing it. Apart from its especially delicate standing in the region, the very idea of foreign investment had become suspect. However welcome investment funds might be in purely financial terms, there was a nervous awareness of conflicts of interest between investor and recipient and a legacy of hostility to the foreign investor, who was presumed to be distorting and retarding a developing economy and indeed to be intent on doing so. In the special case of oil Japan's problem was aggravated by the fact that most known investment opportunities had been pre-empted by the United States or western Europeans. Nevertheless, Japan, accelerating in the 1970s a trend begun in the 1960s, placed considerable sums abroad, particularly in Malaysia, Indonesia, Thailand and the Philippines. Anxious to reduce its dependence on Middle Eastern oil, it engaged in exploration or investment in Indonesia, New Guinea, Australia and Nigeria. Japan's vulnerability in terms of oil was compounded by the fact that Middle Eastern oil bound for Japan passed through the narrow Malacca Strait and so was at the mercy of any unfriendly power in Malaya or Sumatra. The oil hunger of those years focused attention on certain small islands in the South China Sea: the Paracels, seized by China in 1974 by evicting a small South Vietnamese force, and the Spratlys further south, which were claimed by China, Vietnam, the Philippines, the Netherlands and France and some of which were occupied by China in 1988.

Besides his devaluations of the dollar in 1971 Nixon shocked Japan when, without warning to Tokyo, he announced that he had accepted an invitation to visit China. The Japanese government, whose policies had been moulded and constricted by the American alliance and by American policies which, in Asia, were based on hostility to China, was seized with equal astonishment and resentment. What seemed to the rest of the world a sensible move to take some heat out of an overheated quarrel betokened in Japan a reversal of alliances not unconnected with commercial and economic rivalry. Japan feared not only a political volte-face by Washington but also the closing of American markets to Japanese goods, partly at the instance of the American textile lobby but more generally too in order to check the big Japanese surplus in the balance of trade between the two countries. Proposals by Japan to restrict Japanese exports to the United States having produced no result, Nixon took unilateral action, including a 10 per cent surcharge designed to hit Japanese trade. Japanese anger was increased when it became apparent that the rate of growth in 1971 had been reduced to 6 per cent; this interruption in Japan's expansion was blamed on American policy and ill will. The undervalued yen, a source of complaint from all Japan's trading partners, was allowed to float in August 1971 and was in consequence revalued by 16 per cent by the end of the year. Relations between Japan and the United States became, temporarily, bad. They were not sensibly improved by the return of Okinawa to Japanese sovereignty since no limit on the use of the island by American troops was set, nor were nuclear weapons prohibited on it. The emperor visited the United States, his first journey outside Japan since 1921, but the visit was treated as a curiosity rather than a political event. Japan joined the United States' attempt to get the United Nations to retain Taiwan as a separate member when China was admitted, but the attempt failed and Japan's part in it seemed to many Japanese to be misplaced loyalty to a shifty ally. Nevertheless, the drama of Nixon's visit to Beijing exceeded its immediate consequences and neither Tokyo nor Washington wished their economic disagreements to degenerate into serious political conflict. New trade agreements were signed in 1972, Nixon and Sato met at Honolulu and Japan promised to make massive purchases of American (and other foreign) goods to redress the imbalance in foreign trade.

Sato did not long survive the Honolulu meeting. Brother to Kishi and no less pro-American, he had suffered a serious decline in favour, in the country and in his party, and he gave way to Kakuei Tanaka, who immediately went to Beijing and restored diplomatic relations with China. Tanaka was doing only what the United States had done the previous year and many other countries were hastening to copy. China was no substitute for the United States as ally or trading partner; nor was Tanaka markedly pro-Chinese. He was too unpopular to carry through new policies and he retired temporarily into the background during 1972 and was forced to resign in 1974 on being implicated in the bribery of high-level government personages by the Lockheed Aviation Corporation. His successor Takeo Miki survived only until 1976, when the Liberal Democratic Party (LDP) lost its overall majority in parliament for the first time. Miki's vociferous condemnation of corruption – by implication, of his rivals – made him few friends in the party and the 71-year-old Takeo Fukuda took his place. But Miki got his revenge two years later when the party deposed Fukuda and installed Masayoshi Ohira. In an election in 1979 Ohira disappointed the party but survived the vengeful intrigues of its other chieftains for a short space. In 1980 the party found yet another leader in Zenko Suzuki. Throughout these baronial feudings the party retained its dominant position. What made Japan uniquely strange in this generation was the combination of its worldwide economic thrust with static, geriatric political leadership embodied in the LDP.

That direction continued through the next decade in spite of rebuffs: a decline in electoral favour, severe financial scandals, conflict over fiscal reforms, some sparring with the United States, and a diminution of Japan's hitherto unquenchable economic expansion. Elections in 1983, which registered some reverses for the LDP, were followed three years later by a triumphant campaign under the leadership of Yasuhiro Nakasone, who was in consequence accorded an extended hold on the premiership. He was succeeded at the end of 1987 by Noboru Takeshita who, unlike Nakasone, succeeded in imposing on an unwilling parliament a series of reforms to an obsolete tax system – in particular an unpopular consumption tax (3 per cent) – with the aim of redressing the fiscal balance to the advantage of the urban middle class. Simultaneously, scandals exploded over the exceptionally lavish bribery of political parties and personalities by the real-estate conglomerate Recourse Cosmos, and in 1989 Takeshita was forced to resign. His immediate successor quickly fell victim to scandals of a more personal nature but the party succeeded in finding in Toshiki Kaifu a prime minister – the thirteenth since the end of the American occupation – sufficiently reputable and resourceful to hold at bay the Japanese Socialist Party (JSP) led by Takako Doi. In 1989 the LDP lost its majority in the upper house for the first time but since only half of the seats were in issue it remained the largest party. In the next year it retained its majority in the lower house. Kaifu, more durable than had been expected, rebuilt the party's traditional base among farmers, small businesses and women, with the help of a new boom and continuing surpluses in overseas trade.

The comparatively extrovert Nakasone had been second only to Thatcher in praise of Ronald Reagan, but he also visited Moscow, took the initiative in soothing anti-Japanese susceptibilities in South Korea, visited China and South-east Asia, increased Japan's already large aid to the Third World and cancelled some of its more intractable debts. Substantial changes in external affairs were small. A soothing speech by Gorbachev in Vladivostok in 1986, two visits by Shevardnadze to Tokyo in 1986 and 1988 and a visit by Gorbachev in 1991 produced no more than talk about a formal resolution of the disputed Northern Territories. A Russian proposal, first made in 1956, to cede two of the four larger Kurile Islands was repeated by Gorbachev (and later by Yeltsin) but rejected by Japan: these islands, allotted to the USSR at the Yalta conference in 1945, had never been part of Russia and in Japan's view were not part of the Kurile chain ceded by Japan after the Second World War. Japan refused to consider economic aid for Russia unless all four islands were returned. (An agreement over fishing rights in 1998 opened the prospect of wider agreement by 2000.)

In response to American criticism of its trading practices Japan modified some import barriers and eased some of the obstacles in the way of foreign bids for construction contracts in Japan, but the balance of trade between the two countries remained above $50 billion. Under the Omnibus Trade and Competitiveness Act of 1988 the US Congress gave the president authority to designate foreign countries as unfair traders and required him to negotiate the removal of unfair practices and, if he failed, to retaliate. These measures were an indication of American alarm over Japan's surging pre-eminence in industries from automobiles to computers and its advance into superconductors and defence industries. But so long as the Reagan and Bush administrations failed to balance government spending by cutting programmes or raising taxation they remained dependent on foreign borrowing and, since Japan was the biggest lender, American threats of commercial retaliation had limited substance.

Japan's relatively disarmed condition held great advantages and great risks. On the credit side was an enormous saving; even as late as 1980 Japan's defence spending was still less than 1 per cent of GNP. Further, the absence of pressures from military quarters enabled Japan to plan its industrial production and training without the distortions imposed by military exigencies in, for example, the United States and the USSR. Within Japan's military–industrial complex the emphasis was more industrial than military. Japan was naturally reluctant to change a pattern which was helping it to equal or even surpass the United States as the United States had surpassed Britain 100 years earlier. By 1980 Japan had not only overtaken Germany in many leading products but was making more steel and cars than the United States and, by installing more modern equipment, had achieved twice the American output per man. Japanese capitalism was centrally planned, guided and financed and was taken to include education and training and to be an important element in the broad picture of neo-Japanese culture. Even more successful than the France of the Monnet Plan or the German *Wirtschaftwunder*, it allied private business with government and labour. It distrusted the blind forces of the market and the simplistic nostrums in which Reagan's America and Thatcher's Britain were asked to put their faith. Its outward and visible signs included the highest GDP per head in the world, a number of industries which exported 90 per cent of their output and much the largest provision of aid to the rest of the world (passing $10 billion a year). In some aspects it was as distinct from American capitalism as was either from communism.

Initially, these triumphs owed much to the American alliance, which provided the security behind which Japan's energies could be concentrated on the creation of wealth. The efficacy of that alliance was called in question by the American defeat in Vietnam and by episodes to which the United States was especially exposed by its more adventurous foreign policies – for example, its failure to redeem its hostages in Iran. Self-defence, militarily adequate in the context of the alliance, had to be re-examined. It was, in effect, reinterpreted. Already in the 1950s the concept of self-defence had been held to include the pursuit of an enemy to his bases and attacks on those bases. It was also extended to the protection of vital sea routes and, in 1980, to joint naval exercises with other powers. Self-defence was adjudged to be a relative term whose meaning changed with the development of an enemy's military technology and one's own strategic needs. Although Japan's revulsion against nuclear arms was confirmed by its adherence in 1970 to the Nuclear Non-Proliferation Treaty of 1968, the passing of the generation which had known war and defeat was marked by growing support for larger defence budgets. The crisis caused by Iraq's annexation of Kuwait in 1990 gave a precise focus to the debate about Japan's responsibilities in world affairs. A purely financial contribution to the international muster against Iraq seemed unheroic, but a military contribution was unconstitutional and unpopular and Kaifu was obliged to abandon an attempt to change the constitution to permit it. Japan's non-military contribution was nevertheless massive: $9 billion for the general war coffers; a further $2 billion specifically for Egypt, Jordan and Turkey; and mine-sweepers, medical supplies and civilian aircraft to carry refugees. By a narrow majority the parliament later endorsed the use of armed forces in UN peacekeeping operations and Japanese units were sent to UNTAC in Cambodia and in 1993 beyond Asia to Mozambique.

By 1991 Kaifu's time was up. Under his premiership the LDP had done better than expected in elections at the end of that year but had nevertheless lost ground. The economy was still growing but at the rate of 5 per cent, low by Japanese standards.

Stock prices and property values were slumping. He was replaced by Kiichi Miyazawa, another LDP nominee, who weakly confronted the gravest Japanese recession for 20 years and more vigorous complaints from the United States over Japanese ingenuity in keeping foreigners out of Japanese markets. But more was at stake than the distribution of political offices in a system dominated by one party. The end of the Cold War distorted postwar Japan's political system and posed testing questions about Japanese security and economic policies. The LDP's monopoly of office was a function of the dominance of the single issue of anti-communism in the decades following the Second World War. In that period the United States had impressed democratic forms on Japan and had pressed Japan into the Cold War against communism. The United States undertook by treaty the defence of Japan and, so long as the Cold War lasted, tolerated, if with increasing irritation, Japan's refusal to conduct its external economic affairs in accordance with the rules of openness enshrined in the Bretton Woods agreements. The LDP enjoyed power in a multiparty system on the terms that it would cede power to no other party and particularly not to the JSP. Putting profit before pride, Japan accepted a ban on raising (and paying for) its own armed forces and made prosperity the main business of government in the knowledge that national security was guaranteed by the United States. The LDP developed into a cabal of conservative leaders appropriating the highest political posts among themselves (much as leading Roman families had rotated the Papacy and its prizes in the late Middle Ages before its removal to Avignon). It left administration and even policy-making to senior civil servants and filched scandalously large rewards for not interfering too far in government or with business.

This state of affairs was challenged in the early 1990s not from outside the LDP but from within it. In 1992 Mori Hasokawa left the LDP and formed the New Japan Party: he was an aristocrat and grandson of Prince Fumimaro Konoye, one of the outstanding figures in prewar Japan. In the next year two other defectors, Ichiro Ozawa and Tsutomu Hata, formed the Renewal Party: they were members of the largest faction in the LDP, led by Shin Kanemaru, whose ascent to the top office seemed barred by the spectacular scale of his involvement in bribery. But this challenge to the LDP failed. In 1993 it lost a striking number of seats (as did the JSP) but remained the largest party in parliament. LDP dissidents formed the first non-LDP government in Japan's postwar history with Hasokawa as prime minister. But Hasokawa was himself not untainted by financial scandal and the coalition which he led was divided over taxation, electoral reform and defence policy. He was unable to make more than limited progress with plans for less bureaucracy, decentralization of government and the opening of Japanese markets to foreign competition and he was replaced in less than a year by Hata, whose government proved the most short-lived in postwar Japan. The JSP did a deal with its enemies in the LDP to oust the interloping reformers and the LDP recovered power at the price of allowing a socialist, Tomiichi Murayama, to become prime minister for the first time. The economic programme of an uneasy coalition was then battered by the devastating earthquake at Kobe in 1995, whose cost fell mainly on the government, and Murayama resigned at the beginning of 1996, having served the latter half of his 18 months as a prime minister in evident decline. Ryutaro Hashimoto restored the LDP's majority in the lower house, using and then discarding the socialists and outwitting Ozawa's new party, but made only unconvincing attempts to tackle the problems of swollen debt and an overvalued yen. He survived for nearly three years until Japan's economic malaise was converted into alarm by the economic collapses in eastern Asia (see Chapter 18) to which nearly half of Japanese exports went and in which Japanese banks had lent large amounts of money. After devastatingly poor results in partial elections to the upper house in 1998 the LDP turned the office of prime minister over to Keizo Obuchi. Unemployment was at a rate which, officially underestimated by perhaps half, was greater than at any time since the war; debt, also officially obscured, probably exceeded $500 million. Obuchi planned to rekindle consumer demand through tax cuts and consumer vouchers and to rescue selected banks with government funds but with little effect and in 1999 he invited Ozawa, the LDP's chief renegade, to join his cabinet. Obuchi's approach to Ozawa demonstrated the poverty of the LDP and Ozawa's acceptance appeared to mark the reversal of his challenge to it in 1993.

The advent of President Clinton to the White House seemed to foreshadow sharper and more public controversy with Japan (as with the EC) over economic affairs but, whatever Clinton's intentions, his position was initially no stronger than that of Reagan or Bush. The imbalance in the trade between the two countries was still growing, American attempts to gain access to Japanese markets by setting guaranteed targets for selected products was a failure, and the Clinton administration was forced back to the crude expedients of retaliation through tariffs or depressing the value of the dollar against the yen – the one a device generally reprobated by the United States and the other unwelcome to American importers and by no means certain to achieve its aims. In 30 years the value of American exports to Japan had doubled but the value of trade in the opposite direction had quadrupled – in the Japanese view because American exporters (of, for example, cars) neglected to find out what Japanese buyers wanted, in the American view because Japan used complicated bureaucratic procedures to thwart the operations of market forces. At a loss to find a remedy, the United States alternated trade talks with bluster and threats to impose punitive retaliatory super-tariffs. Talks in 1994 produced undisguised stalemate and illustrated the worldwide dangers of bad relations between the United States and Japan as the value of the dollar fell steadily; in 1995 the United States reverted to threats. Nevertheless, neither side seemed to have the stomach for more than rhetorical brinkmanship (that is, using military power to make political threats). The uneasy relations between the world's leading economic powers were also tangentially soured by anti-American protests arising from the continued American military presence on Okinawa and other islands and the behaviour of American forces there. These discontents were met for the time being by raising the rents and agreeing to close 11 of the American bases over five to seven years.

The half-century after the Second World War witnessed no transformation more remarkable than Japan's but towards the end of that period doubts began to nag. Postwar Japan was a one-party democracy in what had been for 2000 years an exceptionally homogeneous society. It had a constitutional monarchy as unobtrusive as its pre-Meiji precursors. Its rise to global economic power was grounded in a financial system and corporate ethos designed for recovery from catastrophe and based on cheap money, government subsidies and a high level of saving. It surmounted with outstanding skill the challenges posed by the oil price rises of the 1970s. But in the 1990s the economic miracle evaporated until in 1998 Japan was technically in recession to the alarm and amazement of the whole world. Rates of growth slumped; the currency was extravagantly overvalued; borrowing became irrational as banks lent lavishly, accepting equity as collateral and so creating a system based on the implicit assumption that equity values would rise indefinitely; Japanese and others were mesmerized by trade surpluses of $100 billion a year and Japan's huge foreign reserves; the banking system was tremulous with debts of the order of $500 million – an economic miracle of the wrong kind. The long boom had been genuine but reckless: borrowing far exceeded the reasonable capacity to repay on time and stock markets reacted by rising as though exponentiality ruled. The resulting crisis was complicated by disagreement over its prime cause. Either the system was structurally unsound (in particular through providing too much cheap money and allowing insolvent banks to flourish) or, alternatively, it was bled by inadequate demand. The appropriate remedies in the one case or the other – tighter monetary controls or monetary stimulus through financial relaxation – were incompatible and the economic failings, whatever their cause, were compounded by the psychological disorders in money markets and stock markets in Japan, in Asia and in the rest of the world. Critics in and beyond Japan questioned more than the economy. They condemned the flagrant corruption which sapped the credit of the ruling party and weakened its ability to tackle serious matters and they wondered whether the stresses of achievement in Japan's schools and universities were not killing personal initiative, industrial inventiveness and social resilience. Some of the wondering was not untinged by *Schadenfreude*. Attempts to reflate the economic miracle were half-hearted and slow to take effect. Japan gave the United States naval facilities during the war in Iraq (Chapter 14) but abstained from wider issues of relations with the US and China.

Japan's ups and downs in the twentieth century were extreme. Its grander enterprises – the attempt to dominate Manchuria, China and South-east Asia, the challenge to the United States at Pearl Harbor, its participation in the Second World War – ended in disaster. But its recovery was swift and spectacular. It became for a while arguably the second power in the world, militarily disarmed but economically rampant. This rise was checked by economic mismanagement and sclerotic one-party politics but it contrived to retain the appearance of boundless potential. It was one of the great powers of the huge Pacific zone but shared that distinction with the United States and China, one or the other of which it had been at war with for most of the century.

CHAPTER 3

China

The triumph of Mao

In 1949, a little over a quarter of a century after its birth, the Communist Party of China won the ancient capital city of Beijing. A movement had become a government. The defeated Kuomintang was reduced to the island of Taiwan where its leader Jiang Kaishek, like the last of the Ming emperors 300 years earlier, clothed himself with imperial pretences reminiscent of the French nobles and Italian bankers who wandered round western Europe in the later Middle Ages calling themselves emperors of Byzantium. The new lord of China, Mao Zedong, was able to declare in January 1950 with only slight exaggeration that all China was his except Tibet.

The vast lands and imperial traditions which fell to Mao after the Second World War had been going begging since just before the First World War. The decline of the last (Manchu) dynasty, which had exposed China to foreign intervention and had almost occasioned its partition in the latter part of the nineteenth century, had culminated in the revolution of 1911. Revolutionary groups and secret societies, partly indigenous and partly fomented among overseas Chinese, effected the disintegration of the *ancien régime*. Faced thereafter with the task of re-establishing the cohesion, dignity and power of China they failed, so that 50 years later China was still potentially a great power but not actually one.

The most notable of these successor groups was that of Sun Yat-sen (died 1925), a nationalist, a democrat and a socialist, who wanted to reform China through his instrument, the Kuomintang. The Kuomintang established a government in the southern capital of Nanking but it never succeeded in bringing the whole country under its obedience. The collapse of the old regime was followed, especially in the north, by the appearance of war lords who created autonomous fiefs for themselves and engaged in civil wars. Even in the south, where the Kuomintang imposed a degree of order and stability, the huge tasks of administrative reform and modernization were tackled but not mastered.

The Kuomintang looked around for outside help and accepted from the new and no less revolutionary government of the USSR the advisory services of Michael Borodin. Under the pressure of circumstances the Kuomintang began to adopt in its fight against the war lords some of the methods (the organization of the party and of party–state relations), though not the doctrines, of European communism, and it also entered into an alliance with the Chinese Communist Party, which had been founded in Shanghai in 1922. The communists consisted of small groups in certain southern provinces. They became a part of the Kuomintang under the overall leadership of Jiang Kaishek, but disputes between communist and other Kuomintang leaders (and between left and right non-communist factions within the Kuomintang) were endemic. There was also confusion among the communists themselves because communist committees in Shanghai gave ill-judged instructions to leaders active in the countryside, and still more because Moscow attempted to direct matters without adequate knowledge of Chinese history and conditions. At one moment Moscow had different emissaries in China advocating incompatible policies. In this atmosphere Mao Zedong gradually became one of the principal leaders in the countryside, often at odds with his superiors in Shanghai and himself still evolving his own ideas and tactics. In 1931 the Japanese attack in Manchuria forced Jiang Kaishek to send troops to the north, but confusion in the communists' ranks prevented them from taking advantage of this distraction of the non-communists and in 1934 they were decisively defeated as a result of adopting ill-chosen tactics which Mao had argued against. The communists set out on their myth-making Long March from south-eastern China, first westward and then northward to the province of Yenan in the far north-west, where they preserved their movement and bided their time. During the Long March Mao rose to ultimate authority. He had been moving away from the classic Marxist strategy of achieving power by fighting the battles of the industrial proletariat and towards annexing communism to peasant indignation (periodically a mighty subversive force in Chinese history); he proposed to set up a small peasant republic and to create peasant armies which would one day be strong enough to seize towns.

Meanwhile, the Kuomintang, having disposed of the communists and made headway against the war lords (it took Beijing in 1928 and secured Manchuria the next year by agreement with General Chang Hsueh-liang, the Young Marshal), was attacked by Japan, first in Manchuria in 1931 and then in China proper in 1937. From this date until 1945 the Kuomintang and the communists were rivals for the honours of effecting the revival of China as a great power and for the prize of ruling it after the Japanese had been defeated. The communist remnants which had reached Yenan grew rapidly into an army of about 100,000, attracting recruits from the peasantry and from youth generally on a nationalist anti-Japanese ticket. In 1941 the Japanese attack on the United States at Pearl Harbor merged this Far Eastern war into a general war which temporarily overlaid China's civil discords. The Kuomintang acquired powerful allies, but its fortunes were not destined to revive. It had failed to arrest economic collapse, its leadership remained narrow and cliquish, its administration became corrupt, high-handed and over-reliant on secret police, and finally its armies disintegrated. By contrast, the communists rose in popular esteem. Their sojourn in the wilderness had

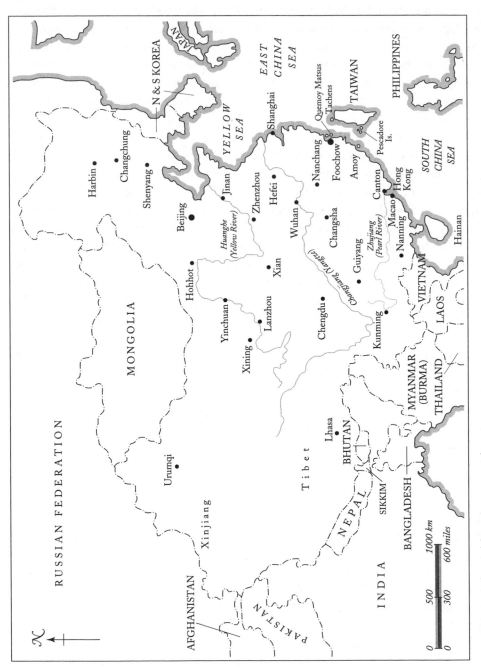

3.1 China and neighbouring countries

given them glamour and concealed the seamy side of their own methods of rule. They had the reputation of fighting the Japanese more seriously than the Kuomintang and when the war ended they were ready to return from the outskirts to the centre. A few years later they were the government of China.

When Jiang Kaishek was chased out of China a generation of civil conflict came to an end and the communists were presented with the opportunity to do what no faction had been able to do since the fall of the empire, and in which the empire itself had failed: to make China strong and healthy enough to maintain its integrity and independence. In the past, threats to the integrity of China had come from the imperial powers of western Europe sailing across the seas, from the Russians approaching over land, and from the Japanese. By 1945 the western European powers were no longer in a position to menace anybody in the Far East, and Japan had been all but annihilated. The Russians, however, had reappeared on the scene, while the Americans, traditional upholders of the integrity of China against interlopers, were despairing of the Kuomintang and were about to revert to an Asian policy centred on Japan, such as they had pursued at the opening of the century.

Continuous Russian expansion into Asia began after the Crimean War. That defeat inaugurated essays in liberalism at home and in Far Eastern adventure, both of which were sporadic. The tsars were more or less permanently preoccupied with the problems of Poland, the Balkans and the Straits, but there was a party at St Petersburg which made a speciality of the Far East. The 1860s and 1870s were a period of expansion; the great Russian proconsul Count N. N. Muraviev established the Amur and Maritime provinces in 1858 and 1860 respectively; Vladivostok was founded in 1861; Sakhalin was acquired (but Alaska sold); the Kazakhs and the central Asian Khanates were subjected. By the 1880s Russia, having reached the borders of Persia and Afghanistan, had been brought face to face with the British in India, while further north a warm water Pacific port and a share in the China trade stimulated imperial and financial imaginations.

War between the Japanese and the Chinese in Korea in 1894–95 brought Japan considerable gains (including Taiwan, the Pescadores and, temporarily, the Shantung peninsula and Port Arthur) and served notice of the decline of Chinese power. Russia, France and Germany intervened in defence of China, although Britain, suspicious of the Russian advance in Asia, now began its pro-Japanese policy as a counter. The Russians, having with the French helped China to pay its war indemnity to Japan, entered into an alliance with China, took Port Arthur and planned the Chinese Eastern and South Manchurian railways. The Russians and the Japanese were vying with each other for Manchuria. In 1904 Japan attacked Port Arthur and in the ensuing Russo-Japanese War the Russians were defeated and forced back into Manchuria and Mongolia. Japan's standing in Asia and the world was immensely increased and the Russian advance across the top of Asia was checked by a Japanese counter-force in Manchuria. The First World War temporarily eliminated Russian power, effected no

Chinese revival, distracted other Europeans from Asian affairs, and left Japan in a situation where, far from curbing the Russians, it had itself to be curbed – and could be curbed by no power except the United States. The Russians recovered positions in Outer Mongolia and Central Asia in the 1920s and came once more into conflict with the Japanese in Manchuria in the 1930s, but they did not seriously return to the struggle for Manchuria until the final week of the Second World War.

For most of the war years Stalin was too much occupied with the Germans to pay much attention to Asia, let alone intervene there. The USSR signed a neutrality pact with Japan in 1941 and before Pearl Harbor Japan sought and received assurances that the Russians would abide by this pact. Up to the Teheran conference of 1943 Stalin asked for nothing in the east, being in no position to ask for prizes until he was ready to give a helping hand against Japan. At the Moscow conference in October 1944 there were hints of a change in the Russian attitude, and at Yalta in 1945 Stalin's terms were set out and accepted by allies who were anxious to avoid quarrels, still overrated Japan's will and capacity to fight on, and were – except for a few initiates – ignorant of the nuclear weapons about to be used. Stalin asked his allies to reverse the verdict of the Russo-Japanese War of 1904–5 and to guarantee him certain positions at the expense not of Japan but of China. The positions lost by the Russians in Manchuria and Sakhalin in 1905 were to be restored; the Kuriles were to go to the USSR too; and the USSR's virtual annexation of Outer Mongolia was to be recognized.

Stalin's policy in Asia was to nibble at the Chinese circumference and to prevent the establishment of any powerful central Chinese government. By declaring war on Japan he secured rights and planted troops in Manchuria and was able to carry off Japanese industrial plant, although not without incurring Chinese resentment. He had already engineered an anti-Chinese revolt in the Ili valley in Xinjiang, where a secessionist republic of Eastern Turkestan sprouted under Russian protection in 1944. Outer Mongolia, nominally under Chinese suzerainty but effectively in the Russian sphere since 1921 and conceded to the USSR by the western allies at Yalta, was abandoned by the Chinese (who had no choice in the matter) by the Russo-Chinese treaty of 1945. It was not recovered for China when Mao succeeded Jiang in 1949.

Stalin's declaration of war on Japan had one further notable consequence in the bisection of Korea, for when the Japanese surrendered it was arranged, as a matter of convenience, that Japanese forces north of the 38th parallel should surrender to the Russians and those south of that line to the Americans.

Russian intervention in the Far East was nicely timed. As the Russians knew, the Japanese were anxious for peace; they were taking soundings in Moscow in the hope of securing Russian mediation to end the war. The first nuclear bomb was dropped on 6 August 1945 on Hiroshima by the Americans, who also knew that there was an active peace party in the Japanese cabinet. The Russian declaration of war followed two days later. On 9 August the second bomb was dropped on Nagasaki. Hostilities ended on 15 August (on which day the Russians signed their treaty with Jiang Kaishek).

Whereas Stalin wanted a weak China and may well have considered himself successful, the Americans wanted a strong China, failed through no fault of their own during the years of transition from war to peace, and later began to see the prospect of China strong indeed but not at all to their liking.

American policies in the Far East were conditioned at the start of the century by the acquisition of the Philippine Islands from Spain in 1898 and by suspicion of the European powers which, having turned most of South-east Asia into colonial terrain, seemed about to carve up China too. With its interests and its moral sense in happy accord, Washington claimed for itself any rights or privileges which any European power succeeded in extracting from the Chinese (the policy of the open door, that is, no commercial preferences between foreigners from different states) and stood up at the same time for the integrity and independence of China.

The American entry on this scene was unexpected and unpremeditated. The war of 1898 against Spain, which began in a muddled way in Cuba, had the incidental result of substituting American for Spanish rule in the Philippines. There ensued a considerable public debate on the politics and morality of expansionism, with the lurking background knowledge that if the United States did not assert its power in the Pacific, either the British or the Germans or the Japanese would. This debate coincided with the manifest decline of China.

The British, alarmed by the trend towards annexations, leases and special commercial privileges for particular groups of foreigners, had sought American co-operation to put a stop to this colonialist rat race, but Washington was not at this point interested and the British thereupon entered a game which they despaired of preventing and began themselves to mark out enclaves and take leases.

The change in the American attitude came with the appointment of John Hay as secretary of state. Hay's first set of notes, condemning spheres of influence and advocating the open door, had little practical effect, although they were popular in the United States; a second set, at the time of the Boxer rebellion and the allied intervention under German command to which the rebellion gave rise in 1900, testified to increasing American concern; so did Washington's mediation in the Russo-Japanese War and the signing of the Treaty of Portsmouth on American soil. But it was some time before American and British policies were brought into harmony. Britain, seeking an ally in eastern waters and apparently rebuffed by the United States, had turned to Japan, while the United States was becoming the protector of China and the enemy at sea of Japan. This discrepancy continued, not without damage to Anglo-American relations, until after the First World War when the Washington treaties of 1921–22 in effect eliminated the Anglo-Japanese alliance, established a three-power naval ratio of 5:5:3, and secured a nine-power guarantee of the integrity of China and the open door. (At the London conference of 1930 the Japanese ratio was raised from 3 to 3.5.) Secretary of state Charles Evans Hughes forced the Japanese to withdraw their troops from the Shantung peninsula and Siberia, but in the 1930s the Americans, undecided as to whether strong action would check or strengthen the expansionist factions in Japanese politics, became less effective and there was little reaction from Washington to the Japanese conquest of Manchuria, the proclamation of the state of Manchukuo in 1932 or to the Japanese occupation of Shanghai later in the same year. Japan withdrew from the Washington and London naval treaties at the end of 1936, claiming parity with the United States and Britain, and embarked on war with China in 1937. At the same time Japan challenged the European powers by propounding a 'new order' for all eastern Asia, and when the Europeans (western and Russian) had made it plain that they wanted no troubles in the east, Washington began to negotiate with Tokyo.

The outbreak of war in Europe in 1939 gave Japan a freer hand against China and new opportunities in South-east Asia. A new and more bellicose government, installed in 1940, decided to attack Indo-China as a first step but hoped to avoid American intervention. This government fell when Hitler attacked the USSR. The foreign minister, Yosuke Matsuoka, who wanted to join in the attack, was dropped, and General Hideki Tojo, who wanted to attack the United States, became the most influential member of the cabinet. He became prime minister in October 1941 and gave the order for the attack on Pearl Harbor in December.

Until the turn of the tide in the middle of 1943 the Americans were in danger of being evicted from the Far East altogether, but the Battle of Midway and the final victory over Japan brought them back with a unique preponderance such as no power had ever previously enjoyed.

The war forced Washington to reconsider its Far Eastern policy. Everything combined to make Americans pro-Chinese – traditional policies, missionary connections, Japanese behaviour, and the appealing (in both senses) Madame Jiang – but the Kuomintang government was not successful and was ceasing to be worthy. Nevertheless, Washington, which renounced extraterritorial rights in China in 1943 as a gesture, determined that China should emerge from the war fully sovereign in the full extent of its ancient territories (including Manchuria, Taiwan and the Pescadores) and a major power with a permanent place in the Security Council.

China was to be the United States of the Asian continent, a vast, united and liberal-democratic power: a view which Churchill, among others, regarded as romantic moonshine. When the shortcomings of the Kuomintang became more and more obvious, General Joseph Stilwell was sent to keep an eye on Jiang Kaishek and to bolster and, if possible, reform the Kuomintang, but the general's comments on the Kuomintang were so critical that he was recalled at the instance of Jiang's friends. General Patrick Hurley, who had been sent to China in August as President Roosevelt's personal representative with the Generalissimo, became the principal vehicle of American policy with the new task of bringing the Kuomintang and the communists together again. Hurley and General George C. Marshall, who succeeded him in 1945, made only slight headway. The Kuomintang and the communists were ineradicably suspicious of each other and discussions for an accommodation broke down on the issue of the amalgamation of their two armies. When the Japanese surrendered the Americans lifted Kuomintang forces by air to take control in north-eastern China, while the Russians who had just entered Manchuria gave the communists arms and opportunities in that area. Until the latter part of 1947 there was an uneasy truce, but civil war was only suspended. The Americans, by now thoroughly distrustful of the Kuomintang, withdrew their units from China but were uncertain whether to withdraw all forms of support. General Albert C. Wedemeyer, sent to China in July 1947, recommended extensive American aid on the basis that the Kuomintang should introduce extensive reforms under American supervision, but by this time China was approaching economic and financial collapse and rioting was common. Nevertheless, interim aid to China was approved before the end of the year and the China Aid Act was passed in April 1948. This was supplemented by a Sino-American agreement and the Kuomintang made a belated effort to put its house in order.

But it was too late. The communists were winning battles in steady succession. All Manchuria was theirs by the end of 1948 and the next year became a roll-call of famous cities conquered for communism. Washington wrote off the Kuomintang. Jiang, who had made the blunder of over-committing himself in the last stages of the civil war, resigned the presidency at the beginning of 1949 and the Kuomintang asked – in vain – for mediation by the United States, the USSR, Britain and France. The communists had no further interest in coalitions or accommodations. A People's Republic was proclaimed in September. On 18 December 1949 Mao arrived in Moscow as a head of state.

The victory of the Chinese communists created problems for both the Americans and the Russians. During the remainder of 1949 and the first half of 1950 the Americans were moving towards diplomatic recognition of the new regime, but possible negotiations to this end were held up by the arrest of the American consul-general in Mukden and his imprisonment with four of his colleagues for a month at the end of 1949, and were then aborted by war in Korea. At some point in this period the United States decided that Taiwan was a necessary part of a line of strategic bases and must be kept out of communist hands. This decision, which was made public, made the United States keep Mao's regime out of the Chinese seat at the UN and made the Chinese believe that Taiwan was being held as a temporary refuge for Jiang Kaishek, pending an attempted reconquest of the mainland. The Korean War also led the Chinese into an overconfident assessment of their military strength, expressed in the picturesque but inaccurate description of the United States as a paper tiger.

Mao's victory proved as awkward for the Russians as for the Americans. The world supposed that the interests and policies of the two principal communist powers must be closely allied. This assumption owed something to the Cold War and was strengthened by the war in Korea between communists and anti-communists; it led to bewilderment and amazement when it transpired a few years later that Moscow and Beijing were quarrelling bitterly. In fact, the interests of the USSR and China were only partly congruent; the communist parties of the two countries had no close emotional bonds;

and in Moscow the Chinese party was regarded as only doubtfully loyal to communist doctrine and to the world movement dominated by the Russians. After the death of Stalin the divergence in policies became more obvious, partly because of the removal of the undoubted leader of the communist world and partly because the passage of time allowed the differences in the circumstances of the two countries to make themselves increasingly felt.

Stalin wanted no powerful China. So long as the government of China was non-communist it was comparatively easy for him to pursue a policy of alliance coupled with pinpricks. The treaty of August 1945 with Jiang had pins stuck into it, since the Kuomintang acknowledged in effect the absorption of Outer Mongolia into the Soviet sphere and failed to regain in Manchuria rights which now passed from Japan to the USSR. The Chinese communists were, for Stalin, another pin with which to lacerate the Kuomintang, until in 1949 they took the place of the Kuomintang and so ceased to be a mere pin. When Mao arrived in Moscow, Stalin had to devise a completely new China policy which would take into account both the USSR's desire to dominate the Asian heartlands and the inescapable expectation of fraternal love and assistance between communist parties. Given the size and potentialities of China, this was a problem which had never previously come up in Moscow.

Mao had to learn too. He knew little about the USSR (or any other major power) before a visit to Moscow where he was made to hang around for two months before a new Russo-Chinese treaty was concluded in 1950. This was a business measure dealing with railways, credits and similar matters. The Russians gave the Chinese a handsome present consisting of the Changchun railway and its installations. The Chinese acquired the right to administer Dalny, though the ultimate fate of this port was to be reconsidered upon the conclusion of a peace treaty with Japan. The USSR provided China with a credit of $300 million over five years at 1 per cent and repayable in 1954–63. Further agreements covered, among other things, joint exploitation of oil in Xinjiang and joint operation of air routes in central Asia. These agreements were the start of co-operation between the two countries which lasted until the late 1950s. They were confirmed during a visit to Moscow by Zhou Enlai in 1952 shortly before the announcement of China's first five-year plan, the formation of a powerful National Planning Commission under Gao Gang and the creation of a Ministry of Higher Education. With the plan, the commission and the drive for higher education the Russo-Chinese agreements were an integral part of Mao's design for a new China.

China and the superpowers

Nine months after the proclamation of the new Chinese republic war broke out in Korea. This unforeseen and, for the Chinese, inopportune event had a deep effect on Asian politics and on the relations between Asians and non-Asians involved in Far Eastern affairs. It forced the Chinese to look to their defences when they could have been concentrating on internal affairs; it dominated American policy at a moment when that policy was in the making; it raised questions concerning consultation and co-operation between the principal communist powers; it threatened to import a cold war into Asia, boosted Indian neutralism and caused Americans to equate neutralism and pacifism with indifferentism and moral perversion.

The history of the Korean peninsula is like the history of any small country wedged between more powerful neighbours. For 1,000 years Korea was ruled by two dynasties separated by a brief Mongol conquest. It suffered Japanese and Manchu incursions in the sixteenth and seventeenth centuries but survived until the end of the nineteenth, by which time it had become a pawn in Sino-Japanese–Russian conflicts. Japan's victories in the war with China in 1894–95 and with Russia in 1904–5 gave Japan a free hand in Korea, which was annexed in 1910. It failed in 1919 to recover its independence although a provisional government was established under the presidency of Syngman Rhee, who had acquired a doctorate at Princeton. Independence was promised by the Cairo declaration of 1943 by Roosevelt, Churchill and Jiang Kaishek.

When the war came to an end in 1945 there was no dispute over the status of Korea, but at the moment of independence an accident deprived it of unity. The Japanese having surrendered partly to the Americans and partly to the Russians, Korea was divided into two pieces along the 38th parallel. This famous line came into existence as a result of negotiations between army officers of relatively junior rank; it was not a creation of ministerial decisions. But administrative convenience hardened into political fact and thereafter all attempts to equip Korea with a single government failed. The cause of this failure was the presence of Russian as well as American troops. Contemporaneously in Poland, for which rival governments also contended, there was only one occupying army and so only one possible answer. In Korea there were two armies and so no answer.

In 1947 the United States took the problem to the United Nations, which appointed a commission (UN Temporary Commission on Korea – UNTCOK) to effect unity through elections. Elections were held in the south in 1948 but the commission was prevented from operating in the north and the result of its activities was the creation of a government which claimed to be the government of all Korea but had no authority or existence north of the 38th parallel. The head of this government was Syngman Rhee, now an elderly, rough, reactionary but legendarily essential and, as it turned out, almost irremovable father figure. In 1949 the Russians (who had nurtured a rival government in the north) and the Americans both withdrew their armed forces, so that Korea became a country with two governments, overhung by the Russians in Manchuria and Siberia and by the Americans in Japan and conscious of the emergence of a new China on its borders.

The first half of 1950 was occupied by new elections in South Korea and propaganda in North Korea for reunification either by elections throughout the country (from which Syngman Rhee and others were to be debarred) or by a merger of the two parliaments. When it became apparent that these gambits were unavailing, northern troops crossed the border on 25 June, capturing the southern capital of Seoul the next day. It is doubtful whether North Korean troops would have taken this action if the US secretary of state, Dean Acheson, had not, in January, excluded Korea (and Taiwan) from the defence perimeter which, by implication, the United States was ready to fight to retain. Kim Il Sung, North Korea's prime minister (1948–72) and president (1972–94), who had spent the war years in Moscow and was Moscow's nominee for his jobs, was encouraged to invade by both Stalin and Mao: the former provided air cover. What perhaps none of them foresaw in June was that the American attitude of January would be reversed by the invasion and that South Korea and Taiwan would prove to be parts of the American defence perimeter after all.

The Security Council met at once at the request of the United States and passed, in the absence of the Russian member, a resolution requiring a ceasefire and the return of northern troops to their own side of the border. Truman instructed MacArthur in Tokyo to support the South Koreans and ordered the US Seventh Fleet to insulate Taiwan. Two days later (27 June) a second resolution of the Security Council called on all members to help South Korea to repel the attack made upon it and to restore international peace. This resolution proceeded upon the basis, subsequently challenged by the Russians, that the fighting between North and South was an international threat, although it was not made clear whether it was international because North and South were two different states or because an admittedly internal and civil war was deemed to have international repercussions. China protested against illegal intervention in Korean affairs.

At first the fighting went in favour of the North. The South Koreans and the UN forces which came to their help were driven to the very tip of the Korean peninsula, but in September MacArthur, in command of UN forces, landed troops at Inchon, 240 km to the north, and as a result of this bold stroke South Korean and other units crossed the 38th parallel in October and pressed on to the Manchurian border. The war seemed to be over. Truman flew to Wake Island to congratulate MacArthur, who gave his opinion that neither the Russians nor the Chinese would intervene. He was wrong about the Chinese, who attacked on 26 November. Exactly a month later they were across the 38th parallel and the South Koreans and their allies were once more in full retreat.

The Chinese attack was a forestalling action. The Chinese, who remembered the Japanese attack on their country via Korea in 1931, suspected that the Americans in Japan were about to repeat that performance. American aid to Jiang under the China Aid Act, MacArthur's visit to Jiang on Taiwan soon after the outbreak of war in Korea, the crossing of the 38th parallel by the Americans in October and their approach to the Yalu River, the open debate on American strategic interests in the Pacific islands and on the possibility of a return by Jiang to the mainland – all these things combined to persuade the new regime in Beijing that the Americans intended an anti-communist campaign similar to the anti-communist interventions in Russia after the 1917 revolution. So the Chinese struck first.

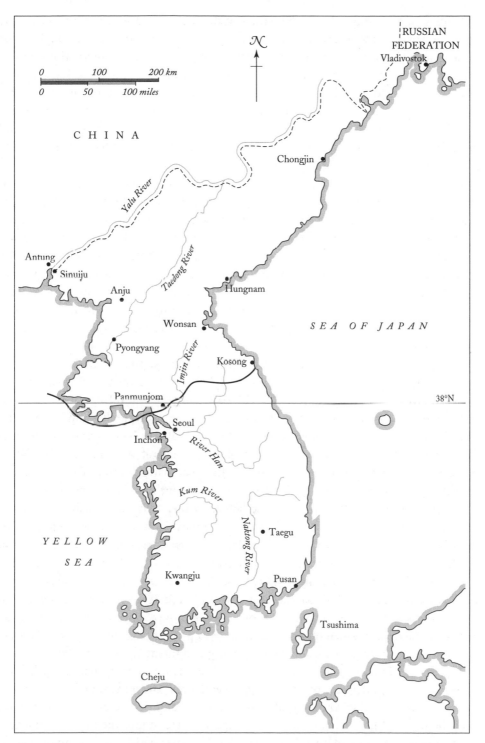

3.2 Korea showing the division between North and South

Chinese intervention altered the nature of the war and gave rise to a fierce debate about how it ought to be prosecuted. From June to November the war, although waged on one side primarily by the Americans, could be represented as an international punitive expedition. After November it became more and more a Sino-American conflict. MacArthur wished to recognize this fact and wage open war on China, using the most effective military means. This meant following Chinese aircraft across the Manchurian frontier instead of breaking off pursuit when this line was reached in combat, and bombing Chinese installations on the Yalu River and elsewhere. This attitude could lead to the use of nuclear bombs in the heart of China itself.

But MacArthur's views did not carry conviction in Washington. The chiefs of staff shrank from the prospect of embarking on a war with China which might drag on for years, while the president and his civilian advisers were extremely loath to re-enter Chinese politics (from which the United States had very recently extricated itself) and well aware of worldwide disapproval of any such adventure. Washington's allies became alarmed. The British prime minister Clement Attlee flew to Washington to express this alarm, especially about the possible use of nuclear bombs in Asia for a second time, and the neutrals began to give neutralism a markedly anti-American inclination; distrust of the United States in world affairs received a fillip which was slow to fade away.

As early as July 1950 Nehru, whose government had supported both the Security Council's resolutions, made approaches to Stalin and Acheson to put a stop to the fighting. His intervention was received with bare courtesy but in December India and other neutrals appealed to both sides not to cross the 38th parallel and during that month the Indian representative at the UN Sir Benegal Rau had a series of conversations in New York with an emissary from Beijing, General Wu Xiuquan. The latter, however, left New York before the end of the year with nothing achieved; a UN ceasefire committee was rebuffed by Beijing; the time for mediation was not yet.

On the first day of 1951 the Chinese launched their second offensive. UN forces were quickly forced out of Seoul and a fresh UN appeal for a ceasefire was rejected. But the Chinese advance petered out. At the UN China was declared an aggressor and in Washington in March a telegram from MacArthur was read to the Senate in which the general in effect urged the United States to strike at China and not simply accept the re-establishment of the 38th parallel as a boundary line. It was now the Chinese turn to retreat, the UN recovered Seoul, the South Koreans once more crossed the 38th parallel and MacArthur issued on his own initiative a peremptory challenge to his adversaries to accept an armistice, coupled with an implied threat of massive retaliation. The challenge was ignored and Truman warned MacArthur that he had exceeded his powers and was pursuing a policy not approved by his government and commander-in-chief. The general tried to appeal to the Congress and people of the United States over the heads of his military and civilian superiors. He sent to the Republican leader in the House of Representatives Joseph W. Martin a letter which was read in the House and which recommended the strongest measures against China, including the use of Jiang's troops. On 11 April he was dismissed by Truman.

The dramatic dismissal of MacArthur caused such a stir that its significance was not immediately assimilated. What it meant was that the Korean War had to be brought to an end by compromise and mediation. The American government rejected the alternative of complete victory by the military defeat of China. Yet it took over two years more before an armistice was signed in July 1953.

The dragging out and winding up of the war can be briefly recorded. Fresh Chinese attacks in 1951 were held and both sides began to feel their way towards a truce. A broadcast in the United States at the end of June by the Russian member of the Security Council J. A. Malik led to negotiations (at Kaesong in July and later at Panmunjon) which were tedious, fruitless and punctuated by fears of a renewal of full-scale operations and by accusations against the Americans of recourse to bacteriological warfare. The most intractable issue was the fate of prisoners of war, many of whom in Southern hands were alleged to be unwilling to return to the North, but an exchange agreement was signed in June 1953 (shortly after the death of Stalin, although no connection between the events can be definitely proved). The agreement was then wrecked by Syngman Rhee, who released prisoners rather than turn them over to the North Koreans, whereupon the Chinese launched a major offensive. Notwithstanding these turbulent episodes, an armistice agreement was signed in July.

A peace conference at Geneva which opened in April 1954 failed to produce a final settlement and Syngman Rhee then went to Washington to try to persuade the United States to sanction a joint invasion of China by South Koreans and Jiang Kaishek's forces. He argued that the regime in China was on the verge of collapse but failed to convince Congress or Eisenhower or Dulles. In the following year American and Chinese troops were gradually withdrawn.

The Geneva conference, although it failed to produce agreement on Korea, demonstrated that the country would revert to the position that ruled in 1949, bisected and freed from foreign occupation. In the same year the United States decided not to intervene at Dien Bien Phu. But also in the same year the United States concluded treaties with Pakistan and Japan and created SEATO. The acceptance of the *status quo ante* in Korea and the refusal to engage in war in Indo-China did not betoken an American withdrawal from Asia. For the next 11 years – until the beginning in 1965 of the American attack on North Vietnam – the United States tried to play a major role in eastern and south-eastern Asia by displaying but not using military power, with the object of halting the territorial progress of communism by conquest or subversion. In Korea communist aggression had failed, but in the American view it was making dangerous strides elsewhere in Asia by means of subversion. Although the opposite was the case in Malaya where the tide was running against the communist insurgents, Chinese power, still supported by Russian aid, made Washington tremble for the successor states in Indo-China and for Indonesia. American policy was thus anti-Chinese because China had become the fount of a new wave of communism, and by the same token it was ideological, claiming virtue for the stand against the evils of communism and imputing wickedness to those who refused to fight the good fight or at least applaud it.

The events of the early 1950s strengthened and prolonged American links with the remnants of the Kuomintang. On the outbreak of the Korean War Truman had given Jiang Kaishek an undertaking to keep the new Chinese regime away from Taiwan and the adjacent Pescadores islands. In view of China's total naval incapacity this commitment was easy to honour but it involved Washington in courses of action not approved by its principal European allies and it contained an awkward ambiguity. When Jiang was evicted from the mainland he retained control of some islands off the coast. Did the American umbrella cover these islands as well as Taiwan and the Pescadores? This was partly a question of the extent of Washington's unwritten commitments to Jiang but it raised further questions: Were these offshore islands necessary for the defence of Taiwan? Must they be retained by Jiang in order to affirm American steadfastness in Asia generally?

The offshore islands were the Tachens, Quemoy and the Matsus, situated off Amoy and Foochow and forming an offshore screen similar to the advance guard which the Pescadores provided for Taiwan on the other side of the Taiwan Strait. In 1954 Beijing began to emit demands for the liberation of Taiwan whereupon Washington retorted that any attack on Taiwan would have to reckon with the American fleet. In September the Chinese bombarded Quemoy as a riposte, it seemed, to the creation of SEATO by the Manila Pact. The Kuomintang fired back and for several weeks this fire and counter-fire looked like the beginning of a more serious encounter. In November 13 American airmen, captured during the winter of 1952–53 when their aircraft came down in Manchuria, were sentenced in Beijing to terms between life and four years for espionage, and in December the United States and the Kuomintang concluded a new treaty, which declared the defence of Taiwan and the Pescadores to be a common interest. In 1955 Jiang abandoned the Tachens under fire from the mainland.

Mao agreed to receive Dag Hammarskjöld to talk about the American airmen but in the summer of 1955 the Chinese bombarded Quemoy again. The Americans had meanwhile decided that no more territory should be ceded and Jiang gradually moved troops into Quemoy until about one-third of all his forces were stationed just off China's mainland coast. The new bombardment died away and there followed a period of easier Sino-American relations, marked by exchanges at Geneva, ambassadorial conferring in Warsaw and the release of the American prisoners. By the middle of 1958 there was even talk of American recognition of Beijing but the Eisenhower–Dulles administration formally denied that it contemplated such a step. This statement was immediately followed by a fresh bombardment and a Chinese demand for the surrender of the islands, which was met by a declaration by Dulles to the effect that the

Americans would fight to protect Taiwan and another by Eisenhower defining Quemoy and the Matsus as necessary for its defence. American escorts for Jiang's troops sailed within a few miles of the coast. War was feared. Washington's allies and sections of American opinion became nervous and after a few days the crisis was deflated by the resumption of the Sino-American talks in Warsaw.

Hazardous though Dulles' policy of brinkmanship had been, it had, during these years, shown that the American decision not to intervene in Indo-China in 1954 did not betoken a general failure of American will. This determination was further emphasized in South Vietnam where the Americans first gave the anti-communist regime economic and military aid and then engaged themselves directly in war on the Asian mainland. This engagement changed the nature of American policies in the Far East. The defeat of Japan in 1945 had given the United States total dominance in the Pacific. The conflict between Truman and MacArthur and its outcome showed that Pacific dominance was still the basis of policy, buttressed by garrisons in the Japanese and Philippine islands and by alliance with Australia and New Zealand (concluded in 1951 as the price of these countries' consent to the peace treaty with Japan). But the collapse of the French attempt to resume empire in Indo-China, coming as it did after the triumph of communists in China, led the United States towards a new policy of Asian rather than Pacific dominance.

Communist China's conflicts with the United States coincided nearly with a sharp decline in its relations with the USSR in the course of quarrels which developed in the late 1950s and were public news by 1960. One of the most startling consequences of the death of Stalin was the clash between the incompatible temperaments of Khrushchev and Mao, which was superimposed upon the sometimes divergent interests of the Russian and Chinese empires and exacerbated by doctrinal dispute. When Mao visited Stalin in 1949 there was an element of obeisance about this encounter between the Chinese leader and the man who, hyphenated with Marx–Engels–Lenin, was more than just a Russian leader. Stalin's power had endured for a quarter of a century, his prestige had been enormously increased by the Second World War, he was a legendary figure, a little like a long-lived and successful Chinese emperor. Mao, however, had disliked the Soviet Union since early encounters with it before the Second World War and, if not yet in 1949, became disposed to discern something superhuman in himself.

When Stalin died there was at first no agreement in the USSR about his successor and even a short-lived view that he had no single successor. A composite Stalin – Bulganin/Khrushchev – replaced the committee rule of the Malenkov interlude and visited Beijing in 1954. Then Khrushchev emerged as the new Russian autocrat and was assumed by many to be *ipso facto* the chief of world communism as well. To Mao, however, this proposition was not self-evident; there was no rule which said that the world's leading communist had to be a Russian nor any disposition in Mao's mind to accept a rumbustious political boss in that role. During his visit to Beijing in

1954 Khrushchev had failed to establish with Mao either a hierarchical or a personal relationship.

For a while relations remained equable. China needed Soviet economic and technical help and remained alive to the need for military support which the outbreak of the Korean War had dramatized. The Russians continued to help the Chinese to modernize their army; the Chinese Fourth Field Army which had entered Korea in 1950 was part of the force which had defeated the Kuomintang and which the Chinese were anxious to transform into a more modern instrument. Resentments, such as the feeling that the Russians had done very little to help the Chinese communists before they won power, were kept in the background. In 1954, with the Korean War clearly over, the Russians left Port Arthur and handed over its installations to China – two years later than the date set in the Russo-China treaty of 1950. They transferred to China their half-share in the joint companies formed in 1945 to exploit oil, non-ferrous metals and civil aviation in Xinjiang and to operate ship building and repair in Dairen, and entered into new agreements to provide financial credits and skilled technicians and know-how.

Deterioration set in about 1956 and acquired a cutting edge in the two following years. At the twentieth congress of the Soviet Communist Party in 1956 Mikoyan, followed by Khrushchev, set about the demolition of Stalin's memory. De-Stalinization involved points of doctrine on which Mao could fairly claim to be heard, but he was not consulted. Khrushchev was still unconfirmed in his new apogee and it would have been at least becoming for him to consult an elder like Mao. In external affairs Khrushchev was showing a dangerous unsureness. One of his first initiatives had been to try to repair the breach with Yugoslavia. Chinese attitudes to Yugoslavia were unsettled in the late 1950s. On the one hand Yugoslavia's independence of Moscow appealed to the Chinese; on the other hand the Yugoslav communists harboured heretical notions. The independence prevailed at first over the heresies, but from about 1957 the heresies seemed to the Chinese more serious. Furthermore, in 1955 Bulganin and Khrushchev demonstrated support for non-communists, notably Asian non-communists, by their visits to India, Burma and Afghanistan. Chinese doubts were next reinforced when revolt occurred in Poland and Hungary. In the Chinese view the Russians mishandled, or nearly mishandled, both emergencies. In the Polish case the Chinese intervened in support of the more independent communist Gomulka and cautioned the Russians against the use of military force; in the case of the anti-communist Hungarian rising they urged the Russians not to withdraw their troops prematurely.

In 1957 in a new agreement on technical aid, Khrushchev (according to the Chinese at a later date) promised China samples of nuclear material and information about the construction of nuclear weapons. This was the year in which the Russians perfected the first intercontinental missile and launched the first sputnik: the whole world drew exaggerated conclusions from this achievement. The Russians were thought to be overhauling the Americans, perhaps even to have done so, and the Chinese expected Khrushchev to exploit this marvellous advantage. The communists had long possessed superiority in sheer numbers; now they were ahead in technology as well. The east wind, in Mao's phrase, was prevailing over the west. The Russian nuclear armoury could be used to pin the Americans to the wall, while the communist states helped their friends to power throughout the underprivileged world; in Asia, Africa and Latin America there were revolutionary movements eager to discard the yoke of capitalist imperialism with the help especially of the Chinese, whose own experiences between 1922 and 1949 had taught them more than anybody else knew about the strategy of revolution in poor, backward, agricultural countries.

There were several points in the Chinese analysis with which Khrushchev and at least some of his senior colleagues disagreed. They may well have been the only persons in the world who knew that the Russian sputnik had not put the USSR ahead of the United States, and therefore they did not believe that they could immobilize the United States by the threat of nuclear annihilation. To some extent they were caught in the toils of their own jubilation, for the more they magnified their technical successes, the more it was supposed that they had won for themselves a much freer hand in international affairs than was really the case. They were therefore disconcerted by the Chinese view that the communist powers could afford more adventurous policies. The Chinese also maintained the orthodox Marxist position that war in some form at some day was inevitable because imperialism made it so whereas the Russians had diluted the basic doctrine of the inevitability of war not so much for reasons of pure logic but rather because their awareness of the frightful consequences of the use of nuclear weapons had led them to discard so baleful a belief; they were thinking specifically of nuclear war and not of war in general. The nuclear danger also caused them to differ from the Chinese in their approach to non-nuclear wars: both Moscow and Beijing endorsed wars of national liberation, but Moscow was more worried than Beijing about the risks of escalation to nuclear war. These divergences were sharpened by the death of Stalin which released a stifled debate inside the USSR. Malenkov pronounced that a world war would be likely to destroy all civilization; during his term of office as prime minister he stressed the imbecility of war and coupled it with his policy of increasing the supply of consumer goods. Khrushchev, while still in competition with Malenkov, attacked the latter for defeatism and for advocating coexistence with capitalists and put forward a hard policy of building up the strength of the USSR. However, when he himself became prime minister he set out to assuage the asperities of the Cold War because, among other reasons, he found the Russian forces ill-organized. At the twentieth congress of the Communist Party he said that war was not inevitable and might not be essential to the worldwide triumph of socialism. This view was repeated in the declaration issued in November 1957 at the end of the Moscow conference of communist parties (the Chinese included), and discussion seemed from this point to be shifting to the question whether all war, not only nuclear war, had become inexpedient. In 1958, however, the Chinese view that the east wind was prevailing over the west turned a theoretical debate into a live tactical issue with the Chinese expecting the Russians to take positive action incompatible with the general trend of the debate since 1953.

At the same time a further cause of dispute emerged. In general the Russians and the Chinese were in accord on the need to turn Asia, Africa and Latin America away from the capitalist camp, but they differed over the means. The Chinese, intent upon multiplying the number of states under communist rule, wanted to help only communists, whereas the Russians, taking the more pragmatic attitude that any anti-western regime was an advantage, were willing to help bourgeois revolutionary movements where communists were non-existent or unlikely to succeed. At the conference of communist parties in Moscow at the end of 1960 this disagreement was temporarily smothered by the adoption of a compromise formula: national democracies were to be helped if they were evolving in a socialist direction.

The Russo-Chinese alliance, already ruffled by suspicion and friction in 1956–57, was completely unhinged in the next two years, during which the USSR showed itself indifferent to vital Chinese interests, or even hostile to them. Jiang's immunity on Taiwan under the protection of the American Seventh Fleet and his possession of the offshore islands were running sores about which the Russians were in Chinese eyes unpardonably lukewarm. The Russians, while sympathizing with Beijing's feelings about unredeemed Chinese territory, were wary of Pacific entanglements and determined not to be drawn into war for Taiwan. They refused to set up a joint command for the Far East and made demands which to the Chinese amounted to impermissible infringements of Chinese sovereignty. Khrushchev seemed willing to establish nuclear bases in China but only on the understanding that they would be Russian and there would be no Chinese finger on the trigger. Some Chinese leaders, including the minister of defence Marshal Peng Dehuai, considered the price worth paying but Peng – incurring the suspicions of Mao, never a man to brook rivalry – was dismissed and disappeared, and the Russian attempt (if such it was) to create in eastern Asia the same sort of strategic position as the American position in western Europe failed. To make matters worse, the Russians poured cold water on the Great Leap Forward at a time when their co-operation was essential to its prospects, adopted a neutral attitude in China's disputes with India in 1959, continued to give large amounts of aid to Indonesia even though Beijing was being driven to protest against the Indonesian government's behaviour to its Chinese population, and set out to improve relations with the United States. The Chinese were being forced to reassess the attitudes of the USSR and the balance of the major forces in the world.

Events in the Middle East may have contributed to this rethinking. In July 1958 the Iraqi monarchy was overthrown and the king, his uncle, his prime minister Nuri es-Said, and other notabilities murdered. For a time it seemed possible that the Americans and British would take up arms against this revolution and so start a war. The Chinese were interested in these events. They demanded to be included in any conference assembled to deal with the situation, and their renewed bombardment of

Quemoy began shortly after the Iraqi coup. They may have calculated that the Russians could be induced to use the nuclear threat against the Americans or even to become involved in fighting. If they were thinking in these euphoric terms, their disillusionment was sharp and they were forced to the profoundly melancholy view that, on the contrary, the Russians were engaging in a conspiracy with the Americans to dominate the world and prevent China from becoming a nuclear power.

When the world learned in August 1959 that Khrushchev was going to the United States and would confer with Eisenhower at Camp David, the Chinese concluded that Khrushchev had rejected Beijing's thesis that the USSR should put forth its strength rather than negotiate from it. Although there had been some signs of Chinese endorsement for the Khrushchev policy, a change of mind in Beijing, coincident with changes in the top ranks of the Chinese Communist Party, had produced an unequivocally tough tone towards the United States and warnings against the naïve amateurishness of those who imagined that it was possible to lie down with imperialist lions. Not only did China's leaders not share the Camp David spirit; the Camp David negotiations appeared to leave out Chinese interests as though China were nothing more than an impediment to a Russo-American *rapprochement*. Shortly after his return from the United States, Khrushchev went to Beijing, a visit which had the almost unparalleled consequence of producing no communiqué. If his hosts asked him what he had said to Eisenhower about Taiwan, it is unlikely that he had a palatable reply, and in the new year both the foreign minister and the prime minister of China made statements which amounted to declarations of no confidence in Khrushchev's foreign policy. At a meeting of the presidium of the World Peace Council (a communist front organization) in Rome in January 1960 the Russian delegation attacked China, and at a communist conference in Warsaw in February the Chinese were observers only, although Outer Mongolia and North Korea were full participants. In April the ninetieth anniversary of Lenin's birth provided both sides with an occasion to expound their views at intemperate length, and a powerful Chinese propaganda campaign brought the quarrelling into the open. Mao, emerging from semi-retirement, made five separate statements explaining the Chinese attitude and pouring scorn on the folly of trusting the Americans.

It was no doubt the Chinese hope to convert or unseat Khrushchev, and the Russian leader, preparing for the Paris summit conference with the United States in mid-May, was in some danger. The Supreme Soviet met on 5 May, there was a reshuffle in the party secretariat, and there were rumours of splits and cabals. But Khrushchev went to Paris and, despite the U-2 incident and the failure of the conference, repeated his belief in peaceful coexistence on and after his return home. In Bucharest in June he attacked the Chinese in a meeting which was supposed to restore harmony and in August Russian technicians in China, to the number of about 12,000, were ordered to pack up and return home, bringing with them the plans on which they had been working. This bitterly unfriendly act, coinciding with the domestic setbacks of the great famine years, seemed to the Chinese tantamount to an invitation to the Americans to invade China and to the Kuomintang to incite a rising against the communist regime.

Correspondence and propaganda continued with increasing acerbity and the conference of 81 communist parties held in Moscow in 1960 was characterized by vituperative debate and a communiqué which too thinly papered a too-large crack. The Russians had the better of the argument when it came to counting heads. By this date the Russo-Chinese alliance was non-existent and doctrinal solidarity a farce. The withdrawal of the Russian technicians was a cancellation of the economic co-operation initiated immediately after the establishment of the Chinese People's Republic, and Khrushchev's approaches to Eisenhower had revealed the strict limits of Russian support for China in external affairs. The attempt to operate a Russo-Chinese alliance in world affairs had run on to the rocks of Khrushchev's American policy.

But at the end of 1964 Khrushchev was overthrown and the second triumvirate which took over power *ad interim* (like the earlier collective leadership after Stalin's death) attempted a reconciliation. Kosygin went twice to Beijing. The Chinese, however, refused to attend a conference of communist parties in Moscow in 1965 and subsequently frustrated Moscow's plans for a world communist conference. The Russian embassy in Beijing was attacked in 1967 and the next year Beijing condemned the Russian invasion of Czechoslovakia and Brezhnev's doctrine on the right and duty of the USSR to act outside its borders for the defence of socialism and the socialist bloc as a whole. In 1969 there were incidents on the Ussuri River, where the possession of a few islands had long been a matter for (not very heated) dispute. Men were killed and there was talk about the possibility of a Russian pre-emptive strike against China before its nuclear capacity assumed deterrent proportions. Russian forces in the east were increased in the 1970s and 1980s from 33 to 56 divisions, and from 1979 the Russian threat to China was magnified by the establishment of Russian naval and air bases in Vietnam. Negotiations in Beijing in 1969–70, to which the USSR sent one of its most senior and able diplomats, were lengthy but unproductive, and renewed talks in 1979 were wrecked by the Russian invasion of Afghanistan (with which China has a border).

Some compensation for the collapse of a grand communist alliance was provided for China by its readmission to the comity of nations. Canada and Italy established diplomatic relations in 1970. In the same year a majority in the UN General Assembly – but not the requisite two-thirds – voted in favour of China's membership and at the end of the year Mao's regime was admitted to be the rightful incumbent of China's permanent seat in the Security Council. China came into the UN on its own terms, which included the rejection of an American–Japanese proposal to retain Taiwan as a separate member alongside China. Most importantly, relations between China and the United States were dramatically altered. In 1971 Nixon reversed American policy towards China when he decided to jettison the two Chinas policy if that were necessary to establish diplomatic relations with Beijing.

This was the culmination of a long, slow process. At Geneva in 1954 Zhou had proposed discussions to ease tensions and a first meeting took place in that city after the release of the 13 captured American airmen. Talks foundered in 1957 over the American recognition of Taiwan as a separate state but were renewed in Warsaw the next year and the United States began to give visas to American journalists who wanted to go to China. The ensuing crisis over the offshore islands froze attitudes on both sides but contacts were maintained and in 1960 Zhou proposed a Pacific non-aggression pact. For some years there was stalemate. In 1966 the US secretary of state Dean Rusk said that the United States would not try to overthrow the government in Beijing by force but the war in Vietnam put an end to even the mildest sign of normal relations until the American withdrawal from South-east Asia revived the situation created in the 1950s by the truce in Korea. The Americans were acknowledging the defeat of their efforts to be a continental Asian power. In 1971 an American ping-pong team, which had been playing in various Asian countries, was invited to China, the first recorded appearance of this sport in high politics. This move was followed by a further relaxation of the American trade embargo (there had been some relaxation in 1969). In July Nixon's adviser on national security, Henry Kissinger, went secretly to Beijing and Nixon himself followed in the next year.

In the next years these American moves coincided with the ending of the Vietnam War and, more importantly, with a reciprocal desire on Mao's part to improve relations with the United States. In the late 1960s China's relations with the USSR had deteriorated so far that Mao feared war between the two countries. Quarrels over overall communist policy in the world were exacerbated by overt military threats on their borders in Mongolia where Soviet forces had been increased from 15 to 44 divisions. China's land frontiers had been a recurrent worry throughout its history. Mao also feared for his domestic position since during the Cultural Revolution his encouragement of the Red Guards to confront the army had led him to anticipate – in his imagination at least – a coup by Marshall Lin Biao with army support. The new accord had little precise content (and a visit to Beijing by President Gerald Ford in 1975 added none) but it was an important political demonstration; a joint warning to the USSR – by the Americans not to take Russo-American detente for granted, by the Chinese not to make big trouble on China's borders; a sign that bipolarity at the summit of world affairs was coming to an end; and the opening therefore of a new view of the future. For the time being, however, China remained militarily well below superpower status. It could not hit the United States or greatly harm the USSR and it had not forced the United States to change its stance on an independent Taiwan.

In the following decade China set out to achieve two things: to become an independent nuclear power and a world leader in a new international of the underprivileged. By 1975 it had set off some 20 nuclear explosions and possessed an estimated 300 nuclear weapons. Some of these were intermediate-range missiles but most could be delivered only by aircraft with a range of 2,400 km. By the end of the 1970s, however, there were good grounds for supposing that China possessed no only the missiles but also the delivery systems needed to attack targets in the European areas of the USSR. Secondly, Zhou Enlai, who had steadily built up China's diplomatic position in Asia from the Bandung conference in 1955 onwards, made a tour of African countries in 1963–64 but China's comparatively modest defence expenditure and its industrial growth pains made it a power of the future rather than a power to be reckoned with in the present. What China achieved in these years of travail was to project so menacing an image of its future power as to make the world take it seriously in the present. This fear was fed by the mysteriousness with which China was cloaked by the outside world's own determination to treat it as not just different but out of this world. It was a product in particular of confusion about Chinese attitudes towards nuclear war and a belief that China's leaders regarded such a war with equanimity on the grounds that China's vast size and few large cities would enable it to survive nuclear attack. The Chinese were, in fact, well aware that a nuclear war would be a universal disaster and that China and the Chinese Communist Party would be among the victims, and although they clung to the not implausible thesis that wars were inevitable, they did not apparently regard nuclear war as inevitable. Like others, they hoped to prevent a nuclear war by a policy of deterrence but, unlike others, they could not in the 1950s and 1960s do the deterring themselves. China in this period was exposed to nuclear threats or preventive war in the same way as the USSR had been exposed between 1945 and 1949.

In this situation the Chinese, like the Russians before them and regardless of whether their ultimate intentions were malevolent or peaceable, had to resort to minor non-nuclear deterrents while being careful to avoid any disastrous provocation of a nuclear power. They challenged and exposed Asia's largest non-nuclear state, India, and came to terms with lesser countries which might have been tempted into an enemy camp. Having taken Tibet because they could (see below) and postponed the conquest of Taiwan because they must, they pursued a policy of limited activity which fitted their limited capacities. The decision of North Vietnam to take an active part in war in the south was, it may be presumed, approved by the Moscow conference of 81 communist parties and by the government of the USSR, which could not resist appeals to communist solidarity and could have no objection to endorsing and even assisting a guerrilla war likely to prove embarrassing to the United States. When in 1963 the United States decided to take a leading part in the war and to raise the level of warfare in order to preserve an independent South Vietnamese state, they in effect served a no-aggression notice on China. The Chinese, faced with a conflict between two principles – the principle that a nuclear power must not be provoked, and the principle that a national liberation movement must be helped – opted for the former.

This dominant principle was further exemplified in Europe. Albania, one of China's few friends, received little more than the rhetorical support which the Russians could be expected to put up with. In any case, the Chinese were only marginally interested in Europe. They were more interested in Africa, which presented, in their view, excellent prospects for revolution. More broadcasting time was devoted to African listeners than even to southern Asians, but the results were disappointing, for by the time that China was ready to play a full part in world affairs, most of the nationalist movements in Africa had won power and independence and, being intent on retaining their power, were anything but insurrectionary. The fall of Ben Bella in Algeria in 1965 was a special setback, similar to the rout and slaughter of the Indonesian communists in the same year.

China was on the way to becoming a regional nuclear power but was also searching for a more than regional role. Its emergence as a future giant power gave notice that the bipolar world of the Cold War was destined to be short-lived. China's first nuclear explosion in October 1964 was followed by a second in May 1965. A year later a first thermonuclear weapon, probably capable of use in submarines (of which China had 30, received from the USSR), was exploded. China's first guided missile test occurred in October 1966 and its first hydrogen bomb was exploded in June 1967. It would soon be formidable for 1,600 km around; it could be expected to have a wide range, if limited stocks, of nuclear weapons some time in the 1970s; and it might spring a surprise by developing ahead of expectations a submarine nuclear armoury to threaten the United States and Latin America from the Pacific Ocean. But unlike the United States and the USSR, it was not becoming the centre of a group. It had failed to detach more than a few, comparatively insignificant communist parties from the main body of international communism which, if faced with a choice, persisted in choosing Moscow rather than Beijing; only the distant and ineffective Albanians and New Zealanders stuck staunchly at Beijing's side.

There is always a certain grandeur about isolation. Britain, Japan and the United States had all at various times dallied with its lures. Communist China made a virtue of its isolation and discounted the dangers by dwelling on a more distant future in which it would ultimately circumvent and discomfit the major powers whose hostility it had to bear in the present. China was used to having powerful enemies. Britain and Germany had been succeeded in this role by Japan, and Japan in 1945 by the United States – especially after the outbreak of the Korean War. The USSR, superficially a natural ally, had turned out within a decade to be an enemy, a foreign power upon whose goodwill China had mistakenly, if for a short space, allowed itself to become over-dependent. In this situation China's leaders seemed to veer towards a nationalism even more intense than might have been expected from a half-century of impotence and revolution, and to seek reassurance in their country's vast size and splendid history, their faith in the revolution which they had made and an optimistic view of world politics. In their eyes Asia, Africa and Latin America were revolutionary, anti-colonial domains where their major enemies – the United States, the USSR and the principal western European states – would get into trouble because of their archaic political attitudes and economic contradictions. Western Europe and northern America would also develop similar revolutionary movements in which the bourgeoisie would be threatened and would finally be supplanted by the proletariat. Meanwhile, China must assemble and develop its resources and – in the view of Mao himself and some of his associates – preserve the ardour of its revolution.

Resurrection

Mao's government was pledged to end corruption in the public services, reverse the economic slide which had overwhelmed the Kuomintang, make China a modern industrial power and introduce sweeping reforms in land-holding and agriculture. These were huge tasks requiring money, authority and peace. Corruption, waste and bureaucracy were attacked in the Three-Anti campaign begun in Manchuria in August 1951 and extended to the whole of China two months later. A Five-Anti campaign followed, directed against bribery, tax evasion, fraud, the theft of state property and the betrayal of economic secrets. These campaigns seemed to betoken, on the part of the government, a real concern to secure the approbation of the Chinese people and, conversely, an equal concern to ensure that the people should not only behave correctly but think correctly. The campaigns were pursued by means of public meetings, confessions, purges, delation and executions. They were indiscriminate and were used for attacks on unpopular or richer classes such as missionaries, merchants and private entrepreneurs. Landlords and kulaks were singled out, partly as an acknowledgement of the debt owed to the poorer peasants who had ensured the survival and eventual success of the communists. The dispossession of landlords and kulaks, which began in 1950, was accelerated and made horrible by the panic which spread in China during the first months of the Korean War and claimed 2 million victims or more: the newly installed rulers, like the leaders of the French Revolution facing the armies of *émigrés* and hostile powers, lived in expectation of a counter-revolutionary uprising which would be supported and exploited by the United States.

Collectivization began slowly in 1951. The example of the USSR in the 1930s, and the inadvisability of disillusioning and antagonizing the peasants who had just become proprietors in place of the vanished landlords, dictated caution. In 1953–54 Mao was ill and Gao Gang – the semi-autonomous lord of Manchuria, pro-Moscow, pro-heavy industry – was temporarily in charge. (He committed suicide soon afterwards.) On his return Mao decided to step up the pace of change, particularly in agriculture. After two poor years the 1955 harvest promised well; he did not want to leave the new peasant proprietors undisturbed for long for fear that a new class of kulaks might emerge from their ranks; the first five-year plan, covering the years 1952–57 (but not published until about half its course was run) was inadequately primed by the Russian pump and needed a further boost that could come only from brigading and driving the peasants into more efficient methods and greater productivity. The basic aim was to sap the peasant's resistance to the state; so long as he owned his land he would keep the will to fight, but as soon as he lost it the spirit would go out of him.

In the earlier years the approach to communal ownership had been cautiously pre-pared through a series of staging points beginning with co-operation on specified tasks at certain seasons; proceeding thence to a distribution of rewards partly on the basis of the size of a man's holding and partly on the amount of work done by him; and so leading to a final phase in which the ownership of the land would be transferred to the communal group (not the state), rewards would be calculated on the basis of work done, and the group's affairs would be regulated by general meetings and elected com-mittees. From the latter part of 1955 this progression was enormously accelerated and in something like two or two and a half years it was all but completed. The speed of this vast economic and social revolution was characteristic of the methods and out-look of China's new leaders, but it also sharpened the discomforts and resentments (especially among the better-off peasants) which such a programme would have evoked in any case.

During these years Mao, whose rapid collectivization was bound to offend the more conservative, also ran the risk of disgruntling the more radical faction by wooing the intellectuals who, though suspect because of their western training and thinking, were useful to the regime. Mao wanted to initiate a real debate which would engender a genuine conviction of the correctness of his policies. The intellectuals, however, were extremely chary of beginning, even after Mao, by coining the slogan of the Hundred Flowers, virtually pressed them to believe that the regime wanted them to think for themselves and express their views with more freedom and less regard for conformity than they had hitherto dared to use. When criticism was evoked, it proved to be too exuberant. The inevitable disillusion which was eroding the high hopes and self-reliant optimism of the morrow of victory had been sharpened by inflation, labour troubles, and shortages of food and consumer goods, and in this atmosphere the hoped-for dis-cussion about how to progress along the communist path extended to more radical questioning of basic communist tenets. A few months after the first mention of the Hundred Flowers the debate released by that slogan was abruptly closed.

It was succeeded early in 1958, at the commencement of the second five-year plan, by the Great Leap Forward and the vigorous introduction of the commune system in country and town. The Great Leap Forward (preceded by an earlier and unsuccessful Little Leap during 1956–57) was an incitement to greater exertions, associated particu-larly with Liu Shaoqi, a leader of the more impetuous school who succeeded at the end of 1958 to the highest position in the state upon the unexpected retirement of Mao from the presidency (but came later to bewail his share in the miseries of the Great Leap). The Great Leap Forward was meant to be a short cut to greater production. After some experimentation it was ordained for the whole country in the autumn of 1958. The principal aims were to mobilize labour, set women free for industrial jobs, establish local industries as an adjunct to larger units of production and introduce country people to industrial processes. One of the most publicized items was the mak-ing of steel in backyards (an idea which produced great but poor steel), however the most important feature was the communes which were rapidly established throughout rural areas to the accompaniment of a propaganda barrage designed to drown criticism in a wave of enthusiasm. Property was brought into communal ownership and individuals were told to look to the community for free food, services and entertainment. In many places results went ludicrously and tragically far; even cottages, trees, fowls and small tools were turned into communal property. The central government had only faulty machinery for ensuring that its wishes were carried out sensibly throughout the vastness of China. It operated through cadres, a non-communist device added by the communists to the system of government. These links between the central government and the people were responsible for much of the inefficiency, cruelty and brutality with which new policies were implemented. Thirty million people, perhaps many more, were killed by starvation or violence as they tried to trek away from famine or succumbed to it. In some areas a third of the population suffered premature and wretched death.

The inefficiencies of the Great Leap Forward were magnified by natural disasters and the whole experiment, intended to rationalize and boost agricultural production, was abandoned. It was a piece of wilfulness on Mao's part which lacked the necessary labour and the necessary enthusiasm on the ground, a vast flop which was for a time concealed by false claims. Although the communes survived as new elements in society and government, by 1960 the small team was once more the basis of the rural economy. The revolution lost face seriously during the great famine years. It had exacerbated an inevitable crisis by grave over-estimates of crop production and it had experimented unsuccessfully with a new communal pattern which the Russians had explicitly derided.

In the 1960s the revolution began to devour its children. China's ruling group was disrupted with a violence more familiar in the USSR than in China, where the only major communist figures to have been purged had been Gao Gang in 1954 and Peng Dehuai in 1959. Obsessed by the fear that his life's work was being eroded by bourgeois backsliding, Mao determined to displace all those leaders whose steadfastness and fervour were in doubt and to revitalize party and populace by turning to youth. After some years of preparation he revealed in 1965 to his principal colleagues plans for a cultural revolution and appointed the mayor of Beijing, Peng Zhen, to direct it. Peng Zhen, however, was soon at cross-purposes with Jiang Qing, Mao's third wife, and some time in the first half of 1966 he was dismissed. In 1966 Mao reappeared in public after an effacement of six months and a few weeks later the Cultural Revolution got publicly under way with a series of rallies, demonstrations and denunciations and a much-publicized swim by Mao in the Yangtze near the provincial capital of Wuhan. It so happened that at this time there was a major breakdown in the educational system, which had forced the authorities to postpone for a year all entries into universities and similar institutions and so discharged millions of young people into temporary purposelessness. They were turned into Red Guards, who were to replace the communist youth organization (which had supposedly gone flabby) and go to work to boost production in field and factory. From these useful, if unacademic, pursuits they were diverted to an ideological crusade and, in an exuberance of anti-revisionist spirits, demonstrated against revolutionary insufficiencies and pre-revolutionary attitudes and symbols, assaulting individuals and destroying property in a movement which spread so extensively that it disrupted communications and brought factories to a halt. Some 20 million young people were said to be involved, most of them in their teens.

'Cultural Revolution' was the misleading name for a reign of terror accompanied by the most revolting cruelty. It had its sources in internal and external problems – economic planning, devolution, consolidation versus forcing the pace of progress, attitudes to the Russians – which had troubled the party in the 1950s and disrupted it in the 1960s. The revolution split the party at all levels. Hundreds of thousands of leaders, from President Liu Shaoqi to much humbler officials, lost their posts, were tortured and killed. Inevitably, the army advanced in power. Lin Biao, who had succeeded Peng Dehuai in 1959 and had invented and distributed the famous little red book, sided with Mao, thus ensuring Mao's victory and confirming the defeat of the pro-Russian faction once represented by Peng. Lin Biao was proclaimed Mao's eventual heir. But in 1971 he disappeared. Rumour had it that he fled to the USSR in an aircraft that crashed in Mongolia, killing him. Two years later at the tenth congress of the Chinese Communist Party he was openly accused of plotting to assassinate Mao and cement an alliance with the USSR. These charges were repeated at the joint trial in 1980 of the leaders of the Cultural Revolution and Lin's one-time closest military associates.

In 1976 Mao Zedong died. He was an extreme example of the individual in whom ideology occludes the intellect, common sense and human emotions and helps a naturally authoritarian man to monstrous abuses of power. After a singularly long and arduous struggle which culminated in the victory of 1949 he saw his visions coming to grief. In order to preserve them he turned to policies which created chaos and brutality on a huge scale, ruined rural China by devastation and depopulation, and destroyed much of the material and spiritual heritage of the oldest civilization in the world. Zhou Enlai died in the same year as Mao and these two deaths released a struggle for power between three main groups. The first beneficiary was Hua Guofeng, who was Mao's choice for the leadership and succeeded Zhou as (acting) prime minister. This was a setback for Zhou's 72-year-old deputy and presumed heir, Deng Xiaoping. Deng, general secretary of the Communist Party in 1956, had been purged during the Cultural Revolution but reappeared in 1974 and in the next year was appointed deputy chairman of the party, first deputy prime minister and chief of staff of the army. Demonstrations in Beijing in Deng's favour led to his disgrace and the further promotion of Hua to be first deputy chairman of the party (next to Mao) and prime minister. When Mao himself died, Hua, temporarily free from attack from the right, moved swiftly against the radical left. The so-called Gang of Four, led by Jiang Qing, were arrested a few weeks later and Hua became chairman of the party. But in the following year Deng made a comeback and for the next three years Hua and Deng shared the principal posts and the limelight, until in 1980 Deng ousted Hua after a campaign in which Hua's position as Mao's successor was undermined in the name of democratic freedom and Mao himself was criticized for having acted autocratically by nominating his successor. At the same time the Gang of Four were brought to trial and linked with Lin Biao's abortive coup of 1971. The effect of the trial, and presumably its purpose, was to represent the Gang of Four as a conspiratorial group in the tradition of China's secret societies; to discredit the armed forces as treasonable and incompetent; and indirectly to implicate Mao himself in the economic and social disasters of the Cultural Revolution.

In Chinese communist terms Deng was a conservative pragmatist. His victory meant a return to traditional types of competitive examination, the rehabilitation of the intelligentsia and other victims of the radical years, the restoration of the profit motive, higher prices for peasants and higher wages in industry and commerce, and wider openings to the west and Japan and even to the USSR. But although a revisionist and modernizer, Deng was no liberal or any sort of democrat. He wanted to modernize the Chinese economy without relaxing the political grip of the Communist Party. The Cultural Revolution had set back modernization and in his declining years Mao had failed in his primary task of bringing China back to its rightful place as the greatest power in the world. Deng and his colleagues elaborated programmes for the modernization of industry, the armed forces, agriculture and science and technology. Large sums were borrowed and spent but programmes were cut back when the financial establishment (bankers returning to posts which they had held before the Cultural Revolution or even before Mao's triumph over Jiang Kaishek) discovered that foreign funding was outrunning foreign revenues (exports, remittances from overseas Chinese, tourism). Growth was strong – with some poor spots in energy production from all sources and in grains – but so too was demand. Inflation rose to 20–30 per cent a year and corruption was magnified as the gap grew between official prices, unchanged for years, and prices on black markets. Price reform was urgent but anticipation of it further accentuated the gap, caused runs on banks as depositors rushed to change their money into goods, and so forced the government to postpone price reform. As in the USSR, the problem of grafting market mechanisms into a command economy generated economic breakdown and bitter disputes between political leaders.

Deng was himself caught in these dilemmas. He both saw the need for liberal measures and feared them. He was alive to his dependence on the army and its ageing and conservative chiefs who had thrown him out in 1966 and restored him in 1975; he much enlarged the armed police force. He oscillated between an innate authoritarianism and a readiness to loosen the reins in order to foster economic progress – and an equal readiness to tighten the reins when relaxation encouraged political protest. His policies engendered therefore their own reversal. He tolerated and seemed to encourage the efflorescence of protest which in 1978–79 took the form of affixing popular complaints and demands on Democracy Wall in Beijing and he was able to combine for several years substantial economic expansion with tolerable political freedoms. But about 1985–86 economic advance faltered while popular demands became, on the contrary, more pressing. The price of economic progress was rising prices, rising inflation, breakdowns and bottlenecks in communications, shortages of capital and energy, and corruption. Economic growth, instead of relieving want, was making it worse and fuelling indignation. Deng imposed import controls and devalued the currency in an attempt to restrain the economy and, in the face of rising student clamour for more and quicker changes, he relaxed censorship and permitted more open political debate. But in 1987, scared by the outcome of this liberalizing trend, he changed course, muzzled liberal academics and compelled the Communist Party's comparatively liberal and comparatively young general secretary Hu Yaobang to resign (as he himself had been compelled by Mao to resign in 1966). After a few months Deng again changed course and reverted to a relatively liberal stance. At the end of the year he fulfilled his frequently announced intention to retire, taking with him into retirement a clutch of old conservatives and leaving at the head of affairs two younger men – Hu's successor Zhao Ziyang and a new prime minister Li Peng. Deng's retirement was more apparent than real and not very apparent.

In 1989 Hu died. His funeral was made the occasion for massive demonstrations in which students from Beijing's universities were especially prominent, voicing protests against the slow pace of change, economic failure and persistent corruption. They were joined by discontented intellectuals and by workers, and suddenly they were making a big impact not only in the capital but also in some 80 other cities all over China. They posed a threat, not necessarily to the Communist Party, but to its elderly ruling clique. To the octogenarian Deng, however, and to others of his generation these two threats were indistinguishable and amounted also to a threat to China itself. Deng equated the party with the revolution which it had made, and the revolution with China. Anybody who opposed the party was therefore a traitor to his country. At this critical moment Zhao, who shared Hu's belief that economic reforms required some political reforms too, happened to be away in Korea. On his return to Beijing he took a conciliatory, even sympathetic and apologetic, line but behind the scenes his more conservative adversaries persuaded the mutable Deng to their side. The students were attacked and maligned in official publications. Over-optimistically, they for their part refused to be intimidated. The resulting confrontation was briefly frozen because of the impending arrival of Gorbachev in Beijing. In Tiananmen Square, which was permanently occupied by huge but well-ordered crowds, the mood turned to hostility against Deng personally. Deng resolved to use force to dispel the crowds. The first moves by troops were blocked by unarmed civilians, the temper of the soldiers appeared uncertain or even friendly to the demonstrators, and two operations were called off; but eventually the drama which had riveted the attention of much of the world from the end of April to the first days of June was brought to its close by massacre. In Beijing alone, several thousand were killed. Governments all over the world expressed outrage, loudly but briefly.

For Deng the Tiananmen massacre was a deplorable necessity which shook his domestic position and set back his external policies. A decade earlier Deng had visited Tokyo and Washington and some years later he had received Thatcher in Beijing and sent his foreign minister to Moscow. An eight-year commercial agreement with Japan, concluded in 1978, was followed by a peace treaty. With the United States full diplomatic relations were established in 1978: Washington agreed to shift formal recognition from Taiwan to Beijing and remove its troops from Taiwan, while China watered down its demand for the complete abrogation of Washington's treaty relations with Taiwan. Reagan angered China shortly after his election by trying to square the new Sino-American concord with a revival of sales of arms to Taiwan but he was quickly forced to abandon this impossible stance. Bush pursued the Nixon–Reagan policy of making friends and contracts in China, overlooking brutal Chinese repression of risings in Tibet in 1987 and 1989 and a personal rebuff when the Chinese government prevented the outspoken critic Fang Lizhi from accepting an invitation to meet Bush at the American embassy in Beijing. At the same time Deng cautiously improved relations with the USSR. Whereas in the 1970s he had advertised his discontent with Moscow by despatching Hua on visits to Romania and Yugoslavia and by publicly advocating a Sino-Japanese–American alliance against the USSR, he responded amicably to Gorbachev's first indications in 1986 that the USSR was prepared to make concessions on border disputes, withdraw troops from Mongolia and Afghanistan and end support for the Vietnamese occupation of Kampuchea. The Chinese foreign minister visited Moscow – the first such visit for over 30 years – and Gorbachev was invited to Beijing. Before going there in 1989 he announced the withdrawal of 500,000 troops from China's borders and a reduction by two-thirds of the USSR's 50,000 troops in Mongolia. Prime Minister Li Peng visited six South-east Asian countries in 1990. Visits to China in 1992 by the Emperor Akihito and Boris Yeltsin put China undisputedly back on the world map in the year in which it had to be carefully wooed over Yugoslavia and other international issues because of its veto in the Security Council. Deng presented the outside world as a field of operations rather than a thicket of hostile forces.

In this world China, like India almost half a century earlier, had an irredentist programme. Its most substantial item was Taiwan, which was under the rule of the Jiang dynasty (Jiang Kaishek followed by his son Jiang Jingkuo) and was protected by the American navy. When Nixon inaugurated Sino-American détente in the early 1970s it seemed possible that the second of these factors might be at least relaxed and Beijing conceived the notion of 'one country two systems' to take advantage of this opportunity. But Taiwan's bounding economic fortunes were making it independent of American tutelage and in the 1980s Reagan sought to revert to the Two Chinas policy which was predicated upon an independent Taiwan. Jiang Jingkuo brought martial law to an end in 1987 and was succeeded by a native Taiwanese, Li Denghui, who, while insisting on Taiwanese independence and sovereignty, promoted economic links with China, encouraged Taiwanese investment in China and permitted elections for the first time since 1948. In 1996 Beijing interrupted this comparatively equable state of affairs by firing four nuclear rockets into the waters around Taiwan, probably a demonstration against Li's repeated references to China and Taiwan as two 'equal states' and by his impending re-election by direct popular vote. The United States, fearful of an invasion of Taiwan from the mainland, despatched a naval battle group and normal disequilibrium was restored.

Further south, at the estuary of the Pearl River, lay the two foreign enclaves of Macao and Hong Kong. Macao was a peninsula and two islands on the western side of the estuary, just over 10 sq. km in extent, first occupied by Portuguese traders in the fifteenth century. It had ranked as a province of Portugal from the conclusion in 1887 of a treaty with China. More than 90 per cent of its population of half a million were Chinese. Riots in 1966 demonstrated the precariousness of Portuguese rule and resulted in the humiliation of the Portuguese governor and in *de facto* power-sharing between China and Portugal. In 1993 China promulgated a Basic Law for Macao, which came into operation on the inauguration in 1999 of the Macao Special Administrative Region of China.

The fate of Hong Kong was largely governed by two special features: a dateline dictated by the fact that the greater part of the territory was held by Britain by virtue of a lease which terminated in 1997, and the remarkable postwar prosperity which made it one of the wonders of the world's economy and swelled its population tenfold. Hong Kong had been acquired by Britain in three pieces: the island in 1841, supplemented by Kowloon across the water in 1860 and by the New Territories (which comprised 89 per cent of the colony) leased in 1898 for 99 years. When the Second World War ended, the colony's population was about half a million. A move by the Kuomintang to occupy it was thwarted, the victorious communists mysteriously stopped short of a similar attempt a few years later and the British returned to an increasingly prosperous exemplar of capitalist commerce and finance with, however, a deadline set by the term of the lease of the New Territories. No Chinese regime accepted the validity of any of the three nineteenth-century transactions. For China the whole of the colony was and always had been sovereign Chinese territory. For the practical realization of this situation Mao and his successors were prepared to take a long view, which would be automatically shortened by the passing of the years. Hong Kong was no use as a base for an attack on China either by the Kuomintang on Taiwan or the United States.

The Macao riots of 1966 were replicated a year later in Hong Kong, synchronized with verbal and physical attacks on the British in Beijing. This aggressiveness alarmed the business community in Hong Kong and the colony's democratic elite, but the governor and police were more resolute than those of Macao and the status quo was substantially undisturbed. However, violence in the colony and the Chinese capital served notice on the British of the approach of 1997, with the extra complication that the need to resolve the future of the colony had somehow to be reconciled with the need to improve relations with a resurgent China. By the mid-1970s the defeat of the Gang of Four and the restoration of Deng made rapprochement with China practicable as well as desirable and at the end of that decade the governor of Hong Kong went to Beijing to initiate talks. Deng, although intransigent on Chinese sovereignty, resurrected the notion of two systems in one state but the advent of Thatcher soured relations. Deng and Thatcher were equally obdurate but Deng was the more realistic, better informed (at least initially) and held practically all the cards. Thatcher, deeply averse to any surrender of British sovereignty and fresh from her triumph in the Falklands, toyed with the idea of a condominium and, even more unrealistic, a surrender of sovereignty so circumscribed as to be no surrender. Proposals for a continuation of British administration after 1997 on the grounds that only thereby could the stability and prosperity of Hong Kong be guaranteed irritated Deng who, after an abrasive meeting of the two leaders in Beijing in 1982, declared that, failing agreement within two years, China would produce its own unilateral plans for the future of the area. In the ensuing impasse confidence and share prices in Hong Kong slumped, the Hong Kong dollar lost a third of its exchange value in a year and panic loomed. The one concrete outcome of Thatcher's visit was Deng's two-year deadline. Before it was out the British foreign secretary announced in Hong Kong and Beijing the abandonment of Britain's proposal for continuing British administration. This retreat cleared the way for the resumption of talks which produced the Joint Declaration of 1984.

This declaration was a compendium which included a statement of principles by China and agreement that China would produce and promulgate a Basic Law for Hong Kong to come into force in 1997, when sole British administration would be replaced by sole Chinese administration. The declaration created a Joint Liaison Group with a vaguely supervisory role in a transitional period before and after 1997 – originally a Chinese proposal but modified in negotiation to restrict the group's authority, delay its inauguration and extend its life to the year 2000. In 1985 China duly established a committee of 82 persons, including 23 from Hong Kong, to draft a Basic Law. Published in 1988 and approved by the People's Congress in Beijing in 1990, it promised Hong Kong a special status for 50 years, an elective element in the legislative council of one-third from 1997 and up to half by 2003, and required Britain not to exceed these limits before handing over. The publication of this grudging enactment, which disappointed the more optimistic illusions fostered by the Joint Declaration, caused dismay in Hong Kong, where fear of the future had been exacerbated by the Tiananmen massacre.

Shortly afterwards a new British governor, Christopher Patten, a Conservative minister who had lost his parliamentary seat at the general election of 1991, arrived to preside over the colony's last years. Patten's hands were tied by the events of 1982–84, which had shortened Deng's temper, introduced the two-year deadline and secured for China the right to legislate for Hong Kong's future with only the vaguest constraints from a set of principles of its own devising. Within these constraints Patten's tasks were to ensure as amicable a transfer of power as possible (London having at least one eye on Anglo-Chinese relations in the indefinite future) and to allay Hong Kong's fears. He resolved also to introduce as much democracy as possible within the severe limitations set by the Joint Declaration. Hong Kong's fears were already manifest in the rate of emigration, which doubled or trebled around 1990, fuelled by the prospects of communist rule and by British niggardliness in admitting fugitives from the colony to Britain. Until 1962 all in the colony had a right to British citizenship and entry into Britain but these rights had been abrogated and Britain was proposing to restrict entry to 50,000 individuals and their dependants. These select few were to be picked on a complicated points system which could not conceal the fact that Britain was fulfilling its obligations not to the people of Hong Kong but to an elite of successful businessmen and colonial servants.

Patten confronted China's constitutional plan with proposals of his own to come into operation at imminent local elections and at the election of a new legislative council in 1995. He reduced the voting age from 21 to 18 (the voting age in China), so creating an electorate of 3–4 million; introduced single-seat, single-vote constituencies; made the two councils for Hong Kong/Kowloon and the New Territories and the 19 district boards wholly instead of two thirds elective; and reformed the 60-seat legislative council by making 20 instead of 18 members directly elected, 10 by local councillors who had themselves been elected to their councils and the remaining 10 by functional constituencies with a broadened franchise. His limit of 20 directly elected members of the legislature conformed with the Joint Declaration's one explicit provision on constitutional change.

For Hong Kong these changes had the advantage of extending, however belatedly, its fledgling democracy but the disadvantage of giving offence to its impending Chinese masters, whose response was vociferous hostility and charges that the governor was in breach of the Joint Declaration and of British undertakings given at the date of that declaration. (Upon his departure from Hong Kong in 1997 Patten let it be known that he had been left in ignorance of these undertakings when he assumed office in 1991 and afterwards.) Patten's reforms, narrowly approved by his legislative council, were a gamble on the chance that China would swallow a little democracy in a small corner of its huge territory whose rich material gains would dwarf ideological and constitutional niceties. But elections in 1995 were ignored by two-thirds of the electorate and China reiterated its intention to dissolve the new legislature in 1997. Patten's gamble was a valiant irrelevance; his aim of giving Hong Kong the beginnings of democracy was honourable but not at that date practicable, even had he not been tripped up by his colleagues in London. On 1 July 1997 Hong Kong reverted to Chinese rule as a

Special Administrative Region under the Basic Law of 1990. The event was marked on the British side by a mixture of post-imperial pageantry and democratic rhetoric and on the Chinese by concessions deemed necessary to maintain Hong Kong's economic momentum without importing democracy. China welcomed a capitalist but not a democratic Hong Kong. This was a unique event: a western imperial colony not liberated but handed over to a communist state.

These and all other matters of consequence were overshadowed by the uncertainties caused by the longevity of Deng Xiaoping. Deng resigned his last formal office – chairman of the Central Military Commission – in 1991 when he was probably 87 years old but he remained a dominating presence. His policy of mending foreign fences was powerfully assisted by evidence of China's economic progress. Growth rates, which had been 4–6 per cent in the late 1980s, reached 13 per cent in the early 1990s, mainly due to developments by private enterprise in coastal areas. Devaluation of the currency in 1990 was rewarded by handsome surpluses on foreign trade. Yet Deng's dash for growth had question marks against it. What might happen when he died was guesswork; his policy of liberalizing the economy while maintaining authoritarian party rule might become an unsustainable contradiction; his faith in market forces ignored the changes which modern communications had brought into markets by making them as attractive to disruptive speculators as to legitimate and honest traders. Post-Maoist, post-communist China was an authoritarian state which contained a thrusting and thriving neo-capitalist economy and also a huge rural population of family farmers: the last a survival from before Mao's revolutions and the other grafted on to them. It was unclear whether this strange, perhaps unique, complexity was good ground for success or not.

The immediate outlook was unpromising. In 1993 tensions turned into serious riots following tax increases, free market pricing, persistent inflation between 25 and 30 per cent, and conflict between the centre and the provinces, cities and the countryside. A massive migration to the cities was fostering crime, tax dodging and corruption (the last pervading civil and military elites). High spirits were mixed with fears and discontent. Whether communism was to be succeeded by a Chinese capitalism or the more familiar Chinese anarchy was an open question. Yet China was approaching the turn of the century as one of the world's largest economies measured by purchasing power, as the country with the world's longest imperial pedigree and as a nuclear power. China's economy was not only growing but being transformed. By the mid-1990s three-quarters of its exports were manufactured goods, a development which caused some unease to its Japanese and Korean neighbours. It had a surplus on trade with the United States second only to Japan's and the value of its current construction contracts with American corporations exceeded $100 billion a year.

With an eye to these present realities and future possibilities President Bush regularly vetoed congressional wishes to deny China most-favoured-nation treatment in consequence of the Tiananmen killings and reports of persistent torture and inhuman labour camps. President Clinton was less circumspect but, in terms of upholding human rights, no more effective. By invoking human rights he not only irritated Chinese leaders but gave them opportunities to display patriotic anti-Americanism as they manoeuvred for power or survival in the post-Deng era. His threats to impose super-tariffs on Chinese exports in retaliation for Chinese disregard of American copyrights and other intellectual property were no more effective against China than they were against Japan: that is to say, they had marginal and probably temporary effect.

In 1997 Deng died. Anybody living in so vast a country as China might be excused for imagining that other parts of the world did not much matter. Deng did not make that mistake. Whether he had an acuter sense of the technical revolutions of the twentieth century, or whether he was needled by the greater successes of Chinese outside China (in Taiwan, Hong Kong, Singapore) he resolved to turn China outwards and chase the great gains to be won by free enterprise. Although in power only at a late age, he lived long enough and laboured unhurriedly enough to set a course which was unlikely to be consciously reversed in the next generation.

The fifteenth congress of the Chinese Communist Party confirmed the triumvirate of Jiang Zemin as president, Li Peng as prime minister and Zhou Rongji as first deputy prime minister. Li reached the end of his non-renewable term in 1998 and was succeeded by Zhou, an engineer of economic and bureaucratic reform within the boundaries of absolute party control – economic reform through wholesale privatization, bureaucratic reform by sacking bureaucrats. China had substantial reserves, healthy external balances and some foreign investment, and it claimed growth at 8 per cent (down from a vertiginous 15 per cent). In spite of migration to cities, 70 per cent of its population was rural and dependent on an agricultural economy which comprised 100,000 state farms, half of them making losses. Much of industry was heavily and unsustainably subsidized, corrupt and short of funds. The new regime began to reduce subsidies to state enterprises, the rescue of insolvent banks and the influence of army chiefs in industry (and so their influence on economic and foreign policies). But its measures were restricted since extensive withdrawal of subsidies and dismissals were bound to cause massive unemployment, more corruption and even revolt. China was remarkable on several counts – its size, its population of 1.2 billion, its ethnic homogeneity, and the scale and variety of its resources awaiting the capital, energy and advanced education necessary for their exploitation. In the late 1990s China modified its asperity towards Taiwan, concluded frontier agreements with Russia and three central Asian states and signed the Comprehensive Test Ban Treaty and the Chemical Weapons Convention (the latter providing for inspections on Chinese soil); but it failed, against American opposition, to gain admission to the WTO. This failure was a relief to China's rural sector, which feared reductions in import tariffs on American products, and, more generally, chimed with an anti-American phase generated by American protests against successful Chinese espionage in the United States and the bombing of the Chinese embassy in Belgrade during the Kosovo war. More telling, if less obvious, was the growing value to China of trade with the United States, which was accounting for nearly 40 per cent of Chinese exports by the end of the century.

China had experienced periods of great power alternating with ages of decay and subjugation. The power had been exercised over a wide but nevertheless delimited area, not in the universal mode familiar in the history of Europe, Islam or the United States. The recovery of power in the latter part of the twentieth century and the prospect for the twenty-first of a coherent Chinese state dominating a worldwide system of states was the outstanding item in any catalogue of the differences between the years 1900 and 2000. It was, however, a prospect which owed much to the fabled inscrutability of Chinese affairs. Among a number of happy economic indicators only one – thriving surpluses on the balance of payments – was concrete. China's economy was dominated by a web of banks and state-owned enterprises (i.e. lending and spending institutions) which were insolvent and prevented by political controls from declaring or remedying their insolvency. Fifty years of communist rule had transformed China's place in the world and the fortunes and hopes of many in China itself, albeit at horrifying cost in human life. The communist hierarchy's determination to remain in control of the future was grounded therefore in two contradictory but equally revolutionary experiences: misery and expectations.

Deng's successors remained wedded to an authoritarian and centripetal political system pursuing cautiously liberal economic policies and, to a greater degree than Deng himself, cautiously expanding foreign policies, the latter through China's permanent seat in the UN Security Council and by exploiting the opportunities provided by a seemingly boundless (but not necessarily permanent) supply of ready cash available for buying foreign friends and the raw materials needed to sustain a domestic economy growing at the rate of 10 per cent a year. China's financial strength was offset by a shortage of raw materials needed for growth at this pace. President Hu Jintao revived Zhou Enlai's tentative and lapsed attempts to win friends in Africa with lavish loans to African governments and a variety of engineering, extractive and other enterprises. He himself toured Africa in 2002 and 2007, and in 2006 hosted a grand summit in Beijing to which a large majority of African heads of state came. This foray was aided by the United States' somewhat lackadaisical and sporadic attention to Africa and by the worldwide distrust aroused by President Bush's botched intervention in Iraq and elsewhere in the Middle East. It risked, however, backfiring through the miserably low wages paid to African workers by Chinese entrepreneurs and their inattention to basic safety measures and African susceptibilities. In general the seventeenth congress of the Communist Party, attended by 2,000 members, was not designed to herald new courses. It looked forward to 2012 more in terms of personalities than policies and the personalities were all established party officeholders.

Xinjiang and Tibet

Despite its size, China claimed to be comparatively free of ethnic problems. But it had two: Xinjiang and Tibet.

Xinjiang, conquered by the Manchu dynasty in the middle of the eighteenth century, had borders in the twentieth with Kashmir, Afghanistan, three Soviet Republics (the Kirghiz, the Kazakh and the Turkoman) and Outer Mongolia. It had in the past been one of those provinces where a governor exercises unusual powers by virtue of his very distance from the imperial centre. He was a semi-independent proconsul who had sometimes looked to the Russian rather than the Chinese empire for help in troubles which he could not cope with himself (as, for instance, during Muslim revolts in 1930–34 and 1937). With China in disarray he could expect little from the east and had to turn west; when, however, the Russians became fully occupied by the German invasion in the Second World War, he faced about and became the friend and ally of the Kuomintang, who were in law his suzerains. In 1944 the Russians helped to foment and sustain a revolt in the Ili district of Xinjiang where an Eastern Turkestan Autonomous Republic was proclaimed, but in the Stalin–Jiang treaty of August 1945 Moscow recognized Chinese sovereignty in Xinjiang and promised not to interfere there – a promise which seems to have been inadequately kept. During the last phase of the Kuomintang the Russians tried to extend their prewar monopoly of civil aviation in Xinjiang and to re-create a Russo-Chinese partnership in economic opportunities. At the time of the collapse of the Kuomintang the former object had been achieved on paper, but not the latter, and after the governor of Xinjiang had gone over to Mao, the Russians opened negotiations with the new regime. In March 1950 agreements were signed for the creation of joint (50/50) companies to exploit oil and non-ferrous metals for 30 years and to operate civil airways for ten. Mao was in no position to hold out for complete Chinese control in the province, indubitably Chinese though it was, but he set about improving its communications with the rest of China by rail and road, including the Tibet–Xinjiang highway (flouting the Panch Shila agreed between himself and Nehru in 1954 – see p. 434). Apart from a sizeable rising in 1962 Xinjiang presented no more than persistent irritation although the Uighurs in the province outnumbered the Chinese by a substantial proportion of its 20 million inhabitants and had kinsmen in self-exile in Kazakhstan, an independent state after the collapse of the USSR. Yet, if less publicly than Tibet, Xingjiang posed a choice between exterminating or accommodating linguistic, religious and ethnic differences. The attempt to exterminate seemed as foolish as unconscionable but it was not certain that Beijing saw it that way.

For China, *Tibet* was an integral part of China and the Tibetans were one of China's 'five races'. The Tibetans, however, conscious of their wholly different culture, religion and language, took another view, partly on the grounds that de facto independence since 1911 had ripened into full independence and partly by construing vague and ancient declarations of Chinese respect as formal grants of independence and not the mere courtesies which the Chinese said they were. The Mongol Khan Kublai, a grandson of Jenghiz, who became emperor of China in the thirteenth century and was converted to Buddhism, bestowed favours and rights on a lama who established in Tibet a local dynastic rule of uncertain radius. A hundred years later a schismatic line of so-called Yellow Hat Buddhists appeared and after a further 200 years supplanted the line installed by Kublai as effective rulers of Tibet. The chief of this line was the Dalai Lama (he claimed spiritual descent from a contemporary of the Buddha in the fifth century BC), and in the seventeenth century he received from the first Manchu emperor in China marks of respect which may or may not have amounted to something approaching sovereignty. In the next century the Chinese entered Tibet to protect the country against Mongols and refused to go away again. They also defended it against a Gurkha invasion later and consolidated their position during the nineteenth century, aided by the tendency (sometimes described as mysterious) of the boy Dalai Lamas to die just before or soon after reaching the age to assume full powers.

The nineteenth century also witnessed the approach of the British and the Russians, and in 1903 Sir Francis Younghusband rapped on Tibet's southern door, proceeded to Lhasa and so served notice of Britain's unwillingness to leave China a free hand in Tibet. This was the period of Chinese disintegration but any British notion of taking China's place in Tibet was soon abandoned. The thirteenth Dalai Lama fled in 1903 to Mongolia and thence to China, where his reception was disappointing. He returned to Lhasa in 1909 but fled again in 1910, this time in fear of the Chinese and into India. The collapse of the Chinese empire in 1911 seemed to open the way to real independence but at the Simla conference of 1913–14 between Chinese, Tibetans and British, the latter proposed a recognition of Chinese suzerainty in return for a Chinese promise of Tibetan autonomy which would include the right to conduct its foreign affairs independently. This proposal, repeated in 1921, was never bindingly adopted. The Simla conference also propounded a frontier between India to the south and Tibet and China to the north and north-east (the so-called McMahon line) in a document which was initialled by the Chinese but never ratified, not because China questioned the line but because its acceptance was linked with a division of Tibet into inner and outer zones and the exclusion of Chinese troops from the inner.

Upon the death of the Dalai Lama in 1933 the Chinese took the opportunity to return to Lhasa. A mission bearing condolences arrived and remained until 1949, when it was ejected as a result of the general collapse of the Kuomintang. Before this exodus China supported a revolt by the regent of Tibet against his ward, the fourteenth Dalai Lama, who was still a child. The Kuomintang patronized and recognized as Panchen Lama a boy who had been discovered in China in 1944 and was still there: the Panchen Lama, another Yellow Hat hierarch with at least temporal superiority over the Dalai Lama in eastern Tibet, was a spiritual and temporal rival of the Dalai Lama. (The previous Panchen Lama had fled to China in 1923 and died there in 1937.)

This last throw by the Kuomintang proved useful to the communists, who took over the new Panchen Lama and set him at the head of a provisional Tibetan government in exile. He lived in Beijing with a Chinese wife but in 1962 he disappeared after refusing to attack the Dalai Lama. He reappeared in 1979, having apparently been severely ill-treated in the interval, and died there in 1989 curiously young. Although inferior in rank to the Dalai Lama, the Panchen Lama had the supremely important function of authenticating a new Dalai Lama. By 1995 the Dalai Lama and the Chinese had discovered the new incarnation in different boys. The former almost immediately disappeared.

During 1950 there were attempts by the authorities in Lhasa to negotiate with Beijing in Hong Kong, Calcutta, Delhi or wherever contact could be made, but late in that year China invaded and soon secured control of the capital and much of the country. Tibet appealed unsuccessfully to the United Nations and the Dalai Lama fled in 1959 to India. The authorities remaining in Lhasa accepted Chinese suzerainty in return for a promise of a measure of autonomy as an Autonomous Region of China but the famine inflicted by Mao on China in 1961–62 killed 25–30 per cent of the population of Tibet's various provinces. After Mao's death Deng and the Dalai Lama exchanged proposals for discussions about the future of Tibet on the basis that nothing except complete independence should be ruled out in advance. But in the years which followed China was less energetic in pursuing proposals than in despatching to Tibet enough Chinese settlers to outnumber its 6 million Tibetans. This annexation by demography was supplemented by the destruction of Tibetan institutions and culture, particularly thousands of monasteries and convents whose inmates were forced to disperse back to their villages or escape to India.

China's forceful subjection of Tibet was based on power and the plausible, if contentious, interpretation of historic treaties. It spurned or understated Tibetan resistance and worldwide condemnation of its harshness. China's Tibet problem had some echoes of Putin's Caucasian problem but Tibet was the more inaccessible to the world at large and China less vulnerable than Russia to international displeasure. By 2008 some 100,000 Tibetans had fled to India and had created at Dharmasala a self-governing community supportive of the authority of the Dalai Lama. The Dalai Lama has recognized on various occasions Beijing's claim suzerainty over Tibet.

Deng and his successors also developed more positive policies, spending large sums of money on improved communications to eliminate Tibet's famous inaccessibility and to make it a honeypot for tourists.

China is the most hugely impressive country in the world. This fact was not obvious in 1945 but 50 years later it was inescapable and troubling. Its sheer size and population were second to none, its recorded history longer than any, its arts and civilization among the wonders of mankind. It claimed a conscious identity derived principally from a secular religion but constrained also by semi-submerged ethnic minorities. It had faced few external challenges during its long history (Mongols and Manchurians had come and gone) until in the nineteenth century Europeans and post-Meiji Japanese had inflicted death and humiliation which too China had eventually overcome, if only after a long time and at great cost. Towards the end of the same century it had suffered one of the most appalling visitations of the plague known to human history. It had lost a dynasty when the emperor and his mother died within one day of each other. It could not play Europeans off against Japanese: in 1905 Japan had decisively marked its rise to power by sinking a Russian fleet but in the same period Europeans began to be distracted from Far Eastern affairs by war clouds over Europe. It experimented disastrously with republicanism and communism for most of the twentieth century and owed its escape from Japanese imperialism in 1945 not to itself but to the United States.

After the Second World War it was judged to be a budding junior partner of the Soviet Union. But not so by itself. By the end of the century it was seeing Maoism as a disastrous interlude but Japan's uneven experience of western exploitation as no less to be avoided. It combined a vast unreformed rural economy with a bounding urban capitalism: the whole ruled, and to remain ruled, by the Communist Party. The government's grip over outlying areas – particularly Tibet and Xinjiang – was imperfect, mainly because it lacked the necessary army of efficient administrators in the service of central government. Tibet posed problems (ethnic and religious) beyond the administrative, and Taiwan even more intractable ones. The former attracted the attention of the world through the evidence of harsh maltreatment and even torture and most particularly because the world could not get a clear idea of what China wanted or what, if anything, might be achieved by bewailing the plight of the Dalai Lama or trying to protect Taiwan, the prosperous offshore relic of an *ancien régime*. Yet the new China had problems commensurate with its achievements and opportunities, particularly perhaps in its apparently most successful enterprise: the phenomenal growth of its economy at around 10 per cent a year. Growth at more modest levels it might achieve out of its own resources but growth by record strides required not only the requisite capital but risk capital which neither a state command economy nor foreign lenders are normally keen to supply. China at the beginning of the twenty-first century was manifesting its greatness in the economic rather than the military or the diplomatic sphere and to that extent its regime was becoming uncommonly dependent on continuing economic progress and economic good behaviour. Behind all these questions lurked another: whether the autocratic rule of the Communist Party would be longer or shorter than the rule of the Communist Party of the USSR had been.

CHAPTER 4

Korea

The Korean War (see p. 117) left North and South deeply hostile to each other and condemned to decades of misrule. The military inferiority of the South was mitigated by American reinforcement – a UN force commanded by an American general remained in the country – and a vastly better economic performance. The UN voted annually in favour of the reunification of the country by way of free elections but these resolutions were without effect. So were talks between North and South from the early 1970s onwards. In North Korea Marshal Kim Il Sung held uninterrupted sway. Opposition dared not show its head. In South Korea Syngman Rhee's ruthless rule, buttressed by a defence treaty of 1953 with the United States, ended in 1960 when he was forced to resign and flee to Hawaii, where he died in 1965 at the age of 90. A military coup in 1961 carried General Park Chung Hee to power, which he held for nearly 20 unlovely years. They were marked by considerable economic success and continuous, if ineffectual, protest against harshness and corruption. In 1963 Park and his principal colleagues transformed themselves into civilians and Park was elected president. He sent a contingent to fight with the Americans in Vietnam. In 1971 one of two United States divisions was removed. Martial law was reintroduced in 1972 with such extreme disregard for human rights that President Carter announced that the remaining American division would also be withdrawn – a decision reversed by Reagan when it appeared that North Korea's large armed forces were being made even larger. In 1979 Park was assassinated by the chief of his intelligence services. The new president Choi Kyu Hwa bade fair to inject a measure of democracy but was quickly rendered powerless by a group of officers led by General Chon Doo Hwan. Demonstrations which turned into a revolt in Kwangju in 1980 were isolated and brutally repressed (perhaps 2,000 were killed) and after nine months as a civilian façade for military rule Choi resigned his office to Chon, who was invited by Reagan to Washington. In 1983 a bomb, almost certainly placed by North Koreans, killed 21 people in Rangoon, including four South Korean cabinet ministers. Chon, the main target, escaped. This outrage disrupted talks on unification. They were, however, resumed in 1984–85. The results were meagre: a few dozen visits in either direction to see relatives but no reduction in frontier fortifications or military exercises. The choice of Seoul for the 1988 Olympic Games induced North Korea to ask for some participation.

The International Olympic Committee offered to hold five events in the North but on terms which North Korea did not accept.

During the 1980s South Korea emerged from a period of economic development behind strong protectionist cover to become a flourishing industrial power in a world-wide and mainly liberal economic order. Reunification of the peninsula and better relations with ideological enemies would offer further economic gains without, however, being essential to them. When Chon's presidency came to an end in 1988 the succession might be by fiat, coup or election. Chon decreed the last and his choice demonstrated the vast change which had come over South Korea from a country focused on war with North Korea to one in competition with Japan and other economic giants. Chon's friend and chosen successor General Roh Tae Woo won the election with 37 per cent of a large turnout and against a divided opposition. The imminence of the Olympic Games may have helped him since South Koreans wanted to avoid disturbances during the Games and were therefore wary of the uncertainties of radical change. Six months of extreme violence had preceded the election, alarming the United States as well as Roh, who adopted a conciliatory tone directed particularly to the middle classes and middle-aged, who were showing signs of sympathy with the seething indignation of radical youth. After his victory Roh established diplomatic relations with China and Russia (on a visit to Seoul in 1992 Yeltsin apologized for the shooting down of Korean Airlines flight 007 in 1983) but he had strained trade relations with the United States, resisted an American request to quadruple his contributions to the costs of American forces in South Korea and refused to send South Korean forces to the Gulf War in 1991. He engaged in new talks, eventually fruitless, with North Korea, approved the admission of both Korean states to the UN and set out to conciliate some of his domestic opponents. These were three: Kim Jong Il, an ex-officer who had played a leading role in the 1961 coup but broke with Park in 1973 and re-emerged in 1980 as leader of the New Democratic Republican Party; Kim Young Sam, leader of the Democratic Reunification Party; and Kim Dae Jung, leader of the largest opposition group, the Party for Peace and Democracy (later the Democratic Party). The first two of these accepted amalgamation with Roh's Democratic Justice Party, jockeying for the role of Roh's favoured successor, and formed with him the Democratic Liberal Party. Kim Young Sam succeeded Roh in 1992 – the first civilian president for 30 years, a cautiously conservative reformer pledged to expose corruption in government and business and an assiduous visitor to Asian neighbours. Ex-president Chon and others were charged with and convicted of treason and peculation and sentenced to death or long prison terms – these sentences being then commuted.

In the 1990s the South Korean economy resumed for a while its vertiginous growth at 8–9 per cent a year but an escalating crisis in 1995–97 exposed its weaknesses, caused widespread strikes and collapses in money markets and was stemmed only by unprecedentedly massive international intervention. More than a million highly paid workers demonstrated against the revision of their terms of employment and the lifetime tenure of their jobs. Banks failed and share prices collapsed; manufacturing industry was found to be floating on excessively large and ill-supported loans; the country's reserves fell below $10 billion against foreign debts perhaps 20 times greater. South Korea's currency, the won, rapidly lost half its exchange value; and foreign lenders were called upon to lend more in order to salvage what they had already imprudently lent and lost. Confidence and credit ratings fell so abruptly that, fear outpacing pride, the government was obliged to accept international intervention and loans totalling in the first place $57 billion: the contributions included $21 billion from the IMF itself, $10 billion from the World Bank, $4 billion from the Asian Development Bank and $20 billion from 13 states. This enormously expensive series of emergency loans, inconceivable if the beneficiary had been poor and secluded rather than rich and globally involved, illustrated the ironical dependence of the American and other developed economies on ill-balanced or ill-managed or corrupt economies in the twilight world between the old rich and the new. Yet it was not enough. A further $10 billion was hurriedly pledged and advanced as the currency continued to fall and businesses found themselves unable to maintain their corporate plans or even sustain their current operations particularly foreign ones. In the private sector, banks in the principal capitalist countries extended loans of around $100 billion, mostly scheduled for early repayment.

South Korea was a country with only modest domestic resources in primary products – in this respect unlike South east Asia – so that its expansion was based on manufacturing and borrowed capital. It was a country where developed countries with money to spare lent with an enthusiasm which turned to the detriment of borrowers and lenders alike when the bubble burst. The crisis of 1997–98 was the harder to confront because of South Korea's record in the 1980s (annual growth at 10 per cent) and the early 1990s (8 per cent). One of the casualties was President Kim Young Sam, replaced by the perennial outsider Kim Dae Jung (in uneasy alliance with Kim Jong Il). His best promise was that things might get straightened out in ten years. Yet in little more than one year South Korea recovered most of its pre-crash growth rate and its external trading surplus, although without doing much to secure itself from similar catastrophes in the future.

In North Korea the government declared in 1985 that it would adhere to the Nuclear Non-Proliferation Treaty but seemed intent nevertheless on countering with nuclear weapons South Korea's superior non-nuclear armoury. Deprived of Soviet support by the turn of events in Moscow, North Korea agreed in 1991 to permit inspection by the International Atomic Energy Agency (IAEA) but then refused to sign the agreement unless the United States withdrew its forces from South Korea. Kim Il Sung hoped for American and Japanese recognition as part of the price for abandoning his nuclear possibilities. He played a teasing game with the IAEA, agreeing to some of its requests, going back on some of his promises, finally driving the IAEA to refer the *impasse* to the Security Council and President Clinton – fearful of Kim's capacities and intentions but fearful too of provoking him into war – to threaten sanctions or even armed intervention. Kim made overtures to South Korea for an economic union or unification but in 1994 he suddenly died, leaving his reclusive son as a semi-designated heir until in 1998 he was named head of state alongside his father, who was posthumously promoted to Eternal President. After the latter's death Clinton secured by a judicious combination of threats, carrots and concessions an agreement whereby North Korea undertook to stop the construction of new reactors capable of producing weapons-grade plutonium, not to reprocess its spent fuel rods and to allow regular inspection by the IAEA in return for the provision by the year 2003 of two new reactors of insignificant military capacity. The United States agreed to establish diplomatic relations, supply oil and remove obstacles to trade and investment; it dropped demands for inspection of North Korea's stock of nuclear weapons. This agreement quickly broke down, with mutual accusations of non-compliance. In 1997–98 North Korea tested missiles with ranges of 1,000 and 2,000 kilometres and fired them over South Korea and Japan and tried unsuccessfully to launch a space satellite. This display of strength was contradicted by other signs when a North Korean submarine ran aground in South Korea and its crew, escaping ashore, were killed – reportedly by their own officers – and when a year later another submarine was found offshore with all its crew dead inside it. Besides losing Russian support with the advent of Gorbachev, North Korea was conscious of fading Chinese goodwill as China's relations with South Korea and the United States improved. Its economy and perhaps its regime appeared to be crumbling and deaths from starvation were said to be running into millions. In 1999 it engaged in talks with the United States in which it tacitly agreed to suspend its missile developments in return for the ending of the sanctions which had been in force against it since the war of 1950–53. By the end of the century North Koreans were starving and their country was friendless. Nevertheless vituperative exchanges continued until North Korea suddenly agreed in 2007 to demolish all its nuclear installations and activities, probably forced into submission by its own ineptitude in taking on a superpower, starving its own population in the process and jeopardizing the support of its mentor, China. Thereupon President Roo Moor-hyun (of South Korea) paid a visit to his northern counterpart which might or might not lead to the re-unification of Korea after nearly 40 years of frosty separation. Later in the same year, however, elections in South Korea for the presidency from 2008 resulted in a victory for a right-wing businessman Lee Myung-lak, likely to be less cordial towards the North or at least in no hurry to lower fences between North and South: rapprochement in Korea could burden the South with some of the problems accepted by West Germany when the wall between East and West came down (p. 252).

North Korea survived military but not economic attack. It was reduced more by isolation and intervention.

Related reading: part two

Avedon, J.: *In Exile from the Land of the Snows* (1984) [Tibet]
Milward, James A.: *Eurasian Crossroads* (2007)
Shilling, Ben Ami: *Politics and Culture in Wartime Japan* (1981)
Spence, Jonathan D.: *The Gateway of Heavenly Peace – The Chinese and their Revolution 1875–1980* (1981)

PART THREE

Europe remodelled

CHAPTER 5

Western Europe

Recovery

Western Europe's recovery after 1945 was robust. Economic recovery, which required the restoration of severely damaged but essentially sound and skilled economies, was powerfully engendered through American financial aid, which was itself impelled both by generosity and by fears of the collapse of countries of vital concern to the United States in the Cold War. The Marshall Plan (1947) was, with the North Atlantic Treaty (1949), a crucial factor in the tempo of western Europe's material repair and spiritual reassurance.

When the war ended the countries of western Europe were in a state of physical and economic collapse, to which was added the fear of Russian dominance by frontal attack or subversion. During the war plans had been made for the relief of immediate needs in Europe. The UN Relief and Rehabilitation Agency (UNRRA) was created in 1943 and functioned until 1947: a European Central Inland Transport Organization, a European Coal Organization and an Emergency Committee for Europe were established and merged in 1947 in the UN's Economic Commission for Europe (ECE). These organizations assumed that Europe's ills could be treated on a continental basis, but the Cold War destroyed this assumption and, although the ECE continued to exist and issued valuable *Economic Surveys* from 1948 onwards, Europe became bisected for economic as well as political purposes.

The immediate precursors of American economic aid were the failure of the conference of foreign ministers in Moscow in March and April 1947 and the Truman Doctrine whereby, in March, the United States took over Britain's role of supporting Greece and Turkey and rationalized it in anti-communist terms. In June General Marshall, then secretary of state, propounded at Harvard the plan which bears his name and which offered to all Europe (including the USSR) economic aid up to 1951 on the basis that the European governments would accept responsibility for administering the programme and would themselves contribute to European recovery by some degree of united effort. The Marshall Plan was a bridge back to normality, to be financed with $17 billion of American money to resuscitate industry, modernize agriculture and ensure financial stability. It required the creation of a European organization; the

Russian refusal of the offer, for the USSR and its dependants, turned the organization into a western European one. Sixteen countries established a Committee for European Economic Co-operation which assessed their requirements in goods and foreign exchange for the years 1948–52 and was converted in April 1948 into the more permanent Organization for European Economic Co-operation (OEEC). Western Germany was represented through the three western commanders-in-chief of occupation forces until October 1949 when German representatives were admitted. The United States and Canada became observer members of the organization in 1950 and subsequently co-operation was developed with Yugoslavia and Spain. At the American end the Foreign Assistance Act of 1948 created the Economic Co-operation Administration (ECA) to supervise the European Recovery Programme (ERP). In the following years the OEEC became the principal instrument in western Europe's transition from war to peace. It revived European production and trade by reducing quotas, creating credit and providing a mechanism for the settlement of accounts between countries. While it was a government-to-government and not a supranational organization, it nevertheless inculcated international attitudes and fostered habits of economic co-operation which survived the ending of the ERP. It was replaced in 1960 by the Organization for Economic Co-operation and Development (OECD) in which the United States, Canada and Japan were full members and which extended the work of the OEEC into the developing areas of the world.

The establishment of the OEEC coincided with the signing in March 1948 of the Treaty of Brussels by Britain, France, Belgium, the Netherlands and Luxembourg (the last three compendiously referred to as Benelux from the time when they formed a customs union in 1947). This treaty, like the Anglo-French Treaty of Dunkirk of 1947, was directed against a revival of the German threat but contained in addition provisions for political, economic and cultural co-operation through standing committees and a central organization and was seen by at least some of its promoters as a step towards a broader military alliance with the United States. Truman, speaking of the need for universal military training and selective military service in the United States, so interpreted it and the leader of the Republicans in the Senate, Arthur H. Vandenberg, proposed and carried a motion in favour of American aid to regional military organizations which served the purposes of American policy: the senator was in essence advocating a military pact between the United States and western Europe, a military counterpart to Marshall's economic plan. The North Atlantic Treaty, signed in April 1949 by the United States, Canada and ten European countries, gave the latter for at least 20 years a guarantee of their continuing independence and integrity against Russian attack by formalizing and institutionalizing the American intention to remain in Europe and play the role of a European power. At this date the Russians, like the Chinese 15 years later, had large and frightening land forces which weighed heavily on all those within their reach but lacked a diversified, modern armament capable of engaging the United States. The North Atlantic Treaty brought American air power and nuclear weapons to bear in order to inhibit the use of Russian land forces in the area designated by the treaty.

The European members of this new alliance were comparatively passive beneficiaries who, in spite of providing 80 per cent of its forces in Europe, were dependent on the far more significant American contribution, without which their own contribution was irrelevant to their main needs and fears. Although in terms the treaty was a collective security arrangement, it was more like the protectorate treaties of an earlier age whereby a major power had taken weaker territories under its wing. The treaty created a permanent organization (NATO – the North Atlantic Treaty Organization) for political discussion and military planning and some of its makers envisaged the growth of something more than a military alliance – a community or union. But nothing of the kind emerged for a variety of reasons: the enormous disparity between the power of the United States and any other member, the failure of the European members to coalesce into a political unit commensurate with the United States, the breadth of the Atlantic Ocean, the unquestioning addiction of Americans to the sovereignty which seemed to them old-fashioned in others, the revival of European power and confidence, and the waning of the Russian threat halfway through the life span of the treaty.

For almost half a century NATO was a principal instrument in the Cold War. Western Europe, with the Atlantic and Mediterranean seas, was its theatre of operations. The European members of the alliance provided the bulk of its forces, the Americans the bulk of the equipment and money. The Europeans were careful to avoid any form of military association among themselves which might seem to weaken the Euro-American link. They were more reluctant than the Americans to acknowledge that an anti-Soviet alliance entailed an early end to hostility with Germans and the integration of West Germany into the alliance but this step was precipitated by events thousands of miles away in Asia: the Korean War. Within little more than a year after the signing of the North Atlantic Treaty the outbreak of this war created substantial calls on the United States' resources and Washington became anxious to convert its allies from passive protégés into junior partners and to build up in Europe itself a counter-force to the Russian armies, distinct from the long-range American air power which, although based in Europe, was under exclusive American command and remained so even when joint NATO commands were created. Britain and France, with much of their forces committed outside Europe, could give little help immediately and were therefore the more easily constrained to accept an American decision to rearm the Germans. In 1950 General Eisenhower returned to Europe as supreme commander of the kind of anti-Russian alliance feared by Moscow between the wars. In the same year Greece and Turkey were invited to co-operate with the allies in the defence of the Mediterranean, although they did not become full allies until 1952: their co-operation helped to establish an eastern flank to protect the allied central sector and to threaten the USSR from the south. In 1952 at Lisbon, the NATO council approved a plan to create by 1954 a force of 96 active and reserve divisions and 9,000 aircraft. Although these targets were never attained, the Lisbon decisions gave the alliance the shape which it ever afterwards retained.

With one exception: the German problem – that is to say, the status of West Germany as a political entity and its role in NATO's planning and operations. With the Korean War, American pressure to accelerate West Germany's sovereignty – and therewith West German rearmament – became irresistible, but France in particular was anxious to find a way to prevent the resurgence of autonomous German military power. René Pleven, the French minister of defence, proposed that German units be raised and incorporated in multinational divisions but that western Germany be allowed no separate army, general staff or defence ministry. Adopting the pattern of the European Coal and Steel Community, which had been launched on French initiative and was about to come into existence (see p. 187), Pleven devised a European Defence Community (EDC) with a council of ministers, an assembly and a European minister of defence. The French aim was to minimize the German military unit and at the same time to integrate the German military contribution, both operationally and politically, in an international organization. British participation was all but essential since without it the proposed international organization would consist only of France and Germany with lesser makeweights. For France a British commitment was the only way adequately to offset the risks inherent in the rearmament of Germany and the reappearance of a sovereign German state, but no British commitment satisfactory to France was forthcoming during the four years in which the EDC was under debate.

In 1952 agreements signed in Bonn and Paris created a complex new structure: six continental European states signed a treaty creating the EDC, the three western occupiers of Germany agreed to end the occupation upon ratification of the EDC treaty, and the NATO powers, including Britain, entered into separate ancillary treaties promising military aid in the event of an attack upon any of the EDC partners. But the French remained uneasy. They wanted British membership of the EDC and not a pledge to help it, and they disliked the provision in the EDC treaty permitting the raising of whole German divisions in place of the smaller units proposed by Pleven's plan. The United States and Britain brought pressure to bear on France, the former by threatening an 'agonizing reappraisal' of American policies if the EDC treaty were not ratified (which was taken to mean the cutting off of American aid to France) and the latter by giving in 1954 a further pledge of military and political co-operation with the EDC. But in that year the French parliament finally came to a vote and refused by 319 votes to 264 to debate the ratification of the treaty.

With this vote the EDC and all the Bonn and Paris agreements of 1952 collapsed. There was anger in Bonn, where Adenauer insisted that western Germany must have sovereignty none the less, and in Washington, where Dulles decided ostentatiously to cut Paris out of a tour of European capitals. In London, more constructively if belatedly, Eden set to work to put the pieces together again by diplomatic labours and a more specific pledge than Britain had so far been willing to vouchsafe. By the end of

1954 the Brussels treaty of 1948 had been expanded to take in the German and Italian ex-enemies and was renamed Western European Union (WEU); this WEU took over the non-military functions of the Brussels treaty organization and became militarily an ingredient in NATO; Britain declared that it would maintain on the continent forces equivalent to those already committed to the Supreme Allied Commander in Europe (SACEUR), that is, four divisions and a tactical air force; the occupation of western Germany was ended; Adenauer undertook not to produce atomic, bacteriological or chemical weapons, long-range or guided missiles, bomber aircraft or warships, except upon the recommendation of SACEUR and with the assent of two-thirds of the council of WEU. West Germany became a full member of NATO the following year. One other loose end was clutched. France and western Germany agreed that the Saar, which France had hoped ever since 1945 to annex in one form or another, should constitute a special autonomous territory embedded in WEU, but the Saarlanders rejected this arrangement by plebiscite and the Saar became a part of western Germany at the beginning of 1957. Thus the first postwar decade closed with NATO in existence to extend American protection over western Europe, Britain as the firmest and most effective of the European members of the alliance, and a nascent German state back in the comity of western Europe.

The weak point was *France*. Whereas Britain had made an energetic recovery from the war and West Germany was on the verge of its economic miracle, France was relapsing into the political instability which had characterized it between the wars, accompanied by economic ineptitude and colonial overstrain. But France too was on the verge of economic revival which was to reanimate agriculture, manufacturing industry and retail trade until the mid-1970s; was about to shed its imperial burdens and (most of) its imperial illusions and, with a radical political somersault, was restating its German problem in terms of partnership instead of hostility.

France had been a major European land power and a major imperial power but had failed in the contest with England for sea power. In the nineteenth century the decline of France's position in Europe had been matched by the acquisition of a second overseas empire to replace the territories lost to Britain in the wars of the eighteenth century, but by the beginning of the twentieth century France, slipping back in the demographic and the industrial race and spiritually still divided between the heirs of the Enlightenment and the Revolution and those who accepted neither, was becoming discouraged and unnerved and unresponsive to central government. The awful sacrifices of the First World War and the no less awful humiliation of the Second, separated by incapacity to face up to the problems of the economic crisis or to Hitler's challenge to basic values, brought France low in its own eyes until the exploits of the Resistance and the leadership of de Gaulle revived and personified the French spirit: de Gaulle's identification of himself with France and his constant use of the first person singular were precisely what was needed after the physical and spiritual lesions of a century.

When the war ended the French tried to strike out into a new world with some of the trappings of the old until they found that this would not work. They adopted a constitution and political methods unhappily reminiscent of the defunct Third Republic, made great efforts to retain or recover their empire in Asia and Africa, tried the old game of weakening Germany permanently, and made treaties with their traditional British and Russian allies. But they also revolutionized their foreign policies by joining the anti-Russian western alliance even though it entailed the rearming of Germany, took the lead in devising new political structures suitable to Europe's altered place in the world, accepted the end of empire and – most important – adopted under the lead of Jean Monnet a successful form of central economic planning for the modernization of industry and agriculture. Monnet's economic philosophy steered between the crudities of a communist command economy and those of free market-eers – or, to put it another way, sought the best of two worlds by a *dirigiste* allocation of resources and entrepreneurial freedom. During the war national production had fallen by 65 per cent but within two years of liberation in 1944 and before the incep-tion of the Marshall Plan, 90 per cent of this loss had been recovered. From 1947 the series of Monnet Plans, elaborated and applied by a modest central government department and using Marshall funds mainly for the reconditioning or transforming of industries, allocated resources, determined priorities and masterminded the restora-tion of the economy sector by sector in association with state-owned enterprises and private businesses. From the date of the second plan (1952–57) socio-economic sectors such as education, research and training were included and led at the next stage to central direction of social policies and a welfare state financed by employers and employed.

The renunciation of empire brought France, over Algeria, to the brink of civil war, from which it was saved in 1958 by the return to power of de Gaulle and the thwart-ing thereby of a right-wing military plan to seize control of the capital and the state. De Gaulle tamed the generals and colonels, disposed of the politicians and the remain-ing colonies and, profiting from a rapidly improving economic situation, rescued France from a position of scorn.

De Gaulle inherited two recent decisions of his predecessors – the decision to become a nuclear power and the decision to join an economic community with avowed political implications. The first of these decisions was congenial to him. He believed that France could be a major power and he believed that power must be modern. Just as he had been an expert in tank warfare when many of his colleagues were still in favour of the horse, so now a generation later he held that there was a choice between nuclear power and no power, and he held too that beyond a certain point there was lit-tle difference between one nuclear power and another: a nuclear power which reached that point became a member of the first league even if it possessed fewer or less sophist-icated weapons than other members of the league. The second decision may have been less congenial to him, not so much because he eschewed all unions or harboured anti-quated notions about the ability of a country like France to go it alone, but rather because his ideas on the nature of useful unions were different from those of the authors of the Treaty of Rome. While aware that the independent states of Europe were no longer what they had been, he did not believe that the minds of Europeans had become supranational. In his view the vast majority of Europeans still responded to the idea of the nation and he therefore based his European policies on the nation (but not necessarily state sovereignty). De Gaulle's *patrie* was not the state (*état*) and might be fitted into a partnership or association which recognized and protected national identities. Further, de Gaulle's pragmatic temper led him to insist on the differences between more and less powerful states and held that any association should be governed or guided by a directorate composed of the former – in this case France and western Germany with or without Italy. Equality between states, with its corollary of one-state-one-vote, he regarded as a vicious pretence, whether portended in the EEC or practised in the UN General Assembly. (The directorate of the five permanent members of the Security Council, however, fitted his theory, subject to putting the right Chinese delegate in the Chinese seat.)

De Gaulle also inherited a position which he found intolerable in a NATO which he found anachronistic. Following his doctrine of directorates, NATO should be directed by the United States, Britain and France, but it was in his view dominated by the United States with a touch of special British influence achieved by British subservience to American policies. Shortly after his return to office in 1958 de Gaulle tried to establish with the United States and Britain a triumvirate within NATO, but his ideas were rejected on the grounds that the formation of an alliance within an alliance would lead to the loss of the other allies. Washington and London, moreover, underrated France at this stage: they derided French nuclear ambitions, did not see how France was to dispose of its Algerian incubus, and failed to see that the status of France was changing and would change more rapidly in the near future.

De Gaulle not only desired the revival of France: he saw that it was happening. He saw too how Europe was changing. The Cold War had passed its peak and must end one day. The Americans could not be expected to stay in Europe indefinitely. Weapons technology was converting the American presence in Europe from a necessary strategic disposition into a dispensable political gesture which would be greatly modified or even abandoned when it became unduly costly. The automatic immediacy of an American response to a Russian attack in Europe had lost some of its credibility when American cities first came under direct threat from Russian intercontinental missiles: either the Russians would not attack or they would do so in a way calculated to avoid an American response.

Immediately after de Gaulle's return Dulles offered France nuclear weapons in return for the right to put American launching sites in France. De Gaulle refused and in 1959 withdrew the French contingent from NATO's Mediterranean fleet. He refused to be ruffled by the Berlin or the Cuban crises and was strengthened by both in his view that there was no pressing Russian danger. In 1962 when Kennedy offered France as well as Britain nuclear weapons he again refused and in 1966 he withdrew French forces from all NATO commands. This policy struck some responsive chords in Europe. The waning of the Russian threat and of the fear of economic collapse, the achievement of the prime purposes of NATO and the Marshall Plan, gave Europeans a new confidence which they translated into a desire to run their own affairs (notwithstanding that for the most part they already did so). This new nationalism was sharpened in the 1960s by resentment at American economic penetration, the debit side of the American investment which gave Americans control over European enterprises and so over the hiring and firing of labour. De Gaulle's anti-Americanism, rooted in Roosevelt's partiality for Vichy and anti-Gaullist French generals and admirals during the war, was not out of tune with Europe's mood – until he gave the impression that he wanted to put an end to the American alliance altogether. For this western Europe was not prepared. The Cold War might be waning but it was not over; it might recur and so long as there was a doubt there had better be an alliance. De Gaulle himself affirmed the need for an alliance more than once, but his desire to see the Americans at a distance from Europe created the impression that the alliance was in the Gaullist view expendable.

France in the 1960s was ready to relinquish, or at any rate relax, an alliance which had been thrust upon it in the 1940s out of economic necessity. The change in France's economic circumstances was as important as its change of ruler in 1958 in producing a change in policy. De Gaulle was not untypical of Frenchmen and many other Europeans in wishing to diminish political and strategic dependence on the United States. At the end of the war de Gaulle and other leading French politicians had wanted France to adopt an intermediate position between the United States and the USSR, but the onset of the Cold War and French military and economic weaknesses forced the French government in 1947 to make a choice and choose the American side. The need for money and for food determined French policy. The Marshall Plan offered salvation and France took it. But – like the Americans themselves – they saw the programme as a short-term rescue operation and – unlike the Americans – assumed that the consequential alignment would also be reviewed at the end of the short term.

The postwar drift from an intermediate to an aligned policy was facilitated by, and to some extent a cause of, the dropping of the communists from the government. From their role as national heroes and active partners in the resistance to the Germans the communists had reverted to a suspect, sectarian position in which the interests of Moscow counted for more than national unity and regeneration. Even before the Marshall Plan and its rejection by the USSR their continuance in government had become next to impossible on account of the Truman Doctrine, the decision to abandon discussions with the Vietminh and fight it, the stern suppression of revolt in Madagascar and of strikes in the nationalized Renault works, and a wage freeze; communists had already been dropped from the Belgian and Italian governments earlier in 1947. At the end of that year the French communists tried to exploit politically serious strikes which had genuine economic sources in the financial policies of the government of Paul Ramadier, but they failed, their representatives were dismissed from the government and the party lapsed into a long period of opposition. Political power shifted to the right and even when it swung back leftward in the mid-1950s it did not re-embrace the communists and France remained for a decade an acquiescent member of the western alliance. But by the 1960s France was ready to reconsider its role, owing to the coup of 1958, and its partial disengagement from the American alliance took place not at the instigation of communists but under the guidance of de Gaulle.

A fourth and principal element in de Gaulle's heritage in 1958 – along with France's nuclear programme, the Treaty of Rome and membership of NATO – was the rapprochement with Germany. The architects of this rapprochement were Robert Schuman and Jean Monnet on the French side and Adenauer on the German. Adenauer proposed in 1950 a Franco-German union, to which Italy and the Benelux states and possibly Britain too might adhere. De Gaulle, then in retirement, welcomed the idea, and ten years later he turned it to good account by concluding a Franco-German treaty at a time when his relations with the EEC and NATO were strained. De Gaulle's return coincided with a weakening of German–American relations. Adenauer's political attitudes were markedly personalist and the death of Dulles had removed the principal bond between him and Washington. He was suspicious of the Camp David spirit and Eisenhower's attempts to find points of agreement with Khrushchev. Towards Britain Adenauer's feelings had been cold since, after the war, a British officer had found him unfit to be mayor of Cologne in spite of the fact that he had held that office continuously from 1917 to 1933. He did not like Macmillan, was caustic about his attempt to play the role of mediator between Washington and Moscow, and was angered by his visit to Moscow in 1959 to discuss a European settlement – affecting above all Berlin – without prior notice to Britain's German allies, who were more closely affected by it than anybody else. Adenauer also resented Britain's aloofness from the EEC and its attempt to block progress by forming the European Free Trade Association (EFTA). He was ready to turn to France and, after some initial hesitation, to find a new personal friend in de Gaulle.

In 1959 Adenauer, after ten years as chancellor and now 83 years old, toyed with the idea of accepting the West German presidency. For a man who was Stresemann's senior and had been considered for the chancellorship of the Weimar Republic in 1921 and 1926 the end was approaching and his colleagues considered that the time had come for him to retire to a less active post. But for Adenauer the transfer was only palatable if it were to be accompanied by a transformation of the presidency from an ornamental into an executive office. He was willing to be a president like Eisenhower or de Gaulle but not a president like his own predecessors or his Italian neighbour. When it became apparent that his compatriots did not relish a presidential democracy he decided to remain chancellor. In elections in 1961 his party, the Christian Democratic Union, lost its absolute parliamentary majority and in the ensuing inter-party negotiations for a new government Adenauer was forced to accept a conditional fourth term of office as chancellor, the condition being that he would retire in 1965 at the latest. During meetings with de Gaulle at Rambouillet in 1960 and in Paris in 1962 – the latter was followed by a triumphant tour of western Germany by de Gaulle – Adenauer opted for a continuing Franco-German understanding in spite of misgivings about de Gaulle's version of European integration and de Gaulle's opposition to a European political union and the inclusion of Britain in the EEC. By 1962 he was further disillusioned with the United States under the new Kennedy administration and with Macmillan's devious approaches to the EEC, and in 1963 he signed with de Gaulle a treaty which formalized the Franco-German entente and sought to make it the core of European politics, a working alternative to or brake upon NATO, the EEC, the Anglo-American partnership, an American–Russian rapprochement or the American–German entente of the 1950s. This treaty was a peak in de Gaulle's diplomacy but he did not remain on it, for the accord was mistimed. Adenauer himself was on his way out and his immediate successors were unenthusiastic about this, among others, of his personal achievements. The Franco-German treaty became almost at once a dead letter. De Gaulle failed to achieve the changes which he desired in the way NATO functioned at the top. He believed that Britain was Washington's Trojan horse within Europe's walls, but he would have been more correct to see Bonn in this role, for whereas Britain was dependent on the United States economically, West Germany remained dependent on the Untied States for its very defence.

By the late 1950s problems over the distribution of power and weapons within NATO produced some bizarre schemes. De Gaulle's own proposals in 1958 for a NATO directorate comprising the three powers with extra-continental interests had been made in response to an American request for ideas about this problem, but they found no favour in Washington or London, where they were regarded as no more than a French claim to equality with the United States and Britain. A year later, after the installation in Europe of IRBM (Intermediate Range Ballistic Missiles) under a dual control or 'two keys' system, the supreme commander General Lauris Norstad stressed the need for a multinational nuclear authority, and in 1960 the United States proposed to install in Europe 300 mobile Polaris missiles on road, rail and river under American control. De Gaulle, asked to accept 50 of these, said he would do so only if France produced its own warheads, thus making French control a condition of acceptance, whereupon the Americans dropped the plan.

These discussions, abortive though they were, showed that, with the elaboration of medium-range nuclear weapons, NATO could not go on for ever on the basis of an American nuclear monopoly. Either the Europeans would themselves produce a deterrent force and so turn NATO into a more equal partnership, or some way must be found of creating a joint American–European nuclear force. The first solution – a distinct European force – presupposed a European political authority to control it, and although Europeans might have liked to have such a force, they showed no signs of evolving the necessary political authority. The solution must therefore lie on American–European lines, and there were two schools of thought, the multinationalist and the multilateralist. The multinationalists accepted national sovereign control and aimed at no more than the retractable commitment of national forces to a NATO commander, together with increased participation by all the allies in strategic planning and political consultation. The multilateralists devised a scheme for mixed forces in which nuclear weapons would be operated by units whose personnel would be drawn from different states. The American administration adopted multilateralism in 1962, not long before the British and French governments demonstrated their continuing addiction to, in the British case, multinationalism as the Americans understood it and, in the French case, a multinationalism which excluded the Americans. Since, however, the Americans hoped that multilateralism would provide the answer to the German question – how to give the Germans a satisfactory share in nuclear operations without alarming the Russians – they persisted with it despite the opposition of their other principal allies. They proposed in 1963 a multilateral force (MLF) of 25 mixed-manned surface vessels, each carrying eight Polaris missiles, three-quarters of the cost to be paid by the United States and West Germany.

Western Germans welcomed the scheme as a means to restore the close relations with the United States which had characterized the 1950s. Distrustful of the American–Russian rapprochement which produced the test ban treaty of 1963, they saw in the MLF a way of securing a special position equivalent to the possession by Britain and France of independent nuclear deterrents. The Russians, for the same reasons, objected stoutly to the MLF and insisted on regarding it as a case of nuclear proliferation. The French ignored it and the British were scornful of its military value but agreed, for political reasons and after strong American pressure, to participate in it. The Italians, Greeks and Turks agreed to join. At the end of 1964 the new British Labour government produced an alternative scheme without obvious appeal or virtue. Thereafter the MLF wilted because the Americans concluded that they did not need to entice West Germany away from France and because they came to believe that Russian objections were genuine and fatal to the attempt to control nuclear proliferation. They fell back on proposals to give the allies a bigger share in planning committees, and in 1966 such questions were temporarily submerged by the French decision to withdraw from all NATO's military organs and expel such organs from France. France remained a member of the alliance but would have no part in its operations so long as it remained unreformed.

Restored sufficiently to semi-withdraw from the alliance, France was shaken in May 1968 by an outbreak of revolutionary violence in Paris. The causes were not peculiar to France. All over western Europe there were deep sources of discontent which overlapped and fused: urban squalor, revulsion against the horrors of the war in Vietnam, overcrowded universities and schools, the fight for higher wages in a period of inflating prices. In France de Gaulle's government irritated the young by its paternalist tone and the liberals by its attempts to direct radio and television and control the press: the progressive element in Gaullism had grown dimmer during the ten years since de Gaulle had returned to save France from fascism and military rule. The position in French universities and schools was far from being the worst in Europe (in some parts of Italy schoolchildren had to attend on a rota system because there was no room for them all at once), but it was bad enough to inflame a generation which had been attuned to political activism by the Algerian war and was politically better organized than anywhere else in Europe. Since the war the number of university entrants had been quadrupled by, among other things, a rising birthrate and the rule that any boy or girl achieving the *baccalauréat* was entitled to go to a university. New universities were being built in Paris and out of it, but they were started too late. The resulting chaos was increased by bureaucratic centralization, the discontent by outdated syllabuses and outdated rules about personal conduct (sometimes enforced by the police). The new university at Nanterre on the edge of Paris became notorious for clashes between students and staff but it was not unique, and it was trouble at the Sorbonne in the heart of Paris which converted such clashes into something like a revolution. After an occupation of university buildings by students the university authorities called in the police and the police behaved with such brutality that opinion in the capital, not normally on the side of students, swung massively in their favour. The troubles culminated in a night of battle in which the police (this time on government instructions) and the students fought one another for control of the Left Bank while the scenes of violence were relayed to France and beyond by radio reporters roaming the streets. The police won the battle but students continued for a time to occupy parts of the university. At the same time workers in Paris and other cities went on strike, occupied factories and set up action committees which began to look like a new government in embryo. The authority of the legitimate government was badly shaken. The prime minister, Georges Pompidou, advised de Gaulle to resign. There was talk of a new French Revolution. But a month later de Gaulle went to the polls and won a sweeping victory.

There were several reasons for this. Although a nucleus among the students had revolutionary political aims, many of them wanted no more than university reform and the strikers were not revolutionary at all. They were not trying to overthrow the government but to get better wages out of it and less unemployment. The leaders of the Communist Party were too much part of the system to want to risk its disruption, were afraid of more left-wing groups and had no sympathy with students. Above all, de Gaulle's nerve held. Although he had to hurry back from a state visit to Romania, he did not let himself be hustled when he got back. Having assured himself by a secret expedition to military headquarters that he had nothing to fear from the army, he correctly weighed up the situation, waited for the university authorities and the trade unions to begin to recover their control in their respective spheres and then, disdaining François Mitterrand's bid to replace him in the presidency, won a sweeping victory by the votes of frightened Frenchmen and dismissed Pompidou. He then backed his minister of education Edgar Faure, who made a radical attack on the problem of higher education in spite of some of his colleagues and of much conservative opinion. Faure introduced joint teacher–student management; abolished the centralized system under which France had in effect a single university and substituted for it 65 universities (13 in Paris), none of which was to have more than 20,000 students; and further decentralized control within each university by creating joint councils for each nucleus of 2,500 students.

But de Gaulle's days were numbered. One of his aversions was the French senate. One of his preoccupations was the reform of the machinery of government by the creation of regional assemblies. He proposed to link this reform with the abolition of the senate and put the two issues together to the electorate by referendum. But the senate was not unpopular and de Gaulle's use of the referendum, coupled with the implication that a no-vote entailed his own resignation, was widely regarded as unfair tactics. A majority voted no. De Gaulle at once resigned. (He died the next year.) The president of the senate Alain Poher assumed the functions of the presidency *ad interim* until a presidential election was won by the Gaullist candidate, Georges Pompidou, on the second round. Pompidou, a banker influenced by fears about the stability of the overextended dollar, had adopted more wholeheartedly than de Gaulle the case for a Franco-German entente within a European union.

Franco-German entente

Konrad Adenauer's rule in western Germany (1952–63) established in Europe a new state which was resuming Germany's economic dominance on the continent. It was built on the economic policies of the western countries (currency reform and Marshall aid) and the division of Germany. Territories lost in the east were less valuable than those retained in the west; refugee labour from the east was opportune for reconstruction and peculiarly mobile. Investment boosted growth without inflation. Growth restored morale. High standards in education, industrial training and discipline, and efficient administration added their quotas. In the four years preceding sovereignty the combined western zones trebled industrial output and raised GNP by two-thirds. The population recovered its prewar numbers and was stabilized in the 1960s at 60 million (eastern Germany's was 17 million). So long as output rose and unemployment did not, generous provision for public services and a welfare state attracted minimal opposition. Material success was matched by political success on two fronts: internally, a democracy which worked and a partnership between capital and labour; externally, acceptance in the world's strongest alliance. Germany was the only country with a substantial population on both sides of the Iron Curtain.

In the first Adenauer years the west meant, overwhelmingly, the United States. Yet in his later years Adenauer edged towards a more European stance, particularly in his relations with de Gaulle. His successors began to probe Germany's traditional associations in central Europe. Adenauer's task had been to reposition Germany in Europe after the disasters of the Nazi years. His alliance with the United States was a precondition for new relations with France and Russia. The first were firmly established but the latter were interrupted by the building of the Berlin wall in 1961, which not only isolated one part of Germany from the other but also cut western Germany off from the USSR. Adenauer's departure was followed by a short postlude with Ludwig Erhard as chancellor until, in 1966, he was forced out of office by his own party. From 1966 to 1969 the Christian Democrats and the Social Democrats governed in coalition, with Kurt Kiesinger as chancellor and Willy Brandt as vice-chancellor and foreign minister. These three years constituted a bridge between the Adenauer era and the almost equally long socialist era to come. The grand coalition abandoned Adenauer's attitude of regarding half Europe as virtually non-existent. The sources of this evolution were détente in Europe and Washington's increasing preoccupation with better relations with Moscow without as much regard for German susceptibilities as had been evinced in the past; the abandonment of the pretence that European security and the German problem were inseparable and that no European system could usefully be studied in the absence of German reunification; the appetite of eastern European economies leading to restiveness against satellite status and a desire for the products of the new technology (computers, for example) which western Germany could provide; and to popular appreciation among West Germans of the barrenness of the promise of reunification via a western alliance, the realization that the road to reunification did not run through Washington. Bonn therefore entered into discussion with eastern European states and in 1967 established diplomatic relations with Romania. This eastern policy quickened after 1969 when Brandt became chancellor and opened discussions with East Germany, Poland and the USSR.

Besides renewing normal relations with wartime enemies Bonn had to negotiate with Czechoslovakia, which was demanding the abrogation of the Munich agreement of 1938, and with East Germany, which was demanding recognition as an independent sovereign state. This last issue was complicated by the problems of Berlin, a divided city in which Germany's four principal conquerors still had special rights. A new four-power agreement on Berlin provided, among other things, easier rail, road and water communications between West Germany and west Berlin and freer access for west Berliners to East Germany for a wide variety of purposes; by a General Relations Treaty the two Germanies recognized each other's sovereignty and frontiers and promised to settle disputes peaceably; and diplomatic relations were established between Bonn and Prague and the Munich agreement was declared invalid. Treaties with the USSR and Poland which included recognition of the Oder–Neisse line were concluded in 1970 and ratified in 1972. Both Germanies became members of the UN (1973). A quirky postlude to these transactions was the claim in 1975 by East Germany for the return to Berlin of works of art removed during the Second World War to safer places further west – some 600 paintings by major artists including 21 by Rembrandt, over

200 drawings by Dürer and Rembrandt, Queen Nefertiti and possibly thousands of Egyptiaca, and more. But that the Hague Convention of 1954 could be held to apply to these circumstances was hardly a political liklihood.

These various agreements resolved much but not all the business which a peace conference in 1945 might have been expected to settle. Berlin was not purged of its anomalies. The four powers maintained their rights in the city, which remained two cities; the movement of west Berliners to the east became easier but not normal; west Berlin remained constitutionally attached to West Germany but physically contiguous only to East Germany. The reunification of Germany was not ruled out, although its attainment by force was. Brandt's Ostpolitik was much criticized by his countrymen and although he strengthened his parliamentary position in 1971, he lost ground in the ensuing years. In 1974 he was forced to resign the chancellorship by the discovery of a spy at work in his private office. He was succeeded by Helmut Schmidt.

Again by coincidence change in Bonn was closely followed by change in Paris. In 1974 Pompidou died. In the ensuing election François Mitterrand won the first round but was defeated in the second by the narrowest of margins by Valéry Giscard d'Estaing. Seven years later Mitterrand was successful and remained president until 1995. In West Germany, Schmidt remained chancellor until 1982 when his government was defeated in the Bundestag and his Free Democratic Party (FDP) partners switched their allegiance to give the conservative Helmut Kohl the chancellorship, which he held until 1998. For most of this long term his opposite number in Paris was Mitterrand.

Mitterrand was a politician of considerable intelligence and self confidence, cunning and patience, essentially non-dogmatic and even non-party. He was also a modernizer and in that sense more radical than conservative but, like many modernizers, somewhat careless of the human costs of modernization. Domestically, his first task was to reassert the socialists' predominance over the communists on the left and as far into the centre as possible. To do so he needed to recover votes which the poorer classes had given to de Gaulle but were not so ready to give to the general's successors on the right; and he needed to make inroads into communist areas in order to make the socialists independent of communist support. These aims were facilitated when Giscard's challenge for the presidency in 1974 in opposition to the Gaullist heir apparent, Jacques Chirac, split the right-wing alliance. Four years later the socialists overtook the communists in all but a few communist strongholds and in 1981 Mitterrand won the presidency. Having worsted the communists he dismayed and fragmented the socialist party, first, by abandoning traditional left-wing policies (partly in order to retain the middle ground and partly because his initial attempts to practise expansionist economic policies foundered on the impracticabilities of socialism in one country) and, secondly, by promoting dispute and intrigue within the socialist party. Although France had attained a higher GNP than Britain's it had weathered the economic storms of the 1970s less well than Germany. Its older industries, in transition, had had to face depression as well as the strains of change; newer industries, successfully fostered, wavered. The political scene was ambiguous. Close-run elections in 1986 saddled the president with a right-wing prime minister (Chirac) whose own hold on his majority and his office was uncertain. In elections in 1988 Mitterrand fared better than expected but the socialists recovered their parliamentary position only narrowly. The exceptionally able Michel Rocard became prime minister but Mitterrand did not like him and injudiciously replaced him in 1991 by Edith Cresson, whose blunders and tactlessness ensured her departure in little more than a year. Pierre Bérégovoy filled the gap before elections in 1993 which were disastrous for the left. Chirac, intent on the next presidential election, evaded the premiership, which was occupied by Edouard Balladur for the short interval to 1995. In these later years Mitterrand's touch with his own party became unsure and with his prime ministers ungenerous, even disloyal. He gave the impression of lassitude (he was a sick man) and became aloof, capricious, nepotistic and (like Thatcher, whom he otherwise resembled not at all) semi-detached from parliament and parliamentarism.

Against this kaleidoscopic background Mitterrand emphasized the role of the presidency as above party and focused on foreign affairs. A pragmatist in the tradition which stretched from Talleyrand to de Gaulle, a political professional rather than a political thinker, he affirmed the Franco-German alliance and accepted a secondary role for France in European affairs – secondary to Germany in order to be secondary to no other country. After Kohl's re-election as chancellor in 1987 he welcomed proposals for closer Franco-German military co-operation, a Franco-German brigade and a Franco-German defence council. The collapse of the USSR and the consequent reunification of Germany created a sharp dilemma. He accepted German unification because he was in no position to do anything else – and likewise the admission to the EU of ex-Soviet satellites – but the reappearance of *Mitteleuropa* as a factor in European affairs after half a century extended Germany's influence into central and eastern Europe and gave it a range of foreign choices alternative to the Franco-German alliance and Franco-German direction of the EU. The accelerated integration of Europe and expansion of the EU were German, not French, policies. They were distasteful to much of French opinion, the more so since they entailed painful anti-inflationary measures (to keep monetary union on course), aggravated unemployment and provoked violent popular clamour for protectionist subsidies, tighter immigration controls and narrower rights to citizenship.

Balladur's mild-mannered conservatism and economic dependability defused some of these troubles, reassured the French electorate and turned him into a candidate for the presidency but he lacked the gifts needed to succeed against the more extrovert and supple Chirac and he came third in a first round which stirred only modest enthusiasm for any of the candidates. The socialist Lionel Jospin, thrust into battle when Jacques Delors ruled himself out, received most votes in a high poll but Chirac won the second round. By temperament he was, like Mitterrand, a man more adept at finding ways round problems than, like Delors, eager to confront them. Constitutionally, he succeeded to a position which for nearly 30 years had been exceptional in western Europe. Fashioned on the American model by and for a great man (de Gaulle), the French presidency had been filled at least adequately by a succession of men but the likeable Chirac was a less able politician and he faced an accumulation of problems, chief among them a high (12 per cent) level of unemployment, corrosive and seemingly immovable. Public opinion accused governments of sacrificing people's needs to a determination to keep pace with Germany's insistence on inaugurating an EMU with a single currency by 1999. This disgruntlement was reinforced by nagging doubts about France's standing in the world, particularly in Africa, where the French experiment in post-colonial influence was coming in the 1990s to seem a sham incapable of mastering African anarchy or countering American influence opposed to France's protégés: second to Germany in Europe, France was simultaneously being relegated to a minor role in Africa. This unease formed part of Chirac's decision in 1997 to try to arrest the decline of the right which had put him in power by holding premature elections before the socialist left could establish Lionel Jospin as Mitterrand's true heir. Chirac's right–centre coalition was soundly beaten. Only the National Front of Jean-Marie Le Pen on the extreme right emerged as a net winner. Jospin became prime minister caught between spending money to reduce unemployment and the more rigorous policies required to meet the Maastricht criteria for joining the EMU. Improvements in the economy – zero inflation and rises in investment and consumer spending – eased the dilemma and the cohabitation between Chirac and Jospin proved more harmonious and successful than had been expected. Political rifts appeared on the right after further losses in local elections in 1998 caused some to toy with the idea of an alliance with the National Front which was anathema to others. Jospin meanwhile straddled the centre from initially a decidedly leftist stance: an endorsement of what had been Mitterrand's, and was to be Blair's electoral strategy.

In Germany Kohl's uninterrupted 16 years as chancellor exceeded even Mitterrand's hold on office but in 1998 the Christian Democrat/Social Union (CDU/CSU) lost elections, soundly beaten in the western Länder, resoundingly in the east. Expectations in the east had been severely disappointed, unemployment throughout Germany was stubbornly high and support for European unity – with the consequential extinction of the powerfully symbolic Deutschmark – was wavering. Kohl's long reign was notable for the unification of Germany, which he had embraced with bold promptitude, if underestimated costing; and for the transformation of European unity which he promoted in constant alliance with France and enlarged from the EEC of the 1950s to the EU of the 1990s. Where Adenauer had foreshadowed a Europe clustered round the Rhineland Kohl was forthright in adopting the more ambitious vision of a European Union embracing *Mitteleuropa* and beyond. As the German capital prepared to revert to Berlin it carried with it two great changes: Germany claimed leadership in Europe but not mastery; and the lands long debated between Germany and Russia were to gravitate not to Germany but to a European union. Schröder was the first German chancellor unequivocally to regard the alliance with France and the integration in the EU of Britain not as alternative ploys in western Europe but as equally basic postulates of a pan-European policy and springboard for further expansion. But Schröder's domestic position was fragile. It was based on a strong swing of the eastern Länder from the CDU to the Social Democratic Party (SDP), on the latter's traditional image as the party of high employment, better pensions and more welfare, and on coalition with the Green Party. But within a year the eastern voters began to desert him; the Greens showed more inclination to fight their coalition partners over specifically green issues than to fight with them against the opposition; and Schröder's economic measures – immediately challenged by his more flamboyant colleague and finance minister Oskar Lafontaine (whom he speedily got rid of) – were more centrist than leftist and angered many of his supporters, the more so since he had failed to make his stance clear before the elections. A series of regional elections in 1999 left him dependent on the CDU in the Bundesrat and forced him to contemplate a Grand Coalition with the right – the opposite of his apparent pre-election purpose. Unlike the British Conservatives at this date, the CDU continued to command much of the middle ground.

Britain on the edge

Britain's recovery from the war was strong, swift but not sustained. Morale at home and prestige abroad were high. War losses had been severe but the financial management of the war had been prudent. Half the costs had been met out of taxation, the other half by selling foreign assets and borrowing. The abrupt end of American Lend-Lease in August 1945, followed by an American loan which was disappointingly low and accompanied by impossible conditions (the convertibility of sterling within one year), presented the new government with a daunting task which was mastered in the short term by a combination of wise management and American aid. Marshall funds, although available for four years, were dispensed with after two. They were used primarily to restore war-damaged industries and to fund an ambitious programme of social reform in education, health and social security – but not for the wider and more radical restructuring of the manufacturing economy which Britain needed to retrieve the position in the world which it had been losing since the late nineteenth century to Germany, the United States and newer competitors. Taxes remained high but interest rates low; unemployment was low and wages were under control; economic growth averaged 4 per cent a year. Prewar production, the prewar value of foreign assets and the prewar level of personal incomes were all recovered by the end of the decade. Simultaneously, education was expanded and a comprehensive social security system was introduced. But Britain did not recover as much of its prewar position as an independent Great Power as it assumed it had.

On the debit side the Attlee governments (1945–51) committed Britain to a nuclear armoury and expensive defence policies which, besides causing the resignation of

Aneurin Bevan and other ministers, had considerable fiscal and budgetary effects for the rest of the century. This burden was the more grievous since Britain's longer-term industrial decline was not mastered and the country remained the more vulnerable to external vicissitudes and domestic mismanagement: for example, rises in the cost of imported raw materials such as were occasioned by the Korean and Vietnam wars, and the huge rises in the price of oil stemming from wars and revolutions in the Middle East in the 1970s. The relaxation of controls and trade liberalization, by removing protection from nascent industries, created from the 1950s onwards serious imbalances on external account and distracted attention and resources from a more radical renewal of the British industrial base. This base had always been comparatively narrow – coal and a few prime industries such as textiles and engineering – and responded only sluggishly to the development of new methods, new competitors and new industries. Adaptation there was, but not enough to shelter the economy from the buffets inescapable in a world economy no longer controlled from Britain. In addition, Britain was losing its primacy in the provision of financial services and other invisible exports. Only rarely throughout the nineteenth century and twentieth did Britain achieve a surplus on trade in manufactured goods but the gap was covered by surpluses on invisibles until the Thatcherite 1980s.

Between the wars Keynes, as mindful as any economist must be of the paramount importance of markets but also deeply perturbed by the social and economic consequences of unemployment, argued that an uninhibited market system could not be relied upon to regulate an economy for the best. He advocated a mixed regime in which governments would use both monetary and fiscal measures to limit or counter blind market forces. He denied that free markets alone could iron out the asperities of trade cycles and that a direct and precise correlation existed between employment policies and price inflation. His great influence established an orthodoxy which depicted the economy as a delicate mobile requiring deft balancing by intelligent and well-informed managers in tandem with market forces. Against this prescription extreme monetarists proclaimed that governments neither could nor should intervene in the economy except by regulating the money supply and that they could and should do this.

The mixed economy required exceptional skills and a benign context. Politically, the central issue amounted to a clash between the two imperatives of stemming unemployment and stemming inflation. The mixed economy adopted short- and medium-term planning, nationalization of selected industries, government investment in traditionally private sectors, partnership between labour and capital, and progressive taxation. Overall the aim was growth to underpin the basic obligations of the state and, additionally, the delivery of postwar social aspirations: financial stability and industrial peace, unemployment without inflation. But it failed to control inflation or wage levels and the emphasis on growth encouraged imprudent financing.

In the aftermath of the Suez disaster of 1956–57 the prime concerns of Harold Macmillan's administrations were foreign: recovery from that defeat, the repair of the

American alliance, decolonization in Africa and relations with the EEC. In domestic affairs these years were, somewhat unkindly, described as a waste of time. The succeeding Labour governments took tentative steps to tighten monetary policy but lost office in 1970 to the Conservatives who, with Edward Heath and Anthony Barber as prime minister and chancellor of the exchequer, created a boom which was, however, a speculative boom which diverted profits and savings into short-term gambles and drove wages up further. Attempts to institute voluntary or semi-voluntary wage restraint were progressively ineffectual and culminated in a miners' strike and the fall of the government. In the 1970s (as in the 1930s, if less so) political leaders were, and mostly felt themselves to be, ill-equipped to understand or cope with multiple economic disorders – the major oil crises of that decade, inflation, wage scrambles, banking collapses – and were then driven to desperate remedies. The Labour governments of Harold Wilson and James Callaghan (1974–79) were disunited or hesitant on major issues, beginning with the exchange value of sterling, which Wilson defended obstinately but ultimately in vain against a number of his cabinet colleagues. (An overvalued currency – a form of financial machismo – was a recurrent malady of the British economy for much of the century.) The Wilson cabinets were disunited also over the government of Northern Ireland, devolution for Scotland and Wales, membership of the EEC, industrial relations and wage policies and monetary management in the face of worldwide inflation and rising domestic unemployment. Over labour relations, sometimes a euphuism for curbing the power of unions and sometimes for keeping wages low, Wilson recoiled when it became clear that he risked splitting his party; one result of this understandable pusillanimity was to strengthen left-wing dissidents against more cautious trade union traditionalists. In 1976 an unforeseen financial crisis obliged the Callaghan government to seek a loan from the IMF in order to stiffen the value of the currency. The pound fell from $2.40 to $1.70; the bank rate rose to 15 per cent and reserves fell alarmingly low; government spending exceeded 45 per cent of GNP. The implications for the standard of living and the balance of payments caused something like panic. Recourse to the IMF was seen as shameful but strengthened the hand of the chancellor of the exchequer Denis Healey – who had been for a time almost isolated in the cabinet – and enabled him to impose on colleagues and country the deflationary measures which many of his predecessors had shirked. No part of the credit made available by the IMF ($3 billion over the years 1977–79) was actually borrowed. The stricter monetary courses adopted by the government and the prospect of uncovenanted profits from North Sea oil lifted the economic clouds but the Labour government did not survive long enough to enjoy the benefits of this stormy episode. With inflation at 10 per cent and rising – lower than it had been but still alarming in the context of a general loss of confidence in the government's handling of labour relations – the electorate opted for a new and bristling broom.

Britain's discomforts were not confined to the domestic and the economic. It was uneasy about its position in the world and uncertain about which part of the world it belonged to. Having lost their continental possessions towards the end of the Middle Ages, the British extolled their island status and fortified it with the Protestant secession and their seafaring gusto. Thereafter, the British fought other Europeans rather less than Europeans fought each other, but this amiable trait was more dismissive than pacific and the sense of distance – not always distinguishable from a sense of superiority – was far from extinct in the twentieth century. In 1945 the view from the island focused more easily on the Commonwealth and the United States than on Europe.

The Commonwealth, originally the British Commonwealth but renamed in the light of postwar decolonization, was a descendant of the British empire and historical accident. The dissolution of British rule in Asia, Africa and the Caribbean began with the retreat from India and Burma in 1947–48, a step long envisaged but not precisely programmed until the end of the war. This dramatic move had unexpectedly precipitate consequences throughout the colonial empire which (with the exception of Rhodesia) was abandoned with good grace and little fuss in the ensuing 20 years. But the emerging Commonwealth was not a power centre, still less an instrument for the exercise of British power. Its headquarters were in London but meetings of its political chiefs sometimes left Britain in a minority – in Thatcher's time in a minority of one – and although the Commonwealth provided Britain with special contacts and opportunities it did not reinforce British power in the world. After the cession of Hong Kong in 1997 Britain still had 16 colonies or dependent territories, most of them very small and only a few – Gibraltar, the Falkland Islands – politically obtrusive. The Commonwealth was transformed from a historical ragbag to a functioning international organization which states with no British connection wished to join because it provided the advantage of sodality without the taint of failure which cumbered more prominent bodies.

Britain's special relationship with the United States was a reality but not one which gave Britain what it thought it was getting. (Washington's only truly special relationship was with Israel.) Before the war Anglo-American relations were poor to bad. During the war they were excellent, but the excellence was due to crisis and to personalities: what was special about the wartime relationship was the unusually close collaboration between Churchill and Roosevelt. After the war many wartime friendships and channels persisted, facilitated by a common language and by shared experiences and ideals, but old divergences – commercial and imperial – reappeared and attempts by British prime ministers on visits to the White House or in reaching for the telephone to play the part of Churchill degenerated into back-scratching. The special relationship deflected British attention from political developments in continental Europe and gave continentals – France in particular – grounds for barring Britain from the European Community.

British attitudes to Europe were essentially unfocused. Britain had absented itself from Europe for so long that the British did not see what was happening there and were not told by their leaders, who themselves did not see: they either signed or did not enter into agreements, in either case on the basis that they did not much matter. As a European union gradually materialized, the British continued ignorant or apathetic as their leaders shirked open debate about its aims and their implications for Britain. Consequently, prejudices and dogma played a depressingly ignoble part in a political transformation as important and startling as any in two centuries of British history: even proponents of closer institutionalized links with Europe continued for years to believe that they might construct the sort of association which was never on offer.

That Britain should be part of the OEEC (the Marshall Plan – see p. 158) was never in doubt. Britain joined it automatically but also ensured that the OEEC should be an association of sovereign states and nothing more. Britain did not join the Coal and Steel Community (the Schuman Plan – see p. 188) which contained in its High Authority a seed of supranationalism. It then backed a Defence Community which was conceived in a moment of desperation and never came into being (see p. 160). Macmillan was the first prime minister to engage with the EEC, as it then was. He was in two minds about it: a weakness for romantic rodomontade interfered with his rational intelligence. Wilson was also in two minds which he did not know how to resolve: he was gradually won over by the economic arguments in favour of joining the EEC but was held back from acting on his conclusions by fears of splitting his party. Heath, although more purposeful and pragmatic, was likewise foiled by party conflicts and by an inability to inform and instruct public opinion. He knew what he was about, but contrived to make it dull, more a matter of necessity than opportunity for Britain. Callaghan, like Major many years later, regarded continental Europeans as people living in a different and less wholesome world. Thatcher was much more vigorous than her predecessors but strangely inconsistent and ultimately disastrous. She signed one of the major stepping stones in the evolution of the EU – the Single European Act of 1985 – but then allowed her prejudices to become an obsession which justified her, in her own eyes, in bypassing her cabinet, wrecking her party and ending her remarkable reign.

When Margaret Thatcher became prime minister in 1979 she was the first woman to hold that office and she held it with exceptional dominance and for longer than anybody in the century. She was determined, vigorous and hard-working – perhaps the most hard-working prime minister since William Pitt but not the most intelligent. She was handicapped by her predecessors' failure to grasp serious long-term economic problems, by a poor sense of the popular mood and by her poor choice of cabinet colleagues. She was deliberately divisive and rude. She spoke with contempt of consensus, degraded local government and manipulated the cabinet system of government to curtail discussion and suppress dissent. Unlike Winston Churchill, whom she frequently invoked, she was no sturdy parliamentarian except in her mastery of the tricks of Question Time in the House of Commons. Her economic recipes were crude caricatures of monetary doctrines, none of her monetary targets was met nor was she able to fulfil her promise to reduce government spending as a percentage of GDP; her policies were quickly, if quietly, dropped from sight. Her more enduring contributions to public affairs were the jolts which she gave to two overblown establishments. She reminded trade union leaders, whose power she (like the miners' leader Arthur Scargill) much exaggerated, that their movement would benefit by defining its business more narrowly and conducting it less violently; she made it easier for second-rate figures in finance and industry to be removed, albeit often at egregious expense; and by boosting the free movement of money she hastened the eclipse of sterling's long international role.

Thatcher came to power in one recession and left it in another. She enjoyed but squandered two uncommon advantages: the yield of North Sea oil, which reached its peak in the 1980s, and the proceeds of her programme of privatization which, whatever might be judged of its merits or its handling, brought the government large sums which were credited to current account and enabled it to present illusorily balanced budgets. She curbed inflation but simultaneously nurtured an explosion of credit and a consumer boom. The pound was kept at a high value with concomitant high interest rates which stifled industry, extinguished viable as well as deservedly moribund undertakings, reduced manufacturing output by a third and so diminished the tax base, rendered Britain incapable of financing its public education and social services and raised unemployment to levels unforeseen by the government itself. During the Thatcher years a nation of savers became a nation of gamblers. Private domestic debt trebled, mortgage debt quadrupled and personal savings – an important and distinctive element in the British economy – sank from 16 per cent of national income to close to zero. There was a return to widespread poverty which, although much less personally distressing than that of the great depression between the wars, was painfully felt and evident and was reflected in a variety of telling statistics such as prosecutions for begging or loitering, which rose to 4,000 a week. By cutting credit controls and taxes Thatcher fuelled speculation, encouraged the nation to live beyond its means and created demand on the economy which could be met only by imports which crippled the balance of payments. Vast amounts of money were lent to speculators and lost.

Thatcher's talents were for combat. She belonged emotionally to the xenophobic tendency in the Conservative Party (there was a significant, if less strident, counterpart on the left). She won applause for her response to the Argentine seizure of the Falkland Islands (see p. 689) and her triumph encouraged her to attitudes of glorious disdain for everybody except the United States. She embarked on a characteristically root-and-branch attack on union power but she was frustrated when tempted to handle foreign and Commonwealth affairs in the same mode. Under her rule Britain's relations with the EC were conditioned by an innate dislike of foreigners, imperfect comprehension of foreign affairs and dogmatic hostility to anything beyond minimal co-operation with the Community and minimal abandonment of formal sovereignty. She fell abruptly from power when half the Conservative members of the House of Commons revolted against her style of government, her disdain of her colleagues, her cavalier attitude to the constitution (particularly her manipulating of the cabinet system), the discord within her administration over the EC and an obsession with an issue – European unity – not of the first interest to the electorate, gathering economic stringencies and, above all, the prospect of losing their seats at the coming general election if she remained their leader. Thatcher was succeeded by John Major, whose apparent modesty and lack of evident disqualification was made by Thatcher's performance to seem a recommendation and who scored an unexpected victory in elections in 1992. Major had a tenacious conviction that, the EC having come into existence and the alternative of a free trade area not being on offer, Britain needed to play a leading role at the centre of the EC instead of denigrating it from the sidelines. But the transition from Thatcher to Major did not give the new prime minister a free hand. Thatcher herself, wounded by dismissal from office by her own party, became a rancorous focus for disunity within it. In the new House of Commons, Conservatives were divided into a faction loyal to Thatcherite attitudes, a faction prepared to follow Major in claiming a constructive role for Britain in European affairs and a third faction as much concerned to find fault with the EC as to try to understand its workings. Major was hampered by taking office at a moment when the oil revenues which had masked Thatcher's budgetary legerdemain were in decline and were forcing the government to raise instead of cutting taxes if it was to avoid a hazardous level of public borrowing and maintain at least adequate public services. The Conservative victory of 1992 was followed by economic recovery which produced growth of nearly 4 per cent but also laid bare the trap created by the policies of the 1980s. With manufacturing output still inadequate, growth stimulated imports to satisfy increasing purchasing power but thereby threatened the balance of payments and the value of the currency and obliged the government to raise interest rates (to the dismay of manufacturers) in order to restrain the growth which it was nevertheless earnestly seeking. In foreign affairs Britain was a country grappling negatively with distasteful problems – large ones in Northern Ireland and the European Union, lesser ones in Hong Kong.

Thatcher gave xenophobia a political point which it had not enjoyed since a much earlier generation of Tories had loved to hate the first Hanoverians. British opposition to the EC was emotional, irrational, poorly informed and yet popular against a background of resentful disappointment. However convinced Major might be of the inescapability of a British commitment to the EC, he failed to extricate himself or his party from the trough dug by Thatcher, who put at risk by her fractiousness London's title to be Europe's financial capital. Thatcher had come to power as the leader of the Conservative Party but she was in spirit the leader of a right-wing section within it. At the beginning of the twentieth century Britain had recoiled from what Lord Salisbury in 1885 called 'the abyss of isolation' but it never (in peacetime) got further than substituting ambiguity for isolation. The Thatcherite minority in the Conservative Party hankered after the unfettered independence which had vanished around 1900 when

Conservatives like Balfour and Lansdowne appreciated that neither politically nor economically was it any longer sensible or safe.

The Thatcherite aftermath was short. Major's surprising victory in 1992 was followed five years later by the most devastating Conservative defeat in British history. The party lost all its seats in Scotland and Wales and won only 164 in England and Major's immediate resignation of the leadership precipitated a contest which further exposed and embittered the party's dissensions. The Labour Party, led by Tony Blair, took power with a massive majority. The victorious party called itself New Labour, which – tactical psychology apart – meant that the party was more inclined than it had been to accept rather than stigmatize capitalism and yet intended at the same time to pursue with more responsibility and energy than the Conservatives principles of fair shares and public service. These were conflicting aims and in seeking to direct them in tandem the new government laid the emphasis on the former as a precondition for the latter. Blair, seeking the widest consensus where Thatcher had derided that word, courted popular approval for the equitable reconciling of incompatibles and for the view therefore of politics as a pragmatic and not a dogmatic undertaking: the crucial test, in Britain as elsewhere, would lie in the rise or fall in unemployment – the collision point of economic and social imperatives.

Blair was an articulate and intelligent politician with an impressive programme of domestic reforms. He dominated British politics for a decade but was undone by a major miscalculation which forced him to resign in 2007. He was convinced of the long-term need for European–American accord and co-operation and of the less complete conviction of many continental Europeans on this point. He felt that Britain had a unique role as a bridge between the two halves of what had been the NATO alliance, applied himself to filling this role but had the misfortune to coincide in office in London with George W. Bush in Washington – and discovered that, his efforts bearing more fruit in bonhomie than substance, his influence with Bush in the crucial crisis of Iraq was inadequate. In particular, his insistence on the need for a clear UN mandate for military action against Iraq without an unambiguous resolution of the Security Council was disregarded.

European union (west)

The European Community was created with two main purposes: to find a solution to Europe's German problem and to make its members richer and more influential in the world as partners than they could be as separate states. In the background to these aims lay Europe's history as the creator of the sovereign state and the home of its most successful examples. The principal obstacle to the development of a European union was the engrained strength, psychological and institutional, of nationalism.

From Bismarck's time to Hitler's Germany was, with only brief intervals, the state which most Europeans most feared. In a European states system Germany was inescapably the most powerful state, for although it was twice defeated in war and might be curbed in the immediate aftermath of defeat, its resources and skills ensured its resurgence. Its neighbours moreover, although they might fear it, depended on a prosperous Germany for their own prosperity. Even before the end of the Second World War a few Europeans, notably Dutch and Belgian, confronting this dilemma of reconciling their economic dependence on German recovery with their fear of German military might, envisaged a new European order in which the sovereign nation state would no longer be paramount. Whereas a states system by its very nature encouraged national aggressiveness, in a partnership each nation – including the German – might develop its resources and preserve its identity and cultivate its pride in a context more conducive to co-operation than aggression. Opinion in the more powerful states – France, Britain – was unsympathetic to anything so radically restrictive of their formal sovereignty and independence, but within a few years of the war's end French leaders became converted to ideas for a western European association which, in economic affairs, would maximize commerce and output and, politically, would circumscribe Germany's predominant power and redirect its ambitions. France abandoned the policy, entertained both in 1945 and 1919, of weakening Germany by partition and disarmament in favour of a policy of supporting and sharing in German recovery. Britain, on the other hand, although – or because – its own economic recovery from the war was at first more emphatic than France's, failed to perceive either the economic advantage or the political calculation behind the movement towards a partnership which would make the sovereign state less than sovereign. British attitudes were partially reversed in the 1960s and 1970s when governments of both the right and the left came to fear the consequences of exclusion from a western European economic association, but in the 1980s Thatcher personified and inflated British atavistic aversion to political association with the result that Britain was cast in the role of a disgruntled, even subversive, member of the Community whose development was bedevilled rather than strengthened by Britain's adherence to it.

On the continent the prestige of the nation state suffered during the war. National governments failed to prevent nation states from being battered or their citizens from being killed, tortured and enslaved. In Britain, however, the institutions of the state were not diminished; they remained intact and functioned with remarkable efficiency and fairness. In British eyes the separation from the continent by the English Channel remained axiomatic. The British were uninterested in giving the lead towards that strong and more permanent association which Britain, uniquely in 1945, had the strength and prestige to offer. The British still thought of themselves as a maritime power and a world power, only peripherally European, unthinkably less than sovereign. For two and a half centuries Britain had had no land frontiers, since even its troubles in Ireland lay beyond the sea. Its principal preoccupations were the freedom of the seas, the movements of commerce, and peace. The first two of these objects it pursued by maintaining a naval lead over the combined strength of other substantial naval powers and by ensuring so far as possible that the European nations which dominated the world should include a number of land powers of the first rank but only one such naval power. In this context the continent of Europe was a place to which negative principles applied: it must not be allowed to distract or threaten Britain, it must not fall under the dominance of one among its principal land powers. British diplomacy was directed to maintaining a balance and preventing a hegemony in Europe; if British diplomacy failed, then British arms had to shoulder the task which, though in a sense negative, was also vital to British interests as they had evolved since the Tudors had laid the foundations for a kind of British power altogether different from the continental imperialism of the Plantagenets. The British therefore developed a state of mind which drew no distinction between the near and the far. Geographers might talk of the 'Far' East and measure the distance to India in thousands of miles, but to many an Englishman Delhi and Singapore and Hong Kong were psychologically no further away than Calais; they were often more familiar, and they were, of course, more British.

In 1945 Britain's innate inattention to European affairs was enhanced by the fortunes of war and the prospect of peace. During the war every continental European combatant, including the USSR, had been overrun and at some point defeated or almost defeated. Britain had been terribly hard-pressed and had been bombarded from the air, but it had not been invaded or occupied or defeated. Its victory vindicated its right to go on as before, since it is the prerogative of a victor to retain its past, whereas its shattered and disillusioned European neighbours were looking for a new start and not for a restoration of an old order which had failed. The British and continental attitudes to the past were therefore completely different, and continentals who expected British sympathy for radical political experiment in Europe were overlooking not only Britain's separate historical development but also its postwar psychology, the intent to repair and improve the structure of British life but not fundamentally to alter or find fault with it.

The advent of a Labour government in Britain in 1945 should have revealed the difference, for the Labour Party, although a reforming party, was no less traditionalist than the Conservatives. It consisted of pragmatic radicals and socialists who wanted to make life happier for the lower classes by continuing the gradual and non-revolutionary adaptation of Britain's social structure to modern notions of social justice. It had no intention of overturning the British apple-cart and not much interest in other people's apple-carts. It was a hard-working middle-of-the-road administration which was trying, in exceptionally difficult economic circumstances (aggravated by the end of Lend-Lease and American insistence on the premature convertibility of sterling), to restore the British economy and reform British society and it did not wish to be diverted from these tasks by unprofitable foreign entanglements. The continent was chaotic and impoverished and, as the transfer of Britain's commitments in Greece and Turkey to the United States showed, could better struggle out of its troubles with American rather than British aid. Moreover, the new leaders in Europe were (quite

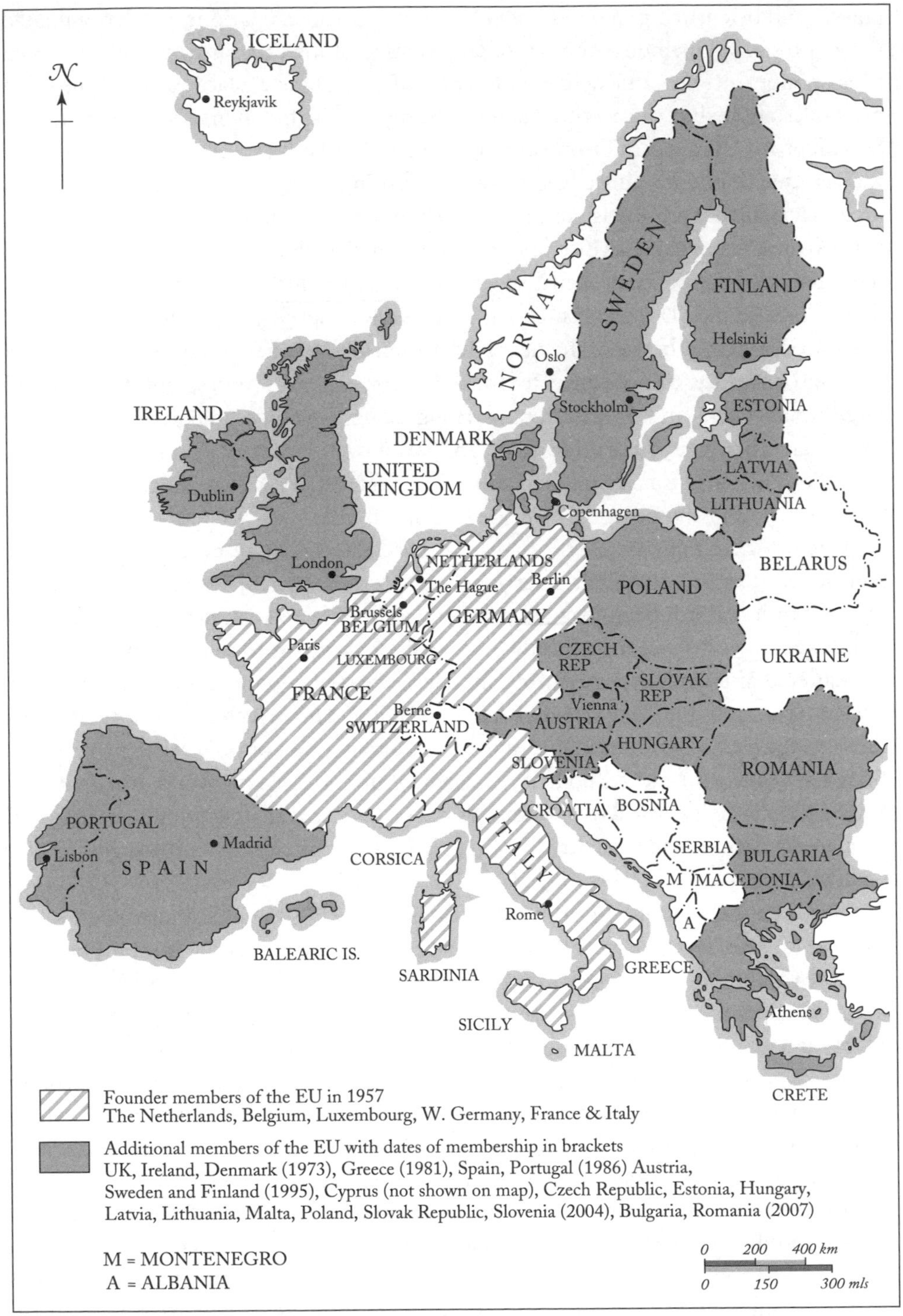
N
ICELAND
Reykjavik
NORWAY
Oslo
SWEDEN
Stockholm
FINLAND
Helsinki
ESTONIA
LATVIA
LITHUANIA
BELARUS
IRELAND
Dublin
UNITED KINGDOM
London
DENMARK
Copenhagen
NETHERLANDS
The Hague
Berlin
POLAND
Brussels
BELGIUM
GERMANY
Paris
LUXEMBOURG
CZECH REP
UKRAINE
SLOVAK REP
Vienna
FRANCE
Berne
SWITZERLAND
AUSTRIA
HUNGARY
SLOVENIA
ROMANIA
CROATIA
BOSNIA
PORTUGAL
Madrid
Lisbon
SPAIN
CORSICA
SERBIA
BULGARIA
M
MACEDONIA
ITALY
Rome
A
BALEARIC IS.
SARDINIA
GREECE
Athens
SICILY
MALTA
CRETE
Founder members of the EU in 1957
The Netherlands, Belgium, Luxembourg, W. Germany, France & Italy
Additional members of the EU with dates of membership in brackets
UK, Ireland, Denmark (1973), Greece (1981), Spain, Portugal (1986) Austria,
Sweden and Finland (1995), Cyprus (not shown on map), Czech Republic, Estonia, Hungary,
Latvia, Lithuania, Malta, Poland, Slovak Republic, Slovenia (2004), Bulgaria, Romania (2007)
M = MONTENEGRO
A = ALBANIA
0 200 400 km
0 150 300 mls

5.1 Growth of the European Union

apart from being foreigners) mostly conservatives and Roman Catholics; opponents, it was wrongly thought, of planned economies, uncomfortable partners for British socialists. In so far as they were attracted by federal ideas, these leaders were regarded as unpractical visionaries. For the British the nation state was one of those bits of the past which practically nobody questioned. That this state had come into existence by a sequence of federal agreements was comprehensively ignored.

Winston Churchill had told the British during the war that they operated in three circles – the Anglo-American, the British imperial and the European – and that this triangularity gave Britain special opportunities and a unique position in the world. Until Harold Macmillan applied in 1961 to join the European Economic Community the European circle was the one which seemed to offer Britain the least. The most important was the Anglo-American. Britain – or at any rate Ernest Bevin, who became foreign secretary in 1945 – saw that the consolidation of Europe under the aegis of a single power could no longer be prevented by British diplomacy or British arms alone, and that if this bugbear of British foreign policy was to be avoided the Americans must be made a European power. NATO was the outward and visible sign of his success, but his endeavours to create an Anglo-American thrust in European affairs, in the place of the expired British power to intervene and rectify, made him suspicious of continental federalists who might hanker after an independent European power to the exclusion of the Americans. Their policies were at best irrelevant, possibly damaging, to his aim of bringing in the New World to create a balance in Europe. Furthermore, those in Britain who were hostile to the United States or wary of its preponderance were not for the most part European federalists. In so far as there was a party in Britain which was thinking in terms of a 'third force' in world affairs, it conceived at this period a third force provided by the Commonwealth rather than by a united Europe. The Commonwealth, together with nuclear weapons and the pound sterling as an international currency, would keep Britain in a separate category.

Britain's change of heart did not begin to occur until some 10 to 15 years after the end of the war and even then it manifested itself more fitfully than the comparable revolution in continental thinking which had been imposed by wartime defeats. Britain continued to think of itself as a worldwide, even if no longer an imperial, power – a somewhat uncritical adjectival substitution. One of the most striking consequences of the war was the British departure from India in 1947 (followed more rapidly than was expected by departure from Africa), but this abnegation of empire took place in such an atmosphere of self-congratulation that the attendant loss of power was overlooked. The loss of India was regarded as a victory for British commonsense, which it was, but not as a curtailment of British power, which it was too. For generations Britain had been a world power because it possessed in Asia an area where it could keep, train and acclimatize armies for use in distant parts of the globe, and this reserve of power was at least as important as the command of the seas in making Britain what it was in the world. The departure from India, coupled with the loss of wealth and strength during the war, sapped Britain's staying power in the Middle East and made Australia and New Zealand turn to the United States for their security. (Britain was not a party to the tripartite Anzus Pact of 1951 which confirmed this lesson of the Second World War and was one of the world's most equable alliances until the 1980s when the return of anti-nuclear Labour governments in both Australia and New Zealand created difficulties over naval exercises. In 1984 New Zealand banned from its ports all nuclear-powered or nuclear-armed vessels.)

Britain did not, however, draw the conclusion that the end of empire and of defence commitments in Asia, Africa and Australia had converted Britain into a primarily European state. The empire had been replaced by the Commonwealth, a more elevating concept perhaps but one of less substance since it lacked the empire's bonds of allegiance to the British Crown, government by a ruling class which regarded itself as all one kin, mutual comprehension through a prodigal exchange of secret telegrams, and a British commitment to the defence of all its territories. The Commonwealth became an association of monarchies and republics of widely differing traditions and inclinations, requiring above all development capital which Britain could not provide, and pursuing independent and even contradictory foreign policies on the basis that this permissive latitude was a necessary price for a continuing association which was still worthwhile. And so perhaps it was, since the Commonwealth proved to be an international organization which worked up to a point. But it contained within itself racial conflicts which posed tests of statesmanship which the British governments of this period failed to pass. In Rhodesia Britain was credibly accused of dealing softly with rebels because they were white and at home the same government exposed itself to even more serious charges. In 1963 Britain had given Asians in Kenya the right to opt for British citizenship, which many of them took. In 1968 the most important element in this right – the right to enter Britain – was summarily removed from them by a government which, in its ignorance of the true facts and figures about coloured immigration, allowed itself to be panicked into slamming the door against some of its own fellow citizens. This unprecedented act, grounded in colour prejudice in a section of British society and in racial discrimination by the government, made nonsense of the Commonwealth ideal – and was later challenged and condemned in the Council of Europe. Even if Britain had in the past thought of the Commonwealth as a source of political strength, Britain's rulers from the 1960s were finding it as much an embarrassment as a support.

Unofficial pressure groups in favour of a European union had been encouraged, not least by Churchill, who spoke more than once during the war of the need for European unity and advocated in a famous speech at Zurich in September 1945 a Council of Europe. These groups organized a convention at The Hague in May 1948 which was held under the sponsorship of many of Europe's leading figures, including Churchill, and which succeeded in persuading the five Brussels powers to set up a Council of Europe consisting in the first place of themselves and Norway, Sweden, Denmark,

Ireland and Italy – to which were shortly afterwards added Iceland, Greece, Turkey, West Germany and Austria. The members were required to respect the rule of law and fundamental human rights. The constitution was a hybrid, an assembly without legislative powers yoked to a committee of ministers; the members of the assembly were appointed by national parliaments, in practice in accordance with the party representation in each parliament; the committee of ministers, which was included in the constitution on British and Scandinavian insistence against the more federalist wishes of other members, ensured that any authority which the Council of Europe might exercise should be subject to the control of national ministers responsible to national parliaments. The assembly never acquired any real authority and at the end of 1951 its president Henri Spaak resigned in despair.

But another and more substantial initiative was under way. In May 1950 the French foreign minister Robert Schuman proposed a *European Coal and Steel Community* (ECSC). Although multinational in scope, this was an essentially Franco-German venture with political as well as economic aims. It marked the conversion of France to a partnership with Germany which became one of the principal features of postwar Europe. Coal and steel were at the heart of Franco-German economic and military competition and by proposing to place these industries under joint international control France was, openly, burying the hatchet and, privately, acknowledging the foolishness of trying to compete: to this degree it accepted, consciously or not, that in the new Europe it would be a junior partner with Germany and that being a junior partner was more sensible than trying to be an independent actor. Britain was sceptical on principle and mildly hostile because it hoped that British steel would undersell European steel. There has been argument about whether Britain refused to join the ECSC or France made it impossible for Britain to do so; the one view does not exclude the other. In April 1951 six states (France, West Germany, Benelux (3), and Italy) signed a treaty establishing the ECSC, which came into existence in the following year. It consisted of a High Authority of nine individuals acting by majority vote with power to take decisions, make recommendations, make levies on enterprises, impose fines and generally control production and investment in the six countries; a court of justice empowered to pronounce upon the validity of the High Authority's decisions and recommendations; a council of ministers; and an assembly entitled to censure the High Authority and by a two-thirds majority to enforce the resignation of the council of ministers. In the late 1950s, when the demand for coal declined, differences arose between the High Authority and the council of ministers, and the High Authority suffered some attenuation in practice of its supranational competence.

By the early 1950s the Council of Europe had been joined on the European stage by the Coal and Steel Community and by an incipient Defence Community, and in 1952 Eden proposed the amalgamation of these three bodies and their parallel institutions. The Council of Europe appointed an ad hoc assembly to work out a scheme on these lines, to include provision for a directly elected assembly and a European cabinet. This was an attempt to build a political association, tentatively called the European Political Community, on the twin bases of economic and military co-operation and it was to embrace most of the non-communist countries of Europe. The prospective membership was large, even though Sweden's empirical neutralism, Switzerland's doctrinaire neutralism and the unpalatable autocracies of Spain and Portugal might exclude these countries in the shorter or the longer run. But the scheme was stillborn. The demise of the EDC in 1954 killed it and even without this blow it is difficult to believe that the rudimentary institutional economic association so far achieved sufficed to support so ambitious a parliamentary structure. As the nation states of Europe recovered from their postwar blues they became less disposed to abandon their identities.

The Coal and Steel Community was from the outset a first step rather than an end in itself. For devotees of European union it was one move in a process of creating a series of functional associations which could later be agglomerated. Coal and steel were no longer the prime sources of energy in a world powered by oil and expecting to be powered by nuclear energy. By 1955 the six members of the ECSC had progressed far enough to be ready to convene a formal meeting at Messina where they resolved to form a *European Economic Community* (EEC) and a *European Atomic Community* (Euratom). The British attended the conference as observers and then withdrew, partly because they thought the new venture would be a failure, partly because they were opposed to a common external tariff which would be inconsistent with what was left of Commonwealth preferences, and partly because they wanted to limit co-operation to forming a free trade area, EFTA – which they proceeded to form and which, unlike the EEC, was a failure.

The treaties establishing the EEC and Euratom were signed at Rome in March 1957 and both bodies came into existence at the beginning of 1958 and began to function a year later. In 1967 they were merged with the ECSC. The Treaty of Rome created a constitution in four parts: a Council of Ministers, a Commission, a Parliament and a Court. The Court of seven was the guardian and interpreter of Community law. The single-chamber Parliament was primarily a debating body. Created at a stroke by treaty between states, it had only embryonic powers of the kind which national parliaments had accumulated through time in their attempts to constrain the executive power. It might reject but not amend the Community's budget and dismiss the Commission in its entirety but not in part; it possessed a limited share in framing legislation but no control over the Council of Ministers. The Commissioners, at first two per member state but after the Community's enlargement only one from each of the lesser members, were fully and exclusively occupied with Community affairs at the Commission's headquarters in Brussels. Most of them had had ministerial experience in their own countries but performed in Brussels functions closer to those of departmental chiefs in a national civil service. Finally, the Council of Ministers, representing the

Community's several member states, was, within the terms of the Treaty of Rome, the Community's dominant organ. It was a replica of the similar Council which had been incorporated at a late stage in the plans for the Coal and Steel Community in order to ensure that that Community should be less a supranational entity than a national collective, and the EEC's Council was even more clearly superior to the Commission in Brussels than the ECSC's Council was to the High Authority of the ECSC. Consequently, the most significant debates and decisions on the EEC's development took place in the Council and revolved not around the distribution of power among the Community's main bodies but around the exercise of power within the Council – which matters might be settled by a majority and which required only a 'qualified' majority. (This was a majority reached after ascribing to each member's vote a weight commensurate with its economic power.)

The first stage in economic integration, which was to be completed in 12 years (and was), was commercial – a customs union with a common external tariff and, internally, the removal of all tariffs and the elimination of quotas. A second and overlapping stage envisaged a broader economic union with, in particular, a common agricultural policy (CAP); free movement of labour and capital; the homogenizing of social policies, laws (especially company law), and health and safety and other standards; and monetary union with a common currency and a single central bank. Political integration, so far as it might be necessary to secure the Community's economic aims, was an inevitable corollary but the Treaty of Rome was silent on this aspect. For some, political integration was an end in itself and a necessary means to strengthen the Community's influence not only in Europe but also in further areas of special concern to Europeans, notably colonial empires on the verge of independence, and the Middle East, whose oil was western Europe's most crucial import. The parallel aims of Euratom, embodied in the separate treaty creating that community, were to conduct nuclear research, construct nuclear installations, work out a safety code and set up a body to own and secure pre-emptive rights over nuclear raw materials.

The first six members were joined in 1973 by Britain, Ireland and Denmark, in 1981 by Greece and in 1986 by Spain and Portugal. Norway's adherence, negotiated alongside Britain, Ireland and Denmark, was rejected by plebiscite, and Greenland, which joined with its Danish parent, seceded in 1986. Of all these additions Britain's was the most important and the most contentious, delayed and later soured by Britain's own ambivalence but also vetoed for a number of years by France.

Britain's scepticism about the EEC had led it to form in 1959 a European Free Trade Association (EFTA) together with the three Scandinavian states, Switzerland, Austria and Portugal. (EFTA was a cut-down version of an organization of the same name but of 17 states, including the six founders of the EEC, which was to abolish tariffs between its members over ten years but not establish a common external tariff or any form of political union.) The British believed that de Gaulle – who returned to power in France at this time – would kill off the EEC, but this was a misinterpretation since de Gaulle intended not to undermine the EEC but merely to delay its development while France's economic recovery gathered pace and France's political weight in Europe increased commensurately. De Gaulle's proclaimed objection to British membership on the grounds that it was a stalking horse for American interests had enough plausibility to carry conviction with other members of the EEC in spite of their anxiety to have Britain as a member to offset German and French dominance. By 1960, however, de Gaulle was ready to consider British membership and publicly proposed it. Macmillan, who had repaired Britain's relations with the United States and the Commonwealth after the Suez debacle of 1956–57, was also anxious to give Britain a stronger European role. His visit to Moscow in 1959 had shown him to be an honest broker in international affairs but not a necessary one; the cancellation of the British Bluestreak missile in 1960 had exposed the difficulties of maintaining an independent nuclear force with a sporadically uneven economy; and in 1961 he responded to de Gaulle's overture and negotiations for Britain's adherence to the Treaty of Rome began that year. These negotiations, although laborious, were proceeding to an apparently successful conclusion when they were overborne by a serious Anglo-French misunderstanding. In June 1962 Macmillan visited de Gaulle at the Château de Champs. What passed between them is uncertain and each may well have mistaken the intentions of the other: an interview between a devious man and a silent one can leave much unclear. It would appear, however, that Macmillan, who had made admission to the EEC a centrepiece of his foreign and economic policies, not only played down current difficulties over Commonwealth preferences and agricultural policy but also left de Gaulle with the impression that Britain was prepared to integrate with its continental neighbours in the military sphere. This integration was a matter of the first importance to de Gaulle, who wanted a Europe independent of the United States but could not envisage a credible European defence force without a similarly independent Britain, which did not in his estimation exist. So his objection to British membership was one of principle, and negotiations for it were pointless.

In France opinion was divided about the admission of Britain to the EEC. Tangled discussions in Brussels over food prices disturbed many Frenchmen and during 1962 the *patronat* became increasingly hostile to British admission. But for de Gaulle these were minor matters if he could get Britain into an association which would be strategic as well as economic. After June 1962 he seems to have felt confident that he could do this. The French elections of November 1962 confirmed his authority by giving him a majority in parliament and a welcome success after a setback in October when his vote in a constitutional referendum had gone down. He was aware of Macmillan's domestic difficulties when the Labour Party came out in October against joining the EEC but he probably saw little reason to suppose that the British government would be defeated. He may have been wrong. Macmillan might have felt constrained to go to the country before so momentous a step as joining the EEC, and he might have lost an election fought on this issue. The main arguments against the EEC, other than the national distrust of over-association with foreigners, were: that the EEC was a bureaucracy and not a democracy, constitutionally speaking, an irresponsible form of government; that the EEC was devoted to free competition and entry into it meant abandoning national planning, not for international planning but for laissez-faire; that parliament would have to renounce its control over vital aspects of British public business; that the EEC was an inward-looking, Eurocentric organization with un-British traditions such as multiparty government and Roman–Dutch law in which British civil servants would be at a disadvantage; and that the process of government by qualified majority – that is, by giving a power of veto to a combination of one major and one minor partner – was a sure way to create disgruntled factions.

Towards the end of 1962, when the British and French leaders seemed intent on getting Britain into the EEC and the American administration was blessing the union, a decision in the Pentagon started a chain of events which led to the rupture of the negotiations. This was the decision to cancel the manufacture of the air-to-ground nuclear missile Skybolt, which the British had contracted to buy from the United States. The decision, taken in November on the grounds of cost, deprived Britain of the instrument with which it had hoped, after the cancellation of its own Bluestreak, to maintain an independent nuclear force up to 1970. By paying half the development costs Britain might have saved Skybolt and its own nuclear programme, but the price was too high and in December Macmillan went to Nassau in the Bahamas to meet Kennedy and find an alternative. He did not, to de Gaulle's disgust and perhaps surprise, turn instead to France and make the failure of Skybolt the occasion for switching from an Anglo-American to an Anglo-French or Anglo-European nuclear association. This demonstration of where Britain's first allegiance lay led de Gaulle to pronounce on 14 January 1963 the exclusion of Britain from the EEC.

At Nassau Kennedy offered Macmillan the Polaris submarine missile in place of Skybolt. Macmillan accepted. Kennedy made the same offer to de Gaulle, thus reversing a decision in the previous year not to offer France nuclear weapons. This decision had been reached after a division between those who hoped to improve Franco-American relations (a course initiated by Kennedy at a successful meeting with de Gaulle in June 1961) and others who argued that it would give a fillip to nuclear proliferation. De Gaulle refused the offer. Both Macmillan and de Gaulle were insisting on their nuclear sovereignty. De Gaulle refused to accept Polaris; Macmillan, while accepting Polaris and committing Britain's bomber and tactical air forces and Polaris units to NATO, insisted on ultimate British command and the right of withdrawal. The one attitude was not very different from the other, and both were essentially nationalist. The Americans, however, were looking for a supranational solution to the problem of nuclear sharing in NATO and they may have believed at Nassau that Macmillan, as opposed to de Gaulle, had agreed to fall in with their plans in return for Polaris.

Macmillan and de Gaulle disappointed each other and the British approach to the Community lapsed. When the Labour Party returned to power in 1964 Harold Wilson renewed the British application. His approach was different. Macmillan had given the impression that the main purpose of joining was to pull British economic chestnuts out of the fire, and that for Britain the economic benefits of joining would be considerable and would outweigh both the loss of sovereignty and the inconveniences of closer contacts with non-British folk. This prospectus was not an appealing one either in Britain or the Community, and the procedure adopted to implement it was the bizarre one of sending a senior minister to Brussels to conduct protracted negotiations over details (unkindly dubbed the kangaroo tail syndrome) and without a firm policy decision on the main issue of whether Britain would in the end want to join or not. By contrast Wilson told the British public that the economic disadvantages of joining would be considerable; he argued only that the advantages were in the long term more considerable. He stated the aim unequivocally: to join the Community, accepting all its rules in advance. He himself, a convert to British membership of the Community, was much influenced by the conflict between the EEC and the United States over the (GATT) Kennedy Round which revealed the vulnerability of an economically isolated Britain in the event of a trade war between continental western Europe and North America. But the chief obstacle remained. Although five of the six were ready and even eager for Britain to join, de Gaulle could still prevent it. Britain's links with the United States, its recurring debits on external account, and its continuing commitments beyond Europe provided arguments, if arguments were needed, for classing Britain as a thing apart.

The question was whether France would continue to insist on these arguments. They had always, even in de Gaulle's mind, been counterbalanced by others, notably by France's uneasiness about a European Community in which two states – France itself and West Germany – outranked the rest and might one day confront each other on a major issue. Britain therefore had two faces. While on the one hand it was, as an American appendage, unacceptable, it was simultaneously, as a counterweight to Germany, desirable. During 1967–69 the latter aspect began to overhaul the former, partly because of developments within the Community and partly because de Gaulle's resignation in 1969 facilitated a change of emphasis in Paris.

In 1969 de Gaulle once more dropped a hint that the time might be ripe for British membership. He invited the newly appointed British ambassador Christopher Soames, who was Churchill's son-in-law, for a general discussion of Franco-British relations in which he talked about closer four-power co-operation in Europe (France, Britain, West Germany and Italy) and an adaptation of the EEC to fit Britain in. These were basic Gaullist ideas of long standing but as a result of a chapter of ineptitudes the exchanges – largely a monologue by de Gaulle – produced a public diplomatic row when the British divulged the tenor of the talks to other governments and allowed the impression to gain ground that France was offering Britain a place in a European directory of major states in return for the suppression of the EEC and perhaps NATO too. Britain's chances of getting into the Community either by the front door or the back receded.

But not for long. That year de Gaulle resigned the presidency and was succeeded by Pompidou. Within a few months a change of government in Britain made Edward Heath prime minister. Heath had been the protagonist of British membership of the EEC at the time of the first application in 1961. In December 1969 the heads of government of the six had committed themselves at a meeting at The Hague to British membership and Heath lost no time in confirming that France, also under new leadership, would back a second application. Heath visited Pompidou in Paris in May 1971 and by treaties signed in January 1972 Britain, Denmark and Ireland became members of the EEC from the first day of 1973. A conference convened in 1972 by Pompidou of the six and these three had resolved to complete a Union, including a monetary union, by 1980. The Norwegian government, which negotiated with the EEC in company with the three, also agreed to join but its act was disavowed by a referendum. In Denmark and Ireland a referendum endorsed the treaty of accession.

The British case was peculiar. The treaty-making power of a British government required no popular or parliamentary endorsement. Nevertheless, a referendum was considered appropriate although it did not take place until two and a half years after the date fixed for Britain's accession. This unusual procedure arose out of the equivocations of the Labour Party. The Labour Party was more seriously divided than the Conservatives over the EEC and Wilson, his natural ambivalence sharpened by fears of splitting his party and ruining its electoral prospects, declared that the terms secured by the Conservatives should and could be bettered. He said that when Labour returned to office these terms would be renegotiated. This was, in effect, a threat to denounce the treaty unless its other signatories agreed to alter its terms. Wilson also promised that revised terms would be submitted to the country as well as the cabinet. Early in 1974 Heath, having narrowly miscalculated his electoral advantage, called an election and lost it, whereupon Wilson's new administration (a minority government until a second election later in the year gave him a slim majority) opened discussions with the EEC in which the main British effort was to get new terms sufficiently different from those in the treaty to show that the Conservatives should have done better. The main issue was the size of the British contribution to the Community's budget, on which the foreign secretary James Callaghan obtained sizeable concessions. The British cabinet approved the new terms with few dissentients. The electorate, certainly confused by elaborate and conflicting economic arguments, probably somewhat bored by this long-drawn-out affair, and not a little impressed by the plea that it would be wrong to undo what a previous government had with all due form and propriety done, said yes to membership in June 1975 by precisely two to one. Thus, 25 years after it could have joined a European community on virtually any terms of its own choosing, Britain haggled its way into the Community which had been constructed without it.

At the core of the Community was the Franco-German entente, tentatively but enduringly established by the Coal and Steel Community. Britain's entry was expected to broaden and strengthen this core but did not do so. If the initiative in creating the entente was French, its affirmation was German. Adenauer's first concern after the formation of the West German state in 1952 was to anchor it to the west by unquestioning association with the United States and membership of NATO, but in his later years he gave increasing attention to Germany's place in Europe. France was becoming, in Bismarck's phrase, more *bündnisfähig* – a more worthwhile ally – and at the same time disenchanted with Britain and freed from postwar wrangles with Germany. The plebiscite in the Saar in 1955 had removed the last serious Franco-German difference from the political agenda whereas Britain's unilateral abandonment under American pressure of the fiasco at Suez had soured Franco-British relations. France was overcoming its reputation for political and economic instability and the firm handling of the Algerian crisis in May 1958 was followed by two meetings between Adenauer and de Gaulle at Colombey-les-Deux-Eglises and Bad Kreuznach which put Franco-German relations on a new footing. Between these meetings a French statement bluntly rejected British proposals (supported by Adenauer's finance minister Ludwig Erhard, but not by himself) for a loose free trade area.

There were, nevertheless, serious divergences between French and German attitudes. France, with Italian support, proposed in 1959 regular meetings of the six foreign ministers, backed by a secretariat to be established in Paris. The Treaty of Rome was silent on political integration and it seemed to the Germans and to the Benelux members of the Community that the French were trying to create in Paris a political organization of an international character distinct from the institutions in Brussels and designed to bypass, throttle or even take over the supranational economic activities which were proceeding there. These suspicions were sharpened in the next year when the French elaborated their plan and proposed a council of heads of government with a secretariat in Paris. Such a 'union of states', successfully pressed by de Gaulle on Adenauer at Rambouillet in July, was incompatible with federalist ambitions. The whole subject was referred by the six to a special committee (the Fouchet, later Cattani, committee), which discussed two successive plans of French origin and the objections to them. These objections amounted in sum to the contention that the plans left out all the principal features of the EEC's own constitution, since they contained no provision for a parliamentary element or for an independent executive or for eventual decision by majority vote. The subject was allowed to fizzle out. Since it had been raised by France this outcome was a rebuff to France but also evidence that France was willing to accept some rebuffs rather than demolish the Community.

Another dispute arose over the elaboration of a common agricultural policy. The principal bone of contention at its inception was the level of uniform prices to be set for cereals. In 1963 Dr Sicco Mansholt, one of the Commission's two vice-presidents and specially charged with agricultural matters, produced a plan for fixing a common price which was to be lower than the price ruling in Germany (and Italy and Luxembourg), so that French eagerness collided with reservations in Bonn which were all the more stubborn because the direction of affairs passed in 1963 to Erhard, who had his eyes on the general election due towards the end of 1965. De Gaulle played on the fact that Erhard, while reluctant to accelerate the CAP, was anxious to establish an agreed EEC position in the coming negotiations under the GATT (the Kennedy Round) in which the six were proposing to bargain as a single team. The American president had been empowered by the Trade Expansion Act of 1962 reciprocally to cut tariffs by as much as half but his powers to do so were to expire on 1 July 1967. The tariffs imposed by the six were mostly bunched in a band ranging from 6 to 20 per cent, whereas American and British tariffs were either much higher or zero. Consequently, the EEC Commission and also the French government pressed for the lopping of the higher tariffs (*écrêtement*) rather than general cuts (in which they were eventually forced to yield when the Americans proved adamant). Some Americans and British had expected and hoped that the six would split among themselves over a common approach to the Kennedy Round but at the end of 1963 compromises were accepted in order to permit both the Kennedy Round and the CAP to proceed.

During 1964, however, differences between France and Germany became worse, with France still holding up agreement on essential preliminaries to the Kennedy Round in order to extract Bonn's acceptance of a uniform cereal price and also to prevent it from joining the MLF (see p. 167). The year ended with another of the compromises for which the Community was becoming noted. The American administration having tacitly abandoned the MLF, Bonn agreed to the uniform cereal price in return for special subsidies (also payable to Italy and Luxembourg) and the postponement of the common agricultural policy from 1966 to July 1967. This was a victory for de Gaulle, but it left Bonn resentful and ready to give a lead against France in the new crisis which de Gaulle's policies evoked in the next year.

The crisis arose out of proposals by Dr Walther Hallstein, the Commission's (German) president, to extend the authority within the Community of the Commission and the Assembly at the expense of the Council of Ministers by, first, expediting the switch in the Council from unanimity to majority voting and, secondly, by channelling agricultural levies directly to the Commission instead of to national governments for transmission to the Commission. These proposals were a challenge to de Gaulle's views and some of Hallstein's colleagues warned him that he was going imprudently fast. Moreover, by presenting his proposals first to the Assembly instead of to the Council as the rules provided, Hallstein gave de Gaulle an opportunity to put his foot down. The French ambassador to the Community was withdrawn and France attended no Council meetings for six months. These tactics succeeded. The crisis of the 'Empty Chair' was resolved at the beginning of 1966 in a series of meetings in Luxembourg (not Brussels) which were, in effect, a governmental negotiation between France and its five partners. By the Luxembourg Compromise the members of the Community accepted informally that any member might insist that a particular proposal which it considered of special interest should remain under discussion until unanimity was reached. France thus secured a veto in circumstances to be judged and defined on each occasion by itself. By accepting this compromise France's partners, although giving little away on paper, acknowledged implicitly that French membership and full co-operation were of the essence of the Community. Thereafter the Luxembourg Compromise receded into the background. It was not invoked by Britain when, in the 1980s, Britain succeeded France in the role of reluctant or recalcitrant partner: by that date a Community which had existed without Britain for decades did not feel its very existence threatened by threats such as those posed by France in the 1960s.

These were constitutional disputes. There were also financial troubles, particularly in connection with the CAP, which by the 1980s was dispensing more on buying up surpluses for resale at a loss than on subsidies to farmers. The Community needed an agricultural policy because so many of its inhabitants were engaged in agriculture and because the Community was not self-sufficient in many foodstuffs, but the policy ran away with itself and instead of turning underproduction into sufficiency turned it into embarrassingly large surpluses. In addition, the Community was propelled into competition with the United States where subsidies to farmers were also producing surpluses which had to be sold or dumped in the same markets as Community surpluses. Financially, the Community's problem was aggravated by fluctuations in exchange rates among its members. In order to reduce the impact of these ups and downs the Community created a special 'green' currency, which was, however, abused by currency dealers.

The main mechanism of the CAP was an annual fixing of prices by the Commission. These prices were set somewhat above world prices in order to give farmers and farm workers an attractive standard of living. The Commission undertook to buy surpluses at fixed prices and it levied import duties on foreign foodstuffs whenever prices fell below prescribed levels. When this system turned production into surplus the Community faced the need to reduce its agricultural acreage. In 1974 Dr Mansholt proposed a ten-year programme to this end but it was rejected by the Council of Ministers who, individually, were afraid of losing votes at their next national elections if they endorsed the plan. There was also a second and more respectable objection to the plan. Cutting agricultural production meant putting out of business smaller farmers who not only commanded emotional and sentimental admiration but were often the economic core of whole communities: an end to farming in a given district could impoverish and depopulate the whole district. Whereas an older industrial revolution had involved a switch from one kind of manufacture to another, agricultural revolution threatened to extinguish one economic activity without replacing it by another.

To finance the CAP the Commission had at its disposal the proceeds of agricultural levies and import duties and 1 per cent of each member's GNP, but these revenues were intended to cover all the Commission's expenditure, not only the CAP. From 1979 the Commission might cover a year's deficit by requisitioning from members a further contribution not exceeding 1 per cent of its receipts from VAT. In the 1980s this further source ceased to bridge the gap, and since the main cause of the imbalance was the CAP, members had strong grounds for demanding a radical review of its subsidies to farmers as a condition for increasing the share of VAT to be transferred to the Commission. But in this respectable endeavour they – particularly Thatcher's Britain – so overdid the rhetoric and underplayed the genuine social obstacles to radical change that little was achieved and in 1984 the VAT ceiling was raised without any serious inroads into the CAP's excesses. Besides the specific problem of the CAP, unity in Europe moved into rougher waters. The main immediate aim of a customs union among six members, all of them comparatively prosperous, was achieved ahead of schedule but was followed by vexing problems: slow economic growth, unemployment rising to 10 per cent of the work force, the admission of new members. The original six had been followed in 1972 by Britain, Ireland and Denmark and by three Mediterranean countries (Greece in 1981, Spain and Portugal in 1986) but the collapse in 1989 of Soviet dominion over half of Europe raised the question of whether Europe really meant all Europe and, if so, how fast. To meet these various concerns in a rapidly changing context not of its own making the Commission produced a series of programmes for assimilating currencies and credit policies – two from Raymond Barre of France and one from Gaston Werner of Luxembourg. All were set aside. The last proposed in 1974 a ten-year period during which fluctuations in currencies would be progressively restricted, movements of capital would become unrestricted, and national economic and budgetary policies would become subject to communal consultation with, at the end of the period, full monetary union with a single currency and a central Community bank. The plan was an economic ineptitude since it proposed a very great deal in an impossibly short time but something like it was attained during Roy Jenkins' presidency of the Commission and through a fresh Franco-German impulse from Valéry Giscard d'Estaing and Helmut Schmidt. The latter formulated a European Monetary System (EMS) with strict limits to currency fluctuations, a reserve currency and a central reserve of $50 billion in gold and foreign exchange.

The EMS, which came into existence in 1979, was created by all 12 Community members but four of them – Britain, Greece, Spain and Portugal – stayed outside the mechanism (the Exchange Rate Mechanism – ERM) devised to operate the system. Its function was to keep currencies fixed in terms of one another, subject to variations not exceeding 4.5 per cent (with greater latitude for Italy) and subject also to annual review and readjustment of the fixed values. The system had two main purposes. Managed exchange rates were a compromise between floating and fixed rates, a way of controlling currency fluctuations whose volatility not only discouraged trade by making future prices peculiarly uncertain but also allowed trading rivals to engage one another in competitive inflation for short-term advantage. Secondly, the system was a step towards a European monetary union (EMU) with a single currency, to be called the ecu (later renamed the euro). Within a year loans were being negotiated and bonds issued in ecus and within ten years ecu loans exceeded in value loans in currencies other than the dollar, the yen, the Deutschmark and the Swiss franc.

The Single European Act of 1985 was another attempt by those who wanted to push on rather than hold back. The outcome was the humbler business of keeping the show on the road by step-by-step advances which made it more difficult to stop or reverse unification. But such signs of progress could not disguise the fact that pro-union campaigners were on the defensive until the situation was transformed by the collapse of Soviet power in Europe in 1989–90.

European Union (east–west)

This collapse was the most portentous event in the fortunes of the Union after its inauguration in 1957. East Germany became *ipso facto* a part of a reunited Germany; reunification made Germany incontestably the most important state in Europe – so much so that Thatcher and Mitterrand (the latter only fleetingly) tried to think of ways to stop or neutralize it; the exit of the Russians doubled the count of the members of the Union. But these consequences were not immediately apparent. One of them was the weakening of the German mark. West Germany's economic success had been an essential ingredient in the EC's economic and monetary integration although the strength of the mark had also been a source of apprehension among other members. With unification the mark became not too strong but too weak. It could not for a time cope with the costs of unification – the conversion of the eastern mark and the salvaging of East Germany's derelict industries and agriculture – and at the same time serve as the anchor of the EMS. Partly in response to generous exuberance and partly to win votes Kohl, overriding the German Bundesbank, promised to redeem the East German mark at parity with the western mark. In theory the West German government had choices about how to guard against the inflation inherent in this open-handedness and in the funding of the rehabilitation of the east, but a devaluation of the mark was regarded as inconceivable and higher taxation as more burdensome than borrowing. Therefore interest rates had to be raised and, given the standing of the mark throughout the EC, interest rates in other parts of the EC had to be raised too – or at least could not be lowered. Put crudely, the rest of the EC was paying in higher interest charges part of the cost of reviving eastern Germany when what they needed was cheaper money to rekindle their own growth. The Bundesbank was caught between the need on the one hand for higher rates to counter inflation in Germany and, on the other, the need throughout Europe for lower rates to counter recession. The bank gave priority to the former as by its constitution it was bound to do. It was in any case unenthusiastic about monetary integration which would shift power from itself to a central Eurobank.

To the question whether to EEC should apply the brake or the accelerator Germany chose to put its weight behind trying to have their contributions reduced. In return the recipients were reminded of their obligations to keep inflation below a given limit, to keep budget deficits below a given percentage of total government expenditure and to keep their borrowing at a sum below a given percentage of their GDP – i.e. to adopt financial and therefore social policies capped by the Union – and to suffer heavy fines if they broke the rules. These conditions were quickly shown to be less than copper-bottomed in the case of existing members when Germany and France broke them with impunity.

In a final step, designed as closing the door on major reviews for some time to come, ex-President Giscard d'Estaing was asked to propose constitutional changes (e.g. voting rights in the Council of Ministers) to deal with the doubling of the Union's membership – which he did with baffling caution. At the end of 1990 five central members of the Community agreed to abolish reciprocal visas and border controls. This so-called Schengen agreement (it was based on a Schengen computer system) was introduced in 1995 by its five originators and Spain and Portugal and was expanded to nine by the adherence of Italy and Austria in 1997 – in which year a rush of Kurdish refugees into the EU, mainly through Italy, gave urgency to the Schengen partners' resolve to elaborate a common policy on political asylum and an integrated police force. It also reinforced the decision of non-Schengen members not to join.

These were the preliminaries to the conference held at *Maastricht* early in 1992. At Maastricht all 12 members of the Community signed a treaty whose main purpose was to give more precision to progress to monetary and economic union and to append to economic policies a series of principles and mechanisms for the co-ordination of policies in other areas. The treaty created a *European Union* in which the Community and its organs were subsumed.

The European Union was a federation in all but name (a federation being essentially a union established by treaty, not by conquest). The draft of the treaty acknowledged this fact but the word 'federal' was deleted in deference to British susceptibilities. This deletion did not affect the substance since in all political associations, whatever they may be called, the inescapable question is the delineation of powers between authorities at different levels. In this matter the treaty affirmed the principle of 'subsidiarity' which ascribed authority to the member state in all cases of doubt or apparent overlap between the state and the Community or Union: this principle had been espoused by three successive chairmen of the Commission – François-Xavier Ortoli in 1975, Roy Jenkins in 1977 and Jacques Delors, who insisted on its inclusion in the Maastricht treaty.

The European Union introduced a European citizenship in addition to citizenship of its several members and gave all citizens the right from 1994 to vote in elections in the state in which they were residing, subject to regulations to be unanimously adopted by the Council of Ministers. (These provisions were similar to proposals made by Churchill to Roosevelt for an Anglo-American union: Churchill also proposed a single currency.) A European Council composed of heads of government and the president of the Commission was created, charged to meet once a year and to present to the European parliament an annual report on the state of the Union. The Union was also charged with the development of common policies in areas outside the Community's immediate concern with economic and monetary integration. In these matters the Union was in effect the Community's Council of Ministers acting in spheres from which the Commission was entirely and the parliament almost entirely excluded. These spheres were foreign and security policies and internal policies relating, for example, to immigration, drugs, terrorism and some other kinds of crime. This part of the treaty amounted to little more than declarations of intention. The treaty did not rescind the Community's competence specifically to negotiate economic agreements on behalf of the Community with states or groups of states outside the Community.

The most concise part of the Treaty of Maastricht dealt with economic and monetary union, of which the first stage was already in place. The second stage, designed to prepare the way for stage three (full implementation), was set to start in 1994. In stage two a European Monetary Institute, an association of members' central banks, was to oversee and try to secure the preconditions for a single currency and a central bank. The essential preconditions were sustainable budgeting practices and machinery for sustaining them. They were defined, as markers but not as rigid conditions, on terms of convergence in four categories: price inflation (5.1 per cent), yields on ten-year bonds (8.5 per cent), budget deficits as a percentage of GDP (3 per cent) and gross public debt as a percentage of GDP (60 per cent). Stage three was to be reached by 1999. From the beginning of 1997 the Council of Ministers might decide that a majority of members (seven) had achieved the necessary convergence and might in that event set a date for the inauguration of a full union by those members. In the absence of such a decision full union would nevertheless be inaugurated from the beginning of 1999, subject to provisions for exemption for members not yet in a condition to join. The first *terminus ad quem* would put pressure on laggards if they wished to avoid the creation of a two-tier Community. This was the only part of the treaty which committed members specifically to anything not contained in the Treaty of Rome or the Single European Act. Britain was expressly exempted from its provisions. More generally the treaty also redefined or extended the Community's commitment to harmonizing policies and law in certain areas such as transport, the movements of funds, professional qualifications and the environment. It was no less important for what it excluded from joint action or consideration: for example, the provision of health services and overall Community principles in relation to such services. The main weakness of this part of the treaty was a yawning discrepancy between the programme for economic unity and the timetable incorporated in the programme.

Social services and the grey areas between economic and social policy became a subject of sharp debate, principally between Britain and the other members. The latter wanted to advance beyond the Social Charter adopted in 1989 but the British Conservatives adamantly opposed this part of the treaty, which was therefore recast as a separate protocol not applicable to Britain. At the root of this disagreement was the continued British disposition (much strengthened by Thatcher) to treat labour relations as a form of combat as distinct from the view, which had played a conspicuous role in the postwar German economic miracle, that economic prosperity required a partnership between capital and labour. Thatcher's successor, John Major, refused to have any truck with a Social Chapter in the hope of asserting his nationalist credentials within the Conservative Party while at the same time reversing Thatcher's disdain of the Community and British alienation from it. The other members were content to put social matters into an optional protocol as the price for keeping Britain in the fold. The protocol itself was a declaration of unexceptionable general principles which might be invoked by the Commission if it were minded to draft relevant directives which might then be approved or not by the Council of Ministers. The protocol covered subjects such as health and safety at work and equal pay for women and men but excluded others such as the right of association among workers, strikes and levels of pay.

The structure of the Community was little affected by the Maastricht Treaty. The Council of Ministers, the stronghold of national governments, retained its domination, although within the Council each member's veto was diluted by the expansion of majority voting in place of unanimity. From 1995 the president of the Commission was to be nominated by member governments after consultations with the parliament and all other commissioners were to be nominated by governments after consultations with the president. The parliament's authority received a marginal boost. Besides being entitled to offer opinions and amend directives it acquired a new right of veto in limited circumstances and it could by a two-thirds majority censure and so secure the dismissal of the entire Commission. It was to be elected by the same method in all states in accordance with regulations to be approved by the Council of Ministers. The European Investment Bank also received a modest boost and a new Regional Committee was created with 169 members and vague advisory powers. It seemed unlikely to have more influence than its equally hazy predecessor, the Economic and Social Committee. All members except Denmark and Britain ratified the treaty by the end of 1992. It was rejected in Denmark in a referendum by 50.7 per cent but this decision was reversed after Denmark was granted the right (already conceded to Britain) to opt out of important sections of the treaty on the pretence that the treaty itself allowed such manoeuvres. In Britain, where accession was made subject to parliamentary endorsement (although strictly only its fiscal implications required the approval of the House of Commons), Major narrowly won the day for ratification after some equivocation and secret deals with Irish parties in the House.

The 1992 Treaty of Maastricht was concluded by making concessions and exclusions in order to enshrine the greatest common factor of agreement at a time when the EU was facing a helter-skelter of applications for membership from ex-communist countries. Existing members hoped to keep the process orderly (i.e. slow) but the momentum of European affairs after 1989 substantially defeated the tactics employed. The applications were sorted into batches: ten central European states (plus Malta, Cyprus and perhaps Turkey) to be in first place, to be followed by Romania and Bulgaria. There were real problems and on paper stiff conditions. The most serious problem was financial. The old Union was financed by six of its members who contributed more than they received. In the new Union the six would still be net contributors and the newcomers would all be added to their financial burden.

The Treaty of Maastricht was quickly followed by the collapse of the ERM and the emasculation of the EMS. The EC had approved in 1989 a plan (accepted even by Thatcher) for economic and monetary integration and this plan was incorporated in the treaty but without time limits for any stage. The plan endorsed the extension of the EMS with its ERM to all EC members and although Thatcher continued to object to it the logic of events obliged Britain to join the ERM in 1990. But it did so at an unsustainable overvaluation of the pound and at a rate set without consulting its German or other partners who might be called upon to sustain it. Britain simultaneously cut interest rates and so raised doubts about its commitment to reducing inflation and pursuing the convergences required for implementing monetary union.

The EMS/ERM was at once a mechanism for regulating the exchange values of its various currencies and a step towards the supersession of these currencies by a single currency. As a mechanism it required periodic readjustments of exchange rates by orderly government agreement rather than by short-term speculators operating in money markets for their own immediate profit. As a stage towards a single currency it encouraged the belief that adjustments should be increasingly infrequent until the need for them faded away: stability became confused with fixity. In its first years the ERM was used, as intended, to make small but frequent adjustments in rates, but from 1987 none; and after the unification of Germany it lost its essential anchor – a central currency not vulnerable to inflation. By 1992 neither the Italian lira nor the pound sterling could be sustained within their prescribed limits. The lira was devalued by 7 per cent and temporarily excluded from the system by speculators to whom the interventionist role assigned to the ERM had been surrendered by inaction. The pound was similarly assailed. Neither Major nor his chancellor of the exchequer Norman Lamont had played a part in joining the EMU (that was done by Thatcher). Lamont disliked the EMU and was determined not to devalue sterling, whose exchange value he aimed to preserve by raising interest rates. He had gravely overrated the extent to which the Deutschmark had been weakened by the unification of Germany. He spurned German offers for a negotiated realignment of currencies. The pound fell below its ERM limit, was suspended and then devalued by 17 per cent; the British exchequer lost billions of pounds. Unwilling to relinquish his office, Lamont was dismissed by Major. There were compensations, particularly for exporters, in this severe and ill-managed adjustment but Lamont's attempt to show that he could run the British economy without regard to Britain's major European partners was neither sensible nor successful. The ERM itself was discredited but further vagaries among currencies were stemmed more quickly than expected and at the beginning of 1994 the European Monetary Institute, the Eurobank in waiting, opened its doors in Frankfurt.

When Delors' tenure of the presidency of the Commission came to an end in 1994 Major vetoed Jean-Luc Dehaene of Belgium as his successor but accepted Jacques Santer of Luxembourg, whose views were virtually indistinguishable from Dehaene's. In the same year Austria, Sweden and Finland became members.

The Maastricht stepping stone towards greater integration, and the post-communist impetus to the extension of the Union into central and eastern Europe, led to a further meeting in Amsterdam in 1997 whose outcome was modest. Shortly before the meeting the rout of the British Conservatives and the unexpected fall of the French government changed the political climate. The new British Labour government, while maintaining some of its predecessor's objections to the way in which the Union was going, abandoned its disgruntled obstructiveness. It declared in advance its readiness to adopt the Maastricht Social Chapter (and to incorporate into British law the European Convention on Human Rights) and claimed in Amsterdam a leading constructive role in the Union while insisting on keeping full sovereign control over immigration and asylum and putting a brake on the evolution of common and defence policies. More disconcerting was the advent as French prime minister of Jospin, apparently caught by surprise by his victory and uncertain how to manoeuvre between Chirac's determination to be part of a single currency in 1999 and his own socialist party's scepticism on this score.

The drive behind the plan for a single currency at the earliest possible moment and with wide participation lay in Kohl's forcefulness and Chirac's concurrence. Kohl in particular was increasingly imbued with fear of renascent German nationalism if the EU faltered. But there were serious doubts whether the Maastricht criteria could be met, even by Germany. Besides the Maastricht preconditions governing the admissibility of each national currency were the further problems of managing the single currency after its inauguration. Germany and France devised a stability pact to safeguard the strength of the new currency by imposing rules – with fines for infringement – to prevent EMU members from slackening their budget practices and so weakening the currency. Any such rules involved some central control over national financial strategies and independence. Kohl was intent on rigorous precision; Chirac and his then prime minister Alain Juppé had been willing to subscribe to the German programme, although not without misgivings about the pact's effects on government spending which the French socialists in particular wanted to be free to expand in order to combat unemployment. At Amsterdam the Germans prevailed, Jospin followed Chirac's lead and the conference adopted the principle that national budgets should be bal-anced in the medium term. The main aim was endorsed by leaving much else unsaid.

At the beginning of 1999 11 member states adopted a common currency, the euro, under the control of a European Central Bank substantially independent of govern-ments and with an initial interest rate of 3 per cent throughout the 11 territories (except Italy, where it was 2.5 per cent). Britain, Denmark, Sweden and Greece delayed their adherence, Greece because it had not attained the Maastricht criteria and the other three by choice. Outside the euro zone opposition to a single currency became more symbolic than economic. A single market did not require a single currency but a single market with fair competition did: the real issue was whether or not a state might be allowed to indulge in unilateral competitive devaluations of its currency.

The euro was conceived with two distinct functions. It was to reflect and further promote the economic and political integration of Europe in the same way as single national currencies had replaced and unified multiple national currencies in, for example, France, Germany, Italy. Secondly, it was to become a world currency in the sense of ready acceptability and widespread use throughout the world economy along-side the dollar and the yen. It was designed not to supplant the dollar but to fortify a world system which the dollar, whose prime function was to serve the American eco-nomy, might not by itself sustain. The test of the euro would therefore come at times when the dollar weakened. Since at the end of the century the American economy flourished and the dollar strengthened, the euro faced in its infancy no such test.

At Amsterdam the Schengen agreement was extended throughout the Union with licences to Britain, Ireland and Denmark to opt out of it. Foreign policies were to be integrated only by inter-governmental discussions – i.e. EU bodies being excluded – but agreed policies would be implemented by the EU subject only to qualified major-ity voting in the Council of Ministers. There was little change in the rules regarding unanimity or majority voting in the Council and no agreement on reform of the Commission (which now had 15 commissioners but fewer realistically distinct depart-ments) beyond providing that, upon the next intake of members, those members with two places on the Commission would lose one of them in return for added weight in the calculation of weighted voting in the Council. After Amsterdam the Commission resumed its approach to enlargement of the Union and the Council of Ministers sanc-tioned the opening of negotiations with – in addition to Cyprus, already approved – Poland, the Czech Republic, Hungary, Slovenia and Estonia on the basis (propounded in 1993) of satisfactory conditions on democratic politics, free market economies, human rights and safeguards for minorities. In 1998 a special conference in London was attended by 11 candidates for admission (but not Turkey) as well as all existing members and in the following year Poland, the Czech Republic and Hungary began negotiations for admission. In 1999 the Commission proposed the opening of negoti-ations with six more states: Latvia and Lithuania, Slovakia, Romania and Bulgaria, and Malta; and that Turkey be recognized as a candidate.

In external affairs the Union had already operated as a single entity in the last (Uruguay) round of the GATT (General Agreement in Tariffs and Trade) (see p. 762). Wars in Yugoslavia reinforced the need for some integration of policies in Europe. In the Middle East too Europeans had powerful reasons for concerting policies: oil and geography. The EU drew more than half of its oil from the Middle East – three times more than American imports from the same region. (EU exports to the Middle East exceeded American exports fourfold.) Further, the Middle East and North Africa occupied half the Mediterranean litoral with Europeans occupying the other half. The widening gap between rich and poor in these regions, besides threatening the stability which was vital for steady oil production and transport, boosted licit and illicit migration to the EU in alarming volume. The EU pursued a programme of commercial agreements with Arab states and Israel which broadened into a policy, endorsed in 1995 by the Council of Ministers, for a general free trade zone designed not only to increase trade but also to ward off the dangers of instability with an as yet unavowed prospect of extending this zone from the Mediterranean to Iraq and Iran – states branded by the United States as terrorist pariahs. Europeans feared that American anti-Islamic rhetoric and commitment to Israel were destabilizing the region and they resented their exclusion by the United States from Israeli–Palestinian peace talks in Madrid and Washington (see pp. 367–70). While they shared with the United States an urgent desire for peace in the Middle East, they distrusted the means and to some extent the motives with which the United States pursued this aim. In the military sphere the proponents of an integrated structure and forces for the EU and the absorption into it of the WEU were disliked by those, particularly the British, who feared any diminution of the role in Europe of NATO and the United States. Joint ventures were limited to a Franco-German force joined by Belgium, Luxembourg and Spain and two (land and air) forces adumbrated by France, Italy, Spain and Portugal. Europeans saw little occasion for the use of armed force within the EU except as reinforcement for the civil power in civil disturbances but the wars in Yugoslavia in the 1990s displayed the need for joint action outside EU territory, the dependence of the EU on the United States and the differences between them, and the need for the EU to be better equipped to run its own affairs. In 1998 France and Britain initiated a plan for a European rapid reaction force with appropriate institutions and intelligence, under the control of the EU's Council of Ministers, within the framework of the UN and consistent with the obligations of the North Atlantic Treaty; and in 1999 the EU created the new post of Secretary-General to the Council of Ministers and High Representative for the Foreign and Security Policy. Mindful of the need not to appear to rebuff the United States, the EU conferred this post on NATO's retiring secretary-general, Javier Solana. Simultaneously, NATO appointed to Solana's post the British secretary of state for defence George Robertson, a staunch Atlanticist and Europeanist.

The EU suffered in 1999 a severe, if salutary, blow when a report commissioned by the parliament on the workings of the Commission was so damning that the entire

Commission resigned. The report's criticisms were most forcibly directed against one of the French commissioners, Edith Cresson, personally and against the president *ex officio* but the parliament, being unempowered to dismiss individuals, brought about the removal of the Commission *en bloc*. The heads of state and government lost no time in selecting as Santer's successor the former Italian prime minister Romano Prodi, who formed a largely new Commission, promised to expunge malpractices and inefficiencies, and faced a new parliament intent on sharpened combativeness. With the departure of Prodi to become Italy's president, Jose Manuel Barroso inherited the problems of constitutional reform necessitated by the expansion of the EU to 27 members. These were eventually resolved by the European Reform Treaty concluded at Lisbon in 2007, which among lesser measures pruned the commission and reduced the exercise of the veto and also – so it was hoped – paved the way to a return to substantive policy issues.

The southern flank

Command of the Mediterranean, although disputed during the Second World War, was not in doubt after it and all the European riparian states (and Portugal) joined NATO over the years and then became members – in the case of Turkey an associate member – of the European Community. Malta and Cyprus, members of the Commonwealth from 1964 and 1961, also became associates of the EC.

Historical accident – its shift into the Anglo-American alliance against Germany in 1943 – and the uninterrupted predominance of the Christian Democrat Party after the war made *Italy* an original and unquestioned member of NATO and of the EC. Italy's retreat from fascism converted it into a parliamentary democracy but did not make it prosperous. Post-fascist governments inherited a situation in which 2 million out of a working population of 20 million were unemployed and nearly half of Italy's workers were employed (or unemployed) in agriculture. By 1970 this proportion had been reduced to 20 per cent but the fundamental problems of economic overpopulation remained, for which the classic remedy was emigration (not new, since Julius Caesar had founded Narbonne in Gaul for this purpose). The chief haven, the United States, had been progressively closed by quotas and literacy tests. Some 150,000 Italians left home every year for Australia, Canada and elsewhere, but there was still not enough work for those who remained (and who, since the leavers were younger, became a senescent population). Schemes for helping the impoverished south failed to check the widening gap between the two halves of the country, and the twin problems of surplus manpower and depressed areas became two of the mainsprings of Italy's postwar European policies. Italy's first postwar democratically elected prime minister Alcide de Gasperi was persuaded that the cure was participation in a European confederation and so Italy joined the European Coal and Steel Community as a founder member in

1951 even though it had no coal and, outside Elba, no ironstone. Instead of growing oranges and lemons for the delectation of richer Europeans beyond the Alps, Italy would emulate them, even if it had to import iron all the way from Venezuela to feed the modern steelworks being constructed at Taranto; and 20 years later Italy was exporting 20 million tons of steel a year. In the 1950s GNP was doubled by modernizing industry, investing in training and making good use of surplus labour; industrial output rose from a quarter to nearly a half of total output. The discovery of natural gas in the Po valley gave an unexpected boost from 1958 although supplies proved limited and this uncovenanted benefit lasted only a few years.

De Gasperi ruled Italy until his death in 1954 as unchallenged leader of the Democratic Christian Party (DC), in close association with the Roman Church at all levels from the Vatican to the parish priest and which in the context of the Cold War prohibited a coalition with the communists, who constituted the second largest party in Italy and the largest European communist party outside the USSR. His successor as prime minister, Amintore Fanfani, disliked clerical interference in matters of state and would have liked to revive some aspects of the prewar corporatist state but he lacked the personal and political dominance of de Gasperi (let alone Mussolini) and was leader not of the DC but of a faction – albeit the largest faction – in it. In 1962 Fanfani, together with the more flexible Aldo Moro, engineered a coalition with the socialists and in 1964 he aimed unsuccessfully at the presidency. (He did so again in 1971 and died in 1999.) From the mid-1960s he reverted to severely right-wing policies as Italian politics became increasingly a field of conflict within one party and – although Fanfani himself set an example of impeccable integrity – became increasingly corrupt (not unlike politics in Japan). Until the elections of 1987 the DC succeeded in retaining power, as the fascists had done immediately after 1922, through alliances with smaller and subordinate parties but, unrelieved by respites in opposition and unwilling or unable to produce a new generation of leaders, it evinced a declining sense of purpose, an incapacity to master economic problems and a laxness in regard to standards of public morality which would have ensured its earlier defeat if its main opponent had not been the tabu communists. These lost some middle-class and intellectual support from the shocks of 1956 and 1968 but retained – again until 1987 – most of their considerable popular following. During the brief pontificate of John XXIII (1958–63) there was a lessening in papal interference in Italian affairs but no abrogation of the Vatican's special right to intervene under the Lateran Treaty of 1929. Pius XII's excommunication of communists was lifted, there was no repetition of the abuse levelled at President Gronchi for visiting Moscow, and although the debate on civil divorce in Italy in 1969–70 led to a recrudescence of clerical intervention, the church-and-state question did not rise above the level of an accustomed, if sometimes exasperating, family dispute. Italian democracy succumbed neither to communism nor clericalism. Nor did it suffer the fate of Greek democracy, although a fascist plot contrived by Prince Valerio Borghese was detected in December 1970. Nevertheless, by the 1970s Italy was in poor health politically as well as economically. The government inspired little faith, public services were regularly breaking down, corruption was an open and even popular topic of conversation, inflation rose and in 1974, year of the first oil crisis, the deficit on the balance of payments reached $825 million (of which $500 million was for oil). West Germany and the IMF came to the rescue but Italy looked like being a permanent drain on the EEC and, particularly after the regional elections of June 1975, a political risk as the communist share of the poll edged up towards that of the Christian Democrats and Italy's allies asked themselves what they would do if the communists came into the government (they had last shared in government in 1947) or if communist successes in elections provoked the right into a coup. The problem was evaded, and thereby prolonged, when in the general election of 1976 the Christian Democrats managed to maintain a small lead over the communists but were forced to form a single-party government without a parliamentary majority and dependent on communist abstentions. The fall of this government two years later revived the arguments for and against a coalition of the two main parties, the Christian Democrat and the communist. Opponents included the United States and the Vatican on the one hand and also the extreme left, which regarded communist participation in such an alliance as treason. Aldo Moro, chairman of the Christian Democrats, was kidnapped and murdered by extremists intent on making this point.

The Italian Communist Party (PCI) was the largest outside the USSR; it played a leading part in Italian national and local politics, whether in power or not; and it had a strong native intellectual tradition which made it less foreign than other communist parties appeared to be. It was at the centre of the Eurocommunism which became a talking point in the 1970s and attracted in particular the Spanish and French parties (PCE and PCF).

Eurocommunism was an assertion that communist parties need not be blindly subservient to an international movement and particularly not to the Communist Party of the Soviet Union (CPSU); it was an attempt to deny the Stalinist past. It was also an attempt to bolster the central communist tradition against the New Left which, still further to the left, was representing communist parties as fossilized anachronisms. The PCI was reverting to the nineteenth-century view that socialism could win substantial victories by democratic means – that fair elections between a plurality of parties could be turned to good account. This view had been submerged in the twentieth century by Lenin's disciplined democratic centralism, by the sight of democrats taking the side of the whites in Russia after 1917, and later by western democrats' preference for fascism over communism. But the older view was never quite lost in Italy.

Palmiro Togliatti was an outspoken critic of the USSR even in the 1950s, and at the conference of communist parties in Moscow in 1969 he alone opposed the Brezhnev theses which sought to justify the Russian invasion of Czechoslovakia and which were accepted even by the Spanish and French parties – the latter without reservations.

Togliatti found an ally for his more nationalist outlook in the Spanish leader Santiago Carrillo, who, after opposing Eurocommunism, was converted and wrote its basic text *Eurocommunism and the State*. The PCI supported the so-called historic compromise in Italy, the alliance of all anti-fascist parties. It approved Italy's membership of the EEC by contrast with the ambivalent PCF, which boycotted the European parliament until 1975 and opposed direct elections to it until 1977. The PCI declared in 1974 that it did not require Italy to leave NATO.

The Italian example carried the Spanish and, more hesitantly, the French parties into a loose Eurocommunist entente but there was little positive substance to it beyond disengagement from the taint of Russian tutelage. Communists in north-western Europe, including France, had next to no prospect of winning power through the ballot box, mainly because of the existence of sizeable socialist parties. In southern Europe they might hope to do better but if they did they would almost certainly be prevented from taking office by inflexibly anti-communist armies.

The Italian political order collapsed with disconcerting abruptness in the years around 1990. The fundamental principle of Italian politics from 1947 had been the exclusion of communists from government. The Christian Democrat Party had ruled, alone or in coalitions of which it was an essential partner, throughout this period and formed the nucleus of a wider governing class which embraced financiers, industrialists, linkmen with their counterparts in the Vatican, the Mafia and other more or less right-wing interests whose common anti-communism and devotion to their several material interests overrode their differences, subordinated the free play of democratic politics and nourished widespread corruption both by the smaller parties, which exacted a price for their part in keeping communists out of office, and by the larger parties, which needed more and more money to keep their allies content and their leaders in a befitting style of living. With the collapse of communist rule in Europe the system's anti-communist lynchpin disappeared. Coincidentally, economic strains, besides threatening the national economy and mood, punctured the political order which was funded by mulcting the public purse. Malpractice which included trafficking by political leaders in the allocation of lucrative public contracts, with the socialist prime minister Bettino Craxi as deeply implicated as Christian Democrat leaders, was so pervasive that the system could not be salvaged for want of sufficiently untainted segments. Courageous action by judges and prosecutors against Mafia bosses was followed by criminal charges against eminent politicians and businessmen. Local and national elections in 1991 reduced the reputable remains of the Christian Democrat Party to insignificance. With thousands of politicians under police investigation, tens of thousands of public servants in fear of prosecution or dismissal, and all the established parties more or less discredited, new parties appeared with promises of radical cleansing of public life and vaguely miraculous cures for a huge public debt which was growing annually by sums equivalent to 10 per cent of GDP. Politics were polarized around an empty centre.

From this complex cataclysm two forces emerged: a new left-wing force whose principal ingredient was the Party of the Democratic Left (formed by the more flexible segments of the old Communist Party) and a right-wing alliance consisting of an old party, a new party and something which was hardly a party at all. The old party was the Movimento Sociale Italiano (MSI), formed in 1946 as a relic of fascism. The party had operated tactfully within the rules of democratic politics, gradually attracted members and votes from other right-wing groups, became a not unimportant minor party and on occasions provided the parliamentary votes needed to keep a Christian Democratic government in office. After nearly half a century its first leader Giorgio Almirante gave way (1987) to Gianfranco Fini who, although ousted temporarily in 1990–93, recovered power in time for the elections in 1994, in which year the party changed its name to Alleanza Nazionale (AN). Fini represented the traditional conservative bulk of a party which also had a radical revolutionary wing. Besides Roman Catholic causes common to many right-wing parties in Europe, the AN–MSI preserved such fascist notions as the corporatist state, Italy's destiny as a Mediterranean power and its claims to territories along the eastern shores of the Adriatic. It was stronger in the south and centre than in the north.

By contrast, the newly created Northern League had little support in south or centre. The League was an amalgam of lesser Leagues, beginning with the Venetian League founded in 1983. It embodied the conservatism of small businesses against the over-mighty conglomerate and the over-intrusive state. It regarded the centre and Rome as a land of corrupt drones and the south as a land of delinquent layabouts and advocated regional devolution in a loosely federated Italy. Its leaders in 1994 were Umberto Bossi and Gianfranco Miglio, leaders of the Lombard League which had overtaken the Venetian League as the voice of northern Italy. To these two parties were added Forza Italia and Silvio Berlusconi, the first little more than a slogan and the second one of Italy's most successful businessmen, president of Fininvest, the holding company of his own creation, whose assets included much of Italy's press and television. Berlusconi's reasons for entering politics on the right (he had earlier supported and befriended politicians of the left) included the demise of the Christian Democrat Party and his wish to step into its shoes, the need to defend his personal business empire (particularly his interests in the media) from any attempt to regulate it, alarm at the country's crumbling economy and political order and prospects of communist electoral victories, and the need for some new party to bridge the gap between the AN–MSI and the Northern League. With these and other parties of the right Berlusconi created in January 1994 the League for Freedom (Polo della Libertà) which won the elections two months later. His political programme was more rhetorical than precise. It promised to liberate private enterprise, diminish government, reduce government expenditure, create a million new jobs and introduce a presidential rather than a parliamentary democracy; but its principal appeal was its novelty.

Berlusconi and his allies won 366 of the 630 seats in the national assembly with 43 per cent of the votes cast; left-wing parties won 213 seats with 34 per cent; centre groups a mere 46 seats. This was victory for the right but not obviously for political cleansing. With Forza Italia emerging as the largest single party in parliament, Berlusconi became prime minister with embarrassingly large promises of lower taxes, more jobs and clean government. To the power which he already had through his newspapers and television he added the endorsement of the ballot box. How far he regarded these two sources of power as compatible was unclear, a question all the more pressing since Forza Italia alone had no majority in the assembly, where it was dependent on the expressly regional interests of the Northern League and the disquieting prejudices of the semi-fascist AN–MSI. As a successful tycoon, Berlusconi was European and internationalist in his outlook but that of his allies was either indifferent to these wider issues or the reverse of his. Berlusconi presented himself as a break with an unsavoury past but his own links with that past were not negligible. The most obvious difference between Forza Italia and the Christian Democrats was the former's weaker links with the Vatican and the Italian ecclesiastical hierarchy – links retained by the rump of the Christian Democrats, renamed Partito Popolare.

Berlusconi's promises all came to nought. He himself came under investigation for corruption (and was convicted in 1998 of bribery); he raised taxes and introduced a budget which was condemned by the World Bank and other international bodies for failing to tackle a frightening deficit; and he refused to relinquish control over his newspaper and television empire. (Berlusconi, it could be said, understood the power politics of his own time as had Pompey the Great 2,000 years earlier. Pompey risked forfeiting the consulship in Rome rather than lay down the command of his army. Berlusconi risked the premiership rather than divest himself of the power which his media empire gave him.) His term in office lasted seven months, less than the average of the 50 ministries which preceded his from the end of the Second World War. He was forced to resign when the Northern League defected from his coalition. His demands for a dissolution of the assembly and fresh elections (in which he hoped to win more seats) were denied by President Oscar Scalfaro, who found in Lamberto Dini a stop-gap prime minister of unobtrusive competence who was appointed at the end of 1994 and stopped the gap for a whole year. Dini was succeeded by Romano Prodi, who served (with interruptions) until 2008 when his patchwork administration disintegrated and Berlusconi returned to power with control of both chambers of parliament but uncomfortably dependent on Umberto Bossi's separatist Northern League which had scant regard for the interests of southern Italy and still less for the EU but was the second strongest group within Berlusconi's coalition.

At the eastern end of the Mediterranean the western alliance secured a lodgement in Turkey and Greece which was strategically important but also embarrassing because of the mutual hostility of these two countries. The fighting against Italians and Germans in *Greece* in the Second World War was sharp but short. The ensuing occupation was exceptionally severe. The mainly agricultural economy was devastated; bridges and railway stock were almost totally destroyed; three-quarters of Greek shipping was lost; starvation in Athens was severer than almost anywhere in Europe. The war engendered a civil war which outlasted the wider war by several years and, following atrocities on both sides, seared the Greek consciousness for a couple of generations. A communist attempt to seize power in 1944 was foiled by British troops. The eventual defeat of the communists in 1949 was effected with American aid which included the first use of napalm. However welcome the outcome, Greeks resented British insistence on the restoration of the monarchy and the American support for the political right which characterized the next 50 years. The royal line, inaugurated by a Danish prince nearly 100 years earlier, was not only tainted with acquiescence in the prewar dictatorship of General Joannis Metaxas but was suspected of a willingness to serve the interests of one foreign power or another. King George II returned to Athens after the war in much the same way as Louis XVIII returned to Paris in 1814 – in the baggage train of foreigners – and although his brother Paul, who succeeded him in 1947, was accepted as a symbol of anti-communist unity so long as a plausible communist threat lasted, the defeat of the communists left him vulnerable to charges of being the tool of the Americans and the Greek right. That defeat was secured by the Yugoslav secession from the Stalinist bloc (Tito needed to mend his fences with the United States) and by the creation of a large, well-equipped and well-trained Greek army with rigorously selected right-wing officers. The continuance of the civil war to the end of the 1940s was an economic and social disaster, partially relieved by American aid, and the major determinant of Greek foreign policy. Greece joined NATO in 1952, an ally of the United States against eastern Europe and the USSR but an uncomfortable partner since the abiding concern of Greek policy was hostility not to the USSR but to Turkey, a valued friend of the United States.

After the civil war and a short period of political instability the conservative governments of Field Marshal Alexander Papagos and Constantine Karamanlis (1952–63) provided the beginnings of economic recovery. Under Karamanlis, who had an unprecedented run of eight years in office, the currency was rescued and tourism, which became a bonanza with the invention of the package holiday, was skilfully developed; but modernization was interpreted as industrialization which, in competition with other industrial countries, had disappointing results and widened the gap between the cities and a neglected countryside. A scarcely disguised Communist Party re-entered the political arena but never got more than 15 per cent of the vote, except in the special circumstances of 1958 when its 25 per cent included a big protest vote against the government's handling of the Cyprus crisis. The centre was fragmented by personal jealousies and remained out of office until, in 1963 and under George Papandreou's leadership, it won more seats in parliament than any other party. During the next few years Papandreou initiated a programme of social improvement, notably in education and health, but he soon got into trouble with the palace, where since Paul's death his young and badly advised son Constantine now reigned, and he aroused the hostility of the class of persons who equate all social reform with communism. This hostility was accentuated by the activities of the prime minister's son Andreas, an economist who had been induced by Karamanlis to exchange an American professorship for a non-party professional post in Athens. Andreas Papandreou was a social democrat of the type found in Scandinavia or the left wing of the American Democratic Party (he had been an active campaigner for Hubert Humphrey); his incursion into Greek politics irritated other leaders more particularly because the Centre Union led by his father was not a left-wing party like the British Labour Party so much as a centre party like the French Radical Socialists. He became a useful bogey for the right, which began to raise the cry that the country was in danger from communism, and in 1965 he was alleged to have become implicated with a left-wing secret society in the army called Aspida – a society which can hardly have been very left-wing if it existed in the Greek army.

So long as king and prime minister worked in harmony there was little chance of a coup, but after an initial amicability these two fell out over the control of the armed forces. The king regarded this control as part of his royal prerogative, to be exercised through a minister of defence acceptable to him. Papandreou, while retaining the palace's man in the post, believed on the contrary that the armed forced should be subordinate to civil control exercised through the prime minister and cabinet. The clash came when Papandreou sought to change the chief of staff and the minister of defence refused to dismiss him or to accept his own dismissal from the government. Papandreou decided to solve the tangle by becoming his own minister of defence but the king refused to appoint him and dismissed him from the premiership. The king had meanwhile been intriguing with some of Papandreou's party colleagues, who were induced to abandon him and so bring the government down in parliament. There followed a period of squalid manoeuvres accompanied by minor demonstrations in the streets and a few strikes, until the moderate elements of both the right and the centre came together to put an end to an unedifying spectacle which had been started by the king's unconstitutional behaviour. But the extremists on the right, assuming, as did most people, that the Centre Union would win the next election, resolved that it should not take place.

This was the immediate cause of the coup of April 1967 by a small group of army officers, a grade below the top ranks and outside the upper crust which had normally monopolized these grades, who owed their advancement to the expansion of the army after the Second World War. They were fanatical, if unintelligent, anti-communist salvationists who saw politics as a simple and fierce contest between good and evil. Their coup was not a conservative one but a radical one, although it had at the start the acquiescence and support of traditional conservatives. Whether the coup also had American support is doubtful. American interference in Greek affairs was undoubted and so was American suspicion of the centre politicians who were ousted by the coup, but of the variety of possible coups under more or less open discussion the Americans may be presumed to have preferred something more traditional than the one which in fact occurred. Colonels Papadopoulos and Makarezos and Brigadier Pattakos were neither particularly eminent in the service nor particularly appealing to the public. What is certain, however, is that the Americans were widely assumed to have had a hand in the plot and behaved afterwards as though they had.

After the coup little was heard of the communist threat which was supposed to justify it, and the seizure of the papers of the left-wing party failed to produce any evidence in support. The coup was a seizure of power by a handful of military bigots. At the end of the year the king attempted a counter-coup which was peculiarly incompetent and after a few hours he fled to Rome. The new regime dismantled the apparatus of the state, purged the armed forces and the Church, annulled Papandreou's social reforms, browbeat the judiciary and established strict control over the press and broadcasting. In addition it resorted to torture and brutality on a large scale and, as an international commission of lawyers subsequently found, as a deliberate instrument of policy. Torture by the police was not unknown in Greece but the extent to which it was practised by the regime appalled the outside world when the facts became inescapable. As a result charges brought against Greece in the Council of Europe by the Dutch and Scandinavian governments for breaches of democratic safeguards were amended to more serious charges under the European Convention of Human Rights and Greece was forced to leave the Council in order to escape suspension from it. The American government, however, viewed these proceedings with no more than embarrassment and after a brief period of indecision gave the regime its accolade in the shape of arms supplies. Greece as a *place d'armes* for NATO seemed more important than Greece as a conforming member of the society of free and democratic nations which NATO was proclaimed to be.

The Greek dictatorship, which began as a triumvirate of colonels, was modified in 1971 when two of them were eliminated by the third. In 1973, following a mutiny in the navy, the monarchy was abolished, and later in that year the army transferred effective power to Brigadier Dimitrios Ioannides, the chief of the military police. The funeral of George Papandreou earlier in the year had provided the occasion for a portentously large demonstration in Athens and students in particular harassed it with an indignant boldness which cost them dear. The regime collapsed in 1974 under the weight of its bungling in Cyprus, where it tried to get rid of Archbishop Makarios and annex the island in the belief that the Americans would prevent Turkey from interfering. The Americans had twice before blocked a Turkish invasion but this time they did not. Makarios escaped, the Turks invaded and the Greek government, having brought upon itself a confrontation with Turkey, ordered a general mobilization for which no preparations had been made. Karamanlis, who had been living in exile in Paris, returned to form a democratic coalition government and consolidated his position by winning for his party a clear majority over all others. The electorate voted by two to one to abolish the monarchy.

Karamanlis knew that Greece needed friends: he renewed the campaign to join the EEC and visited Balkan and other communist capitals. He was anxious to defuse conflicts with Turkey which had become many and acute. He had exceptionally wide popular support and a rare overall majority in parliament. Elections in 1977 reduced but did not destroy this majority and when he ascended to the presidency in 1980 his colleague, George Rallis, moved smoothly into the premiership.

The most pressing of the Greco-Turkish quarrels lay in Cyprus (see Note C at the end of this part) but it was not the only one. There was also a complex of disputes over the Aegean. At the time of the Turkish invasion of Cyprus Greece fortified islands in the eastern Aegean which had been demilitarized by the treaties of Lausanne (1923) and Paris (1947). There were also disputes over territorial waters, the continental shelf and air traffic control.

Territorial waters – that is to say, the reach of sovereignty beyond the water's edge – created no troubles so long as both sides observed, as they did, the traditional six-mile limit. On this basis Greece held sovereignty over 35 per cent of the Aegean, Turkey over less than 10 per cent. If, however, the limit were stretched to 12 miles, the area of Greek sovereignty would be almost doubled, the Turkish would be enlarged only slightly; the points of direct contact between international and Turkish waters would be drastically reduced; and Turkish vessels would be obliged to take passage through Greek waters or stay at home. The international community had not endorsed a 12-mile limit for territorial waters but it moved in that direction when the first international conference on the law of the sea (1958) recommended that for certain purposes (customs, immigration and health control) national jurisdiction be extended from 6 to 12 miles. Neither Greece nor Turkey signed the convention drafted by the conference, but the trend disturbed the Turks.

The continental shelf, a postwar concept introduced into international law by the United States, raised questions about the right to exploit, and the proprietorship of, the seabed beyond the limits of territorial waters. Rights in the shelf carried with them no rights in the waters or the airspace above it. The Geneva Convention, elaborated by the 1958 conference and signed by Greece but not Turkey, defined the debatable area as the seabed beyond territorial waters if no deeper than 200 metres or capable of being exploited for the extraction of minerals. It provided that islands should confer on their sovereign owners the same rights – and Greece had over 2,000 islands in the Aegean. Exploitation of rights in the shelf was, however, to be subject to freedom of navigation, fishing and scientific research. Where two sovereign states confronted each other in such a way as to create overlapping shelves, the median line should normally constitute their submarine frontier. In the disputes over the Aegean Greece maintained that this convention, being declaratory of international law, was legally unalterable and so not politically negotiable. Greece had some support for this contention in decisions of the

International Court of Justice and also for the even more highly contested assertion that islands had continental shelves of their own. All these contentions were opposed by Turkey.

The issue became acute in 1973 when Turkey published a provocative map of the Aegean continental shelf and granted submarine exploration licences to a parastatal corporation. A few months later it despatched the survey ship *Candarli* into the Aegean with an escort of warships. This move was quickly, although coincidentally, followed by the invasion of Cyprus and a consequent exacerbation of the conflict over air traffic control.

From 1952 air traffic control over the Aegean had been exercised by Greece; Turkish flights had to be notified to Athens and Turkish pilots in the area had to take instructions from Athens. But during the Cyprus crisis Turkey claimed the right to take control over the eastern half of the sea. Greece rejected the claim and declared the Aegean airspace unsafe as a consequence of the conflict. Turkey later extended its claim to cover international as well as Greek and Turkish flights and, in the Greek case, military as well as civilian flights.

The years 1974–75 were a tense period, sporadically lightened by bouts of discussion between Greek and Turkish ministers or lawyers. On both sides the parliamentary opposition was more bellicose than the governments. In February 1976 another Turkish ship, *Sizmik I*, carried out a series of surveys accompanied this time by a single warship only. Nerves began to tingle again, particularly when the Turkish government, under pressure from its own opposition, rejected a Greek proposal formally to renounce force as a way of settling the two countries' disputes. Greek approaches to the Security Council and the International Court provided no alleviation. The Court refused to grant an interim protective order or to accept jurisdiction, while the Security Council passed the buck back to the protagonists with platitudinous exhortations to settle their problems themselves. This was marginally a victory for the Turks, who preferred bilateral political discussions to international intervention, juridical or political. Karamanlis and Ecevit met in 1978 and instituted regular meetings at lower levels at the rate of three or four a year. They served to prevent the situation from getting worse but there was no substantial lifting of the clouds until the military takeover in Turkey in 1980, at which point the new Turkish government made a concession on another front.

In protest against its allies' inactivity at the time of the Turkish invasion of Cyprus in 1974 Greece had withdrawn from co-operation with NATO. Karamanlis wanted to return to full partnership but Turkey under civilian rule tried to set conditions, in particular by securing in advance a redefinition of Greek and Turkish responsibilities in the Aegean. These preconditions were dropped by the new Turkish government in return for a Greek promise to exclude no Greco-Turkish issue from future discussions. Greece therefore returned to NATO with all these issues undecided but avowedly negotiable.

The foremost aim of Karamanlis's foreign policy was to join the EEC. His reasons were political and economic. On the political side nearly all Greeks in 1974 found dependence on the United States obnoxious because they believed that the Americans had not only supported the colonels' dictatorship but had helped it to power in the first place. There was no thought, except among communists who had done badly in the elections, of switching to the Russian camp. But in the EEC Karamanlis hoped to find friends against Turkey and a barrier against another lapse into dictatorship in Greece. Economically too Greece needed the EEC. The dictatorship had reversed the favourable economic performance of the 1960s when prices in Greece had been remarkably stable and the booming economy of Germany had provided some relief for Greece's chronic state of economic overpopulation. The dictators, anxious to win support at home, had distributed favours to various classes. In order to do this they had inflated the money supply with the result that the lucky favourites had stimulated an import boom which had seriously upset the balance of payments and produced heavy short-term foreign debts. Inflation reached an acknowledged 35 per cent and was certainly higher.

Greece, as a predominantly agricultural country, faced a basic problem which was politically insoluble without the goad of foreign pressures such as the EEC might provide. Greek agriculture employed 40 per cent of the working population but contributed only 16 per cent of GNP. (By the date of entry to the EEC these figures had changed little: agriculture still provided work for 32 per cent of workers and contributed 14 per cent to GNP.) The land was owned in small and often separate parcels (the national average was about 12 acres), Greek convention and testamentary law promoted fragmentation, and the consequent inefficiency drove peasant proprietors into the towns, whence they neglected their holdings either through absenteeism or because of the family feuds which were a common consequence of the division of property enforced by law. The produce of the land went primarily to the rich foreign markets of western Europe; the domestic market got what was left over and, since demand exceeded supply, the Greek consumer had to pay high prices. The trade, foreign and domestic, was in the hands of middlemen who made their profits not only in exports but also at home, since they bought the whole of a farmer's crop early in the year before domestic prices had begun to rise and sold it (after satisfying export markets) on a rising market. In order to appease the farmers, who were a substantial proportion of the electorate and commanded more sympathy than middlemen, governments disbursed subsidies which condoned the structural shortcomings of the industry and paid for them out of the public purse. While economists believed this to be mismanagement, politicians could see no alternative – unless membership of the EEC were to enforce changes in practices which were incompatible with the EEC's own rules. The Greek case raised wider issues for the EEC's existing members. Apart from Italy (a founder member) Greece was the first Mediterranean country to join and its fragile agricultural economy caused misgivings: these were, however, offset by the desire not to give the Community the air of a rich man's club. Additionally, Greece's admission, with Turkey's assumed to follow soon afterwards, presented the Community with the prospect of conflict between two members which the Community had little power to resolve. The preliminaries to Greek admission were interrupted by the military coup of 1967 but were resumed when Greece was restored to democracy in 1974. The Greek cause was forcefully promoted by France and in 1979 a treaty of accession was signed and Greece became a full member in 1981. Andreas Papandreou's socialist PASOK and the communists boycotted the parliamentary debate on the ratification of the treaty and opposed membership of the EEC, mainly on the grounds that it would inhibit the development of Greek industry and intensify the parasitic relationship of the Greek on the European economy, but when Papandreou came to power later in that year he made no move to annul Greek membership. In the event the economic consequences of joining the EC were disappointing: a big boost for fruit-growers (curtailed after Spain and Portugal joined too) and substantial financial help which failed, however, to prime industrial reorganization, attract foreign investment or alleviate Greece's severe trade and payments deficits.

In 1981 the conservative New Democracy party lost power to PASOK as a consequence of an overwhelming desire for change and of the personality of Andreas Papandreou who, besides being an eminent economist, had all the trappings (and many of the defects) of a commanding pasha. He understood that Greece was not a modern industrial state nor capable of becoming one but a poor country half-way between the wealthy west and a Third World dependent on richer countries. He was aggressively anti-American and promised to close American bases in Greece (but did not). His party had a social programme which amounted to the beginnings of a welfare state, which he proposed to finance by making people pay their taxes and by pruning expenditure on public administration. He introduced sensible and moderate social reforms and had some modest and temporary success in reducing inflation and the deficit on external account. But he did not tackle Greece's cumbrously over-centralized and inefficient government machinery, his rule was autocratic and unpredictable, his social policies were fiercely attacked by the Church and the moneyed classes, and this accumulation of obstacles destroyed his government when, in addition, he was assailed by public and private scandals. These scandals, economic failure and its leader's authoritarian handling of a mediocre cabinet, caused the collapse of the PASOK government in 1988.

In external affairs Papandreou followed the example of Karamanlis in seeking better relations with Greece's Balkan neighbours but not at first with Turkey. Karamanlis had cultivated Greece's traditional friendship with Yugoslavia without, however, going as far as a formal pact and had tried tentatively to promote some form of Balkan entente. He received Zhivkov in Corfu in 1979 and later in that year Greece, Yugoslavia, Bulgaria and Romania all attended a conference on communications in the Turkish capital. Karamanlis became the first Greek prime minister to visit Moscow since 1917 and the first ever to visit Beijing. Papandreou improved relations with Albania but allowed relations with Turkey to rise to nearly boiling point in 1987 over oil exploration in the Aegean. In 1988 the Turkish prime minister made an unprecedented visit to Athens and more temperate relations prevailed.

Papandreou's successor Constantine Mitsotakis had little room for manoeuvre. His victory in 1988 was not decisive, he was forced into alliance with incompatible parties united only in their dislike of PASOK, he secured a (narrow) majority only in 1990 and he was plagued by economic crisis – the highest rate of inflation in the EC, a debt approaching 150 per cent of GDP, failure to meet the conditions prescribed for aid from the IMF and serious strikes against his attempts to tackle overmanning in the public sector. The disintegration of Yugoslavia, the revival of the Macedonian question and the opening of the Greek frontier with Albania (which had been sealed with wire fences by the latter's communist rulers) turned the Balkans into quicksands where it was difficult for Greece not to put its feet wrong. In spite of the brutal behaviour of the Bosnian Serbs, Mitsotakis adhered to Greece's old friendship with Serbia (he later visited Belgrade at the height of the Kosovo crisis to affirm Greek sympathy with the Serbian government) and he also cultivated its other old friendship with Romania in spite of the fact that Iliescu was hardly less of a communist than Ceauşescu had been. He staved off international recognition of the Yugoslav Republic of Macedonia as an independent state under the name of Macedonia but at the cost of adding to the nationalist emotions already too plentiful in the Balkans. Refugees from Albania were at first charitably received by Greeks; they were also welcome for their willingness to do dirty and ill-paid jobs. But as their numbers increased so did thieving and hooliganism by some, with the result that they became widely vilified and many were sent back to Albania unceremoniously and indiscriminately. Frontier questions which had been dormant for more than a generation recovered their relevance together with complaints on the Albanian side of aggressively nationalist behaviour by Greek Orthodox churchmen. In 1993 Papandreou got his electoral revenge on Mitsotakis, whose government was accused of ineffectiveness and nepotism and had no plausible plans for curbing double-figure inflation and unemployment approaching 10 per cent of the workforce, but Papandreou did not long survive this last victory and after his resignation PASOK chose as his successor Costas Simitis. Simitis, whose unexciting style provided a welcome contrast to the unproductive polemics of the recent past, was an unobtrusive modernizer intent on restructuring the Greek economy, joining the EMU and improving relations with Turkey, the EU and the United States.

The end of the Cold War affected Greece profoundly. Greece had been attached to western Europe for the convenience of NATO and cut off therefore from the Balkan region to which geographically it belonged. Karamanlis had strengthened this attachment by taking Greece into the EC in 1981 but this political strategy misfired when Greece became embarrassingly expensive to the EC as well as politically disruptive on account of its hostility with Turkey (and, if less so, its sympathies with Serbia). It became the most isolated country in Europe and correspondingly disorientated and even paranoid. Like Finland and Portugal, it was a lesser nation state but, unlike these two, it lacked regional support. And, unlike Turkey, it had nowhere to go except the EU.

Simitis recognized this fact at least partially. He put all Greece's eggs in the EU basket. He devalued the drachma by 14 per cent in order to join the ERM in 1998 and the EMU with its single currency in 2001. This policy entailed strict monetary measures which were bound to aggravate unemployment, a painful assault on the swollen bureaucracy and the rigid labour market, severe changes in social security and costly development of the infrastructure in order to turn Thessalonica and Piraeus into major ports for the commerce between the rest of Europe and points east – an aim which required also equable political relations with Greece's neighbours, particularly Turkey (which might in an extreme case throttle Thessalonica) and Macedonia and Serbia lying between northern Greece and central Europe. More widely, it entailed recognition of a fact which neither Greece nor Turkey had adequately (if at all) acknowledged for 50 years: that the admission of these two countries to international associations – Truman aid, NATO and the EU – demanded in return the resolution of the quarrels which divided and engrossed them. In 1997, when the government of Cyprus bought from Russia 300 missiles with a range of 1,600 km, Turkey vowed to destroy them. Greece declared this response to be an act of war. They did not come and at the end of the century Greece adopted a more conciliatory mood, which Turkey reciprocated. Greece, which had looked to the EU to redress pro-Turkish inclinations in the United States and the UN, had made itself unpopular with its European partners and become the more aware of the folly of perpetual quarrels with its much stronger neighbour – whatever the rights or wrongs of the case. Elections in 2004 were won by a landslide by the right (Costas Karaminlis), and in 2007 by a whisker.

At the other end of the Mediterranean it had become axiomatic to suppose that nothing much would happen until Franco died. *Spain* had emerged from the Second World War in an ambiguous position. Franco had wanted to join forces with Germany and Italy but had not done so except to the extent of sending a token force to fight with the Germans against the Soviet Union. His price for closer co-operation, which Hitler refused to pay, was a free hand in creating a new Spanish empire in north-west Africa. Spain was denied membership of the UN in 1945 but the Cold War transformed Franco from a quasi-fascist dictator into a staunchly anti-communist associate of the NATO alliance. American bases were established in Spain under agreements made in 1953. Franco's conservative and paternalistic Catholic nationalism included an attempt to make Spain economically self-sufficient. He brought the country near to economic collapse in the late 1950s but was persuaded against his instincts to sanction a more international economic policy to Spain's considerable profit – and his own, since he was given the credit for economic recovery and died in office and in his bed in 1975. His death made Spain a kingdom in fact as well as name. Franco had pronounced

Spain a kingdom in 1947 but he had no liking for the last king's son, Don Juan, and no intention of relinquishing his own quasi-monarchical control. He therefore ignored Alfonso XIII's act of abdication in favour of Don Juan and gradually prepared the latter's son Don Juan Carlos for the succession. Juan Carlos played an equivocal role in an equivocal position, so that on Franco's death his character and political ideas were something of a mystery. His first government was a mixture of Francoists and democrats but within a year he appointed as prime minister the 47-year-old Adolfo Suarez, an able politician who fitted no precise faction. This was a skilful move which alarmed conservatives and the army without giving them distinct cause for revolt and pleased moderate groups on the right and the left which believed that Spain needed change. The appointment of Suarez signified the king's intention to accelerate change and also to be seen as a monarch capable of picking his own man. He was fortified by the approval of the Cortes and a referendum in favour of substantial constitutional changes. Within two years of Franco's death the king and Suarez were strong enough to face parliamentary elections with confidence.

Franco's modernization had been ill-regulated and careless of the poorer classes and the new regime inherited a distorted economy. It also inherited the perennial problem of regional discontent, particularly in Catalonia and among the Basques. The Socialist and Communist parties were legalized, the latter in spite of American and military pressures to the contrary. The socialists, led by Felipe Gonzalez, proved the stronger of the two. The right was torn between those who wanted a new cleansed Christian Democratic Party and those who wanted a broader party including as many old Francoists as possible. In the first popular test in 1977 the communists and the right fared badly and Suarez's centre-right triumphed. In further elections in 1979 the right was routed, the communists staged a small recovery and the voters opted for two broad centre groups, giving Suarez a slight advantage over Gonzalez. But Suarez's handling of economic affairs was tentative and of the Basque separatists insensitive and indecisive (see Note B at the end of this part).

In 1981 the constitutional and democratic monarchy sponsored by the king was challenged by an army coup. The army was dominated by officers with archaic and anti-democratic ideas. They engaged in sporadic plots which, although ludicrous, were also dangerous until an overt but incompetent attempt to overthrow the regime, which included a spectacular assault on the Cortes, forced the king to disavow its leaders and confront the army as a whole with a choice between himself and their Francoist predilections. Suarez, however, did not survive nor did his centre-right bloc. He resigned and was succeeded by Leopoldo Calvo Sotelo, but at the end of 1982 fresh elections brought Gonzalez to power. His supporters included many who wanted Spain to leave NATO (which it had just joined) and he promised to hold a referendum on the question: he subsequently declared himself in favour of continued membership and carried the day in a referendum, although Spain then insisted on the removal of American aircraft by 1992 (Italy agreed to receive them). The Spanish economy flourished within the EC, enjoying wider markets, foreign investment, a share in the world boom and the benefits of relatively cheap labour, but the boom brought its familiar accompaniment of speculation and corruption. In the 1990s Gonzalez was weakened by rising unemployment and dissension in his own party, including a split which occasioned the resignation of his deputy, Alfonso Guerra. Having narrowly won a majority in 1986, he lost it after by-elections in 1990 and called a general election in 1993 in an attempt to revive his authority. He survived in office but only with the support of a small right-wing Catalan party. The conflict with Britain over Gibraltar was unfrozen to the extent that the frontier, recently closed, was reopened and the British government, while repeating its commitment to honour the wishes of the Gibraltarians, agreed that sovereignty be an item in future discussions. Talks in 1987 preserved goodwill without altering either party's stance. Gonzalez lost office in 1996. The conservative José Maria Aznar formed a government with the support of Catalans and Basques and kept his office by enlarging their autonomous powers.

Spain was distinctive in a number of ways. It was the main heir to Europe's clash with Islam but also more knowledgeable about the Arab world and sympathetic to it. It was as self-consciously Roman Catholic as, for example, Poland or Ireland and home to the largest Roman Catholic order founded in Europe since the Renaissance but it was not uncomfortably militant and the political influence of the church – and of the army – was as constrained as at any time since the eighteenth century. It was also the country where the word 'liberal' entered the European political vocabulary. Restored to democracy in 1975, Spain tackled its disgruntled provinces – Catalans and Basques – with enough generosity to avoid the gruesome disintegration of Yugoslavia and the crude separation of Italy's Northern League (p. 210). Its post-Franco politics were a model of democratic correctness. The left made way for Jose Maria Aznar's rightish coalition which in turn ceded power to the left when Aznar's support for Bush's invasion of Iraq cost him votes. After re-elections in 2008 this leftish government had a cabinet with more women than men.

Change in Spain was preceded by change in *Portugal* when, in April 1974, a group of middling and junior army officers overthrew the dictatorship and installed a junta of seven under the presidency of General Antonio de Spinola, a returned and critical African governor. A tussle for power followed within the dominant Armed Forces Movement and between the political parties which took shape after the coup. General Spinola resigned in September and fled the country in the following March after becoming involved in an unsuccessful anti-communist coup. A communist bid for power failed. Elections in April 1975 gave the socialists, led by Dr Mario Soares, 38 per cent of the vote and relegated the communists with 12.5 per cent to third place behind the centre-right Popular Democrats (26 per cent). Portugal seemed on many occasions on the brink of civil war. The Armed Forces Movement and the army itself were split, but a coup in favour of the extreme left misfired and senior officers, alarmed by the prospect of anarchy, combined to support a minority socialist government and the installation of the relatively uncommitted General Antonio Ramalho Eanes as chief of staff.

Elections in 1976 gave no party a clear majority, the most successful being the Socialist Party, which won 107 of the 263 seats. In the presidential election which followed General Eanes won 61.5 per cent of the votes distributed among four contenders. Soares formed a minority socialist government which was attacked both from the communist left and by the right representing not only the old regime but also the poor, anti-communist and conservative farmers of the north. Soares resigned at the end of 1977, formed a new coalition but was dismissed in 1978 by the president, who appointed a government of technicians and, when this faltered for lack of a parliamentary base, another under Portugal's first female prime minister Maria de Lurdes Pintassilgo. The president was trying to find a parliamentary coalition or a non-parliamentary alternative which would stem the country's post-revolutionary swing back towards the right, but this swing became more manifest at the end of 1979 when Francisco Sá Carneiro won nearly half the seats in parliament. He became prime minister but found himself at odds with the president who, using his constitutional right to interpret the constitution, blocked a number of measures whereby Sá Carneiro intended to steer the economy back into the paths of free enterprise. President Eanes won a further term of office in 1980. Portuguese politics continued to oscillate between centre-right and centre-left. In 1983 Soares, having failed to win an overall majority, formed a government with the social democrats to his right but this alliance collapsed in 1985 and Soares resigned. He became Portugal's first civilian president for over 60 years, with the conservative Anibal Cavaco Silva as prime minister – an economist who had twice served briefly as a minister under Sá Carneiro and won a landslide victory in 1987 with more than half the votes cast. Minor changes were made to the constitution to expedite the denationalization of industries and the decollectivization of agriculture. In 1991 Soares was re-elected president for five years with convincing popular approval. Poor by western European standards but orderly and enjoying the benefits of EC membership, Portugal shifted leftward in 1995 when the Socialist Party, led by Antonio Guterres, won nearly half the votes, occupying the middle ground between communists or the left and social democrats and the Popular Party on the right. They retained this position in 1999.

CHAPTER 6

Central and eastern Europe

Stalin's empire

As the Ottoman empire receded (see Chapter 9), pieces of it won autonomy or independence, the adjacent Habsburg and Russian empires calculated what they could get out of it and three forces shaped the future: religion – Christianity, mostly of the Orthodox variety and essentially anti-Turkish; nationalism, pitting one emergent state against another; and a romantic megalomania, dreaming of old empires and carefully oblivious of embedded minorities (Greater Greece, Greater Serbia, Greater Albania). Between the two world wars they were pawns where Germany manoeuvred more successfully than other Europeans for trade and influence. After the Second World War they became Soviet satellites (except Greece) and, with central Europe, constituted unwillingly the eastern half of bisected Europe during the Cold War.

The partition of Europe after the Second World War was the consequence of a trend and an accident. The trend was the decline, accentuated by war, of the European nation states. Europe was a continent which had functioned in the form of comparatively small and comparatively strong entities, capable of maintaining separate existences because of the industrial sophistication of some and the addiction of all to the principle of self-determination. Thus the stronger European states existed because they were strong, while the weaker ones existed because it seemed right to the stronger that they should. But with the waning of the strength of the strong, the basic element in the pattern of Europe disappeared and Europeans ceased to be able, for the time being, to maintain truly independent states. The question was what new forms would be imposed by dependence.

The answer to this question was determined by accident, by the fact that the precipitating cause of the war had lain in the centre of the continent – in Germany – so that the course of war meant a convergence of anti-German forces on the centre from the sides. Despite some plans to the contrary, the Anglo-American and the Russian advances into Germany were in substance separate operations which created separate American and Russian dominances to the west and to the east of Germany. Anglo-American sea power modified this pattern by decreeing that Mediterranean Europe as far as the Aegean should fall into the American and not the Russian sphere. This new

Countries belonging to Warsaw Pact. (Albania formally withdrew from the pact in 1968.)
1989-90 Collapse of the Eastern Bloc; Warsaw Pact ceased in 1990; Comecon ceased in 1991.

Czechoslovakia ceased to exist January 1993; new Slovakian and Czech republics came into existence
October 1990. DDR (East Germany) absorbed by the Federal Republic of Germany.

Russia ceded independence to Latvia, Lithuania and Estonia in 1991 – final withdrawal of
Russian troops completed in August 1994.

June 1991: Slovenia and Croatia unilaterally declared independence; Macedonia and Bosnia-Herzegovina
followed; Macedonia seceded September 1991; April 1992: Serbia and Montenegro became
Federal Republic of Yugoslavia.

6.1 Eastern Europe

distribution of power was recognized by Stalin's abandonment of Greece to Churchill, his refusal to pay attention to the Greek communist revolt or help it, and by the subsequent attachment of Greece and Turkey to NATO. At the other end of Europe Finland fell into the Russian sphere not only because of its strategic importance for the defence of Leningrad but because Anglo-American sea power did not overlap Europe round the north as far as it did in the south. Only Germany and Austria were designated common ground and even here the new principle of Russo-American partition prevailed and created in Germany a partition within a partition which assumed crucial and critical significance in world affairs as the focus of the Cold War. In the rest of Europe the Americans and the Russians let each other be.

It has been argued that the division of Europe and the resulting Russian overlordship in eastern Europe were the consequence not of historical accident but of agreement, notably agreement at Yalta by Roosevelt and Churchill to give Stalin a position of power which otherwise he could not have achieved. This argument cannot be sustained. Roosevelt and Churchill conceded at Yalta nothing that it was in their power to withhold. The Russian armies were already in occupation of positions in Europe from which they could not be expelled and Stalin's postwar dominance in eastern Europe derived from his victories and not from any bargain with his allies. The most that Roosevelt and Churchill could do was to try to get Stalin to accept certain rules governing the exercise of the power that was his. This they succeeded in doing by persuading him to endorse a Declaration on Liberated Countries which promised free elections and other democratic practices and liberties. When, later, Stalin ignored the engagements contained in this declaration western governments could do no more than protest. Action was impossible.

Within the Russian sphere Stalin's problem was the nature of Russian control and its mechanisms. He created a satellite empire in which the component states retained their separate juristic identities – separate from each other and from the USSR – but were subjected to Russian purposes by the realities of Russian military power and the modalities of Communist Party and police rule and unequal economic treaties. There was soon little difference between former foes like Hungary, Romania and Bulgaria, and wartime allies like Poland, Czechoslovakia and Yugoslavia. This indifference was manifested at an early stage: in Poland the Lublin Committee (Polish Committee of National Liberation), a communist-dominated group of leaders formed in 1944 from among the Polish resistance and groomed in Moscow, was established in Warsaw as the government of Poland in order to frustrate the London Poles who had conducted the fight against the Germans from exile; in Romania the king was compelled in March 1945 to appoint a government controlled by communists and to cede to the USSR its Moldavian province (which had been part of Russia from 1812 to 1917). In form the defeated enemies were equated with the allies by the conclusion of peace treaties in 1947 and of further treaties between each of them and the USSR during 1948 (with the allies the USSR already had treaties dating from the war years). The peace treaties cost

Hungary Transylvania, which (as in 1920) went to Romania, and a smaller piece of territory awarded to Czechoslovakia; confirmed Romania's loss of Bessarabia and northern Bukovina to the USSR, and southern Bukovina to Bulgaria; and gave the USSR the Petsamo area of Finland and a 50-year lease of the naval base at Porkkala with an access corridor. The treaties of 1948 provided for mutual assistance against Germany and proscribed any alliance by the one signatory which might be construed as directed against the other.

But Stalin aimed at more than formal arrangements and by the end of the 1940s he had, except in Yugoslavia and Finland, transferred the machinery of government into the hands of obedient communists who were not merely conscious of the realities of Russian power but determined, puppet-like, to serve it. This transfer involved the suppression or emasculation of non-communist parties and the elimination from the communist ranks of communists who were more national than Muscovite. This process was successfully achieved in the short run, unsuccessful in the longer run in that it failed to secure for Moscow a trouble-free zone of influence round the USSR's European borders. Yugoslavia rejected Russian dominance in 1948, Poland and Hungary kicked against it in 1956 and Romania led a campaign against it in the mid-1960s. By the 1970s it was in evident decay but still sustainable, even though the use of force – which was its ultimate guarantee – was becoming more a memory and a bluff than a plausible practicability. The advent of Gorbachev triggered collapse in 1989.

In 1946 Yugoslavia, Czechoslovakia, Bulgaria and Albania had communist prime ministers: Tito, Klement Gottwald, G. M. Dimitrov and Enver Hoxha. In Hungary and Romania the post was occupied by Peasant Party leaders, in Poland and Finland by socialists. All these countries had coalition governments, although only the governments in Prague and Helsinki gave the appearance of a real distribution of power. In Finland the communists were left out of a new government formed after elections in July 1948, in which they fared badly. Elsewhere, communist control was intensified during 1947–48, although in Yugoslavia the communist monopoly of power worked against and not for the Russian interest and culminated in June 1948 in the eviction of Yugoslavia from the fraternity of communist states.

Poland's historic struggle against neighbours reached into Polish communism: Rosa Luxemburg disputed Lenin's peasant policy, and the Polish Workers' Party later deprecated Stalin's campaign against Trotsky. The leadership of the Polish party was wiped out in 1937–38 and the party itself was dissolved by the Comintern when Stalin was laying his plans for his pact with the Nazis. It was resuscitated in 1942 and nourished by the hideous behaviour of the Germans in Poland, which caused some revulsion of feeling towards Russians and communists. The discovery in 1943 of the Katyn massacre reminded the Poles that, for them, the choice between Russians and Germans was a hopeless one, but the Germans were at that time the present pest from which the Russians were future liberators. At the beginning of 1944 the Russians entered Poland in pursuit of the Germans and in July they accepted the Curzon Line as Poland's frontier in the east and sanctioned the Lublin Committee, which shortly afterwards became the country's provisional government. In August the people of Warsaw rose against the Germans in the expectation of swift help from the advancing Russians, which, however, was withheld; the victims included many leaders of the resistance, national communists as well as non-communists. The rising, besides being directed against the Germans, was an attempt by the London Poles and their secret army in Poland to establish their authority in Warsaw before the arrival of the Russians.

The looming Polish problem was twofold: what were to be Poland's boundaries and who was to rule? The Russians wished to shift Poland to the west in order to gain territory for themselves in the east and, perhaps, to perpetuate a pro-Russian and anti-German slant by adding German lands in the west to the Polish state; the Russians were also determined to insist on a government which was wholly or preponderantly communist. By the Yalta conference in February 1945 the Russians controlled Poland. The Americans and British disputed Russian plans at length but irresolutely; they recognized the force of Stalin's arguments about the importance of a reliable Poland between the USSR and Germany, they did not regard the Polish question as the most important on the agenda, and they believed that no great harm would come from leaving the composition of the future Polish government vague since they had Stalin's agreement to the broadening of the provisional government and to fair and early elections after the end of the war. Before the Potsdam conference in July the Poles had been put by the Russians in possession of German lands beyond their old western borders and at that conference Churchill's forebodings and remonstrances were uttered in vain. The British and Americans accepted the accomplished fact provided it were called an interim measure which would be reopened upon the negotiation of a peace treaty with Germany.

Stanislaw Mikolayczyk, chief of the Polish government in exile in London and leader of the Polish Peasants' Party, had been added to the provisional government in Warsaw as a deputy prime minister. The other principal figures in the government came from the Lublin group: the communist Boleslaw Bierut as president, the socialist Edward Osobka-Morawski as prime minister and the communist Wladyslaw Gomulka as a deputy prime minister. The promised elections were held in January 1947 to the accompaniment of every conceivable electoral abuse, which failed, however, to conceal the underlying popular strength of the Peasants' Party. This party was said to have won 10 per cent of the vote and 28 of the 444 seats in the parliament but Mikolayczyk felt obliged to seek safety in flight, as did many others. The rump of the Peasants' Party was absorbed into the Democratic Bloc which, created in 1944, embraced the resurrected Workers' Party, the Socialist Party and others and became in 1948 the United Workers' Party. The Americans and the British protested in vain over proceedings which they had no power to rectify. But within the communist leadership the old division between Polish and Muscovite communism, already visible in the days of Rosa Luxemburg, reappeared with Gomulka, now secretary-general of the single party, as leader of a faction which wanted to make communism more Polish, more popular and less subservient to Moscow. The quarrel between Stalin and Tito gave him an occasion to express support for Titoism, as a result of which he was gradually denuded of all his posts and disappeared into the background for the next eight years.

These events coincided with the transformation of the political scene in *Czechoslovakia*. Before the Second World War, the Communist Party of Czechoslovakia was, unlike its neighbours, neither illegal nor underground. It was the second largest political party in the country. It escaped being compromised by the general communist alliance with Hitler in 1939–41 because Czechoslovakia was already occupied by the Germans and its parties banned. It played a patriotic role during the war and emerged after it as the biggest party owing to the proscribing of the collaborationist Agrarian Party. Its leader Klement Gottwald was therefore the natural prime minister. He and his colleagues had operated before the war in a democratic system and they now co-operated with other parties in what was at first a genuine coalition of all anti-fascist groups. The first postwar elections endorsed Gottwald's position by giving the communists 39 per cent of the vote in a free election, the highest percentage. Eduard Beneš, who resumed the presidency after the defeat of Germany, was the principal symbol in central Europe of the wish to conduct a state in accordance with western values and in friendship with the USSR. This formula, if not intrinsically inoperable, was made so by the evident wish of Beneš and his non-communist colleagues to participate in the Marshall Plan which, seemingly, was first sanctioned but on second thoughts negatived by Stalin. Beneš survived for a few months only. In February 1948 the minister of the interior Vaclac Nosek dismissed eight police inspectors in Prague. The cabinet voted to reverse this step but the prime minister supported Nosek, and a deputy foreign minister of the USSR, Valerian Zorin, arrived in Prague. Nosek declined to reinstate the policemen and 11 ministers tendered their resignations. They were the non-communist ministers, minus, however, the socialists who, although they had voted with the majority of the cabinet against Nosek, were reluctant to break their association with the communists in government – despite the fact that three months earlier they had selected a new leader to replace the fellow-travelling Zdenek Fierlinger. Anti-communist demonstrations occurred in Prague. Police were brought into the capital from outside. Amid fears of increasing tumult Beneš tried to restore calm by accepting the 11 resignations. Two ministers were killed by falling from windows, one of them – Jan Masaryk – having perhaps been pushed out. In June Beneš resigned. He was succeeded by Gottwald. The mopping up operations consisted of amalgamating all Czech parties or remains of Czech parties with the Czech Communist Party, and likewise in Slovakia, whereupon the single Slovak party was amalgamated with the single Czech party to make the National Front. Czechoslovakia became a police state. A similar attempt to extend Russian control in Finland in 1948 was dropped when it ran into difficulties. The Prague coup was a significant event in the Cold War because it rekindled fears of 1945 that Russian communism planned to engulf all of Europe.

Concurrently in *Hungary*, the monarchy having been abolished in January 1946 – nearly 30 years after it had ceased to function – a coalition government was formed with the Smallholders and Socialist parties. The leaders of the former, Zoltan Tildy and

Ferenc Nagy, became president and prime minister and it won 56 per cent of the vote in the first postwar election. In the winter of 1946–47 rumours of a plot against the state were put about, trials were staged and the secretary-general of the Smallholders' Party Bela Kovacs was abducted by the Russians. The Americans and British, partners with the Russians in the Control Commission for Hungary, protested but were helpless. In May 1947 the prime minister went to Switzerland to see a doctor and, while he was away, was asked to stay away and resign. A new plot was discovered. Elections in August were patently rigged. Members of non-communist parties fled or were put on trial, their parties were split and partially absorbed, as elsewhere, into a single National Independence Front. Tildy resigned the presidency in July and was succeeded by a complaisant social democrat, Arpad Szakasits.

In *Romania* the Peasant leader Ion Maniu was accused in 1947 of plotting against the state with American and British agents. He and others were tried and condemned, and the Peasant Party was dissolved. In December the king abdicated. In the following February the Social Democrat Party was merged with the Communist Party, and in March this party won 405 of the 414 seats in parliament. But before this election dissension had struck the Communist Party too and one of its veteran leaders Lucretsiu Patrasceanu was dismissed from the government, arrested, expelled from the party and, according to rumour, lodged in the Lubianka prison in Moscow. In *Bulgaria* the leader of the Agrarian Party Nicola Petkov was arrested with others in 1947 and executed. The Fatherland Front, product of the usual socialist–communist merger, appeared in the next year.

During this period of regimentation Moscow's central purpose was to refashion each satellite in accordance with a general pattern and to attach each of them to the USSR by all means short of incorporation. But there was to be no incorporation. The new fashioned states were to be People's Democracies, not Soviet Republics. Talk of incorporation was dowsed by Moscow, which made it clear that a People's Democracy was different from a Soviet Republic. Communist enthusiasts with visions of admission to an extended Soviet commonwealth were disabused. The reasons for his policy may be found in Stalin's essentially cautious nature; or in his realization that these areas would, if fully absorbed, cease to be a buffer zone; or in the inability of the war-ravaged USSR to make radical changes in its structure in the mid-1940s; or in the knowledge that some of the satellites had enjoyed and expected a higher standard of living and of public administration than the USSR could provide; or in Stalin's desire to avoid unnecessary provocation of the western powers and to hoodwink them by getting the substance of empire without making constitutional changes which they would not stomach.

Stalin prevented the satellites from making political associations among themselves. Everybody visited everybody and piled up bilateral treaties of friendship and mutual assistance, but schemes of a more radical kind withered. Various such schemes were in the air immediately after the end of the war. Czechoslovak minds reverted to the Little Entente with Yugoslavia and Romania; and Hungary, whose relations with

Czechoslovakia were marred by problems of exchanges of population, riposted in some alarm with a plan for a Danubian confederation. (A Danubian conference at Belgrade in 1948 left the Russians in effective control of half the river. The Americans, British and French, outvoted at every turn, protested that the convention of 1921 remained in force in the absence of a universally accepted substitute.) Downstream, the notion of a South Slav federation flourished for a while and produced some talk of a Romanian–Hungarian counterweight. The South Slav federation was the least unlikely of these federative ideas, if only because it was sponsored by two leaders of the first eminence, Tito and Dimitrov, but their plans became too grandiose for Moscow's liking and a Yugoslav–Bulgarian union looked uncommonly like a takeover of Bulgaria by Yugoslavia: the chief city of such a union would be Belgrade not Sofia. In 1947 Tito told the Bulgarians publicly that he looked forward to a monolithic entity of free Balkan peoples and Dimitrov, visiting Yugoslavia to sign four pacts, secretly ceded Pirin Macedonia to the Yugoslav Macedonian Republic. Traicho Kostov, deputy prime minister of Bulgaria, spoke of a union of all South Slavs in the near future, and Dimitrov spoke in the Romanian capital of a customs union leading to a federation which would include not only the South Slavs but also the North Slavs (excluding those in the USSR) and Hungary, Romania, Albania and Greece. At this point Moscow intervened, summoned Yugoslav and Bulgarian leaders and told them that Romania must be left out of their plans, although Albania might later be added to a Yugoslav–Bulgarian state. The Yugoslavs were also told to drop plans for sending troops into Albania. No union of any kind was effected. Dimitrov died in Moscow in 1949, a year after Yugoslavia was expelled from the communist bloc.

Tito had irritated Stalin by his anti-western policies in Trieste and Greece at the end of the war when Stalin was still being comparatively amiable to his wartime allies. These were minor matters but Tito's vision of a Balkan federation under Yugoslav control was more indigestible and was followed by Tito's insistence that Yugoslavia was not only separate from the USSR but different and that communist doctrine and practice were not so rigid as to be unable to take account of the differences. Stalin decided to get rid of Tito by displacing him with one of his subordinates (Andriye Hebrang or Sreten Zujovic) and so secure in Yugoslavia a regime as obedient as any other in eastern Europe. He was not intent on casting off Yugoslavia but on casting out Tito, and the harsh retribution inflicted by Tito on Stalinists (particularly in Serbia) after the breach suggests that the struggle within the Yugoslav party was acute and Tito's victory a narrow one. The dispute ranged over such topics as the proper organization of a communist state, the role of the Communist Party, agrarian policies, Yugoslavia's laxity in liquidating capitalism and the person of the Yugoslav foreign minister Vladimir Velebit, whom the Russians accused of being a British agent. Friction was increased by the presence in Yugoslavia of Russian civilian and military advisers who seemed to the Yugoslavs to represent a Russian claim to superiority and to be paid too much; Russian attempts to put pressure on the Yugoslavs included threats to withdraw these experts.

Throughout the correspondence the Yugoslavs were evidently anxious to avoid a breach, an attitude which may have strengthened the Russian resolve to exact admissions of error on the points in dispute. But the outcome was a Yugoslav refusal to accept the status of pupil and in June the breach was made public by the eviction of Yugoslavia from the Cominform, the international association of communist parties which had been formed in the previous September to ensure ideological conformity.

Tito was a convinced communist but not an obsequious one. He had envisaged the adherence of a Yugoslav communist republic to the Soviet Union but he had also in his younger days been disturbed by the Russian purges of the 1930s, had been shaken by the Russo-German pact of 1939 and had had experience of Stalin's attitude to lesser communist leaders. In 1948 he abandoned the Stalinist mode of international communism out of national and personal pride; his national roots distinguished him from communist leaders who had lived longer in the USSR than in their native countries, and his successful struggles against the Germans had given him self-confidence and a popular following. He was fortunate in that Yugoslavia had no frontier with the USSR and that western aid enabled him to parry communist economic blockade. Yugoslavia became an international anomaly, a communist state dependent on American and other western aid, an ally of Greece and Turkey in the Balkan pact of 1953 and then a protagonist with Nehru and Nasser of neutralism and non-alignment. The Yugoslav secession entailed diplomatic and economic breaches with the Soviet satellites, and shifts in Yugoslavia's relations with its non-communist neighbours. It contributed to the defeat of the communist rebellion in Greece and the settlement by partition in 1954 of the problems of Trieste (Italy finally renounced its claim to the whole Free Territory in 1975). It dispelled the myth that a communist government not subservient to Moscow was a contradiction in terms. It promoted a series of witch-hunts in the satellite bloc, where the Russians proceeded to eliminate communists who might be sympathetic to Tito or tempted to follow in his footsteps.

The most spectacular consequence of the breach was the trial of Laszlo Rajk in Hungary. He and other Hungarian communists were brought to trial on a compendium of charges, to which they confessed and which included spying for the pre-war Horthy regime, for the Nazi Gestapo, for the United States and Britain and for Tito. The trial was an anti-Tito demonstration, all the more forceful in that it ended with the execution of the accused. It established Matyas Rakosi as Stalin's man in Hungary. In Bulgaria the veteran communist Traicho Kostov was expelled from the party, arrested and, along with others, tried and executed. The charges ranged from Trotskyism to Titoism; their essence was conspiracy against the state. In Albania Koci Xoxe, who had favoured a union with Yugoslavia, was eliminated by his anti-Yugoslav rival Enver Hoxha (who survived an inept Anglo-American attempt to unseat him in 1949 and a Russian coup after a quarrel with Khrushchev in 1960, evicted his erstwhile Chinese friends in 1978 and died in 1985). In Poland Gomulka lost his remaining badge of respectability by being expelled, with others, from the central committee of the party after accusations of collaboration with the Pilsudski dictatorship and the Gestapo and of nationalism and deviationism. He was not, however, put on trial. Moscow preferred to strengthen its position in the most important of the satellites by sending the Soviet marshal Konstanty Rokossovsky to Warsaw, where he became a Polish citizen and minister of defence. In Czechoslovakia Tito's secession and the Rajk trial were followed by a purge of suspected pro-Titoists and of communists who had spent the war years in London. The victims included the foreign minister Vladimir Clementis, who resigned in March 1950 but was not made to stand trial. At the end of 1951 communists of the wartime Moscow group, including the party secretary Rudolf Slansky, were put on trial in proceedings which had a distinct anti-Jewish tinge and cast Jews as scapegoats for the unpopularity of the regime.

These trials consolidated police power in the state and Stalin's hold on the satellites. The rejection of the Marshall Plan in 1947 had been followed by the Russian blockade of Berlin and by more militant action by communists in western Europe (particularly in France and Italy), but these ventures had failed and their failure coincided with a challenge to Russian rule in eastern Europe which succeeded in Yugoslavia and looked like becoming contagious. Stalin's response was harsh and practical: he stamped, where he could, on threats to Russian interests and added to the apparatus of communist integration by creating in Comecon an institution for economic assimilation and by creating the beginnings of military co-ordination.

Comecon – the Council for Mutual Economic Assistance – was founded in 1949 as a counter to the Marshall Plan. Its founding members were the USSR, Poland, Czechoslovakia, Hungary, Romania and Bulgaria, which were joined almost at once by Albania and a year later by eastern Germany. It was in form an association of sovereign states: communist propaganda was at this time attacking the Marshall Plan as an American device for overriding European sovereignties. But in Comecon there was for many years no question of any insistence on sovereign rights to dissent, and the dominance of the USSR was underlined by the exclusion of Yugoslavia. For ten years Comecon had no constitution, meagre quarters and a tiny staff in Moscow, and few activities. In so far as it was anything more than an anti-American gesture, it was an adjunct of the Russian policy, chiefly pursued by other means, of using planning to annex the satellite economies to Russian needs and not to develop the area as a whole in the interests of all its parts. The satellite governments were themselves in the process of adopting the rigid communist system of planning by setting national targets and instructing each separate enterprise how much it must contribute to the aggregate (a system which the head of the State Planning Commission in Moscow Nikolai Voznesensky was trying to reform until his dismissal by Stalin in March 1949). Until the crises of the mid-1950s Comecon occupied itself modestly with statistical research, technical exchanges and the promotion of bilateral and triangular trade treaties, but from 1956 considerable changes were introduced. Twelve standing commissions were established in different capitals, Yugoslavia and China were admitted as observers, a constitution was worked out and came into effect in 1960, an international executive was inaugurated in 1962, and meetings of these various organs became regular and frequent. Comecon organized aid for Hungary in materials and credits after the revolution of 1956, promoted joint planning and investment, and expanded satellite co-operation on a broad multilateral basis: for example, for the distribution of electric power and in the construction of oil pipelines. An international payments system was introduced by the creation in 1964 of an International Bank for Co-operation. These developments did not alter the basic character of Soviet economics: namely, autarky, which became autarky of the bloc rather than autarky of each state, and a command economy in which enterprises were required to meet production targets rather than make profits. The communist bloc remained an insignificant element in world trade.

In military matters Moscow exercised control and supervision through officers in the satellite forces who had been trained in the USSR. The despatch of Marshal Rokossovsky to Warsaw was a uniquely overt and elevated gesture but one which had numerous parallels at lower levels. In 1952 this tentacle policy was supplemented by the creation of a military co-ordinating committee with Marshal Bulganin as chairman, and at a conference in Warsaw at the end of that year a combined general staff was instituted with headquarters in Cracow under a Russian general. Military facilities, involving considerable displacements of population, were developed along the Baltic coast, in Poland and eastern Germany and round the Black Sea. The satellites were at this stage contributing something like 1.5 million men to military and security forces, were incurring a commensurate financial burden, and were being obliged to adjust their industries, their industrial revolutions and their economic planning to the military requirements of the bloc as assessed by the USSR. There was, however, no formal multilateral defence treaty until, after Stalin's death, the admission of western Germany to NATO prompted the inauguration in May 1955 of the Warsaw Pact. This treaty, to which the USSR and all its satellites were parties, was expressed as a regional arrangement for self-defence within the meaning of article 52 of the UN Charter: it was renewed in 1975 and 1985. It created joint organizations with headquarters in Moscow. It incidentally regularized the presence of Russian troops in Romania and Hungary, where they would otherwise have had no legal standing after the termination of occupation rights in Austria by the treaty which restored Austrian sovereignty in that year. In general the Warsaw Pact was a formalization of existing dispositions and added little of substance to them. Membership of the alliance became, however, a touchstone of the reliability of Moscow's associates in the Cold War.

After Stalin

Stalin's death in March 1953 stimulated unrest. His death did not initiate it – there were strikes in Czechoslovakia, for example, the previous year – but in June 1953 serious disorders occurred in East Germany which the government was unable to bring under control without the help of Russian tanks. In Hungary tens of thousands were confined in camps in a campaign directed in particular against the peasants, the majority of the population. In 1954 Moscow gave evidence of new thinking about relations with the satellites when it sold to the satellite governments the Russian share in joint companies created after the war for the control of key industrial and commercial enterprises. The liquidation of Beria in the USSR was copied further afield: in Hungary the chief of the security police, Gabor Peter, was sentenced to life imprisonment and the first secretary of the ruling party Istvan Kovacs was forced to confess to unjust arrests and false witness. In 1956 Poland and Hungary gave much sharper testimony to the insecurity of Russian rule.

In June 1956 there were strikes and riots in the *Polish* city of Poznan. They were directed chiefly against low wages for long hours. Industrial unrest coincided with intellectual ferment and with Roman Catholic demonstrations at Czestochowa, the home of an especially venerated shrine of the Virgin Mary. The first secretary of the United Workers' Party Edward Ochab became persuaded that Gomulka must be readmitted to grace and power. During visits to the USSR and China Ochab seems to have convinced the Chinese, but not the Russians, of the need for this reversal. In October the politburo admitted Gomulka and excluded Rokossovsky. A powerful Russian delegation arrived, consisting of Khrushchev, Molotov, Mikoyan and Kaganovich, and Russian troops in Poland and eastern Germany began to move. Gomulka was included in the Polish team chosen to confront the visitors. These were not allowed to attend a meeting of the Polish central committee and after 24 hours they left. Hot words were spoken but rough action was stayed. Gomulka was appointed first secretary. Rokossovsky left for Moscow. He was followed within a few days by Gomulka. The upshot was that the Russians, who had presumably gone to Warsaw with the intention of checking Gomulka and his party, decided after a quick look to accept them. The alternative, a direct use of Russian forces in Poland, was too risky because Russian forces might well have been resisted by the Polish army and a fight in Poland could have led to serious trouble in other countries. Gomulka was a communist and had no illusions about Poland's need to keep on reasonably good terms with the USSR. He did not propose to take Poland out of the Warsaw Pact or to share power in Poland with non-communists. He could be lived with. In December a new treaty gave the Russians the right to retain troops in Poland.

In *Hungary* the revolution which immediately followed the settlement in Poland exceeded the limits to which the Russians were prepared to go. A few weeks after Stalin's death Rakosi, the complete Stalinist, was forced to surrender the post of prime minister to Imre Nagy. This was a rebuff but ambiguous inasmuch as he kept the post of first secretary of the Hungarian Communist Party and his staunchest supporter, Erno Gerö, remained minister of the interior. Two years later, with Malenkov's star in decline in Moscow, Nagy was removed and Rakosi was back in full control but less than one year further on Krushchev led the movement which denounced Stalin's doings (from but not before 1934) and hastened to repair relations with Tito. Satellite leaders found themselves in a quandary. They had to discover the practical implications of the new vogue for collective leadership and how far the restoration of Tito to the communist fold implied new freedoms for all satellite leaders. Rakosi and Nagy became prime victims of these questions. Rakosi was especially obnoxious to Tito, whom Krushchev was anxious to conciliate, whereas Nagy cherished exaggerated expectations of becoming something of a Tito himself. Rakosi lost all his posts. Gerö was promoted to first secretary and Nagy returned to the premiership. But Rakosi's dismissal unleashed opposition which Gerö was unable to master (he lasted only three weeks) and Janos Kádár became first secretary as the Russians discovered that in order to maintain their hold on Hungary they must use military force.

The Russians, in the persons of Mikoyan and Suslov, who were passing through Budapest on their way to Belgrade, appeared to endorse a Nagy government – but perhaps without knowing what sort of government it would be. Nagy announced that he was including in his government two leaders of the suppressed Smallholders' Party, Zoltan Tildy and Bela Kovacs, and on the same day Russian troops which were menacing Budapest began to withdraw. Nagy then announced the end of one-party rule and demanded the complete evacuation of Russian forces. Nagy had now gone much further than Gomulka. By 30 October it seemed that the withdrawing Russian troops were preparing to return. The die was cast either on 31 October when Mikoyan and Suslov were told that Hungary intended to leave the Warsaw Pact, or at the latest on the following day, when Nagy made a public statement to this effect and declared that Hungary would become a neutral. On that day an alternative government was set up by the Russians under Kádár and when, two days later, General Pal Maleter, Nagy's minister of defence, went to negotiate with the Russians over the withdrawal of their troops, he was kidnapped. Budapest was attacked on 4 November (the day on which Gomulka went to Moscow) and thereafter the revolution was quickly suppressed. Thousands of Hungarians were deported to the USSR or executed. Kádár applied himself to running Hungary within the limits imposed by Moscow: no elections and no quitting the Warsaw Pact. He ruled for 32 years. He was on friendly terms with Khrushchev. He proclaimed a general amnesty in 1963, cultivated a comparatively unautocratic style, abated the use of torture and imprisonment, and permitted the discussion and introduction of economic reforms.

Under Rakosi and Gerö Hungary's manufacturing output had at first increased but the productivity of a greatly enlarged industrial workforce did not improve, there was only pitiful investment in plant or technology, and when the workforce ceased to grow manufacturing growth subsided to zero. Investment in roads, housing, education and research was negligible. By the mid-1970s economists were advocating a drastic abandonment of central economic planning, the unleashing of market forces of supply and demand, and schemes for allocating the profits of particular enterprises between workers, the state and reinvestment. These discussions were open and even broadcast on television. But intellectual barriers were coming down faster than the political. Actual reforms were unheroic and the ruling party unadventurous and, unlike its counterparts in Poland and Czechoslovakia, small.

The suppression of the Hungarian revolution of 1956 was one of those brutal acts which damage the perpetrator but are undertaken upon the calculation that graver damage would otherwise result. Communist parties in western Europe lost members on a considerable scale and communist governments shuddered at the display of Russian determination. Before long they found new cause for unease in the Russo-Chinese split. The Chinese were judged to have given Moscow the right advice on Poland and Hungary – that is, to acquiesce in changes and, in Hungary, to use force only after Nagy had given the revolution an anti-communist course – and Zhou Enlai visited Poland and Hungary early in 1957 to consolidate this advantage and stress the need for good Russo-Chinese relations. Khrushchev's subsequent handling of the quarrel with Beijing disturbed satellite leaders who disliked the way in which Khrushchev insisted on bringing it into the open and making communists take sides. In 1960 Khrushchev used a congress of the Romanian party to stage a demonstration against the Chinese, and although in 1961 81 communist parties (Yugoslavia alone abstaining) signed in Moscow a declaration intended to paper over cracks, Khrushchev continued until his fall in 1964 to conduct a public campaign against the Chinese.

On this issue *Romania* took the lead first in persisting with attempts to resolve the disputes and then in refusing to take sides. Gheorghe Gheorghiu-Dej, the virtual ruler of the country since the end of the war (and undisputed ruler after the fall in 1952 of Ana Pauker and Vasile Luca), challenged the Russians in Comecon where, in 1962, Khrushchev proposed to create a supranational planning organ with powers to direct investment throughout the bloc and prescribe what should or should not be done in each member state. The Romanians, who wanted a steel mill but were cast for the role of producers of raw materials, invoked the principle of national sovereignty which the Russians themselves had made much of when Comecon was founded. They displayed their dissatisfaction by entering into a separate agreement with Yugoslavia for a hydro-electric scheme at the Iron Gates on the Danube, by proposing that China be a full member of Comecon and by threatening to leave it. Romanian leaders visited Paris, London, Ankara and other non-communist capitals. After Gheorghiu-Dej's death in 1965 his successor as party secretary Nicolae Ceauşescu also talked of the dissolution of the Warsaw Pact and of the loss of Bessarabia to the USSR 25 years earlier. After a tactful visit by Brezhnev to Bucharest in 1965 the more implausible Romanian proposals abated as the realities of the situation became apparent once more. Romania continued to assert its idiosyncrasy by establishing diplomatic relations with western Germany in 1967.

The year 1968 brought a fresh challenge from a different quarter: Czechoslovakia. The Yugoslav secession had given Gottwald a motive and an excuse for tightening his control (there were more executions in Czechoslovakia than anywhere else) and the bleak years of the Cold War with their talk of American action to liberate eastern Europe put a clamp on all meaningful criticism of the government. Although the government was distrusted, it was not seriously opposed; fear of the police stifled talk and prevented organization. Within the governing party debate was atrophied. The events of 1956 in Poland and Hungary struck no visible spark in Czechoslovakia, which came to be rated as the most docile of the satellites.

Presiding over this inertia was Antonin Novotny, first secretary of the Czechoslovak Communist Party from 1953 and president of the republic from 1957. Novotny was a Czech who despised Slovaks and did not conceal the fact. This became one item in a movement against his leadership which led to his removal from his party post in January 1968, from the presidency in March and from the party in May. Ditched by Moscow, he was succeeded in the first office by the first secretary of the Slovak Communist Party Alexander Dubček and in the second by General Jan Svoboda. The first and more important of these changes amounted to a reversal of power within the party, largely instigated by Slovaks.

Dubček, besides being a Slovak nationalist, was an economic reformer, in government relatively humane and in economics relatively liberal. He presented Moscow with a conundrum and for several months it could not make up its collective mind what to do about him. The new government's first measures were vague and without explicit threat to the communists' monopoly of power or to the Warsaw Pact, but its Action Programme, published in April, and a promise of elections in May put Moscow in a dilemma which it resolved at the end of August by invasion.

Czechoslovakia was an industrial state which was especially hampered by the drawing of the Iron Curtain where it was drawn. Economically, its western half belonged with the western world, even if Slovakia did not. The country's economy made a decent recovery from the war but was stagnant in the 1960s. Its prewar strength in the manufacture and export of consumer goods was undermined by Russian insistence on expanding heavy industries whose products were required by the USSR but had no markets outside the satellite bloc – since in western terms their technology was outdated. Its methods were dangerously polluting. It produced twice as much steel as it could sell. It became isolated from the rest of the world. The standard pattern of central communist direction and control engendered ossification, and a return to consumer goods was obstructed by new vested interests in heavy industry. Czechoslovakia avoided excessive indebtedness to the west on the Polish or Hungarian scale but could not readjust or repair its economy without western capital.

Economists were alive to these dangers. Some mainly ineffective reforms were initiated in 1958 and a more far-reaching programme for decentralizing industrial management, elaborated by Professor Ota Sik, was approved by the Central Committee of the ruling party in 1965. Similar ideas had been discussed in neighbouring countries, including the USSR itself, and more radical measures than Sik's had been adopted in

Hungary. There was in 1968 no compelling reason to suppose that Moscow would veto the kind of economic policy which the Dubček government wished to implement.

But pressure for such changes was accompanied by a second kind of ferment. Decentralization of economic management was equated with liberalization of controls and worker participation (or industrial democracy) and these trends overlapped naturally with demands for more freedom generally, notably freedom of expression in the press and on the radio and the democratization of party politics and the parliament – all of which posed more serious problems for the Russian guardians of the established order. Whereas in January 1968 the Russians had apparently decided that Novotny had lost his grip and was expendable, and that Dubček was acceptable in his place (Dubček proclaimed the solidarity of Czechoslovakia with the USSR and visited Moscow immediately after his appointment), a couple of months later Brezhnev and his colleagues were becoming worried by Dubček's programme and perhaps also by the likelihood of him being forced further in a liberal direction by the enthusiasm released by the change of government in Prague. This change had been followed by a considerable relaxation of censorship, by a number of ministerial changes and by the prospect of political democratization as well as economic liberalization. There was popular pressure on Dubček to make radical internal reforms which would raise questions about Czechoslovakia's external relations. Dubček had taken care to make personal contacts with Russian, Polish and Hungarian leaders before meeting the suspect Romanians and for a couple of months his neighbours evinced no distrust of him or his new course, but from the end of March criticisms began to appear in East Germany and Poland and the Russians had to ask themselves whether the changes in Czechoslovakia were not more portentous than they had at first seemed. The reformers were growing in confidence and were exciting ever greater popular expectations. Their Action Programme contained radical proposals concerning the respective functions of party and government, the rehabilitation of victims of the purges of 1949, the position of Slovakia, the revival of the parliament and some freedom for minor parties (within the National Front which the communists would continue to control). Dubček, who relied injudiciously on his ability to remodel the Communist Party and secure its support for his programme, turned an unwilling ear to warnings of military action by Moscow.

To the Russians the Action Programme was objectionable in itself and doubly objectionable in the wider context of central and eastern Europe. It brought personal and political freedom to the centre of a debate which could hardly be confined to Czechoslovakia. The first major upheaval in the postwar communist bloc had been caused by the example of Yugoslavia in 1948, the second by the examples of Poland and Hungary in 1956. It was vital to prevent Dubček from setting a third bad example. In May Dubček and other leaders of the new course went to Moscow. Two weeks later Kosygin paid a prolonged visit to Prague and so too – at the same time but separately – did Marshal A. A. Grechko, accompanied by Marshal Epishev, the chief of the Soviet army's political intelligence. Kosygin seemed to be seeking an accommodation, the generals to be preparing for action if there were none. In June the forces of the Warsaw Pact held manoeuvres in Czechoslovakia. These had been arranged a long time before, but they were considerably enlarged and the Russian tanks which came with them seemed in no hurry to leave. This hint or demonstration by the Russians coincided with the publication of a new liberal manifesto – the Two Thousand Words – which put further reformist pressure on Dubček and sharpened the tension between demo-cratic and reformist forces in Prague. August saw the publication of new statutes of the Czech Communist Party, which amounted to the ending of democratic centralism and the granting of substantial rights to other parties. Later in the month the maverick Ceaușescu and Tito the bogeyman visited Prague to great acclaim within a few days of one another. The situation was now so dangerously charged that the French and Italian communist parties tried to mediate and the West Germans, equally alarmed by the turn of events, withdrew their forces from the Czechoslovak border in order to belie rumours that they and their allies were instigating a secession from the Warsaw bloc.

Intervention in the affairs of a neighbour was neither new nor ideologically unjustifiable, but the extreme form of military invasion was to be avoided if possible – perhaps to be eschewed altogether on some estimates of the damage that such strong-arm methods might do to international communism and the USSR's place in it. The debate on how and how far engaged the Russian leaders throughout July and half of August. A first meeting at Warsaw, not attended by the Czechs (or Romanians), pro-duced a letter warning them that their proposed reforms were tantamount to allowing power to escape from the Communist Party. They were asked to explain their doings. This meeting was followed by a Russo-Czechoslovak meeting held, on the latter's insistence, in Czechoslovakia – at Ciernanad-Tisou on the Slovak border. It began on 29 July and lasted four days and was immediately followed by yet another meeting, at Bratislava, of all members of the Warsaw Pact except Romania. Before Cierna the Russians issued a threatening statement saying that a cache of American arms had been found on Czech soil and it is difficult to judge whether Cierna was anything more than window-dressing. Bratislava reasserted the military threat. Russian troops moved out of Czechoslovakia. Moscow's propaganda against Prague stopped. But on 20 August the Russians, accompanied by East German, Polish, Hungarian and Bulgarian units, invaded.

The invasion was militarily precise and efficient. The Czechoslovak armed forces offered no resistance, Dubček had said they would not. Dubček was not overthrown. He was seized, flown to Moscow under arrest, possibly drugged and forced to give his assent to a Russian invasion. He did so in the belief that invasion was inevitable and that without his assent it would be uselessly and bloodily resisted by his own people. If the Russians expected the presidium in Prague to displace Dubček and install a new government, they were ill-informed and their dispositions insufficient. They came as conquerors and although their power was overwhelming they negotiated with Dubček and Svoboda.

Twenty years of communist rule had stifled political and cultural life and created economic disaster through sterile bureaucracy on the one hand and unreality on the other – none of the five-year plans had worked as envisaged by the planners. Reformers in the 1960s aimed for a better kind of socialism, which the Russians would not countenance because too much reform anywhere in the satellites was necessarily a threat to the entire Stalinist system. The concrete symbol of this imperative was a treaty signed in October which permitted Russian troops to be stationed in Czechoslovakia in undefined numbers. Dubček was gradually demoted, sent to Turkey as ambassador and then recalled to be expelled from the Communist Party. He was replaced by the more amenable Gustav Husak. From the Russian point of view the invasion was a regrettable necessity, well executed. Reform and the reformers were eliminated. Some western tremors notwithstanding, it created no threat to international peace and it did not halt the course of Russo-American détente: there was no more than a brief interruption in the talks that led to the opening of SALT in 1969 and the agreement with Bonn in 1970. But the invasion forced Moscow to proclaim an extreme doctrine about the limits of sovereign independence within the communist bloc and to make plain that Russo-American détente implied no loosening of the reins of power therein. The invasion and the doctrine unsettled eastern Europe by the violence of the action and the implications of the doctrine, and the use of the ostensibly anti-western Warsaw Pact against one of its own members emphasized the strains prevailing within the bloc 20 years after its consolidation.

These strains had two main sources: nationalism and conflicts of economic interest. Nationalism was in varying strengths endemic throughout the bloc. Bulgaria, at one end of the scale, endorsed the Brezhnev doctrine in a new constitution in 1971 and so elevated socialist internationalism above traditional nationalism and state sovereignty. This was an echo of Dimitrov's old-style international communism coupled with Bulgaria's perennial leanings towards Moscow to offset its uneasy relations with its neighbours. (But in the 1970s Bulgaria sought to improve its relations with Romania and Yugoslavia and even with Greece and Turkey too.) Most eastern Europeans, however, were as loath as western Europeans to subordinate their national identity to supranational organizations or causes. The USSR contributed to this particularism by its heavy-handedness in moments of crisis and by obstructing regional associations within its sphere. Any association had to be all-embracing and must include the USSR.

Of the two principal organs of eastern European integration the Warsaw Pact was little more than an expression and deployment of Russian power. Its forces were commanded by a Russian commander-in-chief and its headquarters were a departmental office of the USSR's high command. It had been created in opposition to NATO and its function was to face NATO's forces in Europe. But whatever their avowed purpose, the Pact's forces had other potentialities, of which the invasion of Czechoslovakia was an uncomfortable reminder. The defence of eastern Europe included, according to the

Brezhnev doctrine, firing shots in anger against enemies within the gates. The doctrine raised questions not about power but about sovereignty. All eastern European countries knew that they had to live with Russian power and observe the limitations which it imposed on their own freedom of action, but they wished at the same time to maintain, even if they might not exercise, sovereign rights. This was for the most part a vain aspiration, a kicking against the pricks exemplified by Romania's continued refusal (maintained in spite of a visit to Bucharest by Marshal Grechko in 1973) to take part in Warsaw Pact activities and by Ceauşescu's symbolic visit to Beijing in 1971 and his reception in Bucharest in 1972 of the presidents of the United States and western Germany.

In Comecon, the second quasi-international body, strains were more concrete. Having come to life in the late 1950s after a somnolent start, Comecon was endowed in 1962 with a Basic Plan of International Socialist Division of Labour. This title proclaimed the intention. In 1971 a second basic document was adopted: the Complex Programme for the Development of Socialist Economic Integration, incorporating a long-range programme reaching 15 to 20 years ahead. (In this year Albania rejoined the organization after a gap of nine years.) Comecon's practical problems were fundamentally no different from those of any international organization trying to reconcile the good of each with the good of all. Its members had divergent views of their interests and the harmonization of these was complicated by the immense preponderance of the power of one member. In eastern Europe the division of labour meant two things in particular: that each non-Russian member should concentrate on one or two economic activities prescribed for it by the organization as a whole (in effect by the USSR), and that the resulting exchanges within the group should largely take the form of trading these prescribed manufactures for Russian primary products – notably oil: Russian exports of oil to other members of Comecon rose from 8.3 million tons in 1965 to a projected 50 million tons in 1975. Such a division of effort within a state would seem natural enough but when applied in advance of political unification it entailed a supranationalism which members distrusted because it removed decisions from national control (the same objections were heard in western Europe) and threatened to reduce particular members to dependence on a single industry or crop, with consequent further loss of political independence. There was also the question of payments, the fear that the terms and benefits of trade with Comecon would be manipulated to the disadvantage of the weaker brethren by arbitrary fixing of unfavourable currency parities. The 1971 Complex Programme acknowledged these fears to the extent of envisaging a common currency or convertible rouble by 1980 after a period in which separate currencies would be equitably and permanently adjusted in terms of one another.

Members of Comecon had a common interest in raising their economic performance and their trade with one another, but particular members also had an interest in trading with, and therefore producing for, countries outside the bloc: some of their needs could be satisfied only by buying from western countries, their trade would expand faster if they dealt with western as well as eastern countries, and there were political advantages in a commercial diversification which would reduce economic dependence on one or two neighbours. The USSR itself set an example which it could hardly denounce in others by concluding with the United States in 1972 an agreement designed to treble Russo-American trade by 1975. (This agreement was terminated by the USSR at the beginning of 1975 after the US Congress had inserted into the Trade Reform Act 1974 an amendment linking the expansion of Russo-American trade with the relaxation of the USSR's emigration policies. The author of the amendment, Senator Henry Jackson, hoped to facilitate Jewish emigration from the USSR but succeeded only in checking trade between the two countries.) From 1973 Comecon engaged in talks with the EEC about agreements between the EEC and particular Comecon members embodying quota reductions and most-favoured-nation clauses. Western countries were particularly attracted by the possibility of increasing their purchases of non-Middle Eastern oil.

But these horizons were not all fair. Increased east–west trade coincided with increased world commodity prices and increased inflation in the west. Eastern Europe, experiencing inflation in its own economies for domestic reasons, including higher wages, was faced with the alternatives of importing a further measure of inflation with western goods and raw materials or of cutting back its trade. When Romania, which had redirected half of its foreign trade to countries outside Comecon, was preparing a new five-year plan in 1975, it altered its first intentions by reducing the share of its trade which it proposed to do with the west; but, loath to retreat into the closed circle of Comecon, it began to explore the prospects for more trade with the Third World and for this purpose applied for and was given membership of the conference of non-aligned states convoked in Lima in that year (but held in Colombo the next year). Even Czechoslovakia, consistently the strongest economy and a creditor country within the bloc, was caught in this dilemma, partly because of the vigour of its trade and industry. Its trade with the west, facilitated by the establishment of diplomatic relations with western Germany in 1973, brought in the world's goods but at the world's inflated prices, and since Czechoslovakia could not abandon incomplete projects which depended on foreign contracts it found itself having to increase the value of its exports to the west by more than 20 per cent if it were to pay for its imports by trade.

In Hungary decentralization in economic affairs troubled the Russians and the more conservative wing of the Hungarian communist establishment, but a visit by Brezhnev to Budapest in 1972 was taken to carry with it continuing Russian support for Kádár and cautious liberalization. Nevertheless, Kádár remained harassed. Hungary's import bill rose vastly, with Russian as well as world prices increasing so much that the government, unable to bridge the gap by greater productivity and exports, was obliged to pass price increases on to the consumer. At the eleventh party congress in 1975 Kádár himself survived criticism but his prime minister Jenö Fock and other senior personages had to resign and new policies of austerity and recentralization were adopted to cope with an unmanageable deficit in the balance of payments.

Much more serious from the Russian point of view was *Poland*, where economic difficulties led to the overthrow of the government by workers' demonstrations, a phenomenon rare in any quarter of the globe and least expected in an authoritarian communist state. Poland was something of a special case in Stalin's empire, for Poles harboured an atavistic national hostility to Russians, whether tsarist or bolshevik, and, as Roman Catholics, were equally hostile to Orthodox Christianity and communism. Increases in food prices provoked in 1970 strikes and riots which the government failed to control. Forty-five people were killed and over 1,000 injured. Gomulka resigned. A new government under Edward Gierek cancelled the price increases, raised wages and social security payments, imported foreign consumer goods (at considerable cost) and purged party and administration by dismissing officials at all levels and placing new men and women in half of the top positions at the centre and beyond. The press was given greater freedom (but was restricted again in 1974) and in 1972 wages and benefits were raised again – the government demanding in return harder and more punctual work – and a new parliament was elected with many new faces but also the standard 99 per cent vote for the communist candidates. By 1973 many economic indicators were so propitious that it was permissible to speak of a boom: industrial and agricultural production up, real wages up, investment up, prices stable. But the cost was a large increase in the import bill and foreign debt, as the government satisfied consumer demand and the needs of industrial modernization by buying abroad and foreign borrowing. By 1974 Poland, like Romania, was doing half its trade with the west. Huge price increases, especially for food, led in 1976 to strikes, riots, deaths and heavy prison sentences. A Committee for the Defence of the Workers (KOR) came into existence to help the families of the dead and imprisoned and to protest against the heavy-handed brutality of the police. Price rises were rescinded, wages in industry and prices to farmers were raised, and Gierek persuaded Moscow to send substantial quantities of food and industrial machinery to Poland. This was a policy of repression tempered by concession. It did not work. The wage increases accentuated the demand for imported consumer goods and so increased inflation and the already unmanageable debt to western trading partners. The deaths of 1970 and 1976 were not forgotten; further demonstrations and hunger strikes forced the government to grant in 1977 an amnesty to those prosecuted for the previous year's disturbances; and Gierek, who held his first meeting with Cardinal Wyszczynski, was seen to be appealing to the Roman Catholic Church for help. The election of Cardinal Wojtyla to the papacy – the first Polish pope since Poland was Christianized 1,000 years earlier – had an immeasurable but far from insignificant effect in a country which regarded itself as the jewel of the Counter-Reformation. Pope John Paul II paid an emotional visit to Poland in 1979, which was another year of bad harvests and mounting foreign debt. Gierek's task was becoming beyond his powers and the industrial workers were moving towards another confrontation with the government.

In 1980 they struck again, bringing the shipyards along the Baltic to a halt against a background of unmanageable foreign debts, soaring prices and severe shortages. Earnings on exports were almost wholly absorbed by the charges on a massive foreign debt of over $20 billion, increasing by $2 billion a year. Meat was alternately unobtainable and prohibitively expensive. Wage increases of 10–20 per cent, granted by the government in the summer, threatened to aggravate inflation without making life tolerable for the recipients. There was nobody to blame except the government, but equally there was no constitutional way of blaming the government. Consequently, the ensuing strikes were inevitably political. Not only could they not be settled by collective bargaining between the workers and their employers; but such bargaining was itself impossible because the workers were permitted no lawful organizations to do the bargaining. The system could solve nothing. If the strikers stayed out the government would have to choose between using force and bypassing the system.

But the government itself was not free to choose. It had to consult the USSR. Gierek flew to see Brezhnev to discover how much rope he was allowed. Neither he nor Moscow wanted a showdown with the strikers (which would rapidly become a showdown with a far wider segment of the population), but the use of force by the USSR could not be ruled out. Gierek had to find out what he might in no circumstances concede, and the agreement ultimately reached with the strikers in the Gdansk yards in August showed what these limits were. In that agreement, signed on behalf of the strikers by Lech Walesa and subsequently copied in similar terms in the Silesian coalfields and other areas, the strikers accepted the leading role of the Communist Party, Poland's socialist system and its membership of the Russian bloc. In return for recognizing these limits Poland's remarkably mature and disciplined opposition leaders won, on paper, astonishing victories: the right to strike; the right to form trade unions independent of the state; wider discussion of the government's economic policies; an abatement of censorship; appointments and promotions on merit and irrespective of party membership; increased wages and pensions; promises on working conditions, housing accommodation and maternity leave; a second day off in the week, and regular broadcasts of Roman Catholic church services. Some of the clauses were vague; others could hardly be implemented without an economic miracle which nobody expected. Nevertheless, nobody doubted that something extraordinary had happened. An officially non-existent opposition, using non-violent industrial muscle, had forced a totalitarian government to meet many of its demands, to change the country's constitution and to reintroduce political dialogue where there had been none for a generation. The immediate and most potent cause of the government's defeat by the worker's movement, Solidarity, was its economic failure, but the workers' demands showed how far discontent spread beyond the purely material sphere to questions of human freedom and dignity such as the right of industrial groups to manage (some of) their affairs for themselves and to express and publish their own views.

Communist control was preserved in diluted form when General Jaruzelski, prime minister from February 1981, was appointed head of the party later in that year. To make assurance doubly sure he then proclaimed martial law. Walesa's control over Solidarity, by contrast, faltered as the government's measures and the arrest of some of its leading members produced divided counsels. When martial law was lifted after a year the main focus of opposition had shifted from Solidarity to the more tractable hands of the Roman Catholic Church, traditionally accustomed and disposed to deal with lay power. An uneasy accommodation was tacitly sealed by a visit by the Pope in 1983, followed by an amnesty for (most) political prisoners, which emphasized the army's confidence. But confidence was misplaced, for there were no answers to accumulating economic problems or to an accelerating flight from membership of the Communist Party, which was the only recognized instrument of government. The murder in October 1984 of Father Jerzy Popieluszko, one of a number of outspoken priests whose sermons praised Solidarity in patriotic terms, revealed the fires beneath the surface. It revealed also the inadequacy of the government's control over its own agencies: Father Popieluszko was kidnapped and tortured to death by the police.

The extraordinary significance of the Polish protest lay in its source – the industrial workers. In the USSR protest against bad government had been endemic for over 100 years, back to the days of Alexander Herzen; but this was intellectual protest, as ineffectual as it was honourable and admirable. It reappeared in the postwar USSR and elsewhere, for example Hungary and Czechoslovakia. But only in Poland – and East Germany (1953) – were there, before the late 1980s, any industrial protests on a politically significant scale. Stanislaw Kania replaced Edward Gierek as secretary-general of the Polish Workers' Party. Poland could either pay its debts or feed itself but not both: the meat which had been at the centre of the summer's discontent could either be exported for foreign currency or released into the home market where, as a result of the wage increases granted before and after the strikes, it was more in demand than ever. Coincidentally, a bad harvest was adding to import bills for grains and feedstuffs, and although Poland's principal western trading partners – the United States and West Germany in the lead – were willing to extend fresh loans, only in Moscow could Poland's new government get credits commensurate with its difficulties. Poland in 1980 was a portent of trouble within the bloc but not, like Yugoslavia when Tito confronted Stalin 32 years earlier, a detachable part of the bloc. As the Poles themselves saw, geography ruled out anything like the Yugoslav secession and, by the same token, the massive financial and political aid from the west which sustained Tito from 1948. The degree to which Kania might succeed where Gierek had failed would therefore be settled in Moscow, whence alone Kania might get the economic aid or concessions needed to maintain the treaty with the strikers – a compromise which Kania could not honour if Moscow did not let him do so. The USSR permitted the August settlement as the least of a number of evils but there was no guarantee of its continuing endorsement, still less of approval for further tinkering with the constitution or with the dominance of the Communist Party.

That the USSR was capable of reoccupying Poland was never in doubt and the examples of Czechoslovakia and Afghanistan showed that the Kremlin did not lack the nerve to use force. There were nevertheless strong reasons for supposing that it was extremely averse to doing so. These reasons derived neither from Poland's fighting spirit, which could be presumed to be as splendid and ineffectual as it had been in 1939; nor from any American deterrent, for an American military threat was not credible and economic sanctions were slow to operate and fairly easy to circumvent. What made the USSR recoil from an invasion of Poland was the prospect of finding there nobody to govern the country – no Kádár as in Hungary in 1956, no Husák as in Czechoslovakia in 1968. Poland's communists, already identified with economic catastrophe and internal repression, could not affront Polish nationalism by playing a similar role, and so a Russian invasion would entail direct Russian rule – as in tsarist times. But this was a policy which had been rejected both by Stalin in 1945 when he poured cold water on the idea that the countries of eastern Europe should join the USSR as Soviet Republics (the three Baltic states alone excepted), and by Brezhnev when he rejected in 1970 Gomulka's plea to use Russian forces to save his falling regime. Therefore Moscow adopted a minimal policy. It wrote off the Polish Communist Party and fell back on the Polish army in the hope that Jaruzelski could, by martial law if necessary, keep Poland a one-party state and in the Warsaw Pact. Failing such an outcome, Stalin's recipe for the control of central Europe was – in Poland's case at least – in ruins. In 1944–45 Stalin had occupied this area as a prelude to establishing in it governments which would both be subservient to Moscow and wield adequate authority each in its own zone. That done, Stalin could withdraw all or some of his armed forces. But if the authority of these governments were to collapse the system collapsed. The USSR would then have to choose between tolerating a multiparty system and reimposing direct Russian military rule. The appointment of General Jaruzelski as prime minister was a makeshift response to a hopeless dilemma. Polish military rule might avoid the extremes of overt Russian dictation and party political competition, but it could solve neither Poland's main problems nor those of the USSR in Poland. Martial law from 1981 to 1983 delayed an inevitable dialogue with Solidarity while further damaging the economy by angering western countries which, venting on Poland their displeasure with the USSR, refused to renew their loans or to extend their trade.

End of empire

In 1985 Gorbachev came to power in Moscow prepared to abandon the Stalinist empire. In 1989 it vanished. Its component satellites had suffered under Russian communist political and economic diktat. They had produced protest movements but none strong enough to dismantle the Russian empire until Gorbachev judged that its preservation spelled more trouble than it was worth. From the turmoil emerged more states than had existed before. Everywhere except in Romania it vanished almost bloodlessly. The East German state disappeared; in central Europe attempts to shore up communist parties by finding less rebarbative leaders for them failed; communist rule was decisively rejected and centre-right governments were installed; further east, in Bulgaria and Romania, the old regime with a new face was not so clearly removed.

In *Poland* Jaruzelski's government tried to stave off economic collapse by imposing painful reforms, but since his government lacked popular legitimacy its programme was rejected in a popular referendum in 1987. Two years later, in April 1989, Jaruzelski, overriding opposition from the military and the communists, legalized Solidarity. He agreed to introduce a multiparty system, remove censorship of the press and broadcasting, and hold elections for the Senate and the Seym (the lower chamber), reserving however for communists and their minor allies two-thirds of the seats in the Seym. Two months later elections were held and the communists routed. After the second round of voting Solidarity had won 99 of the 100 seats in the Senate and the maximum open to it in the Seym (162 out of 460). In the reserved seats many official communist candidates failed to win the 50 per cent of votes required for election on the first ballot. This outcome produced consternation in ruling circles and astonishment practically everywhere. Jaruzelski, having resigned his party post, was elected to the state presidency by the two chambers of the parliament but the communists failed to form a government acceptable to parliament and their minor allies switched to Solidarity, which found itself propelled inexorably, but not wholly willingly, into government. After tortuous negotiations one of its leaders, Tadeus Mazowiecki, was made prime minister, most of the communists in the Seym voting for him. His appointment was welcomed by Gorbachev. But the economy continued to plummet so disastrously that the European Community established a special emergency fund to buy food for Poland and provide three-year subventions from the EC itself, its principal member states, the United States and Japan. During the decade wages lost a fifth of their purchasing power, inflation came near to 500 per cent a year, and Poland's debt to the west of $35.5 billion was much the largest of the satellites'. (Hungary's at $13.7 billion at the beginning of 1989 was higher per head of population. Others were: East Germany $7,600 million; Bulgaria $5.4 billion; Czechoslovakia $4 billion; Romania $3.9 billion but then paid off almost entirely at Ceauşescu's quirky resolve. Yugoslavia owed the west $17.6 billion.) In 1990 Jaruzelski extricated himself from a hopeless position by prematurely resigning the presidency, which was thereupon contested between Lech Walesa with demands for speedier but unspecified action and, on the other hand, the more prosaic but more reflective Mazowiecki: the man of destiny who had challenged the communist order, against the man who seemed better equipped to pick up the pieces. The contest between them was bizarrely confused by the incursion of a third candidate, Stanislaw Tyminski, who had spent the previous 20 years in Canada and

Peru making himself (so he said) a millionaire and who promised to do the same for countless Poles. He beat Mazowiecki into third place on the first round and although overwhelmed on the second by Walesa secured a quarter of the votes cast.

Shock therapy for the economy imposed all but intolerable burdens in order to cope with the huge debts incurred in the 1970s and 1980s to the Paris Club of western lenders and private bankers. The United States, followed by Britain and France, wrote off two-thirds of its debts as a contribution to, and reward for, democracy; the EC concluded a helpful association agreement, and the IMF provided funds in return for drastic reductions in government expenditure. In the 1990s the economy grew at about 6 per cent a year, unemployment fell, foreign investment was encouraging, hyperinflation was reduced; but these improvements came too late and too incompletely to save Walesa. He and the parliament were at odds over remedies and over the distribution of power: Walesa, having played the central role in getting rid of communist rule, found it uncongenial to adapt to parliamentary democracy. Parties proliferated. Of 67 taking part in elections, 29 won seats – pluralism with a vengeance. Mazowiecki's Democratic Union and the (ex-communist) Democratic Left Alliance (SLD) were in first and second place. Walesa failed to get himself made prime minister as well as president. In 1993 the SLD with its allies of the Peasant Party (PSL) won elections and the latter's leader Waldemar Pawlak became prime minister. But Walesa's unaccommodating personality, insistence on controlling senior appointments and eagerness to be re-elected in spite of declining popularity made for political instability. Pawlak was forced out of office after little more than a year, replaced by the ex-communist Josef Oleksi. Presidential elections in 1995 were narrowed down to a contest between Walesa and the SLD's Alexander Kwasniewski – young, intelligent but a former communist who had held office in Poland's last communist government. During the campaign Walesa recovered much of his lost popularity but in spite of aggressive support from the Roman Catholic hierarchy, which focused attention on past ideological battles rather than current economic problems, he was narrowly defeated by opponents who were better organized and more forward-looking. Two years later the SLD/PSL coalition was defeated by the more right-wing Solidarity Electoral Alliance (AWS), consisting of the two main strands of the old Solidarity movement – trade unions and free marketeers – with some 30 smaller groups. The SLD vote held up but the PSL lost much of its rural vote. Poland's politics were developing as a two-bloc rather than a two-party system.

Poland's external affairs were equable but complicated by its position in the middle of Europe. By recognizing Poland's existing frontiers Walesa and his successors removed contentions to the east and hoped to secure Poland's postwar gains in the west. Its frontiers with Russia had been drastically reduced, there were no Germans left in Poland and ethnically it had become singularly homogeneous. It joined the OECD in 1996 and hoped to join the EU soon after 2000. Its membership of the EU was strongly championed by Kohl in spite of German fears of a substantial flood of Polish workers into a difficult German labour market. Eastward olive branches were extended to Russia but Poland's more immediate concerns were with Lithuania, Belarus and Ukraine. With Lithuania historical conflicts were overcome by mutual awareness of a common plight, but economic failures in Belarus and Ukraine constricted their trade with Poland.

In *Hungary*, in the same month as the Polish elections of 1989, the body of the murdered Imre Nagy was brought to Budapest and given a reburial which turned into a vast popular demonstration against the regime. Kádár's 32-year rule had been brought to an end the year before (he died in 1989). He had advocated economic reforms before the advent of Gorbachev in the USSR but after that event his concept of reform was made to seem too lame and was overtaken by a new momentum. His successor as general secretary of the ruling party Karolyi Grosz came into collision with his colleagues over the scope and pace of change – notably with Miklos Nemeth, the prime minister, and Imre Poszgay, the regime's economic expert, who wanted to accelerate economic reform and introduce radical political changes such as the abandonment of the communist monopoly of political power. Elections in a multiparty system were promised for early in 1990 and the party set about salvaging some of its power by changing its name and putting on a new public face: the Hungarian Socialist Workers' Party became the Hungarian Socialist Party. Two main opposition parties emerged: the Hungarian Democratic Forum, a centre-right party akin to the Christian Democrats of western Europe, and the Alliance of Free Democrats, the vehicle primarily of urban intellectuals. Fifty other parties appeared too. The non-communists defeated the communists (who were reduced to 10 per cent of the vote) and formed a coalition which, however, remained intact for only a few months. It was replaced by a centre-right coalition under the unobtrusive but firm guidance of Josef Antall who, until his death in 1993, was the chief begetter of the least turbulent transition from communism to democracy in the former Soviet satellites. His party won nearly half the seats (with a quarter of the popular vote) but could find no miraculous economic cures and was embarrassed by an extreme right-wing minority – two burdens which contributed to its defeat in 1994 by a resurgent, largely ex-communist, socialist party led by Gyula Horn. With nearly a quarter of Hungarians living outside Hungary – 2 million in Romania, 1 million in Slovakia, Serbia and Ukraine, smaller numbers in Croatia and Slovenia – Horn's policy was to agree frontiers in return for guarantees of minority rights. Under successive governments in the 1990s Hungary's main aim was economic revitalization with western help, bearing in mind, however, that it had a substantial interest in healthy economic relations with countries to the south and east – its near neighbours in the Balkans and Ukraine. Its strengths lay in a booming agriculture, tourism and the development – for which foreign partners and investment were necessary – of steel and chemical industries, car manufacture and assembly and, more distantly, oil. Its weaknesses included a falling and ageing population (a mere 10 million) and uncomfortably large budget deficits.

Hungary played an elliptical role in the next act of the year's drama. In May *East Germans* began to desert their state in a mass emigration when Hungary, in a gesture with no special reference to German affairs, removed restrictions on its frontiers with Austria. East Germans on holiday in Hungary found that they had an open road through Austria to West Germany, where they had automatic rights of access and citizenship. They took the road at a rate initially of 5,000 a day. This exodus was swollen a few months later when Hungary abrogated an agreement with East Germany and virtually constituted itself a transit area for mass emigration of the discontented and the desperate. Others in East Germany staged huge anti-government demonstrations in Leipzig, Berlin and other cities and under these pressures – and with the example of events elsewhere in central Europe seen on West German television – new escape routes to the west were fashioned through Czechoslovakia, from Poland through East Germany in special trains, and eventually direct from East to West Germany. By the end of the year about half a million had left and they were still leaving at the rate of 2,000 a day.

At the beginning of the year Erich Honecker's inclination had been to hold on to power, if necessary by force, and to treat his people as Deng had treated the Chinese in Tiananmen Square. Honecker's position, however, was in one crucial respect the weakest among communist leaders since the state which he ruled was a Russian creation without a national identity of its own. The USSR was the ultimate source of the ruling party's power (as it was throughout the satellite empire) but also, and uniquely in the German case, the USSR was the source of the state's legitimacy or *raison d'être*. When, therefore, Gorbachev arrived on a visit to Berlin in October 1989 his appearance in the midst of a crisis not only recalled his appearance in Beijing in similar circumstances six months earlier but also underlined the essential difference that, whereas in Beijing he had been an accidental observer, in Berlin he held a key to future developments. In terms which were at once guarded and unmistakable he warned Honecker against the dangers of not moving with the times and privately made it clear that the East German regime must expect no help from the USSR in suppressing violent demonstrations. He may have gone even further, thwarting Honecker's assumed willingness to use East German forces in the manner of Deng and encouraging Honecker's removal from power. In a flurry of unforeseen events Honecker was replaced as general secretary of the Socialist Unity Party by Egon Krenz, a younger but not much less tarnished member of the inner core of the communist elite; and Krenz, who barely outlasted the year, was himself replaced by Gregor Gysi, under whose guidance the party renounced its monopoly of political power, changed its name and prepared for multiparty elections. Hans Modrow, mayor of Dresden and a comparatively respectable communist, became prime minister in an interim administration formed to conduct negotiations with non-communist groups which were pupating into political parties. These parties, campaigning under the management of their West German counterparts, submerged but did not obliterate the communists in elections in which nearly half the votes were cast for the right, fewer than a quarter for socialists and 16 per cent for communists. The Berlin wall was demolished and the city united as men and women from east and west were once more free to pass from one side to the other.

The dismantling of the Berlin wall by its people precipitated the reunification of Germany. The consequences were controlled by Kohl and Gorbachev. Kohl seized his opportunity. After some initial hesitation and prodded by Washington, he welcomed the fall of the wall, annexed East to West Germany and went on to put into the pockets of East Germans real for valueless marks at the rate of one for one. The East German state was turned into five Länder of the Federal Republic and the four occupying powers abrogated their powers in Berlin. Gorbachev tried but failed to secure the neutrality of the new enlarged Germany but at a meeting with Kohl in the Caucasus acquiesced in its membership of NATO in return for the right to keep Russian troops in what had been East Germany until the end of 1995, a substantial German contribution to their costs and an undertaking that no German units committed to NATO or any NATO units stationed in Germany should be deployed in the former German Democratic Republic. Mitterrand and Thatcher, among many others, were taken by surprise by reunification: the former quickly acknowledged the fact and recovered his poise but Thatcher's more fervent anti-Germanism was mollified only with difficulty by Bush. The Poles, who had the most cause for concern, asked for no more than a reaffirmation of their postwar frontiers, which they secured by a treaty signed on the first anniversary of the piercing of the wall. East Prussia remained part of the USSR, so that the new state was not prewar Germany. These events amounted to the settlement which had not taken place in 1945 between the combatants of 1941–45 in eastern Europe and it was effected by them.

More had crumbled than the wall. The East German economy had too. Wages in the east soared to western levels, completing the destruction of eastern industries, while the costs to the Federal Republic were unexpectedly severe (they verged on $200 billion a year) and the East Germans who received Deutschmarks also lost their jobs. Unification was a misnomer. Eastern Germany was not only far weaker but much smaller than its western counterpart. Seventeen million people were merged with 63 million and even after ten years and massive subsidies production in a united Germany was only 10 per cent above West Germany's, and the contribution of unity to exports was a mere 2 per cent. Unification weakened Germany in the short run and after the initial euphoria gave rise to disenchantment and tensions on both sides of the erstwhile divide. The Federal Republic, desperate to prevent mass migration from east to west – flight from what was not only a police state but also economic disaster – had undertaken to convert East German marks to Deutschmarks at parity (there were exceptions) but this promise inflated the West German money supply by 14 per cent and nothing could prevent the collapse of East German industries. The plight of the east was revealed as even direr than expected and was in some ways worsened by the radical medicine applied to it: unemployment soared as industries stopped work because they could find no buyers for their shoddy goods. The Federal government was obliged to pay a heavy price in subsidies, rising interest rates and budget deficits in order to sustain the east at subsistence levels short of anarchy. A special office, the *Treuhandanstalt*, created to sell into private ownership 14,000 enterprises as quickly as possible and at whatever cost in job losses, found many of them so overmanned and environmentally noxious as to be unsaleable. (Its first chief was assassinated and it was wound up in 1994.) Yet the government kept control of the situation and, in spite of jagged ups and downs, the economy of the eastern Länder showed modest, if irregular, growth as their infrastructure was modernized, their command economies were unravelled and the rescuable parts were privatized.

With reunification Germany regained its Bismarckian position as the weightiest state in Europe – its weight but not, so it seemed, its ambitions.

In *Czechoslovakia* revolution came last but in the end fast. Opposition had crystallized around Charter 77, which was a staid statement of basic rights and a specific protest against the persecution of a rock group. It carried 1,250 signatures. It was followed by the more broadly based Civic Forum, which sought discussions with the government on the release of political prisoners and the removal from office of certain communists accused of inhuman behaviour in 1968 and later repressions. It was able to control demonstrations involving 1,000–2,000 people. The Communist Party, aware of its unpopularity, apathy in its own ranks and the winds of change blowing from Poland and the USSR, narrowly preferred discussion to force. It discarded Gustav Husák as its general secretary (an office which he had held, together with the presidency, since 1968) and appointed a group of more conciliatory communists, led by Ladislas Adamec, to discuss changes with representatives of Civic Forum, led by Vaclav Havel. The communists were, however, offering too little and when it became evident that Gorbachev, on a visit to Prague in 1987, preferred Havel to Adamec the latter threw in his hand. Marian Calfa, a member of Adamec's government, assembled a coalition in which communists and their docile allies held only 11 of 18 posts. The dour Milos Jakes, who had succeeded Husák in the presidency, resigned in favour of the more emollient Karel Urbanek as a rising tide of popular demonstrations accelerated the dissolution of the old regime, bloodlessly but decisively. At the end of 1989 Havel, who had served more prison terms than any triumphant national hero since Mahatma Gandhi, became president. His position was confirmed by elections in 1990 although it was less solid in Slovakia than in the 'historic lands' of Bohemia and Moravia. Dubček reappeared and was rewarded for his past endeavours and sufferings with the post of chairman of the parliament. Uniquely in the former satellite states the Czech and Slovak communists decided not to change the name of their parties. By agreement with Moscow the 70,000 Soviet troops in Czechoslovakia were to be withdrawn by 1991 (Gorbachev had already agreed to withdraw his 50,000 troops from Hungary by that date).

In *Bulgaria* Todor Zhivkov had risen through the ranks (first secretary 1954, prime minister 1962, president 1971) and had ruled longer than even Kádár in Hungary. Bulgaria had limited economic success in the 1970s with tourism and exports mainly within Comecon of agricultural machinery and computer components but the 1980s were bleaker. Zhivkov tried to bolster his position in 1983 by dismissing his deputy Chudomir Alexandrov and embarked the next year on an ill-calculated campaign against Bulgaria's Turkish and (Bulgarian-speaking) Pomak minorities, who numbered about 1 million. In 1950 Bulgaria had asked Turkey to grant visas to 250,000 Turks in Bulgaria, and under an agreement of that year 154,000 left Bulgaria for Turkey without their relatives, who were, however, allowed to emigrate under a second agreement of 1968. At that point the Bulgarian government declared that there were no Turks left in Bulgaria and that all remaining Muslims were the descendants of Bulgarians who had been forcibly converted to Islam. In 1985 these Muslims were required, for the purposes of the census, to adopt Bulgarian names. This decree revealed massive discontent and even panic, and in the face of Bulgarian obduracy Turkey opened its frontier to all would-be migrants without requiring visas. The result was an exodus. Although Bulgaria refused to allow males of military age to leave, at least 300,000 persons did so, whereupon Turkey reintroduced visas. Bulgaria evicted some 2,000 Muslims into Romania and Yugoslavia, whence most of them proceeded to Turkey. After the revolution of 1989 the remaining Muslims were given the right to choose their own names and many refugees returned in order to claim expropriated land. The final blow to the Zhivkov regime was delivered not by Muslims but by a conference of environmentalists in Sofia which was turned into demands for *glasnost*. These were met by police brutality of a kind that had served its purpose in the past but led now to the ousting of Zhivkov by his rattled colleagues. Like Honecker, Zhivkov was arrested and charged with crimes against the state. Under his successor Petar Mladenov the Bulgarian Communist Party changed its name to Socialist, renounced its political monopoly and began negotiations with other parties – the Agrarian People's Party and the Union of Democratic Forces, the latter an assemblage of anti-communist groups – to form a transitional government. These talks having led nowhere, the communists remained in office and contrived to win what appeared to be reasonably conducted elections, but the ensuing popular clamour forced Mladenov to resign the presidency to Zhelu Zhelev, the ex-communist leader of the UDF. Political power wavered between the renamed communists and their opponents. A split in the communist–socialist party and bounding inflation cost the prime minister Andrei Lukanov his majority and then his office. His successor Dimitru Popov won a close election with the help of a Turkish party and imposed severe economic measures. But in 1994 the left, whose better organization outweighed memories of cast-off ideologies, recovered enough lost ground to win overall control of parliament. The new prime minister Zhan Zidenov was typical of the new breed of left-wing leaders which was in the ascendant throughout much of the former satellite empire: young men with more open minds, better educated and disposed to pursue left-wing aims within a democratic system and a capitalist economy. But they had to find answers to pressing economic problems in a country which could no longer sell its tobacco to Russia and had moribund industries, a worthless currency and a people faced with starvation. Violence and counter-violence by the police forced Zidenov from office and elections in 1997 finally removed the communist survivors. Failures and scandals were making the country ungovernable, demonstrations were verging on civil war, and the impasse over Kosovo was ruining commerce along the Danube or across Serbia to the Adriatic. Ex-king Simeon II of Bulgaria, who had earlier failed in a bid for the presidency, became prime minister largely because he bore no responsibility for this state of affairs.

In *Romania* the fall of the communist dictatorship was accomplished only with sickening bloodshed but communist power was not immediately extinguished. Nicolae Ceauşescu had used the Romanian Communist Party, never large, as a base for converting Communist Party rule into a family tyranny of intense malignity, supported by delation, a private army, a ruthless police and driving megalomania. Like Stalin, whom he admired, Ceauşescu was obsessed with getting things done and damning the human cost. He aimed to modernize and aggrandize Romania by the force, not so much of communist doctrine as of his own authority and personality, but, like many a dictator, he failed to draw the distinction between Romania and himself and embarked on spectacular enterprises reminiscent of those of the madder Roman emperors. Both at home and abroad he won for a time a measure of approval through anti-Russian policies and gestures, including his refusal to co-operate in the Warsaw Pact or allow foreign troops on Romanian soil. He was rewarded with lavish praise from, among others, George Bush and with a British knighthood and was received effusively in countries as diverse as China, India and Israel. At home, however, he denuded the economy and ordered the destruction of 7,000 villages, whose inhabitants were compelled to migrate in search of a livelihood and were employed in building ostentatious palaces in the capital on starvation wages. Serious riots were first recorded from Brasov in 1987, and at Timisoara in Transylvania at the end of 1989 the army refused to fire on demonstrators who turned out to protest at the persecution of a fearlessly outspoken Protestant cleric Laszlo Tokes. This spark lit a fire which Ceauşescu, returning from a visit to Teheran, was unable to quench. His security police or private army was opposed by the regular army as well as by large unarmed crowds, and thousands were killed before Ceauşescu and his wife took to flight. They were captured and executed after the merest formality of a trial. Paradoxically, Ceauşescu, the least satellite-minded communist leader, paid the grimmest price in the debacle of the Soviet empire. His removal allowed other communists, who had been plotting a palace revolution, to take power. As the National Salvation Front they declared a transitional government which won internationally supervised elections and thrust its leader Ion Iliescu into the presidency. He was re-elected in 1992 but defeated in 1996 by Emil Constantinescu, who formed the first non-communist administration. Under a variety of post-Ceauşescu governments the standard of living fell disastrously and violent demonstrations threatened civil order. At the end of 1999 Constantinescu dismissed the prime minister Radu Vasike, who refused to recognize his dismissal. Post-Ceauşescu governments were fleeting and feeble, caught between the minimum conditions for aid from the IMF and the refusal of Romania's citizens/consumers to accept them. The dissolution of the USSR impinged on Romania through declarations of independence by the Moldavian SSR with its partly Romanian population and by the Ukraine, which had been given a part of Romania in 1939. Attempts to reconstruct the oil, gas and coal industries with a view to making them profitable by 1996 attracted only disappointing amounts of foreign capital but in 2000 Romania was promised an accelerated track to EU membership.

The year 1989 witnessed revolutions in the grand tradition – the assertion of separate identities, civic rights and human values – but they were sustainable only through economic improvement. They were revolutions against tyranny, corruption and incompetence. Since communist parties had been responsible for these evils, the revolutions were also revolutions against these parties and against communism itself. The parties were demoted from their privileged positions and removed from power in most places for (probably) a long time, but they were not eliminated and might be expected to find some place in the spectrum of multiparty politics, mostly under a new name. The principal features in the overthrow of the Stalinist empire in Europe were economic disaster, Gorbachev, persistent intellectual and popular protest over decades, and the rulers' lack of a plausible claim to legitimacy. The principal consequence was articulation in both senses of the word: the expression of opinion triumphing over suppression, and the re-emergence of the half-buried pattern of sovereign nation states. Gorbachev saw that the Stalinist system was an expensive millstone round Moscow's neck and had lost the strategic rationale which had been its prime justification after 1945. Forty years later an American attack on the USSR, which was in any case far less probable than Stalin might himself have imagined, would bypass the satellites by passing miles over their heads instead of through their territory. Gorbachev's disenchantment with Stalin's system was not concealed from the regional satraps whose business it was to operate it. They could see that they were no longer wanted. They had become proconsuls in a defunct empire and they could not look to their fellow citizens for support since they had grossly abused their power and, besides destroying basic freedoms, had allowed whole economies to moulder. Although in the 1950s economic growth had reached 10 per cent in the more favoured parts of the zone, by the 1980s it was zero or nearly zero practically everywhere. Hence hardship, indignation, tensions, demonstrations, repression (often extremely brutal) and so to revolution. The revolutions were swift and thorough: second-rank communists who were thrust into leading positions disappeared almost as soon as they appeared. Most portentous was the standing of Gorbachev, the president of the USSR which had imposed the regimes that were being discarded. Instead of being reviled he was acclaimed by crowds which chanted his name with grateful enthusiasm and seemed to regard the United States and other western democracies as peripheral. Yet Gorbachev, however crucial his role in the transformation of European affairs, was not the only begetter of the revolutions in central and eastern Europe. These were not as sudden as many bewildered observers imagined. They were part of a sequence (to which they owed much) of abortive risings reaching back to the first postwar decade: 1953, 1956, 1968, 1980. All these commotions, including the formation and early achievements of Solidarity in Poland, antedated the elevation of Gorbachev and were made by people – some of them out of the ordinary, but many of them people commonly dubbed ordinary – who won attention for their indignation and their values and eventually triumphed on the streets in the tradition of the barricades. Solidarity, for example, ignited a jet of popular pressures which could not be capped. The destruction of the imperial superstructure by the fires of revolution uncovered the perennial alternative: a *Mitteleuropa* articulated into separate states, conceived as nation states but in reality conglomerates of greater or less coherence. In the eyes of the new men and women these states were real and legitimate. The old rulers had lacked legitimacy – in East Germany the state itself did too. Revolution therefore had strong nationalist ingredients. For these peoples the decades after the Second World War had been not a Cold War between the superpowers but a waiting war between Soviet imperialism and nearly a dozen separate nationalisms.

The revolutions did not solve economic problems. By the standards of western Europe the material state of these countries was pitiable. Yet most people in central and eastern Europe were materially better off than most people in Asia or Africa. Their economies suffered from distortion, not from sterility. They possessed agricultural and mineral resources and experienced growth in output, reaching in some places 10 per cent a year – albeit growth from a low postwar base and increasingly in the wrong directions. In Poland's large agricultural sector, four-fifths of it in private hands, output rose throughout the postwar decades but investment was inadequate and the agricultural workforce failed to contribute to GNP commensurately with its numbers or to feed the population. Investment in Polish industry increased output but not productivity; exports declined and foreign debt accumulated. Czechoslovakia, with a lengthy history of good education, good administration and technical skills, with the highest income per head in central Europe, with a flourishing export business and enviable natural resources, was converted under communist rule from the things it did best (notably medium industries such as making shoes) to serving the satellite bloc's appetite for heavy industrial goods and armaments. It lost old skills and concentrated on products which, with the end of the Cold War, were wanted neither at home nor abroad. Hungary, the smallest of this central European trio, possessed rich and well-watered agricultural land and significant mineral resources, although these were not – with the exception of its bauxite – of the first quality. Postwar modernization boosted output and industrial exports, but the economy was neither adequately capitalized nor efficiently managed, returns on investment were low, foreign debt high. In all three states much effort brought little reward. Food and consumer goods became dearer and scarcer. Industrial pollution was the worst in the world. Eastern Europe fared no better. Romania embarked on an ambitious, even ruthless, attempt to modernize its economy on the basis of its coal, oil and other minerals, its chemical, hydroelectric and metallurgical industries, and its underpaid and overworked labour force. Ceauşescu's megalomania turned failure into catastrophe. In 2000 the presidency was contested between an old-style communist and an anti-semitic nationalist; the former, Ion Iliescu, won by 2 to 1. In Bulgaria a similar, if less ruthless, expansion of industry increased output, much of which was unsaleable because of its poor quality. In sum, considerable efforts to catch up with western Europe left central and eastern Europe further behind, impoverished, polluted and verging on hopelessness.

Recovery was disappointingly slow and complicated. The first fruits of liberation were clear enough: freedom from hostile foreign domination, from the police state, from economic subjugation, from fears which were always nerve-wracking even when not immediately acute. They got self-rule, membership of NATO and the promise of joining the EU. But much was uncertain, including how to reconnect with the past and how far to embrace the different political and economic patterns of western Europe whose embrace was the outstanding factor in their severing of their links with Russia.

Poland had once constituted (with Lithuania) one of the largest purely European empires of modern times. It had also, uniquely, been obliterated twice – in the eighteenth and twentieth centuries – by its neighbours. Polish nationalism was – again uniquely – stirred by the stimulating papacy of John XXIII and the role of the Roman Catholic Church in the first effective steps to free Poland from Russian rule. To some degree therefore the conventional distinction between foreign and domestic affairs persisted as more clear-cut than in other European countries which were experimenting with the new tripartite division into foreign, domestic and European affairs. Polish nationalism was deeper – but by the same token less frenetic – than that of the fringe nationalist parties elsewhere which were the flotsam and jetsam of fascism. Poland was a large country but not amongst the largest in Europe. It was uncertain how much punch it carried and uncertain how much its recollection of horribly bad times in the past could be tucked away in the history books, and unable to match the economic aggressiveness of its neighbours. In 2005 the brothers Lech and Jaroslav Kaczynski won a landslide centre-right victory which revived fears of a Polish nationalism focused on the Russo-German pincer which had destroyed Poland in the past but their rule (as president and prime minister) lasted little more that a year and was followed by an equally emphatic centre-left victory. Poland became once more pivotal in Europe. After the First World War it emerged from obliteration to become immediately a battleground between Russian communism hoping to conquer Warsaw (and Berlin) and nationalists hoping to recover something of its glory days in alliance with Lithuania and Ukraine. After the Second World War it was engulfed by Russian communism but escaped upon the collapse of the Soviet empire and joined the novel European Union with its commitment to an expanding democratic Europe.

Unlike Poland, Czechoslovakia had no ancient history as a state. The union of Czechs and Slovaks was comparatively recent and imposed, first by the victors of the First World War and then by the Soviet Union after the Second. The Czechs had been part of the Austrian part of the Habsburg empire and Prague had been briefly the empire's capital city. The Slovaks had been a second-class peasant citizenry ruled by Hungary. The union did not survive liberation. Havel's heroic star waned. He was succeeded as prime minister by Victor Klaus who was confronted by demands for autonomy by his Slovak counterpart, Victor Mecias, a communist turned nationalist. Mecias asked for more than Klaus was prepared to concede and the Czechoslovak state split into two. Havel became president of the new Czech Republic. Klaus made a dash for western free marketry which led to economic growth rates near zero, wage cuts, commercial and financial collapse, evaporating foreign currency reserves and his resignation in 1998. Slovakia, a poor relic of 5 million inhabitants, slid in economic terms from central to eastern Europe although it formed part of the Visegrad group with Poland, Hungary and the Czech Republic. (This group was more a convenient geographical term than an active association.) Mecias became increasingly autocratic, was twice removed from office, recovered with a striking victory in Slovakia's first general election (1994) when he outdistanced 20 other parties with lavish promises on the economy and attacks on Slovakia's Hungarian minority, its Czech neighbours and western capitalism. In 1998 his opponents joined forces to defeat him.

Hungary, the smallest of the central European trio, was the most continuously battered in the twentieth century. From being an equal partner with Austria in the Habsburg empire, it declined by taking the wrong side in two world wars, through its abortive attempt to escape from the Soviet empire in 1956 and by emerging into independence with half of all Hungarians living outside its borders. Economically it struggled for the rest of the century; politically its policies delivered more deadlock that progress. But it mended historic enmities with Romania and Serbia and began by the end of the century to stabilize and expand its economy. It possessed well-watered land and significant mineral resources although these – except its bauxite – were not of the best quality and had been inadequately capitalized and incompetently managed. At elections in 2006 the prime minister Ferenc Gyurescy won the rare prize of re-election.

For all the peoples of central and eastern Europe the events of 1989 constituted a revolution. The basic facts were matched by bewildering uncertainties. The Kaczynski interlude in Poland suggested that prewar nationalism was alive but only just, the fading of Havel suggested that Thomas Masazyk's western liberal republic was not the popular choice of Czechs. Not the for first time in European history revolution posed the question what was to follow the defeat of an *ancien régime*. In the revolution which erupted in France in 1789 the issue was debated between the Three Estates, more realistically between the Third Estate and the other two but also between the Three Estates and outsiders – the Sans-Culottes and the Babouvistes – who were easily nullified. (In the premature English revolution in the seventeenth century the winners had beheaded the king, i.e. the constitution, without knowing what to do next.) In the nineteenth century Macaulay had discerned in the Press a Fourth Estate but by the twentieth century the Press had either failed to live up to this role or trivialized it and the onward march of democracy on the left wing of European politics was still in search of an effective, attractive and responsible voice, particularly perhaps in central Europe as it emerged from a regime neither liberal nor democratic. In western eyes the revolution looked like a joyous espousal of liberalism, meaning a form of democracy constrained by the rule of law, individual human rights and intermittent participation in a parliamentary process (elections), a prospect insufficiently democratic in a conflict between the Third Estate (now called the elite) and the People. Communism, which might have played a part, was in the circumstances of 1989 ruled out of consideration, leaving an incompleteness in the political spectrum in the east which besides perplexing the old–new eastern countries also misled their western affiliates.

The elimination of Russian dominance over half of Europe was a challenge for the European Union. From an association of six states it became within a short time an agglomeration of 27 and for the first time a entity living up to its name. This transformation aggravated political and constitutional problems. Nevertheless new members were admitted without excessive delay until only the hard cases remained. These included Cyprus, opposed by Turkey but admitted, and Turkey itself. The ex-Soviet satellites were graded and put in a queue, a practice which gave them the assurance of acceptance but not at first a firm date. Russia was not a candidate and did not ask to be. Although it had played a major part in European affairs (in the partitions of Poland and the Napoleonic wars) there remained the question in European minds whether Russia was 'really' part of Europe. More significantly the United States did not want to see it in the EU. Nor did its former satellites and if there ever was a chance of more formal relations between Russia and Europe it evaporated swiftly in the 1990s so that after the troubled times of Gorbachev and Yeltsin Putin consolidated the new Russian state in decidedly nationalist and sovereign mode.

If Russia was different and so outside Europe Britain was by its own choice also different but yet in Europe. It cherished a shrinking – but not wholly unreal – belief in a special relationship with the United States, a residual sequel to the special relationship between Churchill and Roosevelt (between them rather than between the two countries) in the Second World War. British leaders, with negligible exceptions, did not aim to create an Anglo-Russian opposition to the EU but cast themselves as linkmen between the United States and continental Europeans mistrustful of American policies, particularly trade policies and American subservience to Israel. This balancing act suffered a serious setback, however, when British influence failed to prevent the attack on Iraq which had little to do with Europe and was widely condemned by it. As the war subsided the United States took steps to improve its relations with Germany's and France's new leaders, Angela Merkel and Nicolas Sarkozy.

At Lisbon in 2007 all 27 members of the EU approved a European Reform Act which, in particular, gave the EU Council of Ministers more the appearance of a national state executive by restricting the veto powers of its separate members and creating the post of President of the Council somewhat along the lines of the French Président du Conseil. The Lisbon treaty was designed to formalize such agreements as could be achieved on administrative and constitutional matters and to give more attention to the EU's place and performance in the world.

CHAPTER 7

Yugoslavia and Albania

Federated Yugoslavia

Tito lived for 32 years after his rift with Stalin in 1948. After Stalin's death Khrushchev paid two conciliatory visits to Yugoslavia. The first, in 1955, was tantamount to a confession of error and an apology for the Russian stand in 1948. The second, in June 1956, followed the twentieth congress of the Communist Party of the USSR at which, earlier in the year, Khrushchev had indicated that relations with the satellites needed to be put on a new basis; it followed also the dissolution in April of the Comintern, the body which had pronounced Tito's excommunication. But Russo-Yugoslav relations remained distrustful, if less bitter. Internally, Tito, having won the right to tackle his problems in his own way, did so only tentatively, although the introduction of workers' management in industry in 1950 and the abandonment of collectivization in the countryside in 1953 attested a willingness to moderate doctrinal rigidity. The constitution of 1945 had nationalized all industrial, commercial and financial enterprises, limited individual landholdings to 60 acres, and organized the surplus agricultural land into collective farms. The first five-year plan was an immensely detailed, voluminous and bureaucratic blueprint for a Russian-style command economy. It was gradually dismantled in the 1950s, mainly because it was hopelessly cumbersome. In 1950 and again in 1961 industrial control was devolved on to workers' councils with wide powers of management, including the right to allocate investment funds and to decide what to do with profits. In the early 1960s new lines of credit were made available through local banks (as opposed to the central bank) and the system of fixing prices centrally was relaxed. A new constitution in 1963 introduced real but limited decentralization without, however, removing ultimate power from the party or Tito himself. These half-measures failed to give industry the expected stimulus, the economy remained stagnant, inflation rose and so did Yugoslavia's dependence on aid from the IMF and the United States. There was a brief reaction in economic policy but the liberalizing and decentralizing strands were – also briefly – resumed. So in fits and starts the economic sector was fragmented into tens of thousands of autonomous units. Whether the psychological stimuli of decontrol and self-management outweighed losses in efficiency and productivity was inconclusively debated. More

7.1 Yugoslavia and its republics, 1991

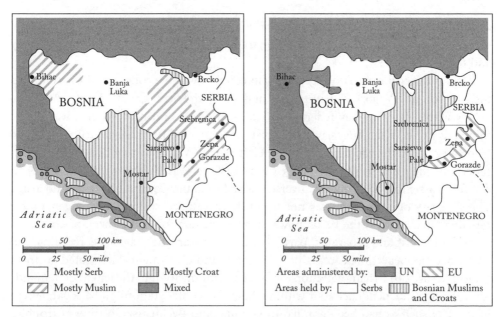

7.2 The Vance–Owen plan (April 1993)

7.3 The Contact Group proposal (July 1994)

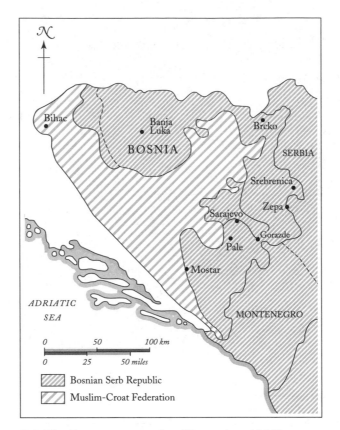

7.4 The Dayton peace plan (November 1995)

certainly, these industrial changes created a new base for political power by opening careers for talents in industry besides the traditional ladders of the Communist Party and the armed forces.

Besides the economy Tito's second main concern was the cohesion of the state and the creation of a Yugoslav identity over and above the Serb, Croat and other nationalisms within the Yugoslav federation. Tito, half Croat and half Slovene, was determined to preserve the Yugoslav state which had emerged from the destruction of the Habsburg and Ottoman empires in the First World War. He was aided by the camaraderie of the partisan warfare of the Second World War, during which he had been careful to assemble an ethnically diverse leadership in the Communist Party and army. The integrity of Yugoslavia was not seriously threatened so long as this generation remained in charge. By the 1970s, however, a new generation had grown up, which was more nationalist and separatist, partly because the wartime magic was receding and partly because peacetime competition for goods and investment exacerbated far from forgotten sores. In Croatia agitation for more autonomy went to the length of demands for sovereign independence (but within a Yugoslav confederation) and a separate seat in the UN such as had been granted to Ukraine and Byelorussia. A time of troubles loomed – with Tito close on 80. In 1971 Tito decided to stamp on his aberrant younger colleagues. He made it plain that he was the judge of when enough was enough, and that in his judgement Croat separatism was unpardonably threatening the integrity and welfare of the Yugoslav state. Once he resolved to intervene he carried the day. The Croat elder statesman Vladimir Bakarić stood by him. The younger leaders resigned. Tito then repeated this performance in Serbia, where the younger politicians were no less nationalist; and in Slovenia and Macedonia (but here dissent was not purely nationalist).

Separatism was an extreme form of the continuing problem of decentralism which called in question the powers of the central government and the central organs of the Communist Party. In the 1950s and 1960s both centralism and permanent communist rule were questioned. Centralism was attacked on grounds of efficiency and offended local patriotism. Criticism was open and lively. It raised the question of how political authority could be dispersed without denting communist control. The decentralizers argued as technocrats, managers and grassroots politicians. Their arguments either skated around the consequences for communist control or, as in the case of Djilas, accepted the conclusion that the Communist Party had no automatic right to permanent power. They became a double source of offence to the centralizers who, pre-eminently the security and police chief, Alexander Ranković, not only preferred central to dispersed authority for its own sake but also saw in decentralization a menace to the communist monopoly of power. Tito allowed the debate to flourish until it seemed to become dangerously disruptive. He was not an enemy of limited debate, but he did not intend that either side should win. In the liberalizing atmosphere of the 1950s the first need was to curb the liberalizers. Djilas was persecuted and imprisoned. Ranković remained in office – and was even promoted – until his anti-liberal campaign overstepped the bounds and he was found to be spying on Tito himself, whereupon he was dismissed. At the end of this phase Tito devised a new constitution which created an Executive Bureau or Presidential Commission consisting of two representatives of each federal republic and one from each autonomous district, with Tito as permanent federal president. (After his death the presidency was to revolve.) This arrangement was intended to signal a compromise but it left the realities untouched and conflict no more than deadened.

The outcome of the separatist and decentralizing currents of the 1950s and 1960s was to block secession but at the same time allow a federation with a strong centre to evolve towards something approaching a looser confederation of sovereign entities on the model of Switzerland. And the state remained a communist one. In 1958 the Communist Party had been renamed the League of Communists. This change was taken to indicate that the party might not always be the right organ for running local government bodies or industrial plants. But the party, or League, remained unique, so that the unity of Yugoslavia remained linked with communist rule rather than the development of a Yugoslav nationalism. Older nationalisms survived and flourished and, when Yugoslav federalism disintegrated, leaders in the several republics transformed themselves from communists into strident nationalists, reanimating the ethnic and religious hatreds which had served to get rid of alien overlords (Turkish, Austrian) in living memory and were now aligned against one another.

At Tito's death in 1980 Yugoslavia was unique. It was the only communist neutral in the world. But it was also fragmenting and indigent. It was no more cohesive as a communist federation than it had been as a triune kingdom. The task of the tail end of the Karageorgević dynasty had been to compound Serbs, Croats and Slovenes into a Yugoslav state and nation, but this task was no more than half-achieved before the Second World War reopened old divisions, particularly between the Serbs and Croats, whose grisly wartime leader Ante Pavelic tried to create a separate Croat state, buying Italian support by ceding marginal Croat lands to fascist Italy (which was looking across the Adriatic for its version of *Lebensraum – spazio vitale –* in Albania and Dalmatia). On the other hand, the communist resistance to Italians and Germans produced an aura of Yugoslav confraternity which, after the war, Tito sought to enhance by giving ethnic minorities – Montenegrins, Macedonians, Albanians (in Kosovo), Hungarians (15 per cent in Vojvodina) – equal or approximately equal status with the three original constituents of the Yugoslav state. But Tito could not give these different groups anything approaching economic equality. Their national and religious differences – within Christianity and, for Muslims, beyond it – were not offset by any economic fruits of federation. Aid from the west which followed the rift with Moscow was used mainly to develop industries. The consequent drift from the countryside to towns was at first a welcome relief for rural overpopulation insufficiently tempered by emigration, but in the longer run it weakened agriculture without commensurate benefit from industry, which faltered when reforms in management and financing were applied too slowly and without turning the right to manage into competent management. Western helpers lost interest when they lost money and when aid to Yugoslavia lost its political edge with the cooling of the Cold War. Foreign debt piled up, so that paying the interest on it became a burden on the Yugoslav economy greater than the benefits conferred by the loans in the first place. In 1989 the federal prime minister Ante Marković, a Croat, aiming to strengthen the economy in order to stave off Serb, Croat and Slovenian nationalism, instituted a convertible currency, commercial banks, a stock exchange and other apparatus of a capitalist market economy. He won little international support. Inflation was reduced from 2,000 per cent to zero in a matter of months and exports and the reserves rose but at the price of catastrophic unemployment and bankruptcies and dire want. Endemic tensions between the several republics were accentuated.

Dissolution: Serbs, Croats and Slovenes

At one level – the popular level – Yugoslavia was a country in whose towns and villages one marriage in three united a couple from different ethnic and religious communities. At another level – the political – it was a country whose several republics were run by politicians who promoted themselves by emphasizing their communal roots and divisive loyalties – which is to say, that they built their power by abusing other communities. Personal neighbourliness and political communalism were at odds and those who led or wished to lead saw the latter as the better route to power. They were perhaps hollow men but they were also noisy men and from Tito's death or earlier Yugoslavia displayed signals of strains portending either constitutional change towards a looser federation or, in default of adjustment, its disruption and war. The most powerful of the six republics was Serbia, both home to the largest group and the one with the largest numbers outside its own republic: 2 million Serbs in Croatia and Bosnia besides 10 million in Serbia. Serbian leaders also had the support of the Orthodox Church in and beyond Serbia – particularly in Greece and Cyprus. Religion was still a part of nationalism in the Balkans, and the intersection of secular and religious paranoia gave these conflicts a ruthless inhumanity all but banished from most of the rest of Europe. Most important of all to Belgrade was its control of the Yugoslav federal army of 135,000, officered predominantly by Serbs.

The temper of the Serbs was embodied in Slobodan Milosevic, who rose through the Serbian League of Communists to become president of the Serbian Republic. He was a Serb nationalist and a skilled politician with minimal loyalty to the idea of Yugoslavia. He had extinguished in 1989 the autonomous status of the two regions of Kosovo and Vojvodina – the former nine-tenths Albanian in population and the latter significantly, although not as preponderantly, Hungarian. The issue in Kosovo went back to the Middle Ages when Kosovo had earned a hallowed place in the mythology of Serb nationalism (the six hundredth anniversary of the fateful battle of Kosovo which had extinguished Serb independence fell in 1989). Milosevic encouraged Serbs in Croatia who were agitating for an autonomous Serb region; revived Serb claims to parts of Bosnia; obstructed the routine advancement of the Croat Stipe Mesić to the federal presidency; and in the Krajina district of Croatia condoned Serb activities reminiscent of the provocative disorders stirred up by Konrad Henlein and the Sudeten Germans against the Czechoslovak state in 1938. He advocated the maintenance of the Yugoslav federation within its existing borders and so won the goodwill of the EC and the United States, which wanted to nip troubles in the bud and thought Milosevic was the man for that job – for instance, by getting Mesić smoothly installed as president and pacifying rather than inflaming ethnic conflict in Kosovo. But while for those outside Yugoslavia the federation represented continuity and stability, to Slovenes and Croats it looked like a menacing Greater Serbia. In June 1991 Slovenia and Croatia declared themselves independent of Yugoslavia, repudiating not only the existing federation but any modification of it.

The Yugoslav government sent federal forces into both countries. They failed to prevent Slovene secession but fought a largely successful war against Croatia. Slovenia, compact, homogeneous, peripheral and with a mere 1 million inhabitants, possessed – like each Yugoslav republic – its own defence force distinct from the federal army, whose units in Slovenia were isolated from one another and from their supplies. These were checked and repulsed. Milosevic, intent on concentrating the federal army against Croatia, was content to see Slovenia go and it became independent for the first time in its history. There was, however, a crucial difference between Slovenia and Croatia. In Slovenia there were few Serbs but in Croatia, which covered one-fifth of Yugoslavia, with a population of 4.5 million, there were 600,000, mainly at its eastern end (eastern Slavonia) and in the Krajina between the Adriatic coast and Bosnia. The Serbs won control of a third of Croatia. In eastern Slavonia the federal army's devastation of Vukovar won the Croats international sympathy and helped them to win international recognition of their independence – which they had lost in 1102. In the Krajina the Croats were worsted by the local Serbs. (The Krajina was originally a Croat–Serb buffer zone or Hadrian's Wall created in the sixteenth century by the Habsburgs against the Turks, the Serbs being refugees from the Ottoman empire. In more modern times the Krajina was extended southward to include Knin and its surrounding area peopled by Serbs more militantly anti-Croat than the Serbs of the Krajina proper had been wont to be.)

International intervention in Yugoslav wars had two motives. The first was to stop the fighting for fear that it would spread to the whole of Yugoslavia and beyond. Such fears were well-grounded: the independence of Slovenia and Croatia was likely to produce similar demands in other republics because Serbia and Macedonia contained ethnic minorities and Bosnia consisted only of minorities; and because conflicts in Yugoslavia attracted nervous attention and inflamed national susceptibilities in Albania, Greece and (to a lesser degree) Bulgaria. The UN imposed in 1991, in the first or Serbo-Croat phase of the wars, an embargo on the delivery of arms to any part of Yugoslavia. The EC – later the EC jointly with the UN – tried by diplomacy to negotiate a settlement between the combatants. This might involve recasting the existing Yugoslav federation – a solution abandoned before the end of 1991 – or accepting its dissolution. A *troika* of EC foreign ministers was succeeded by a single negotiator (Lord Carrington, Lord Owen, Carl Bildt in succession). The UN appointed first Cyrus Vance and then Thorwald Stoltenberg to work with Owen until this effort was superseded in 1994 by a Contact Group of five (United States, Russia, Britain, Germany and France). All these eminent persons strove to secure ceasefire agreements and to devise a generally acceptable territorial apportionment of Bosnia within its existing boundaries but with a new constitution. The ceasefire agreements were adopted and broken with sickening cynicism while the territorial proposals were all dismissed by one faction or another with a flippancy which paid scant tribute to the arduous and mainly sensible labours of their authors.

The second branch of international intervention was the succour of victims of war and the protection of those providing these services. It was pursued by various agencies, including UN agencies, and by a UN Protection Force – UNPROFOR – recruited from over 20 countries and despatched to aid and protect the aiders but not to become involved in the hostilities. UNPROFOR was not a peacekeeping force. A UN peacekeeping force was sent to Macedonia but UNPROFOR was established, first in Croatia and later in Bosnia, to protect aid agencies, to succour victims in various areas where peace had not been secured and to keep out of the fighting. It was despatched for humanitarian purposes but in breach of the UN's normal practice of sending peacekeeping or humanitarian missions only to areas where hostilities had been reliably suspended. UNPROFOR was partly a gamble on getting such a suspension and partly a reaction to the unexpectedly fearful atrocities which accompanied the fighting. It was put into a war situation without the authority or capacity to make war and in the hope that it might perform its tasks in spite of the wars being waged in its zones of operation: this was an operation of a kind never before undertaken by the UN Security Council. In many areas and various ways UNPROFOR was successful but it was always a pawn waiting to be seized by one belligerent or another. Its fortunes were inextricably entangled with the parallel diplomatic attempts to take war out of the situation.

The EC's diplomatic effort to pacify Yugoslavia, grounded in fear of spreading disorder and sharpened by horror at the stupefying brutality used by the combatants, was flawed from the outset. EC members discerned an opportunity to assert – or at least test – their collective power but neither the Community as such nor its several members had given much thought to a crisis which had been in the making for a decade or more. Nor was the EC merely unprepared. It had as a Community no standing outside the territory of its members, no armed forces, no community of purpose and no established machinery for concerting Community foreign policies. It was, on the contrary, only embarking on the first steps towards creating such machinery and fell into the error of supposing that one way of doing so was to act as though it already had what it hoped to concoct. The EC was not a regional organization for Europe in the terms of article 52 of the UN Charter. Attempts to invest it with authority from the OSCE (an even more embryonic body with likewise no armed forces) were an unconvincing subterfuge, the more so since Yugoslavia was a member of the OSCE, with a veto on its more positive actions. The EC pressed for the acceptance of Mesić as Yugoslav president, a three months' suspension of the Croat and Slovene declarations of independence, the withdrawal of all armed forces to barracks and a conference on the future shape of Yugoslavia. It achieved none of these things and although it negotiated a series of Serb–Croat ceasefire agreements, these were routinely disregarded. The fighting in Croatia was halted only because the Serbs had conquered most of what they wanted and Bosnia claimed the attention of both Serbs and Croats.

The EC – and notably Germany – took the lead in arguing for immediate and unconditional recognition of Croat and Slovene independence. This was a political act. In law a people or nation has no right to secede from a sovereign state by invoking the principle of self-determination, although other states may, using established diplomatic criteria, choose to recognize a claim to statehood. Slovenia satisfied the broad criteria of international practice but Croatia did not. An adjudicator consulted by the EC – Robert Badinter, a former French minister – reported that the state of affairs in

Croatia did not warrant immediate recognition. Croatia neither offered nor was it required to offer guarantees to its large Serb minorities; Croats were not reminded that if Croatia seceded from Yugoslavia Serbs in Croatia might with equal force claim a right to secede from Croatia; and there was no Croatian government with control over the whole of the territory claimed by the new state. Croatia was granted recognition as an independent state in the slipstream of Slovene independence and in the hope of preventing the spread of war into Bosnia and beyond. The opposite view, expressed by the UN secretary-general, Boutros Boutros-Ghali, was that recognition would do nothing to check Serb–Croat hostilities and would evoke a declaration of independence by Bosnia–Herzegovina and its invasion by Serbs and Croats in temporary alliance. Bosnia–Herzegovina satisfied the criteria for independence even less than Croatia.

Milosevic's position in Serbia came under some threat in 1992. Milan Panic, who had returned from the United States after making a lot of money there and had been appointed prime minister of the Serbian republic, was disenchanted with Milosevic. So too was Dimitri Cosic, an eminent Serb nationalist who had been appointed to the vacant Yugoslav presidency. At a conference in London, Cosic struck a bargain with the Croat president Franjo Tudjman: Serbia would recognize Croatia's independence and its right to the Krajina in return for internationally guaranteed rights for Serbs in Croatia. This agreement was a setback for Milosevic – if only because it had been negotiated by somebody else. He was faced with the choice whether or not to endorse it at the cost of antagonizing the more militant Serb nationalists in Serbia and the Bosnian Serbs led by Radovan Karadzic and his military counterpart General Radko Mladić, who had purported to annex the Krajina to Bosnia. Milosevic used a dispute over control of the army to secure the dismissal of Cosic, decisively defeated Panic in a presidential election and affirmed his authority in parliamentary elections – in which, however, Vojislav Seselj, campaigning for the eviction of all non-Slavs from the whole of Bosnia and Kosovo, won 20 per cent of the vote and so presented Milosevic with a challenge as the standard-bearer of the purest nationalists. Seselj and Karadzic, who declared an independent Serb republic in Bosnia in 1992, were for Milosevic rival Serb chieftains who had to be kept in order or outmanoeuvred.

For the time being Milosevic had consolidated his position and became the key figure in the search for peace by negotiation. Outsiders had to choose between seeking a deal acceptable to him or making war on him with economic weapons and perhaps more. Since by this date he had invaded Bosnia with rapid success (see below), the only available deal must include some acceptance of Serb conquests in Bosnia as well as Croatia, both of them now internationally recognized sovereign states. Slovenia escaped further turmoil and began a slow approach to EU membership. The choice or risk of military war against Serbia raised the prospect of lengthy, costly, bloody, possibly ineffective operations with ill-defined purposes, unforeseeable wider consequences and, most telling, disagreement among strategists on what kind of operations and what weight of force would be appropriate. One of Milosevic's main strengths was his awareness that no such war was at all likely over Bosnia. He was little disturbed by the arms embargo imposed by the UN in 1991 on all parts of Yugoslavia since the ban hurt other parties more than the well-armed Serbs; and economic sanctions, imposed on Serbia in 1992 by the EC and the UN, had yet to make their mark. From mid-1992 into 1995 his central problem was how much of Bosnia to annex in the face, on the one hand, of growing international hostility and sanctions and, on the other, the successes of the Bosnian Serbs, whose calculations and ambitions might not accord with his own. Serbs in Serbia were prepared to suffer for Greater Serbia but not necessarily for a Greater Serbia with Radovan Karadzic as its hero. The architects of Greater Serbia were in Belgrade, not Bosnia; they were Milosevic and the Serb Orthodox hierarchy, not Karadzic and Mladic.

Partition: Bosnia–Herzegovina

Bosnia–Herzegovina was distinct from Serbia and Croatia not merely as a separate Yugoslav republic but as a political entity which, within varying boundaries, had been accepted as such formally since the sixteenth century and in practice for many generations earlier. Many of the inhabitants had affinities with Serbs or Croats; others were different because they were Muslims. The Bosnian Serbs accounted for less than a third of the population, the Bosnian Croats for about a sixth, the Muslims for nearly half. All these people were Slavs by race and tongue as a result of invasions in the early Middle Ages by Slavs of various kinds who overlaid Iberian, Celtic and Avar peoples and other trace elements. Among these invaders Serbs and Croats were the most prominent and they penetrated into Bosnia as well as establishing principalities of their own on three sides of it. They arrived in the Balkans as pagans but became Christians, and although they were often allies against the dominant but declining power of the Byzantine empire they were divided by giving their allegiance to rival Byzantine and Roman ecclesiastical authorities. Relatively inaccessible, Bosnia became a patchwork of lordships, great and small, which were relatively independent of outside domination until the conquest of the whole area by the Ottoman Turks after the battle of Adrianople in 1463. The Bosnian church was Catholic, not Orthodox, but was suspected of heresy in Rome where nobody knew much about it. The weakness of the ecclesiastical link, the growth of towns under Turkish rule and the simple good sense of adopting the new rulers' faith contributed to the unusually wholesale conversion of Bosnians to Islam. By about 1600, half of them were Muslims. Peasants trying to get a living with the minimum of interference from superiors, merchants anxious to maintain and extend their commerce in the new environment of Turkish administration, Turkish law and Turkish favours, found little embarrassment in putting off one faith and putting on another – or the reverse, when expedient.

From beginning to end of the Turkish domination, Bosnia's fortunes were conditioned by the frequent wars between the Ottoman and Habsburg empires. Its frontiers were fixed by the treaties which punctuated those wars in the eighteenth century. As the next century progressed the Turks lost control and Bosnia was up for grabs. With Serbia and Montenegro becoming independent states and clients of Russia, Austro-Hungary became more worried about the Russians than about the Turks and Bosnia became more vulnerable to expansionist neighbours. After the Russian defeat of the Turks in 1877 the European powers gathered at Berlin to redraw the map of the Balkans. They decreed that Bosnia should pass to Austro-Hungarian administration (converted into annexation in 1908 but lost to Vienna at the end of the First World War, which started in the Bosnian capital Sarajevo). Between that war and the next there was wide agreement on the idea of a Yugoslav state but no agreement on the division of powers between its central government and its provinces. Bosnia was, with Croatia, opposed to centralization which meant, in effect, power to the Serbs. The problem was unsolved when the Second World War broke out and it was no more than suppressed, partially, by Tito who as a communist was a centralizer but as a Slovene–Croat was not. In Tito's Yugoslavia, Bosnia became one of the federation's more depressed areas. One consequence was increased communal tension; another was the departure of many Bosnian Serbs to Serbia, a flight which made the Muslims much the largest of the three main communities in Bosnia. Tito encouraged the Muslims to think of themselves as a distinct community and they were formally so recognized in 1971. But they were split between communist and anti-communist Muslims. Ilia Izetbegovic, future president of Bosnia–Herzegovina, was a prominent anti-communist leader.

In 1990 the government of Bosnia–Herzegovina (Herzegovina was its small southwestern corner) was a coalition formed after elections in that year. It contained Muslims, Serbs and Croats but the Serbs left the coalition – their first step towards a distinct Serb state in as much of Bosnia as they might be able to conquer. When fighting in Croatia began President Izetbegovic was faced with a choice between remaining in a new Yugoslavia shorn of Slovenia and Croatia, or claiming independence as Slovenia and Croatia had. He chose the latter. He feared Serb and Croat designs on his republic's territory and wanted to be in a position to appeal for outside help in protecting it. He was accorded international recognition and membership of the UN early in 1992 but not before the UN, reacting to the doubling of Serb regular forces in Serbia (normally around 45,000) and the growth of Serb irregular units, had imposed its embargo on the supply of arms to all parts of Yugoslavia, including Bosnia. Serbia treated these events of the spring of 1992 as a signal for open hostilities by regular and irregular forces. They gained control of half Bosnia in a few days, using the metamilitary weapons of savagery and massacre and so changing the nature of UN intervention in Yugoslavia which, originally confined to protecting aid agencies and civilian victims in need of food and medicines, became entangled in the fate of a million refugees congregated and besieged in lethal enclaves and clamorous to escape from Bosnia rather than be succoured in it. At this point Serbia and Montenegro together proclaimed a new Yugoslavia consisting of themselves, another new state.

There were now several new states in what had been Yugoslavia and two of them were at war with one another: Bosnia–Herzegovina and the new, reduced Yugoslav federation. What had been a civil war in Yugoslavia had been converted into a war between two sovereign members of the UN and the Security Council could have branded Serbia an aggressor. If the war was in any sense a civil war it was a civil war in Bosnia, not a civil war in Yugoslavia. There would have been no case for applying an embargo to Bosnia had it not already existed. But a one-sided lifting of the embargo implied an engagement in the hostilities which in 1992 no government seemingly contemplated, partly because to do so must jeopardize UNPROFOR's tasks and put an end to the EC/UN's mediatory diplomacy and partly because the Bush and Clinton administrations set their faces against the kind of UN intervention which must entail active American involvement on the ground. The result was equivocation at the international level and covert arms supplies to all parties.

In 1992–94 the EC/UN negotiators and the Contact Group produced a series of plans for partitioning Bosnia into Serb, Muslim and Croat segments within a continuing Bosnian entity. These plans were accepted at one time or another by all the principal parties in Bosnia but never simultaneously and with more partisan guile than pacific fervour. They accepted the principle of division but not the divisions proposed. The Muslims regarded them as outrageously unfair invitations to commit suicide while the Serbs regarded them as inadequate recognition of their conquests and ethnic entitlements. In this phase sanctions, tightened in 1993, were causing considerable distress in Serbia, where unemployment engulfed half the workforce and the economy was cut off from international aid and investment. (Greek, Cypriot and Russian attempts to circumvent the sanctions were no more than marginally effective.) Milosevic was forced to consider reining back the Serbs in Bosnia by applying his own sanctions on supplies to Bosnia – especially oil – and by closing Serbia's borders with Bosnia, but divisions within the EC and the indecisiveness of the United States relieved his fears and emboldened him to pursue his plans to create a Greater Serbia by conquests. Karadzic, presumably with Milosevic's approval, rejected a Contact Group plan giving him control over 49 per cent of Bosnia and demanded a larger slice of eastern Bosnia, access to the Adriatic in the west and half Sarajevo. He was more inflamed than chastened by international intervention which, on the scale represented by UNPROFOR, excited derision. For three years the Bosnian Serbs had known only success but their brutal excesses prodded the Security Council into designating in 1993 safe areas (on the analogy of the safe havens proclaimed in Iraq in 1991 but in very different circumstances) and authorizing UNPROFOR to use force to prevent them from being bombarded. Since, however, the Council's members did not provide UNPROFOR, already overburdened, with the means to discharge these new functions, the safe areas – all of them peopled by Muslims and threatened by Serbs – were safe only so long as the Serbs refrained from attacking them. There were six of them: four in eastern Bosnia close to the border with Serbia and strategically important for communications between Serbia and Bosnia; Sarajevo; and Bihacs in north-western Bosnia, athwart a main railway and adjacent to the main pocket of Serbs in Croatia. (The town of Bihacs and its surrounding area were Bosnian enclaves vulnerable to attack from three quarters – Krajina Serbs to the west, Bosnian Serbs to the east and dissident Muslims in the north, led by an eccentric entrepreneur, at odds with the Muslims in Sarajevo and with visions of establishing a state of their own.)

The UN was not the Serbs' only adversary. There were also the Croats, with whom Serbia had warred in 1991. In Bosnia Croatia had a choice. It might conspire with Serbia to partition Bosnia or make an alliance with the Muslims against the Bosnian Serbs. The semi-independent Croatia created by Italy and Germany during the Second World War had included most of Bosnia and in 1993 the governments of Croatia and Bosnia agreed to form a Muslim–Croat federation with looser confederate links with Croatia, leaving a Bosnian Serb rump to make similar arrangements with Serbia. The Croats bided their time. Tudjman unostentatiously reorganized and re-equipped his army before launching offensives which recovered the Krajina with unexpected efficiency and expelled some 200,000 terrified Serbs who, fleeing eastward, constituted the war's biggest forced migration and one of its most atrocious human calamities. Aid agencies and their UN protectors were overwhelmed. Croat forces also recovered most of eastern Slavonia, which they had lost to Serbia in 1991. These reverses for the Serbs, combined with the UN's attempts to throw a safety net over selected areas, precipitated fresh joint action by Milosevic and Karadzic.

The creation of safe areas which were unsafe was a disaster which nevertheless marked a stage in the ending of the fighting. During 1994 the United States and Milosevic circled round a possible compromise whereby Milosevic would recognize an independent Bosnian state and ditch Karadzic in return for the cession to Serbia of Serb enclaves in eastern Bosnia, including Srebrenica and other safe areas. But Milosevic decided to back Karadzic, overrun with him these enclaves and revive the siege and bombardment of Sarajevo. The Bosnian capital was reduced to starvation, almost the whole population of Srebrenica was massacred and some 400 Dutch and Ukrainians serving in UNPROFOR were taken hostage and humiliatingly evicted. The United States resolved that defeating the Serbs was a necessary preliminary to peace.

The United States had the power but was undecided how to use it, unsure of the co-operation of its European allies, vexed by the prospect of picking a quarrel with Russia and determined to avoid putting American lives at risk. This last concern meant using air power but not ground forces.

One source of differences between the United States and EC members was their aims. The overriding, almost exclusive aim of the EC was the restoration of peace whereas the United States was seriously troubled about securing justice for non-Serbs, particularly Muslims. By 1993 Europeans reckoned that the Serbs had won the war in Bosnia and it was futile to encourage the Muslims or a Muslim–Croat alliance to continue it. France and Britain, which provided the largest contingents for UNPROFOR, determinedly opposed any measures which might provoke attacks on it, necessitate its withdrawal together with the aid agencies and delude the Muslims with vain hopes. Americans, on the other hand, were impelled towards a policy of helping the Bosnian government to redress the military balance by removing the arms embargo and using air power to halt Serb aggression and defend the safe areas. Finding that a resolution to raise the embargo would be defeated in the Security Council, Clinton decided instead to recall American vessels from the patrol in the Adriatic which was enforcing it. The practical effect of this step was small but the wider implications of disavowing a resolution for which the United States had lobbied and voted in the Security Council were graver. Clinton's decision – which was taken, but not announced, before the Democrats' heavy losses in the mid-term elections in November – meant backing Muslims and Croats against Serbs and risking overt Russian support for the Serbs. As in the civil war in Spain in the 1930s, the Bosnian war was being covertly internationalized. The United States and Russia were providing encouragement and more than encouragement to different belligerents while Islamic states in the Middle East were vying with one another in supplying or promising aid to the Muslims. (Some of these countries had been sending charitable aid since as far back as the 1970s. In the 1990s more robust commodities entered the pipelines.)

American advocacy of air power was no less contentious. Air power meant NATO air power since there was no other readily available. It was contentious on political and tactical grounds. The Russians, on whom the Contact Group counted to persuade Milosevic to compel Karadzic to accept its latest peace plan, found it hard to stomach the introduction of the quintessentially anti-Russian NATO into the Bosnian tangle, regarded it as a ruse to bypass the Security Council and the Russian veto in it, and were privately indignant about bringing NATO into the battle on the side of the Bosnian government against the Serbs. Europeans fretted against the American refusal to incur casualties in ground operations and, together with some American strategists and commanders, contested the efficacy of air strikes on the grounds that targets in Bosnia were difficult to find and still more difficult to hit. Over Bihacs they appeared to be justified. When the Serbs, having countered over-optimistic offensives against them, held the town at their mercy, their adversaries invoked air retaliation but it proved dubiously useful and was discontinued. Elsewhere, however, Serbs around surviving safe areas were attacked by NATO air units and by the artillery of a new Rapid Reaction Force created by France, Britain and the Netherlands. The air operations, which were the largest in NATO's entire history, were undertaken without informing Yeltsin. In substance, the United States overruled its European allies, humiliated Russia, sidelined the UN – and got results. One result was to damage the UN as seriously as the League of Nations had been damaged by Britain and France in the Ethiopian crisis of the 1930s.

But the main result was a prospect of peace. The United States effectively took the field against the Bosnian Serbs without going through the formalities of condemning them at the UN as a threat to international peace and hoping to drive a wedge between them and Milosevic. It convoked the presidents of Serbia, Croatia and Bosnia–Herzegovina to talks at an air base at Dayton, Ohio, and kept them there for three weeks until they accepted terms which were presented to them. The Bosnian government, which had the most reason to reject the terms, accepted them under the threat, implied or explicit, that the American aid which had enabled them to fight on would cease. The Bosnian Serbs, who were not invited to Dayton, accepted the terms with unconcealed repugnance. Milosevic abandoned the Bosnian Serbs' leaders but not the prospect of Greater Serbia. In substance these terms followed earlier proposals for the partition of Bosnia–Herzegovina into two roughly equal halves (a Bosnian Serb republic and a Croat–Muslim federation) within a sovereign Bosnian state with a weak central government and a weakly integrated capital, Sarajevo, under overall Croat–Muslim control. Each of the two halves was to be entitled to raise its own army; it was a state in all but name. Persons convicted of war crimes were to be debarred from holding public office; some 50 persons, including Karadzic and Mladic, had been named by the prosecution at the tribunal established by the UN but only one had been apprehended and arraigned; the rest were beyond the tribunal's reach and had a good chance of remaining beyond it. An international implementation force (I-FOR), substantially American and outside UN control, was raised to police the Dayton agreement.

From the international point of view these wars in Yugoslavia were on balance a fiasco. Much was done to succour victims from the accustomed hazards of war and from the heightened horrors of ethnic vengeance. The first round between Serbs and Croats was brought to a halt through international mediation but also because the combatants had reasons of their own to desist: the spread of the war to Bosnia suspended their conflict for three years. It was also the real test for international intervention.

The chief aim of the main international bodies most of the time was to stop the war. They failed because, initially, they were not prepared to deploy the necessary force and, later, because they could not agree among themselves what kind of force to use. The discredit for these failures fell on the UN as an organization but the blame attached more properly to the principal members of the Security Council: they ducked the issue by trying to use UNPROFOR for purposes for which it was neither intended nor equipped by them and, having recognized Bosnia–Herzegovina as an independent sovereign state, they refused to act as though they had done so. The Security Council was not asked to treat the war in Bosnia as a threat to international peace (which it clearly was) or to authorize consequential measures as prescribed by the UN Charter. The UN was further diminished when the United States, having resolved to take effective action, preferred to do so not by giving a lead in the UN but through NATO, whose members could be relied on to mute their objections to American strategies.

All external states grievously misinterpreted the purposes of Milosevic and underestimated the ruthlessness of the Bosnian Serbs. In the Bosnian round of the Yugoslav drama the Serbs made the running until checked by the Croats. Preferring international diplomacy to international action the EC and, for a time, the United States wrongly assessed, first, the readiness of the belligerents to heed reasonable proposals for peace and, later, the capacity or willingness of Milosevic to control the Bosnian Serbs, in particular Karadzic, who was a potential rival for the chieftainship of Serbian nationalism.

The introduction of UNPROFOR in the absence of a ceasefire was an unprecedented gamble which, despite some promise in Croatia in the first round, went disastrously wrong in the next. The early initiatives of the EU were impelled by good intentions unaccompanied by equivalent good judgement.

The solution finally imposed by the United States had a strong air of non-finality. It gave Serbs and Croats much of what they wanted and had acquired illicitly and brutally. Although not invited to Dayton, the Bosnian Serbs had the least cause to complain since they were allotted more of Bosnia than demography dictated and their territory was denominated a Serb republic. Formally, the Dayton agreement preserved a single Bosnian state but in reality it consisted of two parts waiting to be annexed by Serbia and Croatia. The Muslims, the largest community, retained some leverage in half the new state but none in the other half. About a quarter of a million people were destitute as a direct result of wars of aggression and ethnic cleansing. In a world accustomed to talk of sending the 'right signals' this outcome looked terribly perverse. It gave victory of a sort, at least temporarily, to small cliques which had annexed religio-nationalism to their selfish ends.

Much of this mediocre performance could be ascribed to the relative unimportance of south-east Europe compared with, for example, the Middle East, whose economic and strategic importance had, almost simultaneously, predisposed major powers to go to war and pay for it. With the partial exception of the war in Korea 40 years earlier there was no clear precedent for UN intervention in an international war such as, given the recognition of an independent Bosnia–Herzegovina, this war was. More fatefully, forceful American intervention when and where and how it mattered – that is to say, on the ground – was not made available through the UN or otherwise.

Neither Croatia nor Serbia felt satisfied with the outcome. Tudjman died in 1999, was mourned as the father of independent Croatia but losing influence through his intolerance and nepotism, he left a country without foreign friends and with an economy in decline; nor was it the Croatia he had fought for. He had been forced into an unwelcome anti-Serbian alliance with Bosnia's Muslims when he would have preferred a straight deal with Milosevic to absorb part of it in Croatia. Milosevic too, for all his political skills, was weakened by the war in Bosnia. The Dayton settlement marked a setback for Serbian attempts to annex parts of Bosnia; Greater Serbia did not come into existence. Economic sanctions racked Serbia as wages fell in a few years to a third of their prewar levels and in 1998 the currency was devalued by 45 per cent. Elections in 1996 were followed by persistent demonstrations which forced Milosevic, implicitly admitting electoral improprieties, to cede control of Belgrade and other city councils to opponents. These were, however, an assortment of incompatibles whose alliance did not hold: the new mayor of Belgrade Zoran Djindic was a liberal democrat (who was soon forced into hiding), whereas the more prominent Vuk Draskovic was an anti-Milosevic nationalist who made his peace with the latter and became, if only briefly, a deputy prime minister. In 1997 Milosevic promoted himself to the presidency of the reduced Yugoslav federation but he failed in repeated elections – made void by turnouts below 50 per cent – to install his nominee in his old office or president of Serbia. In 1998 the extreme nationalist Radical Party of Vojislav Seselj more than doubled its parliamentary strength and demanded the incorporation of Kosovo in a unitary Serbia and the eviction from it of all Albanians. Milosevic made Seselj – another rival for the leadership of Serb nationalism – a deputy prime minister and gave his party half the seats in the cabinet.

The Bosnia fashioned at Dayton did not come into existence. In the Serbian segment the Serbs split. Karadzic, now an indicted war criminal, lost his majority in the assembly and a faction willing to accept the Dayton agreement briefly prevailed; but in 1998 Karadzic's heirs regained control until the next year, when the international administrator appointed at Dayton, Carlos Westendorp, dismissed their leader Nikola Poplasen. The Bosnian Croats refused to play their allotted role in the central administration at Sarajevo and reduced to vanishing point their alliance with the Muslims, who were reduced to a potentially revolutionary indigence. In Montenegro, now attached only to Serbia whose population outnumbered Montenegrins by 6:1, independence became increasingly attractive. The presidency was won by Milo Djukanovic against Milosevic's candidate but events in Kosovo threatened to disrupt the country as NATO included Montenegrin installations in its targets: the port of Bor was one of Serbia's main supply routes. Montenegro became roughly equally divided between partisans of independence and of continuing special links with Serbia, the former gradually gaining ground.

Kosovo

Milosevic went to Dayton with an ace up his sleeve and when the conference ended it was still there. Nothing was said about Kosovo. The Americans feared that pressing for undertakings about the province would scupper any settlement over Bosnia; in 1996 the EU affirmed the integrity of Yugoslavia and so implicitly Kosovo's status as part of Serbia, and sanctions against Serbia were removed. The Kosovars were left on their own. For the Serbs Kosovo was a magic name which, with some history and more legend, had been exalted into the birthplace of the Serb state and the epitome of Serb valour against the Ottoman Turks and Islam in the fourteenth century. Serbia tried to appropriate Kosovo during the Russo-Turkish war of 1877–78 and did so in the Balkan wars of 1912–13. Politicians and academics continuously advocated over a century and more the incorporation of Kosovo into Serbia and the expulsion of its overwhelmingly

Albanian population. Both before and after the Second World War Serbian governments tried to secure the deportation of large numbers of Albanians to Turkey. In 1989 Milosevic abrogated the limited autonomy granted to Kosovo 15 years earlier and repeated the policy of expelling all Albanians. The Albanians retorted with an ineffectual declaration of independence in 1992, which the Serbs ignored. Thereafter neither Serbs nor Kosovars were willing to go back to the autonomy of 1974–89. Some Kosovars were willing to contemplate a form of autonomy in the new Yugoslav federation equal to that of Montenegro but most no longer had faith in anything except independence. The Kosovo Democratic League (KDL) led by Ibrahim Rugova and the Kosovo Liberation Army (KLA or UCK) were divided less by aims than by means – whether to resort to arms. The KLA had grown from small beginnings in 1983 into an active rival of the KDL and had acquired arms when the Berisha regime in Albania (see below) was overthrown and its stores were breached and dispersed.

The problems of Kosovo became actively internationalized when Milosevic was seen to be moving military and paramilitary units into the province, repeating his invasion of Bosnia in 1992, with the prospect of atrocities such as the massacres at Srebrenica and elsewhere in Bosnia. The United States, Russia and European states were agreed on the need to force Milosevic to withdraw these forces but Russia strongly objected to the use of NATO as the means. All these states approved a Security Council resolution requiring Serbia to withdraw its forces and cease its depredations and they together convened a meeting with Milosevic and the KLA and other Albanians at Rambouillet, near Paris (1995), to consider – and accept – terms which included the withdrawal of all Serb forces (with minor exceptions), the disarming of the KLA, the introduction of a substantial international peacekeeping force and a corps of 2,000 unarmed monitors from the OSCE, the initiation of negotiations about the future of Kosovo, and the return of Albanian refugees to their homes (or what might be left of them). The Albanians accepted this programme conditionally upon the acceptance of the whole of it by Milosevic and in spite of the omission of any direct reference to the possibility of independence for Kosovo. Milosevic did not go to Rambouillet and responded to the Rambouillet ultimatum by intensifying his operations, which included murder, rape and arson, in order to hurry the Albanians out of Kosovo. War followed – a war waged by NATO against which Russia protested, not because it was pro-Serb (as Milosevic may have imagined) but because it was anti-NATO.

The war lasted ten weeks. It failed to protect the Albanians of Kosovo but it forced Milosevic to capitulate. The NATO allies, having assembled a force of (initially) 450 aircraft, fought it – largely at American insistence – with air power only and with aircraft flying above 15,000 feet. The NATO forces suffered no casualties: all the dead were Serb or Albanian. The outcome appeared to confound the numerous sceptics who maintained that air power alone must be inadequate but after a tentative start, and in spite of a few deplorably disastrous mis-hits, the bombing of Belgrade and other Serbian cities put an end to the fighting. On the other hand NATO air power had ground support (including intelligence) from the KLA and a growing possibility of international intervention by ground forces may have played a part in Milosevic's surrender. The death and destruction inflicted by air power were peculiarly indiscriminate and did not end with the fighting since the country was littered with unexploded cluster bombs.

Milosevic accepted terms of surrender put to him by Finland's president Martti Ahtisaari on behalf of the NATO alliance and by Yeltsin's special envoy Victor Chernomyrdin. These terms were largely, if not precisely, those presented at Rambouillet: Serb forces to leave Kosovo in ten days, international civilian and military regimes to be installed, Albanians to be allowed back to their homes, the KLA to be demilitarized. They were a blow not only to visions of a Greater Serbia but also to Serbia itself, for although nothing was said about the ultimate fate of Kosovo its least likely future was reunion with Serbia: it faced an indefinite period of inchoate international tutelage by (chiefly) European states which had failed to find a durable solution for it in 1913 and had not even tried to do so in 1995. Two-thirds of the Serbian parliament accepted the terms of surrender against the votes of Seselj and his Radical Party; he resigned from the government. The refugees – some 900,000 – flocked back to what was left of their homes and began the search for what might be left of their families. The war threatened the stability of the neighbouring Macedonian, Montenegrin and Albanian republics but did not last long enough to cause immediate upheavals. Milosevic and others were indicted for war crimes and crimes against humanity, with possible charges of genocide held in reserve. After failing to annex Bosnia, Milosevic had lost Kosovo. He also lost his position in Belgrade (2000), was arrested and arraigned at The Hague and died in prison in 2006. He was succeeded by the moderate nationalist Vojislav Kostunica.

The war, uncomfortably for both NATO and Russia, raised the question of post-Soviet Russia's place in Europe. There were those, particularly but not exclusively in the United States, for whom Russia was a failed superpower of no real consequence; others, particularly in Europe, recalled that Russia, although no world superpower, had played for more than two centuries a major role in European affairs. Russia, while supporting international measures against Serbia, was adamantly opposed to the expansion of NATO eastward to Russia's borders and its active use in European affairs. To some of the Russians in Yeltsin's ramshackle and fluctuating administrations these moves denoted American attempts to threaten and humiliate Russia and bypass the UN Security Council and the veto – the first judgement was a wild exaggeration, the second broadly true. To the United States, on the other hand, NATO forces, which had already been used in Bosnia, were not so much an alternative to the UN as the only readily available war machine in the absence of regional (i.e. EU) forces and institutions. As the war ended the NATO allies welcomed Russian participation in peace negotiations and the enforcement of the terms of surrender but insisted on the inclusion of Russian units in a unified command, which would be NATO. The Russians, demanding a separate zone in Kosovo and independence from NATO, deftly moved troops from

Bosnia through Serbia and onto Kosovo's main airport, which they reached ahead of NATO. This unexpected gesture made the point that Russia could not be left out of account, but it had little impact on the course of events. It disclosed rifts in Moscow between, broadly speaking, the civilian and military branches of Yeltsin's administration and a lack of authority which was in itself alarming. The Russians had to back down and be content with a small and widely dispersed contribution to the NATO peacekeeping force (K-FOR), to drop their demand for a separate zone of occupation and to accept a mutually satisfying formula of meaningless complexity for the chain of command. K-FOR secured the KLA's agreement to hand in all its weapons except side arms, cease wearing uniforms, dismantle its check-points and help in the clearing of minefields: the future of these units remained, however, uncertain.

The war was an unlawful war with a just cause. NATO's action lay outside the terms of the North Atlantic Treaty and was a breach of the UN Charter. In the longer prospect it strengthened, if only by its example, the arguments for international action (by the UN) against a sovereign state on humanitarian grounds. It was undertaken on account of crimes against the person, all of them committed within Serbian territory. Such crimes were not novel but they had previously been prosecuted only in the context of other offences: at Nuremberg in the context of aggressive war, against Galtieri's Argentina and Saddam Hussein's Iraq in the context of crimes against property (the invasions of the Falklands and of Kuwait). Secondly, the war strengthened arguments for joint EU military institutions and forces, substantially independent of, although not entirely divorced from, the United States – a fundamental revision of the North Atlantic Treaty. It strengthened too the case for a permanent international court with criminal jurisdiction, more universal than the ad hoc court at The Hague covering crimes in Yugoslavia and more powerful than the court created at the conference in Rome in 1998 (see Chapter 30). Twelve years after Rambouillet Kosovo had become more than a regional imbroglio: a testing ground in manoeuvres between the US/EU and Russia. Neither was primarily interested in Kosovo itself, which declared its independence in 2008, thereby creating in effect a second Albanian state.

The severing of Kosovo from Serbia was a foregone conclusion not only because nine out of every ten of its inhabitants were Albanian but from the American decision in 1998 to bomb Kosovo and Serbia in an attempt to pacify what had become one of the most inflamed parts of Europe. Yet a sizeable minority of EU members held back from recognizing Kosovo's independence, at least partly because they felt bound to maintain the established rule of international law that international boundaries may be altered only by international treaties. So Kosovo, landlocked and friendless, became a shipwrecked freak under the continuing tutelage of the EU but with next to no prospect of joining it. In Serbia, the extreme nationalists (whose leader Seselj was in prison at The Hague awaiting trial) were expected to profit from these developments and came close to winning the presidency but elections on 2008 gave pro-Western and pro-EU leaders an unexpected, if narrow, advantage.

Macedonia and Albania

In *Macedonia*, whose very name conjured up powerful emotions in Greece and Bulgaria, the tensions of these years were internationalized by paranoid reactions, not least in Greece, where ancient history was invoked to bolster modern nationalism – and win elections. When in 1389 Sultan Murad I extinguished the Serbian empire at the battle of Kosovo he anaesthetized for five centuries what was to become the Macedonian Question. The Macedonian name went back to antiquity and to the warrior kings who conquered Greece as a preliminary to conquering much of the world known to them. Macedonia was later to be defined in territorial or linguistic terms. These two approaches were inconsistent and neither was precise. There has been no Macedonia for over 2,000 years and no agreement on whether Macedonian is a distinct language or a Bulgarian dialect. The Macedonians of recent times are Slavs but whether closer kin to Bulgars or Serbs has been much disputed – the Bulgars pointing to linguistic affinities, the Serbs to common cultural rituals unknown among the Bulgars. The quickening reflux of Ottoman power in Europe in the nineteenth century resuscitated ancient Serb and Bulgar principalities, revived separate Serb and Bulgar churches anxious to assert themselves against the Hellenic patriarch of Constantinople, and created between Serbia, Bulgaria and Greece tensions which were focused particularly upon Macedonia and the port of Thessalonica. Whereas in political terms the separatism of the emergent Slav states was anti-Turkish, in religious terms it was anti-Greek. After the Russo-Turkish war of 1877–78 the Treaty of San Stefano, imposed by Russia, gave Bulgaria all Macedonia but not Thessalonica. The Treaty of Berlin, by which the other Great Powers insisted on curbing this Russian victory, restored Macedonia to the Turks and divided Bulgaria into two pieces (which succeeded in coalescing in 1885). In the last decade of the century Bulgaria fostered ambitious Macedonian organizations but these quickly split on their tactics and strategy and by the time the progressive decline of the Ottoman empire led to the Balkan wars of 1912–13, Serbia and Greece had discovered a common purpose in preventing Bulgaria from getting Thessalonica. The second stage of the Balkan wars ended with the Treaty of Bucharest, by which Macedonia was divided in such a way that Bulgaria received only one-tenth of it, the rest being allotted to Serbia and Greece, with the latter securing a larger share than Serbia and also Thessalonica. There was some consequent migration and more after the First World War, more or less voluntary. These movements left only a small Slav-speaking population in Greece but an abiding fear among Greeks of a revival of plans for a distinct Macedonian state which would remove from Greece its most fertile province and 1.5 million of its inhabitants.

After the Second World War plans for a union between Yugoslavia and Bulgaria were scotched by Stalin and Tito's reorganization of prewar tripartite Yugoslavia into a federation in six parts created the Yugoslav Republic of Macedonia. Forty-five years later this Republic, with a population of 2 million, a quarter of whom were Albanians concentrated in the north-west corner and the rest divided into a dozen categories, had a crumbling economy, virtually no industry or purchasers for its principal crop (tobacco), no currency apart from the Yugoslav dinar and no army. The writ of Kiro Gligorov – an ex-communist who became president in 1992 – ran but feebly beyond the capital, Skopje. In 1991 the Macedonians confirmed by plebiscite a declaration of independence but the Albanian part of the electorate boycotted the voting and the Greek government prevented for two years international recognition of the country's independence and maintained for most of 1992–94 an economic blockade of it. The Albanians of Macedonia fared better than their kinsfolk in Kosovo but were all but excluded from the republic's government and army and hankered after autonomy or independence or union with an enlarged Albania – which Albania itself was in no mood or condition to promote.

Greek concern about the new state had several sources. The most recent was the Greek civil war, when many Slavs had been recruited into the ranks of Greek People's Liberation Army (ELAS). There were deep-seated suspicions of meddling in anything with the name Macedonia attached to it; exaggerated reactions to the appearance in Skopje of ancient but provocative maps showing Macedonia extending over parts of Greece; fears that a Macedonian state on Greece's border might engender claims for Albanian and Turkish minorities. Finally and most prominently, political leaders in Athens revived romantic illusions about the continuing relevance to modern affairs of the career in the third century BC of Alexander of Macedon, whom the Greeks of those days had regarded as more barbarian than Greek. Greece's membership of the EC ensured a degree of attention for chauvinist posturing which might otherwise have gone unremarked. Macedonia was obliged to adopt the unwieldy nomenclature of Former Yugoslav Republic of Macedonia (FYROM) before it was admitted to the UN. It remained uneasily at peace with the help of a small UN peacekeeping force (to which in 1993 the United States contributed units) and in spite of limited outbreaks of violence in 1995. Less volatile than Bosnia, it had, however, borders with four unfriendly and more securely established states – Albania, Bulgaria and Serbia as well as Greece – and was itself landlocked. In 1995 Gligorov narrowly escaped assassination. He had won recognition from all his neighbours and Turkey but the triumphs of Serb and Croat states militated against the idea of the state as a multi-ethnic state such as Macedonia must be. After elections in 1998 power shifted from centre-left to centre-right, to more determined post-communist economic reforms and to improved relations with Greece and Bulgaria, but the flood of 275,000 battered it and destitute Albanians from Kosovo and the interruption of its trade with Serbia created economic chaos and ethnic alarm. Gligorov held off a challenge by supporters of the idea of a Yugoslav federation including Macedonia. He lost his office in 1999.

Albania, bordered by Montenegro, Serbia, Macedonia, Greece and the sea, won independence in 1912 with a German prince as king (for a few months). The new state embraced only half the Albanians. The other half was allotted in 1913 to Serbia and Montenegro and, in smaller numbers, to Greece. These Albanians were principal losers in the post-Ottoman apportionment of the Balkans. On various occasions from 1878 onwards Greece claimed what it called northern Epirus, a variable area amounting to about a third of Albania and inhabited by a substantial Greek minority. Of 3 million Albanians living outside Albania after the Second World War 4–500,000 were in the Macedonian Republic of Yugoslavia, 50,000 in Montenegro and as many in Greece, and others in Turkey, Italy, the United States and Canada from old and more recent migrations. Two-thirds of the Albanians in Albania were Muslims of diverse sects, the remainder Orthodox or Catholic Christians, the Orthodox outnumbering the Catholics by two to one. Ethnically, the principal minorities were Greek and Vlach. The number of Greeks was put at 40,000 or 100,000 according to political viewpoint: official censuses recorded religious, not ethnic, affiliation and a number of Albanians spoke Greek in Turkish times because the Turks forbade the teaching and use of Albanian but not of Greek.

During the First World War it appeared likely that Albania would be partitioned between Greece, Italy and the new kingdom of Yugoslavia, but such plans were vetoed by Woodrow Wilson. A southern boundary, first delineated by an international commission in 1913, was endorsed by the League of Nations in 1921 and accepted by the states concerned, including Greece and Italy, in 1926. After the war Albania was chaotic until Ahmet Zogu asserted his rule over most of it and made himself king in 1928 (he died during the Second World War). In 1939 Italy invaded it in order to attack Greece but Albania succeeded, with German help, in gaining territory from Serbia and Montenegro, if only temporarily. Resistance to the Axis occupiers was led by Enver Hoxha with aid from Britain. Hoxha, who was a middle-class paranoiac partly educated in France and Belgium, established a Stalinist dictatorship. He eliminated Koci Xoxe and other close associates whom he plausibly suspected of being attracted by Tito's schemes to absorb Albania into the Yugoslav federation. Another close associate Mehmet Shehu, a veteran of the Spanish civil war, was prime minister until 1981, when he committed suicide and was attacked *post mortem* as an agent of both the CIA and the KGB. Hoxha became hostile to Khrushchev's USSR and severed relations with it in 1961. He lauded Mao's China until 1978, when he attacked it for revisionism. He isolated and impoverished Albania by pursuing modernization and revolution with ruthless incompetence, wasting its substantial mineral resources (chrome, copper, nickel) and hydro-electric potentialities. He died in 1985 after a period of senility during which Ramiz Alia was effectively the country's ruler.

Confirmed in power, Alia gave some signals of reform but they were feeble and the communist regime began to disintegrate. Law and order broke down; the underlying north/south division between Ghegs and Tosks was complicated by violent feuds within these broad societies; many Albanians took flight to Italy and Greece. Alia was forced to permit elections in 1991. They were well conducted, the turnout was remarkably high and the ruling Party of Labour (later renamed the Socialist Party) polled strongly in rural areas and won twice as many seats as all the opposition parties combined. Alia became president under a new constitution with, briefly, Fatos Nano as his first prime minister. But failure to get expected aid from the United States, the EC and the IMF, and mounting disorder and destitution showed that affairs were beyond his control and fresh elections in 1992 reversed the previous year's result as the new Democratic Party, led by Sali Berisha, won nearly two-thirds of the seats. Berisha became president.

By profession a heart specialist and in politics an observant communist turned fervent anti-communist, Berisha pursued with more zest than foresight economic policies pressed upon him by foreign advisers and allowed the economy to be hijacked by speculators and racketeers. Prices soared; gangsterism and corruption, to which the United States and other well-wishers turned a blind eye, flourished; the Democratic Party split; aggressive politicking by the Orthodox Church and a visit by Pope John Paul II did not help to stem discord; foreign aid still did not appear in more than a trickle; Berisha became increasingly authoritarian; an attempt, supported by the United States, to strengthen his constitutional powers was rejected; in 1996 he emerged victorious from elections which were, however, caustically denounced by OSCE observers. Fraudulent get-rich-quick schemes whose competitiveness pushed the promised rewards to a ridiculous 150 per cent collapsed, ruining some three-quarters of the population, precipitating a renewed exodus to Italy, Greece and Yugoslavia and sparking an uprising which bisected the country. Berisha lost control of the south and formed a temporary coalition government with his rival Fatos Nano. Under Italian leadership, European countries sent a small force as a rudimentary means to inject a measure of order and security into selected towns. At further elections in 1997 Berisha and his party were trounced and he resigned and was succeeded by Nano. While the advent of Berisha had marked the end of communist dictatorship, his decline and fall were marked by confusion in the United States and the EU, where he had been cast as the acceptable face of post-communist Albania – the man who might stabilize the country, strengthen American designs to stymie Serb expansionism and prevent Albania from serving as an outpost of aggressive Islamism. In Albania itself Berisha remained powerful in the north as the Nano government failed to assert its power over the whole country. Berisha resorted to emergency powers but was forced in effect to abdicate. Economic chaos, political fragmentation and flourishing crime ensued.

The wars in Yugoslavia in the 1990s and their outward ripples were a stage in the lengthy reordering of south-east Europe in response to the withdrawal over centuries and the ultimate disintegration of the Ottoman empire. At different stages other states intervened in this process, usually in a spirit of mutual hostility. The conflicts of the 1990s were a reminder to the peoples of the region that their endemic disputes were of concern to more distant and powerful forces. They also testified to the much-reduced hostility among those who felt minded to intervene. These wars destroyed Yugoslavia. The chief loser was Serbia where Milosevic played his hand like La Fontaine's frog. Only its eastern border remained intact. To the north-west Croatia and Slovenia became sovereign states. To the west and south-west Bosnia–Herzegovina retained a precarious and, in part, an ambiguous attachment to Serbia, as did Montenegro. To the south Macedonia became independent. The most intractable segment was Kosovo, wedged between Serbia–Montenegro, Macedonia and Albania. Given its overwhelmingly Albanian population, outsiders, with the exception of Russia, wished it to become another new state: Russia's opposition might be ascribed to historic links and Slavic affections or to Putin's search for pawns to play in his diplomatic moves against the USA and NATO. A union of Kosovo with Albania was shunned by everybody. Kosovo was left under temporary UN occupation similar to the ill-omened fate of Danzig between the two world wars. It declared independence in 2008 and was quickly recognized by the USA and most (but not all) EU members.

Notes

A. Northern Ireland

Northern Ireland, frequently but wrongly called Ulster, was that part of Ireland which remained part of the United Kingdom when the rest of Ireland broke away from the union created in 1800. During the winter of 1921–22 there were two principal issues in debate between the English and the Irish. The partition of Ireland was widely regarded as inevitable but the status of the Irish state was hotly debated. The English insisted and a narrow majority of the provisional Irish parliament agreed that it should be a Free State within the British Commonwealth and empire, owing allegiance to the British Crown and presided over by a British governor-general. In Ireland a republican minority pressed its case to the point of civil war but lost, and Ireland, although a separate member of the League of Nations from 1923, did not become a fully independent republic until 1937.

In the north-east a border was agreed in 1925. The new province of Northern Ireland inherited from the Act of Union of 1800 the right to elect members to the parliament at Westminster and was given by the Government of Ireland Act 1920 a bicameral legislature and an executive with a considerable degree of internal autonomy (extended in 1948). The province was governed until 1972 by a Protestant oligarchy dominated by landowners but embracing in later years representatives of the more prosperous urban and professional classes, one of whom, Brian Faulkner, became its last prime minister. The power of this oligarchy rested on the electorate in which Protestants outnumbered Roman Catholics by two to one. This religious division was, however, not the only one.

There was also conflict between proponents and opponents of a united Ireland and – a more recent division – between bosses and workers, rich and poor. The bosses were mostly Protestant but not all the Protestants were bosses. The partisans of a united Ireland were mostly Roman Catholics but not all Roman Catholics wanted Ireland united; or not immediately; or not by force. The aim of the dominant class was to remain in control, making such reformist concessions as seemed necessary (opinions differed as to which these might be). The aims of the opposition ranged from the unification of Ireland to the ending of anti-Catholic discrimination and in 1969 the IRA (descendants of the Irish Republican Army formed to evict the English from Ireland) split. The larger group, adopting a Marxist interpretation of the situation, aimed to enlarge its base among the deprived Roman Catholic minority by enlisting the support of the poorer Protestants: this group put socialism first and abandoned violence in favour of propaganda. The other group, called the Provisional IRA, maintained the traditional policy of uniting Ireland by the eviction of the English by violence: their interpretation of the situation was not class conflict but national war and their appeal was to nationalism and Roman Catholicism. English aims, finally, were negative. The English had lost the will to remain in any part of Ireland but felt an obligation to stand by the established order in Northern Ireland. Both Conservative and Labour governments saw the need to push the provincial oligarchy into civil and political reforms, as a matter of expediency and as a matter of justice. Both believed, or acted as though they believed, that no more than this was necessary, a delusion from which they should have been disabused by the events of 1969–72.

In these last years of the old order the province had three prime ministers. Disorders, particularly on historic or religious festivals, were a normal feature of political life but not normally lethal. In 1966 disorder had been aggravated by a spate of killings by the newly formed (Protestant) Ulster Volunteer Force, but the authorities regained control until in 1969 political murder reappeared. In that and the next year the number of victims was small (13 and 20 respectively) but they sufficed to induce the British government to send troops – a reaction necessitated not by the scale of the troubles but by the fact that the local forces of law and order – the Royal Ulster Constabulary supplemented by the B-Special Constables – were composed of Protestants and were regarded by Roman Catholics as instruments of the Protestant sectarian supremacy. Their use to suppress disorders was incompatible with a policy of recognizing and rectifying Roman Catholic grievances but, conversely, the dissolution of the B-Specials and the disarming of the RUC on which the British government insisted in 1970 intensified Protestant apprehensions for their own fate and reinforced their intransigence.

Having intervened thus far, the English, anxious to retire again as soon as possible, pressed the provincial executive to introduce reforms to satisfy those among the Roman Catholics who were agitating for civil rights. Successive prime ministers, Terence O'Neill and James Chichester-Clark, were willing in principle but inhibited by their own supporters, who regarded reforms as a prelude to further concessions leading to the unification of Ireland with dire consequences for Protestants and the economy of the northern counties. The hold of such leaders over the Protestant majority was further weakened by the emergence of new leaders whether, like Ian Paisley, eloquent anti-papalists of a kind no longer found outside Northern Ireland or, like William Craig, protagonists of the right of the majority to have its way and fight for it. Nevertheless, a number of reforms were enacted. They were years too late. They divided Protestants and no longer satisfied Roman Catholics whose attention was being diverted from civil rights to sectarianism by the Paisleyites on the one hand and the Provisionals on the other. Killings multiplied (173 in 1971) and a new prime minister, Brian Faulkner, resorted to detention and internment without trial. In one night 342 persons were arrested. Some were clearly the wrong persons, and not one of them was a Protestant. This was not surprising since the object of the operation was to break the IRA.

But the operation strengthened the Provisionals. It swung Roman Catholic opinion, which had at first welcomed British troops as protection against Protestant militants, over to the IRA and forced the official IRA to join the Provisionals in denouncing the British government, without whose endorsement Faulkner could not have acted. Stories of brutality and torture by the English, subsequently endorsed by the European Commission on Human Rights, added fuel to the flames. The Protestants were both emboldened and alarmed: emboldened because Faulkner had not ventured to intern even the most militant UVF leaders and alarmed because they felt denuded in the face of increasing IRA violence and the emasculation of their own means of securing law and order. A new Protestant self-help force appeared, the Ulster Defence Association, as a counterpart to the Provisionals. The provincial executive became ineffective and in March 1972 it was suspended. The British government assumed direct responsibility. It also lost its credibility when 14 unarmed Roman Catholics were killed by British troops in Londonderry.

Direct rule from Westminster involved Britain in confrontation with the opposition, which was no longer only the Roman Catholic parties or civil rights movement but also the Provisional IRA. Nevertheless, the Heath government set to work to find a constitutional answer to Northern Ireland's problems. The policy had two pillars and they were incompatible. The one was power-sharing, an insistence on Roman Catholic participation in government at all levels, including a restored provincial executive which was to be permanently a coalition and, secondly, democratic endorsement by the province's electors. By 1972 the Protestant majority was prepared to endorse no such thing. Protestants were enraged by the murderous activities of the Provisionals, and Protestant militants took to killing twice as many civilians as the Provisionals (who directed their fire more particularly at the British troops). Thus the British government's policy, enshrined in 1973 in a White Paper and apparently triumphant at a conference at Sunningdale, was for a second time foredoomed by unreality, and the addition at Sunningdale of a gesture towards unification by the creation of a Council of Ireland (north and south) made its rejection doubly certain. The British general election, unexpectedly called by Heath in 1974, gave the electors in Northern Ireland a chance to show their mind and they decisively rejected the Sunningdale scheme. The restored executive survived for a while but was brought down by Protestant demonstrations and a general strike against power-sharing, leading to the declaration of a state of emergency. London's answers were to fly in more troops and resume direct rule: the two things it least wanted to do.

From the winter of 1972–73 both sides within the province had produced groups which were trying to reach out to one another but they were too tentative and submerged to be much heard amid the clash of arms and rhetoric. Truces were arranged but were imperfect and short. The English put a brave face on their helplessness and justified their presence by predicting, with some superficial plausibility, a blood bath if they were to leave. That they would leave one day seemed obvious to all but themselves: a repetition of the blindness of the French to the realities of their tenure of Algeria. That they should do so sooner rather than later was an argument which the larger part of them was emotionally unprepared to entertain. In 1980 two new prime ministers, Margaret Thatcher and Charles Haughey, were trying to devise a way round the blockage created by the claim of the Protestants – accepted by all British governments – that, being a majority within the province, they had a democratic right to veto constitutional change. Discussions continued after a switch in Dublin from Haughey to Garret Fitzgerald but the two governments were far apart, not because of divergent attitudes to violence but because of their presuppositions. Dublin saw no end to the troubles without significant political change; it did not seek immediate or even early change but the various changes which it advocated at one time or another all pointed in that direction. Thatcher, on the other hand, believed that the first task was the conquest of violence by force and her readiness to consider change, even in the long term, was strictly circumscribed by her argument – familiar from the Falklands, although less inflexible in Gibraltar and discarded in Hong Kong – that British policies must be subordinated to the wishes of the majority in the territory concerned. When in 1984 the New Ireland Forum, an association of Irish Republic parties, proffered a series of possible formulas for political manoeuvre pointing towards unification or a condominium in the north, Thatcher dismissed them with marked asperity. Nevertheless, a year later she and Fitzgerald agreed by the Hillsborough agreement to establish a standing joint body or 'ministerial conference'. The immediate practical purpose of this agreement was to improve police co-operation and border control. Its larger purpose was to marginalize the IRA. Its unavowed implication was a growing role for the Irish Republic in the affairs of Northern Ireland. The British government, looking to Dublin for help on the first count, was willing to allow the Republic to become associated in some of the affairs of the province. Irish governments felt constrained to co-operate with the British since the status quo was from the Republic's point of view less hazardous than the alternatives: either, on the one hand, war in the North leading to victory for the Protestants or the extreme right; or, on the other hand, a union which would saddle the Republic with a million Protestant dissidents and bankrupt it.

Revelations of serious miscarriages of justice in the English courts which neither Fitzgerald nor Haughey (who returned to office in 1987) could easily overlook made the agreement unexpectedly awkward for the Irish government but its main impact was on the Unionists, who saw it as a derogation from British sovereignty in Northern Ireland and an abandonment of British support for entrenched Protestantism. The Unionists set themselves to destroy the agreement by making further discussion conditional on its abrogation. Profoundly hostile to Dublin's involvement in the province's affairs in any shape or guise, Unionist leaders hoped to nullify the agreement by non-cooperation with the British secretary of state. The British government never convincingly affirmed a resolve to keep the province in the United Kingdom and although the agreement provided that the 'status of Northern Ireland' would not be altered without the assent of a majority in the province, the Unionists retorted by pointing to the article in the Irish constitution which described the whole island as the territory of a single nation – a provision which had been interpreted by the Supreme Court in Dublin as laying upon the Irish government a duty to reintegrate Ireland. To Unionists the British government had been hypocritical when it signed the Anglo-Irish agreement without securing, or even asking for, the abrogation of this article. One effect therefore of the agreement was to marginalize not the IRA but the Unionist parties. These, however, were mistaken in their belief that they could wreck the agreement, since the British refused even temporarily to suspend its projected joint conferences of ministers and officials. The agreement achieved little by way of policing the border in ways not available without the agreement. It failed to stop or reduce the murderous activities of the IRA in Ireland or in England, and it froze – at least for a number of years – attempts to bring direct rule to an end. The IRA's campaign – which included an attempt to kill Thatcher and other ministers at Brighton in 1984 and intensified violence with imported weapons and explosives from 1988, and which was met by British attempts to pick off and kill leading IRA activists – kept the conflict alive but with scant prospect of the success sought by the IRA. Despite its name, the IRA was not an army and it could not dislodge the British army, which needed to send to Ireland no more than 15–20,000 troops (briefly increased to some 30,000 for a special operation in 1972).

From the late 1980s a section of the nationalists which included Gerry Adams, president of Sinn Fein – the political aspect of Irish nationalism – became convinced that their political aims were not being furthered by military action. They also became persuaded that the British government no longer harboured strategic or economic reasons for preserving British power in Northern Ireland, although Britain would not relinquish power against the wishes of a majority of the people of the province. The British, however, were profoundly distrustful of the nationalists and, coincidentally, John Major's government became dependent on Irish Unionist votes in the House of

Commons after elections in 1992 left it with a precarious majority in debates on the Treaty of Maastricht. The Northern Irish representation at Westminster had been more than doubled by Callaghan (largely on the urging of the ex-Conservative turned Ulster Unionist, Enoch Powell) and the Unionists used their parliamentary power to block proposals for joint Anglo-Irish administration in Northern Ireland. They were suspicious of London's attempts to stop the fighting through concessions to Dublin, attempts which were far from unpopular in Britain, where sympathy with the Protestants dwindled as they, in 1992 for the first time, murdered more Catholics than vice versa. In the longer term, the Unionists were obliged to contemplate a demographic shift as Catholics looked forward to overhauling the Protestant majority in not much more than a generation. Finally, in the province itself the age-old religious backing for armed conflict was weakening, politics were becoming secularized, leaders could rely less on sectarian demagogy and fears, and northern Protestant distrust of Catholics was beginning to be allayed as political power in the Irish Republic slipped away from an over-mighty and over-secretive church to a secular political class.

In Dublin a revolt against Haughey in 1991, although initially a failure, secured his departure and replacement by Albert Reynolds as leader of Fianna Fail and Taoiseach (prime minister). Elections dented Reynolds's position in the Dail so far that he was obliged to give substantial weight in his cabinet and the ministry of external affairs to the Labour Party, led by Dick Spring. This coalition broke up acrimoniously in 1994 and a new government was formed by John Bruton, leader of Fine Gael, in coalition with the Labour Party and the small, new and socialist Democratic Left. Behind these changes Irish leaders persisted in pursuing what they saw as an opportunity for a truce and permanent peace. Hopes were stimulated when a series of meetings between Adams and John Hume, leader of the (Roman Catholic) Social Democratic and Labour Party in Northern Ireland and a member of the British parliament, produced an (unpublished) set of proposals for peace. In oblique response the British and Irish prime ministers issued a declaration which amounted to an offer of discussions provided the IRA first renounced violence unequivocally and permanently. In what looked like prevarication the IRA asked for clarification, which the two governments refused to give without a prior renunciation of violence, and advanced the proposition that constitutional changes in Ireland should be submitted to the Irish people as a whole and not separately to a plebiscite in the north. This argument was clearly unacceptable to the British and failed, if that was its purpose, to drive a wedge between London and Dublin even though Dublin was convinced, as London was not, that Adams was in earnest and capable of delivering an agreement for peace. Major's cautious procrastination had the general support of the British Labour Party and he succeeded in winning the trust of James Molyneaux, the leader of the province's largest Protestant party, thus diminishing the abrasive and unco-operative Ian Paisley and his faction. When in 1994 the IRA proclaimed a ceasefire Major's tactics seemed for a while to be justified.

The gradual transformation of the situation rested, however, on a major change which carried with it fresh obstacles. As the 1990s progressed, it became clear that the driving force was the establishment of continuing and close accord between the British and Irish governments, which was regarded by the Protestants in the North as the mechanism for concessions to Irish nationalism and the looming abandonment by Britain of the union with Northern Ireland. For two years governments worked laboriously on a joint document to be presented to all parties as a basis for discussions about the future government of the province. It was published in 1995 and shocked not only Paisley's party but also Molyneaux's Ulster Unionists (UUP) because of its proposals for joint Anglo-Irish authorities to co-ordinate such administrative problems as border controls. The British government represented this 'framework' document as no more than a basis for a conference at which all parties might table other proposals. It stressed the safeguards for Unionists in the document's insistence that any agreed proposals must be endorsed by the North's political parties, by a referendum in the North and by the British parliament. But the Unionists, whose bargaining positions rested on their voting power in a finely balanced House of Commons whose term was running out, were alarmed by pan-Irish elements in the framework document and by the evidently declining sympathy for them in the rest of the United Kingdom, where they were portrayed as mock militarists flavoured by Protestant fundamentalism. Between the protagonists – the British government and the IRA – there was little trust, so that progress was slow and became slower as an issue crucial to both – the prior surrender of arms – reached the agenda. On this point Major took a stance which, since it was compatible with surrender rather than negotiation, was completely unacceptable to the IRA and therewith Major forfeited the opportunity which he had done much to create: his dependence on Irish Unionist votes in the House of Commons was a sizeable element in his dilemma. The principal positive outcome of Major's term of office was the internationalization of the problem of Northern Ireland, first, through his affirmation of the closest attainable cooperation with the Irish government and, secondly, by recruiting an international committee with a former US senator (George Mitchell) as chairman to help to get all-party talks started and to conduct them.

The IRA's ceasefire lasted 17 months in 1994–95. It covered major acts of violence in Ireland and Britain but not so-called punishment beatings of individuals – ruthless, vicious and numerous, and perpetrated by both sides – nor was it reinforced by continuing political momentum or any disarmament. In 1995 Molyneaux resigned the leadership of the UUP to be succeeded by David Trimble, a politician with his roots in the Orange Order, the symbolic fellowship devoted to the celebration of ancient Protestant victories. Trimble was intelligent and relatively young but his following was divided, none of his party colleagues in the British parliament had voted for him, he was wary of losing votes to Paisley's and other Unionist parties and he was by temperament as well as circumstances more inclined to manoeuvre than to boldness. Since

Protestants were deeply distrustful of IRA promises and ceasefires and refused to see that any nationalist surrender of arms before negotiations was a phantom, Trimble was in an exposed and weakening position.

Blair's main aim on assuming office was to get talks started. He established sound relations with a new Irish prime minister Bertie Ahern; fixed a date for the beginning of talks; insisted that Sinn Fein would not be admitted to them if the IRA did not declare and maintain a credible ceasefire; adopted with Ahern the new principle that disarmament should proceed in tandem with the talks; and proposed a separate commission with a Canadian chairman to advise how it might be brought about. In the summer of 1997 the Orange Order made a significant contribution to peaceful palaver by abating its claims to stage provocative marching (which it called walking) through Roman Catholic areas and the IRA proclaimed a fresh ceasefire which enabled the British government to invite Sinn Fein to the talks due to begin a few weeks later. Trimble did not like the proposals on disarmament since they guaranteed the surrender of no single weapon but (unlike Paisley) he was reluctant to exclude his party from the talks. For Unionists the focus of the entire problem was the IRA, which they regarded as an illegal armed force which aimed to end the union of Northern Ireland with Great Britain, unite it with the Irish Republic and so end the dominance of the Protestant community. Their fixed resolve was to defeat any Anglo-Irish plan which might pave the way to a united Ireland outside the United Kingdom. In the winter of 1997–98 the projected talks came close to abandonment as the parties prevaricated and killing began again but, thanks mainly to determined diplomacy on the British side and reluctance by the Northern Ireland parties to appear responsible for a return to civil war, all parties were brought together and presented jointly by the British and Irish governments with (fairly) fresh constitutional proposals. These were: a new parliament or assembly in Northern Ireland with legislative powers and guaranteed participation for Nationalists as well as Unionists, a standing cross-border body at ministerial level with executive powers in limited spheres, and an overall council comprising representatives of the United Kingdom, the Republic of Ireland, Northern Ireland, Scotland and Wales. In broad terms this refurbished initiative recognized that the attempt to solve the problem by an Anglo-Irish approach had failed and sought instead to dissolve it in an enlarged context. The proposals in effect ruled out a united independent Ireland in the near future. The chairmanship of George Mitchell, the active determination of the two prime ministers acting (most of the time) in tandem and war-weariness produced an agreement over the constitutional status of Northern Ireland and the distribution of power in it: the Good Friday agreement of 1998. The province was to remain part of the United Kingdom until a majority of its electorate decided otherwise. Power would be shared; the Protestant monopoly ended and a new regime begin under a coalition of the Ulster Unionists and the Social Democratic and Labour Party (SDLP) (and perhaps other smaller parties including Sinn Fein), major decisions would require the support of 60 per cent of both Nationalists and Unionists in the parliament. The Irish Republic would abandon the claim to Irish unity inscribed in its constitution. It acquired instead a special position in relation to Northern Ireland through membership of a North–South Ministerial Council which, while something of an anomaly in the relations between sovereign states, looked more like a committee of administrative workhorses than a seedbed of political union. The Council of the British Isles remained in the mists in which it had been conceived. All political prisoners were to be released within two years provided that the bodies to which they belonged did not resort to violence. Disarmament was to begin within a month or two but few supposed that it would get far. This was a plan for ending armed conflict and for ending anti-Catholic discrimination. It did not settle, nor did it engage, the question of Irish unity. Nationalists found it more acceptable than did Unionists. Most Nationalists now hoped to achieve their aims through demographic change rather than violence: the proportion of Roman Catholics in the province had already risen to 45 per cent. Among Unionists, however, probably more than half disliked the agreement for one reason or another but did not dislike it enough to vote against it in the referendum which followed its conclusion. The agreement bought time. A peculiarly appalling atrocity by a minor nationalist group at Omagh further discredited violence but was also a reminder of the continuing readiness of nationalists to resort to it or at least retain the power to do so. The greatest threat to the agreement lay in the fact that the best-armed faction – the IRA – had least reason to be pleased with it since it did less than nothing to advance the unification of Ireland.

It took two years to achieve the Good Friday agreement and another 18 months to put it into operation by establishing a devolved government. The crux was the surrender of arms. The IRA, which was not a party to the proceedings, refused to surrender its arms and the Unionists of David Trimble refused in consequence to form an executive inclusive of Sinn Fein on the grounds that the decommissioning of arms by all paramilitary groups was a covenanted precondition of the creation of an executive and that Sinn Fein was with the IRA an intrinsic part of the Nationalist movement. The Ulster Unionist Party split between those insisting on the letter of the formula 'No decommissioning, no devolution' and others seeking a compromise to save the Good Friday agreement. Trimble won a less than resounding majority of his party's Council for the immediate creation of a devolved government and the IRA appointed an emissary to the decommissioning commission chaired by the Canadian General Jean de Chastelain. These moves sufficed to bring about devolution but the Unionist Council hedged its endorsement of Trimble's policies by insisting that, if after three months no serious progress had been made with decommissioning, the devolved executive might be dissolved. A North–South Council of Irish Ministers met for the first time and a seven-party Council of the Isles – adding Scotland and Wales, the Isle of Man and the Channel Islands to the new constitutional structure – was inaugurated. But peace still depended on securing an adequate appearance of demilitarization within a short time.

The Good Friday agreement was welcomed by the very many people whose main wish was peace but it was abhorred by those in the IRA who perceived it as an affirmation of the English position in the north of Ireland. Since the IRA was not a party to it the agreement was neither inclusive nor conclusive. It was none the less a big stride away from the mentalities of belligerence and towards habits of negotiation and co-operation.

It was the beginning of the end to a crisis which had lasted for more than half a century. Northern Ireland was to remain, perhaps for at least another half century, a part of the United Kingdom. The IRA had failed to drive the British out of Ireland and create a united Ireland. The principal turning point had been the decision of two British prime ministers – Major and Blair – to stand by the principle that Great Britain would not leave Northern Ireland against the wishes of its people and that this determination would be made clear to the IRA and to the Irish government discreetly and credibly; it put an end to the suspension of the rule of law, torture and too much political rhetoric. The IRA lost by its own gangsterism some of the sympathy it had enjoyed in the province as a whole while within its ranks some leaders began to acknowledge that the British could not be driven out by force. The Irish government too, particularly Ahern himself, became convinced of the honesty and immoveability of the British government. Probably the British always had more cards to play than the IRA. Certainly they learned to play them intelligently and patiently. (For torture etc. see further Chapter 14 on the Iraqi war.)

B. The Basques

The Basques are a people of obscure origins and sharp self-consciousness. They have preserved a cultural identity based on an unaffiliated language and romantic historical claims. Straddling the occidental Pyrenees, they have been acquiescent in France but effervescent in Spain. A nationalist movement in the late nineteenth century claimed for the Basques in France and Spain independence under the name of Euzkadi. Repression by Franco's regime led to a split between those willing to accept a state within the Spanish state and those prepared to insist on independence, if necessary by violence. The secessionists created in 1959 'Basque Homeland and Freedom' or ETA. This split was aggravated by prosperity which, as in the 1890s, caused an influx of non-Basque workers competing for the jobs on offer in Burgos and thereabouts. After violence in the late 1960s 16 persons, mostly from the middle class and some of them priests, were put on trial in 1970 before a military court in Burgos, charged with murder, bombings, illegal possession of arms and illicit propaganda. The trial lasted several years and gave a boost to ETA, which in 1973 carried its war into the Spanish capital and assassinated Franco's prime minister Admiral Carrero Blanco. After Franco's death the new regime enacted a new constitution (1978) which divided Spain into regions, two of them with especially wide autonomy – Catalonia and the Basque country. ETA's political wing, Herri Batasuna, won 12–14 per cent of the vote in Basque areas in successive elections in the 1980s and 1990s while activists continued to pursue independence by violence which, met by police brutality, created a semi-suppressed civil war. In 1998 ETA, influenced apparently by the pacific turn of events in Northern Ireland, declared a permanent cessation of violence but after 14 months it reversed this gesture.

C. Cyprus

In 1878 Disraeli, prompted by British military opinion, contemplated the seizure of Cyprus but contrived to secure it by diplomacy. On the eve of the Congress of Berlin he entered into an agreement with the Turks to defend their empire against Russia upon being permitted to occupy Cyprus, which was for the British of those days the key to western Asia. Britain, contemplating the collapse of the Ottoman empire or alternatively the substitution of German for British influence at the Sublime Porte, was on the lookout for vantage points in the eastern Mediterranean. The occupation of Cyprus in 1878 was followed a few years later by the occupation of Egypt. The British remained in both for the best part of three generations.

Cyprus was annexed by Britain in 1914 on the declaration of war between Britain and Turkey, and British sovereignty was recognized by Turkey by the Treaty of Lausanne in 1923. Between the wars British rule was challenged by the partisans of *enosis* or union with Greece but was never seriously threatened. For the British Cyprus was a colony which could gradually be granted the degree of self-government compatible with its usefulness as a staging-post and a base in the British imperial scheme of things. For the Greek section of the population, however, the British themselves and their programme of limited development were an affront to their rights. The Turkish minority was a spectator of Anglo-Greek conflict. At the end of the Second World War the British estimate of the value of Cyprus rose as a result of retreat from Palestine and the weakening of the British position in Egypt. The British assumed that they should therefore remain sovereign over Cyprus. The Greek Cypriots, however, expected a reward for their loyalty to Britain during the war and regarded the British withdrawal from Egypt as a prelude to a negotiated review of the British position in Cyprus.

Cypriots were not in general hostile to Britain or much attracted to the alternative of rule from Athens but they insisted on their right to vote on their status at some prescribed, but not necessarily immediate, date; they were willing to permit British military bases on the island. The British were handicapped by much ignorance about their subjects' feelings, by the inadequacy of a badly neglected police force and by fears that concessions to Cypriots would have troubling consequences in other outposts of empire. They insisted on retaining full sovereignty indefinitely and unquestioned, and they mistakenly believed that they could prevent Greece from raising the Cyprus issue at the UN by appeals to Anglo-Greek amity and veiled threats of bringing Turkey into the equation. Active resistance to Britain was fostered by nationalists in Greece (including Athens radio), by the more militant Orthodox clergy and by the intransigence which alienated the bulk of passive Cypriots who abhorred violence but were at one with the activists in demanding at least an acknowledgment of their right to bring British rule to an end.

In 1946 the exiled bishop of Kyrenia returned to the island and in 1950, at the age of 37, he was elected to the archiepiscopal throne which had been vacant during the years 1937–47. He took the regnal name of Makarios III and became at the same time ethnarch or national leader. In common with all Greek Cypriots he looked to Greece for support in arguments with Britain or, failing their satisfactory outcome, in internationalizing the issue by taking it to the UN. No Greek government could deny this patriotic duty, however reluctant it might be to impair good relations with Britain. In 1950 a plebiscite organized by the church returned the inevitable (but not, as the British deludedly imagined, faked) response in favour of *enosis* and the Greek prime minister General Nicholas Plastiras equally inevitably responded to it in a tone of mixed encouragement and moderation. About the Greekness of Cyprus no Greek bothered to think twice. Four Cypriots in five were Greek by race, tongue and religion. Whether they supported the left-wing party AKEL (Progressive Party of the Working People) or the right-wing KEK (the Cyprus National Party) they shared a common nationalism, for which they were soon to fight together in the insurrectionary movement of EOKA, the National Organisation of Freedom Fighters.

The Turkish section of the population (18 per cent) was no less alive to the Greekness of the island but drew opposite conclusions from the same facts. They feared Greek rule. These fears were not great in the first postwar years but they were latent and easily inflamed. The Turkish state, as opposed to the Turks of Cyprus, also feared *enosis* because Cyprus was only 60 km from the Turkish coast, because postwar Greece seemed for a short while to be exposed to communism, and because Greece might still cherish the ambition to conquer Constantinople and the coasts of Asia Minor (which it had tried to do immediately after the First World War). Turkish governments showed, however, little inclination to intervene in Cypriot affairs until encouraged to do so by Britain.

In 1951 the Greek government sought a way of satisfying its Cypriot compatriots and its British allies by offering Britain bases in Cyprus – and also in Greece itself – in return for *enosis*, but Eden was not interested in a solution which could have saved much later bloodshed. In 1953 he exacerbated the situation by declaring that there was no question of a British withdrawal. This statement forced Greeks to decide between an indefinite acceptance of the existing position and a resort to violence to change it. Makarios tried an intermediate course. In 1954 he went to Athens to get the Greek government to raise the Cypriot question at the UN. Eden repeated that no discussion was possible and the colonial secretary affronted the Greek government by arguing that Greece was too unstable to be allowed to extend its sway to Cyprus. The Greek government then raised the question of self-determination for Cyprus at the UN but half-heartedly and without pressing the case, which was shelved. The disappointed enotists organized demonstrations which evoked an excessive British counter-reaction (including measures against schoolchildren). The British in Nicosia and London believed that the *enosis* movement was a bubble blown in their faces by a small and unrepresentative group of irresponsible agitators who had succeeded in cowing the bulk of a pro-British population. This was, at the very least, a serious misreading, just as the British appreciation of the value of Cyprus as a base was also seriously mistaken: Cyprus, though valuable as a command headquarters (HQ Middle East Land and Air Forces was transferred there in 1954) and as an air staging point, was a poor country with meagre resources, no adequate naval base (Famagusta being too shallow) and a manifest vulnerability to Russian nuclear attack. The Suez War of 1956 proved that it had some value for the Royal Air Force but no other.

In 1955 Eden and his foreign secretary Harold Macmillan brought the Turkish government officially into the matter. The Greek and Turkish governments were invited to a conference in London where the latter opposed every solution acceptable to the former. The results included a collapse of Greco-Turkish relations, atrocities against Greeks resident in Turkey, a Greek boycott of Balkan Pact meetings and NATO exercises, the despatch of British army units to Cyprus and an escalation of anti-British violence there. In Cyprus the governor and the archbishop met for the first time, a British colonial secretary appeared in the island also for the first time and a new governor was appointed – Sir John Harding, field-marshal and former Chief of the Imperial General Staff. The policy entrusted to him was to separate the ethnarch-archbishop from the insurrectionary movement which had come into the open in 1954, to negotiate with the one and to extirpate the other. This policy, pursued until the end of 1957, was based on false premises and poor information and was at one point abandoned by the British. The Harding–Makarios negotiations were proceeding early in 1956 towards a conclusion when the British government intervened and decreed the deportation of the archbishop to the Seychelles. Eden appeared to have been swayed at this juncture by pressure from the right wing of the Conservative Party, by the dismissal of General Glubb by the king of Jordan (which Eden interpreted as a deliberate slight to his government) and by the failure to manoeuvre Jordan into his prized creation, the Baghdad Pact. He resolved to teach his enemies a lesson, foremost among them Makarios and Nasser. But Makarios was released in the following year, much to the annoyance of the Turks and without any compensating advantage since the archbishop refused to return to Cyprus and took up residence in Athens.

British attempts to quell the insurrection were equally unsuccessful. This revolt was led by Colonel Grivas, an officer of the Greek army and a Cypriot by birth, who set himself to evict the British by a combination of military skill, faith and ruthlessness. Grivas had fought on the same side as the British in two wars and was outraged to discover that, despite the UN Charter and frequent British promises in the past, Britain had no intention of allowing the Cypriots to choose how and by whom they should be

governed. Like Cavour after the Crimean War, Grivas took the view that his compatriots had paid for self-determination with their blood, and when he saw that the
British view was different, he set about shedding more blood. He decided, according to
his own account, to resort to violence in 1951 but he laid his plans with professional
care, carried out an extensive and open reconnaissance of the terrain and waited until
1954 before making his first purchase of arms and setting up a headquarters in a sub-
urb of Nicosia inhabited chiefly by British families. He launched his revolt in 1955,
survived a drive against him at the time of Makarios's deportation in 1956 and immediately struck back. His main weapons were bushcraft, discipline and terrorism, his
victims frequently Greek civilians, his armoury and front-line manpower always small.
He provoked the British into retaliatory measures which failed – collective fines on villages, high but ineffective bribes, hangings and torture. He defeated the policy which
Harding had been sent to implement.

In the course of the year in which Makarios was in the Seychelles and the
Harding–Grivas duel was taking place, the first Greco-Turkish riots occurred and the
British government began, although unintentionally, to transfer the initiative from
London to Ankara and Athens. During 1956 Eden produced a plan by which Cyprus
would be allowed self-determination after ten years of self-government, but instead of
applying his scheme he submitted it for approval to the Turkish and Greek governments. The Turkish government rejected and so killed it. Later in the year new proposals, elaborated by an eminent British judge Lord Radcliffe, were in the same way
submitted to the Turkish and Greek governments. The Radcliffe plan rejected self-
determination and mentioned partition. It was accordingly rejected by the Greeks,
while Turkey was emboldened to suggest that either half of Cyprus or the whole of it
should be annexed to Turkey. The Greeks, thoroughly alarmed, threatened to leave the
western camp. In 1957 General Sir Hastings Ismay, the secretary-general of NATO,
offered to mediate, but although the Turks were willing the Greeks were not. The Turks
believed that a majority of the members of NATO were sympathetic to Turkey; the
Greeks that their cause would prevail in the UN but not in NATO. There was deadlock
and continuing disorder and murder. The government of Harold Macmillan reviewed
Eden's Cyprus policy and, faced with the threat to NATO's eastern flank, decided that
Britain no longer needed to be sovereign in the whole of Cyprus. Sovereign bases
would do and the Greek and Turkish governments must be brought to accept independence for the rest of the island. For Turkey independence was acceptable, since
it automatically excluded *enosis*. Upon Greece independence might be forced, since
Greece abominated partition and was afraid that in the absence of a settlement Greeks
in Istanbul and other parts of Turkey would be stripped of their property and either
killed or expelled.

In December 1957 Harding was replaced by Sir Hugh Foot, who produced a new
plan: self-government as a colony for a period followed by self-determination, with the
proviso that *enosis* would need Turkish approval. The mention of *enosis* was too much

for the Turks and demonstrations were organized in Ankara when Selwyn Lloyd (now foreign secretary) and Foot visited that capital. The Foot plan disappeared. It was succeeded by the Macmillan plan, which was a further step away from undiluted British rule. Macmillan proposed to introduce representatives of the Greek and Turkish governments alongside the British governor and to create a mixed cabinet and separate Greek Cypriot and Turkish Cypriot local administrations. The last provision was unacceptable both to Makarios and to the Greek prime minister, Constantine Karamanlis. The Turks riposted by instigating riots to put pressure on the British to apply their plan none the less. The revolution in Baghdad in July 1958 may have inclined the British government, threatened with the loss of its Iraqi ally and the collapse of the Baghdad Pact, to lean further to the Turkish side and Macmillan set out on a tour in the course of which he slightly modified his plan, failed to reconcile Makarios or Karamanlis to it, but resolved to apply it. Violence increased horribly.

The spreading communal hatred shocked and alarmed the Greek and Turkish governments into an accord. They agreed that Cyprus should be independent. Britain would be accorded sovereign rights in certain military bases. The new state would have a Greek president, a Turkish vice-president with a veto in certain matters, and a cabinet of seven Greeks and three Turks; this 7–3 proportion would be repeated right down the administrative ladder. The Greek and Turkish states would station small armies of 950 and 600 men respectively in Cyprus. This scheme was accepted with the greatest reluctance by Makarios, who declared it unworkable. He was, however, threatened with abandonment by the Greek government and on 1 March 1959 he returned at last to Cyprus. Grivas, infuriated by the politicians' betrayal of the cause of *enosis*, was fêted, promoted and sent back to Athens. Instead of driving the British out and making Cyprus part of Greece, his campaign had ended with the British still in possession of sovereign bases and Cyprus still not part of the Greek kingdom. Cyprus became independent and a member of the UN and member of the Commonwealth (1960–61).

The Zurich settlement was an attempt by frightened men to prevent the situation from getting completely out of control. That was its one merit. But Makarios was right in regarding the constitution as unworkable. Each of the five principal towns was to have two separate municipal bodies, though this concession to communal distrust produced such absurdities in practice that it was never implemented. Discussions for an improved system broke down and the Greek majority in parliament rejected a Turkish proposal to extend the existing arrangements for a year. The constitutional court pronounced both the Greek and Turkish cases to be wrong, and in 1963 Makarios made proposals which were meant to force the Turks into further discussions but were taken by them to be a breach of the constitution and an attack on their safeguards. Serious fighting developed and attempts by leaders on both sides to arrange and enforce ceasefires broke down. Moreover, the progenitors of the Zurich agreement had by now passed from the scene. Both the Karamanlis government in Athens and the Menderes government in Ankara had fallen. The former had been replaced by a government under George Papandreou which began its existence without a parliamentary major-ity, while in Turkey a military coup had overthrown the parliamentary system in 1960. General Gürsel, who was successively provisional head of state and then in October 1961 president, installed a coalition government, but the new military regime was assailed by an abortive coup from within its own ranks in 1963 and by the recrudes-cence of Menderes's Democratic Party under the new name of the Justice Party. When fighting broke out again in Cyprus, the veteran Ismet Inönu had just resigned the premiership and been persuaded to retain it, albeit with a majority in parliament of only four.

Some 200 Turks were killed in this new bout, Turkish jet aircraft flew menacingly over Nicosia, a Turkish naval invasion was thwarted by the American Sixth Fleet prowl-ing in the vicinity, the Greek and Turkish forces in Cyprus took up hostile battle posi-tions, and the British colonial secretary Duncan Sandys abandoned his Christmas holiday to fly overnight to Cyprus. After four years of independence Cyprus had brought Greece and Turkey to the verge of war.

Britain tried to transfer the Cyprus problem to NATO. The Greek and Turkish governments were willing to accept NATO intervention but Makarios was not; nor were other members of NATO anxious to become embroiled. In February 1964 a second Turkish invasion threat was unostentatiously foiled by the American fleet and Britain accepted the need to invoke the UN. The raising of a UN force coincided with a third invasion scare, but by mid-March the Canadian advance party of a UN force reached Cyprus. It was followed by units from Eire, Sweden, Denmark and Finland which, together with British units transferred to UN command, constituted a force of 7,000 which gradually asserted control, although occasional outbursts continued to occur – and led to reprisals against the Greeks in Istanbul.

In addition to the peace force the UN secretary-general appointed a mediator to seek a political solution, but no incumbent of this office was able to find a solution acceptable to both sides. The United States, alarmed by the consequences of Greco-Turkish conflict, took a hand through the former secretary of state, Dean Acheson, who produced a scheme for *enosis*, excluding an area in north-eastern Cyprus which would go to Turkey. The Turks thereupon asked for a larger area and so converted the plan into partition in a new form. Acheson then revised his plan and proposed that the north-eastern area should merely be leased to Turkey for 20 to 25 years. At this point the plan became unacceptable to everybody and the Turks, already disappointed in their hopes of NATO and frustrated by the American fleet, turned tentatively towards the Russians (who may at this time have sensed a possibility of undermining the entire Baghdad Pact since Pakistan was also disappointed by the United States and Iran was internally unstable and internationally plastic). Early in 1965 the UN mediator pro-posed a demilitarized independent Cyprus, debarred from *enosis*, in which the Turkish minority would be protected by a UN guarantee and a resident UN commissioner. A new government in Ankara rejected the idea.

With the UN force preventing a resumption of civil war, the basic political fact reasserted itself: namely that Turkey, Cyprus's nearest neighbour and a country with three times the population of Greece, was capable of preventing *enosis* but was not capable of achieving the conquest of the island. Hence the independent status of Cyprus, an independence resulting from a balance of external forces which was countered by an opposite balance of internal forces. Externally, power lay with the Turkish and not with the Greek state; internally, power lay with the Greek and not with the Turkish community. The power of the Greek community was limited by the power of the Turkish state, and the power of the Turkish state was limited by forces which were not native to the area. Cyprus therefore was an international problem-child destined, so long as these circumstances prevailed, to independence tempered by ungovernability. The UN stopped the killing but could not resolve the underlying dispute. The best it could do was localize it.

Year after year, the mandate of the peacekeeping force was renewed by the UN which recoiled from the consequences of saving money by removing the force. Talks between the two communities started and stopped more than once. Any whiff of *enosis* from the Greek side was met with Turkish talk of double *enosis*, a new name for partition and the attachment of northern Cyprus to the Turkish state. In 1971 Grivas was back in Nicosia. The only new element in the situation was the worsening relations between Makarios and the military junta which had seized control of Greece in 1967. The junta supported Grivas's heirs, now called EOKA B, against Makarios, whom they regarded as a troublesome red priest. They tried to force him to change his government (and did succeed in making him remove his foreign minister) and they incited his fellow bishops to bring charges of simony against him for combining the presidential and archiepiscopal offices. They were anxious to score a popular victory by forcing the pace in Cyprus in order to be able to pose as Greek patriots who had united Cyprus with the Greek heartlands. But Makarios was re-elected president in 1973 without opposition, routed the bishops and had them unfrocked for good measure, and struck back at Athens in 1974 by demanding the recall from Cyprus of the officers of the Cypriot National Guard who were doing the junta's bidding and subverting rather than protecting the Cypriot state. At this point the junta acted. Makarios was attacked in his palace by the National Guard but escaped in a helicopter with British help and was flown to England. The insurgents proclaimed Nikos Samson president in his place, a choice as unwise as it was unsuitable, as Samson had been a notorious EOKA gunman and had to resign at the end of a week.

The independence and integrity of Cyprus had been guaranteed by Greece, Turkey and Britain. Greece was in the process of destroying both. Turkey saw in Greece's foolhardy action an opportunity to occupy at least a part of the island. Britain was unwilling to do anything, partly because of the difficulty of finding reinforcements for its units in the British bases but more emphatically because intervening meant intervening against Turkey and so on the side of the Athens junta and the equally unattractive

Samson. Consequently, Turkey invaded Cyprus five days after the coup against Makarios. A ceasefire was imposed two days later and the next day the junta in Athens collapsed. The Turks remained.

The three guarantors met at Geneva. Turkey's attitude was threatening but realistic: either there must be a new constitution acceptable to Turkey or Cyprus would remain de facto partitioned. The constitution proposed was a loose confederation not far short of independence for the components, and the proposal was accompanied by an ultimatum. The talks were broken off. The Turks attacked again, occupied 40 per cent of the island in two days and turned 200,000 Greeks into refugees. The American ambassador in Nicosia was murdered by Greeks who took American inaction to betoken complicity with Turkey. The British were criticized violently in Cyprus and in Greece for not doing more, as a guarantor, to help Cyprus escape the plight brought upon it by a Greek government; it was, however, restrained by the United States, which was anxious to preserve its intelligence installations in the north of the island. Makarios returned at the end of the year. Cyprus was, in effect, partitioned but nobody was prepared to say so and its affairs were therefore back to inter-community talks, hampered by the emotions of war, charges and counter-charges of atrocities, the plight of refugees, economic disruption and the unreality of any attempt to restore the integrity and independence of Cyprus with a Turkish army in control of a large part of it. Makarios, who died in 1977, was succeeded as president by Spyros Kiprianou.

Both the UN, which tried to mediate from 1977, and the Greeks had tacitly to accept federalism as the basis for any possible settlement. In discussions between the two communities within Cyprus, and between the Greek and Turkish governments, the Greeks were intent on securing a strong federal centre, together with a substantial Turkish withdrawal from the territories which they had conquered. At the end of 1983, however, the Turks forced the pace by declaring the northern part of the island independent. The UN secretary-general, Javier Perez de Cuellar, who had considerable personal knowledge of Cypriot affairs, contrived to persuade leaders from both sides to discuss a loose federation: the Turks, in possession of 37 per cent of the territory, seemed willing to reduce their share to 29 per cent and to accept a Greek, not a rotating, presidency; the Greeks seemed willing to allot to the Turks 30 per cent of the seats in a lower and 50 cent in a second chamber. Progress was, however, imperceptible. In 1986 the Turkish regime accepted a UN plan for reunification but the Greeks, hoping for better terms, countered with a different plan. Talks continued, punctuated in 1987 by the election of a new president of Cyprus George Vassiliou, who promised progress towards agreement but could not make any. Bush tried to mediate in 1991 but the moment was ill-chosen. Elections in Turkish Cyprus strengthened the separatists, elections in Turkey itself produced a hung parliament, and the Greeks in Athens and Cyprus were stiffly opposed to a demand by the Turkish Cypriots for an entrenched right to secede from any federation which might be set up. Further talks in 1997 served only to affirm the intractability of the situation as the (Greek) government of Cyprus bought a missile defence system from Russia and Turkey threatened to use force to prevent its delivery. Economic considerations pointed to compromise, political fears and prejudices denied it. Cyprus was Europe's Kashmir, a seemingly insoluble clash frozen by the UN's interdiction of war – at peace, but not too bothered by partition and waiting for a new generation to make a better job of cohabitation.

Related reading: part three

General

Gillingham, John: *European Integration 1950–2003 – Superstate or the New Model Economy* (2003)
Jenkins, Philip: *God's Continent – Christianity, Islam and Europe's Religious Crisis* (2007)
Judt, Tony: *Postwar – A History of Europe since 1945* (2005)
Mazower, Mark: *Dark Continent* (1998)

Particular

Barnett, Corelli: *The Audit of War – The Illusions and Reality of Britain as a Great Power* (1986)
Bloomfield, Kenneth: *A Tragedy of Errors – Government and Misgovernment in Northern Ireland* (2007)
Glenny, Misha: *The Balkans – Nationalism, War and the Great Powers 1804–1999* (2001)
Sampson, Anthony: *The Essential Anatomy of Britain* (1992)
Stern, Fritz Richard: *Dreams and Delusions – The Drama of German History* (1999)
Weber, Eugen: *Peasants into Frenchmen – The Modernization of Rural France* (1976)
Wilson, Duncan: *Tito's Yugoslavia* (1979)

PART FOUR

The Middle East

CHAPTER 8

Islam

The independence of the Arab world reintroduced religion as a political force in the Middle East. Islam, the third and last of the great religions derived from Zoroastrianism, spread with astonishing rapidity from the Arabian peninsular to triumphs in western Asia and northern Africa in the century following the death of its founding Prophet in AD 632.

Checked at either end of Europe by the Byzantine emperor Leo the Isaurian and the Frankish King Charles Martel it continued to expand to become in modern times the professed faith of some 1.2 billion people and perhaps the world's most dynamic religion. The Dar ul-Islam or House of the Faithful – the name means submission – quickly lost its purely Arab character, split into numerous branches and, like Christendom before it, confronted the problem of how authority should be shared between its ecclesiastical and secular members. Christendom, whose first major schism became permanent in the eleventh century AD after a long series of temporary breaches, attempted two solutions to this problem, neither of which worked well. Byzantium turned its secular emperor into a sacred person with ambiguous and contested authority over patriarch and councils of the church, while western Christendom developed a doctrine of the Two Swords, a partnership which produced more conflict than concord under the weight of its unreality. The idea of a single secular–religious polity evaporated to be succeeded by a patchwork of territorial secular states (misleadingly called nation states). Within Islam the first major split, more personal than doctrinal, occurred when the Prophet's son-in-law and his followers seceded from the main body. They became the Shi'a, the preferred variant of minor groups, more inclined to doctrinal rigidity and even violence but limited to about 10 per cent of the Dar ul-Islam except in Iran where it eventually attained overwhelming majority.

As primacy passed from the relatively sparse Arabs to Iranians, Mongols and Turks the resulting Muslim empires came into contact with alien empires and ideas. The last great Muslim empire, that of the Ottoman Turks, was brought to an end by the First World War, having already gradually lost hold over its European extension. The dissolution of its empire in Asia was more abrupt, leaving much of the Arab world under British or French control. The Second World War destroyed this ambiguous form of empire (the mandate system) but substituted in a small corner the Jewish state of

Israel, widely regarded by Arabs as an affront and as an outpost of yet another imperial regime by which the United States would inherit power over the Middle East.

The Middle East meanwhile had changed in two ways. New political ideas, partly derived from the French Revolution and partly from western models and ambitions for economic development, had been percolating into the Arab world or sections of it. These were often politically, socially or religiously unsettling and they coincided with something even more unsettling – the arrival of affluence through the discovery of oil. This phenomenon, starting at the beginning of the twentiethth century and accelerating spectacularly after its middle years, created destabilizing divisions between rich and poor, introduced lifestyles deeply offensive to many Muslims (particularly clerics) and above all created the conviction that the United States was intent not only on displacing Britain and France but also on imposing American dominion either by implanting obedient but unpalatable governments on Arab states or by force of arms, if necessary. Oil created hostility of two kinds: jealousy on the part of indigenous oil owners quick to denounce the greed of foreign invaders and fear that oil, having become not merely a valuable commodity but also a vital need of these unwelcome invaders, would cause war. This fear was far from illogical. The increasingly obvious fact that the world demand for oil and the lack, at any rate in the short term, of an alternative to oil, combined with the further fact that two-thirds of the world's known stock of oil lay in the Middle East, exposed the region to attacks by any country which needed the oil and believed itself powerful enough to impose a new order on the Middle East – specifically, the United States. The fact that the United States possessed such power but had no idea how to wield it made the situation the more menacing. In the context Islam – or rather Middle Eastern Islam – produced alarmingly violent movements. They were not unique: Islam's Judaic and Christian cousins had done no less in the course of their longer careers but the twentieth century setting gave Islamic violence and anti-Islamic rhetoric a fearful virulence.

Throughout the second half of the twentieth century the Middle East maintained its preponderance in the possession and export of oil and around the year 2000 alternative sources of supply ran out and the world's appetite for oil sharpened. The political weight of Middle Eastern suppliers, hitherto often exaggerated, began to be underestimated as China, India, Australia and other aspirants to industrial development threatened seriously to upset the balance between supply and demand. Within the Middle East too, instability in Iran precipitated by the Khomeini revolution and by the devastation of Iraq by the United Sates and its allies shifted the balance of oil power to Saudi Arabia, an authoritarian autocracy whose stability rested principally on the difficulties of perceiving any alternative regime. A deficient or uncertain supply of energy raised genuinely serious alarm such as had not been felt since coal had ceased to be king or, even more remotely, timber had ceased to fuel life.

CHAPTER 9

Turkey

The Ottoman empire in Europe reached its limit with the failure to take Vienna in 1683 and the ensuing treaty of Carlowitz (1699) which marked the beginning of a long and convulsive recession leaving it with little more in Europe than the city of Istanbul. Strategically, however, Turkey in the twentieth century had potentially a role as a link between Europe and a renascent Arab world.

Modern Turkey, stretching 1,000 miles from west to east, bounded by seas, Arabs and Iran, was created after the First World War by Mustafa Kemal – Ataturk – as a secular state inhabited by Muslims: Sunni Turks and a Sunni Kurdish minority, once persecuted but by the end of the twentieth century shifting in relatively small numbers from their south-east homeland to Istanbul and beginning to prosper there. (For the Kurds see p. 417.) Ataturk gave Turkey a new capital, Ankara, in the centre of the country but his state retained Istanbul in its European fringe, once the greatest city in Europe. Turkey was a state between three worlds: the Arab world which it had ruled for centuries; the central Asian republics inhabited by Turkic kin which had been conquered by imperial Russia but won independence upon the collapse of the Soviet empire; and Europe. The Cold War enhanced its links to the west through its strategic importance to the United States. It was specifically an object of the Truman Doctrine, was included in the Marshall Plan, became a member of NATO, sent troops to the Korean War of 1950, and allowed the United States to use its territory in the Lebanese crisis of 1958 and the Gulf War of 1991. Europeans, however, were less comfortable than Americans with close relations with Turkey and shillyshallied over its admittance to the EU. It joined OPEC but its relations with Arab states and Iran were uneasy. It was a lonely state.

When Ataturk died in 1939 he was succeeded as president and leader of his Revolutionary People's Party (RPP) by his friend and comrade-in-arms Ismet Inonu (president 1939–50, also prime minister 1961–65). But he left his programme incomplete. About half his country had not accepted modernizing, westernizing and democratic trends which he had set in motion or his belief that the right place for clerics was in the mosque and not in government. A second political party split from the RPP in 1950 with the name Democratic Party (DP), but although the two treated one another as adversaries many Turks regarded their politicking as a charade and remained attached to an older Islamic tradition. Turkey was as deeply riven as Russia in the century after Peter the Great, the modernizing tsar. Politicians and the political system were further weakened when their modernizing ambitions failed to deliver economic rewards for more than a small minority of the people. One consequence was the dominant influence of the army, itself twice modernized (by Ataturk and by the Americans after the Second World War), broadly anxious to maintain the democratic parliamentary system and unwilling to assume the responsibilities of government except at critical moments.

With the end of the Second World War the DP, a splinter from the RPP, all but extinguished the latter. Its leaders Celal Bayar and Adnan Menderes became president and prime minister. They enjoyed the first flush of the Marshall Plan, encouraged private industries, subsidized agriculture and sought to curb the political power of the army. The DP's modernizing zeal improved the economic infrastructure and expanded Turkey's industrial sector but at a cost and pace and with a dogmatic hostility to planning which drove the country into bankruptcy, from which it was rescued by the IMF and accommodations with its foreign creditors. Economic mismanagement was compounded by Menderes's increasingly crazy despotism and the latter half of the decade was punctuated by demonstrations and riots, including indiscriminate attacks on Greeks and their businesses. After a carefully prepared coup in 1960 the army arrested all the DP's members of parliament, dissolved the party, put nearly 600 persons on trial and executed three of them including Menderes. General Cemal Gürsel became head of a ruling National Unity Committee of 38 with Colonel Alparslan Turkes – a Cypriot and something of a cultural, religious and nationalist fanatic – as (temporarily) the power behind the throne. This regime was weakened by plots within the military and produced a new constitution which was greeted at a referendum by a surprisingly large adverse minority. The dissolved DP was revived as the Justice Party – one of a dozen new parties – and came a close second to the RPP at elections in 1961. It regained power in 1965 with its new leader, Suleiman Demirel, a self-made engineer, cautious conservative and powerful speaker with a common touch. In or out of office Demirel became the outstanding political figure in Turkey for the rest of the century.

To the perennial problems of economic stability and progress the 1970s added that of internal order, threatened by dissidents of both left and right and by Kurdish separatism. In coping with these problems Demirel and his principal adversary Bülent Ecevit, who succeeded to the leadership of the RPP in 1972, were hampered by the proliferation of parties at both ends of the political spectrum, notably the Islamic and nationalist Grey Wolves formed by Turkes. Parliamentary majorities became more difficult to secure and military interference more unpredictable. The constitution of 1961 had given the military a special status within the state but military interventions took a perplexing variety of forms, from the declaration of emergencies and imposition of martial law to the creation of temporary military authorities alongside and in ill-defined tandem with civilian bodies. Demirel and Ecevit moved in and out of office while the economy plummeted and public order evaporated. After 1977 neither of the two principal parties had a parliamentary majority. Demirel formed a coalition with Turkes but defections from his own party forced him to resign. Ecevit was obliged to introduce martial law in 1978 and to resign in his turn in 1979. Anti-communist measures – the term communist being very loosely interpreted – included the suppression of press and academic freedoms, arrests by the thousand and the recourse to terror and torture as a routine. Disorder was compounded by fatuity when more than 100 ballots failed to elect a new president in 1980. Disorder also destroyed hopes of economic recovery (which was further retarded by the oil price rises of the 1970s), stimulated the more militant tendencies among the Kurds, turned to political assassination and compelled the army once more to assume direct rule in order to fend off anarchy. All parties were dissolved, local as well as national politicians and thousands besides were arrested; political discussion was banned. General Kenen Evren was proclaimed head of state, order was restored with a ruthlessness rendered acceptable to many by the fears which had preceded the coup; and in 1983 the army installed a new civilian regime.

The new man was Turgut Ozal, another engineer and an economist who had worked in the United States and for the World Bank and as an adviser to Demirel, who promoted him to the cabinet in 1979 with special powers over the economy. Ozal formed the Motherland Party and in 1983 won a clear victory over all other parties, including one preferred by the army and led by a general. He curbed inflation and rectified the balance of trade and payments by rigorous monetary controls, deflation, high interest rates, low wages and reduced subsidies. The outcome was mixed but on balance favourable: on the one hand substantial growth in GNP and exports, useful public work on roads, irrigation and telecommunication and a boost for tourism; on the other hand an explosion in speculation and corruption and a calamitous fall in living conditions for all but a small number of entrepreneurs. The Motherland Party was an uncomfortable amalgam of modernizing westernizers and Islamic purists and nationalists and Ozal was no more successful than his predecessors in pruning the bureaucracy or imposing taxes and making people pay them. Remittances declined alarmingly as distrustful workers in Germany and elsewhere preferred to keep their money where they were. Financial scandals and allegations of nepotism eroded Ozal's personal standing and public confidence in his doctrinaire market capitalism. He secured in 1987 after laborious negotiations a fresh economic and defence agreement with the United States and readmission to the Council of Europe, from which Turkey had been expelled when its constitution was abrogated in 1980. Ozal was gradually replaced by the evergreen Demirel. Ozal moved in 1989 from the premiership to the presidency – the first civilian president for 28 years. He was followed in each office by Demirel. He died suddenly in 1993.

Demirel faced a worsening Kurdish situation and the Gulf War against Iraq. The latter aggravated the former, which was already peculiarly intractable because the

Kurds in Turkey refused to become Turks while the Turks refused to contemplate a Turkish–Kurdish state. In Ottoman days Turks and Kurds were alike Muslims (and so allies against the persecuted Armenians) but in Kemalist and post-Kemalist Turkey the religious bond was less of a counterweight to their ethnic differences and in the aftermath of the Gulf War of 1991 Turkey's Kurdish problem clashed with the wider international aspects of Kurdish nationalism. Turkey co-operated with the American policy of aiding Iraqi Kurds against Saddam Hussein while at the same time fearing that the United States wanted to create a Kurdish state, anathema to Turkey. Kurdish refugees from Iraq were forcibly repulsed, the Turkish army violated the frontier with Iraq in punitive pursuit of Turkish Kurds and kept up to 35,000 troops on Iraqi soil, and the toll of Kurdish dead surpassed 25,000 without quelling Kurdish militancy.

Both Ozal and Demirel were intrigued (as Enver Pasha had been in the early years of the century) by the opportunities offered by the emergence of new national Turkic states in central Asia out of the dissolution of the USSR (see p. 499). Ozal visited them and invited their leaders to Ankara. For Demirel these were alternative possibilities: an association with them and with Iran in an Islamic block, or a Turkic association without and to some degree against Iran, which was Shi'ite, theocratic and not Turkic. Awkwardly, Turkey, although kin with all these new states (except Tajikistan) had no borders with any of them. It was by long tradition wary of Russia and Iran but this wariness was balanced by their importance as markets for exports and sources of necessary imports: Russia was Turkey's largest trading partner and Iran was a crucial source to mitigate Turkey's severe energy shortage. Turkey promoted a Black Sea Economic Co-operation Treaty, which was signed by 11 states in 1992, a similar Caspian Sea Organization and an Economic Co-operation Treaty with Iran and Pakistan. Turkey was especially anxious to ensure that central Asia's prospective oil exports should flow through Turkish pipelines rather than through the Caucasus to Russia's Black Sea ports.

In the 1990s a general sense of failure afflicted the ruling True Path Party, led by Turkey's first female prime minister Tansu Ciller, so that the Rafeh or Welfare Party led by Necmettin Erbakan – another engineer but also a populist distrustful of and distrusted by the army's chiefs, anti-tycoon and anti-Israel – scored startling gains with calls for a return to Muslim traditions and behaviour patterns. Founded by Erbakan in 1983, Rafeh was not the first explicitly Islamic party. Erbakan had himself formed two similar parties, both of which were dissolved by the Constitutional Court for transgressing the constitution's commitment to secular rule. Erbakan was banned from political activity from 1980 to 1987 but Rafeh flourished, helped by revulsion against corruption in high places, and a vision of a new Islamic role for Turkey instead of the seemingly fruitless bid for membership of the EU. After elections in 1995 it was the biggest party in parliament and the next year it formed a government with Erbakan as prime minister in coalition with Ciller. Alarmed at Erbakan's success and annoyed by Ciller's opportunist alliance with him, army chiefs publicly reiterated their support for a secular regime and the Constitutional Court dissolved Rafeh and imposed a fresh ban on Erbakan and his principal party colleagues. Ciller was passed over for the succession, which went to an old Motherland Party chief Mesut Yilmaz, who lasted until 1998.

Relations with the EU were a constant irritant. Turkey became in 1964 the first associate member of the EC, but got no further until the conclusion in 1995 of a customs agreement. Loans from the EC/EU were gradually diminished by the competitive claims of Greece, Spain and Portugal as these states became full members, and were interrupted after the coup of 1980. There was little demand in western Europe for Turkish products. Western Europe, uneasy about the effects of free movement of labour in an EU with Turkey as a member, woke up to the fact that Turkey would be the Union's second most populous member with commensurate weight in its councils. Turkish disenchantment was crystallized by the opening in 1997 of negotiations for Cyprus's membership of the EU, by much expanded Greek purchases of foreign arms in the same year and by more clamorous European criticism of Turkey's disregard of human rights. Turkey retaliated with threats to veto all new admissions to NATO if it were denied membership of the EU. Europeans continued to regard Turkey as an anomaly in Europe, overlooking the fact that in south-east Europe it was, although territorially exiguous, the most powerful regional state.

Turkey had become a part of Europe by virtue of the politics of the Cold War. In a Europe dominated by the American conflict with the USSR Turkey was unquestionably a strategically valuable member of NATO, but in the post-Cold War Europe of the EU Turkey – geographically peripheral, economically a likely burden, politically an embarrassment – tended to revert to what it had occupied in history books and atlases: an ambiguous status between two worlds. This dichotomy was sharpened in the 1990s. Although Turkey was finally acknowledged in 1999 as a candidate for EU membership and Ecevit made an appearance at a conference of heads of state and government in Helsinki, the United States was fashioning an extended role for Turkey in the Middle East, where American policies were not well regarded by most EU members. In the 1990s the United States secured the use of Turkish airbases for American (and British) attacks on Saddam Hussein and brokered an alliance between Turkey and Israel. Israelis favoured this orientation, which gave Israel the right to use Turkish airfields and posed a threat to Syria as well as Iraq, but in Turkey it was both welcomed and distrusted – welcomed in as much as it sanctioned Turkish incursions into Iraq in pursuit of Kurds but distrusted because Turks suspected that the United States supported the creation of a Kurdish state and was pushing Turkey into an unacceptably pro-Israeli stance.

At the turn of the century Turkey's established political pattern was looking frayed. The contest between Ataturk's secular legacy and the clerical culture of much of the country outside its main cities had little meaning for a new class of successful businessmen and technicians who were mostly pious but moderate Muslims and regarded the existing parties as marginal elites. From the 1990s the economy, slowly at first but accelerating around 2000, emerged from the doldrums and grew vigorously, if patchily. The rate of growth reached 10 per cent, inflation was brought down from 70 to 10 per cent and foreign investment waxed (but unemployment remained high). In 2001 Recep Erdogan, formally of the Welfare Party, formed the Justice and Development Party (AKP), won elections in 2002, introduced social reforms (including women's rights) and began to shift Turkish politics towards a central consensus in place of two-party jousting. With Abdullah Gul, who became foreign minister in 2003, Erdogan sensed an opportunity to make Turkey strong enough to do without the embrace of either the Muslim world or of the EU: the rise of Islamic parties in the Arab world and Iran was distasteful and potentially a threat to stability in Turkey and European opposition to Turkey's membership of the EU was stiffening. Historical conflicts (as with Greece) were reinforced by human rights objectors, by the scale of Turkish migration into Europe and, most seriously, by the outspoken opposition of new German and French governments led by Angela Merkel and Nicolas Sarkozy. In 2007 the US Congress added acrimony to honest doubt by formally describing Turkish persecution of the Armenians in 1915 as genocide.

When in the same year a presidential election loomed Erdogan was dissuaded from standing. He nominated Gul but Gul's candidacy had a mixed reception because he had in the past shown sympathy for the idea of a Muslim state. Army chiefs, self-appointed guardians of Ataturk's legacy, expressed alarm. Gul was elected narrowly on a third ballot. The army restated its position but did nothing more drastic. Erdogan and his party scored an emphatic victory – a vote for accommodation with the Kurds as against the army's preference for invading Iraq's Kurdish provinces, and a victory for Kemalist secular democracy. But these successes were offset by the continuing failure to make progress towards EU membership and uncertainty whether the economic climate would continue fair.

CHAPTER 10

The Arabs and Israel to the Suez War

In the seventh century AD the Arabs surged out of the Arabian peninsula and created an empire which stretched at its zenith from the Pyrenees, along North Africa, through what was later called the Middle East and deep into central Asia. The successors of Mahomet, or caliphs, failed to preserve the unity of this vast and increasingly polyglot realm and the Arab conquerors became, in their turn, subject for 1,000 years to Kurds, Turks, British and French. But they never lost the powerful links of a common language and a common faith, and when they began to recover their independence these links served to revive visions of a renewed unity. The collapse of the Ottoman empire in Asia in 1918 offered to its Arab subjects a prospect altogether different from that offered, by the more gradual withdrawal of the same empire in Europe, to the racially and linguistically divided Christians of the Balkans.

But in 1919 the Arabs were disappointed. The Ottoman empire was virtually partitioned between the British (who already held Egypt and Cyprus) and the French, and one effect of this Balkanization of the Middle East was to foster separate Arab particularisms (Syrian, Iraqi, Jordanian) and dynastic feuds at the expense of Arab unity: the Arab world was more united under the Turks than without them. The new rulers from the west, lured by international politics and by oil back to the scene of their crusading adventures, became obstacles both to Arab unity and to Arab independence, not least because of the deadening effects of their overwhelming power on the Arab will to struggle for these aspirations; a second world war was needed to get the westerners out. French rule was eliminated by the British when the French authorities in Syria and Lebanon declared for Vichy; British rule, on the other hand, was maintained and even temporarily strengthened in spite of powerful anti-British currents in Egypt and an attempted pro-German coup in Iraq in 1941. The veiled occupation established in neighbouring Iran by Britain and the USSR did not immediately affront the Arabs, and when the war ended the British were the sole surviving target of Arab nationalism, whose temper was sharpened by Britain's administration of the mandate over Palestine where, in consequence of Britain's endorsement in 1917 of the Zionist aim of a Jewish National Home (the Balfour Declaration), a new non-Arab and non-Muslim community had gradually taken hold and was claiming the right to be not a home but a state.

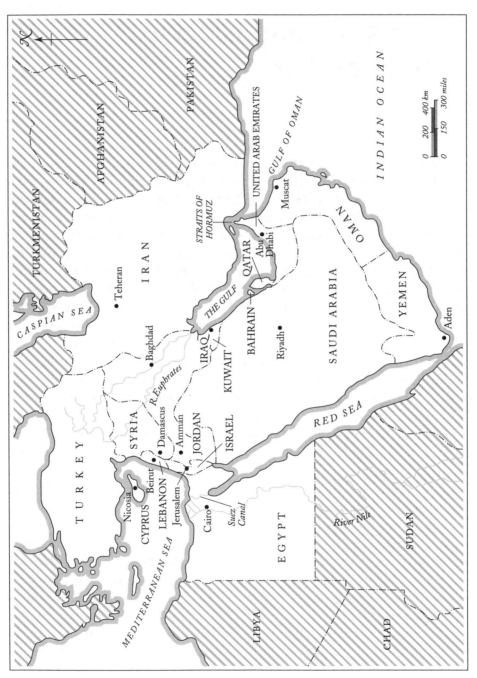

10.1 The Middle East

Faced with this powerful and stubborn remnant of the imperialist centuries, and with the vigorous new threat of Zionism, the Arabs were exceptionally divided among themselves. At the level of power monarchs, Saudi and Hashemite, were divided by inherited rivalries; more important, there was a rift between an old order, largely monarchical and traditionalist in its views on society and religion, and a new order which, with its beginnings in Arab intellectual movements of the nineteenth century, aspired to modernize religious and political thought and forms and to reduce the huge differences between the style of living of the very rich and the very poor. This revaluation inevitably produced within the Arab world internal conflicts and strains which enfeebled the Arab capacity to remove the British or defeat the Jews. The British were able to leave in their own time and the Jews established their state of Israel.

The creation of Israel

The British had struggled for a generation to reconcile their pledges to the Jews and to the Arabs (the latter reinforced by Britain's desire to be on good terms with the oil-producing Arab states and to retain bases in the Arab world), but the two were irreconcilable and the attempt to find an accommodation passed imperceptibly into a hand-to-mouth evasion of the most urgent current complications until the whole responsibility of the mandate was abandoned in 1948. At one point Britain tried partition. The Peel Commission proposed (1937) a tripartite division into an Arab and a Jewish state, leaving Britain with a mandate over a reduced area which would include the holy places of Jerusalem and Bethlehem with access to the Mediterranean. But upon closer inspection this scheme proved impracticable and Britain, forced by the approach of war in Europe to choose between the two sides, chose the Arabs and undertook, in the White Paper of 1939, to keep the Jewish element in the population of Palestine to one-third of the whole (it had risen since 1919 from 10 to nearly 30 per cent) and so to stop Jewish immigration after a further 75,000 Jews had been admitted. Thus Hitler cast upon Britain the odium of refusing asylum to Germany's persecuted Jewry because the imminence of a war against Germany made Britain even more sensitive to the need for Arab friendships: grand strategy, as well as oil strategy, dictated the terms of the White Paper. The Nazi Holocaust then transformed the fortunes of Zionism. The misery and optimism of the survivors achieved what Theodor Herzl and his successors had never come near to achieving.

After the 1939 White Paper Zionists had switched their main effort from Britain to the United States, abandoning their hope of achieving their aims by persuasion in London in favour of an actively anti-British policy to be financed (after the war) with American money. During the war the political effectiveness of Zionism was greatly enhanced in the United States and the Zionist cause was embraced by the two most powerful Americans of the 1940s, Presidents Roosevelt and Truman. This American involvement set the United States and Britain in opposition to each other. The prime

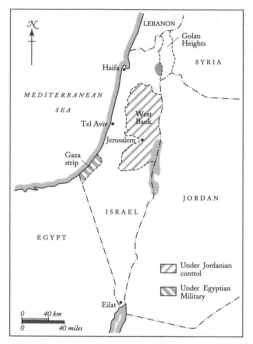

10.2 Israel – armistice lines, 1949–67

10.3 Israel – 1967, after the Six Day War, showing territorial gains

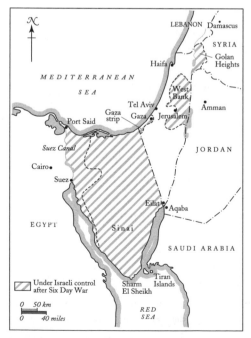

10.4 Israel – 1975, after the Sinai interim agreement with Egypt

10.5 Israel today

American concern was to persuade Britain to admit Jews to Palestine as generously and quickly as possible. On the assumption that some 100,000 Jews had survived the Nazi abomination, the United States adopted David Ben-Gurion's plea, made in August 1945, for the issue of that number of entry permits. Both Churchill and Attlee, themselves men of generous disposition and proven sympathies for the Zionist cause, wished to do something for the unhappy survivors and hoped to secure at the same time American support for British policies in the Middle East as a whole. But this co-operation was not to be had. The Americans wanted to help the Jews without becoming entangled in British positions of a suspiciously imperialist nature (the British only became respectable allies in these parts in American eyes in terms of a Cold War threat from the USSR); they failed to appreciate the extent of Britain's difficulties in Palestine concurrent with the surrender of power in India in 1947 and the challenge to the western position in Berlin in 1948.

The campaign to get Britain to issue the 100,000 entry permits was regarded in London as an extravaganza based on irresponsibility and inspired by ulterior motives. It was especially resented when the Jews took to terrorism in Palestine immediately after the end of the war. Nevertheless, the British government opted for a joint Anglo-American approach to the problem, and in October 1945 a committee of six Britons and six Americans set off to take soundings in Palestine, five Arab states and the European camps where the survivors of Nazism were waiting. Its report, published in April 1946, endorsed the estimate of 100,000 homeless Jews in Europe and the plea for their immediate admission to Palestine; it also rejected partition, recommended the continuance of the British mandate and – besides urging massive Jewish immigration – proposed the abolition of existing limitations on the purchase of land by Jews. The committee had hoped to produce an acceptable package deal, but Truman endorsed only the plea for 100,000 entry permits and the Arabs and the British government rejected the proposals as a whole. The appearance of the committee's report coincided with a Jewish terrorist attack in Tel Aviv which provoked counter-terrorism from the British side which indicated that the British nerve in Palestine, no less than British tempers in Whitehall, was beginning to break. While it was still widely supposed that Jewish atrocities were the independent work of special units (the Stern Gang and Irgun Zvai Leumi), undertaken without the approval of the main Jewish defence force (Haganah) or established political bodies (the Jewish Agency and Zionist organizations), there was already evidence that the case was otherwise and that the British authorities were faced with a concerted nationalist attempt to remove them. In June 1946 a part of the King David Hotel in Jerusalem was blown up and 91 persons were killed.

After the rejection by Britain of the report of the Anglo-American committee the idea of partition was revived. Ambassador Henry Grady for the United States and the British home secretary Herbert Morrison produced in July a plan for two autonomous but not sovereign provinces, and the issue of 100,000 permits a year after the establishment of this hybrid state. Truman rejected the plan and the British tried the expedient of a round table conference, but the Jews refused to engage in anything except bilateral discussions with Britain. The repetition by Truman of his support for the 100,000 permits during his campaign for the presidency was not a help. Discussions nevertheless continued sporadically between September 1946 and February 1947. They were abortive. The realities of the situation were reflected by increasing terrorism and the execution by hanging of the young Jew Dov Grüner, the first victim of British exasperation. In February 1947 Britain announced that the problem and possibly the territory would be transferred to the UN. A special session of the General Assembly created the UN Special Committee on Palestine (UNSCOP) and its 11 members set off for Jerusalem. In the same month 4,544 refugees aboard the *Exodus 1947* arrived at Haifa after being collected at Sète in the south of France and furnished with travel documents for Colombia. They were refused permission to land by the British authorities and were shipped back to Sète whence, again refused permission to land, they were directed with horrible insensitivity to a German port. *Exodus 1947* was one of 60 or more shiploads of illegal immigrants organized by the Jewish Agency. Few of them reached the Promised Land but their very failure helped to ensure the creation of a Jewish state. In July the toll of innocent suffering was dramatically increased when two British sergeants were hanged by an Irgun band. Unable to solve their problems, or to keep order, or even to defend themselves, the British were now more than ready to go.

UNSCOP produced, by a majority, a new partition plan of ridiculous complexity (three Arab and three Jewish segments linked in a sort of economic union with Jerusalem under international trusteeship), and this plan was adopted with modifications by the UN in November. It was accepted with misgiving by the Jews and rejected by the Arabs. Jewish acceptance was misleading: the Jews were willing to accept publicly the promise of a Jewish state whatever their reservations about its size and shape, but they did not accept the corollary of a Palestinian Arab state and contrived or condoned the annexation of the designated Arab sections by the emir Abdullah of Transjordan. The prevention of a Palestinian state was a cornerstone of Israeli policy for a generation and more. The UN plan, whatever its validity (the UN had no authority to make states), was quickly made irrelevant and the Jews won their state by conquest. Fighting began before the end of 1947 with attempts by the Jews to get control of the segments allotted to them. There were also disorders in Arab towns. The British were impotent and lost even the reputation for fairness which they regarded as one of their special contributions to public morality. In December they declared that they would surrender the mandate on 15 May 1948.

Fighting increased. The Jews managed to procure arms in substantial quantities to meet the expected invasion by the regular armies of neighbouring Arab states. The last British official left Palestine on 14 May. A state of Israel was proclaimed by Ben-Gurion, whose long years of dedication to a persecuted people earned him the plaudits of Jews everywhere and many Gentiles. He became Israel's first prime minister with

Chaim Weizmann, the veteran leader of Zionism, as president, despite the fact that in the previous December the twenty-second Zionist Congress had marked the passing of his influence and had even exposed him to some ruderies. Truman immediately – but against strong opposition from his secretary of state George Marshall – recognized the new state and Stalin was not far behind.

Five Arab states marched against Israel but their action was no index of their keenness for a fight or their effectiveness in it. The Syrians did little and the Lebanese less; the Iraqis retired early and the Egyptians arrived late; the Jordanians were thwarted by the Jewish defence of Jerusalem. The UN intervened by appointing the Swedish Count Folke Bernadotte to mediate. He effected a truce which lasted a month and was then murdered by the Stern Gang. The truce was used by the Israelis to raise large sums of money in the United States to buy arms for their regular and irregular forces, which were numerically superior to their diverse, ill-organized and unmotivated adversaries. They were decisively victorious in renewed fighting. The state of Israel was firmly established and transformed demographically. On the eve of the declaration of independence in May Israeli forces had contrived at Deir Yasin in the outskirts of Jerusalem a massacre which set in train an exodus of refugees who were to constitute, with their as yet unborn progeny, one of the bitterest bones of contention between Arabs and Jews and one of the sorriest spectacles of the times. The massacre of Deir Yasin (the name was later changed to Givat Shaul) was used to swell a tide of terror.

In its fledgling years American arms and aid were crucial to Israel's survival. It formed a secondary but similarly enduring alliance with Iran, which provided asylum for Jews fleeing from Iraq in the late 1940s and recognized Israel in 1950. This alliance was strengthened in the ensuing decades by commercial ties and exchanges of military intelligence and, surviving the fall of the shah, contributed to Ayatollah Khomeini's resistance to Iraqi attack on Iran in 1980. Its cement was hostility to the Arabs which had been a persistent theme in Iran's history and became the determining factor in Israel's fight for survival. Arab states, as distinct from Palestinians, never had much appetite for a war with Israel but Ben-Gurion and other Israeli leaders put their faith in military dominance. During the war Ben-Gurion rebuked his commanders for not driving more Palestinians out of Palestine and in the two years 1948–50 Palestinian property was systematically wrecked. When King Farouk of Egypt tried during the war to open negotiations his advances were rejected and when, after seizing power in Syria in 1949, Husni Zaim proposed peace and homes in Syria for 300,000 Palestinian refugees Ben-Gurion (who rightly regarded Zaim as unstable) did not respond or pursue these proposals with Zaim's successors. Ben-Gurion resigned his office in 1953 and retired to a kibbutz. He was succeeded by his foreign minister and one-time close associate in the Zionist movement Moshe Sharett, who initiated secret peace talks with Nasser's new regime in Egypt. These negotiations were sabotaged by a number of Sharett's cabinet colleagues and by the supposedly retired Ben-Gurion, who had retained, besides his exceptional prestige, a way back through a claim on the reversion to the ministry of defence which meanwhile was occupied by Pinchas Lavon. Ben-Gurion believed that one more war was necessary. Sharett refused to believe that aggression could guarantee Israel's continuing existence. Sharett had perhaps half the leaders of the ruling Mapai party behind him but he lacked Ben-Gurion's ruthless resolve and he permitted the militant General Ariel Sharon to use his special units against border incidents with provocative indiscrimination. At the end of 1955 Ben-Gurion reclaimed the office of prime minister, dismissed Sharett and adopted a policy of confrontation and provocation. A year later the Suez War broke out. It set a pattern for the rest of the century.

One of Israel's weaknesses was not exorcised. It contained too few Jews, notably too few if it were to expand into yet further Arab lands. The solution, obvious to its first leaders, was dual: Jewish immigration and Arab emigration. Israel was a haven for the persecuted and the visionary but it failed to attract more than a trickle from west Europe or North America (lands where Israel's main attraction was the vision of the kibbutzim, whose role in the new state gradually faded). Over the treatment of the Palestinian Arabs fierce controversy persisted and was accentuated in a later generation by charges by, among others, Israeli historians, of unconscionable harassment and wanton spoliation. The question of what to do about the Arabs of Palestine was not faced in Israel any more than it had been within the Zionist movement before the creation of the state. Gradually the plight of the Palestinians acquired international repercussions of greater consequence for Israel than the attitudes of Arab states.

The creation of the state of Israel was an extraordinary phenomenon. Israel came into existence as a result of the tenacious memories of a persecuted people whose misfortunes in various parts of the world had given them an intense addiction to the words of their holy books; as a result of atrocious crimes perpetrated against European Jewry in sight of Europe and the world; and as a result of the exertions of leading Jews who captured a piece of territory not their own, fortified by a conviction that their end was one of those which justifies every means. The state which they founded was as exceptional as its origins. By adopting the principle that the door to it must be open to all Jews everywhere, it became a mixture of tongues and cultures and unequal skills, held together by the unifying power of a Hebrew revival and by a community of race and of hope (though not of religion, since the Jewish religion meant little to many Israeli citizens). The Law of Return of 1950 gave all Jews the right to come to Israel. The Law of Citizenship of 1952, however, conferred on them Jewish, not Israeli, citizenship and Arabs in Israel were designated persons of Arab nationality, not Israeli citizens. These Arabs suffered certain disadvantages – for example, in the acquisition and holding of land. Israel was dependent on external aid, which it received liberally from American and other Jews and, by way of reparation, from the German Federal Republic. Its life was conditioned by external hostility, since the Arabs refused to accept its existence and insisted that, as an imperialist subterfuge for the maintenance of Anglo-American power in the Middle East, it must be dismantled. It adopted, in spite of its economic and military stringencies, a mainly democratic form of government.

Externally, however, it developed policies, shaped by its victories on the one hand and its continuing precariousness on the other, which secured no more than the prospect of more victories. To defend its frontiers it retaliated promptly, vigorously and often indiscriminately against every assault great or small through the special units commanded (initially) by Sharon. This escalation of violence was effective in the short term but at the cost of sharpening the aggressive psychology of the new state, prompting counter-action by Arabs and prolonging a chain of defensive and offensive operations against hardened enemies. That these operations were against Arab states helped to obscure the centrality of the Palestinians who were without a state.

Arab revolutions

Arab states, humiliated by their ineffectiveness and division, refused to recognize the state of Israel and continued hostilities by closing the Suez Canal to Israeli shipping and to goods going to and from Israel. This action was condemned fruitlessly by the Security Council which, equally fruitlessly, asserted that Israel should either readmit Arab refugees or compensate them. Since these refugees outnumbered the Jews in Palestine, Israel argued with much plausibility that it could not be expected to readmit them so long as Arab states continued to proclaim their intention to extinguish the Israeli state. The Arabs themselves did little to integrate refugees in their places of refuge since politically the most important point about a refugee was his refugee status and plight. From 700,000 in 1949 their number doubled in the following decades and they became no less a danger to the states which harboured them than they were to Israel.

To Arabs the fact that Jews had suffered at the hands of Christian Europeans through the ages seemed a poor reason for allowing them to expropriate a part of the Arab world and drive three-quarters of a million Muslims out of it. The failure of five armies to prevent this injustice caused Arabs to round on the leaders who had so conspicuously failed. Observers who thought or hoped that time would heal the acerbities of this conflict had to retreat to a more pessimistic view as officially sponsored Arab propaganda maintained a vicious anti-Zionism and the new generation in the refugee camps was nourished on visions of a return to Palestine after a gloriously successful war which would erase Israel from the map. Zionist nationalism and extremism were matched by Arab nationalism and extremism. Although the situation remained frozen by external factors – in particular, the Tripartite Declaration of 1950 by which the United States, Britain and France undertook to maintain a balance of armaments between Arabs and Jews and to consult together over any infraction of frontiers – basic attitudes within the area changed little. What did change was power in Arab states. In Syria Husni Zaim seized power in 1949 and held it for a few months before being ousted by Sami al-Hinnawi, who ruled until 1954. In 1963 the Ba'ath Party, founded in 1940 by Michel Aflaq (a Christian) with pan-Arab, socialist and cross-religious visions, came to power but its leadership was woefully divided and in the course of disputes various sections wooed different ethnic and religious groups in Syria. One of these sections formed an alliance with the Alawis, a Shi'ite minority (11 per cent of the population), strong in western Syria and favoured by the French during their mandate. This alliance led to an Alawi dominance which lasted to the end of the century – at first precariously but consolidated in 1982 when Hafiz as-Assad defeated a Sunni backlash and killed some 50,000 Sunnis in and around Hama. In Jordan Emir Abdullah, having transformed Transjordan into the kingdom of Jordan, was murdered in 1951 as he entered the Al Aqsa mosque in Jerusalem. His grandson, Hussein, ruled in his place until 1999. The most profound of the changes of these years occurred in Egypt in 1954 when the monarchy was overthrown by officers who had bitterly resented the ineptitude of their country's operations in 1948 and now despatched the last representative of Muhamad Ali's line into exile.

The titular leader of the Egyptian revolution of 1952 was General Muhammad Neguib but the real leader was Colonel Gamal Abdel Nasser, who became prime minister in 1954 and supplanted Neguib as president of the new republic a few months later. Nasser was a young man of 36 who had made a career in the army from origins in what might be called the lower middle class. He had the necessary impetuousness and indignation to make a nationalist revolutionary, but he had also qualities of coolness, shrewdness and humour which keep the revolutionary sane after success. He was sufficiently quick-witted to keep more or less abreast of the problems which assailed him when he found himself required to elaborate policies in world affairs. The first of these problems was the unfinished business of getting rid of the British. In addition, he had to find his place in the Arab world, African as well as Asian, and take a stand in the Cold War for or against the west or the Russians or neither.

The British occupation of Egypt began in 1881 with a debt-collecting expedition but its real motive was strategic – to secure control of the eastern Mediterranean, the route to India and the east, and the Nile valley. Egypt remained formally a province of the Ottoman empire under the hereditary rule of the heirs of Muhamad Ali, but it became in effect semi-independent under the British instead of semi-independent under the Turks. When Britain and the Ottoman empire went to war in 1914 Britain proclaimed a protectorate over Egypt which was converted in 1922 into a treaty relationship. Britain secured in 1936 the right to station 10,000 men in the Suez Canal zone for 20 years, an arrangement acceptable to the Egyptians because this base could serve to protect Egypt against the ambitions of Mussolini who was engaged in conquering Ethiopia. During the Second World War Churchill resolved to maintain and strengthen Britain's Middle Eastern position. Arabs had shown certain pro-German proclivities which threatened to give Germany dominion in the Middle East after the conquest of the Balkans and Crete in 1941. The British therefore occupied Syria, Lebanon and Iran and wooed Turkey (unsuccessfully until 1944, when Turkey severed relations with the Axis – it entered the war the following February); they also forced the pro-British Nahas Pasha on King Farouk as prime minister. Nahas hoped that in return the British would give Egypt after the war the independence which they had promised 60 times since 1881, but the king, preferring a tougher to a waiting game, dismissed Nahas in 1944.

At this time Eden was preparing a postwar British position in the Middle East based on an association of pro-British states, particularly the Hashemite monarchies of Iraq and Transjordan. He encouraged Nuri es-Said in Iraq to revive the concept of the Fertile Crescent as a political entity with Baghdad as its capital and embracing autonomous Zionist and (Christian) Maronite communities and he promoted a pro-British League. But the Arab world was no more united by Arabism than Europe by Europeanism. Egypt, the most populous, sophisticated and influential member of the League and by virtue of its printing presses and radio the most ubiquitous, was hostile to any suggestion of a Hashemite bloc and peculiarly hostile to Britain so long as the British continued to occupy the Canal Zone and other points where the Union Jack had been hoisted during the war. For Egypt the main adversary was Britain, not Israel. After the war and the departure from India, Britain – more precisely, the Chiefs of Staff and the Foreign Office under Bevin's direction – focused on the Middle East as the centre of a revised version of British world power to be exercised from a vast *place d'armes* in the Canal Zone. This outlook overlooked the costs (Britain was about to give up its leading positions in Greece and Turkey because they cost too much), miscalculated American willingness to support a quasi-imperial scheme and confirmed Britain (not Israel) as Egypt's chief adversary. Britain owed Egypt £400 million (and a further £70 million to Iraq) and these debts were only a part of the strains which were intensified by the abrupt ending of American lend-lease, the disorders in and retreat from Palestine and the Berlin air lift. Nevertheless, Bevin set about negotiating new treaties with Egypt, Iraq and Transjordan. He quickly succeeded in the last case (1946), although Emir Abdullah was much criticized for allowing British troops another 25 years' lease of Jordanian soil. With the Egyptian and Iraqi governments Bevin succeeded in reaching agreements which were accepted by Sidky Pasha for Egypt and Salih Jabr for Iraq but were rejected by their parliaments and people because they did not provide for complete British evacuation.

In the early 1950s the political scene in the Middle East was transformed by the war in Korea and the Cold War. The United States and its allies were anxious to create there an anti-Russian bastion similar or ancillary to NATO. The American, British, French and Turkish governments produced plans for a Middle East Defence Organization (MEDO) which would include Egypt and the Canal base; the British would evacuate the base but the allies, adapting an idea once entertained by Bevin, would have the right to return in certain eventualities. This scheme, rooted in world affairs, ran foul of Egypt's conception of a foreign garrison on the Canal as a symbol of indignity. Egypt, unmoved by the fear of the USSR which animated the west, rejected MEDO and denounced the Anglo-Egyptian treaty of 1936 which had five years to run. In January 1952 anti-British riots in Cairo caused extensive damage and accelerated the evacuation of the Canal

Zone. When Neguib and Nasser seized power a few months later they were confronted not only with the problem of the British, whose occupation of Egyptian soil was a standing national affront, but also with the new problem created by the desire of the west to enlist Egypt in the Cold War and make the Canal Zone an anti-Russian arsenal.

In the two years after the revolution Egypt and Britain settled outstanding differences. They began with Sudan, which had been an Anglo-Egyptian condominium since its recapture from the Mahdists in 1899. Egypt wished to restore the union of Egypt with Sudan because of the vital importance of the Nile waters and because of ancient pharaonic vistas of the unity of the Nile valley. The British, effective rulers of Sudan for half a century, insisted that the Sudanese must decide their future for themselves and the Egyptians, wrongly believing that Sudan would opt for unity with Egypt, agreed. In the event Sudan chose independence in spite (or because) of Egyptian propaganda and became a sovereign state in 1956. Nasser accepted this reverse with pragmatic acquiescence. Agreement on the Canal Zone was reached in 1954 on the basis that the British would depart in 20 months but would have the right to return if any member of the Arab League or Turkey were attacked by any outside foe except Israel. Iran was not included in the reverter clause in spite of British attempts to put it there. This treaty represented considerable, if sensible, concessions by Britain, which were unpalatable to a section of the ruling Conservative Party but were accepted by the government, partly on the grounds that the existence of nuclear bombs had turned the base into a death trap, and partly in response to pressure from the United States, where continuing bad relations between Britain and Egypt were regarded as a serious impediment to the Middle Eastern segment of the American policy of containment. But for Egypt the agreement of 1954 with Britain was not a preliminary to alignment with the west. The west, on the other hand, believed that better relations with Egypt implied such an alignment. Consequently, the better relations soon took a turn for the worse.

In 1955, the year of the Bandung conference of neutralists, Egypt became wedded to non-alignment. The issue did not arise in the first postwar years because alignment meant alignment against the Russians and there was as yet no Russian presence in the Arab world to be aligned against. The traditional Russian spheres of activity in the Middle East were the non-Arab states of Turkey and Iran, and in both the USSR had experienced and apparently accepted rebuffs at the end of the war; claims for the return of Kars and Ardahan (lost to Turkey in 1921) and for the revision of the Montreux Convention governing passage through the Straits of Constantinople were ineffective, while the attempt to subvert the regime in Iran by sponsoring an Azerbaijani republic and a Kurdish bid for independence was defeated by the astuteness of the Iranian prime minister Qavam es-Sultaneh and the firm reactions of the United States and Britain. The prompt Russian recognition of Israel was not followed up and seemed to have been regarded in Moscow as a blind alley. The Korean War was regarded by Arabs as no concern of theirs: at the UN General Assembly all Arab members refrained from voting on it. Nasser's route to neutralism and the Bandung spirit was charted by the influence on him of Nehru – especially during K. M. Panikkar's embassy in 1953–54 – and by the western powers themselves.

Egypt and Iraq stood for different brands of Arab unity long before the revolution in Egypt in 1952 made that country a socialist republic by contrast with the traditional monarchy which lasted in Iraq until 1958. Both before and after 1952 Egypt's leaders aspired to leadership in parts of Africa as well as western Asia while Iraqis, before and after 1958, focused on the dream of a large Arab domain east of Suez. This dream was rendered singularly unrealistic by ancient rivalries between Damascus and Baghdad, the imposition of the mandates regime in the northern parts of the Middle East after the First World War and the destruction in the south of the power and pretensions of the Hashemite dynasty by Ibn Saud. Yet the vision persisted. Hashemites came to reign in Damascus (briefly), Baghdad and Amman, and the Hashemite regent of Iraq, Abd ul-Ilah, hoped to become king in Damascus after he ceased to be regent in Baghdad. Had this part of the dream materialized a large Hashemite kingdom or league of Hashemite kings might have followed, but such a development was never welcome in Syria. After the first postwar Syrian revolution Husni Zaim inclined to Iraq but later in his short period of power veered towards Egypt and Saudi Arabia; his successor Sami al-Hinnawi favoured an Iraqi–Syrian union but by so doing precipitated his own fall; and his supplanter Adib Shishakli (1949–54) – the strong man of the Middle East before the advent of Nasser – rejected any close association with Iraq because it was monarchical and pro-British. The overthrow of Shishakli by the Syrian army, helped by Iraqi gold and by British moral support at least, revived the prospect of an Iraqi–Syrian alliance but opposition among Syrians to the Iraqi royal family and its British connections killed it.

The United States was less preoccupied with these matters than with the Middle East as a theatre of superpower conflict. Its overriding concern in the 1950s was to devise a Middle East policy as part of the containment of the USSR. This took the form of a new anti-Russian rampart stretching from the Bosphorus to the Indus, the so-called Northern Tier, and it involved arming Turkey and Pakistan. It did not at first include any Arab state since the collapse of the MEDO project had persuaded John Foster Dulles, Eisenhower's secretary of state, that Arabs were valueless allies against the USSR as well as enemies of the United States' protégé Israel. But as plans for a Northern Tier progressed Iraq came to be included, with two important consequences. British involvement was all but indispensable but Britain was torn between resentment over what it regarded as an American takeover of its political and economic interests in the Middle East and the realities of the superpower struggle. The addition of Iraq to the Northern Tier shifted Britain to a more wholehearted alliance with the United States in the region because, among other things, it offered Britain a fresh chance to refurbish its relations with Iraq through a new treaty to replace that due to expire in 1957 which Bevin had failed to prolong. But, secondly, the inclusion of Iraq was a crucial mistake.

Iraq was not a natural member of the Northern Tier. Besides being Arab it had no frontier with the USSR and its inclusion was seen in Cairo as a manoeuvre to disrupt Arab solidarity and strengthen Iraq against Egypt (as India regarded the arming of Pakistan as a threat to itself in Kashmir rather than a threat to the USSR).

The first formal step towards the Baghdad Pact complex was a treaty of April 1954 between Turkey and Pakistan. It was followed within weeks by American military aid agreements with Pakistan and Iraq and in 1955 by a Turco-Iraqi mutual assistance treaty (the Baghdad Pact itself) which was declared open to all members of the Arab League and other states interested in the peace and security of the Middle East: Pakistan and Iran adhered that year but no other Arab state followed Iraq's lead into the Middle East branch of the western camp. Syria swung the bulk of the Arab world to Cairo and away from Baghdad and a counter-alliance was formed by Egypt, Syria and Saudi Arabia. Attempts to improve relations between Egypt and the west came to a halt. Within the Arab world polemics became strident. Nasser set out for Bandung where, in obedience to the prevailing anti-colonialist and neutralist wind, Iraq was censured for joining the Baghdad Pact and Pakistan for joining its equivalent, SEATO (South-East Asian Treaty Organization).

The Suez War

Besides the division within the Arab world Nasser was concerned with the fact that Israeli retaliation against Arab propaganda and raids was being turned against Egypt. Early in 1955 Egypt experienced an exceptionally sharp Israeli attack in the Gaza area, ordered by Ben-Gurion who had recently returned to power from retirement and was, to Nasser's knowledge, seeking arms from France. This Franco-Israeli association, although never a formal alliance, became one of the principal ingredients in the Suez War of 1956. The Tripartite Declaration of 1950, designed to prevent an arms race in the Middle East, was circumvented by Israel, which found in France sympathizers ready to help Israel in secret. French motives were various: there was a feeling of obligation to the Jews as a people who had suffered too much; a feeling of admiration for what they had achieved in Israel; a feeling of socialist solidarity between Guy Mollet and Ben-Gurion; above all the conviction that Nasser's aid to Algeria was a prime factor in the revolt there. Some Frenchmen shared Eden's view that Nasser was a menace like Hitler and must be brought down before it was too late. French policy, traditionally pro-Arab, was pulled in a new direction and France agreed in 1954 to supply Israel with fighter aircraft.

On his return from Bandung Nasser too began to look for arms. The signatories of the Tripartite Declaration refused to supply Egypt or Syria with all they requested. Syria turned to the Russians, who had become interested in playing a more active role in the Middle East since the Gaza raid had exposed Egypt's weakness. But Nasser was reluctant to buy Russian. After trying Beijing (where he got a hint to try Moscow) and then Washington and London once more, he finally took the Russian plunge and announced in September 1955 that he was to receive Czech arms without strings. It was now Israel's turn to be alarmed. By the Czech deal Egypt was to get a wide range of weapons including 80 MiG 15s (the fighters used in Korea), 45 Ilyushin 28 bombers and 115 heavy tanks equal to the best in the Russian army and superior to anything which Israel had. Israel pressed France to revise the agreement of 1954 by supplying Mystère 4 jet fighters instead of Mystère 2s. France complied and Israel received in April 1956 a contingent of the best fighter aircraft in Europe. Their arrival just after the French foreign minister Christian Pineau had paid a visit to Cairo evoked an indignant anti-French outburst from Nasser and destroyed what chance there was of the Arab wind prevailing over the Israeli in the French cabinet.

Like most countries, Egypt wanted both guns and butter. Nasser faced the question of whether he could get economic aid from the west after accepting military aid from the communist bloc. The answer proved to be no. The test was the Aswan High Dam, and it showed that not only France but also Britain and the United States were turning against Nasser.

The high dam was designed to transform Egypt's economy and society by adding 860,000 hectares to the area of cultivable land, making the Nile navigable as far south as the Sudanese frontier and generating electricity to service industrial plants which would provide the growing population with a living. It was to cost $1,400 million, including $400 million in hard currency, of which the World Bank would advance $200 million and the United States and Britain $56 million and $14 million respectively at once and the remaining $130 million between them later. During 1955 negotiations seemed to be proceeding without more than normal hitches, but during the first half of 1956 they petered out. Britain and the United States decided not to help. Nasser's credit, in both senses of the word, was running down, especially as a result of his purchases of communist arms.

In 1956 he recognized the communist regime in Beijing – a step which caused special irritation in Washington, even though his real reason may have been his fear that the new Russian leaders might be persuaded to join the western powers in a new Middle Eastern arms embargo. The Czech arms deal had broken the 1950 embargo, to the general delight of the Arab world, which resented it as a clog on their sovereignty, but it could be reimposed if the Russians were looking for goodwill in the west, and in that event Beijing would be the only alternative source of supply. In addition the cotton lobby in the American Congress disliked laying out American money to help Egypt to grow more cotton to compete with American cotton. Egypt was blamed for not coming to terms with the other riparian states along the Nile (Sudan, Ethiopia and Uganda) and for pledging for arms purchases money which would be needed to service its foreign loans. Americans argued that it was imprudent to allocate so much money to a single project since the United States would then have to refuse all other requests for aid to Egypt for many years, leaving the Russians to step in and say yes. But behind all these reasonings lay the plain fact that Washington and London did not like

Nasser and thought (like the French for a different reason) that it would be salutary to snub him and cut him down to size. This attitude was strongest in Britain where it found vent in the obsessive misinterpretations of Eden, who mistook Nasser for a fascist dictator and thought he could be easily replaced. (Eden's animosity had been sharpened in March by the dismissal of General Sir John Glubb and other British officers from Jordan's Arab Legion, of which Glubb was the commanding officer. Fortuitously, this move by King Hussein coincided with a visit to Cairo by the British foreign secretary Selwyn Lloyd. Eden saw it as a deliberate affront contrived by Nasser.)

On 19 July 1956 Dulles informed the Egyptian ambassador in Washington that the Anglo-American offer to finance the dam was revoked. The French ambassador in Washington Maurice Couve de Murville had predicted that Nasser would retaliate by seizing the revenues from the Suez Canal. On 26 July he did.

The Suez Canal was indubitably a part of the Egyptian state but it was also the subject of two, very different, instruments – a concession agreement and an international treaty. The former, granted to Ferdinand de Lesseps by the khedive or viceroy of Egypt Said Pasha and confirmed by the Ottoman sultan, conceded the right to operate the canal for 99 years from its opening, which took place in 1869. The concession had passed from de Lesseps to the Universal Maritime Suez Canal Company, which was an Egyptian corporation with headquarters in Cairo and Paris and with a diversity of shareholders, including the British government and a host of ordinary French *rentiers*. The concession had 12 years to run in 1956. Thereafter, the operating rights would revert to the Egyptian state. Nasser's action amounted to the nationalization of the company's rights, but since he promised compensation he had done nothing illegal or, in the twentieth century, unusual – although the company might well ask where the compensation money was to come from. Nasser would, however, be on the wrong side of the law if he broke the terms of the second instrument – the convention made in 1888 between nine powers, including the Ottoman empire, which was at that date suzerain over Egypt. The parties engaged themselves to keep the canal open to all ships of commerce or war, in times of war as well as peace, and never to blockade it. Should Nasser fail to keep the canal open, he would be in breach of the convention and the signatories would be entitled to take measures to reopen it. There was some ill-judged expectation that if the canal pilots were withdrawn, the canal would cease to function and the right to intervene could be said to have arisen, but in the event the canal continued to function smoothly until bombarded by the British and French, even though the company's pilots were nearly all withdrawn under pressure by outside powers.

The nationalization of the canal company gave Britain and France an excuse for the forcible action which they wished to take against Egypt. The British cabinet allocated £5 million (imperialism on a pittance) and resolved to use force within a week, only to discover that Britain's military preparedness was such that nothing could be ventured before the middle of September or without calling up the reserves. This delay enabled the United States to intervene. Eisenhower and Dulles agreed with the British and

French governments in wishing to put the canal under international control but, although they had little love for Nasser, they were opposed to the use of force until all methods had been tried and had been seen to have been tried. Eisenhower, who made his position clear in letters to Eden and in public statements, was temperamentally averse to force and was also convinced that force was inexpedient because it would lead to sabotage of pipelines, encourage other leaders (for example, Jiang Kaishek and Syngman Rhee) to claim American support for the use of force in their quarrels too, and turn the uncommitted world against the west. Eisenhower sent a special emissary to London who reported in July that the British were intent on using force, and thereafter a duel developed between Eden and Dulles, enemies since the crisis of 1954 in Indo-China, with Eden manoeuvring to get American sanction for a forward policy and Dulles sidestepping and playing for time.

First the British and French, with American support, convened in London a conference of the canal's principal users and presented a plan for a new operating board to ensure international control of the canal. The conference did not approve this plan unanimously; it was criticized as an unjustifiable infringement of Egyptian sovereignty. Nevertheless, the Australian prime minister Robert Menzies and four other members, representing the majority view, went to Cairo to present the plan to Nasser, who turned it down and pointed out that the canal was functioning normally. Next Dulles, perhaps merely in order to keep talking and avoid shooting, propounded a Suez Canal Users' Association with the right to organize convoys and take tolls from the vessels in them. This plan appealed to the British, who saw a chance of running a convoy through the canal against Egyptian opposition and so putting Egypt in the wrong in American eyes. Dulles then killed the scheme upon becoming suspicious that Britain and France might use it to start shooting; he pointed out that the American government had no power to force the masters of American vessels to pay tolls to the association instead of the Egyptian government. Britain and France referred the dispute to the Security Council while explicitly stating that they reserved the right to use force. When the Council met on 5 October Egypt proposed negotiations, while Britain and France produced a plan for international control of the canal. Unofficial negotiations outside the Council made substantial progress but Egypt persisted in its refusal to accept international control and the Anglo-French plan was defeated by a Russian veto.

The French became increasingly exasperated with the British. Joint Anglo-French commands had been set up at the beginning of August but the prospect of action by the slowly assembling hosts diminished as the British wavered between their desire to keep in step with the French and their anxiety not to get out of the Americans' good books. By late September or early October the French were reverting to their line of co-operating with Israel, from which they had been distracted by the lure of a joint Anglo-French operation in response to the nationalization of the canal company.

Israel had powerful reasons for making war on Egypt. Raids into Israel by *fedayeen* based in the Sinai peninsula had become more audacious and frequent. Land near the

frontier was becoming too dangerous to farm and the Israeli government feared out-
rages even in the centres of its cities. Only a spectacular gesture could end this murderous nuisance. Further, Israel wished to break the Arab blockade of the gulf of Aqaba
and so win a sure outlet to the countries of Asia and Africa from the port of Eilat,
which was languishing at the head of the gulf; even Israel's air links with Africa were
insecure. The opening of the straits of Tiran at the entrance of the gulf would compensate Israel for the Egyptian refusal to allow ships bound to or from Israel to use the
canal. But Israel's capacities were not the equal of its intentions. Egypt's new Russian
bombers were in a position to bomb Israel's cities and cause panic among the newer
immigrants who had not yet become tempered to life in a besieged state. Israel's air
force was barely able to defend these cities even with its new French fighters, or to protect Israeli land forces operating in the open desert, and it was unable to bomb
Egyptian airfields and so prevent the Egyptian air force from taking off. In June 1956
Israel concluded with France an agreement for the provision of weapons and intelligence which settled the Israeli determination to go to war but still fell short of an assurance of victory. Israel needed French fighters operating from Israeli airfields to defend
Israel's cities and also bombers to attack Egyptian airfields. For the second purpose the
only aircraft available locally were British bombers on Cyprus.

The French set about engineering this combined tripartite operation and succeeded.
During October French ministers divulged Israel's plans to British ministers; on
16 October the French and British prime ministers and foreign ministers met in Paris
with nobody else present. The British ministers were reluctant to embark on any but
the most furtive co-operation with Israel because of the repercussions in the Arab
world. But Ben-Gurion insisted on a formal commitment from the British, whom he
did not trust, and this he secured at a secret meeting at Sèvres where the British foreign secretary joined French and Israeli ministers, subsequently authorizing the signature of a secret tripartite treaty. At this point the Israeli commander-in-chief altered his
battle orders, which had envisaged an Israeli raid in force similar to earlier raids but
bigger, and proposed instead to commit his forces to the open desert upon the assumption that British attacks on Egyptian airfields would give the Israeli troops immunity
from air attack.

Israel attacked on 29 October and duly received the anticipated support of Britain
and France (the French also prevented the Egyptian fleet from attacking the Israeli
coast), but the Egyptian air force was in any event incapacitated since the Russians,
who were still in operational control of the Ilyushin 28s, ordered their pilots out of
the battle area. Britain and France issued an ultimatum to Israel and Egypt requiring
both sides to withdraw 16 km from the canal. This was a ruse intended to preserve
the fiction that Britain had not colluded with Israel. Neither side paid attention to the
ultimatum, Egypt because the canal was 160 km within its own frontiers and Israel
because its forces were some way from the canal and were not intended to go there. The
Israeli campaign was virtually over on 2 November when its principal objectives – the

clearing out of the *fedayeen* bases, the opening of the straits of Tiran and a resounding victory against Egypt – were assured.

A few hours after the initial Israeli attack the Security Council met to consider an American resolution requiring the Israelis to return to their borders. Britain and France vetoed this resolution but the General Assembly, convoked under the Uniting for Peace resolution (a procedure adopted in 1950 on western initiative to enable the Assembly to consider and make recommendations on matters on which the Security Council was stultified by a veto), adopted in the early hours of 2 November an appeal for a ceasefire. At the UN a small group which included the secretary-general Dag Hammarskjöld and the Canadian minister for external affairs Lester Pearson, worked to stop the approaching Anglo-French sea and land attack on Egypt (which, unlike the Israeli, had not yet been launched) and to recover control over an alarming situation by imposing a ceasefire and despatching an international peace force to the area. The Anglo-French attack began with a parachute drop on 5 November. On the next day a seaborne armada from Malta landed troops but on the same day Britain cried halt and France after some hesitation desisted too.

The British decision was the result of an accumulation of pressures. Britain, more than France, was split. The parliamentary opposition, much of the press and a substantial part of the public were opposed to the government's policy. Eden's own party and a majority of the country as a whole supported him consistently except on the use of force, for which there was never a popular majority. The existence of doubts within the government was common knowledge. The independent members of the Commonwealth were also split; Australia and, less enthusiastically, New Zealand supported Eden, but Canada and the newer dominions did not (there were as yet no independent African members). This opposition had, however, been foreseen and discounted and for that reason the usual processes of Commonwealth consultation were omitted and Commonwealth governments, like senior advisers in Whitehall and all the pertinent British ambassadors abroad, were kept in the dark. But the decisive reason for calling off the operation was the failure to secure American endorsement and the failure to foresee what American opposition entailed.

The attack on Egypt caused the biggest financial crisis in Britain since 1945. Britain lost on balance $400 million during the last quarter of 1956; withdrawals were probably half as much again but were partly offset by one or two exceptional influxes which were credited during the quarter. Sterling was healthy and the reserves more than adequate for ordinary purposes, but losses of this order could only be borne for a number of weeks without external aid to preserve the exchange value of the pound. It became clear that Britain would have to borrow to save the pound (which, apart from the war, was not threatened) and that neither the United States nor the IMF would lend the necessary sums until the fighting was called off. The prophesied run on the pound which panicked Eden and many of his cabinet colleagues did not occur but the situation was exaggerated by the chancellor of the exchequer, Harold Macmillan (who was to emerge from the debacle as the next prime minister), and, without warning to its allies, Britain abandoned the enterprise. (One consequence of this disaster was to make Eden's successors more insistent on Britain's right to a place at the top table of world affairs, to the detriment of its attention to European affairs.)

There was in these calculations one subsidiary element which may have had some effect on some people. This was the entry of the Russians upon the scene. Until 5 November the Russians were too much preoccupied with the suppression of rebellion in Hungary to take a hand in Middle Eastern affairs, but on that day they proposed to Washington joint action to force Britain and France to desist and threatened vaguely to use rockets against Britain and France. They also indicated that they might allow volunteers to go to the Middle East but statements to this effect were made only after the fighting was over, except in one case when Khrushchev made, at a diplomatic party in Moscow, remarks about volunteers which were not reported in the Russian press. The Russian threat to use rockets – which was taken seriously by British intelligence for a few weeks – was countered by an American threat to retaliate, after which no more was heard on this subject. By their intervention the Russians gained a sizeable propaganda victory in the Arab world; it is improbable that they ever intended anything else.

Israel's gains included the extirpation of the *fedayeen* on its borders with Egypt and the freeing of the port of Eilat which, from a village of fewer than 1,000 inhabitants, grew to be a flourishing port of over 15,000, trading all over the world and rendering the blockade in the Suez Canal harmless. In the next decade Israel became a nuclear power, maintained its French alliance and won fresh undertakings from the United States and Britain. These states declared in 1957 that they regarded the straits of Tiran as an international waterway and would take action to ensure free passage through them into the gulf of Aqaba. (The straits were indubitably territorial waters but international law required riparian states to permit innocent passage for all vessels through them if they led to international waters or to the territory of another state.) The Arabs continued to talk of eliminating Israel but the rhetoric began to sound like a mask, hiding a conviction that Israel had come to stay. Yet there ensued no peace, only a suspension of war with growing debate on both sides about the need for another round.

The Suez fiasco dramatized the evaporation of British power in the Middle East. Postwar plans to fashion a new relationship with Egypt and the area generally ran counter to British capabilities and the British mood. The causes were chiefly financial but included also the end of empire in Asia and the reversal of the British and American roles in the world of oil. The British retreat began, if imperceptibly, in the 1940s with the renunciation of the Palestine mandate and the transfer to the United States of the British position in Turkey by the Truman Doctrine. By 1956 the Middle East was dominated not by the British or any other empire but by American strategies in the Cold War and the commitment to Israel.

CHAPTER 11

From Suez to the death of Nasser

Reassessments

The Suez War raised Nasser's prestige high. He had secured the leadership in Egypt only in 1954. Suez confirmed him in it and made him a popular as well as a military ruler. He had kept his head and his dignity, had emerged intact from an imperialist onslaught and an Israeli invasion, and had demonstrated his power in the Arab world when even Nuri es-Said, Britain's staunchest friend in the Middle East felt obliged to condemn Britain's action and propose Britain's eviction from the Baghdad Pact. Jordan too rejected its traditional British links and the subsidies which went with them, denounced its treaty with Britain and joined instead the Egyptian–Syrian alliance of 1955 (to which Saudi Arabia and Yemen also belonged). Nasser kept the canal and showed he could work it and got the dam too. The Americans, who might be said to have precipitated the whole affair by abandoning the dam project, had supported a regime which they had notoriously ceased to admire and were left in the aftermath without a policy. The Russians were jubilantly claiming all the credit and getting much of it, and they undertook to finance the Aswan Dam in place of the Americans and British.

While the debris was still flying the United States tried to make a fresh start with the Eisenhower Doctrine. This venture proceeded from the assumptions that, with the defeat of Britain, it had become necessary for the United States to take an initiative and fill a vacuum which would otherwise be filled by the USSR. Between $400 and $500 million were to be disbursed in two years in economic and military aid to willing recipients who would enter into agreements with the United States authorizing and inviting the use of American arms to protect the integrity and independence of the signatory if threatened with overt aggression from any nation controlled by international communism. Neither Egypt nor Syria was expected to conclude such an agreement but Eisenhower sent a special emissary to tour the Middle East and get as many takers as possible. His only success was in Lebanon where, more out of courtesy than enthusiasm, a Christian leader entered into the requisite agreement – and was later to suffer for this decision. King Saud of Saudi Arabia was polite and paid a visit to Washington but evaded signing any agreement. In Jordan there were anti-American riots. The

Eisenhower Doctrine was a new version of the old plan of constructing an anti-Russian front in the Middle East, and its failure was due to the spread of neutralism among Arabs who realized, especially after the Suez War, that they were no longer helpless against major outside powers and that the decline of Britain might be followed not by a fresh foreign domination but by none.

The Russians reacted hopefully to openings in Syria and Iraq but with disappointing results. With Syria, whence came exaggerated reports of spreading communism, the USSR concluded economic and military agreements, while Syria expelled three American diplomats and carried out a purge of the army. Turkey, disturbed by these pointers, concentrated forces on its southern borders. Egypt sent troops, which were received in Damascus with acclaim. The tension was temporarily eased but in January 1958 some Syrian officers went to Egypt and asked Nasser to declare a union between the two countries in order to avert a communist takeover in Damascus. The pan-Arab nationalists of the Syrian Ba'ath Party had become alarmed at the growing influence of the Russians and of Syria's principal, and somewhat lonely, communist Khaled Bakdash. Preferring Egyptians to communists, they instigated a political move which Nasser, though hesitant, felt unable to reject upon being faced with the argument that an Egyptian refusal would leave no alternative to communism. The creation of a United Arab Republic, consisting of Egypt and Syria, was proclaimed on 1 February 1958. Yemen became loosely attached to it in March.

In Iraq the Hashemite King Feisal II, with his Jordanian cousin, retaliated with an Arab Federation but this union was short-lived for on 14 July 1958 Feisal, other members of his family and Nuri es-Said were murdered in a military rising led by Generals Abdul Karim Kassim and Abdul Salem Aref. The revolutionaries included communists, whose presence at the centre of power alarmed the west and enticed the Russians. The Americans and British, dismayed by this revolution at the centre of the Baghdad Pact, at once moved forces into Lebanon and Jordan, as President Camille Chamoun of Lebanon invoked the Eisenhower Doctrine and King Hussein of Jordan the Anglo-Jordanian treaty. (Jordan's request to Britain to intervene was drafted in London.) In Jordan British force saved the monarchy at a time when its fall would have produced turmoil, laying it open to attack from Israel. In Lebanon there was a civil war in progress which was threatening the religious equilibrium on which the prosperity of the country had been based for decades. The Lebanese government had invoked the United Nations in May, but by the time of the revolution in Iraq in July the dangers of increasing civil and religious strife had become so great that the marines sent in by President Eisenhower were welcomed by a large majority. In both countries, therefore, foreign intervention was a stabilizing factor and was not held against the interveners, especially as they contrived to get themselves out again rapidly with the help of Hammarskjöld. In Lebanon a new president General Fuad Shehab a member of an old Maronite family, was able to re-establish the country's traditional equilibrium.

The Baghdad revolution looked at first sight like another link in the chain of Russian opportunities which included Arab hostility to the Baghdad Pact, the Czech arms deal, the Suez War, the financing of the Aswan Dam, Russian attendance at the Afro-Asian conference in Cairo in 1957, and a visit by Nasser to the USSR in 1958. Iraq left the Baghdad Pact (which was renamed the Central Treaty Organization – Cento – and moved its headquarters to Ankara). But Kassim was himself no communist, the Iraqi communists failed to consolidate their advantages and Iraq became more or less a neutralist state where the Russians were as unwelcome as any other major power. The Russians, who had been careful not to offend the nationalists by committing them-selves to the communists, swallowed their disappointment and reverted to more famil-iar ground. They tried (unsuccessfully) in 1959 to inveigle the shah of Iran away from the western camp and began to show an interest in better relations with Turkey after the fall of Menderes in 1960, in which attempt they were later assisted by Turkish dis-appointment over the American interdiction of a Turkish invasion of Cyprus. The USSR recognized Kuwait in 1963 and Jordan in 1964, and the presence of Khrushchev at the opening of the Aswan Dam in 1964 reasserted the usefulness of the Russian pres-ence in the Arab world.

The Iraqi revolution also occasioned intervention by China in the affairs of the Middle East or, in Chinese terminology, west Asia. Until this time American and Russian interests in the Middle East had been openly antagonistic. Russian policies in Iran in 1945 on the one hand, and on the other the Truman Doctrine, the Baghdad Pact, American bases at Dhahran in Saudi Arabia and Whelus Field in Libya and the US Sixth Fleet in the Mediterranean, turned the Middle East into an annex of the Cold War. In 1956, however, the Americans and Russians found themselves in agreement on the need to thwart the British and French at Suez and the Iraqi revolution of 1958 strengthened the view that some of the superpowers' interests in the Middle East might be the same. This accord was not to the liking of the Chinese and when an interna-tional conference on Middle East affairs was mooted Beijing objected to the holding of it without Chinese participation. The conference never took place. Although Chinese effectiveness in the Middle East was minimal, China began in 1958 to venture there. It gave exclusive support to Iraqi communists when the Russians were advocating more ambiguous policies; gave aid to Yemeni republicans; and, more anti-Israel than the Russians, received the Palestinian leader Ahmed Shuqueiri in Beijing almost as a head of state and promised him military aid. Zhou visited Cairo in 1963 and 1965. But the Chinese were remote and no better liked than other outsiders.

Within the Arab world the Iraqi revolution, which was wrongly expected to entail the early disappearance of the monarchy in Jordan, created a new pattern by shifting Iraq from the traditionalist monarchist category into the revolutionary republican one. The years 1958–63 were a period of weak government. Iraq produced no equivalent of Nasser. The predominant military power and the civilian political world were split within themselves as well as being opposed to one another. The first military leaders,

Abdul Karim Kassim and Abdul Salem Aref, were mutually hostile and divided on many issues, notably relations with Nasser's Egypt and the burgeoning United Arab Republic. Of the main civilian parties the Ba'ath was hostile to Kassim, who tried therefore to use the communists to maintain what became an unsuccessful balancing act. The Ba'ath tried to kill Kassim in 1959, secured his downfall and murder in 1963 by a coup orchestrated by the CIA, and elevated Aref to a presidency designed to be more decorative than executive. A year later Aref seized full power with an openly military regime but in 1966 he was killed in an accident and succeeded by his weaker brother Abdul Rahman Aref. The Arefs were an interlude between Kassim and Saddam Hussein, for after two years the Ba'ath returned to power under the presidency, however, of the Ba'athist general Hassan al-Bakr and so with the military and not the civilian politicians in apparent control. Under cover of the new president's favour Hussein set out to create a powerful modern professional army and turn Iraq into a totalitarian autocracy in the grasp of himself and his extended family. Hussein's vision of Iraq was not, however, merely clannish, for he also aspired to use his personal power base as the motor for a nation state which would become a major actor in the Middle East through military power, economic wealth and nationalist emotions: for some years he courted Shi'ite as well as Sunni Muslims.

The decline of Nasser and the Six Day War

During the early 1960s Nasser's prestige declined from its post-Suez peak. The revolution of 1952 had had a strong socialist strand among officers who were largely of peasant origin and had high, if vague, hopes of the benefits to come from land distribution and agricultural co-operatives, but disappointing results led to a shift to industrial development, nationalization and state controls. In external affairs the fall of the senior (Iraqi) branch of the Hashemite line had brought no gain to Egypt. The union with Syria was not a success: Egypt and Syria had no common frontier; Nasser and the Ba'ath had too little in common beyond a superficial socialism; and the influx of Egyptians into Syria and Nasser's policies of land reform and of forcing all political parties into a single movement or front strained a union which had been a shot-gun marriage from the start. Syrians swung back to the idea that a union with Iraq would suit them better (especially after the Iraqi Ba'ath helped to oust Kassim). In 1961 a revolution in Syria brought about the dissolution of the union.

In Yemen, loosely attached to the United Arab Republic, an attempt to overthrow the imamate and install a republic led to a civil war in which Nasser backed the republican leader Brigadier Abdullah Sallal without realizing that he was thereby entangling himself in Yemen for several years and to the tune ultimately of 50–60,000 troops. The imam was supported by Saudi Arabia, so that the Yemeni civil war developed into a vicarious contest between two of the principal Arab states. After two years both found the effort unrewarding and in 1965 Nasser travelled to the Saudi capital to meet King

Feisal (a relatively progressive member of his house who had displaced his brother Saud the year before), put an end to the civil war and even effect a rapprochement between Egypt and Saudi Arabia, the protagonists of the opposing socialist and traditionalist tendencies in the Arab world. Earlier in the same year he had initiated a rapprochement with Jordan.

This re-emergence of the theme of Arab unity owed as much to apprehension about Israel's plans for diverting the Jordan's waters as to war-weariness in Yemen. An American plan in 1955 for an equitable apportionment of these valuable waters had been rejected by the Arabs on political grounds, whereupon Israel had started to construct engineering works which would take water from the Galilee region in the north to the Negev desert in the south. Israel maintained that the quantities to be pumped out of the Jordan's main stream would neither exceed the Israeli quota in the 1955 plan nor leave the lower reaches of the river unduly salty. The Arabs denied both these propositions. Foreseeing that the Israeli engineering works would be completed in 1964 they convened a conference in Cairo, attended by traditionalist monarchies and progressive republics, in order to concert counter-measures. These included the diversion of two of the Jordan's tributaries, the Hasbani in Lebanon and the Banias in Syria – the latter at points within sight and range of the Israeli frontier; secondly, the creation of a unified Arab High Command which, with a useful ambivalence, could be construed either as a means of preventing Israeli attacks on the work on the Banias or as a covert way of keeping the Syrians, the most unpredictable of the Arab allies, from starting anything on their own; and, thirdly, the promotion of the Palestinian Arabs to something approaching sovereign status with a Liberation Organization (PLO), an army and a headquarters provisionally in Gaza. (Al Fatah, created by Yasser Arafat in the aftermath of the Suez War, became the principal element in the PLO, which was formed in 1964. Arafat became its chairman in 1969. Its headquarters were in Jordan until 1970, Lebanon until 1982 and Tunisia until 1994.)

Arab unity was as superficial as ever. The Palestinians in Jordan were a threat to that state and its monarchy. Feisal turned out to be a dubious ally: the agreement of 1965 on Yemen came to nothing and Feisal began to create a traditionalist or Islamic bloc within the Muslim world. He paid visits to the shah of Iran and king of Jordan and ordered arms from the west in alarming quantities. Arab unity and Nasser's role as its leader were in reverse. The flashpoint proved to be Syria.

Syria's stance in the Middle East was inhibited by its domestic politics. The alliance of the Ba'ath Party with an Alawi group of army officers led by General Salah Jadid (see p. 324) was a marriage of convenience which glossed over some uncomfortable differences. The army disliked Marxist and atheistic elements in the Ba'ath but approved its anti-parliamentary leanings and valued its provincial organization. In 1966 Jadid led a coup which was successful but he gradually lost ground to his more subtle colleague and defence minister General Hafiz as-Assad. Jadid lent a friendly ear to the Palestinians in Jordan, who were fearful of being attacked by King Hussein and his army, who, in their turn, feared that the Palestinians aimed to take over Jordan with Syrian help. Jadid was willing to help the Palestinians but the more circumspect Assad sent tanks but not aircraft, with the result that the Jordanians were able to cripple the unprotected Syrian tanks and force them into a humiliating retreat. As Jadid tried to lay the blame for this rebuff on Assad the latter carried out a coup, imprisoned Jadid and kept him in prison until be died there more than 20 years later. Hussein quelled the Palestinians who, militants and unarmed civilians alike, fled into Lebanon a year later.

Uncertainties and forays on Israel's borders with Syria and Jordan contributed to rumours that Syria was moving troops for an attack on Israel. These reports were untrue. Their provenance and purpose – probably Russian – were uncertain. But in May 1967 they caused a war. Nasser did not want a war and did not much like the Syrian government but he was (as in 1958) ill-informed about affairs inside Syria and he was unhappily aware of his own declining prestige: he felt he must do something. So he acted. He demanded the withdrawal of the UN Emergency Force (UNEF) which had been in Sinai since 1957 and despatched Egyptian forces to harass UN positions. Two days later, his demand having been rejected by the UN commander, who said that he had no authority to entertain it, Nasser repeated it to U Thant. After consulting his advisory committee on UNEF, U Thant complied and UN forces pulled out of Sharm es-Sheikh, leaving Egypt in control of the straits of Tiran. On the previous day Nasser had declared that the straits would be closed to vessels flying the Israeli flag and to contraband of war on whatever vessel (but not to Israeli commerce in non-Israeli ships).

Israel had withdrawn from Sharm es-Sheikh in 1957 in reliance on western promises to guarantee free passage through the straits, the opening of which had been one of Israel's prime objectives in making war on Egypt in 1956. Israel had stated that the closing of the straits would constitute a *casus belli* and on the day when UNEF departed the Israeli prime minister Levi Eshkol publicly called on the western powers to implement their guarantee. Washington and London issued statements about international waterways and the British foreign secretary George Brown propounded a maritime declaration whose bearing on the crisis appeared, however, remote. De Gaulle proposed four-power talks but the Russians refused. Although Israel had not been provoking war there were Israelis who saw advantages to Israel from a fresh encounter. The pros and cons had been openly canvassed along lines which, broadly, divided military hawks from more cautious civilian politicians. When matters came to a crisis Israel's main preoccupation was to ensure that the United States would not intervene against Israel as it had in 1957. The Americans were neither prepared to help Israel militarily nor asked to do so, but they were not opposed to Israeli action and this amber light was good enough for Israel.

Nasser's first moves, taken from a sense of obligation, had engendered in Egypt and beyond a flood of enthusiasm which carried him further afield, brought King Hussein to Cairo to sign a treaty and establish a joint command (which Iraq joined a few days later) and smothered Russian warnings to go carefully. The result was disaster. Israel struck the first blow. It destroyed the Egyptian air force on the ground and so rendered the Egyptian forces in Sinai defenceless: 15,000 of them were killed. The whole of the Sinai peninsula was occupied by Israel. Jordan's quixotic entry into the war cost it all its territory west of the Jordan river and its half of the city of Jerusalem. Syria was dealt with a few days later no less summarily, losing the Golan Heights as Israeli forces advanced almost to Damascus. Nasser, who had moved back to the centre of the stage only to collapse as humiliatingly as Farouk 20 years earlier, resigned but other scapegoats were found (and executed) and Nasser survived to fall in a later war.

There was much debate over the legal correctness and political consequences of U Thant's decision to withdraw UNEF and to do so speedily. UNEF had been deployed with Egypt's agreement, which was required because the operation was launched under chapter VI and not chapter VII of the UN Charter. But Hammarskjöld had made an agreement with Nasser and the question arose whether, by this agreement, Nasser had abrogated to any degree Egypt's sovereign right to require the removal of the force. On the one hand it was argued that the effect of the Nasser–Hammarskjöld correspondence was to make the stationing of UNEF on Egyptian soil terminable only by mutual consent; on the other hand, that this limitation applied only so long as UNEF was fulfilling its original role of bringing the hostilities of 1956–57 to an end, which role had been completed long before 1967. (It was never part of UNEF's role to keep the straits of Tiran open. This was an obligation of the western powers, if anybody's.) But whatever the true construction of the relevant documents, U Thant had to consider practical matters. His Advisory Council was divided, the UN's forces in the field were being forced out of their positions, two of the governments supplying forces indicated that they would withdraw whatever U Thant decided. In these circumstances U Thant had no choice. Had he prevaricated and delayed, as some of his critics maintained, he would have done no more than get some of his own force killed.

Israel's new conquests made it safer and fortified its gritty resolve and, in some quarters, the divinely providential element in Israeli nationalism. Although its territory was larger, its frontiers were shorter. Its troops stood beside the Suez Canal and the straits of Tiran and on the commanding Golan Heights, Many Israelis hoped that they now had the power and the counters to force their neighbours to make peace and recognize a state of Israel with frontiers not very different from those existing before the war. The one gain to which they intended to cling with non-negotiable tenacity was the emotion-sodden old city of Jerusalem. The Golan Heights and Sinai might be traded for formal peace and recognition. Nasser was amenable to such a deal but was not prepared to act unilaterally and in the absence of effective moves from either side the opportunity was let slip. By August, when Arab leaders met in Khartoum, their stance was intransigent. Saudi Arabia and Kuwait agreed to make good to Egypt its losses from the closing of the canal and to Jordan its losses from the capture of all its lands west of the Jordan river, which included the revenues provided by tourists and pilgrims visiting Jerusalem. In return Egypt agreed to quit Yemen and to make no fuss about the ending of the ineffective and burdensome boycott which the oil-producing countries had applied against western customers. Unofficial sanction was given for separate and secret discussions by Jordan with Israel. Various peace terms were mooted, including free passage for the Israeli flag through the straits of Tiran and the Suez Canal and eventual Egyptian recognition of Israel. But this piecemeal approach did not satisfy Israel, which remained intent on a formal peace conference and direct Arab–Israeli negotiations without intermediaries (as opposed to the so-called Rhodes formula by which each side would communicate with the other through a UN or other mediator). Fighting began again. The USSR, which had lost prestige as well as, vicariously, materials of war, decided to rearm Egypt. In October an Israeli destroyer was sunk by Egyptians using Russian weapons. As the exchanges of fire across the canal increased, Israel resolved to force Egypt to revert to a ceasefire by massive and deep retaliation but Egypt, instead of complying, called for and got more Russian help. The Russian position in Egypt was fortified; the Americans were correspondingly alarmed.

On the Jordanian front the principal changes effected by the war of 1967 were, in addition to the shifting of the frontier, the influx of a further 250,000 Palestinian refugees into Jordan, a more effective organization of Palestinian guerrilla forces and the conversion therefore of Jordan into a primary target for Israeli attacks. The humiliating collapse of the regular armies of Arab states had intensified the Palestinian belief that it was futile to rely on these states for the recovery of the lands which they had lost in Palestine. They had, however, a compulsively emotional appeal through much of the Arab world and believed themselves able to block Arab–Israeli deals which would neglect their irredentist demands. Their principal weapon was the threat to disrupt the Jordanian kingdom where, besides constituting half the population and spreading from the countryside into the capital and other cities, they now had armed forces. Militarily, they posed no threat to Israel – a further reason why they chose to threaten Jordan – but their guerrilla tactics provoked Israel to retaliations which fell upon the countries which harboured them. In 1968 a section of the Palestinians took to hijacking aircraft to advertise their cause and vent their anger. An aircraft of the Israeli El Al line was forced to land at Algiers, where its Israeli passengers were held until released through Italian mediation, and the Israeli air force destroyed 13 aircraft on the ground at Beirut in response to an attack by Palestinians on another El Al aircraft at Athens.

In Israel the shock and recovery of 1967 produced a rigidity which characterized the rest of the century and also a confidence in its ability to defeat any Arab threat and in American support for almost anything it might choose to do. In November 1967 the UN Security Council adopted its Resolution 242/67 which condemned the acquisition of territory by force, required Israel to withdraw from its recent conquests and advocated a settlement which would include recognition of Israel and a fair deal for the Palestinian refugees. This resolution was endorsed by the Arabs (other than Syria) after some hesitation but rejected by Israel. This unaccustomed solidarity among major powers was facilitated by the fright of Washington and Moscow at finding themselves on opposite sides in a shooting war which, fortunately for them, lasted only six days. The United States wanted stability in the Middle East but was hampered by what seemed to Arabs increasingly servile commitment to Israel. The cessation of American aid to Egypt in 1966 (including free food under Public Law 480) had cast Egypt into the arms of the USSR even before the disasters of the 1967 campaign but Russia too wanted stability in the region: specifically, for the reopening of the canal for the passage of supplies to North Vietnam and for the flotilla established as a permanent symbol of its expanding reach in the Indian Ocean. France, no longer dependent on Middle Eastern oil after the opening of the Algerian and Libyan oilfields, had extricated itself from the Israeli alignment into which the Mollet government had led it and, alarmed by the growth of Russian naval power in the eastern and (prospectively) western Mediterranean, tried to break the Russian monopoly in the Arab world and give Arabs some freedom of diplomatic and commercial manoeuvre by offering to sell arms to Iraq and Libya. As in 1956, so in 1967, France's main concern in the Middle East was the implications of events there upon the balance of power in the western Mediterranean. Britain, still dependent on Middle East oil and still enmeshed in the Persian Gulf, wanted peace on general grounds and particularly for the commercial convenience of reopening the canal. But Resolution 242/67 brought neither peace nor stability.

In 1970 Israel resolved to put a stop to a two-year war of attrition on the Suez front by making air raids into Egypt to within a few miles of Cairo. In response the USSR bolstered Egypt's defences with missiles, pilots and rocket crews: by the end of that year the USSR had stationed 200 pilots and 15,000 men in missile crews in Egypt and were manning 80 missile sites in addition to earlier sites manned by Egyptians but equipped with Russian missiles. Israel was forced to desist. Fighting was once more confined to the canal and its environs. The United States and the USSR pressed their clients to start talking instead of fighting. Israel agreed to talk on the basis of a withdrawal to pre-1967 limits and Nasser said that Egypt would recognize Israel. Israel agreed that talks might be indirect (through a UN negotiator, the Swedish ambassador to the UN Gunnar Jarring) or direct. The United States produced a plan for a ceasefire as a preliminary to negotiations over an Israeli withdrawal and Egyptian recognition of the Israeli state. Israel disliked this plan, as did the Palestinians; Nasser rejected it – and went to Moscow, where he stayed for two weeks. But a 90-day ceasefire and standstill agreement was concluded: within an area of 50 kilometres on either side of the canal fighting would stop and no fresh units would be introduced, and talks would begin under Jarring's auspices. This agreement was renewed in November 1970 and February 1971, but it was infringed by Egypt moving missiles into the standstill zone. Israel quit the Jarring talks and demanded massive American aid. It got only part of its demands, waxed indignant with Washington and was forced back to the talks before the year ended. The talks were an attempt to find a peace settlement on the basis of Resolution 242. They came to nothing, largely because the Arabs believed that Israel had accepted

242 to the letter (American negotiators gave them that impression) whereas Israel regarded 242 as, at best, a starting point for general discussions about all matters in dispute.

The Palestinians were alarmed. They foresaw an Israeli–Egyptian deal, followed perhaps by an Israeli–Jordanian one, which would leave them out in the cold. George Habash's Popular Front for the Liberation of Palestine, a small but especially militant group, impatient with Arafat's leadership, resorted to violent tactics which included plots against Hussein's life and the hijacking of American and British airliners. Hussein decided on a trial of strength with the Palestinians, who were turning his country and capital into an armed camp and exposing it to enemy attacks. His army inflicted heavy casualties on the Palestinians but the Arab world, shocked by the spectacle of fratricidal war, intervened and forced him to sign what was, in effect, a treaty of peace with Arafat, who was thus accorded the status of a head of state without the inconvenience of having a territory to defend or control. The king committed himself to supporting Palestinian aims, although he soon afterwards entered into discussions with Israel which were unlikely to produce terms of peace acceptable both to Israel and Palestinians. One consequence of Jordan's internal war was the sudden death of Nasser from a heart attack caused by his exertions in restoring peace in Jordan. He was succeeded with constitutional smoothness by vice-president Anwar as-Sadat.

The death of Nasser removed from the scene the first Egyptian to rule in Egypt since before the days of Alexander the Great. The movement which brought him to power had complex sources. It sought national emancipation, spiritual revival, social reform and economic and military modernization. Nasser wanted to rid Egypt of a parasitic monarchy and upper class, to extinguish British domination over Egypt and Sudan, and to raise the miserable standard of living of the Egyptian people by a more equitable distribution of land, the extension of the cultivable area and the promotion of industries. He acquired the further aims of leading all Arabs against Israel and against Arab regimes deemed reactionary.

The revolutionary movement, in which he was at first only one among a number of leaders, was predominantly but not exclusively a military collectivity in which Nasser soon came to be the leading figure by force of personality and the elimination of possible rivals. The enemies of the old regime had included elements – the Muslim Brotherhood on the right and the communists on the left – which constituted distinct centres of power. They were suppressed almost as quickly as the pashas of the old order. Political parties were banned. Nasser outmanoeuvred the nominal leader of the coup, Neguib, who was suspected of being insufficiently implacable against some pre-revolutionary elites. The monarchy was abolished; the big landowners were stripped of some of their land; rich business entrepreneurs were hobbled by nationalism; in 1954 Nasser negotiated the removal of British forces from the Canal Zone and British rule from Sudan. The stage seemed set for the economic reforms which would convert the coup of 1952 into a social and economic revolution.

Egypt's economy was weak at home and abroad. Egypt had too little cultivable land, a one-crop economy (cotton), a stagnant agriculture, negligible mineral wealth, a very small share of international trade, little industry, little capital with which to develop industries and a population growing at the rate of 3 per cent a year. The relatively small sector of modernized industry was in foreign ownership. There was, however, a native bourgeoisie with some capital resources and Nasser aimed at first to get its co-operation in the development and diversification of the Egyptian economy. But this class had no faith in the new regime and preferred to put its money into unproductive savings at home or abroad rather than venture it in industry. By the end of the 1950s massive unemployment and crushing poverty had been scarcely affected and Nasser turned to other ways. The western refusal to finance the Aswan Dam and the Anglo-French attack on Egypt in 1956 had given him cause to seize the assets of foreign companies, and in the early 1960s he went further and established state control over the greater part of the economy (other than retail trade). He also extended land reform from modest and largely ineffective first steps of 1952 (when a limit of 200 feddan had been set on individual holdings, a reform which was evaded by various devices such as transferring parts of estates to relations: this reform did not apply to state or religious lands). A five-year plan for the years 1960–65 aimed to increase GDP by 7 per cent a year and did in fact increase it by 5.5 per cent, but this improvement was hardly felt by the working population, whose numbers increased in the same years by 4 per cent.

Nasser's economic problem was never an easy one and it was made impossible by his foreign policy. He may well have intended in 1954 to devote more of his attention and resources to domestic affairs, but the resolution in that year of his differences with Britain was almost immediately followed by a more aggressive Israeli policy and by Britain's adherence to the Baghdad Pact, which Nasser interpreted as British and American intervention in Arab politics on the side of adversaries intent on stifling Egypt's revolution. So Nasser found himself increasingly concerned with foreign affairs. The authors of the revolution had always intended to create a stronger, more efficient and better equipped army than Farouk's and this aim was intensified by the need to defend the country against Israel and the revolution against Nuri's Iraq and its British friends. Nasser's consequent search for arms – and for the means to pay for them – first pushed Egypt's defence spending up beyond all normal percentages of national income and then forced Nasser into borrowing sums which Egypt had little prospect of repaying. Aid and other resources which might have gone into development were appropriated to finance a deficit on external account which increased alarmingly from 1961 onwards. The war in Yemen made matters worse. The continuing war with Israel deprived Egypt of American aid and free food. At the time of Nasser's death Egyptians were materially hardly better off than they had been 18 years earlier (though there had been some improvement in living conditions in towns); and Egypt itself was in the west's black books and in pawn to the USSR.

CHAPTER 12

The destruction of Lebanon

When Nasser died in 1970 the politics of the Middle East (excluding Iran) were dominated by a bipolar pattern: Israel–United States versus Egypt–USSR. Within a few years they looked very different. The Russian alliance with Egypt was broken. The United States, while not abandoning Israel, was increasingly embarrassed in its role of protector, which was barely compatible with the role of peace-maker which it also cherished. The Palestinians acquired a new strength, only to see it gravely jeopardized. The Arab oil exporters gave a startling demonstration of the efficiency of economic sanctions. The Lebanese state was all but destroyed.

Sadat, like Nasser, found himself under pressure from Moscow to reach some accord with Israel on the assumption that Israel was under equivalent pressure from Washington. Both the United States and the USSR were oscillating between putting pressure on their clients and acceding at least in part to their demands for aid and arms: by the end of 1971 American aid to Israel, after being reined back, was again substantial. After the fighting in Jordan in 1970 and the death of Nasser, Egypt, Syria, Libya and Sudan agreed to form a new federation of Arab republics, but Sadat's diplomacy was multifaceted. He wished to improve Egypt's relations with the Saudi and Jordanian monarchies and also to effect a reconciliation between Syria and Jordan, which had been within an ace of fighting each other over the Palestinians. He was well equipped for these exercises since he scared the heads of other states less than Nasser had done, and although he made the mistake of assuming that he would bring the Arab–Israeli matter to the point of decision within a year, he contrived not only to establish himself at home but also to edge towards a bilateral agreement with Israel. He offered in February 1971 to open the canal to Israeli cargoes in return for a partial Israeli withdrawal or the convoking of a conference to be attended by the four major outside powers, but neither in this wise nor in the Jarring talks was any progress made during the year. In the next year Sadat twice went to Moscow, found he could not get the help he wanted, concluded that Brezhnev had betrayed Egypt by promising Nixon to keep Egypt on short commons, and with unexpected boldness told the Russian specialists and advisers in Egypt to leave. They did so in a matter of weeks.

The Yom Kippur War

In 1973 Sadat waxed even bolder. His Arab fence-mending complete but his hopes for a bilateral settlement with Israel soured by Israel's obduracy, its persistence with (illegal) settlements in occupied areas and increased American aid to Israel, he adopted a policy of diplomacy by gesture. He decided to take with Syria offensive action designed, in particular, to recover the Sinai peninsula and, in general, to provoke active intervention by the United States in Middle Eastern affairs. On 6 October Israel and the rest of the world were taken by surprise by an Arab attack on two fronts. The Egyptian army attacked across the Suez Canal and pierced Israeli positions while the Syrians advanced against the Golan Heights. Each combatant had separate and limited aims which were, however, poorly co-ordinated. Egypt's attack in the south, which stopped a few miles beyond the Canal, was too limited to inhibit Israel's riposte against the Syrians. In response to Syrian pleas Sadat incautiously ordered further advances, which carried his armies beyond air cover and enabled the Israelis (who had disbelieved warnings of the joint offensive) to seize the initiative, divide the Egyptians and surround an Egyptian corps. The Americans rushed aid to Israel and the Russians, not to be outdone, did likewise to Syria, Egypt and Iraq, but both superpowers were primarily concerned to stop the fighting which was carrying both of them a step too far. Sadat's stroke was stymied and Syria's was repulsed after two days, marginal help from Iraq, Saudi Arabia and Morocco notwithstanding. Israel, having survived a nasty shock, was content to be halted although its forces were well on their way to Cairo.

Stalemate suited the United States and the USSR, the latter as soon as it became clear that the Arabs were not going to win and the former because, once Israel had been saved, the principal American concern was to prevent an Israeli counter-attack which would provoke a more forceful Russian riposte. The United States and the USSR jointly presented to the Security Council a resolution requiring a ceasefire, implementation of Resolution 242/67 and peace talks under 'appropriate' auspices. Egypt and Israel accepted this resolution and it was adopted by the Council. The Russians had privately proposed to the Americans that American and Russian troops be sent to the Middle East but Washington rejected this idea emphatically. It was, however, reintroduced by Egypt either spontaneously or at Russian instigation, and the USSR then publicly supported it. The American reaction was extreme. All American forces throughout the world were brought to the most advanced state of alert, whereupon the USSR retracted. Washington had demonstrated implacable opposition to the arrival of Russian units in the Middle East; but some European allies were disturbed by what they deemed American overreaction, provoking in return some acid American comments on their nerve and reliability.

A conference to wind up the war was convened at Geneva at the end of 1973 but the ensuing year was devoted primarily to personal diplomacy by the US secretary of state

Henry Kissinger, while the conference was held in abeyance like a net under an acrobat. A first Israeli–Egyptian disengagement agreement was reached in January 1974; both sides withdrew and a UN force took station between them. On the northern front negotiations were slower because Israel insisted on proper notification of the numbers, names and fates of Israelis captured by the Syrians, which the Syrians either would not or could not give, and because it was impossible for Israel to withdraw more than a mile or two without endangering its entire strategic position and its settlements within range of the Golan Heights. Nevertheless, Kissinger, by persistent shuttling between capitals, succeeded in getting a first agreement here too. (Both agreements were extended in November for six months and then again for another six months.) At the next stage the main crux was the status of the PLO and its demands. Israel refused to recognize the PLO as anything but a terrorist organization or the Palestinians as anything but refugees or to consider territorial retreat except in the context of a general peace agreement. The PLO's proclaimed position was that it did not accept the existence of the state of Israel, but it was supposed to be willing to negotiate on the basis of the pre-1967 borders. It insisted on being a principal party in negotiations as opposed to having the Palestinians represented by some Arab government. Israel wanted a series of bilateral arrangements beginning with Egypt (and sidelining the Palestinians). Sadat was disposed to seek such an agreement provided it were quickly followed by similar agreements between Israel and its other neighbours, so that Egypt might not be accused of breaking Arab ranks or leaving the Palestinians in the lurch. Kissinger wanted an Israeli–Egyptian agreement as quickly as possible; the United States and not an international conference to be the peace-maker; and to fortify the American–Egyptian link without too greatly offending Israel or American Jewry: everything else could wait. Kissinger saw an Israeli–Egyptian peace as a stage towards peace in the Middle East and he did not believe that peace in the Middle East could be attained except by stages. Peace, moreover, was increasingly important for the United States, whose attempts to get away from a policy focused on support for Israel had been encouraged by Sadat's break with the USSR and then made urgent by the Arabs' use of oil sanctions during the war. The weakness of Kissinger's tactics was his emphasis and dependence on Egypt, which he was pressing into a bilateralism offensive to Egypt's Arab allies and into a disregard of the Palestinians, whose claims remained none the less more central to the Arab–Israeli conflict than purely Egyptian–Israeli questions. In order to succeed Kissinger had to get Sadat to divorce Egyptian–Israeli issues from wider Arab–Israeli issues and above all from the Palestinian cause. He risked therefore damaging his new Egyptian friend throughout the Arab world.

The Arabs were in no mood to abandon the Palestinians, however much they might wish that the Palestinians had never been heard of. The Palestinians brought trouble and danger, but at an Arab conference in Rabat in October 1974 even King Hussein, who had been firing on them four years earlier and had forced 15,000 of them to flee from Jordan to Syria, joined with everybody else in acknowledging that the PLO represented Arab Palestine; and from Rabat Yasser Arafat proceeded to the UN General Assembly, which received him as though he were a head of state and adopted a strongly pro-Palestinian resolution affirming the rights of the Palestinians to sovereignty inside Palestine and to be principals at a peace conference. In winter 1974–75 it seemed likely that the PLO would declare itself a government in exile and be recognized by a majority of the United Nations, despite the lesions which weakened its claim to represent all Palestinians and despite the extremism of splinter groups whose indiscriminate kidnapping and killing shocked most people.

If the war of 1973 gave the Palestinians a boost and a chance to recover from their drubbing in Jordan in 1970, it also boosted Arab morale and hopes in other ways. Quite apart from showing that the Egyptian army had become a match for the Israelis (at least for a week), it demonstrated Arab power against greater states. The Arab oil producers, banded together in the Organization of Arab Petroleum Exporting Countries (OAPEC, a division of OPEC), shocked the whole of the developed world by cutting off oil and raising its price fourfold. For the oil-producing states oil was a weapon as well as a source of revenue – for some the only or overwhelming source. All of them were concerned to safeguard and increase their oil revenues and in 1971 they had made, at Teheran and Tripoli, agreements to secure these ends for the next five years. They insisted through OPEC in 1972 that purchasing countries which devalued their currencies should revise the terms of these agreements so that the producers should not lose by the devaluation. They also changed their attitudes towards the way in which they would take their profit. Whereas hitherto they had done so mainly by fiscal measures, by taxes on offtake at the wellhead, they now moved towards participation or part ownership of operating companies and resolved to appropriate 25 per cent of the share capital of major companies, rising to 51 per cent by 1982. They felt that what they set out to get they would get because – even before the war of 1973 – the developed world was worrying about an energy shortage amounting to an energy crisis. This crisis began to push up prices alarmingly in 1970–71 and made the producers more conscious of the advantages of restricting production: restrictions on output would prolong the life of reserves of an irreplaceable asset, put the screws on customers, and yet maintain producers' revenues if prices were raised – as they easily could be in a seller's market – to compensate for a lower volume of sales. Importing countries were vulnerable either way. Restrictions, let alone a stoppage, would jeopardize their industry and their daily life; price increases would disfigure their balance of payments. The companies, however, were not in the same position as the importing countries. They suffered only one way. Restrictions and stoppages harmed their profits, higher prices did not.

When the war began the Gulf producers raised their prices by 70 per cent. OAPEC threatened to cut deliveries by 5 per cent a month until Israel undertook to evacuate Arab territory and accede to the legitimate rights of the Palestinians. Saudi Arabia cut deliveries by 10 per cent; to the United States and the Netherlands, Israel's main champions, totally. Iraq nationalized parts of certain foreign companies and Libya talked of total expropriation. As a result of this multifarious, if ill co-ordinated Arab action oil prices in Iran, Nigeria and elsewhere shot up. The EEC expressed sympathy for the Palestinians, Britain stopped supplies of arms to Israel and Japan reversed its pro-Israeli proclivities. Arab threats did not fully materialize – it was, for example, not possible to boycott the Netherlands when oil despatched to other countries could be transshipped to Rotterdam – and within the Arab world there were some who feared the effects on themselves of harming western economies which were their principal customers. But the point had been made. Primary producers were no longer the exploited but could call the tune and use economic leverage for political ends. The change was so startling to opinion in the industrial world that it was greeted with cries of 'Blackmail!' For the Middle East it meant that so long as there was an energy crisis Arabs could not be trifled with. Oil was the most important item in the world economy, the source of growth and optimism. The use of the oil flow and price in retaliation for the United States' protection of Israel created gloom and fear.

Thus the Kissinger–Sadat axis was a brittle one. The arguments which Kissinger could bring to bear on Sadat without discountenancing him in his own country were limited by so efficacious a new weapon and by the enhanced prominence of the Palestinians. Nor were the Israelis, on their side, to be pressured so easily. They had not been defeated. They had, on the contrary, satisfied themselves that in spite of initial reverses they had been on the way to another victory. But they had been severely shaken by the failure of intelligence services which, in so small a country, were vital to prevent instant obliteration. In elections at the end of 1973 the government parties lost six seats; the gains were on the right but there was increased support too for doves critical of Israel's Arab policies. The chief of staff and other senior officers resigned. Moshe Dayan, ultimately responsible for national security as minister of defence, lost some of his hero's image and was left out of the new government formed in April 1974 when General Yitzhak Rabin succeeded Mrs Golda Meir as prime minister. The spectacle of an American president touring Arab capitals in June was a disturbing one, even though Nixon came to Jerusalem too. The speed with which the USSR more than made up Syria's and Iraq's losses in arms was disturbing, even though the United States did the same for Israel. At the end of 1974 Syria, by proposing a new joint military command with Egypt, Jordan and the PLO, emphasized the underlying unity among Israel's neighbours and their commitment to the Palestinians. Perhaps Israel had never been so unsettled. This was not a situation in which an American secretary of state could wield too big a stick, certainly not in public view.

Kissinger renewed his shuttle diplomacy early in 1975 with the aim of getting a further Israeli–Egyptian disengagement agreement. At first he was unsuccessful, owing mainly to Israeli obduracy. Sadat, after a meeting in May with President Ford at Salzburg, announced the reopening of the Suez Canal and in September a new agreement was reached. Fresh front lines and force levels were accepted; the keeping of the agreement was to be monitored by a string of early warning stations, some of them manned by American civilians; Israel abandoned the Mitla and Giddi passes and Egypt's oilfields in Sinai, in return for which it was promised massive American aid and the passage of Israeli cargoes (but not vessels) through the canal. This was the crown of Kissinger's exertions and by comparison it seemed to matter little that on the northern front the greater acerbity of the adversaries and Israel's persistence in planting new settlements in occupied territory prevented any equivalent relaxation. Yet it was in this area that the next crisis was about to occur.

Civil war

One of the recurrent features of Middle Eastern politics from 1919 onwards was the attempt to forget about the Palestinians. From the time when Emir Faisal and Chaim Weizmann talked at the Paris peace conference without troubling about them, the Palestinians had been overlooked or worse, but they refused to disappear or lose their identity. By 1975 there were rather more than 3 million of them, of whom close on half lived in Israel, or under Israeli occupation. Of the remainder 750,000 were in Jordan, 400,000 in Lebanon, 200,000 in Syria. Through half a century they had persistently posed political problems, tugged at consciences (non-Arab as well as Arab) and resorted to violence to draw attention to their grievances. After their pounding in Jordan in 1970 the centre of these activities was Lebanon.

Lebanon has been called the Switzerland of the Middle East. This meant two things: first, that the Lebanese were good at making money, richer than their neighbours and rich because of the services they rendered rather than from domestic natural resources; and, secondly, that the country was a patchwork of communities held together by political skill and tolerance in the service of material self-interest. The patchwork was imposed by geography as much as history, and the cohesion of the patchwork was a condition of the survival of the state. Two parallel ranges of mountains, one close to the sea and the two separated by a narrow valley, cut the country into vertical strips which were again divided by transverse barriers, and within this grid separate communities had preserved their individualities and mutual hostilities. These had been sharpened by religions – Muslim and Christian – and by further divisions within religions: Sunni, Shia and Druze; Maronite, Greek Orthodox and Greek Catholic (Uniate). They had also been sharpened by varieties of economic experience, for not all Lebanese were rich. The richest group were the Maronite Christians, who held in addition the presidency, given to them by the constitution and at a time when Christians as a whole outnumbered Muslims. The other Christian communities were neither so rich nor so powerful, but so long as Lebanon presented the appearance of a prosperous mercantile community in the guise of a state, by so much was it Christian rather than Muslim.

The largest of the Muslim communities were the Shia, but the Sunni, who monopolized the post of prime minister by constitutional right, were more influential politically. The Shia, many of whom had drifted from being poor countrymen to becoming poor townspeople, felt themselves equally neglected by Maronite Christians and Sunni Muslims. They were most exposed to Israeli incursions. The Druzes, on the other hand, who still preserved much of the fierce exclusiveness which had marked their origins in the eleventh century, were confident and assertive because, though for the most part poor and frequently indignant, they formed a compact and well-knit society in a hereditary mountain homeland and under a hereditary leader, Kamal Jumblatt, who commanded their loyalties and expressed an appropriate left-wing have-not philosophy.

Into this delicate cat's cradle of criss-crossing confessional and economic tensions had come in 1948 refugees from Palestine who, by 1975, numbered about 400,000, mostly housed (an ironic word) in dreadful camps. They included some 5–6,000 active gunmen, whose aim was the recovery of lost lands in Palestine by any effective means and the extinction – if that were necessary, as it was assumed to be – of the Israeli state. Since such an aim could never be attained by a few thousand armed men it had to be prosecuted through Arab states, which had to be induced to make war on Israel. Since these states were only half willing to do so, and since when they ventured they got beaten, the Palestinians had a survival problem which led them to look even further afield for aid and sympathy, notably to the leading left-wing powers, China and the USSR (although the latter preferred to put its money on governments rather than on movements which were attacking governments), and to universal left-wing opinion which would rally to dispossession and destitution and not be too gravely offended by the use of terror as a weapon justified by desperation. Within Lebanon Palestinians could count on support, not from the political and mercantile elite, which regarded them as a nuisance, but from other sections of the population, which had to recognize them as fellow Arabs and underdogs. By the 1970s the Palestinians were more than a nuisance. Their militant organizations, encamped on Lebanese soil, regarded themselves as being at war with Israel, which was Lebanon's neighbour and did not hesitate to strike back when attacked from Lebanon. The Maronites in particular, as conservative Christians, disliked and feared the Palestinian organizations because they were left-wing, militant, Muslim and a threat to the stability of the state which gave the Maronites their wealth and their influence. It was an important coincidence that the Maronite position in Lebanon was already under some threat from a decline in the proportion of Christians in the population and from the nemesis which haunts a too prosperous exclusivity.

In 1975 a group of Muslim fishermen, aggrieved by a concession granted to a group of Christian fishermen, staged a demonstration which turned into an affray. Some Palestinians took sides with the Muslims. Christians saw in this episode a writing on the wall: the Palestinians, already a standing incitement to Israeli aggression against Lebanon, were now interfering in the balance of internal Lebanese politics. Anti-Palestinian incidents followed, caused by the Phalange, a right-wing Christian faction. Violence escalated; the government, always weak in a crisis because of conflicting loyalties implanted in it by the constitution, fell; the army, small and itself divided, failed to keep order. The disorder, which had begun as faction fights, turned into a battle for territory. The Palestinians, who had arms in plenty, became more and more involved (against the wishes of some of their leaders) and their opponents more and more provocative. There were innumerable truces of insignificant duration. Battle having been joined, opportunity beckoned to both sides. A left-wing alliance of Druzes and Palestinians seemed set to take over the country, the Druzes in order to supplant the existing ruling groups and the Palestinians in order to make Lebanon safe for Palestinians and a base against Israel. On the other side the Maronites and their allies sensed the chance to do to the Palestinians in Lebanon what King Hussein had done to them in Jordan: expel as many as possible, kill some leaders and perhaps even exterminate them with Israel's help.

As the civil war threatened to entail the destruction of the state Syria had to consider what to do. Lebanon had been a part of Syria (as had Jordan and Palestine) under Ottoman dominion and before, but Syria hesitated to intervene for a number of reasons. If the Syrian army were to go into Lebanon the Israeli army would most probably do so too and a new conflict would be staged, unwelcome to Syria and to Syria's Russian patrons. Nor would Jordan, with which President Assad had been improving relations, take kindly to any move which looked like a step towards recreating Greater Syria. The same argument applied to Iraq. Syria therefore, though inclined to favour the Druze–Palestinian side, was more concerned to end the fighting and put the Lebanese state back on its feet; and Assad concentrated on finding a way of restoring the constitutional proprieties under a Maronite president (though a new one), even if this entailed attacking the Palestinians. Syrian intervention therefore took an anti-Palestinian and pro-Maronite flavour which outraged other Arab states which, suspicious of Syrian designs, tried to substitute pan-Arab for Syrian management of the crisis by introducing a mixed Arab force and an Arab League mediator. But these moves had little substance. Assad chose his moment to put his own troops in and imposed a provisional settlement whereby the Maronites would retain the presidency *de jure* but the president would no longer choose the prime minister and the Muslims would have equal representation with Christians in the parliament. This was a restoration which amounted to a defeat for the leftish Shi'ites and Druzes (Kamal Jumblatt was killed, probably murdered), who had scented power only to be denied it by foreign intervention; and it was a defeat for the Palestinians, who had made common cause with the Druzes and other anti-Maronite elements and in doing so had backed the losing side and been battered first by the Maronites and then by the Syrians. It was also a defeat for the Russians who, having perforce shifted their pivot in the Middle East from Cairo to Damascus, saw Syria acting with a degree of independence and in a direction unpalatable to Moscow. Yet Moscow gave no help to Jumblatt or Arafat; its influence in the crisis was minimal. Assad, not Arafat, had become the dominant force in the state. Lebanon itself was in ruins and in tutelage. It could eject Syria from its system only at the price of letting loose new conflicts between the private armies of Maronites, Druzes and others, which no purely Lebanese army could control. The Maronites, although rescued by Syria, were no less hostile to it and remained prone to flirt with Israel in spite of the fact that this flirting fatally divided them. The Palestinians, having been attacked by Jordan and by Syria, having lost their stronghold in Lebanon, and conscious that Sadat's sympathy for them was offset by Egypt's contrary interest in peace with Israel, had once more nobody to rely on but themselves. Arafat had looked for support in the wrong quarter. Disillusioned with Arab governments and nervous about leftish breakaways from his own movement, he had formed an alliance with the Arab left and so become a target for Arab governments determined to annihilate it.

The civil war in Lebanon, which lasted from April 1975 to November 1976, cost 40,000 lives and huge material and commercial damage. The new president Elias Hrawi, less committed to the Maronite ascendancy in its old form than his predecessor Suleiman Franjieh, lacked the authority and the armed power to make his government's writ run. The fighting was brought to a stop by the Syrians but Assad's position in Lebanon was both taxing and embarrassing. Syria was reviled by the rest of the Arab world; Iraq cut off oil (but Saudi Arabia provided credits to fill the gap). Assad had neither the means nor probably the wish to take the whole responsibility for Lebanon's affairs. He reverted to negotiation. At Shtoura in July 1977 Syria, Lebanon and the PLO reaffirmed a Lebanese–PLO agreement made in Cairo in 1969 whereby the PLO would withdraw its armed units from Beirut and the frontier zone in the south. This disarming of the Palestinians was put in train in Beirut but not in the south, where fighting started again between Palestinians and Lebanese Christians. The Israelis invaded and with their help Major Saad Haddad established (in a largely Muslim area) a semi-independent Christian state of Free Lebanon. Neither the Lebanese army, always helpless in the face of communal strife, nor the UN Interim Force in Lebanon (UNIFIL) could counter this creation of an Israeli puppet state, while in the rest of the country private armies resumed their battles and assassinations. There were about 40 armies or armed bands in this small state. In 1980 battles between the two principal Maronite forces resulted in victory for the Phalange and the Gemayel family over the National Liberal Party of the Chamoun and other prominent Maronite clans. The victors were the more determined to remove from Lebanon all Palestinians, civilian refugees as well as armed units, and they had Israel's armour to help them. A new no-go area, like Major Haddad's and beyond the reach of the government, was created in and around Beirut, a Phalangist autonomous canton.

Camp David

This disintegration of Lebanon was promoted by Israel. South Lebanon was part of the lands claimed for Israel by Zionist irredentism, but this claim might have remained muted if the area had not become during the 1970s a refuge of Palestinian revanchism.

Israel was determined to eradicate the militant arm of the Palestinians by force, and most Israelis regarded any aggressive action for this purpose as a legitimate exercise of the right of self-defence. In its earliest days the threat to Israel's existence came from Arab states. Israel believed that, by its superior efficiency and American aid, it could always defeat enemies who would be perpetually at odds with each other. At this stage the Palestinians were no more than a minor instrument of the Arab states, useful mainly for propaganda purposes. But they became the central issue, evolving a fighting force of their own, attracting international sympathy and commanding the (limited) support of Arab states – a reversal of roles which turned them into a more persistent danger to Israel than any Arab government.

Israel's increasingly aggressive response was a recognition of this change. Whereas Arab states could not be destroyed, the political power of the Palestinians might be if enough Palestinians could be killed or dispersed. A change of government in Israel helped to put this reasoning into practice. During 1976 the Labour-dominated coalition struggled in vain with economic problems and disorder on the West Bank. Splits developed within the coalition and within the Labour Party itself. At the UN the United States was increasingly alone in vetoing anti-Israeli resolutions in the Security Council and eventually joined the majority in condemning Israel's ruthless and illegal behaviour in the West Bank. Rabin resigned when his wife was accused of a currency offence but his successor, Shimon Peres, did not survive a general election and in 1977 Menachem Begin, veteran fighter against the British and biblical fundamentalist, formed Israel's first government without the Labour Party. He declared that Israel must keep the West Bank and should accelerate the creation of new settlements there. President Carter, among others, called these settlements illegal. He proposed that the Geneva conference be reconvened (with Russian participation) and that the PLO be invited to attend it on condition that it recognize Israel's right to exist. Begin was willing to see Palestinians at a conference but adamant that he would never negotiate with the PLO, thus allowing Arafat to avoid giving a straight answer to Carter's question. In November Begin, to general amazement, took up an offer by Sadat to go to Jerusalem. Sadat badly needed peace. He had fought a four-day war with Libya on his other flank; the Egyptian economy was in tatters; and domestic disaffection had turned into riots.

Addressing the Knesset with a directness which attracted worldwide praise, Sadat deplored delays in reconvening the Geneva conference and appealed for peace between Egypt and Israel, Israel's withdrawal to its 1967 frontiers and the right of self-determination and statehood for the Palestinians; he did not mention the PLO by name. Before the year ended talks between Egypt and Israel began in Cairo and Begin visited Ismailia, where he spoke of an autonomous Palestinian entity with an Israeli military presence for 20 years. His formal proposals for the West Bank, published at the end of the year, envisaged continuing Israeli control of security and public order, a choice for the inhabitants between Israeli and Jordanian (but not Palestinian) citizenship, Arab immigration in 'reasonable numbers' to be agreed between Israel, Jordan and the new authority of the autonomous territory, and freedom for Israelis to buy land. Carter approved this response, thus opposing the creation of a Palestinian state.

This was the beginning of the process which ended the war between Egypt and Israel but did nothing for the Palestinians. Begin, while he might be induced to relinquish valuable forward positions and defences in Sinai (although it was for him divinely appointed Jewish land), had no intention of abandoning control over the West Bank; he proposed on the contrary to accelerate its demographic transformation by encouraging settlements regardless of their strictly military justification; the Jewish population of the occupied West Bank quadrupled in three years of his government. Egypt needed peace and the return of the territory and oilfields in Sinai, lost in 1973. Sadat, pessimistic about any deal with Begin, once more invoked American intervention and got a ready response from Carter who, having failed to reactivate the Geneva conference, became an eager champion of an Israeli–Egyptian accord as a first piece in a series of agreements between Israel and all its surrounding enemies.

The United States assumed the role of principal negotiator in this cause and at a tripartite conference at Camp David in September 1978 Carter got Begin and Sadat to subscribe a 'framework' for a general Middle East peace: Israel was gradually to leave the West Bank and Gaza, creating an autonomous Palestinian entity with a temporary Israeli presence, all other problems to be deferred for five years. Alongside these aspirations were two precise conclusions, the one positive and the other negative. Egypt recovered the Sinai peninsula (subject to demilitarization) but the Palestinians got neither recognition nor land at any foreseeable point in time. Sadat had proclaimed his determination to heed and pursue Palestinian rights but he was not deeply committed to them, he did not like the Palestinian leaders and at Camp David he wilted under Begin's sticky fundamentalism and Carter's eagerness not to let either Sadat or Begin leave the meeting without signing a formal agreement. Sadat was fiercely attacked throughout the Arab world for failing to make his settlement with Israel contingent on an equitable deal for the Palestinians. He lost his Saudi subsidies, became dependent on American charity and was assassinated in 1981. He did, however, receive jointly with Begin the Nobel Peace Prize which, as in the case of Kissinger and Le Duc Tho a few years earlier, was thus bestowed on warriors who mended their ways rather than on more exemplary men of peace.

The euphoria generated by Sadat's appearance in Jerusalem in 1977 lasted about a year. American pressure on Jordan and Saudi Arabia to applaud what had been done failed. The Arabs were divided into the hostile and the very hostile. Israel continued its economic decline (its rate of inflation became one of the highest in the world) and pursued its tough policies on its northern borders and the West Bank. Begin's cabinet lost its more eminent members and its popular support; General Dayan, who had crossed the floor when Begin won the election of 1977, deserted him over his government's insistence on promoting settlements which had a political but no strategic purpose, and General Ezer Weizmann did so too on similar grounds. But although Begin's unyielding manner lost him friends, there were few signs that his basic objectives had become unpopular. The election of the outspokenly pro-Israeli Ronald Reagan to be president of the United States was a relief for Israelis, who had begun to ponder the future policies of an American administration forced to choose between its devotion to Israel and its material and strategic interests in Saudi Arabia and the Gulf. And the war launched by Iraq against Iran in 1980 readvertised the fissures among Israel's enemies as some Arab governments supported Iraq and others did not.

At Camp David Begin had bought off Egypt, a rare diplomatic feat in Israel's history of military triumphs. But he secured his southern flank as part of an expansionist policy in other directions. Israel kept its hold on the occupied West Bank with little difficulty. Although it was obliged to use harsh measures which did it no good in the outside world, internally there was minimal Israeli criticism of either the occupation or its seamier side, and Begin used his freedom of manoeuvre to the south and east to launch a war northward into Lebanon. A narrow electoral victory in 1981 left him dependent in the Knesset on small and myopic religious parties. Israel's creeping colonization of the West Bank became more brutal and precipitate – the Jewish population was to be increased from 20,000 to 120,000 by 1985 – and the Israeli air force displayed its muscle by destroying a nuclear installation near Baghdad in June and raiding Beirut in July: a left and right against Iraq on the one hand and Syria on the other. The former exploit, designed to pre-empt or delay the emergence of Iraq as an offensive nuclear power, was condemned at the UN even by the United States, which delayed, by a few token weeks, the delivery to Israel of new military aircraft. The attack on Beirut was prompted by discord within Lebanon between Syrian forces and the Christian Phalange. When at the end of 1980 the Syrians had evacuated Zahle to the east of Beirut the Phalange forestalled the regular Lebanese army and occupied it. The Syrians supported the army's attempts to oust the Phalange. Fighting spread. Israel saw its opportunity. Besides raids into southern Lebanon it flew demonstrative sorties over Beirut and when Syria introduced ground-to-air missiles it attacked them. Israel hoped to propel President Bashir Gemayel, a Maronite Christian and son of the founder of the Phalange, to take sides with that militant body and so entrench a Christian and anti-Syrian statelet in parts of Beirut and its surroundings. But President Gemayel was persuaded by Syria and other Arabs to denounce an Israeli–Phalange alliance. Torn between Syria and Israel, the Maronites were on the slippery slope to the loss of their once dominant role in Lebanon.

At the end of 1981 the Saudi prime minister Prince Fahd presented a plan for peace which required the withdrawal of Israel to its 1967 borders and implied the recognition of the Israeli state within those limits. This plan was anathema to Israel but was aborted by the Arabs themselves when Assad refused to go to a conference at Fez to discuss it. King Hussein strongly supported the Saudi initiative, patched up his quarrel with Morocco by his first visit to that country for five years, but displeased Reagan by his insistence on including the PLO in any peace process notwithstanding the refusal of the Palestinian National Council formally to abate its demand for the elimination of the Israeli state.

Reagan was clinging to the view that peace could be achieved without the concurrence of the PLO but his commitment to Israel and to his predecessor's Camp David programme received two knocks at the end of 1981. In October Sadat was assassinated. More of a hero outside his country than in it, Sadat offended many Egyptians by his style as well as his policies. The peaceful transfer of power to Hosni Mubarak demonstrated the comparative stability of Egypt's political system. The new president, although too cautious to make any abrupt changes of policy, was concerned to garner the full fruits of the Camp David agreement so far as they related to Israel's retreat from Egyptian soil (which was completed in April 1982) but also to mend Egypt's relations with the rest of the Arab world, which had been wrecked by Camp David's evasion of Palestinian claims. Where Sadat had flaunted western ways Mubarak was decorously Islamic; he relaxed Sadat's (and Nasser's) repression of political opponents, won foreign aid for Egypt's public services and quietly restrained military expenditure. (By 1984 he felt strong enough to legalize a revived, if fairly tame, Wafd Party and allow it to take part in a general election.) Reagan, secondly, was obliged to recognize some linkage between different parts of the Middle East and so implicitly to modify his belief that the Palestinian issue could be kept in a tight compartment. Concerned by the extension of the Iraqi–Iranian war to the Gulf he agreed, and narrowly persuaded the Senate to agree, to the sale of AWACS intelligence aircraft to Saudi Arabia (see Chapter 14) but at the cost of giving Israel still more military aid, an agreement for 'strategic co-operation' and an enhanced capacity for independent adventures. By the same token the American room for manoeuvre in the Middle East was becoming more inhibited even before Israel marginalized all peace plans by launching on 6 June 1982 a full-scale invasion of Lebanon.

Israel's invasion of Lebanon

The ostensible object of this operation was to root out the Palestinians from southern Lebanon who were harassing Israel but there were deeper causes and wider ambitions. Long before there were any Palestinians in Lebanon Ben-Gurion had planned to disrupt it by seducing its Maronite Christians and either annexing its southern part or creating a satellite state there. For Menachem Begin and Zionists of his kind parts of Lebanon belonged to Israel by divine and biblical right. The spark for the invasion was provided by the attempted assassination of the Israeli ambassador in London. Begin told the Knesset and the world that Israel's forces would advance no more than 45 km beyond their frontiers but Sharon, with or without the knowledge of all his colleagues, had concluded six months earlier plans for co-operation with Lebanese Christians and Israeli forces advanced rapidly from the south to the outskirts of Beirut, which they bombarded for two months. The object of this operation was the eviction of the Palestinians from Beirut. The Israeli government shrank from a direct assault on and capture of Beirut because it would entail heavy Israeli casualties and American displeasure, but in July east Beirut was taken with Christian help and the Palestinian men of fighting age agreed to leave: they were evacuated by sea. In September President Gemayel was assassinated, perhaps with Syrian connivance or instigation. He was succeeded by his brother Amin. Israel attacked west Beirut. In revenge for Bashir Gemayel's death and after the departure of Palestinian fighters the Christian Phalange, with Israeli support, massacred 1,000, perhaps 2,000, helpless Palestinians in two camps at Sabra and Chatila. The perpetrators were Phalangists but Israelis were present at Phalangist headquarters throughout the three days and nights of atrocities which continued ceaselessly with Israeli help. Subsequently, an official inquiry in Israel, forced upon a reluctant Israeli government by international outcry and internal disquiet, censured a number of highly placed Israelis for their responsibility in these doings.

By invading Lebanon Israel put at stake the virtually unconditional support which successive American governments conceded to it. Whether the invasion alone would have permanently eroded that support is questionable but the massacre made a mark on an American view of Israel which, ever since the foundation of the state in the wake of the Nazi Holocaust, had permitted a double standard to be applied to the more dubious Israeli actions. In Israel itself the shock was sharp but perhaps short. More tellingly, Israeli deaths in the occupation of southern Lebanon over the next few years created at least the beginnings of a revulsion against the more unacceptable features of Israeli aggressiveness, a suspicion that Israel's policies were in the long run hopeless, and some disinclination to accept the majority view that only the Palestinians were blameworthy. The bombardment of Beirut and the massacres in the camps gave Israel's resoluteness in the search for self-preservation a taint of lunatic atrocity which even the use of napalm in earlier clashes had not earned for it.

A multinational peacekeeping force of American, French and Italian units, later joined by a minute British contingent, had arrived in Lebanon before the massacres in order to oversee the evacuation of the PLO and Syrians from west Beirut. Casualties at this stage were around 15,000 (mostly Lebanese civilians). At the same time Reagan produced another peace plan. Since it included a ban on Israeli annexations, an end to Israeli settlements on the West Bank and an autonomous West Bank state in association with Jordan, it was immediately rejected by Begin. Reagan's simultaneous plea for the mutual withdrawal of Israeli and Syrian forces was ignored by both and was a dead letter from the start. The Arabs produced their own plan, which again implicitly recognized an Israeli state (within the 1967 frontiers) but also demanded a Palestinian state with Jerusalem as its capital: this was a refurbishment of the Fahd plan of the previous year (Fahd had become king in June on the death of his brother Khaled). Lebanon's faction fighting continued and the Syrians and Israelis remained in the country. The Palestinian fighters (about 7,000) were dispersed in ten different directions, half of them to Syria, but Syria failed to promote an effective alternative to Arafat as the Palestinians' outstanding leader.

The Syrian position was initially precarious but was gradually consolidated, mainly because neither the Israeli–American front nor Syria's Arab enemies had anything viable to offer. The Israelis were overstretched and unhappy, the Lebanese army impotent, the multinational force decamped when it got caught in the crossfire of Lebanese politics: 239 US marines were killed in a single suicide raid in 1983 after the US navy bombarded Shi'ite and Druze positions from offshore. Begin resigned in 1983 from a combination of personal grief on his wife's death and political frustration, leaving Israel militarily, politically and morally weakened. President Assad on the other hand, having survived two rounds of risings against him in the first months of 1982 (although only at the cost of massacring his domestic enemies to the number of perhaps 10–20,000) was left locally in control. In Lebanon Amin Gemayel had nobody but Assad to turn to and when in 1983 Gemayel tried to secure an Israeli withdrawal by direct negotiation with Israel his partners in the Lebanese government denounced his efforts and Assad forced him to cancel the deal which he had made. Gemayel's task of piecing together a coalition from his country's warring forces was repeatedly frustrated by one or another of them and Gemayel himself was reduced to insignificance.

The Israeli withdrawal was completed during 1985 but the Israelis took with them 1,000 Lebanese captives, hostages for Lebanese good behaviour, and kept for another 13 years control over southern Lebanon through the dependent South Lebanese Army, a Christian force in a predominantly Muslim region. Lebanon became a country without effective government, its political parties divided against each other and within themselves, its regular armed forces pitted against each other and its capital fractured among rival irregular forces whose principal weapon was hostage-taking. First among these last forces was al-Jihad, whose main purposes were the return of the 1,000 Lebanese captives in Israel and the release of 17 Lebanese imprisoned in Kuwait. Al-Jihad was to some degree controlled by Hizbollah, which was affiliated to the movement of the same name in Iran (see Note C at the end of this Part) and aimed to create an Islamic state in Lebanon as a springboard for war with Israel and the recapture of Jerusalem. It hijacked an American B 747 on its way from Athens to Rome, brought it to Beirut and, with the assistance of the Shi'ite leader Nabih Berri, bartered its passengers for the 1,000 captives in Israel. To recover the 17 Lebanese in Kuwait it seized American, British and French citizens in Beirut. Their governments declared their joint refusal to buy hostages from terrorists but the Americans and, later, French broke ranks and did so largely for domestic electoral reasons – and, in the American case, in the course of selling arms to Iran for money for the war in Nicaragua which the US Congress was refusing to fund (see Chapter 28). The British government, which happened to have no elections impending, stood by its engagements. International agreement over hostages broke down because national perceptions and circumstances differed and no adequate machinery existed for ensuring a common foreign policy.

Hostage-taking proliferated and the cost of redeeming them soared. (The Lebanese captives in Kuwait were freed by Saddam Hussein's invasion in 1990. The UN then negotiated with Iran the release of the remaining hostages in Beirut and subsequently an exchange of Lebanese captives in Israel for Israeli captives in Lebanon.)

Syria failed to pacify or unite Lebanon. The PLO, buffeted but not eradicated, rebuilt its positions in the camps round Beirut to which the PLO's fighting men returned after 1982 to protect their families. Syria, abandoning its policy of restoring the Maronite–Sunni ascendancy, promoted an alliance of the Shi'ite Amal Party of Nabih Berri with the Druzes, led by Jumblatt's son Walid, which, although it failed to evict the Palestinians from their camps, evicted the Maronites from west Beirut. Among the Maronites Gemayel was, from the Syrian point of view, a broken reed since by attaching himself to Syria he antagonized half his own community, half the Phalange and half the (Christian) Lebanese army – all bodies where Syria was as much disliked as Israel. The Phalangist Samir Geagea, commander of the Lebanese forces, challenged Gemayel's authority but the Maronites, fearful of these divisions among themselves, created a Salvation Council as a means of getting rid of Geagea and retaining their hold on east Beirut. Another leading Maronite, Elie Hobeika – a former commander of the Lebanese forces, who had been displaced by Geagea in 1986 – threw in his lot with Syria and agreed to a truce with the Shi'ites and Druzes and to Syria's political programme: parity between Christians and Muslims, a reduction in the powers of the Maronite president, and a special relationship between Lebanon and Syria. But these moves failed to restore unity in Lebanon or to stop the fighting. Gemayel, who had not been consulted, repudiated the agreement with Berri and Jumblatt, and the Maronites disowned Hobeika in favour of Geagea. In 1987 Maronites murdered the Sunni prime minister Rashid Karami and developed in east Beirut a single-minded and militant hostility to the Syrians, who returned in force.

Lebanon was divided three ways and then four. In the south Israel supported its puppet regime under Christian military control. The rest of the country had rival governments headed by Karami's successor Selim al-Hoss (a Sunni) and Michel Aoun (Christian commander of the Lebanese army). Aoun's main aim was the eviction of Syria's 30,000 troops, in which he had help from Syria's perennial foe, Iraq. Fighting increased. In 1989 a rump of the Lebanese parliament elected in 1972 was assembled at Taif in Saudi Arabia. Its aim was to give Lebanon a new start after 15 years of civil strife, foreign invasion and progressive disintegration. It recognized the main shifts in Lebanese politics by leaving the presidency to the Maronites but giving more powers to the Sunni prime minister and more parliamentary seats to the Shi'ites, the largest single community. President Elias Hrawi dismissed Aoun but his army remained loyal to him. Aoun and Geagea fought one another until Aoun was bombarded into surrender in 1990 by Syrian missiles: the battles between these two Christian forces marked the schismatic disintegration of Maronite power. Geagea withdrew his forces from Beirut, leaving Hrawi's government ostensibly, Syria effectively, in control of the capital and most of the country. Israel retained its indirect control in the south through the puppet South Lebanese Army and through its evident readiness to use force – as, for example, in 1993 when heavy bombardment propelled half a million refugees to Beirut in an attempt to compel Lebanon to expel Hizbollah units from its territory. The attempt was unsuccessful and Israel's actions made Hizbollah more popular than it otherwise would have been. Israel's attempt in 1982 to dismember Lebanon and annex part of it turned it into a satellite of Syria.

Elections in 1992 demonstrated the strength of the Shi'ites but also their division between the main body of Nabih Berri's Amal and Hizbollah, each with its own private army. Al-Hoss was succeeded as prime minister by Rafiq al-Hariri, a richly successful businessman who mastered inflation, kept taxes and unemployment reasonably low, brought the balance of payments into surplus and secured a measure of foreign aid and investment. He restored some vigour to the urban economy but could neither arrest rural decline nor diminish the load of 4–500,000, mostly homeless, Palestinians alongside a Lebanese population of 3.5 million. In the south Hizbollah developed from a sectarian to a national anti-Israeli movement supported by Druzes and Christians. It intensified its operations and caused rifts in Israeli governments and opinion over whether to remain in occupation or retreat. This dilemma was compounded when General Emile Lahoud, elected president of Lebanon in 1998, declared that there could be no negotiated Israeli withdrawal from Lebanon without a simultaneous withdrawal from the Golan Heights.

The events of the 1980s and 1990s destroyed the political structure of Lebanon created after the Second World War by Sunni Arab nationalists and Maronite Christians on the basis of a division of offices and power between these two groups (with a slight advantage to the latter) but put nothing new in place of the old. For 20–30 years Lebanon flourished on a compromise which, however, sidelined the mainly rural Shia who constituted one-third of the population. The progressive disintegration and impoverishment of Lebanon were rooted in this exclusion which offered opportunities to disruptive outsiders (Syrians, Iranians and others); by the seemingly permanent presence of the Palestine refugees; by the civil wars of 1975–90 with their death toll of around 150,000; by the accumulating discontent and fears which were concentrated and nourished in Hizbollah; and from 2001 by the policies of the Bush administration which poured cold water on attempts to find a road to peace in the Syrian–Lebanese–Palestinian–Israeli sector of the Middle East. Hariri was assassinated at the end of 2005 and the Maronite leader Pierre Gemayel a few months later. Elections in 2007 marked the progressive shift of Lebanon's politics away from an historical multifaceted pattern to a bilateral conflict between those accepting close links with Syria (preferably without Syrian troops) and on the other hand Christians and Shi'ites led by Aoun and intent on keeping Syrian interference to a minimum. Thus Syria, backed by Iran, was dominating Lebanese politics and hoping thereby to put an end to the uncomfortable isolation of the years following the unreal union with Egypt.

But Syria, even with Iranian support, was unable to subjugate Lebanon, and could only paralyze it. Hizbollah's influence waxed as the Lebanese came to see it as the real opposition to Israel (like Hamas in Gaza) and as the United States was weakened by the fiasco in Iraq, but the Sunni government of Fuad Siniora supported by the Druze Walid Jumblatt retained its formal status. In 2008 the balance of power shifted when Hizbollah staged a coup, seized control of western (Muslim) Beirut and virtually imprisoned the leaders of the government.

CHAPTER 13

Towards a Palestinian state

King Hussein's diplomacy

In the wake of the Israeli invasion of Lebanon, King Hussein resumed his efforts to find a settlement between Israel and its Palestinian neighbours. The rebuff to Israel in Lebanon and the worsting of the PLO by Syria revived the king's hopes of an agreement whereby Israel would cede territory in exchange for peace. These hopes were shared by Shimon Peres, leader of Israel's Labour Party and joint head of a coalition formed in 1984 with Likud, led after Begin's resignation by Yitzhak Shamir; under a power-sharing agreement Peres was prime minister from 1984 to 1986 when he switched posts with Shamir and became foreign minister. These hopes were, however, unreal. Each side had a non-negotiable item unacceptable to the other. Likud, while ready to discuss some form of autonomy for Palestinians, insisted on keeping control over all territory conquered in and since 1967 and on negotiating only with Jordan. From its earliest days Israel had refused to countenance a distinct Palestinian state and it refused to enter into talks with the PLO or with a mixed Jordanian–PLO team. Hussein, on the other hand, believed that no peace was possible without the direct participation of the Palestinians and that the PLO was their proper representative. In this view he was supported by western European governments, while the United States, obedient to Israeli insistence, interpreted direct talks to mean talks between Israel and Jordan only, with no wider international conference. Since one main element in any peace talks must be the cession (or other disposition) of territory occupied by Israel, not to Jordan but to Palestinians, the pattern was lopsided unless Jordan were to abandon its plea to include the PLO and the PLO were to give Hussein a free hand to negotiate the fate of the Palestinians independently of themselves. Hussein's task in these circumstances was to reach the conference room by some dexterous fudging and, not surprisingly, he failed.

He began by reaching agreement with the PLO on the principle of territory-for-peace and on convoking an international conference which would include all five permanent members of the UN Security Council, Israel and a joint Jordan–PLO delegation. This formula buried the PLO in a large assembly but it implicitly rejected Israel's form of direct negotiation and, by making no reference to the Security

Council's Resolution 242, affronted Israel's demand for prior recognition of Israel's right to exist as a state. Hussein got no support from other Arab states apart from Egypt. In 1985 he made one of his repeated visits to Washington in order to assure the United States that the PLO would endorse Resolution 242. He also asked for American arms. Reagan refused to modify the American–Israeli formula for direct negotiations but alarmed Israel by agreeing to supply Jordan with missiles and aircraft. His rejection of Hussein's plans for a peace conference was the penultimate nail in their coffin and later in the year they foundered when even moderate Arabs such as King Fahd refused to attend an Arab meeting to discuss them.

Hussein blamed the PLO for this setback. Encouraged by their partial recovery in Lebanon the more militant Palestinians were keen to draw attention to their cause by startling and violent acts. In one incident in Cyprus they killed three Israelis. Later in 1985 four Palestinians boarded at Genoa the Italian *Achille Lauro* as it set out for a cruise in the eastern Mediterranean. They intended (so they later said) to leave the ship at Ashdod in Israel and there execute some spectacular destruction of Israeli property and lives. They were, however, discovered on board before reaching Ashdod and thereupon – and apparently on the spur of the moment – seized the liner and issued a demand for the release of a number of Palestinians held captive in Israel. One of the hijackers murdered an American passenger. Alarmed by this turn of events, Palestinian leaders – notably Abu Abbas, an associate of Arafat, if not always in total accord with him – ordered the hijackers to return the liner to its captain and come ashore in Egypt on being assured that they would thence be conveyed to a safe place. This resolution of the incident was made possible by Mubarak, who provided the means of getting the hijackers off the *Achille Lauro* and out of Egypt. But the Americans, incensed by the murder of the hapless passenger, intercepted the Egyptian aircraft carrying the hijackers and Abu Abbas to Tunisia and, by threatening to shoot it down, forced it to land in Sicily, where armed Americans from a NATO unit tried to seize its passengers. This last part of the exploit was foiled by the Italians, who arrested and charged the hijackers but allowed Abu Abbas to escape to Yugoslavia. The consequences of these adventures included the fall of the Italian government (subsequently reinstated); the weakening of Mubarak, whose mediation brought him the humiliation of having one of his aircraft brought down by the Americans; the raising of illegal violence to higher levels, not only by the PLO but also by Israel, which bombed the PLO's offices on Tunisian soil; and the final abrogation of Hussein's peace plans.

In the next year (1986) the United States tried to reflate the peace process by offering to accept the PLO at a broad international conference if it would accept Resolution 242 and forswear violence – a belated conversion to the defunct Hussein plan. But Hussein, increasingly occupied with the war in the Gulf between Iraq and Iran, washed his hands of the PLO; Peres came to the end of his term as prime minister and was succeeded by his partner Shamir, who did not like his dealings with Hussein; and the PLO retorted to the American initiative by demanding that the United States publicly endorse the Palestinians' right to self-determination – that is, to a state of their own. In 1987 the Palestinian National Council abrogated the 1985 accord between Arafat and Hussein and affirmed its demand for an independent Palestinian state and separate representation at any peace talks.

As 1987 ended the Palestinians under Israeli occupation surprised everybody, including the Israelis, by staging a rising – *intifada* – on their own account. It began with a traffic accident in Gaza, where the Palestinians' living conditions were peculiarly disgraceful and Israeli police brutality peculiarly barbarous. Stones were thrown, mostly by children, and the Israelis retaliated by opening fire and killing people. The rising spread to the West Bank and Jerusalem and evoked from the startled Israelis a riposte so harsh that Israel's already tarnished reputation was severely damaged throughout the world and even governments protested publicly. Israel failed to suppress the *intifada*. The *intifada* failed to achieve anything more concrete than the violent advertisement of Palestinian grievances. The arrival in the late 1980s of thousands of Jews from the USSR hardened attitudes on both sides: 200,000 immigrants in 1990 and the tide still rising presented Israel with demands for housing and jobs which it could not satisfy. Israel was losing its grip on southern Lebanon and the crisis over Kuwait was to add to its worries by allowing Syria to come in from the cold and win some (grudging) goodwill in Washington by contributing to the American assemblage of armed force in Saudi Arabia against Iraq (see Chapter 14).

The United States, which was by this stage providing Israel with financial and military aid up to and beyond $2 billion a year (in spite of laws which forbade aid to governments which flouted human rights), was embarrassed by Israel's behaviour and the foundering of the peace process. It decided in 1989 to talk for the first time officially and directly to the PLO but its fundamental determination to protect and secure Israel on its own terms foiled the American search for peace and enabled Shamir to block with impunity all moves towards a settlement which did not satisfy every Israeli condition and exclude the Palestinians from negotiations and recognition. Shamir reaffirmed Begin's position at Camp David. The Likud declared that it would trade no land for peace, would continue to expedite Jewish settlement of the West Bank, would never give votes to Arabs in east Jerusalem and would attend no conference so long as the *intifada* lasted. In the next year Sharon increased the pressure for bold Zionist policies by resigning from the cabinet. The Likud–Labour coalition broke up and, after lengthy bargaining by both major parties with minor religious parties, Shamir was able to form a new government but one dependent on the fanatic fringe. The Labour Party was divided between adherents of Peres and of Rabin. Arafat, under similar pressure from colleagues, also took refuge in a regression to extreme positions. The United States tried to use Mubarak as a mediator but with no success.

Iraq's invasion of Kuwait deflected attention to more urgent conflicts. It was also one more setback for the always tenuous prospect of Arab unity. Arabs were no more united, or more likely to unite, than other kindred. But since the waning of Ottoman power, and more specifically since the creation of the Arab League in the 1940s, they had made a point of the search for unity and had been correspondingly downcast among themselves and mocked by others when it eluded them. The late 1970s had been a bad time by these standards. Egypt, the most prestigious Arab state, was made an outcast by Sadat's Camp David policies and was not even invited to attend the Arab conference at the end of 1980. Syria was cast as another deviant on account of its intervention in Lebanon, supported only by Libya and Algeria in the remote west and by South Yemen in the remote south. In the first Gulf War Saudi Arabia, carrying with it all the Gulf states, supported Iraq against Iran, whereas Syria supported Iran; Jordan took Iraq's side with unexpected directness. When the war ended King Hussein embarked on another attempt to refashion the politics of the Arab world. His aims, interrelated, were pacification in the Middle East and the preservation of his own kingdom. To the north and west the king faced enemies in Syria and Israel; to the south was the Saudi monarchy, hereditary enemy of the Hashemites; to the east was Iraq, waxing strong under a leader as ambitious as he was unpredictable, but a man for whom the king had feelings of friendship and misplaced trust; and further off was Egypt, which was readmitted to the Arab League in 1989. During his arduous but fruitless efforts to inaugurate peace talks between Palestinians and Israel, the king had become disenchanted with the United States and, if to a lesser degree, Britain and the more convinced that the Arabs themselves must take a concerted and purely Arab initiative. At his invitation, the presidents of Iraq and Egypt – and of the newly reunited Yemen at Saudi Arabia's back door – met in Amman early in 1990. But a few months later both his main guests torpedoed his plans and endangered his throne, Saddam Hussein by invading Kuwait and Mubarak by precipitately joining the forces being assembled by the United States in Saudi Arabia. The king denounced the Iraqi invasion and Iraq's taking of hostages, insisted on an Iraqi retreat and the restoration of Kuwait's independence, and supported UN sanctions; but he continued to import Iraqi oil out of necessity and advocated the continued supply of necessary food and medicines to Iraq. He also continued to champion an exclusively pan-Arab resolution of the crisis. His attitudes were popular in Jordan but nowhere else, and in attempting once more to play the role of honest broker he found himself snubbed by Bush and received by Thatcher with the barest courtesy. The Kuwait crisis demonstrated that he was the most well-intentioned but least effective statesman in the Middle East.

Israel's dilemma

The second Gulf War, together with the extinction of Russian influence in the Middle East, encouraged the United States to seek a comprehensive peace settlement. It sought to mollify Arabs by opposing the development of Israeli settlement in the occupied territories and by supporting the principle of land-for-peace, and it secured Israel's participation in a peace conference by a mixture of concessions (no independent

Palestinian state) and coercion (delaying a $10 billion guarantee for financing the settlement of Soviet Jews). The Likud government was divided on the issue of land-for-peace but united in refusing to admit a separate Palestinian delegation to peace talks and making only vacuous proposals for Palestinian autonomy. After much wrangling a conference opened in 1991 in Madrid, whence it was transferred to Washington, where disputes over seating arrangements reduced the talking to encounters in corridors. These talks were little more than a charade and the killing of the Hizbollah leader Sheikh Abbas Musavi by Israelis in Lebanon at the beginning of 1992 created fresh, if temporary, obstacles, but American hopes revived when, later in the year, the Israeli Labour Party won a general election (winning 44 seats in the Knesset to Likud's 32) and Rabin succeeded Shamir as prime minister.

Israel's main aims remained the same – to come to terms with Jordan and Syria and isolate and divide the Palestinians – but the tactics changed inasmuch as Rabin declared himself willing to discuss with Syria Israel's occupation of the Golan Heights. But this overture, which seemed designed to win a quick deal with Syria, failed when it turned out to mean a thinning out of Israeli forces but not their withdrawal or any cession of occupied territory. On Palestine Rabin proposed a five-year experiment during which a Palestinian local authority would have limited powers over (mostly) social services but little political authority or policing power. Discussions about Jerusalem were ruled out and the position of the PLO in Israeli eyes was left unresolved.

Neither Rabin nor Arafat was in a strong position. Neither had enough support to deliver a meaningful agreement, nor was it clear that either wished to. Arafat and the PLO were gravely devalued by their stance in the Gulf War on top of their persistent failure over years to secure a Palestinian state. Arafat's prestige had been highest in the 1970s when he succeeded in achieving a status approaching that of a head of state and in establishing formal links with the European Community (1974). But he was weakened five years later when the Camp David accords, which were applauded by the EC, gave the Palestinians nothing beyond vague phrases. He recovered some of his political stature when the EC reasserted at Venice in 1980 its support for Security Council Resolution 242 but he was a performer on a narrowing stage, diminished not only by more militant groups but also by the *intifada*, whose leaders within Israel appeared – to Israelis in particular – to constitute an alternative Palestinian leadership. Arafat in the early 1990s was a leader uncertain of his next move. He was, however, still the Palestinian leader of international consequence; and the Palestinians still outnumbered Israelis in the Middle East and accounted for nearly a fifth of the inhabitants of Israel.

Rabin's electoral victory (to which recent immigrants from Russia had made a decisive but not necessarily lasting contribution) had left him short of a majority in the Knesset and he was likely to lose it if he made any but the smallest concessions to the PLO. Since, in addition, he distrusted and disliked the PLO and its leaders, he hoped to find alternative interlocutors to Arafat: externally Jordan and even Syria, within Israel other Palestinians with whom he might negotiate a strictly limited kind of autonomy in a strictly limited area. But Palestinian leaders in Israel could not be persuaded to act independently of the broader Palestinian movement and the real opposition to the PLO was not the leaders of the *intifada* but the relentlessly militant Hamas. This extremist group of Sunni Muslims, unashamed of violence and bent on the extinction of Israel, came into prominence around 1990 and grew in strength with each display of lawlessness or brutality by Israel (for example, the expulsion in 1992 of over 400 indiscriminately arrested Palestinians from Gaza into the barren and freezing wastes of southern Lebanon in breach of international law). Rabin was forced gradually to the conclusion that his only choice was between talks with the PLO and an increasingly insecure status quo. He was also under American pressure to resume the negotiations which had foundered in Washington. Their resumption took a curious turn. Fresh talks began in Oslo, engineered by an unofficial Norwegian body on the initiative of the PLO and welcomed by a number of Israelis but without the knowledge of the United States or, initially, of Rabin. The outcome was a formal written agreement which was accepted by Rabin with some reluctance and blessed by a ceremony on the White House lawn in Washington (1993). Israel recognized the PLO as representative of the Palestinians and the PLO recognized Israel's right to exist and agreed to denounce violence. On this basis the Oslo plan extended over six years (1993–99) in three stages: first, an Israeli withdrawal from the Gaza strip and seven cities in the West Bank and the transfer of powers to the PLO; second, the transfer of intervening villages in the West Bank, elections within three months and free movement between the transferred territories; and ultimately discussions over the future of the 140 Jewish settlements in the territories and of Jerusalem. In spite of much imprecision, implementation of the first stage proceeded but the further stages were bedevilled by distrustful sparring between the two sides, by the hostility of Hamas seeking to discredit Arafat and destroy the PLO, by Rabin's unwillingness to move faster than he felt compelled to and by Israel's accelerated confiscation of lands in the occupied territories for further settlements. For Israel the cession of Gaza was good riddance of a destitute and violent area from which it drew no profit and some discredit, an area, moreover, whose transfer to the PLO would expose Arafat's shortcomings as a putative head of state. The cession of Jericho, on the other hand, and other cities on the West Bank, was unwelcome, since it gave great offence to many Israelis and, so far as it portended further territorial cession, raised questions of the security of the state as well as the future lives of those settled there. The West Bank was to be divided into areas under Palestinian control, areas of continuing occupation and areas of conflicting authority.

A second stage was concluded, albeit partially and more than a year behind schedule, when six cities and several smaller towns or villages were transferred to (limited) Palestinian administration – excluding, however, Hebron, the principal city in the south, overwhelmingly Palestinian but with a vociferous and armed Jewish minority and special links with the biblical patriarchs, and the scene in 1994 of the killing of

29 Muslims in a mosque under the eyes of Israeli police. A subsequent agreement, Oslo II, provided for the transfer of Hebron and other places over an 18-month period from the beginning of 1997. The resulting ambit of Palestinian authority was a patchwork, not an economic and barely a political entity, in which the cities were separated from one another, their supplies of water and other necessities were controlled by Israel, and the Israeli police and army retained rights to operate in the intervening spaces, which comprised two-thirds of the West Bank. The Palestinian police (30,000 strong) were denied the right to arrest Israelis and 100,000 Israeli settlers were menacingly marooned within a complex reminiscent of South Africa's Bantustans.

Rabin pursued this process without the optimism consistently expressed by his foreign minister, Peres. With more conviction Rabin sought peace with Jordan. Israel and Jordan had not engaged in hostilities for nearly half a century but Israeli strategists were perennially nervous about the possibility of attacks from Jordanians or by other Arabs using Jordanian territory. Rabin and Hussein shared an aversion to Arafat and just as Ben-Gurion had negotiated with Hussein's grandfather for Jordan to appropriate lands allotted to a Palestinian state, so Rabin sought Hussein's co-operation against Palestinian claims to Jerusalem by conceding to a religious body in Jordan rights of guardianship over Muslim holy places in Jerusalem. On this basis the two leaders issued (1994) a declaration ending the state of war between their countries. It was not popular in Jordan and its significance was somewhat diminished by Clinton's insistence on staging the publicity for it in Washington rather than in the Middle East.

But the key to Israel's quest for peace lay not in Jordan but in Syria. Jordan had no valid or plausible claim to any part of the old mandated territory of Palestine, whereas Syria had. The treaties made during and after the First World War carved up not only the Ottoman empire but also Syria, which under Ottoman rule was, although subjected, nevertheless intact and included the whole of Israel and Lebanon and parts of Jordan. Whereas Assad's first aim was to recover the Golan Heights, Syria's older, if vaguer, ambition was the reconstruction of Greater Syria. Assad, a politician as cautious as he was ruthless, a skilled practitioner of the arts of inactivity rare in the Middle East, knew – as too did Rabin – that Syria had alternatives to peace with Israel. It might co-operate with Iran or perhaps Pakistan or even the old enemy, Iraq, to create a second nuclear power in the Middle East which would eliminate Israel's monopoly and puncture its defence strategy. Israel's survival rested, as it had rested for half a century, on arms and American money. Its military expenditure exceeded $7 billion a year and it had fortified itself with a nuclear armoury. But American subventions could not safely be expected to continue at current levels and Israel's nuclear weaponry was causing Arab and other Muslim countries to follow it into a regional arms race and mutual bankruptcy. Yet Rabin's policy seemed no different from that of his predecessor Shamir, who avowed his aim to spin out peace talks with the Palestinians for ten years, and Rabin faced only slowly the case for making peace with Syria by surrendering the Golan Heights. His tortured and hesitant search for a way to combine security and peace ended in 1995 when he was shot dead by a young Israeli (by origin a Yemeni Jew) who had no doubt that his victim's probings were misguided and sinful.

Peres, once more prime minister, resolved to fortify a precarious position by an early election. His gamble failed. He had come to the conclusion that Israel could not for-ever stifle Palestinian aspirations or hostilities by force alone but he was unable to per-suade the electorate that he had an effective alternative. Hamas, as determined as Israeli extremists to wreck the Oslo agreements, staged a series of murderous attacks which killed hundreds of civilians in Jerusalem and Tel Aviv. Peres, anxious to assert his for-titude, ordered retaliation with ground and air strikes against Arabs in southern Lebanon in which 200 civilians were killed, including women and children in an ambulance and in defiance of protests of UN units on the spot which asserted that the targets were not what the Israelis said they were. This incident had uncomfortable repercussions for the United States when, failing to get the UN's report on the events suppressed, it blocked the condemnation of Israel in the Security Council and hard-ened its resolve to prevent the re-election as UN secretary-general of Boutros-Ghali (who was proving too independent-minded). Peres none the less lost the election, albeit by the tiniest margin.

The new prime minister Binyamin Netanyahu had as his prime aim the demolition of the Oslo agreements which had been formally concluded before the election. The United States backed these agreements but it did so not on account of what they con-tained but because they offered, however tenuously, a prospect of stability in the area. When Netanyahu's rejection of them extinguished this prospect the United States was obliged to seek an alternative way to stability which amounted in practice to discover-ing and accepting Netanyahu's irreducible terms for a new Israeli–Palestinian settle-ment. The United States ceased to refer to the Oslo agreements, preferring to talk of a 'peace process'. Netanyahu's concessions were minimal: an autonomous Palestinian entity much smaller than that envisaged by Oslo, permanently barred from enlarge-ment, economically dependent on Israel and formally deprived of the normal attri-butes of sovereignty. He was, it later transpired, prepared to withdraw from Lebanon, even though his senior military chiefs were still talking of occupying part of it for 1,000 years. (Israel began to withdraw in 1998.) On the Golan Heights he appeared intransigent.

Netanyahu had been directly elected to his office by popular vote, the first prime minister of Israel to enjoy this enhanced authority under a constitutional amendment of 1992. He was, however, at odds with leading members of his party, the Likud. He adopted a combative stance by affirming Israel's determination to maintain and multiply settlements in occupied territories, by provoking Hamas and other militants to violence in order to lay on them the blame for the abrogation of Oslo, and by mak-ing contemptuous offers to the PLO and Arafat who, without effective weapons or allies and without the trust of many of his own colleagues, had a threadbare bargain-ing position. The principal effect of these offers was to transfer 7 per cent of the West

Bank under joint control to the PLO and 2 per cent of the territory under Israeli control to joint control, thus giving the PLO over 10 per cent instead of 3 per cent of the total area in the hope of postponing indefinitely any reduction in Israel's control over the remaining 90 per cent. He was also particularly concerned to annul the Oslo provisions about east Jerusalem which, since its capture in 1967, had been incorporated into the state of Israel as conquered, not occupied territory; its 160,000 inhabitants were swamped by building new housing for Jews only, public and private land in and around the city was confiscated, Palestinians were evicted and prevented from coming back to work or pray in the city without special permits, which the new government ceased to issue. Most provokingly, Netanyahu ordered the construction on Har Homa between Jerusalem and Bethlehem of 6,500 homes for 32,000 Jewish settlers – a political act which was also a strategic manoeuvre which completed the encirclement of Jerusalem by Israeli strongholds. In the contest over Hebron he aborted Oslo II by insisting that the protection of its 400 Jewish inhabitants among 20,000 Palestinians required rights of access for Israeli armed forces.

Netanyahu's abrasiveness was a calculated gamble on American acquiescence which was virtually assured of success in the short term but held dangers in the long run. He broke a fundamental strand in Israel's foreign policy. Whereas Ben-Gurion had felt obliged in the last resort to yield to pressure from Washington and Rabin had followed that example at Camp David and over the Oslo agreements, Netanyahu persisted in independent and aggressive courses in the face of American disapproval. He calculated that the disapproval would not be translated into significant action but he also made patent the American dilemma between attachment to Israel and concern for stability in the Middle East. This dilemma, combined with Clinton's need for foreign successes to distract domestic attention from scandals in the White House, led the president to try to force the pace. In 1998 he summoned Netanyahu and Arafat to the United States and, after strenuous personal endeavours, forced them to sign an agreement – the Wye River Memorandum – which neither of them wanted or was likely to implement. Israel undertook to withdraw from a small amount of occupied territory in return for Palestinian promises of greater diligence in preventing attacks on Israelis. The basic questions of a Palestinian state, its size and borders, and Jerusalem were set aside. The immediate result was to weaken Netanyahu in Israel and Arafat among Palestinians. Netanyahu repeatedly delayed submission of the agreement to his cabinet, which ultimately approved it by only a thin majority and after unilaterally altering its terms. There was one novelty. The new agreement introduced the CIA into the security problem. Arafat agreed that his measures to prevent Palestinian attacks on Israel and Israelis should be monitored by the CIA, which would also report on Israel's complaints about Palestinian laxity in arresting assailants. This arrangement placed the United States in a more central and exposed position than ever before and was profoundly unpalatable among both Palestinians and Israelis. All Palestinian groups except Arafat's Fatah denounced the Wye agreement. Further attempts by Clinton in person, who flew to the

Middle East in the week when his impeachment became inescapable, failed to rescue the so-called peace process. Since Clinton was the first president of the United States to set foot on Palestinian territory or to address the Palestinian National Council, Arafat was in obliging mood but Netanyahu, whose hold on his office was no less precarious than Clinton's, was characteristically belligerent. These were three weak men temporarily in charge of a singularly portentous issue.

The weakest of the three was Netanyahu. He denounced the Wye agreement a few weeks after signing it. Nevertheless, he was censured by the Knesset, where left and right joined to vote against him. Like all his predecessors, he was concerned first and foremost with the survival of the state of Israel which, as it celebrated its fiftieth birthday, was as insecure as it ever had been. His deep hostility to the Oslo agreements and their derivatives overrode Israel's dependence on American goodwill (for its military hardware, its standard of living and its evasion of near-total isolation in the world). It pleased right-wing nationalists and religious extremists but only at the cost of making such forces, Muslim as well as Judaic, more vociferous and influential. By his policies and his personality Netanyahu made too many enemies and at elections he and the Likud were decisively beaten. A new Labour leader, ex-general Ehud Barak, won the prime-ministerial election by a surprisingly wide margin. Both major parties – Labour as well as Likud – lost seats in the elections for the Knesset, where the number of parties rose from 10 to 15. Seven of them were accommodated in Barak's cabinet (but not Likud). Third in strength in the Knesset was Shas, the religious party more concerned with orthodoxy in Israel than the expansionist or pro-settler activism whose champions lost votes. Barak promised a speedy withdrawal from Lebanon, where Israel's position had become untenable with the disintegration of the South Lebanese Army and the growth of Hizbollah's power. But withdrawal was risky and had wider implications. It would enable Hizbollah to advance to Israel's borders and bombard Israeli towns and settlements within Israel unless Syria could be persuaded to interdict such operations. Barak agreed to resume talks with Syria broken off by Netanyahu. Syria demanded the immediate and entire restitution of the Golan Heights, home to 17,000 Israelis (some of whom had been there for more than 30 years) and a significant source of Israeli revenues. In return Barak hoped to secure from Syria peace on Israel's borders with Lebanon as well as Syria. With many in Israel Barak believed that peace in these areas was a vital Israeli interest and that Israel's capacity to achieve it on acceptable terms was in decline. For the Palestinians Barak had little to offer. He might wish to freeze Israeli settlements in the West Bank but was not prepared to evict the 400,000 settlers; the rate of construction of new homes for Jews in the occupied territories rose under his government. He promised to honour and implement the Wye agreement but wished to negotiate modifications to it. While appearing to accept the inevitability of a Palestinian state he was determined that it should be disjointed, less than sovereign in practice and dominated by Israeli forces free to operate over more than half of the West Bank. Negotiations with Arafat over the details of a modified Wye agreement left the Palestinians in control of the same extent – 40 per cent – of the West Bank. Barak made minor concessions on a right of passage between the West Bank and Gaza, a street in Hebron and aid for the creation of a port in Gaza but the main issues were postponed: the acceptance and date of a Palestinian state, the right of Palestinians to return to it, the Israeli settlements and Jerusalem. By the end of the year Barak was in danger of losing his pivotal coalition ally – Shas – and his majority in the Knesset, mainly on account of his efforts to make peace with Syria. The 1990s were a decade of failure and death. The will to succeed by compromise was weaker than the fear on both sides that no settlement in sight could be achieved without dangerous concessions. Violence persisted: Palestinians and Israelis were dying in thousands and in the proportion of 3:1. Israel remained in occupation of 60 per cent of the West Bank and 30 per cent of Gaza.

In 2001 the veteran hardline Ariel Sharon became prime minister. Implacably opposed to negotiations with the Palestinians he had nevertheless adopted a policy of conceding to a Palestinian authority an area of occupied territory on the West Bank. This territory was to be delineated by him and to be defined on the ground by a huge wall 400 miles long. Not all Israeli settlements would be removed; some were to be enlarged and protected by detachments of the Israeli army, the settlers themselves were being surreptitiously armed, and the new Palestinian territory would be not only surrounded but penetrated by roads reserved for the Israeli army. Four years later Sharon suffered a stroke which left him hopelessly incapacitated. His successor Ehud Olmert was an ex-hardliner who, like Sharon and many others, had come to accept, in principle, the necessity for a Palestinian state but, unlike Sharon, was prepared to discuss with (suitable) Palestinians how this might be achieved. He was encouraged by the change in the Palestinian leadership from the hated Arafat to the more pliant Mahmoud Abbas but he was also weakened when the democratic process, constantly appealed to by Bush, severed Gaza from the West Bank and installed in the former – which contained 40 per cent of the displaced Palestinians – a Hamas government with no faith in anything short of the defeat and destruction of Israel. Olmert was also weakened by a series of charges of financial impropriety and by an ill-conceived and unsuccessful Israeli invasion of Lebanon which he had promoted and which deprived him of the charismatic Sharon's ability to manipulate the Knesset, still a markedly cynical opponent – but necessary co-signatory – of any deal with the Palestinians.

Ignoring these obstacles Bush, hoping to find in this corner of the Middle East some antidote to the disaster in Iraq, visited Israel for the first time in his presidency and convoked a conference in Annapolis in the United States (2007) in which he declared his conviction that Olmert and Abbas would reach a solution by the end of 2008 and then departed leaving the two sides to issue a similarly vague declaration. Rocket attacks on Israel from Gaza underlined the hollowness of talks which excluded Hamas while the increasingly desperate plight of the Gazans added to the impact of anti-Israeli propaganda around the world and forced Egypt to allow Gazan refugees to flood into Egypt.

In 1999 King Hussein died after a reign of 47 years during which the Jordanian state and its Hashemite dynasty became accepted parts of the political map of the Middle East. Without Hussein neither was secure. In the last weeks of his life the king switched the succession from his brother Hassan, Crown Prince for most of Hussein's reign, to his son Abdullah, partly as a result of palace intrigues. The new king could count on the loyalty of his armed forces but lacked the prestige and experience which enabled his father to confront and in some measure control a restless press and the stirrings of democratic opposition to his autocracy. Its Arab neighbours, Syria and Iraq, were no better than fair-weather friends; its relations with the United States were governed by its attitudes to Israel; and its economy was at best stagnant, with unemployment above 20 per cent of the workforce and budget deficits and foreign debts unmanageable without aid from the IMF and World Bank, whose conditions were unpopular and divisive.

CHAPTER 14

Iran and Gulf Wars

Iran is in traditional parlance a part of the Middle East but it is emphatically not part of the Arab world. It remembers the Arab conquest of the seventh century more resentfully than the Mongol which is more recent by 600 years. It is the stronghold of Shia Islam, the tense and high-pitched deviant from Sunni orthodoxy: unique because the Shia, although a majority in Bahrain, Iraq and perhaps Oman too, are everywhere except in Iran subject to a Sunni dynasty or ruling class. Iran is rich in oil but, unlike the Arab world, not only in oil. Its dominant Iranians rule over a heterogeneous variety of races and religions. It has never since Alexander the Great been subject to western imperialism, although it has been obliged on occasions to humble itself before them, particularly the British and Russians. The world's thirst for oil has given it the means to turn itself into an industrial and military power without equal in its surrounding region.

Iran vaunts its descent from one of the oldest empires in the world. Founded by the Persian King Cyrus in the sixth century BC out of a conglomeration of Asian peoples it briefly embraced Egypt and was only prevented from expanding from Asia Minor into Europe by the extraordinary victory of a coalition of Greek states at Salamis in 480 BC. It recovered from Alexander's counterattack to become the main thorn in the flesh of the Roman and Byzantine empires. In the seventh century it was converted to Islam when the Arab conquests spread from the Arabian peninsular into Africa, Asia and Europe but adopted the Shi'ite branch of the new faith – a personal rather than a doctrinal variant – and therewith an obsessive distrust of its neighbours. (The Shi'a comprise only about 10 per cent of the Dar ul-Islam but within Iran about 90 per cent of the population.) Successive dynasties have cherished imperial memories and at times longings and in the twentieth century Iran was a state striving to modernize in pursuit of power, particularly after the discovery of oil early in the twentieth century, but psychologically overweighted by its mighty military past. Geography and race made it a loner among states and religion reinforced its separateness. Its awareness of its past (glory) and present (oil) encouraged it to look to nuclear power to enhance its fortunes and its belief that it could go it alone, if not in the world then at least in the Middle East. To these attitudes was added an uncompromising hostility to the existence of Israel.

During the Second World War both Great Britain and the Soviet Union occupied Iran on the plea of strategic necessity (the Iranians resisting for three days), and enforced the abdication of the founder of Iran's new dynasty Reza Shah Pahlavi, who was exiled to Mauritius and died in South Africa in 1944. His son and successor Muhammad Reza Pahlavi had neither time nor opportunity to make a mark among his people by the time the war and the occupation ended. The treaty of 1942, which sanctioned foreign occupation, provided for the withdrawal of the British and the Russians six months after the end of hostilities. The Russians made an attempt to retain influence in the province of Azerbaijan, comparatively rich, traditionally hostile to the central government and situated on the borders of the USSR. They also lent support to Kurdish separatism and may have entertained hopes of establishing a Russian sphere of influence stretching southwards from the Kurdish republic of Mahabad through other Kurdish territories to the Persian Gulf. They were assisted by the Tudeh Party, an amalgam of Marxist communists with an older liberal tradition which had infused the Constitutional Movement earlier in the century.

British troops left Iran punctually in 1946 but Russian troops had to be manoeuvred out by the Iranian government. The astute elder statesman Qavam es-Sultaneh, who became prime minister in January 1946, visited Moscow in February on the heels of an Iranian complaint to the newly established Security Council and contrived to persuade Stalin that Russian aims in Iran could better be attained through good relations with the Iranian government than by the continued presence of Russian troops in north-western Iran. The Russians, who were as keen on an oil agreement with the central government as on fostering separatist movements against it, withdrew their troops only a few weeks late. Qavam entered into discussions about an oil agreement but evaded any conclusive step on the plea that, constitutionally, the ultimate decision lay with the parliament which was about to be elected; he also delayed the elections. Qavam simultaneously played a double game with the Tudeh Party. Having taken some of its members into his cabinet in order to mollify the Russians, he then welcomed (to put it mildly) a revolt by powerful southern tribes which demanded the dismissal of Tudeh ministers and other Tudeh members in prominent positions. The new Majlis (the lower house of the Iranian parliament) duly censured Qavam for engaging in discussion with the Russians for an oil agreement and declared it null and void. In spite of these oblique achievements Qavam was defeated and resigned at the end of the year. Having outwitted the Russians and seen the British depart, he was embarking on a policy of co-operation with the United States, whence he hoped to get financial aid and diplomatic support in Iran's traditional search for means of keeping both the Russians and the British at arm's length.

Oil and nationalism

Qavam's successors were, nevertheless, to be sharply engaged with the British in a quarrel in which the United States, after some hesitation, gave Britain firm support. Anglo-Iranian relations were soured by the existence of the Anglo-Iranian Oil Company, which had a monopoly of Iran's proven oilfields and in which the British government itself held a substantial number of shares. This unusual connection gave the company a political tinge and involved the British government in commercial affairs, two developments which were, in Iranian eyes, neither natural nor welcome consequences of the grant of a concession to a private individual early in the century. Iranian discontent was increased by the suspicion that the company sold oil to the British navy on unduly favourable terms, by its secretiveness about the extent of these sales and about its accounts generally, by its failure to publicize in the rest of Iran the good wages, working conditions and other benefits which it provided for its labour force. On the other hand the company's shortcomings were not all its own fault: its failure to advertise its own virtues was due to the fact that, since it was practically unique in complying with the labour laws, it could not claim credit where credit was due without casting aspersions on other employers.

Foreign concessions in mining, banking, railways, the telegraph, tobacco, etc. had excited hostility from the middle of the nineteenth century. The concession inherited by the Anglo-Iranian Oil Company had been granted in 1901 to W. K. D'Arcy and acquired by the company before the First World War. The Iranian government had bargained to receive a percentage of the company's net profits, but this bargain turned out badly for Iran since the Iranian share was rendered dependent on the level of taxation in Britain. It was further affected by the slump between the wars and in 1932 Iran purported to cancel the concession. As a result of negotiations between Reza Shah and the company a new agreement, duly ratified by the Iranian parliament, gave the company a new concession running for 60 years from 1933 (instead of 60 years from 1901) over a substantially diminished area, and gave Iran royalties to be calculated on the quantity of oil extracted. By 1950 this output was 32.5 million metric tons, three times the amount produced in 1938; Iran was the largest producer in the Middle East and had at Abadan the largest refinery in the world.

The revenues from the oil were much needed. After the Second World War Iran embarked on economic expansion and a plan adopted by the Majlis in 1947 envisaged the expenditure of $651 million, of which $242 million were to come from oil. But oil revenues in 1947 and 1948 were a disappointment in spite of huge increases in the company's profits and the company, sensing trouble, concluded a supplemental agreement under which the royalty rate was raised by 50 per cent and the company agreed to pay £5.1 million at once out of its reserves and to make further payments out of reserves annually instead of waiting until 1993, as the 1933 agreement provided. This agreement was favourable to Iran but it was also complicated to the point of incomprehensibility and was unacceptable to a group of nationalists who wanted to terminate the concession entirely and take the management and profits of the oil industry into purely Iranian hands. General Ali Razmara, who became prime minister in 1950, refrained for a while from pressing the supplemental agreement on the Majlis. When he recommended its adoption – largely on the grounds that Iran was short of qualified technicians – the Majlis special oil committee demanded the nationalization of the oilfields and refinery, and the prime minister withdrew the agreement. The company, unexpectedly made aware of terms being offered by the Arab American Oil Company (Aramco) to the Saudi Arabian government – terms which were more favourable (in good years) and above all easier to understand – prepared to reopen discussions and simplify the supplemental agreement. Razmara produced a series of reports by experts who opposed nationalization but he was assassinated in 1951 by a fanatic nationalist belonging to the semi-religious Fidayani-Islam. On the next day the Majlis approved the oil committee's proposals and a few weeks later it nationalized the oil industry.

General Razmara was succeeded by Husain Ala, a friend and nominee of the shah, who wanted to avoid appointing the chairman of the oil committee Dr Muhammad Musaddiq, in which attempt the shah failed. Dr Musaddiq began at the end of 1951 a spell of power which lasted tumultuously until August 1953. Musaddiq was a rich and aristocratic hypochondriac who appealed to xenophobic chauvinists, religious fanatics, communist and non-communist radicals, the old landowning aristocracy to which he belonged, and all those who distrusted the shah's attempt to resurrect the authority of the dynasty which had been abased by his father's abdication and the foreign occupation during the war. His political stock-in-trade was a nationalism which, though it may have been intended as a screen, became the substance of his political actions. If Musaddiq intended to combine the nationalization of the oil industry with the continued employment of foreign technicians and continuing foreign finance, he was soon defeated by his own extreme professions and supporters. Musaddiq became almost a figure of fun to the world at large, certainly to the western world, but in his own country he roused genuine popularity (quite apart from the bought support of the capital's mobs) and even his political opponents were to acknowledge his success in reducing corruption in public affairs. He failed, however, to retain control over the course of the oil dispute or to retain his own confidence in himself, he became the prisoner of his own rash attitudes, and he underrated the effectiveness of the economic sanctions which the British government was able to deploy against him.

The oil nationalization law expropriated the British company and created a new Iranian company to take its place. Throughout the ensuing controversies Dr Musaddiq insisted on British recognition of the validity of the nationalization decree as a prerequisite for any negotiations on compensation for the British company. The British, on the other hand, maintained that the decree was illegal and inoperative, that the company's title remained intact, and that the concession agreement of 1933 could not properly be revoked by unilateral act of one party to it even if that party was a sovereign state. Consequently, Britain claimed not only compensation for the loss of the benefits secured to the company by the concession agreement but also a further sum representing damages for a wrongful breach of contract.

The controversy involved not only the British company but also the British government, which was responsible for the safety of British citizens (who might be endangered by nationalist frenzy) and wished to safeguard its own financial stake in the

British company; it was also concerned to stand firm in defence of British rights for fear that weakness in one part of the Middle East might provoke attacks on British interests elsewhere. During 1951 various attempts were made to negotiate with Dr Musaddiq – by the British company, by a special emissary of President Truman and by a British delegation led by a cabinet minister. The American administration chose the British side after some hesitation. Its sympathy for the British case was tempered by its desire to attract Iran into the western camp but Musaddiq's histrionics alienated Americans.

The dispute was not in the last resort ruled by the legal rights and wrongs but by the British government's unwillingness to use force (except to protect British citizens); by the Iranian company's inability to sell Iranian oil in face of obstacles interposed by the British company and the lack of solidarity among producers; and by the economic collapse of Musaddiq's regime which, deprived of its revenue from the British company, was unable to find alternative sources of cash. Having failed to raise loans from the United States or the World Bank, Musaddiq called in the renowned Dr Hjalmar Schacht, who judged him, after a few days' acquaintance, to be one of the wisest men of the age but was unable to help him. Meanwhile, some of Musaddiq's allies were wavering. He was reappointed prime minister in July 1952 after a routine resignation upon the convening of a new Majlis, but the members showed some reluctance to grant him the full powers which he asked for. When the shah refused to give him the war ministry he resigned. But Qavam, who succeeded him, was only able to stay in office for four days and then had to take flight; the mob demonstrated in Musaddiq's favour, the Majlis voted him full powers, and the throne itself seemed to be in danger. Only the army had the capacity to unseat him, and a year later it did.

Musaddiq's triumph had exposed his political dependence on the mob without lessening his financial dependence on the British, which in turn was conditioned by his dependence on the extreme nationalist mullah Kashani, who had become president of the Majlis and would countenance no approach to the British. By the end of 1952 Musaddiq and Kashani had fallen out. In the next year Musaddiq triumphed over Kashani and dismissed the Majlis but failed to prevail over the shah. In August the shah dismissed Musaddiq and appointed General Fazullah Zahedi in his place. Three days later the shah and the general were both in flight, but whereas the shah fled to Rome, the general withdrew only a little distance and within a week of his original appointment he returned to put an end to the Musaddiq regime with not inconsiderable help from the CIA and the British secret service. The shah returned too. The helping hand of the United States was barely concealed and was not forgotten when the shah was once more forced into flight a quarter of a century later.

Peace was soon made in the oil dispute. New agreements were worked out on the basis, ironically, of recognizing the validity of the Iranian nationalization decree. The Iranian oil company remained in being and in possession of the oil. A consortium of eight foreign companies – British, American and French – was created. The British company accepted, not without demur, a 40 per cent share in this consortium and received from its seven associates £214 million for the remaining 60 per cent, which they bought between them. The British company was also to receive £25 million, spread over the years 1957–66, from the Iranian government in compensation for its losses since nationalization. The consortium was given effective control over the Abadan refinery and the principal oilfields for 25 years, with a series of options of renewal, and undertook to pay the Iranian government 50 per cent of profits. Thus nationalist doctrine was satisfied, the consumers were assured of their requirements and the producers of their revenues. Full diplomatic relations between Iran and Britain were restored in 1954. Musaddiq spent the next two years in jail.

The shah and the ayatollah

The fall of Musaddiq was a victory for the shah. Musaddiq's left-wing supporters were persecuted with a thorough ferocity and the shah gradually asserted the paramountcy of the throne, first through military rule which lasted until 1957 and then through a series of prime ministers who were either submissive or turned out. The death of the shah's only brother in 1954 jeopardized the dynasty and obliged the heirless shah to divorce his second wife and marry a third, who bore him a son a year later. Thus fortified, the shah began to implement a policy of land distribution and reform which proved so unpopular with the landowning classes and the Majlis (in which they were well represented) that the shah dispensed with parliament for the two years 1961–63. In 1963 he felt strong enough to hold a plebiscite, which confirmed his personal ascendancy and the decline of the power of the provincial notables. The worlds of the urban politician, the tribal chiefs and the educated young remained for diverse reasons disgruntled, but oil revenues increased and Iran's gross national product began to register annual increases of the order of 7 per cent.

In 1952 Iran became the first recipient of American Point Four aid (Truman's contribution to international co-operation announced in his inaugural address in 1949 and based on his appreciation of the role of European capital and technology in the development of the United States). In 1955 the shah decided to join Cento (as the Baghdad Pact had become) and in 1959 he paid a state visit to London and received President Eisenhower in Teheran. After a short period of frigidity, Russo-Iranian relations improved and in 1963 President Brezhnev too was officially received in the Iranian capital, a reminder that the traditional suspiciousness between the two countries had to take account of the fact that Iran had a long undefended frontier with the USSR and looked to northern trade routes for the export of the produce of its northern provinces. The shah undertook not to permit the installation of nuclear missiles in Iran and, without abandoning Cento or joining the unaligned group, he moved towards a more independent position in world politics. By 1969–70 he was able to play a decisive role in shaping the political future of the Persian Gulf after the departure of the British and, relishing the role of a crowned entrepreneur, to use mineral wealth and a bounding economy to turn Iran into a considerable military and industrial power.

The shah's bent was growth at all costs and the key was oil, although oil was not the country's only resource. It was rich too in natural gas, other minerals and agriculture and was establishing industry as fast as 50 per cent illiteracy and a wretched educational system would allow. When in 1973 war in the Middle East gave the oil producers the excuse to push up prices the shah insisted on maximum increases, against the wishes of more cautious Arabs who hesitated to damage western countries which were their best customers. In two years the Iranian government's revenue per barrel was multiplied by ten and its total annual oil revenues rose from $2.3 billion to $18.2 billion. In the year after the oil price rise of 1973 GNP rose by 42.5 per cent. Spending rose too, particularly defence spending, which also multiplied by ten in the half decade and passed the $10 million mark; by 1975 Iran was spending on defence a larger proportion of GNP than any country in the world except Israel. The results of this explosion were not all happy: 1975 saw a deficit in the balance of payments of nearly $1 billion. Waste and corruption flourished commensurately; inflation took hold. Those hurt by inflation and least able to make a profession of corruption had to be compensated and wages were nearly doubled in 1974–75 with the usual cyclic nightmare: demand for goods, inadequate supply, rising prices and further wage demands. The shah, who had dealt roughly with the landed aristocracy in the early 1960s, showed signs of imperial displeasure with the new, ostentatious and corrupt rich, and toyed with schemes for handing over half the ownership and profits of industry to the workers. Yet wages remained derisory and Teheran became a shanty town of 5 million for whom housing was shamefully inadequate. His regime's weaknesses were the uncertainty surrounding an autocracy with an infant heir, the opposition of the conservative mullahs, the opposition of radical students and other protesters, which even one of the world's most ferocious secret police apparatuses could not mute, and his own refusal to listen to others. He was obsessively concerned with left-wing conspiracies but blind to the threat from clerical radicalism and he became dangerously ignorant of the state of his own country, where the savagery of his police, SAVAK (trained by Americans and Israelis), and blatant inequality alongside ill-gotten wealth ensured that when the tocsin sounded thousands of civilians rushed unarmed into the streets, prepared to face his fearsome military machine. Between his return in 1953 and his second flight in 1979 the shah worked a revolution in Iran, using the country's wealth to create prosperity and strength; but the headlong pace and fearful inhumanity of this revolution united conservatives, radicals and liberals against it and so generated a counter-revolution. When in January 1979 the shah asked Dr Shahpur Bakhtiar to assume the premiership, Bakhtiar consented only upon condition that the shah leave the country.

The beneficiary of these events was Ayatollah Ruhollah Khomeini. Khomeini was an extraordinary figure: a redoubtable scholar, personality and politician. He excited enmity and near-idolatry. Although an eminent Shi'ite cleric, he did not hesitate to scorn his fellow theologians and he was rootedly hostile to the ruling dynasty and its material values. He became a leader of those – particularly numerous among the younger generations – who opposed secular government and the modernization of Iran in the American mould, and after harshly suppressed riots in the early 1960s he had fled in 1964 to Turkey and thence to Iraq and finally to France, whence he continued to animate opposition to the shah – with a personal bitterness after the shah refused to allow him to return to Iran for the funeral of one of his sons. When, a month after enforcing the flight of the shah, Bakhtiar too fled, Khomeini, now an ageing and obdurate moralist and nationalist, entered upon an autocratic rule which lasted unchallenged until his death ten years later.

Khomeini proclaimed an Islamic republic and instituted a regime even more intolerant than the shah's, although possibly less murderous. He appointed as prime minister Mehdi Bazargan, a liberal Muslim intellectual with a scientific education who had been imprisoned by the shah, but there was in fact no central government. Bazargan was harassed from left and right, by Kurdish and Arab minorities, and by conflicting pronouncements from the ayatollah himself, who retired to the holy city of Qum, dominated the scene by sporadic utterance and allowed a kind of religious hooliganism to prevail. Local Islamic committees spent their time rounding up and executing those whom the hazards of denunciation exposed to their indiscriminate wrath. The shah's authority and partisans had evaporated with his flight, which turned him into a figure of suspicion. Restored to his throne in 1953 by the Americans and thereafter showered with American aid, he was widely regarded as an American creature and when, via Egypt and Mexico, he reached the United States in search of the best medical treatment for the cancer which would soon kill him, many in Iran feared that his arrival in New York augured another American attempt to put him back on his throne.

In November 1979 radicals in Teheran invaded the American embassy and took 53 of its inmates hostage. This coup was partly directed against Bazargan, who finally succumbed, but more overtly against the United States. It incidentally, but portentously, alarmed the Russians, who feared retaliatory American action in Iran at a time when their own hold over their puppets in neighbouring Afghanistan was becoming insecure (see Chapter 19) and it was useful to Khomeini in rallying the splintered fragments of Iranian society behind himself. At every turn over the next 12 months the ayatollah supported the hostages' captors, whose urge to lay hands on the shah and humble the United States overrode the milder counsels of those – Bazargan and, after him, Abolhassan Bani-Sadr, appointed president in January 1980 – who wished to restore normal relations with Washington, if only to unfreeze Iranian assets in American banks and get spare parts for weapons. Bani-Sadr was forced into flight by a fresh wave of terror in 1981, of which his successor was an early victim, one of many.

Imperial powers have been wont to accept with a certain equanimity the disasters which befall their servants in foreign lands. But not so the more sensitive American public. There was no evidence that the hostages were ill-treated but the mere fact of their detention was regarded as a slur and disgrace not to be borne. Their fate became an obsession and the situation was further inflamed by the Russian invasion of Afghanistan a few weeks later. On the one hand the United States had an interest in preserving Khomeini's rule because he seemed to be the one man who could prevent Iran from falling to pieces; civil war in this area was not only to be feared on general grounds but also because it might provide the USSR with a legitimate excuse to intervene under its treaty with Iran of 1921. On the other hand the United States saw politicians like Bani-Sadr as its natural allies and wished to strengthen them against the coalition of extremes represented by the ayatollah and the radicals. Washington calculated that it would reinforce the moderates by imposing severe sanctions, for which, however, Washington needed European and Japanese collaboration. But this strategy was vitiated by a latent contradiction. Bani-Sadr was trying to negotiate goods-for-oil agreements with Europe and Japan, so that American attempts to get these countries to impose sanctions on Iran hampered Bani-Sadr, whom the Americans were hoping to bolster.

For their part, Washington's allies had little faith in sanctions but were disposed to fall into line, partly in order to show solidarity with Washington against a blatant breach of diplomatic practice and partly to prevent Washington from resorting to force to free the hostages. Force, they reckoned, would not succeed and it might lead to the closing of the Gulf and the loss of shipments of oil more important than Iran's. Iran responded to this threat of sanctions by making economic agreements with the USSR, East Germany, Czechoslovakia and Bulgaria. These agreements were economically marginal but, for the west, politically disturbing.

Early in January 1980 President Carter told the US Congress that the use of force to rescue the hostages would almost certainly fail and might lead to their deaths. In April he made the attempt. It was a gamble and it failed. Eight Americans were killed and six helicopters and one troop carrier lost. The hostages were not killed but they were dispersed. American prestige suffered. The allies, in the course of preparing sanctions which were to be an alternative to force, were vexed at not being told that force was after all to be used. Moscow was pleased that the world should have another military incursion to talk about besides Afghanistan. Muslim countries felt obliged to rally round Khomeini, whose personal power was strengthened by this episode, and again at the end of the year, when Iran was attacked by Iraq (see the next section).

Khomeini died in 1989. He had established a theocratic state and become the symbol of active opposition to the seamier side of western civilization but he had also imposed on his country a tyranny as repulsive as the shah's and a war which entailed vast slaughter and economic catastrophe: inflation at 30–40 per cent, plummeting production, negative investment at home and abroad, loss of crucial oil revenues. Like the first Safavid shahs 500 years earlier, the Pahlavi shahs had tried to recreate an Iranian empire on the basis of Shi'ism and modernization, only to be unseated by Khomeini, who pronounced the two incompatible. Nevertheless, Iran, with or without Khomeini – and possibly stronger without – remained the spearhead of a cultural revolution which, with echoes in Arab lands, challenged the western culture whose leadership had passed to the United States but which had been attacking the Islamic Middle East since Europeans checked the Ottoman Turks in the seventeenth century at Vienna.

Khomeini's death fell between the end of Iran's war with Iraq and the international assault on Iraq in 1991. From the latter Iran emerged the greatest winner since the war eliminated Iraq for the time being from the politics of the Gulf, forced Saudi Arabia into a controversial role and inordinate expenditure and so helped Khomeini's successors to repair the damage suffered by Iran in the earlier war. The new president Ali Akbar Rafsanjani consolidated his relations with the military and won a comfortable victory in elections for the Majlis in 1992. In that year he felt strong enough to rekindle conflict over the island of Abu Musa in the Straits of Hormuz by requiring the Arab Emirates except Sharjah to present special permits before entering the island. (Iran and Sharjah were joint sovereigns under an agreement made before the creation of the Union of Arab Emirates in 1971.) He mollified western governments by helping in the release of hostages in Lebanon and manoeuvred to attract western bankers and industrialists scrambling for a share in new enterprises and contracts. Yet Iran remained a regional power unable to exercise its regional power to the full. After Khomeini's death it was an uneasy diarchy. Khomeini was not replaced either formally or in popular parlance. His successor as leader, Ayatollah Ali Khamenei, lacked Khomeini's personal magic, his religious credentials and his reputation for learning; he was neither referred to as the Imam nor accorded the supreme rank of *marja* until after his promotion to ayatollah. He was the keeper of the true Islamic flame in succession to Khomeini, the senior figure in a land where the spiritual crown at least vied with the constitutional and, unlike the president, the occupant of an office with no fixed term; but he owed his position to Khomeini's dying preference over his rival Ayatollah Hossein Ali Montazeri, and maintained his influence with the discreet support of Rafsanjani. The outside world interpreted this diarchy as a sharp ideological antithesis between extremists and moderates, dogmatists and pragmatists, but the reality was less clear-cut and less confrontational. Power in Iran, like power in most states, was shared. Khamenei and Rafsanjani both belonged to the same broad constituency but whereas the leader was head of the clerical establishment, the president was charged by virtue of his office with the tasks of repairing the economy and Iran's capacity to play the role of a major regional power.

The economy continued at first to wilt: foreign debts accumulating and unserviceable, the currency losing value faster than almost anywhere in the world, industry more than half-closed, foreign investment negligible, and inflation causing widespread despair, to which the government's counter was shriller anti-western propaganda and blatant support for extremist regimes (Sudan) or subversive groups (in Egypt). On the credit side, education, whatever its quality, and literacy were greatly extended; so were the public services, expectations of life and basic incomes. But free speech and a free press were bounded by a prudent self-censorship, penal sanctions were brutal and indiscriminate, the young were kept in what their elders considered to be their place, women were discriminated against as a matter of course and most so-called ordinary Iranians found it hard to make ends meet. The Majlis remained in being and a variety of parties was tolerated but legislation was subject to the scrutiny and veto of the 12-man Council of Guardians, which also vetted candidates of all parties for election to the Majlis. In external affairs Iran was as verbally abusive of the United States as vice versa. It made no secret of its support for the Hizbollah in Lebanon but denied wider charges of subversion and terrorism, evidence for which eluded the Americans who sought it. Clinton branded Iran a threat to the Middle East and the world and imposed sanctions on companies (of whatever nationality) which traded with or in Iran. Iran aimed to assert its regional power by rebuilding its armaments after the war with Iraq and pressing its interests in Central Asia as well as in traditionally debatable areas in the Arabian peninsula and the Gulf. It barely concealed its intention to develop a nuclear armoury, thus challenging Israel's monopoly in the Middle East and the will of the United States to sustain it.

When Rafsanjani's term ended in 1997 he was succeeded by Muhammad Khatami, who surprisingly defeated Khamenei's favoured candidate by a large margin and was evidently disposed to relax internal tensions rather than impose the rigorous conservatism of a dogmatic and intolerant minority. He had strong support from the rising generations and the unemployed, who numbered a quarter or more of the workforce, but his clerical opponents were entrenched in the Majlis and the judiciary, the National Security Council and the Council of Guardians. Khatami improved relations with the Arab world and Europeans and even made approving remarks about some aspects of American culture, but he remained constrained by the religious right and by the slump in the price of oil, which provided 90 per cent of Iran's export earnings.

Khatami was replaced by the more fiercely nationalist Ahmedinejad whose popularity as the mayor of Teheran carried him to the presidency in 2005. Iran resumed its nuclear conversion programme, asserting its right to develop nuclear power for civil purposes, accepting limited international supervision but convincing few that it did not intend to proceed to the manufacture of nuclear weaponry. Distrust between Iran and the United States was total. Ahmedinejad attended the UN General Assembly and visited Presidents Chavez and Morales in South America, perhaps in an attempt to break out of isolation, but in 2007 Khameini asserted his superior status and trimmed Ahmedinejad's sails by dismissing two members of his government. These manoeuvres were followed by a visit to Teheran by Putin, the first by a Russian head of state since Stalin attended the three-power conference against Nazi Germany in 1943. In Washington Bush's counter-rhetoric was blunted when US intelligence reported that Iran had probably abandoned its nuclear weapons programme some years earlier and when it was seen to be driving Iran into the arms of Russia. What Qavam es-Sultaneh had fended off in 1946 (p. 377) the Bush administration was bringing about whether Ahmadinejad remained president or not.

Saddam Hussein

In Iraq the Aref regime (p. 338) had been overthrown in 1968 by a coup which put General Ahmad Hassan al-Bakr in the presidency. This was a victory for the Iraqi branch of the Ba'ath Party and more particularly for Saddam Hussein Takriti, the brutally strong man of the new regime. Saddam Hussein remained half in the background until 1979, when he took open control after a plot of obscure origins (probably by a disgruntled rival clan within the Sunni establishment). He looked south rather than west. His first ambition was to reassert Iraq's position in the Gulf. His chief adversaries therefore were not Syria, Egypt or even Israel but Iran and Saudi Arabia, and since both of these were supported by the United States he turned to the USSR and concluded in 1972 a treaty for, among other things, the supply of arms. But Saddam Hussein did not intend to get hitched to the Russian wagon and three years later he concluded an agreement with France for the supply of a nuclear reactor and set up a nuclear research establishment with a large staff of engineers. Iraq, which had signed the Nuclear Non-Proliferation Treaty, maintained that all the safeguards prescribed by the International Atomic Energy Agency were being observed, but Iraq's adversaries – particularly Israel – feared that it was preparing to produce nuclear weapons: the plant where the reactor was being built in France was sabotaged, material destined for Iraq was sabotaged at Toulon, an Egyptian nuclear physicist in Iraqi service was murdered in Paris. Iraq also turned to Italy for help in training naval and air officers and for the delivery of ten vessels of war. Given Iraq's geography, these could be used only in the Gulf. Contacts outside the USSR and eastern Europe, particularly with West Germany and Japan, were intensified after displays of Russian power in Aden and Ethiopia in the late 1970s. In 1980 Iraqi nuclear installations were bombed by Israel.

Iraq's development was not purely military. The government embarked also on literacy and other educational programmes, technical training, industrial expansion and an agricultural plan designed to enable Iraq to produce all its food instead of a mere quarter. All these measures were based on oil. Oil provided 98 per cent of Iraq's export revenue and financed 90 per cent of the government's investment. Output reached 2 million barrels a day in 1973 and 2.5 million in 1977, and hit a brief peak of 3.7 million before the end of the decade. Iraq became the world's second biggest exporter.

In 1980 Iraq attacked Iran. The causes of this war included the temptation to score off Iran in its hour of weakness after the fall of the shah; Hussein's profound dislike of Ayatollah Khomeini, whom he regarded as a religious lunatic; unease about Khomeini's Shia intrigues among the Iraqi Shia, who staged serious riots at the end of 1979; a suspicion that Khomeini had been involved in the unsuccessful coup of that summer against his regime; and, finally, the perennial question of the Kurds, a sizeable minority in Iraq (18 per cent) with awkward claims in the oil-bearing region of Kirkuk and an even more awkward propensity for allowing themselves to be used by Iran against Iraq.

Hussein hoped that he had settled the Kurdish question in 1975 (for its antecedents see Note A at the end of this part). After admitting Kurds to the Iraqi cabinet in 1973 and granting autonomy to the Kirkuk region in 1974 Iraq bought from the shah in 1975 a promise to stop Iranian aid to Kurdish dissidents. But Hussein could not be sure that the shah's promise would be honoured by Khomeini and in any case he resented the price he had had to pay for it and wanted to go back on his own promise. This was the immediate cause of the war. It concerned the respective rights of Iraq and Iran in the Shatt al-Arab.

The Shatt al-Arab carries the waters of the Euphrates and Tigris to the Persian Gulf. These rivers, whose headwaters are in Turkey, flow through Iraq to the Shatt, which marks the frontier between Iraq and Iran. Halfway along its course of 200 km it is joined by the Iranian river Karun. The Shatt is Iraq's only outlet to the sea and also carries the traffic of the Iranian ports of Khorramshahr and Abadan in the province of Khuzistan, whose population consists of Iranian citizens of Arab race. The Gulf into which the Shatt debouches leads, not directly to the open sea, but to the Straits of Hormuz, which are 800 km from Iraq and easily commanded by Iran. When in 1971 Iran had seized the small islands in the straits (the Tunbs and Abu Musa), which Britain had wished to transfer to two of the Arab emirates, Iraq was unable to do more than break off diplomatic relations with Iran and expel Iranians from Iraq.

The first treaty concerning the frontier between the Iranian and Ottoman empires along the Shatt al-Arab was signed in 1555. It had many successors. No treaty ever satisfied both parties to it and the complexities were increased by shifts of the terrain, waterways and islands and (eventually) by the discovery of oil. At the beginning of the twentieth century the Ottoman empire had secured control over almost the whole of the Shatt and this position was inherited between the two world wars by Iraq. It was, however, challenged by the resurgent power of Iran under the Pahlavi dynasty, which claimed that the frontier ran down mid-channel. In 1937 a new treaty considerably improved the Iranian position, notably by making the Shatt freely usable by naval and merchant vessels of both states. After the Second World War, and particularly after the 1958 revolution in Iraq, Iran began to put pressure on Iraq. In 1969 Iran abrogated the 1937 treaty. Iraq riposted by declaring the whole of the Shatt to be Iraqi territorial water but Iran's support for Kurdish revolts against Baghdad forced Iraq in 1975 to accept a deal whereby the shah would abandon the Kurds in return for recognition of the mid-channel frontier. In 1978 the fall of the shah again transformed the situation. Iran lapsed into something like chaos and lost the American support which had been so conspicuous an element in the expansion of Iranian power. Iraq, on the other hand, had been gathering strength since the coup in 1968. In 1980 Saddam Hussein abrogated the 1975 agreement and invaded Iran.

He miscalculated. The war was not the walkover which he hoped for. Khomeini's Iran did not fall to pieces and Iraq became committed to wearing operations which exposed its weaknesses as well as its ambitions. The Iranians stemmed the Iraqi attack despite the disorganization of their country and the reluctance of the clergy to give the army – a possible rival for power – a free hand. Saddam Hussein, like Ayub Khan in Kashmir in 1965, failed to get the quick victory which was the only kind of victory worth having. The war entered upon years of ding-dong slaughter and Iraq's vision of dominating the Gulf and the Arab world faded. Khomeini was able to throw thousands of conscripted Iranians into battle with religious ruthlessness, insisting that he would accept no terms for peace short of the overthrow of Saddam Hussein.

Iraq all but won the war in the first few weeks, but then made a fateful pause in the false belief that it had done so. Iran held the main Iraqi offensive and an extension of the front northward to Desful; retaliated by attacking Basra from the sea and targets as far north as Mosul by air; achieved limited successes over the next two years; emboldened Syria to block the flow of Iraqi oil through Syria to the Mediterranean; and proclaimed in 1982 war aims which amounted to a demand for Iraq's surrender – the replacement of the Iraqi regime and substantial reparations for aggression. But Iran's military successes were too modest to match these aims. Year after year small gains were made at hideous cost in death, mutilation and destruction, but without denting Iraq's resolve. Iraq, thwarted on land, developed a new twofold strategy: it attacked Iranian oil installations (oil exports were crucial in financing Iran's war effort) and internationalized the war by raising fears of an oil shortage as a consequence of damage to shipping in the Gulf and the closing by Iran of the strait of Hormuz. Iran's export earnings were significantly curtailed but it reacted cautiously to this escalation of the war and refrained at first from interfering with foreign shipping. In 1985 Iraq launched a second major land offensive – the first since the beginning of the war – but this attack and an Iranian counter-offensive made small impact and confirmed the stalemate on land. Even when Iranian forces crossed the Shatt in the following year and subjected Baghdad to regular bombardment no military decision seemed to be in sight; and a further Iranian offensive against Basra in 1987 was equally inconclusive.

In the Gulf, however, Iraq had some success with its economic warfare and its policy of goading Iran into activities which would invite international intervention. Iran's economy was more susceptible than Iraq's to the loss of oil revenue, since Iran was financing the war largely by exporting oil in excess of the quotas prescribed by OPEC, whereas Iraq – although it had lost one of its main oil outlets at the outset of the war – was sustaining its war effort with subsidies from Kuwait and other Arab states: Kuwait, although traditionally hostile to Iraq, which had territorial claims against it, was nervous about possible Iranian subversion among Kuwait's Shi'ites, who numbered nearly a third of its population. Iraq's new strategy presented Iran with the problem of scaring Kuwait into desisting from aiding Iraq without at the same time scaring western states into active participation in the Gulf against Iran. This was a particularly delicate operation since the war presented President Reagan with an opportunity to settle old scores with Iran over the taking of American hostages in Teheran and new scores over the humiliating exposure of the arms-for-hostages traffic in which the United States had been engaging. Reagan, hoping to succeed where Carter had failed, tried to get Iran to secure the release of American captives in Lebanon in return for the supply of American and Israeli weapons. This covert manoeuvre was contrary to the United States' principle of never negotiating with hostage-takers or terrorists. It was later justified on the grounds that its aim was to encourage so-called moderates in Iran, but these moderates were for the most part mythical and in so far as they existed their influence was diminished when the American proposals and furtive visits to Teheran were revealed.

By opening a second front at sea Iraq aimed to inveigle the United States into blockading Iran and even perhaps into hostilities against it. The initiative was taken by Kuwait which, economically dependent on the free flow of oil through the Gulf, asked the United States to protect Kuwaiti tankers by allowing them to fly the American flag (contrary to the Geneva Convention of 1959) and to send a substantial naval force to the Gulf, where it was likely to become engaged in hostilities with Iran. This request followed an attack on the US frigate *Stark*, which was hit by an Exocet missile (albeit launched by Iraq, not Iran) and it was reinforced by reports of the installation of Chinese ground-to-sea missiles at Hormuz and by a Kuwaiti appeal to the USSR for the use of the Soviet flag which raised American fears of an expanded Russian naval presence in or near the Gulf.

The involvement of the United States in the Gulf made it impossible for Iran to win a war which Iraq had already failed to win in spite of considerable foreign aid in arms, intelligence and finance. Ending the war became a matter of time and diplomacy. The Security Council unanimously approved a call for a ceasefire in terms which side-stepped Iran's demand that Iraq be labelled the aggressor. Iran therefore prevaricated while Iraq stalled in the hope of increased American support in weaponry, training, intelligence and military sanctions against Iran. But the United States shrank from out-right war in support of the Iraqi aggressor and the war went on until 1988. Neither side had defeated the other. The main issue of rights in the Shatt was resolved only when Hussein, having precipitated a different crisis, abruptly conceded to Rafsanjani all that he had fought for against Khomeini. Hussein's invasion of Kuwait was an even bigger miscalculation than his war against Iran.

Kuwait and the Gulf War

On 2 August 1990 Iraq invaded Kuwait. The sheikhdom of Kuwait was something of an anomaly in the Gulf. Much smaller than Iran, Iraq or Saudi Arabia, it was, however, more populous and richer than the Gulf's other minor states and was a long way away from them: it was a solitary small state surrounded by larger ones. It had been part of the Ottoman empire under the autonomous rule of a family which established itself in the eighteenth century. It was the subject of special treaties between the Ottoman and British empires. Unlike the rest of the Gulf, Kuwait concerned Britain not because of the piracy which impeded British commerce, but because of fears of German or Russian expansion to the Gulf by means of railway concessions and Ottoman favours. To allay these fears treaties were concluded in 1899 and 1913, and after the First World War Kuwait became a British protectorate. In the 1930s the new state of Iraq claimed that Kuwait, as a former part of the Ottoman pashalik of Basra, belonged by right of succession to Iraq. More particularly, Iraq laid claim to the islands of Bubijan and Warbah at the head of the Gulf and to the tip of the Rumeila oilfield which, mainly in Iraq, extended beneath the frontier into Kuwait. These claims were not in themselves substantial. The islands were barren, without oil, partly submerged for part of the year, and no help or hindrance to Iraq's commerce to or from the Gulf. Kuwait's extraction of oil from the Rumeila field amounted to about 1 per cent of its yield. But the claims could be used to stalk bigger prizes in northern Kuwait.

In 1961 Britain left Kuwait, which became independent and a member of the United Nations. Kassim repeated Iraq's traditional claims and the ruler of Kuwait, afraid of an Iraqi attack, appealed to Britain for help. A small British force was expeditiously landed, the Iraqis (who had remained a long way from the frontier) subsided, the British troops were quickly withdrawn and were replaced for a short time by contingents from other Arab states. Two years later Iraq recognized the independence and sovereignty of Kuwait, which became a member of the Arab League.

Upon the Iraqi invasion in 1990 the emir of Kuwait and his family fled, a puppet administration was installed and Kuwait was declared to be a province of Iraq. It was also despoiled. Hussein's motives were greed and need. He had been rearming on credit after his war with Iran and his suppliers had stopped his credit. He spent or pledged perhaps $100 billion on war in a decade, most of it in purchases in countries bound by UN resolutions not to supply him. On the eve of his invasion of Kuwait his debt to non-Arab creditors was about $35 billion, much of it owed to commercial companies but underwritten by governments and so ultimately a charge on the public. Kuwait's wealth was fabulous, Iraq's postwar needs were urgent and Hussein may have believed that Kuwait was ripe for the taking. In 1986 the emir had disbanded the Kuwaiti parliament and in 1989 he rejected pleas to reinstate it; half the emirate's population were immigrants without citizenship or full civic rights; nomadic Bedouin were denied rights because they could not prove fixed residence, as too were Palestinians and others, even if born in Kuwait. But if Hussein was counting on some sort of a welcome he was greatly mistaken. He was no less mistaken about Arab and international reactions. The invasion was an incontestable act of aggression by one member of the UN against another and by one Arab state against another, and unlike Iraq's equally blatant aggression against Iran a decade earlier the attack on Kuwait was also a threat to the interests of the United States and other countries. The appropriation of Kuwait's oilfields would considerably increase Iraq's weight in OPEC and its influence over the pricing of oil worldwide. It might furthermore be a prelude to an attack on Saudi Arabia, which could place virtually all Arab oil under Iraq's control, cause widespread political chaos by unseating the Saudi monarchy and weakening other Arab regimes, and precipitate universal economic instability and recession if, with or without an attack on Saudi Arabia, oil prices doubled or trebled.

Hussein's action was therefore a massive miscalculation which created an impressively broad coalition against him and, given the gravity of its possible consequences on the one hand and his own stubbornness on the other, a confrontation not easily to be dispelled without war. Over previous decades Iraq had enjoyed western and Soviet help in creating powerful, partly modernized armed forces. To Iraq's aggression against Iran the United States, Britain and other countries had turned a blind eye; some had given significant direct or indirect aid to the Iraqi war effort, as had a variety of Arab states. Leaders in most of these states had disregarded Hussein's slaughter of thousands of Kurds with chemical weapons; in the United States attempts to chastise Iraq through economic sanctions had been thwarted in Congress and the White House. To Hussein's delusions therefore about the international effects of his aggression foreign states had themselves contributed and one of Washington's principal concerns in the months after the invasion of Kuwait was to drive home the message that this act was not to be condoned as Iraq's earlier misdeeds had been. In addition, the context in 1990 was changed as well as the stakes. Since the fall of the shah in Iran the United States had become determined to prevent a similar fate overtaking the Saudi monarchy. The Cold War had come to an end. Arab governments which had supported Iraq against Iran were angered by Hussein's attack on one of themselves and feared his pretensions to leadership in the Arab world – pretensions nourished by a view of himself as successor to Michel Aflaq, who had died in 1989 in Paris after long years in exile.

The American response was two-pronged: invocation of chapter VII of the UN Charter and a distinct and massive American military expedition into the Middle East. But although the American response was swift and vigorous its motives were confused. The occupation of Kuwait provided justification, even an obligation, to take international action to reverse the invasion by embargo, extending if necessary to blockade and the implementation of these measures by force, under articles 41 and 42 of the Charter (see Chapter 30). But the occupation of Kuwait was not the prime cause of the distinct American action, and the reversal of the occupation was not the United States' sole object. Since similar infractions of international law by Iraq (and others) had evoked no such response the despatch to the Middle East of a quarter of a million troops could not plausibly be attributed to Kuwait's fate alone. The cause of this vast effort was plainly something more than solicitude for international law or for the emir of Kuwait. The cause was fear of further aggression by Iraq against Saudi Arabia coupled with the opportunity to overthrow the Iraqi regime under cover of the liberation of Kuwait. This proliferation of aims, besides necessitating the doubling of the

American forces in Saudi Arabia, delayed the American readiness to strike since the forces deemed adequate to free Kuwait and defend Saudi Arabia remained for months inadequate to conquer Iraq. Bush – apparently taken by surprise in spite of some timely warnings – committed himself to a display of force which cast doubt on the sincerity of the UN prong of his two-pronged strategy (which was the centrepiece of his appeal for international support), sowed seeds of uneasiness about his aims, and created trouble for himself on the home front both by declaring that this obviously offensive capacity was strictly defensive and by committing the United States to huge expenditure and a humiliating need to tout for foreign contributions. He succeeded in rallying international support at the UN and for his fighting forces on Saudi soil: active Saudi alliance was a *sine qua non*. His problem lay in keeping either coalition together when his purposes appeared to be different from theirs. The forces assembled in Saudi Arabia comprised, besides the essential Saudi contribution, units from Egypt, Syria, Morocco, Britain, France, Pakistan, Bangladesh and more. But this heartening multiplicity created its own problems. Iraq's aggression meant different things in different places. The alliance's common aim was the restoration of Kuwait's independence. Americans, however – and the Thatcher administration in Britain – wanted total Iraqi defeat to be followed by the overthrow of Hussein and the destruction of Iraq's weaponry, including weapons which, however horrible, were not proscribed by international law and were manufactured, held and supplied by a number of states. To Arabs on the other hand, from King Fahd of Saudi Arabia to President Hosni Mubarak of Egypt, Hussein's offence was his flouting of the principles, proclaimed by himself in 1980, that no Arab state should attack another and that Arab issues should be settled by Arabs. By flouting these principles Hussein put his fellow Arab leaders in the awkward position of having to choose between acquiescing in Iraq's unprincipled abuse of power and allying themselves with the Americans, whose behaviour and very presence in force in the Middle East were offensive to many Arabs and Muslims. Even those Arabs who chose the latter course were having misgivings a few months later. In November the king of Morocco revived the notion of an Arab conference; by December Saudi Arabia was secretly discussing through Arab intermediaries a possible revision of the Iraqi–Kuwaiti frontiers; Kuwaitis in exile revived an old proposal for a long lease of Bubijan and Warbah to Iraq; in January Mubarak was to be seen in the unlikely company of Qadafi, whom he visited in Tripoli along with Assad; and no Arab was untouched by the prospect, floated by Hussein and cautiously approved by sundry Europeans and the USSR and China, of an international conference on the Middle East which would embrace Israel's occupation of the West Bank, Gaza and Jerusalem and be held in tandem with a settlement of the Kuwaiti crisis or soon thereafter.

The initial flurry of diplomatic and military activity was followed by a pause lasting several months, necessitated partly by the very nature of action under chapter VII of the UN Charter, partly by American determination to launch nothing less than an immediately crushing blow and partly by genuine, if tenuous, hopes of scaring Hussein out of Kuwait by demonstrations of military might but without bloodshed on an unpredictable scale. Between the Iraqi invasion on 2 August and the recourse on 29 November to article 42 of the Charter the United States held its coalition together while accumulating more and more force in the Middle East in the hope of ensuring that, in the event of war, a first blow against Iraq (whether in Kuwait or in Iraq was understandably left uncertain) would achieve its purpose without unbearably long and costly operations. Publicly, the United States sidestepped the question of whether these purposes warranted a war whose cost in lives, money, general economic disruption and long-term influence in the Middle East might prove disastrous. It also played down, to the point of trying to expunge, that part of the first Security Council resolution which required – besides complete Iraqi evacuation of Kuwait – a negotiated settlement of the crisis: negotiation, for the United States (and Britain) meant negotiation after the end of the crisis and not in order to end it. For his part Hussein played a militarily weak hand with some dexterity but limited success. He seized foreigners in Kuwait (who numbered several thousands and came from two dozen countries) and transported some to Iraq, where about 340 were dispersed to likely targets in and outside Baghdad as a shield against armed attack; he prevented foreigners in Iraq as well as in Kuwait from leaving the country; he threatened to set Saudi oilfields and installations ablaze and to attack Israel if he were attacked by the United States; he tried with minimal success to sow discord among the United States' associates and to inflame anti-American Arab and Muslim emotions; he mended his fences with Iran in the hope of securing a sizeable gap in the UN's economic cordon. His refusal to allow foreigners to leave Iraq or Kuwait and his planting of them in and around sensitive installations (in violation of the Geneva Convention on the treatment of civilians) provided ammunition for extended denunciations of his law-breaking but the presence of these possible victims was an embarrassment to their governments, which had to present themselves as undeterred as well as outraged and criticized unofficial rescue attempts by assorted emissaries – Kurt Waldheim, Jesse Jackson, Edward Heath, Yasuhiro Nakasone, former US Senator John Connally, British MP Tony Benn – whose motives governments tried obliquely to impugn. Women and children were permitted to leave from September, and in December Hussein declared that all who wished might be home for Christmas.

On 29 November the Security Council approved a resolution – the culmination of 12 – authorizing the use after 15 January 1991 of any necessary measures to secure the removal of Iraq from Kuwait and the restoration of its former rulers. This legitimization of the recourse to war was passed by 12 votes to two (Yemen, Cuba) with one abstention (China). The firmness of the Arab with the non-Arab members of the anti-Iraqi alliance was bolstered by American and British somersaults in their attitudes to Syria, whose anti-Iraqi credentials cancelled its earlier ostracism as a paymaster of international terrorism; and by subventions to Egypt, which, while gravely damaged by truncated tourism and loss of remittances from Egyptians forced to leave their jobs in Kuwait and Iraq, was compensated by substantial remission of foreign debts and the provision of large new credits (mainly from the United States and Saudi Arabia). Hussein continued to insist that his occupation of Kuwait was irreversible. Bush adopted increasingly exclusive eyeball-to-eyeball tactics, complaining repeatedly that the obstacle to a peaceful implementation of the UN's resolutions was Hussein's failure to understand the American position. In what he described as a last effort to save the peace Bush proposed talks in Washington and Baghdad on the basis, however, that such talks must be exploratory only and entail no negotiation. Hussein prevaricated. The foreign ministers of the two states met in Geneva. Neither gave way. The UN secretary-general Javier Perez de Cuellar made a despairing attempt to fend off war, meeting Hussein in Baghdad two days before the date set by the Security Council for the use of force. On the previous day the US Congress authorized Bush, albeit by narrow majorities, to go to war. The broader aims of the United States, whatever their virtues or legitimacy, were incompatible with a peaceful settlement, within the terms of the UN's resolutions, of the crisis provoked by the Iraqi aggression.

When 15 January was reached the United States wasted no time and opened hostilities during the night of 15–16 January: it did so without informing the secretary-general of the UN, in whose name the hostilities were launched. But for a further six weeks these hostilities were muted while the United States and its allies assembled ever larger forces and attempted to win the war by bombardment at long range and without recourse to the hazards of general land warfare. The Iraqi air forces were reduced to impotence and put to flight, seeking refuge in Iran, where they were interned; the navy fared no better; Iraqi ground forces, armour and communications were severely pounded and Baghdad was subjected to destruction greater than anything which it had suffered for 700 years. Iraq countered with largely ineffective missiles aimed at Saudi and Israeli cities and by devastating Kuwait City and barbarously maltreating its inhabitants. As the contest's extreme inequality became obvious Hussein was driven to attempt negotiations but did so equivocally and obliquely. Bush responded by insisting on unconditional compliance with all pertinent UN resolutions, by inviting Iraqis to revolt against their government and by adding conditions of his own in order to maintain pressures for unconditional surrender. Attempts, notably by the USSR, to broker an Iraqi withdrawal from Kuwait on acceptable conditions were rejected by the United States, which evaded their discussion by the Security Council and on 23 February, a date chosen ten days earlier, converted the war into a general onslaught on Iraq which was intended to remove or kill Hussein without dismembering the country – which Bush explicitly disavowed but was nevertheless a likely sequel.

The final stage, lasting less than a week, was little more than a *promenade militaire* and a massacre of fugitives by unopposed air power. Kuwait was liberated and its ruling dynasty resumed its sway. An unsavoury regime in Baghdad was humiliated. Some 50,000 Iraqis were killed, perhaps twice that number. The infliction of undeniable defeat on a cruel dictator was widely welcomed but since the American purpose was neither avowed by the United States nor licensed by the United Nations the former stood accused of being two-faced and the latter, made use of rather than involved, was weakened.

The financial and political costs of the war were heavy. The US secretary of state and the British foreign secretary toured the Middle East and other capitals soliciting contributions and succeeded in collecting sums equal to about four-fifths of their costs. They demonstrated, however, that they had embarked on a war which they could hardly afford and, by sidelining the UN, had been obliged themselves to undertake the business of levying contributions which would otherwise have been performed by the secretary-general. The political costs included evident but less than fatal strain on the Soviet–American détente and a pronounced accentuation of anti-Americanism from Morocco to Iran, but one more clamorous than enduring. The war did not make the Middle East more stable. American intervention to protect Saudi Arabia exposed its inability to defend itself and the American presence introduced practices and ideas – from democracy to sexual licence – profoundly repugnant to Arab rulers and ruled. Jordan's support for Iraq unified the country but bankrupted it. Saudi–Yemeni hostility was sharpened. Kuwait itself was pushed into an unconvincing experiment in tempering absolutism with a degree of democracy. In the Gulf Iran moved closer to recovering its dominant position. To the north the use of Turkish air bases recalled Turkish claims on northern Iraq. In spite of missile attacks on its cities, Israel, pressed and generously rewarded by the United States, refrained from entering the war and used this forbearance to extract large subventions: the fact that this money was to be recouped from Saudi Arabia and Kuwait did not go unremarked in the Arab world. Israel saw its principal enemy battered and humiliated and the PLO, which had denounced Iraq's aggression but otherwise backed Iraq, discredited and weakened.

Egypt was a major beneficiary and increasingly open convert to the western side. Mubarak was paid in cash for adding the weight of the Arab world's most populous and prestigious state to the anti-Iraqi alliance. Twenty billion dollars of its foreign debts were written off and another $20 billion rescheduled, and Egypt received economic and military aid from the United States beginning at $2.1 billion a year and later tapering off gently. Mubarak was re-elected president for a third term in 1993. In spite of a background of anti-Americanism, he had no difficulty in winning the requisite votes of two-thirds of the members of a parliament almost monopolized by the National Democratic Party, which two years later won 95 per cent of the vote in a general election. A few small parties existed on sufferance but applications to start new parties had to be vetted by a select committee which, since its creation by Sadat, had never approved such an application. The Muslim Brotherhood and other Islamic groups, never strongly supported (least of all in rural Egypt), were losing ground steadily. Police oppression and violations of human rights were pervasive but not too blatant; violent demonstrations such as the killing of several tourists at Luxor in 1997 were sporadic and ill-concerted. The economy was diversified – oil exports, remittances, canal dues, tourism – and registered during the 1990s annual growth around

5 per cent, tiny budget deficits and reassuring reserves of foreign currencies. The privatization of state enterprises and scrapping of bureaucratic controls were accelerated and completed a picture which had much appeal to the IMF. On the debit side foreign investment and domestic savings were meagre and the gap between rich and poor widened, food prices surged as subsidies were cut, public services – including education and health – ceased to be free and became impossibly costly for many. But from a distance Egypt seemed by Middle Eastern standards stable.

The most important sequel to the attack on Iraq in 1991 was that it did not end there. Bush publicly encouraged Iraqi Kurds and Shi'ites to accomplish what he himself had failed to do by rebelling against Hussein but Hussein's military power had not been demolished and it was used against them ruthlessly. The Kurds in particular suffered in battle and in flight misery and death on a scale unusually bitter and devastating even for them. (For more on the Kurds see Note A at the end of this part.)

Iraq was attacked and defeated because it had invaded Kuwait and was supposed to be intent on invading Saudi Arabia too, but the latter threat was not to be removed by substituting one Iraqi regime for another. Iraq's aggressiveness, whatever its scale, raised one of the central issues in international politics in the second half of the twentieth century: how to ensure the supply of essential resources lying outside the territorial confines of powerful and avid consumers. The United States and other powerful states were dependent on Middle Eastern oil but unable to secure it by occupying or dominating the relevant areas in the manner of the Ottoman empire or the Anglo-French mandates system. (The Kuwait war was fought to assert the rule of law forbidding one state to appropriate the territory or resources of another.) The alternative to this outmoded imperialism was to secure national interests through international peace and stability and the operation of market forces. When that order broke down, as it did upon Iraq's annexation of Kuwait, force had to be used and the UN Charter so provided. But the *casus belli* was the infringement of national sovereignty, not the interruption of trade or threats to trade. Consequently, legitimate international action in defence of national supplies depended on a simultaneous breach of the law relating to sovereign independence. The United States showed that it could and would fight for its interests. The display of American will, no less than the display of immense technical competence, both logistical and operational, was a major event in international affairs but there was a proviso: that there had to be a legal loophole, which in this case was provided by the violation of Kuwait's sovereign independence. How the United States would act in the face of a threat to its interests arising from domestic upheaval and not from international aggression was not only dubious but also peculiarly germane to the Middle East, where conflict (Israel apart) came from internal threats to governments rather than hostilities between them. Until Iraq attacked Kuwait in 1990 no Arab state had attacked another in 70 years and if the Kuwait war were to restore that pattern, the occasion for American or other foreign intervention would be limited to aggression by or against Israel. Furthermore, the American will to act in a crisis was thrown into some doubt in the same year when the United States hesitated for long before taking effective action in Bosnia.

The Security Council remained committed to two matters in Iraq: the protection of minorities and the destruction of weapons of mass destruction. The Council ordained safe havens and no-fly zones in north and south Iraq, created a body, United Nation Special Commission (UNSCOM) for the discovery and destruction of weapons of mass destruction and imposed economic sanctions to ensure compliance with these and other terms for the cessation of hostilities. The Kurds in the north and the Shi'ites in the south were regarded as victims in need of protection against Hussein's disregard of human rights but Iraq's enemies were loath to overthrow Hussein with no alternative to him in sight, the Kurds were disunited among themselves, Kurdish areas of Iraq were exposed to invasion from Turkey in pursuit of Turkish Kurds, and the Shi'ites might seek protection from Iran or get it uninvited. American policy amounted to a kind of semi-anarchy and within a few years Hussein reasserted much of his authority. The Kurds, having discovered the limits of American support for them, patched up the differences among themselves in order the better to strike a deal with Hussein. By the 1990s the United States was switching its anti-Hussein manoeuvres from Kurds and Shi'ites to Sunni malcontents and, by the Iraq Liberation Act 1998, the Congress made $97 million available to entice (mainly discordant) groups into some form of unity and finance a civil war.

Sanctions inflicted considerable misery without unseating Hussein. Infant mortality trebled and the general expectation of life fell by 15–20 years. The Security Council exempted food and medicines but since it also blocked exports of Iraqi oil except in limited quantities through the UN, it deprived Iraq of the money to buy these things: only half of the proceeds of permitted exports was made available for imports and none for the maintenance of the oil industry's installations. In 1998 the Council more than doubled the quota, bringing it to two-thirds of prewar levels, but this concession was illusory since Iraq was unable to deliver the additional quantities from its dilapidated industry. After some years Russia openly denounced the continuance of sanctions, France and China began to vacillate and others became uneasy with measures which bore heavily on innocent people without commensurate political effect: the ineffectiveness and cruelty of sanctions against Iraq discredited the view that these weapons might be a comparatively civilized way of making war. Equally ineffective were various measures directed specifically against Hussein himself: incitement to insurrection by minorities, to mutiny in the army, to intrigues among his relatives and assassination plots. In 1995 two of his sons-in-law fled the country, denouncing the dictator, but they were enticed back and executed. Covert attempts to kill Hussein instigated by the CIA miscarried. He was emboldened to make in 1994 an armed *promenade militaire* towards Kuwait. Interpreted by the United States as a fresh threat to Kuwait, it was more probably a taunt and it was quickly reversed in the face of American resolve.

More disturbing was the problem of Iraq's possession and manufacture of weapons of mass destruction – nuclear, chemical, biological. Such weapons existed in the Middle East but Iraq's were special because of the terms on which the war against it had been stayed. By Resolution 687 of 1991 the Security Council granted Iraq a ceasefire on conditions which included the renunciation, disclosure and destruction of such weapons and international inspection of the necessary processes – all of which were to be completed in 40 days. This resolution was supplemented by Resolution 707 authorizing aerial reconnaissance to spot concealed sites and suspicious movements and Resolution 751 requiring independent monitoring of Iraq's manufacturing capabilities. Iraq was never going to comply with these undertakings so long as its principal enemies in the region, Iran and Israel, possessed weapons of mass destruction or appeared likely to acquire them. In association with the International Atomic Energy Agency (IAEA) UNSCOM located and eliminated much of Iraq's nuclear weaponry and launchers but Iraq refused to deliver any of the inventories required by Resolution 687 and obstructed by mendacity, clandestine moves and physical confrontations UNSCOM's attempts to find chemical and biological stocks and information about Iraqi manufacturing capacity and programmes. This search for information, as distinct from the search for stocks, required good intelligence, with which UNSCOM was not provided. It turned therefore to likely sources, particularly the Iranian and Israeli secret services: operational sense but political dynamite. Iraq argued that UNSCOM was trying to ferret out Iraqi state papers which it had no right to see and accused American among other UN inspectors of passing information to Israel and to Americans who later used it to bomb targets in Iraq. For four years the two sides played hide-and-seek. Iraq accepted the UN's right to information about dual (i.e. civil/military) activities and gradually handed over documents by the thousand – but only under pressure until in 1995 Hussein's obstructiveness and deceit impelled the United States to renew the war, for which large forces were assembled in the Gulf. For this course, however, the United States could find no support in the Middle East or among its European allies, except Britain. Kuwait was a partial exception, reversing a refusal to allow its territory to be used by American troops in return for the despatch of substantial ground forces to defend it against Iraqi counter-attack. Even Israel was far from enthusiastic about a new war in which civilians might be a target of Iraq's terrible weapons. The prime American purpose – to get rid of Hussein – was widely but discreetly approved but American methods were not. Claims for the accuracy of the latest long-range weapons were heard with cynicism; the inevitable killing of thousands of Iraqis was repugnant; the use of overwhelming force to get inspectors onto a handful of sites seemed dubiously appropriate besides being a breach of the long-established rule of international law that any use of force must be proportionate to the offence to be chastised. As in 1991, the Americans hesitated. The disintegration of their grand alliance of 1991–92 took the edge off their resolve. When it was proposed that the UN secretary-general Kofi Annan should go to Baghdad, they reluctantly acquiesced, with the face-saving proviso that his mission was not to negotiate but to ensure unequivocal compliance with UN resolutions.

The background to Annan's mission was the presence in the Gulf of large American forces but a declining expectation that they would be used. He defused a crisis without changing what had created it. A formal agreement signed by him and Hussein (subject to endorsement by the Security Council and therefore by its Permanent Members) affirmed UNSCOM's right to unfettered access to all sites which it wished to inspect, including those from which it had been debarred on the grounds that they were offices of the Iraqi state, or presidential palaces. Besides vague phrases about the dignity and sovereignty of Iraq Hussein secured one new provision. Annan agreed to appoint additional individuals of his own choice to accompany UNSCOM teams on visits to the disputed buildings. Outside this agreement Hussein gained by his challenge to the United States which, having personalized the conflict, failed to win the duel. He had caused the UN secretary-general to go to his capital and won extended publicity for the malignity of sanctions. UNSCOM's work had been validated but the Middle East was no more stable than it had been, the American alliance was manifestly insecure, the use of force had become less credible and the American claim to be acting on behalf of the 'world community' was exposed as empty when the United States refrained from seeking the Security Council's support for military action because the Council was unlikely to give it. The Annan–Hussein agreement was endorsed by the Council with sharp but imprecise warnings to Hussein not to infringe it, but without the express mandate sought by the United States and Britain to make war on him without further recourse to the Council if he did. In 1998 he did.

After the Annan–Hussein encounter the general expectation was that UNSCOM would be allowed to fulfil its mission (or much of it) and that sanctions would be removed at the end of the year, but these expectations left out the question of whether the United States would be satisfied with any conclusion which did not include Hussein's downfall. The prospective removal of sanctions was played down by the United States and Hussein reverted to his obstructive tactics. The United States reassembled its military forces. Iraq's Arab neighbours declared that it must resume co-operation with UNSCOM but refused to back military action or welcome military forces on their soil. Hussein had succeeded in driving a wedge between the United States and most of its one-time associates but by his abrasiveness he had allowed the United States to override the Annan–Hussein agreement and resume its (almost) single-handed attacks on Iraq. The United States was in an all-or-nothing situation. It had been slow to realize that its policies after 1991 were not working. Sanctions had become a boomerang and the attempt to neuter a conscienceless dictator had done more to diminish American influence in the Middle East than to undermine Hussein. In the ensuing brinkmanship both protagonists went over the edge. Hussein invited an attack which he expected to evade and the United States retaliated with four nights' bombing of targets in Baghdad and elsewhere. Executed without effective opposition, this operation caused considerable damage, mainly to public buildings and army quarters (which had been evacuated) but did not remove Hussein. Legally, the air attacks were a breach of the UN Charter and, less obviously but probably, of customary international law as being a use of force disproportionate to the aims sought. Politically, their aims were not attained, the operation was censured openly or more discreetly throughout the world, and governments in the Middle East well disposed to the United States were embarrassed and weakened.

For the United States Hussein's dictatorship was not only loathsome – there were others in the same category – but alarming because it threatened the stability of the Middle East in two special matters of prime importance to the United States: the survival of Israel and the politics of oil. Support for Israel was still axiomatic in Washington and had gone to the lengths of condoning Israeli policies which ran counter to American policies (the repudiation of the Oslo agreements, expansion of settlements in occupied territories, refusal to adopt international conventions on the manufacture or use of weapons of mass destruction). On the other hand, the United States could not get tough with Israel until it had finished off Hussein. In 1998 Clinton went surprisingly far towards recognizing a Palestinian state, but he needed to balance that step by demolishing Hussein's regime. Secondly, as in 1990–91, Iraqi oil was a significant element in Middle East oil production. The removal of UN sanctions, the restoration of Iraq's oil industry and exports – and in the background a possible renewal of Iraq's attempt to gain control of Kuwaiti oilfields – would enable Iraq to manipulate the world price of oil, even to reduce it very substantially by breaking OPEC quotas. He would become more than an Iraqi president, an oil king capable of affecting the economics of developing new fields in the Caspian region. These fields were for a time believed to be abundant enough to challenge the primacy of the Middle East and so a boon to the United States second only to the disintegration of the USSR. Early American estimates of reserves around 200 billion barrels were reassessed to a more prosaic 30 billion but the challenge to the Middle East remained. It was dependent, however, on intricate financing of development and transportation costs. The Caspian fields were located in and surrounded by various states which were politically unstable and at loggerheads with one another and few, if any, oil corporations were prepared to invest the huge sums required without the reasonable prospect of a world oil price unlikely to be sustained unless all major Middle East producers set and kept strict annual production quotas.

The destruction of Iraq

At the end of the century UN inspection and monitoring operations in Iraq had been thwarted by Hussein and the Iraqis were being starved and routinely bombed by the United States and Britain in the name of the UN to no purpose and with the dwindling attention of the rest of the world. Then, on 11 September 2001, a small group of Muslims (mostly Saudis) delivered an enormous shock to the United States. With two hijacked aircraft the twin towers of the World Trade Center in downtown New York were rammed and demolished and around 3,000 people were killed. A third airliner hit the Pentagon in Washington. The coup was masterminded by Osama bin Laden's al-Qaeda organization. The horror and outrage were magnified by astonishment at an event with the psychological impact of Pearl Harbor in 1941 but much closer to home. The explanation had to be proportionately cataclysmic: Islam had declared war on the United States, this was a clash of civilizations.

There were few more unlikely allies in the Middle East than Osama bin Laden, a religious fundamentalist and puritan, and Saddam Hussein, a secular powermonger. But bin Laden's wild and wildly successful venture, directed from the remote wastes of Waziristan, was a weighty element in Washington's resolve to make war on Iraq in breach of international law and the UN Charter and with amazingly scant consideration of the consequences. The pretext for war was the alleged possession and manufacture in Iraq of weapons of mass destruction. There were no such weapons. The purpose of the war, however, was the destruction of Hussein's regime, for which there was some sympathy even in the Middle East. The Bush administration was anxious to have international support for action and acquired it from Britain and, if modestly, from other countries. All these potential allies wanted to secure UN endorsement. The United States argued controversially that existing Security Council resolutions had given this endorsement but it was prepared to do without it. Tony Blair, who was anxious both to legitimize the use of force and to preserve Anglo-American relations on wider issues and to steer clear of the endemic anti-Americanism of many EU members, overrated his influence with Bush and found himself yoked to a policy and to action which became more and more unpopular in Britain. By 2007 even the United States was looking for ways to retreat without making the situation worse.

In the north the total destruction of Saddam's regime gave the preponderantly Kurdish regions a considerable degree of autonomy but not independence (which not all of them wanted); in the south Iranian influence was boosted but the Iraqi Shi'a were divided between those in favour of more or less Iranian interference; in the centre the Sunnis, who were uniquely stigmatized as comprehensively part of the fallen regime, recovered enough resilience to make a monkey of the American occupation but not enough unity among themselves to form an effective government over the centre, let alone over the country as a whole.

Further afield the war and ensuing chaos in Iraq influenced two relatively dormant battlegrounds. In the borders between northern Iraq and Turkey, Turkish Kurds of the PKK (p. 417), now divided between militants seeking to accelerate Kurdish independence and gradualists preferring a policy of wait-and-see, set out to provoke a full-scale invasion of Iraq by the Turkish army (the air force was already bombing Iraq) and the parliament gave the government almost unanimous approval for military action in spite of pleas by Bush not to do so. Yet further afield Pakistan – a nuclear power at odds with most of its neighbours – ceased in effect to be an ally of the United States,

Musharraf was undermined and forced to install a civilian regime of doubtful stability and implausible democracy (p. 451).

Thousands of deaths, looting and torture severely affected American (and British) prestige and credit around the world and handed to Russia a rare diplomatic opportunity. Putin visited Teheran, the first senior Russian leader to appear in a benign role in the region since Kosygin acted as mediator between Pakistan and India in 1966 (p. 438). The place of the United State in world affairs was also weakened by failure and by an accentuation of the 'war on terror' which drove the Bush administration to abandon the constraints of the rule of law (domestic as well as international) on the plea that exceptional danger justified the vesting of overriding powers in the president: examples of recourse to such desperate argument range from Q. Fabius Maximus to Robespierre with Bush's emotive 'war on terror' echoing *Hannibal ad portas* and *la patrie en danger.*

Hopes – or at any rate plans – for fresh Israeli–Palestinian talks were compromised as Israel hardened its anti-Hamas stance in Gaza and took steps to reduce the extent of a possible Palestinian state in order to defend its settlements on the West Bank; while on its side Hamas saw no advantage in abandoning its anti-Israel aggressiveness.

Finally, one aim of US policies in the Middle East and Asia – to stem the proliferation of nuclear weapons – was rendered more remote. India and Pakistan had already broken the barrier (p. 450) and so too had Israel. Iraq was found not to have any but Iran, whatever its settled intentions, if any, was judged to be at least capable of making nuclear bombs and delivering them in the near future. Washington's refusal to discuss Israel's nuclear armoury remained steadfast but it was becoming increasingly difficult to justify an American–Israeli monopoly or to avoid admitting that the regime established by the Nuclear Non-proliferation Treaty of 1968 (p. 38) had ceased to exist.

The Iraq war was arguably the direst upheaval in world affairs since the Second World War and its aftermath posed a challenge no less testing than the problems faced by the post-First World War conferences (Versailles, Lausanne) in this part of the world in 1919–23. Since it had been in nobody's interest to create such a situation, the inception and conduct of the Iraq war was a severe blow to hopes that human beings were getting better at understanding and controlling events. It illustrated not so much the perils of villainy as the pitfalls of intellectual insufficiency and, in the perhaps profitless weighing of the one against the other, left that question undecided.

The allied invasion and subsequent treatment of Iraq and American actions at Guantanamo and elsewhere breached international law, most flagrantly in the recourse to torture as defined and outlawed in a number of instruments of international law. They pleaded necessity on the grounds of security, a political imperative. In doing so they made a stark choice but one which had a price: by overriding the law they forfeited the right to protection by the law and the right to claim without hypocrisy that they were acting to strengthen the rule of law. They were denying the universality as distinct from the relativity of law and morality. In sum the United States waded crassly into the

Middle East with formidable force to win a swift and easy victory without considering, or apparently thinking it necessary to consider, what to do next. It substituted fighting for thinking. But its problem, which was real, was not just the removal of a single regime but the reshaping of the Middle East in order to secure whatever oil might be needed for the American economy and American foreign policies for the next generation at least. That was the main issue and American actions in and after 2003 made these aims even harder to achieve than they already were. The incidental killing of 100,000 Iraqi civilians was, among other acts of destruction, probably criminally justiciable.

CHAPTER 15

The Arabian peninsula

The Saudi kingdom

The Saudi kingdom is a historical alliance which has lighted on a crock of gold. In the eighteenth century the Saudi clan and the puritan sect of the Wahabis formed an alliance which was so successful that it got possession, early in the nineteenth century, of the holy places of Mecca and Medina and pushed its tentacles as far afield as the areas now called Syria and Iraq. Success was temporary, for with the help of Egyptian arms the Ottoman sultan threw the Saudis back into the desert whence they had erupted and for the rest of the century they had to struggle with neighbouring clans to stay alive. They barely did, but fortune returned to them with the young Abdul Aziz ibn Saud (c. 1880–1953), whose sword created a new realm, called from 1932 the kingdom of Saudi Arabia. The crown of this kingdom belongs to the family of Saud, all the sons of a deceased monarch having claims over grandsons. Abdul Aziz was succeeded by four sons: Saud (1953–64), Feisal (1964–75), Khaled (1975–82) and Fahd; and in 1995 there were in existence some 30 or more princes of this generation and perhaps 6,000 adult princes related to Abdul Aziz in lesser degrees. Territorially, the kingdom was nearly coextensive with the Arabian peninsula, bounded by the strategic waterways of the Persian Gulf and Red Sea; but to the east and south a number of principalities and republics impaired the tidier pattern which seemed to have been designed by nature but was not yet accomplished by Saudi man. The departure of the British in 1971 from the Gulf and Aden removed one great power from the area without substituting another.

Saudi Arabia was a country of great size and, after the Second World War, vast wealth. But in human terms it was a small state. Its population towards the end of the century was no more than 6–7 million, but some estimates made it much smaller, and about a third of the inhabitants were not Saudis. The richer it grew the more tempting its riches (which lay in the north) to a predator. It was therefore driven by prudence to seek a powerful ally and to build powerful armed forces. The ally – and main supplier of the hardware for these forces – was the United States.

American penetration of the Middle East began in Saudi Arabia, where the American oil company Aramco concluded in 1950 with the Saudi government a

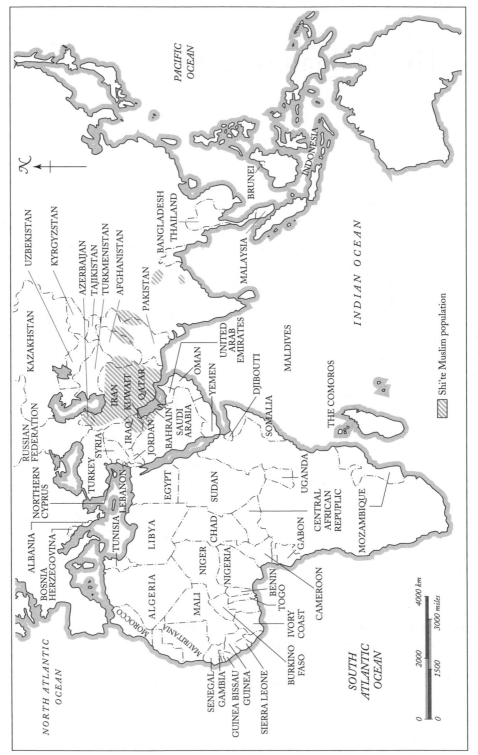

15.1 The Islamic world, members of the Organization of the Islamic Conference

50–50 deal which was considerably more generous than the terms traditionally vouch-safed by British and French companies and was designed to enable American companies to compete with and ultimately displace the British. From this commercial vantage point the United States developed a political relationship with the dependably anti-communist Saudi royal house. This alliance lacked the fervour of Washington's commitment to Israel or the thrust of its alliance with the shah of Iran, but it was the one abiding feature of its relations with the Arab world and had special strategic connotations which increased with the growth of Russian naval power. For much of the postwar period Americans contrived to shut their eyes to the fact that the Saudis were deeply opposed to both Israel and Iran, the two principal pillars of the Middle Eastern policies of the United States. They were no less firmly opposed to democratic and other principles which Americans wished to infuse into their foreign policies.

One legacy of the creation of the Saudi kingdom was its opposition to the Hashemite descendants of the sherif of Mecca whom Abdul Aziz had evicted from his temporalities and spiritualities alike. These descendants ruled in Jordan and (until 1958) Iraq. They were also the butt of Nasser's reformist drive and so provided a bond between the conservative Saudi monarchy and revolutionary Egypt. Abdul Aziz's successors were anxious to escape from an isolation which was no longer safe for a country so rich but so under-equipped in human and material terms; and they began in Cairo. The association was, however, half-hearted. Nasser was anti-American but King Saud was not. Egypt and Saudi Arabia took opposite sides in the civil war in Yemen. King Saud's conservative instincts proved stronger than his anti-Hashemite inheritance, so that in Jordan in 1957 he supported King Hussein against a Nasserist opposition. An ambitious ten-year pact between Saudi Arabia, Egypt, Jordan and Syria, concluded in 1957, faltered from the start and quickly went the way of the numerous inter-Arab pacts of these years when Arabs were finding it difficult to decide which of their kin were friends and which were not.

After Nasser's death in 1970 King Feisal, who had been the power behind the throne even before he came to occupy it in 1964, moved towards the leadership, which had been slipping from the more exuberant Nasser – particularly after the war of 1967 with Israel and the failures of the Egyptian expeditionary force in Yemen. Feisal strengthened Saudi links with the United States and improved relations with the shah; he visited Iran in 1965 and concluded an agreement on the ownership of the possible submarine wealth of the Gulf; and in 1968 the shah went to Mecca. Feisal's leadership in the Arab world was evident at the conference of Arab states at Rabat in 1969, where he succeeded in institutionalizing, by the creation of a standing Islamic Conference, an idea which he had cherished for some years. Egypt became part of this scheme when Sadat evicted the Russians from Egypt in 1972 and, more conservative than Nasser, stemmed at the centre of the Arab world the revolutionary current which had characterized it from the early 1950s. But Egypt forfeited its place in the Muslim family by its separate peace with Israel at Camp David and was not invited to the Islamic assembly which, at Taif and Mecca itself early in 1981, brought together 42 monarchs and other heads of states covering northern Africa and southern Asia from Morocco to Indonesia – an imposing advertisement of slowly maturing Saudi tactics.

The war of 1973 further enhanced Saudi Arabia's international importance. For the first time an economic weapon – oil – was brandished almost as frighteningly as tanks and aircraft. Saudi Arabia cut its production by 30 per cent, more sharply than any other exporter. By this action it put its anti-Israeli before its pro-American policy. The price of oil shot up from $3 to nearly $12 a barrel in a few months. Saudi Arabia's GNP rose by 250 per cent in a year (and went on rising: oil revenues of $4 billion in that year passed $40 billion four years later). Saudi action made the rest of the world digest the implications of a cutback in oil exports, while at the same time Saudi Arabia's great wealth rose to legendary proportions. By 1980 one-third of the financial reserves of the whole world outside the USSR and its satellites belonged to Saudi Arabia. Nor was this a fleeting boom, for Saudi Arabia possessed a quarter of the world's known reserves of oil, was producing 9.5 million barrels a day at comparatively low cost and could increase this production by about 70 per cent with little effort.

Saudi Arabia was therefore more of a prize than ever. But the world in which it lived was becoming progressively less tranquil and there were doubts about its own internal stability. This stability was threatened most by an increasingly numerous class with wider horizons than the monarchy, but not necessarily much less conservative.

The rule of the royal family, however bizarre or anachronistic in western eyes, was assured so long as the princes maintained the historic alliance with Wahabi Islam and established a fresh understanding with the classes, civilian and military, which worked the new institutions engendered by wealth and power. The princely house was, on the whole, successful in these tasks and in preserving its own discipline. The royal family was extensive, powerful and very rich. Its stability was maintained by a strict hierarchy. Which prince would be the next king was well known, and which would follow after him. The thousands of lesser princes had their allotted places in what was in effect a regalian *nomenklatura*. Rarely did any of them step out of line but it was evident that the system would be more difficult to operate, the hierarchy more difficult to define, when the first generation of the sons of Abdul Aziz was followed by the next generation of far more numerous cousins. Nevertheless, the monarchy had a nasty shock when in 1979 250 Oteiba Bedouin seized the Great Mosque at Mecca and held it for two weeks in protest against the worldliness and corruption which were gaining ground in Saudi society – in spite of draconian enforcement of rigorous laws. This incident coincided with riots, stimulated by Khomeini's successes and precepts in Iran, among the Shia minority – a small minority of 120,000 but a major component of the workforce in the oilfields. Saudi society was vulnerable by reason of its lack of professional and technical skills, which obliged it to employ large numbers of workers from other Arab countries and east Asia (Korea, Thailand, the Philippines) and to devote to education as large a share (15 per cent) of government spending as it allotted to defence in the five-year plan for 1975–80 and thereafter.

Saudi Arabia was embarrassed by the failure to resolve the Arab–Israeli dispute and the consequent divergence between itself and the United States. Saudi Arabia kept out of the more militant aspects of this dispute but it was in a sense more committed than any state. In politics most things can be compromised, even frontiers, but the Saudi claim against Israel was religious: the demand by the custodian of holy places for the return of Jerusalem, another holy place, to Muslim hands (but not to Saudi Arabia itself). No Saudi prince was willing to abandon this claim, which the west consistently failed to take seriously, and it united the Saudis with King Hussein of Jordan, whose grandfather had been murdered in the Al Aqsa mosque in Jerusalem. At the conference in Baghdad summoned to protest against Camp David Saudi Arabia tried to moderate the more extreme Arab reactions to Sadat's separate peace with Israel and at the same time retain the leading role which Iraq might snatch out of the heat of Arab indignation.

In the wider conflict between the superpowers the advent of the Russians to Aden and the Horn of Africa created a war zone in the Indian Ocean with all eyes trained on the strait of Hormuz, traversed by 140 ships a day, three-quarters of them oil tankers. Saudi Arabia's traditional border concerns acquired an added international dimension, a foretaste of the testing challenges of the Gulf Wars of the 1980s and 1990s. In the war of 1991 against Iraq the Saudi dynasty played a conspicuous role on the international stage, presented in public a united front and demonstrated its immense wealth by undertaking to pay a lion's share of the costs of the anti-Iraqi allies, including the United States. On the other hand, two Gulf wars seriously depleted the country's reserves and, concurrently with falling oil prices, halved its revenues and forced the regime to cut its expenditure in 1994 by 20 per cent. Saudi Arabia was still the world's largest producer of crude oil, the possessor of a quarter of the world's proved oil reserves and, although not a modern industrial power, a financial power backed by a large part of the world's most essential industrial commodity. But oil was not enough to secure the stability of a regime whose two main supports, the dynasty itself and the prosperous middle class, were both growing larger but not more coherent: the former counted dozens of princes in an upper echelon whose number created opportunities for discord, while the latter was not immune from doubts about the regime. There were pressures for some degree of social reform and financial modernization, particularly from the growing number of Saudis educated abroad; the labouring class, also growing, was increasingly foreign, and the kingdom's close relationship with the United States was potentially unpopular, not least with sections of the Muslim establishment. King Fahd made conciliatory gestures to his Shi'ite minority, proclaimed an amnesty for political offenders, convoked a new (advisory) Majlis and instituted regional councils under the authority of princes of the royal house. But he refused to tolerate a Committee for the Defence of Legitimate Rights set up in 1993 and its chairman Muhammad Masari fled to London in the following year. Prodigious overspending, including the costs of two Gulf wars, presented the government with unfamiliar economic problems. After a heart attack, the king briefly transferred effective powers to his half-brother, Abdullah, at the end of 1995, a shift in power rather than policy and a postponement of whatever crises might be latent within the existing order.

The southern fringe

Yemen, part of the Ottoman empire from 1872 to 1919, was ruled until 1962 by hereditary imams whose rule was one of the least amiable in the world. The population was divided between Sunni and Shi'ite Muslims (the latter being of the Zaydi persuasion). Yemen had a coastline stretching northward from the Bab el-Mandeb along the Red Sea but no access to southerly waters. By the Treaty of Sanaa in 1934 Britain recognized the Imam Yahya as sovereign and accepted an adjournment until 1974 of territorial disputes arising out of Yemeni claims against British-protected sheikhs and the colony of Aden. Yahya's policy was to temporize, but his son, Ahmad (who became imam shortly after his father's assassination in 1948), revived Yemeni claims and argued that constitutional changes in the British colony and protectorates were in breach of the Treaty of Sanaa inasmuch as they prejudged matters which were to be settled in 1974 and created an anti-Yemeni group designed to disrupt Yemen, which Britain had recognized. Border affrays resulted and the imam concluded in 1956 the Treaty of Jidda with Egypt and Saudi Arabia and in 1958 a federal association with the United Arab Republic. The absolute rule of the imams was terminated by a military revolt in 1962 and Ahmad died the next year. His son Muhammad al-Bakr was deposed and Yemen became a republic with Brigadier Sallal as its first president. He invoked Egyptian help under the Treaty of Jidda, while the imam invoked Saudi help under the same treaty. There ensued a mixed civil and international war with each side backed by a foreign state (in the manner of the Spanish Civil War of the 1930s). At Riyadh in 1965 Nasser and Feisal agreed to discontinue their aid and withdraw their troops; the Yemenis were to install a coalition and hold a plebiscite to decide their country's form of government. But this agreement was abortive, troops were not withdrawn and Nasser later said that Egyptian forces might stay indefinitely. After the war with Israel in 1967 he had to change his mind again and withdraw them. The war ended in 1970 in compromise. The republic prevailed but royalists joined its government.

At precisely this time the adjacent *Aden* protectorates and colony were being vacated by Britain in the course of its retreat from global power, a retreat which affected the Persian Gulf as well as Aden and the command of the southern entrance to the Red Sea.

The port of Aden was in the possession of the East India Company and then of the government of India from 1839 to 1938, when it became a British colony. It was given a legislative council in 1947 and elected members were introduced in 1955; under a new constitution in 1958 the elected members became a majority of the council. During the period of Indian government (first as part of the Bombay presidency and finally for a few years as a separate province under the direct control of Delhi) Adenis complained that they were a neglected outpost of the Indian empire. After the transfer of their affairs to the British colonial office nationalist demands for independence waxed. Important as a port for 2,000 years, Aden became in the middle of the twentieth century the site for a big new oil refinery and for the headquarters of Britain's Middle East Command. Conservative ministers therefore decided, and stated with incautious boldness, that nationalist aspirations could not be allowed to go to the lengths of independence. The nationalists, led by Abdullah al Asnag, the secretary-general of Aden's trade unions, proceeded to press their views by strikes which seriously threatened a base dependent on native Adeni and immigrant Yemeni labour, and by boycotting the electoral processes with which Britain had hoped to satisfy local political aspirations.

The adjacent Aden protectorate consisted of 23 sheikhdoms divided for administrative convenience into a western protectorate embracing 18 sheikhdoms and an eastern containing the other five. All had entered into protection agreements of some kind with Britain between 1839 and 1914, and Britain had performed a useful pacificatory role in this part of the world. After the Second World War Britain negotiated new treaties under which British political officers were appointed to advise the sheikhs, who agreed to accept the advice given them except in relation to Islamic law and customs. In the western principalities the appointment of a new sheikh had to be confirmed by the British governor of the colony. The sheikhdoms and the colony constituted a geographically compact, religiously homogeneous area, but the colony differed from its surroundings in being populous, comparatively rich and hostile to the monarchical principle. The nationalists in the colony envisaged a union with the protectorate territories, and ultimately with Yemen also, but not under their existing rulers.

Aden was a small and neglected world of its own until Britain's departure from the Suez base in 1956. In that year a British minister told the colony's legislative council that his government foresaw no possibility of changes in Aden's affairs and was confident that this immobilism would be welcomed by a vast majority of its inhabitants. Later in the year the blocking of the Suez Canal by Nasser caused unemployment and strikes in Aden. At the same time the sheikhs became aware of the threat to their way of life. In 1958 the sultan of Lahej decided to take the road to Cairo, while in 1959 six of the western sheikhs, caught between the devil of Adeni nationalism and the deep seas of Yemeni subversion, formed the federation of Arab emirates which the British had been working for in vain since 1954. This group, renamed the Federation of South Arabia in 1962, was gradually enlarged but never embraced all the sheikhs in spite of British grants 50 times bigger than those previously provided.

Britain, intent on retaining Aden as bases in Kenya, Egypt and Cyprus vanished or became unreliable, decided in 1963 to attach the colony to this new federation, uniting the sheikhs and the merchant class and circumventing the nationalists. Under this scheme Britain retained its sovereignty in the colony; it undertook not to extract the whole colony from the federation, although it might withdraw parts; during the seventh year of this symbiosis, but not before or after, the colony might of its own volition secede, but if it did it would have to revert to colonial status and could not become an independent state; whereas each normal member of the federation had six seats in the Federal Council, Aden was to have 24. This bizarre concoction intensified nationalist agitation. The Adeni nationalists refused to co-operate with Britain or recognize the federation, turned to Egypt for help and took to violence to accelerate the British departure and ensure the collapse of the rest of the British plans. The federated sheikhs tried to get promises of continuing military support, which the British Labour government was unwilling to give since they would virtually negate the policy of with-drawal and retrenchment and would entangle Britain in Arab feuds: by accepting a military commitment while abandoning political power Britain would get the worst of two worlds. The British government preferred to accelerate departure. Aden and its hinterland became in 1967 the People's Democratic Republic of Yemen (PDRY). The departure of the British, who had provided most of the jobs, and the closing of the Suez Canal in the same year plunged the new state into economic distress which accentuated its inherent instability. It was at odds with its northern neighbour, the Yemeni Arab Republic (YAR), whence it was invaded with Saudi help in 1972. A short war ended with talk – but no more – of amalgamating the two Yemeni states. The island of Socotra, south of Aden, a British colony from 1880 to 1967, became part of the PDRY.

From the Saudi point of view a union, or federation, of the PDRY and YAR would be an advantage only if the resulting entity were right-wing. Saudi Arabia wished to exercise control over the YAR and seduce the PDRY from Russian influence. In 1976, after secret meetings in Cairo, Saudi Arabia established relations with the PDRY. This move was made possible by the termination in the previous year of the rebellion against the sultan of Oman in his Dhofar province, in which Saudi Arabia and the PDRY had been on opposite sides. Thereafter Saudi Arabia and the USSR vied with each other in offers of aid to the PDRY.

In the YAR the president Colonel Ibrahim al-Hamdi was assassinated in 1977 after three years of power and was succeeded by Colonel Ahmad al-Ghashni, who was assas-sinated a year later. Although these murders seemed motivated in the main by tribal feuds there was some reason to suspect al-Hamdi of trying to play a separate game of his own with the PDRY, and in 1979 the PDRY invaded the YAR in company with dis-contented refugees from the YAR. In the same year President Abdel Fattah Ismail of the PDRY concluded a 20-year treaty with the USSR. He was succeeded in 1980 by his prime minister Ali Nasser Muhammad, who wanted to find a way of reconciling the Russian connection with better relations with the YAR and Oman. The two Yemeni states were united in 1990 under the presidency of President Ali Abdullah Salih of the YAR. Leaders on both sides saw the advantages of unity but neither wanted the other to enjoy or share them. The new state, whose capital was at Sanaa, had burgeoning oil revenues, mostly in the north, but the two armies were not merged and in 1994 an attempt, instigated or supported by Saudi Arabia, to re-establish a separate southern

state led to the conquest of the south by the north. President Salih settled his contentious borders with Oman and maintained peaceful relations with Saudi Arabia.

The sultanate of *Muscat and Oman* was ruled from 1932 to 1970 by Sultan Said bin
Timur, whose main aims were to keep foreigners out and keep public monies to him-
self. A coup in 1970 brought his son Qaboos to power after a civil war in which Britain
and Iran helped him against the People's Front for the Liberation of Oman and the
Arab Gulf (PFLOAG), which had some but inadequate Russian and Chinese support.
The new sultan was as open-handed as his father had been parsimonious.

Britain and the Persian Gulf

Between the powerful American fleets in the Mediterranean and the South Pacific lay
a gap. For 25 years after the Second World War this gap was filled by the British who,
up to the mid 1960s, insisted that they would go on filling it. The Defence White Paper
of 1957, the first to appear after the fiasco of the Suez War, contained a mixture of old
and new ideas. It still envisaged local forces not only in Aden and Cyprus but also
in Kenya (which, however, on becoming independent in 1963 granted Britain only
limited facilities by an agreement of March 1964); it also envisaged a carrier group in
the Indian Ocean. The Kuwait operation of July 1961 (see p. 391) reinforced arguments
in favour of local garrisons for acclimatizing troops, since between a quarter and a
half of the men flown to the scene of that action from temperate climes had been
quickly prostrated by the heat. On the assumption that such operations remained an
inescapable part of Britain's lot in the world, tropical bases seemed essential. The White
Paper of 1962 reiterated the need for a British presence to assure stability and with it
the need to maintain forces in Aden and Singapore. But the arguments and assumptions of the framers of Defence White Papers were challenged by those who counted
the cost of these establishments (especially after the Labour victory of 1964 in the middle of a financial crisis) and by those who believed that bases in Arab territory created
political ill will out of proportion to their military usefulness.

If Aden was the outward and visible sign of the British presence in these waters
its focus was the Persian Gulf, an arm of the Indian Ocean which makes a long and
narrow penetration into the Middle East, dividing Arabia on the one hand from Iran
on the other. This arm is at its narrowest at the strait of Hormuz which divides the
Persian Gulf from the Gulf of Oman and the ocean. The whole of the eastern shore of
both gulfs is Iranian territory, but the opposite shore counts 14 sovereigns. At the head
of the Persian Gulf is Iraq and next to it Kuwait, separated by 560 km of Saudi coastline from the other principalities – the island of Bahrain, the promontory of Qatar, the
Trucial States and lastly the corner state of Muscat and Oman. Kuwait's political and
business affinities have been with its Arab neighbours to the north and its sons have
gone to Cairo or Beirut for their education, whereas the links of the remaining Gulf

states have been rather with Pakistan and India and their sons have gone to school in Karachi.

Britain's initial concern in these waters was to secure a monopoly or dominance over the routes to India and to protect British trade from the depredations of sheikhs who, at the southern end of the Persian Gulf, lived off piracy and earned for this strip of land the name of the Pirate Coast. From 1820 onwards the British imposed a maritime peace by a series of treaties or truces with these Trucial sheikhs and in 1861 extended the system northwards to Bahrain by an agreement which pledged Britain to protect Bahrain in perpetuity. Later in the century Britain negotiated control over the external policies of the sheikhdoms and also of Kuwait and Qatar. Finally, as pearling and oil made these states important for their own sake and not merely as adjuncts of important commercial waters, a series of twentieth-century agreements gave Britain exclusive rights in the commercial exploitation of local riches but without control over internal affairs.

Throughout most of this period the landward frontiers of these states, lying vaguely in uninhabited and supposedly worthless country, were of no concern, and the obligations contracted by Britain as a consequence of the maritime truce remained for a long time unquestioned since Britain had additional reasons for remaining in the Persian Gulf and was undisturbed by commitments to local rulers in an area which it intended to go on policing by naval and air forces for the complementary purposes of the new traffic in oil.

In the endless traffic between Europe and Asia the Middle East must either be crossed or circumvented, and in this context the Arab nationalism of the twentieth century affected Europeans in the same way as the Muslim conquests which prompted the crusades and the voyages round Africa. In the heyday of British power in the Middle East the British travelled freely across it, but after the Second World War the direct central route was lost as one Arab government after another denied to Britain the special rights and facilities which it had previously enjoyed by treaty or by occupation. The withdrawal from Palestine and the Canal Zone, the revolution in Iraq in 1958 and the abrogation of the Anglo-Jordanian treaty at the time of Suez in 1956 eliminated this route and made it necessary to find a southern or a northern detour. The southern route lay through Libya and Sudan to Aden, but in 1964 the Libyan government sought a revision of its 1952 treaty with Britain and in the same year Sudan attached virtually prohibitive conditions to overflying rights. Going south meant flying across central Africa or even southern Africa, both routes being politically awkward as well as expensively long. The northern alternative, by Turkey and Iran and the Persian Gulf, remained valuable but no longer essential since technical developments were opening up a new, if arduous and expensive, route from Britain westward to Singapore.

Communications therefore provided an argument, effective though not conclusive, for staying in the Persian Gulf a little longer, provided it was understood that the days of the British presence were numbered. Oil provided only a weaker argument. The importance of Middle Eastern oil to Europe was undeniable, but the policy of ensuring supplies by a physical presence seemed increasingly anachronistic. Europe, unlike the United States, had become dependent on Middle Eastern oil. Britain, for example, which before the Second World War imported more than half its oil from the American continent, was by 1950 importing half its needs from Kuwait alone, and it was estimated in 1965 that Europe's annual consumption of 300 million tons would rise in 15 years to 750 million tons, despite the greater use of natural gas and nuclear power. Important discoveries of oil in the Sahara in 1956 and Libya in 1959 might decrease the proportion of Middle Eastern oil in Europe's consumption but not the total amount of Middle Eastern oil required. Oil was thought likely to remain cheaper than gas or nuclear power or submarine hydrocarbons, and Middle Eastern oil was cheaper than other oil, but this European dependence was not as frightening as it seemed to a number of European statesmen since Middle Eastern producers were, for their part, heavily dependent on their European customers. By the mid-1960s, when a British retreat became a reality, the oil revenues of the states concerned exceeded £2 billion and provided between 70 and 95 per cent of the budgetary income of the several producers. Neither the increasing demand from Japan nor the prospect of China's entry into the market seemed likely to counter the need of the Middle Eastern producers to sell their oil to Europe, and if this were so, military bases were as irrelevant to the flow of oil as to the supply of any other commodity.

There was, however, a further argument – political rather than economic. The British, it was said, had gone to the Persian Gulf to keep the peace and provide the stability without which commerce is endangered and they had done so. A British withdrawal could be followed by disorders which would interrupt the flow of oil. These disorders might be the result of sabotage or of frontier disputes between the states of the region. Sabotage is not a thing which regular military units are particularly suited to prevent, while one of the more usual causes of sabotage is nationalist resentment against the presence of foreign garrisons. Frontier disputes were numerous: Iran claimed Bahrain; Iraq claimed Iran's province of Khuzistan and Kuwait; Saudi Arabia had disputed frontiers with some of its smaller neighbours, many of whom were at feud with one another. So long as such disputes persisted Britain might claim to be rendering a service by remaining in the area and performing a policeman's task.

In the Trucial States Britain tried but failed to promote a federation as a first step towards release from its perpetual obligations. Britain was not supposed to interfere in the internal affairs of these states but often felt obliged to do so because of their mutual disputes, the shortcomings of some of their rulers and the aid which the poorer ones required. The rulers, though no longer in need of protection from the seaward, felt the need for protection against Saudi Arabia or their own not very numerous subjects. The ruler of Qatar (which had loosely formed part of the trucial system in the early nineteenth century but had left it in the 1860s) asked for British help against internal troubles in 1963 but was refused it. The principal problem, however, was the relationship between the sheikhs and Saudi Arabia. Britain wished neither to let the sheikhs down nor to prop them up indefinitely.

Britain's relations with the Saudi royal house had been friendly and strong, notably in the days of King Abdul Aziz, although less so after the accession of his son Saud in 1953 and much less so after the substitution of American for British influence in Saudi Arabia. Britain was embarrassed by the apparently complete imperviousness of the Saudi regime to the slightest touch of modernity, except in the accumulation of oil royalties which were expended by the royal family on ventures frequently more lavish than useful. It did not seem right to abandon states once redeemed from piracy to the mercy of a big neighbour still noted for slavery. Moreover, in 1955 a running dispute over the Buraimi oasis led to military confrontation. This oasis, a collection of ten villages partly in the possession of the sheikh of Abu Dhabi and partly in that of the sultan of Muscat, was coveted by Saudi Arabia, whose claims had been rejected by Britain for a generation. The dispute, which involved the two powerful forces of honour and oil, was referred to an arbitral tribunal at Geneva but the Saudis, having too little faith in their cause or in the tribunal, bribed witnesses on such a scale that Britain was moved to public protest. The Saudis also sent troops into the villages, whence they were forcibly expelled by the British. Yet Britain was loath to pursue the quarrel, which died down once more.

As in India, so too in the Middle East, the positions of power vacated by Britain were transmitted to no single successor. The post-British regime in the Gulf was the outcome of negotiations between Britain itself, Iran and Saudi Arabia. The shah renounced the Iranian claim to Bahrain, which became in 1970 a fully independent member of the United Nations. Populous and wealthy enough to stand on its own feet, it was unwilling to become a member of the proposed new federation of Gulf states, unless it were accorded an equivalently overwhelming representation in the projected Union of Arab Emirates. This federation came into being at the beginning of 1972 but without Qatar and Ras al-Khaimar (one of the seven Trucial States), both of which chose independence. All existing treaties with Britain were abrogated. Iran, pleading strategic exigency, seized the islets of Abu Musa and the Tunbs in the narrows between the Persian Gulf and the Gulf of Oman, causing Iraq to break off diplomatic relations with Iran and expel Iranians from Iraq. The new order rested essentially on agreement between Iran and Saudi Arabia, on the latter's inability to secure at this stage full control over the western shores of the Gulf to match Iran's control on the other side, and on the fortuitous absence of Egyptian and Iraqi voices, owing to the former's defeat in 1967 and the latter's continuing war with the Kurds and other internal weaknesses; but none of these factors was necessarily permanent. The assassination of Feisal in 1975 and the peaceful succession of his brother Khaled did not disturb the pattern, but in the same year Iraq began to recover its freedom of action. The Gulf Council, created in 1981 on Saudi initiative, was part of the Saudi effort to counter both Iraqi and Iranian influence: it embraced Saudi Arabia, Kuwait, Bahrain, Qatar, the United Arab Emirates and Oman.

Notes

A. The Kurds

The Kurdish peoples trace their tribal names further back in time than any other people in the world and their presence in western Asia for 4,000 years. Their fortunes reached a peak in the days of the twelfth-century sultan known to Europeans as Saladin. In more recent centuries they have been divided between the Ottoman empire and the Safavid and Qajar empires in Iran and further divided since the First World War among the Turkish and other successors of the former. They were promised statehood by the Treaty of Sèvres in 1920 but denied it by the substituted Treaty of Lausanne in 1923. In religion most Kurds are Sunni Muslims but in Iran many are Shi'ites and in Turkey about a third are Alawis. By the mid-twentieth century they numbered about 25 million – half of them in Turkey, 7 million in Iran, 4 million in Iraq and smaller numbers in Syria, the Armenian SSR and Soviet central Asia. The last tried without success to get recognition as an autonomous republic in Gorbachev's Russia.

In modern Turkey the Kurds number about a fifth of the population. They were concentrated in south-east Turkey, an area of agricultural decrepitude with its capital at Diyarbakir, and, like the Turks, were divided between a secularist view of the state and a Sunni clericalism. An increasing number of them spread to Istanbul and other essentially Turkish cities, where some of them prospered, intermarried with Turks and became more assimilationist than nationalist. Between the wars there were serious risings in 1925, 1930 and 1937 as Ataturk's centralized and secularist regime played down a distinct Kurdish identity and discriminated and maltreated Kurds. After the Second World War – and particularly during 1950–60, when the Democratic Party was in power – relations eased but discontent and repression smouldered and in 1984 the Kurdistan Workers' Party (PKK), a partly nationalist and partly communist party founded a few years earlier by Abdullah Öçalan, started a guerrilla war which stoked hatred and brutality on both sides, wrecked thousands of villages and drove refugees off their lands into Diyarbakir (its population trebled) and other cities further west. Some 750,000 migrated to western Europe, where they added their voices against Turkey's admission to the EU. Öçalan, who directed operations from Syria for many years, fled in 1999 to Europe and then Africa, where he was captured in Kenya, extradited to Turkey, tried and sentenced to death.

In Iran the Kurds were harried by Reza Shah between the wars and then led up the garden path by the Russians, who paid diligent attention to Kurdish notables during the war, fostered Kurdish nationalism and supplied a separatist movement with arms. In January 1946 the Kurds proclaimed the independent republic of Mahabad, but for the Russians the Kurdish movement was no more than a useful appanage of the separatist Azerbaijani republic which they had contrived in Tabriz at the end of 1945. The Mahabad republic was an expression of genuine non-communist local feelings, whereas the Azerbaijani republic was a communist artefact. Attempts to ally the two were never more than superficially successful although the Kurds, dependent on Russian support, were half-tied to the Azerbaijanis. After the Russian withdrawal from Iran in 1946 the Azerbaijanis negotiated, without reference to the Kurds, an autonomy agreement with the Iranian government but a few months later prime minister Qavam es-Sultaneh, having evicted communists from his government in Teheran, sent the Iranian army to destroy the communist local government in Tabriz. The Mahabad republic was then at the mercy of Iranian arms. It was annihilated, its leaders fleeing or being hanged.

The fate of the Kurds in Iraq was largely in British hands when, after taking Baghdad in the First World War, British forces went on to Mosul and installed the Kurdish leader Mahmud Barsandji as governor. The Kurds hoped for an independent Kurdistan as a reward for their anti-Turkish services during the war and in the first postwar years the British were primarily concerned to prevent the return of Mosul to the new Turkish state. The abortive Treaty of Sèvres of 1920 (which provided for an independent Armenia) gave the Kurds no more than a promise of autonomy which the Iraqis, a protected or mandated state on its way to independence, were determined to limit or annul. His hopes disappointed, Barsandji declared an independent Kurdistan. The British deported him to India but then (1922) reinstated him as governor in Mosul. A year later he fled to Iran. The Treaty of Lausanne (1923) annulled the Treaty of Sèvres and therewith its provisions for Kurds and Armenians. The new Turkish state claimed Mosul but in 1925 the League of Nations endorsed the British claim that it was part of Iraq. Five years later Barsandji returned to Iraq in an attempt to win some Kurdish advantage out of sporadic clashes between Kurds and Iraqis but he was thwarted by British air power and with the end of the British mandate over Iraq the Kurdish region became a part of the sovereign state of Iraq.

Towards the end of the Second World War a new Kurdish leader, Mustapha Barzani, led a revolt which was crushed: some 10,000 Kurds fled to Iran and Barzani fled to Moscow. The revolution of 1958 in Baghdad destroyed the alliance between the three anti-Kurdish states of Iraq, Turkey and Iran and substituted for the Iraqi monarchy a republic of 'Arabs and Kurds'. Barzani returned from Moscow and was honourably and even munificently received by President Kassim, who looked with favour on the Kurds because of the left-wing tendencies among them. In 1960 a Kurdish Democratic Party was allowed, but the Kurds were divided in their views on Kassim and even their left wing disliked the communist ideas which gained ground in Iraq after the revolution. After some internal dissension the Kurdish Democratic Party became definitely anti-communist, rapidly lost Kassim's favour, was persecuted and officially extinguished.

In 1961 the Kurds rebelled. Kassim claimed that they were receiving military supplies from Britain and the United States. He turned for arms to the USSR, which found it opportune to forget its earlier support for the Kurds in the hope of finding a more useful ally in Kassim. The Iraqi army started a full-scale campaign against the Kurds with napalm bombs and rocket-carrying aircraft. In February 1963 Kassim was over-thrown and killed and the pan-Arab nationalists of the Ba'ath Party took control of the government under the presidency of General Aref, who engaged in discussions with the Kurds and gave them to understand that they would get something like autonomy. Later in the year, however, the discussions were broken off by the seizure of the Kurdish negotiators and the Iraqi army, supported in the field by Syria, where the Ba'ath had also come to power, embarked on an even more ferocious campaign against the Kurds than the operations of 1961–62. But the Ba'ath anti-communist nationalism had alien-ated the communist world, which raised the cry of genocide. Early in 1964 a truce was negotiated. It proved fragile, but in 1970 President al-Bakr and his vice-president Saddam Hussein renewed it and Barzani won a fresh agreement on autonomy which, however, again collapsed for a variety of reasons, including the disputed status of Kirkuk. When Iraq and Iran joined forces against the Kurds, Barzani fled to the United States.

The Iraqi revolts of 1958 and 1963 were unwelcome to the shah. The shah wanted Shi'ite Muslims to have a share in the government of Iraq and if the Shi'ites were to be so treated the Kurds would have to be so too. He refused to help Aref's anti-Kurdish operations even when Kurds took refuge in Iran and he gave Iraqi Kurds surreptitious – and not so surreptitious – help. His rapprochement with King Feisal of Saudi Arabia in 1965 encouraged him to think in terms of a Persian Gulf regulated by a Saudi–Iranian compact without the need to accommodate Iraq. In 1980 Iraq turned the tables on Iran by supporting Kurdish separatists within Iran and when Iraqi Kurds appealed for support from the exiled Khomeini, Saddam Hussein slaughtered them with chem-ical weapons. In and after the Gulf War of 1991 the Americans hoped that Kurds and Shi'ites would revolt against Hussein and the incautious language of President Bush was interpreted by them as incitement to do so. Not for the first time these Kurds misread ambiguous signals emanating from greater powers. Bush's Turkish allies were opposed to Kurdish independence or autonomy anywhere and his Saudi allies were equally opposed to similar recognition for Shi'ites. Hussein's crushing defeat at the hands of the United States and its allies did not prevent him from savaging Kurds and Shi'ites. The latter's homelands in southern Iraq were drained to make them an easier prey and many were killed by Iraqi forces or driven to flee into Iran.

The Iraqi Kurds were only tenuously united. The Patriotic Union of Kurdistan (PUK) split from the Kurdish Democratic Movement (KDM) in 1975, advocated more active opposition to the central government and refused to support Iraq in its war with Iran, whereas the KDM – and Kurds in Iran – sided with Iraq. After the Gulf War the PUK's leader Jalal Talabani responded positively and disastrously to Bush's call to revolt, whereas the KDM and Masud Barzani (son of Mustafa) were more cautious. The two leaders' following among Iraqi Kurds was about equal. Hussein, dealing with each separately, produced a draft law for autonomy which satisfied neither and in the aftermath of their abortive rising 1.5 million Kurds fled into Iran and half a million to

Turkey. In 1992 fresh proposals which included an elected Kurdish assembly and an autonomous executive in an (imprecisely defined) zone were accepted by both the KDM and the PUK, but their co-operation lasted no more than two years. International attention and commitment flagged. UN members failed to keep up their contributions to UN aid and supervision, diseases took hold, Iraqi harassment increased and so too did fighting between the Kurdish parties. In 1996 Barzani rounded on Talabani with Iraqi help; Talabani riposted by seeking help from Iran; and American visions of an independent or autonomous Kurdistan were at least temporarily wiped out.

B. The Shi'ites

The Shi'ites, who separated from the main Muslim stock over 1,000 years ago, comprise about a tenth of Islam. They revere the Prophet's son-in-law Ali and his two sons, Hassan and Hussein, as the originators of the true line of divinely inspired imams (leaders). Most of them await the reappearance of the twelfth imam, who disappeared in AD 880, but some of them await other reappearances. They are widespread in Islam but strongest east of the Euphrates. They dominate Iran where they have had the control of power for 500 years, outnumber other groups in Iraq and Lebanon, and constitute important minorities in Syria, Pakistan and elsewhere. Khomeini's successes boosted their standing wherever they were to be found but also scared non-Shi'ites, particularly Arabs who distrusted Iranians and Sunnis who disliked clerical intervention in government. Their faith is imbued with suffering and persecution, a bottled bitterness directed chiefly against Sunnis, whose faithlessness to the true line has been further sullied by western – notably American – modernism and immorality; also against Jews and Baha'is. The legitimacy of violence is more obvious to Shi'ites than to Sunnis or most Europeans.

C. Sectarian violence

The Muslim Brotherhood, founded in Egypt in 1928 by Hassan al-Banna, who died in 1949, asserted what it held to be basic Muslim values and particularly opposed the separation of church and state (as those terms were understood in the west) and foreign influences on Islam. Its prime aim was the reassertion of Islamic law (the shari'a) and the paramount authority of shari'a courts. Hassan al-Banna preached patience but not all his followers achieved it. The Brotherhood murdered the Egyptian prime minister Nokrashi Pasha in 1948, was dispersed and dissolved, revived in the anti-British climate of the 1950s, supported the movement which brought Naguib and Nasser to power but was discarded by them, tried to kill Nasser, suffered thousands of deaths in prisons but recovered after Nasser's death. Sadat, who was more partial to religious groups, tried to split the Brotherhood into violent and anti-violent wings but his pro-western policies alienated both and narrowed the gap between them. The Brotherhood was saddled with responsibility for his murder and again suffered arrests on a large scale. The murder in 1990 of Rifaat al-Mahgoub, the chairman of the Egyptian parliament, provoked a similar operation against religious revolutionaries. Similar movements in, for example, Syria, Sudan, Algeria and Pakistan built up parties within the state with the aim of subordinating the constitution to fundamental Muslim tenets, codes, courts and practices. Although banned from party politics in Egypt the Brotherhood was active in middle-class professional bodies and attracted a new class of follower among the social and economic victims of accelerating urbanization. During the Gulf War Islamic movements became a recruiting ground for Americans anxious to find and finance anti-Russian guerrillas in (for example) Afghanistan but when the Russians retreated from Afghanistan these recruits returned to Egypt where, discarded and unemployed, they joined groups – Hamas el-Islamiya, Jihad al-Islam – which were violently hostile to American support for Israel and Mubarak's support for the United States. Unable to eliminate them, the Egyptian government jailed, tortured or murdered many of them and inflamed the rest.

Conflicts within Islam interlocked with the Arab–Israeli feud and Arab responses to Israel's existence and its oppression of Palestinians: a number of anti-Israeli bodies resorted to violence. In the 1970s the Popular Front for the Liberation of Palestine (PFLP) and its leader George Habash took to hijacking in order to draw international attention to the grievances of Palestinians. In 1970 the PFLP hijacked four aircraft, destroyed one of them on the ground at Cairo and three in Jordan, released all those on board and secured in exchange the release of PFLP prisoners from British, German and Swiss jails. In 1972 Japanese sympathizers opened fire at Lod airport in Israel, killing 25 people including three of themselves. In 1973 the Israeli air force forced an airliner to land in Israel in the mistaken belief that Habash was on board. In 1976 the PFLP hijacked a French airliner with a number of Jews on board and forced it to land at Entebbe in Uganda in an attempt to secure the release of Palestinians from Israeli jails; after the non-Israeli passengers had been released by the hijackers the remaining 100 were rescued by a daring and efficient Israeli raid on the airport. The 1980s saw no diminution in violent protest, but it took a variety of forms, adding the taking of hostages to murder and suicide. In 1983 pro-Iranian Shi'ites attacked public buildings and the American and French embassies in Beirut; among 21 persons arrested were three Lebanese. In response, hostages – mostly American or French – were seized in Beirut and a Kuwaiti aircraft was seized at Teheran and two American passengers murdered. In 1985 a handful of Palestinians hijacked the cruise ship *Achille Lauro* as a means to get 50 Palestinians out of Israeli jails; one passenger, an American, was killed (see p. 365). The hijackers surrendered at Port Said where they were put on an Egyptian aircraft for Tunisia, which was forced by the American air force to land in Sicily. The Italian government refused to hand them over to the United States and they escaped to Yugoslavia. A group led by Sabri el-Banna (Abu Nidal) appeared to combine fiery indignation with an eye to the main chance. Besides the attempted murder in 1982 of the Israeli ambassador in London (which Israel tried to pin on the PLO and Arafat), attacks on passengers for Israel at Rome and Vienna airports and hijacking an Egyptian aircraft, which was forced down at Malta, where an Egyptian attempt to recover it caused 57 deaths, Abu Nidal appeared willing to work for sundry Middle Eastern governments (including perhaps Israel's). For its part, Israel intercepted and forced down an aircraft in the mistaken expectation of finding Palestinian leaders and taking them hostage.

In 1986 the United States with British help bombed Libya on the plea that the killer of an American soldier in a Berlin night club had been a Libyan; the United States sought to justify this act as self-defence. In 1988 the Hizbollah in Lebanon captured and hanged an American colonel serving with the UN; a Kuwaiti aircraft was flown by hijackers to Mashad in Iran, thence to Beirut, where it was refused permission to land and then to Cyprus, where its passengers were released; and an American airliner was destroyed over Lockerbie in Scotland and all its passengers and crew were killed (p. 523). In 1989 Israel kidnapped from Lebanon Sheikh Abdul Karim Obeid in another tit-for-tat operation. In the 1990s the most noticeable group was Hamas, a small group of Palestinians who, like the even smaller Islamic Jihad, turned to violence to vent their rage against the Israeli state. Its origins went back to prewar years. After the Second World War, and especially after the war of 1967, it developed schools, mosques and hospitals as well as a military wing dedicated to the destruction of Israel. It was invigorated around 1978 by Sheikh Ahmed Yassim, who was later seized and imprisoned in Israel. It attracted widespread, but largely passive, support among Palestinians in Gaza and the West Bank who were losing faith in the PLO and distrusted Arafat's negotiations with Israel. The high-handedness of Rabin's and Netanyahu's governments strengthened Hamas and enabled it to pose as a significant alternative to the PLO in the struggle for an independent Palestinian state. After the massacre in 1994 of 29 Muslim worshippers in a mosque in Hebron under the eyes of the Israeli police, Hamas abandoned its proclaimed policy of killing soldiers but not civilians. Unlike Hizbollah in Lebanon, Hamas was neither Shi'ite nor apparently funded by Iran.

Muslim militancy became increasingly anti-American as well as anti-Israeli in the last decade of the century, notably after the Gulf War of 1991, when the United States negotiated the right to station troops in Saudi Arabia for the duration of the war but failed to withdraw them afterwards. Saudis, particularly opponents of the Saudi regime, objected that this continuing American presence was an infringement of their country's independence and, for the more puritanical Muslims, an affront to decency. The American base at Dhahran was attacked in 1996 and two years later the American embassies in Nairobi and Dar-es-Salaam and nearby buildings were damaged and people killed in attacks apparently organized and financed by Saudis.

In these years the term fundamentalism – a term borrowed from Christianity – came into use as one of the more mischievous oversimplifications of the age. A fundamentalist is one who believes the totality of what he is told to believe. Islam, more thoroughly than any other major religion, retained sway over the hearts and minds of its adherents and these were attracted into parties prepared to use violence and justify it, whether the cause were religious, nationalist, social or a compound of these. Muslim fundamentalism was used not only to describe these various and sometimes dangerous groups but to imply that Islam was essentially violent and that parties claiming a special allegiance to Islam were part of a single unified and menacing force. Islamic fundamentalism, a catch-all phrase coined in the west, stressed the more disruptive aspects of a cultural revolution of long standing. From one standpoint it denoted a conservative reaction against assorted political and social ideas which had been reaching Islam from the west for centuries and created intellectual movements opposed by traditional establishments. To outsiders these movements, active not only in the Middle East but also from west Africa to South-east Asia, were vengeful enemies of the west and were condemned because they were Muslim as much as because they were violent. Most Muslim fundamentalists, like Christian or Jewish fundamentalists, eschewed physical violence. The bogey of a general Islamic conspiracy to subvert and terrorize the forces of law and virtue was as mischievous and ridiculous as the invention of a Zionist conspiracy of equal malevolence, but the suppression by despots of more constitutional oppositions allowed violent religious groups to monopolize the role of opposition. Prominent among these was al-Qaeda, the creation of Osama bin Laden, who established training camps in Afghanistan impelled by religious fervour and intense hatred of the USA and its associates who were portrayed as humiliators of Muslim and a brand of evil.

Related reading: part four

Hourani, Albert: *Arabic Thought in the Liberal Age 1798–1939* (1962)
Kinzer, Stephen: *All the Shah's Men – An American Coup and the Roots of Middle East Terror* (2003)
Mahfouz, Naguib: *Palace Walk* (1990)
Ruthven, Malise: *Islam in the World* (1984)
Vital, David: *The Future of the Jews* (1990)
Wasserstein, Bernard: *Divided Jerusalem* (2001)
Yergin, Daniel: *The Prize – The Epic Quest for Oil, Money and Power* (1991)

PART FIVE

South Asia

CHAPTER 16

The Indian sub-continent

The half-century preceding the departure of the British from India had seen a series of reforms, evolved by the British and leading logically and explicitly to Indian independence; the growth of divisions within India which led to the partition of 1947; and a growing awareness of world politics, in which, nevertheless, the new rulers were, for the most part, but imperfectly versed. In the nineteenth century India, though less closed to the outside world than China or Japan, had a view of the world which was overshadowed by the British presence; and the principal episode of the century was the Sepoy Revolt or Mutiny of a part of Britain's subjects against British rule. This view was changing by the end of the century. The Russian advance towards Afghanistan; Curzon's preoccupation with the north-western frontier and Tibet; the extension of British Indian power into the Middle East; the alliance of Britain with Japan in 1902, followed by Japan's defeat of Russia in 1905; revolutions in Turkey, Iran and China – all these turned the Indian mind – or part of it – outward. Although in 1947 Jawaharlal Nehru was the only member of his cabinet with any claim to expert knowledge of foreign politics, his colleagues and many others among his compatriots had grown up with the feeling that, if India's special problem was the defeat of the British raj, there were also other problems and other powers to be reckoned with. Even though many Indians misjudged the nature of the problems, deceiving themselves with the belief that their cause was the British presence and their cure would be the British departure, this mistake was a matter of misinterpretation and not of cloistered ignorance. Within India nationalism, which was one of the by-products of the Hindu and Muslim intellectual revivals of the nineteenth century and took visible shape in the founding of the Indian National Congress in 1885, was inevitably anti-British. Like most nationalist movements, it came to be divided into more and less militant factions (led by B. G. Tilak on the one hand and G. K. Gokhale and then M. K. Gandhi on the other), but, unlike others, it was also divided in a more enduring way before the day of victory. As independence approached, the ability of Hindu and Muslim to live together diminished until it proved impossible to maintain a single successor state to the British raj and at independence the two great religious communities feared and hated each other as much as they feared or hated the British.

Britain had long envisaged the surrender of empire in India but without formulating a timetable. The Second World War imposed the timetable. At the beginning of that war the viceroy made the inept mistake of declaring war on India's behalf, as he was entitled to do, without consulting a single Indian. Congress ministries, in office under the constitution of 1935, thereupon resigned. In 1942, Sir Stafford Cripps was sent by the British cabinet to India to offer it dominion status with the right to secede from the empire, but the exercise of this option and all other internal advances were to be postponed until the end of the war. The Congress, which may have misjudged British intentions and certainly – if recruiting figures meant anything – misjudged Indian sentiment, decided to have no part in the war and to use it to wage a Quit India campaign against the British. In 1944 Britain, now sure of victory in all theatres, appointed a new viceroy, Lord Wavell, and released imprisoned Indian leaders. After the general election of 1945 the Labour government sent three cabinet ministers to India to try to get agreement between the Congress and the Muslim League as a preliminary to independence, but relations between these bodies had deteriorated during the war (the reverse of the experience of the First World War) and the British attempt failed. The League and its leader Muhammad Ali Jinnah were convinced that Britain was partial to the Congress; in August 1946 Jinnah inaugurated Direct Action by the League to secure a separate sovereign state for Muslims; and the winter of 1946–47 was marked by violent communal riots. Early in 1947 the viceroy came to the conclusion that no single Indian central authority could be constituted and he accordingly advised the British government either to retain power for at least a decade or to transfer it, fragmented, to the several provinces.

The first partition

The British government rejected this advice, replaced Wavell by Lord Mountbatten and announced that Britain would abdicate in June 1948. It proposed to resolve the dilemma by neither of the methods recommended by Wavell but to partition India and hand over power to two separate governments. The 562 princely states, which were not part of British India, were to be cajoled into one or other of the new states. Their relationship with the British crown was regulated by the doctrine of paramountcy. Britain did not propose to transfer its paramount rights to the new India or Pakistan but declared that paramountcy would lapse, with the result that each ruler would be free in law to accede to India or Pakistan or neither – and free in practice to accede to India or Pakistan. Junagadh made the impractical choice of acceding to Pakistan, with which it had no border; the ruler was forced to see his error, departed for Pakistan and left his state to become part of India. Three states toyed with independence: Travancore, Hyderabad and Kashmir. Travancore's ambitions were quickly seen to be illusory: Hyderabad had first to be blockaded and then (in 1949) invaded. Both became part of India. With Kashmir we shall be further concerned.

Britain's shock tactics were intensified when Mountbatten reported that even June 1948 was too late for the transfer of power. He concluded that violence would become uncontrollable before then, and the British cabinet accepted his view. By advancing the date to August 1947 it left scant time for settling the biggest issue; the lines of partition between India and the two widely separated segments of Pakistan. A boundary commission was created, consisting of two Hindu and two Muslim judges with Sir Cyril Radcliffe as chairman. On most contentious points the two Hindu and the two Muslim voices cancelled each other out and Radcliffe was left to take, in two months, a series of detailed decisions on localities which he did not know and had no time to visit. The new borders did not serve to contain the peoples within them. Fear drove millions across them and in the course of this mass exodus millions were slaughtered. Sikhs, quitting the homes in the Punjab in which they no longer felt safe, attacked Muslims moving westward for the same reason; Muslims retaliated; atrocities were multiplied over a wide area reaching to Delhi itself. Two million men, women and children may have died, 10–15 million survived only as refugees, and this horrible feast of violence was capped in January 1948 by the assassination of Gandhi himself, Hindu apostle of non-violence killed by a Hindu fanatic.

In the new state of *India* two men took control – first and foremost Jawaharlal Nehru and with him Vallabhai Patel. Nehru became prime minister and held that office until his death in 1964. Patel, to whom fell the task of consolidating the Indian federation of former British provinces and princely states, died prematurely in 1950. The Congress Party chose Purshottandas Tandom to be its president but in 1951 Nehru enforced Tandom's resignation by resigning from the Working Committee which was the Congress's power house. Nehru remained president of the Congress until 1955, when he handed the office to a reliable subordinate. In general elections in 1952, 1957 and 1962 the Congress received a slightly rising share of the vote (45–48 per cent) and a consistently massive majority in the federal parliament, despite internal divisions and growing criticisms from right and left. Its principal adversary, the Communist Party, won 3.3 per cent of the vote in 1952 and around 10 per cent in the two following elections, but this vote was concentrated in a few areas. In Kerala the communists won power on a minority vote and formed a government, but it was dismissed by the central government in 1959 and an anti-communist alliance won elections in 1960, despite a rise in the local communist vote to 42.5 per cent. The Sino-Soviet quarrel produced a rift in the party; its secretary A. K. Ghosh attacked China in 1961, and the Chinese invasion of India in 1962 further discomfited the party in general and its Chinese wing in particular.

But Indian political life was less disrupted by party conflict than by other divisive forces, linguistic and religious. India's 60-odd languages included a great many derivatives of Sanskrit, predominant in the north; a group of non-Sanskrit languages, including four principal ones, in the south; and a kind of *lingua franca* in Urdu/Hindustani. Some of these languages generated a devotion so ardent as to provoke bloodshed. Hindi, one of the northern Sanskrit derivatives, had enthusiasts who wished to make it the single official language of the country, an ambition opposed not only by those who realized the value of English but also by Bengalis proud of their own tongue and by southerners affronted by any implied denigration of Tamil, Malayalam, Kanada or Telugu. In the south the language question became an ingredient in a Tamil separatist movement and all over India pressure grew to redraw the map on linguistic lines. A new province, Andhra, was created on this basis in 1953, and in Bombay a serious crisis between Marathi-speakers (who were a majority in Bombay city) and Gujarati-speakers forced the central government to choose between an avowedly bilingual state or the promotion of Bombay city to be a state on its own. The government chose the former course and displeased everybody, until in 1960 the Marathi-speakers were able to insist on a partition and the transfer of Bombay city to the state of Maharashtra. In the Punjab, where religion was a greater threat to unity than language, the Sikhs campaigned for a Punjabi-speaking Sikh state which would have entailed a division of the Punjab. Despite fasts by their leader Master Tara Singh they were not successful. Nor were they pacified. In the north-east Nagas and Mizos presented similar dilemmas.

In external affairs Nehru was determined to remain in the Commonwealth (especially if Pakistan did) while adopting a republican constitution and conducting a foreign policy which might be not merely independent of Britain's but contrary to Britain's. He succeeded in persuading the other prime ministers of the Commonwealth (as the British Commonwealth was significantly renamed at this period) that India might remain a member even though it became a republic. Without this revolutionary step the expanding postwar Commonwealth, with its strong republican tendencies, could hardly have taken shape. In 1949 a Commonwealth conference accepted an Indian plan to declare the British sovereign head of the Commonwealth and leave each member free to adopt a monarchical or republican constitution. India itself became a republic at the beginning of 1950, and within a few years there were more republics than monarchies in the Commonwealth. The independence of each member of the British family of nations had been accepted for a generation but none had so far consistently pursued a foreign policy which ran counter to Britain's. This Nehru set out to do without impairing relations with London, and he was substantially successful. Although Britain was a committed protagonist in the Cold War, Nehru held that it was none of India's business and that the two camps were behaving with equally deplorable folly. Having taken a part in bringing the Korean War to an end he went on to elaborate a posture of neutralism in the hope of keeping sizeable powers out of the Cold War, of limiting its evil effects and paving the way for its eventual termination. In 1995 he visited Moscow, and India received a return visit from Bulganin and Khrushchev (who made the mistake of making the anti-British speeches which Indians were capable of making themselves but did not countenance in others). In the following year the Anglo-French attack on Egypt and the Russian intervention in Hungary confirmed

Indian belief in the wickedness of all major powers, even though Nehru himself was less censorious of the Hungarian episode than of Suez (perhaps because of the latter's implications for Commonwealth solidarity). Nehru's determination that Asia should give the rest of the world an example in sanity caused him to pursue the myth of Sino-Indian friendship with an unrealistic tenacity which, when China attacked India in 1962, gravely weakened his prestige.

One source of the refusal of many Indians to give the Chinese menace sufficiently serious attention was the all-consuming quarrel with *Pakistan*. Even India's claims against western colonial powers like France and Portugal were emotionally trivial compared with the animosity against Pakistan. (These claims were admittedly small in territorial extent. France ceded Chandernagore – virtually part of Calcutta – in 1951 and its remaining possessions – Pondicherry, Karikal, Mahé and Yanan – in 1954. Portugal adopted in India, as in Africa, the device of converting its colonies into provinces of metropolitan Portugal, but this nominal metamorphosis was of short avail and in 1961 India took the Portuguese territories – Goa, Danan and Dia – by a show of force.) Unlike India, Pakistan lost its father figure early. Jinnah, who had become governor-general on independence, died in 1948. Liaqat Ali Khan, Pakistan's first prime minister, was assassinated three years later. For several years Pakistan wasted much of its tenuous substance on barren constitutional disputes while public figures succeeded each other in high offices, corruption became scandalous and the army wondered how long to let it go on. Khwaja Nazimuddin succeeded Jinnah as governor-general and then succeeded Liaqat Ali Khan as prime minister in 1951; in 1953 his own successor as governor-general, Ghulam Muhammad, dismissed him and installed Muhammad Ali Bogra in his place.

These changes, which involved attempts to preserve a balance between West and East Pakistan, were accompanied by a gradual collapse of authority and by rioting. In 1954 the Muslim League was severely defeated in provincial elections in East Pakistan and the central government, humiliated and jeopardized by this reverse, despatched General Iskander Mirza to East Pakistan as military governor. This appointment was the beginning of the movement towards military rule. In the next year General Mirza became governor-general on the death of Ghulam Muhammad and appointed Chaudri Muhammad Ali, an able and honourable civil servant, to be prime minister. He, however, resigned in 1956 and was succeeded by Firoz Khan Noon, a distinguished veteran. A constitution was finally adopted in 1956, but in 1958 parliamentary democracy came to an end after the deputy speaker of the East Pakistan parliament had been hit on the head with a plank during a debate, so that he died. Martial law was proclaimed with General Ayub Khan as administrator and subsequently as Mirza's successor as head of the state. Political parties were banned. A new constitution was introduced in 1962 based on the American presidential rather than the British parliamentary system.

Pakistan's instability gave India the excuse to justify its fears of its neighbour on the grounds that there was no knowing what governments in such straits might do next. When unstable government was succeeded by military government, Indian fears were merely transposed into a different key and it was alleged that an efficient junta was even more of a danger than an inefficient civilian regime. The ill will between the two countries was concentrated on Kashmir, but Kashmir was not its only cause. The massacres of 1947 had given a spectacularly bad start to a relationship which was almost foredoomed in that it arose out of the inability or refusal of India's two communities to live on good terms with each other. The tendency in India to treat partition as an ephemeral aberration was an additional source of irritation in Pakistan. There were also disputes over the distribution of the waters of the Indus and its tributaries, and over the property of those (about 17 million) who had fled from one country into the other and found themselves unable to sell the pieces of land which they had left behind. Further, the division into two parts of what had been a single economy produced economic tensions which developed into a trade war and reached a high pitch of acrimony when India devalued its currency in 1949 in step with Britain but Pakistan refused to follow suit until 1955. But worst of all was Kashmir.

The state of *Kashmir* consisted of Kashmir proper; Jammu; an upper tier running from the north-west to south-east and consisting of Gilgit, Baltistan and Ladakh; and a western fringe which included the small territory of Poonch. Kashmir had suffered centuries of oppression by a variety of tyrannical overlords. It was under Afghan rule when it was conquered by the Sikh prince Ranjit Singh in 1819. The same prince shortly afterwards installed Gulab Singh as ruler over Jammu, and Gulab Singh duly added Ladakh and Baltistan to his realm. In the 1840s all these territories, Gilgit in the far north-west still excepted, became part of British India as a result of the two wars between the British and the Sikhs for the mastery of the Punjab. The Sikh princes remained in power as maharajahs of Kashmir and Jammu, and in 1947 the British were turning a blind eye to the notoriously unsatisfactory rule of the rich and incompetent Hari Singh. This maharajah's Muslim subjects, four-fifths of the total, were solidly opposed to his rule and so were many of the Hindu minority. Muslim opposition was divided between the Kashmir Muslim Conference, to which no Hindu could belong, and a larger organization, led by the intelligent and open-minded Muslim Sheikh Abdullah, which, following the example of the Indian National Congress, included members of both creeds.

As independence approached in 1947 the maharajah prevaricated, partly because he was toying with the notion of an independent Kashmir and partly because his interests lay in directions other than statecraft. The small territory of Poonch purported to secede and was immediately invaded from Pakistan. The maharajah appealed to India, which refused to come to his help unless he formally acceded to India. This he did just in time to enable Indian troops to be flown into Kashmir to forestall the capture of its capital Srinagar by the invaders. India referred the situation to the UN Security

Council and Pakistan sent regular army units into Kashmir which recovered some of the ground occupied by the Indian army. The Indians removed and in 1949 deposed the maharajah and Nehru made the first of a number of promises to hold a referendum. A UN mission proposed a ceasefire, which came into effect on the first day of 1949, and a plebiscite, which was never held. The ceasefire hardened into partition along an adventitious line. Parts of Kashmir became integrated with Pakistan; these were the west, including Poonch, and Baltistan and Gilgit. The rest of the country, including Ladakh, was ruled by Sheikh Abdullah as prime minister under the nominal authority of a member of the princely house as head of state, until in 1953 the Indians, suspicious that Sheikh Abdullah too wanted an independent Kashmir, put him in prison and replaced him by Bakshi Ghulam Muhammad, with whom they proceeded to work out a new constitution for Kashmir as a fully integrated part of the Indian federation.

During the 1950s a number of abortive attempts were made to supplement the ceasefire by a political settlement. The American Admiral Chester Nimitz, who was appointed to supervise the plebiscite, never even went to Kashmir. A UN conciliation commission (UNCIP) abandoned its task at the end of 1949. An Australian judge, Sir Owen Dixon, was appointed UN mediator but was obliged to announce failure. Talks in 1951 between Nehru and Liaqat Ali Khan also failed. Dr Frank P. Graham took over Sir Owen Dixon's task with the same result. After the dismissal of Sheikh Abdullah in 1953 there were new talks between Nehru and Muhammad Ali but again fruitlessly. Then in 1954, at the time when Kashmir's constitution and status were being altered, the United States and Pakistan entered into an agreement which provided for American military aid to Pakistan. From the American point of view this was an anti-Russian move, part of the American policy of containment or encirclement, but from the Indian point of view it was a powerful reinforcement of India's principal enemy. Nehru made it the occasion explicitly to go back on his promise to hold a plebiscite in Kashmir. At the beginning of 1957 Pakistan asked the Security Council to order the withdrawal of all troops from Kashmir, to send a UN force there, to organize a plebiscite and to require India to abandon the new constitution which was about to integrate Kashmir into India. India opposed UN intervention and the USSR vetoed the resolution. A year later Dr Graham made similar proposals to India, which rejected them.

Northern borders: Tibet, Kashmir, the Himalayan states

In the 1950s Indians became aware of Chinese activities on India's northern borders. Besides the subjugation of Tibet (see p. 145) there were incidents in Ladakh, a polarization of politics between pro-Indian and pro-Chinese parties, and clashes in India's north-eastern corner. Sino-Indian frontiers run for 1,600 km through some of the most daunting territory in the world from Ladakh (where Kashmir pushes a wedge between India and Tibet), past Nepal, Sikkim and Bhutan, and on to India's North-East

Frontier Agency (NEFA) and Burma. In 1954, in the context of a commercial treaty about Tibet, India and China proclaimed five principles for the conduct of their mutual affairs. These principles, the Panch Shila, were: respect for each other's sovereignty and territorial integrity, non-aggression, non-interference in each other's internal affairs, equality and mutual benefit, and peaceful coexistence. On Nehru's side the Panch Shila reflected certain basic aims of his foreign policy: to eschew war, to give the rest of the world an example in international behaviour and to get on well with China in spite of ideological differences. India protested to China over the use of force in Tibet, but to the Chinese argument that Tibet was part of China the Indian government had no reply and Nehru pursued his endeavours to reach amicable and rational solutions to current problems. The Sino-Indian commercial treaty on Tibet dealt with the rights of traders and pilgrims, transferred to China postal and other services previously operated by India, provided for the withdrawal of Indian military units from Yatung and Gyantse, and recognized Chinese sovereignty in Tibet. Nehru and Zhou met for the first time as the latter returned to Beijing from the Geneva conference on Indo-China and Korea, and Nehru went to Beijing. Like the British before and the Americans after this period, Nehru was primarily interested in his relations with China; the status of Tibet and the fate of the Tibetans were items in a larger picture. American and British governments periodically expressed sympathy with the Tibetans but both gave the Dalai Lama the brush-off when they became engaged in improving relations with China – in the American case after Nixon's visit to China, in the British when Thatcher was trying to get acceptable terms for the surrender of Hong Kong.

In the late 1950s there were a number of incidents leading to Chinese complaints of Indian troops crossing into Tibet and Indian complaints of Chinese troops found south of the frontier. These aberrations could be accounted for by the difficulty of knowing exactly where one is in such country and the Indians in particular, anxious to prove that India and China could coexist peaceably in Asia, were not on the lookout for more sinister explanations. The possibility that the two sides had radically different ideas of where the frontier ran on the map was evaded. Yet by the mid-1950s the Chinese had entered the Aksai Chin or Soda Plains in Ladakh. This area, between the two mountain ranges of the Kuen Lun and the Karakoram, had long been disputed ground because it had never been agreed which range marked the Sino-Indian border. To the Chinese the Aksai Chin was important because it lay in the path of a road which they wished to build to link the Tibetan capital with their western province of Xinjiang. This road they now proceeded to build. Their operations can hardly have been concealed from the Indians. Conceivably, knowledge of what was going on did not immediately reach Nehru himself owing to myopia among Indians whose obsessive animosity against Pakistan blinded them to the extent of Chinese activities which implied a claim to 30,000 sq. km of Indian territory. But the capture of an Indian patrol by the Chinese in Ladakh brought the issue into the open and in 1958 the Indian government formally expressed surprise and regret that Beijing had not seen fit to consult Delhi about the highway.

In 1959, when Tibetan discontent mounted into a serious anti-Chinese revolt, the Dalai Lama fled to India and Nehru wrote privately to Zhou to express his concern. He received no answer until six months later when a public Chinese reply laid claim for the first time to extensive stretches of Indian territory. In the interval Moscow agreed to give India financial aid and Khrushchev, before setting out for the United States, adopted a neutral instead of a pro-Chinese posture. India likewise was maintaining a neutral position between China and the United States and refusing to take an anti-American line. The Chinese accused India of stirring up trouble in Tibet and border incidents which had been going on for several years without attracting wide attention produced casualties, publicity and bitterness. An Indian policeman was killed at Longju at the eastern end of the Sino-Indian frontier and several Indians were killed in a skirmish in the Changchenmo valley about midway along the north–south border between Tibet and Kashmir and on the Kashmiri side. It was no longer possible to conceal the fact that the dispute was not about who was where on the occasion of a particular clash, but about where the frontier itself was supposed to run. Up to 1960 Nehru refused to discuss border problems with China. In 1960–61 officials conferred in Beijing but failed to agree. Nehru neither pressed matters nor prepared his armed forces to meet any attack in what was becoming a dangerously contested area but in 1962 China put troops across the McMahon line (separating India from China) and skirting Bhutan to the west entered a part of India which was peculiarly difficult to reach from the rest of India. Nehru, who had consistently admitted that the frontiers were ill-defined and needed to be discussed, refused to begin talking unless the Chinese first withdrew behind the line. The Indian army in the north-east had been reinforced during 1962 but its intelligence and logistical services were poor and when the Chinese attacked in earnest India was humiliatingly defeated.

China's vigorous action was at variance with its approach to frontier disputes with Pakistan and Nepal: it had proposed discussions with the former and concluded an agreement with the latter in 1961. In India, however, counsels were divided. Nehru himself and his army chiefs had been opposed to a forward policy which might precipitate the frontier issue but there was an opposing view which regarded forceful action as opportune and Chinese retaliation as unlikely. If, as may be supposed, Nehru became converted to this view he was bruisingly undeceived and the riddle of Chinese moderation in victory would be explained on the hypothesis that China wanted to do no more than stop Indian infiltration into the disputed areas (by pushing forward police posts) and put the frontier problem back on ice until India was prepared to negotiate about it. China offered to negotiate but the humiliation of defeat prevented Nehru from accepting: the Indian army had lost 3,000 men killed and 4,000 captured. Following a ceasefire at the end of the year a group of India's fellow neutralists – Burma, Sri Lanka, Indonesia, Cambodia, the United Arab Republic and

Ghana – offered to mediate, but they did so in so neutral a spirit that many Indians were indignant, hoping for greater sympathy and support. This attempted mediation produced no resolution and the crisis petered out.

The coincidence of this short war with the Cuban crisis prompted speculation about deeper Chinese calculations and more dramatic international pressures behind the scenes. While it is exceedingly unlikely that Moscow took Beijing into its confidence over Cuba, it is not unlikely that the Chinese were kept informed by the Cubans. That being so, the Chinese could have seen in the possibility of war between the USSR and the United States an opportunity to force out of Delhi a cession of the territory in Ladakh which they had occupied. Even larger motives could be imputed to them: to inflict severe defeats and losses on India, to bring Nehru's government down, to help Indian communists, to strike at India's economic planning. But for such grand designs there is no firm evidence.

Nehru's standing in his own country was both weakened and strengthened. He had been forced to seek military aid from the United States and Britain and his neutralism had led India into acute danger – because a neutralist, more perhaps than anybody else, needs to be prepared and strong – but he himself seemed more irreplaceable than ever and he was in no danger of losing office. The British government hoped to use this shock to India to bring about a settlement with Pakistan over Kashmir, but once the Chinese attack had been suspended, the shock to Indian security became less than the shock to Indian pride, so that India was in no mood to compound its differences with Pakistan, whose attitude towards India during the critical weeks had been the reverse of soothing. India, moreover, believed that Britain was on Pakistan's side. Conversations took place but produced nothing, and at the end of the year relations between the two countries were inflamed by the theft of a hair of the Prophet from its shrine at Hazratbal in Kashmir. This incident produced riots in both countries and led Nehru, aware that his life was approaching its end, to make an endeavour to resolve the Kashmir problem. He released Sheikh Abdullah, who had talks with both Nehru and Ayub Khan. These were fruitless. In May 1964 Nehru died. He possessed the two qualities inseparable from any claim to statesmanship: personal integrity and intelligence. He gave the new state of India a sense of identity, a commitment to religious tolerance and democracy, and the foundations of high-quality modern education. Nehru was succeeded by Lal Bahadur Shastri. Pakistan, convinced that nothing short of force would serve, was preparing for war. It feared that the time for success in war was running out. On the other side India was worried by Pakistan's American arms and its overtures to China: Ayub Khan visited Beijing early in 1965. Both governments were suspicious and weaker at home than they had been.

Attention was temporarily diverted from Kashmir to a desolate and uninhabited mudflat called the Rann of Kutch. This unattractive area, under water for part of the year, was regarded by India as part of the state of Kutch which was undeniably part of India, but Pakistan claimed that the border ran through the middle of the Rann on the

principle that boundaries in watercourses lie in midstream. The dispute, in itself somewhat ridiculous, brought the two countries to the verge of fighting but abated after an
offer of British mediation. In 1968 Pakistan got by arbitration one-tenth of its claim.
More serious was the arrest of Sheikh Abdullah. Since his release the Kashmiri leader
had visited Britain and a number of Muslim countries and he was about to go to
Beijing. The Indian government took the view that he would be better back in prison,
whereupon Pakistani troops crossed the ceasefire line which had been established and
kept under UN observation since January 1949. The Pakistani air force conducted
some successful operations but the crucial land attacks were held by the Indian army
and India retaliated by invading Pakistan itself. Thereafter the fighting came to a
stalemate. China delivered a threatening note to India but took no effective action
in support of Pakistan. U Thant went in person to Asia and secured an (imperfectly
observed) ceasefire. The USSR offered to mediate if Shastri and Ayub Khan would
meet Kosygin in the Uzbek capital of Tashkent. Britain and the United States urged
both sides to stop fighting and there were at least implications that economic aid and
military supplies would be stopped if they did not.

Pakistan had hoped to score a quick victory as a preliminary to negotiations from a
position of strength. Its political aims probably entailed the cession to Pakistan of considerable areas of Kashmir, including perhaps the central Vale of Kashmir with or without a plebiscite. These hopes were frustrated by the Indian army, whose performance
surprised all who were judging it by its failures against the Chinese three years earlier.
India's successes in the fighting were matched by stubbornness on the political front.
Having agreed to a ceasefire, India, which remained in occupation of a slice of
Pakistani territory, showed no more inclination than it had after 1949 to proceed to a
political settlement. Sentiment apart, India had two substantive grounds for its continued refusal to treat with Pakistan. The first was strategic. The only serviceable road
for the Indian army to use to reach Ladakh ran through the Vale; the abandonment of
the Vale would cripple India in any encounters with the Chinese in Ladakh. An alternative road skirting the Vale could be constructed but only at considerable cost and
over a period of years. Secondly, Indians were genuinely averse to a settlement on a
religious basis. A plebiscite in Kashmir meant counting Muslims and Hindus and
determining the political future of a territory by reference to the religion of the majority of its inhabitants. India (unlike Pakistan) was a secular state, firmly committed to
non-confessional politics. It could hardly accept any procedure in Kashmir which was
also acceptable to Pakistan without betraying this principle and also – a matter of practical urgency – endangering the 100 million Muslims in India whose property and lives
could well be jeopardized if they were regarded as adherents of Islam rather than
citizens of India.

The brief war in Kashmir enabled India to re-establish its military prestige and score
a modest diplomatic point against the feeble intervention of the Chinese. India was not
obliged to cede anything to Pakistan. Pakistan failed to secure its objectives and gave

its larger neighbour an opportunity to demonstrate the strength of its negative position over Kashmir. China had felt compelled to do something in support of Pakistan and had chosen to do the least. The USSR was embarrassed by a possible renewal of the Sino-Indian conflict and by the possibility of having to take sides between India and Pakistan. India, intrinsically the more important of the two countries if only because of its size, had been cast by the USSR as a useful adjunct in the Sino-Russian conflict, was in receipt of Russian aid and had been championing the USSR's claim (rejected by China) to be an Asian country and a proper member of Afro-Asian conferences. The USSR therefore had powerful reasons for not offending India, but it wished also to have good relations with Pakistan. It disliked Pakistan's recent tendency to look for aid and comfort to Beijing, from whose lukewarm cajolements Pakistan ought, in Moscow's view, to be weaned. Further, the Kashmir war had disenchanted Pakistan with the United States. Pakistan had accepted SEATO and Washington's general alliance system but when the crunch came in Kashmir the Americans had failed to give Pakistan the support which it supposed itself to have bought and paid for. Consequently, there was at least a possibility of detaching Pakistan from the American system as well as from the Chinese flirtation. More than that, the similar disenchantment of the Turks, whom the Americans had prevented from invading Cyprus (p. 301), and the perennial fluidity of Iranian politics, where too the shah might be glad of a friend uncommitted to the Arabs, gave Moscow the exciting prospect of dissolving the Northern Tier. But since Russian diplomacy in Pakistan must not lose sight of more important Russian interests in India, it was essential for Moscow to reduce Indo-Pakistani animosities to the minimum. The Tashkent meeting, which took place at the beginning of 1966, was designed both to present the USSR in the role of peace-maker and to clear the complex channels of Russian diplomacy in Asia. The meeting stayed the expiring war and boosted Russian prestige but produced no answer to the problem in Kashmir.

Britain's position during the Kashmir war was that of a friend who is so impartial that he has become useless to both sides and distrusted by both. India and Pakistan each believed Britain to be committed to the other side under a cloak of pious objectivity. In India Britain's position was made worse when Harold Wilson deplored India's invasion of Pakistan without having previously deplored Pakistan's original act of aggression. (Although Pakistan had attacked in Kashmir and not in other parts of India it transpired that there had been a slight incursion into other Indian territory by Pakistani forces.)

In India itself the war in Kashmir, coming the year after Nehru's death, intensified debate about his foreign policy. The central point of a country's foreign policy is its own security, elaborated in national defence forces and foreign alliances. The weakness of India's foreign policy in the age of Nehru was that it decried these traditional concerns and gave more attention to the exercise of influence upon the conflicts between major powers which affected Nehru's vision but did not directly affect India's independence or integrity. In order to play this role in world affairs India needed exceptional prestige (to command the attention of the great and to collect a following of the less great, without which India by itself would be of comparatively little account) and exceptional detachment. Nehru personally provided both and so succeeded in winning for himself and his country a position which, if not always popular with the great or the less great, was nevertheless gratefully used by the great on such occasions as the ending of the Korean War and the Indo-China settlement of 1954 when Indians were accepted as impartial chairmen or mediators. But Nehru's detachment, and his refusal to allow his policy of non-alignment to be prejudiced by arms deals and alliances, was only compatible with India's own prime requirements upon the basis that its relations with its neighbours were good. And this was not the case. Both India's most powerful neighbours were hostile: China and Pakistan claimed territory under Indian control, and the attacks delivered first by the one and then by the other forced India to consider whether a policy of non-alignment between the United States and the USSR was not at least irrelevant, and possibly a hindrance, to the defence of its Himalayan borders and the retention of Kashmir. Could India be non-aligned and safe? Could it, as Nehru had believed, be safer non-aligned than dependent on one great power and forced into hostility to the other? Perhaps non-alignment remained the wisest attitude, but if so, must not India become a nuclear power as well as a neutral one?

Nehru's successor – after Shastri died suddenly at the end of the Tashkent conference – was his daughter Indira Gandhi, under whose rule India entered a phase in which internal affairs increasingly overshadowed the world role which had engrossed Nehru. The contradictions within the unwieldy Congress Party led to splits which foreshadowed a reformation of Indian political patterns. After elections in 1967 a number of provinces were governed by unstable coalitions and within a year five of them had been placed under president's rule. The central government faced threats to law and order from strikes, students and the continuing failure either to come to terms with the insurgent Nagas and Mizos in the north-east or to silence them.

The eastern sectors of India's northern borders were more sensitive than the western inasmuch as they provided easier access into India. They included the unratified McMahon line; Nefa, where Nagas and Mizos were in revolt against Indian rule, tying up Indian forces and damaging India's moral standing and prestige as stories of vicious Indian tactics leaked out to the world (the Mizos became eventually in 1986 India's twenty-third state); and the weak Himalayan states. Sikkim, the central and smallest of these, received from India in 1950 a guarantee of internal autonomy and a subsidy in return for Indian control of its defence and foreign policies. India was allowed to station troops on Sikkim. In 1974 India turned the Chogyal (ruler) into a figurehead (in the name of democracy) and Sikkim into an associate state of the Indian republic with representatives in both houses of the Indian parliament. China was upset and so was

Nepal. The Chogyal committed suicide two years later. Bhutan, the easternmost of the three principalities, agreed in 1949 to accept Indian guidance in foreign affairs in return for Indian promises of non-interference in its internal affairs but Gurkha immigration from Nepal threatened to submerge the Bhutanese in their own country and take it either into India or into a greater Gurkhaland centred on Nepal. In both Sikkim and Bhutan India was continuing the policies of the British while in the background was a Chinese claim to Bhutan rejected by Britain early in the century and the uncomfortable fact that Sikkim, governed by a minority of Tibetan stock, had been virtually part of Tibet in the eighteenth century.

Of the Himalayan states much the largest, and the only fully independent, was Nepal, the home of the Gurkhas who had provided famous battalions for the armies of Britain and India. It had been a refuge for Hindus fleeing from the Mogul conquest and had become a separate state in the mid-eighteenth century. From the middle of the nineteenth century to the middle of the twentieth it was under the dual control of a royal family without power and the less than royal but more powerful family of the Ranas, who ruled it much as the mayors of the palace had ruled Merovingian France or the shoguns ruled Japan until the Meiji restoration of 1867. By the middle of the twentieth century the dominance of the Ranas was threatened by a recrudescence of the royal power and by Congresses on the model of the Indian National Congresses, of which there were two: the Nepali National Congress, founded in 1947 in Calcutta and led by B. P. Koirala and his relatives, and the Nepali Democratic Congress, founded in Calcutta in 1949 by a member of the royal family. In 1950 King Tribhuvana provoked a constitutional change by fleeing first to the Indian embassy in Kathmandu and then to India itself. The next year he returned, entered into an unofficial compact with the Ranas, introduced a parliamentary regime and installed a coalition government which included Ranas and Koiralas.

These dissensions were embarrassing to the Indian government, whose object was to dominate Nepal politely and keep it out of the news. India recognized Nepal's sovereignty in 1950. The Ranas had tended to look to China as a counter against India, and Nehru therefore wanted correct and amicable relations with the king. It was also important for Nehru that the king and the Koiralas should co-operate, since in any clash India's natural sympathies would be with the National Congress rather than the monarch and such a clash might induce it to turn to China.

King Tribhuvana was succeeded in 1955 by King Mahendra, who proceeded to visit Moscow and Beijing and to receive in his own capital not only the Indian president and prime minister but also Zhou Enlai. Alive to the possibilities of exploiting his strategic position, he sought economic aid from all quarters and concluded with China in 1961 a border agreement which gave Nepal the whole of Mount Everest. He also agreed to the construction of a road by the Chinese from Lhasa to Kathmandu. He died in 1972. Over the next 20 years India gradually took over Nepal. Mahendra's son, King Birendra, was regarded by Indians as not very intelligent, his queen and her family as grasping. A Nepali arms deal with China in 1988 alarmed India and when in the following year an Indian–Nepali trade agreement expired, India closed 13 of the 15 border points between the two countries, thus imposing an embargo which caused much economic distress in Nepal and fuelled disgruntlement with the king's absolute rule. Riots in Kathmandu in 1990 reminded the king of his regime's dependence on India and also impelled him towards a measure of constitutional change which reduced his powers and his divinity. Elections in 1994 were won by a party which professed loyalty to the king and to market economics. In 2001 the king and other royals were assassinated by the crown prince who also killed himself. The new king Gyanendra reinstated absolute rule in 2005 but two years later a motley association of republicans won power and the ancient monarchy came to an end.

The second partition

By the end of the 1960s Ayub Khan's rule in Pakistan had gone on too long with too few results. In East Pakistan secessionist feeling grew and the leader of the Awami League Sheikh Mujibur Rahman was arrested. In West Pakistan there was resentment against Punjabi domination. Leaders emerged to crystallize political and social discontents which forced Ayub Khan to step down in 1969: his most enduring mark was the enlargement of the army and the modernization of its equipment. He was succeeded by General Yahya Khan, who proposed to guide Pakistan along much the same lines but perhaps a little faster. Elections were held in 1970 for a constituent assembly to be charged to produce a constitution within 120 days. Ayub Khan's selective democracy – a form of indirect choice based on local elections and proceeding upwards by stages by the election at each stage of delegates to the next – was set aside and universal suffrage permitted. The result in East Pakistan was an overwhelming victory for Sheikh Mujibur, in West Pakistan a somewhat less decisive victory for Zulfikar Ali Bhutto, who had been Ayub Khan's foreign minister in the years 1963–66 and formed the Pakistan People's Party (PPP) in 1967. Sheikh Mujibur's victory had been predicted, though its proportions had not; they were probably inflated by a hideous cyclone which, among other things, demonstrated the incapacity of the central government to organize relief and so accentuated East Pakistan's conviction that the government in the west did not care about its problems. The success of the Awami League was primarily an expression of Bengali separatism. East Pakistan, the more populous of the two halves of the country, objected to its status (under Ayub and Yahya) as one of five provinces, the other four all being in the west; it wanted a generous measure of autonomy in a loose federation in which the central government's authority would be confined to defence, foreign affairs and some currency matters. Both Yahya and Bhutto envisaged a stronger centre. After the elections talks began between Bhutto and Mujibur, who could now point out that he was the leader of the largest party in Pakistan's parliament. In the background was the fact that the ultimate repository of power was the army and the army was largely western. But recourse to the army to coerce the east could mean the disruption of Pakistan.

The Bhutto–Mujibur talks got nowhere and in the east Mujibur began to act like the head of an independent administration. He was again arrested. The president gambled on stopping secession by jailing the seceders, but he provoked instead full-scale fighting. It lasted two weeks. India, moved as some thought by anti-Pakistan venom but more certainly by fears of an anti-Indian left wing coming to power in West Bengal, and by a flood of Hindu fugitives estimated at 10 million, intervened in arms and the Pakistani forces in the east were forced to surrender: 90,000 men were taken prisoner. American and Russian warships appeared briefly in the Bay of Bengal. India also over-ran the Rann of Kutch and a slice of Azad (Pakistani) Kashmir. Pakistan suffered substantial losses in men and material on land, at sea and in the air. Yahya resigned and Bhutto took his place. Mujibur was released to become the prime minister of the new state of Bangladesh (president in 1975). By invading East Pakistan India exposed a growing awareness of a serious contradiction in the UN Charter: the contradiction of state sovereignty and on the other hand the imperative in some circumstances to protect and enforce human rights regardless of frontiers. The inviolability of the state was violated when, for example, Tanzania invaded Uganda in 1979 to unseat Idi Amin (p. 588). Earlier in the decade India's armed intervention enabled thousands of Bangladeshis to return home.

The outlook for the new state was bleak in the extreme. Mujibur was popular but weak and during 1972 he was away ill in England for two months. Postwar chaos was aggravated by a catastrophic wave of disease and death, and then by general disorder, crime and corruption on such a scale that a distracted government had to proclaim a state of emergency in 1974. A year later Mujibur was murdered in a coup which was followed by a struggle for power between sections of the army. The economy was in ruins in spite of $1 billion of foreign aid. China, acting in support of Pakistan, vetoed the admission of Bangladesh to the UN for three years. Relations with Pakistan, the unravelling of the foundered association of what had been West and East Pakistan, and the release of prisoners and return of fugitives were hampered at the outset by Bangladeshi talk of war crimes trials (which never took place). After the assassination of a second president, General Hussein Muhammad Ershad became president in 1983. He possessed the reputation of being neither corrupt nor violently Islamic, but in 1985 he made Islam the state's religion (85 per cent of the population were Muslims). He introduced a measure of stability but little hope of relief for a country crushed by war, poverty and frequently by nature: appalling floods in 1988 put three-quarters of it under water. Opposition, divided between 20 groups of which the two most prominent were led by the widow and daughter of former presidents (whose mutual animosities were hardly less acute than their hatred of Ershad), was rendered the more ineffectual by its habit of boycotting such elections as the government ordained. After elections in 1986 Ershad lifted martial law but a year later he reimposed it and dissolved the parliament. He won fresh elections in 1988, but mounting popular disorder and waning support in the armed forces (which he failed to appreciate) undermined his position and he was obliged to resign in 1990. He was arrested and charged with corrupt practices. Elections in the following year were a contest between Mujibur's daughter and his successor's widow. The latter, Begum Khaleda Zia, won and became prime minister of a country of outstanding poverty and vulnerability to natural disasters. A military takeover in 2007 landed both women in jail.

For Mrs Gandhi the bisection of Pakistan was no bad thing. India's decisive intervention in Bangladesh was popular in India. She crushed opposition to herself in the Congress Party at elections in 1971, winning 40 per cent of the vote and making her opponents look like clueless has-beens, but she produced no solutions to the prime needs of a huge population growing at the rate of 2.5 per cent a year or to those of India's industries stifled by bureaucratic state controls. Food problems became acute and some goods and commodities disappeared altogether. With overconfidence in herself and her politically inept and authoritarian son Sanjay, she espoused such unwise measures as compulsory sterilization. In 1975 a High Court judge started a chain of unexpected events by ruling that she had offended against the Corrupt Practices Act in the elections of 1971 and by imposing on her the statutory disqualification from political activities for five years. The Supreme Court granted a stay and suspended the disqualification pending appeal but two days later Mrs Gandhi declared a state of emergency, arrested hundreds of her political opponents and introduced stiff censorship. She explained that a conspiracy against progress and democracy had been discovered but no convincing evidence of so serious a threat was provided and her action looked more like an attempt to impose a dynastic despotism masquerading as benevolent autocracy: more dynasty than democracy. She was ousted in 1977 by the Janata, a coalition formed by the austere and elderly Morarji Desai, who had been an unsuccessful candidate for the premiership in 1964 and 1966, had been slighted by Mrs Gandhi and had formed a new party in opposition to her authoritarianism and her promotion of Sanjay. But the Janata lapsed into squabbling and survived only two years. In 1980 Mrs Gandhi won sweeping victories and resumed her rule. A few months later Sanjay was killed in an air accident. His elder brother Rajiv was adopted by their mother as heir apparent.

Mrs Gandhi was assassinated in 1984 by Sikhs, with whom she had developed something of a personal feud. The Sikhs were a would-be nation in a vast conglomorate federation. They had ruled the Punjab between the decay of the Muslim Moguls after 1700 and the arrival of the British in the mid-nineteenth century. The partition of India in 1947 entailed the partition of the Punjab and the flight of the Sikhs of (Muslim) West Punjab eastward to where the dominant Akali Sikhs hoped to create a Sikh state or quasi-state. They agitated for greater autonomy in Punjab, the incorporation into it of Chandigarh (shared with the neighbouring state of Haryana) and a reallocation of river waters. These were political claims arising out of the Sikhs' religious identity. Mrs Gandhi's hostility was directed to the former, which smacked of separatism, not to the latter, which gave no offence in a secular and multireligious state. The Sikhs aggravated their offence in Mrs Gandhi's eyes when the Akali Dal made common cause with the Janata in 1977, and after her return to power she sought to discredit it by allowing extremists among the Sikhs latitude for their wilder ways. Under a militant leader, Sant Bindranwale, they occupied and stocked with arms nearly 40 Sikh shrines, including the Golden Temple at Amritsar. Faced with this threat of insurrection, Mrs Gandhi ordered the army to clear the shrines and in the course of the main operation at the Golden Temple 1,000 Sikhs were killed, including Bindranwale, who was thus promoted to martyrdom. A group of 300 Sikhs later recovered possession of a part of the Golden Temple in defiance of their own leaders and the army again resorted to force to evict and arrest them. The army's operations, which included the use of tanks, appeared incompetently crass and unnecessarily destructive. In revenge two Sikhs of Mrs Gandhi's bodyguard killed her.

At the invitation of Congress leaders Rajiv Gandhi took over the premiership in a remarkably smooth transition. Known as a retiring man without political ambition or experience, he was regarded as a convenient but temporary figurehead whose presence could forestall chaos. Within a year he became a leader in his own right who impressed Indians and others by a quiet determination and obvious integrity but this unexpectedly auspicious start was not maintained. Although he held his ground at the centre he lost it in many provinces. He had some success in economic affairs; growth rose to 9 per cent a year and consumer goods became more plentiful. He was genuinely opposed to religious factionalism but alienated both Muslims and Hindus. He distanced himself from the crusty barons of the Congress Party but replaced them by personal cronies. He bewailed corruption but failed to deal forthrightly with scandals. His good sense did not suffice to solve the Sikh problem or prevent him from publicly slighting India's Sikh president Zail Singh. His effort to prevent massacre and civil war in Sri Lanka was not rigorously thought out (see p. 502).

His most urgent problem was Punjab. He sought and gained an accord with the Sikh leader Sant Harchand Singh Longowal, giving Punjab the city of Chandigarh in return for the cession of a number of villages to Haryana and an allocation of river waters vaguely favourable to Haryana. Although Sant Longowal was then assassinated by Sikh militants the agreement stood the test of provincial elections in Punjab, which were won by the Akali Dal, campaigning for its endorsement. In Haryana, on the other hand, the proposed loss of Chandigarh gave great offence to Hindus and led to a crushing defeat for the ruling Congress Party in 1987. Nor did the agreement itself survive. Disputes over its detailed application gave the more militant Sikhs the excuse to disavow their leaders, pull down parts of the Golden Temple on the grounds that it had been polluted by Hindus, and proclaim their separate state of Kalistan (1986). The Golden Temple was recovered from the militants but the underlying conflicts persisted, among Sikhs and between Sikhs and Hindus. Violent disorder occurred from time to time but Sikh separatism was dented.

The setback to the Congress Party in Haryana was preceded, if less dramatically, in other provinces – West Bengal, Kerala. Gandhi's personal standing was tainted by the resignation of his defence minister V. P. Singh in protest against the government's reluctance to explore financial scandals, particularly those relating to defence contracts with Bofors of Sweden, and continuing dissension within the ruling party caused further electoral losses at by-elections in 1988. Huge trade deficits, as exports declined and imports rose, added to the feeling that the government was as precariously in control of the country's economy as of its cohesion. On the credit side, Gandhi pacified Assam's discomfort over the influx of Muslim refugees from Bangladesh; a fence was built to stem the flood while plans were made to send refugees back. On balance, however, Gandhi's performance in domestic affairs began to look like honourable inadequacy. Abroad, he improved relations with China but achieved no concrete settlement of the two countries' frontiers. He reaffirmed India's good relationship with the USSR and made some improvement in relations with the United States; he got credits from the one and technical aid from the other. He was a principal author of the South Asian Association of Regional Co-operation (SAARC), an association of seven states – India, Pakistan, Sri Lanka, Bangladesh, Nepal, Bhutan and the Maldives – which by deftly avoiding all contentious issues engineered some useful co operation in commercial and technical matters and transport: it established a headquarters in Kathmandu. In the all-important direction of Pakistan, Gandhi met both President Zia ul-Haq and Bhutto's daughter and political heir, Benazir, to demonstrate goodwill as a cautious prelude to reducing mutual fears and suspicions. But in 1989, his virtues having been overtaken by his shortcomings, he lost a general election to a coalition, led by V. P. Singh, and stretching from the Bharatiya Janata (BJP) on the Hindu right to communists on the left. The Congress Party fared particularly badly in the northern states but it remained the largest party in the Lok Sabha and Gandhi was re-elected its chairman. Singh commanded a majority only so long as the extremists of right and left continued to support him. He jeopardized this majority with proposals for positive discrimination in the job market for the lower castes and he lost it in 1990 when he ordered the arrest of Lal Krishna Advani, leader of the BJP, who was conducting a long march across northern India with the aim of building a Hindu temple on the site of a disused Muslim mosque at Ayodha in Uttar Pradesh. Chandra Shekhar, who was Singh's colleague and adversary in the Janata Dal, took the opportunity to split the party and succeed Singh by winning from Gandhi a promise of parliamentary support.

The rise of the BJP was an additional element in a disorderly political scene plagued by an accumulation of economic reverses: interest rates at an unprecedented level, repeated devaluations of the rupee, a foreign debt exceeding $70 billion, a population growing so fast that it seemed likely to match China's in 100 years. In 1991 Gandhi, India's most solid politician, was assassinated by a Tamil in the course of an election tour in southern India. Although the Congress Party then won 225 of 544 seats in the Lok Sabha, the BJP, which had a mere two seats in 1984, won 119 with 20 per cent of the vote. The BJP, whose strength was mainly in the north and west, was an expression of militant Hinduism organized by religious zealots and led by demagogues who traded on respectable antecedents as anti-British nationalists in order to transfer this hostility to Muslims, trade unions and much else. The BJP aspired to be what the Congress Party had long been: the party of government and the soul of India. This role belonged to the Congress in the anti-British age of Indian nationalism but the Congress and its principal opponents, the communists, were in decay and the BJP appealed to a deeper and remoter strand grounded not in the British raj but in endemic myths and sentiment. So long as neither party could win control of the Lok Sabha India was obliged to experiment with the uncertain play of coalition government, with, therefore, the irritants as well as the virtues of truly multiparty democracy. In 1992 a party of BJP zealots succeeded in destroying the mosque at Ayodha with, it seemed, the blessing of the BJP provincial government. This affair was partly a motley demonstration from the wilder shores of Hindu nationalism and partly a BJP stunt. The state of Uttar Pradesh was placed under central government for a year, at the end of which the BJP was beaten in elections. It remained, however, a significant element in the kaleidoscopic politics of the centre. The Congress Party returned to government with concessions to right and left and with Narasimha Rao as a relatively featureless but unexpectedly enduring prime minister and, as finance minister, Manmohan Singh, who rescued India's finances. He devalued the currency, reduced inflation, lowered tariffs, introduced tax reforms, adopted modified market policies, replenished the reserves, won favourable deals from the World Bank and IMF and made India talked about with more attention than despair. In provincial elections in 1993 the BJP suffered severe losses and split, retaining substantial popularity only among middle classes in Delhi and other big cities. But Rao failed to do more than check the decline of the Congress. He turned a blind eye to corruption in government and party, and politics became a series of manoeuvres to keep the BJP out of power. The BJP rebounded and after elections in 1998 its leader Atal Bihari Vajpayee formed a coalition by brigading 18 smaller parties (many of them little more than projections of personalities). But a year later Vajpayee was defeated by one vote in the Lok Sabha upon the defection of one of these parties on a trivial issue. In the ensuing interregnum, which lasted six months, the BJP made and lost friends but Vajpayee himself enhanced his standing as a man of consequence and competence, whereas the Congress Party – having chosen Sonia Gandhi, Rajiv's Italian-born widow, as its standard-bearer – barely held on to its popular vote and lost seats in areas of special importance to it. The BJP remained in power and remained also dependent on allies of unpredictable loyalty to it and one another.

The abiding sore in the sub-continent was the hostility between the two biggest states. In spite of some conciliatory moves, this hostility, evidenced by Kashmir and made more feverish by the development on both sides of ballistic and nuclear weapons, got worse. In 1972 Indira Gandhi and Zulfikar Ali Bhutto had concluded a comprehensive agreement in direct talks in Simla and by the end of that year had fixed a provisional Line of Control in Kashmir (thinly supervised by a UN mission) and had begun the process of repatriating prisoners of war taken in the war over Bangladesh, which had seriously shaken attitudes in both countries. It caused Mrs Gandhi to abandon her father's cherished non-alignment and conclude a treaty with the USSR to offset American partiality for Pakistan. Pakistan had lost not only face and half its territory but also half its domestic market, a major part of its raw materials and manufactures, its overseas markets (which had been supplied by East Pakistan) and foreign earnings; and the constitutional problems, unsolved since 1947, remained, although temporarily laid to rest by the adoption of a new presidential system. More generally, the loss of Bangladesh drew Pakistan more obviously westward to the core of the Islamic world.

Bhutto was an able politician with few scruples, the determination to build a new Pakistan with himself at the helm, a combination of patrician hauteur with demagogy, and some of the panache of an army leader but without army backing or the trust of the middle classes. Falling short of his self-made image, he was brutally punished by the ferocity of Pakistani politics and in 1977 ousted by the army and later hanged. Butto set Pakistan on the nuclear road. He sought French help, which was promised but revoked on American remonstrance and he succeeded, at first secretly, in starting a programme under the charge of a Pakistani scientist who had acquired the necessary expertise in the Netherlands. His expressed attitude was that, since Hindus, Jews and Christians had nuclear weapons, there should be an Islamic bomb too. Washington tried by pressure and cajolery to stop Pakistan's progress; it cut off economic aid as required by the Foreign Assistance Act 1976, refused to relax debt repayment terms and offered Pakistan modern fighter aircraft if it would apply international safeguards to its nuclear activities. Washington's dilemma was how to make Pakistan a secure ally without fatal injury to American relations with India.

In 1977 the Pakistani army installed General Muhammad Zia ul-Haq as president in place of Bhutto and inaugurated a cruelly repressive regime. In external affairs Zia continued Bhutto's policy of equipping Pakistan with a nuclear option, took Pakistan out of the moribund Central Treaty Organization (CTA) alliance and made it a member of the non-aligned group, but he was at first more of a stop-gap than an autocrat. He belonged to neither the Punjabi aristocracy nor the Sindi plutocracy, he favoured the relatively unpopular intolerant fringe of Muslim fundamentalism and the army, which had made him president, showed no signs of keeping him in that post for long. But the Soviet invasion of Afghanistan in 1979 consolidated his personal position by making changes temporarily impolitic and abruptly reversed his relations with the United States, where he was suddenly hailed as a champion of democratic values. Zia set himself successfully to use the invasion as a lever to recover American military aid and funds. The Soviet action, although a costly blunder, was interpreted in the United States as a dangerous increase in Soviet power which – the shah of Iran having been overthrown – could be checked only by arming Pakistan and using it as a channel for arming opposition to the USSR in Afghanistan. Zia lent himself to this policy with enthusiasm. He received profuse American aid, notwithstanding American dislike of Pakistan's nuclear programme and its role in the drug trade, and notwithstanding too the Symington Amendment, which prohibited aid to states manufacturing nuclear weapons.

By 1983 the remission of fears of Russian aggression against Pakistan revived pressures within the country for an end to military rule. In an attempt to preserve his position Zia surprisingly announced at the end of 1984 that he would hold a referendum to test popular approval of his policies and of himself as head of state, with the corollary that, if approved, he would serve for another five years and intensify the Islamicization of the constitution and the application of severe Koranic penalties for infringements of religious rules. The votes cast were almost all in his favour. Martial law was removed at the end of 1985 – a show of moderation which, however, was preceded by an act of indemnity for past actions and a substantial increase in the presidential powers, including the extension of Zia's own term of office to 1990.

Zia had done nothing to lessen tensions between Punjabis on the one hand and Sindis and Baluchis on the other and the return to Pakistan in 1988 of Bhutto's daughter Benazir increased bitterness. The economy was burdened by the profligacy of a military regime which allocated 40 per cent of the budget to the armed forces, ran huge deficits on the budget and external account, and allowed foreign debts to escalate ominously: defence costs and the service of the foreign debt together absorbed 85–90 per cent of the budget. Zia was constrained to seek a large loan from the IMF, for which he had to submit his country to severe austerity, higher prices, new taxes and collapsing social services and roads (the health budget was cut to less than one-fiftieth of the defence budget). Zia's problems were multiplied by declining remittances from Pakistanis in the Gulf and other foreign parts (these reached $25 billion a year at their height and were largely squandered by Zia's regime), by a sequence of crop failures, by the stream of refugees from Afghanistan, and by the private armies of drug syndicates which operated even in the capital, where Pathan immigrants clashed with the non-Pathan inhabitants. Opposition to Zia therefore grew but it was not co-ordinated. After her return Benazir Bhutto pulled discordant groups together, but not seamlessly. The first local elections after her return disappointed her followers. She was handicapped as a woman and a Sindi, particularly in the dominant province of Punjab (which contained over half the population); by a personality in which intelligence was not unmixed with arrogance; and by an inauspicious marriage arranged by her mother. The government had some success in denigrating and marginalizing her PPP until two events in 1988 transformed her position: Zia abruptly dismissed his civilian prime minister Muhammad Khan Junejo, who dissented from the army's espousal of total support for the *mujaheddin* in Afghanistan, and Zia was himself killed in an air accident. Two other generals and the American ambassador died with him.

These events were the prelude to a phase dominated by bitter and futile party political hostilities, by the accentuation of Pakistan's Islamist fundamentalism and nuclear programme, and by the impact of its involvement in Afghanistan. Elections which followed Zia's death were fought between two consolidated groups: the Islamic Democratic Alliance, which consisted of the Muslim League and minor associates, and the PPP and its associates. In a low poll the PPP won much the larger number of seats but not a majority and it failed to win in any province except Sind and the North West. Benazir Bhutto was installed as prime minister and the army performed one of its periodic retreats into the background. But not for long. In varying degrees the army, the president and a majority of the provincial governors were hostile to Bhutto and were waiting for a chance to get rid of her. Her heritage of corruption, drug trafficking, Afghanistan, economic decline, inter-provincial squabbles and growing Islamic fundamentalism was too much for a government which controlled only two provinces and was ultimately dependent on army officers whom she could neither conciliate nor subordinate. Accused, not without all reason, of incompetence, corruption and nepotism, her government was dismissed by the president, using the pretext of its failure to master endemic violence in Sind between Sindis and *muhajirs*. (The latter were post-1947 immigrants from India who had become a relatively prosperous community in Karachi at odds not only with Sindis but also with Punjabis and Pathans and had started fighting among themselves.) Fresh elections later in the year were won by the Islamic Front, an amalgam of nine parties with a strong flavour of religious intolerance and the backing of the army. The Front and its allies controlled two-thirds of the parliament but the president Ghulam Muhammad, a Pathan, quarrelled with and in 1993 dismissed his prime minister Nawaz Sharif over the right to appoint the commander-in-chief of the army. Sharif was reinstated by the Supreme Court but in ensuing elections Bhutto got her revenge and became once more prime minister until, in 1996, she was dismissed by the new president Farouk Leghari, partly on account of her failure to cope with provincial feuding, economic failings, corruption and other crimes and, more precisely, because the army's chiefs told the president to remove her. A year later elections reduced her PPP to a rump. The country's effective rulers were a new National Defence Council dominated by generals who set stability a long way above democracy but secured neither. Sharif returned. He tried to bolster his position by moving from the moderate Islamicism enshrined in the constitution to a more intolerant version demanded by zealots.

In 1990 President Bush refused to certify that Pakistan had no nuclear weapons – a certificate which was a precondition for economic and military aid. Throughout the 1970s and 1980s the United States had discounted reports that India was developing research into plutonium or manufacturing nuclear weapons in an attempt to restrain Pakistan's parallel activities: Pakistan was the United States' principal base and conduit for aid to the Afghan *mujaheddin*, including the Taliban. But by 1990 Pakistan was believed to possess half a dozen uranium 335 warheads, to be building a plutonium reprocessing plant and to be importing plutonium. In 1998 India carried out five nuclear tests. Pakistan riposted with six and at least connived at an invasion of Kashmir (see below). The United States thereupon cut off aid, triggering an economic crisis in Pakistan. The value of the currency halved in a few months and inflation and the budget deficit rose sharply. (Sanctions were not the only economic problem. Pakistan had one of the world's most rapidly swelling populations.)

Sharif's worries were compounded by the successes in Afghanistan of the Taliban, whose more fanatic leaders condoned massacres of Shia Muslims. These massacres embarrassed the United States and outraged Pakistan's own Shi'ites, who amounted to a fifth of the population. In 1998 the United States fired missiles over Pakistan's territory without notice to its government in an attack on the Saudi dissident Osama bin Laden, who had taken refuge in Afghanistan and was suspected of complicity in attacks on American embassies in east Africa.

Finally, Kashmir: in the late 1980s there was intermittent fighting between Pakistan and India over the possession of a glacier north of Kashmir and from 1989 the central Kashmiri issue was once more inflamed. Sheikh Abdullah having died in 1983, his mantle had fallen on his son Faruq Abdullah (a lightweight character too close to New Delhi for the taste of most Kashmiri Muslims) and his son-in-law Ghulam Muhammad Shah, and the family disagreements of these two compounded political feuds and led to disorders in 1989–90 in which a number of people were killed. India blamed Pakistan for the disorders, dropped Faruq and resorted to direct rule from Delhi. In Kashmir the anti-Indian and increasingly violent Jammu and Kashmir Liberation Front gained popular support, while in reply the Indian authorities fell back on harsh reprisals, including the random torture of innocent victims. In 1993 the temple of Hazrat Bal in Srinigar, which possessed a hair from the Prophet's beard, was surrounded by Indian troops upon rumours of a plan by Muslims to remove the hair. Muslims were outraged by this show of force, which non-Muslims deplored as unwisely provocative. Kashmiri dissidents were divided between those wanting independence and those preferring incorporation in Pakistan, a division which Indians were glad to observe and possibly foment. In 1994 Rao retaliated against Pakistani meddling in Kashmir by claiming the return to India of Kashmiri territory annexed to Pakistan.

Tensions were heightened in 1998 when both India and Pakistan carried out tests which established beyond doubt that both possessed nuclear weapons and the means to deliver them over large distances – in India's case into China as well as Pakistan. In 1999 a body of Pakistanis and Afghans numbering 6,000 or more invaded Kashmir over a 90-km front. The Indians were taken by surprise and suffered over 1,000 fatal casualties but retaliated with heavy artillery and the determination neither to concede anything to Pakistan nor to allow fighting in Kashmir to endanger India's route to

Srinagar and Ladakh, which must be crucial in the event of renewed conflict with China over the Aksai Chin – occupied by China in 1962. On the Pakistani side, the venture was a failure, brought to a halt not only by India's riposte but also by American pressure, which ominously marked a swing in the United States away from Pakistan and towards India. Sharif was a dictator in the making who failed to recognize that in Pakistan generals, not civilians, dictate. He had in 1997 dismissed the president and diminished the presidency and although he had allies in the army, the chief of staff General Pervez Musharraf was not one of them. When, in the wake of the Kashmir humiliation, Sharif tried to blame and supplant the general he was himself removed in a coup which the world condemned in the name of democracy but Pakistanis, laying on the prime minister the blame for a collapsing economy and soaring corruption, did not disapprove. Pakistan was suspended from the Commonwealth (at the same time as Nigeria was reinstated on its reversion to democracy) but this rebuke – entailing exclusion from meetings but not loss of membership – was the least of Musharraf's problems. He refrained from imposing martial law, completed the disengagement from Kashmir, distanced himself from Muslim extremists in Pakistan and Afghanistan and resumed dialogue with the IMF, without whose aid economic collapse was inescapable. Pakistan had been brought to the brink of a crisis greater than any since the secession of Bangladesh. Its political, administrative and judicial apparatuses were rotten and seen to be rotten; its religious fabric, enshrined in the constitution as well as in the hearts of Pakistanis, was scarred by tensions between traditional Sunnis, extremist Sunnis and a (20 per cent) Shi'ite minority. Only the army might claim to be a united and nationwide body, although even here Musharraf could not count forever on the solidarity of the officer class or on popular trust in the country's fourth military regime. Musharraf was no fanatic but army leaders of his generation were closer than their predecessors to Islamic parties in Pakistan and Kashmir and to the Taliban in Afghanistan. Pakistan's 50-year alliance with the United States was virtually abrogated by such shifts and by American hostility to Islam and its adherents in the Middle East, while the development by both Pakistan and India of nuclear weapons was creating in Asia a second Cold War. On the assumption that these were an ultimate but ultimately unusable deterrent, the Indo-Pakistani conflict over Kashmir could become for Pakistan one in which it might step up its brinkmanship; but, secondly, Pakistan might in relation to India inherit the role of the Soviet Union in relation to the United States, courting total ruin before the economic absurdities of modern warfare could commensurately destroy its enemy.

Musharraf started with weaknesses which eventually caught up with him. He was not a native-born Pakistani but a *mojahir* (born in post-partition India). He nevertheless rose to the top of the military tree. He was the architect of an offensive into Kashmir which failed. He allied Pakistan with unpopular American policies in Afghanistan, permitted the United States to conduct more or less overt operations in his country and lost control of the border region of Waziristan in unsuccessful operations against bin Laden. He lost again when in a tussle with the Chief Justice Iftikar Chaudury he tried to forbid the return of Nawaz Sharif to Pakistan. Sharif returned but was immediately deported to Saudi Arabia. Next Bhutto returned to wild acclamation, no little distrust and an attempt on her life. Sharif returned again under the aegis of Saudi Arabia which preferred him to the less radically conservative Bhutto and the rapidly waning Musharraf. Musharraf renounced his military office and apparel and secured re-election as a civilian president. Bhutto was assassinated. Elections reduced Musharraf's parliamentary support to a rump and his presidential authority to a shadow and left the two principal civilian parties dominant provided they could abate or conceal their mutual hostility.

A suitable person was found to occupy the post of prime minister in a coalition. The chief justice and other judges were set free. Musharraf promised to cooperate with the new government. Never had Pakistan's political institutions seemed more artificial, but never had political crisis been so acute, and there were favourable elements. Pakistan was prospering. In the first years of the new century it achieved growth rates which exceeded in percentage terms anything achieved in Europe and the established pattern of power as monopolized by the military and feudal landlords was being diluted by liberal and democratic voices, notably in cities and universities.

At the end of the century India had emerged as much more than half of what had been India before 1947. After the Second World War the world had wondered at economic miracles in Germany and Japan. Economies in South-east Asia had burgeoned miraculously, if sometimes with less discipline. But the Indian sub-continent was generally regarded as a disaster area. None the less, India achieved its own miracle by handling economic, sectarian, administrative and technical problems, most of the time, in a democratic and secular framework protected by the rule of law. At independence the word 'India' denoted a vast and disjointed segment of the British empire – ethnically, religiously and linguistically diverse to the point of incoherence. At the century's close India was a state smaller than that British sphere but still one of the largest political entities in the world. It had mastered the language question, Sikh separatism and religious discrimination: its presidents had included both a Muslim and a Sikh. It had become self-sufficient in food, doubled the level of literacy and created first-class schools of management and technology, and it was half in love with modernization and effective financial and business institutions. On the debit side, much of the country was shockingly poor, 500 million people (up to 50 per cent of the population in some areas) were illiterate, advances in public health and communications were patchy, deep corruption reigned in provinces and at the centre, and – the focus of domestic and international criticism – the economy had failed to match the achievements of Asian competitors. Growth over the first 30 years of independence had averaged about 3 per cent. In the next decade it accelerated incontinently to 7 per cent or more, with consequential problems for budget and external balances and inflationary fears. Only in the 1990s did relaxation of bureaucratic state controls, lower taxes and tariffs, and rigorous financial policies begin to promise rates of growth at once encouraging and sustainable.

Unlike China India never constituted a single political unit. In spite of the secession of Pakistan in 1947 it remained one of the largest states in the world and ethnically and linguistically as diverse as any. Gandhi and Nehru gave it the trappings of a tolerant secular democracy but Indira Gandhi found it difficult to steer between these ideals and, on the one hand, a big state's need for authoritative government and, on the other, the conflicts of ancient cultures and religions. The governments which followed hers were weak and unstable, leading to six years of rule by the Hindu nationalist BJP, serious violence (particularly in Gujarat in 2002), a resurgence of communist fortunes in elections in 2004 and an erosion of the confidence which characterized the closing decades of the twentieth century. That confidence was nourished by astonishing economic growth but growth very unevenly spread and painfully absent in India's vast rural stretches. Despite its successes India remained a poor and illiterate country where prosperity frequently contributed to social and economic divides which recalled the persistent widening of the gap between rich and poor set off in western Europe by the Industrial Revolution.

CHAPTER 17

The Indo-Chinese peninsula

The most turbulently disputed postwar arena in South-east Asia was Indo-China. This area, put together by the French, contained the protectorates of Annam and Tonkin and the colony of Cochin-China (Annamite by race, Chinese by culture, and together called the three Kys) and the protected kingdoms of Luang Prabang or Laos, and Cambodia (Thai by race, Hindu by culture). The Khmer forebears of the modern Cambodians ruled an empire which, at its peak in the twelfth century, reached from sea to sea and included the southern parts of Burma, Siam, Laos and Annam. In Laos invading Thais had established an ascendancy in the thirteenth century. By the nineteenth Cambodia and Laos were threatened by Annam but were saved by the French.

The French established themselves in Asia later than other European powers. Their defeats in the Franco-Prussian War had deprived them of territory, valuable resources, population, prestige and self-respect, and although recovery was rapid, the acquisition of a new colonial empire in the 1880s was in some sense a compensation. It took the form of entering the competition for whatever might be made out of the disintegration of the Ottoman and Chinese empires. Tunisia was virtually annexed. Madagascar was occupied, and the three Kys were made the nucleus of an Indo-Chinese dominion which might provide a way into southern China and was extended by taking Cambodia and Luang Prabang under the French wing. The acquisition of Annam and Tonkin led to an unpopular war with China, while the western and Hindu-ward move brought France into competition with the British in Burma, where they were checked by the viceroy Lord Dufferin (who feared – or perhaps invented – a French threat to India), and also into a more enduring hostility with the independent kingdom of Thailand. French power remained substantially unshaken until 1940.

During the Japanese occupation in the Second World War the three Kys became the autonomous state of Vietnam and upon the Japanese withdrawal Ho Chi Minh, the leader of a communist-dominated nationalist coalition, proclaimed the independent republic of Vietminh. As in Indonesia and Korea practical considerations determined the course of events with more far-reaching effects than were contemplated at the time. When the war ended the British took control south of the 16th parallel and the Chinese north of it. Both withdrew during 1946 but the former had first cleared the way for the

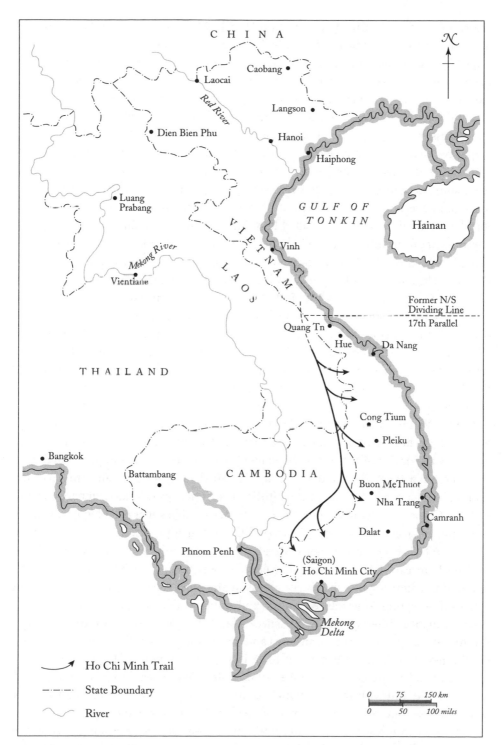

17.1 Vietnam, Cambodia and Laos

return of the French, who arrived to find Ho Chi Minh in control in the north, with the Annamite emperor Bao Dai, who had abdicated in 1945, as his chief counsellor.

France did not have the nerve to take the extreme but simple step taken in India by the British Labour government. The French began by recognizing Ho's government as autonomous within the French Union but refused to accept his demand for the union of the three Kys. Towards the end of 1946 French policy stiffened as a result of right-wing pressure. Haiphong was bombarded and Hanoi was attacked by the Vietminh, convinced that France intended to overthrow Ho: some 40 Frenchmen were killed and 200 abducted. This was the beginning of a war which lasted seven and a half years. After some hesitation the French decided to give up further negotiation with Ho and to switch instead to Bao Dai, to whom they offered the union of the three Kys which they had refused to Ho. The so-called Bao Dai experiment was an attempt to separate communists from other nationalists and to preserve with Bao Dai's complaisance a general French overlordship throughout Indo-China. An agreement signed in Along Bay in 1948 embodied this policy (which was to be reflected in the south in the next decade by the Americans with President Diem as the anti-communist nationalist) and a new state of *Vietnam* was formally constituted in June 1949. Bao Dai, who had been in France during the negotiations, returned to his own country as head of state. Vietnam was proclaimed an Associated State in the French Union and Laos and Cambodia were given the same status. Among those who refused to co-operate with Bao Dai was the Roman Catholic leader and future president of South Vietnam Ngo Dinh Diem.

But the Vietminh did not give up and the victory of the Chinese communists across the northern border transformed the situation. The attempt of the French to retain power by the device of the semi-independent Associated State led to protracted bickering between themselves and Bao Dai and failed to achieve its aim. In 1950 five months' conferring at Pau about constitutional advances exacerbated all parties, while in Indo-China the Vietminh took the field under its able general Vo Nguyen Giap. A Vietminh offensive was strikingly successful. Marshal Alphonse Juin was sent to the scene. Bao Dai also returned. Pierre Mendès-France and others began to say that it was time for France to clear out of Asia. The French government, which had been resolutely opposed to admitting that the situation was in any sense international, relented to the extent of accepting American economic and military aid; to fight for French supremacy brought neither sympathy nor success, and the only way to continue the fight was to call it a fight against communism and invoke the aid of anti-communist friends. On this new basis General Jean de Lattre de Tassigny was appointed high commissioner and commander-in-chief in December 1950. With a new general to raise morale, with American aid and with the negotiation of a political settlement of the status of the Indo-Chinese states within the French Union, the French made their final effort.

But the Vietminh struck first and showed that it was capable of waging open war as well as guerrilla operations. Within a year the French lost de Lattre, who was invalided home, a dying man. Bao Dai's Vietnamese army was coming into existence with extraordinary slowness, and the private armies which complicated the picture were not being reduced to his control. Chinese aid to the Vietminh was increasing. During 1952 French losses in men, material, morale and prestige were considerable, and in 1953 the Vietminh carried the war into Laos, threatened the royal capital of Luang Prabang and forced the French to divert forces from Vietnam to the Plain of Jars in Laos. In Cambodia King Norodom Sihanouk raised the political stakes by asking for a status in no way inferior to that of India and Pakistan in relation to Britain, and then embarrassed the French by temporarily decamping to Thailand. Amid this scene of disintegration the French could do no more than offer to review the constitution of the French Union and begin yet another round of negotiations with Bao Dai as well as the Laotian and Cambodian monarchs. (Sihanouk had succeeded to the throne in 1940 at the age of 18. In 1955 he abdicated in favour of his father, who reigned until 1960 with Sihanouk as prime minister. In 1956 Zhou Enlai and Sihanouk signed a non-intervention agreement. Sihanouk visited Beijing, Moscow, Prague and Belgrade; also Madrid and Lisbon. He adopted a policy of the widest diplomatic contacts and aid from as many places as possible. He seemed, however, to have a preference for China, which he again visited in 1958 and 1960. In 1960 he resumed the top place in the state with the title of Head of State.)

There was by this time nothing left for the French in Indo-China except a need to salvage pride. They were preoccupied with the revival of German strength, beside which the strength of the Vietminh seemed both inconsiderable and irrelevant to France's position in the world, and had entrusted affairs in Indo-China to generals who, often unrealistic and at odds with one another and their civilian colleagues, had fought and lost an old-style colonial war. If the Vietminh mattered to anybody, it mattered to the Americans, who were already paying for it indirectly and saw it as a new-style anti-communist war. It required only a climactic event to make France acknowledge that what it really wanted in Indo-China was to get out. This event occurred at Dien Bien Phu, a small garrison or camp in a bowl in the north-west. Its possession was important in relation to the Vietminh's threats to neighbouring Laos, which were themselves important inasmuch as they demonstrated French inability to protect a protectorate and at the same time diverted French forces from the defence of the strategically and politically central Red River delta and Hanoi. Dien Bien Phu had changed hands more than once during the war. It was taken by the French in November 1953 and after some hesitation they decided to stay there.

General Navarre, now in command of French and Vietnamese forces which considerably outnumbered the Vietminh, believed that if he could force the enemy to battle he could inflict upon them a major defeat and permanently reduce their operations to minor guerrilla scale; he believed that the Achilles' heel of the Vietminh was in numbers and that the Chinese or Russians, though willing to supply arms and equipment, would not send fighting men across the borders for fear of American retaliation. Dien

Bien Phu was therefore to provide the setting for the battle which would cripple the Vietminh.

Early in 1954 agreement had been reached among all the principal powers concerned to hold an international conference on Indo-China and Korea, and as the preparations went ahead it became increasingly clear that the outcome at Dien Bien Phu would have a powerful influence on the course of negotiations. It also became clear that the French, so far from delivering a knock-out blow, were being surrounded and pounded by an unexpectedly large force and were in danger of having to capitulate. What was not so clear in these circumstances was whether France's allies would be well advised to make a special effort and intervene. The Americans, who had been opposed to any such involvement, began to have second thoughts and to propound the view that the loss of Indo-China would be a fatal blow to all South-east Asia and even further afield. Dulles appealed for united international action to prevent the imposition of communism on South-east Asia. Congressional leaders and allies were sounded on joint intervention in Indo-China and retaliation against China itself in the event of a Chinese counter-strike. The response was unfavourable.

The Korean War had left the United States with little appetite for Asian adventures and the allies had not recovered from their distrust of MacArthurism, which they detected reviving in the views of Admiral Arthur Radford, the naval chief of staff, who advocated American air strikes. Eisenhower was prepared to give his consent to Radford's policy if Congress were to agree and the United States were not the only intervener, but General Ridgway, chairman of the chiefs of staff, opposed intervention on the grounds that it would force the Chinese to enter the war, as they had done in Korea. Eisenhower, who had campaigned for the presidency on a promise to stop the war in Korea, may have known that his conditions for intervening were most unlikely to be met, but he allowed Dulles to pursue the question of allied co-operation. After discussing intervention in London and Paris, Dulles returned to Washington under the impression that he had secured agreement for a general conference to devise a plan but Eden, with whom his personal relations were bad, denied this interpretation of their talks and refused to send a representative to a preliminary discussion. Dulles returned to Paris with a proposal for unilateral American air intervention and Eden, who was also in Paris on his way to Geneva, flew back to London, where a Sunday meeting of the cabinet refused to give its endorsement. Eden communicated this decision to Georges Bidault, the French foreign minister, at Orly airport on his way to Geneva and so acquired the reputation of being the man who saved the world from being plunged into a new world war by American temerity at Dien Bien Phu. It seems, however, truer to judge that American intervention had already been dismissed because of the opposition of the American chiefs of staff (Admiral Radford alone excepted), American congressional and public opinion and Eisenhower's personal disinclination. Within a short time the view that Indo-China was essential to the free world had been dropped and the fate of Vietnam was once more being treated as a local affair.

The Geneva conference, convened to discuss Korea and secondarily Indo-China, opened on 26 April. Dien Bien Phu fell on 7 May. The French government also fell and Mendès-France became prime minister with a promise to reach a settlement in Indo-China by 20 July or resign. On 23 June Mendès-France and Zhou Enlai had a private discussion in Berne before the latter set off for Beijing during a break in the conference. At the same time Churchill and Eden visited Washington to discuss a variety of topics and repair the damage to Anglo-American relations caused by the Dulles–Eden misunderstandings. Soon after the conference resumed three armistice agreements were signed. Vietnam was partitioned roughly along the 17th parallel (a compromise choice), the Vietminh agreed to withdraw from Laos and Cambodia, and three armistice commissions were constituted with Indian, Polish and Canadian members to supervise their implementation. The conference marked the defeat of France and its withdrawal from all of Indo-China. It purported to proclaim the creation of three new independent states: Laos and Cambodia, which were to be safeguarded against their hereditary enemies in Vietnam and Thailand by guarantees by China, France, Britain and the USSR; and Vietnam, which had won independence but not integration.

In *Laos*, although the Geneva settlement provided for the withdrawal of Vietminh forces, there were other forces to keep revolt going. The Pathet Lao, created in 1949 by Ho as an adjunct of the Vietminh, with a member of the Laotian royal family, Prince Souphanouvong, among its senior leaders, had established control over the two northern provinces of the country. In 1956 this prince visited Beijing and Hanoi and in the next year he negotiated a coalition with his half-brother Souvanna Phouma (who was prime minister), on the basis that Laos would be neutralized. But this coalition lasted only until 1959, when Souphanouvong and other Pathet Lao leaders were arrested. (Later coalitions in 1962 and 1973 were equally evanescent.) The United States, having adopted the domino theory that communism would engulf the whole of South-east Asia if it won a victory in any part of the region, was not prepared to tolerate neutralism and decided to exclude not only the communist prince but also the neutralists. It began to pour money and other aid into Laos with an abandon which produced much corruption and two years of civil war. A new government in Laos, making the most of North Vietnamese incursions, asked for a UN mission and a UN force. Hammarskjöld visited Laos in person and sent a special representative to observe and report and so gain time for temperatures to fall, but in December 1959 General Phoumi Nosavan staged a successful coup which had the opposite effect. It also evoked, a few months later, another coup led by Captain Kong Le, a rather naïve symbol of the irritation of ordinary men who were fed up with feuding and corruption. Souvanna Phouma declared his support for Kong Le, became prime minister once more and contrived briefly to reconcile the general and the captain, again on a neutralist ticket. But his solution did not last, largely because the Americans were able to rebuild a right-wing front under General Nosavan and Prince Boun Oum, a distant relative of the reigning family and mediatized ruler of Champassak (in the south). Souvanna Phouma fled to Cambodia, whence he was transported in a Russian aircraft to confer with his half-brother and Kong Le. He was also courted by Boun Oum and Nosavan but preferred to set off on a world tour. Meanwhile, Kong Le had inflicted a defeat on Boun Oum and Nosavan. In 1961 the three princes met in Switzerland and agreed that Laos should become a neutralized state without military alliances. In Washington a new president, J. F. Kennedy, was more inclined than Eisenhower had been to accept a neutral Laos, partly through disenchantment with the Laotian right and partly because of the failure of direct military intervention at the Bay of Pigs in Cuba. War was brought to an end when the United States and China reached agreement behind the scenes on a neutralized Laos and the evacuation of foreign troops – that is, American troops which China feared and the United States felt to be engaged in a worthless cause. But Laos continued to be used by Ho for supplies into South Vietnam, the authority of the Pathet Lao spread and the American forces were replaced by an active communist army – part Laotian and part Vietnamese – which numbered 60,000 or more. In 1963 the Laotian coalition dissolved and the country became virtually partitioned with the Pathet Lao ruling in the north-east and Souvanna Phouma the rest. From 1964 the United States reversed its policy of withdrawal, built up large ground forces and used its air forces in operations by the Laotian government against the Pathet Lao. Laos became an important American theatre of war, ancillary to the waging of the war in South Vietnam and to the protection of American forces of about 50,000 in Thailand. The Americans dropped a greater weight of bombs on Laos than had been dropped on Germany from beginning to end of the Second World War.

In *Vietnam* the 1954 Geneva settlement gave Ho Chi Minh half the country and the expectation of the rest in less than two years if the terms of the settlement were fully accepted and implemented. The Geneva agreement was an armistice agreement signed by generals on behalf of France and the Vietminh. It drew a line, imposed a ceasefire, and made arrangements for the regroupment of military forces and the resettlement of civilians on either side of the line. The conference also produced a number of declarations, including a final declaration propounded but not signed. The United States and South Vietnam dissociated themselves in particular from this declaration's provision for elections throughout Vietnam by the middle of 1956; they believed that such elections were bound to transfer the whole of the country to communist rule since the part north of the armistice line contained a majority of the population – which was, in addition, likely to vote with that 90 per cent solidarity characteristic of authoritarian regimes. The government in South Vietnam, which had been established in Saigon by the authority of Bao Dai before the Geneva conference, considered itself bound by nothing that was settled there.

For the French the armistice agreement was a means of escape. They were able to conclude a war which they were losing. Thereafter, they watched with an excusable but irritating smugness as the Americans repeated in the next phase many of the mistakes which they had made between 1945 and 1954. For the Russians and the Chinese the settlement was a political arrangement which they pressed upon Ho, the Russians because they wanted France to stifle the nascent European Defence Community, and the Chinese because they wanted to remove western forces and influence from a country on their borders; both may have supposed that Ho would soon rule as effectively in Saigon as in Hanoi and were faced with fresh problems when this did not happen.

For the Americans the Geneva settlement marked the end of a French presence in Asia which, however obnoxious on general anti-colonialist principles, could have been rendered useful in anti-communist terms. Having decided in 1954 not to buttress French rule any longer, the United States sought an alternative anti-communist and anti-Chinese force. They disapproved of the Geneva settlement because it not only failed to constitute such a force but also threatened to accelerate Chinese communist expansion by giving Ho the whole of Vietnam in two bites — the north by the armistice agreement and the south through elections: they regarded Ho as a satellite and discounted his chances of becoming the Tito of Asia. They resolved therefore to maintain the independence of the anti-communist regime established by Bao Dai in the south, and also to create a new anti-communist alliance to check China in Asia as NATO had checked the USSR in Europe. Accordingly, the South-East Asia Collective Defence Treaty (the Manila Pact, establishing a South-East Asia Treaty Association – SEATO) was signed in September 1954 by three Asian and five non-Asian states: the Philippines, Thailand, Pakistan, the United States, Australia, New Zealand, Britain and France. These signatories bound themselves to take joint action in the event of aggression against any one of them in a designated area, and to consult together in the event of threats from action other than armed action (namely, subversive activities). The designated area was the general area of South-east Asia including the territory of the signatories and the general area of the South-west Pacific to 20 degrees 30 minutes north; the area included therefore Vietnam, Cambodia and Laos but not Taiwan or Hong Kong.

SEATO never became an impressive organization. No purely Asian state of substance joined it except Pakistan, which, distant from China and not really concerned about Chinese expansion in South-east Asia or anywhere else, joined for ulterior reasons – to please the United States and get American support against India. France became an increasingly cynical member; Britain became an increasingly embarrassed one, balancing the obligations of a loyal ally (with a special interest in the area so long as it retained obligations to Malaysia) against the wish to keep out of Vietnam and the temptation to criticize American mistakes there. SEATO was no more than the United States writ differently. Its purpose was to ensure the independence of South Vietnam but it could not save that ill-governed country from the dilemma of either collapsing or surviving as an American protectorate. (SEATO was dissolved in 1975.)

Ho had accepted the Geneva armistice reluctantly and under Russian and Chinese pressure. It may be surmised that only the prospect of elections in 1956 persuaded him to come to terms with France when he was entitled to expect not only the surrender of Dien Bien Phu but the collapse of the entire French position in the same year. He soon saw that his hopes were to be falsified and that the 17th parallel was another armistice line destined to harden into a political frontier. It was, moreover, a line of graver consequence than the division between the two halves of Korea, for in Vietnam the south fed the north and the perpetuation of the division entailed economic problems as well as disappointment over the denial of reunification. In the period of uncertainty between the signing of the armistice and the date fixed for the elections which were never held, Ho initiated a programme of agrarian reform and sought also to expand industry and exploit North Vietnam's mineral wealth, but the agrarian reform, modelled on Chinese collectivization, provoked a peasant rising which provoked a reign of terror which got out of hand and caused some 50,000 deaths. Industrialization required help from advanced countries such as the USSR and Czechoslovakia rather than China, and after the Sino-Russian split in the 1950s Ho had to balance between Moscow and Beijing. At first he allowed relations with the latter to deteriorate and in 1957 he received Voroshilov in Hanoi, but this partiality displeased some of his colleagues. Ho himself had associations of a lifetime with the USSR and Muscovite communism, and General Giap, backed by the North Vietnamese army, expressed the traditional Vietnamese distrust of China, but other leaders were pro-Chinese, including Truong Chinh, whose strength lay in the Lao Dong Party (founded in 1951 and essentially a communist party although it embraced a few non-communist notables). Ho spent two months in Moscow in 1959, returning to Hanoi via Beijing. By this time fighting had been resumed in the south and the problem of getting rid of the French was succeeded by the far bloodier problem of getting rid of the Americans. He lived just long enough to see it happen, dying in 1969.

American policy during the Eisenhower and Kennedy administrations rested on the proposition that South-east Asia mattered to the United States because of the domino theory. This theory, which turned out not to be valid, seemed the more plausible in the 1950s and 1960s owing to the strength of the communists in the huge country of Indonesia and the introduction there of Sukarno's Guided Democracy (see Chapter 18). The American resolve to stem the anticipated communist flood assumed that it could be attained without committing American forces to battle on the Asian mainland. The crisis in Vietnam during the Johnson administration was precipitated when this assumption was seen to be untrue because the Diem government in South Vietnam was unequal to the task of defeating the north. The domino theory invested Vietnam with a signal significance beyond its intrinsic importance. The Americans, besides portraying Diem's regime with marvellous inaccuracy as a democracy, misjudged their man.

South Vietnam started its independent career comparatively peacefully and prosperously in spite of the arrival from the north of nearly a million refugees (two-thirds of whom were Roman Catholic Christians). Its prime minister Ngo Dinh Diem, a northerner and a Roman Catholic, eliminated Bao Dai, who was deposed in 1955 (and retreated to France, where he died in 1997), and a year later inaugurated a republic with himself as president. Although the last French troops did not leave until 1956, American aid was transferred from the French to the Diem government from the first day of 1955. Diem was an anti-French intellectual, not particularly pro-American and in no way a democrat. He treated South Vietnam as a personal or family demesne which he administered through a network of secret societies, nepotistically, intolerantly and unintelligently. He antagonized the Buddhists, the dominant religious group, and the hill peoples who, although only a small minority of the population, inhabited more than half of the countryside in which subversive movements might be sustained. In the cities too Diem and his relatives, who included five brothers, became increasingly unpopular. The cities became generators of inflation and vice while the countryside became an open field for the settlement of private grudges and for extortionate demands which drove the peasants into the arms of the communist opposition.

A first coup against the regime in November 1960 failed but three months later the opposition was strong enough to attack Diem's palace from the air. At about the same time Ho decided to give material aid to the forces gathering against Diem in the countryside. Despite American pressure Diem had refused to supply food to North Vietnam in the mistaken belief that the northern regime was about to collapse under the weight of peasant revolts. Thus Ho was given an economic as well as a political motive for reopening the war. At the time of the Geneva armistice the communists in the south, many of whom retreated to the north, had concealed their arms against a possible resumption of fighting. An active communist opposition to Diem had come into existence under the name of the Vietcong – originally a term of opprobrium, like Whig or Tory. In 1960 a National Liberation Front (NLF) was formed and in 1962 the International Control Commission, an observer group established at Geneva eight years earlier, reported that North Vietnam was intervening in civil war in the south in support of the NLF.

In 1963 Buddhist hostility to the Diem regime reached a climax. Buddhist monks burned themselves to death in gruesome protest against persecution. The authorities retaliated by sacking pagodas and torturing monks. The Americans cut off aid to Diem and instigated a coup against him. Diem and his most markedly unpopular brother, Ngo Dinh Nhu, were killed, the regime collapsed and General Duong Van Minh ('Big Minh') became the head of the first of a series of transient military governments. In the next 18 months half a dozen coups took place. General Minh was forced into the background within two months of Diem's end. General Nguyen Khanh, more militant in relation to North Vietnam but no more secure in Saigon, was opposed by Buddhists and students demanding an end to military rule. He was displaced early in 1965 by the yet more militant general Tran Van Minh ('Little Minh'). From the latter part of 1965 the rising men were General Nguyen Cao Ky, the most militant of the generals to gain power and the most determined to carry the war beyond the 17th parallel, and General Nguyen Van Thieu.

The United States had two incompatible aims. It was determined to prevent communist government in Vietnam and not to become directly involved on the Asian mainland. The failure of France's Bao Dai experiment and of Bao Dai's non-communist successors created a dilemma which the United States resolved by rating its first aim above its second, with disastrous results. It believed that its choice lay between non-intervention and modest military intervention and, choosing the latter, became progressively involved in one of the major conflicts of the second half of the century. During the early 1960s the Americans became alive to the weaknesses of their policy of supporting weak South Vietnamese regimes and also more committed to it. One of Kennedy's early decisions on taking office in 1961 had been to increase American aid in men and material but without committing combat troops. He accepted the advice of General Maxwell Taylor, a former chairman of the US chiefs of staff, to build up American forces and by 1962 American aircraft were flying combat missions and the CIA was conducting more or less underground operations, but a few months before his assassination in 1964 he ordered a gradual retreat to culminate in complete withdrawal by the end of 1965. However, the initiative was slipping from the Americans to the Vietcong, so that an American withdrawal was becoming more problematical. The Vietcong, aided by the misrule of Diem, the confusion among his successors and by North Vietnam and China, had extended its control until the South Vietnamese and American forces were in danger of being driven into a few fortified footholds. The policy, copied from Malaya, of isolating villagers from guerrillas was unsuccessful because the differences between Vietnamese villagers and Vietnamese guerrillas were insignificant compared with the differences between Malay villagers and Chinese guerrillas in Malaya. The Americans, seeing that the Vietcong was winning, decided to increase their military effort and their control over the direction of the war, and at first the position of the Vietcong rapidly worsened. Thereupon the government of North Vietnam began to send regular divisions to its rescue. The war became, with scant disguise, a war between the United States and North Vietnam. In the south the Americans aimed to subjugate the whole country. Ultimately, they failed and, with hindsight, it could be said that they would have been wiser to have adopted General Salan's strategy of holding the centres of population from which no enemy could have dislodged them, and of securing and sealing off the rich, easily defensible and ethnically distinct Cochin-China. Instead American forces were multiplied year by year: from 23,000 at the end of 1964 to 390,000 two years later and 550,000 by the beginning of 1968. When American withdrawals began in July 1969 these forces had lost 36,000 dead. At their peak the combined American, South Vietnamese and allied forces numbered 1.25 million, backed by a mighty air force. Against them General Giap proved himself a brilliant guerrilla commander who knew how far to follow and how far to deviate from the strategic teachings of Mao Zedong.

In July 1964 the US destroyer *Maddox*, operating with South Vietnamese sea and land forces against North Vietnam, was twice attacked in the Bay of Tonkin. President Johnson used this episode, tendentiously explained, to obtain from Congress authority to use US forces in open naval combat: he grasped at the possibility of quick victory by air bombardment. A successful attack on an American garrison at Pleiku near the armistice line early in 1965 was followed by sharp American bombing reprisals. But the quick victory was prevented by Russian aid to Ho, notably for the anti-aircraft defence of Hanoi, and as the American bombardment became fiercer, and napalm, poison gases and defoliants were introduced, so opposition to the war within the United States developed vociferously and violently. The home front, mobilized by television, took the part not just of an enemy vilely massacred but of its own kith and kin involved in these horrors.

Johnson began to bid for peace. He offered to treat unconditionally with North Vietnam for a cessation of hostilities on the basis that South Vietnam would be an independent and neutral state; and he offered $16 billion in aid to South-east Asia, including North Vietnam. But he was not willing to accept the Vietcong as a party to the negotiations. In reply Ho enunciated a set of conditions which were not irreconcilable with the American proposals and Johnson implicitly but not explicitly opened the door of the negotiating chamber to the Vietcong as well. He was, however, unwilling to stop all bombing immediately (a bombing pause in May lasted only a few days) or to agree to withdraw all American troops before negotiations began. At the beginning of 1966 Johnson conferred with Ky and Thieu in Honolulu. Bombing was interrupted for several weeks and negotiations seemed not improbable, but the war went on, increasing in intensity and horror. Vietcong adherents and others were slaughtered by the most up-to-date weapons. They were hunted by and thrown out of helicopters, tortured, raped and murdered. In a celebrated instance at My Lai in 1967, which later led to a criminal trial and conviction in the United States, 300 civilians were killed by a US army unit.

By the end of 1967 the United States was bombarding the north heavily from the air but American casualties were severe and at a meeting with Kosygin at Glasboro in New Jersey, Johnson tried unsuccessfully to enlist Russian help to end the war. In South Vietnam Ky fell foul of the Buddhists and the Ky–Thieu government split and was reformed as a Thieu–Ky government (which lasted until 1971, when Thieu prevailed). A truce was declared for the festival of Tet in January 1968 and in Hanoi the foreign minister Nguyen Duy Trinh made pacific statements but his remarks, while welcome to some in Washington, were also regarded there as a feint to cover an impending offensive. Both interpretations were valid, for counsels in Hanoi were divided. Optimistic hawks believed that they could seize Saigon and other southern cities, win the active support of the urban populace and cause Thieu's armies to collapse. The attack was launched, caught the Americans unprepared but failed in all its main aims except the capture of Hue by the NLF, which held it for two months. The attack was, however, successful in an unexpected way. Although it did not destroy the Thieu regime it caused a loss of nerve in Washington. Two months later Johnson announced that American bombing was to be substantially curtailed and that he himself would not stand for re-election as president. Peace talks between the United States and North Vietnam opened in Paris. South Vietnam and the Vietcong joined the discussions. But they led nowhere. North Vietnam had discovered that it could survive the American onslaught and maintain the supply of men and material to the south by using routes and methods which, being comparatively primitive, were never wholly disrupted by aerial bombardment. North Vietnam had also discovered that the Americans really wanted to get out and either turn the war over once more to the South Vietnamese (whose army was brought up to a strength of over 1 million and given the most modern equipment) or end it. Johnson could neither win a victory, since he was not prepared to use nuclear weapons, nor negotiate a peace, since North Vietnam preferred waiting to negotiating. He was pursuing incompatible aims – to get out and to secure the existence of a separate, non-communist South Vietnam. North Vietnam was not convinced that it need concede the latter in order to get the former, and when the Democrats went down to defeat in November the new president Richard Nixon found himself in the same dilemma. Although he had pledged himself to end the war, he immediately sanctioned the extension of American bombing to Cambodia in another vain hope to find the quick victory.

So *Cambodia* was brought into the field of war. In March 1970 Prince Sihanouk was unseated by a coup by his own prime minister General Lon Nol. Sihanouk had ensured comparative peace and quiet from 1955 to 1965 but forfeited American friendship by his neutralism and his friendship with Zhou Enlai. Cambodia, like Laos, had been used by North Vietnam without much regard for its neutrality and Sihanouk had been reproached by some of his compatriots for putting up with too much infringement of the country's rights. The new Cambodian government asked for American arms to defend itself against intruders. It got instead American armies, accompanied by South Vietnamese forces (hereditary enemies) and by all the devastation of which the American military machine was capable. The American command in Vietnam was justifiably anxious to counter the use of Cambodia by the North Vietnamese and unjustifiably convinced that it would capture vast communist stores and major headquarters. The operation was militarily successful, though doubtfully necessary; politically it was at best irrelevant. It was stopped by the US Congress, which refused to vote funds for troops or advisers in Cambodia and, in 1973, by the same means stopped Nixon's resumed bombing of the country. Lon Nol protested that he had never been told that American and Vietnamese forces were to enter Cambodia.

Although American bombing of North Vietnam was resumed in 1972 these operations were the last lashes of the frustrated American giant. The withdrawal proceeded steadily and only 25,000 Americans remained at the end of the year. Since 1970 the governments of the United States and North Vietnam had been secretly in contact through Henry Kissinger and Le Duc Tho and in January 1973 representatives of the

United States, both Vietnams and the Vietcong met in Paris and agreed on a ceasefire, to be internationally supervised, and on the creation of a Council of National Conciliation in Vietnam to prepare elections. These agreements endorsed the American retreat but did not bring peace. There was heavy fighting in the latter part of 1973 and throughout 1974, with Thieu expressing confidence that his new army of a million men could win the war. He expected American aid but did not get it. His army disintegrated in the face of 200,000 North Vietnamese and 100,000 Vietcong adversaries. In 1975 he resigned and Big Minh returned from the shadows to surrender what authority was left in Saigon. The war was over. About 2 million people had been killed. In Laos, which had been invaded in 1971 by South Vietnam with American air support, North Vietnam won decisive victories and fighting came to a stop in 1973 on the basis that yet another coalition would be constructed and all foreign troops withdrawn. The new government came laboriously into existence in 1975 and perished the same year. The monarchy perished too. Prince Souphanouvong, now president, and the Pathet Lao had won the internal battle. Laos became a dependency of Vietnam under the name of the Lao People's Republic. In spite of its name its first elections were not held for 14 years.

For Cambodia the end of one war meant the beginning of another. Sihanouk, upon being displaced by the Americans and Lon Nol, had shifted to the left and allied himself with the Khmer Rouge, thereby transforming a comparatively insignificant faction of about 3,000 active members into a militant body ten times that size. Its leader Saloth Sar, better known as Pol Pot, was a zealot of about 50 years who had spent time in left-wing circles in Paris and later in China during the Cultural Revolution. His revolutionary programme included the abolition of religion and money, the creation of a rural populist communism and the extinction of cities; his revolutionary performance killed a million people or more in a sickening reign of terror after the United States abandoned Lon Nol and the Khmer Rouge took Phnom Penh a few days before the North Vietnamese entered Saigon. The Americans bombed Cambodia (now Kampuchea) once more in 1975 when the Khmer Rouge captured the US intelligence vessel *Mayaguez*, but the war was now between Kampuchea and Vietnam. It was provoked by the Khmer Rouge, which attacked Vietnam in debatable borderlands and in indisputably Vietnamese territory. Vietnam retaliated with a successful invasion of Kampuchea at the end of 1978 and installed a subservient government with Heng Samrin as president and Hun Sen as foreign minister, later also prime minister; both of them were Khmer Rouge renegades with a heavy responsibility for past atrocities. Hun Sen, albeit unbalanced and corrupt, introduced some beneficial reforms, including land distribution and encouragement for small businesses, and permitted wider freedom of speech and religion, but his rule was brutal. The Khmer Rouge offered little resistance, retreating to the north-west where it was pursued by the Vietnamese invaders. Kampuchean troops and refugees escaped into Thailand, whence the troops were able to filter back and fight again.

The war between Vietnam and Kampuchea was of concern to China for reasons both ancient and modern. China's traditional enmity towards an independent

Vietnam had been overlaid during the 1960s and 1970s when the Sino-Soviet split created competition between China and the USSR. China helped the Vietcong in order to pre-empt Russian aid and influence, but this amity did not last. The Cultural Revolution, derided by the Vietcong, severely curtailed Chinese external activity, and Nixon's visit to China and the subsequent Sino-American rapprochement were bitterly resented in Vietnam. North Vietnam's victory over the United States, the unification of north and south in 1975, this new state's large army, its alliance in 1978 with the USSR (when it became also a full member of Comecon) and its conquest of Kampuchea – all these factors ignited China's hostility. Vietnam's invasion of Kampuchea posed a threat to the hegemony in Indo-China which China had pursued for 1,000 years, while Vietnam's links with the USSR betokened a dependence which, occasioned by the exhaustions of war, economic mismanagement and a sharply rising population, heralded a Russian dominance in Indo-China even more distasteful to China than Vietnamese or American dominance. Russian influence in Vietnam was part of a threat manifest also in northern Asia and Afghanistan.

There were two other irritants: territorial conflict in the South China Sea and the treatment of Chinese in Vietnam. There were about a million Chinese in Vietnam, most of them in the south. These Hoa, as they were called, were economically success-ful and commensurately unpopular. Their nationality was open to argument and their loyalties to doubt. In 1977 many Hoa, including some from the remote south, trekked into China in what the Vietnamese described as migration and the Chinese as expul-sion. Whether or not incited by China, this trek acquired a momentum of its own and continued for two or three years. More enduring was conflict in the South China Sea. Old disputes were fanned by the belief that there might be oil under the waters of the Gulf of Tonkin. This belief enhanced the value of contested groups of islands to which both China and Vietnam laid claim. In 1974 a Chinese evicted a Vietnamese force from the Paracel islands, whereupon South Vietnam occupied the Spratly islands – small, numerous, uninhabited and further south. Both these groups, lying about halfway between Vietnam and the Philippines, were within the 200-mile offshore limit recog-nized by China and Vietnam. In 1988 the growing Chinese navy took possession of some of the Spratly islands and (in 1994) the Mischief Reef in the archipelago, in spite of Philippine claims. Malaysia and Brunei also had claims in the area. In 1996 China joined the Asian Regional Forum (see p. 490) and backed ASEM – Asian–European Meetings – in an expansive mood which spelled opposition to exclusive Japanese–American regional dominance. China's preoccupation with Vietnam gave Kampuchea a powerful friend. China berated Vietnam's aggression and Deng Xiaoping, on a visit to the United States, threatened to teach Vietnam a lesson. The USSR came to the help of Vietnam by vetoing its condemnation by the Security Council and, when Chinese troops invaded northern Vietnam, sent a flotilla which included a missile carrier into Vietnamese waters. But China's demonstrative riposte across its frontiers with Vietnam – which did much damage but also cost the invaders unexpected casualties – did not stop Vietnamese forces from sweeping across Kampuchea as far as the Thai border. More persuasive in Hanoi were the burden of keeping 250,000 troops in Kampuchea, the evaporation of Soviet aid, and the difficulties of restoring relations with the United States so long as 230 American soldiers missing during the war remained unaccounted for and Vietnam continued to occupy Kampuchea. By 1987 Vietnam had resolved to get out of a troublesome and costly situation. It announced that its forces would begin to withdraw at once and would all be evacuated by 1990. They left in 1989.

Simultaneously discussions began for a new government. Sihanouk and Hun Sen had a number of meetings in France and Indonesia, encouraged by China (to a limited degree, for China was not wholly averse to a war which was a drain on Vietnam's resources and on the popularity of its government at home). But neither Sihanouk nor Hun Sen nor both of them together could construct an effective regime without the Khmer Rouge, which had substantial armed forces as well as Chinese – and some American – support: the United States, like China, was prepared to give at least one cheer to any enemy of Vietnam and had been urging Sihanouk since the early 1980s to make common cause with the Khmer Rouge and with Son Sann, a former prime minister under Sihanouk and the leader of the third effective anti-Vietnamese force. (Sihanouk and Son Sann each commanded perhaps 10,000 armed men, the Khmer Rouge 30,000 at the very least. Hun Sen's army amounted to about 40,000, including a number of Vietnamese who remained in or returned to Kampuchea because they saw small prospect of a decent living in Vietnam.)

Partly at Australian prompting, the idea of overthrowing Hun Sen was replaced by attempts to unite all the main factions in a Supreme National Council in which Hun Sen would have six seats and the three opposition groups two each. At a late stage Sihanouk, the chairman-designate, insisted on being the thirteenth member of this Council, thus raising his contingent to three. This obstacle was surmounted by proposing that Hun Sen be deputy chairman to Sihanouk, with a seat of his own additional to his six nominees. The plan envisaged a gradual return to normal political activity after 18 months of supervision and administration by the UN, but Hun Sen's distrust of Sihanouk and his Chinese backers, and his fear of Khmer Rouge preponderance, made him prevaricate in the hope of getting some international recognition for his own regime without being forced into a coalition. A UN force was despatched to lay the base for elections by preparing electoral registers, assuring voters that it was safe to vote, organizing the return of some 250,000 refugees from Thailand and keeping the various parties to their engagements. UNTAC (UN Transitional Authority in Cambodia) came close to being an interim government for most of Cambodia and so a new kind of UN intervention. Although small – about 20,000 persons – it was markedly successful in its main tasks. It could not prevent Sihanouk from moodily retreating once more to Beijing or the Khmer Rouge, in occupation of a tenth of the country where it supported itself by sales of timber and precious stones through corrupt Thai entrepreneurs and army officers, from threatening to disrupt and then boycotting the elections. But elections were duly held in 1993 in a generally orderly way and with 90 per cent of voters taking part. Contrary to expectations, Hun Sen's Cambodian People's Party (CPP) with 38 per cent of the vote was defeated by its rival Funcinpet led by Sihanouk's son Prince Rannarith, which won 45 per cent. Sihanouk, mindful of the continuing strength of the Khmer Rouge, exerted himself to bring Funcinpet and the CPP together even though he had to concede to the latter an equal share in government and a blocking power in the parliament. This was a victory for the defeated Hun Sen, who became joint prime minister with Rannarith. Sihanouk reassumed the regal style which he had laid aside in 1955. But the Khmer Rouge could not be written out of the plot and a year later it recreated enough chaos to bring about the disintegration of the new government and the destruction of much of UNTAC's work. As in Angola the UN relied perforce on a minimum of goodwill and good faith and was powerless when these failed. In 1997 Hun Sen rounded on Rannarith and drove him from his share of power and from the country.

One persistent aspect of the travails of Vietnam after its victory over the United States was a stream of refugees trying to escape from the miseries of life in Vietnam under an incompetent and harsh regime compounded by an American economic embargo. They went by sea, many of them being attacked, despoiled, raped and killed on the way. Most of them came from the north of the country but the tally of refugees from the south increased during the 1980s. Around 57,000 of them reached Hong Kong, where they were most unwelcome and were detained and confined in insanitary pens. All but a fifth of them were adjudged by the colonial government of the already overcrowded island to be economic refugees (a new term) and not genuine political refugees whose return to Vietnam was precluded by international conventions. In 1989 the government of Hong Kong announced a scheme for the voluntary return of these refugees with one aircraft a month, but few were willing to go. At the end of the year 51 men, women and children were sent back against their will in a night-time operation which occasioned such an international outcry that the scheme had to be abandoned. In the next year the British and Vietnamese governments and the UN High Commissioner for Refugees concluded an agreement for the repatriation of refugees 'not opposed' to it. Britain, while it did not abjure its claim to be entitled to repatriate economic refugees by force, enlisted the help of the UNHCR in persuading them to go and hoped that many would do so after discovering that their treatment in Hong Kong was as bad or worse than anything which they might have to suffer in Vietnam. The return of these boat people to Vietnam was accelerated by the British in the prelude to the cession of the colony to China.

In 1993 the raising of the American embargo gave a fillip to the Vietnamese economy which, albeit belatedly and from a wretchedly low level, set out to emulate other east Asian economic 'tigers'. Diplomatic relations between the United States and Vietnam were fully restored only in 1997. Commercial relations were declared normal in 2006.

CHAPTER 18

South-east Asia and ASEAN

The term 'South-east Asia' is used to describe the countries which lie between India, China, Australasia and the open expanses of the Pacific Ocean. Diverse by race, religion and wealth, they had before the Second World War one nearly common feature: with the solitary exception of Thailand all were ruled by foreigners. The British, French, Dutch, Americans and Portuguese had spread over the area and appropriated varying amounts of it. This state of affairs was viewed with dissatisfaction within the region and also by the Japanese, whose New Order had been expanded into the Great East Asia Co-Prosperity Scheme under the direction of a special ministry in Tokyo. When war brought the Japanese to South-east Asia they came as anti-imperialist liberators, promising to remove European overlords, an operation which proved astonishingly easy. Three days after the attack on Pearl Harbor the Japanese sank the British warships *Prince of Wales* and *Repulse* (10 December 1941); Singapore fell in February 1942 and Corregidor in May; western dominance finished.

It was succeeded by a short Japanese phase in the course of which the new overlords, like Napoleon in Germany, found that nationalism is not a commodity that can be turned on or off at will. Some Japanese genuinely believed in the co-prosperity theme and wished to help the peoples of South-east Asia, but more were simply new imperialists who quickly alienated the local nationalists. As the fortunes of war turned against the Japanese, so did the nationalists, preparing to achieve their ends partly by services rendered to the former colonial powers and partly by a new strength that would not be overborne by war-weary Europeans. In Burma and the Philippines the end was easily achieved, in Indonesia less easily. In Malaya independence was delayed by an insurrection that was more communist than nationalist. Indo-China (see the previous chapter) was fated to suffer the long war which assumed international proportions and whose settlement posed further international problems in the successor states of Vietnam, Laos and Cambodia.

Throughout this region, the Philippines apart, the predominant power as the war ended was the British, represented until 1946 by the supreme commander in the South East Asia Command, Lord Mountbatten. The British expected to resume their former status in Burma, Malaya, Singapore and smaller territories and to restore the French, Dutch and Portuguese in Indo-China, Indonesia and Timor and the white rajah of Sarawak.

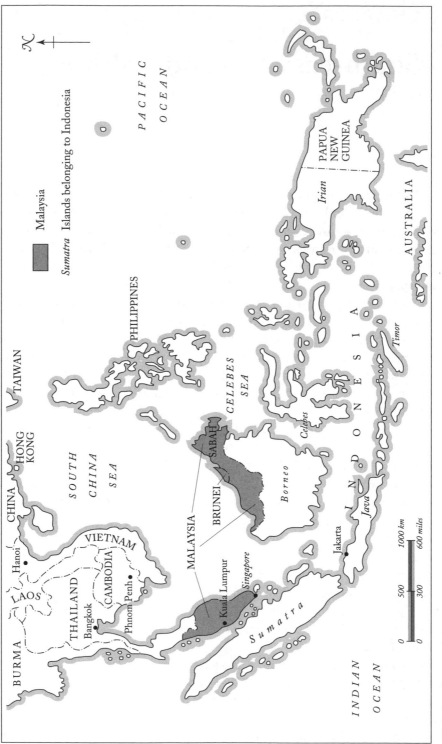

18.1 South-east Asia

Burma, renamed Myanmar in 1989, became independent in 1948 after a brief post-ponement on astrological advice and as one of the world's most ethnically complex countries. It became also one of the most isolated so that its people were impoverished and its rulers ignorant. Before the Second World War Burma was supplying nearly half the world's exported rice, selling valuable minerals and timber, producing oil and acquiring a modern infrastructure. It was also invaded by foreign marketeers and speculators and experienced a subversion of its values and its monarchical and religious institutions – an upheaval comparable with Ataturk's revolution in Turkey with the added infelicity that the engineers of change were alien. Long governed by an absolutism tempered by anarchy, Burma received a veneer of constitutional and economic modernization which fostered, besides anti-colonial resentments, a conflict between more modernization in an opening world and a retreat into conservative traditionalism.

In wartime Burma a group of nationalists without much knowledge of the outside world, pro-Japanese at the beginning of the war but later anti-Japanese and supplied with British arms, were associated together in the Anti-Fascist People's Freedom League (AFPFL). As the war came to an end there was doubt among the British whether to recognize and deal with the AFPFL. The government in London was opposed to re-cognition but the supreme commander, faced with the problems of installing a new administration without adequate resources of his own, favoured it. The Labour victory of July 1945 and the surrender of the Japanese in August produced a decision to recognize. The new British governor, who wanted to arrest the nationalist leader Aung San, and nearly did, was replaced, the AFPFL was treated as an embryonic government, and although Aung San and other leaders were assassinated in July their surviving colleagues achieved their goal of independence from Britain on 4 January 1948. There was no fighting. The British, strongly influenced by their pledge to leave India and by the impossibility of using the Indian troops of South East Asia Command against the Burmese, retired, leaving the AFPFL to struggle with huge war damage, its own internal divisions and with the hill peoples round the central Burmese plain whose traditional distrust of Rangoon (Yangon) created a string of separatist problems. The AFPFL included communists who split off from it and among themselves and waged separate campaigns against government; assassination had robbed Burma of a number of coming leaders during 1947 and 1948; revolt in Arakan along the west coast, added to troubles in the east (from the Karens spread across central Burma, the Shans – a Thai people – wedged between Thailand and China, and the Kachins in the far north), threatened independent Burma with disruption. There were Muslims in most parts of Burma, the majority of them in Arakan where, known as Rahingya, they had been since the seventh century AD.

In 1950 a new danger was introduced when 4,000 Kuomintang troops crossed into Burma from China under General Li Mi and gave rise to fears that the new Chinese regime would follow its retreating enemies. But Beijing made a point of not blaming

Rangoon and after a while General Li Mi and his followers were removed by air to Taiwan by the Americans. Nevertheless, Burma felt it wise to edge politely and circumspectly away from its British and American connections. Although the Chinese in Burma numbered only about 300,000 Burma's frontier with China was straddled by the Kachins (300,000 in China, 200,000 in Burma and a small number in India). In 1953 the Burmese government intimated that it did not wish to renew the expiring Anglo-Burmese defence treaty or retain the British military mission which had been in the country since independence; it also informed Washington that it wanted no more American aid. Zhou Enlai visited Rangoon on his way back to Beijing from Geneva in 1954 and the Burmese prime minister U Nu returned the visit later in the year. Further meetings led to the initiation of frontier discussions which were completed when General Ne Win displaced U Nu (who returned to power in 1960 but was again displaced by Ne Win in 1962 and this time imprisoned for six years).

Ne Win was a general with a taste for philosophical and socialist discourse which he combined with the suppression of parliament and the imprisonment of his political opponents. His seizure of power was, in the first place, a response to the threat of disintegration posed by the country's dissident movements. The demands of the Shans in particular (in later years the most persistent dissidents and the most successful drug dealers) for a new federal and looser constitution created a fear that the refugee Kuomintang forces in the north-east might, with American help, launch an invasion of China which would turn Burma into a battlefield (like Korea), while the existence in Burma of at least three different communist rebel movements made a Chinese invasion not improbable. The new regime, being overtly military, looked less feeble but it too failed to eradicate the various rebellions. It watered down U Nu's socialism but also watered away democracy: political parties were suppressed and universities closed in 1964. Burma's traditional fear of China and the Chinese persuaded Ne Win to visit the United States, but the American war in Vietnam was all but universally regarded in Burma as unjustifiable and ominous interference in Asian affairs.

In economic matters Ne Win was even less successful than his predecessors. Under the Japanese occupation the acreage under rice had been halved and although this area was increased after the war, production was ruined by civil wars and anarchy. Exports fell to one-tenth of their prewar figure and by 1966 domestic consumption was rationed. Desperate measures, such as the remission of all agriculture rents, did little good. The overall decline of the country's economy left farmers with nothing to buy even when they were paid for their produce, so that they had no incentive to produce more than they could themselves eat. Rice, once the source of Burma's wealth, was no longer worth growing, let alone exporting. Inflation, accompanied by static wages, impoverished the bulk of the population. Grandiose enterprises turned to dust; democratic forms were supplemented by intimidation; poverty and disease killed hopes as well as people. Burma became an economic dependency of China, obliged to import oil and gas at steeply rising prices.

N

INDIA

CHINA

VIETNAM

Myitkyina •

LAOS

Haka •   Sagaing
           •
         Mandalay   • Taunggyi

• Magway   • Loi-Kaw

Sittwe •

THAILAND

BAY OF
BENGAL

Bago •   Hpa-an •

Yangon
(Capital)   • Mawlamyine

Paithein •

GULF OF
THAILAND

Glossary
Current Name   Former Name

Current Name	Former Name
Myanamar	Burma
Yangon	Rangoon
Tanintharyi	Tenasserim
Bago	Pegu
Magway	Magwe
Ayeyarwady	Irrawaddy
Dawei	Tavoy
Pathein	Bassein
Bamar	Burman
Kayin	Karen
Mawlamyine	Moulmein
Hpa-an	Pa-an

ANDAMAN
SEA

• Dawei

Name Change: On 18 June 1989
the name of the country was
changed to the Union of
Myanmar. The English spelling of
many towns, divisions, states,
rivers and nationalities was
changed.

0	250	500 km
0	150	300 miles

Mountains

ARAKAN STATE

18.2 Myanmar (Burma)

In 1977 an attempt on Ne Win's life was followed by discrimination against Muslims, torture and killing. A massacre in Arakan caused flight into Bangladesh. Ne Win, who assumed a new term of office in 1978, became autocratic, secretive and out of touch and in 1981 he made way for General San Yu, who ruled in his shadow rather than in his place. The various peripheral wars continued in the north-east and south-east, with the Burmese communists joining in where they were welcome. The economy deteriorated to such an extent that Burma graduated downward to the status of a Least Developed Country (LDC – eligible for especially soft international loans) and in 1987 the state cancelled all notes below a certain face value, thus extinguishing the savings of countless people. Discontent spread from the poor to the middle classes and the army. Demonstrations were brutally repressed by the police, and General Sein Lwin, noted for his ferocity, was thrust into the presidency which Ne Win had resumed but now once more abandoned. Continuing riots forced Sein Lwin to resign after a few weeks and were not abated by the installation of the civilian Maung Maung, who lasted two months. The army resumed power, dissolved parliament and ruled through a State Law and Order Council (SLORC). When fresh elections were promised, some 200 parties appeared but only those acceptable to the government were licensed. Aung San's daughter Aung San Suu Kyi returned from exile in England to lead a National League for Democracy but was arrested. The League claimed a massive victory in 1990 but the official results of the elections mirrored the government's wishes rather than the voters' choices and the government remained unmoved. Aung San Suu Kyi was put under house arrest until 1995, when she was unexpectedly released. SLORC was transformed into the SPDC (State Peace and Development Council) with, mostly, new faces. But the ruling caste was divided with Ne Win still looming in the background with uncertain aims, the SPDC's attempts to entice foreign businesses and tourism failed and the economic crisis in Thailand in 1997 threatened Myanmar with the reflux of thousands of workless refugees. Efforts by the EU through a German–French–Finnish mission to mediate between the regime and Aung San Suu Kyi testified to the range of the former's interests rather than any pliability in Myanmar's internal affairs.

A fresh uprising in 2007, again led by students and Buddhist monks, was swiftly and ruthlessly crushed with a number of protesters dead and at least hundreds imprisoned. In 1980 Idi Amin's tyranny in Uganda had been overthrown by an armed invasion from Tanzania (p. 588) but in 2007 nobody was prepared to take such drastic action to rescue the people of Myanmar from the weirdly robotic Than Shwe, the current dictator of this peculiarly fissile country, although an emissary from the UN secretary-general was allowed to visit Aung San Suu Kyi twice.

Myanmar had become independent after 60 years of British rule with only the semblance of a state. It was an amalgam of antagonistic ethnic groups of which the Burmans constituted the most central and the largest. Within the Burman sector the failure of Aung San's democratic venture left untrammelled power with the military.

The army was largely and increasingly officered by Burmans, General Ne Win derived additional authority as chief of the Burman nation and an almost uninterrupted series of civil wars around the state's borders set the seal on Burman military authority. Ne Win's successors wrecked their own dominance, among Burmans as well as non-Burmans, by economic policies of outstanding ineptitude. Themselves increasingly reclusive, they also isolated the state from its international commerce to such an extent that all sections of the population were grievously impoverished and the ensuing protests were joined by thousands of Buddhist monks. The authorities' response was brutal and in the short term successful. The outside world, which had paid little heed to this tale of incompetence and misrule, was forced to protest and western countries, particularly the United States, took action to the extent of imposing economic sanctions but these measures did little more than accentuate the government's own policy of isolation and were in any case incomplete: India, China and South-east Asia declined to give up importing from Myanmar goods which they wanted from it.

In *Malaya*, a conglomeration of principalities plus small British colonial territories, the British had no easy way out. The naval base on the adjacent island of Singapore (itself a British colony) created arguments for staying which did not exist in Burma, and the strength of the Chinese (in Malaya a substantial minority and in Singapore a majority) made many Malays less resentful of British rule than apprehensive of the local Chinese, whose leaders – replacing prosperous prewar leaders compromised by their collaboration with the Japanese invaders – had taken to the jungle and to communism. Among the active opponents of the Japanese the largest group had been Chinese and most of these were communist rather than adherents of the Kuomintang, but by the very fact of their racial and doctrinal distinctiveness they could not claim to be a nationalist movement like the AFPFL in Burma.

An initial bid for power was checked by the British after some hesitation. The British then tackled the racial problem and proposed a Malayan Union in which citizenship would be obtainable by any person who had lived ten years in the country. The Malays opposed this plan, which would have made citizenship, and so political power, available to a large section of the Chinese population. The British thereupon proposed a Malayan Federation in which the powers of the Malay sultans were greater than in the proposed Union and the opportunities for the Chinese to become citizens were restricted.

In 1948 the Chinese communist insurrection began and an emergency was declared which was to last for 12 years during which the insurgents baffled 50,000 troops, 60,000 police and a home guard of 200,000. In 1950 General Sir Harold Briggs, the director of operations, realized that the key to the situation lay in the silent support given to the insurgents, often out of terror, by the great mass of the population, and he therefore made plans to assemble and protect the people in resettlement areas where they would be immune from blackmail and would cease to supply the insurgents with food. General Sir Gerald Templer, who arrived as governor in 1952 in succession to the murdered Sir Henry Gurney, continued this policy and developed at the same time political measures designed to bring the Malay, Chinese and Indian communities together as a prelude to independence. Malaya became independent on 31 August 1957 under a constitution which established a revolving presidency tenable by the Malay sultans in turn. It entered into a defence agreement with Britain but did not become a member of SEATO and refused in 1962 to allow Malayan territory to be used by British units which might be called upon to help Thailand in the event of a threat to that country from Laos.

Singapore, with a population three-quarters Chinese, was set on the road to independence by the usual British process. A new legislative council with an unofficial and elected majority was installed alongside a nominated executive council. This machinery of government then evolved into a legislative assembly and a council of ministers under a chief minister, most of whose colleagues were chosen by the assembly, the governor retaining certain reserved powers. Full independence came in 1959 subject to the retention of British rights in the naval base. The prime minister Lee Kuan Yew was anxious for closer links with Malaya but since a union would place the Chinese in a majority the Malays were reluctant unless the union were at the same time extended to other and less Chinese territories. Such territories existed in Sarawak, North Borneo and Brunei.

In 1946 the rajah of *Sarawak* Sir Charles Brooke ceded the principality, which his family had held since 1841, to Britain and in the same year Britain assumed in *North Borneo* the rights and responsibilities which had belonged before the war to the British North Borneo Company. Both Sarawak and North Borneo became crown colonies. *Brunei*, a third territory along the northern side of the island of Borneo (most of which formed part of Indonesia), resumed its prewar status as a British protectorate.

In 1963 Sarawak and North Borneo (now *Sabah*) joined Malaya and Singapore to form a Greater Malaysian Union, despite protests from the Philippine Republic, which had claims in North Borneo, and from the Indonesian Republic, which regarded the scheme as a plan to create a western-orientated state capable of checking Indonesian ambitions. Brunei refused to join and a revolt against the sultan, who was believed to favour accession, gave the Indonesian President Sukarno the idea that the federation was unpopular and might be destroyed by inexpensive guerrilla operations, persistence and propaganda; and that he might be able to add the rest of Borneo to Indonesia. The ensuing Indonesian confrontation forced Malaysia to appeal for British and Australian military help and frustrated the British intention of getting out of the region after creating Malaysia. The confrontation abated when Sukarno was demoted by his army in 1965–66, but Malaysia was a contrived constellation whose components had been forced into federation for external and adventitious reasons and upon the assumption that the territories tacked on to Malaya could not exist on their own. After its creation

Malaysia's largest ethnic group was Chinese (43 per cent) with Malays the next largest (40 per cent). In the Malayan peninsula Malays were 50 per cent and Chinese 37 per cent of the population.

Brunei had rejected the assumption that the smaller territories in the region could not exist on their own and Singapore rebutted it. Brunei, vestigial survival of an empire which had once reached to the Philippines, fabulously rich in relation to its size and population and virtually the private estate of its sultan, attained internal self-government in 1971 and complete independence from Britain in 1984, when it joined the UN, the Commonwealth and ASEAN (see below). Singapore, having joined Malaysia at its inception, broke away. Its socialist People's Action Party (PAP) was opposed by the conservative Malayan Chinese Association on the issue, among others, of whether Malaysian politics should be conducted essentially on class or racial lines. Both parties were largely Chinese but the PAP wanted politics throughout the federation to be organized around the needs and interests of economic classes. Across the water in Malaya Tunku Abdul Rahman, who was a conservative Malay nobleman as well as party leader and prime minister, was alarmed by the attitudes of the PAP and its leader Lee Kuan Yew, and was determined to ensure that no Chinese Singaporean should become prime minister of the federation. He decided to evict Singapore from it. Lee Kuan Yew had no wish to secede, but tensions between the two territories and their two leaders convinced him that an early and reasonably amicable divorce was imperative. Singapore developed an outstandingly successful mixed economy. Foreign capital flowed in; income per head trebled in the first decade after the breach in 1965; and the PAP reaped the benefits by remaining in power for a generation. Singapore had for several years uneasy relations with Indonesia, inflamed by incidents such as the execution in Singapore of two Indonesian soldiers and the refusal to recognize Indonesia's conquest of East Timor in 1975 (see pp. 484–5), but disagreements were contained and eased within the framework of ASEAN.

In *Malaysia* – thus constituted with the Malay states, Sarawak and Sabah but without Brunei or Singapore – the principal political problem was relations in the Malay peninsula between the rural Malays, numerically superior, and the urban Chinese, economically predominant. Elections in 1969 were tumultuous and the army had to be used to restore order. Abdul Rahman resigned in the wake of this setback to hopes of peaceful communal development. He was succeeded by Tun Abdul Razak, who enjoyed the fruits of an impetus to the economy which brought benefits to Malays through economic growth rather than economic redistribution at the expense of the Chinese. Although the second Development Plan (1971–75) made a faltering start and was temporarily upset by the world oil crisis in 1973–74, Malaysia's diverse economy successfully withstood the buffets of the mid-1970s. The risk of racially polarized conflict was avoided. Abdul Razak revived the United Malayan National Organization (UMNO), which had been created in 1946 as a focus for Malay nationalism against the British and the assertion against the Chinese of the Malay nature of Malaya. He reconciled factions within UMNO and coaxed it into alliance with the Malayan Chinese Association (MCA – founded in 1949) and the Malayan Indian Congress (founded in 1954). By the early 1970s all parties of consequence in Malaysia were associated in a multicommunal alliance, in which UMNO was the largest component.

Tun Razak modified Malaysia's pro-western stance in the direction of non-alignment. He visited the USSR and China and after 1975 he favoured the inclusion of Vietnam in ASEAN, but he died in 1976. His successor Dato Hussein Onn, who was prime minister until 1981 when his health gave way, faced economic deceleration, renewed threats to communalism from Malay nationalism (and assertive Muslims), allegations of corruption and fears – unrealized – of secession by Sabah; but economic recovery helped his National Front of ten parties to convincing victory in elections in 1978. His deputy prime minister and successor Muhammad Mahathir was a more controversial politician who had first made his mark by criticism of Abdul Rahman and later adopted a robust stand against undue and unnecessary deference to British interests. As prime minister, Mahathir's political fortunes were erratic. His position was tainted by rumours of financial scandals, in spite of which he won unexpectedly clear victories in federal and state elections in 1986. In the next year he almost lost the presidency of UMNO and in 1988 the Supreme Court declared UMNO an unlawful organization on grounds of procedural delinquencies, but Mahathir circumvented this damaging judgment by going to war with the judiciary. The Chief Justice was suspended and then dismissed; five other senior judges were suspended and two of them dismissed; the Court nevertheless confirmed its original ruling. On the political stage Mahathir was opposed by two of his most eminent former colleagues, Tunku Razaleigh Hamzah and Datuk Musa Hitam. The latter accepted an ambassadorial appointment and in a general election in 1990 the former was decisively defeated. Mahathir consolidated his position as leader of a ruling coalition of 14 parties dominated by UMNO. In elections in 1995 some local opposition persisted in Sabah and the Muslim Parti Islam Se Malaysia (PAS) retained a foothold in Kelantan in the north, but the principal opposition party, the Democratic Action Party, was beaten even in its stronghold, Penang. The economy, growing at the rate of 8 per cent a year, was as buoyant as any among Malaysia's ASEAN partners and rather more soundly grounded in natural resources (oil and gas) and manufacture. Between 1970 and 1995 the agricultural sector's contribution was reduced from 30 to 14 per cent and 80 per cent of the enhanced manufacturing output was exported. Nevertheless, growth was so far dependent on foreign borrowing that the economy was vulnerable to speculative attacks on the currency such as struck the region generally in 1997 (see below). Mahathir angrily denied that the ensuing crisis was due to defects in Malaysian financial institutions or management and blamed the principles and practices applied to international economic affairs by the world's leading economic states and the international bodies which they dominated. He dismissed his finance minister and probable successor Ibrahim Anwar – a possible rival in times of trouble, accused of gross sexual and other crimes and convicted amid massive demonstrations in his favour, which did him no good – and he called an early election which he won, although not without some disturbing omens. His ruling coalition lost 20 seats, five of them held by cabinet ministers, and the Malaysian Islamic Party, already in power in Kelantan, won control of neighbouring Trengganu. In 2006 Mahathir chose the more affable Abdullah Badawi to share power with him in the newly created post of prime minister. By the fiftieth anniversary of its creation the Malaysian federation had recovered from the economic setbacks of 1997 (p. 490) and, more coherent than its neighbours in South-east Asia and with a manageable population of 30 million, was able to project steady economic growth for the next several years.

South of the British possessions in Burma, Malaya and Singapore lay in 1945 the former Dutch empire in *Indonesia*. When the British returned to South-east Asia after the defeat of the Japanese, their actions were dominated by their decision to leave India. South-east Asia (with the exception perhaps of Singapore) was for Britain an adjunct of India and it was hardly conceivable that the British could for long pursue in South-east Asia policies that were plainly at variance with their chosen course in India. No such considerations affected the Dutch, whose position in Indonesia was not regulated by any other positions in Asia. For them the question was the basic question which the British put to themselves in India – whether to go or to stay – and not the secondary question which confronted the British in Burma – whether to stay in spite of the departure from India. The Dutch proposed to revert more or less to their prewar positions and they looked to their British allies to help them.

The return of the Dutch to Indonesia was generally assumed in 1945, but for practical reasons the British supreme commander was unable to undertake extensive operations and dealt with the nationalist leader Sukarno in the key island of Java. Dutch forces arrived to take the place of the token British occupation, but found themselves opposed by a comparatively well-organized and well-equipped movement under leaders of ability and sophistication whose foreign contacts and travels had given them an insight into the wider forces affecting the continuance of European rule in Asia. The British tried to mediate and by the Linggadjati agreement of 1946 the Dutch recognized the de facto authority of the self-proclaimed Indonesian republic in Java, Sumatra and Madura and agreed to withdraw their forces from these areas; a union between the Netherlands and Indonesia was to be created by the beginning of 1949. But this scheme failed to please anybody and the situation degenerated into chaos. In 1947 the Dutch resorted to force in what came to be called the First Police Action. A respite was secured by the Renville agreement but fighting recurred, the situation was brought before the Security Council, and after a Second Police Action in December 1948 the Dutch, who were impeded by the anti-colonialism of the United States and its representatives in Indonesia, found themselves obliged to compromise. Independence was conceded in 1949, subject, however, to the acceptance by the new Indonesian

Republic of a shadowy union with the Netherlands (unilaterally abrogated by Indonesia in 1956); to the exclusion of West Irian (western New Guinea); and to a federal constitution of seven states, converted into a unitary state a year later, although not without sporadic fighting and abortive secessions from central Javanese control. Under the influence of Nehru the Indonesian Republic, of which Sukarno became president, adopted a non-aligned stance in international affairs and enhanced its standing by playing host in 1955 to the first conference of non-aligned states at Bandung. In south Asia the Bandung conference was regarded as a retort to the previous year's Treaty of Manila, whereby the United States seemed to plan to extend the Cold War to Asia and the Pacific. Zhou Enlai's appearance at Bandung helped Indonesia to establish good relations with China and gave Indonesia's non-alignment a communist rather than a western tilt.

At its visionary widest an independent Indonesia had included Malaya, Singapore, North Borneo and New Guinea. More practically, it included all the Netherlands East Indies. West Irian fell into this category but the other half of New Guinea was Australian (either part of the Australian Commonwealth or a Trust Territory administered by Australia). Fears of the extension of Indonesian power throughout New Guinea caused the Australian government to support the Netherlands' retention of this corner of its empire, but the logic of events – measured in miles from Holland – forced the Dutch to abandon in 1962 a last outpost to which they had succeeded in clinging on the plea that the inhabitants were not Indonesians and were unlikely to get a fair deal from Indonesia. The prolongation of this question for 13 years after independence kept nationalist spirits on the boil and strengthened the position of Sukarno, the country's most eloquent and popular nationalist, in spite of the gradual collapse of parliamentary democracy under his rule and economic recession (aggravated by the eviction of the Dutch and the nationalization of their enterprises). In 1959 Ahmed Sukarno, supported by the army and the Communist Party (PKI), transformed the state into a Guided Democracy, a euphemism for personal dictatorship and a bravura performance which, however, left him sandwiched between the army and the PKI. His determination to secure West Irian drove him closer to China and the USSR and so earned him British and American distrust as a possible conduit through whom the communist powers might get control of South-east Asia's largest and richest state. The PKI encouraged Sukarno in his opposition to the creation of a Malaysian federation, which he presented as a device for preserving British influence. He backed a revolt in Brunei in 1962 against its merger with the federation – it was suppressed by the British in a few days – and kept up confrontation with Malaysia by border forays and protests at the UN and other international gatherings until the end of his rule.

Although gravely weakened by war, revolution, civil war and (90 per cent) illiteracy Indonesia was, by virtue of its size (over 13,000 islands and a population of 200 million) and natural wealth, a power of a different order from any other state in South-east Asia: a possible counter to Chinese influence and expansion or an adjunct to them. The PKI under its leader A. K. Aidit was one of the most effective communist parties in the world, and pro-Chinese. In spite of a membership believed to exceed 10 million it had failed in 1945 to win a monopoly of power by a coup at Madiun in Java but had won 18 per cent of the vote in elections in 1955. In 1965 a false report of Sukarno's death became the signal for a communist putsch. Six generals were cruelly mutilated and murdered but others escaped and the coup failed. In a counter-coup, supported if not engineered by the American and British governments and secret services, something like half a million communists (including Aidit) and suspected sympathizers were killed, several millions more were imprisoned for decades and the army established its control over Sukarno and the country. The former was gradually stripped of his powers, resigned in 1967 and died in detention in 1970. His successor T. N. J. Suharto, a peasant's son in general's clothing, was a deft political operator who turned Indonesia into a centralized economy run by and for himself and his very extended and extensively enriched family. Suharto was elected president for seven successive terms stretching to 1998. He kept vast numbers of opponents in detention (some were transported to a convenient offshore island) but the national economy prospered with American and Japanese help. Although earnings from the export of rubber fell, Indonesia's oil and its enviable variety of other minerals more than redressed the balance. In the 1970s and 1980s the economy was growing at the rate of 7–10 per cent a year – much of it, however, squandered on ostentation and senseless manufactures as unsaleable as anything produced in the USSR's satellites in Europe. This growth was checked in the late 1980s by declining revenues from oil and the rising cost of imports from Japan and debt service to it, and the currency was devalued. In 1989 Indonesia resumed formal relations with China after a breach of 24 years and Suharto visited Moscow after an equally long period of tepid contacts. Suharto was re-elected unopposed in 1998, but the economic turmoil which surfaced the previous year (see below) brought him down. Half the population was in dire need, the Chinese were fleeing the country with their money and Suharto's attempts to blame economic catastrophe on foreigners – and to refuse their aid – were deplored by many in Indonesia as well as by its neighbours and principal creditors (Japan, the United States, Germany). Suharto's successor B. J. Habibie was distrusted by the army as a civilian and by civilians as the army's figurehead. In elections in 1999 the ruling Golkar Party had the unfamiliar experience of coming second. The winners were the new Democratic Party and its leader Megawati Sukarnoputri, Sukarno's daughter. At this point the constitution imposed an interregnum which events in East Timor converted into a catastrophe.

Indonesia's constitution provided that the president be elected by the parliament enlarged for this purpose by representatives of regions and minorities. The presidential election was not due to be held until three months after the parliamentary elections, with the result that uncertainty clouded the prospects of Megawati and Habibie and the attitude of the army to each of them. Suharto's fall had prompted the East Timorese to expect the independence for which they had been fighting for a quarter of a century and Habibie publicly conceded that there should be a referendum on this issue, apparently without consulting the army's chiefs, who were appalled by the prospect of a vote which was bound to favour independence and stimulate other secessionists in northern Sumatra and West Irian (New Guinea) and ultimately perhaps elsewhere.

Timor, the last major island in the chain between continental Asia and Australia, had been divided by the Dutch and Portuguese in almost equal sections. The eastern, Portuguese half was detached from Macao at the end of the nineteenth century to become a separate colony, which it remained after the western half had become part of the Indonesian republic. The overthrow of the military regime in Lisbon in 1974 exposed East Timor to engulfment by Indonesia, which was, however, opposed by two groups, the one pro-Portuguese and the other demanding independence. Civil war broke out in 1975, the Portuguese left and Indonesia invaded and annexed the territory, devastating it with modern weapons, killing half the inhabitants and incarcerating many of the survivors in camps. Portugal and Australia implicitly acquiesced. The rest of the world hardly noticed. The president and his deputy were assassinated in 1979. Continuing resistance was met by ruthless ferocity powered by arms supplied by western manufacturers under licence from western governments, primarily the American and British. Resistance to Indonesia died down in the 1990s but revived with the death of Suharto. Habibie's decision to allow a referendum on independence or continuing integration with Indonesia was followed by the despatch of a UN Assistance Mission (UNAMET) to organize and supervise the referendum. It produced a remarkably large turnout and a four-to-one vote for independence. These developments precipitated an onslaught by militias – special army units in disguise – which killed about 30,000 Timorese, drove hundreds of thousands to flight and impelled the UN Security Council into despatching a (mainly Australian) force into East Timor under chapter VII of the Charter.

This intervention deeply affronted the army's leaders, who remained, however, undecided how to respond and whom to support in the coming presidential election. The one other centre of authority in Indonesia – the Islamic notables – were divided between a conservative and a liberal tendency and likewise shocked into indecision. The economic consequences were more pronounced. The beginnings of recovery from the reversals of 1997–98 were blocked as the Timorese crisis destroyed Indonesia's credit in every sense of the word. The parliament formally accepted the secession of East Timor and passed a vote of censure on Habibie, who thereupon withdrew from the presidential competition. Once independent East Timor was left to its own devices and descended into extreme poverty with unemployment at 80 per cent. Fredelin, the old independence party, won the most seats in elections in 2006 but not a majority. It adapted blocking tactics, its leaders lost their erstwhile prestige and the new generation produced no personalities of equal calibre.

In Indonesia the national assembly elected as president Abdurrahman Wahid, an ailing but respected and skilful Javanese Muslim notable with moderate views. This choice occasioned violent demonstrations and the next day Megawati was elected vice-president. Wahid assembled a broad coalition government whose most urgent tasks were to keep Indonesia in one piece and to prevent the imposition of a military despotism. Regional conflicts were all but inevitable in so huge a country and particularly acute in the province of Aceh in Sumatra. In 2002 Indonesia got a new president in Susilo Bambang, followed by a taste of violent Islamic protest in the bombings of Bali and Jakarta (2003) and a share of the terrifying visitation of the tsunami which overwhelmed a large corner of South-east Asia in 2004.

Thailand had the unique experience of escaping the European conquest which embraced the rest of South-east Asia. It was left as a buffer between the British, who advanced from India into Burma, and the French, who advanced from Annam and Tonkin into Laos and Cambodia. Unlike Burma, Laos and Vietnam, it had no frontier with China and it had succeeded in assimilating a substantial part of its Chinese population of 4 million (12 per cent of the total), but it shared the general apprehensiveness of all South-east Asia concerning the revival of Chinese power and welcomed an American alliance as an insurance. It became the one genuinely Asian member of SEATO (the Philippines and, even more so, Pakistan being but peripheral members of an alliance termed South-east Asian). The army, which had imposed limits to royal absolutism in 1932, ruled directly from 1938 to 1973 through a succession of strong men – Marshals Pibul Songgram, Thanarat Sarit and Thanom Kittikachron – with an interlude of civilian rule (1944–46) under Nai Pridi Panomiong who, on being worsted by Pibul, retired to China and there revived his wartime Free Thai movement, which did not this time amount to much. Rich in rubber, tin, teak and rice, Thailand stood in less need of foreign aid than most of its neighbours but it became expensively embroiled in the wars to the east. Threatened in 1962 by communist units on its borders with Laos, it was offered and accepted the help of American troops. Two years later it permitted the establishment of American air bases for use in the war in Vietnam, and this counter-aid to the United States was gradually expanded to six major bases accommodating forces of 50,000. By the 1970s the strains of war, and the awareness that the war was being lost by the Americans, fostered discontent, which was accentuated by the general corruption, inefficiency and uncertain policies of military rule. The American alliance and the consequent involvement in Vietnam were increasingly criticized and after riots in 1973 civilian rule was restored. This change marked a partial reversal of external policies as well as a desire to clean up public life, which had been corrupted by oligarchic government and the inflation and vices attendant on a foreign military presence. The American forces began to leave in the same year but another product of the war remained in the shape of the Patriotic Front which, with some Chinese support, had for ten years maintained guerrilla groups a few thousand strong among the Meo peoples who (numbering in all about 300,000) lived astride the Thai–Laotian border. In 1976 an increasingly bewildered civilian regime was again replaced by the military behind a military–civilian façade, whose main worry was the advent of Vietnamese power to the borders of Thailand; but the moderate right regained control.

Vietnam's conquest of Kampuchea (Cambodia), for long the buffer state between Thailand and Vietnam, threw thousands of refugees into eastern Thailand and forced it to look for help to counter Vietnamese expansion and restore Kampuchea's independence. Thailand's friends and allies in South-east Asia did not provide the kind of support required by Thailand, which turned to China and the United States. Both supplied arms, the latter in large quantities and on condition that these arms might be available for use by the United States as well as Thailand. With economic growth around 10–12 per cent a year, industrial investment and output growing, tourism also growing and external payments in balance, Thailand prospered. Within its monarchical framework it was governed by interlocking and mutually beneficial associations of the army and the business community, headed by generals but marginally constrained by a parliamentary constitution and the residual powers and considerable prestige of the monarchy. In 1988 General Prem Tinsulanonda gave way at the age of 82 to General Chatichai Choonhaven, but four years later the choice of General Suchinda Kraprayoon as the next prime minister without parliamentary approval caused riots, led by ex-General Chamlon Srimuang, on a scale which prompted King Bhumipol to intervene, snub the military and install a civilian prime minister. Besides quarrels between generals the regime was marked by outstanding peculation and, mainly in the west and south, disturbances caused by Muslim or communist insurgents or organized opium dealers. The financial turmoil in the region (see below) in 1997–98 caused no political upheaval beyond constitutional amendments and attempts to limit the amounts of money spent at elections. But in 2006 a military coup, designed to check the creeping advance of democracy, unseated the prime minister who fled to London. The king appointed another civilian prime minister.

The Philippines (about 7,000 islands), overrun by the Japanese during the war, were recovered by the United States in 1945 and given their independence in the next year. The terms of the transfer of sovereignty included a lease of bases to the United States for 99 years, reduced in 1966 to 25 years from that date. The central problem of the new government was authority. The country had become a gangland in which different groups, including the police, had become laws unto themselves. Violence was endemic and rose in a crescendo at or near election times. Prominent among the forces in the state were the Hukbalahaps, originally anti-Japanese guerrillas supported during the war by the Americans but, the war having ended, now expendable or worse: their leader Luis Taruc proclaimed himself a communist. He surrendered in 1974 but his movement persisted in the north, where its New People's Army (NPA) governed substantial areas with some support from the local population. The NPA's sphere was near enough to the American air and naval bases at Clark Airfield and Subic Bay to cause the United States some uneasiness and ensure support for a series of presidents judged capable of containing the insurgents. There was also dissidence in the south, where an established Muslim majority found itself becoming a minority and formed the Moro National Liberation Front. In the capital, Manila, ostentation flourished alongside the debris of war.

In 1962 President Diosdado Macapagal exhumed the Philippines' claim to Sabah (North Borneo), which forms one side of the Sulu Sea, otherwise enclosed by Philippine islands. He broke off relations with Malaya and refused to recognize the new state of Malaysia, of which Sabah had agreed to become part. But this issue was allowed to drop by his successor Ferdinand Marcos (president 1966–86), who, although elected as a reformer, became preoccupied with attempts to retain the presidency beyond the constitutional term and a fabulous enrichment of himself and his family. A referendum in 1973, following the imposition of martial law in 1972, allowed him to prolong his hold on office. Martial law was annulled in 1981 and Marcos unsurprisingly won a presidential election in the same year. His rule was tyrannical and his wife, who became a political personage in her own right, was no better. They plundered their own country, calculating that its strategic significance to the United States would make Washington turn a blind eye. In 1983 Benigno Aquino, the most eminent opponent of the regime (who had been imprisoned in 1973 to keep him from winning an election and was released in 1979 to seek medical treatment in the United States), was assassinated as he set foot on his native soil from an aircraft, killed by a hired gunman who was himself immediately shot dead. A subsequent inquiry pointed the finger at a group which included the chief of army staff General Fabian Ver and two other generals, but they were officially exonerated. With fresh elections due in 1986 and increasing unrest verging on civil war, the Americans were forced to ask themselves whether Marcos was not a rapidly wasting asset, but the more vulnerable he became the more the Americans found themselves trapped between him and what was to them an even more unpalatable, increasingly left-wing alternative. Having lost Vietnam and its base at Camranh Bay to allies of Moscow, they were fearful of seeing the Philippines with their even more important bases go the same way. They sustained Marcos until he became unsustainable and then switched their support to Aquino's widow, Corazon, who campaigned against Marcos for the presidency and forced him to decamp two weeks after a further re-election – and the Americans to change sides – under the pressures of huge peaceful demonstrations and a few highly placed desertions to her side. Marcos died in the United States in 1989.

Mrs Aquino, although president by popular acclaim, was none the less dependent on the army, personified by Juan Ponce Enrile and Fidel Ramos. Her vice-president Salvador Laurel had been her rival for the presidency. She inherited a 20-year-old insurrection in the south, an external debt of $25 billion, a debt service which absorbed a third of foreign earnings, declining domestic production and an agreement with the IMF which was on the verge of being abrogated for non-compliance with its terms.

She negotiated a new agreement but recovery was sluggish. Discord in the insurgent provinces persisted and discord within the government soon made its appearance, particularly from army officers critical of her inability to repress the NPA and the Moro Front. Forced to dismiss Enrile, she found herself the more dependent on Ramos; vice-president Laurel deserted her for Enrile at local elections in 1987. A series of revolts advertised her uncertain control, prevented her from embarking on much-needed land reforms and increased her dependence on American goodwill. In spite of earlier support for those demanding the closure of American bases, she stood by the agreement permitting their presence until 1991, while obtaining Washington's assent to quinquennial reviews, which were a way to raise the rent. She concluded with Reagan an agreement whereby the two presidents undertook to use their best endeavours to ensure payment to the Philippines of $962 million for two years, but the US Congress approved only $365 million for one year. Any extension of the bases beyond 1991 would require endorsement by two-thirds of the Philippines' senate and possibly a referendum. The bargaining power of the Philippines was far from inconsiderable since the bases were not wholly replaceable except at staggering cost and their evacuation would impose on the United States a thorough and painful strategic review. A new draft treaty was rejected by the Philippine senate in 1991 in spite of the considerable sacrifice in jobs and revenues at a time of severe and worsening poverty. President Aquino, after initially contesting the senate's resolution, required the withdrawal of the Americans within three years. In 1992 Aquino was succeeded by Ramos, who conducted a more coherent administration, made peace with the principal insurgents, directed a more prosperous economy but failed to do much for most Filipinos. In 1998 he was succeeded by Joseph Estrada, a popular entertainer turned populist politician, who campaigned on the theme that nobody else really cared about the poor. He was removed by the army in 2001 and jailed for life on charges of corruption: much of his instability came from vicious conflicts over the country's rich and diverse minerals. Estrada's successor, Gloria Macapagal Arroyo, assailed by separatist, Islamist and communist guerrilla forces, proved unable to sustain her government's authority in this straggling state.

The countries of South-east Asia other than those in Indo-China formed in 1967 the Association of South East Asian Nations (*ASEAN*). The first members of this association were Indonesia, Malaysia, Singapore, Thailand and the Philippines. Their aims were to attack poverty, disease and other social ills; improve their commercial and economic weight in the world; secure their independence by reducing the sources of domestic upheaval and the temptations to outsiders to meddle in their affairs; and keep foreigners away. There were to be no joint military planning or exercises nor any other kind of military collaboration. This was a mutual aid association, economic and social, but not without some silent hopes that it might curb Indonesia's potential capacity to overawe the region. Indonesia contained almost half of ASEAN's population.

ASEAN was not the region's first postwar essay in co-operation. In 1961 Thailand, Malaya (as it then was) and the Philippines formed the Association of South-east Asia which, however, disintegrated as a result of the rival claims of the last two to Sabah. In 1963 these two and Indonesia projected a different tripartite association which never came to fruition. There were at this period two major obstacles: tensions arising out of the creation of Malaysia and the pro-communist attitudes of Sukarno in Indonesia. The removal of Sukarno by the Indonesian army was a necessary precondition for the creation of a broad South-east Asian association, as too was Indonesia's willingness to collaborate. Sukarno's successors were willing. Confrontation between Indonesia and Malaysia faded away and the quarrel between Malaya and the Philippines, although it produced a diplomatic rupture, also died down after Sabah voted in 1967 to join Malaysia: President Marcos visited Kuala Lumpur a year after his inauguration. Relations were again soured that same year after a mysterious massacre of Muslim soldiers on Corregidor (possibly by their own officers) and by a brief revival of the Philippines' claim to Sabah, but the claim was put on ice by Marcos who, although unwilling to take the unpopular step of finally abjuring it, rated it below the new regional solidarity. President Aquino later made a formal renunciation.

The British departure from South-east Asia and the Americans' war in Vietnam tested this solidarity. The announcement in 1968 of imminent British withdrawal from Malaysia and Singapore prompted these two states to conclude with Australia, New Zealand and Britain a new agreement (to which Brunei later adhered) replacing the existing Anglo-Malayan defence agreement and then in the same year to join their partners in ASEAN in proposing that South-east Asia be declared a zone of peace, freedom and neutrality. If these two steps were barely consistent with each other, the inconsistency was the price paid for transition from a colonial world to regional co-operation for the better securing of national independence. The American war in Vietnam was an affront to that independence until its conclusion in 1973. For the ASEAN states the most disturbing sequel to the United States' failure in Vietnam was Nixon's rapprochement with China and the opening given to China to exercise in South-east Asia the power role abandoned by the United States, with the further problem of deciding whether the prime enemy in the region was communist China or communist Vietnam. The threat from Vietnam was made the more acute by Vietnam's invasion of Kampuchea.

Members of ASEAN were divided. At the UN in 1970 Malaysia and Singapore had voted to give the Chinese seat in the Security Council to the communist regime in Beijing, the Philippines had voted against and Indonesia and Thailand had abstained. Most members of ASEAN hoped to add Vietnam to their association in spite of its communist regime, but by invading Kampuchea Vietnam offended against one of ASEAN's basic tenets – respect for national sovereignty and independence. Vietnam's treaty with the USSR was another count against it since another of ASEAN's tenets was its resolve to keep major powers away. The dilemma was most acute for Thailand.

Thailand wished to act in concert with its ASEAN partners but it was more directly threatened than they were by Vietnamese expansion into Kampuchea and was well aware that ASEAN had no military might to oppose Vietnamese aggression, whereas China had. In fighting terms the anti-Vietnamese effectives were the Khmer Rouge and China. For other ASEAN members on the other hand, in particular Indonesia, China was the main threat to the region in the long term and China's incursion into northern Vietnam in 1979 was a sinister omen. In these circumstances ASEAN's survival was a tribute to its leaders, but these strains were not relieved until the Vietnamese withdrawal from Cambodia and the Russian withdrawal from Vietnam.

Enlargement was implicit in ASEAN's name. It was nurtured by a desire for geographical tidiness – it would have liked to reach its eponymous natural limits by the year 2000 – and by an equal desire to keep China and Japan at arm's length. The original members were joined by Brunei in 1984, by Vietnam in 1995, and by Cambodia, Laos and Myanmar in 1997, although Hun Sen's coup in that year caused Cambodia's admission to be deferred. That Myanmar should be admitted when Cambodia was not illustrated the illogicality of political choice, for Myanmar was not merely an autocracy openly disdainful of democracy (its ruling junta held elections and then ignored them) but also one of the world's prime transgressors of human rights; on the other hand it was peculiarly vulnerable to Chinese pressures. In matters of defence the members were disturbed by Singapore's grant of military facilities to the United States in 1989 in breach of ASEAN's commitment to keep the region a zone of peace; they were assured that nothing more than repair and maintenance were involved. In 1993 regular talks on security were expanded into an Asian Regional Forum embracing 15 states and the European Union. It was joined by India in 1996. Both India and China were suspicious lest so wide an organization fall under the dominance of the United States or Japan or become a focus for a struggle for power between them.

In economic affairs completely free trade was envisaged by 2003 and a wider economic union with unrestricted movement of capital by 2020. The emergence in 1989 at Australian initiative of APEC (Asian Pacific Economic Cooperation) portended a larger zonal group which might absorb ASEAN. APEC embraced China, Japan, the United States and Australia and in 1996 this group of 12 was joined on the scene by the 25-member ASEM (Asia–Europe Meeting), more a recurrent conference than an organization. ASEAN itself was shaken, and shook the world, by severe economic failures beginning in 1997 in Thailand. What had made ASEAN a world cynosure was its success measured in terms of growth, and what had grown spectacularly were elementary education in the labour force in place of an illiterate peasantry and urban sweatshops, a high level of savings, lavish foreign loans (up to 50 per cent of GDP) and credit – with its obverse debt and its concomitant corruption. In the early 1990s, although exports were still growing at 20 per cent in places, financial hazards were beginning to take a toll: notably, competition from China, which devalued its currency in 1994 and was under pressure to devalue further as the Japanese yen declined, and an obstinate persistence in keeping currencies pegged to the US dollar in spite of the yen's decline against the dollar. Large export surpluses were being turned into deficits by reckless financing. In 1997 the linkage between the Thai baht and the dollar was abandoned and the baht was floated and lost a quarter of its dollar value in two weeks. Companies which had borrowed dollars to invest in (often highly speculative) operations reconverted into dollars at high losses; the companies themselves were halved in value on stock exchanges and sacked half their workers; bank failures followed. Thailand used its reserves to shore up its currency and, having failed to do so, was left with no reserves. Other currencies were quickly affected by fears of similar sequences of disaster although circumstances in the region's various countries were not entirely alike. In Malaysia imprudent loans had been made largely by domestic banks, while Indonesia's excessive instability and corruption carried economic panic into revolution. There were similar shocks and falls in the Philippines, South Korea and Hong Kong and secondary alarms throughout the world.

The largest external debt in the region was Thailand's $10 billion. Businesses, already insolvent, were suddenly shown to be irredeemably doomed to extinction or to be picked up cheap by foreign foragers or local *mafiosi*. Property and share values, having soared senselessly, were brought down to reality crudely and painfully by nimble speculators and panic-stricken innocents. The possibility of insurrection loomed with millions of unemployed footloose in the region. The IMF orchestrated with eight countries emergency credits totalling $17 billion to stem the collapse of the baht and shield western lenders from catastrophic sequels: their conditions included restraining Thailand's growth to 4 per cent a year. An even larger support programme for Indonesia followed ($43 billion) as the ruppiah lost four-fifths of its value in two months. Yet these were not feeble economies. Their growth had created heady expectations which, when deflated, caused alarm and even panic, but people as a whole remained better off than they had been less than a generation earlier and the impact of these vagaries on the world at large was below 10 per cent. The region embraced sizeable economies which had been mismanaged. Intervention by the IMF and foreign states might stay the fall of currencies but could not by itself rehabilitate frayed systems. Like Japan, South-east Asia had treated success as though it required no reckoning, and when a reckoning was called for success was found to contain a large element of exaggeration, which was paid for in deflating currencies, share prices and financial institutions. In a number of cases collapse was accentuated by mendacity and corruption. Regimes were shaken but – Indonesia apart – survived.

Economic recovery required two things: the creation of stronger domestic economies in place of spectacular but unsound growth, and governments sufficiently intelligent and honest to direct this transformation. Governments had proved incompetent at controlling markets, curbing imprudent growth and preventing unconscionable speculation – a weakness not confined to Asian governments but mirrored, for example, in parts of Latin America where too governments were failing in their duty to protect their peoples. The crisis put a large question mark over ASEAN's founding proposition that the region was strong enough to prosper by its own (united) efforts and assert its virtual autonomy in a global economy. The members of the group were more divided than united by their shared misfortunes, about whose causes and remedies they differed; and by the extreme turbulence in Indonesia, ASEAN's richest member.

CHAPTER 19

Afghanistan

The identity of the modern state of Afghanistan began to be formed by Ahmed Shah in the eighteenth century after the assassination of Nadir Shah of Iran, whose empire had extended over Pathans, Turkomans, Uzbeks and Hazars (descendants of the Mongols) who lived between the deserts of eastern Iran and what was to become the north-west frontier of the British in India. In the nineteenth century the British, after defeating the Sikhs, extended their rule westward and came into collision with Amir Abdur Rahman of Afghanistan who, having consolidated his position after a time of troubles, was moving in the opposite direction. In 1893 the Durand line, named after the foreign minister of India and running through Pathan country, was drawn but the nature of this line was not precisely defined and successive Afghan governments denied that it was ever meant to be an international frontier.

Between 8 and 9 million Pushtu-speaking Pathans live on either side of the Afghan–Pakistani frontier. On the eve of Pakistan's independence in 1947 and after it Afghanistan tried to persuade first Britain and then Pakistan to agree to the creation of an independent Pathan or Pushtu state which would not, however, include the Pathans living in Afghanistan (who were alleged to desire no change) but would stretch from Chitral in north-western Kashmir down to Sind and might embrace parts of Baluchistan and Sind and even Karachi. Pakistan rejected the notion. For some years there was border fighting – associated in particular with the faqir of Ipi, a persistent thorn in Pakistan's flesh – and a series of domestic protests and flurries. An offer by the shah of Iran to mediate in 1950 was accepted by Pakistan but never eventuated. Shortly afterwards the dispute died down, but it continued to affect relations between Afghanistan and Pakistan and, together with the former's tradition of friendly relations with the USSR, was a factor in keeping Afghanistan out of the negotiations for the Baghdad Pact, sponsored by the west. From 1953, when it became the first non-communist recipient of Russian aid, Afghanistan moved into the Russian sphere, but its dependence on the USSR remained discreet for 25 years. Afghanistan stayed off the international map.

Modern Afghanistan has been governed by the Pathans of the south-east with the reluctant acquiescence of other races, among whom the more important were the northerners who, although quick to stigmatize the Pathans as idlers, found in the comparative richness of their own lands and herds compensation for their disproportionately low political influence. Afghanistan was a country with few natural resources and a medieval fiscal system. Since the parliament refused to impose any but the lightest taxes on land, public revenue was derived from customs duties which were necessarily small. Smuggling was a major economic activity. Muhammad Zahir Shah, who came to the throne in 1935, was well-disposed to modest progress but obstructed by a parliament which he, unlike his neighbour the shah of Iran, was not strong enough to dismiss or manipulate. He was deposed in 1973 while on a visit to Europe, the monarchy was abolished and a republic inaugurated under the presidency of one of his relations, Muhammad Daud Khan. During the 1960s foreign aid (Russian, but also Chinese and French) was used mainly for road building. Some of this activity, notably the road and tunnels built by Russian engineers from Mazar-i-Sharif near the frontier with the USSR and over the Hindu Kush to Kabul, had obvious strategic significance, particularly alarming to Pakistan.

Muhammad Daud had been helped to power in 1973 by a section of the (more or less) communist People's Democratic Party (PDP) which came into existence in 1965 and then split into the Khalq, led by Nur Muhammad Taraki and Hafizullah Amin (broadly rural and Pathan), and Parcham, led by Babrak Karmal (predominantly urban and stronger among Tajik and other non-Pushtu-speaking peoples). Parcham supported Muhammad Daud and was rewarded with places in his cabinet. Daud was trying to play off east against west, sought aid from the shah of Iran, persecuted both Parcham and the Khalq and in 1977 put their leaders in jail. Both factions, however, made headway in the army and in 1978 the tables were turned and Daud was ousted. This was a victory chiefly for the Khalq which, after a brief spell of co-operation with Parcham, despatched Karmal and other Parcham leaders into dignified exile as ambassadors. When later summoned to return home they preferred not to.

Taraki and Amin quickly came to grief. Their impulsive reforms enraged landowners and the clergy and precipitated rioting in which many were killed (including the American ambassador, whose role behind the scenes, if any, has remained a mystery). In what may have been an abortive coup against the government some 50 Russian advisers in Herat, close to the Iranian frontier, were gruesomely murdered. Taraki's star waned and Amin tried to recover control by ordering ferocious razzias in the countryside and killing his enemies by the thousand. Alarmed by these disorders, by seething Islamic opposition provoked by Amin's persecution and the example of neighbouring Iran, and perhaps also by events in Iran which constituted both a temptation and an excuse for an American armed coup there, the Russians resolved to get rid of Amin and tighten their grip on Afghanistan. But as Taraki, with Russian encouragement, was about to remove and kill Amin, Amin removed and killed him. Amin, who was proving less subservient than Moscow required, lasted another three months, at the end of which the Russians, having tricked him into asking for their help against the rebellion which he could not master, invaded the country in the closing days of 1979. Amin was executed, Karmal reappeared and was installed as president.

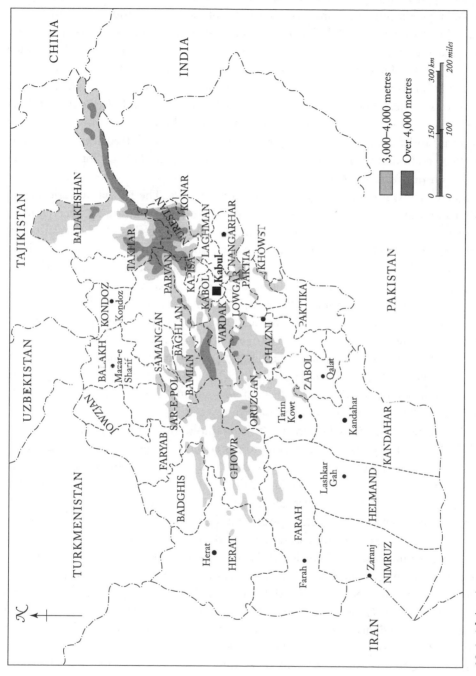

INDIA

TAJIKISTAN

BADAKHSHAN

NURESTAN

KONAR

LAGHMAN

TAKHAR

PARVAN

KAPISA

KABOL

Kabul

NANGARHAR

PAKTIA

KHOWST

KONDOZ

• Kondoz

UZBEKISTAN

BALAKH

Mazar-e
Sharif •

SAMANGAN

BAGHLAN

VARDAK

LOWGAR

PAKTIKA

PAKISTAN

JOWZJAN

SAR-E-POL

BAMIAN

GHAZNI

ZABOL

Qalat •

FARYAB

ORUZGAN

Tarin
Kowt •

Kandahar •

GHOWR

BADGHIS

KANDAHAR

TURKMENISTAN

Lashkar
Gah •

HELMAND

FARAH

Herat •

HERAT

Farah •

Zaranj •

NIMRUZ

IRAN

3,000–4,000 metres

Over 4,000 metres

300 km   200 miles

0   150   100

0

N

19.1 Afghanistan

This act of aggression was interpreted in Washington as a calculated move in Russian global strategy rather than as a response to the dangerous flounderings of an incompetent puppet. From Moscow's point of view Taraki and Amin had created chaos in a frontier zone and, if Moscow's interpretation of events was to be believed, were playing into the hands of Moscow's enemies in Iran, Pakistan and the United States. This trouble area had, moreover, a special characteristic. It was a Muslim and largely Turkic country which bordered on republics of the same texture within Soviet central Asia where, as every member of the politburo could recall, *bashmak* or robber insurgency had been endemic for half the lifespan of the USSR. Here were sufficient grounds for the invasion which a majority of the politburo endorsed at the prompting, as it seemed from outside, of its military members, influenced by leading personalities in the central Asian republics.

But the consequences were wider than these motives. The Russian invasion coincided with the post-revolutionary disarray in Iran and with continuing uncertainty in Pakistan where, shortly before the invasion, General Zia ul-Haq had advertised his insecurity by cancelling elections and all party political activities. Moscow had been accusing both Iran and Pakistan of interfering in Afghan affairs and these charges, whether or not true, might herald further acts of aggression. The invasion brought Russian armed forces to within an hour's flying time of the Persian Gulf and the Indian Ocean and to Baluchi country: the Baluchis had been fighting against their Iranian and Pakistani overlords from 1973 to 1976 and many had fled into Afghanistan and to the USSR. After the initial phase of the invasion two-thirds of the Russian invaders were located in south-western Afghanistan, where they could not fail to be seen in Washington as a threat to Iran and the Gulf. Movements of American vessels of war to the Gulf had in Moscow the same message in reverse.

The United States played up the frightening implications of an invasion which was a blatant act of aggression and a blow to American prestige severely dented by the continuing captivity of the hostages in Teheran and by the fall of the shah. The shah in person had been portrayed as a major bastion of American strength and Washington was accused – by, in the first place, dismayed Americans themselves – of having failed to stand by a friend. The American position in and around the Gulf was weakened by this charge, even though Arabs secretly rejoiced over the discomfiture of a non-Arab monarch whom none of them loved. President Carter had a legitimate interest in switching the international limelight from his own dilemma over the hostages to the enormity of Russian behaviour in Afghanistan and he was supported by the Muslim world. The Islamic Conference (an institution created in 1969 by the Saudi monarchy) held an unprecedented emergency meeting at which Khomeini inveighed against the USSR as almost as satanic as the United States and all Arab members joined in condemning the invasion. The Gulf states were more emphatic than the anti-Israeli Confrontation Front (Syria, Algeria, Libya, South Yemen and the PLO) but even the latter could not forbear to curse.

In terms of action, however, Carter's range was limited. Earlier in the year he had announced the formation of a Rapid Deployment Force of 100,000, but no such force yet existed. Nor was it clear what it would do if it did. The president was therefore thrown back on measures such as stopping the export of grain to the USSR (unpopular with American farmers who sold the grain to Argentineans, whence it found its way to the USSR) and trying to orchestrate international displeasure by a boycott of the Olympic Games in Moscow, which annoyed the Russians but did them little harm and evoked a mixed response from the rest of the world. The principal immediate consequences of the invasion were that the USSR committed some 90,000 troops to pacify a country already in its sphere of influence and saw this large force fail. The substitution of Karmal for Amin improved the regime's domestic standing but boosted opposition by endowing it with American funds and modern missiles. Karmal's government reintroduced religious instruction in schools, allowed religious programmes on television and even built mosques, thus winning the allegiance of younger mullahs. It also wooed tribal leaders. Its opponents, collectively known as the *mujaheddin*, controlled about two-thirds of the country but were seriously divided between seven groups based in Peshawar and eight in Iran. The lion's share of American aid, channelled through Pakistan and allocated with Pakistan's advice, went to Muslim Sunni fundamentalists who were distrusted by Shi'ite groups operating in the western parts of the country with Iranian support, by more intellectual or secular leaders, and by partisans of the ex-king (who lived in Rome and showed no wish to leave it). A small number of individuals enriched themselves by trafficking in arms and drugs, while much larger numbers of brave men fought and died in frightful warfare which was kept going by the superpowers.

From 1982 the UN issued annual pleas for a ceasefire, for a timetable for the expeditious withdrawal of Russian forces, and for agreements between the Pakistani and Afghan governments to stop aid to the *mujaheddin* through Pakistan and to return the thousands of Afghan refugees who had fled to Pakistan. Pakistan and the United States were unco-operative so long as the *mujaheddin* appeared to have a good chance of overthrowing the communist regime in Kabul, and the Reagan administration was also reluctant to forgo the advantages of exploiting the discomfiture which Moscow had brought upon itself by invading.

The advent of Gorbachev to power transformed the situation, if only slowly. Gorbachev was determined to get out of a venture which was disastrously costly in money and lives. He wished to preserve the communist regime in Kabul, but if he had to choose between saving it and evacuation he would choose the latter. In 1986 he offered an immediate token withdrawal and total withdrawal as soon as hostilities against Kabul were abandoned. A year later he dropped the condition and announced total withdrawal within ten months. In the interval he tried to strengthen the Afghan government by jettisoning Karmal, who died in Moscow in 1996, in favour of Muhammad Najibullah, a tough Pushtu police chief, who became the general secretary of the ruling People's Democratic Party and later head of state. Najibullah had the dual task of controlling the factions which made up the PDP and of enticing the opposition (or some of it) into a broad coalition with a newly elected parliament and under a new constitution. But his conditions, which included the reservation of a leading role to the PDP and a special relationship with the USSR, were unacceptable to the *mujaheddin* who were at this point given doubled American aid and more bigger weapons. The net result of this phase was the exclusion of the Russians, the revival of the conflicting warlords and the rise of the Taliban.

The Russian invaders departed on schedule. Their departure was followed by twelve years of civil war. The government in Kabul did not, as expected, collapse and the *mujaheddin* failed to take Jellalabad and other key points in the east, Najibullah contrived both to stay in power in the capital and in much of the country and gradually to come to terms with a sufficient number of guerrilla groups for peace under a broad-based government. But in 1992 he lost his nerve and took refuge in a UN encampment. (He was later gruesomely tortured to death by the Taliban.) The new president Burhanuddin Rabbani, a Tajik, courted his fellow Tajik leader, Ahmed Shah Masud, and the Uzbek Abdul Rashid Dostum, who exercised firm control in the north round Mazar-i-Sharif, but the next year Rabbani appointed his principal adversary, the Pushtu Gulbuddin Hekmatyar, prime minister, whereupon Hekmatyar forged a new alliance with Masud and Dostum and shelled Kabul. The UN laboriously persuaded the principal factions into a broad alliance but the emergence of a new force, the Taliban – virulently puritan Sunni Pushtu zealots united by impatience with the feuds of everyone else and supported by the United States and Pakistan – took Kandahar, then Herat, then (in 1995) Kabul, and put Hekmatyar to flight. They were checked in the north by Dostum until 1997 when he fell out with Masud (who was killed in 2001) and other Tajik allies and fled. The Taliban entered Mazar in triumph on the way to completing their conquest of the north-east and the Wakhan panhandle with its access to China and Kashmir, but by this time their fanaticism and cruelty had made them hugely unpopular and an anti-Taliban alliance supplied by Iran, Uzbekistan and Tajikistan reformed and twice drove the Taliban out of Mazar and in 1999 out of Kabul too. However the Taliban consolidated their control over nine-tenths of the country.

In 2001 the United States invaded Afghanistan under the aegis of NATO and with the support of Britain, other NATO members and Australia and with the purpose of destroying Osama bin Laden's al-Qaeda organization in the borderlands between Pakistan and Afghanistan. Having failed to purify politics and society in Saudi Arabia and Sudan, bin Laden had established himself and his headquarters in this inhospitable region. His impulse, originally more moralistic than religious, was increasingly expressed in religious terms (as was western counter-rhetoric) and in political action such as attacks on United States embassies in east Africa, not implausibly laid at his door. But attempts to kill him and dismantle al-Qaeda were thwarted by the nature of his chosen battleground and this failure soured United States relations with Pakistan and complicated the anti-Taliban activities of President Karzai and his NATO protec-tors. Karzai's writ did not run far beyond his capital. By 2007 Karzai and the British, who had been given the task of defeating the Taliban in southern Afghanistan, were being forced to consider diplomatic attempts to sow discord among Taliban groups rather than treat the Taliban as a unified force which might be militarily defeated. Unification and pacification of Afghanistan remained remote. The economy remained dependent on opium (over 90 per cent of GDP), abhorred but irreplaceable so long as the war lasted and sedulously harvested by the Taliban.

Notes

A. Central Asia

From the collapse of the Soviet Union and the Russian empire in Asia emerged five new sovereign states with a population, unevenly distributed, of 50 million, the great majority of them Turkish by race and language and Muslim by religion, the largest minority being some 8 million Russians, mostly in the northern half of Kazakhstan. Previously called with political ambiguity Russian Turkestan, this block of states, all of which declared independence in 1990 with the borders which they had had as Soviet Republics, had frontiers with Russia, China, Pakistan, Afghanistan and Iran but none with Turkey. None had access to the sea. In the northern part of the area was the huge state of Kazakhstan, the size of India and twice the size of the other four republics combined, but with a population of only 17 million of whom 40 per cent were Kazakhs and 40 per cent Russians (but there was a considerable exodus of the latter after inde-pendence). To the south were the two lowland states of Turkmenistan and Uzbekistan and the much smaller Tajikistan and Kirghizia – renamed Kyrgystan – in the high mountains to the east of Uzbekistan. Most populous of the five and the most homo-geneous ethnically was Uzbekistan. There were sizeable Uzbek minorities in the states to the east of it and in the area as a whole Uzbeks were much the most numerous (Russians came second). The entire area was predominantly Turkish except Tajikistan, which was 60 per cent Iranian; and predominantly Sunni Muslim with some Shi'ites in the southern belt. Kazakhstan, the richest in mineral resources, in first place oil, marched with Russia. Its oil reserves were believed to be so copious as to challenge the dominance of the Middle East (for the politics of oil pipelines see p. 72). Turkmenistan, especially rich in gas, oil and other minerals, marched with Iran and Afghanistan; Uzbekistan, also endowed with oil and gas, a lifeline after the collapse of world prices for its cotton and wheat, marched with Afghanistan; Tajikistan with Afghanistan, Pakistan and China; Kyrgystan with China. All these new states had considerable but underdeveloped resources alongside weak economic infrastructure, weak administrative machinery, rapidly increasing populations, disputes between and within themselves and artificial boundaries laid down by Moscow in the 1920s and

1930s when they had become Soviet Republics. After independence their governments ceased to call themselves communist but remained autocratic: in Turkmenistan, for example, elections in 1992 gave almost 100 per cent of the vote to the former communist Saparmurad Nigazov, who ruled with extravagant eccentricity until his death in 2006. His Uzbek counterpart was equally dictatorial, if less eccentric. Iran and Turkey eyed new areas of possible influence. Visits were exchanged between leaders of the four Turkish states and President Özal of Turkey. There were similarly calculated courtesies between them and Iran, which took the lead in establishing in Teheran a Caspian Council (Iran, Russia, Azerbaijan, Turkmenistan, Kazakhstan) and an Economic Co-operation Organization (Iran, Turkey, Pakistan, Afghanistan and the five new states). These bodies were suspected of cloaking semi-imperial Iranian ambitions. A Black Sea Economic Co-operation Treaty, promoted by Turkey, was signed in 1992 by 11, mostly Asian states. Non-Muslim China and India also displayed eagerness to establish commercial links and regular communications from telephone services to air schedules. Russians and others feared the spread of specifically Islamic parties. In Tajikistan, where 20 per cent of the population was Uzbek, ethnic and religious conflicts amounted in 1992 to civil war. President Rakhmon Nabijev was forced to flee but was restored by Russian and Uzbek intervention after a brief interval in which the Islamic Renaissance Party, which had support from the communist Najibullah regime in Afghanistan, formed a coalition government pledged to more religion in a nevertheless secular state. On Nabijev's return 100,000 or more refugees fled into Afghanistan (which contained a Tajik population of 3 million).

B. Sri Lanka

Ceylon gained its independence from Britain in 1948 as a consequence of the British departure from India. In 1972 it became Sri Lanka and a republic.

It was governed alternately by two main families and the parties which they formed: the United National Party led in turn by D. S. Senanayake, his son Dudley Senanayake, and his nephew Sir John Kotelawala, and the Sri Lanka Freedom Party, founded by Solomon Bandaranaike, a defector from the UNP, and after his murder in 1959 by his widow Sirimavo. The UNP governed from 1948 to 1956, from 1965 to 1970 and from 1977 to 1989; the SLFP the rest of the time. The most important election campaign was that of 1956 in which Bandaranaike defeated the UNP by running on a combined racial and religious ticket, pro-Sinhala and pro-Buddhist. His success was followed by persecution of the Tamil minority (a quarter of the population) and a permanent increase in the political influence of the Buddhist establishment, which had subsequently to be courted by the UNP as well as the SLFP. Alongside the contest for power between these two parties opposition was provided by a variety of left-wing parties of which the most notable was the Lanka Sama Samaj Party, founded in 1935 as an expression of anti-colonialism and a member of the Trotskyist international until 1963 when it joined Mrs Bandaranaike's government (this alliance was dissolved in 1975). Mrs Bandaranaike also brought the pro-Russian Communist Party into government and since other left-wing groups had lost ground her coalition was expected to win the elections of 1965. That it did not was mainly due to an economic situation which neither main party had contrived to control but which had deteriorated alarmingly during the SLFP's years of office in the 1960s.

After independence, as before, the economy of Sri Lanka was heavily dependent on the export earnings of tea, coconut and rubber estates owned by British companies. The revenue from these products fell steadily while at the same time the import bill rose, the largest single item being for food. This was a typical Third World situation in which the economy was dominated by increasingly less remunerative dealings with the former metropole and an increasing inability to feed a growing population without ruinous expenditure of foreign currency or, when that failed, foreign borrowing. The population was rising fast. It roughly doubled between independence and 1975. In the 1960s alone the external debt quadrupled. Unemployment rose from around 40,000 at independence to something near to 700,000 when, at the next turn of the electoral wheel, Mrs Bandaranaike and her associates handsomely won the elections of 1970 and re-formed the coalition that had been defeated five years earlier. In April 1971 it was severely shaken by a carefully prepared, well-armed peasant rising.

This rising, which came as a surprise, was organized and directed by the Janatha Vinukhti Peramuna (JVP) or Popular Liberation Front, formed in 1965 as a splinter from the ailing Maoist Communist Party. It regarded the SFLP and UNP as two virtually indistinguishable aspects of a post-imperialist and neo-colonialist bourgeoisie which was prevented by self-interest from tackling the country's basic economic problems and social ills. The emphasis of its doctrine and its practice was on the peasants and it attempted to use the peasants to strike a blow at the government and the system. There was later the usual insoluble squabble about who struck the first blow, but there was no doubt about the outcome. After seven weeks the government had prevailed but the challenge to it was such that the number of people killed in the process of asserting its authority ran into tens of thousands. A most unusual constellation of states supported Mrs Bandaranaike materially or orally. They included the USA, USSR and China; India and Pakistan; Britain, Australia and Egypt. Mrs Bandaranaike maintained until 1977 the state of emergency proclaimed in 1971 but was then defeated by the UNP under Junius R. Jayawardene, who became prime minister in that year and president under a new presidential constitution the next. This swing to the right was marked by a dash for growth to emulate the fortunes of Singapore, Hong Kong and Taiwan, but economic ambitions were wrecked by acute racial and religious conflict in which the government became involved with the Tamil minority, once the country's rich ruling class, 18 per cent of its population and mostly Hindu.

The Tamils constituted a majority in the north and parts of the east. Distinct in race and religion they sought autonomy or independent statehood from the Sinhalese

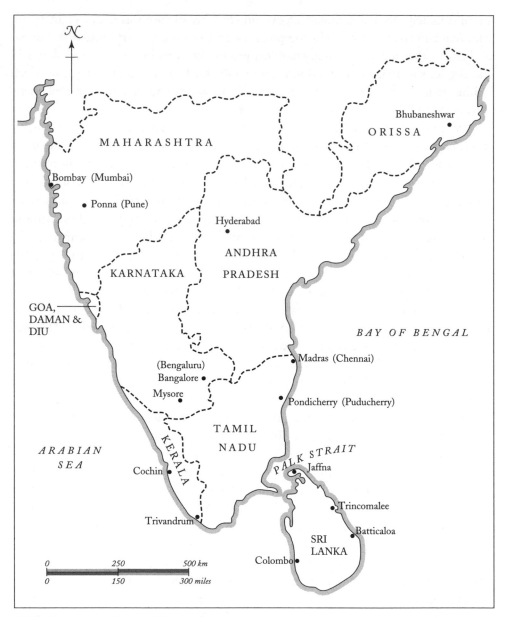

19.2 Southern India and Sri Lanka

Buddhist majority which had established a powerful central government but had failed to use its power to allay Tamil separatism. Jayawardene underrated the Tamil problem, forced Tamil members out of parliament in 1981 and resorted to force which led to civil war and Indian intervention. The more militant Tamils formed the Liberation Tigers of Tamil Eelam. Both sides committed atrocities. Rajiv Gandhi could not ignore

the outrage felt by the Tamils of Tamil Nadu in southern India and in 1986 the governments of India and Sri Lanka agreed that the Tamils of Sri Lanka should be granted
autonomy but could not agree on the area of the autonomous province. Jayawardene
decided to extirpate the Tigers. He failed, and Gandhi intervened to stop massacres of
Tamils by the Sinhalese army. Jayawardene was obliged to let the Indian army into Sri
Lanka to protect Tamils. But the Tigers, who were set on independence and therefore
opposed and ignored the Indo-Sri Lankan agreement, refused to surrender their arms
as envisaged by that agreement, with the result that the Indian force, whose original
complement of 15,000 was doubled within a few months, found itself trying to enforce
the surrender of Tamil arms instead of protecting Tamils. To do so it had to abandon
its peacekeeping role and use force, whereupon India was accused of planning to
detach northern Sri Lanka and annex it to India. In 1988 Gandhi declared that he
would withdraw his force the next year. For his part Jayawardene was accused of
opening the way to Indian imperialism and also of having made undue concessions to
Tamil autonomy. As the Indian forces prepared to depart – the last of them left early in
1990 – the government engaged in talks with the Tamil Tigers but these broke down
and fighting was renewed. The Tigers had boycotted the 1988 elections with the result
that seats in Tamil areas were won by the Eelam People's Revolutionary Party, backed
by the Tamil National Army. The Indian intervention had strengthened the more
intransigent and militant Tamils.

Jayawardene's tribulations were aggravated by a revival of the JVP, which had
abandoned its communal character and turned into a right-wing Sinhalese nationalist
movement. Massacres and political assassinations multiplied, in the south as well as
the north. In 1989 Jayawardene resigned and was succeeded by his prime minister
Ramasinghe Premadasa, who won a three-cornered contest in which his principal rival
was once more Mrs Bandaranaike, whose civil rights had been restored in 1986 after
several years' suspension. Premadasa, an autocratic political fighter, narrowly escaped
impeachment in 1991 and was assassinated two years later by a Tamil. In 1994 the UNP
was defeated by a left-wing coalition led by Mrs Chandrika Kumaratunga, the lively
and articulate daughter of Solomon and Sirimavo Bandaranaike, who promised tough
action against corruption, retribution against right-wing gangs terrorizing and killing
helpless peasants, and talks with Tamils, the standard recipe for dividing the opposition. She inherited a surge in economic growth and low demographic growth (below
1.5 per cent) and also the melancholy reality of enviable wealth afflicted by the abrupt
dislocation of a traditional rural society and by religious ethnic conflicts as vicious as
any in the world. In 1995–96 the army inflicted serious reverses on the militant Tamil
Tigers and captured the Tamil capital, Jaffna, incidentally turning hundreds of thousands of non-militant Tamils into refugees, but failed to bring the militants' leaders to
the negotiating table. Rising military expenditure destroyed budget estimates and
absorbed the economic gains of earlier years but growth continued. Kumaratunga was
re-elected at the end of 1999 but the Tamil Tigers remained fighting fit and the mood

on the government side hardened. The election in 2005 of Mahinda Rajapaksa to the presidency exemplified this dismal trend.

Related reading: part five

Chaudhuri, Nirad C.: *The Autobiography of an Unknown Indian* (1987)
Chang, Jung: *Wild Swans – Three Daughters of China* (1991)
Iriye, Arike: *The Cold War in Asia* (1974)
Levy, Adrian and Catherine Scott-Clark: *Deception – Pakistan, the United States and the Secret Trade in Nuclear Weapons* (2008)
Mistry, Rohinton: *A Fine Balance* (1996)
Moon, Penderel: *Divide and Quit* (1997)
Peterson, A. D. C.: *The Far East – A Social Geography* (1949)
Sheehand, Neil: *A Bright Shining Lie* (1988) [Vietnam]

PART SIX

Africa

CHAPTER 20

General

In the 1950s and 1960s Africa produced a phenomenon of unparalleled extent: the emancipation from foreign rule of enormous areas. This was on the whole unexpected. When the Second World War ended there were only three fully independent states in Africa: Ethiopia, Liberia and South Africa. The next ten years were a decade of preparation for the liquidation of the French, British and Belgian empires, and a further ten years later most of Africa was free. Since France, Britain and Belgium came to accept with versatile swiftness the need to go, these decades witnessed struggles over timetables rather than principles. Compelled by calculation rather than by force, the imperial powers abandoned with unexpected ease vast areas whose governance they had acquired in the previous century with equal facility. The process of decolonization was, however, halted in the southern tip of the continent by the stubbornness of the Portuguese in Angola and Mozambique and by the ruthless determination of the semi-independent white settlers of Southern Rhodesia. The self-preservative resistance of the latter, and the refusal of the former to calculate in the same way as the French, the British and the Belgians, were decisively influenced by the existence still further south of the South African stronghold of white supremacy, where the white minority was comparatively much larger (one in four) than elsewhere and was fortified by riches, by modern technical power, by having nowhere else to go, and by a doctrinaire racialism which permitted extremities of repressive injustice and cruelty.

The northern fringe of the African continent has been made by history a part of the Arab–Islamic civilization and has been more conscious of affinities with the Middle East than of its ancient economic or current political links with the rest of Africa. Moreover, the European overlordship exercised from Casablanca to Suez through protectorates, unequal treaties, military agreements and direct annexation was different in kind from the colonial empires established by Europeans south of the Sahara. But North Africa is at the same time part of Africa; the ethnic line between the Arab–Berber and Bantu races runs through Sudan and gives trouble there which other states on either side of the line cannot ignore; Egypt and Morocco have played prominent parts in African affairs and associations; Tunisia had a leading voice in the Congo's early troubles; Libyan ambitions and arms have troubled not only Central but also West Africa. The desert is no longer the barrier that it used to be since the aeroplane and the radio have enabled people to transcend it; language is no more a barrier between Arab Africa and Bantu Africa than it is within these two areas; and religion provides points of contact between Muslims and Christians on both sides of the divide. The North therefore, though still distinct from the rest of the continent in special and enduring ways, will be classed here as more African than Asian, with the sole exception of Egypt, whose postwar African role has been consistently subordinated to its Asian and not the other way round.

Although most of Africa became independent with unexpected speed, resentment against the retreating imperials persisted well beyond the generation which had known them and created outside Africa a certain impatience with what came to be counter-resented as an excessive, even perverse harping on the past. For Africans, however, the past was not so very distant or merely historical, particularly when it became apparent that the commanding heights of the economy had not passed into African hands; banks and other foreign corporations and UN agencies seemed insufficiently alert to African needs, insufficiently attentive to African arguments, suspected of continuing foreign domination by new means. In the first post-war years Africa attracted outside attention as a secondary arena of the Cold War (Chapter 26) but the attention was sporadic and unrelated to African needs. Later, Africa came to be stigmatized as a region of incompetent and corrupt government, a place where aid was more likely to be wasted or looted than used to good effect – a judgement sharpened by the catastrophic rule of Robert Mugabe in Zimbabwe (pp. 611–12) extended into the twenty-first century – nor was Mugabe the only available whipping boy. As late as 2007 a European–African conference convened in Lisbon to plan a grand scheme for European aid to Africa generated more recrimination than co-operation. The last generation of British and French rulers in Africa set out to equip the colonies that they were about to leave with liberal constitutions, good government and the rule of law but they were no more than partially successful. Half a century after decolonization much of Africa was plagued by weak government (or dictatorship), corruption and the evil activities of drug and arms traders.

CHAPTER 21

North Africa

The Maghrib

The core of the Maghrib and its principal players are Morocco, Algeria and Tunisia. It contains also two peripheral areas with their own sub-plots: Libya to the east and Mauritania and the western Sahara to the south-west.

The French invaded Algeria in 1830 and declared it a part of metropolitan France in 1848. As a consequence of their occupation of Algeria they became involved in the monarchies of Tunisia to the east and Morocco to the west, then under the nominal suzerainty of the Ottoman sultan. By the Bardo Treaty of 1881 they established a protectorate over Tunisia, a poor and relatively small country with a population in 1945 of only 3 million. In Morocco the evanescence of the Ottoman sultan's power coincided with the decay of the Moroccan sultan's own authority, thus creating an invitation for foreign intervention, but French power was not so easily substituted owing to the ambitions of other European states. In the first years of the twentieth century France obtained a free hand in Morocco by conceding the same to Italy and Britain in Libya and Egypt, by defeating a claim by Germany (which accepted compensation in Central Africa) and by allowing Spain to appropriate the northern strip whence the Arabs had invaded Spain 1,200 years earlier. The Treaty of Fez with the sultan in 1912 crowned these diplomatic successes and established a protectorate of the same kind as the French protectorate over Tunisia, although the whole country was not brought under effective French control until the 1930s. Tangier became an international zone and a fiddlers' paradise. The Italians reaped the reward of their complaisance when they were allowed in 1911 to take Tripolitania from the Turks on the eve of the Balkan wars.

During the Second World War the whole of northern Africa became a battlefield or, in the case of Morocco, a military rear area. Equally important were the politics of the war, especially the Atlantic Charter, the eviction of France from the Arab countries of Syria and Lebanon, and the appearance on the scene of the Americans, including President Franklin D. Roosevelt himself, who had a much publicized interview with the sultan of Morocco, Muhammad V ben Yusuf. The Tunisian nationalist leader Habib Bourguiba was released from a French prison in 1943, went to Cairo in 1945 and thence to the United States, and settled in his native country once more in 1949. The Moroccan leader Allal al-Fasi, who had been in prison from 1937 to 1946, also went in 1947 to Cairo and then settled temporarily in Tangier. In 1947 the newly created Arab League established a Maghrib Bureau (Maghrib means 'West' in Arabic; the Maghrib comprises at least Morocco, Algeria and Tunisia, sometimes Tripolitania as well), thus institutionalizing the Arab interest in the affairs of North Africa.

Both France and Italy had been defeated during the war but ended up on the winning side. In North African terms Italy paid the price of defeat while France won the rewards of victory; Italy lost its African colonies while France was reinstated in the Maghrib. Aware of the need for change, France sought modifications within the framework of the Bardo and Fez treaties, but the nationalists aimed to terminate the protectorate status altogether. The French had encouraged immigration, so that there was a considerable French population settled on the land or in business alongside the French administrators who ran the government of Algeria and had come to do much the same in Morocco and Tunisia in spite of the sovereignty of sultan and bey. French education had nurtured an elite which appreciated French culture, as the French intended, but also became attracted to the idea of independence. These modernizing nationalists found themselves allied with traditionalist malcontents who resented the French presence from a conservative and Muslim standpoint. Caught between these currents, the bey of Tunis wavered ineffectually until he was more or less captured by the French, to his eventual discomfiture, while the much younger sultan of Morocco wavered more purposefully, attached himself to the nationalist movement and was exiled by the French, to his eventual benefit.

The governments of the Fourth French Republic were all coalitions which contained ministers who wanted to meet nationalist movements more than halfway and other ministers who did not want to make life unpleasant for the settlers. This was an impossible combination which rendered France ineffective, allowed Tunisia and Morocco to achieve their aims and drove the largest group of settlers, the Algerians, to revolt against the government of France. The first French plan, the French Union, conceived in 1946, created the new category of Associated States with Morocco and Tunis, and also Vietnam, Laos and Cambodia, in mind, but whereas the Asian trio accepted this new status, the African pair refused it. There were reasonable hopes of a settlement with *Tunisia* after the return of Bourguiba in 1949 and until his arrest in 1952. Robert Schuman, prime minister of France, spoke in 1950 of the ultimate independence of the protected states; internal reforms of a democratic nature were seriously discussed; Bourguiba's Neo Destour Party was represented in the bey's government. But many nationalists regarded the reforms as inadequate except possibly as a first step, whereas the French regarded them as a long step with no immediate next step in sight. By the end of 1951 the dialogue had turned into rivalry for the support of the bey, who was himself so uncertain of his better course that he appeared sometimes to be a nationalist and sometimes a puppet of the French. At the beginning of 1952 a tougher line gained ground in Paris. Bourguiba was arrested and the prime minister Muhammad Chenik was dismissed. The bey accepted the French programme and a number of nationalists fled to Cairo. Constitutional changes, which had been meant to please the nationalists, were imposed by authority against their will. The attempt to reach agreement bilaterally had failed, for the acquiescence of the bey was unimportant by contrast with the disagreement of the nationalists, who now carried the debate into the international sphere. In 1954 Pierre Mendès-France, after his blitz peace in Indo-China, insisted that the Tunisian problem must be solved no less radically. He flew to Tunisia, accompanied by the right-wing Marshal Juin, to propose full internal self-government. He fell from power in 1955 before his initiative had borne fruit, but his successor Edgar Faure pursued the negotiations and Bourguiba accepted the French proposals as a step towards independence and returned to Tunisia. Nine months later, on 20 March 1956, Tunisia became fully independent and concluded a treaty with France which included provision for the stationing of troops in the country. Bourguiba remained president until 1987 when, increasingly venerable but senile, he was replaced by Zayn al-Abdin Ben Ali. Distinct political parties were allowed but no specifically religious party.

The *Moroccan* case was not very different. A period of genuine negotiation revealed to both sides the gap between the French programme of democratic gradualism and the nationalists' determination to get independence very soon. The principal difference between the Moroccan and Tunisian cases lay in the temper of the ruler. Muhammad V had shown signs of allying himself with the Istiqlal (Independence) Party at the end of the war, and by so doing he had destroyed the basis of government in Morocco which, during the seven-year term of office of General Noguès as resident-general, had rested upon the good personal relations between the two men – the *dialogue sultan–résident*. A second major factor was the isolation of the French settlers from the outside world during the war years 1940–42, an isolation which had larger consequences in Morocco than Tunisia because the French community in Morocco was also isolated from the surrounding Muslims by Marshal Louis Lyautey's prewar policy of siting new French towns away from the traditional centres of Moroccan life. From 1947 to 1951 Marshal Juin was resident-general, but in spite of his somewhat forbidding presence a new *dialogue* Paris–Fez was initiated and the sultan visited Paris in 1950. The French, however, believed that they had an alternative to treating with the nationalists, whom they and some Moroccans were tempted to write off as uncharacteristic and irresponsible townees, of less significance than traditional personages like the pro-French, and anti-sultan, pasha of Marrakesh, el Glaoui. The sultan was persuaded – he subsequently said coerced – into signing in 1951 decrees initiating the reforms which the French were prepared to introduce, but the consequent agitation in Morocco and elsewhere in the Arab world caused him to swing away from the French and for a year there was increasing uncertainty and disorder, culminating in December 1952 in barbaric anti-white outbursts in Casablanca. In the following February the sultan was sent into exile. His absence, however, did not serve to restore order or strengthen French rule, while in Spanish Morocco an assembly of notables refused to recognize the exiled sultan's uncle

Muhammad ben Arafa, whom the French had placed on the throne. In 1955, follow-ing the settlement with Tunisia, the sultan was brought back and before the end of the year France had agreed to concede full independence. It took effect on 2 March 1956. Both Morocco and Tunisia became full members of the Arab League in 1958.

Muhammad V was succeeded in 1961 by his son Hassan II, who ruled for the next 38 years with a highly successful blend of virtues and vices. He combined ostentatious wealth and unconcealed autocracy with political astuteness. He commanded the trust of his army and exploited the nationalism which animated Moroccans of all parties and classes. All patronage, political and religious, was in his hands. Political parties, which had been allowed from 1977 to take part in elections, accepted nominal demo-cracy at the price of good behaviour. Muslim fundamentalism was curtailed in spite of not inconsiderable popular support. Left-wing parties, when not destroyed, were pen-etrated by the secret police. His policy in the Sahara (see below) was not questioned, but its success encouraged opponents of the royal autocracy whose voices had been muted out of patriotism. In 1993 he conspicuously displayed his self-confidence by opening a huge new mosque and permitting the first elections for nine years (for two-thirds of the parliament). Opposition parties made some gains but not enough to disturb the king or dent his belief in his divine right to rule as he thought fit. Although he had no qualms about eliminating opponents or mere suspects with a cruel ruth-lessness, he combined crude power with political skill which secured for his regime uncommon stability and even popularity and he swung Morocco to an American alliance which served both him and the United States well. In association with the IMF he introduced from the early 1980s reforms which, however, bore heavily on a rapidly growing population and he bequeathed to his son Muhammad VI (who succeeded him in 1999) an autocratically controlled society with high illiteracy and unemployment, increasingly crowded in seething cities without basic services (water, electricity). The new reign saw a gradual shift of power between the monarchy and Istiqlal in favour of the latter and confirmed the comparative insignificance of Muslim fundamentalism. Good economic growth was offset by disproportionate distribution.

The revolt of *Algeria* against France began with hostilities in the Aurès mountains in 1954 which were at first regarded as a fresh instalment of familiar colonial troubles but developed into a war which involved the flower of the French army, the full panoply of military rule and censorship, and terrorism and torture, three separate white French challenges to the authority of Paris, the fall of the Fourth Republic and the achieve-ment by Algeria – uniquely in Africa until Zimbabwe – of independence by force of arms. The situation was without any parallel in Africa. The European population had been a part of the country for much longer than any other settler community, it was nearer to the mother country, and in the main cities it was as numerous or almost as numerous as the Muslims; its services to Algeria were conspicuous. Juridically too the situation was peculiar since Algeria was constitutionally a part of metropolitan France, so that Frenchmen who failed even to envisage a severance were maintaining an un-reality which was nevertheless no fiction. The legal position contributed to a stubborn psychological attitude which caused outsiders to wonder why it was that Frenchmen alone in the world were unable to see that their days as rulers in Algeria were num-bered. The French, moreover, like the British in the Middle East after the retreat from India, hated the thought of further surrenders after the collapse of their empire in Indo-China; just as Africans were encouraged by the ending of French and British rule in Asia, so in reverse were the French and British influenced in their African policies by their postwar experiences in Asia, making in Algeria and Egypt in particular mistakes of timing and understanding which they might have avoided if they had not felt that their descent from the first rank was proving too hasty for dignity or safety.

In Algeria, additionally, senior French officers developed in the shadow of the defeat in Indo-China a sense of mission so strong that it distorted their sense of proportion and led them in the end to jettison their oaths of allegiance. These officers convinced themselves that they belonged to the gallant and prescient category of the saviour with the sword, that they alone appreciated the full import of the communist threat to civilization, and that theirs was the honourable destiny of leading the resistance to the hosts of darkness and opening the eyes of woolly-minded sluggards to the dangers and responsibilities of the twentieth century. This apocalyptic determinism was accompanied by an almost equally passionate emotion. The day-to-day business of administering large tracts of Algeria had become the responsibility of the army, and in the course of govern-ing their localities officers had acquired a proficiency, knowledge and sympathy for the people in their care which, they judged, would not easily be supplied by anybody else.

There was a foretaste of revolt at Sétif in 1945. Like a similar rising in Madagascar in the same year, this revolt was suppressed with brutality. France in 1945 was in no mood to do things by halves; for the killing of 100 Europeans about 6,000 Algerians were killed in retaliation. The nationalist leader Ferhat Abbas was arrested and the French community was given the incentive and the excuse to arrogate to itself an authority which belonged rightly to the government in Paris. The weaknesses of the governments of the Fourth Republic allowed this authority to be exercised and enhanced until the return to power of de Gaulle in 1958 put it to a test which it failed. There was, however, no effective nationalist threat to French rule during the decade between the Sétif rising and the revolt in the Aurès mountains at the end of 1954, which forced France to deploy half a million troops. During these years French ministers and governors-general tried to temper the repression of nationalism with economic advancement and democratic reform, but they failed to mollify the nationalists, whose aim was not reform but independence, and they antagonized the European community, whose preoccupation with repression left little room for anything else.

This dilemma was illustrated vividly during the first stage of the revolt. The defeat of the Faure government in November 1955 had been followed by a general election and the installation of a minority government led by Guy Mollet. The new prime minister attempted to find a way to bring the fighting to an end. Yet when he went to Algiers he was pelted with garbage by Europeans, while approaches to leaders of the insurrectionary Front de Libération Nationale (FLN) were entirely unproductive. Mollet appointed General Georges Catroux, a widely respected and liberally minded proconsul, to the governor-generalship, but Catroux resigned his office within a week and without leaving France. In 1956 Mendès-France resigned from the Mollet government on the grounds that it was not doing enough, while the prime minister probably felt that if he ventured more boldly he would provoke a trial of strength between Paris and the Europeans in Algeria, which Paris would not win. The weakness of Paris was dramatically illustrated, and its position with regard to the FLN seriously damaged, when five FLN leaders, including Ahmed Ben Bella, were kidnapped when returning by air from a meeting with the sultan of Morocco. The aircraft in which they were travelling, which was registered in France and piloted by a Frenchman although operated by a non-French company, was diverted from its destination to Algiers without the knowledge of the government in Paris. During the next 18 months political attitudes remained irreconcilable, the French army and the FLN secured positions in which neither could defeat the other, terrorism increased on both sides and spread to Paris and other cities in France, torture became a regular instrument of government and was seen to be, and any lingering intention of applying the new compromise constitution called the Algerian Statute of 1947 was finally abandoned.

Morocco and Tunisia were drawn into the conflict. The sultan had been deeply offended by the kidnapping of Ben Bella, who had been his guest an hour or two earlier, but in 1957 he and the bey offered to mediate in Algeria. The next year, however, the bey was angered when the French, irritated by the FLN's freedom to use Tunisian and Moroccan soil as asylum, attacked Sakiet in Tunisia from the air and killed 75 people. In May 1958 Algeria rebelled and two weeks later Pierre Pflimlin, the last civilian prime minister of the Fourth Republic, resigned. The rebel government in Algiers planned to seize power in Paris. Almost the whole of Corsica, the stepping stone, had accepted the rebel regime and half the commanders of the military regions in France were believed to be disloyal. Only one obstacle to success in the capital remained – a Frenchman of enormous prestige and outstanding political skill. On 1 June de Gaulle was invested with full powers. On 4 June he flew to Algiers.

By a mixture of authority and ambiguity de Gaulle took control of the situation and gradually acquired the power to impose a solution upon it. This took him nearly four years. By doing enough to retain the initiative, but not too much to reveal himself, he prevented potentially hostile groups from acting against him until it was too late. He began by patching up relations with Tunisia and Morocco, agreeing to withdraw French forces from both countries (except from the naval base at Bizerta). He moved from Algeria many senior officers who, even were they minded to object to their postings, could not gainsay the legitimacy of an order from *the* general. General Raoul Salan, leader of the revolt in Algiers, was permitted to remain temporarily in his command, but he was relieved of his civilian functions, which were once more divorced from the military command. After these preliminary moves de Gaulle prepared his first major statement on the future of Algeria and made his first bid for peace with the FLN. In September 1959 he formulated a choice between independence, integration with France and association with France, the choice to be made within four years from the end of hostilities, defined as any year in which fewer than 200 people had been killed in fighting or by terrorism. This pronouncement precipitated a second white revolt. It was a failure. Energetic action by the French government showed how the authority and power of Paris had grown during the past 18 months.

Support for de Gaulle within France, more widespread and positive in 1960 than in 1958, was partly due to a feeling that the war had gone on too long and partly to restiveness over the methods which were being used to wage it. Henri Alleg's book *La Question* focused attention on the use of torture by the French army. The trial of Alleg in 1960, followed by the disappearance and (as it was correctly surmised) murder of the French communist university lecturer Maurice Audin, the trial in 1961 of the Algerian girl Djamila Boupacha, protests by the Roman Catholic cardinals occupying French sees, and a manifesto signed by 121 leading intellectuals, all contributed to turn French opinion against the French community and army in Algeria. Towards the end of 1960 the leaders of the revolt were put on trial. But there was still one white rebellion to come. It came in April 1961. It was led by four generals and it lasted four days. Two of the four were subsequently sentenced to death *in absentia* and the other two, who surrendered, to 15 years' imprisonment – all sentences being eventually reduced. Out of the failure of this rebellion arose the Organisation de l'Armée Secrète (OAS), which resorted to terrorism, and, by creating among the European population fears of reprisals by an independent Algerian government, provoked an exodus which deprived the country of much-needed skills in administration, education and other public services.

De Gaulle's victory on the white front was not at first accompanied by any improvement in the nationalist quarter. In September 1959 the FLN had proclaimed a provisional Algerian government with Ferhat Abbas as prime minister and the imprisoned Ben Bella as his deputy, and Ferhat Abbas had left Tunisia for Cairo, which was to be the seat of government for the time being. De Gaulle temporized after the defeat of the white revolt; the FLN turned for help to Moscow and Beijing; opinion among non-combatant Algerians moved towards the FLN and its unequivocal demand for independence and not towards any middle position between the FLN and the Europeans. De Gaulle began therefore to move more purposefully towards negotiation with the FLN. A first secret encounter at Melun was a failure but after discussions between de Gaulle and Bourguiba, between FLN leaders and Georges Pompidou (still at this time a private banker) and between the FLN and Moroccans, Tunisians and Egyptians, a conference opened at Evian in May 1961. But suspicions and difficulties proved at this stage too great; the latter included the FLN's claim to be recognized as a government, the right of the imprisoned Ahmed Ben Bella to appear at the conference, guarantees for the French who might wish to remain in Algeria, continuing French rights in the naval base at Mers-el-Kebir, Saharan oil, and the conditions under which the proposed referendum on the status of Algeria would be held. When the conference failed, de Gaulle publicly and unequivocally accepted Algerian independence. But the rest of the month saw a series of setbacks. Franco-Tunisian relations suffered a relapse when Bourguiba demanded a complete French evacuation of Bizerta (effected in 1963 after Tunisia laid its complaint before the UN); the FLN took a more assertive position when Yusuf ben Khedda succeeded Ferhat Abbas as head of the provisional Algerian government and supported Bourguiba over Bizerta; the OAS made an unsuccessful attempt on de Gaulle's life and OAS activities increased throughout France as well as Algeria; and there were rumours of the proclamation of a dissident French republic under General Salan in northern Algeria. Ben Khedda proposed a new round of negotiations.

A second Evian conference in March 1962 achieved a ceasefire, agreed terms for a referendum and, on the assumption that the result would be in favour of independence, further agreed (among other things) that French troops would be withdrawn progressively over three years except from Mers-el-Kebir, which France was to be permitted to occupy for at least 15 years; that France might continue its nuclear tests in the Sahara and retain its airfields there for five years; that France would continue its economic activities in the Saharan oilfields; and that French technical and financial aid to Algeria would continue undiminished for at least three years. On 3 July 1962 Algeria became an independent sovereign state for the first time in history. But its leaders did not hold together. Ben Bella, returning to the scene after six years' absence in prison, won power but alienated colleagues and followers by moving too fast, by trying to reorganize the FLN on communist lines and by trying to play a leading and radical part in African and Afro-Asian affairs to the neglect of urgent domestic problems. In June 1965 he was overthrown when he was on the point of ousting his minister of defence Colonel Houari Boumédienne, who succeeded him. Ben Bella was imprisoned until 1978 and a fugitive until 1990.

Boumédienne's policies included a new structure of government, state capitalism, the nationalization of natural resources, vigorous exploitation of oil and gas deposits, and industrialization; and, in external affairs, cautiously good relations with the USSR, continued collaboration with France, a Maghrib entente, and active association with the Arab states against Israel. He ruled through a Council of the Revolution with himself as chairman and its further membership undisclosed. He created in 1968 regional authorities for economic and social affairs and made them elective a year later. Dissatisfaction – sharply evinced by an abortive army revolt led by Colonel Tahar Zibri – focused on the failure to partition big estates at once or give workers in industry as much control in management as many of them wanted. His hostility to communists inclined him to be soft on right-wing extremists. He concluded a series of agreements with France for the development and nationalization of mining and other industries, securing both French aid and Algerian control. He also secured the return to Algeria of

300 works of art removed by the French. In 1967 France evacuated its remaining land bases in Algeria and next year the naval base at Mers-el-Kebir. Boumédienne visited Moscow soon after his accession to power, broke off diplomatic relations with Britain over Rhodesia, declared war on Israel and sent troops to fight it, and broke off relations with the United States. When a first pan-African cultural festival was held in Algiers in 1969 it was attended by the president of the USSR and the French foreign minister as well as a concourse of African and other notables.

Boumédienne ran a one-party state for 13 years, during which the FLN dissolved into cliques, became staggeringly corrupt and lost its authority in the army. He was removed in 1978 and replaced after an interval by the more cautious Colonel Chadli Benjedid, who had to find an alternative to the FLN. He asserted civilian rule and introduced political reforms but failed to stem corruption, remedy poverty or avert growing cynicism and fear. The economy suffered as the oil price rises of the 1970s were reversed: 70 per cent or more of the workforce was unemployed and in 1988 demonstrations turned into riots which were quelled by open and brutal army intervention as an ageing elite struggled to maintain itself in a country where three-quarters of the population were under 25 and nearly half under 14, and where the Berber majority which had contributed much to the eviction of the French was discriminated against. (Berber-speakers were only a quarter of the population but large numbers of Arabic speakers were or felt themselves to be Berbers.) He sketched a vision of a federated Greater Maghrib and, as a first instalment, concluded in 1983 a treaty with Tunisia to which Mauritania later adhered. With Morocco, however, Algeria's relations remained difficult on account of the two countries' differences over the western Sahara (see below). In 1989 Benjedid introduced a new constitution which made Algeria a multiparty state. One of many new parties was the Front Islamique du Salut (FIS), part of a large but diffuse movement which was initially a political protest movement but was destined to develop a religious fundamentalist wing of peculiar viciousness. The FIS, quick to use the new constitution, scored impressive gains in local elections within two years of its introduction and went on in effect to win a general election at the end of 1991: it won nearly half the votes and over 80 per cent of those seats which were settled in the first round. The government, which had won only 16 seats in the first round, cancelled the second. Benjedid was forced to resign; the FIS was outlawed and thousands of its adherents were imprisoned; and an improvised Council of State persuaded Muhammad Boudiaf, a hero of the war of independence, to return as president from Morocco where he had taken refuge after being condemned to death by Ben Bella in 1964. Boudiaf was a devout Muslim and a champion of non-religious, non-military government but within a few months he was assassinated and the army installed General Lamine Zeroual in his place. Boudiaf, and after him Zeroual, was in a quandary between trying to crush or split the FIS in which perhaps a majority sought more rigorous Islamic rules of behaviour but only a segment wanted a theocratic state on Sudanese or Iranian lines. Zeroual, who was a 'conciliator' rather than an 'eradicator', held talks in 1994 with a number of party leaders, excluding the FIS, but these parties were unwilling to agree measures for the establishment of a democratic order without the co-operation of the FIS. Later in the year a conference convened in Rome was attended by the FIS but was consequently boycotted by the government. It produced a National Contract which the FIS accepted but the government rejected. In the next year, and with the FIS still banned, Zeroual – civilianized – was re-elected. His victory lay less in his share of the vote than in holding an election at all. The country was in a state of anarchy; parts of it were outside governmental control and in other parts this control was exercised only through murder; army chiefs were divided to the point where some were suspected of murdering others; and hundreds of people were being killed every day in vendettas and other feuds which were as much about private debts as politics or religion; the business community, the IMF and Algeria's foreign creditors were engulfed in gloom. Zeroual repeated his electoral victory in 1997 with qualified endorsement by UN observers. Another new constitution extended his presidential powers but ultimate power belonged to the army, where hawks were prevailing over doves. The massacre toll rose as the insurgents slaughtered whole villages and police stations were turned into grim scenes of torture and extermination centres. In 1998 Zeroual, whose support among army chiefs was waning, declared that he would not seek re-election in the coming year. Seven candidates appeared, six of them withdrew on the eve of the poll and Abdulaziz Bouteflika, a former foreign minister who had been in exile for 20 years, won the presidency with 74 per cent of the electorate who ventured to vote: the turnout was officially said to be 60 per cent and was probably around 24 per cent. The number of violent deaths in 1992–99 may have reached 100,000 in seven fearful, wasted years.

Bouteflika's task was to establish the state which the FLN had failed to maintain, to conciliate or defeat the Islamic movements of varying militancy which had disrupted Algeria in reaction to the FLN's inefficiency and corruption, and to revive a potentially rich economy strangled by civil disorder and crime, headlong urbanization, the vagaries of oil prices, and foreign cold-shouldering. Chirac became the first French president to visit Algeria since its independence. Bouteflika was over whelmingly re-elected in 2006 but disorder on a reduced scale persisted in the capital and the south.

The French colony of *Mauritania*, peopled by descendants of the Almoravids who had once ruled all Morocco and half Spain, began its independent existence with disputes with the latter and proceeded thence to disputes with the former. The object of the first of these disputes was Rio de Oro, one of a cluster of Spanish possessions in the north-west corner of Africa. In 1956 Spain ceded Spanish Morocco to Morocco, retaining, however, the towns of Melilla and Ceuta and three other small enclaves whose population was mainly Spanish. In 1957 Spain sent troops to Ifni in south-west Morocco but ceded it to Morocco in 1958 as far south as latitude 27 degrees 40 minutes. There remained the Canary Islands, which stayed part of Spain, and Rio de Oro, claimed by both Morocco and Mauritania. These rival claimants were united in opposition to the

Spanish presence in a territory where the world's richest phosphate deposits had been found in 1945. Morocco, heavily dependent on the export and therefore the world price of phosphates, would have liked to acquire the whole of Rio de Oro but was prepared to concede part of it to Mauritania rather than see the creation of a new state, possibly with a Hispanophile monarch and extensive Spanish aid and tutelage. Mauritania wished to thwart the creation of a Greater Morocco. Spain, having announced its departure in 1974, wished for a referendum which would produce a majority for a new independent state. Morocco fought off this prospect by getting the UN to ask the International Court of Justice who had owned Rio de Oro before the Spanish got there. The Court answered in 1975 that the status of Rio de Oro must be decided on the basis of self-determination and not by reference to past history.

While the Court was still deliberating Morocco reached a preliminary agreement with Mauritania over the exploitation of the phosphates and in 1975 King Hassan personally led 350,000 Moroccans a few miles into Rio de Oro in a demonstration designed to force Spain to negotiate with Morocco and Mauritania and not hand over to any third authority. Spain agreed at the end of the year to transfer Rio de Oro to the two African claimants jointly and they, five months later, partitioned it: two-thirds to Morocco and one-third to Mauritania.

This disposition was opposed by the Popular Front for the Liberation of Saguiet el-Hamra and Rio de Oro (Polisario), which came into existence in 1973 as, initially, an anti-Spanish and, in response to the course of events, became an anti-Moroccan movement. The Polisario claimed that Rio de Oro belonged neither to Morocco nor Mauritania. It proclaimed in 1976 the *Sahrawi Arab Democratic Republic*, which drove the Mauritanians, whose economy was unable to maintain the struggle, out of the field. The Mauritanian army removed President Ould Daddah and gave up the fight (1978) but Morocco was not so easily disposed of. The Polisario had support from Algeria and Libya: Algeria, because of its general hostility to Morocco and to any settlement in the region which might block its access to the Atlantic; Libya, out of a general sympathy with militant underdogs. Libyan support lapsed when Qaddafi, on a visit to Rabat, bartered away his pro-Polisario stance for a Moroccan promise to keep out of his imbroglio in Chad (see the next section – this deal was denounced by King Hassan three years later because it displeased the United States). Algeria's support for the Polisario weakened because of Algeria's domestic troubles. A year after buying off Qaddafi King Hassan and Chadli Benjedid came to an agreement whereby the Sahrawis, although allowed to retain their quasi-government in Algiers, lost Algerian funds. The conflict between the Polisario and Morocco became a stalemate in the latter's favour, for whereas the Polisario made no significant gains Morocco was slowly pushing it back by the inglorious but effective strategy of building walls of sand across 3,000 km of desert. This moving line, punctuated by forts 5 km apart and manned by 100,000 troops, created enclaves which were then peopled by Moroccan settlers.

Morocco's chief concern was to asphyxiate a Sahrawi republic and retain the Atlantic seaboard and its hinterland. Hassan rejected a plea by the OAS to talk to the

Polisario but appeared willing to back a referendum which, it was assumed, would give him – or could be made to give him – those disputed areas which mattered to him at the cost of letting others become an independent Sahrawi state. He invested money in the coveted areas as well as moving hopefully pro-Moroccan settlers into them, calculating that he would thereby win any referendum which might be forced upon him. In 1991 a ceasefire was brokered by the UN as a preliminary to a referendum on independence or integration with Morocco. A team of 2,000 observers and peacekeepers under the United Nations Mission for the Referendum in Western Sahara (MINURSO) was assembled but its work was bedevilled for ten years by disputes over who was qualified to vote and how those qualified might be identified. Many inhabitants of the area were nomads of no fixed abode; others were alleged to be immigrants with no previous connections there. In 1996 an Identification Commission set to work in regional centres but found no way round the problems. In 1999, however, the UN secretary-general Kofi Annan persuaded both sides to accept the year 2002 as the date for a referendum. He failed, however, to get them to agree in advance to accept a verdict which they did not like. In 1999 signs of a rapprochement between new rulers in Morocco and Algeria – Muhammad VI and Bouteflika – foreshadowed the political isolation of the Polisario, leaving it perhaps with a degree of autonomy under Moroccan sovereignty. The UN appointed a special envoy – former US secretary of state James Baker – to devise a peace plan. Morocco rejected it.

Mauritania, having cut its losses to the north, was beset with troubles at home and to the south. Economic stringencies, including an encroaching desert, exacerbated class and ethnic tensions. Mauritania comprised paler and darker (Beydane and Haratine) Moors and black Africans. The Beydane constituted a ruling caste but the Haratine, descended from slaves, were twice as numerous, while the black Africans – about a third of the total – were akin to the Fulani, Wolof and other peoples across the border in Senegal. Under the brutal rule of Colonel Masouiya Ould Taya, who seized power in 1984, thousands of Mauritanians were killed in a series of massacres in 1989–92 and tens of thousands fled into Senegal. The arrival of these (non-Muslim) refugees provoked a counter-expulsion of some 70,000 and created for a while a threat of war. (There were about ten Mauritanians in Senegal for every Senegalois in Mauritania.) Ould Taya espoused a multiparty system and used it in a string of elections in 1992 to reinforce his autocratic rule as the various parties quarrelled with each other. Elections in 2003 showed that he and his faction in the ruling class were the better political tacticians. His military junta remained in power.

Libya and Chad

The postwar fate of Italy's North African colonies was to be resolved by the four principal victorious powers by September 1948, failing which the problem would be transferred to the United Nations. The British and Italian governments devised a plan (the Bevin–Sforza plan), whereby an independent Libyan state would come into existence at the end of ten years and during the interval its three parts would be under British or Italian tutelage: the Fezzan (which was coveted by the French as an addition to Tunisia) under Italian trusteeship, Tripolitania in the middle under British administration for two years and Italian trusteeship for eight, and Cyrenaica further east under British trusteeship for the whole ten years. This plan was objectionable to the Arabs and to the Russians, who proposed a five-year UN trusteeship (they also proposed UN trustee-ships of five and ten years for Eritrea and Italian Somaliland). The General Assembly rejected the Bevin–Sforza plan and there followed a period of negotiation and investiga-tion by a UN commissioner (Dr Adrian Pelt), as a result of which the whole of Italy's North African empire was converted into a constitutional monarchy under the emir of Cyrenaica Muhammad Idris as-Sanusi as King Idris of Libya. The new state came into being on the first day of 1952 and shortly afterwards entered into an agreement with Britain which gave Libya economic aid and arms and gave Britain military rights in the small post of El Adem. The Americans subsequently established a larger base at Wheelus Field. In 1969 the king was ousted by army officers disgruntled by corruption in high places. Their leader Colonel Muammar Qaddafi disdained diplomatic conven-tions by interfering wherever possible to help (notably the Palestinians) or harry (oil companies, communists, Israel and established governments, especially monarchies). Within the Arab world Qaddafi projected a series of unions which were insubstantial and increasingly derided: with Egypt and Sudan in 1969, extended to Syria in 1970, but never effective; with Egypt and Syria again in 1971, equally without consequence; with Egypt in 1972 upon the eviction of the Russians from Egypt but followed in 1973 by complete diplomatic rupture; with Tunisia in 1974, the most short-lived of these attempts at fusion since it was denounced by Bourguiba two days after it was pro-claimed; with Syria in 1980; and with Chad at the beginning of 1981. In the last case union appeared to be a euphemism for at least partial annexation. Qaddafi's contempt for conventions led him to organize the killing of political opponents who had fled to foreign countries, even using his diplomatic missions for this purpose.

Within Africa Qaddafi not only played a leading part in the troubled affairs of Chad but was suspected of much wider ambitions. Arid and sparsely populated (about 4 million inhabitants), athwart the dividing line between Arab- and Bantu-speakers and Muslims and Christians, with six international frontiers and presumed wealth in uranium, gold, oil and other precious commodities, Chad was endemically unstable and a standing temptation. Its first president François Tombalbaye, a representative of the educated southern elite, was unsympathetic towards the Muslims of the north, whose opposition to his government he insisted on regarding as banditry. It was also a threat to the tourist traffic which he hoped to encourage. By 1966 he was challenged by FROLINAT, the National Liberation Front of Chad movement with headquarters in Libya. He turned for help to France, with which Chad, like other former French colonies, had a defence agreement. (France had some 6,000 troops in West and Central

Africa in these years, distributed over 13 states.) This help began with supplies but expanded in 1968–70 to direct intervention with paratroops and aircraft which secured Tombalbaye's position until 1975 when he was assassinated. His successor Felix Malloum gradually lost the war against FROLINAT. Meanwhile, the leaders of FROLINAT's several armies fell out. The French withdrew, Qaddafi backed Goukouni Oueddei who was willing to cede – or to promise to cede – the northern Aozou strip and its supposed uranium deposits to Libya. His rival Hissen Habre formed a brief alliance with Malloum before turning on him and seizing power in the capital Ndjamena in 1979. Libya, Sudan and Niger engineered a superficial accord between Goukouni and Habre but in 1980 Libya, driving its Russian tanks across the desert with surprising efficiency, enabled Oueddei to put Habre to flight. In 1981 Qaddafi and Goukouni announced a union of their two countries. Qaddafi then agreed to pull his troops out in return for a French undertaking to do likewise, but when the French withdrew the Libyans remained in occupation of the Aozou strip. Elsewhere, Habre regained and consolidated his position but his impoverished government was weakened by falls in the price of cotton which fuelled popular discontent. A peace conference at Brazzaville in 1984 was unsuccessful but thereafter Habre's fortunes revived, particularly from 1986 when Libya, having failed in a fresh offensive, abandoned Goukouni and Goukouni himself split with one of Habre's other opponents, Acheikh Ibn Ommar. In 1987 Habre's forces won a convincing victory in the north although without recovering the Aozou strip. After this victory many of Habre's enemies either came to terms with him or fled to the Sudan, but in 1989 a coup against him (which failed) demonstrated the turmoil beneath the surface. The plotters, led by an old associate Idriss Deby, resented favours dispensed to erstwhile enemies, personal or tribal, in order to seal this reconciliation. They had help from Libya and in 1990 they tried again and were successful. France, which had intervened on several occasions to protect Habre, refused to do so again. American patronage and his Israeli guards were not enough to save Habre, who fled to Cameroun. Deby imposed a degree of stability. His was the largest minority in a fractured state but a compromise which he achieved with the comparatively rich south was short-lived. Chad's almost ceaseless civil wars were used by the United States, Egypt and Iraq – strange conjunction – to make trouble for Qaddafi in Libya.

When Reagan took office in 1981 the new administration in Washington, understandably irritated but extravagantly obsessed by Libya's often outrageous behaviour, sent warships into the Gulf of Sirte and shot down two Libyan aircraft. The United States also imposed economic sanctions and in 1983 and 1984 sent Airborne Early Warning and Control (AWACS) intelligence aircraft to Egypt to deter Qaddafi from adventures in that direction: Qaddafi had threatened to march into Egypt and he had a hand in an abortive plot to overthrow President Nimeiry by dropping bombs on Khartoum as a prelude to a coup by Sudanese officers. In 1986 the Americans delivered a massive air and naval attack on Tripoli and Benghazi which failed to kill Qaddafi. In a smaller attack in 1989 two Libyan aircraft were destroyed after the United States had accused Libya of building a plant for the manufacture of poison gases.

Africans were alarmed by Qaddafi's activities and by his visions of a great Islamic Saharan empire which would point a menacing finger at the wealth of Zaïre, overawe Sudan and Uganda, and cut a swathe westward from Chad through Mauritania, Mali and Niger to the Atlantic in Senegal, the Guinea and Ivory Coasts and the Bight of Benin. The murder of President Luiz Cabral of Guinea-Bissau, the overthrow of President Sangoule Lamizana of Upper Volta, a coup which failed against President Seyni Kountche of Niger (who endured almost annual coups after seizing power in 1974) – all these events in 1980 were ascribed to Libyan machinations. So too was an abortive coup in Gambia which was suppressed by prompt Senegalese intervention. The remoter Central African, Cameroun and Gabon Republics also felt a Libyan current blowing their way and privately wished that France might send troops back to Chad. Gambia, Senegal, Ghana and Gabon severed relations with Libya and Nigeria threatened to follow suit.

Yet Libya was in no position to create an empire. It was more aggressive than powerful. Its population numbered no more than 4 million, its army about 40,000. During the crisis in Chad in 1980 Egypt mustered more than twice that force on its border with Libya alone and breached the frontier with impunity. What Qaddafi had was an alarming political style and oil. He used the oil partly to twist the arms of customers to whom he chose to sell at half price or less, and partly to buy Russian arms. But in the 1980s Libya's oil production fell to a quarter of its peak in the previous decade, and although Qaddafi turned Libya into the largest *place d'armes* of Russian origin outside the USSR and central and eastern Europe much of this weaponry was either unsuited to his foreign ventures or left inadequately tended in places where it quickly deteriorated. His interventions in Chad were inconsequential. After declaring himself the champion of the Muslims he helped non-Muslims to power. The uranium which he was supposed to covet had no proven existence. (The Aozou strip had been assigned to Chad by a Franco-British agreement of 1899. An unratified Franco-Italian agreement of 1935 assigned it to Libya. Tombalbaye allegedly sold it to Libya in 1973 by an agreement of which no record has been produced. In 1989 the Organization for African Unity (OAU) persuaded both countries to refer their dispute to the International Court of Justice which ruled in favour of Chad.)

Although hostile to Islamic fundamentalism, Qaddafi supported Iran against Iraq. During the Gulf War of 1991 he denounced both Saddam Hussein's invasion of Kuwait and the intervention of the United States and its allies against him. After the war he began to repair his relations with Egypt, where President Mubarak was receptive in the hope of breaking earlier links between Libya and Sudan (which sheltered Egyptian fundamentalists) and of getting an interest in Libyan oil.

In 1988 an American airliner was destroyed in flight over Scotland. The dead included many Americans. There were grounds for suspecting that this crime was the work of Iranians retaliating against the destruction of an Iranian airliner over the Persian Gulf by American fire, but the American, British and French governments suspected two Libyans, whom they identified, and demanded their extradition for trial in the United States or Scotland. The relevant international convention – the Montreal Convention of 1971 – provided that in the absence of applicable extradition treaties there was no obligation on the suspects' country to hand them over but the three governments used their weight in the UN to procure in 1991 a resolution of the Security Council demanding that Libya should do so. Two years later the same three states secured the imposition of economic sanctions against Libya when it did not comply. Libya refused to arrest or hand over the suspects for trial in what it regarded as hostile territory, but ten years after the catastrophe a novel compromise was reached by which they would stand trial before a Scottish court sitting in the Netherlands. This judicial arrangement, however, did not dispose of the political aspects of the case. Ostensibly, it concerned two individuals but in 1988 the plaintiff governments were more concerned to indict Qaddafi and his regime and even ten years later they had an interest in his condemnation if only to justify the economic sanctions visited upon his country. Negotiations for the trial were therefore protracted. A single defendant, Ali al-Megrahi, was convicted and jailed and although doubts about the verdict persisted Libya acknowledged its responsibility for the crime. UN sanctions were lifted (the US and France abstained on the vote in the Security Council). In a volte-face in 2003 Qaddafi renounced any intention to obtain nuclear weapons and promised to increase Libya's oil production in the hope seemingly of better relations with members of the European Union and the Arab League.

CHAPTER 22

West Africa

Independence

Europeans were interested in Africa long before they occupied it. In the century after the death of the Prophet Mahomet North Africa mounted the greatest threat to European Christendom which it ever faced, and although that threat was parried by Frank Charles Martel and the Byzantine emperor Leo the Isaurian, Spain remained for centuries partly under an alien rule buttressed on occasions by fresh support from Berber Africa. When the Christians finally drove the Muslims out of the Iberian peninsula, their momentum carried Spanish and Portuguese adventurers into and around Africa and made Cape Horn a station on a new route to the east. In more modern times Africa became a place where Europeans got things: slaves for plantations in the west, food for industrialized countries whose peoples were leaving the land for the factory, precious minerals like gold and copper and diamonds and uranium. At first only the coastal areas were exploited, but later the rumoured wealth of the interior tempted organized expeditions to follow in the footsteps of adventurers and missionaries. Although checked at first by the unexpected strength of African kingdoms, white power eventually prevailed – especially when curiosity and enrichment were reinforced by inter-white competition. So, in a final phase of European penetration, Africa was partitioned by official emissaries, part soldiers, part administrators, making territorial claims and fighting for them because traders demanded protection and each European state was afraid that others would take what it did not annex for itself.

By the last quarter of the nineteenth century Europe had acquired a great part of Africa in a short space of time, and there was some danger of fights between European states as a result of the uneven distribution of the spoils. The Europeans proceeded to settle these matters reasonably amicably among themselves. There were many wars in Africa during the colonial period, but none of them were fought between European states except as an adjunct of a European war, and even the most menacing disputes (for example, for the control of the Nile valley or the possession of Angola) were settled without the sort of conflict which in a previous century had attended the ambitions of the European powers in Asia and North America.

The Europeans took possession of Africa at the height of the Industrial Revolution. The technical disparity between Europeans and Africans was enormous. The cultural gap was no less great. Europeans remained almost without exception ignorant of African history (they often assumed there was none) and customs, while Africans acquired few of the benefits of the technically superior civilization of their new masters. There was no attempt at a partnership between the races until nearly a century later when the Europeans were in retreat and seen to be. Meanwhile, very large numbers of Africans died unnecessarily and painfully, especially in the areas ruled by Belgians and Germans; the French and British versions of civilization were less lethal in spite of wars, forced labour and the pains of mineral concessions. Economically, occupied Africa stagnated until well into the twentieth century when the Second World War and the incipient successes of nationalist leaders produced some startling changes – the first by creating a demand for African raw materials and the latter by making an impact on colonial authorities who, although vaguely concerned about the welfare of their territories from the end of the First World War, did next to nothing about it until the beginning of the Second. Exceptions to this economic stagnation were provided by the gold and diamond mines of South Africa from the 1870s and by the copper of Northern Rhodesia and Katanga in the twentieth century. Towns and their appurtenances sprang up and work was provided (at special non-European wages and in circumstances even worse than those of Victorian England) for increasing numbers of Africans. The effect of industrialization was heavily adverse for the African. The benefit to the new industrial workers was small since industry operated on cheap labour. The expectation of life among miners was low; they returned to their homes young and dying, useless and often infectiously diseased. A new class of migrant was created, the countryside was ruined, and the extremes of poverty were – as the Royal Commission on East Africa noted in 1955 – to be found in the main areas of European settlement. The European occupation had created an appalling economic problem, which itself created grave social problems (especially in cities), which in turn encouraged white observers to despise and shun the Africans. On their side the more indignant Africans accused the whites of exploiting and debauching the blacks.

African political leaders drew inspiration from both India and America. They formed National Congresses in imitation of the Indian National Congress; many of them were attracted by Gandhian ideas of passive resistance; and the independence of India in 1947 had an effect in Africa which had not been foreseen. From the American continent, and notably the Caribbean, Africans gained confidence and dignity and a habit of meeting together. A first pan-African conference was held in 1900, followed by a second in Paris during the peace conference of 1915. These first meetings were dominated by West Indian blacks but the sixth, held in Manchester at the end of the Second World War, was attended by the principal African leaders – Kenyatta, Nkrumah, Akintola, Nyerere, Banda. It voiced demands for independence which would have seemed totally unreal five years earlier. A mere ten years later West Africa was leading the way to independence from European rule.

In Accra, the capital of the British colony of the *Gold Coast*, riots in 1948 were started by ex-servicemen in protest against high prices. The colonial authorities were taken by surprise, and a commission of inquiry produced a radical report which said, in effect, that the colony's newly proposed constitution was out of date before being introduced: to give Africans a majority of the seats in the legislative council was no longer enough. A new commission of Africans, with an African judge as chairman, was appointed to devise a new constitution. These developments coincided with the appearance of a new nationalist leader Kwame Nkrumah who, aged probably 38, had returned to his country from the United States in 1947 and was determined to press for independence more energetically than older leaders such as J. B. Danquah. Nkrumah demanded immediate self-government. He seceded from Danquah's party, formed the Convention People's Party, earned the distinction of a prison sentence and won electoral victories in 1951, 1954 and 1956. After the first of these the British governor Sir Charles Arden-Clarke summoned him from prison and made him chief minister, thereby adopting the view that the colonial problem was not how to prolong colonialism, but how to make the best use of what time was left, to swim (not drift) with the tide and not uselessly to fight against it.

The British method, in the Gold Coast and elsewhere, was gradually to increase the elective and African elements in legislative and executive councils. Legislative councils in British territories progressed from assemblies dominated by appointed officials to assemblies containing a majority of elected members, and at the same time the governor's executive council was similarly transformed by the introduction of leaders of the main party in the legislature. The governor retained at first extensive reserve powers but later this association between the colonial authority and nationalist movements was carried a stage further by converting the nationalist leader from the governor's chief minister into a prime minister of a self-governing territory. At this point the territory was on the verge of independence, and with independence the governor disappeared. If the territory decided to remain in the Commonwealth, it might accept the British queen as its titular head with a governor-general as her representative on the spot, or it might become an independent republic within the Commonwealth but without any direct link with the British crown. The new state would, in any event, establish diplomatic relations with the British government (as distinct from the British crown) through representatives called high commissioners if the Commonwealth link were maintained, or ambassadors if it were not.

Given this method, the main problem was to regulate the pace. This was an exercise in compromise between an irresistible flood and a removable power. The Gold Coast became self-governing in 1955, independent under the ancient name of Ghana in March 1957 and a republic in 1960. It led the way for Africans into the Commonwealth. Nkrumah, influenced by India's example, calculated that the Commonwealth association would be a help to new states coming naked into international society.

The second West African state to become independent was French *Guinea* (1958). The French had been slower than the Spaniards or the Portuguese to enter Africa and

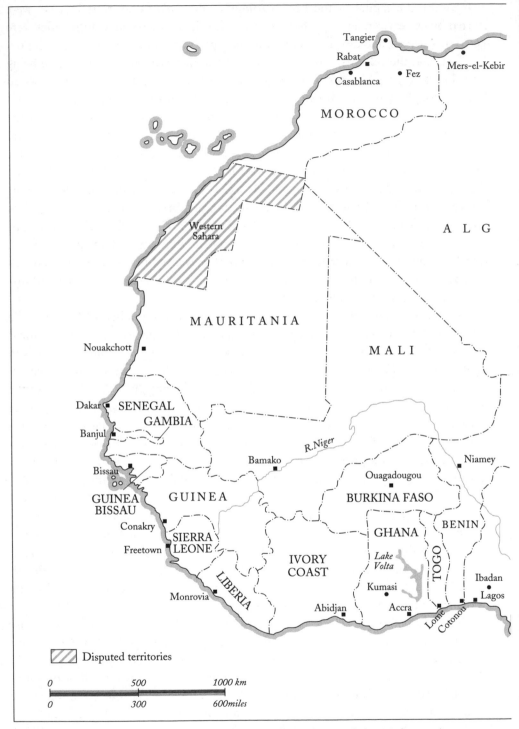

22.1 North-west Africa (with inset of Nigeria at the time of the Biafra war)

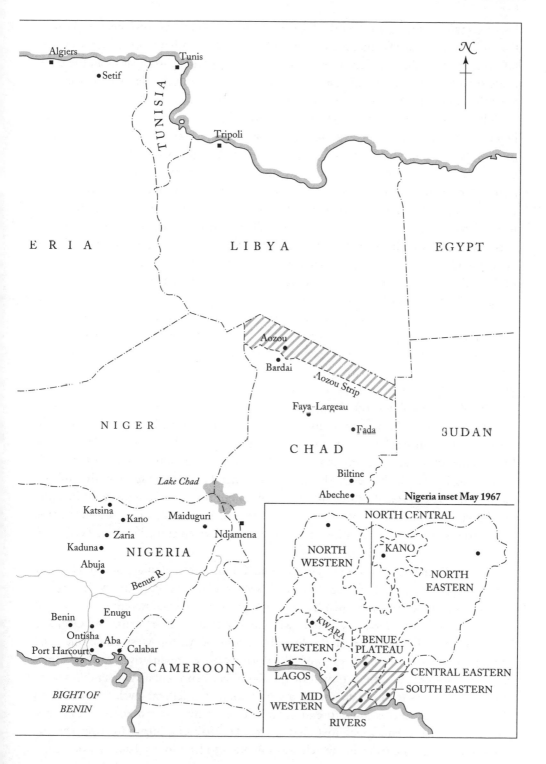

N

Algiers

Tunis

Setif

TUNISIA

Tripoli

E R I A

LIBYA

EGYPT

Aozou

Bardai

Aozou Strip

Faya-Largeau

N I G E R

Fada

SUDAN

C H A D

Biltine

Lake Chad

Abeche

Nigeria inset May 1967

Katsina

Kano

Maiduguri

Zaria

Ndjamena

Kaduna

NIGERIA

Abuja

Benue R.

NORTH CENTRAL

NORTH
WESTERN

KANO

NORTH
EASTERN

Benin

Enugu

Ontisha

Aba

KWARA

Port Harcourt

Calabar

WESTERN

BENUE
PLATEAU

CENTRAL EASTERN

CAMEROON

LAGOS

SOUTH EASTERN

BIGHT OF
BENIN

MID
WESTERN

RIVERS

less successful at first than the British or the Dutch. When in the seventeenth century they followed the new fashion their motive was emulation rather than any large expectation of gain. In the eighteenth century, however, they were participating in the slave trade on a large scale, extracting at one time as many as 100,000 slaves in a year, and after the abolition of the trade in 1815 and of slavery itself in 1848 (14 years after its prohibition in British territories) French merchants turned from human goods to ivory and rubber and French explorers and missionaries began to penetrate inland and so stimulated ambitious dreams of a vast and compact empire stretching from the west coast to the Nile and from Morocco to the equator. In the event France acquired 3 million sq. km by the end of the century, something between a fifth and a quarter of the whole continent. Almost the whole of the great African bulge came under French rule; it was formed into the governor-generalship of French West Africa in 1895 and comprised eventually eight separate colonies and, after 1945, the two trust territories of Togo and Cameroon. Four equatorial territories were similarly federated in 1910. Only in the valleys of the Niger and the Nile were the French worsted by the British. In 1900 French advances from Morocco in the north, from Senegal in the west and from the Congo in the south, where the great explorer de Brazza left his name, converged at Lake Chad. France also acquired in the First World War the enormous island of Madagascar; most of the German Cameroons, leaving a small slice which passed to the British, who administered it with the eastern province of Nigeria; and half of Togoland, which was also originally German and was divided in 1919 between France and Britain as the owners of the adjacent territories of Dahomey and the Gold Coast.

After the fall of France in 1940 French West Africa opted for Vichy until the invasion of north-west Africa by the Americans and the British in 1942. An attempt by the Free French and the British to seize Dakar, the capital of Senegal, in 1940 failed. In Equatorial Africa, however, the governor-general Félix Eboué, a native of the Caribbean, took the Gaullist side in August 1940 and introduced a number of imaginative social and political reforms. At a conference at Brazzaville in 1944 the Africans were promised more participation in mixed Franco-African councils, more decentralization and a wider franchise.

The first French constitution of 1946 was liberal from the colonial point of view but it was rejected by the French people and the second constitution of that year was less far-reaching. It created the French Union, comprising the French Republic, Associated States and Associated Territories (there were also Overseas Departments and Overseas Territories, which were part of the French Republic). All the West and Equatorial African territories became Associated Territories with representatives in the French National Assembly and the Council of the Republic. Representative assemblies were also established in each territory with a grand council at federal level. From 1947 to 1954 France had a succession of predominantly conservative governments, but in 1956 the Mollet government, which included Gaston Defferre as minister for overseas territories, introduced a *loi cadre*, which was intended to lead to a substantial degree of internal autonomy by way of universal franchise, elected councils and the Africaniza-tion of public services. The *loi cadre* marked the abandonment of the policy of integration or assimilation in favour of a freer federation in which the African territories, while still associated with France, would increasingly order their own affairs and develop their own services and personalities. The *loi cadre* was elaborated by a series of decrees which endowed the 12 West and Equatorial African territories with assemblies elected on a common roll and with councils of government elected by the assemblies. Considerable powers were reserved to the governors, the West or Equatorial high com-missioners, or the metropolitan government, but nationalist demands had secured the elimination of special votes for whites and every constituency in every territory had a majority of black voters. The Rassemblement Démocratique Africain, the principal nationalist party which operated throughout French West Africa, won the ensuing elections in Guinea, Soudan, Ivory Coast and Upper Volta.

These political changes were, however, offset on the economic side where French policy remained integrationist and, in return for French aid and guaranteed markets in France, proposed to make French Africa a highly protected area serving French metropolitan economic interests. In the following years Africans became increasingly restless about economic policy in this franc zone. They claimed that a system which allowed free trade in the zone but erected barriers round it profited the stronger members rather than the weaker, impeded economic growth in the African territories, and pre-vented them from diversifying their economies. In addition the *loi cadre* accentuated differences among African leaders. Some, of whom Félix Houphouët-Boigny of the Ivory Coast was representative, seemed well satisfied with the French proposals, while others, among whom Sekou Touré of Guinea was the most eminent, suspected the *loi cadre* of being not a stage to sovereign independence but a device to postpone it indefinitely.

When de Gaulle returned to power in 1958 he faced the West Africans and Equatorial Africans with a choice: either autonomy within a *communauté* in which France would retain control of the economic levers, or independence – which was a polite term for expulsion into a francless world. All but Guinea made the first choice. Guinea became an independent sovereign state in October 1958, humiliatingly discarded by its French mentors and forced to look to communist powers for the wherewithal to sustain its independence. The association was not a happy one and Touré was forced to change course (see Chapter 26) before he died in the United States in 1984 after a heart attack, his position already undermined by discontent which came to a head in a coup which put Colonel Lansana Conte in his place to cope with a legacy of repression, corruption and bankruptcy. Conte's position was strengthened by the failure of a counter-coup but he faced persistent popular grievances grounded in tribal rivalries and the standard IMF medicine administered to impecunious countries and swallowed with revulsion by its chief victims, the poor. Ethnic tensions, serious trade deficits augmented by falls in the price of bauxite, loss of IMF support and the decline and collapse of basic public services so weakened Conte that he was obliged to concede elections in 1993 which he won by the narrowest of margins and he did so again in 1998 and 2003: stability of a sort but change inevitable and uncertain.

France's other West African colonies, which had chosen autonomy within the projected *communauté*, did not long remain content with their status. In 1959 Senegal, Soudan, Upper Volta and Dahomey decided to federate under the name of Mali and ask for independence. The two latter changed their minds under French pressure and although Senegal and Soudan persisted the resulting federation lasted only a couple of months, after which Senegal too withdrew, leaving Soudan with the new name of Mali; it moved into the Guinea–Ghana orbit. The idea of a Mali federation had been unpopular not only in Paris but also among French African states further south, especially in the Ivory Coast where Félix Houphouët-Boigny riposted by forming with Niger and the detached Upper Volta and Dahomey an association called the Council of the Entente and asked for and got independence in 1960. Houphouët-Boigny wished to fortify the Entente by introducing dual nationality in it, but it was weakened by coups in Upper Volta and Dahomey in 1961 and by persistent suspiciousness in these and other states (including Togo, which joined in 1966) of Houphouët-Boigny, who was regarded as unduly hostile to Nkrumah and too partial to Tshombe in the Belgian Congo (see the next chapter). The net result of these centripetal and centrifugal forces was to solidify the several French colonies as separate sovereign states.

The independence of the Entente countries in 1960 deprived the *communauté* of any meaning although in theory it continued to exist as an association comprising France, Madagascar and the Equatorial states. These latter – Gabon, Chad, Ubangi-Shari and French Congo (the last two renamed the Central African Republic and Congo-Brazzaville) – produced a plan for a federation which was, however, abortive; they too became independent as separate sovereign states in 1960. In 1963 the Senegal river states (Senegal, Mali, Guinea and Mauritania) planned an association, though this was frustrated by political differences: the notion was revived in the late 1960s.

The huge British territory of Nigeria also became independent in 1960, followed in 1961 by Sierra Leone, the British colony wedged between Guinea and Liberia, and in 1965 by Gambia, the northernmost and last remaining British territory in West Africa, a narrow enclave within the embrace of Senegal. Of the trust territories in West Africa the French Cameroons and French Togoland became independent republics, while the British Cameroons and British Togoland were attached to Nigeria and Ghana respectively. Portugal and Spain were slower to divest themselves.

The coastal loop from Senegal to Benin

Ten states with a combined population not much larger than Britain's occupied the West African coast between the Senegal and Niger rivers. In *Senegal* Leopold Senghor

– poet and scholar, the first African *agrégé*, a Christian leader in an overwhelmingly Muslim country, a leader in whom charisma was an addition to and not a substitute for intelligence – ruled for 21 years before making way voluntarily and peacefully in 1981 for Abdou Diouf, who was confirmed in his position by a convincing electoral victory two years later. Diouf, however, failed to stem sectarian rivalries, escape the control of elderly and conservative local bosses, or retrieve an economy overburdened by unwanted groundnuts and afflicted by drought. Unemployment rose, living standards fell, regional feuds and Islamic fundamentalism reared their heads. External debt charges rose to approximately half the national income, recourse to the IMF entailed painful austerity, and ventures such as phosphate plants, the Dakar shipyards and the Senegal River Plan languished, as did agriculture. Foreign aid cushioned these failures. Senegal enjoyed strong French and American support and Diouf was able to win further elections in 1988 by hook or by crook but the disorder which followed obliged him to impose martial law and he was further weakened by economic decline, new austerity measures, the devaluation of the Central African (CFA) franc (see p. 550) and signs of French reluctance to bail him out unless he gave Senegal's democracy more reality. At the next elections (1993), Senegal's first multiparty contest, Diouf won only a disappointing 58 per cent, further reduced the next year. Senegal's foreign relations with its neighbours, Mauritania and Gambia, were uneasy, leading in the first case to undeclared war (see the preceding chapter).

Gambia was a stranger neighbour since it was entirely embraced within Senegal. This smallest of the British colonies in West Africa led at first an equable existence after independence. With an economy which enabled it to dispense with British aid after 1967, Gambia experienced nothing worse than rubs in its attempts to work an 'association' with Senegal until in 1981 President Dawda Jawara was forced into the humiliating expedient of calling in Senegalese troops in order to retain his office. He accepted a confederation with Senegal – by which Gambia hoped to have the benefits of independence and of partnership with a larger economy. But relations were soured by the prevalence of Gambian smuggling and Senegalese suspicions of Gambian intrigues among malcontents in Senegal's southern province of Casamance, where the mainly Wolof speakers maintained a secessionist movement (which appeared to have support also from Mauritania and the adjacent Guinea-Bissau). In 1989 Senegal renounced plans for the integration of Gambia with Senegal. In 1994 Jawara's long and honest rule as prime minister and then president ended when an army coup by Lieutenant Yahya Jammeh (aided by Nigeria's dictator Sani Abacha) forced him to flee. His departure ended the longest stint of democratic rule in independent Africa and the dominance of Gambia's largest ethnic group, the Mandinka. Gambia was dependent on international aid but got much of what it wanted. Its economy was abnormally distorted by migration from the countryside to the town.

Between Gambia and Guinea, in Portuguese Guinea – *Guinea-Bissau* – a liberation movement (PAIGC: African Party for the Independence of Guinea and the Cape Verde Islands) founded in 1956 by Amilcar Cabral, started a rising in 1959 and full-scale war in 1963, in the course of which the Guineans gradually established their control over the greater part of the country. In 1970 Portugal was implicated in an invasion of the neighbouring state of Guinea, where PAIGC had its headquarters. An inquiry by the UN found that 350–400 invaders had been landed by ships manned by white men; the Security Council censured Portugal. In 1973 Cabral was murdered in the Guinean capital Conakry. Guinea-Bissau and the Cape Verde islands became separate states in 1975 with plans for a union which was not consummated. The islands, ten of them 320 km from the mainland, provided sustenance for no more than a third of their inhabitants. They were isolated and kept politically stable by the tight control of a ruling group until the early 1990s when Cape Verde adopted a democratic constitution. In Guinea-Bissau Joao Vieira turned multiparty democracy to his advantage by winning an election in which opposition parties were so numerous that none had a chance of winning. A revolt in 1998 developed into a civil war in which both sides drew support from Senegal. Guinea-Bissau became a principal staging point in the drug trade between the New World and the Old.

South of the Guinea Coast *Sierra Leone* (pop. 6 million) began its existence as a colony with a split personality: freed slaves established by Britain in the coastland and a distrustful hinterland of peoples conquered by Britain soon afterwards. It was ruled after the Second World War by the brothers Margai – Sir Milton until his death in 1964 and the more radical Sir Albert until his plans for constitutional change cost him the elections of 1966. The army intervened briefly, chiefly in order to keep Siaka Stevens from power, but in 1968 Stevens became prime minister and in 1971 president of the newly proclaimed republic of Sierra Leone. Stevens turned the country into a one-party preserve, an economic catastrophe and a paradise for corrupt tycoons who sucked it dry while waiting for the aged Stevens to depart. He resigned in 1985 after 17 years' rule and was succeeded by General Joseph Momoh with promises to end the corruption and misrule which had characterized the government of which he had himself been a member for over a decade. Momoh had difficulty in dissociating himself from the unsavoury pillars of the old regime; the business world became a battlefield between old-established Lebanese operators and immigrant Israelis (some backed by South Africans). Internal conflicts were aggravated by rival foreigners attracted by the glint of diamonds and other prizes. Momoh's term was abruptly ended by junior officers who forced him to flee. The youthful leader of this coup, Captain Valentine Strasser, jailed some of Momoh's ministers, secured the cancellation of about a fifth of the country's foreign debt to a dozen creditors in return for a promise to restore civilian rule by 1996. However, he failed to set a date for the elections which were supposed to bring his transitional authority to a democratic conclusion, and failed to establish his rule in eastern and southern parts of the country where the Revolutionary United Front (RUF), an expression of regional and tribal dissension which mixed elevated aims with atrocious behaviour, got aid from neighbouring Liberia and Guinea, seized the principal mines and took native and foreign hostages. The country was atomized by the indiscipline of an army suddenly enlarged tenfold, by the forays of irregular forces intent on opportune loot and by the no less opportunistic manoeuvres of foreign organizations dabbling in a vastly expanded arms trade. Strasser was ousted by his second-in-command Brigadier Julius Maada-Bio, who was quickly supplanted by Ahmed Tejan Kabbah, duly elected but inexperienced and in turn evicted in 1997 by Major Johnny Paul Koroma, who then made common cause with the RUF. Sierra Leone was suspended from the Commonwealth, and Economic Community of West African States (ECOWAS) (see p. 549) established a group of four led by Nigeria to restore Kabbah with imperfectly concealed aid from foreign mining companies. Freetown was blockaded and shelled and Kabbah restored in 1998. He wreaked vengeance but not extermination and the RUF returned to ravage Freetown before a truce was imposed in 1999. Peace talks began in Togo. Kabbah's position was strengthened when the newly elected president of Nigeria Olusegun Obasanjo reversed his predecessor's decision to recall Nigerian troops. A peace agreement was reached in Togo in 1999. A UN Mission in Sierra Leone (UNAMSIL) was created to supervise disarmament and other provisions. Kabbah retained the presidency with his main enemy, the RUF's leader Foday Sankoh as nominal but prudently absent vice-president. But fighting continued until Britain decided to send troops to stop it. Kabbah was restored. Fifty thousand out of a population of 5 million were dead. Rescuing the economy proved as difficult as pacification. Sierra Leone was one of those countries – Guinea Bissau, Liberia and Somalia were others – so splintered by tribal fragmentation as to cease to be a state, but in none of them did a tribal splinter become a state.

Liberia, virtually an American preserve until the 1970s, was disrupted in 1980 by the violent removal of the dominant Tolbert family and the ruling True Whig Party by Sergeant (later General) Samuel Doe. Doe's support was predominantly tribal and although he survived for ten years, protected by an Israeli-trained guard and the Israeli secret service, he never established his authority throughout the country. Economic disaster supplemented tribal animosities and in 1990 invasion from the north-east started a chain of massacres and civil war in which tens of thousands were killed and about a million made homeless. The United States, which deplored Doe's demolition of the Tolbert regime but came to terms with him and used Liberia as an intelligence centre, cold-shouldered him when his prospects dimmed. Five West African states assembled a military force, Economic Community of West African States Monitoring Group (ECOMOG), to stop the fighting between the rebels and Doe (beleaguered in the capital) and between rival rebel sections fighting one another. But ECOMOG failed to protect Doe, who was seized, tortured and killed after taking refuge with it. Doe's executioner, Prince Johnson, an alcoholic psychopath, seized control temporarily in the capital but most of the country was dominated by Charles Taylor, who had served in Doe's government before being charged with embezzlement and driven into temporary exile in the United States, where he was imprisoned. Taylor recruited exiled Nigerians and Ghanaians, thwarted ECOMOG's efforts to make peace, invaded Sierra Leone and fostered suspicions that ECOMOG was being used by Nigeria to pursue quasi-imperial ambitions in West Africa. (Nigeria met four-fifths of ECOMOG's costs and supplied two-thirds of its 15,000 troops.) ECOMOG slowly prevailed against Taylor with the apparent aim of forcing him to come to terms with the feeble government in Monrovia protected by ECOMOG under the increasingly phantom presidents. The task of conciliation was aggravated as factions split and multiplied and ECOMOG's Nigerian and Ghanaian principals grew worried about the costs of their intervention. A fragile ceasefire was negotiated at the end of 1994 and converted the next year into a power-sharing agreement but Taylor, having won Nigeria to his side, emerged as the effective winner by virtue of more money, better arms and better organization. He presented himself as a reformed character and conciliator and the war wound down, having cost 150,000 lives and incalculable suffering and damage. ECOMOG left in 1999. Liberia, like Sierra Leone, was a state in which ethnic groups fought for power with an eye to sympathetic kin over the state's borders. Taylor, the ablest of the errant warlords of the region, seemed at times intent on creating a regional power centred on Monrovia and capable of looking Nigeria in the face, but his power was essentially military and despotic. His end came in 2002 when multiple pressures proved too much for him and he fled. He was succeeded by Ellen Johnson-Shirleaf, Africa's first female head of state, who had worked as an economist at the World Bank.

Ivory Coast was the most successful of West African states in the first decades after independence. Superposing good management on good fortune (a benign climate and no real desert) its government designed, first and foremost, to intensify and diversify the rural sector; secondly, to give measured encouragement to industrialization, including opportunities for private enterprise within a state-controlled system and assurances to foreign capitalists wishing to invest and earn a fair profit; and, thirdly, to avoid heavy spending on defence and other forms of ostentation. The national product grew steadily at the rate of 3 per cent a year and the average annual income of the country's 8 million people rose from less than $100 before independence to about $800 by 1980. But this average increase owed more to the rapid enrichment of the few than to the spread of prosperity to the many, and after 1980 growth faltered. Oil began to flow in 1984 but with limited effect on the economy, offsetting recession rather than enhancing growth. Collapsing cocoa prices, due to overproduction worldwide, undermined the commodity which still in the 1980s provided (with coffee) half of Ivorian foreign earnings, and this shortfall combined with high borrowing at high cost to create an economic crisis. In 1987 Ivory Coast suspended payment on its foreign debts (which amounted to 150 per cent of GDP) and exports of cocoa; two years later it halved the price paid to cocoa growers. Private businesses were owed more than $1 billion by the state and private banks were collapsing. Loans from the World Bank expiring in 1989 were not renewable and the country was not poor enough to qualify for special debt remissions. Cuts in public services and wages – the IMF demanded cuts up to 75 per cent in salaries in the public sector – provoked strikes and demonstrations but failed to rectify the country's deficits. As Houphouët-Boigny, confessedly 80 but nearer to 90, approached the end of his natural span he took few steps to ensure an orderly succession. A constitutional amendment introduced in 1980 had designated the vice-president as heir but nobody was appointed to that office and five years later Houphouët-Boigny announced that he would remain in office until he died. In 1990 he so far bowed to domestic anxieties and to the new wind of change in Africa as to sanction the forma- tion of more than one political party, but his main concern in his declining years was the construction at unconscionable cost of a vast church in his native village and getting the Pope to sanctify it, which the Pope did. Houphouët-Boigny was re-elected president. Some two dozen parties, newly established, contrived to field only one candidate, who nevertheless received 18 per cent of the votes cast in elections held under the control of, and not without manipulation by, the ruling party. Rises in cocoa and coffee prices in the mid-1980s were not sustained and austerity and bureaucratic pruning caused some distress. Houphouët-Boigny died in 1993 after 33 years in power and leaving no designated successor. The president of the national assembly Henri Konan Bédié moved deftly to win the succession but not without splitting his party. He inherited a position of strength in one of Africa's more stable societies but chose to adopt an assertive style, even disfranchising non-Ivorian residents, who constituted a third of the electorate. In 1995 he was comfortably re-elected, most of his adversaries ducking the contest at the last moment. He accelerated privatization in the economy and its diversification, seeking to diminish its dependence on cocoa, attract foreign investment to its variety of minerals and establish it as a financial centre with a stock exchange for all West Africa. The IMF and World Bank smiled on his plans: the former granted a low-interest loan of $395 million (on terms which included reductions in price controls and overstaffing in the public sector) and the latter gave a guarantee of $30 million to facilitate the development of energy supply. Foreign debt remained heavy but was rescheduled. But even in this once exemplary African state the palmy days were over, standards of living were falling, wages in the public sector were unpaid, riots in the capital marked the end of the century and the president fled. The turn of the century was marked by conflict between north and south, French troops (4,000) helping a revolt in the south. Peace was slowly restored by Nigerian and South African mediators. Ivory Coast was a leading member of the West Africa Economic and Monetary Union (UEMOA) created with Senegal, Benin, Togo, Mali and Burkina Faso (and joined in 1997 by Guinea Bissau).

In *Ghana*, the pioneer of West African liberation, the personal leadership of Nkrumah turned into a febrile autocracy which passed step by step beyond a struggle to maintain the unity of the new state and modernize it, and became perverted into a struggle to assert the authority of Nkrumah himself. Nkrumah wished to propagate his vision of African unity by accelerating the independence of other territories and consolidating the energies of Africans and Africanism in the service of African dignity and African effectiveness in the world; but his methods and his personality did not always commend him to other African leaders, whose own pan-Africanism was filtered through their several national experiences and ambitions. Like Nasser's pan-Arabism, Nkrumah's pan-Africanism was suspect. The exuberance which had contributed so much to make him the first ruler of a sub-Saharan republic was a drawback in a new situation which demanded the arts of diplomacy as much as the *élan* of leadership.

Nkrumah's second ambition was to make Ghana a modern industrial state. This ambition was impeded by a complex of regionalism, conservatism and political jealousies and by a serious drop in the world price of cocoa, Ghana's principal source of revenue. The Convention People's Party, whose main strength was in the coastal areas, was opposed by chiefs whom it regarded as a divisive and reactionary force and by the United Party led by K. A. Busia and J. E. Appiah. Above all, his showpiece failed him. He revived an abandoned British plan to build a dam across the river Volta and he concluded an agreement with an American corporation to build a smelter which would buy and refine Ghana's large deposits of bauxite. The World Bank would lend the money to build the dam on the strength of Ghana's prospective profits from the sale of bauxite but the contract with the American Kaiser corporation failed to provide that the bauxite to be used in the smelter should be Ghanaian bauxite and the corporation imported bauxite from elsewhere. The dam was built but Ghana's profits from the smelter were minimal and a country which had started its independent existence with enviable reserves began to slide into debt. Other foreign companies enticed Ghana into expensive projects of which the most notorious was the enlargement of the Accra–Tema road into a four-lane highway with all the appurtenances of a British motorway. To these extravagances Nkrumah contributed by grandiose building. Bloated economic activity carried with it a grievous load of corruption. Nkrumah's failure to meet his promises of a better life for all was compounded by an increasingly dictatorial and suspicious manner. The illiberality evidenced, for example, by the removal of the chief justice after the delivery of an unpalatable verdict in a treason trial, coupled with increasing corruption and profligacy in the administration, destroyed Nkrumah's attempts to get foreign friends and finance and created an opposition to him in the army which, by a bloodless coup in 1966, unseated him while he was away on a visit to China.

In the world at large Nkrumah wished to follow a policy of non-alignment. His circumstances were exceptionally favourable. Upon independence Ghana's resources and reserves – at £200 million the latter were larger than India's – gave it a material base for a measure of independence which might the more easily be maintained since the Cold War had not at that date reached Africa. But in practice Ghana under Nkrumah never achieved non-aligned status in the eyes of outsiders. For half the period 1957–66 it appeared pro-western, for the other half pro-eastern. Ghana remained in the Commonwealth, was visited in 1961 by Queen Elizabeth II and its leader welcomed in Washington by President Eisenhower, but the crisis in the Congo and particularly the murder of Lumumba, for which he blamed the west, turned Nkrumah against the western world, while the elaboration in theory and practice of his 'scientific socialism' with the inauguration in 1962 of a one-party system turned the western world against him. In contradistinction to Nasser's evident pragmatism, Nkrumah became increasingly ideological and illogical, evolving a form of economic planning akin to communist models but nevertheless dependent on western capital for its success. The coup which removed him was managed by the CIA.

Nkrumah wasted Ghana's enviable heritage and belied his own vision. He reduced the country to bankruptcy and initiated the corruption which subsequent regimes failed to master. With one two-year interlude, his fall was followed by four military governments of varying incapacity. The first of these, led by Colonel Ankrah, found that Nkrumah's extravagances had run the reserves down to £4 million and the external debt up to £279 million and created a deficit on external account of £53 million. Ankrah made some improvements to this dismal tale before relinquishing power in 1969, but economic growth remained below 1 per cent a year, the population was increasing by 3.5–4 per cent annually, the standard of living had been cut by a severe devaluation and the first attempts of the new prime minister Kofi Busia to secure an alleviation of the external debt were only moderately successful. By the beginning of 1972 Busia had been defeated by his predecessors' legacy, by an imprudently liberal policy which permitted an inflow of foreign goods which crippled the balance of payments, and by a drastic devaluation which doubled the external debt at a stroke. He was ousted while away in London by the (military) National Redemption Council under the chairmanship of Colonel I. K. Acheampong. This well-intentioned group struggled, not always harmoniously, with economic problems which were being aggravated by steep rises in the price of oil and other imports and by consequent rises in the cost of living. Ghana's creditors gave it some relaxation on the repayment of debts but not as much as it hoped for. In 1978 Acheampong was ousted by General F. W. K. Akuffo, who lasted less than a year against a rising tide of indignation. He too was removed and, together with Acheampong and six others, executed after a coup led by Flight-Lieutenant Jerry Rawlings, who promised to end corruption, reverse economic decline and restore civilian rule. In his three months in power he succeeded only in the last, completing an electoral process which had already been set in motion and which installed Dr Hilla Liman as president of a country with a collapsing economy and aggravated social tensions. At the end of 1981 Liman was ousted and Rawlings returned, struggled against the economic slide and sporadic plots and riots, pulled away from his more radical associates and introduced substantial deflation and a number of devaluations in order to get help from the IMF. Having attacked Liman for being willing to deal with the IMF and having failed to get economic aid elsewhere, Rawlings switched to a policy of IMF-led growth and had some qualified success: inflation fell from 100 to 20 per cent, the budget was balanced and growth reached 6 per cent. But revenues from cocoa and timber declined (gold sales, however, went up); foreign debt remained a throttling burden; the cost of imported oil, which had quintupled in the decade preceding Rawlings's return, absorbed nearly half the country's foreign earnings; the devaluation of the cedi in 1983 from 2.75 to 1.62 to the dollar caused great distress; promises of an early return to civilian rule and of popular consultation were not kept; the ruling Provisional National Defence Council was a clique with good intentions but no sound constitutional standing; opposition in politics or in the administration became a road to jail but this treatment did not deter Rawlings's enemies at home and abroad (mostly in Ivory Coast and Togo) from keeping up their intrigues against him. Rawlings forfeited the support of radicals, introduced measures which hurt the many more than they hurt the few at the top, and risked the disgruntlement of junior officers which had kindled more than one coup in Ghana's history. Such a coup in 1989, although unsuccessful, was the more ominous for coming from his own Ewe people. Yet he was set to remain in power for the rest of the century.

By 1990 Rawlings was being nudged towards constitutional reform by international forces, foreign finance and the regional fashion for more democracy, while remaining averse to a multiparty system or at any rate to more parties than two. Unexpectedly, in 1991 he announced a programme for a return to civilian rule and at the end of the following year he was re-elected president by a majority of two to one. Parliamentary elections were boycotted by a cynical and divided opposition, whose refusal to enter the multiparty fray gave Rawlings 189 seats in an assembly of 200 and, in effect, turned Ghana into a one-party state with a multiparty constitution. It was also a state with rosier economic expectations than had been the case when Rawlings seized power for the second time 11 years earlier. With the help of about $2 billion of foreign aid, government spending had been axed, inflation had been reduced to 15 per cent, growth in the agricultural sector had averaged 2.5 per cent since the early 1980s, new sources of revenue had been developed in, for example, fishing and there was even talk of Ghana emulating the Tigers of East Asia in Taiwan, South Korea and Hong Kong. On the other hand, continued economic progress depended on rising foreign aid and rising rates of growth, whereas the economy remained heavily dependent on cocoa and gold, corruption in the private sector persisted, there was no domestic and disappointingly little foreign money for investment, strikes were on the increase, and forecast budget and trading surpluses were unfulfilled. But the balance of these political and economic gains and losses, together with discord in Nigeria (see below), encouraged Rawlings to play a stronger role in African affairs as chairman of ECOWAS (whose francophone members trusted Ghana more readily than Nigeria), as elder statesman in the eyes of new men in Sierra Leone and Gambia and a respected visitor to a string of southern African states. He comfortably defeated an assortment of old enemies in 1996 – the rural vote was solidly for him – but in parliamentary elections opposition parties did well enough to start lining up for the presidency in 2000. His successor John Kufuor maintained his run of stability and economic progress.

In *Togo*, where the first president Sylvanus Olympio was assassinated in 1963 and the second Nicholas Grunitzky displaced a few years later, Gnassingbe Eyadema maintained himself in power against substantial – largely regional and ethnic – unpopularity and frequent plots. The president's political strength lay in the north, whence came a large proportion of the army's officers. Matters turned to open crisis when, after riots in 1991 and a conference lasting two months to ventilate accusations of fraud and murder in high places and proposals for constitutional reform, the president rounded on his prime minister, Joseph Kokou Koffigoh, dismissed the army's commander-in-chief (both Ewes) and cancelled projected elections. The army, whose attitude had been uncertain, rallied to the president in alarm at spreading disorder – some of which was allegedly incited by the president himself to keep the army on his side. Further serious riots in 1993 prompted half a million Togolese to flee to Ghana and Benin, whereafter Eyadema allowed elections to proceed and was declared the winner. In co-operation with the IMF Togo developed a niche economy, self-sufficient in food, fostering tourism and a modest manufacturing sector, and serving as entrepôt for its landlocked neighbours to the north. Eyadema died after 35 years as president. His death was followed by unexpected chaos until his son took his place with the help of the army.

In adjacent Dahomey, renamed *Benin* in 1972, a country living under the shadow of Nigeria and without jobs or resources, the military were in and out of government, displacing one civilian president and installing another until in 1970 they forced three past presidents to work together on a rota system which proved to be no more than a two-year interlude before military rule. In 1972 Colonel Matthieu Kerekou seized power, survived a series of attempts against his life – including one in 1977 allegedly launched from Togo with French, Moroccan and Gabonese help – was re-elected in 1984 and (narrowly) in 1989, made a tour of communist capitals including Beijing (1986) and then turned cautiously back to the French connection. The opposition to his rule was divided, consisting of young people without jobs, junior officers without promotion, unions, and ethnic rivals in the south. He saw his country become a small exporter of oil and also an entrepôt for drugs from Asia to the west. But by 1990 his days were numbered and Benin led the way in West Africa to multiparty systems. Kerekou, like Kaunda in Zambia a year later, accepted his dismissal peacefully, and was succeeded by Nicéphore Soglo, who released political prisoners, abstained from strong-arm rule and introduced economic changes calculated to win foreign (mainly French) aid. Conversely, however, his economic reforms put large numbers of people out of work and nearly 100 parties appeared. Soglo, whose ruling coalition was mainly Fon, southern and Christian, lost in 1996 to a revived Kerekou, who had meanwhile abandoned Marxism for an enthusiastic Christianity and won the support of Nigeria's Sani Abacha.

Landlocked: Mali, Burkina Faso, Niger

Behind the arc of states stretching from the mouth of the Senegal river almost to the mouth of the Niger lay three large, arid and landlocked countries: Mali, Burkina Faso (formerly Upper Volta, the smallest of the three) and Niger. In *Mali* Modibo Keita, one of the architects of the abortive Malian federation, was ousted in 1968 by General Moussa Traore, who ruled for 23 years. In his search for foreign aid he vacillated between the communist states of Europe and Asia (which he visited in 1986) and the readier, if unpalatable, succour of the IMF. Mali had trouble from the Tuareg, Berber desert-dwellers who lived also in Burkina Faso, Niger, Algeria, Libya and Chad. As decolonization loomed in the 1950s the Tuareg hoped to secure with French help a state of their own. After independence – and largely on account of drought – they dispersed into neighbouring countries, notably Libya, where they enlisted in Qaddafi's wars in Chad, whence, however, they began to return to Mali around 1990, causing fighting in Mali and Niger. Traore was trying to bring this fighting to an end when he was ousted by his army. A transitional government concluded with Algerian help an agreement with the Tuareg which conceded them regional autonomy but did not satisfy a more militant group; fighting went on with increased viciousness. An outburst of democracy produced 20 political parties to contest elections in 1992. Alpha Konare was elected president, survived a coup in 1996 for the restoration of the Traore dictatorship, grappled with droughts, corruption and crippling debt and was re-elected in chaotic elections in 1997. From 2002 Amadou Toure gave Mali a welcome stretch of civilian rule – a general turned civilian and in search of a party.

Part of Mali's pre-independence heritage was a border dispute with *Burkina Faso* which was aggravated when Captain Thomas Sankara took power there in 1983 (ousting a three-year-old civilian regime which had succeeded the military regime of General Saye Zerbo). Sankara was attractively efficient, young and honest, but his authority rested on an amalgam of discordant elements. He developed good relations with Benin and projected a union with Ghana but this trend alarmed Mali, which launched a short and ill-conducted war in 1985. Two years later Sankara was murdered and succeeded by a close friend, Blaise Compaore, who, less radical than Sankara and more autocratic, presided over a multiparty regime in which his party held the biggest stick and did not shrink from brandishing it against unions, students and others with views of their own. Compaore was routinely plagued by friction or worse with neighbouring Ivory Coast.

Niger too suffered plots and disorders, generally instigated by military dissatisfaction with the efficiency or honesty of civilian rule. These coups were effected with the minimum of violence and amounted to an accepted, if not very satisfactory, way of changing a government which had failed but which had no ready-made successor in a one-party state. Niger's first ruler Hamami Diori had won his position with strong French help against a rival, Djibo Bakary, who leaned rather to the left and to the Islamic north of the country. During the civil war in Nigeria Diori supported the central government in defiance of France's support for Biafra and he paid the price in 1974 when the army turned him out: a drought in the previous year, extreme even by Niger's standards, had weakened his position. His successor Seyni Kountche inaugurated military rule and remained president until his death in 1987. He was followed by Colonel Ali Seybou who would, it was hoped, display a less offensive lifestyle than Kountche, but did not. A new constitution restored civilian rule in 1993 but produced stalemate between president and prime minister should they fail to agree. They did and President Ousmane Mahamane, a Hausa, was forced into competition with prime minister Amadou Hama for support from the second largest group, the Songhai. A coup in 1996, in which Abacha's hand was again discerned, handed the presidency to the self-styled non-political but autocratic General Ibrahim Bara Mainassara, who was assassinated in 1999. Niger had too many ex-presidents for comfort. It had too a Tuareg minority comprising a tenth of the population which felt excluded from jobs and education but failed to muster an effective rebel force of more than 2,000. Mainassara included Tuaregs in his government. Niger's uranium made it a cynosure of French attention so long as uranium was believed to be a scarce mineral but French aid was markedly reduced in the 1990s.

Nigeria

Nigeria was a twentieth-century creation. The colonies of Lagos and South Nigeria were united by the British in 1906. The former was the home of the Yoruba, whose society was based partly on tribal chiefs and partly on cultivated cities. The dominant people in the latter were the Ibo, who had neither chiefs nor cities but were the more easily united as a nation and displayed a thrusting vigour which carried many of them long distances from their homes in eastern Nigeria and into the western and northern parts of the federation created by the British when, in 1914, they joined northern Nigeria to the two southern colonies.

The north was in a state of flux when the British reached it at the end of the nineteenth century. Early in that century the Islamicized Fulani had established their authority over a medley of pre-existing Hausa states and so created the empire of Usman dan Fodio and his descendants. Conflict between Fulani and Hausa and others persisted and the British assumed the task of mastering it as a prelude to uniting all their territories in this part of the world, but the federation which they created was an uneasy amalgam of states and cultures without a national consciousness or unity. After the Second World War the southern half of the country pressed for independence, while the north hesitated for fear of being reduced to dependence on the south with its coastal windows on the outside world's commerce, skills and manners. The north even toyed with the idea of a separate state with access to the sea either down a river corridor along the Niger or through Dahomey or the Cameroons on the one side or the other. Before independence, riots with racial and religious overtones gave warning of the dangers which the new state would run, but the advantages of unity seemed to make the experiment worthwhile and in 1960 Nigeria became independent with a constitution based on three regions. The federal premiership went to a northerner, Sir Abubakr Tafewa Balewa. The eastern leader Namdi Azikiwe became president and his party co-operated with the principal northern party in the government at the centre. It was Azikiwe's belief that a country as big and heterogeneous as Nigeria could only be governed by a coalition of all its main groups within a federal structure, but the western leader Chief Obafemi Awolowo preferred to form an opposition in the federal parliament.

The accord between east and north did not last long, nor did the cohesion of the west. The Ibos annoyed their northern partners by trying to win parliamentary seats in the northern region. In the west Chief Samuel Akintola challenged Awolowo and succeeded in getting him and other leaders tried and imprisoned. Akintola was not satisfied with Awolowo's policy of forming an opposition at the federal level. He preferred a policy of alliance with the north, displacing the Ibos and getting for his own people a share in the power, perquisites and finances of central government. In 1963 a fourth, mid-western region was formed. In 1964 a census showed a total population for the whole country of 55.6 million, of which 29.8 million were in the north – more than half. This demographic preponderance of the north increased the attractions of an alliance with the leaders of that region and, together with charges that the census had been faked, also increased political tensions. Elections in the western region in 1965 produced allegations of flagrant malpractice. In the next year more serious fighting began in the north. The country's uneasy tripartite constitution broke down with, first, a mainly Ibo insurrection; then a coup which provoked an attempt to create an independent Ibo state; and eventually successive redivisions of the country into more and more constituent states.

In 1966 a group of young Ibo officers rebelled, partly in protest against bad government and partly as a demonstration against the north and its allies in the west. The federal and northern prime ministers, Sir Abubakr Balewa and the Sardauna of Sokoto, were murdered along with Chief Akintola and many more, but senior officers stepped in to arrest further developments and the junior officers. General Johnson Ironsi was proclaimed head of state with the mission of keeping the country from breaking up and providing competent and honest administration. Ironsi was an Ibo. He was well intentioned but not otherwise well equipped for the delicate task of holding the country together and when he incautiously suggested that a unitary constitution might be better for Nigeria than a federal one, northern fears of attempted Ibo dominance flared up into another coup and he was murdered in his turn. He was replaced by Colonel Yakubu Gowon, a northern Christian, who released a number of imprisoned civilians, including Awolowo, and expressed the usual hopes for an early return to civilian rule. A conference at Lagos agreed on a loose fourfold federal structure, but it coincided with a counter-massacre of Ibos in the north and the flight of the survivors back to the eastern region.

After the first coup in 1966 Lieutenant-Colonel Odumegwu Ojukwu had been appointed military governor of the eastern region. He concluded that the salvation of the Ibos could only be secured by secession and in May 1967 he proclaimed the independent state of Biafra and war began. Attempts at mediation by the OAU (at Kinshasa in 1967, Algiers in 1968 and Addis Ababa in 1969) all broke down. The federal army, expanded from 10,000 to over 200,000 men, gradually prevailed in spite of tough Biafran resistance. While Britain and the USSR supplied arms to the federal government, France supplied Biafra and two of France's closest African associates, Ivory Coast and Gabon, recognized the secessionist state – as too did Zambia and Tanzania. The suffering in Biafra, overcrowded and virtually besieged, was appalling and widely reported throughout the world. By January 1970 it had become decisive. In that month Biafra was forced to capitulate and, as such, ceased to exist. Gowon proved a statesmanlike victor. He preached reconciliation and practised it. Nigeria's economic growth was resumed at a great pace. It became one of the world's largest producers and exporters of oil, besides being rich in coal, tin and other minerals, and in agriculture. But the government was none the less overspending its revenues and internal problems were not washed away by this wealth. The rich got richer and the poor mostly stayed poor or, with inflation, got poorer. The huge army and a large police force of 30,000 became notorious for corruption, as did the more affluent sectors of civilian life. There were strikes and unemployment. The constitutional problem was unsolved. After the civil war the country was divided into 12 states (later increased to 19) but Gowon incautiously indicated that there might be more, on an ethnic basis which, if seriously applied, could produce up to 300–400 states. The census of 1973 returned a total population of 79.76 million, a growth of 43.5 per cent since 1963 and an average annual increase double that of the fastest growing populations in the world. Nobody believed the figures although some people in some areas liked them. The fact that increases varied suspiciously from state to state forced Gowon to say that they would not be used as a basis for any political decisions. By 1974 it was announced, to the relief of many Nigerians, that the return to civilian rule promised for 1976 would be postponed. Gowon's too evident inability to grasp the nettle of corruption led to his displacement in 1975 while he was out of the country. He was allowed to go with his family to England. His successors Generals Murtala Muhammad (assassinated after a few months) and Olusegun Obasanjo were more vigorous in their attacks on corruption and other problems. The latter, who refrained from styling himself president, promised to restore civilian rule in 1979 and after prolonged constitutional debate which produced the bulkiest constitution in the world Alhaji Shehu Shagari became president of a new federation of 19 states.

Nigeria was a giant among African states in more than size. It had wealth. Like Zaïre and South Africa, it had the potential to become the economic powerhouse of a vast region by allying its resources with foreign capital and expertise. It was among the first half-dozen oil producers in the world and had a GNP at the end of the 1970s of about $35 billion ($460 per head) and a growth rate of 6–7 per cent a year. At its peak in 1974–76 oil production exceeded 2 million barrels a day. But this bonanza engendered an orgy of activity which got out of control. Nigerian oil, exceptionally expensive to produce, happened to come into world markets in large quantities in the same period as Alaskan and North Sea oil, with the result that demand slackened, the price had to be cut and production held back to 1.5 million barrels: the balance of payments, which had shown a surplus of over 4 million naira in 1974, went suddenly into the red in 1977, reserves fell by two-thirds and inflation rose to 40 per cent a year. But Nigeria's credit remained high and it was able to borrow large sums to put it back on to sounder courses. Its basic problem was not how to balance its books but how to apply its enviable revenues. It was at this stage an immensely wealthy country whose inhabitants nevertheless saw nothing of this wealth but continued to live in a colonial, mainly agricultural society which was using no more than half its cultivable land and, as a result of neglect, inefficiency and incompetent investment, was importing food. The country was also frighteningly lawless and blatantly corrupt; its ethnic divisions and mistrusts had not evaporated; its army (although reduced from 230,000 to about half that number in 1980) was an expensive and unsettling legacy of civil war. But it was a measure of the new civilian government's resources and optimism that it felt able to produce a five-year plan for 1981–85 which aimed to make Nigeria self-sufficient in food and manufactured goods by the end of that period.

Both the outgoing military regime and its civilian successor intended Nigeria to play a positive part in African affairs, perhaps in world affairs too. It forced its way on to the Security Council in 1976 against the candidature of a fellow African state (and neighbour) nominated by the OAU. It put a lot of energy and money into the 1976 Festival of African Arts in Lagos, a prestige jamboree which partially rebounded because of organizational chaos and scandals about overspending. It so dominated the Economic Community of West African States (ECOWAS) that this organization would have been boneless without Nigeria. Lagos became a necessary port of call for British, American and other politicians trying to resolve the Rhodesian crisis. As a member of the OAU, the Commonwealth and OPEC, as well as the UN, Nigeria was active in a unique sample of international organizations.

On the last day of 1983 the army returned to power. Major-General Muhammad Buhari became head of state in place of Shagari. There were many reasons for an upheaval which displeased few Nigerians: blatantly rigged elections in the previous year; even more blatant corruption; soaring food prices; an economy no longer buoyed up by oil, whose price had been cut by 10 per cent and production by nearly 25 per cent; interminable constitutional wrangles; religious disorders in the north, notably in

Kano where thousands were killed in suppressing riots by the Muslim Maitatsine at the end of 1980 and again in Borno and Gongola states in 1982 and 1984 respectively. The new government was akin to its predecessor, conservative and pledged to produce prosperity without corruption. For some, including junior officers waiting their turn and Muslims of a puritan turn of mind, it was too like the Shagari regime with too many of the same businessmen and chiefs in the seats of federal and provincial power. It was threatened within a few months by rumours of fresh coups, which were suspected by some of being fabricated in order to enable the government to forestall action from within the army's middle ranks, dissatisfied by dilatory measures against profiteers. When the government did take action it bungled. The most notorious of the alleged profiteers, Umaru Dicko, had taken refuge in London, where he was kidnapped by three Israelis and a Nigerian with ill-concealed Nigerian government involvement and more than a little suspicion of official Israeli participation: this coup was foiled when British police extracted Dicko from a packing case in which he was about to be flown to Nigeria.

The Buhari government was an all-round failure. It denounced corruption without abating it, savaged criminals without reducing crime, intensified economic austerity without any countervailing benefits and forwent aid from the IMF (to bolster its foreign creditworthiness) by refusing to devalue the naira. It irritated its partners in OPEC when it cut its oil prices without giving OPEC notice in advance: oil revenues had sunk to half their 1980 value and the Buhari government was nervously aware of the part played by oil in the decline and destruction of the Shagari government. Within two years (in 1985) Buhari was evicted by one of the principal members of his gov erning council, General Ibrahim Babangida, a recurrent figure in Nigeria's political crises but one who had hitherto avoided the first place and its responsibilities (1985).

Babangida's main tasks were to rescue the economy, restore civilian rule within a reasonable time and prevent Nigeria's regional conflicts from turning into a religious war between north and south, Muslims and Christians. Nigeria's economic problems arose not from lack of resources but from its over-optimistic use of a single source of wealth (oil) whose value had suddenly plummeted for reasons outside Nigeria's control. The collapse of the oil boom stunned Nigeria the more forcibly because it had been riding so high on the crest of the wave that was now spent. With the end of the boom the naira was floated and quickly lost 70 per cent of its value. Inflation, wage freezes and penal interest rates hit both the poor and the flocks of *nouveaux riches* born of the boom. Average income per head dropped in five years from over $1,000 to $250. Babangida needed to restore confidence within Nigeria and to recapture international confidence and funds, but his attempts to do so evoked strong criticism from those – including Obasanjo – who inveighed against an economic policy which made the poor poorer and gamblers richer without reversing industrial recession. As a prelude to the restoration of civilian rule a constituent assembly was elected in 1987 with, however, limited competence: it was precluded from considering the federal principle, the two-party system, the ban of former politicians, or religion. Babangida's confidence in himself was shown by two striking acts in 1989. When an electoral commission approved six political parties from which the government would select two, Babangida rejected all six and licensed two others of his own devising. Secondly, he intervened in the succession in the sultanate of Sokoto. The death in 1988 of the aged sultan provoked a politico-religious tangle which developed into an issue in relations between the sultanate and the federal government. A son of the deceased sultan was proclaimed sultan in his father's place but the government interposed a veto and appointed instead an eminent Muslim, Ibrahim Dasuki, a direct descendant by a junior line of Usman dan Fodio. No less disturbing than these economic constitutional and religious problems was demography. The population was projected to reach 250 million by 2020 in the absence of birth control, of which there was only the most modest prospect. This was a problem widespread in Africa but peculiarly alarming in Nigeria, which would, on existing trends, become one of the most crowded countries in the world and drastically short of food, schools, hospitals and other crucial services.

Babangida ruled by corruption, oppression and deceit. He repeatedly promised and postponed a return to civilian rule. In 1991 he cancelled a presidential election for the third time but later in the year elections were unexpectedly held for governorships and assemblies in the several states, which now numbered 29: the newly licensed Social Democratic Party won majorities in 16 of the assemblies and the National Republican Convention the largest number of governorships. Demands for Babangida's resignation multiplied as a comprehensive breakdown of law and order loomed with riots in Lagos and other cities (chiefly against price rises) and looting and religious clashes in the north and north-east. Babangida's term of office was extended to August 1993 but powerful personalities inside Nigeria and its principal foreign creditors – the United States, Japan, Germany – were no longer concealing their opinion that he ought to go. The foreign debt had reached $30 billion, corruption was blatant, Nigeria was becoming a major international drugs entrepôt and its very existence as a single state was once more being questioned. A presidential election in 1993 was cancelled when it appeared that the winner would be Chief Moshood Abiola, millionaire Yoruba leader of the Social Democratic Party (SDP). Abiola fled to England and was imprisoned when he returned. Babangida's plans for a fresh election were rejected by the SDP. The SDP and National Republican Party (NRC) offered to join an interim government with the military but their offer was rejected by Babangida. Apprehensions among senior officers caused splits, as a result of which Babangida was discarded and replaced by his deputy General Sani Abacha, with Ernest Shonekan as a figurehead who resigned after a few months. In 1994 Abacha, a deranged tyrant, sanctioned a Nigerian occupation of the Bakassi peninsula in Cameroun, which commanded the approaches to the Calabar and Cross rivers, areas rich in oil; he supported anti-democratic forces in Benin, Gambia and Niger and plunged into the civil war in Sierra Leone. Notions of Nigeria as a stabilizing force and economic dynamo in West Africa vanished as it accelerated towards disintegration, religious discord and terror. The execution in 1995 of the writer and political activist Ken Saro-Wiwa with eight other protesters from the oil-bearing Igoni lands after a blatantly unsatisfactory trial and on the eve of a Commonwealth conference evoked worldwide condemnation but no effective action. Nigeria's membership of the Commonwealth was suspended (that is to say, not cancelled) and the United States and other purchasers of Nigerian oil refrained from depriving themselves of it by any international ban.

Abacha promised to restore civilian rule by October 1998 and prepared for it by perfecting a novel form of multiparty democracy: five parties, all of which nominated the same individual – himself – for a civilianized presidency. But suddenly he died. Adventitiously, Abiola died too after years of solitary confinement and ill-treatment of uncertain brutality. Abacha's successor was his second-in-command Abdulsalam Abubakr, a northern Muslim like most of the officer corps. His elevation did not have the approval of all his fellow generals, who were divided over a transfer of power to civilians but elections were held in 1999 and ex-General Obasanjo became civilian president. The elections were certainly rigged but probably unnecessarily so. Obasanjo, a Yoruba, had strong support, not only from senior officers, but also in northern and eastern regions – not, however, in the Yoruba west, where the Alliance for Democracy made a clean sweep (but failed everywhere else). Nigeria was by this time the world's pre-eminent example of a riches-to-rags story, as divided as ever by race and religion, ravaged by outrageous corruption and by overdependence on the wayward price of its oil. Obasanjo won a further term in 2002 but could not bring stability to the north where Muslims and Christians fought from time to time or to the south where nearly half the population of the Delta region died in violent disorders.

A quarter of a century of political instability, economic disaster and misrule left West Africa with the independence which it had won from the colonial powers but few of the anticipated fruits of independence. Spirits were low, expectations reduced, disappointment bitter, tempers frayed. A number of the states of West Africa hoped to alleviate their economic plight through federal associations. Sixteen of them created in 1975 the Economic Community of West African States, a halfway house between national sovereignties and the pan-African OAU. The first aims were to increase trade among the members and to fund co-operative developments in agriculture, communications and education, with further economic co-operation to follow, but ECOWAS, initially fearful of Nigeria's economic dominance, became rather a tool of Nigerian political designs through its involvement in Liberia and Sierra Leone. Nigeria's affluence gave the members hope but Nigeria's power gave them pause, more especially the francophone members, six of which created a community within a community: CEAO – Communauté de l'Afrique de l'Ouest. (CEAO had counterparts in Central Africa in CEEAC – Communauté Economique des Etats de l'Afrique Centrale – and UDEAC – Union Douanière et Economique de l'Afrique Centrale – whose names sufficiently indicated their ambitions. All six members of the latter belonged to the former, whose ten members included English and Portuguese states as well as French speakers.) In 1948 France had instituted a franc zone by undertaking to buy local currencies at the fixed rate of 50 CFA francs for one French franc, an increasingly expensive way of securing political influence and an increasingly disruptive arrangement as the several currencies diverged from one another. The French franc became extravagantly undervalued, labour became more and more expensive, French investment was diverted to anglophone countries where real rates of exchange prevailed, and a busy trade grew up in smuggling goods to francophone countries in return for local currencies convertible into French francs at the fixed rate, which remained unchanged for nearly half a century. In 1994 the French government of Edouard Balladur devalued the CFA franc by half in terms of the French franc (and the associated Comoro franc by one-third). The aims and hopes of this devaluation were increased investment and liquidity and – a necessary precondition – a change of mood among creditors, who might be induced to write off part of their debts. Some debt was written off but creditors already committed to cancelling the debts of the former Soviet satellites in Europe were reluctant to tackle African problems with equal vigour. Inflation running at 30–40 per cent in most of the zone was halted and then reduced to around 10 per cent. Overall growth in West African states at 4–5 per cent was stronger than the negligible rates in Central Africa, where growth depended too greatly on mere optimism. Domestic liquidity rose, mainly through repatriation of capital which had fled abroad, but the money remained in banks instead of being invested, partly because would-be borrowers recoiled from the rates of interest demanded by the banks and partly because the banks distrusted the applicants.

The members of both ECOWAS and CEAO also concluded defence agreements: ECOWAS in 1981, Mali, Guinea-Bissau and Cape Verde abstaining; CEAO by stages from 1977, Togo joining the original six. The signatories of CEAO's defence pact were divided between some who regarded it as a first step to getting rid of French troops from West Africa and others who were far from ready to approve such a step. These defence arrangements were of much less consequence than economic agreements. The economic agreements were, on the other hand, hampered by the inescapably worldwide nature of the problems which they addressed.

West Africa's political problems were largely home-grown and blamed on the new rulers. The colonial past bore some responsibility, but a receding one. Colonialism had by its very nature destroyed the ruling class and its institutions. Even where the colonial rulers practised indirect rule and so made use of the indigenous system, this system and its protagonists were downgraded. Moreover, the new nationalists who led the successful campaigns for independence – unlike the leaders of the National Congress in India, which had been founded in the nineteenth century – had minimal experience of government and precarious authority. Their authority was personal. It derived from charisma or rank, so that the choice for the people, so far as they had a choice, lay between the demagogue and the general. Some were good and some were bad, but all lacked systematic political backing and they were obliged, therefore, to rely on their wits or their swords. The natural outcome was either an entrenched tyranny or constant shifts. In West Africa there was more instability than tyranny. Freedoms were curtailed or abused on the plea that the autocrat or the one-party state would be more efficient, but such regimes failed to deliver the goods.

West Africa – and in this respect its lot was repeated through most of sub-Saharan Africa – saw a modest economic advance in the 1960s, checked in the 1970s and reversed in the 1980s. In the course of the twentieth century Africa's population was multiplied by nearly ten (from 100 million to an expected 1 billion or not much less) and it moved into cities. Migrants became refugees. The demand for food created by the first of these trends was magnified by the second, as the migrants became non-producing consumers of food. The countryside became denuded, the cities insanitary and dangerous. The food deficit was further aggravated by the post-independence view that the road to prosperity was industrialization. The application of this nostrum created more debt than success, increased Africa's manufacturing output only marginally (it remained about 1 per cent of world output), exposed the lack of adequate managers and fanned the corruption inherent in a chase after contracts. Aid was misused and often the misuse was encouraged by ignorant or greedy donors. Industrial and commercial failures were visited on other sectors: roads, schools and universities decayed and health deteriorated. Only half the children went to school; half the teachers were unqualified. Corruption in business was barely severable from corruption in government, which extended to bullying the judiciary and the press. Wars, drought, famine and adverse terms of trade in a world governed by the wealthier countries made matters worse. Some states were woefully small (nine had fewer than 1 million inhabitants at independence) and some were unmanageably big. Nearly all were multilingual, multi-ethnic, multireligious, multicultural – not the unities which they seemed to be on the map or which outsiders took them to be. Their boundaries, at first decreed sacrosanct, gradually ceased to be so. Foreigners turned their backs on investment in Africa and ignored its tourist attractions. Yet much of the continent possessed excellent agricultural land, valuable minerals and plentiful sources of energy. The economic balance sheet was not wholly negative but the remedies for centuries in an economic backwater, followed by decades of bad policies and bad government, required harsh sacrifices which must fall mainly on the numerous poor, making them not only poorer but also ill-disposed to trust their governments. The IMF's recipe for salvation was two-edged. On the one hand international institutions provided funds but on the other they required devaluation of currencies, liberalization of trade and increases in productivity which more often than not could be achieved only by sacking people, raising prices and cutting services. This was medicine which cured the community by killing its members. Plans to offset the painful side effects were, again more often than not, either feeble or sidestepped. The World Bank, in a review in 1989 of the well-known ills of poor agricultural performances, industrial decline and excessive debt, noted their political as well as their economic sources – the precariousness of the rule of law, the absence of a free press. The World Bank and the IMF had previously tied aid to economic plans and economic performance, setting terms which spelt severe hardship or worse for small business and individuals. These institutions, by identifying good government as a central economic requirement, tried in addition to promote or reward good government.

The instability of the African state, and therewith its disappointing performance, were due to more than the shortcomings of its leading personalities. The post-independence population explosion negated economic growth and powered poverty, corruption and crime in swollen cities. It shifted the balance between town and countryside at a rate which cities could not handle. It contributed to failures amounting often to collapse, in education at all levels, health services and standards, transport and other public services. Ill-conceived and ill-managed economic policies produced crippling external debts out of all accepted proportion to GDP or export revenues. But beside these handicaps the state itself lacked the essential attributes of a state: definition and authority. In 1964 the OAU resolved to sanctify the borders delineated by and inherited from the colonial powers in order to avoid disputes likely to lead to war, but this sanctification was also petrification and most African states harboured in consequence ethnic conflicts within themselves or ethnic minorities with kin across the border: they were arenas, not agoras. Political groups or parties tended to be factional rather than national, armies alone being more nearly national. The multiplication of political parties in the name of democracy tended to produce quinquennial crises and to institutionalize ethnic conflicts to the advantage of an aggressively dominant group determined to monopolize power. In the last quarter of the century regional wars, endemic and violent conflicts within states and ever-increasing debt were destroying societies and their future. The most telling figures were the reduction of resources allotted to education from 10–12 to 3–4 per cent of government spending, as – in the worst cases – states dissolved into open territories for rival bands taking turns to loot.

Africa in the second half of the twentieth century was notable above all for the decolonization which trebled the number of independent states in the world. The Cold War affected these new states through the interplay of the superpowers, but they themselves had no more than a marginal role in that conflict. They had, however, a more subtle role in international affairs. They owed their independence to the almost universal view that they ought to have it but they were forced to realize that they remained dependent in crucial ways – the prevailing of economics over political theory and popular will. Correspondingly, the stronger of the world's states were brought to use their power not to occupy or physically belabour weaker states but in order to require by economic armlock standards of domestic behaviour in return for economic aid – blending moral purpose with brute force in defiance of the doctrine of the immunity of the state from foreign interference. The proliferation of states (mainly in Africa) modified theory and practice regarding the nature and privileges of the state which, developed in Europe, was exported to other continents in a period when that framework was ceasing to be axiomatic.

CHAPTER 23

Central Africa

Congo–Zaire–Congo

West Africa became independent without anything that could be called an international crisis. East Africa was to follow suit in the next few years. But the independence of the Belgian Congo produced not only internal chaos and civil war but also a serious international crisis. African states were divided among themselves, and the United Nations was called upon to play expected and unexpected roles in the course of which it was attacked by some of its principal members and its secretary-general was killed. The sources of this catastrophe were, first, the hurriedness with which the Belgians took their departure from a colony which they had hardly at all prepared for independence; secondly, the very great size of the Congo and its ethnic and tribal diversity; thirdly, the revolt immediately after independence of the Force Publique or army, whose mutinous conduct left the new central government powerless; next, the attempt to detach the rich southern province of Katanga and make it a separate state; and finally, the fact that the United Nations was required to perform a multiplicity of barely consistent tasks and was hampered in them by the inadequacies of its own machinery and by the hostility and independent actions of certain governments, notably the Russian and the British.

The Belgian Congo was a territory of over 2.5 million sq. km inhabited by many different peoples, some of which constituted tribal federations: the Bakongo in the west, including the capital of Leopoldville, and also in the neighbouring territories of Angola and Congo-Brazzaville; the Baluba in southern Kasai and northern Katanga; and the Balunda in southern Katanga. In spite of its great size the Congo touched the ocean only at the end of a corridor between Congo-Brazzaville and Angola. Its modern history began with the ventures of explorers along the Congo river. It became famous as a result of H. M. Stanley's expedition in 1874 and was at once an object of international competition among the principal European powers. Britain, already well endowed and busy elsewhere, did not enter the lists on its own account but pushed the claims of its old friend, Portugal. France and the three-year-old German empire were not so altruistic and in 1876 an international conference reached a temporary compromise by creating the International African Association, which was to act as a sort of composite cultural mission to enlighten the darkest heart of Africa and find out what was there. This conference met, not by accident, in Brussels, convened by the Belgian king Leopold II.

The International African Association did not eliminate the ambitions of the European powers, and in the early 1880s there was widespread fear of war as a result of their jealousies in West African from the Niger down to the Congo. In 1884 a conference in Berlin, engineered and presided over by Bismarck, sorted things out on the basis that there was enough for everybody and no need to fight: Europeans would do best to recognize one another's possessions and tacitly sanction in advance further acquisitions of anything not yet under a European flag. The Congo was handed over to the Congo International Association, which was the International African Association under a new name, and, in effect, Leopold II in person. The king thus became the largest private estate owner in the world, although he did not yet know how rich his property was. His obligations were to extirpate the slave trade, permit free trade and secure free passage for all on the Congo river. He defaulted in his first obligation until an outcry in Britain and elsewhere compelled him to abolish the trade – and to resort to forced labour instead. His administration of his estate became one of the most notorious scandals since Cicero's denunciation of the proconsulship of Verres, and in 1908 the Congo was transferred from Leopold to the Belgian state, which despatched a governor-general to rule with the help of a Belgian civil service. The interests of Africans were to have priority over the exploitation of the domain, but this principle was not in practice found to involve any advancement for Africans or any but the most rudimentary mingling of the races.

Shortly before the First World War the mining of copper in Katanga began and brought with it two potent changes. Katanga gradually became twice as rich as the whole of the rest of the Congo; should the Congo ever become independent the Katangans would be in a position to demand first place in the state or to leave it and set up on their own. The second change was the transformation of the territory into a booming partnership between the administration, Belgian finance houses and the Roman Catholic Church. And so it remained for nearly half a century. Some attention was paid to the economic well-being of the Africans but no political activity was tolerated and education above the elementary level was reserved for few. In so far as Belgians thought about the future they imagined a slow advance by Africans to a level at which a new form of association might have to be devised, but a transfer of power to Africans did not enter into their calculations and no steps were taken to train even an elite.

This view began to be questioned in the 1950s. Missionaries became alive to the pressures of nationalism and uneasy about the assumptions on which the territory was being ruled. In Brussels, where a left-wing coalition came to power in 1954, the liberation of French and British territories could not be ignored; de Gaulle's offer of autonomy for France's colonies was made at Brazzaville just across the river from Leopoldville. African leaders, some of whom met one another for the first time at the

Brussels Fair of 1958, began to espouse independence and many of them attended the Pan-African Conference of the same year in Accra, where they received encouragement from fellow Africans and were reinforced in their determination not to get left behind. A few days after the end of the Accra conference there were riots in Leopoldville.

The recently appointed governor-general Maurice van Hemelrijk believed that acceleration was the only sensible policy. He advocated a parliament for the Congo by the end of 1960 and independence in 1963 (reduced, by the end of 1959, to independence in 1960), but he was forced by conservative protests in Belgium to resign in September 1959. His successor Auguste de Schryver found he had to go even faster. Tribal fighting began before the end of the year and in January 1960 the Belgians assembled in Brussels a conference at which, to their surprise, the Africans unitedly asked for immediate independence. The Belgians agreed to leave the Congo at the end of June. Never had so much been conceded so quickly. The frontiers of the new state were to be the same as those of the colony, and when Sir Roy Welensky suggested that Katanga should leave the Congo and join the Rhodesian federation, the Belgian government was much displeased. The internal structure of the new state was, however, left undecided, while the distribution of top posts was also unsettled pending elections, which were held in May. The Belgians made some attempt to remedy their sins of omission by running a crash training programme for Africans in Brussels and by enlisting Ghanaian help in the training of more Africans in the Congo.

The most prominent of the Congolese politicians, and the favourite of the Belgians, was Patrice Lumumba, one of the founders in 1958 of the Mouvement National Congolais which was the Congo's main non-tribal party. Lumumba and his principal associates, Cyrille Adoula and Joseph Ileo, demanded the Africanization of public services and professions with a view to ultimate independence. At the Accra conference Lumumba struck up a friendship with Nkrumah and, although he became more extreme in his demands during 1959 and was eventually imprisoned, he retained his good standing with the Belgians until the eve of independence. He wanted a strong centre rather than a diffuse federation, in contradistinction to his opponents, who were essentially the modern equivalents of tribal and local chieftains: Joseph Kasavubu, the more sedate and aristocratic leader of Abako, which was founded in 1950 among the Bakongo with the aim of restoring the old Kongo empire but which became converted to the idea of a Congo state provided it was a federal one; Moise Tshombe, the rich middle-class *évolué* and leader of Conakat, through which the Balunda aimed to exercise power in Katanga either within a federal Congo or independently; and Jason Sendwe, whose Balubakat eyed the Balunda to the south with considerable suspicion and prevented Conakat from speaking for the whole of Katanga. Lumumba's tendency to quarrel with other leaders in his own party, and a change of attitude in Brussels, led to attempts to create an anti-Lumumba front, but the attempts failed, Lumumba's party emerged from the elections as the biggest and Lumumba was installed as prime minister of a broad coalition government with Kasavubu as president.

Independence was proclaimed on 30 June 1960 and the official celebrations lasted four days. Forty-eight hours later occurred the first mutinies in the Force Publique. The soldiers expected that independence would instantly improve their pay and open their way to the officer grades, which were entirely filled by white men. When nothing happened they decided to replace their officers. This indiscipline was accompanied by some violence and rapes, much multiplied in the telling. An African sergeant Victor Lundula was appointed commander-in-chief and the situation seemed to have been brought under control in a couple of days but fresh mutinies and more serious violence quickly followed. There was, however, no killing until after Tshombe's proclamation of the independence of Katanga on 11 July.

The mutiny of the Congolese army was the main source of all the Congo's woes. It deprived the Congolese government of power and authority. It caused a panic among Europeans, and the Belgians announced that, with or without Congolese consent, they would return to protect their nationals. The immediate consequence of Tshombe's unilateral act of secession was to infuriate Lumumba, who became suspicious of a Katangan–Belgian plot to subvert the independence of the new state and detach its richest province. Subsequent events strengthened his suspicions. Although he remained for a time willing to discuss with the Belgians the maintenance of law and order, he was not willing to do what Tshombe had done and ask for their help in suppressing the mutinies. Since there was no other force immediately available to him, this rift between Lumumba and the Belgians enabled the mutinies to spread and take hold. At the same time the rift between Lumumba and Tshombe made Lumumba more anxious to maintain than to disarm the Congolese army, with the result that when UN forces arrived to restore order Lumumba dissuaded them from taking the essential step of disarming the mutinous units.

These were not the only consequences. The Belgians, who occupied Leopoldville with parachute troops on 11 July, in effect abrogated their recently signed treaty of friendship with the Congo and switched to Tshombe, whom they provided with a Belgian armed force and commander-in-chief. They thereby annulled not only the Belgian–Congolese association but also the unity of the Congo. This unity was already precarious and the attempts to re-establish it form one of the two principal strands in the complex story of the next three years. The other strand was the conflict over the powers and duties of the UN forces which began to arrive in Leopoldville on 14 July to restore order and displace the Belgians – but without agreement on whether the restoration of law and order included the subjection of Katanga to the authority of the central government.

Lumumba and Kasavubu began by working in harmony, but in September they broke with each other and Kasavubu dismissed Lumumba and appointed a new government. The parliament supported Lumumba, who maintained, with some justice, that the president's action was illegal. In the ensuing crisis Hammarskjöld's representative in Leopoldville Andrew Cordier closed airports and radio, thereby giving an advantage to Kasavubu by denying to the more popular Lumumba the opportunity to state his case in different parts of the country or make his voice heard on the air. This action was bitterly resented within the Congo and beyond and led to fierce Congolese attacks on the UN with Russian support. Lumumba remained in Leopoldville in his official residence. Cordier's successor Rayeshwar Dayal refused to assist him, and he became, in effect, the protégé of the UN (which was now attacked for being pro-Lumumba) until he fled from Leopoldville at the end of November, hoping to reach Stanleyville by car. He was overtaken with the help of aircraft and was lodged in jail in Thysville, whence he fled to the Katangan capital of Elisabethville on 17 January, only to be captured again and murdered.

Shortly after the Lumumba–Kasavubu rift in September Colonel Joseph Mobutu, the chief of staff of the army (the commander-in-chief Victor Lundula was not in the capital) began his rise to the power which, with the help of the CIA, he was to turn into a despotic and avaricious dictatorship between 1965 and 1997. He ejected both the parliament and the Russian and Czech embassies and, when attempts to recon-cile Lumumba and Kasavubu failed, declared for Kasavubu, who acquiesced in the colonel's usurpation. Mobutu introduced a new constitution and some degree of order and efficiency, but although supported by the west, he failed to establish the sort of military regime which other soldiers were successfully establishing in Asian and Arab states at this time. The provinces did not respond; the resources available to him – communications, trained personnel – were totally inadequate; the army was divided, with General Lundula and the forces in Orientale province remaining pro-Lumumba, as did many politicians and, so far as was ascertainable, the popular favour.

In February 1961 it was apparent that the Mobutu–Kasavubu team had failed and a new government was appointed under Ileo. It lasted six months until August, when Ileo was succeeded by Adoula, who remained prime minister until 1964. During this period the Lumumbists, led by Antoine Gizenga in Stanleyville, and the Katangans, led by Tshombe and Godefroid Munongo in Elisabethville, were separate and often separ-atist factors in the situation. Various attempts were made to bring all three sections together but hopeful moves in the direction of Stanleyville usually caused Elisabethville to shy away, and vice versa.

The Stanleyville secession was never formalized in the same way as the Katangan. It developed after the break between Lumumba and Kasavubu and gathered strength after the murder of Lumumba, when the Russians seemed to be on the verge of recog-nizing the Stanleyville party as the government of the Congo and of supplying it with arms. But if the Russians expected to secure a foothold in Africa by exploiting the emo-tions roused by Lumumba's death, they miscalculated; their faces were as white as any Belgian's, their intervention was in principle as unwelcome, and instead of pleasing they shocked Africans by the ruthlessness with which, upon their arrival in Orientale, they proposed to set about the anti-Lumumbists. They were seen off by a small party of UN troops. Gizenga meanwhile equivocated over his relations with Ileo, watching the state of Ileo's relations with Tshombe, but when he was appointed deputy prime minister to Adoula he accepted the post on the understanding that Adoula would use force to put an end to the Katangan secession. He accompanied Adoula to the conference of non-aligned nations in Belgrade in September 1961. The failure of the operations against Katanga, about to be related, revived his suspicions and he returned to his own base in Stanleyville, thereby recreating the tripartite pattern. Attempts to induce him to return to the capital having failed, he was brought there under arrest in January 1962, lodged in jail and expelled from the government.

The Katangan secession was a formal, if illegal, state of affairs with a precise beginning and a precise end. It was proclaimed by Tshombe on 11 July 1960 and renounced by him on 21 December 1961. Its inception thus coincided with the mutiny of the Force Publique and Belgian intervention, and it was accompanied by an appeal to Belgium and a refusal to allow Kasavubu and Lumumba, the federal president and prime minister, to go to Elisabethville. As a result of these moves Katanga was for the time being protected from the chaos developing in other areas, and while the UN was trying to re-establish order in Leopoldville province the Belgians did so in Katanga. They also provided Tshombe, at his request, with administrative services and ran the mines and paid royalties to Tshombe instead of to the central government. These payments were a direct breach of the pre-independence agreement (the *loi fondamentale*) which had been signed by the Belgian government and accepted by, among others, Tshombe; but they enabled Tshombe to enlist and pay an army of foreigners with which to oppose his Congolese adversaries and, if need be, the UN.

The UN came to the Congo in response to three appeals by Kasavubu and Lumumba on 10, 12 and 13 July 1960. They appealed first for technical aid, including aid in the organization and equipment of security forces. In their second and third messages they appealed for help against Belgian aggression. Hammarskjöld, taking the initiative under article 99 of the Charter, asked the Security Council to consider technical aid for the Congo and the problem of law and order. The Council authorized the despatch of military aid to the Congolese government with the proviso that force should not be used by UN troops except in self-defence. The council was divided on whether to require the Belgians to withdraw, Britain, France and China abstaining from the vote. Hammarskjöld asked African states north of the Congo for military and other help, an appeal later extended to certain European and Asian members. The first troops reached the Congo on 14 July and four days later a force of 4,000 had been assembled. The air lift was provided by the United States, Britain and the Soviet Union. Differences of opinion about the functions of the UN troops arose at once. General Alexander, in command of the Ghanaian contingent, began disarming the mutineers of the Force Publique. Had he been allowed to continue to do so, all might have been very different, but Lumumba insisted on stopping the process, partly because he was suspicious of outside interference and partly because he wanted to use the Force Publique against Katanga.

The Security Council met again on 20 July and resolved unanimously that the Belgians should withdraw and that other states should refrain from aggravating the situation; it confirmed the authority already given to Hammarskjöld and commended what he had done. The Belgians began to withdraw on the 20th and by the 23rd they had left the Congo again – except Katanga. Ghana and Guinea then threatened to withdraw their troops from the UN force and place them at the disposal of the Leopoldville government in order to help evict the Belgians from Katanga and force the province to accept the authority of the Kasavubu–Lumumba regime. Consequently, the UN had to consider most urgently whether its own force was entitled to enter Katanga to achieve these objects and, if not, whether it should now be empowered by new resolutions to do so. Hoping to bypass this difficulty, Hammarskjöld flew to Brussels and the Congo to secure the entry of UN units by negotiation and announced on 2 August that a first contingent would do so in three days' time. But the Katanga authorities said they would resist and Ralph Bunche, despatched to Elisabethville to discover if they really would, advised postponing the move. Rather than use force, and uncertain whether he was empowered to in these circumstances, Hammarskjöld returned to New York to seek further instructions from the Security Council. This check was accounted a victory by the Katangans. It further infuriated Lumumba, who decided that the UN had let him down and that he should seek African support for a campaign against Katanga.

The Security Council's next meeting took place on 8 and 9 August and (France and Italy abstaining) repeated the injunction to the Belgians to leave immediately, authorized the entry of UN forces into Katanga and reiterated that these forces were not to be used to influence the internal conflict. The last part of the resolution was but doubtfully consistent with the second, since the essence of the conflict was the authority of Leopoldville over Elisabethville, and the entry of UN troops into Katanga, even if designed only to compel the departure of the Belgians, could not fail to have an effect on the balance of domestic Congolese forces which were in conflict. Hammarskjöld returned to the Congo and to his policy of getting UN forces into Katanga bloodlessly. He entered Katanga with a token force but refused to take a representative of Lumumba with him, thus further antagonizing Lumumba, who became convinced that the secretary-general was embroiled in a plot against him. For his part, Hammarskjöld became convinced that Lumumba's main aim was to get rid of the UN presence. Tshombe, meanwhile, used the breathing space afforded by these quarrels to consolidate his position. A fourth meeting of the Security Council on 21 August produced an ominous sign when a resolution of strong support for Hammarskjöld was opposed by the Soviet Union and Poland.

Throughout August the situation in the Congo deteriorated, with every prospect of a clash between the Congolese and Katangan armies. A conference of 13 African states in Leopoldville failed to give Lumumba the support he wanted and advised against an attack on Katanga, but Congolese troops were taking matters into their own hands and contrived a massacre of Baluba, who were trying to establish a state of their own. (They had already suffered a massacre by the Balunda since Tshombe could not establish his predominance in Katanga as a whole without this radical alteration of the numerical balance.) At this point Kasavubu's resolve to get rid of Lumumba, whose unpredictability had grown alarmingly and whose reputed pro-communism was embarrassing, gave Tshombe a second breathing space; the projected attack on him was called off, and his Belgian troops took the opportunity to move north and establish a second secessionary state in Kasai under the short-lived presidency of Albert Kalonji. A separate state, backed by the Belgians, had come into existence in the south, while in the north-east the Russians were playing with the idea of another separate state, backed by themselves.

The Congo seemed to be about to break up into three warring units, two of which would be foreign bases. The situation was aggravated upon the opening of the UN General Assembly in September, when Khrushchev arrived in person to attack the secretary-general and two rival Congolese delegations competed with each other for seats in the Assembly and the ears of its members.

This session of the Assembly was notable for the admission of 17 new African members. They refused to support the Russian attack on Hammarskjöld and joined with the western bloc to isolate the communist states. But they did not agree with prevailing western views on the Congo, nor did they remain united among themselves. In Britain, France and the United States the Katangan case, propagated by a lavishly supplied promotion lobby, made many converts in political and business circles on the plea that Katanga was an oasis of peace and sanity in an otherwise barbarous and increasingly communist Congo. This thesis found no accepters among Africans, who unanimously condemned Tshombe and his ways, while being divided on what to do. One group turned against the UN and reverted to Lumumba's plan for a joint African invasion of Katanga. Another group remained attached to the idea of UN action, though dissatisfied with the action apparently contemplated; this group became a pressure group at the UN with the object of persuading the secretary-general and other members that a policy of reducing Katanga by negotiation was hopeless and should be replaced by direct action. A third group of Africans, consisting of recently emancipated French colonies, placed its faith for a time in the Mobutu–Kasavubu alliance and the gradual radiation of law and order from Leopoldville out into all the provinces. The temporary decline of Mobutu, the murder of Lumumba and the installation of Ileo provided a depressing background to events in the last months of 1960 and the beginning of 1961, during which successful attempts were made by Hammarskjöld to get the Russians and the Belgians to stop their independent bolstering of Stanleyville and Elisabethville.

On 21 February 1961 the Security Council explicitly authorized the UN forces to use force in the last resort to prevent a civil war. It did not, however, authorize the use of force against Katanga, or for the removal of the Belgians, or to secure a political solution. This development marked a return to better relations between Hammarskjöld, the independent African states and the west – or at any rate the United States, where

Kennedy had just assumed the presidency – but it alienated not only Tshombe but also the Kasavubu–Ileo government, which suspected the UN of being in western pockets, disliked any increase in its pretensions and now began to draw closer to Tshombe. At a conference at Tananarive in March Tshombe persuaded Ileo to accept a plan for a loose confederation of sovereign Congolese states. No Lumumbist had attended the conference, whose proceedings they regarded as a western ruse to give legitimacy to Tshombe by manipulating the ex-French colonies in his favour. Ileo, however, quickly repented of having moved so far in the direction of Katanga, set about repairing relations with Gizenga and the UN and, at a further conference at Coquilhatville, ordered and effected the arrest of Tshombe.

In July the Congolese parliament assembled at Lovanium, the university town near Leopoldville, in order to patch up a grand coalition. Tshombe was released, Ileo gave way to the honest and respected manager of men, Adoula, and Gizenga joined the government. On the UN side the replacement of Dayal by the Tunisian Mahmud Khiari and the Ghanaian Robert Gardiner helped to improve relations between the government and the UN. But the grand coalition was not achieved. Tshombe was now odd man out.

There followed the military operations against Katanga. By now Katanga was in African terms a formidable power, equipped since the beginning of the year with men, supplies and even aircraft from Belgium, France, South African and Southern Rhodesia. A few specified Belgians had been removed as a result of laborious negotiations, but the UN representatives on the spot were convinced that Tshombe was only playing for time and had no real intention of dismissing his Belgian and other mercenaries or of coming to terms with Leopoldville. These suspicions were reinforced when UN forces seized about 100 foreign officers who had been declared undesirable aliens by the Adoula government. Tshombe acquiesced but the local UN representative Conor Cruise O'Brien agreed that in order to minimize personal affronts the details should be handled by the Belgian consul in Elisabethville, who guaranteed the voluntary departure of the officers but then failed to honour his word. Moreover, other foreign officers not in Elisabethville remained untouched. This attempt to evict some officers was doubly unfortunate for the UN since its failure encouraged Katangan obduracy while its legality was strongly attacked by British representatives in the Congo and New York. Britain became for a while as useful an ally for Katanga as Belgium or France.

In the face of this rebuff the UN had to decide whether to take further steps or to acquiesce. Khiari and O'Brien, believing that Munongo was the real kernel of resistance, hoped to separate Tshombe from Munongo and to get Tshombe to Leopoldville, where Hammarskjöld would come to talk him into a more amenable frame of mind. But Tshombe refused to be enticed and O'Brien, believing that he had Khiari's authority to use force to round up the foreign officers in Katanga and put an end to the Katangan secession, planned a second military operation, which included the virtual kidnapping of Tshombe. It failed. The Katangans were better prepared and the British government, by refusing to allow Ethiopian jet aircraft to fly over Rhodesia to the Congo, presented the Katangans with a decisive advantage. UN forces captured the post office and radio station at Elisabethville, but Tshombe took refuge with the British vice-consul and then in Rhodesia. The UN operation had produced bloodshed which, much exaggerated in the reporting, shocked and antagonized those who thought that a peace force must achieve peace without force, and Tshombe had been let slip. Hammarskjöld arrived in Leopoldville to find an utterly unexpected situation – confusion and stalemate in Katanga, stubborn and effective hostility from Britain and, if in smaller degree, from the Belgian and American governments also. He determined to seek out Tshombe and talk to him. He left for Ndola in Rhodesia by air on 17 September and was killed when his aircraft crashed *en route*.

This appalling calamity – for Hammarskjöld was one of the most outstanding personalities in postwar international affairs – was followed by a ceasefire and the return of Tshombe to Katanga. After the appointment of U Thant to serve the rest of Hammarskjöld's term of office, the Security Council returned to its familiar dilemma: whether to try to reconcile Adoula and Tshombe or to bring the latter to heel. On 24 November the Council, Britain and France abstaining, authorized U Thant to use force to expel foreign mercenaries and political advisers from Katanga, thus implicitly endorsing O'Brien's policy, although he himself was removed from the scene. UN forces were still in Elisabethville but they were awkwardly placed since Tshombe's mercenaries were manifestly keen to provoke a next round of fighting, in which they would surround and destroy the UN forces. The UN representatives in Katanga decided to take action in order to prevent their scattered units from being picked off piecemeal before the arrival of reinforcements, but they were again handicapped by Britain which, having promised to deliver a supply of 100-lb bombs, succumbed to right-wing pressures and cancelled its undertaking. Fighting was inconclusive and when Tshombe agreed to meet Adoula, U Thant ordered a new ceasefire. On 21 December 1961, at Kitona, Tshombe renounced secession. The Kitona agreement was endorsed by the Katangan assembly two months later.

But the troubles of the Congo were not so easily assuaged. During most of 1962 Adoula and Tshombe were engaged in fruitless discussions concerning the implementation of the Kitona agreement, which was opposed in Katanga by Munongo and European secessionists. Tshombe, who interspersed his meetings with Adoula with secret visits to Welensky in Rhodesia, seemed unable to make up his mind. He eventually departed for a prolonged stay in Europe. Although Adoula took three Katangans into his cabinet in 1963 no genuine reconciliation was brought about. The central government continued to be oppressed by problems of economics and law and order, and early in 1964 a more serious revolt broke out in Kwilu under the leadership of Pierre Mulele, who had recently made a trip to China. This outbreak was the more ominous because the UN troops were departing. The last planeload left at the end of June, the fourth anniversary of independence.

The balance sheet of these four years of international endeavour, sometimes co-operative and sometimes competitive, is not easily struck. At the outset the UN, through sticking to the letter of the law, desisted from disarming the mutinous Force Publique, a major source of continuing disorder. There were mistakes and misunderstandings in the handling of relations with the legally appointed, if personally difficult, prime minister Patrice Lumumba, and the resulting suspiciousness affected not only the UN's own standing and operations but also relations among African states and relations between them and other states. In Katanga the UN earned the hostility of certain powers and suffered from the criticism that UN forces had come to secure order but had shed blood in the name of peace. Apart from the fact that all police operations must envisage the use of force as an ultimate sanction, the blame for the ambiguities over Katanga belonged primarily to the members of the Security Council, whose instructions were not sufficiently precise. Further, a joint operation such as the UN operation in the Congo was bound to run into difficulties as soon as there appeared among UN members any serious discrepancy of aim.

The successes of the UN were considerable. It achieved almost immediately its first aim of displacing (except from Katanga) the Belgians who had returned when the Force Publique mutinied. Its intervention prevented intervention by individual states on their own account and enforced in one case, the Russian, a retreat; fears that Africa would become a major Cold War theatre were allayed. The UN succeeded in keeping the Congolese economy going, providing elementary administrative services, and preventing famine and epidemics. It could take credit for staving off civil wars in the Congo which would almost certainly have been worse but for the UN presence and became worse when that presence was removed. Finally, when the UN forces departed in 1964 Katanga had not seceded. But it was still, as it was bound to be, richer than the whole of the rest of the country, economically so dominant that its leaders were in a position either to play a separatist hand or to claim a dominant position in the central government.

The central government's lack of authority became patent immediately after the departure of the UN forces. Civil war started again. The Adoula government was first reconstituted and then replaced by a new administration under Tshombe, who returned from Europe as the UN departed. Tshombe tried to form a broad coalition and to enlist the support of the OAU, but Gizenga (whom, among others, he released from prison) formed a new opposition party and the OAU – in spite of creating a reconciliation commission under Kenyatta's chairmanship – failed to find a remedy for the Congo's ills. Tshombe was too greatly disliked to be able to control the situation except by arms and he began, soon after his return, to enlist a new force of (mainly) Belgian and South African mercenaries. This force was quickly successful and rebels who had taken Stanleyville found themselves threatened with the loss of all their principal strongholds. They had meanwhile taken hostages, and in an attempt to rescue these hostages Belgian parachute troops were flown in American aircraft from the

British island of Ascension to Stanleyville, which was recaptured from the rebels. About 200 hostages were killed in spite of this operation (or, as some maintained, because of it), in addition to some 20,000 Congolese who lost their lives in the furies of this rebellion. Africans outside the Congo were divided between those who took the easy course of denouncing the Belgians, Americans and British as imperialist recidivists and those who, stifling their dislike of Tshombe, defended the right of the Congolese government to ask for outside help if it wanted to. Tshombe, who had already in July been refused an invitation to the OAU's conference of heads of state in Cairo, was kept out of the conference of non-aligned states in the same city in October. Upon his arrival in Cairo he was escorted to a hotel and kept there until he decided to return to Leopoldville.

Both in Leopoldville and Stanleyville Congolese leaders were divided among themselves. Rebel unity did not survive reverses and Kasavubu's appointment of Tshombe as prime minister had not betokened any real reconciliation. Although Tshombe was successful in elections in April 1965, Kasavubu shortly afterwards dismissed him. The president failed, however, to construct a new government without Tshombe and in November the army, in the person of Mobutu, stepped in, dismissed the president and established military rule. With this revolution the army, which alone had had real power since independence, assumed responsibility as well. Mobutu, who had once been a Lumumbist, defeated Mulele's revolt in 1966 and next year survived an attempt, assisted by mercenaries, to restore Tshombe. He reshaped the political map by reducing the number of provinces from 21 to 12 and then to eight, and he reduced the likelihood of secession by nationalizing the assets of the (Belgian) Union Minière. He repaired relations with Belgium, which he visited in 1969, concluded financial and technical agreements and played host to King Baudouin in Kinshasa. Although he had to imprison large numbers in the process, he brought a semblance of peace and some prospect of economic improvement to an exhausted country. In 1970 he became president for seven years. He felt strong enough at home to give his attention to wider African problems, meeting President Ngouabi of Congo-Brazzaville (relations between the two countries began a much-needed improvement) and also Presidents Kaunda and Gowon. He introduced civilians and younger men into senior government posts in place of Adoula, who fell ill, and other senior figures, who were sacked. He consolidated his personal power, renamed the country Zaïre and set about turning it into the Iran of Africa with himself as its shah.

In 1977 the Lunda peoples of Zaïre and neighbouring Angola, organized as the Front de Libération Nationale Congolaise (FLNC), staged a revolt in Shaba (ex-Katanga). The west assumed that Cubans, who were helping to train refugees from Zaïre in Angolan camps, had promoted the revolt but Castro swore that he had, on the contrary, tried to restrain it and there was no evidence to gainsay him. The wealth of the province – cobalt, uranium, diamonds and copper – made it a matter of concern to the outside world and in spite of the embarrassment of going to the aid of a regime as corrupt as Mobutu's had become France transported, largely at Saudi Arabian expense, 1,500 Moroccan troops to stiffen a Zaïrean army which was widely regarded as useless. A year later a second revolt took place. One hundred and thirty Europeans were killed and in order to save further lives 700 French and 1,700 Belgian paratroopers were flown to Zaïre in American aircraft. Having evacuated 2,500 Europeans, they were replaced by a mixed African force recruited from Morocco, Senegal, Ivory Coast, Togo and Gabon. This African intervention was to be coupled with a wider international effort to rescue Zaïre from the bankruptcy into which it had been plunged by the collapse of the world price of copper, the closing of its principal rail outlet (to Benguela in Angola) and Mobutu's malpractices. But aid from the IMF and the EEC was dependent on internal reforms and resident IMF supervision, and since Mobutu postponed the one and cold-shouldered the other, the plans came to nothing. Some sections of the economy prospered but the state piled up huge debts and was shored up by western countries which valued its minerals and superficial stability. Over the three decades in which Mobutu ruled most Zaïreans became progressively worse off and the life of the average Zaïrean ended at 40, while Mobutu himself and his family became prodigiously and ostentatiously rich. For most of this period Mobutu seemed irremovable but by 1990 bazaars and universities were seething and open opposition was flaring up from time to time even in the capital. Serious disorders culminated in a massacre at Lumbumbashi. Mobutu promised constitutional changes but granted none. He espoused a multiparty system, hundreds of parties appeared. He proposed to legitimize three of them, but these were mere manoeuvres. The reality was two governments in the capital, provincial governors who were virtually independent proconsuls, and everywhere lawlessness. By promoting one prime minister after another Mobutu weakened all of them and when the Supreme Council appointed a prime minister (Etienne Tsishekedi, who had been a minister in Kasavubu's time) Mobutu installed another. He kept a subservient parliament in being beyond its proper term. The economy continued to dissolve, prices soared, salaries were unpaid, education, transport and other services collapsed, swindlers flourished openly, great numbers of people lived in fear, parts of the army were out of control. In serious rioting, possibly incited by the government, shops and factories and private property were ransacked and Mobutu was forced into seclusion but not out of office. He kept parts of his army of 50,000 paid, using the assets and printing presses of the central bank to ensure its loyalty as well as to support his imperial style, but unpaid units resorted to terrorism and racketeering. He recovered some of his frayed international standing by helping to mediate in Angola and by trading on international fears of accelerating chaos, but cancer and explosive insurrection in eastern Zaïre undid him. In distant Kivu province Laurent Kabila had maintained since the 1960s a popular and ostensibly socialist bailiwick. This realm began to expand in the 1980s and by the 1990s Kabila was one of a number of leaders looking for ways to overthrow Mobutu and succeed him. He was given a boost when the Banyamulenge – Tutsi who had been settled in Kivu for a couple of centuries but whom the government in Kinshasa wished to expel and had deprived of their citizenship in 1981 – joined forces with him. This conjunction led to a regional war and thence to the rapid collapse of Mobutu (1997 – he died a few months after his defeat) and his regime. Kabila arrived in Kinshasa with unclear intentions, few obligations, a variety of opponents and a good deal to hide. He declared his wish to install a democratic order at the end of two years and offered posts to other political personalities, excluding, however, Tsishekedi whom, along with other rivals, he imprisoned. But he had no democratic credentials, his own troops were not better controlled than Mobutu's had been, and he was saddled with involvement in massacres of Hutu in the east. The country's ethnic and political divisions were magnified by the ruin of the economy and Kabila's victory accelerated its disintegration. It was renamed the Democratic Republic of Congo but Kabila established control over no more than half of it. He owed his victory to help from Uganda and Rwanda but affronted Presidents Museveni and Bizimanga, who, additionally, fell out with one another: their interests differed, since the former was chiefly concerned to prevent hostile incursions over his frontiers and into the mineral areas thereabouts, while the latter was intent on pre-empting by wholesale violence any renewed assault by Hutu exiles on himself and the Tutsi dominance of Rwanda. Against these erstwhile allies Kabila had help from Zimbabwe, Angola and Namibia, without which he would have lost his capital to mutinous elements in his own army. But the presence of these foreign forces was not popular and they showed no wish to go away again. Ceasefire agreements signed in 1999 by dozens of greater and lesser commanders did not much change the situation.

Impoverished by Mobutu, ravaged by the overspill of Hutu–Tutsi conflicts (pp. 567–8), this once affluent region was further confused by the fitfulness of United States policies, unclear about whether they should have policies about Africa beyond, in the case of Zaïre, calculating whether Mobutu or Kabila might better serve their purposes. Assassinated in 2001, Kabila was succeeded by his son Joseph who joined forces with Mobutu's son Francis and the veteran Gizenga and sufficiently pacified the country to hold and win elections in 2006 and begin the huge task of repairing the disintegration of Zaire and restoring basic public health and personal safety.

Rwanda and Burundi

Rwanda and Burundi, formerly German colonies, were placed under Belgian mandate after the First World War. The population consisted of the Hutu; the Tutsi, supposedly descended from warrior invaders who had arrived in the sixteenth century and become a semi-divine ruling minority; and the pygmy Twi, a distinct but small minority despised by both Hutu and Tutsi. Hutu and Tutsi spoke the same language, intermarried and looked much alike, but were differentiated by occupation: the Hutu were mainly agriculturalists who grew bananas and other crops, the Tutsi raised cattle. This distinction was increased during the 80 years of colonial rule when the Tutsi were treated as and turned into a superior administrative caste. In 1959 the Hutu of Rwanda revolted. The Tutsi monarch, or Mwami, who had succeeded on the mysterious death of his half-brother, was deposed in 1961 and fled to Uganda. A republic was proclaimed under Grégoire Kayibanda, a Hutu. In 1962 the Belgian mandate was terminated, and Rwanda and Burundi ceased to be jointly administered, Rwanda became an independent republic and Burundi an independent (Tutsi) monarchy. In both countries special groups – rulers, army officers, clerisy and clergy – revived latent prejudices and hatreds and so impelled masses of ordinarily innocuous people to torture and massacre.

In *Burundi* the ruling Tutsi were viciously assailed by Hutu in 1965 and the monarchy was overthrown a year later but the Tutsi retained power until 1972 when the Hutu rose again, many Tutsi were slaughtered and some 200,000 fled to Tanzania. In 1987 a new president, Pierre Buyoya, allowed the Hutu a bare majority in his cabinet and the post of prime minister. He risked hostility from both Tutsi (a mere 16 per cent of the population) who feared that concessions were the thin end of the wedge, and from Hutu who branded the Hutu prime minister a collaborator but he survived attempts on his life and an invasion from Tanzania and was succeeded in 1993 by a Hutu, Melchior Ndadye. Ndadye was killed by Tutsi officers and his successor died in the attack which killed the Rwandan president Juvenal Habyarimana (see below). From 1994 Burundi's Tutsi army overshadowed the civilian government and at least condoned scattered massacres. Hutus were herded into camps called villages, from which a number emerged at night to take revenge. Buyoya was reinstated in 1997 but the country was in a state of semi-submerged ethnic war. A power-sharing agreement was devised in 2003; the Hutu and Tutsi shared the seats in the lower house of parliament 60:40 and in the senate 50:50.

In 1964, shortly after independence, the Hutu of *Rwanda* perpetrated a genocidal massacre of Tutsi and many Tutsi fled to Uganda. The Hutu of Rwanda were divided among themselves as well as from the Tutsi: the division was partly regional but also over relations with the Tutsi. President Kayibanda, a southern Hutu, was overthrown in 1973. He was replaced by General Juvenal Habyarimana from the north, who repelled a Tutsi invasion from Uganda in 1990 with French help but at the price of agreeing to share power with Tutsi. To support himself against rival Hutu who distrusted his attitudes he created a Hutu youth movement which became a sinister force supplied with arms by the government and incited by the radio to massacre Tutsi and the more moderate Hutu. The former were regarded by many Hutu as a fifth column ready to join with Tutsi exiles in Uganda to exterminate the Hutu but in 1993 Habyarimana, largely in response to foreign pressures, agreed at a conference at Arusha in Tanzania (implementing an earlier agreement at Kinshasa in Zaïre) to create a two-nation government. This agreement alienated and alarmed those Hutu who wanted a purely Hutu state and felt safe in no other. Habyarimana consequently dithered until threatened with economic sanctions by the World Bank and the IMF. In 1994, returning from a further conference at Dar-es-Salaam, he was killed, together with his fellow president of Burundi, when his aircraft was destroyed as it was landing at his capital.

This was a signal for an invasion of Tutsi exiles from Burundi. Half a million Hutu were gruesomely massacred and two or three times that number fled into neighbouring countries, mainly Zaïre. International attempts to protect refugees were frustrated by the refusal of governments (except the French) to provide either forces or funds in aid of African states which were willing to intervene. A French attempt to succour refugees in the south-west corner of Rwanda was discontinued when the relatively small force involved came under military threat. Civilian aid agencies were unable to persuade the refugees in camps on Rwanda's borders with Zaïre, Burundi and Tanzania to return to their homes and untended crops since these camps contained not only a million or more destitute refugees but also armed and vengeful Hutu whose single prospect was to fight their way back to power by marshalling the hapless refugees at gunpoint against the Tutsi. The UN and other agencies were left with a choice between abandoning the refugees who were dying in thousands or continuing supplies of food in the knowledge that much of it would be appropriated by the gangs which dominated the camps. An attempt by the new Tutsi government to persuade refugees back to their homes by appointing as prime minister the Hutu Pasteur Bizimanga fell short of the needful reassurance. In Rwanda the Tutsi, having suffered perhaps a million deaths by violence became a yet smaller dominant minority, more embattled, more vulnerable and more intransigent. After a year the government of Zaïre resolved to force the unwelcome Hutu encamped on its territory back across its borders but most preferred to take flight deeper into Zaïre, where they became trapped between Kabila's anti-Mobutu forces and their dread of returning home. In 1996 Banyamulenge units attacked some 40 refugee camps in Zaïre, killing or scattering the occupants: most of the survivors were driven back into Rwanda or Burundi, where their presence rekindled the slaughter. The massacres of the 1990s were the clearest instances of genocide since the adoption in 1948 of the Genocide Convention – with the possible exception of the campaigns in Guatemala against its indigenous people (p. 712).

West Central Africa

Between Nigeria and Congo lies a wedge of smaller territories. In Cameroun – home to two-thirds of the population of these territories and a relatively successful adjuster of linguistic tensions – France intervened to sustain the friendly government of Ahmadu Ahidjo against a revolt whose causes were mainly economic. Ahidjo resigned suddenly in 1982, to be succeeded by Paul Biya, who proved to be disappointingly ineffective. Sharp falls in the prices of Cameroun's principal exports – coffee, cocoa, cotton – produced crippling debt, left public servants unpaid, encouraged corruption and smuggling, dictated recourse to the IMF and austerity, and stimulated political infighting which Biya failed to master. He refused to appoint a prime minister until forced to do so. He won a narrow and suspect victory in elections in 1992 and was re-elected president after deferring elections while opponents squabbled over the selection of single candidate. He was re-elected again in 1997 when a Commonwealth observer team delivered a damning report on electoral malpractices (Cameroun had joined the Commonwealth in 1994). Biya's repeated successes reflected his popularity in the more densely populated northern parts of the country. He won a fourth successive seven-year term in 2002.

In *Gabon* hopes turned to disillusion. Potentially one of the richest states in Africa, Gabon was ruled by Presidents Leon M'Ba (deposed in 1963 but restored by French troops) and Albert Bongo, who changed his first name to Omar upon conversion to Islam in 1973 and completed the country's transition to a one-party state. In spite of natural wealth which included a quarter of the world's known store of manganese, Gabon was struck by economic crisis in the 1970s and 1980s, so that the government had to levy a forced loan on salaries and reschedule its foreign debts as the only way to avoid default. Serious riots in 1990 forced Bongo to introduce a multiparty system faster than he would have liked. After elections in which his Parti Democrate Gabonais comfortably outpaced its challengers he formed a new government of six parties, the PDG retaining the principal ministries but taking only a minority of places in the cabinet, and he himself was re-elected president in 1993 – by the proverbial whisker and against a challenger with support from Cameroun.

In *Congo-Brazzaville* the first president Fulbert Yalou was overthrown by revolution, France refusing to intervene in a situation which it recognized as one of well-founded popular indignation. Alphonse Massemba-Debat and then Marien Ngouabi took the country to the left but the latter was assassinated in 1977 and the former shortly afterwards executed. Denis Sassou-Nguesso (president 1979–92) of the Parti Congolais du Travail kept both pro-Chinese and pro-Russian parties down but not wholly out. His ill-planned use of public funds and extravagant spending on projects of little merit, coinciding with falls in oil production and the oil price, debilitated the economy, encouraged a self-defeating drift to the towns, exacerbated ethnic rifts and increased imports and foreign debt. When the army refused to quell riots in 1985 the president saved himself only by the use of the presidential guard and six years later he was cut down to size, albeit escaping retribution and keeping his position and some of his powers. Elections in 1992, local and then presidential, led to the installation of Pascal Loussaba as president but Nguesso recovered power in 1997 after vicious fighting in which he had support from President Bongo in Gabon (his father-in-law) and other neighbours and from American and French oil companies. French troops were withdrawn that year. Sassou-Nguesso became a survivor.

In the landlocked *Central African Republic* a coup by Colonel Jean-Bedel Bokassa similar in its origins to military coups in Burkina Faso, Benin and Niger, led, however, to enormities when the colonel declared himself emperor and went to insane lengths of ostentation and cruelty. France, after becoming embarrassingly associated with one of the period's most indecent tyrannies, assisted with its overthrow in 1979. An attempt by Bokassa to return in 1983 failed. After a short transitional period André Kolongba, a dependant and relative of President Mobutu, ruled for 12 years. He resisted the trend towards a multiparty state for as long as he could, received aid from Iraq until the Gulf War of 1991, only partially replaced it with aid from Taiwan and, most importantly, lost the favour of France, which still had (until 1999) 3,500 troops in the country. Unable to stave off elections any longer, Kolongba was eliminated in the first round, tried to cancel the second but was replaced in 1992 by André-Félix Patasse (re-elected in 1999). He lost his grip and (in 2002) his office to Francoise Bozize, who promised civilian democratic government.

The Spanish island of Fernando Po in the Bight of Biafra – renamed Macias Nguema island – together with Rio Muni, an enclave in Gabon, became the independent state of *Equatorial Guinea* in 1968 and shortly thereafter a family autocracy characterized by economic calamity and mass murder. President Obiang Nguema, who replaced Francisco Macias Nguema in 1979 and relied for protection on his Moroccan guards, was not much of an improvement on his predecessor but was propelled in the 1990s towards a multiparty order. A plot involving freelance buccaneers from South Africa, Britain and elsewhere in 2004 was foiled. The plotters' aim was to take over the country and install a subservient government in the expectation of substantial financial gain from its presumed natural resources.

The islands of *Principe* and *Sao Tomé*, 200 miles west of Gabon in the Gulf of Guinea, which had been first seen by the Portuguese in the fifteenth century, became independent in 1975 and moved in the same democratic direction when President Aristide Pereira was trounced in elections in 1991 by Antonio Mascarenhas Monteiro but were engulfed by accelerating unemployment, inflation and foreign debt. A coup by junior officers in 1995 against President Miguel Trovoada failed in spite of compliance from Prime Minister Carlos de Graça.

CHAPTER 24

East Africa

Sudan

The history of Sudan in modern times is an alternation of subjection and self-rule. From 1820 to 1881 it was a part of the Ottoman empire in name and of its autonomous Egyptian pashalik in fact. From 1881 to 1898 it was ruled by the Mahdi Muhammad Ahmad Abdullah (died 1885) and his successors. From 1899 to 1955 it was subject in theory to an Anglo-Egyptian condominium, in practice to Britain. In 1956 it became an independent state, and then a member of the Arab League and the United Nations.

The Anglo-Egyptian condominium reflected no Anglo-Egyptian agreement about Sudan. The administering powers agreed in little and did not bother to co-operate. After the Anglo-Egyptian treaty of 1936 the British allowed a greater degree of Egyptian penetration, but although Sudan was coveted by Egyptian governments it attracted few Egyptian administrators. Sudanese nationalism gathered strength in the 1930s under the leadership of Ismail al-Azhari, who became secretary of the Graduates General Congress, formed in 1938. Owing to the active role of Britain and the comparatively negative role of Egypt Sudanese nationalism was at first more anti-British than anti-Egyptian and looked to Egypt to help displace the British. This anti-British streak was intensified during the Second World War, when nationalists raised the issue of Sudan's postwar status and received unsympathetic answers from the British, who were occupied with present and pressing realities in the campaigns against the Italians in Ethiopia and against the Italians and the Germans in North Africa. The Egyptians sensed the opportunities in this situation and welcomed the formation by Azhari of the Ashigga Party, which aimed at the union of Sudan with Egypt. He had the support of Ali el-Mirghani, one of Sudan's two principal religious leaders. As a direct response the Umma Party was created to work for the independence of Sudan under the leadership of Sudan's other principal religious leader Abd al-Rahman al-Mahdi, the posthumous son of the famous Mahdi. The Umma Party was suspected of dreaming of a revival of the Mahdist monarchy with British help.

The conflict between Britain and Egypt, which existed independently of Sudan, was intensified by these moves and when the British administration took a step towards

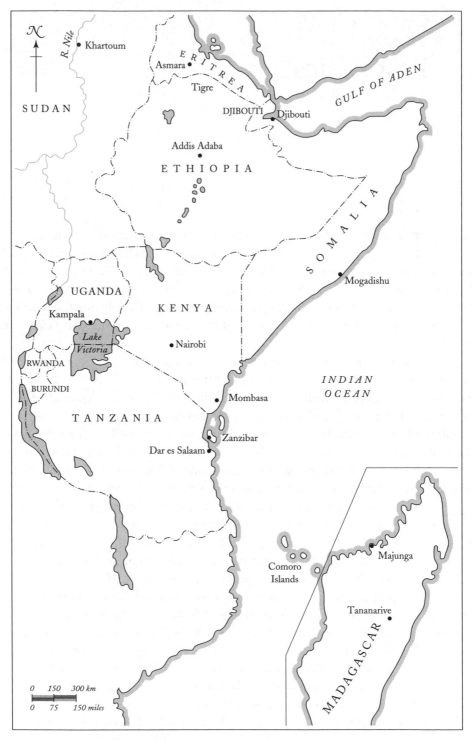

24.1 The Horn and East Africa

Sudanese self-government by creating an advisory council for northern Sudan, the Egyptian prime minister, Mustafa al-Nahhas Pasha, resurrected the slogan of the unity of the Nile valley. The British antagonized northern and southern Sudan by omitting the south from the new councils; the south was affronted, while the north suspected Britain of planning to annex it to Uganda. This conflict, which was to lead to severe fighting on the eve of independence, was religious, racial and economic. The south comprised the three provinces of Bahr al-Ghazal, Upper Nile and Equatoria, with a population of rather more than 3 million out of a total population of 10 million. These provinces, bordering upon five African states (the Central African Republic, Congo, Uganda, Kenya and Ethiopia) looked to their African neighbours rather than to the Arab north. The inhabitants, although they included some 40 per cent of Muslim Africans, were predominantly negroid and pagan; some of the tribes continued to display the weaknesses inflicted by slavers from the north who had systematically removed the best men and women; the poverty of the south was worse than the poverty of the north. After the war the British, who had in the past been accused of accentuating the divide between north and south, adopted a policy of unification, but a conference held in 1946 contained no southern representatives and gave the south cause to complain that unification was really subordination. After a further conference at Juba in 1947 northerners claimed that the south had agreed to unification, while southerners denied this interpretation and continued to ask for separation from the north or a federation with guarantees.

This internal dispute was partly obscured by the larger dispute between Egypt, insisting on the unity of the Nile valley, and Britain, insisting on Sudan's right to decide for itself after a period of self-government under the British aegis. In 1947 Egypt accepted the principle of self-determination in the mistaken belief that it would produce a union of the two countries, but Britain and Egypt were still unable to agree on the immediate constitutional changes and in 1948 Britain introduced a new constitution without Egyptian concurrence. Legislative and executive councils covering the whole of Sudan were established but the elections for them were boycotted by the pro-Egyptian parties. After anti-British demonstrations Azhari was arrested. Egypt was at this time embroiled in the Arab–Israeli war and its immediate aftermath.

In 1951 the British governor appointed a commission to consider further constitutional advances. Sudan was plainly moving fast along the road through self-government to self-determination, and Egypt thereupon carried out a threat, uttered in 1950, to abrogate the condominium agreement of 1899 and the Anglo-Egyptian treaty of 1936. King Farouk was declared king of Egypt and Sudan. But in 1952, as a result of the revolution in Egypt, he became king of neither.

A few months earlier Britain had produced a self-government statute for Sudan which the new Egyptian government, whose new chief General Neguib was half-Sudanese, accepted with certain modifications which curbed the governor's special powers in the south. All the main Sudanese parties issued pro-Egyptian declarations and the amended statute was embodied in an Anglo-Egyptian agreement of 1953 intended to lead to independence not later than 1961. Elections, preceded by vigorous Egyptian campaigning, were held at the end of 1953 and gave overwhelming victory to Azhari's refurbished party, now called the National Unionist Party. Azhari became prime minister in 1954. Neguib lost his position in Egypt in the same year.

In 1955, on the eve of independence, the south exploded.

The south was affronted by the new government's allocation of posts and by its persistent rejection of the south's demand for the right to secede or autonomy in a loose federal system. An army section which turned upon its Arab officer sparked violence which spread rapidly and was only mastered when the prime minister invoked the aid of the British governor and moved substantial forces from the north into the south. The south, submitting, claimed that it had done so in reliance upon British mediation and was subsequently let down. Repression was thorough and brutal. Southerners were executed in their hundreds and deported to the north in their thousands and fled to neighbouring African territories in their tens of thousands. The south became a closed area whence reliable information was difficult to obtain and gruesome reports emanated.

The revolt accelerated independence which came on the first day of 1956. It was followed by the break-up of Azhari's party, a coalition under him and then a coalition without him. New parties formed. Abdullah Khalil, who succeeded Azhari in 1956, grappled for two years with economic problems (lightened by an aid agreement with the United States in 1958) and with reviving fears of Egypt. In 1958 Egypt sent troops into two disputed areas on the Egyptian–Sudanese border, but this tactless demonstration recoiled on Cairo at elections in the same year which gave the Umma Party the largest number of seats. Nevertheless, Khalil was afraid of an alliance between Azhari and Nasser and he was suspected of being privy to an army coup by which he and his government and the constitution were all to be swept away. General Ibrahim Abboud took power with a supreme council of officers.

Military rule lasted for six years, during which the situation in the southern provinces deteriorated drastically. The Sudanese government pursued a policy of Arabization and looked with suspicion on the foreign Christian missionaries whom it suspected of being anti-Muslim agents of a western policy of separatism. The Missionary Societies Act of 1962 restricted their activities and induced a number to leave; the surviving 300 were expelled in 1964 after the resumption of full-scale insurrection by the separatist Anya Nya movement and brought with them to the outside world tales of extensive massacres by government troops. In 1964 General Abboud's military regime was overthrown and after a few weeks during which he ruled in conjunction with a civilian administration he resigned. Ser el-Khatim Khalifa formed a transitional coalition of intellectuals and re-emergent politicians which was replaced early in 1965 by a more normal coalition of politicians in which the Umma Party had the largest voice. A southerner, Clement Ngoro, held the ministry of the interior and north–south negotiations took place both in Sudan and in Nairobi with a number of leading southern exiles. A further conference planned for February at Juba was post-poned owing to a refusal by the Anya Nya to surrender in advance, but discussions were resumed in Khartoum in March. With the south demanding a federal constitu-tion and northern politicians inveighing against separatist plots little was achieved. Fighting continued and southern opinion moved increasingly away from federation and towards independence, with both sides seeking support from neighbouring states. The Sudanese government exerted itself to improve its relations with Ethiopia, Uganda and the Central African Republic, and the Sudanese African National Union appealed to African opinion through the OAU and its Liberation Committee in Dar-es-Salaam.

In 1969 a group of military officers led by General Gaafar Muhammad Nimeiry seized power and established a more left-wing and pro-Egyptian government. The coincidence of similar coups in Somalia and Libya gave rise to vague projects for a union of all these countries with Egypt and the creation of an Arab bloc of north-east African states. This plan was expanded to attract South Yemen and Syria, thus linking it with the defunct union of 1958 with Egypt as a pivotal common factor, but these schemes came to nothing. In Sudan they were attacked as distractions from more urgent domestic problems, especially the civil war in the south. Nimeiry survived a series of attempts to unseat him which were at least assisted, if not instigated, by Libya and Ethiopia. In 1977 Sudan moved close to war with Ethiopia as a result of the help which it was giving to the Eritrean revolt against Addis Ababa. At home a reconcilia-tion between Nimeiry and his principal opponent Sadiq al-Mahdi, marked by the latter's election to a vice-presidency of the Sudanese Socialist Union, brought Muslim fundamentalists into the government and thereby split the Muslim Brotherhood between those prepared to share power and others who insisted on holding out for comprehensive theocratic rule. The coalition crumbled in 1979.

Throughout the early 1980s Nimeiry's fall was confidently predicted. His troubles in the south revived, his economy went from bad to worse, students and other malcon-tents demonstrated against him, his suppliers – mainly Saudi Arabia and the United States – began to ask themselves whether they would not be better without him; and his borders were crossed by hordes of destitute and starving refugees from Ethiopia and Chad. He reacted by imposing and savagely implementing Islamic laws and penal-ties, calling himself Imam (although a third of his countrymen were not Muslims) and by granting valuable concessions to Saudi and other tycoons. Sadiq al-Mahdi opposed the severity of the application of the Shar'ia and was put in prison in 1983 but released the next year. By 1985 about a fifth of the population was starving, maladministration had brought public services and basic works (irrigation, for example) to a standstill, the special security police were justly loathed, the foreign debt service exceeded the value of exports, foreign loans were obtainable only at ruinous cost, the south was again in arms against Khartoum and to all intents and purposes autonomous.

In April Nimeiry, away on a visit to the United States, was removed by the army after what amounted to a strike by the professional classes – a pre-emptive coup by the military to forestall more radical action. The succeeding military government proved only a stop-gap while traditional political parties argued their way to a civilian coalition with al-Mahdi as prime minister. But al-Mahdi, weak and inconsistent, gave hostages to fortune by espousing (contrary to his campaign rhetoric) Islamic fundamentalist policies and fell out with his allies of the Democratic Unionist Party by failing to stop – or not trying hard enough to stop – the war in the south. He was accused of sabotaging peace moves. The DUP left his government in 1988 and he became dependent on the National Islamic Front (NIF). The army feared defeat in the south, was impatient with his dithering and fearful of economic collapse. The war, resumed in 1983, had cost at least half a million dead and 1.5 million refugees. The external debt had risen to $7 billion; discussions with the IMF broke down; food riots became frequent. In 1989 the army resumed overt power under General Omar al-Bashir, a more circumspect but hardly less convinced Islamicist than his predecessor, but the army had by this time become permeated by the NIF and al-Bashir was a figurehead masking the power of Hassan al-Turabi, the NIF's leader, who succeeded in claiming for himself and his party a perverse monopoly of Islamic orthodoxy. Besides its appeal to army officers, the NIF had made converts among businessmen and in the public services in reaction against the striking incompetence and outrageous corruption of earlier governments but it failed to check inflation, attract foreign investment or stop the war in the south – in spite of continuing divisions in the south over whether or not to accept anything short of full independence and a split between the (mainly Nuer) section led by Riak Machar and the (mainly Dinka) forces of John Garang's Sudanese People's Liberation Army. The government in Khartoum was widely vilified for its conduct of the war, further alienated Egypt and Ethiopia by complicity in an attempt to kill President Mubarak in Addis Ababa in 1995 and soured its relations with Saudi Arabia by its sympathies with Iraq. It discarded its military trappings in 1993, converting al-Bashir and others into civilians but leaving al-Turabi's role unaltered (but impaired by an accident): this partnership began to fray. War, drought and the obstruction by Khartoum of international relief services created a mounting tide of famine and a humanitarian calamity outstanding even in the records of East Africa. Khartoum itself was attacked by the United States, which destroyed targets – probably the wrong ones – in retaliation for attacks on American embassies elsewhere in East Africa by anti-American Islamic militants. George W. Bush strengthened US economic sanctions and in 2005 the war between north and south was declared over. Garang became first vice-president of Sudan. The death toll was put at 1.5 million. The status and temper of the south remained uncertain. The border between north and south was undefined as were the borders between Sudan and its Kenyan and Ugandan neighbours.

Darfur

Darfur – the home of the Fur – lodged between Sudan and Chad was in the seventeenth century the successor state of a number of small independent and prosperous states which early in the twentieth century was absorbed into the Sudan. On Sudan's independence in 1956 it became part of Sudan, involved tangentially in its north/south civil wars (1956–72) and still a place of unrest when those wars ended: it was also embroiled in the conflict between Chad and Libya (pp. 521–4). Upon the seizure of power in Sudan by General al-Bashir (p. 576) the new government in Khartoum embarked on war in Darfur in the name of Islam and with arms supplied by China. The United States was alarmed by these upheavals which coincided with attacks by al-Qaeda on American embassies in Kenya and Tanzania. The Sudanese government sought to veil its seemingly genocidal operations by acting through semi-detached militias, the Janjaweed, but reports of atrocities became so horrifying that the African Union was persuaded to despatch a force, grudgingly accepted by Khartoum, to relieve the situation. This force was, however, too small to be effective, so that the UN Security Council felt obliged to provide an international peace-making force of 20,000. By this time deaths in Darfur had risen to several hundred thousand with many times that number homeless, starving and waterless and too terrified to go home even if they could, and various groups among the Fur were fighting one another. As some fled westward into Chad President Deby invoked foreign aid, insisting that it should come from neither the UA nor the UN but from the EU where he could be assured of a sympathetic French presence. A peace agreement concluded in 2007 was a first step towards the salvation of surviving victims but only partially effective since the predatory forces had split into fragments, many of which could not be included in formal agreements. Conditions in so-called camps remained barbarous and so dangerous that many charities were forced to abandon their work. The International Court of Criminal Justice resolved to indict President al-Bashir.

The Horn

The ancient *Ethiopian* kingdom, an amalgam of races, languages and religions, retained its independence even in the nineteenth century and therewith a certain immunity from the modernizing trends which normally accompany both colonialism and anti-colonial movements. Subjected for only five years in the twentieth century (1936–41), it resumed its hallowed way of life under its astute monarch Haile Selassie, who had first mounted the throne in 1930 at the age of 38. The emperor was a cautious innovator whose reforming proclivities were in advance of the landed feudatories and wealthy churchmen who were the most eminent and powerful people in his realm. An attempted coup at the end of 1960, followed by army mutinies in March 1961 and a reported conspiracy in August of that year, revealed the existence of discontent among the educated young and junior officers who looked to Prince Asfa Wossen for more spirited progress, but the emperor re-established his control with awe-inspiring ease and continued his policy of slow internal advance. He also cultivated good relations with the emerging states of Africa (perhaps as an insurance against traditional Muslim hostility towards his predominantly Christian power base); in 1958 his capital became the headquarters for the UN Economic Commission for Africa and in 1963 the Organization for African Unity came into being there. For both these organizations the emperor caused spacious quarters to be built.

Ethiopia's especial external concern was with the neighbouring and non-Bantu *Somalis* who, unlike the Ethiopians, were not only conquered by Europeans in the nineteenth century but also partitioned among them. The Somalis, Muslims but not Arabs, appeared in the Horn of Africa towards the end of the European Middle Ages and subsequently joined in Muslim attacks on the Christian kingdom of Ethiopia. They were subjected in the latter part of the nineteenth century, first by the French in the 1860s and then by the British and the Italians (who also took Eritrea – so named by the Italians in that century – flanking the Red Sea to the north of Ethiopia) in the 1880s. The British colony of Kenya extended northwards over a predominantly Somali area, and Ethiopia appropriated in its Ogaden province territory to which the Somalis laid claim. Relations between Ethiopia and the Somalis were therefore inherently bad and British relations with both were uneasy, since the Ethiopians suspected Britain of partiality to Somali claims against Ethiopia, while Somalis found Britain unsympathetic to their claims against Kenya.

In 1935 the Italians, dissatisfied with the barrenness of their part of Somaliland and their imperial fortunes in general, exploited an incident at Wal Wal in the disputed Ogaden in order to conquer Ethiopia. They were suspected of toying with the idea of a Greater Somalia which would annex British Somaliland, but their defeat by the British in 1941 revived the independent Ethiopian empire (to which was added Eritrea in 1952 after a period of British trusteeship) and left the Somalis still subject and divided. At the end of the war Ernest Bevin proposed a Greater Somalia consisting of British and Italian Somaliland and parts of Ethiopia, but this notion antagonized Ethiopia without profiting the Somalis. Discussions on the Ethiopian–Somali frontier proceeded sluggishly until 1959 when a conference in Oslo with Trygve Lie as arbitrator produced a compromise agreeable to neither side. In 1960 Italian Somaliland, to which the Italians had returned in 1950 to administer a ten-year trusteeship, became independent, and as this date approached the British, who had become nervous of Egyptian interference in British Somaliland, hurried their own colony forward so that it could be joined with Italian Somaliland to make the independent republic of Somalia – large but poor, racially mixed, ill-prepared, and distrusted and menaced by its Ethiopian and Kenyan neighbours.

At the Lancaster House conference on Kenya in 1962 the Somalis asked unsuccessfully for a plebiscite in the Northern Frontier District of Kenya (an area of over 260,000 sq. km) and its union with Somalia. Later in the same year Kenyan politicians discussed with Somalis an East African federation which would embrace not only Somalia and the British East African territories but also Ethiopia; in the event of such a development the Kenyans made it plain that they intended to keep the whole of the Northern Frontier District for themselves. In December a boundaries commission recommended that the district be divided into two regions, both to be included in the new Kenyan state. This recommendation, which was accepted by the British government, produced riots and a rupture of diplomatic relations by Somalia. Kenya was able to get other African states on its side and a Kenyan delegation walked out of an Afro-Asian conference at Moshi in Tanganyika in 1963 when the Somalis raised the border issue. At a further conference in Addis Ababa a number of Africans chided the Somalis for again raising the question.

The Somalis did not accept the treaty of 1897 by which Britain had ceded part of British Somaliland to Ethiopia; between Italian Somaliland and Ethiopia there was no established border. On independence the Somalis had refrained from challenging a neighbour which possessed American equipment. Ethiopia too, conscious of the racial divisions within its own borders, avoided a clash. But the Somali claim against Kenya alarmed Ethiopia owing to its affinity with Somali claims on Ethiopia's Ogaden province. Fighting developed unofficially along the border during 1962. In the next year the Somali president Abdurashid Shermake visited the USSR, Egypt, India, Pakistan and Italy. He got little help or encouragement. Kenya's independence at the end of that year saw the conclusion of a Kenyan–Ethiopian defence treaty, and a few months later open fighting began between Ethiopia and Somalia. The Russians offered their mediation and a deputy foreign minister of the USSR went to Mogadishu, thereby evincing Russian concern, if not for the Somalis, at any rate about possible American or Chinese influence in the Horn. More effective mediation was proffered by the president of Sudan and the king of Morocco, and after talks in Khartoum hostilities were suspended. But the underlying problem was not resolved and further discussions between Kenya and Somalia in 1965 were abortive. Sporadic fighting continued until 1967 when a new Somali government asked President Kaunda to mediate. Diplomatic relations were restored the next year.

In French Somaliland a movement in favour of amalgamation with the Italian and British territories was circumvented by a vote in the assembly at *Djibouti* to continue as an Overseas Territory of the French Union, but in 1975 France decided to leave (retaining, however, an armed force of 4,000) and in 1977 the independent Republic of Djibouti came into existence. It included the port of Djibouti and the west shore of the Bab el-Mandeb, was coveted by Somalia and vital to the external commerce of Ethiopia, and was divided between Afars, who had kin in Ethiopia and Eritrea, and Issas, who were Somalis. (After the fall of Mengistu in Ethiopia Djibouti adopted (1992) a multiparty constitution which did not, however, alter the essentially ethnic nature of its politics. President Hassan Gouled Aptidon, an Issa, was accused of manifold atrocities against Afars, which lost him French support and isolated him from Djibouti's neighbours in East Africa and the Arabian peninsula.)

The Horn of Africa acquired international significance in the context of the Cold War. It provided at the southern end of the Red Sea a bridge from Africa into Asia hardly less important than the complementary passage through Sinai, and eastward it faced the wider waters of the Indian Ocean. The United States established influence and bases in Ethiopia. The USSR responded in Somalia, where it supplied arms for the Somalis to use against their neighbours in return for storage and communications facilities, intelligence posts and a large air base. In 1974 these manoeuvres were inflamed and transformed by revolution in Ethiopia.

Haile Selassie was pressed by friends and relatives to abdicate in 1973 when he reached the age of 80. He was old and much burdened – his heir had a stroke in 1973; his alliance with Israel crumbled in that year of war in the Middle East; American cordiality was waning; students were rioting and workers striking – but he refused to resign. He made a move to loosen the lid which he had clamped on his country but the past blew up in his face. A group of army officers mutinied. This mutiny led to a further revolt by privates, NCOs and junior officers, to the dethronement of the emperor (who later died in prison, possibly murdered or maltreated) and to numerous political assassinations. The deadening influence of the aged, if once noble, emperor had produced intolerable strains (between regions and classes and even within the army), conspiracies, corruption, misgovernment and stagnation, all of which were worsened by the drought and famine which afflicted much of Africa in the early 1970s and by the contrasting affluence of the court and nobles. The first mutiny was followed by a series of short-lived governments and by the formation of a loose amalgam of groups called the Dergue (or Committee), whose membership seemed to be fluid and was largely unknown but which became the real power in the capital.

The dominant figure in the new regime was Colonel Haile Mariam Mengistu, a clever manoeuvrer who defeated his main rivals in the Ethiopian People's Republican Party with the help of the socialist Meison, which he then routed. Mengistu and his Alyotawi Seded secured control in Addis Ababa but not over the whole country and, most particularly, not in Eritrea in the north or in the disputed lands in the south. For the next 17 years Mengistu was at war on several fronts, and without foreign help he would have lost one or all of these wars. He got help from the USSR and its Cuban surrogates when, in 1977, Moscow decided to back Mengistu, jeopardizing and forfeiting its alliance with Somalia in order to displace the United States in Ethiopia. Cuban arms saved Harar and Diredawa for Ethiopia and repulsed the Somalis, who had been on the verge of conquering the Ogaden. This relief enabled Mengistu to hold his own against the Eritreans until, once more with Russian and Cuban help, he could mount a counter-offensive. For the time being Mengistu was saved – and the USSR committed to supporting the Christian Amharic empire of Haile Selassie in its new colours under the Dergue. Besides his conflicts with Eritreans and Somalis Mengistu faced revolts in Tigre in the north-west and by the Oromo or Galla peoples of the south (the latter constituting about half the country's population).

Somalia was switched by these events from Russian to American protectorship. But it too was a deeply divided country. In the last third of the nineteenth century French, British and Italian colonizers had asserted patchy rule over a network of pastoral clans and sub-clans which reasserted themselves after independence in 1960. The clan system operated within a broader, if vaguer, framework of townees versus the rest, which was accentuated – particularly in Mogadishu – by an influx of job seekers in the colonial years and a second migration of refugees from the wars with Ethiopia. In 1969 Shermake was assassinated. He was succeeded after an interregnum and a military coup by Colonel Siad Barre, who belonged to the Marehan clan, which was a section of the Darode peoples, who were sandwiched between the Issas to the north and the Hawieh to the south. Barre aimed to centralize Somalia around Mogadishu and himself. Besides strengthening links with the USSR and the Arab world he promulgated an eccentric socialist programme, benefited after 1977 from American favours and invaded Ethiopia with groundless hopes of American military support. When his forces were quickly repulsed by the Ethiopians with Russian and Cuban help his own position was seriously undermined by his misconceived and humiliating adventure. He became a harsh and nepotistic autocrat, lost the support of allied sub-clans and in spite of a rally to his leadership against an Ethiopian invasion in 1982, became enmeshed in a civil war which accelerated the disintegration of the state and caused famine, rapine and the flight of 2 million terrified and starving people. At one point the Red Cross was devoting one-third of its worldwide resources to Somalia and 20 other humanitarian agencies were involved there. One of Africa's few homogeneous countries was transformed under Barre's rule into a maze of hostilities sharpened by a flood of undiscriminating American aid which, although often allocated to inappropriate and uncompleted projects, created nevertheless pots of gold. The northern, formerly British, part of the country purported to secede as the Republic of Somaliland but its president Muhammad Egal won no international recognition (except by Djibouti in 1997) and little foreign aid.

Accumulating opposition forced Barre to flee in 1991, whereupon clan leaders who had joined forces against him resumed mutual hostilities. The most prominent of these was Muhammad Farah 'Aideed', who (like Barre) was an Italian-trained soldier and policeman, had been kept in prison by Barre for years but was released when his talents were needed by Barre against Ethiopia. He narrowly missed becoming Barre's successor when, through a tactical error, he allowed Mogadishu to fall into the hands of his rival Ali Mahdi Muhammad, who assumed the title of president. To compensate for this failure Aideed sought allies among other groups, including Islamic zealots who rallied to him when the United States singled him out as a special enemy and tried to kill him. There were in Somalia two separate but interlocking calamities. The one was the chaos and mayhem which followed the collapse of Barre's regime; the second was drought, famine and disease due in the first place to natural causes. The first gravely aggravated the second. The first was felt mainly in the capital and along the coast, the second most severely 160 km inland. The first required international mediation or more forceful international intervention to pacify and disarm the warring factions; the second required food, medicine and protection. The worst of the famine was over by the middle of 1992 but relief agencies continued to be robbed of 10–20 per cent of their supplies and at the end of that year a UN mission (UNOSOM) was despatched to supervise and improve the distribution of international aid to those for whom it was intended. UNOSOM was given neither the authority nor the means to disarm the factions which were robbing the agencies, although the UN secretary-general Boutros-Ghali argued strongly that disarmament was a necessary precondition for UNOSOM's tasks. This disagreement, essentially between the UN and the United States, led to further divisions and to disasters which caused the United States to refuse to provide ground forces for later UN operations. (In Bosnia and Kosovo it insisted on resorting to NATO. The international force sent to East Timor was almost entirely Australian.)

UNOSOM's initial force of 500 Pakistanis with severely limited powers was quickly expanded into a neutral multinational peacekeeping body and thence into an active combatant in the Somali factional fighting with the addition of armed conflict between the United States and the Aideed faction. The United States contributed units to UNOSOM and also despatched a separate Rapid Deployment Unit of 1,300, which was independent of the UN. UNOSOM's forces were commanded by a Turkish general with an American second-in-command. The commander of the Rapid Deployment Unit, Admiral Jonathan Howe, was made special representative of the UN secretary-general when the first holder of that post (the Algerian Muhammad Sahoun) resigned in protest against American militancy. In the enlarged UNOSOM of 28,000 the United States provided 8,000, with Italian and French contingents taking third and fourth places after the Pakistanis in second place. The first American arrivals were welcomed by Aideed, whom the United States seemed to favour above Ali Mahdi, but during 1993 the United States abandoned the policy of bringing the warlords together and decided instead to eliminate Aideed politically and, if necessary, personally. Aideed became anti-American and anti-UN and his followers killed 25 Pakistanis in an affray which the Americans blamed on him but he described as an American attempt to seize his radio station. The United States retaliated by sending a second American force (mainly teenagers) to seize Aideed, but this force captured only two of his adjutants, killed 500 Somalis and wounded perhaps 1,000 more, lost two helicopters and had to be rescued by UNOSOM's Pakistani and other units. Eighteen young Americans were killed. Clinton decided to pull out. American troops left during 1994, followed by UNOSOM. No progress had been made towards reuniting or pacifying Somalia, which after three years remained divided between tribal coalitions manoeuvring against one another and pretending to ignore the detached fiefdom of President Egal in the north. After Aideed was killed in 1996 his rivals concluded an alliance – the Sedere Pact – against his son Hussein, with Ethiopian encouragement. Somalis remained without a government – an area rather than a state, in which 20 chieftains vied for power locally, weaponry was the one commodity in plentiful supply and brigandage a major activity of numerous armed forces. From this chaos two main forces emerged, the one, under Colonel Ahmed Yusuf, with headquarters at Baidoa whence it aimed to proceed with Ethiopian help to Mogadishu, and the other – the Union of Islamic Courts (denounced by the United States) – which seized control of Mogadishu and so foiled Yusuf's venture. The ethnic mixes along the borders between Somalia and Ethiopia added to the ambiguities and conflicts in the region. The United National Liberation Front (UNLF), created under Ethiopian auspices, aimed to detach parts of Somalia or at least participate in Somalia's civil wars, and Ethiopia deployed military force on a large scale to assert its claims to debatable areas and invaded Somalia.

In Ethiopia Mengistu's government was able to cow the Western Somali Liberation Front and to check, but not defeat, the Eritrean People's Liberation Front (EPLF). Sudan and Saudi Arabia tried to unify minor Eritrean groups – three of which signed an agreement in Jeddah at the beginning of 1983 – as a prelude to a broader accord with the EPLF, whose leftward inclination they distrusted, but these moves were ineffectual and the EPLF demonstrated its vitality by inflicting serious defeats on Ethiopian government forces in 1983 and again in 1988. The United States reclassified the EPLF as a democratic liberation movement instead of a Marxist insurrection. The revolt in Tigre waxed and waned with the fortunes of the Eritreans and the government suffered serious defeats in Tigre in 1989. Russian aid was tapering off and Mengistu felt obliged to offer Eritrea autonomy in a federation. A coup against him misfired but the army, on which he depended, had had enough of war and pressed for any agreement with Eritrea short of independence. Talks began in 1989 with the former President Carter as intermediary. In 1991 Mengistu fled and the capital and central government were taken over by 'Meles' Zenawi, now an ex-communist, as chief of the Ethiopian People's Revolutionary Democratic Front (EPRDF: its main components were the Ethiopian People's Democratic Movement, the Tigray People's Liberation Front and the Oromo People's Democratic Organization). Chaotic elections followed a year later, less chaotic ones in 1994. The EPRDF retained dominance although the Oromos and others, wary of Amharas, wanted secession or at least a loose Ethiopian federation. Afars were similarly divided. The EPRDF swept the board in central and regional elections in 1995 which were boycotted by the principal opposition parties. Ethiopia, landlocked but with rights of access to Eritrea's Red Sea port of Assab, adopted a policy of devolution over five years to a number of regions (originally 14 but reduced to ten), whose ethnic identity threatened, however, to turn devolution into fragmentation. For all the peoples of the region the horrors of seemingly endless wars were compounded by famines so lethal that the world put them at the top of the news and was briefly stirred to raise its support for impossibly overworked and underfunded relief agencies. In external affairs Meles was hostile to the Islamic Front in Sudan (particularly after the attempt on Mubarak's life in Addis Ababa in 1995), to Kenya and the Aideed faction in Somalia. He balanced good relations with the United States by visiting China.

In Eritrea the EPLF acted as though the country were already independent – which it became in 1995, with Issayas Aferworki as president of a state with 3 million people divided about equally between Islam and Christianity, speaking a dozen languages, short of food for a decade or more, struggling to provide for large bodies of displaced persons and demobilized soldiers, to extend its inadequate schools and devise a new-fangled market economy. Its frontiers with Ethiopia were uncomfortably uncertain and in 1998 an Eritrean invasion of debatable ground followed by an Ethiopian counter-attack caused heavy fighting and flights of refugees. Both sides armed themselves with modern weapons bought mainly from Russia and ex-Soviet satellites in Europe. The war spread militarily and diplomatically. Ethiopia supported Eritrean dissidents in Sudan; Eritrea sent aid to Ethiopians opposed to the ruling Tigrayan minority in Ethiopia and to Hussein Aideed in Somalia.

Uganda, Tanzania, Kenya

The preponderant power in East and South Central Africa had been the British, but the first Europeans to arrive were the Portuguese. Bartolomeu Diaz touched land in East Africa on his journey from the Cape to India and back again. On this coast the Portuguese came in contact with the Arab world, establishing ports of call and repair where Arabs were already trading: Kilwa, Zanzibar, Mombasa, Malindi. The nature and extent of Portuguese rights were vague and fluctuating, and they were gradually reduced by the Arabs and then by the British and the Dutch until only the territory of Mozambique remained to them.

The British interest in East Africa was twofold. To the dominant power in the Indian Ocean the coastal territories were a natural bait, while Britain also became a continental African power in the course of establishing control over inland regions which were deemed necessary to safeguard British strategic interests at the Cape and in the valley of the Nile. A northern thrust from the Cape bypassing the Boer republics and continuing into Rhodesia combined with a southern thrust from Egypt and Sudan to create the strategic importance of Uganda and the route of access to it through Kenya. In a particularly colourful chapter of the history of exploration Britain acquired Uganda and Kenya at the end of the nineteenth century, adding Zanzibar in 1890 (in exchange for giving Heligoland to Germany) and Tanganyika in 1919 as a mandated territory after Germany's defeat in the First World War.

British power was not at first territorially deployed. Preferring, as usual, the indirect approach, Britain chose to exert influence on the coast through the sultan of Zanzibar, an Arab potentate who was also sultan of Muscat in Arabia but had moved his capital to Zanzibar in 1840. (Zanzibar and Muscat were separated again in 1861, two sons of a deceased sultan setting up separate states and dynasties as the result of mediation by the viceroy of India, Lord Canning.) Inland, British governments left the business of expansion to commercial concerns until the last quarter of the nineteenth century, when the failure of the companies chartered to exploit parts of Africa, coupled with the competitive expansion of European powers in Africa, induced Britain to shift to policies of territorial annexation. The failure of the British East Africa Company, for example, led Lord Rosebery's cabinet to endorse a British protectorate over Uganda, the prime minister's doubting colleagues being over-persuaded by strategic arguments about the intentions of other European powers, particularly Italy and Belgium, in the regions of the headwaters of the Nile. After the capitulation of the Italians at Adowa in 1896 to the Emperor Menelek II, Britain feared that Ethiopia would make an alliance with France or with the Mahdists in Sudan, and Lord Salisbury pressed the construction of the Uganda railway as a step towards reconquering Sudan. No less important was the contest with Germany, whose determination to become an African power had been made manifest at the Berlin Conference of 1884–85.

The Germans had staked out claims in South West Africa and then in East Africa to the embarrassment of Britain, which disliked German expansion in Africa but was in need of Germany's friendship in Europe during the period of bad Anglo-French relations from 1880 to 1904. Britain consequently acquiesced in the German occupation of South West Africa, while taking the precaution of securing Bechuanaland against possible German (or Boer) aspirations which might interfere with the railway from the Cape northwards. In East Africa Britain likewise acquiesced in a German presence and gave up using the sultan of Zanzibar to make things difficult for the Germans in Tanganyika, while at the same time leasing from the sultan in 1887 a coastal strip 16 km long (including Mombasa) and developing British power in Uganda and Nyasaland so that the emerging German empire might be contained within limits compatible with essential British interests. The First World War eliminated the German factor, but the early part of the twentieth century saw an enterprise which was to produce its own problems. This was the development of Kenya by white settlers. While the removal of great power complications enabled the Foreign Office to dismiss East Africa from its mind, the emergence of new complications of a different nature did not trouble the Colonial Office until too late, for whereas the Devonshire Declaration of 1923 had affirmed the primacy of African interests, the settler community assumed, and was allowed to go on assuming until the eve of independence, that its own powers and privileges were not threatened within the foreseeable future. Even in the 1950s both races believed that a white government's devotion to the principles of self-determination and majority rule would stop short at putting a substantial white community under black rule.

East African independence followed West African but – partly because it came later – was achieved by a telescoped sequence of the established pattern of evolution from nominated to mixed councils and so to the fully elected parliaments which accompanied self-government and presaged independence. Tanganyika became independent in December 1961, Uganda in October 1962 and Kenya in December 1963, but in spite of their geographical closeness the circumstances of the three territories were different.

The special features of *Uganda*'s progress to independence were the country's complex political structure. The Uganda protectorate included a number of monarchical entities, of which the most important was Buganda under the rule of its kabaka Frederick Mutesa II. Others were Bunyoro, Toro, Ankole and Busogo. Moreover, between Buganda and Bunyoro there was a territorial feud of long standing. The existence of these principalities gave Uganda a relatively strong nationalism of a traditionalist kind which was antagonistic both to British colonial rule and to the more democratic and anti-monarchical forms of nationalism. The comparative weakness of these latter strands tended to cast the colonial administration for a progressive role in opposition to the conservatism of the kabaka, who was concerned to preserve his traditional powers and the separate identity of his principality. In 1953 a British minister let fall in London an ill-timed remark about an East African federation, which was taken by the kabaka – and many other Africans – to betoken a British scheme to create a large new political unit for the better preservation of white rule. A central African federation was being formed at this time and East Africans feared that the white settlers in Kenya were to be given throughout East Africa the powers which Southern Rhodesia's white minority was in the process of confirming in its own country and extending to Northern Rhodesia and Nyasaland. A quarrel ensued between the kabaka and the governor, and the kabaka was despatched into exile for failing to observe the Uganda agreement of 1900, by which he was obliged to accept British advice on certain matters.

The kabaka's exile lasted until 1955. A commission under Sir Keith Hancock worked out a new constitution which the kabaka accepted by the Namirembe agreement and by which he agreed to turn Buganda into a constitutional monarchy and recognize it as being an integral part of Uganda; the Buganda parliament, or lukiko, was to send representatives to sit in the Uganda parliament (though it began by refusing to do so). The kabaka was thus restored, but the principality to which he returned was a budding democracy within a larger democracy and the British aim to create an independent Uganda which was a unitary parliamentary democracy and not a federation had been significantly advanced.

Britain failed, however, to resolve Buganda's feud with Bunyoro. This quarrel went back to 1893 when the British under Sir Frederick Lugard and the then kabaka had made war on Bunyoro. Buganda had taken from Bunyoro five counties and two parts of counties and this transfer had been sanctified by Britain in the Uganda agreement of 1900, since when Britain had turned a deaf ear to all Bunyoro complaints until, in 1961, it appointed a commission (the Molson Commission) to try to resolve the quarrel before independence. The commission recommended a compromise which was only partially implemented. Buganda was confirmed in its possession of four counties allotted to it by the commission, but a decision on the rest of the disputed territory was postponed. In 1964, after independence, the government of Uganda conducted the plebiscite which had been recommended by the Molson Commission and which conclusively restored these areas to Bunyoro.

Constitutional change in Uganda had begun in 1950 when the legislative council was given an equal number of official members (that is, colonial servants) and unofficial members. Of the latter eight were African, four Asian and four European in recognition of an ethnic problem which did not, however, impede the advance to independence, owing to the fact that the European settlers were too few to think of retaining political power and the Asians judged it expedient at an early date to conciliate rather than antagonize the African majority. A similar balance of official and unofficial members was established in the executive council in 1952. In 1954 the size of the legislative council was doubled. In 1961 Uganda was given self-government and Benedikto Kiwanuka became its first prime minister, but Bugandan separatism continued to delay full independence. The lukiko, which had petitioned the British crown in 1957 for greater autonomy and refused in the following year to play its allotted role in a general election, declared Buganda independent. The Uganda People's Congress, which had been formed by Milton Obote to fight for independence, entered into an alliance with the Bugandan home rule party Kabaka Yekka in order to win a parliamentary majority. Obote took Kiwanuka's place. Independence followed in October 1962. In the following year Uganda became a republic in the Commonwealth and the kabaka accepted the ornamental office of president. But the alliance between Obote and the kabaka did not last. Early in 1966 rumours of scandals in high places weakened Obote's position. He assumed emergency powers, dismissed and arrested a number of his ministers and dismissed the president. Two months later he introduced a new constitution which precipitated a fresh clash between himself and the lukiko and made himself president. Recurrent rumours of Bugandan plans to resort to force induced him to act first. The kabaka's palace was sacked and the kabaka, barely escaping, was driven once more into exile. No kabaka resided in Buganda until 1993.

Obote was overthrown by an army coup while he was attending a Commonwealth conference in Singapore in 1971. He had antagonized not only traditionalists in Buganda but also the property-owning classes by mildly left-wing pronouncements and intellectuals by authoritarian scorn. After surviving an attempt on his life in 1969 he tried to curb the power of the army and its commander Idi Amin, but failed to do so. Amin took his place. Hailed at first as a good sound army type (and boxing champion) with a respectably British background, Amin instituted a reign of terror, especially after an unsuccessful attempt by Obote in 1972 to invade Uganda from Tanzania with a force of about 1,000 men. Amin was not reluctant to play a part in international affairs. He proclaimed himself a friend of Israel but then changed sides and became a strong partisan of the Palestinians.

He made a particular stir by giving notice to Uganda's 70,000 Asians to leave the country within three months, though he later exempted those of them who were Ugandan citizens. Since most of them were British citizens Amin's move greatly embarrassed the British government which, having foolishly failed to take up an earlier offer by Obote to discuss this problem, now found itself caught between its evident obligation to allow

British citizens into Britain and the clamour against allowing them in if they were numerous and black. Amin also evicted the British military mission and high commissioner whom he accused of complicity in Obote's attempted counter-coup. In the following year he began the takeover of hundreds of foreign, mostly British, businesses while throughout the country the roll of Ugandans, distinguished and undistinguished, who disappeared increased gruesomely to 500,000 by the time he was overthrown in 1979. Amin was what ordinary people call mad. (Coincidentally, 1979 saw the disappearance of two other mad monsters, the emperor Jean-Bedel Bokassa of Central Africa and President Macias Nguema of Equatorial Guinea. All three had received more support than was decent from the three antecedent colonial powers.)

Amin's fall was effected by a Tanzanian invasion, the only practical step by any African state to rid the continent of a barbarous tyranny. A Tanzanian force, accompanied by a Ugandan National Liberation Army, seized the capital without difficulty and installed a provisional government under a former vice-chancellor of Makerere university Dr Yusufu Lule. After a mere two months Lule was deposed by his National Consultative Council and was replaced by Godfrey Binaisa, a lawyer who had held ministerial office under Obote. Binaisa was himself deposed by the army and placed in detention while a pro-Obote council took over the government. These changes, together with Nyerere's known partisanship of Obote, who soon reappeared in Uganda, presaged the latter's return to power, and at the end of 1980 his popularity in the northern half of the country and the active support of the civil and military authorities carried him back to the presidency by a narrow and disputed margin. His rule, which lasted until 1985, was disastrous and hardly less bloody than Amin's. With ethnic feuds unabated and the army out of hand, mass slaughter was reduced only by mass flight – mainly to Sudan and Zaïre. Those who ousted Obote were soon fighting one another. The ultimate victor was the National Resistance Army of Yoweri Museveni which, having defeated Obote's forces and the succeeding military government of Tito Okello, put an end to organized opposition by the defeat of General Basilio Okello in the north (but mopping up continued for three years). Museveni became the new president at the age of 40 with a reputation for decency and political acumen, an appalling legacy of savage destruction and no obvious way to convert foreign sympathy into economic aid. The country's infrastructure had been destroyed, foreign debts and their servicing shackled an economy which was also saddled with the costs of an overblown army, and the north and other regions hankered after a decentralized federalism. Museveni was committed to the one-party state but was obliged to concede the principle of pluralism. He was somewhat compromised by his supposed involvement in 1990 in the invasion of Rwanda by Tutsis from Uganda – a fiasco – but elections in 1996 gave him clear, if not universal, popular approval. Armed disaffection in the north and west, aided by Sudan and Mobutu, was diminished but not eliminated by the weakening of the former and the overthrow of the latter. In concert with Tanzania, Ethiopia and Kabila's new regime in Zaïre, Museveni promoted COMESA (Common Market for

Eastern and Southern Africa) which aimed to maximize co-operation in the large sweep of territory from the Red Sea through the region of the Great Lakes to Africa's southern tip and to bolster its member states against unwanted foreign interference but all these partners were in other matters divided.

Tanganyika proceeded through official–unofficial partnership in government to self-government and independence, but the British authorities tried to give a special multiracial twist to events by espousing the equality of races as opposed to the equality of individuals. This concept was enshrined in a constitution of 1955 which provided that the electors in each constituency should all elect one member of each of the three races, but a party formed to apply it, the United Tanganyika Party, never secured much support and was eclipsed by the Tanganyika African National Union (TANU) formed by Julius Nyerere in 1954. In 1957 Nyerere, who had been asking for independence in 25 years' time, was appointed a member of the legislative council together with Rashid Kawawa, but he soon resigned in order to press the pace and urge independence by 1969. In elections spread over a period in 1958–59 TANU won all the seats which it contested, and in 1960 it extended its victories throughout the country. The multiracial experiment was given up after a change of governor and colonial secretary in 1959, and Tanganyika attained independence in 1961. It chose to be a republic and a member of the Commonwealth.

Tanganyika did not have the buried riches which some African countries possessed but it did have two distinctive, if elusive, advantages: it had no dominant ethnic group and it had in Julius Nyerere a leader uncommonly intelligent, principled and humane. Its peculiar vexation was the problem of Zanzibar.

By an act of union with the islands of Zanzibar and Pemba in 1977 Tanganyika became *Tanzania*. In Zanzibar, when still a British dependency, the Afro-Shirazi Union staged a successful coup at the beginning of 1964. This party, which represented the bulk of the African population of about 200,000 (the Arabs numbering some 44,000) had suffered a setback in elections in 1961 which had given control to a coalition of the Zanzibar National Party and the Zanzibar People's Party; and in 1963 the British, ignoring warnings from Tanganyika, had transferred power to the sultan and the Arab minority, with the result that Zanzibar had carried into independence an inbuilt racial conflict in which the scales had been artificially tipped in favour of a minority. The Afro-Shirazi Union wanted neither the sultan nor any kind of Arab dominance. Its leaders – Abeid Karume, Abdullah Hanga, Othman Shariff – led what was essentially an anti-Arab revolt and proclaimed a republic with the first two as president and vice-president. Their allies included a minor Arab party, the Umma Party, led by Abdul Rahman Muhammad Babu, the local correspondent of the New China News Agency, and a soldier of fortune styled Field-Marshal John Okello, who was said to have fought in Cuba but was soon sent into exile when the value of his services proved less than the embarrassment of his presence. The Afro-Shirazis and their friends were quickly branded by a startled world as tools of China.

Alarm was felt in Dar-es-Salaam and on 17 January Nyerere sent armed police to Zanzibar to gain control of the situation. On 20 January troops in Dar-es-Salaam mutinied; a second mutiny occurred at Tabora in central Tanganyika on the following day. Similar acts of insubordination took place in Uganda and Kenya on the 23rd and 24th. In all these places order was restored with the help of British troops who were still stationed in Nairobi (they were not due to leave until the end of the year). The mutineers asked for better pay and the replacement of British officers by Africans; they were using violence to protest to their leaders, not to overthrow them. But in the light of events in Zanzibar rumours circulated of a widespread communist plot, reinforced by Okello's presence in Dar-es-Salaam on the eve of the first disturbances. The British left a week after their arrival and Tanzania came into existence with Nyerere as president and Karume as senior vice-president. The association proved unhappy. Nyerere was denied influence in Zanzibar and even access to it. Karume established an autocratic and scandalous regime and managed in 1969 to exact from Nyerere the return to Zanzibar of political enemies who were thereby consigned to their deaths. He was assassinated in 1972.

Nyerere tried to steer an even-handed course between the protagonists in the Cold War but won in return little from the communist side and only grudging aid from the west. He tried to promote the health and wealth of his country by applying socialist ideals to rural society and agricultural productivity but failed to persuade or coerce country people into collectives and bequeathed to his successor Ali Hassan Mwinyi an economy which, partly by bad management and partly from bad luck and its own inherent weaknesses, was faced with famine, rationing, a declining standard of living and unpayable debts: 40 per cent of tax revenues had to be spent on servicing public debt. He resigned the presidency in 1985 but remained chairman of Tanzania's ruling party, Chama cha Mapindusi (CCM), and was re-elected to that post in 1997 for a further five years. He criticized his successor's economic policies as Mwinyi turned for help to the IMF and secured large credits at the price of devaluing the currency by 50 per cent and accepting the standard IMF package of funds in return for austerity – the policy which Nyerere had opposed. Mwinyi had also problems in Zanzibar, where he had been president. His successor there, Abdul Wakif, was a figurehead and Zanzibaris feared outright annexation; they took to the streets and people were killed. After elections Mwinyi appointed a new prime minister John Malecela, who became thereby the designated next president but Nyerere and the CCM preferred Ben Mkapa, who won chaotic elections in 1995 which reflected little credit on multiparty democracy (which Nyerere had consistently opposed) and weakened the presidency. Nyerere died in 1999, a statesman outstanding for his uprightness and moderation in tandem with a passionate devotion to the freedom of individuals and peoples. His successors made the best of what little the country had. Its chief asset was the absence of a tribal pattern.

One of the most important elections in the history of British decolonization was held not in any colony but in Britain itself. In 1959 Harold Macmillan was returned to power by the British electorate and one of his first undertakings after this refreshing experience was a journey through Africa which made manifest a new attitude to colonial affairs. Macmillan had felt the 'wind of change' and had determined to let it blow him along. His new colonial secretary Iain Macleod was immediately faced with the most difficult of all the East African situations, Kenya.

In *Kenya* unofficial members of the legislative council began to be given ministerial appointments immediately after the end of the Second World War. They were, however, not black but white, representatives of the British settlers who had been coming to Kenya since the beginning of the century and had been acquiring and developing, in good faith and with intelligent toil, the excellent agricultural land in what came to be called the White Highlands. This community became also politically powerful. It hoped either to rule Kenya in lieu of the colonial authorities or to share in governing a multiracial state on a scale appropriate to its wealth and sophistication rather than to its numbers. It was, in other words, an aristocracy with scant prospects in a democracy and it was suddenly faced with the problems, more familiar to historians than to farmers, of the aristocracy which is required by events to come to terms with a non-aristocratic future. In 1953 this community and the colonial regime were faced with a savage outbreak among the Kikuyus who lived in and around Nairobi and had long nourished grievances against the white settlers as well as hostility to black neighbours.

The Kikuyu and Luo were Kenya's two main ethnic groups, led respectively by Jomo Kenyatta, one-time student of anthropology at London University and president of the Kenya African National Union (KANU), who had returned to Africa in 1947, and Oginga Odinga. The British refused to allow them to form political parties in central Kenya and promoted as a counterweight an association of smaller tribes (the Kenya African Democratic Union – KADU). Shortly after Kenyatta's return the Kikuyu formed a secret society called Mau Mau, whose activities – known to the authorities but not made much of – were the militant expression of a deep-seated nationalist or xenophobic movement. Mau Mau administered oaths and performed secret rites and cherished apocalyptic fancies, all of which were anti-European and anti-Christian. With time the society became extreme in its ambitions and barbarous in its practices. It took to murder – mostly of other Kikuyu – and finally developed a campaign of violence and guerrilla warfare. The government declared an emergency, called for military reinforcements from neighbouring territories and from Britain, arrested thousands of Kikuyu, including Kenyatta (who was sentenced in 1954 to seven years' imprisonment for organizing Mau Mau), and gradually suppressed the rising. It also initiated a programme for the psychological reorientation of the detainees, although in other departments it succumbed to the infectious passions roused by the Mau Mau and became responsible for ugly beatings of detainees, notably at the Hola camp where gross inhumanities and murders were disclosed at a coroner's inquest in 1959. The African victims of Mau Mau numbered about 10,000; the number of Europeans killed was 68. Suppressing the insurrection took the British five years and 50,000 troops.

The British government realized that Mau Mau could not be made an excuse for abandoning constitutional advance and in 1956, the year of the termination of the emergency, it introduced changes in the legislative council. The guiding principle was that of multiracialism or partnership between the races, a theory of government which found almost no support among the Africans, who demanded a majority in the legislative and executive councils and refused to accept parity with the European elected members in the former or a minority of seats in the latter. To Africans multiracialism was a device for giving the whites unfair shares. The Africans also insisted on being given a date for independence, whereas the British government, unwilling to accept the evidence of an accelerating tempo throughout Africa or to affront the Kenyan settlers by naming a date acceptable to Africans, tried to proceed towards independence at an unrevealed pace without losing control of the situation. In 1959 this policy was abandoned (along with the current colonial secretary) and Kenyatta was conditionally released; in 1961 he was given full freedom of movement and then allowed to stand for and be elected to the legislative assembly.

A constitutional conference was held at Lancaster House in London in 1960 and shortly afterwards the leader of government business in the assembly Ronald Ngala was upgraded to chief minister. But the African political leaders were divided among themselves. Many of them represented tribes rather than a nation and they failed to create the single unified independence movement which was characteristic of other emergent African countries. The weaker tribes combined to oppose the stronger Kikuyu and Luo and to press for a federal constitution in which important powers would reside in regions rather than with the central government. Constitutional conferences became contests between KADU, the proponents of regionalism led by Ngala, and KANU, which objected that too much regionalism would make the constitution unworkable and that Kenya had neither the money nor the trained administrators to be able to afford the complications and duplications of a federal system. The advantage lay with KANU, under the leadership of Kenyatta, who became prime minister in June 1963, and the British government was forced to amend constitutional proposals of a federal nature which had earlier been accepted by all parties: KANU's electoral success earlier in the year enabled it to face the British government with the choice between revising the constitution on the eve of independence or seeing it changed immediately afterwards. The British preferred to give way in the hope of sparing Kenya a constitutional crisis on the morrow of independence, even though the cost of concession was a not implausible charge of bad faith from KADU. Kenya became independent on 12 December 1963. It became a republic in 1964, whereupon Kenyatta removed the constitutional safeguards for minorities and regional rights and, by absorbing KADU into KANU, created a centralized one-party state. He removed his principal rival Oginga Odinga from the vice-presidency and put him in detention but in a contrary mood he favoured the political career of the able young Luo Tom Mboya. (In 1969 Mboya was assassinated.)

Kenya under Kenyatta was a relatively stable country run by a progressively more corrupt black elite. Nairobi became a magnet for the rural unemployed who congregated in shanty towns, which were sporadically destroyed by the authorities. Kenya's relations with its neighbours deteriorated. Its rumbustious capitalism grated with Tanzania's possibly more salubrious but less successful socialism and these ideological differences turned in the 1970s into bickerings, mutual expulsions and the closing of the frontier. With Uganda a border dispute initiated by Amin almost led to war. Kenyatta's senescence was another source of worries. His family and familiars were expected to make a bid to retain power and affluence when he died but in the event (1978) vice-president Daniel Moi stepped smoothly into his place with promises of continuing the country's good fortunes and erasing its less estimable features.

Moi had been a useful servant of KANU and was promoted by Kenyatta to home minister and then vice-president. His advancement indicated that Kenya was to have a tribal coalition government and Kikuyu dominion. He displayed unexpected authority and gave Kenya a second instalment of comparative political stability. He withstood a semi-covert challenge from Charles Njonjo (one of Kenyatta's more ebullient colleagues and a standard-bearer of the Kikuyus) and he survived an attempted coup in 1982, but his position was sapped by Kikuyu resentment at his elevation – he came from the minor Kalenjin tribe – and by economic recession. He harassed independent bodies (lawyers, for example) and resorted to strong-arm rule, imprisonment and torture, while he himself became a flagrantly rich man surrounded by mediocre cronies. Kenya's ambition to be the Ivory Coast of the east – a thrustingly successful capitalist state – lost its momentum, unemployment rose, wages fell, landless cultivators flocked to the capital, which became one of the more dangerous cities in Africa, and by the mid-1980s corruption had led to financial scandals, collapsing banks and secret police intrigue. The importance of Kenya's ocean coast (a tropical paradise) attracted the United States, which built bases there, dispensed lucrative contracts and provided funds for strategic and less serious ancillary services. Kenya's relations with its neighbours were poor, particularly with Uganda: each country harboured refugees from the other. The murder in 1990 of the (Luo) Robert Ouko, foreign minister and possible successor to Moi, and the arrest in 1991 after accumulating accusations of gross peculation of the former economics minister Nicholas Biwott, increased clamour against the government but not coherence in the opposition. Serious disorders approaching civil war ravaged the Rift Valley as Kikuyu and Luo were killed or driven out of their homes by Kalenjin, Moi's people. Ethnic divisions were compounded by class divisions as Moi manoeuvred between new rich landowners and tycoons on the one hand and less wealthy traders and speculators in rapidly growing towns. By 1992 elections – the first multiparty elections of the Moi era – could no longer be deferred, KANU suffered severe losses, 15 ministers lost their seats; but the opposition lost their opportunity and much of their credit. Foreign governments suspended aid as reports of corruption and breaches of human rights multiplied. Like Nigeria on the opposite side of the continent,

Kenya might be either dynamo or demon. It hoped to play a leading part in the Common Market for Eastern and Southern Africa – an association of 20 countries with a population of over 300 million, which aimed to become a free trade area by the year 2000 and a complete customs union by 2004. (See also SADC, p. 636.) But Kenya had few friends among its neighbours. It negotiated in 1992 a considerable programme of loans from the IMF for help in servicing its foreign debt (over $6 billion) and for domestic economic and social developments: it was short of capital, skills, material and educational infrastructure (particularly roads and irrigation) and good government. It implemented the greater part of a privatization programme agreed with the IMF and enjoyed thriving exports and economic growth (with tea, coffee and tourism leading) but forfeited in 1997 a substantial part of IMF aid for failing to take steps to check corruption. Moi felt strong enough to defy the IMF, play off one opposition party against another and bring Biwott and other discredited friends back into government. The Kikuyu, especially important on account of their numbers (22 per cent of the population) and business acumen, played hard to get between government and opposition, while the fall of Mobutu in Zaïre encouraged dissidents of diverse kinds from tribal adversaries to younger generations to demonstrate more brazenly and even threaten anarchy. None of which prevented Moi from securing another term of office in 1997.

In 2002 Moi was succeeded by Mwai Kibaki (a Kikuyu) who promised to investigate and eliminate corruption and conciliate other tribes but failed on both counts. After indications that he would create the post of prime minister to share power with himself as president and give this new post to Raila Odinga, son of the Luo leader Oginda Odinga, he succumbed to partisan pressures, gave Odinga a minor post and then fired him. The prosecution of criminal corruption charges was halted. Odinga formed a coalition of opposition parties, seemed to be cruising to victory in 2007 but was declared the loser by a narrow margin and to general disbelief. The United States accepted the validity of Kenya's electoral commission's verdict but European observers did not. Nor did the voters themselves. Violent protests scorched various parts of the country. Hundreds – perhaps 1,000 – were killed in the first week after the elections and 250,000 people were in flight from their homes. The shock and dismay occasioned by these events were all the sharper since post-colonial Kenya had been adjudged a success story. Yet it was a success story in a country of considerable size of which less than half was productive, where loyalties remained tribal rather than national, where the largest tribe (the Kikuyu) had spread beyond its traditional boundaries by entrepreneurial skills but also by conspicuous corruption, where the population was set to double every 50 years (unless ravaged by the plague which was already in evidence in the form of AIDS). The immediate problems were patched up through mediation by the former UN secretary-general Kofi Annan and other African personalities but the basic problem remained. Kenya was caught in a transitional stage between a loose tribal association which was being filtered through colonial rule towards European-style statehood (for the European sovereign state see Appendix p. 800) while at the same time joining at a bound the economic development which had started centuries in the past in Europe with the invention of the letter of credit.

Before and after independence these three countries toyed with schemes for closer economic integration or even federation. In 1963 Kawawa and Obote went to London to try to persuade Britain to hurry Kenya into independence (delayed by Mau Mau) and shortly after their return leaders of all three countries declared their intention to federate. Uganda, however, had reservations about a federation since Obote feared that Buganda would insist on being a full member of such a union instead of a component part of Uganda. Kenyatta subsequently disclaimed any serious intention to federate, declaring that the plan had been no more than a means of pressing Britain to hasten Kenya's independence. Perhaps Nyerere alone was wholehearted. The proceedings were certainly dilatory. Obote failed to attend a meeting held in Nairobi to discuss the scheme, and the Kenyans established an awkward system of being represented by KANU at one meeting and KADU at the next. There were also genuine difficulties such as the location of the federal capital, the choice of a federal president (the promotion of Kenyatta, the obvious candidate, would unleash an inopportune contest for the Kenyan presidency), the division of powers and other constitutional matters, opposition from Ghana to any regional associations likely to hamper Nkrumah's pan-African schemes, and Tanganyika's trend to the left in its domestic and external policies. In the end Tanganyika, regretfully but firmly, insisted on a decision and the scheme thereupon collapsed.

The three East African territories made some attempts to integrate their economies. Under British rule they had had a common currency and certain common services (posts, railways, medical services) and had constituted a common market. Tanganyika and Uganda complained, at intervals and with some justice, that Kenya took the lion's share of the resulting benefits and in 1960 the Raisman Commission was appointed to report on these dissensions. It recommended that the links should be retained subject to some reorganization in favour of Tanganyika and Uganda. In 1964 Kenya offered further concessions in order to prevent the disruption of this partial union and in 1968, after a fresh inquiry and report by a Danish expert, the three states signed a Treaty of East African Co-operation. It became a dead letter as the three partners pursued divergent social and economic policies and their relations became strained, and it was finally dissolved in 1977.

CHAPTER 25

Africa's deep south

The legacy of Cecil Rhodes

Towards the end of the nineteenth century the British in Cape Colony, hemmed in by the German occupation of South West Africa on the one hand and the Boer republics across the Orange and Vaal rivers on the other, ventured northwards in order to rule out a junction between these two potential enemies and to secure a passage for a railway to the north through British territory. In 1844 Britain declared a protectorate over Bechuanaland, huge and largely desert, but for the rest of the century it was a British citizen rather than any British government who directed the British advance. That citizen was Cecil Rhodes and one reason why he was able to direct policy was that he was able to finance it.

Rhodes struck north into Bechuanaland with his eyes on the Zambezi river – and possibly even the Nile. His company, the British South Africa Company, was chartered by the British government in 1889 to administer Bechuanaland and in 1896–97 he conquered the Ndebele Shona and so became the ruler of what was later to be called Southern Rhodesia. In 1896 the failure of the Jameson raid into the Transvaal wrecked his ambition to rule in Johannesburg too and resulted in a reassertion of British governmental control over policy towards the Boers: in 1899 it was the British government and not Rhodes who made the Boer War. From Southern Rhodesia he continued across the Zambezi and, with questionable legality, won concessions from the sovereign, or litunga, of Barotseland and other African chiefs. He added Nyasaland to his empire but did not reach Katanga, a likely next candidate. The British government gave the South Africa Company mineral rights (which turned out to be extremely lucrative after the opening of Northern Rhodesia's copper mines) but limited its administrative powers. In 1923 Britain transferred control of internal affairs to Southern Rhodesia's white settler community. The alternative of uniting it with South Africa was mooted but rejected by the white settlers in Southern Rhodesia. The question of forms of association between various British territories was already in the air but in 1929, when the Hilton Young Commission reported on this area, Northern Rhodesia and Nyasaland were expected to consort with Tanganyika rather than Southern Rhodesia, and in 1930 Britain accentuated the differences between the two Rhodesias by declaring that in protectorates native interests were paramount. Nyasaland had been a protectorate since 1907 – it was first penetrated by Scottish missionaries rather than militant pioneers – and Northern Rhodesia became a protectorate in 1924. In Southern Rhodesia the Land Apportionment Act of 1930 pointed in the opposite direction.

Rhodes had been chiefly interested in mineral rights. By the so-called Rudd Concession signed by the Ndebele monarch, Lobengula, Rhodes acquired for £1,200 a year mineral rights (which his company sold in 1933 to the government of Southern Rhodesia). Also from Lobengula he acquired indirectly through a certain Lippert for £1,000 a year 'land' rights which later gave rise to a long controversy as to whether his company had bought the whole of the surface of Southern Rhodesia. At the time of self-government the company, which had previously resold 31 million acres, transferred a balance of 45 million acres to the new government. In 1914 21 million acres had been 'reserved' for the native population and a royal commission had judged this to be enough. In 1930 the whole of the country was divided by the Land Apportionment Act into European Areas, Native Purchase Areas, Unoccupied Areas and Forests, but the division was regarded by the Africans as unjust since the Europeans, who constituted less than a fifth of the population, were allotted a slightly larger share of the whole, and all the towns; in this area no African might own land. The 1930 division therefore sharpened instead of allaying resentments about how the land had been acquired in the first place, and showed that in Southern Rhodesia native interests would be anything but paramount. In 1938 the Bledisloe Commission rejected closer union between the two Rhodesias and Nyasaland on the specific grounds that divergences in native policies and the hostility of the Africans made it impracticable. It recommended no more than a Central African Council consisting of the governors of the protectorates and the prime minister of Southern Rhodesia to collaborate on matters of common concern. This council was created in 1944, but the protagonists of closer union were not discouraged and nine years later they secured the creation of the Central African Federation. Throughout these years Southern Rhodesia was pursuing a policy of association with Northern Rhodesia in preference to association with South Africa: it was not contemplating a separate existence although a minor white group wanted dominion status in the Commonwealth.

White leaders in Northern and Southern Rhodesia were wary of one another. Roy Welensky in the north, where the riches lay, suspected Godfrey Huggins in the south of wishing to take over Northern Rhodesia for the benefit of the more numerous white population of Southern Rhodesia. On the other hand, Southern Rhodesia, although poorer, had a higher degree of quasi-independence, which the whites in Northern Rhodesia (excluding the colonial administrators) coveted for themselves and wished to secure through the Southern Rhodesian back door. These attitudes were to the fore at a conference at Victoria Falls in 1949 which, with no African present, became a tussle between Huggins and Welensky, with the latter falling back on the position that there should be no federation without a referendum. The northerners were suspicious of the

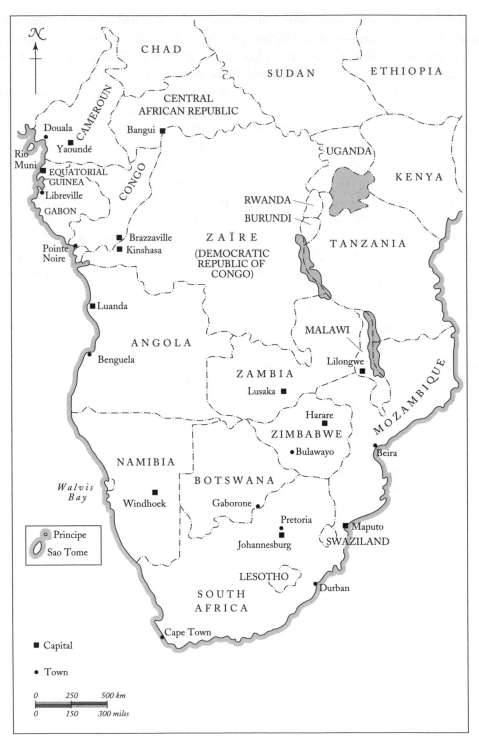

25.1 Equatorial and southern Africa

federal idea, but the conference put it on the map and made it the central talking-point of the next few years. This conference was followed in 1951 by a conference in London of officials from the three territories and the two British departments of state concerned (the Colonial Office and the Commonwealth Relations Office). Their report, while again recognizing African opposition to federation, hoped that it would evaporate under the impact of the economic advantages which they listed. At a further conference in the same year at Victoria Falls the politicians (who included the two British secretaries of state), senior officials and white Rhodesian leaders accepted the greater part of the officials' arguments. This conference was attended by Africans from Northern Rhodesia and Nyasaland, but they were less impressed by the economic advantages of a federation than by the fear of coming under the rule of the white minority in Salisbury.

A change of government in London from Labour to Conservative shifted the balance in favour of federation. Whereas Labour ministers had come to look favourably on federation but were unwilling to go forward without first discovering more about the wishes of the African population, Conservative ministers were more emphatic in their approval, considered that it was impossible to discover what the Africans really thought, ascribed African opposition to irascible and ignorant factiousness, and believed that it was in any case the duty of government to do what was best even if some people did not yet see how good it was. Yet another conference assembled, this time at Lancaster House in London (the maternity ward for emergent constitutions). It was boycotted by the Africans of the two northern territories, but the Southern Rhodesian delegation included Joseph Savanhu and Joshua Nkomo, who acted as uneasy camp-followers until the end of the conference. The outcome was a federal constitution with temporarily significant reservations. The federation was to have three separate territorial administrations and assemblies as well as a federal government and parliament, the retention of the British protectorate over the northern territories, the proviso that the federation should not be granted dominion status without the consent of a majority of the population, and the creation of an African Affairs Board with blocking powers designed (unsuccessfully as it proved) to prevent racially discriminatory legislation. The federation came into being on 1 August 1953. Huggins became the first federal prime minister with Welensky as his deputy and a cabinet of six; Huggins also became the leader of a newly formed Federal Party with branches on both sides of the Zambezi. In Southern Rhodesia he was succeeded by Garfield Todd as prime minister and leader of the United Party.

The *Central African Federation* lasted ten years. It was accepted with misgiving by some whites in Southern Rhodesia who feared cheap black labour and opined that the connection with the British protecting power in the north would act as a drag on their plans for dealing with the racial situation. But on the whole federation was welcomed by the whites, who believed that within it they would conserve their privileged standards of living, excitingly expand the material things which they were already doing well, and somehow find a way of fitting a small African middle class into the existing order. The idea of partnership, which was written into the constitution and salved a lot of uneasy consciences in London, meant at best a half share in power for Africans in a barely discernible future. Like the Belgians in the Congo, they regarded the African as an economic man who could be satisfied with a material competence (however assessed) and, apart from a few overeducated eccentrics, had no real interest in politics. Nationalism they grievously underestimated, and also the force of human indignation over inequality and injustice. Ideas were not their stock-in-trade and so they failed to realize that ideas were at the root of the refusal of the Africans to accept their rule. From the prime minister downwards they insulted and humiliated their black fellow citizens with remarks about living in trees and with the practical application of segregation in public places like post offices and restaurants, and so quickly confirmed the Africans' conviction that partnership was to be not an endeavour but a pretence.

The life of the federation was violent and short. The Africans began the violence. Most of them were never interested in the economic aspects of federation or never understood them; the more sophisticated judged them bogus. The partisans of violence, aided by circumstances and by exaggerated white reactions, became increasingly prominent. An incident provoked by thieves in the night at Cholo in Nyasaland in 1953 caused the death of 11 Africans and injuries to many more and led the authorities to magnify the prevalence of hooliganism and subversion. It was also a curtain-raiser for more significant events in Nyasaland.

Nyasaland was included in the federation because the British insisted, unwilling to keep it on their hands as a separate dependency with little hope of becoming anything but a drain on the British exchequer. It was an African country with a white population of only 1 in 500, no settlers or industry, its people dependent on Southern Rhodesia and South Africa for the jobs which had not been created in their own country. It had a charismatic figure beyond the horizon in Dr Hastings Banda, who had spent most of his life practising medicine in the United States, Scotland, Liverpool, Tyneside and Ghana.

Dr Banda arrived in Nyasaland in 1958 to lead an anti-federation crusade in conjunction with nationalists of a younger generation who were glad to enlist under this famous elder figure. As in many similar cases differences of aim and outlook were submerged by the single paramount objective of seceding from the federation and establishing an independent sovereign state. A secret and confused palaver between nationalist leaders early in 1959 was represented as a conspiracy to kill a number of Europeans and seize power. Banda was not present at this meeting and either knew nothing of it, or did not mind what happened at it, or knew all about it and chose to turn a blind eye. He himself was a man of considerable, even violent, oratorical powers who preached non-violence, but the situation was one of growing violence and jumpiness and the governor of Nyasaland asked for Rhodesian troops to help keep order. Southern

Rhodesia sent 3,000 troops and took the opportunity to declare a state of emergency in its own territory. The governor of Nyasaland followed suit a week later. Between 2,000 and 3,000 Africans were rounded up in the federation, the African National Congresses in all three territories were dissolved and Banda and his chief associates were among those lodged in jail. The British colonial secretary Alan Lennox-Boyd said that he had evidence of an impending massacre.

These dramatic events evoked scepticism as well as alarm, and the British government appointed a commission under a High Court judge Sir Patrick Devlin to verify the allegations with which these emergency measures had been justified. The commission was unable to find evidence of any murder plot and specifically exonerated Banda. It found that the governor of Nyasaland had got into a position where he had either to abdicate or reach for emergency powers and troops, and that, in consequence, Nyasaland had become temporarily a police state in which it was unsafe to express approval of the policies of the Congress to which the great majority of Africans adhered. This report, by exploding a myth propagated by authorities in London as well as Salisbury, gave a fillip to the anti-federation campaign and discredited the bona fides of their opponents. Shortly after its appearance the Colonial Office was placed in the charge of a more liberal member of the Conservative government, Iain Macleod, and the prime minister Harold Macmillan began a series of moves designed to give British colonial policies a leftward shift. These moves were to include his tour of Africa, his 'wind of change' speech at Cape Town during that tour, the appointment of the Monckton Commission, and Macleod's first visit to Kenya – all in 1960.

The federal constitution of 1953 had left the three territorial constitutions untouched. It had also made clear that the federation could not hope for independence or dominion status until they were touched. In 1958 there were elections for the federal and the Southern Rhodesian parliaments. In the former Welensky, who had succeeded Huggins (now Lord Malvern) in 1956, scored an overwhelming victory; few of the qualified Africans bothered to register or vote, partly because they disliked the existing two-roll franchise and partly because they were afraid of the police. In Southern Rhodesia Todd was forced to resign by his cabinet colleagues, who refused to accept a wage increase for Africans, which had been recommended by the Labour Board. They regarded the comparatively liberal Todd as an electoral Jonah. He was allowed a seat in the new cabinet formed by Sir Edgar Whitehead but was soon dropped and in the elections his new United Rhodesia Party won not a single seat. Whitehead scraped in, although the Dominion Party, led by Winston Field, campaigning in favour of independence by 1960, got more votes. This eclipse of Todd was in part a white reaction to the reanimation of the African National Congress by George Nyandoro and Robert Chikerema in 1957 and was also the first of a series of moves which placed the premiership in the hands of ever more extreme politicians, who were gradually forced to be more explicit about the basic white demand for independence from Britain as the only way of ensuring that power would remain in white hands for as long as anybody cared to look into the future. In Northern Rhodesia a new constitution preceded elections in 1959 which gave victory to the United Federal Party (the new name for the local version of the Huggins–Welensky party); the party was, however, almost universally rejected by Africans in spite of the support it received from the whole press. These elections showed that the enchantments of federation were not working even before the alleged murder plot and the judgments of the Devlin Commission.

From about 1960 there was, in effect, a race between the forces which wanted to extract independence for the federation out of the British government and the forces which wanted to break up the federation and establish black rule in its several parts. The British government, caught in this crossfire, resorted to the expedient of sending a commission to look into the situation. Welensky opposed this manoeuvre in private but acquiesced in public. The Africans boycotted it. The commission, presided over by Lord Monckton, an eminent Queen's Counsel and former Conservative minister, produced an ambivalent report in which a majority extolled the principle of federation but judged it unworkable. The commission's work inevitably raised the question of the right to secede from the federation, although the white leaders in Rhodesia and their friends in Britain contended that the commission had no power to consider the matter and that the British prime minister had promised that it would not be raised; a majority concluded that there was no legal right to secede but that, as a matter of practical politics, the issue should be placed on the agenda of a federal review conference and that Britain should declare its willingness to permit secession after the passage of a defined trial period of federation. This recommendation placed federation on probation. The commission's report marked the turning of the tide in favour of the break-up of the federation, even though the commission gave more attention to reforms designed to make it work (such as parity between Europeans and Africans in the federal parliament, a broader franchise, and immediate advances towards self-government in Northern Rhodesia).

A federal review conference assembled in London at the end of 1960. The federal constitution did not require such a conference at this date but in the judgement of the British government it had become necessary. Yet it achieved nothing and was adjourned *sine die*, to be followed by a Northern Rhodesia constitutional conference which produced backstage fighting in which Welensky (who, like Cecil Rhodes, relied partly on a group of members of the Westminister parliament) was worsted by Macmillan and Macleod. Each side suspected the other, perhaps correctly, of being about to use force and Welensky called up troops. The constitutional proposals which emerged would have made it impossible for Welensky to secure control of the Northern Rhodesian parliament but a White Paper made some slight concessions to Welensky. Kenneth Kaunda and other leaders of the United National Independence Party (UNIP) accused the British of tinkering behind the scenes with the agreed outcome of the conference; there were violent demonstrations in Northern Rhodesia and the concessions were reversed. These swingings and swayings reflected the divided mind of the British Conservative Party and cabinet; it was reasonably clear that the federation was doomed, although nobody was prepared to say so; and although Welensky and his white followers had fervent friends in London, there was a growing body of opinion which recognized the greater expendiency of being friends with Kaunda and the many African states which stood behind him. A third set of proposals was propounded which ensured that neither UNIP nor the Federal Party could get a parliamentary majority and was in any case too complicated to be understood by anybody but a constitutional maniac. It was rejected by Kaunda.

During this period another conference went through similar travail to produce a new constitution for Southern Rhodesia. Its proposals, which guaranteed a larger minority parliamentary representation to Africans but also removed nearly all the residual powers of the British government, were accepted by Nkomo at the conference but repudiated by him immediately afterwards because he came to believe, again probably correctly, that if he accepted the increased number of seats, the British government would immediately grant independence to Southern Rhodesia under its white rulers, who would then either arrest or reverse the advance towards African majority rule. The British government had hoped to find a formula containing a large enough element of agreement to enable it to give independence with a good conscience and get out of a hopeless situation, but African insistence on the magic formula of majority rights – echoed by many in Britain itself – baulked its efforts and kept it on the hook.

The following year, 1962, saw an abortive British plan to carve up Northern Rhodesia by elevating Barotseland into a separate state under its traditional and conservative ruler, the litunga, and by giving a further slice of it to Southern Rhodesia. The only effect of this bizarre notion was to create bad blood between the nationalists and traditionalists. R. A. Butler was then appointed to a special office of Central African Affairs. His business was to assuage the internal feuding in the Conservative Party and to wind up the federation. By the end of the year Nyasaland had been promised self-government and the right to secede from the federation. In Northern Rhodesia UNIP was asked to join the government in 1962 and the right to secede from the federation was acknowledged in 1963. With the secession of Northern Rhodesia there was no federation left. It expired on the last day of 1963.

Nyasaland and Northern Rhodesia, independent from July and October 1964, became the republics of *Malawi* and Zambia (both of them within the Commonwealth) with Banda and Kaunda as their presidents. Banda developed into a conservative dictator, intolerant of opposition but successful both in surviving threats of civil war and in developing Malawi's agricultural economy to the point where he was able to raise in 1978 a Euroloan of £14 million. Under a plausible plea of economic necessity he made a commercial agreement (1967) and established conventional relations with South Africa and he supported Renamo in Mozambique (see p. 614) until about 1986.

Autocratic, sharply anti-communist, morally intolerant, Banda had some of the traits of the South African Nationalists. As age dimmed his wits his authority passed to Cecilia Kadzamisa and her uncle John Tembo, who became Banda's heir apparent in a situation of deepening uncertainty. In 1993 a referendum on constitutional change, followed by brain surgery on Banda in South Africa, strengthened opposition to a regime approaching its conclusion. When elections came, Banda's party held some seats in the central segment of the country but north and south were swept by two different parties and the winner in the south – the United Democratic Front – emerged with a clear parliamentary majority. Its leader, Bakili Muluzu, became president with, however, a need to conciliate the north. The aged Banda and his closest associates were charged with murder and other crimes. He died in 1997, nearing 100, so far as could be made out. Malawi entered upon a sad economic slide with weak government, two-thirds of its people in poverty and disputes with the IMF over the level of public sector wages. Matters began to improve after elections in 2005 brought to power a new government led by Bungu wa Mathiriku.

Zambia's fortunes were diametrically different. Zambia became independent with healthy resources and exports and a favourable balance of payments. First among its assets was copper, but it was rich also in other minerals, water and agriculture. A boom in the later 1960s fortified hopes for prosperity together with progress in education and other social services; but the 1970s were a bitter disappointment, particularly after the closing of the frontier with Rhodesia in 1973. The Tanzam railway (see p. 660) failed to come up to expectations. Copper prices slumped in 1975; some mines became unprofitable; whites began to leave the Copperbelt; blacks lost their jobs and their troubles were compounded by a shortage of maize. Kaunda's popularity waned and there were plots or at least rumours of plots against him. With the ending of war in Rhodesia (see p. 610) it became apparent that Zambia's misfortunes could not wholly be blamed on that war. One of Africa's potentially wealthier countries and the recipient of a fair share of western financial and technical aid, Zambia had lapsed into perilous economic straits because development had been grievously mismanaged. The poor got poorer and lacked basic goods; agriculture was neglected while an elite of city dwellers flourished. Kaunda, his personal rectitude unsullied, was none the less criticized for picking mediocre advisers, for refusing to face economic facts and for presiding over a saddeningly inept decline in his people's fortunes. To secure re-election in 1978 he resorted to disqualification of rivals in advance and in 1980 he took emergency measures against an alleged conspiracy to overthrow him. To secure essential foreign credits through the IMF he cut subsidies on foodstuffs with the inevitable result that prices soared and there were serious riots in the Copperbelt in 1986. Whether or not these riots were inflamed by South African agents South Africa applied economic and military sanctions against Zambia, which had become a principal headquarters and base for the campaigns of the Africa National Congress (ANC) against South African apartheid. Economically, Zambia's dependence on South African routes and ports had been intensified by disorders in Mozambique and Angola which atrophied the alternatives. In 1987 the South African air force attacked Lusaka and killed a number of Zambians and in 1989 Kaunda restricted the ANC's presence in Zambia, disowned its militant tactics and embarked on a dialogue with South Africa's incoming president F. W. de Klerk. Mounting popular discontent, allied with growing uneasiness in the army and the churches, forced Kaunda to abandon in 1990 his opposition to the multiparty system which he had abrogated early in his rule. Parties had in fact sprung up and the one-party system was dissolving of its own accord. Elections in 1992 produced an overwhelming victory for the Movement for Multiparty Democracy (MMD). UNIP won all the seats in the eastern provinces but few anywhere else. Kaunda immediately resigned and Frederick Chiluba became Zambia's second president. Kaunda returned to politics in 1995 as Chiluba's coalition collapsed and his popular support crumbled (along with the price of copper) but Kaunda was debarred from running for the presidency in 1996 by a constitutional amendment disqualifying candidates whose parents had been born outside Zambia and was arrested in 1997 on charges of plotting against the state. Turnout in elections in 2001 fell to 30 per cent. Politics became bitter. Economically, Zambia's main hope lay in selling to foreign corporations the government's majority holdings in the copper mines as the country sank into sad social and moral dejection accentuated by stark poverty and epidemic AIDS: 1 million children were said to be orphans.

In *Southern Rhodesia* the constitution of 1961 had left only one political issue between the Southern Rhodesia and British governments: independence. Winston Field had envisaged an independent Rhodesian dominion consisting of Southern Rhodesia and most of Northern Rhodesia, with Barotseland and Nyasaland as separate states under high commissioners appointed by the United Kingdom, but this scheme had been overtaken by events. In 1963 he began negotiations with Britain on the bare issue of independence and was confronted with five conditions: unimpeded progress towards majority rule; guarantees against regressive amendments of the 1961 constitution; an immediate improvement of African rights; an end to racial discrimination; and a basis for independence acceptable to the people of the country as a whole. Ian Smith, who ousted Winston Field in 1964, tried to meet the last and most intractable of these conditions by assembling an *indaba* of chiefs who, having been fêted by the government and given nice trips abroad, said exactly what was expected of them – but without convincing anybody in Britain that this was a demonstration of the popular will. The advent of a Labour government in London at the end of 1964 caused despondency among whites in Salisbury and increased the demand for a unilateral declaration of independence, but the new British government, beset by economic crisis and possessing only the thinnest parliamentary majority, decided to keep talks with Salisbury going to gain time. There was, however, no basis for agreement since the government was pledged to conditions which ran counter to the fundamental demand of the great majority of the white community in Rhodesia: the indefinite preservation of their minority rule. The government proposed the appointment of a royal commission under the Rhodesian chief justice Sir Hugh Beadle to examine ways of testing the popular will, but this proposal was rejected by Smith and on 11 November 1965 the Smith government declared the country independent. The government was thereupon dismissed by the governor Sir Humphrey Gibbs. It remained, however, the effective government of Rhodesia within its borders.

The British government was determined not to use force except in the event of a major breakdown of public order. The situation was one in which British governments had not hesitated to use force, but the Rhodesian case was different in two decisive ways: first, because Rhodesia, although technically a colony, had been administered and, in effect, governed by its own white population for more than 40 years, and secondly because the rebellious government was white and not black, so that a recourse to force in what the Rhodesian whites had made a racial issue would bitterly divide opinion in Britain and could even face British army officers with a test of obedience which they might not pass. The British government was left therefore with two courses, negotiation and economic coercion.

For a year it pursued both courses. It imposed oil sanctions and secured a Security Council resolution banning the supply of arms to Rhodesia and requesting an international economic boycott. Over 40 countries complied with this request. In 1966 the Security Council, at Britain's request, authorized the use of force to implement oil sanctions and later imposed mandatory sanctions over a wide assortment of commodities. Eighteen months later this ban was made total. But despite hardships, which took time to take effect, the Smith regime was able to maintain itself thanks to the South African government (which supplied credit and goods and facilitated the export of Rhodesian products), thanks to Rhodesia's capacity to retaliate economically against Zambia (which was dependent on Rhodesia for coal for its copper mines and in other ways), and thanks also to the British government's reluctance to intensify economic measures so long as it could go on hoping for a negotiated settlement. Rhodesia's exports were substantially blocked, its reserves were depleted, its government had to resort to internal loans, it became virtually a dependency of South Africa, but the regime was not compelled to capitulate and the economy adjusted itself.

In applying sanctions Britain was intent not on destroying the Rhodesian economy or even the Smith regime but on forcing Smith to come to terms. These aims did not commend themselves to most of the Commonwealth, which suspected the British government of being bent on a deal with Smith even to the extent of betraying its predecessor's and its own pledges. At a Commonwealth conference in Lagos Britain succeeded in buying time but not in retrieving the trust of its African partners in the Commonwealth, and at a further conference in London Britain was obliged, by a nearly unanimous show of resolution by members from all continents, to promise to ask the Security Council to apply selected mandatory sanctions if negotiations between London and Salisbury did not produce a return to legality by the end of the year. By the first anniversary of the unilateral declaration of independence the futility of these negotiations had become manifest, and Britain faced a lengthy economic battle which, if pursued, was bound to develop into a contest between the overwhelming majority of the United Nations on the one hand and South Africa and (less resolutely) Portugal, whose policy was to keep the battle going until Rhodesia's opponents got bored and ceased to enforce sanctions. Two attempts to exorcize the problem by personal negotiations between Harold Wilson and Ian Smith – the one on board HMS *Tiger* in 1966 and the second on board HMS *Fearless* in 1968 – failed, principally owing to the obduracy of Smith, but the return of the Conservatives to power in Britain in 1970 revived the prospect of a settlement and rekindled African mistrust.

An unofficial exploration of the chances for a settlement by Lord Alport produced a pessimistic answer but Sir Alex Douglas-Home, back at the Foreign Office in London, opened a dialogue with Smith through Lord Goodman and produced a plan for a return to constitutionality subject to his being satisfied that it was acceptable to the people of Rhodesia as a whole. A commission under Lord Pearce went to Rhodesia in 1972 to find the answer to this question and reported that the majority of Africans rejected the plan. Inside Rhodesia guerrilla operations, which had been unsuccessfully started a few years earlier, increased but were contained by Smith's forces with South African help. Attempts by the OAU to heal splits among black Rhodesian leaders were unsuccessful, but the collapse of Portuguese rule in Mozambique in 1974 transformed the situation by dealing strategic and psychological blows to the white Rhodesians (the frontiers to be defended became several hundreds of miles longer) and by posing new policy problems for South Africa. The leaders of neighbouring countries – Zambia, Botswana, Mozambique, Zaïre, Tanzania – wanted the overthrow of Smith without a war. They were willing to talk, and to try to persuade black Rhodesians to talk, about a short transitional period before majority rule and about guarantees for the lives and property of whites. They were encouraged by the shift in South African policies, notably by a speech at the UN in which the South African representative spoke plainly about the existence of apartheid in South Africa, deplored it and looked forward to a time (unspecified) when it would be removed. This surprising statement was subsequently qualified, presumably for internal consumption, by President Vorster, who said that it did not mean one-man-one-vote or a black parliament. Vorster's balancing act was plain for outsiders to see and Kaunda sent an envoy to talk with Vorster, who seemed keen to compass a change of regime in Rhodesia without bloodshed. In December 1974 Smith released the two principal detained nationalist leaders, Joshua Nkomo and Ndabaningi Sithole, as a preliminary to a ceasefire and a possible constitutional conference, and in the following September Smith, at Vorster's prompting, attended a conference with nationalists on a bridge over the Victoria Falls, Vorster and Kaunda themselves also attending. The conference was a failure, technically because of a dispute about the terms of reference already agreed between Vorster and Smith, substantially because Smith was not prepared to discuss any constitutional proposals except his own, which did not then include a transfer of power to the majority. The notion of a constitutional conference was kept alive by Smith and Nkomo but the prospects were dimmed by white intransigence and by renewed splits among black leaders who had been temporarily persuaded into a show of unity. The collapse of the Vorster–Kaunda initiative left little in prospect except war. In Rhodesia the stalemate continued but around it two big changes had occurred. For Vorster the Rhodesian situation represented a wolf at the door, but the wolf had changed its colour. The failure of the Victoria Falls conference completed the alienation of Vorster from Smith: the main danger for South Africa was no longer the disappearance of white rule but its persistence in hopeless circumstances. Smith was no longer a shield but an Achilles' heel. Secondly, Russo-Cuban intervention in Angola brought the United States into the tangle. The chief American concern, besides the removal of Cuban armies from Africa and checking the spread of Russian influence, was stability, which in Rhodesia was unachievable without the eclipse of white power.

Smith did not see the writing on the wall. Sanctions were a farce. The Beira naval patrol, maintained by the British for ten years (until Mozambique became independent in 1975) at a cost of at least £100 million, prevented the delivery of crude oil to Rhodesia through Beira, but nothing was done to stop the supply of refined products through Lourenço Marques or other routes. Portugal and South Africa made little secret of their assistance to Smith to circumvent sanctions. American compliance was imperfect: the import of Rhodesian chrome and other minerals was legalized in 1971. And it subsequently became clear that Smith was plentifully supplied with oil, mainly by British and associated companies which were assiduous in devising means to help Smith – in which they were able to count on the benevolence of British officials and ministers who turned a blind eye to traffic which was too bulky to be invisible. (Even when this discreditable story became public knowledge no prosecutions were launched against companies or individuals who, in breach of the law, had conducted a foreign policy at variance with their government's commitments and ostensible objectives.)

Smith was also encouraged by the dissensions among his black adversaries. His tactics were to exploit these differences with the aim of saving white control through a deal with one or more of the black leaders, preferably Nkomo. It was a classic policy of divide and rule. But Smith aimed too high, clinging too long to white minority rule and then, when forced to come to terms with Bishop Muzorewa and others, drove a bargain too good to stick.

Negotiations between Smith and Nkomo broke down by the early part of 1976. Guerrilla operations, although still relatively ineffective and confined to border areas, were increasing, with Robert Mugabe emerging as the one leader whom most guerrillas trusted: he alone was uninterested in wheeling and dealing with the whites. Mugabe eschewed the politicking which was second nature to Smith and he also divined that the conflict was one which would be settled by other means. Smith, unable to distinguish one kind of left-winger from another, was over-confident of his ability to represent Mugabe as a Muscovite stooge and over-contemptuous of the guerrillas.

The collapse of Portuguese rule and the Russo-Cuban intervention in Angola obliged the United States to review policies, which had been predicated on a stability which no longer existed. Kissinger's first cursory look at southern Africa in the early 1970s had led him to the conclusion that Washington should and could improve its relations with both black and white regimes in order to prevent the USSR from doing likewise; and he assumed that the regimes which he saw there would remain there. The collapse of Portuguese rule undermined this policy. By cutting all but the South African outlets for Rhodesia's commerce it rendered Rhodesia both more dependent on South Africa and less attractive to South Africa as an ally; it dramatically reduced Smith's chances of survival. To the east it not only closed Rhodesia's routes to the sea but also opened a new guerrilla front. To the west it created in Angola an international crisis by which the USSR secured a toehold in southern Africa. The immediate American ripostes, all of them misconceived, were to switch aid from the Portuguese to the two Angolan liberation movements, which failed, and to instigate a South African invasion, which also failed. When Kissinger returned to Africa in 1976 he announced a sharp pro-black turn by declaring himself in favour of majority rule not only in Rhodesia but in Namibia and South Africa too. This pronouncement was, however, only the rhetorical prelude to an uneasy alliance with South Africa to put pressure on Smith. Vorster stopped military aid to Smith and allowed his surviving economic channels to the outside world to become clogged. Kissinger went to South Africa for a tense meeting with Smith, who was forced to yield to superior power. He accepted majority rule within two years together with a transitional plan which included a black majority in the cabinet and a black prime minister.

Guerrilla war became a major factor during 1976. It spread into the heart of the country; its strains on the economy and manpower became visible and painful; it gave a boost to white emigration. But in his own mind Smith was far from surrender. He insisted on interpreting majority rule to mean not black but responsible majority rule; that is to say, he rejected one-man-one-vote. While announcing the end of white rule he contrived to give the impression that white control would continue. He succeeded in tearing up the Kissinger plan. Kissinger had implied to both sides more than had been agreed by either. He allowed Smith to think that the details which he sketched had been affirmed by the African Front Line presidents and by the guerrillas' leaders, when this was not the case. The Front Line presidents complained in their turn that they had been misled by Kissinger; they regarded as negotiable terms which Smith held to be part and parcel of the bargain which had been forced upon him by Kissinger. It was therefore easy for Smith to declare himself released from that bargain unless no letter of it were altered. The Kissinger plan was exposed as a set of imprecise undertakings which fell far short of agreement. A conference of all interested parties in Geneva failed to rescue the plan. So did a subsequent British diplomatic trot around the continent.

At this point the deadlock seemed worse than ever but the guerrilla leaders had meanwhile agreed to co-operate, militarily and politically, as the Patriotic Front. Brittle though it was, this alliance was to win the war. Nor were external powers prepared to remain inactive. Britain, the United States and South Africa were committed to replacing the Smith regime by something else. So too were the Front Line presidents, whose countries – particularly Zambia and Mozambique – were suffering severely from the economic consequences of the war and from Rhodesian retaliatory strikes against guerrilla camps in their territory.

On assuming office in 1977 President Carter appointed Andrew Young to handle African affairs. London had in David Owen a new foreign secretary, and after a joint tour of African capitals these two produced a fresh plan for ending Unilateral Declaration of Independence (UDI) by the transfer of power to the black majority after a brief resumption of British authority and elections to be held under international supervision. The plan failed chiefly because Smith was outraged by its provision for one-man-one-vote and the prospect of losing white control of the armed forces and security. Smith flew to a secret meeting with Kaunda, once more in search of an alliance with Nkomo – which again eluded him. He turned therefore to a second-best version of the same tactics: a deal with other African leaders in order to pre-empt victory for Mugabe. After acrimonious bargaining with Muzorewa, Sithole and Chief Jeremiah Chirau, Smith accepted one-man-one-vote but secured the white position by entrenched rights in the constitution. Britain and the United States endorsed this scheme with a reservation which made nonsense of it: they approved it provided the Patriotic Front were brought in. But it was a plan to keep the Patriotic Front out.

After much heart-searching the Rhodesian whites approved the new constitution in a referendum in 1979. Elections with a commendable turnout gave Muzorewa the victory and he became prime minister of the aptly named Zimbabwe-Rhodesia. But this settlement was unconvincing. The whites remained in control for an indefinite period and the new government failed to introduce even eye-catching reforms to alleviate, much less remove, racial discrimination.

Fortuitously, the Rhodesian elections coincided with elections in Britain which returned the Conservatives to power under a prime minister suspected of having more sympathy for Smith than most British politicians. Mrs Thatcher appeared from her public statements to favour recognition of the Muzorewa government and the immediate removal of sanctions. But British pragmatism prevailed. The Patriotic Front was by now too effective to be affronted with impunity; it was the winning side. At a Commonwealth conference in Lusaka Britain continued to withhold recognition from the Muzorewa–Smith settlement until one more attempt could be made to reconcile the warring parties. Britain prepared a new constitution, purged of the more blatant pro-white provisions of the 1978 document, and presented it to both sides at a conference in London at the end of 1979 on a take-it-or-leave-it basis. The new foreign secretary Lord Carrington threatened to recognize Muzorewa if the Patriotic Front did not accept his constitution, while on the other side Mugabe and Nkomo were under strong pressure from the Front Line presidents to reach agreement. This combination prevailed. The whites and Muzorewa, although disappointed and angry, had no alternative to acceptance because what they had constructed was unsound. The conference, contrary to initial expectations, reached agreement. A British governor went to Salisbury for four months. Elections, fair and free in the view of some, the reverse in the view of others, gave Mugabe and his party Zimbabwe African National Union (ZANU) a decisive and overall majority and he became the prime minister of the independent state of *Zimbabwe.*

Independence transformed the conflict between black and white from a struggle for power into disputes over land and sharpened the conflict between Shona and Ndebele, personified by Mugabe and Nkomo. The latter was expelled from government in 1982, fled to England, returned for elections in 1985, made his peace with Mugabe in 1987 and became a vice-president but also a back number: a founding father of a modern African statehood whose achievements were disappointed being a minority leader. The Ndebele were numerous enough to disrupt the state but too few to create on their own a constructive society in a hostile environment. During the 1980s they were progressively alienated and alarmed, ZAPU tightened its hold over Ndebeleland and Mugabe established what was in effect a one-party state in a constitutionally multiparty one. The high hopes invested in Mugabe himself were clouded as internal violence led to illegal detentions without trial, rampages by army units and the diversion of food from, and consequent starvation in, politically selected areas. Not all Mugabe's senior colleagues withstood the temptations of power and in 1988–89 scandals forced five ministers to resign and one to kill himself. Mugabe's unconcealed preference for state socialism in a one-party state was unpopular not only with western opinion and governments but also within his own party, where each section feared that in a one-party state another section of the party would become the single ruling group. An impressive economic plan which initially attracted international support was rendered precarious by drought, political instability, poor transport and distribution, a flight from the land to overcrowded towns with inadequate housing and no jobs, an intolerable foreign debt service, declining foreign revenues as world prices fell, and inflation which went up and down but a national product which went only down: all of which weakened the personal position of the man whose pre-eminence had made him peculiarly vulnerable to the twists and turns of fortune.

Two special factors aggravated this situation. The first was war in Mozambique. Zimbabwe formed in 1982 a Special Task Force to defend the oil pipeline to Beira on the Mozambican coast against the Renamo guerrillas, and this comparatively modest venture led Zimbabwe deeper into Mozambique's civil war. In 1986 Renamo declared itself at war with Zimbabwe, thus bringing hostilities to Zimbabwe's eastern province of Manicaland and leading to the creation in 1989 of the Zimbabwean Unity Movement by disgruntled members of ZANU – chief among them Edgar Tekere, whom

Mugabe had dismissed from his government. Secondly, the acute problem of land ownership – i.e. the occupation in the past by whites of the best farmland at derisory cost – was allowed to fester. Britain had offered to contribute £75 million towards a resettlement but insisted at a late stage in the independence negotiations that there should be no expropriation for ten years. A promise to underwrite half the cost of an eventual settlement did not dispel black distrust. Families evicted from their lands after 1980 – the more massive evictions had taken place in the period 1930–60 – were promised recovery, but the new state also undertook to pay compensation in foreign currency to evicted white owners at a rate applicable to sales between a willing seller and a willing buyer. A first plan to settle 162,000 families in five years reached only a third of its target, partly because of practical difficulties such as the need to make new roads, partly because too little land was made available for the landless, and partly because the government insisted that newcomers must first renounce their title to land (if any) which they were leaving. Although Mugabe's term of office ran to 2001 and his party regularly won nearly all the seats in parliament, Mugabe lost ground personally: his despatch of troops to help Kabila in Congo (see p. 566) cost lives and money, his policy of alliance with Kabila and dos Santos seemed both ideologically and pragmatically threadbare, corruption and ostentation in high places were blatant, wages and employment fell, accelerating economic decline reduced the external value of the currency by three-quarters. By 2000, having alienated many among his own Shona people as well as the Ndebele and white minorities, he had little prospect of retaining power without fraud and violence. But, having no adversary of comparable eminence, Mugabe refused to designate a successor within his party. Apparently convinced of his popularity although forced to resort to repression and brutality, he held on to power with no greater inconvenience than expulsion from the Commonwealth (2003) while hyperinflation raged and his people starved and late in 2007 he announced his intention to seek another term in office. Elections in 2008 for the parliament and the presidency produced victory for Morgan Tsvangirai and his party and a severe political crisis. The results of the voting were not disclosed for a month. The electoral commission then proclaimed after a series of re-counts that the MDC had won a narrow parliamentary majority and, after further delay, that Tsvangirai had won more votes than Mugabe for the presidency but not enough to secure office. Meanwhile Tsvangirai and some of his colleagues fled the country and Mugabe, with what could most charitably be called a comprehensive disconnection from reality, refused to recognize his loss of power and office and scorned efforts by neighbouring heads of state to negotiate a way out of the impasse. Mugabe accepted the need for a second round of voting for the presidency and Tsvangirai did so too in spite of patent indications that Mugabe was determined to win by terror if necessary. The MDC then changed its mind and decided not to contest further elections for fear of provoking insensate violence. Mugabe therefore won the presidency once more but he has suffered the sort of shock from which a dictator seldom recovers.

Mozambique–Angola–Namibia

Until 1974 Africa's southern cone was flanked by the Portuguese territories of Angola and Mozambique. The Portuguese record in Africa was first in, last out: the first colonists and last imperialists. This small European country first ventured into strange continents 500 years ago and it acquired in Africa an estate 23 times its own size. Bartolomeu Diaz rounded the Cape of Good Hope in 1487, followed by Vasco da Gama in 1498. The Guinea trade, of which Portuguese Guinea was a relic, flourished during the sixteenth century but the Portuguese were gradually pushed out of West Africa by the Dutch, the British and the French, and they were to find their biggest prizes further south. Luanda, the capital of Angola, was founded in 1576 by a grandson of Diaz; it was held by the Dutch for a short time in the seventeenth century but was recaptured by the rich Brazilian adventurer Salvador de Sá, who became its governor and restored Portuguese rule. In the seventeenth and eighteenth centuries Angola provided slaves for Brazil. The trade was abolished in 1836 and slavery itself supposedly from 1858. During the most intense phase of the European scramble for Africa Portugal was supported sporadically but ineffectually by Britain, but by nobody else. Germany coveted Portuguese territories and hoped to succeed to them by lending Portugal more money than it could repay and then foreclosing. A Portuguese dream of linking Angola with Mozambique by a land strip never materialized. Although Mozambique was settled in the 25 years before the First World War, the Portuguese evinced only tepid interest in Africa, while their laxity in the suppression of slavery earned them a scandalous notoriety, especially after the publication in 1906 of H. W. Nevinson's *A Modern Slavery*.

Major risings in Angola in 1922 and 1935 were ruthlessly suppressed but also nurtured nationalist movements. Lisbon began to see that its rule was threatened less by white home-rulers than by black nationalism, even though the nationalists were in the short term hopelessly hampered by illiteracy, tribal divisions and the overwhelming might of the Portuguese police and army. In 1952 Portugal's colonies were renamed overseas provinces and the 1950s saw a burst of public works and development plans. The change of name enabled Portugal to claim that it was under no obligation to submit reports to the UN under article 73(e) of the Charter. This subterfuge was supported by Portugal's American and British allies and its Brazilian kinsmen but in 1963 the United States and Britain voted for a resolution of the General Assembly urging Portugal to accelerate self-determination; only Spain and South Africa voted against; France abstained.

Portugal practised a policy of assimilation as a means of gradually expanding the franchise but increasing immigration from Portugal in the mid-1950s altered social and economic patterns, reinforced the colour bar and reduced many Angolans to unemployment or semi-employment. Tens of thousands went into exile, mostly in the Congo, and nationalist movements established their headquarters in Leopoldville. The emancipation of British and French West African colonies and the Belgian Congo brought the modern African problem to Portugal's doorstep and in 1961 there were riots in Luanda, partly stimulated by the adventures of Captain Henrique Galvao, who seized the liner *Sta. Maria* and was expected off Luanda in the role of liberator. There were also disorders in the north and an invasion from across the Congolese frontier. The Portuguese were taken by surprise, suffered casualties of 1,400 and responded to barbarities in kind. African casualties were of the order of 20,000 and a stream of hideously wounded refugees over the next years blackened the Portuguese name. By 1970 colonial wars were forcing Portugal to allot half of its budget and over 6 per cent of its GDP to military spending, to raise the largest armies ever raised in Portugal's history and to conscript young men for four years. The absence of a politically active public opinion shielded the government from what had been one of the strongest of the decolonizing factors in London, Paris and Brussels, but ten years of costly and unsuccessful fighting in three widely separated territories sapped the will of the Portuguese military. Liberation movements won popular support, extending their areas of control and getting arms from abroad. The Portuguese tried bombing and barbed wire but the first was ineffective against guerrillas and the second failed to separate them from the populace. The governor of *Guinea-Bissau*, General Antonio de Spinola, convinced of the hopelessness of the struggle, resigned in 1973 and went back to Lisbon as an outspoken opponent of continuing colonial rule. His actions and writings contributed to the overthrow by the army in 1974 of the dictatorship founded in 1926. The Armed Forces Movement which won control in Lisbon declared itself in favour of independence in Portugal's African colonies.

In *Mozambique* a liberation movement, Frelimo, had begun an armed rising in 1964 but suffered in 1969 the assassination of its leader Eduardo Mondlane. The Portuguese persisted with a programme of economic development in association with South African, European and American concerns (which would thereby acquire a vested interest in Portuguese rule). This development, focused on the building of a hydro-electric barrage at Cabora Bassa which would add a million persons to the white population, was clearly political since Mozambique already had six hydro-electric schemes. The political implications – and lobbying by African states – caused some of the participants to think again and – in the cases of Sweden and Italy – to withdraw. Upon independence the main threat to Mozambique came from South Africa, which played a double game there during much of the 1970s and 1980s. President Vorster publicly accepted Frelimo's victory in 1974 and wished the new government of Samora Michel well, but South Africa's overriding concern was to protect its flank against the ANC – which had bases as well as friends in Mozambique – either through anti-ANC deals with the Mozambique government or by aiding that government's insurgent enemies, Renamo (or both). In 1984 South Africa concluded at Nkomati an agreement whereby it undertook to cease supplying Renamo and end economic warfare against

Mozambique in return for Mozambique's abandonment of the ANC, but in spite of later confirmation of these promises Renamo continued to receive aid from South Africa. President Botha's interest in a pacified southern Mozambique (whence came a quarter of the workers in South Africa's mines) did not extend to the north: Renamo was a useful thorn in Machel's side so long as it did not force Machel into the arms of the USSR. But in spite of aid from South Africa and from Portuguese sympathizers Renamo failed to create anything like a rival government. Equally, however, Machel's government failed to suppress it and this failure was due not only to outside aid for Renamo but also to two internal factors: Mozambique was a large country divided into numerous areas suspicious of one another and of central authority, and Machel's government tended to ride roughshod over traditional customs and local susceptibilities in its drive to modernization. Machel was killed in an air crash in South Africa, probably accidental, in 1986. His successor Joaquim Chissano was, at 49, representative of a younger generation which criticized many of Frelimo's old guard for military incompetence and personal corruption. Chissano preferred diplomacy to war, if only because his government might contain Renamo but could not extinguish it so long as South Africa chose to sustain it. On the government's side morale and discipline were low as the cost of living rose and pacification appeared to be out of reach. Chissano steered a reforming course, away from communist centralism and towards a multiparty system, and communist Mozambique abandoned the one party state sooner than its non-communist neighbours in Malawi, Zambia and Tanzania. The Roma agreement, negotiated with South Africa in 1990 with the help of President Kaunda, established a ceasefire and a plan for the reduction of forces and their concentration in specified areas. Renamo later denounced the agreement on the grounds that Zimbabwean forces had not been withdrawn from Mozambican territory. The government was weakened by a (failed) coup against Chissano in 1991, whereas Renamo was strengthened when its leader Alfonso Dhlakama was received by the Pope and Portuguese and other European leaders. Fresh agreements were signed and the UN agreed to field 7,000 observers under the United Nations Operation in Mozambique (ONUMOZ) but Renamo remained obstructive as its position steadily improved in northern and central areas alienated from the government by distrust of its predominantly southern (Shangaan) complexion. In 1992 the old enemies agreed to a ceasefire and apart from localized disputes the fighting died away. The economy recovered but the gap between rich and poor widened. In 1995 Mozambique became the fifty-third member of the Commonwealth, the first without a pre-independence British connection, and began to repair its ruined fortunes by attracting investment from foreign companies eyeing the prospects of tourism, beaches and gambling and from white farmers fleeing a black South Africa. Chissano lost office in 2005 when his term constitutionally ended, leaving his country better governed and better respected than when he took over.

In *Angola* there was no single equivalent to Frelimo and when, on the eve of independence, Holden Roberto's National Liberation Front (FNLA) attacked Agostinho

Neto's Popular Movement for the Liberation of Angola (MPLA) South Africa invaded Angola in support of a third movement, Jonas Savimbi's National Union for the Total Independence of Angola (UNITA). But Neto appealed to Fidel Castro (on Cuban intervention see Chapter 26) and the South Africans were forced for the time being to retreat although they continued to arm Savimbi, who succeeded in winning control over a substantial part of the country, particularly in the inland highlands traditionally hostile to and feared by the coastal peoples of mixed race who favoured the MPLA. The United States supported UNITA but in doing so undermined the MPLA's ability to dispense with the Cubans whose removal was Washington's main aim. Reagan dubbed Savimbi a democrat and sent him huge quantities of aid in defiance of the Clark Amendment of 1974 which specifically forbade it. South Africa's military incursions were dubiously valuable. Tracts of Angola were occupied, devastated and then abandoned. In 1985 Angola, fortified by fresh Russian military equipment, took the offensive against UNITA and South Africa accepted the challenge to rescue it. Both sides failed. A joint UNITA–South African onslaught on the strategic base at Cuito Cuanavale in 1987–88 was thwarted and the South African air force humiliated. UNITA, although battered in the south, was re-established in Zaïre by the United States, but this was only a tactical move as talks were begun in London between South Africa, Angola and Cuba with American blessing (but with UNITA left out in the cold). In 1991 the Bicesse agreements provided for the withdrawal of South African and Cuban troops: the former left during 1989, half the Cubans in the same year and the remainder by mid-1991. The civil war was brought temporarily to a halt.

The UN, which had supervised the Cuban withdrawal through the United Nations Angola Verification Mission (UNAVEM I), was asked to oversee the implementation of the Bicesse accords (UNAVEM II) and, subsequently, general and presidential elections. By the accords Savimbi recognized José dos Santos (Neto's successor as the MPLA's leader) as president and the two leaders agreed to withdraw their troops to 50 specified points and to fuse them into a joint army of 50,000 – a quarter of their combined strength. Political parties were formed by the dozen and elections were held under UN supervision in 1992. Thanks largely to UNAVEM they were peaceable, fair and strikingly popular – over 90 per cent of those entitled to vote did so. But Savimbi, contrary to his expectations, found that he was not the winner. UNITA won 34 per cent of the votes against the MPLA's 54 per cent and, although dos Santos fell narrowly short of the 50 per cent required for confirmation as president, Savimbi won only 40 per cent. Disappointed and distraught by his failure but still buoyed by American support, Savimbi restarted the war which through most of 1993–94 exacted 1,000 or more deaths a day. UNAVEM III, with a mere 400 persons and starved of funds and other resources, was powerless to prevent the destruction of its hard-won achievements. Attempts to stop the fighting – notably by the Lusaka protocol mediated by Zambia, frequently broken and a dead letter by 1997 – were negated by Savimbi, who refused to yield territory won in the latest battles. He demanded a refurbished UNAVEM, which the Security Council refused to provide unless UNITA first accepted the Lusaka agreements. UNAVEM III was dissolved and replaced by the even weaker UNOMA (UN Observer Mission in Angola). Savimbi remained obdurate, angling for support from Mobutu and Kabila in Zaïre and from the rival rulers in Brazzaville (Nguessou and Lissouba) but in the closing months of 1999 UNITA suffered severe losses in the south and in 2002 the civil wars which had lasted for nearly half a century ended. Savimbi was killed in battle and Angola's natural wealth helped it to a notably swift recovery.

Angola was devastated for so many years because it was rich. The war in which each side spent $1–2 billion a year on arms was financed by oil and diamonds – oil which enabled the government to borrow abroad (thus mortgaging the future) and diamonds which UNITA sold to the international cartel managed by de Beers. A sub-plot in Angola's drama was provided by the comparatively small province of Cabinda, which had been of little account before oil was discovered there in 1966. Its population of 100,000 included a secessionist movement. It was coveted by Zaïre but Mobutu was bought off by Neto in 1978.

The independence of Angola in 1975 transformed the situation in South West Africa, which in little more than a decade became the independent state of *Namibia*.

South West Africa, huge, rich and underpopulated, the most barren expanse in Africa except the Sahara, came under German rule at the end of the nineteenth century because nobody else wanted it. In the 1870s the Cape Colony had expressly considered and rejected annexation and even the Berlin share-out of 1884 left South West Africa as *res nullius*. In the concluding years of the century, however, the Germans moved in, first as allies of the Bantu Herrero against the Nama (an aboriginal people second in antiquity only to the Bushmen) and then as settlers and farmers. Rebellions by the Herrero and later by the Nama led to savage repressions amounting to genocide, and by 1907 the territory had been devastated, subdued and handed over to German farmers together with the surviving Africans, who became little better than slaves. In the First World War it was conquered by General Botha and a South African army in a matter of weeks, but after the war it was – together with all other German possessions outside Europe – placed under international mandate instead of being treated as the spoils of the conqueror. The mandate was entrusted by the Principal Allied and Associated Powers to King George V to administer through his government in South Africa but without any transfer of sovereignty. The mandate agreement provided, among other things, for the suppression of trade in slaves, arms and liquor; prohibited the establishment of military bases and the military training of Africans; guaranteed freedom of religion; and required the mandatory power to submit annual reports to the Permanent Mandates Commission of the League of Nations and to forward to the League complaints and petitions from the inhabitants. In its execution of the mandate the South African government treated the new order as tantamount to annexation.

Attempts were made to convert South West Africa into a fifth province of South Africa and although these attempts were successfully resisted by the League the character of the territory was profoundly altered by an influx of white South Africans who acquired land cheaply and became a ruling class complete with an elected parliament. In the north areas were reserved for Africans. White immigration was prohibited in these areas, which were ruled by a governor-general appointed by South Africa acting through African chiefs who received salaries if they were complaisant but were deposed if they were not.

After the Second World War Smuts repeated pleas for the integration of the territory with South Africa on the grounds of propinquity and economic advantage; he denied that, as the mandatory power, South Africa was under an obligation to negotiate a trusteeship agreement with the United Nations; and he argued that the inhabitants of the territory were happy and prosperous and wanted to be part of South Africa. Smuts was obliged to drop his attempt to secure integration and he agreed to submit to the UN reports on conditions in the territory, but after 1948 the Nationalist government stopped the reports and also allotted six seats in the South African lower house and four in the senate to representatives of South West Africa's 53,000 European inhabitants (the non-Europeans numbered 400,000).

The International Court of Justice ruled in 1950, in an advisory opinion (which was elaborated on subordinate points in further opinions of 1955 and 1956), that the mandate was still in force, that South Africa was not obliged to place the territory under trusteeship, but that it was obliged to submit reports and transmit petitions. From this time the Herrero, Nama and Damara tribes made their views known to the world through their spokesman, the Rev. Michael Scott, who presented on their behalf a picture of their conditions and wishes very different from the official South African line. South Africa offered to negotiate with the United States, Britain and France, as the survivors of the Principal Allied and Associated Powers of the First World War, an agreement to place South West Africa under the administration of the International Court, but this novel idea was rejected by a special committee of the United Nations and was withdrawn in 1955. In 1957 the UN appointed a good offices committee of three (Britain, the United States and Brazil) which visited Pretoria the next year and recommended that either the Trusteeship Council or a new body consisting of former League members should receive reports from the mandatory power, but South Africa maintained that the mandate had lapsed and that it was gratuitously continuing to administer the territory in the spirit of the mandate. South Africa next suggested a partition whereby the southern part of the territory would be annexed to South Africa and the northern part (where there were no whites) would be under South African trusteeship and administratively part of South Africa. The General Assembly rejected this scheme. The territory was in practice progressively absorbed into South Africa's administrative system and became subject also to the politics and practices of apartheid.

In 1959 a report by the UN Committee on South-West Africa comprehensively condemned South Africa's execution of the mandate and in the following year a number of African states initiated a substantive case before the International Court of Justice, claiming that the mandate agreement had been violated. Ethiopia and Liberia, former members of the League and the senior independent states of the continent, petitioned the court accordingly and engaged an eminent American lawyer, Ernest Gross, to argue their case at The Hague. In 1960 the court accepted jurisdiction by the narrow margin of eight judges to seven. After protracted and expensive proceedings the court in July 1966 non-suited the plaintiffs and, in spite of its preliminary decision in 1960, ruled by the president's casting vote that they had no standing in the matter before the court. This refusal to entertain the substance of the case caused universal astonishment and was considered all the more unsatisfactory in that the outcome was plainly due to accidents of death and ill-health, without which the judgment on this point would have gone the other way. The immediate effect, besides jubilation in South Africa and some discrediting of the role of law in international affairs, was to return the South West African issue to the arena of politics (where it was bound to end up in any case).

In October 1966 the General Assembly, brushing aside the notion of further recourse to the court, resolved by 114 votes to 2 with two abstentions that the mandate was terminated and the UN must assume the administration of the territory. A special committee was appointed to consider how the second part of this resolution could be made effective. Essentially, the majority in the Assembly was searching for a course of action in which Britain (which had abstained on the resolution) and the United States (which had voted for it) would participate. The committee and a subsequent special meeting of the General Assembly in 1967 were divided between those who asserted, without contradiction, the enormity of South Africa's proceedings and those who asked, without reply, what was to be done about it. In 1968 the UN created a Council for Namibia (as the territory was henceforward called). This Council was not in a position to do anything. In 1970 the Security Council declared South Africa's occupation of Namibia illegal on the ground that it contravened the terms of the mandate. In effect the UN annulled the mandate. The Council's western members abstained but cast no veto.

While the case before the International Court was still in progress the South African government appointed the Odendaal Commission to make recommendations about South West Africa. This move was prompted by more than international interference, for in 1960 a South-West Africa People's Organization (SWAPO) had been formed and had declared itself at war with South Africa, initiating disorders in the territory of unpredictable consequence. The Odendaal Commission reported in 1964 in favour of dividing the territory into one white and ten black areas and spending £80 million over five years on communications, water and other schemes. The black areas would have certain local government powers but matters such as defence, internal security, frontiers, water and power would be reserved to the central authorities. The habitable land and the known minerals fell within the white area. The consideration of this report was postponed pending the decision of the International Court.

Angola's independence gave Namibia a frontier with a sovereign black state and gave Swapo bases within easy reach of that frontier. South Africa abandoned its policy of annexation for the alternative of transferring authority to an anti-Swapo alliance likely to be responsive to South Africa's needs and susceptibilities. Discussions in the Turnhalle in Windhoek during 1975–77 led to the formation of the Democratic Turnhalle Alliance (DTA), an inter-racial association of racially based parties. It was opposed by the multiracial Namibian National Party (a coalition of five parties) and by white segregationists. The Turnhalle conference produced a plan for transition to independence at the end of 1978 together with a draft constitution so complex, and a fragmentation of the territory so excessive, that it sharpened suspicions that its main object was to leave all effective power in Pretoria. The plan, whose essential aim was to put an acceptable Namibian government in place before elections and before independence, was stillborn because it was unacceptable to the UN, which was concurrently elaborating other plans. Vorster, having abandoned annexation, abandoned the Turnhalle alternative. He substituted no new policy but formally annexed the port of Walvis Bay, which had never been part of the mandated territory, and 12 offshore Penguin Islands.

The initiative passed to the UN which, by Security Council Resolution 435 of 1978, adopted its own programme and also established a 'contact group' consisting of the United States, Canada, Britain, West Germany and France to negotiate with South Africa. The UN programme required a ceasefire, release of prisoners, return of fugitives to Namibia but retention of Swapo guerrillas in their bases in Angola, withdrawal of all but 1,500 of the 20,000 South African troops, the despatch of a UN force, elections for a constituent assembly, supervision of the whole process by a Special Representative of the UN and by a UN Transitional Assistance Group (UNTAG), and so to independence on the last day of 1978. South Africa accepted this plan provided that Walvis Bay were expressly excepted, and that an effective ceasefire supervene before the withdrawal of South African forces began. Swapo was worried by the deployment of the remaining South African forces, which it wished to see concentrated in the south, and about the ill-defined co-operation between the South African and UN representatives. While discussion on these points was still in train South Africa delivered heavy attacks on Swapo's bases in Angola and Swapo broke off the talks. The murder of Chief Clemens Kapuuo, an enemy of Swapo and pillar of the DTA, and the South African Administrator's harsh repression which followed, all but wrecked the negotiations. They were, however, resumed after strong Zambian and Tanzanian pressure on Swapo to keep talking and the UN was able to convoke a conference of all interested parties in Geneva at the beginning of 1981. Besides the protagonists – South Africa and Swapo – the five western and six black African states attended as observers.

The conference was brought to naught by South African design. Namibia's independence was further delayed by two changes: the succession of P. W. Botha to the leadership of South Africa and the arrival of Ronald Reagan in the White House in Washington. Botha conducted for some years a more vigorous regional policy than his predecessor; Reagan tied progress in Namibia to the removal of the Cubans from Angola.

The result was stalemate. The DTA was flagging, its leader Dirk Mudge resigned from the council of ministers, and a new association of anti-Swapo groups – the Multi-Party Conference (MPC) – came into being. In 1984 South Africa declared itself ready to give independence to a government of national unity, but a conference at Lusaka attended by Swapo and the MPC produced no unity, Swapo refusing to co-operate with the MPC except on the basis of a precise timetable for independence. In 1985 South Africa devolved some powers to a transitional government but the key to the situation was outside the territory in Angola. As part of the Brazzaville Agreement of 1988 for the withdrawal of troops from Angola the South African and Angolan governments agreed on a joint military patrol of the Angolan border with Namibia. The execution of this agreement and the preparation and supervision of elections were undertaken by the UN (UNTAG). In elections in 1989 Swapo got 57 per cent of the vote – fewer than the two-thirds of the seats which would have given it virtually unbridled power in framing the constitution. The DTA got 29 per cent of the vote and 21 seats. A constitution was quickly adopted in 1990 and Swapo's leader, Sam Nujoma, was elected Namibia's first president. Swapo proved itself conciliatory, made no attempt to monopolize power or posts, succeeded in combining a multiparty system with stability and respected the independence of the judiciary and the press. Walvis Bay was conveyed to Namibia in 1994.

South Africa

Bantu peoples reached the southern tip of the African continent in the eighteenth century and there met the Dutch, clashed with them and were gradually subdued and turned into hewers of wood and drawers of water. The Dutch, who had followed the Portuguese to the Cape and were at first confronted only by the Hottentots, enjoyed a brief dominance until, their home country having become a part of the French revolutionary empire, they became fair game for the British in the Napoleonic wars and lost the base at Cape Town which they had founded in 1652. In the 1830s they packed up and trekked and set up new independent states – successfully beyond the Orange river and the Vaal but unsuccessfully in Natal where, although they defeated the Zulus, they were again pushed on by the expanding British who annexed Natal in 1843. The British colony of the Cape grew politically, economically and demographically; it was granted constitutions in 1853 and 1872, receiving on the latter occasion the right to a prime minister of its own.

In the latter part of the nineteenth century South Africa achieved an unexpected prominence in British thinking for two separate reasons. The first was the discovery of its wealth – diamonds in the 1860s and gold in the 1880s. The second was the conviction that South Africa was a vital link in Britain's imperial communications and that therefore Britain must keep firm hold not only of Cape Town and Simonstown but also of the hinterland. This second preoccupation turned the Dutch, or Boers, into potential enemies, since they might invite other European powers to occupy the sensitive hinterland or cause trouble for the British in Cape Colony by an alliance with their kinsmen in the colony. Moreover, attempts by the Boers to reach the coasts in Portuguese territory and to trade with the outside world through Portuguese ports threatened the monopolistic profits of British traders at the Cape. The British began to expand more purposefully than before. They took Basutoland from the Boers and made it a colony in 1868. They annexed Kimberley, the diamond city, in 1871 and the Transvaal in 1877. Brought up against the Bantu, they fought a series of wars (notably the Zulu War of 1879) and in 1880–81 they went to war with the Boers, whom they incidentally accused of maltreating the Bantu. A British Liberal government, perplexed by the graver practical and moral dilemmas of the Irish question, was divided about the right attitude to adopt towards the Boers, and, after the battle of Majuba in 1881, adopted a policy of conciliation, restored the Boer republics of the Transvaal and Orange Free State and so implicitly recognized the existence of a valid Boer nationalism.

Cecil Rhodes became prime minister of Cape Colony in 1890 and for a few years his voice rather than London's was the decisive one. Within the colony his policy was one of co-operation with the Boers for the paternal rule of the Africans, but any extension of this policy to form an Anglo-Boer entente in a wider field was prevented by British fears about the political and commercial policies of the Boer republics. Rhodes developed and paid for the Cape–Bechuanaland–Zambezi axis which put the Boer republics in jeopardy, countered the German threat from South West Africa and forestalled a possible anti-British alliance between the Germans and the Transvaal. In 1895 he overreached himself. With the connivance of a part of the British government he stimulated a rising against President Kruger of the Transvaal and sent Dr Jameson raiding into Boer territory to sustain it. The result was a rebuff for the raiders and for the British government when the German emperor sent Kruger his moral support by telegram. But although Kruger triumphed and Rhodes fell, the British government, which resumed the dominant role, adopted Rhodes's basic aim of preventing the emergence of a Boer South African state comprising the Boer republics and the British colonies. By winning the Boer War in 1899–1901 Britain postponed this eventuality but did not scotch it, for it came to pass in 1961. Britain earned the hatred of the wounded Boers but failed to appreciate its depth.

After the Peace of Vereeniging in 1902 the British pursued two barely compatible lines of policy. On the one hand they busied themselves being fair and generous to the defeated Boers, often forgetting the Africans in the process. The Transvaal and Orange

Free State were granted self-government in 1906–7, and the constitution of 1908 provided for an all-white parliament which, while meant as a symbol of Anglo-Boer reconciliation, looked in retrospect more like a pledge of African exclusion. On the other hand the British entrenched British supremacy by insisting on the extinction of the sovereignty of the republics and the dominance of the English language, so that the Boers planned for the day when the balance of power in South Africa would shift in their favour and they would be able to turn the tables on the British. By creating the Union of South Africa in 1910 the British government tried to confederate the two self-governing Boer republics and the two British colonies as an independent dominion within the British empire, but this South African dominion was fundamentally different from the three other old dominions by reason of the persistent non-British culture of the Boers (or Afrikaners) and the existence of an African majority in the shadows. When the European war broke out in 1914 the dominion joined in hostilities and sent forces overseas; the Boers, however, revolted, refusing – as they were to refuse again in 1939 – to be counted simply a part of a South African nation. They saw themselves as a people or Volk and not as a state.

The persistence of a distinct Afrikaner nationalism which ultimately triumphed through the electoral victories of the Nationalist Party was accompanied by the growth of an African nationalist movement which was frustrated by the Afrikaners. The Afrikaners had to resort to increasingly stringent measures and extreme ideologies in order to preserve and justify their newly won supremacy, and by the middle of the century South Africa had become an oligarchy ruled by a particular racial group without the consent of the majority of the governed, who – to make matters worse – were a different colour.

The Afrikaners' attitude to colour was an extreme instance of a common prejudice. It had played a part in their decision to trek out of Cape Colony, where the British were putting more liberal ideas into practice and where the coloureds (the offspring of white alliances with black servants) were given the vote in 1853 subject to certain educational tests – a right which they retained until 1956. But the African was an essential factor in the state since his labour was needed in industry and could be had cheaply owing to the scarcity of work in the native reserves (which, comprising one-tenth of the surface of the state, were supposed in theory to accommodate all the Africans but were incapable of supporting more than half of them). Colour became equated with economic degradation; a black man was a labourer who could be had for a low wage. And economic degradation led to social degradation as the Africans were crowded into slummy locations which bred self-disgust and crime. Whereas in Europe the victims of the Industrial Revolution were the more unfortunate members of society, in South Africa the revolution which exalted mining and heavy industry above agriculture found its victims in a separate society, alienated and increasingly hostile. Natal possessed an additional element in the Asians who first migrated there in search of work in the nineteenth century.

The Nationalist Party was built up by General James Hertzog, who was supported by the Labour Party (the representatives of white labour) and opposed by the British section of the electorate and by the moderate Afrikaners led by Louis Botha until his death in 1919 and then by Jan Smuts. Hertzog was prime minister from 1924 to 1939. He and Smuts joined forces in a coalition government in 1933 but upon the outbreak of war in Europe in 1939 they again separated and Hertzog drifted back towards D. F. Malan, who had founded a new Nationalist Party rather than follow Hertzog into alliance with Smuts. The Nationalists refused, however, to ally themselves with the fascist Ossewa Brandwag led by Oswald Pirow. In the first postwar elections (1948) the United Party was ousted by the Nationalist Party, which embarked on an extended period of power under a series of prime ministers – Malan, J. G. Strijdom, H. F. Verwoerd, B. J. Vorster, P. W. Botha – who turned South Africa into an independent republic outside the Commonwealth and a police state based on racial discrimination.

The policies of the Nationalist Party were based on the contempt, fears and hatreds of a minority faced by a majority of a different race and colour, and on a theory elaborated in this context. To the Afrikaner the African, especially the urban African, was an uncivilized barbarian unfit for public responsibility or private intercourse; or alternatively the African, especially the rural African, was a tame, happy and rather lazy servant whose chief desire was to remain in his undemanding, if servile, state. The mingling of the races was biologically evil. Logic therefore, as well as prejudice, dictated the attempts to separate the races which collectively amounted to the policy of apartheid. Although the races must remain in some contact with one another for a transitional period, the aim was the segregation of the black Africans in separate territories – dubbed Bantustans – which would be racial enclaves, economically self-sufficient, within a single South African polity. Scientists, including South African scientists, rejected the biological assertions at the basis of the policy of apartheid; economists demonstrated that the native areas could never become viable except at a cost unacceptable to the white population, and that the white community could not do without black labour: the African was to be returned to a semi-industrialized countryside while the white urban centres nevertheless craved for his services. The theory also overlooked the strength of human feelings of righteous indignation, and the political awareness of Africans who knew what was happening elsewhere in Africa. Finally, many of the protagonists of apartheid underestimated the extent to which their policies forced them to rule by violence and fraud and would attract worldwide condemnation. Prisons filled, floggings became a habitual part of the process of government, executions took place at the rate of one a day, the mail ceased to be private, spies and informers multiplied, an inevitably brutalized police force became a law of assault unto itself, and the regime felt obliged to build up a white citizen army with a potential strength of 250,000 in addition to a part-time commando force of 50,000 (based on four years' compulsory service) and a police force of 20,000 and police reserve of 6,000.

On the other side the African nationalist movement also took to violence. A Native Nationalist Congress, later renamed the African National Congress, had been formed in 1912. The object of its first leaders – chiefs and then lawyers – was to secure a place for the black African in South African society without upsetting any apple-carts, but both the leaders and the rank and file began to have doubts about their prospects during the Hertzog period. The Nationalist victory in 1948 sharpened African apprehensions. The Congress leaders pursued a policy of strikes and civil disobedience to draw attention to demands formulated in 1955 by the Kliptown Charter. The government responded by charging the leaders with treason. One hundred and fifty-six persons were indicted in a trial which lasted four years and ended with the acquittal of all the accused. In 1957 an increase in bus fares produced a bus boycott in which Africans, by trudging long miles to work every day, demonstrated their poverty and their discipline, but violence also grew and in 1958 outbreaks in the Transvaal were fiercely repressed. In 1959 a section of the African National Congress broke away to form the Pan Africanist Congress, led by Robert Sobukwe.

On 21 March 1960 a crowd of Africans, 3–4,000 strong but subsequently inflated by reports to much larger dimensions, converged on the police station at Sharpeville. It was one of a number of similar crowds which were doing the same thing all over the country in protest against the pass laws, which required adult Africans always to have their identity documents upon them. In organizing this demonstration Sobukwe told Africans to leave their passes behind and present themselves at police stations in an orderly manner and unarmed. The crowds were in cheerful holiday mood. At Sharpeville, where a small police force of 75 was nervously on duty, somebody fired a gun and within minutes dozens of Africans had been killed and many more wounded; the wounds of the victims were, according to hospital testimony, almost all in the back. At Langa in Cape Province there was a similar scene and altogether that day 83 Africans were killed and about 350 wounded. Sharpeville became a household word throughout the world. Statesmen of all colours denounced the bloodshed, flags were flown at half mast and formal tributes of silence were paid to the dead. In South Africa a state of emergency was declared as protests against the pass laws continued, the militia was called up and thousands of Africans were put in prison.

Nevertheless, the principal African leaders – Chief Albert Luthuli (shortly afterwards awarded the Nobel Peace Prize), Nelson Mandela, Walter Sisulu – continued the struggle by non-violent means. A successful three-day strike in 1961 was followed by preparations for countrywide non-co-operation and Mandela went underground to organize the campaign. As their leaders, their activities and organizations were progressively proscribed both Congresses produced more militant offshoots in the Sword of the Spirit and Poqo (founded in 1961 and 1962 respectively, the latter using murder as a weapon). In 1963 the government arraigned Mandela, Sisulu and others in a further mass trial at Rivonia and sentenced them to long terms of imprisonment.

The government did not hesitate to use force but it preferred, like any government, to provide its actions with legislative cover. In the first place were a number of statutes affecting the individual in his private capacity. Sexual relations between Africans and Europeans had been a criminal offence since 1927. In 1950 this prohibition was extended to relations between Europeans and coloureds, and in 1949 the Prohibition of Mixed Marriages Act (unlike many other Acts) did precisely what its title indicated – partly in response to the marriage of Seretse Khama of the Bamangwato to an English girl (see p. 663). Also in 1950 the government enacted the Popular Registration Act, described by Malan as the basis of apartheid, which prescribed registration and classification by race. The position of the individual before the law was also affected by the Native Laws Amendment Act 1957, which gave the authorities power to exclude Africans from such places as churches on the grounds that they might cause a legal nuisance (the Dutch Reformed Church protested and then complied); by the Separate Amenities Act 1953, which declared that separate amenities for blacks and whites need not be equal, as the courts had tended to insist; by the General Law Amendment Acts of 1961, 1962 and 1963, which stringently reduced the rights of the individual against the police, introduced house arrest for periods up to five years and sanctioned the indefinite detention of suspects; and by the Bantu Laws Amendment Act 1963, which legalized the eviction of any African from any urban area no matter how long he had lived there and turned him into a squatter on sufferance, who was allowed to work but not to settle.

A second category of statute formalized nationalist control over the machinery of the state. In 1949 separate Indian representation in parliament was abolished and the government launched its attack on the coloured franchise in the Cape province. Its Separate Representation of Voters Bill 1951, removing the coloured voters from the common to a separate roll, was declared unconstitutional by the courts because it took away rights which were entrenched by the South Africa Act 1909, and could not therefore be validly removed without a two-thirds majority of the two houses of parliament sitting together. The government thereupon brought in the High Court of Parliament Bill 1952 to give a committee of members of parliament power to override a decision of the Court of Appeal, but it too was voided by the courts. Malan dissolved parliament, increased his majority but failed to win the two-thirds majority which he needed. He won over some United Party members in the lower house and summoned a joint session of the two houses to consider a bill to amend the South Africa Act. This move failed in spite of a measure of United Party support and Malan was replaced by J. G. Strijdom, who abandoned Malan's legalistic tactics in favour of packing the judiciary and altering the constitution of the senate. By these means he secured, first, the passage by the requisite two-thirds majority of the South Africa Act Amendment Act 1956 (which validated the Separate Representation of Voters Act 1951) and, secondly, judicial endorsement of the Senate Act 1956.

This long tussle stimulated extra-parliamentary but still mainly non-violent opposition among liberal whites as well as among Africans. The Torch Commando, the

Black Sash movement and the bus boycott were its principal manifestations; but the principal consequences were the extinction of the lesser opposition parties (the Liberal and Progressive Parties), the increasing resort to house arrest and detention without trial, and a vigorous use of the communist bogey to brand all opponents of apartheid as subversive agents of an international conspiracy. The South African Communist Party had, after some internal disagreement, taken up the cause of the black worker which the Labour Party refused to espouse, but the communists had been as much hampered in South Africa as elsewhere by the twists and turns of Moscow and they had not greatly prospered. In 1950, however, the Malan government secured the passage of the Suppression of Communism Act, which was important, not because it proscribed communist activities and the relatively feeble Communist Party, but for its definition of communists and for the powers given to the executive to deal with such people. A communist was defined as any individual whom the minister of justice chose to call a communist, and in so determining the minister was to take the widest possible view since any person seeking to promote political, industrial, social or economic change by unlawful acts or omissions, or the threat of them, was to be considered a communist, as were various other broad categories of people. The Act was an instrument for eliminating every kind of opposition in parliament, trade unions, schools, universities and elsewhere, and at the same time a piece of propaganda meant to exaggerate the communist menace.

In the field of labour Africans had been forbidden to form unions since 1937. A ban on strikes imposed during the war remained in force after it, and the Native Labour (Settlement of Disputes) Act 1953 repealed these bans on unions and strikes and kept labour relations under white control.

Further statutes dealt with education. The Bantu Education Act 1953 showed the government's awareness of the crucial fact that children do not naturally adopt racial antagonisms (juvenile loves and hates being otherwise motivated), and also of the crucial need to give Africans a qualitatively different education if they were to form a permanently separate and inferior community. The Act created a new division of the Department of Native Affairs which was to direct Bantu education and displace the religious missions which were running most of the schools for Africans. Some churches handed over their schools willingly, others unwillingly; the Anglicans preferred to close their schools in the Transvaal and the Roman Catholics decided to carry on and bear the cost themselves. In the new nationalized schools education was geared to the place of the African in South Africa: that is, an unskilled worker in industry or a docile rustic in the special territories to be allotted to him. A further Bill to permit the exclusion of Africans from universities had to be withdrawn in 1957, but two years later the university college of Fort Hare was taken over by the state and separate (but well-equipped) university colleges for Africans were created. Africans remained entitled to apply for admission to white universities if they could show that they were qualified to attend courses not available elsewhere, but in practice such pleas were always found by the authorities to lack substance and the liberalism of the universities themselves was thwarted by executive action.

The kernel of the nationalist programme was the territorial separation of the races. The South Africa Land Act 1913 had allocated 87 per cent of land to whites and left open the question of what to do with the remaining 13 per cent, which was regarded as a labour reservoir. The Group Areas Act 1950 prescribed racial segregation in terms of residence, business and ownership of land. One of its immediate effects (completed by the Natives Resettlement Act 1954) was the wholesale removal of Africans from areas of Johannesburg which were needed by the whites. Some of these areas were slums, others were not; to the Africans they were places where they had been able to own property. This Act was followed in 1951 by the Bantu Authorities Act which sought to recreate chieftainship as a basis for the management of the African population. Chiefs, appointed and paid by the government, were to exercise authority in tribal areas, which would be grouped in regions, which would be grouped in territories, over which the Minister for Native Affairs would have ultimate control. This scheme was carried a stage further by the Promotion of Bantu Self-government Act 1959, which (besides depriving the Africans of the right to elect whites to represent them in parliament) consolidated the African reserves into Bantustans. (See Note C to this part.) The Tomlinson Commission, appointed by the government, had reported in 1955 that the cost of implementing the Bantustan policy would be £104 million spread over ten years and that the African population in 1960 was likely to be 21.5 million. The government promised £3.5 million for the development of the Bantustans and established in 1959 a Bantu Investment Corporation with a capital of £500,000 to develop Bantu industries.

South Africa's racial policies became the chief determinants of its external relations and led to something approaching isolation. Even with Britain, a close associate and an ally in the Second World War, relations became awkward as, for example, over the conclusion of a new alliance in which one of the sticking points was special guarantees over the treatment of black employees in the British naval base at Simonstown. The Simonstown agreements, concluded in 1955, were the fag end of several years of discussion in which neither Britain nor South Africa got what it wanted from the other. Britain wanted South African co-operation in the defence of British interests in the Middle East. South Africa wanted a broad alliance of (white) states similar to NATO for the defence of South Africa against communist attack or subversion and, second, the transfer of Simonstown to South African sovereignty. Both Britain and South Africa expected too much. The agreements of 1955, one of which – on staff talks – was secret, transferred Simonstown to South Africa in return for its indefinite use by Britain in peace and war and its use by Britain's allies in war, and in return also for the expansion and modernization of the South African navy with materials to be supplied by British shipyards. Beyond these provisions everything was vague: agreement in principle on the desirability of an African Defence Organization (which never came into being) and

South African agreement, also in principle only, to contribute to the defence of Africa and the Middle East gateways to it (a meaningless phrase). If Britain had felt uneasy but no more in its dealings with the governments of Malan and Strijdom, with Verwoerd (who succeeded Strijdom in 1958) and his foreign minister Eric Louw the gap was wider. It was widened by events such as Sharpeville and the exclusion of South Africa from the Commonwealth.

The Sharpeville calamity fell shortly before a meeting of Commonwealth prime ministers at which South Africa intended to seek assurances that it would remain a member of the Commonwealth if it became a republic. This change had been a prominent item in the nationalist programme and it was not expected to give rise to any difficulties, since the Commonwealth had already adapted itself to the presence of republics. Formally, however, the change required endorsement and the Commonwealth included members to whom South African racial policies were so repugnant that they might grasp at an excuse to withhold their assent. Verwoerd was unable to attend the conference owing to an attempt on his life by a white farmer, and South Africa was represented by Louw. The question of apartheid was kept off the formal agenda on condition that individual prime ministers might express themselves to Louw in private. Louw was forced to appreciate the strength of their feelings and to accept a communiqué which hinted that an application to remain in the Commonwealth, unaccompanied by reform of South African racial policies, would be rejected. The Commonwealth side-stepped the unpleasant and unprecedented step of expulsion and left the initiative with South Africa. A referendum was held later in the year with the expected republican result and South Africa thereupon left the Commonwealth.

Sharpeville also had repercussions at the United Nations. The General Assembly had been concerning itself with apartheid for some years. A commission appointed in 1953 had reported that the situation was harmful to peaceful international relations. In succeeding sessions the Assembly regularly passed resolutions asking South Africa to review its policies in the light of the UN Charter and deploring its failure to do so. After Sharpeville the Security Council resolved that the situation in South Africa might endanger international peace and security, called on South Africa to mend its ways and instructed the secretary-general, in consultation with the South African government, to take measures to uphold the Charter. Hammarskjöld went to South Africa in 1961 but his visit was as fruitless as the Assembly's resolutions. The next year the Assembly asked members to break off diplomatic relations with South Africa, close their ports and airports to its shipping and aircraft, prevent their own ships from calling at South African ports, boycott all South African products and suspend exports to South Africa. In 1963 the Security Council recommended the suspension of all sales of military equipment. Throughout these proceedings the African members were pressing for UN action partly out of genuine attachment to the idea of collective international action as embodied in the Charter and partly because they had no prospect of achieving anything effective on their own against the vastly superior military and economic strength of South Africa. They were embittered by the refusal of Britain and other powers which were capable of exerting economic pressures but reluctant to do so.

The campaign for mandatory economic sanctions developed as the wave of independence in Africa came up against its most formidable obstacle in Africa's deep south. Here was a white minority fortified by an authoritarian and non-egalitarian theology totally different from the secular libertarianism and egalitarianism which, even if subconsciously, informed the policies of the principal colonial powers. This minority, strong and rich, was not a colonial offshoot but a people at home with no thought of going anywhere else. The new African states, powerless to do anything against apartheid, were compelled to turn to those who could – Britain and the United States. They hoped that these countries would be both outraged by the enormities perpetrated by the South African regime and convinced that apartheid was a danger to international peace; they wanted international economic sanctions which would either force the Nationalists to parley with the Africans and give them a share of political power, or cause a disintegration of the regime and the emergence of something new which could in no event be worse.

The British and Americans were not prepared to agree that the practices of apartheid were a threat to international peace within the meaning of article 39 of the Charter. Their reasons were many. Both countries were preoccupied with problems which seemed to them more urgent. The United States gave unhesitating priority to Vietnam and to Latin American affairs, not to mention the Cold War. Britain was more intimately involved because of the old Commonwealth connection and Britain's much longer acquaintance with Africa, but in Britain's financial situation even the relatively small profit on trade with South Africa could not lightly be forgone; British exports to South Africa earned about £150 million a year, 4 per cent of total British exports, while imports from South Africa cost £100 million, 2 per cent of the import bill, leaving a favourable balance of about £50 million. In addition about two-thirds of South Africa's gold went into western reserves and were largely handled at a profit by the London market. In both Britain and the United States vested interests and pressure groups worked with articulate assidulity against intervention. British investments in South Africa were valued at about £1 billion. Britain was also held back by fears of reprisals against its dependencies of Bechuanaland, Basutoland and Swaziland, by the residual importance of the right to use the naval base at Simonstown, and by a postwar mood of getting out of things rather than into them. Public opinion was largely unaroused; the committed minorities were too small to have electoral significance.

The variety of other international commitments made London and Washington hope that an upheaval in South Africa could be postponed, but equally weighty were doubts about the effectiveness of sanctions and the immediate consequences of applying them. The South African economy had been expanded rapidly but had become more self-sufficient; oil and other materials had been accumulated. Experts disagreed on how long South Africa would stand a virtual siege, and on the effectiveness of the naval blockade which would be necessary for a short, and possibly a long time. On the legal side it was argued that the preconditions for such action laid down in article 39 of the Charter (namely, a threat to international peace) existed and had been acknowledged by the Security Council, which resolved in 1963 that the policies of the South African government 'disturbed' international peace. But the substitution of the word 'disturb' for the word 'threaten' was a precise gauge of the political temperature, for it enabled members of the Council to say one thing and yet avoid the consequences of their words. Britain and the United States could no longer bring themselves to deny the substance of the allegations made by African states but they were determined not to be embroiled with South Africa and so insisted on using a word which was not part of the language of article 39. Nor was this simply hypocrisy, although it may have been unwise inasmuch as it postponed an issue which was getting worse: those who had the power were unwilling to use it so long as they could see so little of its probable effects. Sanctions would require a blockade and a blockade would lead to a war. Within South Africa the collapse of the regime could produce anarchy, bloodshed and misery. Ought they to take this responsibility? Since they did not want to the question was not too difficult to answer.

Nevertheless, South Africa could not isolate itself from external affairs. It was directly affected by the independence crisis in Rhodesia, by the challenge to its discharge of its mandatory obligations in South West Africa (see pp. 617–21) and the grant of independence to black regimes in the British protected territories of Bechuanaland, Basutoland and Swaziland (which lay on or within its borders – see Note B to this part). The South African government aimed to preserve white supremacy by economic and military power and did not doubt its ability to do so. It had to consider whether white supremacy could be preserved beyond its own borders and, secondly, how it should conduct relations with established black states. White supremacy was strengthened by the waning of the old feud between the Afrikaner and English-speaking minorities and the feeling that the Afrikaner Nationalist victory in 1948 had become irreversible. The growth of the South African economy blurred the old dividing line between an Afrikaner country party and an English urban one. Afrikaners, while continuing to constitute a country party, were also penetrating the upper reaches of the industrial and financial plutocracy and sharing its bounding standard of living. This change in Afrikaner fortunes created a possible dilemma for the future, when affluent Afrikaners might have to choose between the rigour of their racial doctrines and the maintenance of their standard of living by easing job reservations. This prospect gave some comfort to optimistic liberals who hoped that economic pressures would enforce a gradual abandonment of the practices of apartheid. Externally, the South African government appeared to conclude that white rule in Rhodesia and the Portuguese territories could not be indefinitely maintained and that new black states could be induced by necessity to respond to a show of amicability and so breach the unanimity of black Africa's hostility. South Africa supported the illegal Smith regime in Rhodesia not so much because it believed in the permanence of white rule there but because of white South African sympathy for it and in order to show that economic sanctions could not work even against the much weaker Rhodesian economy. At the same time Verwoerd and Vorster pressed Smith to come to terms with Britain but they misjudged the obduracy of the Rhodesian whites. In the longer view South Africa, strong but beleaguered, would look out towards a hostile world over an expanse of satellites which would one day include also a black Rhodesia, Angola and Mozambique. The model was Malawi (see p. 603).

As the Nationalist Party became strong enough to afford internal dispute without risking loss of power, a hard-line or *verkrampte* section took issue with the enlightened or *verligte* wing (a comparative term) but was severely defeated at the polls. The *verligte* majority proceeded to develop its economic relations with African states, concluded an economic agreement with the Malagasy Republic in 1970 and was encouraged by the response of such diverse African leaders as Houphouët-Boigny and Busia, Kenyatta and Bongo. More importantly, South Africa hoped to secure from a new Conservative government in Britain a reversal of Labour's refusal to sell it arms. Vorster played on the Conservatives' vision of world affairs in primary Cold War colours and their reluctance to consummate Britain's withdrawal from those military vantage points in Asia and the Indian Ocean which in the 1950s had been vaguely termed the gateway to the Middle East. The British withdrawal from the world beyond Europe had faltered in the 1960s (partly because Britain was filling a gap which the United States was in no hurry to man) and British power had remained in evidence in the arc stretching from the Red Sea to Singapore, but after the departure from Aden in 1968 economic stringencies led the Labour government to announce that British forces in the Persian Gulf and east of it would be withdrawn as early as 1971. This development coincided with the growth of Russian naval power and the nightmare that it might take the place of British power in eastern and southern waters. Although impeded by the closing of the Suez Canal by the 1967 war, the Russians were able to establish in the Indian Ocean a small but permanent naval force supported by bases in Socotra, Mauritius and the Andaman Islands (in the Bay of Bengal). This extension redoubled American opposition to British withdrawal and caused Britain itself to enlarge what had become receding horizons.

During the British election campaign of 1970 Sir Alec Douglas-Home, the putative foreign secretary, said that a Conservative government would reverse the Labour policy of not selling arms to South Africa. Conservatives were not partisans of apartheid but they wished to be friends with South Africa in spite of apartheid and because they could see no state nearer to the Indian Ocean that was both strong and anti-communist. After the Conservative victory Sir Alec set about implementing this declaration. He was supported by the new prime minister Edward Heath, who resisted all contrary arguments largely, it seemed, on emotional grounds: that election promises must be kept and that British policy decisions must rest in British hands (a proposition that nobody had denied). While Heath treated arguments by African leaders as attempts to push Britain around, Douglas-Home treated African politics as a department of the Cold War. On the other side it was argued that a Russian naval threat, should it develop, could not in any event be met by a relatively small British–South African naval force; that the focus of such a threat, essentially a threat to the oil traffic, would not be in the southern oceans but round and about the southern shores of the Middle East; and that the British alignment with South Africa – a political demonstration – would create for the Russians political opportunities in Africa far greater than any military benefits likely to accrue to the anti-Russian side. Just as conflict in the Middle East and the ensuing arms race in that area and the American attachment to Israel had created a Russo-Arab front, so would a British alliance with South Africa throw African countries, however reluctantly, into the arms of the USSR; the USSR could look forward to a political windfall on the African continent. Within South Africa these arguments kept alive the illusion that South Africa would be welcomed into a southern counterpart of NATO in a global anti communist strategy. Yet South Africa, mainly for technological reasons, was becoming unnecessary for any such strategy and, mainly for political reasons, was an unacceptable ally. The Anglo-South African agreement for the use of the Simonstown naval base was allowed by the British to expire in 1975.

In 1978 half-veiled scandals and illness shifted Vorster to the presidency of the South African Republic. He was succeeded as prime minister by P. W. Botha. Vorster had ruled for 12 years. He was heir to an insoluble problem and handed it on unresolved but not unchanged. The task of South Africa's leaders was to defend not a state but a state-within-a-state and a racial system hated by many at home, reviled throughout the continent and abhorred in the world at large. Vorster tried to shift South Africa's regional and global positions but did not significantly improve them. In terms of power these two positions were diametrically different. Regionally, South Africa was a dominant power but globally it was of secondary importance at best. Even at the height of the Cold War South Africa failed to persuade more than a handful of conservatives (mostly in Britain and the United States) that South Africa mattered more to them than they did to it. South Africa was rich in resources but dependent on the outside world for capital to exploit these resources, vulnerable therefore to financial pressures or sanctions, and geographically and strategically more marginal than it liked to think. So long as defending South Africa meant defending apartheid South Africa found few friends and those whom it did find (Israeli and Taiwanese arms dealers, for instance) were merely mercenary. Vorster perceived the hopelessness of trying to ally white South Africa with the principal western powers and addressed himself to the region, particularly after the abdication of Portuguese power in Angola and Mozambique and the collapse of white rule in Rhodesia exposed his landward flanks. In an attempt to come to terms with the transition in Rhodesia he sought the co-operation of President Kaunda to pre-empt a victory for the armed guerrillas in Rhodesia and he offered independent Mozambique friendship and economic aid. But in Angola he made war.

He did so ineptly. His invasion of Angola in 1975 had no clear political or military aims and if he counted on western support because of the Cuban presence he was wrong or at least easily deceived about the extent and decisiveness of (mainly American) help. South African casualties, although not severe, shocked South Africans, who had not been told that they were engaging in war. This setback was compounded in 1977 when other clandestine operations came to light. The government's Department of Information had been authorized to engage in deception and bribery in order to win friends and disarm criticism and in the course of its campaigns much of the money provided for these purposes had been misused or appropriated by officials of no mean standing.

Finally in the Vorster years, a special event both symbolized South Africa's bedevilled situation and further soured its relations with the west. It became a nuclear power, but its added military might was irrelevant to its particular problems and alienated its potential friends. In 1977 preparations for a nuclear test in the Kalahari desert, about which the United States was informed by the USSR, led to strong protests from the principal powers. South Africa denied that the Kalahari site was designed for a nuclear explosion but the denial was not widely believed and South Africa continued to refuse to adhere to the Nuclear Non-Proliferation Treaty. The United States, which had been supplying South Africa with enriched uranium, adopted in 1978 legislation prohibiting such sales to any state which did not permit inspection by the International Atomic Energy Authority. (Reagan later found ways of circumventing this ban.) In 1979 a phenomenon inexplicable except as a nuclear explosion was observed by an American intelligence satellite over the ocean between South Africa and the Antarctic. In 1987 South Africa abruptly changed its attitude to the Non-Proliferation Treaty and agreed, under threat of expulsion from the IAEA, to adhere to the treaty. By this time South Africa had at least the capacity to make and use nuclear weapons, even though it had no rational use for them. Against its neighbour they were unnecessary, against its own townships and internal enemies unusable.

P. W. Botha inherited a situation which was intrinsically daunting and tarnished by recent failures within and beyond South Africa's frontiers. He ruled (1978–89) for nearly as long as Vorster. He won the leadership by a narrow margin and only because Vorster's obvious successor, Connie Mulder, was eliminated by the scandals and divisions which precipitated Vorster's retreat. Botha was a politician from the Cape and not from the boilerhouse of Afrikanerdom in the Transvaal. He had held the defence portfolio for 11 years and had the respect and confidence of the military; although victorious within the Nationalist Party he was not strong enough to offend the hardliners. Stubborn and cautious but increasingly domineering, he was determined that South Africa should know the firm smack of government and should stand on its own feet rather than being beholden to allies who laced their friendship with offensive homilies about its internal affairs. Serious riots in Soweto in 1976 and the emergence of the Black Consciousness movement led by Steve Biko – until he was beaten to death by police in 1977 – showed that the will to live dangerously and fight against fearful odds had not been extinguished. These trends illuminated the refusal of a new generation to come to terms with the whites; here were two communities with no way of talking to each other and not much wish to do so. Nevertheless, Botha accelerated the abatement of petty apartheid: football teams and audiences, for example. He toured the Homelands or Bantustans. He hoped to conciliate and detach from the black majority a small black bourgeoisie with a marginal share in the country's prosperity. He tried to prevent Indians and Coloureds from making common cause with the black peoples in return for limited internal autonomy. Separate assemblies of whites, Indians and Coloureds would be created; a mixed electoral college with an overall white majority would choose a president who would appoint three prime ministers, who would pick their own cabinets; and there would be a multiracial council of ministers with a white majority. There was no place for black Africans in this scheme since their numerical preponderance would have destroyed the commanding position which, on arithmetical principles, the whites were able to use against the Indians and Coloureds. These were gestures which changed nothing of substance. The Homelands had become evidently nonsensical and the constitutional tinkering was first spurned by Indians and Coloureds and then only half-heartedly accepted.

Other varieties of federal and confederal solution were canvassed. They were more academic than practical. Talk of partition into a black state and a white was revived, but no line of demarcation conceivably acceptable to both sides could be devised; fairness, in terms of an equitable division of wealth, could not be achieved in any way likely to secure peace between them. The Zulu chief Gatsha Buthelezi, who had revived the Inkatha movement (founded in 1928) and aimed to turn it into a vehicle for negotiating a non-violent settlement with the whites and some sort of autonomy for the Zulus proposed a National Convention to discuss non-violent progress towards majority rule in a unitary state. This proposal seemed to offer little prospect of agreement between blacks and whites in their prevailing moods. Nor was it clear how far Buthelezi could speak for the younger generation of Zulus.

In elections in 1981 Botha lost votes but not seats; his plans were checked but not abandoned. In the following year the right wing of the Nationalist Party, led by Dr Andreas Treurnicht, having failed to gain control of the party, left it, leaving Botha freer to proceed with his constitutional changes. These were approved by the white electorate by a 2–1 majority in a referendum at the end of 1983 and accepted, after some hesitation, by the Coloured and Indian communities, who were thereby embraced in the new tricameral legislature with 85 and 45 representatives to 178 whites. The blacks were excluded but were promised some relaxation of the minor indignities of apartheid and some participation in the local administration of their own communities. The black response was overwhelmingly cynical, as was that of the outside world. The banned ANC intensified its activities both within South Africa and on its borders.

In regional affairs Botha was as ambivalent as Vorster. The Nkomati agreement with Mozambique was initially ambiguous and then dead; the forward policy in Angola was abandoned, resumed and abandoned again; none of Pretoria's shifts in Namibia advanced its interests. Botha resuscitated the concept of an association of all states in southern Africa. Verwoerd had toyed with the prospect of an African commonwealth stretching up to (and even possibly including) Zaïre and under South African economic control. Botha's version was called a 'constellation' but it was too nebulous to attract serious attention and was regarded by black states as no more than a design to increase their economic dependence on South Africa. South Africa's economic strength served to scare rather than unite the area. Distrust and aversion to South Africa were profound and black states were more intent on lessening their dependence on an overmighty neighbour than on going into partnership with it. They created therefore a countervailing Southern African Development Co-ordinating Council (SADCC) of nine black states which, at conferences at Arusha in 1979 and Lusaka and Maputo in 1980, evolved ambitious plans for regional economic co-operation and secured promises of $670 million from outside sources – priority being given to husbandry and communications. SADCC was an essay in regionalism by sovereign states with a population of 60 million, considerable natural resources but inadequate capital, technology or managerial skills. Its members suffered from sporadic drought, direct attacks from South Africa, increasing defence expenditure and an overall decline in output of 15–20 per cent in the first half of the 1980s. First steps were modest but the organization gained international regard and at its fifth congress in Harare in 1986 37 states were represented. So long, however, as South Africa was out of bounds, SADCC could not itself generate sufficient resources to attract the foreign capital which it needed. In 1994 South Africa joined and SADCC changed its name to South Africa Development Community – SADC – which with the further additions of Congo and the Seychelles expanded to 14 members and into Central Africa and the Indian Ocean and to a population of 200 million. It established a Southern Africa Power Pool and a Parliamentary Forum, committed itself to internal free trade by 2005 and negotiated an agreement with the EU to take effect on the expiry of the last Lomé convention in 2000 (see p. 781). Expansion brought complications. SADC overlapped with COMESA (see p. 594) which had 24 members at the end of the century and ran into conflicts, notably over the Congo after 1988, where Mugabe wanted to use SADC to give military aid to Kabila but Mandela and others wanted to confine it to development projects.

In 1985 Botha announced a relaxation of the rules of apartheid governing sex and marriage but not the restrictions imposed by such centrepieces of apartheid as the Group Areas Act or the Bantu Education Acts. He envisaged some devolution of authority to blacks locally but was adamantly opposed to any black share in power at the top. As violence led to scenes reminiscent of Sharpeville in 1960 and Soweto in 1976, South Africa's principal trading partners – including this time the United States – took fright and began once more to talk about mandatory economic sanctions. Western capitalists began to run down their investments, the rand collapsed temporarily and the white business community in South Africa expressed dismay when Botha's riposte was more rod than olive branch. South Africa seemed to be on the edge of an explosion but it had so often been there before that whites and their foreign friends stubbornly insisted that white power could be preserved by superior force, superior intelligence and changes which would include no concessions on the Group Areas Act, the Reservation of Separate Amenities Act or the constitutional dominance of the white vote. Yet there was a new element over and beyond the steady accumulation of pressures and discomforts: an acceptance – albeit by a small section of the whites – that there must be negotiation with the ANC. The biggest obstacles to this change of mind had been, first, the almost universal (white) belief that there was no need to talk to the ANC or any other black body and, second, the equally widespread belief that the ANC was merely a stalking horse for the communists and black power – a prelude to rule from Moscow. The second belief, buttressed by the presence among the ANC's leaders of a sizeable minority of communists, remained strong, but the first had become a subject for discussion. During 1985 white leaders of industry and banking held a formal meeting with ANC leaders outside South Africa and at the end of the year the creation of a new Congress of South African Trade Unions emphasized the government's problems in retaining control over organized labour. The government imposed censorship over the reporting of black riots and police brutalities but although these measures impeded foreign journalists they did not stop the disorder or render the principal black townships less ungovernable. Nevertheless, the overriding change of these years was the arrival at the top of the political agenda of the questions how, when and within what limits to treat with the blacks. As the white state-within-a-state lost moral authority and relied more and more on force, as the whites themselves became more nervously divided, and as the blacks remained capable only of harassing the white regime without supplanting it, so chaos seemed a not impossible prospect.

Painfully and slowly minds were changing within the white South African community. Broadly speaking, the 1970s had witnessed a surprising level of confidence; the 1980s questioned this confidence. In the 1970s whites, who had become used to facing external criticism, fancied that they saw as the threats to their position diminishing. The ease with which economic sanctions against Rhodesia were defeated by western corporations with governmental connivance reduced to insignificance the threat of similar action against South Africa. The late 1970s saw too an economic recovery unforeseen a few years earlier. Growth exceeded forecasts, partly export-led but also nourished by domestic consumer demand. The boom in the price of gold filled the country's coffers and enabled it to pay off foreign debts; taxes were cut; the balance of payments improved. South Africa was not merely surviving but prospering in spite of internal tensions and external vilification. It was becoming less of a 'windfall' economy (although the gold boom belonged to that category), more self-sufficing and independent. Its principal weaknesses were its dependence on imported capital and fuel, shortage of skills, and the uncertainties surrounding the black labour force. Capital continued to flow in spite of the political risks, and the development of oil from domestic coal advanced so rapidly that the cessation of critical supplies of oil after the Iranian revolution of 1979 imposed no more than minor restrictions on private consumption. But the labour market, skilled and unskilled, posed more serious problems. The shortage of skills compelled the abandonment of many promising projects and increased unemployment. The unionization of black labour was potentially a source of effective militancy, by strikes or violence; it was unclear how the whites could keep control of black labour. Whether unemployed or organized in labour unions, the black urban proletariat could become allied with traditional black nationalism.

The 1980s darkened this side of the picture. GDP declined; foreign investment virtually ceased; inflation rose above 20 per cent a year; the economy was ceasing to generate profit to finance its future; the reserves were running down. Discontent was manifested in five by-elections in 1985 when the ruling party lost votes to the hard right in very different constituencies. The ANC had been badly harmed without being smashed: the raids on neighbouring countries failed to scare them into expelling the ANC. Attempts to control the black townships by tens of thousands of arrests and the declaration of a state of emergency shook confidence, particularly the confidence of the business community. Even South Africa's undoubted military strength was less reassuring than it had seemed in earlier years. South Africa, although neither a world power nor a superpower, was a fully modernized power capable of spending about 2 billion rand (about £1 billion) a year on defence and vulnerable only to a direct attack assisted by a superpower, or to a prolonged guerrilla war assisted by a major internal rebellion. Yet it was dependent on outside sources for the maintenance and further development of its heavier equipment and advanced technology; its expanding forces were short of officers, NCOs and instructors; and its perimeter was uncomfortably long.

To retain the goodwill, or negate the ill will, of the west South Africa boasted invaluable minerals which, it believed, the west could not do without. These minerals were, in a number of cases, irreplaceable except by recourse to the USSR as the only other known major repository. In manganese, essential and irreplaceable in steel making, South Africa dominated world production and reserves; in vanadium it was a major producer and possessed enormous reserves; in uranium it had considerable reserves and although other countries also had reserves most of these had no exportable surpluses, so that western Europe and Japan could be seriously upset by any cut in supplies from South Africa (and Namibia); in platinum, whose diverse uses embraced the chemical, electrical, glass and petroleum industries, the United States was dependent on South Africa. This dependence might be lessened by stockpiling and the search for substitutes but the haphazardness of nature in endowing these two areas – southern Africa and the USSR – with such large shares of the world's known deposits of a variety of strategic minerals was a significant factor in how white South Africans assessed their prospects.

International economic sanctions had mixed effects. Their efficacy rested on inter-twined sets of calculations: on the one side their economic consequences and their impact on the political will of intended victims and on the other side the solidarity and political aims of those imposing the sanctions. Reagan and Thatcher espoused a policy of business as usual, arguing that prosperity would soften racial asperities and enable the whites to keep control of a situation which, if it was deteriorating under white rule, would deteriorate faster without it. To Thatcher the ANC was a terrorist organization while Reagan hoped to defeat it by helping UNITA and Renamo, which he regarded as romantic freedom fighters. Thatcher tried to thwart but succeeded only in snubbing her Commonwealth partners when they voted in favour of tougher economic measures. By way of compromise the Commonwealth despatched an Eminent Persons Group to South Africa. Simultaneously, and perhaps not coincidentally, South African attacks on Botswana, Zimbabwe and Zambia scotched any usefulness that it might have had and a mission by the British foreign secretary Geoffrey Howe in the following year met blunt and resentful rebuff: both missions hoped to set a diplomatic ball rolling by securing the legalization of the ANC and PAC and the release of Mandela. Within South Africa sanctions aggravated the existing economic problems of an expanding and sophisticated economy dependent on the international economy, in a period of worldwide stringency. Commercially, they obliged South African enterprises to redir-ect their business away from Britain and the United States and towards West Germany and Japan, but this search for new markets was in itself no bad thing and with the aid of subtle and not so subtle evasions of the obstacles imposed by sanctions South African trade suffered no serious net loss. Particular losses were mitigated, if not fully compensated, and South Africa learned to live with the marginal loss in the short term. Financially, the withdrawal of foreign companies gave South African companies the chance to buy, often at bargain prices, the plants and operations left behind by depart-ing foreigners; some individuals became very rich in the process. More serious was the reduction in the flow of foreign funds. In common with other countries South Africa experienced in the mid-1980s a payments crisis which it surmounted by rescheduling its debts but which was nevertheless a disturbing reminder of long-term dependence on foreign capital. Psychologically, the shock sharpened fears for the future which had political repercussions, first among financiers and industrialists and so among politi-cians forced to face the fact that the white business community needed to participate in the world economy and feared isolation. While the poorer whites might be driven by sanctions to support extreme and racist attitudes, the business classes were driven in the opposite direction. Within the space of a few months in 1989 the Commonwealth and the UN not only asserted the efficacy of existing sanctions but also treated them – and the promise of their remission in return for fundamental changes in South Africa – as a major instrument for the social and constitutional reforms which by that date some Nationalist leaders had espoused but were introducing with tantalizing slowness.

In these cross-currents two facts stood out. The Afrikaner political and intellectual elites were losing their faith in the apartheid which had sustained them since the Nationalist Party came to power in 1948. But although they were shedding their ideology they were not ready to shed power. The blacks on the other hand were unimpressed by shifts in attitudes which seemed to betoken no change in the realities of everyday life. Events spoke louder than the conferences where a few leaders on both sides were beginning to know one another. The death of Steve Biko was only the most flagrant of a stream of incidents which were creating martyrs for the black cause and making a peaceful settlement less and less likely. Each martyr was a figure to whom his surviving compatriots owed a debt which they felt could not be compromised. The generation of the under-30s equated South African capitalism with exploitation, apartheid and police rule; and it was uninterested in any dialogue with the whites, even liberal whites.

This situation was changed by F. W. de Klerk. Botha's political failings, his unattractive personality and ill health combined to embolden his colleagues to get rid of him. Of the candidates to succeed him de Klerk was the most conservative but he transformed the political atmosphere. He saw that South Africa was isolated and that isolation meant economic disaster. He stopped trying to appease the hard right and set out to curb (even if with scant success) the security forces and police, which were acting as though they were a law unto themselves. He abandoned the policy of destabilizing neighbouring states; he permitted protests and orderly demonstrations; he initiated secret talks with Nelson Mandela and released from jail Walter Sisulu and other black leaders; and early in 1990 he released Mandela himself. These measures indicated a determination to negotiate a treaty with black South Africans, represented first and foremost by the ANC, and to give South Africa a new constitution.

Mandela was an even more striking figure. With Oliver Tambo and Walter Sisulu he had been one of a trio of black youth leaders. In 1963 he had been sentenced at the Rivonia trial to imprisonment which seemed likely to last as long as his life. He was vice-president of the ANC, the president being Tambo, who had escaped imprisonment but was by 1990 seriously ill in Sweden. Mandela was a complex man who nevertheless radiated a simple message and honest personality. The ANC, originally the creation of a black liberal elite, had expanded its popular base in the 1950s and thereafter but its leadership remained urban and middle-class. It had looked to the USSR for financial help and became closely associated with the South African Communist Party (SACP) in spite of some distrust of that white organization. It preferred non-violent tactics but endorsed violence when non-violence got it nowhere. Unlike, for example, Black Consciousness (a product of the hopeless 1970s), the ANC did not disdain white support and was not dogmatically anti-white. On emerging from prison after 27 years, Mandela was revealed as a man of extraordinary composure and dignity. If de Klerk had created a new situation, Mandela was the man without whom a new starting point would be of no avail.

Both men had the task of finding common ground for working out a new constitution. Both realized that beginning to talk was an initial portent and the merest prelude to an eventual agreement which might lie some way ahead. Both had the daunting problem of securing adequate consent from his own constituency by marginalizing extremists. The ANC was insistent upon one-man-one-vote. The government had to find a way of reconciling democratic majority rights with safeguards for the apprehensive white minority, part of which was viciously hostile to any relaxation of white rule. The ANC accepted a multiparty system and a mixed economy (so too did the SACP) but was wedded to more government control over the economy than white politicians or businessmen approved. Public order was an immediate issue. De Klerk tried to get Mandela and the ANC to forswear violence, which they were unwilling to do so long as the only actual changes in the country were the release of Mandela and others and the president's evident sincerity and willingness to talk. The ANC agreed, however, in 1990 to suspend violence in return for the gradual release of all political prisoners and the termination of the state of emergency which gave the authorities extensive powers of arbitrary arrest and indefinite detention. The government limited its removal of the state of emergency by excepting Natal, which was the scene of violence of a special kind – violence between blacks. While the ANC was countrywide the undoubted representative of the black community, in Natal this position was contested by Inkatha and Buthelezi. Inkatha had solid support in rural Natal but was losing ground in the towns to the ANC (or, before the ANC was legalized, to the United Democratic Front, which was the ANC in disguise). The resulting contest took the form of hideous violence between Zulu and Zulu in which thousands were killed. The violence spread beyond Natal, in particular to the Transvaal, where it pitted Zulus against non-Zulus. The ANC complained, with more than a little plausibility, that the police were helping Inkatha by standing by instead of intervening to keep or restore order, and even positively encouraging violence in order to impede the government's talks with the ANC. Police revelations (suspected as a fabrication) of a revolutionary conspiracy between blacks and communists were assumed to have the same disruptive purpose, but de Klerk and Mandela kept to their common purpose. De Klerk declared that membership of the Nationalist Party should become open to blacks, thus creating the prospect of two mass parties – the NP and the ANC (already open to whites) – as the principal political pillars of a non-racial democratic South Africa in which the white minority would not be sequestered in a permanently minor party.

The main business of the years 1991–94 was the elaboration and inauguration of a new constitution, non-racial and democratic. A Convention for a Democratic South Africa (CODESA) was convoked. It included more than 20 parties. The context was past passions, persistent violence and fears of civil war to come, counterbalanced, however, by an overriding commitment by the leadership of the Nationalist Party and the ANC to continue their struggle without violence and without fateful delays. The essence of this struggle was the safeguards whereby the (white) minority might enjoy a blocking power short of a veto. The principle of majority rule, meaning black rule, was not negotiable but the limiting conditions of its exercise were negotiable. The negotiations were clouded by the existence of numerous groups besides the two protagonists: white extremists of varying degree; the PAC and other black groups (some of them within the ANC) distrustful of Mandela's drive; and the Inkatha Party, whose power was overrated both by its leader Mangosuthu Buthelezi, who envisaged an autonomous Zulu domain, and by de Klerk, who hoped to construct with Inkatha a right-wing alliance in the new political system.

On the black side Mandela's position was never seriously threatened. The ANC's first national conference for 33 years – in Durban in 1991 and attended by 2,234 delegates – tested and confirmed his authority. His personal dominance preserved unity in the ANC in the face of differences over the handling of the discussions, the tone of propaganda and the use of violence, which many in the ANC believed to be justified by disclosures of aid given to Inkatha in money, arms, training and even incitement to fighting by blacks against blacks. On the opposite side, de Klerk's position was strengthened by a referendum in which whites supported with unexpected emphasis – 69 per cent of a turnout of 89 per cent – accelerated power-sharing under a new constitution; and by his opponents' recourse to violence which, by its failures, discredited them, dissolved their alliance and killed off any prospect of a right for whites to secede from the South African republic. De Klerk, however, was weakened by a refusal by the United States to come out in favour of white demands for a blocking power equivalent to a veto, and by evidence that he was much less than fully in control of his security and armed forces or, alternatively, that he had connived at breaches of the law and of police instructions.

The ANC responded to pressures on de Klerk by producing precise timetables of its own which envisaged an interim government by mid-1992, general elections in the first quarter of 1993 for a constituent assembly, a mixed cabinet by the middle of that year and a new constitution in operation one year later. By insisting that timetables were as important as substance, the ANC forced de Klerk substantially to abandon his hopes of keeping many of the more intransigent whites in the Nationalist Party or of forming an alliance with Inkatha to serve as a counterweight or alternative to his current alliance with the ANC. The ANC did not get all that it was asking for but it gave up fewer of its aspirations than did the government. The ANC successfully jostled the government.

It did so partly because it held a stronger hand from the moment that de Klerk felt obliged to release Mandela from prison and partly because the opposition to CODESA's initiatives was more damaging to the government than to the ANC. This opposition came from whites and blacks, united by their common aim to secure the greatest possible degree of devolution or even the right to secede, but divided over the means to do so – particularly over a resort to force. They combined uneasily in a Freedom Alliance which embraced the Afrikaner Volksfront led by General Viljoen, the

Conservative Party led by Ferdie Hertzenberg, the AWB of Eugene Terre-Blanche, Buthelezi's Inkatha, the presidents of two Homelands – Bophuthatswana and Ciskei – and another 20 smaller groups. Having exerted little influence on the constitutional debate, these groups confronted the question of whether to participate in elections or try to wreck them. The two more important leaders – Viljoen and, at the eleventh hour, Buthelezi – decided to participate. Viljoen parted company with the AWB and other extremists after an affray in Bophuthatswana when Chief Lucas Mangope invited the Afrikaner Volksfront to help him stay in power and the AWB took the opportunity to join in riotously. Mangope was overthrown and Viljoen turned his back on violence and formed a new party with defectors from the Conservative Party. In Ciskei, Brigadier Oupo Gqoso resigned after conflict over police pay and pensions and both these Homelands were, in effect, taken over by the South African army. Buthelezi, who possessed the greatest capacity for disrupting the elections, was in a cleft stick, incapable of winning more than a fractional vote even in Zulu areas and equally incapable of extracting from Mandela and de Klerk more than a fraction of the demands which he had been making over the terms of the constitution or the timing of elections. A week before the elections he reversed his refusal to take part in exchange for face-saving declarations concerning the status of his nephew, the Zulu king (who had shown signs of being irked by his uncle) and promises by Mandela and de Klerk of international mediation over autonomy for KwaZulu-Natal. These promises remained unfulfilled.

Nineteen of CODESA's participants agreed in 1992 on a programme which provided for a Transitional Executive Council operating alongside the existing Nationalist cabinet; elections by adult suffrage in April 1994; a federal state with nine regions, a president and up to two vice-presidents (nominated by parties winning more than 20 per cent of the vote); an executive of not more than 27 to which parties might nominate members in the proportion of one for every 5 per cent of votes won; a legislature consisting of an assembly of 400 (half elected from national lists and half from regional lists) and a senate of 90, 10 from each province; regional legislatures with, depending on population, 30 to 100 members; a Bill of Rights and a Constitutional Court. Senior military leaders declared their loyalty to these arrangements. The government and the ANC agreed that there would be a single army, no dismissals from the civil service and no confiscation of land. The conclusion of these arrangements was due to the persistence of Mandela and de Klerk and to the fact that each needed the other because both feared anarchy. The elections in 1994 were largely undisturbed by violence but seriously disrupted and eventually prolonged by administrative muddles. They were declared to be substantially free and fair and this verdict was accepted by the principal parties in spite of widespread suspicions of grave misdemeanours by Inkatha in KwaZulu-Natal. The ANC scored a sweeping victory but fell narrowly short of a two-thirds majority – 62.6 per cent of the vote, 252 seats in the assembly. The National Party won 20.4 per cent and 81 seats, Inkatha 10.5 per cent and 43 seats. Three other parties won seats in the assembly but failed to qualify for places in the cabinet, of which the ANC occupied 18, the National Party six and Inkatha three. In seven of the provincial assemblies the ANC held majorities but the National Party won in the Western Cape (with the help of the Coloured vote) and Inkatha won in KwaZulu-Natal. These elections ended an era but did not open a new one. The next few years constituted a transitional period which saw the gradual dissolution of the partnership which had guided the end of white rule. The proceedings of the Truth and Reconciliation Commission established to heal sores by discharging consciences produced damaging revelations about the apartheid regime, split the Nationalist Party and eventuated in the resignation of de Klerk in 1997. (Similar commissions established in Chile after the end of the Pinochet dictatorship, in Guatemala and El Salvador after the abatement of civil wars, and in Brazil, Argentina and Uruguay experienced the same clash between the desire for a harmonious future and retribution for past crimes.) The victorious ANC managed the transition more successfully than the Nationalists. Mandela, aged 80 in 1998, was succeeded by Thabo Mbeki as party president in that year and as state president in 1999. Elections in 1999 affirmed the dominance of the ANC. The Nationalist Party was almost eliminated, Buthelezi's Inkatha lost ground, the new Democratic Party led by Tony Leon (white) became the official opposition with only 10 per cent of the vote. But there were no economic miracles. Public services – water, electricity, housing – were vigorously developed but left needs and expectations only sparsely fulfilled. Extreme poverty and high unemployment persisted with inevitably widespread disappointment, disorder and crime. South Africa joined the Lomé association and discussed free trade with the EU but investment and exports languished as the economy remained dependent on a world economy emerging only slowly from recession and then shocked by economic turmoil in East Asia. What had occurred was a revolution in which one society prevailed over another. These were societies which had been bitterly hostile, divided by fear, hatred and contempt – emotions which could not be dissolved overnight or even over a single generation. Deep material divisions persisted and so too, if less obviously, did the spiritual legacy of a nasty history. With Mbeki as president the ANC retained its dominance but lost momentum. Mbeki's style in domestic and inter-African affairs was mediating, unostentatious and in some respects (particularly his diagnosis of AIDS) wrong-headed, so that in 2007 he lost the presidency of the ANC to Jacob Zuma, formerly vice-president but dismissed by Mbeki four years earlier. This result pointed to the election in 2009 of a new state president, more out-going than Mbeki, more in tune with the spirit of the ANC as a militant liberation force but also seriously ensnared in allegations of corruption and immorality.

CHAPTER 26

Russians, Cubans, Chinese

Communism made no great impact in Africa but the Cold War did. The United States supported some frightful regimes because they were anti-communist. The Russians riposted with some, mostly inept, interventions.

What the Russians knew about Africa when the Second World War ended was little. A few nineteenth-century travellers in the Nile valley, a comic opera invasion of Somaliland and Ethiopia in the 1880s and some marginal activity by the Orthodox Church were all that tsarist Russia had to put against the stores of knowledge acquired by western traders, explorers, missionaries and colonial governors; and since almost none of Africa was independent Russia had no diplomatic missions to observe and report about it. The Bolshevik revolution gave a spurt to African studies but these were quickly submerged under the pressure of more urgent cares. As the Second World War ended Stalin put in a bid for a share in Italy's conquered colonies, but it failed. In the 1950s African studies were expanded, an Africa Institute was founded in Moscow (1959) under the direction of an eminent historian, I. I. Potekhin, and the USSR began to send representatives to Afro-Asian conferences. In 1960 the People's Friendship University, later renamed Lumumba University, was founded in Moscow.

African leaders, being anti-colonialist, were anti-western. Most of them professed to be socialists. This was for Moscow a promising background, but it proved less fruitful than expected: the anti-colonial struggle was unexpectedly short and peaceable; African leaders, beginning with Nkrumah, espoused non-alignment; the familiar paths to London and Paris remained well trodden; Soviet aid never matched western aid; African socialism derived at least as much from western socialism as Russian communism. Its principal vehicle had been the French and not the Soviet Communist Party and although the Rassemblement Démocrate Africain (RDA) – established in October 1946 at Bamako – had in Gabriel d'Arboussier a secretary close to communist thinking, its president Félix Houphouët-Boigny was hostile to it. Another founder of the RDA, Sekou Touré, was typically unhelpful to the USSR. Evicted from the French trade union federation of the General Confederation of Labour (CGT), he had joined its African counterpart, the CGTA (later General Union of African Workers [UGTAN]), in which communists were in a minority, and he became the first of a number of African presidents to evict Russians from his country.

Moscow's first venture into African politics south of the Sahara was a reaction to an opportunity. Guinea, pitched into independence in 1958 upon refusing to join de Gaulle's *communauté*, was born in desperate straits. A poor and thinly populated state, it had, nevertheless, a strategic position on the south-west corner of upper Africa, a port nearer than any other to mid-Atlantic, about a third of the world's bauxite and massive grievances against the west. Moscow was quick with diplomatic recognition, credits (140 million roubles in 1959), offers of trade and Czech arms. Sekou Touré was invited to Moscow. Khrushchev promised to visit Conakry and Brezhnev did. Daniel S. Solod, who had served with credit as ambassador to Syria and Egypt, was transferred to Guinea with the purpose of turning Conakry into a centre of regional Soviet influence.

Mali and Ghana fell fortuitously into this picture. Mali (or Soudan, as it still was) was the poor relation of the short-lived union with Senegal which collapsed in 1960 under the weight of its incompatibilities. Huge, arid and landlocked, it had nothing to offer an ally, but Modibo Keita, a socialist of the Sekou Touré brand, was brought by Guinea into the Soviet sphere by a similar friendlessness. He was offered credits of 40 million roubles and Bamako airport was made available to Aeroflot. Ghana, already independent three years earlier, was offered 160 million roubles at this time, although Moscow had at first shown only perfunctory interest in Ghana and sent no ambassador there until 1959. Nkrumah was a strong Commonwealth man, candid about his need for western aid and – in Soviet eyes – a typical product of the wrong section of the African bourgeoisie, which was ready to do deals with the British. But Nkrumah had also been the first to hold out a helping hand to Sekou Touré, he gave aid and a home to the revolutionary Union Populaire du Cameroun, and he became bitterly anti-American after the murder of his friend Lumumba. He was a pendulum swinging in the right direction for Moscow. Like Sekou Touré and Modibo Keita he was to receive the Lenin Prize.

Yet within a few years there was nothing left of this pro-Russian constellation in West Africa. Upon the fall of Nkrumah in 1966 General Ankrah expelled all Soviet experts (about 1,000 of them), the bulk of the Soviet, Cuban and Chinese diplomatic missions and the entire East German trade mission; relations with the USSR degenerated into a slanging match. Modibo Keita survived until 1968 (when he was removed by the army and kept in prison until he died) but the Russian connection languished almost from the start, Russian aid came to a full stop and although a Russian group was reported in the 1970s to be prospecting for minerals in northern and eastern Mali the common belief was that the USSR was more interested in landing grounds for aircraft or paratroopers. The initial association with Guinea turned sour even more swiftly when, in December 1961, Solod was told to pack his bags and leave, accused of complicity in a conspiracy against Sekou Touré. Moscow sent no less a personage than Anastas Mikoyan to try to patch things up but he failed and in 1962 Sekou Touré took a first step towards a more neutral position by accepting $70 million of American aid. During the Cuban missile crisis he refused to allow the Russians to use Conakry airport, which they had built. The first jet aircraft to land there was French.

The main consequence of these failures was a fillip to new thinking in Moscow about Africa. The Russian ventures in Guinea, Ghana and Mali were partly fortuitous and partly ideological. Their principal instrument, however, was economic: money plus expert advice. Russian credits (made available on exceptionally easy terms) were to be used to finance mutually approved capital projects, meet the balance on trading accounts so far as Russian imports were not paid for by Guinean bauxite or Ghanaian cocoa, and contribute to the training of West Africans in the USSR. Moscow sought in this way to detach these states from the western economic embrace, to secure control of their exports and to plant Russian experts in them. But the experts turned out to be more numerous than welcome – 3,000 in Guinea alone at their peak. They tended to recommend showy rather than useful works – such as a big stadium and theatre in Conakry – and they promoted collectivization of agriculture, which was so unpopular that it led in Guinea to unrest which the government had to suppress. Excessive quantities of Russian goods were imported; bills and resentment piled up. And if money was to be the main political instrument the United States had more of it.

Worst of all from Moscow's point of view was the growing feeling that the Russians were interested only in driving crassly selfish bargains. This was not entirely fair. Over the 1960s the USSR paid rather more than the world price for Ghanaian cocoa. The USSR was for Ghana an assured and steady purchaser and when world prices fell Russian purchases stayed the fall by reducing the supply to other markets. The Russian contract kept prices in Ghana's traditional markets more buoyant than they would otherwise have been. In Guinea, on the other hand, the Russian appetite for bauxite ran far ahead of anything resembling generosity or tact. After deposits at Kindia had been prospected by Russian experts a so-called joint company was formed; it was owned and run entirely by Russians. This company's profits were allocated in the first place to a clearing account to offset Guinean purchases of Russian arms and other goods but were juggled in the worst neo-colonial manner. In addition, the USSR contrived to pay a beggarly $6 a tonne for bauxite all the way to 1976 when the price was raised to $16 – still a mere two-thirds of the world price. The ill will so generated was compounded by the Russian refusal to help Guinea build a fishing fleet or to part with any of its own catch in Guinean waters, a foolish niggardliness in sharp contrast with the East Germans and Cubans, who were willing to hand over some – in the Cuban case the whole – of theirs. In sum Guinea, Ghana and Mali served no practical Russian purpose and did less than nothing for the USSR's image in Africa.

But they were a testing ground as, in the aftermath of Stalin's death, Moscow developed an intellectual ferment which Khrushchev's temperament encouraged. The dogmatic categories of Stalinist communism were loosened and Khrushchev, an unintellectual old man in a hurry, was more than willing to stir the pot without caring too much where the spirit of inquiry might lead. Africa, always towards the bottom of any Russian agenda, was not a precipitating cause of this new mood, whose main foreign source was probably the new rulers' determination to find ground for ending the quarrel with Tito. But there were implications for African policy too. The search for friends in Africa need not be confined to leaders whose credentials could pass the tests of Stalinist orthodoxy, which no leading African did. Nationalists, provided they were moving in a socialist direction, became acceptable allies. The path of 'non-capitalism' – a usefully vague phrase which was a favourite with Khrushchev – became respectable. In this context links could be made with Sekou Touré, Nkrumah and Keita without doing violence to basic Russian postulates and although these particular links led only to disappointment the policies underlying them survived. Moscow broadened its field for diplomatic manoeuvre.

Moscow was also becoming better informed. The Africa Institute in the Academy of Sciences was expanded and in 1965 the directorship went to V. G. Solodovnikov, an economist (and from 1965 ambassador in Zambia). Solodovnikov was also put at the head of a Co-ordinating Council for African Studies, created by the Academy in 1966. By 1970 the USSR had 350 scholars working on African ethnography, economics, law, philology, history and geography and when Solodovnikov left the Institute he was succeeded by the son of A. A. Gromyko. There were similar developments in Leningrad and in universities in eastern European countries.

Whether or not for these reasons there was a marked difference in Moscow's handling of the crises and opportunities of the two major civil wars of the 1960s in the Congo and Nigeria. In the former the USSR began by endorsing UN intervention, partly because Lumumba – Belgium's own choice to lead the new state – fitted Moscow's identikit of an African socialist of the right sort; but when Lumumba was ousted and later killed Moscow attacked Hammarskjöld's handling of the situation and threatened unilateral military intervention in support of Lumumba's heir Antoine Gizenga, who, however, lacked adequate support in the country or on its borders (Sudanese hostility sealed the fate of his revolt in Orientale province); his rebellion created a temporary alliance between Kasavubu and Tshombe, which was detrimental to Russian aims; and the final outcome – the establishment of Mobutu, the USA's great black hope – was accompanied by the forcible closing of the Russian embassy in Kinshasa. The USSR retired hurt by its own miscalculations. It had also offended the great majority of the members of the OAU, which was brought into existence in 1963 largely as a consequence of war in the Congo.

By contrast, Moscow strengthened its position in Nigeria during the civil war in that country. This was a victory for pragmatism over ideology. The USSR had been slow to pay attention to Nigeria. Although a Nigerian ambassador went to Moscow a few months after independence in 1960, Moscow did not return the compliment until 1964. Its instinctive sympathies did not lie with the dominant north, or with a general such as Johnson Ironsi who was regarded as a member of a feudal, pro-British class. But disillusion with civilian leaders in West Africa led Moscow to see virtue in military men who might be expected to provide more stable government and to prove themselves more predictable friends. Theory accommodated itself to practical necessities by depicting the military as a popular and progressive force, sweeping away bourgeois capitalist hangovers. Gowon, Ironsi's successor, was not a northerner and showed some signs of making an alliance with Awolowo, who had found favour in Moscow's eyes when he became the first leader of the opposition in the federal parliament: Moscow hoped, wrongly, that Gowon might make him prime minister. Moreover, as Ojukwu moved towards the Biafran secession it became clear that an overwhelming majority of the OAU opposed him. Moscow did not propose to offend them. It decided to back – and arm – Gowon.

The negotiations were conducted the more easily because Nigeria was already negotiating with the USSR for economic aid. Nigeria's development plans were so extensive that it could not get all the aid it required from the west and so, overcoming its profound anti-communism, it turned also to the USSR and eastern Europe. In 1967 a small five-man team of Russian experts spent four weeks in Nigeria travelling over many parts of the country and studying possibilities for a steel industry (for which, with other projects, the USSR eventually advanced $140 million at the end of 1968). But with the outbreak of war Gowon's problems had been reduced to one: getting arms. Britain and the United States refused to give him what he wanted and he turned to the Russian ambassador Alexander Romanov, an adept and sensitive negotiator who did not try to drive an over-hard bargain (Lagos was, in any case, ready to pay cash) and understood that although Nigeria could not be made communist it might be made friendly. Within weeks of the beginning of hostilities Russian and Czech arms began to arrive and Russian support for Gowon persisted firmly and openly. This was a policy which achieved its limited aims. Successive Nigerian governments, all of them strongly anti-communist, preserved the equable relationship with the USSR established during the civil war.

For ten years after the Second World War the USSR failed to find a point of entry into northern Africa. Opportunity came in a roundabout way. Nasser wanted arms which he could not get from the west. He did not know Stalin's successors but on his way to Bandung he met Zhou Enlai at Rangoon airport. Nasser explained his predicament and Zhou suggested he try Moscow and promised to put in a good word for him. After discussions in Cairo and Prague the Russians gave Nasser to understand that he could do what he liked with the Egyptian communists: it would be no part of an arms deal that these should benefit from the pact. When a year later the Americans declined to help with the financing of the Aswan Dam Nasser declared that he would go ahead all the same. He counted on Russian help. This was a chance for the USSR and after some hesitation Moscow took the plunge to the extent of offering finance for the first stage. When France and Britain encouraged Israel to invade Egypt and joined in the attempt to overthrow Nasser Moscow's position was consolidated.

This marriage of convenience ran smoothly enough so long as it was personified by Nasser and Khrushchev. The USSR provided Nasser with transport for his expedition to Yemen in 1962 and two years later Khrushchev attended the celebrations at Aswan. This was a few months before his fall. Already his colleagues were charging him with undue adulation of Nasser. Doubts were strengthened when Nasser refused to back the USSR against China in the row over whether the former was an Asian power and so eligible to attend a second Bandung Conference. During the Israeli attack on Egypt in 1967 Cairo accused the Kremlin of giving only feeble military and diplomatic support. When Nasser died in 1970 the Russian presence in Egypt had become as uneasy as it was large. In 1972 Sadat demanded the immediate withdrawal of 20,000 Russian advisers and experts. They left in seven days. Sadat appropriated all their installations and equipment.

Nasser and Khrushchev were both plain-spoken heads of state, able to cut through the suspicions inevitable in a dialogue between two states so unfamiliar to each other as Egypt and the USSR. Their successors lacked this knack. Sadat suspected the Kremlin of intriguing with his domestic adversaries. He suspected Brezhnev of wanting to do a global deal with Nixon which would incidentally stop aid to the Arabs from either superpower for the struggle against Israel. He resented having to make two begging trips to Moscow in one year and getting little in return. For his part Brezhnev suspected Sadat, whom he rightly regarded as much less radical than Nasser, of unsavoury transactions with rich Saudis and Americans. In the 1973 war the USSR, swallowing its pride in an attempt to recover lost ground, rescued and rearmed Egypt, but this was only an interlude in Sadat's progression away from Nasser's Russian alliance and to the Camp David powwow with Carter and Begin. In 1976 Sadat abrogated the treaty he had made with the USSR in 1971. The Kremlin had lost its greatest prize in Africa.

The USSR stumbled in Sudan too. Moscow was prompt to recognize and welcome Sudanese independence; it classified Abboud, when he took power in 1960, as a progressive soldier and was further encouraged by the Nimeiry coup of 1969. Nimeiry gave the communist Muhammad Ahmed Mahgoub a cabinet post, and the coincidence of similar coups in Somalia and Libya created the pleasing illusion of a left-wing bloc of these three countries with Egypt. But the next year Nimeiry expelled Mahgoub from Sudan and, when he came back and stirred up a revolt, had him executed. This was particularly embarrassing for Moscow, which acclaimed the coup in the belief that it had already succeeded.

More important than Sudan and hardly less alluring than Egypt was Algeria. Mers el-Kebir was almost as attractive a naval base as Alexandria and, by its position westward in the Mediterranean, offered opportunities for outflanking NATO as NATO outflanked the USSR in Greece and Turkey. But Russo-Algerian relations were never easy. Moscow was half-hearted about the FLN, whose leaders seemed to stand at the wrong end of the socialist spectrum, and it hesitated to offend the French Communist Party and its Algerian offshoot, both of which were hostile to the FLN. Russian recognition of the FLN as a government did not come until 1960 (China recognized it in 1958), and Russian backing remained restrained until the failure of the French generals' coup in 1961, followed by the second Evian conference in 1962, set the seal on the FLN's success. Moscow then gave Ben Bella enthusiastic support until his fall in 1965 when, with indecent haste, it sought Boumédienne's friendship with equal zeal.

Algeria's problem was to get the best of two worlds, the USSR and France, and to sup with a long spoon with both. It expanded its trade links with the USSR by a series of commercial agreements, sent hundreds of young men to study in the USSR and accepted some 2,000 Russian technicians and as many military advisers. But it employed as many French and other technicians; made a point of honouring heterodox leaders like Tito and Ceaușescu; and took the line that both the Russian and American fleets should get out of the Mediterranean. Algeria became a prime example of the USSR's main difficulty in Africa. Ideological sympathies led to military aid but not much else. The Russian and Algerian economies were not complementary; their several needs and resources did not mesh. Morocco could supply the USSR more copiously than Algeria with the phosphates which it needed for its chronically sick agriculture; but Morocco was ideologically opposed to the USSR and also at odds with Algeria.

In East Africa the USSR had an unhappy time. In Tanzania Nyerere distrusted Moscow as much as Washington. In Kenya the USSR made a bad tactical mistake when it backed Oginga Odinga who, at independence in 1963, seemed to be Kenyatta's favoured number two but overplayed his hand and was disgraced in 1966. Although Kenya had no arms agreement with the USSR, Russian and Czech arms arrived in the country and were found on Odinga's land. Kenyatta accused Moscow of financing a conspiracy against him and Odinga of being a communist agent. Russian and other communist diplomats were expelled. The best that Moscow could do was keep on better terms with Uganda, which it did even with the atrocious Amin (to whose court a deputy foreign minister Alexei Zakharov was sent as ambassador in 1972). But Uganda, coastless, was the least promising of East African states in geopolitical terms.

Compensation was found further north. In 1963 the USSR made a first agreement with Somalia, offering credits and grants up to $35 million. The connection was strengthened after the coup of 1969 which brought Siad Barre to power. The payoff was the development of a naval base at Berbera, an air base at Hargeisa, storage for missiles and other weapons, and facilities for intelligence and telecommunications. In 1972, when the USSR's positions in Egypt and Sudan were becoming dubious, Marshal A. Grechko, the Soviet minister of defence, paid a visit to Somalia. He was followed two years later by President N. V. Podgorny, who concluded a ten-year treaty of friendship which, among other things, expunged the Somali debt to the USSR – an unusual piece of generosity. By 1977 Russian military aid had reached $250 million, there were 2,000 Russian military technicians in the country and the value of the bases and equipment available for Russian use was about $1 billion. The Russian stake was considerable.

All this had more to do with the Indian Ocean than the continent of Africa. Before 1917 Russian access to this segment of the world's main maritime highway was blocked by the Ottoman empire and Persia. Thereafter a variety of Arab states, and their western sponsors, stood in the way, until in 1955 the arms deal with Egypt opened a door into the Middle East and, via the Red Sea, to the Indian Ocean. In 1971 Aden, at the further end of the Red Sea, became part of the independent and left-wing state of South Yemen – a strategic outpost of great significance if, under Russian tutelage, it could be fitted into a more comprehensive group of client states. As its positions in Egypt and Sudan degenerated, the USSR became commensurately concerned to counter the American dominance in Ethiopia, which, since its virtual annexation of Eritrea in 1952, commanded 1,500 km of the coast of the Red Sea (the opposite coast being under the control of Washington's even stauncher friend, Saudi Arabia).

During the 1960s the United States evolved the A3 Polaris missile with a range of 4,000 km. Launched from vessels in the Indian Ocean, this new weapon would be able to hit Soviet cities. Moscow's first reaction was a proposal to declare the Indian Ocean a nuclear-free zone. When this idea fell flat Admiral S. G. Gorshkov, the father of the modern Russian navy, sent a token force from Vladivostok to the Indian Ocean and established during the 1970s a permanent patrol there. Thus the development of Russian naval power took effect in waters where much of the United States' imported oil and two-thirds of western Europe's were at risk.

In the mid-1970s events offered Moscow a chance greatly to enlarge its sphere of influence in this part of the world. In 1974 Haile Selassie fell. The United States, already shifting from its Ethiopian base at Kagnew to a new strongpoint on Diego Garcia in the Indian Ocean, continued for a while to provide Ethiopia with financial aid, arms and training. The USSR was pulled two ways: its Somali ally was hostile to Ethiopia, but the chance for Moscow to supplant the Americans there was appealing. Moscow had long been mindful of Ethiopia's significance. In 1959, when the country was firmly in the American camp, Moscow had sent the head of the African department of the foreign ministry A. V. Budakov to be ambassador in Addis Ababa. It had extolled Haile Selassie's part in the creation of the OAU, depicted his antiquated regime as progressive, and given him a generous measure of aid. After his fall Moscow found itself possessed of a weapon which Washington did not have. It might arm the new regime: Washington would not.

Arming Ethiopia put the Somali alliance at risk, but Moscow hoped to have it both ways. In 1977 it resolved to take the plunge. Mengistu had emerged as the man to back but he would have to be backed against foreign as well as internal enemies – in particular against Somalia. Moscow turned to Castro to persuade Siad Barre to drop his quarrel with Ethiopia and join a left-wing constellation to be formed round Ethiopia, Somalia and South Yemen.

Castro's sympathies lay with the Somalis (and the Eritreans) rather than the Ethiopians: there had been a Cuban training mission in Somalia since 1974. Yet he accepted Moscow's charge. But he failed to persuade Barre to forgo the golden opportunity to annex the long-disputed Ogaden from Ethiopia. Castro thereupon obliged

Moscow a second time. He placed his armies at the disposal of Moscow and Addis Ababa to defeat his erstwhile Somali friends. First contingents were flown from Cuba to the USSR and thence to Africa. Later units followed by air and by sea from Angola. They saved Harar and Diredawa from capture by the Somalis, halted the Somali advance and then repulsed it. The Russian contribution to these operations was a gigantic air lift via Aden which, beginning in October 1977, comprised 550 T54 and T55 tanks, at least 60 MiG 17s and 21s and 20 MiG 23s, SAM 2 and 3 ground-to-air missiles, BM 21 rocket launchers, 152 mm and 180 mm artillery, self-propelling anti-aircraft systems, armoured personnel carriers and much else. For the USSR this was not only a strategic move but also a display of strength, efficiency and confidence. It was all the more remarkable since never before, even to protect its positions in Egypt, had the USSR resorted to the direct use of force in Africa. But, having saved Ethiopia from Somali attack, the USSR did not permit an Ethiopian counter-attack upon Somalia itself – a measured restraint probably dictated by a determination not to provoke the United States too far and to avoid open superpower confrontation. But even with Russian aid Mengistu could do no more than stave off his enemies and ask for more aid. By the time Gorbachev came to power Mengistu was more expensive than he was worth. He was told that Russian aid and Cuban troops would fade away.

Upon the fall of Salazar in Lisbon in 1974 the USSR sent V. G. Solodovnikov, its leading African academic, to Zambia as ambassador. He was reputedly given high rank in the KGB. Approachable, genial but a notable absentee from the diplomatic cocktail party round, he had the task of making Lusaka a centre of Russian influence and intelligence such as Cairo and Conakry had failed to become. Solodovnikov was as much concerned with ZAPU in Rhodesia and Swapo in Namibia as with Zambian affairs. At the same date the USSR established a surprisingly large embassy in Botswana.

During the rest of the decade the USSR pursued a low-risk policy in southern Africa, in contrast with its forward policy in the Horn. It gave minimal support to insurgent movements in Rhodesia and Namibia, enough to keep them going and keep them sweet but no more. In Angola it contrived to interfere only by proxy. But it became increasingly alert. In 1976 General (later Marshal) S. L. Sokolov travelled as far south as Mozambique in the course of an African tour. Next year a group of no fewer than 11 Russian generals was spotted in southern Angola and another year on General V. I. Petrov visited Angola and Mozambique. The calibre of these explorers was notable. Sokolov was a member of the highest group in the military hierarchy, a group of four. Petrov was the number two in the ground forces, had seen service in the Far East and had been the controlling genius of the operations in Ethiopia and the Horn. The group of 11 included specialists in planning, training, supply, air transport and radio and electronic intelligence; both the ground forces and the air forces were represented. Their surveys led to no operations. They were, however, symptomatic of the Kremlin's awareness that such operations might one day become desirable.

A little earlier, and a little further off the map, a prestigious delegation from the Africa Institute visited (1976) Madagascar and Mauritius to testify to Russian interest in these parts. In 1975 Madagascar took a sharp turn to the left with the advent to power of Didier Ratsiraka, while in the Comoros Ali Soilih (murdered in 1978) also took his country to the left. So did France-Albert René in the Seychelles in 1977.

But the weightiest developments in southern Africa in the 1970s were the sequel to the collapse of Portuguese rule. In Mozambique Samora Machel established, against virtually no initial opposition, a one-party state which was distinctly left-wing in its domestic affairs, although non-aligned in external relations. In Angola the fight for the succession was more closely contested and produced one of the strangest intrusions in the history of the continent: the arrival in force of the Cubans. This astonishing move was prompted by Fidel Castro's personal temperament but would have been impossible without Russian aid and sanction. It gave Moscow a vicarious instrument in a zone where it was reluctant to operate directly and (like Washington) was probably still too ignorant to operate to good effect. It led also to the use of Cuban forces in the Horn.

As a result of American economic sanctions against Cuba Castro had become critically dependent on the USSR: a series of economic disasters on the home front put him at Moscow's beck and call. But Moscow would hardly have called him into Africa if the idea of doing things there had not been his in the first place. Africa always beckoned to Castro. Cuba was too small for him; his attempts to spread his revolution in Latin America were failures; and when he recalled that 'African blood flows in our veins' and spoke of Africans as his brothers and sisters he was expressing something that was real to him, as well as romantic. He wanted to help. Within two years of coming to power he sent instructors to help train guerrillas in camps in Ghana. Two years later, in 1963, a second training mission went to Algeria. But here training spilled over into something more. When Algeria became involved in border fighting with Morocco Castro sent Ben Bella three shiploads and an aircraft load of equipment, accompanied by Cubans who knew how to operate it. These Cubans would almost certainly have become involved in the fighting if it had not stopped just before they reached the firing line. The combat troops were then withdrawn but the training mission remained until the overthrow of Ben Bella.

Castro was also involved in the Congo. Advisers and a small fighting force of about 200 men with Che Guevara in person went to the aid of Lumumba's heirs, but Mobutu's coup in 1965 put an end to their adventure. A few of the advisers crossed the Congo river to Brazzaville but when, next year, the Cuban mission in Ghana was withdrawn upon the fall of Nkrumah, Castro's African expeditions seemed to have proved as futile as those he sent to Latin America.

But he did not lose interest. The toehold at Brazzaville was matched by another in Conakry – the nearest African capital to the Caribbean and a centre for training guerrillas to fight the Portuguese in Guinea-Bissau. Castro also organized an internal security force and bodyguard for Sekou Touré and others for Presidents Alphonse

Massemba-Debat in Brazzaville and Siaka Stevens in Sierra Leone. (In the 1970s he branched out into South Yemen, Oman's Dhofar province and the Golan Heights.)

The Angolan scene was perplexing. Dozens of movements came into being before and at independence but these sorted themselves out into three major forces: Agostinho Neto's MPLA, Holden Roberto's FNLA and Jonas Savimbi's UNITA. The FNLA looked consistently the most effective but Roberto was anti-communist and closely linked with Mobutu. He got aid from various quarters: Zaïre, China, Romania, Libya and the United States (which stuck to Portugal to the last minute but switched the bulk of its aid to the FNLA early in 1975). The USSR backed Neto, but only sporadically; in the year before the fall of Salazar Russian aid had dwindled so far that Neto turned in desperation to Scandinavia and Cuba. But six months after the Lisbon coup Moscow reinstated its aid and, when the FNLA attacked the MPLA in 1975, saved Neto by rushing supplies and weapons to him by air via Conakry and Brazzaville and within a few months by sea. China had retired from the game, unable to match Russian aid to the MPLA which – according to the CIA – had by then received from the USSR and eastern Europe arms worth $80 million. Romania also retreated, but the United States, after some hesitation, persisted and wasted a lot of money.

These successes of the MPLA settled nothing because four weeks before the date fixed for independence South Africa invaded the country. The MPLA declared itself a provisional government; other Africans rushed to recognize it and to denounce the South African invasion and its American sponsors; and Nigeria gave Neto $20 million. Nevertheless, Neto's position was precarious. This time he was saved by Castro.

Castro and Neto had become personal friends. Cuban aid had helped to fill the gap when Moscow turned cold on Neto in 1973–74. Several hundred Cuban advisers arrived in MPLA camps during 1975 and when Neto appealed to Castro for combat troops to fight the South Africans he did not appeal in vain. The first unit arrived by air two days later. It consisted of 82 men in civilian disguise, the forerunners of what was to become an army of 20–30,000. Seaborne reinforcements followed, making over 40 ocean crossings of nearly 10,000 km during the ensuing six months of active hostilities. At one point no fewer than 15 ships were simultaneously at sea on an eastward course, the biggest procession of men and material across the Atlantic since the Americans had sailed to North Africa to make war on Hitler. The seaborne effort was supplemented by an air lift in which Cuba's antiquated Britannias, after landing at Barbados, flew to Guinea-Bissau and Brazzaville. When the Barbados staging point was cut out, under US pressure, by a refusal to refuel the aircraft, an alternative was improvised in the Cape Verde islands.

The Cuban expedition to Angola was a gamble. Its failure would have put paid to the Cuban presence in Africa and perhaps to Castro's rule in Cuba itself, but for decades the MPLA achieved no final victory over its rivals, nor did the expedition develop as Castro intended. He hoped to have his troops back home in six months and was still expecting to accomplish this as late as March 1976. In the event, his overseas force, which absorbed a considerable proportion of Cuba's entire army of 160,000, was obliged to remain in Angola in order to keep Neto and (after his death in 1979) José Eduardo dos Santos in power. Even though the Russians paid the bills, Castro's quixotry imposed strenuous demands and sacrifices on thousands of Cubans – fighting, dying or bereaved. Unlike the Piedmontese sent by Cavour to flounder in the mud of the Tchernaya, they could not comfort themselves with the thought that they were paying for the independence of their own country.

Nobody has been generous to Africa, and the Russians have been among the least generous. If economic aid is a major diplomatic instrument, then the Russian use of it was surprisingly feeble. At the end of the 1970s the total of Russian overseas development aid was equivalent to 0.02 per cent of estimated GNP. The more generous givers were Sweden, the Netherlands, Norway and France, with respectively 0.99, 0.85, 0.82 and 0.6 per cent. Britain managed 0.38, the United States 0.22, Switzerland 0.19. (Italy failed to reach 1 per cent.) Of the net flow of aid to Africa from all sources, national and international, the USSR provided less than 3 per cent. Economic aid therefore was treated by the USSR, not as a major tool, but as a minimum political investment.

On the other hand the effects of Russian aid may have been greater than such figures suggest because it was concentrated in relatively few countries. Certain recipients stood out: Egypt, Algeria, Morocco, Guinea, Somalia. They were picked for political reasons and liable to be dropped for the same reasons. Within them the USSR – like other donors – showed a preference for big industrial projects rather than for rural development: in Egypt, for example, the Aswan Dam, the Helwan steel works, the Nag Hammadi aluminium works. Russian technicians were similarly concentrated; of some 34,000 in Africa in 1977 only 5,000 were south of the Sahara.

The proportion of loans to grants in Russian aid was about 2:1. Rates of interest were low at 2.5 per cent or even nil; but repayment dates were comparatively short, normally 10 to 12 years where a western loan would be repayable over 30 or 40 years. The USSR proved even more reluctant than other creditors to cancel or reschedule debts, although Somalia was so favoured in 1974. Repayment was normally in goods at fixed prices, a practice which led to much grumbling by borrowers who were prevented from reaping the benefits of rising world prices.

In terms of trade the USSR was doing a mere 2 per cent of its trade with African countries, but this insignificant proportion was not entirely inconsequential since the USSR was running a surplus on its trade with Africa which was more than sufficient to offset the deficit on its trade with the west. For Africa the USSR had little commercial importance: only Egypt and Guinea ever did more than 10 per cent of their trade with the USSR.

Military aid fell into two broad categories. There was the provision of material and training given as part of the business of making friends in likely quarters; and there were special efforts made for a particular strategic gain. The statistics of military aid showed therefore jumps at crucial points. During the early 1970s Russian and eastern European military aid to Africa averaged $300–350 million a year. It was fairly widely spread: more than half of Africa's air forces acquired Russian aircraft. In 1977, principally on account of Angola, military aid reached $1.5 billion and in 1978 a further $1 billion was expended on Ethiopia alone. These were, in Russian terms, big figures, a reflection of Moscow's preparedness to take a plunge in Africa and pay for it.

Invitations and grants to students were another kind of aid. Its pitfalls are well known. Students were frequently disappointed in their hosts and the Russians were no more successful than westerners in avoiding the slights inflicted by colour prejudice. The USSR opened its arms to foreign students as far back as 1922 when the first Mongolians were welcomed to Moscow, but substantial programmes were developed only after the Second World War. In the first postwar decade nearly all of them came from the European satellites but with the decolonization of Asia and Africa, and the Cold War's competition for the goodwill of the Third World, steps were taken to attract students from these countries and Latin America too.

Few knew any Russian. They spent therefore a preliminary year learning the language (for which 4,500 teachers were recruited) and doing a course in 'scientific socialism'. The second half of this programme was sometimes resented but perhaps less so than westerners liked to imagine. When Kenyan students went on strike in Baku in 1965 and asked to be sent home their grievances included indoctrination; but communism was part of what the USSR had to offer and many students approached this course with at least a modicum of initial curiosity. Of the substantive courses the most popular were in medicine and engineering.

Foreign students in the USSR were offered 100 roubles a month – twice the grant given to a Soviet citizen – plus cheap lodging at about 2 roubles a month, free medical treatment and an annual vacation grant of 100 roubles for spending in the USSR. About half of all Third World students were at the Patrice Lumumba University and more than half of them came from Africa. According to Russian sources there were in these years some 50,000 foreigners studying in universities and technical colleges, not counting others doing vocational courses at lower levels or postgraduate work at higher levels. This total was supplemented by universities and specialist schools in eastern Europe – for example, schools in Budapest and Berlin set up to train Africans in trade unionism and journalism respectively. In purely numerical terms this was a useful and welcome contribution to one of Africa's most urgent needs but (again merely numerically) it was only a minor addition to more familiar educational routes. In the 1960s and 1970s Britain alone had twice as many African students as the USSR and all eastern Europe combined, and – to take a particular example – at the end of ten years of independence Nigeria had about 15,000 students studying abroad and nearly all of them were in Britain.

Foreign students in eastern Europe, like their domestic counterparts, were granted much less freedom than students in the more permissive west; their daily round was bleaker, although East Germany provided some of the bright lights and carefree style sought by young people embarked on a foreign adventure; they were more supervised, even segregated, and men experienced more than the usual unpleasantness when claiming the attention of local girls. In 1963 Ghanaian students demonstrated in Moscow's Red Square after the death of one of them in a punch-up, and in a particularly bothersome incident 250 Egyptian students were flown from the USSR to the United States after complaints about their living conditions and indoctrination courses. There was a debit side to the account.

For the immensely larger number of Africans who stayed perforce at home the USSR gradually built up its foreign broadcasts. By the end of the 1970s it was broadcasting to the world at large for 2,000 hours a week in 80 languages (China was using only half that number). But Africa, excluding North Africa, which was served by the distinct Middle East service, was not a prime target. In 1979 it was allotted 147 hours per week, the same as in 1966. The leading languages in use by the African service were French, Swahili and Hausa, which occupied 66.5 hours, leaving 80.5 hours for 11 other languages. Apart from its African service the USSR was broadcasting in English around the clock and many of these programmes could be heard in Africa. Among other eastern Europeans broadcasting to Africa the East Germans were the most prominent. The substance of the programmes was the familiar mixture of news laced with music, but the music was not the latest thing and probably turned more sets off than listeners on. Africans seemed to like rather more western decadence than Russian (or Chinese) broadcasters could bring themselves to provide. The quality of news and feature programmes improved considerably after the 1950s, when unfamiliarity with the target areas and their culture gave rise to much factual error and poor judgement, but – to the western ear at least – these broadcasts remained crassly slanted and the Russian and Chinese broadcasters devoted a tedious amount of time to abusing one another.

All these general adjuncts of foreign policy reflected the marginality of Africa in the Russian scheme of things. Only perhaps in South Africa did Russian aid in deliveries of arms and money to the ANC and the Communist Party make a material impact by enabling blacks to maintain forceful opposition to their powerfully armed foes. The rest of Africa was worth some study and some effort and some expenditure but most of the time it was not even a secondary field of action. The attention devoted to it indicated that Moscow had in mind that one day it might be. There were exceptions – areas and occasions where the effort assumed much more significant proportions (Egypt, Ethiopia) – but the motive in these cases could be found in the Middle East rather than the African continent itself. Meanwhile, Moscow accumulated knowledge through its diplomatic missions, its secret services, the journalists of Tass and Novosti, and academic bodies in Moscow and elsewhere. This work coincided with the striking increase in Russian capabilities which characterized the Brezhnev years. Under neither Stalin nor Khrushchev was the USSR a truly world power. Stalin turned it into a nuclear power sufficiently menacing to be a counterpoise to the USA in a bipolar world. Khrushchev inherited this position and, by the failure in the Cuban missiles crisis, demonstrated that Moscow's reach was still limited. But in the 1970s the continuing growth of Russian power and technology put the USSR on the map everywhere. Thenceforward the question, in relation to each part of the map, was what it might decide expediently to do there.

Gorbachev saw that what was being done in Africa was expensive and fruitless. In Ethiopia, as in Vietnam and Afghanistan, the commitment was a ruinous folly which cost too much and bought no political gain. Even the relatively small subsidies given to the ANC were money wasted so long as the ANC relied on violence to destroy *apartheid*. Gorbachev preferred to put Soviet weight behind the Front Line states. He improved relations with Zimbabwe, where his predecessors had made the mistake of backing Nkomo against Mugabe. He reduced the Russian presence to the political, rhetorical and covert, and waited for others to make mistakes instead of making them himself.

Throughout these decades the Chinese played a sporadic *disobligato* to Russian and Cuban performances in Africa. China's achievements in Africa were prodigiously exaggerated. Africa is even more remote from China than from the USSR. By the end of the 1970s China still had no direct link with Africa by air or sea (Aeroflot was flying to 29 African airports). Trade, totalling about $400 million a year, was mutually negligible.

Yet China arrived in postwar Africa not far behind the USSR and at the same point: Egypt, where a Chinese embassy was opened after the Bandung conference in 1955. The main motives – international recognition, admission to the UN and to friends in the Third World – were extraneous to Africa. After the break with the USSR came the desire to make difficulties for Moscow, notably by outbidding its revolutionary fervour at a time when the USSR was shifting towards more pragmatic diplomacy. But the rapid spread of independence undermined Beijing's emphasis on subversion; and although Zhou Enlai visited ten African countries in 1963–64 (the revolts in Kenya, Tanganyika and Uganda curtailed his tour), the Cultural Revolution caused an almost complete withdrawal: in 1966 China's 18 ambassadors were all recalled. To Africans the Chinese appeared to be nice people from a long way away who behaved more agreeably than Russians or Americans but had much less to offer.

China recognized Sudan and Ghana in 1956 and 1957 but had to wait for three and two years respectively for counter-recognition. It was the first to recognize the FLN as the provisional government of Algeria in 1958. It was prompt to offer aid to Sekou Touré: Guinea was one of the few states in Africa with a sizeable Chinese population (4,000 – the others being Mauritius, Madagascar and South Africa). But Chinese credits for Guinea ($26 million), Ghana and Mali ($19.5 million each) were a long way short of Russian offers. Terms, however, were extraordinarily generous: no interest, repayment over long periods, even (in the case of Kenya in 1961) no repayment at all. But when the Cultural Revolution reduced aid to a trickle only about 15 per cent of Chinese credits had been taken up.

To the smiling face of communism was added revolutionary zeal. From Conakry China supported a group of Ivorian exiles and, until his assassination in 1960, Félix Moumié's exceptionally savage Union des Populations du Cameroun. China gave Lumumba £1 million and supported Gizenga until he joined the Adoula government. In 1963 it intervened in Burundi's troubled waters when Tutsi refugees from Rwanda were plotting a return to their country. The Chinese backed the Tutsi but the expedition was a disaster and the Burundi, suspicious of Chinese meddling, evicted the newly arrived Chinese diplomatic mission. A bigger mission in Congo-Brazzaville, established in 1964, also came to grief after a military coup in 1966.

China's steadiest friend in Africa was Tanzania. The Chinese arrived there by the back door as a result of the revolution in Zanzibar in 1964. One of its leaders, Muhammad Babu, had good enough connections with China to raise a loan of $14 million and when Zanzibar was united with Tanganyika (paradoxically, Babu opposed the union) the Chinese won the goodwill of Nyerere. Zhou Enlai and Nyerere exchanged visits in 1965 and the head of the African department of the Chinese foreign ministry was sent to Dar-es-Salaam as ambassador. Then came the Tanzam railway, China's showpiece in Africa.

There were at independence no rail links between Tanganyika and Zambia. Kaunda was anxious to create a passage for Zambian minerals avoiding Portuguese territory, and both he and Nyerere saw the railway as a means to develop neglected areas in their two countries. China, which in 1964 offered aid for building railways inside Tanzania, next year extended the offer to an international line. Both African presidents were seeking western aid and turned to China only when they failed to get it. A first agreement was signed in 1967 after a visit by Kaunda to Beijing. Final agreement followed in 1970 and work began that year.

The Tanzam railway was a single-line track of nearly 2,000 km with 91 double-line stations. It was finished two years ahead of schedule and became the property, in equal shares, of the Tanzanian and Zambian governments. Fifteen thousand Chinese were employed in its construction. They set a good example at work and behaved themselves when off. There was some propaganda byplay but after complaints by the African governments this was restricted to handing out the works of Mao – a latterday version of the distribution of bibles by Christian missionaries. The building of the railway did the Chinese a lot of good for a short time, but maintenance was poor, services degenerated and the Dar-es-Salaam terminal became clogged. For these shortcomings the Chinese were not responsible but their repute suffered none the less when the railway ceased to be one of the wonders of modern Africa.

Chinese penetration of Africa was facilitated by French recognition of the communist regime in Beijing in 1964. Most of francophone Africa followed suit. On their return to Africa after the Cultural Revolution the Chinese took over embassies previously occupied by the regime in Taiwan, often in countries where entry could have been difficult if the Taiwanese had not got these first. Chinese broadcasts to Africa, which began in Arabic at the time of the Suez crisis in 1956, were gradually expanded but did not match the Russian either in hours per week or in their range of languages. In the 1960s and 1970s the Chinese instigated no revolutionary change, largely because they picked the wrong people to support or supported them too feebly; a guerrilla leader in search of arms was better advised to ask Moscow. In 1982, nearly 20 years after Zhou's continental tour, a new prime minister Zhao Ziyang visited ten African states in a gesture of continuing interest which was, however, not much more insistent than planting a flag in the Antarctic. (For a more purposeful policy in the next century see p. 144.)

Notes

A. The Malagasy Republic and the Indian Ocean

The island of Madagascar, lying off the Mozambique coast, came under French rule at the end of the nineteenth century. In 1947 a revolt against the postwar restoration of that rule was rudely repressed, but independence was nevertheless not long delayed. Within the island the Hova dominant minority wanted independence at the earliest possible moment, whereas a larger nationalist group preferred a short delay in order to be sure of gaining power for itself. This group, led by Philibert Tsirinana, succeeded in its aims. Madagascar became the Malagasy Republic in 1958, remaining in the French Union. Tsirinana became president and full independence followed in 1960. Tsirinana steered a pro-French course and became a prominent supporter of black dialogue with South Africa. Although re-elected in 1972, he was forced that year to hand over real power to General Gabriel Ramanantsava, the nominee of the army, to whom he resigned the presidency after a referendum which approved the army's action. Ramanantsava was displaced three years later by Colonel Richard Ratsimandrava, who was assassinated within a week and succeeded by Captain Didier Ratsiraka. French troops left the island in 1973. Ratsiraka nationalized French concerns without compensation and disputed with France the ownership of the Iles Glorieuses, Juan de Nova, Bassas da India and Europa in the Mozambique Channel. The riots which removed Tsirinana in 1972 were repeated and savagely defeated in 1985. Asians were assaulted and many fled. Outside the capital mob rule prevailed. Elections due in 1988 were postponed to the end of 1989 when Ratsiraka retained the presidency but grave riots broke out again and after ruling for 17 years Ratsiraka was replaced by Albert Zafy. A new constitution in 1992 reduced the presidential powers enjoyed by Ratsiraka but produced an assembly in which 25 parties were represented. The party of the prime minister Francisque Ravony had only two seats. A plan by the World Bank and the IMF to rescue the economy, encumbered with $5 billion of foreign debt, was so stringent that it was rejected by the assembly and the president. Madagascar was a country in which the population but little else was rising. Ratsiraka, although increasingly enfeebled by illness, retained his office in 1997 by the thinnest of whiskers.

At the northern end of the Mozambique Channel lie the Comoros. Mayotte, the southernmost of them and traditionally bent on independence from the group, chose to remain in the French Union when the Comoros became independent in 1976. Their first president Ali Soilih, a man of the left, was murdered two years later and the islands became a base for right-wing mercenaries and their commander Bob Denard, dubiously styled colonel, who gained control of this small fiefdom after various adventures in Africa and Asia and maintained his rule by useful contacts with French and South African covert agencies, by the ruthless savagery of his small private army and by adopting the Muslim faith. The Comoros became a staging post for the supply of South African and Saudi military aid to the insurgent Renamo guerrillas in Mozambique less than 300 km away across the water. Denard removed Soilih's successor President Ahmed Abdallah in 1975, restored him in 1978 and had him killed in 1989. Denard returned to the attack in 1995 when he once more invaded the islands, seized President Said Djohar and transferred Muhammad Taki Abdulkarim from prison to be co-president with himself. French troops removed Denard a few days later (he died in 2007). The Comoros experienced coups at the rate of about one a year.

To the north-east of the Comoros lay the British island of Aldabra, famous for its giant tortoises, and beyond that the Seychelles. This group, about 1,500 km from the African coast and twice as far from Bombay, was a British colony from which Britain detached the Aldabra and Chagas groups (mostly uninhabited) to form in 1965, for strategic purposes, a new colony called the British Indian Ocean Territory (BIOT). The rest of the Seychelles were given a constitution in 1967, revised in 1970, and became in 1976 a member of the Commonwealth. In return for the islands detached to the BIOT, Britain built on Mahé, the capital island, an airport to help the Seychelles to become a tourist area. The first president James Mancham was soon ousted by his prime minister Albert René, more to the left. René survived an invasion by white mercenaries connived at by South Africa in 1980. A second such attempt in 1983 was, however, stopped by South Africa. In 1986 René pre-empted a coup fostered by the CIA with British and South African assistance. He subsequently improved his relations with these enemies, chiefly in order to expand the islands' tourist industry. But a decade later government overspending had run the economy down.

Yet further to the north-east the Maldives – 1,200 small islands rising only a few feet above water and lying some 1,300 miles south of Sri Lanka – became independent of Britain in 1965, granting to Britain a lease for 21 years on Gan, where the British were building an air base. Britain also bought for £3 million the island of Diego Garcia from its colony of Mauritius (east of Madagascar) before giving Mauritius independence in 1966. In 1971 Britain secretly leased Diego Garcia to the United States to build a naval base there. Its inhabitants were removed, mostly to the slums of Mauritius, and were given £650,000 (later raised to £4 million) against promises never to go back. A few years later Mauritius laid claim to Diego Garcia. The claim was subsequently toned down but not abjured. Mauritius was a French-speaking British colony with a racially mixed population in which Indians were in a majority. Originally acquired in order to pre-empt France, it was turned into a sugar plantation when its strategic importance evaporated and was worked by imported Indian labour. Indians came to own more than half the land and were opposed politically by French-speaking Creoles who had the support of a small Chinese minority (about 3 per cent of the population). Mauritius was an economic success and it hoped to increase its prosperity by economic links with the Seychelles and the Malagasy Republic. It was wary of its neighbour Réunion, still a French dependency, and of French plans for a francophile association of Réunion, Mayotte and the Comoros. An attempt in 1988 against the life of the prime minister Aneerood Jugnauth, a low-caste Hindu, failed.

An Indian Ocean Commission for economic co-operation on the lines of ASEAN brought old adversaries closer: Madagascar, Mauritius, the Seychelles. Increased air traffic, investment and trade by South Africa suggested that South Africa was displacing the EC as the region's main external prop. Proposals for a demilitarized zone were advanced with an eye to reducing American military activity on Diego Garcia, which had been used by the United States in the Gulf War of 1991.

B. Botswana, Lesotho, Ngwane

The three territories of Bechuanaland, Basutoland and Swaziland became protectorates of the British crown in 1884, 1868 and 1890 respectively. Their transfer to South Africa, which had been envisaged in the South Africa Act 1909, was mooted by Malan during the Commonwealth conference of 1949, during a visit to South Africa by the Commonwealth relations secretary Patrick Gordon-Walker in 1950, again in 1951, 1954 and 1956. But the developing policy of racial apartheid and the intensification of police rule in South Africa eliminated the possibility of British compliance. The Tomlinson Report included all three territories among South Africa's Bantustans but Tomlinson himself acknowledged a few years later that there was no likelihood of their transfer. In 1960 a transfer under the terms of the South Africa Act became a constitutional impossibility, since that Act required an order by the king in council upon the receipt of addresses from both houses of the South African parliament – an impossible procedure after South Africa became a republic. More important, the British parliament had been given assurances, frequently repeated, that there would be no transfer without a debate at Westminster and consultation of the wishes of the inhabitants.

But Britain's neglect of the territories had left them economically dependent on South Africa; and Britain's traditional predilection for conservative chiefs retarded the advance of self-government without reconciling the traditionalists who, fearful of the newer type of nationalist, found some attractions in South African schemes for separate African territories based on the authority of chiefs. British weakness in regard to South Africa was demonstrated when Seretse Khama, the hereditary chief of the Bamangwato in Bechuanaland, married an English girl in 1949. Under pressure from outraged South Africans, the British banished both Seretse and his uncle, the talented and efficient Tshekedi Khama, on the plea that the tribe was split on the question of whether to accept Seretse with a white wife as chief. Seretse remained in exile until in 1956 he renounced his claims and those of his descendants. He subsequently formed the Bechuanaland Democratic Party and after a general election in 1965 became prime minister. Bechuanaland – huge, underpopulated and largely desert – became independent under the name of Botswana in 1966 but its poverty made it dependent either on outside aid or on its big neighbour, and it seemed doomed by past neglect and present stringency to become a satellite of South Africa with all the consequent threats to the moderate and democratic rule which Seretse and his party hoped to give it. Under Seretse, president until his death in 1980, Botswana allowed the Rhodesian guerrillas to set up training camps and joined the group of Front Line states whose aim was to secure majority rule in Rhodesia with the least possible extension of violence. Seretse was succeeded by Quetumile Masire, who continued to provide tolerant and moderately democratic government, albeit essentially one-party rule in an ostensibly multiparty state. In 1997 he announced that he would retire the following year, clearing the way for his vice-president Festus Mogae to succeed him. Botswana was one of the few places in Africa where people in general became better off: a big country with varied resources and good government but devastated by AIDS.

In Basutoland, a landlocked territory of 2 million people, the paramount chief Constantine Bereng, later King Moshoeshoe II, who succeeded to his office in 1960 after an education in England, led a moderate nationalist party (the Maramotlou Party) which was sandwiched between the traditionalists in the Basuto Nationalist Party, led by Chief Leabua Jonathan, and the more forthright nationalists of the Basuto Congress Party, led by Ntsu Mokhehle. In 1965 the Nationalists defeated the Congress but then lost ground. The opposition to them, suspicious of Nationalist links with South Africa, where Chief Jonathan was regarded as the lesser evil, pressed Britain to strengthen the powers which the paramount chief would have as monarch after independence and to conduct fresh elections before independence. The British government was unmoved by these pleas and in 1966 Basutoland became independent Lesotho with a narrow balance of domestic political forces and a tenseness in the political atmosphere which boded ill for Chief Jonathan's government and suggested that if it ran into difficulties it would turn to South Africa for help. Riots which occurred at the end of the year gave Jonathan the opportunity to exact from Moshoeshoe a pledge to keep out of politics and to confine him to his palace. In 1968 some chiefs who had sided with Jonathan appeared to be switching their allegiance to the king and when Jonathan seemed to be losing the elections held in that year he cancelled the proceedings and suspended the constitution. The king retreated into exile but returned in 1970. Jonathan survived until 1986, by which date South Africa, concluding that Jonathan was no longer the best bet from its point of view, applied economic pressures and encouraged the army to take over. General Justine Lekhanya, who had been dismissed by Jonathan in 1964, put an end to the 20-year rule of the Nationalist Party. The king was dispossessed by the military in 1990, went into exile again and was replaced by his son

Letsie III, but retained partisans in and outside the army. In 1994 the comparatively left-wing Congress Party won a comfortable victory in a general election but was attacked by a section of the army demanding the ex-king's recall. Diplomatic activity by (the new) South Africa, Botswana and Zimbabwe resolved this conflict. Moshoeshoe was reinstated as a constitutional monarch with Mokhehle as prime minister, but was killed in a car accident a year later and Letsie resumed his reign – distrusted by Mokhehle and the Congress Party, who regarded him as a tool of the Nationalist Party and the army. Subsequent elections in which the ruling party won all but one of the seats inflamed the opposition and junior officers. Disorders amounting in some instances to mutiny were met by an incursion of South African troops under the aegis of SADC (see p. 636) which was ill-prepared, disproportionately destructive and rescued the regime without strengthening it. Mokhehle suddenly resigned from the Congress Party in 1997 to form a new Lesotho Congress for Democracy which overwhelmingly won the next elections and, Mokhehle having died, made Bethuel Mosili prime minister.

Swaziland, later Ngwame and the smallest of the three territories and the last to attain independence, had an elderly paramount chief Sobhuza II, who was advised by a singularly conservative council. Between 1960 and 1973 he experimented with a modest degree of democracy. At elections in 1964 his Mbokodo Party formed an alliance with the United Swazi Party, the organ of the white farming and business community of 10,000, and routed an assorted opposition of divided and ill-prepared nationalists. Under the constitution prepared for independence in 1968 the monarch was given a dominant position: he could nominate enough members of the parliament to block measures which he did not like, was not bound to act on ministerial advice in all matters in which a constitutional monarch is normally so bound, was given control over Swaziland's principal asset (its minerals) subject only to advice from his traditional council and not from his ministers, and his party was entrenched in power by an electoral system in which the towns, and therefore the nationalists, were submerged in large rural constituencies. Control over the minerals was, however, taken away from him on the eve of independence. The death of Sobhuza in 1982 at the age of about 83 was followed by multiple intrigues in and around the royal family and by a regency under a queen mother who was quickly deposed in favour of another queen mother. Under South African pressure the ANC was proscribed. A new king Mswati II, aged 18, was installed in 1986. He opposed partisans of democracy and the ANC but when he tried to repress his adversaries by widespread arrests and treason trials he was rebuffed by the acquittal of those indicted.

C. *The Homelands or Bantustans*

Four Homelands were established in South Africa and six more were projected:

Transkei: a geographically almost coherent agglomeration of 2.5 million Xhosa-speaking peoples, self-governing from 1963 and 'independent' in 1976; 45,000 sq. km of (largely neglected) agricultural and timber-bearing land; 1.7 million Xhosa-speakers outside the Homeland lost their South African citizenship. Transkei broke off relations with South Africa – it had none with any other state – over the latter's refusal to incorporate East Griqualand in the Homeland and over the dumping of unwanted Xhosa-speakers in it. In 1979 South Africa stopped the main source of this forcible migration – the bulldozing of Crossroads in Cape Province. Transkei's first president Kaiser Matanzima (subsequently imprisoned) gradually lost ground to the left personified by General Bantu Holomisa and Chris Hani, chief of staff of Umkhonto na Swize and general secretary of the South African Communist Party (assassinated in 1993).

Bophuthatswana: a Homeland for about half of the Tswana peoples not in Botswana which, since the migrations to the goldfields in the nineteenth century, has contained only a minority of them; 'independent' in 1977; over 40,000 sq. km in seven different segments without a capital but with the world's largest platinum mines.

Venda: an almost coherent Homeland of 6,500 sq. km incapable of supporting its 1.3 million Vhavenda (kin of the Shona); an area of poor agriculture but, being only 10 km from Zimbabwe, some strategic importance; 'independent' in 1979.

Ciskei: a poor and unruly area of 5,500 sq. km and 500,000 Xhosa-speakers who crossed the Kei in the nineteenth century; claimed by Transkei; self-governing from 1972. The Ciskei and the 'white corridor' leading to East London (where the jobs were) were mutually dependent – and hostile.

The designated Homelands comprised *Kwazulu*: a Homeland intended for 4 million of the 5.5 million Zulus and comprising 31,000 sq. km in ten (originally 48) segments; included one-third of Natal, of which the Zulus claim the whole. *Lebowa* and *Qwagwa*: for the North and South Sotho; small and arid; the former self-governing from 1972. *Kangwane*: north of Ngwane; 3,700 sq. km in two segments for 250,000 Swazis (one-third of the total). *Gazankulu*: 6,300 sq. km in four segments for 350,000 Shangaan; arid but possibly covering minerals. *South Ndebele*: extracted from Bophuthatswana.

By 1990 all four established Homelands were demonstrating their rejection of government policy and support for the ANC. In Bophuthatswana there were demonstrations against President Lucas Mangope. In Venda President Frank Ravele was forced out of office. In Ciskei Lennox Sebe, president for life, was ousted by the local army, which renounced independence and aligned itself with the ANC. In the oldest of the Homelands, Transkei, a similar coup removed two chief ministers in 1987. All the Homelands ceased to exist as such upon the adoption of South Africa's new constitution in 1994. This was an experiment in divide-and-rule which failed.

Related reading: part six

Godwin, Peter: *When a Crocodile Eats the Sun* (2007) [Zimbabwe]
Malan, Rian: *My Traitor's Heart* (1990)

PART SEVEN

Latin America

CHAPTER 27

South America

General

South America in the nineteenth century was isolated from world politics not – as were Africa and much of Asia – by the muffle of European imperialism but by the heritage of post colonialism. The South American republics were also largely isolated from one another. The twentieth century witnessed an accelerating reversal of this pattern, accompanied by spasmodic attempts to assimilate the democratic and industrial revolutions which were the hallmark of the experiences and successes of western Europe and the United States of America: to implant, that is, democratic political forms and social values in narrow oligarchies, and to develop manufacturing industries where trade in primary products had hitherto sufficed for the needs of the ruling classes.

In a century and more after independence South America had become a byword for political instability and social immobility. It was notorious for civil wars, revolutions, coups, political assassinations and short-lived constitutions alongside entrenched social and economic injustice. Its basic needs were the reverse of its experience; namely, political stability and social and economic change. It was in these respects not unique but its ills had been aggravated by time until they posed a daunting dilemma: could it get social and economic change without revolution? Or political stability without perpetuating social and economic stagnation? The underlying conflict between the few and the many was not mediated by a middle class such as had tided western Europe over the bar of oligarchy without intolerable violence.

The government of South America after the end of Spanish and Portuguese rule devolved upon a social elite consisting of big landowners supported by the Roman Catholic Church and by a military caste aspiring to the same social status. By 1945 the traditional power of the upper classes had been destroyed nowhere south of the Panama isthmus and ten years later only in Bolivia (1952). Nevertheless, the oligarchy's props were weakening. Within the religious and military establishments there were growing doubts about the immutability and propriety of its monopoly of power and profit and some concern, expressed with varying degrees of sincerity, over the plight of the rural poor, the growing urban proletariat and the suppressed Indians. An awareness of gross inequalities was stirring consciences and fears and so enlisting in the service of the underdog those two powerful political forces: indignation and the recalculation of expediencies. Churches began to shift their attention and their political weight somewhat to the left, and there appeared in the armed forces officers with some of the instincts of populists and a taste for demagogy.

Through South America a great part of the population was extremely poor, illiterate, unproductive and virtually outside the state. Many states were not merely run by an oligarchy but also owned by it in the sense that the land and what grew on it and what lay beneath it were the private property of a small number of individuals: in various countries 60 to 90 per cent of agricultural land was owned by a tenth of the population. Quite apart from abstract notions of fair or unfair shares, this distribution was a cause of inefficiency. Many landowners, possessing more land than they needed to cultivate, left much of it untilled and untended, but were firmly opposed to any redistribution to other proprietors who might be more disposed to cultivate it. Forcible redistribution produced the opposite evil of a multitude of economically intractable plots: in Colombia, for example, more than two-thirds of the land was uncultivated while much of the cultivable area had been broken down into holdings of a few acres. Bountifully supplied with cheap labour, the big landowners had no need to invest their profits in their land, modernize their methods or increase production.

The rural poor remained poor to the verge of destitution and beyond, and either endured short lives of useless and hopeless misery or drifted to towns where they were not much better off, since they were not fitted to take jobs. Public education in South America as a whole was so meagre that less than a tenth of the population completed a primary course and illiteracy rates of 50 per cent were not uncommon, 90 per cent not unknown. If they were Indians, the peasants who went to the towns invited incomprehension and ridicule by their strange speech and attitudes. Moreover, if the peasants had little to offer, the towns too had little to offer. Industry cannot flourish in places where half the population is too poor to buy its products. South American industries were handicapped by the lack of a domestic market, with the result that the South American countries continued to import goods which they could have been making for themselves. Hence the towns to which the peasants migrated, so far from needing their labour, already contained unemployment; in some of them a third of the inhabitants might be unhoused. And this unemployment was growing not only for economic reasons but also because the population explosion was greater than anywhere else in the world: the population was in the process of doubling every quarter century.

There existed therefore in most parts of South America a revolutionary situation. This situation was accentuated by awareness of it, since an assumption that a pattern cannot last much longer is itself a potent factor for change. The forces making for change, besides the relatively passive rural and urban proletariats, were activists who, out of dissatisfaction with the existing state of affairs, might make common cause with the masses some or all of the way towards revolution.

27.1 South America

The growth of a South American middle class had been stunted by the slow pace of industrial development just as industrial development had been stunted by the self-sufficiency of a ruling class capable of maintaining its standard of living by exporting primary products and using the proceeds to import all the necessities and luxuries which it wanted from the outside world. This economic pattern had social and political con-sequences, since a small middle class is less likely than a large one to adopt distinctive social habits and political aims of its own, and in South America the small middle class, imprisoned within the oligarchic system, was relatively effortlessly seduced into gravitating into the upper reaches of a system which it had no power to subvert. Here again South America was not unique but the standing of the middle class was altered when the Second World War deprived South America of its habitual imports and so promoted domestic development. After a pause in the immediate postwar years the demands created by the Korean War gave a fresh fillip to industrial expansion. These events external to the sub-continent's own affairs altered its economic course, although without seriously altering its social hierarchy. The industrial middle class prospered in some centres, notably in Brazil, but for the most part it came nowhere near to sup-planting the traditional ruling class in the exercise of political power.

The rise of a middle class is commonly associated with the growth of democracy as the middle class, annexing a part of the power wielded by a landed aristocracy, points the way to a yet further expansion of the political system. But South America was liberated from European rule in a peculiar way. Napoleon's subjection of Spain had caused Spanish power in the New World to evaporate, so that the Liberators had stepped into a vacuum as inheritors of the abandoned authority of the Spanish crown rather than as champions of European revolutionary principles or Enlightenment: they were not so much democrats as – like George Washington and his associates a generation earlier – rulers who had seceded from *anciens régimes* based on the sanctity and privileges of (landed) property which they continued to uphold. In these new states the military caste, if second in rank and prestige, came first in terms of power. But after the wars of liberation South American armies engaged in few wars among themselves and faced no enemy threat from beyond the sub-continent. Their officers assumed therefore a domestic role rather than the function of national defence. Some opted for life in the social elite, others for a career in politics, yet others – in later times – for the sweets of business in the arms industry or tourism or the drugs trade. Many saw themselves as the guardians or godfathers of the state (which they often equated with the status quo) and used their power against unduly inefficient or corrupt politicians whom they replaced by others or themselves; but as armies expanded they acquired officers from different backgrounds, so that an awareness of social issues and mild support for reform found their way into the military establishment. Officers of this tendency came to be dubbed *nasseristas* (as opposed to *gorillas*). They spread the notion in the late 1950s and the 1960s that national politics and national armies should become both more professional and more socially conscious. But if the first impact was the destruction of old-style dictators and some diminution of old-style officers, it did not follow that government by civilians was to be the new rule, for the civilians might fall short in efficiency or integrity of what was desired of them, or press ahead with social reform faster than the progressive officers' own assessment of what was healthy.

Alongside this regrouping of domestic forces, whose outcome was likely to differ from one state to another, there was a search for political forms which led the more inquiring minds to consider two foreign models, each of which seemed to have something to contribute: western democracy with its emphasis on freedoms and human rights, and communism with its reputation for economic growth and its claims to equality. The South American intellectual who could discover how to get the best from both these two worlds would perhaps have found the synthetic short cut to prosperity and justice. But he too was faced with a dilemma. He knew that, for economic reasons, South America needed foreign funds; he knew that, for historical reasons, it wanted to steer clear of foreign aid; and he had to face the fact that if, in his search for the synthetic short cut, he looked for aid and inspiration to both western and communist strongholds he would be unpopular with both.

South America's approach to the outside world was conditioned by its need for foreign capital against a background of ill-regulated foreign aid in a previous generation. Towards the end of the nineteenth century and at the beginning of the twentieth the principal capitalist nations had lent money to South America to excess and at high rates of interest to mutual dissatisfaction. The South Americans felt that they had been exploited and the lenders resented many a subsequent default and the expropriation of enterprises which they had built up. The Second World War eliminated export markets. Domestic markets were small because impoverished and intra-American trade meagre. Banks and other financial institutions lacked the mechanisms and habits necessary for providing credit for substantial economic expansion. The poor were too poor to save and the rich frequently invested or banked their wealth abroad. International agencies insisted on onerous undertakings: stable currencies, balanced budgets, rigorous limits to government spending. Industrialization was weak or delayed for many reasons: ruling elites opposed import tariffs and quotas which infant industries needed but rich customers did not like; the several domestic markets were too small and attempts to combine them rudimentary; industries tended to excess capacity, their products to high costs; technology was either local and behind the times or foreign and therefore strange and expensive. Transport and other public services were poor or non-existent, except near big cities. Half the population was drawn into cities of 20,000 or more, overcrowded, dirty, violent and a prey to property speculators. The economic gap between town and country was widening. The land provided status, wealth and a way of life for the few; the towns failed for the most part to become engines of new economic activity. The need for land reform was manifest and a number of countries passed relevant laws, but little practical action followed except in the wake of revolutions. Workers on the land were ill-paid, underemployed and growing in numbers in spite of the drift to the towns. Without credit or adequate communications or, in many areas, water, small proprietors would get neither seeds nor fertilizers nor machinery for what was economically productive land.

Regional associations were one way of seeking economic betterment. Nine South American states and Mexico created in 1960 a Latin American Free Trade Area (LAFTA) whose first aim was to create an agricultural common market. It was succeeded in 1980 by a Latin American Integration Association (LAIA) with wider economic aims and the same members minus Brazil and plus Bolivia. In 1969 an Andean Pact of four states – Peru, Chile (which left in 1973), Bolivia and Ecuador – formed a similar but more compact venture in agricultural and industrial co-operation. In 1985–89 Argentina and Brazil concluded a series of agreements designed to promote economic co-operation and bury hatchets; Uruguay became an observer and then a member of this body. More significantly, over the period 1991–93 these three states, together with Paraguay, by the treaty of Assuncion and the Protocol of Ouro Preto, created the Southern Common Market (MERCOSUR) to form a common market with a population of 200 million, an association more populous than any of the kind except the EU, NAFTA and ASEAN. Bolivia and Chile joined it in secondary capacities. MERCOSUR's initial impulse was political: to smooth hostility between Argentina and its big neighbour Brazil, and also with Chile, with which Argentina had seemed on the verge of war in the 1960s. It brought substantial economic gains in trade and cross-border investment.

Another kind of regionalism – pan-American – barely entered into practical consideration before the last years of the century. The United States was the largest potential source of capital for economic development but relations between the two halves of the continent were dominated by uneasy, sometimes hostile, currents. South America differed from North America not only by its Latinity but also by its fragmentation. While the south became divided into many states, North America did not. From the days of the Liberators, when the sub-continent was Balkanized by post-imperial wars and politics, there were hankerings for the sub-continental solidarity of the great Spanish viceroyalties. A surviving cultural community and a geographical compactness promoted in time an inter-American system, but the contrast between south and north could not be eradicated. In the north the United States had shown an amazing capacity to accommodate a hotchpotch of races and preserved its unity in spite of the disruptive social and economic forces which produced the Civil War, while Canada succeeded in keeping its British and French populations under a single political roof. These two states were bigger and more powerful than any South American state; South Americans became fearful of US preponderance and imperialism; Canada, which might have served as a makeweight, steered clear of conflicts between the United States and Latin states.

The United States fed Latin American suspicions. During its years of expansion the United States was uncertain of its attitudes towards its neighbours in Central America and the Caribbean, and as it became a world power it frequently acted as though these states were something less than sovereign. Just as Britain in the twentieth century found it hard to think of Middle Eastern countries as independent or deserving independence, so the United States in an overlapping period felt much the same way about a group of states which were supposed to have a special impact on North American vital interests. When President Monroe forbade the expansion of European territorial dominions in the New World, Spain and Portugal had already lost theirs and the British, French and Dutch had little interest in challenging Monroe's unilateral declaration: the one serious attempt to do so – France's attempt to turn Mexico into a new Habsburg empire during the American Civil War – was a catastrophic failure. By this time the United States had itself annexed one-third of Mexico, had evinced interest in an isthmian canal and was about to toy with the idea of acquiring the large islands of Cuba and Hispaniola.

The Monroe Doctrine, enunciated in 1823, was the basis of a policy of turning America into an island by purchases (Louisiana, Florida, Cuba, Alaska) and by barring all European powers from recovering their possessions or extending their influence in the continent. It was inspired equally by fears of Russia in the north-west and other Europeans to the south-east. For more than a century the doctrine required little exertion on the part of the United States and it was not seriously called in question until, in the Second World War, the remaining French and Dutch colonies came within the legal grasp of Nazi Germany and, in the Cold War, the Russians dared to establish a base in Cuba. Britain made no attempt to enlarge its West Indian empire and during the decades after the breach between Britain and the new United States British naval power served to buttress rather than challenge the Doctrine. Geography having placed no islands between the British Isles and the seaboard of the United States, the initial post-independence period was one of estrangement but not conflict. (It is hard to believe that conflict could have been avoided, especially during the Civil War, if the North Atlantic had been dotted with islands which the two powers would have competed to occupy.) In the event the possession of a common language and common traditions was not countered by territorial disputes (except over Canada which, illuminatingly, failed to get robust support from London), and when by the end of the century the power of the United States had grown to significant proportions the goodwill between the two countries prevailed over occasional conflicts and led in the next century to an alliance which pulled Britain out of a European and into an American orbit.

In the middle of the nineteenth century, when the United States first began to think of a canal across Nicaragua to link the Atlantic and the Pacific, British assent and co-operation seemed essential. Britain had territories and claims along the nearby coast (in British Honduras, the Mosquito Coast and the Bay Islands); the United States negotiated favourable treaties with Nicaragua and Honduras. By the Clayton–Bulwer Treaty of 1850 the two countries agreed that neither should acquire exclusive control over any canal or special privileges in it; and, further, that neither should occupy or fortify or colonize or assume or exercise any dominion over any part of Central America. This treaty, concluded at a time when the United States was the weaker of the two parties, became an obstacle to later plans to construct a canal without British collaboration and acquire dominion over its course and banks, but by the end of the century British interest in this part of the world was small compared with British interest in the Middle East and southern Asia and in 1901 the Clayton–Bulwer Treaty was replaced by the Hay–Pauncefote Treaty which reaffirmed the principles of neutrality and free and undiscriminating use, but otherwise removed the limitations set by the earlier treaty. The United States then entered into discussions with Colombia for a grant of territory at Panama. A treaty was negotiated but rejected by the Colombian senate, whereupon in 1903 the United States promoted a revolt at Panama and the secession of the area from Colombia. A new Panamanian republic was created and, for $10 million and an annual rent of $250,000, granted to the United States perpetual sovereignty over the so-called Canal Zone and the right to intervene in Panama's internal affairs. The United States made use of this right by despatching troops on a number of occasions.

No less important to the United States than Panama was the large island of Cuba, closer to the United States than any other Latin American country except Mexico. The United States tried on various occasions to buy Cuba from Spain but without success. In 1868 the Cubans rose against Spain and waged war for ten years. They were defeated but rose again in 1895. Feelings in the United States were enraged by the cruelty which the Spanish authorities used to defeat the revolt and by concern for American investments, but the government took no action until, in 1898 and in circumstances which have remained unexplained, the battleship USS *Maine* was sunk in harbour at Havana. Washington delivered an ultimatum and, although the terms were largely accepted and the war virtually over, declared war on Spain. Fighting, which extended to the Pacific, lasted three months and ended with the defeat of Spain and the cession to the United States of the Philippine Islands, Guam and Puerto Rico in return for $20 million. Cuba passed under the tutelage of the United States and so remained until 1933. In 1901 the United States asserted by the Platt Amendment (an amendment to the Army Appropriation Bill) that it would not withdraw its military forces unless its right to intervene for the preservation of good government were embodied in the Cuban constitution. US forces were stationed in the island in 1906–9 and 1912–13 in support of corrupt military regimes, and a naval base was built at Guantanamo.

Within a few years of the Cuban War the United States intervened in the Dominican Republic (1905). Fearful of European intervention as a consequence of the default of the Dominican government on its debts, President Theodore Roosevelt formulated the Roosevelt Corollary to the Monroe Doctrine, by which the United States arrogated to itself the right to intervene in Latin American countries in order to keep governments in order. US forces reappeared in 1916 and for the next eight years the country was under the direct military rule of the United States with a US officer as president. A similar occupation of the neighbouring Haitian republic, also intended to forestall European creditors, lasted from 1915 to 1934. On the mainland the United States intervened openly in the Mexican revolution and civil war by a naval bombardment in 1914 and an unsuccessful army expedition in 1916–17; and US forces, sent to Nicaragua in 1911 to support a favoured president, kept the liberal opposition quiet until 1933 when, upon their departure, the dictatorship of Anastasio Somoza was inaugurated.

This policy of direction and control sustained by sporadic military descents was abandoned by President Franklin D. Roosevelt and his secretary of state Cordell Hull. In his first inaugural address Roosevelt promulgated a good neighbour policy based on non-intervention, and his undertaking was repeated at the Pan-American Conference of 1936 at Buenos Aires. The Platt Amendment was repealed. The right to intervene in Panama's internal affairs was abrogated by treaty. The withdrawal of US marines from Haiti was accelerated. The president accepted the right of the Mexican government to nationalize oil properties within its territory. Latin American hopes were also raised by the passing of the Reciprocal Trade Agreements Act of 1934, which gave the president power to reduce tariffs by as much as 50 per cent, and by the establishment in the same year of the Export-Import Bank for lending US public funds to foreign governments. Before the outbreak of the Second World War Hull, mindful of Germany's attempt in the First World War to get Japan to attack the United States through Mexico, tried to persuade Latin America that Nazism and fascism were present dangers against which the whole American continent should take joint precautions. At Havana in 1940 the American states agreed that no non-American state should be allowed to take over any piece of American territory, but this new enunciation of the Monroe Doctrine was to be upheld by joint American action; the United States was given no invitation to intervene on its own against any external threat. It was rather to supply its neighbours with the arms and equipment to do so. Consequently, one result of Washington's fears for the defence of the hemisphere was the strengthening of the military class throughout the area. Small Brazilian and Mexican forces were sent overseas during the war, but American military supplies affected the structure of politics within Latin America far more than they affected the course of the war.

After Pearl Harbor, Mexico, Colombia and Venezuela broke off relations with Japan, Germany and Italy, and all the Central American and Caribbean republics declared war. When the end of the war was in sight the American states, meeting at Chapultepec in Mexico in February 1945, declared themselves in favour of collective defence against internal as well as external threats (this arrangement was placed on a more permanent footing by the Inter-American Treaty of Reciprocal Assistance, concluded at Rio de Janeiro in 1947), but Washington's concern to create a continental anti-communist alliance found little response among states which were still used to thinking of the United States and not the USSR as the prime intervener in their internal affairs and were more worried by postwar economic problems than by communism. The military classes, which were the most immediately affected by joint defence schemes, were less interested in co-operation than in strengthening their own forces. They looked to the United States for more, and more modern, equipment. The United States on the other hand became increasingly trapped between policies of pre-empting communism by economic aid to its neighbours and interfering in their affairs to suppress communists or anybody who looked like a communist from Washington.

In 1951 the Mutual Security Act was extended to Latin America and from 1952 the United States concluded a series of bilateral defence agreements. If the United States (and Latin American civilians) had qualms about this further reinforcement of the military class, Washington felt constrained by the veiled threat that armies unable to satisfy their needs in the United States might go shopping elsewhere. An inter-American police academy was established at Fort Davis in the Canal Zone in 1962 for the study and practice of techniques of counter-insurgency, but otherwise inter-American military co-operation was not fruitful or popular.

The conferences at Chapultepec and Rio were the seventh and eighth in a series of inter-American conferences which had been inaugurated in Washington in 1889. The ninth of these meetings was held at Bogotá in 1948 and created new institutions and continuing machinery for pan-American consultation and action (Canada still, by its own wish, excluded until 1989). Ostensibly pan-American, but in some minds a Latin counterweight to northern power, the Organization of American States (OAS) had for its objects the maintenance of peace within the area of its members, the peaceful settlement of their disputes, joint action against aggression and co-operative development of economic, social and cultural interests. For Latin America this association with the United States was welcome chiefly on account of the prospect of an economic outpouring like the Marshall Plan for Europe, but this prospect proved a mirage since Washington viewed Europe and Latin America in very different lights: Europe had been ravaged by war and was deemed to be in danger of imminent economic collapse and vulnerable to Russian advances. These arguments applied little, if at all, to Latin America. Disenchantment grew on both sides. The Korean War sharpened Washington's global anti-communism and altered its priorities in Latin America where it focused on political rather than economic issues – the overthrow of President Guzman in Guatemala (see Chapter 28) and, less successfully, of Fidel Castro in Cuba (see Chapter 29). While Washington considered that the anti-communist war in Korea required all states to stand up and be counted Colombia alone sent troops from Latin America.

In 1958 Vice-President Richard Nixon, on a tour of Latin American countries, was received with insults and even violence. In Peru and Venezuela, where dictators (albeit recently displaced) had received the Legion of Merit from Eisenhower, Nixon found himself the target of popular indignation against US approval of dictators. The United States agreed to the creation of an inter-American Bank and an inter-American Fund for Social Development and in 1960 Eisenhower undertook a Latin American tour as part of an attempt to improve relations. Although the eleventh inter-American conference, due to be held in Quito in 1959, was postponed, the foreign ministers of the American states met once in that year at Santiago and twice in the following year at San José. The first of these meetings was mainly devoted to denouncing Rafael Trujillo of the Dominican Republic and Fulgencio Batista of Cuba, matters on which it was not difficult to get a wide consensus. In 1960 a Venezuelan allegation that Trujillo had instigated an attempt to murder President Betancourt produced an inquiry, a condemnation of Trujillo and the eviction of the Dominican Republic from the OAS, but when the United States proposed economic sanctions and internationally supervised elections in the Dominican Republic its associates drew back for fear of setting a precedent for intervention in their own affairs. There was also a clash between the United States and the rest over Cuba: the conference was on the whole anti-Cuban but was not prepared to express itself directly. A proposal for inter-American mediation between the United States and Cuba gained no ground. On the perennial problem of economic co-operation an attempt by President Kubitschek of Brazil to obtain United States aid for an 'Operation Pan-America' produced little response in Washington.

The next year, however, President Kennedy sounded a new note. Addressing himself to Latin America as no president of the United States had done since Franklin D. Roosevelt, Kennedy proposed an Alliance for Progress, massive and long-term co-operation between the United States and its Latin neighbours for the improvement, at the expense of the United States, of their economies on condition that they would also introduce certain fundamental reforms. The United States would provide $20 billion over ten years to pay, in effect, for economic and social reform. Although Latin American governments preferred bilateral to multilateral aid, and although they presumably preferred aid without strings to aid tied to reform, the Alliance for Progress was the sort of intervention which they had been seeking even since the inauguration of the Marshall Plan for Europe, as opposed to the sort of intervention which they habitually feared or said they feared. Later in the same year, at Punta del Este in Uruguay, all the members of the OAS except Cuba subscribed to a charter giving effect to Kennedy's proposals.

The Alliance for Progress was a bold psychological stroke, important for its impact upon the citizens of the United States as well as on the peoples further south, but it was imperfectly thought out in advance and the practical results proved disappointingly meagre. The reasons for the disappointment were many. First, Kennedy's death came all too soon after his inauguration; there had been little time to get results. But, secondly, there were more material reasons. The sum pledged was large but it was questionable whether it could do more than hold a deteriorating situation. US government funds were expected to attract private spending, but the volume of the private spending did not come up to expectations and some of the government funds had to be diverted to unforeseen short-term purposes owing to a fall in Latin American revenues from primary products. Thirdly, there was confusion about the purposes and priorities of the Alliance from Washington's point of view. Was it designed primarily to alter social structures, or to alleviate immediate poverty, or to promote a state's economic progress, or to facilitate inter-state economic integration, or to combat communism? Unless priorities were established it was difficult to know where to begin or what to approve. Finally, there were misunderstandings and pitfalls: whether funds were to become available immediately or only conditionally on the introduction of democracy; whether funds should be given to a reactionary or unconstitutional regime. Cutting off aid meant damaging the hopes of the blameless poor; continuing aid might mean financing backward regimes instead of encouraging progressive ones.

The essential feature of relations between Latin America and the United States was imbalance. So long as the Cold War provided the context within which this inequality had to be handled the United States was looking for reliably anti-communist friends, allowing their ideological attitudes pride of place over their less admirable qualities such as dictatorship, torture and mass murder. With the end of the Cold War the United States became more concerned with stemming the international spread of drugs and promoting democracy – co-operative ventures which, however, were not without high-handedly abrasive intrusiveness.

Forms of government in Latin America shifted perplexingly. During the 1950s there was a clatter of falling dictators, beginning with the fall of Juan Domingo Perón in Argentina in 1955. The following three years saw the withdrawal of Manuel Odria in Peru and the displacement of Presidents Gustavo Rojas Pinilla and Marcos Perez Jimenez of Colombia and Venezuela. The trend in these years was for the military to retire from sight and the autocratic *caudillo*, interested in his personal power and unencumbered by ideologies, came to be represented south of the Panama isthmus only by Alfredo Stroessner in Paraguay who survived until 1989. (He died in exile in 2006. His party retained the presidency until 2008 when Fernando Lago, a recruit for the Chavez camp (p. 697), ended one of Latin America's longest sequences in exile. In 1996 General Lino Oviedo Silva staged a coup which failed and landed him in prison. Barred from the elections of 1998, he successfully backed Raul Cubas Grau against Luis Argana Ferraro. Argana was murdered; Cubas was impeached, resigned and fled; Oviedo too fled. Paraguay was additionally afflicted by the devaluation of the Brazilian currency and reviled by the United States as an adjunct of the drugs trade.) But the military were provided with a *raison d'être* – and with new weapons – by the prevalence of guerrilla movements which carried on in various forms in spite of the blow to morale occasioned by the death of Che Guevara in Bolivia in 1967. The development of anti-guerrilla techniques under the surveillance of US officers enabled governments to defeat movements which had never been numerically strong and were only fleetingly united. Protest found different and less romantic forms. The guerrilla *foco* was replaced by urban kidnappers – the Uruguayan *tupamaros* and their like, who in Argentina, Brazil and elsewhere specialized in the capture of diplomats as hostages. One of the more notable exploits of the *tupamaros* was the capture of the British ambassador in

Montevideo, but although they held him for eight months they gained nothing by doing so. Urban tactics were no improvement on the *focos* and in elections in Uruguay in 1971 the Frente Amplio or Broad Left ran third to the two traditional parties of Blancos and Colorados. Juan Bordaberry, installed as president in 1972 after intricate and disputed calculations, was – like his predecessors – more concerned with the task of finding for Uruguay, once rich on its exports of wool, an economic future in a world which had invented rayon. He was unseated by the military but in 1980 the Uruguayans, with unexpected temerity, rejected a new constitution proffered to them by this regime in anticipation of a more obedient vote and from 1985 Uruguay returned to the peaceful civilian ways for which it had long been noted.

Optimists hoped that such trends would become increasingly characteristic of the closing years of the century but no trend could be counted on to persist, nor could generalizations applicable to the whole sub-continent easily be found. Two crucial elements were economic growth and institutional reform. In the early 1990s economic growth was evident in many countries but uneven. Most – Brazil was the principal exception – sought to handle their immediate financial troubles by privatizing state enterprises and properties in order to raise money to service foreign debts, give budgets a healthier complexion and stave off tax increases: Argentina's plan to denationalize its state oil corporation was the most extensive measure of this kind; in Chile and elsewhere similar transactions were pursued, but in Peru and Venezuela they were suspended. The obstacles were not only the wayward will of ruling classes but also the weakness of the financial and administrative institutions needed to formulate and carry through complicated economic transformations.

With the turn of the century a new mood was gaining ground. Its principal ingredients were a romantic-democratic assertion of a pre-Colombian past; a rejection of militarism and military dictators; uncertainty about whether to mould a Latin American or South American society of nations; a more solid hostility to the USA ranging from distrust to hatred; a search for economic association with world bodies provided that their character and constitutions were re-fashioned to diminish the dominance of major world powers (see in particular Venezuela, p. 696). The satisfaction of such a vision would require in the first place financial stability.

Brazil had become independent as an empire, which lasted from 1822 to 1889 when the second emperor was displaced by a bloodless revolution led by a professor of mathematics. It possessed enormous natural resources and a vast internal market, occupied one-third of Latin America and accounted, with Mexico and Argentina, for nearly two-thirds of its products. According to the census of 1970 its population had grown by a third in ten years and had reached more than 93 million. Thanks to its vast and varied resources, it was able to make economic progress both during and after the First World War. In 1930 Getulio Dornelles Vargas, mildly liberal, was put in power by the army, which was dissatisfied with the traditional conservative oligarchy. He began the modernization of Brazil. He strengthened the central government, nurtured industry and introduced state economic planning. He became both more autocratic and more popular. The army grew suspicious of him on both counts. It feared his new power base in the poorer classes and in 1945 he was forced out of office. But he was returned to power in 1950 by popular vote and with the support of younger army officers. The army, hoping to control him and reluctant blatantly to flout a fair election, allowed him to take office but by 1954 it had had enough of him and was about to evict him – on the grounds of incompetence – when he committed suicide.

The next decade saw the running down of the Vargas era under three presidents. The election of 1955 was won by Juscelino Kubitschek with Julio Goulart as his vice-president. The armed forces, divided in their attitudes towards this result, interposed no objection and allowed the successful pair to take over. They thereby demonstrated the new president's dependence upon them, and he in return tacitly acknowledged the relationship by raising pay and providing funds for military equipment. Some officers wanted more than this and hoped for a reforming administration which would attack corruption, incompetence and the grosser manifestations of social injustice, but they were not willing to endorse any very radical measures nor did they have the satisfaction of observing a good administration at work, for President Kubitschek embarked on extravagant enterprises (such as the building of the new capital, Brasilia) and in the course of an energetically misguided administration opened up huge opportunities for private speculation and peculation.

In 1961 Jânio Quadros, with Goulart still as vice-president, succeeded, but he resigned after seven months, leaving Goulart to take his place under the eyes of a divided and increasingly dubious army and a solidly conservative navy and air force. In these circumstances Goulart's powers were limited and he quickly reached the limits. Where Quadros had preferred to quit, Goulart chose to forge ahead; he rode for a fall. He proposed a wide extension of the franchise, land reform and a neutralist foreign policy. He appealed to the people against the armed forces and congress, accepted communist support at home, established relations with the USSR and opposed the eviction of Castro's Cuba from the OAS (but joined the United States naval blockade of Cuba during the missile crisis). These measures won him some popularity but also evoked fear and hatred, enabled communists to infiltrate into central and state administrations and trade unions and, as different provinces lined up on different sides, produced a threat of civil war, at which point the army intervened.

Having evicted Goulart, the army leaders forced the congress, after a pause in which constitutional propriety was observed by recognizing the president of the chamber of deputies as president, to install General Humberto Castelo Branco as president for the remainder of Goulart's term. The general was succeeded by Marshal Costa e Silva and he by Generals Garrastazu Medici, Ernesto Geisel and João Baptista de Oliveira Figueiredo. Political parties were banned, with the exception of two new ones of no independent vitality. The regime turned a hard face towards trade unions, peasants and students. It made little progress with land reform and halted literacy programmes, which seemed to it dangerous: Brazil remained a country of unused land and unused talent. Faced with growing opposition, it resorted to strong-arm methods, including widespread and appalling cruelty to the political prisoners who were thrown in increasing numbers into the jails.

On the other hand, the military regime claimed credit for its handling of the economy. Having inherited galloping inflation, it not only reversed the trends of the lean 1960s but achieved for a while (1968–74) a growth rate of 10 per cent a year, much in excess of anything seen in the previous 20 years. The main instrument was exports, which were quadrupled, assisted by heavy borrowing from foreigners impressed by Brazil's natural resources and disciplinary government. But 1974 was a year of reckoning in Brazil, as elsewhere in the world. The healthy world markets which had taken Brazil's exports became unhealthy. Internal developments financed from abroad slowed down and Brazil turned to import controls and import substitution. The beneficiaries of the boom began to grumble, its victims to assert themselves. The latter were numerous. In spite of the boom nearly half the population was worse off than before – 40 per cent were sharing less than 10 per cent of the national income. Regional as well as class tensions were aggravated, as the underprivileged north-east waxed indignant about the fat cats in the south. With the advent in 1979 of President Figueiredo the government set about the dual task of restructuring the economy and humanizing the regime. Censorship was relaxed, torture probably diminished and a wide, though not total, amnesty decreed for political prisoners. In the economic sphere special effort was put into the search for alternatives to foreign oil: prospecting for offshore oil (which proved disappointing), the search for substitutes and a nuclear programme. The last raised the usual questions about whether Brazil intended to develop nuclear military power as well as a nuclear-powered economy.

Brazil in the 1970s was not the leader in nuclear development in South America. Its old adversary, Argentina, was ahead. Brazil had not signed the Nuclear Non-Proliferation Treaty but had signed, with reservations, its regional equivalent, the Treaty of Tlatelolco (1967). Argentina signed neither. (Mexico, also in the nuclear race, signed both.) In 1975 Brazil, after a rebuff from the United States, turned to West Germany for help in accelerating its nuclear programme. In return for part-payment in Brazilian uranium, Bonn agreed to supply Brazil with eight reactors, a fuel-processing plant and uranium enrichment technology. Brazil's aim was to have no fewer than 73 reactors by the end of the century. Although the main purposes of this programme were industrial and civilian, the processing plant and the German technology pointed to a military capability. The safeguards embodied in the agreement were stringent but less than total. Brazilian and Argentinean programmes created the possibility of a nuclear arms race in South America similar to those between Pakistan and India or Israel and Iraq but the two countries abjured this insanity in the course of a comprehensive improvement in their political and economic relations over the century's last two decades.

Brazil's size made it a giant among Latin American states. Its potential wealth made it a potentially mighty giant. Its Portuguese background differentiated it from its Spanish-speaking neighbours and gave it a more cosmopolitan flavour, which was accentuated by its awareness of its African origins. Brazil was both a part of South America and turned its back on South America. It was no less detached from North America, determined to assert its independence from the United States and not to play second fiddle to Washington, even when the two countries shared conservative outlooks. It sought closer links with the rising stars of Africa and Asia – Nigeria and Japan – and also with Iraq, another country with plausible ambitions and the supplier for the time being of the greater part of Brazil's imported fuels. Its weak points lay in the excessive growth of its population, heavy foreign debts and the extremes of poverty and wealth within it. As the dreams of the 1970s turned thin, congressional and provincial elections in 1982 gave the government unaccustomed reverses; the IMF insisted in 1983 on painfully classic measures as conditions for its help; and in 1985 the military deemed it prudent to take a back seat after 23 years of political power. Tancredo Neves was elected president but immediately collapsed and died, leaving a little-known deputy and successor José Sarney to cope with daunting economic and social problems. Sarney abandoned monetarist recipes for economic rehabilitation, partly because they fomented misery and even revolution, partly because Brazil's inherent strengths enabled it – or seemed to enable it – to negotiate with its creditors for relief and with the IMF for funds to support a moderately expansionist economic plan. In spite of its huge debts Brazil was able to pay the interest on them punctually. It was also able to imply that without outside aid the Sarney regime would founder, leaving the creditors without hope of interest or the repayment of their capital and confronting the world with the abhorrent possibility of either a reversion to military rule or a regime much to the left of Sarney's. But Sarney lacked political anchorage. His government was a coalition in which the largest partner, the Brazilian Democratic Movement, gave the president full support only when he least needed it. The Movement scored an overwhelming victory in federal and provincial elections in 1986 and then, with the introduction of painful economic measures, bickered with Sarney. These measures excited opposition without stemming inflation, which was growing to astronomic proportions. Elections in 1989 gave a clear majority to Ferdinando Collor de Mello who, at the age of 40, won nearly twice as many votes as his main rival. Collor, governor of the north-eastern province of the country, made the Sarney regime look boring, was fortunate in having to contest the second round of the election with the more extreme candidate of the left and had spent a great deal of money on his campaign. He introduced severe measures which curbed inflation at the price of curbing everything else too. Bank accounts were frozen for 18 months, thus removing about $80 billion from the economy; the currency was devalued; public services were drastically reduced; tax changes shifted money from the private to the public sector. Unemployment soared, businesses collapsed, tax revenues disappeared and the weaker classes were driven to penury and despair. And Collor turned out to be outrageously corrupt. After he and his cronies had stolen about $1 billion he was impeached and replaced by vice-president Itamar Franco pending elections which were held in 1994 and won by a right-wing coalition led by Francesco Cardoso, a former minister of finance and left-wing rebel turned right-wing free marketeer. Cardoso reduced inflation from 1,000 per cent to single figures, imposed hefty tax increases, cut wages in the public services, accelerated privatization and was rewarded by growth in exports in agriculture and manufactures. But the currency, pegged to the dollar, was still overvalued; budget deficits, foreign debt and internal interest rates continued to rise with inevitably aggravated poverty, crime and disorder; illegal occupation of rural land verged on insurrection. He judged nevertheless that the balance of economic recovery over social pain was sufficiently in his favour to justify him in seeking and getting a constitutional amendment to enable him to run in 1998 for a second term, which he won. (This constitutional tinkering found favour in Argentina and Peru too.) But Brazil's much-predicted and regularly deferred march towards the bright economic future which its great size and economic resources seemed to predict was defeated by a combination of external and domestic misfortunes. Collapses among its foreign customers (South-east Asian, Russian) and Cardoso's failure to curb government spending and extravagant borrowing (much of it short-term) resulted in budget deficits around 10 per cent of GDP, recrudescent inflation and a run on the reserves of 10 per cent a month in spite of interest rates of 50 per cent. The IMF and World Bank, fearful of the spread of economic disorder throughout South America (one-third of its GDP was supplied by Brazil), organized credits of $41 billion to protect the currency which, however, unpegged from the dollar, lost half its value in the first weeks of 1999 as $60 billion fled the country.

In 2002 change appeared on the horizon. Luis Ignacio da Silva ('Lula'), the perennial hope of the Brazilian left, was elected president with 46 per cent of the votes cast and took office in a crisis (severe inflation, excessive public spending and fearsome domestic and foreign debt) and rising violent crime. The president was forced to shift somewhat to the centre. A trade agreement with China helped to steady the economy – perhaps a portent of South America's economic relations with the rest of the world. He was re-elected president in 2006 but violent criminal disorder continued to characterize one part or another of this huge country, countered however by a steady if not spectacular rate of growth, four-digit inflation reduced to a tolerable level, the discovery of oil on a scale capable of taking Brazil into the top league of oil exporters, other exports as diverse as iron, ethanol and coffee, and improved prospects of foreign capital for manufacturing and infrastructure – all these factors earned for Brazil (not for the first time) the status of a country apparently on its way to health, happiness and power.

Argentina, the second in extent of South America's states, achieved its independence from Spain at the cost of losing territories which formed the new states of Uruguay,

Paraguay and Bolivia. It was only gradually and painfully consolidated but from the latter part of the nineteenth century it prospered with the development of its lands, largely by immigrants from Europe. The government was in the hands of upper-class conservative and moderately radical politicians who competed for power and sporadically permitted an admixture of democracy, especially between 1916 and 1930. The country's population, its agriculture and its railways expanded steadily and with the introduction of refrigeration it became one of the world's major exporting countries before the First World War; but it lacked minerals and the capacity to develop industry alongside agriculture and commerce. It was severely hit by the slump of 1929 and suffered, partly in consequence, a revolt in 1930 in which army officers (including a 35-year-old Juan Domingo Perón) had the support of the possessing and the dispossessed classes. This event was followed by a period of autocratic conservative rule, buttressed by the army and renewed prosperity. At the same time urbanization and immigration were producing a more politically conscious and socialist working class.

During the Second World War the presidency was held by the ultra-conservative Ramón Castillo, acting president from 1940 to 1942 and president for a further year. Castillo refused to break off relations with the Axis powers, partly because he had fascist leanings himself and partly in despite of the United States, towards which Argentina's governing classes were traditionally hostile. In 1943 the army intervened in what was more than a transfer of power. Its leaders had a programme one of whose aims was Argentina for the Argentineans: a rejection of the role of foreigners in the Argentine economy who promoted useful enterprises but took all the profits away, and a vote of censure on a ruling class which aped foreign, mainly French, fashions and spent half its time in Paris. Another aim was to make Argentina a power whose voice would be heeded in international affairs. And thirdly, the new men, including Perón, wanted social justice at home, by which they meant a less blatant maldistribution of wealth and a less extreme concentration of power in the capital at the expense of the provinces.

A series of generals occupied the presidency in the next two years. In 1944 Argentina broke off relations with Germany and Japan, less out of a change of heart than from a well-calculated need to stand well with Washington as the war in Europe approached its end. In the next year Argentina declared war. (All the independent states of South and Central America and the Caribbean declared war on Germany and its associates between 1941 and 1945. Argentina was the last to do so.) During this period Perón held a number of official positions, developed good relations with union leaders and great popularity with the *descaminados* (the shirtless or destitute), but earned the jealousy of many of his brother officers. Dismissed in 1945, he created a new political party, which won elections in 1946. Perón became president partly through this expression of the popular will but no less through the wave of extra-parliamentary enthusiasm displayed by the crowds of *descaminados* who invaded the political arena. Throughout this contest Perón was openly and vituperatively opposed by the US ambassador.

Perón ruled for nine and a half years crammed with legislative and other measures designed, mainly by authoritarian methods, to turn Argentina into a modern and just country. Banks and other enterprises were nationalized, foreign concerns were bought out with wartime profits, public services and popular education were expanded, industrialization was accelerated, the centralized buying and selling of agricultural products was introduced in order to cushion the effects of price fluctuations. But the pace was too hot for the economy and for the propertied classes, and Perón gave grave offence to the Church. Although the programme was trimmed in the later years Perón made too many mistakes and too many enemies, and in 1955 the navy and the air force, with the Church in the background, tried to bomb him out of the presidency. The army remained loyal to him during the abortive coup and did not feel obliged to replace him after it. Perón dismissed some of his ministers who were most obnoxious to the conservatives and set about safeguarding his position by organizing and arming the *descaminados*. This latter move turned the army against him and a successful coup put another general in his place.

The oligarchy had closed ranks in order to put an end to economic policies which were harming the country and social reforms which were harming them. They had the support of intellectuals who, although they might approve of Perón's social aims, disapproved of his authoritarian methods, particularly censorship; for Perón's advocacy of social reform did not include freedom of expression. The fall of Perón halted the reform movement and raised the hopeless question of what to do when the need for reform is urgent but the readiness of the powers that be for change is restricted. The supporters of Perón – and of the vivacious Eva Duarte, whom Perón married just before his triumph in 1942 but who died in 1952 – did not disappear. They represented a force which, if it could not be wooed away to some other movement, must either be disfranchised or be allowed to resume the *peronista* course.

Meanwhile, the army ruled. It installed General Eduardo Lonardi in the presidency, in which he was later succeeded by General Pedro Aramburu pending elections in 1958 when Arturo Frondizi, a representative middle-class politician and leader of the Radical Civic Union, became president with army consent. Perón's followers remained numerous and the Radicals split over political alliance with them, Frondizi opting for an alliance through which he hoped to seduce *peronistas* to his party. This gamble failed. The persistence of *peronista* feeling was demonstrated at elections in 1960 when, with the *peronistas* barred from putting up candidates of their own, a million voters abstained. In 1962 the *peronistas* were allowed to vote once more. Officers of the three services, angered by Frondizi's miscalculation, discarded him and took counsel among themselves on the basis that the first article of government was the continued exclusion of Perón (in exile in Spain) and his like. The navy, Perón's stoutest opponents, insisted on the simple course of not having elections, and they were supported by a section of army officers known as the *gorillas*. Other army officers, however, backed by the air force, preferred to revert to the system of holding elections, as required by the constitution, but with the *peronistas* disfranchised. Fighting ensued and the latter group won. New elections were held and the moderate army group made Arturo Illía president. The armed forces, having refused to accept the electoral verdict of 1962 or to find a constitutional way of excluding Perón, had resorted to unconstitutional manoeuvres which had further exposed the divisions in their own ranks. In 1966 they removed Illía and substituted Juan Onganía. In 1970 they removed Onganía and substituted Roberto Levingston, who was removed in his turn in 1971 to make way for General Alejandro Lanusse. None of these governments could master inflation or keep order. Disorder increasingly took the form of kidnapping for publicity and ransom – for example, the seizure and murder by a Trotskyist group of Fiat's director-general in Argentina.

In 1972 Perón, now 77 years old, returned amid speculation and apprehension. His arrival was undramatic and his stay short. He endorsed the candidacy of Hector Cámpora in the approaching presidential election and went back to Spain after a few weeks. Cámpora won the election in 1973 with 49.6 per cent of the vote and his party – the Frente Justicialista, alias *peronista* – won 20 out of 22 governorships and control of both parliamentary chambers. But Cámpora was unable to control violence and kidnapping. Perón reappeared, Cámpora resigned, the Frente nominated Perón and his third wife for the presidency and vice-presidency and they received 61.8 per cent of the vote. Perón introduced heavy taxes, bearing especially on the rich but also – in the case of VAT at 16 per cent – on other classes too. He died in 1974, leaving his widow to face the problems of inflation and public order, in dealing with which she was no more successful than her predecessor. She and her government were removed in 1976 by the army, which put General Jorge Rafael Videla in her place but could think of nothing more useful to do than imprison and kill its critics in the name of anti-communism. Many army officers wanted some democracy but not the kind of leader – i.e. Perón – whom democracy promoted.

The military regime, which continued with the presidencies of Generals Eduardo Viola and Leopoldo Galtieri, lasted until 1982, when it was undone by the humiliating outcome of the Falklands War. Under its aegis and by its agents some 30,000 Argentineans were tortured and killed, many of them by being dumped alive into the sea out of aircraft. Inflation exceeded 250 per cent, the foreign debt increased by a factor of six, production and industry collapsed. Clutching at a straw, Galtieri tried to redeem this record by capturing the Falkland Islands on the 150th anniversary of their occupation by Argentineans. He thereby started a war for which Argentina was militarily, economically and psychologically unprepared.

The ownership of the Falklands had long been in dispute. The islands were discovered by John Davis at the end of the eighteenth century. The French colonized East Falkland in 1764, the English West Falkland in 1765. The Spanish bought the former and seized the latter a few years later but then yielded West Falkland to the British, who promptly abandoned it. The Spanish subsequently abandoned East Falkland. In 1829 a new colony was established in the name of the United Provinces of Rio de la Plata, successors in title to the Spanish empire in South America and predecessors of the Argentine Republic. Britain registered a verbal protest. It had established in 1820 a symbolic presence which was destroyed in 1833 by the United States, whereupon the British came back, evicted the few remaining Argentineans and established a colony embracing both East and West Falkland. Argentina persistently challenged the British title, which Britain offered on several occasions to submit to the International Court of Justice, an offer always rejected. Argentina also claimed sovereignty over South Georgia, the South Orkneys and other territory in the South Pacific and Antarctica. This claim clashed with Chilean as well as British claims, of which the latter dated from early in the twentieth century.

In 1979 the British Foreign Office, uneasily but not urgently alive to the dangers, elaborated a plan for relinquishing sovereignty over the Falklands and leasing them back. This plan was presented to a committee of the cabinet which gave it scant attention although the approach of the 150th anniversary of the British reoccupation was a likely source of trouble: a full-scale invasion was not envisaged even after Galtieri's promotion to the presidency at the end of 1981 was followed by rumours and suspicious acts. After bilateral ministerial talks in New York at a relatively low level in 1982 the Argentine government issued a brusque declaration which the talks' pallid conclusions did not seem to warrant, and in the next month a party of Argentinean scrap dealers was sent to South Georgia under naval protection to dismantle an abandoned British station. This probe was not unconnected with the well-advertised withdrawal in the previous year, on grounds of expense and against the advice of the Foreign Office, of the British survey vessel *Endurance* – a symbol of the British presence whose removal led Argentineans to believe that Britain's position throughout the South Pacific was no longer greatly prized in London. Two weeks after the arrival of the scrap dealers in South Georgia Argentina seized the Falklands, undeterred by last-minute attempts by the United States to prevent this blatantly illegal act of aggression. President Galtieri was able to make a triumphant visit to Port Stanley, the islands' capital.

The British government's failure to assess Argentinean intentions until too late left it with few choices. These were negotiation from a position of weakness or war. Ostensibly, it professed to be using force to secure negotiation but once a naval armada had been assembled and despatched there was little prospect of anything except war: peace-makers were up against a time limit and entrenched national obduracies. The British government may have toyed with the notion of a deal whereby – provided the invading Argentinean force were voluntarily removed – Britain would reintroduce its rule for a short time only and then transfer sovereignty to Argentina; but the dominant British resolve was not to treat with the enemy but to beat him, and in this mood negotiation – and all third-party negotiators – were merely impediments. The British expedition was sent into action swiftly but only precariously protected – its air cover was inferior to that provided for any British squadron since the *Prince of Wales* and *Repulse* had been sunk by the Japanese in 1941. It won a resounding victory, but by a whisker and not without grievous loss. It recovered the Falklands, caused the fall of a hateful dictatorship and saddled Britain with the defence of the islands for an indefinite future and at greatly increased cost.

In the course of this victory one episode stood out: the sinking of the Argentinean cruiser *General Belgrano* on 2 May. The loss of life (368 dead); the circumstances in which the action was authorized; the suspicion, in Britain, that the specially constituted war cabinet had not exercised proper control over naval operations; the allegation, again in Britain, that the torpedoing of the *Belgrano* was an item in the determination to torpedo current peace negotiations – all these factors made a big stir in Britain. The last two charges appear to be incompatible. The ensuing controversy was of little interest outside Britain.

The attempts to keep the peace while the British force was sailing south consisted, first, of some hectic diplomacy by the United States secretary of state Alexander Haig, whose main aim was to persuade Galtieri that the British force was no mere bluff and would recover the Falklands by force if no agreement were reached before the expedition reached the islands. This attempt had failed by 29 April and the chief consequences of the failure were two: the United States, which had failed to condemn Argentinean aggression as the UN Charter required, abandoned its neutrality in Britain's favour; and, secondly, the war cabinet in London abated its opposition to the Royal Navy's pleas for more hostile action. For professional but also political reasons (the economic axe was threatening the navy more severely than the other services) naval chiefs wished to demonstrate their unique value to the nation. Proposals for an attack on South Georgia having been rejected, the navy wanted to bag a scalp in the shape of a major Argentinean warship, preferably the aircraft carrier *25 de Mayo* or alternatively the *Belgrano*. The collapse of the first stage of Haig's diplomacy cleared the way and on 2 May the war cabinet, at a strangely slapdash meeting at the prime minister's rural retreat of Chequers, changed the rules of engagement laid down earlier and authorized an attack on either vessel. By the prevailing rules Britain had publicly given notice that it would engage and sink any Argentinean vessel within 12 miles of the Falklands. On 2 May this rule was changed to permit action anywhere outside Argentinean territorial waters although, unlike the defining of the exclusion zone, the new rule was not made public until 7 May.

The sinking of an enemy ship in war is not normally an event to cause surprise. The sinking of the *Belgrano* became controversial on two grounds: first, because it was allegedly unnecessary, and, second, because it destroyed the second of two attempts to preserve the peace by Peruvian diplomacy.

The case for the sinking of the *Belgrano* was that it posed a threat so long as it was at sea and regardless of its position or course. The case against the sinking was that the *Belgrano* was known to have changed course for port, was not – as the defence secretary and the prime minister told the House of Commons and the prime minister repeated a year later – closing rapidly on the British force, and had ceased to pose any threat. (In a strange volte-face seven months later the chief of defence staff said that the only threat came from the *25 de Mayo*.) By a stream of contradictory and sometimes false statements British ministers dug pitfalls for themselves, revealing a disconcerting ignorance of important details and some tardiness in correcting mistakes after the true facts had become available. Victory absolved them from retribution for these sins.

The second matter of controversy was the connection, if any, between the sinking of the *Belgrano* and the proposals for peace which were being canvassed by the UN's secretary-general and the government of Peru. Haig subsequently wrote that both he and the Peruvian President Belaúnde had received from both belligerents general approval of these proposals before the sinking of the *Belgrano* and were working on the details, all of which were known to British officials. The British government denied this account. The British foreign secretary Francis Pym flew to Washington on 1 May and reported to London on the state of negotiations late on 2 May, after the sinking. That negotiations were in progress was known to all. That the sinking of the *Belgrano* put an end to them is sufficiently evident. That the British war cabinet instigated the sinking as a means to abort them is an imputation supported by no evidence. Thatcher, determined on the arbitrament not of politics but battle, was hostile to the UN/ Peruvian initiative but chose to leave Galtieri to block it, which he did. Galtieri misjudged the delicate balance in Washington between pro-British and pro-Argentine sympathizers. He also underestimated the crucial importance of naval intelligence which Thatcher received from Reagan and from Pinochet in Chile (which was already engaged in hostilities with Argentina over the Beagle Channel – see p. 695).

Three days after final British victory Galtieri was dismissed. Civilian rule was restored after a short interval. In Argentina civilian rule meant popularism but without liberalism and with a dose of corruption as an acceptable instrument of government. Elections were won by the Radical Party, whose leader Raoul Alfonsin became president with the tasks of repairing the economy, investigating the disappearance of thousands of victims of the military regime, keeping the military in order, and repairing relations with Britain without abandoning Argentina's claim to the Falklands.

Alfonsin had decency but little else in his favour in politics. He was distrusted by the military, whose overweening style survived the Falklands fiasco, by the Church, by the unions and eventually by the populace which had acclaimed him but turned away from him when prices began to double every month. He survived scattered military mutinies at the cost of giving in to demands to abandon trials of officers accused of enormities against civilians during the military regime. At mid-term elections a revived Peronist Justicialista party won 16 out of 20 state governorships and in the presidential election of 1989 the Peronist candidate Carlos Menem, one-time Peronist and son of a Muslim immigrant from Syria, easily won the popular vote. During his campaign Menem praised Castro and Stroessner; deployed the familiar Peronist rhetorical style; made extravagant promises to the poor but seemed to have no idea how to redeem these promises; and was fierce in his resolve to recover the Falklands. The economic state of the country on the morrow of the election was so alarming that Alfonsin was persuaded to resign in order that Menem might be inducted in June instead of November. He quickly authorized exploratory talks for the resumption of diplomatic and commercial relations with Great Britain (which proceeded slowly in the face of British lack of enthusiasm) and embarked on an economic programme similar to that of President Collor in Brazil. He ditched controls over prices and wages; the former rose steeply and the latter were halved. Businesses and employment collapsed. So too did the currency. Retailers took to pricing their goods in US dollars, whose value quintupled in two months. Hyperinflation was reduced to inflation at about 60 per cent a year but then rebounded into the thousands. Menem tried to sell off state enterprises but had difficulty in finding buyers. His government could raise no money by issuing bonds since nobody would buy them. He reduced the armed forces by a third and gave senior officers pardons for their crimes against human rights. Mid-term elections in 1993 for half the seats in the lower house left the *peronistas* without a majority but Menem secured an amendment to the constitution to enable him to run in 1994 for a second successive term as the man who had killed inflation, made the rich richer without making the poor poorer, and shown an unerring ability to change his politics to fit his circumstances at the shortest notice. Relations with Britain took a turn for the better with an agreement over oil, which was believed to exist superabundantly around the Falklands (though the oil proved to be less abundant than the claims). The two governments agreed to divide the proceeds of exploitation in one area 50/50 and in another 75/25 in Britain's favour. On sovereignty both governments expressed themselves decisively, openly and in diametrically opposite senses.

In 1997 Menem lost control of the Congress. A revival in industry, agriculture and exports was offset by unemployment at around 20 per cent, financial scandals, charges of cronyism and continuing obstruction of every attempt to probe the disappearances of the 30,000 persons made away with during the years of military dictatorship. Menem failed to secure another amendment to the constitution to permit him to run for a third term and in 1999 the Peronist party was severely defeated. Menem himself had by this time swung from *peronista* populism to free market dogmatism which, although it pleased some special interests, reduced half the population to desperate poverty, began to scare the middle classes and left Argentina with external debt of $70 billion repayable in the first years of the coming century.

From the turn of the century Argentina was engaged in a protracted quarrel with the IMF over how far it should accept IMF criticism of its policies in order to secure international credits. It lost the greater part of its borrowing facilities and was obliged to devalue the peso by 40 per cent and then to float it. Economic growth recovered in 2003/4 and passed 8 per cent but, to the poor, not noticeably. In 2005 Argentina undertook to repay its large debts to the United Nations by the end of that year but the necessary measures inflamed public opinion. Nestor Kirchner, an inconspicuous clean broom, was elected president in 2003 and was succeeded two years later by his wife. Their grip on government was less than certain as protests against poverty and corruption persisted.

Chile's history in the nineteenth century had been one of material progress only briefly interrupted by civil war in 1891 and based on rich mineral resources and successful wars against Peru and Bolivia. In the twentieth century Chile had its share of political instability and inflation, its difficulties being accentuated by competition from artificial nitrates. The landed oligarchy lost its hold on power after the revolt of 1891 and Chile moved towards a more democratic order. In 1938 elections gave power to a popular front which included communists and was not debarred from office by the armed forces. A period of orderly civilian government, conservative rather than radical, followed. In 1964 two forces competed for the succession to President Jorge Alessandri – a centre-left alliance led by Salvador Allende and a Christian Democratic Party led by Eduardo Frei Montalvo, who won far right votes and enough of the centre ground to win an absolute majority for a programme of anti-communism blended with reform.

By the end of his term Frei had to his credit a considerable advance in education, a noticeable drop in illiteracy, some industrial development and new housing, and the introduction of graduated taxation. But inflation was not mastered, wages remained low, the number of landless peasants high – so high that they began to occupy lands, from which many were evicted by force and some killed – and Frei alienated a substantial part of his constituency by his land reforms, which extended to expropriation. He thereby split the right, so that in 1970 his party came bottom of the poll and Allende narrowly defeated the conservative Alessandri.

Allende's coalition had in broad terms a clear programme but it had no clear popular or parliamentary majority, its six constituent parties quickly became an uneasy team and it had the support of only some of the country's senior military figures. The coalition's broad aim was to create a socialist state on an established democratic base; the means were to be state control over foreign and domestic capitalist power centres, extensive nationalization, land reform leading to higher agricultural productivity, redistribution of wealth through tax reforms, full employment and an acceleration of Frei's educational and social programmes. These reforms, particularly the redistribution of wealth to create new purchasing power and the stemming of the outflow of profits to the United States and other foreign parts, would generate the necessary finance – an optimistic calculation.

Of the principal government parties the oldest was the Radical Party, a typical nineteenth-century, progressive, anti-clerical party which had emerged from the possessing classes (landed and mine-owning) and was in the throes of debating whether it was Marxist or not. The Chilean Communist Party was the largest and best-organized communist party in South America and was predisposed to co-operation with other parties. Allende's Socialist Party had started as a diverse group of intellectuals who attracted votes from small businesses and the teaching and other professions but were divided on the legitimacy of the use of force. Allende had some of the talents of the conjuror but after a promising start they failed him. In his first year the price of copper went up, temporarily; wages rose while prices remained stable, also temporarily; inflation was held back, again temporarily. Expropriation of US copper companies and domestic banks was popular, as was land reform until it impinged on medium as well as large proprietors. By 1972, however, economic strains caused rifts in the government between those who wanted to move faster and those who urged a touch on the brakes. Allende tried but failed to win support from the Christian Democrats. He persuaded senior officers to join his cabinet but without conciliating enough of them. He had support from the Cardinal Archbishop of Lima but not from most senior clerics. By 1973, when he was more than halfway through his term of office, his economic difficulties became critical with a lurch into serious inflation and food shortages. He alienated many by a style of living out of keeping not only with socialism but also with a usage observed by Frei, Alessandri and other presidents who had followed a Chilean tradition of living as simply in office as out of it. The parliament refused to vote tax increases or funds for subsidies or welfare, and the government's alternative – printing the money – made things worse. Restlessness in the navy and army culminated in a coup in which General Augusto Pinochet Ugarte seized power with US help. Allende committed suicide. Pinochet consolidated his success in a referendum in 1980 which gave him the presidency for a further eight years from 1981. His regime restored economic order by putting Allende's measures into reverse. It also earned for Chile international opprobrium for its fearful barbarity. Churchmen became uneasy about their association with an appalling regime; military and police chiefs became uneasy about keeping order against rising indignation and outrage; businessmen wondered whether they might not do better without Pinochet than with him. The threat to Pinochet came from these groups which wanted Pinochet's Chile without Pinochet.

In 1988 Pinochet failed to obtain a renewal of his rule beyond its term in the following year. Some 20 parties entered the lists in the ensuing elections but the effective choice lay between going back to Frei or back to Alessandri. The centre and left united round Patricio Aylwin Azocar and defeated a splintered right. Pinochet's long reign, the longest in Chile's history, ended. (He remained commander-in-chief until 1988, when he became a senator for life with immunity from prosecution in Chile for misdeeds during his presidency. For attempts to prosecute him elsewhere see p. 758). Aylwin inherited a foreign debt of $16 billion, a decline in the price of copper which accounted for half of Chile's foreign earnings, and discontent among a population which had seen the gap between rich and poor widen over Pinochet's 16 years in power and wages halved. But Pinochet, an ardent modernizer not unlike the shah in Iran, also bequeathed to his successor a promising economic legacy and Aylwin was able to hold unemployment at politically tolerable levels while achieving an annual growth rate around 5–7 per cent. The attitude of the army remained, however, ambiguous and the drift into cities foreshadowed continued instability. At elections in 1993 Frei's son defeated Alessandri for the succession to Aylwin and formed a four-party coalition, the Concertacion Democratica. Somewhat lacklustre by 2000 and internally disputatious, it lost disgruntled voters to an opposition led by Joaquin Lavin but managed to install Ricardo Lagos in the presidency, the first socialist president since Allende. In 2006 Michelle Bachelet Jeria, also a socialist, became Chile's first female president.

One item which Aylwin did not inherit from the Pinochet regime was Chile's ancient quarrel with Argentina at the southern tip of the American continent where the Beagle Channel leads from the Atlantic Ocean to the Pacific. The question was where the one ocean began and the other ended. The dispute concerned islands lying at the eastern, or Atlantic, end of the channel. In 1977 an arbitral award gave these islands to Chile but Argentina refused to accept it and staged naval and air demonstrations, to which Chile responded in kind. In 1979 both sides agreed not to prosecute their claims by force and to accept the mediation of the Vatican. In 1980 Chile again sent armed forces to the disputed area. The quarrel was settled in 1984, substantially in Chile's favour.

The three major states of South America, while occupying almost the whole of the south and east of the sub-continent, left room for seven other successors of the Spanish empire (joined in 1966 by the new state of Guyana – see the Note at the end of this part). In the north-west, where Bolivar had hoped to create a single grand Colombia, three states resulted: Colombia and its two offshoots, Venezuela and Ecuador. Colombia and Venezuela possessed exceptional wealth in two very different forms, cocaine and oil. To the south Peru and Bolivia (formerly Upper Peru) also possessed considerable mineral wealth. Bolivia lost its coastal regions to Chile in the nineteenth century.

In *Venezuela* the ruling establishment was displaced in 1945 by a coup from within itself: an alliance of army officers frustrated by the professional stagnation of their class with the mildly radical Accion Democratica led by Romulo Betancourt. Its slogans were modernization and change. It lasted three years. It achieved an initial measure of land reform but its education policies gave offence to the Church, which regarded education as an ecclesiastical preserve, and it was divided over economic policy: its more cautious members preferred to modernize agriculture rather than encourage industries which would create a politically significant urban proletariat. It was overthrown in 1948 by a counter-coup led by General Carlos Delgado Chalbaud, which inaugurated a military dictatorship that lasted for ten years, proscribed political parties and trade unions, suppressed the free press and sponsored grandiose building programmes while leaving the gap between rich and poor to widen. The most effective of the dictators of this period was Marcos Perez Jimenez (1952–58) who benefited from increasing oil revenues but failed to cope with recession in the late 1950s. A military revolt which failed was followed by strikes, fighting, the flight of the president, a transitional regime under Admiral Wolfgang Llarazabal and elections which brought the Accion Democratica and Betancourt back to power. There followed a period of civilian rule under Betancourt and five successors from, in turn, Accion Democratica and its chief rival the Social Christian Party (COPEI), the Venezuelan equivalent of Christian Democracy. All these presidents were peacefully elected and served five-year terms. This equable regime was interrupted when Perez returned to power but reverted to autocratic rule under the cloak of democracy, became embroiled in corruption, was impeached and forced to resign in disgrace. After two interim presidencies, ex-president Rafael Caldera, who had fallen out with his party, COPEI, and formed a new one, broke the mould by defeating in 1993 candidates from both COPEI and Accion Democratica. Five years later these parties joined forces to defeat Colonel Hugo Chavez Frias, who had been imprisoned after an unsuccessful coup in 1992, launched a second unsuccessful coup from jail in 1994, campaigned in 1998 with a mixture of populist and right-wing oratory and won. The older parties were becoming discredited. Chavez was a popular alternative, whose ability to check unemployment, inflation and corruption was, however, obscure. He followed the example of Fujimori in Peru by declaring liberal and democratic principles and convoked in their name a National Assembly to revise the constitution. He won nearly all the seats, secured an enabling act which allowed him to ignore the parliament, won control over the Supreme Court by dismissing some of its judges, made sweeping inroads into provincial governments and picked quarrels with Colombia (by seeking talks with the insurgent FARC – see below) and Guyana (by reviving Venezuelan claims to disputed border territory). His natural venturesomeness was dependent on the price of oil which, when high, enabled him to subsidize sympathetic politicians in other countries but, when declining, threatened Venezuela's own stability

Venezuela's mainly civilian governments secured political stability so long as they enjoyed considerable revenues from oil, iron and other natural resources, kept the goodwill of the army and – if sometimes grudgingly – the business community, and reached a compromise with the Church over education. But they produced disappointingly meagre social change, did little for labour on the land, created new jobs in manufacturing and service industries which went largely to skilled foreigners, and fell victim to the familiar boom-and-bust sequence characteristic of states whose fortunes were linked to the international price of oil. Oil was nationalized – a few years ahead of the end of existing concessions to foreign companies – but economists were divided over whether to use oil wealth to diversify the economy or to invest ever more heavily in oil and petrochemicals. In spite of growth rates of 10–15 per cent huge foreign debts were incurred and large enterprises were begun which depended for their completion on something over which Venezuela had no control. When the oil price rebounded domestic prices soared amid complaints of inefficiency in the nationalized businesses, wastefulness and corruption in the highest places, neglect of education and health, and persistent poverty. The 1990s brought serious unemployment, inflation bordering on 40 per cent, popular discontent reaching riot levels, a crime wave and the populism of Chavez, which in many ways recalled that of Perón in Argentina half a century earlier.

Elected president in 2002 Chavez was removed by the army with American encouragement but recovered his position in a few weeks. In 2003 he evicted the US military advisers who had been invited into Venezuela by his predecessors and suspended the regular discussions with the US which had been taking place for half a century. His main problem was how to outmanoeuvre the political establishment without violating the constitution or causing violent civil strife. He achieved his aim, at least temporarily, by winning election to the presidency as a preliminary to changing the constitution either by winning also the requisite parliamentary majority or – failing such a majority – by convoking a constitutional assembly to draft a revised constitution to be put to a referendum. Whatever the legal niceties such a programme was thought to make political sense. It was followed in Bolivia by Evo Morales, elected president in 2006 and in Ecuador by Rafael Correa after his election as president in 2007. In all these cases the prime motives were democratic socialist reforms (including enfranchisement or empowerment of the indigenous Indians) and hostility to the United States. This trend, together with a similar but more constrained mood in Brazil, portended a change in the political climate of Latin America but was vulnerable if it failed to bring prosperity as well as power to the people. Chavez in particular, as president of a potentially rich country, could not afford to jeopardize the wealth brought to Venezuela by its oil industry and depended for survival not only on popular acclaim but also on the price and production of oil and its sale to the United States. Venezuela's wealth worked both for and against him since, in Venezuela as elsewhere in the world, wealth tended to widen the gap between rich and poor and to nourish conspicuous corruption. While Chavez remained overwhelmingly popular with the poor he alienated not only the business class and the church but also normally left-wing students and was accused of authoritarianism – a new caudillo albeit different from the army officers and populists of an earlier generation. In 2007 Chavez failed to carry constitutional changes by referendum which would have entrenched his political position but his immediate acceptance of the result did much to blunt the charges that he was aiming for dictatorial powers. Chavez continued nevertheless to alarm enemies who accused him of fostering revolution in Latin America and squandering Venezuela's wealth on quixotic political ventures.

In external affairs successive presidents tried unsuccessfully to resolve border disputes with Colombia and Guyana and then played them down. Betancourt and his first successors made a point of alliance with democratic regimes against dictatorships but in the expansionist and ambitious 1970s Perez, who restored diplomatic relations with Cuba in 1974, cast Venezuela for a leading role in the South American–Caribbean region and the Third World. It had been a founder member of OPEC in 1960 and joined LAFTA six years later. Less happily, it was becoming by the 1990s involved in the world of the international drug trade whose centre was in neighbouring Colombia.

Before the Second World War *Colombia*, a rich country, covering over 1 million sq. km, enjoyed a reputation for political stability and measured economic progress. The latter was based on coffee, cocoa, a variety of manufacturing enterprises and a manageable foreign debt. The ruling class was divided into two parties, conservatives and liberals, and shared power on a roster system until menaced by left-wing insurgents and the dictatorship of Rojas Pinilla (1953–58). The 1950s were a time of ferocious violence, *la violencia*; in 1949 the province of Marquetalia, not many kilometres south-west of Bogotá, declared itself independent and was recovered in the 1960s only with the help of the United States. The Cuban revolution led to hopes of aid for the flagging revolutionaries, but these hopes were falsified and the Colombian revolutionaries fared only marginally better than their Venezuelan comrades. At elections in 1974 the liberal candidate Julio Cesar Turbay Ayala beat the conservative and an assortment of candidates of the left. He was succeeded by Alfonso Lopez, the first president of the Frente Nacional, an alliance of liberals and conservatives formed to defeat both the *violencia* and military dictatorship. In 1978 the conservative Belisario Betancur beat a divided opposition but was reduced by further elections in 1983 to governing with a hostile parliament. Facing the Caribbean and Central America as well as the Pacific and South America, Colombia was drawn into the politics of the area to its north and drifted into measured criticism of Reagan's policies in and around Nicaragua. By formal agreements with rebel forces Betancur tried to put an end to civil wars which had been going on for 36 years but his pacific policies did not command universal approval and a spectacular attack on the Supreme Court, in which many were killed before the attackers were forced to surrender or kill themselves, was variously interpreted as a last act of desperation by the insurrectionary M-19 movement or the recrudescence of civil war on a fiercer scale.

Civil war was waged principally by two forces: the Revolutionary Armed Forces of Colombia (FARC), formed in 1945, predominantly communist and a home-grown challenge to the established political order; and the National Liberation Army (ELN), formed in 1965, inspired partly by Castroism and partly by liberation theology and led by priests. These forces, heavily financed by the drug trade, criminal extortion and a form of regular taxation, became strong enough to carve out a state within the state but not strong enough to overthrow the legitimate state. From the mid-1980s another force emerged: small anti-guerrilla groups, mainly in the north, which ten years later coalesced as the Colombian Self-Defence Force (AUC), loosely, if at all, allied with the government and notorious for committing appalling massacres. The disintegration of the state and its authority contributed largely to the independence and prosperity of the drug cartels which became Colombia's most successful enterprise. Their chiefs established themselves not only as men of enormous wealth ostentatiously displayed but also as another, or overlapping state within the state in the north-western parts of the country, including the cities of Medellín and Cali, where they ruled with the help of Israeli, British and other mercenaries and provided more jobs and better pay than did the government in its own sphere of competence. The economic empire of these drug barons depended primarily on their markets in the United States where, for a time, US agencies were less alive to the dangers of flooding the market with poisonous drugs than to the opportunities of taking part of the profits to finance US policies against Nicaragua: many blind eyes were turned until the murder in 1989 of Luis Carlos Galan, likely to be the next president of Colombia, concentrated attention on the slide, not into anarchy, but to the capture of the state by a sinister cartel whose single aim was money. President Virgilio Barco Vargas promised tough action and President Bush promised lavish help, but the former was reluctant to accept the latter's offer of military support, which was distasteful to many Colombians. Some 12,000 persons were arrested but hardly anyone of consequence. The United States pressed for the extradition of senior malefactors but the barons replied with a threat to kill judges, magistrates and children for every operator extradited. Since more than 50 judges had already been murdered the threat was plausible. In 1987 the Supreme Court of Colombia invalidated an extradition treaty of 1979 with the United States. The question of whether to negotiate with the insurgents became an overriding issue in Colombian politics. The main antagonists – the government and the FARC – reckoned that neither could win outright victory. The FARC and ELN had become more than guerrillas, but although they were winning battles they were still unable to capture cities and had little or no prospect of supplanting the government. President Cesar Gaviria Trujillo (1990–94) promised to do no deals. President Ernesto Samper (1994–98) was accused by the United States of being in their pockets and berated by his own chief of staff General Harold Bedoya for treasonable dealings with them. In the presidential election of 1998 Bedoya won only 2 per cent of the vote and the winner, Andres Pastrana Arango, lost no time in seeking a deal with the FARC. He accepted the FARC's pre-conditions: withdrawal of all government forces and police from a large zone to the south of Bogotá and active government operations against the AUC. Pastrana had support from Clinton although much congressional and public opinion in the United States continued to brand the FARC as stereotypical communists and terrorists up to their necks in the drug business while the legitimate government was becoming irrelevant to a civil war between the FARC and the AUC. The election in 2002 of the comparatively young Alvaro Uribe Velez, a former mayor of Medellin, to the presidency and his re-election in 2004 and 2006 seemed to presage a return to law and order in what had become a country split into two.

Southward from Colombia the Andean republics of Ecuador, Peru and Bolivia displayed the troubled swings between civilian and military rule and the scarcely less troubled problems of joint military–civilian alliances. *Peru* had an extra-parliamentary governing class and a parliamentary world of political parties; it had also a modern or modernizing economic sector and an impoverished economy distinct from this sector. These political and economic worlds were themselves divided. The governing class, held together by a common conservative outlook and by marriage, comprised army officers and large landowners and the more eminent bankers and businessmen. The army, however, contained a radical wing which did not subscribe to all the values of the conservative establishment. The outstanding political party was the Peruvian Aprista Party (APRA), founded in the 1920s with a semi-socialist programme, regarded by conservatives as deeply dangerous and tainted with a willingness to resort to violence. By 1945 it was forswearing violence and moving towards the centre, partly because its stance in the 1920s and 1930s condemned it to nearly permanent opposition and partly in order to compete for votes with the less radical Accion Popular. These parties manoeuvred for power against one another and also with, but at arm's length from, the holders of military and economic power, who were frequently in two minds about whether to use their power indirectly through a political party or directly by occupying the presidency and other public offices. The mainstays of the economy were agricultural (cotton and sugar) but oil was becoming increasingly important. Their development required foreign, in effect United States, capital, which was as unpopular as it was necessary. Nearly half the population were Indians, deprived and despised, and another third mestizos.

In 1948 a military coup led by General Manuel Odria ousted the APRA government of José Luis Bustamente (president from 1946) and forced the Aprista leader Victor Raul Haya della Torre to flee for safety to the Colombian embassy where he remained for several years before departing into exile in Italy. After holding power for eight repressive years, Odria allowed elections to precede the transfer of power to Manuel Prado, a member of one of Lima's most exalted banking families, but a surprising number of votes were cast for Fernando Belaúnde Terry, an architect by profession and leader of Accion Popular, who was presented as a new force between the old APRA left and the military–oligarchic complex. When presidential and congressional elections came round again in 1962 Belaúnde stood against Odria and Haya della Torre. None of the candidates won outright; the army stepped in to block both Odria and Haya della Torre and declared the elections fraudulent for no discernibly adequate reason. After an interval of rule by a military junta the elections were rerun and Belaúnde was declared the winner in a close contest between Accion Popular and APRA. Belaúnde was no conservative but from the army's point of view he was a safe man and political opinion within the army had been shifting for an accumulation of reasons: contempt for corruption in the civilian business elite, a desire for modernization in the armed forces and also outside them, alarm at the persistence of guerrilla risings, the drift of the destitute to Lima and riots in the capital, seizures of land in the interior. The elections of 1963 registered, if still tentatively, a new political configuration with a section of the army willing to back significant change and Belaúnde willing to enlist military support for a progressive programme.

Risings in the 1950s had been scattered and easily suppressed. Their leaders were divided and, as in Venezuela, the communists among them were averse to guerrilla operations – in this case partly because the most notable guerrilla chief, Hugo Blanco, was a Trotskyist and partly because the communists were split between Russian and Chinese factions. But in the 1960s insurrection revived, so much so that in 1965 the United States intervened with a special military corps, much resented by the Peruvian military. Belaúnde's government failed to defeat or appease the rebels. His economic programme, another failure, forced him to devalue the currency in 1967 by 40 per cent. Most conspicuously and ultimately fatal was his inept handling of the oil problem.

The International Petroleum Company (IPC) was the most prominent example of the importance of foreign capital for Peru and correspondingly offensive to Peruvian pride. Earlier governments had tried to milk the company without going to the lengths of expropriating it (and having to run it). Its presence was the one issue on which the far right, the far left and government could speak in unison, laying blame for poor economic performance on foreigners. The company had been established in Peru soon after the First World War under an agreement which was probably made in breach of Peruvian law but was nevertheless plain as between the company and the Peruvian state. The resulting legal imbroglio gave rise to a series of disputes with the United States as well as the company. Belaúnde struck a deal with the company on outstanding disputes but so secretively and open to misinterpretation that its formal adoption by the Act of Talara was greeted with scandalized outrage and was discussed by a conclave of generals who decided that Belaúnde must go. By this time Belaúnde had been forced to seek a coalition with APRA and in doing so had split his own party as well as forfeiting his military support. He fled the country. The succeeding regimes wrecked the Peruvian economy.

This time the army did not look for a civilian partner but decided to shoulder the entire responsibility of government. General Juan Velasco Alvarado, with the enthusiastic support of a group of radical colonels and the more measured support of disillusioned conservatives, took power with promises of economic and social reform and greater efficiency and integrity, but his government came under immediate strain from the inherited IPC issue and, opting for complete expropriation, lost its less radical component. It antagonized the United States by declaring a 200-mile fishing limit and firing on a United States vessel in the course of enforcing it. Social reform, which was presumed to include an extension of political power and economic well-being to the poorer classes, was another source of uneasiness between the radicals and others; it was also dependent on economic growth from, in particular, exports of copper and other minerals, which failed to come up to expectations.

The Peruvian course from 1968 was an experiment, under strongly centralized and military direction, to introduce economic planning and a measure of social reform within a capitalist framework (from which, however, foreign capital had been extruded) with the emphasis on technological and managerial innovation in the service of industry and exports. Velasco himself was a nationalist hostile to US penetration of Peru, a man of the mild right but born outside the dominant oligarchy. A number of his army and civilian supporters were radicals as hostile to the oligarchy as to the United States. The regime had therefore an innate instability which afflicted it when its first achievements gave way to ideological division and were clouded by economic strains. In spite of initially broad agreement on a programme of nationalization (which included the IPC) and land reform, Velasco lost the support of the principal political groups which had helped him to power and felt compelled to seek instead a popular base outside the political establishment. In moving to the left he lost more than he gained, particularly because land reform, although far from insignificant, fell short of expectations and so prevented him from winning peasant and student suffrages. By 1973 both these groups were joining in riots against the government which stiffened their right-wing enemies within it. Conservatives, encouraged by the Pinochet coup in Chile, were further alarmed by the economic consequences of world recession which, in 1974, hit Peru at a time when the president fell seriously ill. The piling up of foreign debt in earlier years and a sharp deterioration in the balance of payments were countered by disagreeable measures which were blamed on left-wing incompetence. A bloodless conservative coup removed Velasco in 1975 and promoted his prime minister General Francisco Morales Bermudez to the presidency. But the military were tiring of grappling with the tasks of government and taking the blame for its failures. A return to civilian rule seemed expedient and after an election in 1980 Belaúnde returned to the presidential palace from which he had fled 12 years earlier. But the 1980s were a bad time to shoulder public responsibilities. Rising inflation and other economic pains fostered discontent among the middle classes and the Indian peasantry and created the Sendero Luminoso – a small army of about 5,000 recruited chiefly among the rural poor and led by a rigid Marxist and visionary mestizo Abimael Guzman Reynoso, called President Gonzalo. In 1985 APRA captured the presidency and announced that it would limit debt-service charges to a fixed percentage of the national product. The new president Alan Garcia set a centre-left course flavoured with anti-Washington gestures. But the dirty war went on with multiple murders, torture and unaccountable 'disappearances' of people whom the army or police did not like. Economic distress went on too: inflation at incalculable levels, a large budget deficit, and the suspension by the World Bank and the Inter-American Bank of their lines of credit. Garcia was soon at odds with the army. He proposed to give it one instead of three places in his cabinet, to reform military administration and cut the army's share (40 per cent) of government spending, and to investigate the massacre of 300 persons in a Lima prison allegedly by the army. The armed forces and the political right, with covert United States support, undermined Garcia's government and then overthrew it. Few regretted it, for Garcia had alienated the poor as well as infuriating and alarming the rich.

Garcia (president 1985–90) left Peru in even worse shape than it had been when he was elected president. With his own party, APRA, discredited and his most eminent opponent, Belaúnde, offering nothing much, the country hankered for a new man. In the elections it got a choice between two: Mario Vargas Llosa, well-known man of letters who had moved from left- to right-wing indignation, and Alberto Fujimori, politically ambiguous businessman of Japanese descent. Vargas won a slight but insufficient lead in the first round but after a peculiarly vicious interval Fujimori soared to a convincing victory. Vargas failed to attract the Peruvian *homme moyen* and scared many potential supporters by visions of austerity to come. Fujimori promised solutions to Peru's main problems without being too specific about the means. Once elected, he reversed Garcia's refusal to honour foreign debts, reversed Peru's decline in output, reduced inflation from the astronomic to the merely large, and put Gonzalo in prison. He also suspended the constitution, dispensed with parliament, interfered with the judiciary, arrested political opponents and suppressed the press. In 1995 he was re-elected, obliterating the former UN secretary-general Javier Perez de Cuellar. Fujimori's unexpected successes pointed to changes in Peruvian society which had gone unnoticed and were submerging the established party pattern. The parties faded away. So too did the Sendero Luminoso. But urban revolt did not. In 1997 Peru commanded worldwide attention when the Tupac Amaru, a small group of urban guerrillas, invaded a party at the Japanese embassy in Lima and took hundreds of guests hostage in an attempt to secure the release from jail of 400 of their fellows. Fujimori refused to meet their demands and was dissuaded from storming the embassy, which was besieged for two months with a dwindling number of captives inside in considerable discomfort. His resolution won him popularity which he forfeited by authoritarianism and corruption, becoming increasingly dependent on the goodwill of the army. He was emboldened to repeat his (unconstitutional) re-election by changing the rules before the next election in 2000. A majority of the judges on the Supreme Court complied; the rest were dismissed. But Fujimori overplayed his hand and was forced to flee. A commission of inquiry (2003) into Peru's misfortunes severely criticized three past presidents and put deaths in civil strife in recent years at 69,000.

Bolivia's social configuration differed from its neighbours' because Victor Paz Estensoro had led as early as 1952 a successful revolt in which communists, Trotskyists and non-communists (including junior army officers), appalled by corruption and inefficiency, injustice and poverty, had participated. The regime nationalized Bolivia's extensive tin mines, broke up large estates, gave Indians (60 per cent of the population) the vote and attempted to diversify the economy in order to reduce the country's dependence on mining, but it quickly ran into economic trouble aggravated by a slump in the price of tin and the leadership split. Paz was succeeded in 1956 by his one-time ally Hernan Siles Zuazo; he returned to office in 1960 but was exiled in 1964 after a coup by General Alfredo Ovando Candia. In 1967 the existence of guerrilla activities was made world-famous by the arrest and trial of the French writer Regis

Debray (committed to prison for 30 years) and the death in Bolivia of Che Guevara. Government was weakened by conflict between Ovando and the titular civilian president René Barrientos and in 1969, a few months after the latter's death, Ovando installed a purely military regime and embarked on policies partly borrowed from Juan Velasco Alvarado's populist regime in Peru. Military rule over the next 15 years was marked by feuds among the generals themselves, their growing involvement in the drugs trade and frequent coups. Only General Hugo Banzer provided (1971–78) some stability at a price (brutality and censorship). In 1978 he permitted elections which marked the beginning of a return to civilian rule. The veteran Siles won the election but was not permitted to take office. In the next year Bolivia had its first female president in Lidia Gueiler Tejido, who was expelled in her turn by a coalition of right-wing officers and drug traffickers who, under the aegis of another two military presidents, conducted a fresh regime of terror and torture. In 1982 Siles returned, half-applauded by the United States. He was again followed by Paz and then by General Sanchez de Lozada campaigning with an Indian vice-presidential partner. Hyperinflation was tackled by methods which produced hyper-unemployment and in 1997 Banzer – now a civilian – became president once more after an election in which his mere 22 per cent of the votes sufficed to defeat his numerous opponents. The growth in the 1980s of the drug business caused the United States to send troops and detectives to suppress it – an intervention much resented, particularly by coca farmers and their friends in the army. United States material and financial aid was much less resented, particularly in the same quarters. In the most significant change since 1952 Evo Morales was elected president in 2006, pledged to end poverty and the dominion of rich Hispanics, a recruit to the new wave of indigenous Indian power. But by 2008 Morales was facing demands for autonomy or independence from the less impoverished provinces of his country and a campaign to secure the revocation of his presidential office.

In *Ecuador* the military seized power in 1976 but held it only briefly, making way in 1979 for a left coalition led by Jaime Roldos Aquilera, who was killed in an air accident two years later. Political power oscillated between left-centre and right-centre as no party commanded a parliamentary majority and the austere rectitude of market economics provoked popular discontents and riots. Ecuador disputed with Peru an area believed to contain valuable minerals and oil. This dispute had been settled by a treaty in 1942, which was denounced by Roldos in 1960. The borderlands remained unruly. In 1992 President Fujimori of Peru on a visit to Quito accepted a proposal for mediation by the Vatican but in 1995 Peruvian forces provoked serious armed clashes. In the same year financial scandals caused the flight of the vice-president and fears for the continuance of civilian rule. Elections in 1996 made Abdala Bucaram Ortiz president. His roots were thin (he was of Lebanese origin) and regional (in the coastlands but not in the Indian uplands) and his undignified eccentricities enabled his enemies to label him mad: one of these eccentricities was to call himself mad. He was forced to flee after a year. In 1998 President Jamil Mahuad Witt settled the dispute with Peru but was overwhelmed by economic problems created by his predecessors' improvidence, falls in the price of oil and natural calamities. After a futile attempt to maintain the currency by spending $200 million the link with the US dollar was temporarily abandoned and the exchange value of the currency halved in a week. Inflation approached 50 per cent but the president's attempts to get help from the IMF were thwarted as the parliament tried to insist on a spendthrift budget and Ecuador defaulted on its foreign debts. The net results of these troubles were chaotic disorders, an increase in the political power of the army and encouragement for the militancy of the disgruntled Indian half of the population. The election of Rafael Correa to the presidency aligned Ecuador with the reforming regimes of Venezuela and Bolivia and increased friction with the United States over the use of bases by US forces. As South America's second exporter of oil (mainly to the US) Correa's Ecuador inclined to the brisker pace and brasher tone of domestic radicalism and foreign confrontation, subject however to the caveats which applied to Venezuela.

South America, nearly twice the size of Europe, and divided into only ten states, continued nevertheless to play a secondary role in world affairs, engrossed in domestic problems (social and economic) but active in the United Nations whence it might with changing preoccupations venture more weightily upon the global field as North America did in the proto-globalizing era which followed the American Civil War.

CHAPTER 28

Central America

Mexico, like Canada, may be destined for embrace in a North American economic zone dominated by the United States but between Mexico and the United States there is a historic feud which is more easily forgotten in the latter than in the former. Mexico lost Texas to the United States in 1836. Ten years later US troops occupied Mexico City. One-third of what was then Mexico became the southwestern United States. In 1862 a French debt-collecting expedition (with British and Spanish encouragement) turned into an imperial adventure and created a short-lived Mexican empire with an Austrian archduke as emperor. This regime was followed after a short interval by the dictatorship of Porfirio Diaz, which lasted from 1876 to 1910 with only one four-year interlude. His remorseless, modernizing rule ended in revolution and seven years of civil war in which the United States intervened on the side of counter-revolution and a war between Mexico and the United States was only narrowly avoided. The long dictatorship of Diaz was succeeded by the even longer rule of a single party called, eventually, the Partido Revolucionario Institucional (PRI) and committed to social mobility and economic reform. But the years eroded the party's revolutionary zeal, it never grasped the nettles of taxing the rich and reforming a notoriously inefficient agriculture, and it became the political vehicle of the well-to-do. In 1938 President Lazaro Cardenas nationalized oil reserves and the oil industry. Presidents succeeded one another decorously and constitutionally and by the end of the Second World War Mexico was a stable country under civilian rule. Relations with the United States had proceeded to a dignified wariness.

Mexico declared war on Germany, Italy and Japan in 1942 and sent an air contingent to the Philippines. After the war it played a leading part in establishing an inter-American security system: by the Treaty of Chapultepec (which is in Mexico) the American states agreed to mutual consultation if the borders of any one of them were infringed and envisaged joint action up to and including the use of force; the Treaty of Rio in 1947 made more precise provision for the peaceful settlement of disputes and collective defence; and these agreements culminated in the creation in 1948 of the Organization of American States (OAS). Foreign leaders paid attention to Mexico. All United States presidents from F. D. Roosevelt onwards visited it and so did all French presidents from de Gaulle onwards. In regional affairs Mexico ostracized Cuba in 1962 but reversed this attitude in 1975; it joined Venezuela and other American states in attempts to restore Cuba to inter-American respectability and to settle the war in Nicaragua; it condemned Pinochet's Chile and sympathized – sometimes sided – with left-wing movements in Central America; its professed aims included the reduction of United States and Russian influence south of the Rio Grande; it refused to accept a US military mission (1951) and openly criticized US actions and judgements in Guatemala, Cuba and Nicaragua; it was a sponsor of the Treaty of Tlatelolco in 1967, which essayed to ban nuclear weapons in the sub-continent; and, principally as a consequence of its oil wealth, it established links with other oil producers, notably Nigeria, while refusing to become a member of OPEC.

From around mid-century the Mexican economy was transformed by a policy of industrialism, urbanization and an extended internationalization designed to reduce the country's dependence on foreign economies while at the same time securing the external finance required to promote and sustain industrial growth. Employment in manufacturing industry passed the level of employment in agriculture. Foreign earnings grew with oil exports but these accounted for no more than a third of the total, in which cotton, coffee and sugar were substantial earners. Growth, already substantial during the war years, continued and enabled Mexico for a time to take an unprecedented demographic explosion in its stride. It was accompanied by a shift from military to civilian rule but not any relaxation of the entrenched single-party regime of the PRI. During the 1970s, however, progress was assailed from many quarters: world recession and domestic inflation, inadequate creation or investment of domestic capital, inadequate training or recruitment of skilled labour, a serious decline of food production, heavy external indebtedness and debits on external trade, increasingly obvious maldistribution of wealth, particularly in the south, where most of the Indian population lived without a sight of the benefits of economic growth: something like nine-tenths of the country's wealth was owned by fewer than half a million persons out of a total of 85 million.

These failings were partially masked by oil. By 1980 Mexico was producing 2.5 million barrels a day, exporting more than half of it (and half of these exports to the United States), had proved reserves of 60 billion barrels and actual reserves three or four times larger, and ranked sixth among the world's oil giants. But the lure of oil enticed governments into an extravagant pursuit of growth and, when the oil boom stopped booming, into debt. Distress and discontent, which exploded shockingly with a massacre of young demonstrators at Tlatelolco in 1968 on the eve of the Olympic Games in Mexico City, combined with economic disappointments and general unease to compel a thorough review. This produced in 1982 a devaluation of the currency by 70 per cent, the nationalization of the banks, a reduction of real wages by nearly half over the next five years, cuts in education, health and other public services and a culture increasingly attuned to short-term speculation rather than long-term growth. Miguel de la Madrid Hurtado, a gifted politician and economist and Harvard graduate,

28.1 Central America

elected president in 1982 at the age of 47, faced a collapsing peso, rising unemployment, clamps on public capital spending and oil-fed corruption. He was able to strike
a bargain with the IMF which secured to Mexico a loan of $3.4 billion and the resched-
uling of half of its external debt of $96 billion, but Mexico failed to meet the conditions
attached to the agreement and the IMF was about to rescind it when in 1985 an earthquake of appalling force struck Mexico City and made any tightening of the screws
temporarily inopportune. Even with half its debt rescheduled Mexico would need for
the rest of the century about $6 billion to cover interest on, and piecemeal repayment
of, the other half – sums which would have to come, by agreement or default, from
foreign creditor banks in so far as oil revenues failed to provide them. Relief, assessed
at $3.6 billion a year for 30 years, was provided by an agreement reached with its

creditors in 1990 under the Brady Plan (see Chapter 5). President de la Madrid was succeeded by Carlos Salinas de Gortari, another Harvard graduate, who had the misfortune to see the ruling party lose a provincial governorship for the first time in more than half a century. The PRI's hold on power began to seem questionable but for a time Salinas achieved a degree of popularity denied to his predecessors. Although mechanization and modernization of industry and poor education kept unemployment high, and privatization enriched only a privileged oligarchy, Salinas pruned foreign debt and the state's overblown involvement in inefficient enterprises, reduced inflation below 10 per cent and turned the budget deficit into an unprecedented surplus. The projected North American Free Trade Area (NAFTA) offered Mexicans legitimate opportunities for work north of the Rio Grande. President Bush delayed action on it during his election campaign in 1992 to the chagrin of the Mexican government, whose economic programme, including growth at 6 per cent a year, depended heavily on US investment in Mexico, but Clinton succeeded in securing Congressional approval for it. Initially, Mexican exports to the United States grew faster than trade in the opposite direction but its benefits were unevenly distributed geographically and barely apparent to smaller businesses.

Although a moderate reformer, Salinas was also involved in, or connived at, some of the vices which he wished to reform – corruption, torture, political murder and the use of Mexico by Colombian drug dealers – and when his term ended in 1994 he betook himself to Ireland. In that year the Mexican regime was badly bruised by two events: open revolt in the southern province of Chiapas and the assassination of the PRI's candidate for the presidency, Luis Donaldo Colosio. Chiapas had been in ferment for many years. At the core of its troubles were the destitution and despair of recently emancipated serfs and landless peasants, mostly Mayas. Their sense of grievance and isolation was accentuated by their speaking little or no Spanish and their poverty by the collapse in 1989 of the price of coffee. Their plight won support from the Bishop of S. Cristobel Samuel Ruez and generated in 1992 the Zepetiste National Liberation Army (ZNLA) which, led by Subcomandante Marcos, demanded land reform and civil rights and implementation of the 1917 constitution. Marcos was ambivalent about the use of violence but protest was inflamed by the evident growth of corruption, drug trafficking and the mismanagement of the public finances which, after the murder of Colossio, forced the government to close financial markets and the United States to extend a credit of $6 billion quickly and publicly.

A few months later the PRI retained the presidency and a majority in the parliament although with a bare majority of the popular vote and amid open cynicism about the working of Mexican democracy. The new president Ernesto Zedillo Ponce de Leon, although belittled as less exciting than his predecessors, seemed a safe choice in troubled times. The economy, however, was more troubled than safe and confidence in the government's handling of it low. Zedillo was at heart a reformer but reform created recession and severer unemployment. Financial institutions, including the banks, were shaky. His recourse to the IMF entailed promises to limit wage increases and redress the budget deficit by privatizing public enterprises – promises easier to make than fulfil when trade unions were clamouring for better pay and purchasers of state industries were few and mean. A spate of imports was playing havoc with the balance of payments, an unexpectedly sharp devaluation of the peso at the end of 1994 was interpreted as panic and interest rates rose to 40 per cent. Devaluation was accompanied by the issue of dollar-linked securities (in exchange for short government bonds) but the total of these *tesobonos* quickly exceeded the country's foreign reserves. To prevent the collapse of the peso, of United States banks involved in Mexico and of United States exports to Mexico, Clinton contrived with the IMF and the Bank for International Settlements a supporting guarantee of $50 billion to which the United States promised $20 billion, secured on Mexican oil reserves. But the Mexican crisis called in question the ability of international finance to meet such a crisis and therewith the willingness of financiers worldwide to support Latin American governments pursuing economic policies dependent on foreign loans and investment. The collapse of the Mexican peso dismayed all Latin American countries, where economic growth was desperately needed for its own economic ends and as a prerequisite for political stability. In Mexico the gap between rich and poor widened, that between poverty and starvation closed and insurrection became more widespread and better armed. This dual instability threatened the future of a country whose problems, although massive, were also easily intelligible since they proceeded not from inherent poverty but from the mismanagement of potential wealth and the sclerosis of almost a century of one-party rule. The PRI blocked moves towards anything more than the appearance of a multiparty system and in 1997 it lost its control of the Congress (winning only 38 per cent of the vote) and the mayoralty of Mexico City to Cuauhatemco Cardenas Solorzano, half-Indian descendant of the famous former president. Insurrection spread from Chiapas to other provinces, abuses of human rights became more frequent and severe, the country was playing a growing role in the international drug trade and the political power of an army increased to 175,000 became more prominent. The multiplication of parties increased the opportunities and the temptations for the exercise of military power in politics and decreased the likelihood of a clear victory for the PRI in the elections due in 2000. However the party made unexpected gains and Vicente Fox Quesada continued the run of PRI presidents, but in 2005 its candidate Andres Obrador, a former mayor of Mexico city, was narrowly defeated into third place and Felix Calderon of the National Action Party (PAN) became president with what consequences remained to be seen. The Mexican constitution barred a president from a second consecutive term.

As Mexico narrows southward almost all of its land border is shared with *Guatemala*. (British Honduras, independent as Belize from 1981, has a short border with Mexico as well as a longer, disputed border with Guatemala.) For over 100 years (1838–1944) Guatemala was ruled by four military dictators with short intervals of civil governments.

In 1944 the army was divided and a group of junior officers supported a comparatively left-wing candidate, Juan José Arévalo, who was president until 1950. Continuing division in the army was represented by the rivalry between two majors, Francisco Xavier Arana and Jacobo Arbenz Gúzman. The former was assassinated in 1949 and the latter won the election of 1950. This victory caused alarm in the United States, where the new regime was regarded as pro-communist and a threat to the Panama Canal. It was an enemy of foreign capitalists and especially of the United Fruit Company, which, as the owner of a tenth of the country's land, exercised even more economic power in Guatemala than the Anglo-Iranian Oil Company in Iran and stood in the way of essential land reform.

The Guatemalans, 10 million people, of whom over half were of Indian stock, suffered from extremes of poverty, disease and social inattention, which were rendered the more intolerable by the prosperity of a small minority and the economic omnipresence of foreign enterprises, which owned not only an abundance of land but also the railways, docks and public utilities. Arbenz accelerated his predecessor's reform programme; he nationalized uncultivated land and supported strikes against foreign concerns. These moves were interpreted in Washington as the beginnings of a fully fledged communist policy, notwithstanding that communists were greatly outnumbered by anti-communists in the Guatemalan government, parliament and civil service and that power lay with an anti-communist army. So long as Truman was president the United States waged veiled economic war but refused to go further. Eisenhower and Dulles, however, resorted to (vicarious) armed force. At the tenth inter-American conference at Caracas in 1954 Dulles tried to get a condemnation of the Arbenz regime but discovered that no other state accepted Washington's interpretation of events in Guatemala. The conference passed a general resolution condemning communist domination of any American state but refused to single out Guatemala, and Dulles thereupon left Caracas abruptly and turned to conspiring with disaffected Guatemalans who were preparing to invade their country from Honduras and Nicaragua. These two countries, having complained of communist incursions from Guatemala, were provided with arms from the United States, while Washington tried to prevent Guatemala from getting arms by appealing to its allies not to supply them and by intercepting communist shipments from Europe. Three months after the Caracas conference Guatemala was invaded and Arbenz was forced to resign. The leader of the invasion, Colonel Carlos Castillo Armas, succeeded him and retained office until he was assassinated in 1957. The annual rate of growth of the Guatemalan economy fell from 8.5 per cent (over 1944–54) to 3 per cent and under Castillo's successors Guatemala lived in a state of suppressed civil war.

Castillo was succeeded by General Miguel Ydígoras Fuentes, who was duly installed as president in 1958 after two disorderly elections. His power was confirmed by a fraudulent election in 1961 but riots, repressed by the army, demonstrated a dependence which he was not wise enough to acknowledge. Military opinion turned against him on the grounds that he spent too much money on himself and too little on the armed forces. In 1962 the army defended him against an attempted coup by the air force, but turned against him when he allowed Arévalo to return to Guatemala and campaign for the presidency. Arévalo, who seemed certain to win a fair election, was regarded as a reincarnation of Arbenz, and in 1963 the army ejected Ydígoras and suspended the constitution. The army tolerated the election in 1965 of the comparatively liberal Julio Cesar Mendez Montenegro, but he was no more able than his more oppressive predecessors to pacify the country. A motley and divided opposition, consisting of communists, Trotskyists and guerrillas who were neither, staged unsuccessful risings and resorted to murder and kidnapping when their risings failed. US forces helped the government. A US ambassador was among those assassinated.

In the 1970s nominal control was shared between the army and civilian parties, with left-wing parties proscribed. A number of officers went into business and became rich, thus earning the jealousy of other officers and attracting charges of corruption. Elections in 1974 were contested by three candidates, of whom the youngest – Colonel Efrain Rios Montt, a passionate Protestant – won but was shouldered out of the way by his elders. The military were divided between hardliners who saw only guerrillas and, on the other hand, a more enlightened minority who saw also widespread poverty and injustice and, at the centre, corruption. Faction was added to violence, corruption and economic collapse. Abuses of power became so gross that in 1977 Carter stopped US aid (it was resumed in 1981 by Reagan). Elections in 1978 gave the presidency to Romero Lucas Garcia, a right-wing general of peculiar brutality who eradicated villages but not guerrillas: his brutality was directed with apparently genocidal purpose against the Indian half of the population. He was ousted in 1982 by Rios Montt, who promised to end private murder, civil war and financial scandals but was himself ousted in the next year with these promises unfulfilled. He was followed by General Oscar Mejia Victores, who devoted himself to the suppression of the left in his own country but showed less interest in conflicts beyond his borders, for which, indeed, Guatemala had limited resources to spare. A nominal reversion to civilian rule in 1985 left the army unfettered, President Vinicio Cerezo being little more than a figurehead who might be saddled with the blame for economic chaos. He edged away from Washington's anti-Sandinista policy in Nicaragua and collaborated with other Central American presidents in seeking peace with the Nicaraguan regime, reconciling President Duarte of Salvador with President Ortega of Nicaragua and ending the Contras' use of Costa Rica as part of a pincer attack on Nicaragua. In elections in 1990 a dozen candidates took the field, ranging from extreme right to centre-right. Rios Montt, declared constitutionally ineligible by the Supreme Court, backed Jorge Elias Sarrano, a Protestant and the candidate of middle-class business, who won on the second round with fewer than half the votes cast. In 1993 he clashed with the vice-president and the military and fled to Panama. Ramiro de Leon Carpio, a civil rights leader, emerged as the next president. He failed to stem the excesses of ordinary criminals or psychopathic officials and officers. In 1995 Rios Montt was again disqualified. His protégé Alfonso Portillo lost the election but won in 1999. Civil war subsided but did not end. Its roots had been planted in the mid-1950s by young people who, under mainly Christian leadership, set out to establish rural communities on reclaimed land but were converted by official persecution into a partly missionary, partly militant movement. It was brutally attacked by the army, which deployed 40,000 troops, destroyed 4–5,000 villages, killed tens of thousands of people and rendered at least half a million homeless. After the most punishing attacks in 1980–84 the militants were reduced to about 2,000, the visionaries lost their illusions of bringing peace to Guatemala and the country was split between bitter indignation and brutal repression. In 1996 President Alvaro Arzu took the crucial step of talking to rebel leaders and so brought these wars to a formal conclusion. But bitterness and mistrust remained. Another bishop, a supporter of groups trying to heal by laying bare the enormities of the past, was murdered. Some 200,000 persons had been killed in what was not so much a war as a series of military razzias against Indians and middle-class civilians over more than thirty years.

On the Pacific coast of Central America south of Guatemala the small and once wealthy state of *El Salvador* was wrecked by civil strife. A standard military dictatorship under General José Maria Lemus was modified in 1961 by the installation of a middle-of-the-road government under General Julio Rivera which adopted a programme of social reform and economic investment which, if inadequate in the eyes of the left, nevertheless made a substantial step away from the narrow conservatism of past rulers. But the modest hopes raised by this change proved illusory and during the 1970s violence erupted between the government and left-wing guerrillas of the Farabondo Marti Liberation Front (FMLF), the militant arm of a broad political left moved to extreme action in protest against a narrow oligarchical style and economic failings. The inauguration in 1977 of President Carlos Humberto Rovero was boycotted by the clergy in protest against the violence and torture practised by the regime itself and in 1979 a coup by junior officers installed a new government pledged to moderate agrarian reform and the nationalization of selected financial and commercial concerns. But this mildly right-wing government failed to control extreme right-wing terrorism. The murder in 1980 of the archbishop of San Salvador typified growing anarchy and a polarization to extremes which left the government stranded in the middle. The United States, fearing that the extreme left might prevail, supported the government as a lesser evil and tried to persuade Guatemala and Honduras to intervene should the government collapse and the extreme left take power, but neither country was keen to denude its domestic position by sending troops abroad.

With the election of Reagan in 1980 El Salvador became a piece in an obsessive US policy of overthrowing the government of Nicaragua and helping any Central American government of the right. The FMLF was stigmatized as a terrorist organization and Reagan certified, in the face of ample evidence to the contrary, that the Salvadorean government's record in human rights was satisfactory and its army under government control. But in spite of increased American aid President Napoleon

Duarte was unable to suppress the Front or break free from the extreme right which in 1982 won more seats than the president's party of the less ferocious right. Robert d'Aubuisson was elected president but was persuaded under pressure from Washington to give way to the more respectable Alvaro Mangana. Another election two years later was similarly indecisive between Duarte and d'Aubuisson. Mounting guerrilla successes during 1984 were countered by more American aid in money, helicopters and weaponry. If, as seemed to be the case, Duarte genuinely wished to treat with the insurgents and introduce some reforms he was thwarted by continuing civil war of a peculiarly nasty kind in which the greater proportion of the killings were the work of right-wing squads belonging to the army or more loosely connected with it. In 1985 Duarte prevailed over the extreme right and so won room to manoeuvre for peace with the left, provided the terms were acceptable to the holders of ultimate power, the army. But he remained uncomfortably wedged between two extremes, his authority more nominal than real, a spent force (in health as well as politically) and the ineffectual arbiter of a war which cost his small country at least 50,000 lives in 12 years. The guerrillas, in spite of maintaining a threat, failed to incite a broad popular revolt and were reduced to a few thousand against an army of 50,000 with US aid amounting to $1 million a day. The military and political wings of the left were divided on whether to negotiate with Duarte; on the right the military and their paramilitary accessories or death squads were out of control and perpetrated indiscriminate massacres. Attempts from 1986 to arrange a ceasefire came to nothing. Elections in 1989 were won by d'Aubuisson's Arena Party, which installed Alfredo Cristiani as president but lost its parliamentary majority in 1991. The death squads were no more responsive to Cristiani than they had been to Duarte. US aid was increased but failed to ensure either of its professed aims – stability and democracy. In 1991–92 UN intervention secured a ceasefire, disengagement of armed forces and an agreement for the creation of a new police force and the absorption of the guerrilla units into the regular army. The FMLF gradually demobilized under UN supervision. Elections in 1994 gave Arena a comfortable win, endorsed by the UN; but three years later the FMLF came only one seat short of Arena and was able to form a left-centre government; in 1999 power swung back to the right but the FMLF fragmented and Arena won a comfortable victory in 2005. This instability reflected repeated economic disappointment rather than ideological mutations.

Internationally, the gravest commotions in Central America occurred in *Nicaragua* following the collapse in 1979 of the dictatorship of the Somoza dynasty which had lasted for nearly 50 years. This dynasty stemmed from General Anastasio Somoza Garcia, who seized power with the help of the United States in 1930. He and his son Luis, who succeeded him in 1956, ruled in alliance with the prosperous landowning and business classes but after the latter's death in 1967 his brother Anastasio Somoza Debayle alienated and even scandalized these allies by the brutality and corruption of his rule, notably his appropriation of large sums out of foreign aid sent to Nicaragua after a serious earthquake in 1972. Armed resistance had begun in 1961 by guerrillas calling themselves the Sandinista Front after Colonel Augusto Cesar Sandino, assassinated in 1934 after leading a rising which was suppressed with the help of troops from the United States. The Sandinistas remained for many years few in number since they failed to win widespread support among the peasantry or the urban working class, but Anastasio II's misrule earned them more sympathy among the professional classes and the Roman Catholic clergy and the murder in 1978 of the editor of Managua's principal newspaper, *La Prensa*, was the signal for serious attempts to put an end to one of Latin America's most outrageous dictatorships.

President Perez of Venezuela took the lead and tried to persuade President Carter to intervene. Carter was torn between his revulsion against the tortures and other abuses prevailing in Nicaragua and his fears that Somoza's excesses would lead to the opposite extreme and a second Cuba in Central America; and, on the other hand, his reluctance to intervene in the internal affairs of a neighbouring sovereign state, particularly to intervene with force. While these issues were being debated and various forms of economic pressure discussed, the chance to replace Somoza by a moderate and democratic regime slipped by. Washington's indecision hardened the determination of the Sandinistas and their allies, domestic and external (Cuba supplied arms through Costa Rica), and in 1979 Somoza was forced to flee.

The victorious alliance immediately fell apart. Promises to hold quick elections and install a multiparty system were shelved. The Sandinistas' clerical and professional allies dribbled away. Reagan began a covert war which eventually put about 12,000 men – the Contras – into the field against the new government. These Contras, dubbed by Reagan 'freedom fighters', consisted of old and newer opponents of the Sandinistas, reinforced by mercenary bandits of no fixed political views except that they were anything but democrats. Their main bases were in Honduras, where the United States built a large air base and increased its aid to the Honduran government tenfold. These exertions failed, however, to overthrow the Nicaraguan government; provided it with excuses to maintain and tighten its authoritarian regime and further postpone the promised elections; alienated anti-Sandinista elements which reprobated Reagan's support for the Somozistas in Honduras and Florida; and gradually converted Nicaragua's neighbours from auxiliaries in Reagan's war to active proponents of a peace which would include the recognition of the Sandinista government.

The attack on Nicaragua, although mainly directed from Honduras in the north, had also a pincer arm in Costa Rica in the south. Costa Rica has been a committedly pacifist state which, after a century and more of turbulence had gone to the lengths of abolishing its army in order to have more to spend on public services and utilities. But it remained poor and dependent on the United States and after the Sandinista victory in Nicaragua in 1979 it responded to Washington's appeal to play a part in containing and eradicating communism in Central America. Eden Pastora, a Nicaraguan social democrat who had joined forces with the Sandinista Front in the early 1970s, quickly changed his mind and broke with it, was then persuaded to rejoin it in 1976, became its commander-in-chief under the sobriquet of Comandante Zero two years later, again defected soon after the victory of 1979 to become leader of the anti-Sandinista forces in Costa Rica, and finally in 1988 abandoned his opposition to the Sandinista government out of disgust with Reagan's tactics. His shifts and changes symbolized the confusion and perplexities among anti-Somozistas who were half disenchanted with the Sandinistas but no less disheartened by United States policies. The governments of other Central American countries oscillated in the same way. Anything but left-wing, they nevertheless came round to preferring the Sandinistas to Reagan's war.

Washington's rooted dislike of any left-wing government in Central America was sharpened in the case of Nicaragua by the fact that, however exaggerated Washington's propaganda about their links with Cuba and the USSR, the Sandinistas got arms from Cuba. This Cold War aspect of the upheavals following the fall of Somoza became a ruling, and to some considerable extent a blinding, element in the United States after the advent of Reagan. The Reagan administration took office resolved to give high priority to Central America as a critical zone in the global conflict of the superpowers. Its endemic troubles, economic and political, had been exacerbated during the preceding decade. Its economic growth, which had been nurtured on an expanding middle class, was brought to a halt by the general world recession, with the result that this class became divided in its political allegiances and the poorer classes became poorer: the middle class was drawn on the one hand to the old oligarchies which represented, even when they could no longer command, the settled order dear to middle-class enterprise and money-making but, on the other hand, this class was alienated from the oligarchs by their selfish brutality and by the suspicion that their days were numbered. The poor had been emboldened by glimpses of a juster order and hardened by the renewed hardships of the late 1970s. The consequent upheavals were, however, regarded in Washington as something more sinister and any inclination by liberal America to welcome Central America's belated revolutions was overlaid by the conviction that they were more than half provoked and extensively supplied by communist Cuba and the USSR. Nicaragua was seen as a Soviet satellite in the making, all the more dangerous than Cuba for being on the mainland. Reagan was therefore easily persuaded that he must ensure the defeat of the guerrillas in El Salvador, stifle any other leftish movement which might arise in the area and, above all, overthrow Nicaragua's Sandinista regime. The means were military, covert and open, and they failed. Besides organizing, training and paying for anti-Sandinista forces in Honduras and Costa Rica, the United States navy staged demonstrations off the Nicaraguan coasts in 1983 and in the next year mined Nicaraguan ports on the Atlantic and Pacific oceans; this mining in contravention of international law was censured by the Security Council (but the United States vetoed the resolution) and condemned by the International Court of Justice.

Further hostile action was impeded by the US Congress, which refused funds requested by the president for the Contras – a refusal circumvented by a number of subterfuges such as selling arms to Iran and diverting the proceeds or part of them to the Contras with, it can hardly be doubted, the connivance of the president (see p. 53).

In 1983 four states – Mexico, Venezuela, Colombia, Panama – formed the Contadora Group, an outer ring of states concerned about the manifold disorders in Central America. Their purpose was to bring about a general pacification in Central America on the basis of recognition of all governments actually in place, self-determination and the reduction of armaments, but the group was distrusted in Washington on account of its even-handedness, which would recognize and probably validate the position of the Sandinistas in Nicaragua. Under pressure from Washington, Honduras, Guatemala and El Salvador refused to attend a conference which the group proposed to convene in 1985. But the group persevered and produced in 1986 a detailed programme (the Carabellada Declaration) for talks between Central American governments. This programme was irremediably opposed to Reagan's insistence that peace must be achieved through talks between the Sandinistas and the Contras and that the former must first introduce political reforms within Nicaragua. To all appearances Reagan put the removal of the Sandinistas above peace, while the Contadora Group envisaged a pacification which might leave the Sandinistas in power. Washington described the Contadora proposals as a threat to the region and to the United States.

But Reagan recoiled from the open military intervention which alone could achieve what he wanted and his support for the Contras was hampered by the revelation, on the eve of mid-term elections in 1986, of the Iran arms deals. The United States was able to keep the Contras in the field in Honduras but in spite of a strength of 15–20,000 and of lavish modern equipment they took no sizeable town in Nicaragua. Honduras, which harboured them and was well paid for doing so, received no support from any other Central American government, while on the southern front Costa Rica abandoned the war when Oscar Arias succeeded Alberto Monge as president and produced a plan (for which he was later awarded the Nobel Prize for Peace) which was subscribed by five Central American presidents including Nicaragua's. It proposed that presidential, national and local elections should be held in Nicaragua in 1990, preceded by the removal of press censorship and of obstacles to multiparty political activity. This scheme was viewed askance in Washington and with premature optimism elsewhere. Nicaragua took quick action by releases from jail, by allowing *La Prensa* to reappear and by annulling its state of emergency and its ban on political parties – but it was criticized for not doing more. Other signatories squabbled over whether they too had done what was required of them in their countries. Nevertheless, the Arias plan was a portent, if only because it pointed in a direction which doomed Reagan's policies and forced his successor George Bush to review and ultimately slide away from them. In 1989 the five presidents pressed their initiative by demanding the disbandment of the Contras and their reintegration into Nicaraguan society.

In 1990 Nicaraguans were allowed their first elections since 1984. Then they had given the victory to the Sandinistas, but this time they did not. The Sandinistas remained the largest single party but they were beaten by a coalition led by Mrs Violeta Chamorro, widow of the murdered editor of *La Prensa*. Although the US attack by means of the Contras had been an expensive failure, US sanctions had wrecked the Nicaraguan economy and Nicaraguans wanted a new government which would end the sanctions and ensure them a decent standard of living. Moreover, the Sandinistas' good record in such matters as health and education was offset by economic incompetence, corruption and in a broader sense by the mournful consequences of taking on the United States in a war which had cost tens of thousands of lives. Although over half the land and over a third of the principal industries remained in private hands, government had nationalized the banks and taken control of wages, prices and imports with disastrous results. Foreign aid, most of it from the USSR and East Germany, was considerable but wasted. Real wages fell during the 1980s by nine-tenths of their value, industrial output declined by a fifth each year and domestic product per head sank to $300 a year, the lowest in the region. Mrs Chamorro formed a government in which place was found for some Sandinistas but none for any of the Contra leaders. Scrapping between Sandinista and Contra bands became endemic, fuelled by steep price rises and unemployment. Chamorro's election, coinciding with Reagan's departure from the White House, allowed the war to come to an end. But sporadic fighting did not, as armies dissolved into bands which found no alternative to violence as a way of life. Elections in 1996 were won by a right-wing coalition led by Arnoldo Aleman Lacajo but his government began to dissolve the next year. He was convicted of fraud (2003) and handed over the leadership of his party to his wife. In Honduras the attempt to return to normality included the appointment of the archbishop of Tegucigalpa as head of the police. Chaotic elections in 2005 created an interregnum which ended with the installation of Manuel Zelaya Rosales as president.

In *Panama* President Arnulfo Arias Madrid set a record of three depositions from office (1941, 1951, 1968). His successor on the third occasion was Colonel Omar Torrijos Herrera, a popular mestizo who had army support and engineered a boom by encouraging foreign banks to do business in Panama and foreign commerce to make the fullest use of its free port. He negotiated the treaties of 1977 by which the United States agreed to hand over the Panama Canal in 1999 on condition that it be permanently neutral and that the United States have the permanent right to defend it. The canal was becoming less strategically important to the United States but remained economically vital to Panama, whose economy rested on the rent paid by the United States, the commerce of the free-trade zone, the traffic in flags of convenience, and offshore banking in the Canal Zone. In 1981, after he had relinquished office but was still commander-in-chief, Torrijos was killed in an air crash. From 1982, following a military coup, a sequence of lustreless generals ruled and power accumulated in the hands of General Manuel Noriega Morena, second in command of the army. Noriega was a likely president, but in 1984 Arias was re-elected against the wishes of the army. Funded by the CIA in spite of his known role in the drug trade, hailed in the United States as a democrat, Noriega remained in the background organizing the torture and murder of his opponents, enjoying an income said to be $100 million a year from making Panama the chief channel for the traffic in drugs between Colombia and the United States, helping the United States to arm the Nicaraguan Contras and rising to be chief of the army. He was dropped by the United States when scandals became too open and he was publicly accused of drug trafficking, electoral fraud and murder. In 1988 Washington urged President Eric Delvalle to dismiss Noriega from his army post, whereupon Noriega dismissed Delvalle from the presidency. In the next year he cancelled the election which had all but certainly elected Guillermo Endara Galimany to that office. He was indicted on drug charges in the United States and Washington tried also to bribe him to leave Panama and live in Spain, but he refused to go. All else having failed, Bush resolved to invade Panama and seize Noriega, which he succeeded in doing in an operation which – depending on the point of view – was either hilarious or humiliating. Noriega was taken to jail in Florida where he remained for 18 years. Endara was installed in his place but lost the presidency in 1994 to a Noriega henchman Ernesto Perez Balladares, who proposed to extend his term into the next millennium, if necessary by changing the constitution, but was foiled by the parliament. In 1999 Mireya Moscoso de Gruber, widow of the long-serving President Arnulfo Arias, became Panama's first female president by defeating Martin Torrijos Espinosa (son of Omar Torrijos), although in parliamentary elections a coalition led by the latter decisively defeated another led by Moscoso.

In the disorder after the Second World War Central America was in the course of transformation, becoming part of the wider world, looking to world markets and scrutinized by international corporations. This revolution had consequences for landownership, the structure of politics and the organization of labour which the ruling elites failed to master or even perceive. They found themselves opposed by liberals and by more strenuous radicals who were, however, divided against one another partly on class lines and partly by opposing views on the morality and expediency of the use of violence. In decades of strife the firepower and traditional authority of the elites prevailed to the extent of thwarting insurrections, so that the 1990s witnessed a return to a more pacific political order based on weariness and the end of the Cold War. By 1997 all the region's civil wars were officially over and a veneer of peace was spread over the area. This was a blessing but it produced expectations not easily met. Economic recovery was sluggish, commercial links between states minimal, hopes of joining NAFTA dowsed by the United States and Mexico, and attempts to find a livelihood (outside crime) for demobilized fighters not very successful. The end of the Cold War induced the United States to take a more relaxed view of the left and look less indulgently on the excesses of its right-wing associates, even to see the traffic in dangerous drugs as a greater menace to the United States than the traffic in dangerous ideas. The drugs trade, in which Central America and the Caribbean played an important role between south and north, had grown by the 1990s to be one of the world's most successful businesses with a turnover worldwide of $400 billion, users approaching 200 million and profits so large that it could lavish bribes on South American politicians and military chiefs and on United States law enforcement agencies and customs officials. It gave Latin America a greater importance in the world than it had ever had, for the drug business was not only successful but manifestly out of the control of the state and international bodies. Attempts by the state to diminish the trade by criminalizing it added to its powerful profits by taking it out of the tax system and suborning and seducing its officials: a bizarre form of market competition. As in the case of alcohol in the United States after 1919, the use of the criminal law failed in its purpose and exempted its targets from the normal activity of the fiscal system. Its leading practitioners were national, even international, figures of consequence. In Colombia, for example (see p. 699), they detached large areas of the country from the authority of the state, creating what was in effect a separate state which both enriched its governors and provided public services, including education and welfare. (In Myanmar the government negotiated with the principal drug baron an alliance for the suppression of all drugs businesses except his.) Primary producers, notably in parts of South America and South-east Asia, were even more dependent on the industry for their livelihood than were its controlling entrepreneurs and exploiters. Organic drugs based on cocaine, heroin or cannabis were being supplemented by manufactured alternatives which could be produced more easily and cheaply and anywhere in the world.

CHAPTER 29

Cuba and the Caribbean

The island of Cuba, the largest of the Antilles, thrusts its western end into the jaws of the Gulf of Mexico almost midway between the peninsulas of Florida and Yucatan, from which it is separated by channels about 160 km wide. Cuba is of all the West Indian islands the nearest to the mainland of north and central America. Its affairs have been a special concern of the United States from the middle of the nineteenth century. Its liberation from Spain at the end of the century proved to be no more than a change of masters, and it entered upon a period of colonial rule without the benefits of a colonial administration. Far ahead of its Caribbean neighbours in educational standards and facilities, and as well-endowed with a middle class as the most advanced Latin American country, it endured nevertheless a record of bad government uninterrupted from its liberation up to and including the Castro regime. The abrogation in 1933 of the Platt Amendment (see p. 676) coincided with the end of the odious rule of Gerardo Machado, which had rested to some extent on US support. Machado had transferred the presidency to Manuel de Cespedes but a revolt by non-commissioned officers (including Sergeant Fulgencio Batista) and students overturned the regime and inaugurated a period of 20 years during which a number of presidents held office. Batista, who ruled from 1940 to 1944, refrained at first from infringing a constitution which prescribed four-year terms with a ban on immediate re-election, but in 1952 he made himself permanent dictator and introduced a reign of terror. On 26 July of the next year, a date which gave its name to a movement, Fidel Castro led an attack on the Moncada barracks in an unsuccessful attempt to supplant Batista. After 18 months in prison, Castro emerged to prepare in Mexico a second attempt, and in 1956 he led an invasion band of 84 which was swiftly defeated. The survivors, who numbered only 12, escaped to the Sierra Maestra, where they turned from the tactics of a *coup de main* to guerrilla warfare which they waged for two years. In 1958 Batista attacked the growing forces of rebellion, but his campaign was a failure and served only to accelerate the disintegration of his regime. On 1 January 1959 it collapsed and Castro triumphed.

Castro's victory was a revolutionary event different from the usual run of Latin American revolutions. The reforming zeal of the new government was powerful and unrestrained. Secondly, it was meant for export. Thirdly, Castroism became allied with

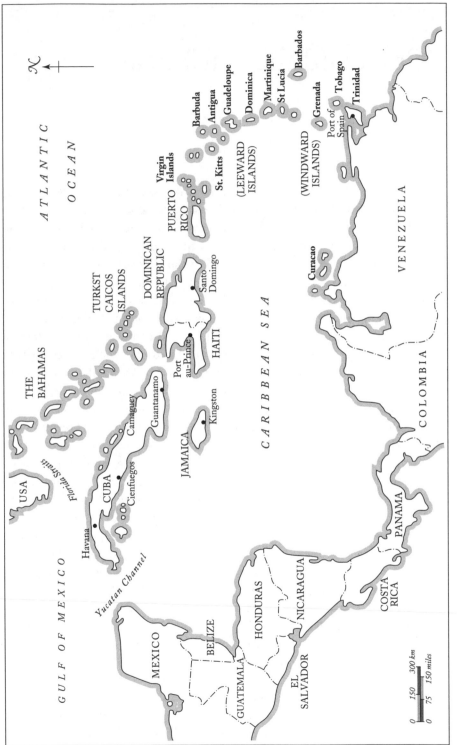

29.1 The Caribbean

Cuban communism, and, fourthly, Cuba entered into alliance with the USSR. These developments led to direct US involvement in counter-revolution and an invasion of Cuba in 1961, and a year later to the direct and open clash between the United States and USSR which has been described in an earlier part of this book.

Fidel Castro did not immediately assume any office. The presidency was conferred upon Manuel Urrutia Lleo, who almost immediately sought to resign it and succeeded in doing so a few months later; he was succeeded by Osvaldo Dorticós Torrado. The premiership went in the first place to José Miró Cardona, who first resigned it in a matter of days and finally resigned after a few weeks; he was succeeded by Fidel Castro. These hesitations and marks of no confidence by moderate reformers betrayed the uneasiness with which they observed a transfer of power which had been accompanied by summary trials and a bloody revenge. In the years before coming to power Castro had issued a number of statements of a moderate character, but he and his principal lieutenant Ernesto 'Che' Guevara, son of well-to-do Argentineans, were determined to effect real reforms and not to play at reforming in the half-hearted manner of so many Latin Americans. Unlike them, Castro did not bother to pay formal respect to the constitution or to hold meaningless elections. He set to work to change things. Moreover Cuba, again unlike so many Latin American republics, was a relatively prosperous country with a relatively diversified economy. Its principal weakness was its dependence on sugar, and thereby on the United States, for its foreign exchange. Castro and Guevara were therefore tempted, by circumstances as well as by their temperaments, to move fast and, relying upon a certain economic strength, to attack without delay the special link with the United States which represented a form of economic servitude and was also politically charged with memories of a generation of US dominance. At the same time, and with an equal disregard for immediate practicalities, Castro tried to extend the benefits of revolution and reform to the peoples of neighbouring countries. He became involved in subversive activities in the Dominican Republic, Haiti, Nicaragua, Panama and Venezuela and alarmed all those whose liberal instincts were less active than their love of law and order (or at any rate order) by giving money to left-wing groups and by broadcasting to Latin America a Castroist message as disturbing as the voice of Nasser in the Middle East.

Castro needed foreign aid, or credits and customers to replace the United States. He made the obvious move. In 1960 Mikoyan visited Havana and concluded a trade agreement with Cuba which, among other things, enabled Cuba to buy Russian oil. In the same year Guevara made a tour of eastern Europe and Cuba established diplomatic relations with Moscow and began buying arms from the communist bloc. Castro inveighed against US rights in the Guatanomo naval base (occupied by the United States for an annual rent of $2,000) and against United States dominion over the sugar plantations; he proposed to nationalize lands, including land in US ownership, took over US and British oil refineries when they refused to refine Russian oil, and seemed intent on spreading his revolution throughout central and southern America. These measures combined to anger and alarm the Eisenhower administration, which, aware of Batista's growing unpopularity, had at first viewed Castro's victory with something less than dismay, and in late 1960 Eisenhower endorsed a policy of getting rid of Castro in favour of some alternative which was neither Castroist nor Batistist (but which did not exist). The United States hoped to bring pan-American pressures to bear but a conference of American foreign ministers at San Jose, while condemning Russian and Chinese intervention in Latin America, refused to refer to Cuba by name. Washington decided to act on its own. It stopped further purchases of Cuban sugar and, after Castro retaliated by nationalizing US property, imposed a complete commercial boycott and severed diplomatic relations (1961).

From early in 1960 the United States had been helping and encouraging Cuban refugees in two places, both under the aegis of the Central Intelligence Agency. In Florida exiled politicians were formed into a political committee which hoped to become a government of Cuba; it included men of very different views who were only held together by their common opposition to Castro and by their US managers. In Guatemala a force was trained against the day when it would return to Cuba in small bands and start guerrilla warfare; at first there was no thought of US military parti-cipation in the adventure, but as time went on the original tactics were transformed from piecemeal infiltration to a single invasion thrust with US air cover, and the exiles were allowed to assume that the United States would back their ground operations with force rather than let them fail. When Kennedy was apprised of these activities immediately after his successful campaign for the presidency, he was troubled by them but did not veto them. The operation was in train; the chiefs of staff, his most awe-inspiring advisers, were in favour of it (but his secretary of state Dean Rusk was not); he did not want to let down several hundred Cubans, with whom he sympathized, nor did he know what to do with them if they were to be disbanded; the expectation that Castro would soon have Russian jet aircraft would make it very difficult, if not impos-sible, to sponsor such an invasion at a later date. Kennedy reaffirmed the ban on the involvement of United States forces but overrode the opposition of Senator William Fulbright and other advisers who advocated the containment of Cuba in preference to direct action which would be contrary to the charter of the OAS and all too consonant with Washington's reputation for imperialism and hypocrisy in its dealings with its southern neighbours.

On the night of 14/15 April 1961 a force of 1,400 men – nine-tenths of them semi-trained civilians – supported by B-26 bombers operating from Nicaragua with Cuban pilots landed in the Bay of Pigs, only to discover that, contrary to the assurances of the CIA, the US administration was not prepared to back them up and that expected risings in Cuba itself were not materializing. The Cuban government's riposte was more effective than had been anticipated and after 48 hours all was over. Castro imprisoned several thousands of his fellow citizens, thus seizing the opportunity to silence, demoralize and in some cases extinguish his opponents. His prestige beyond Cuba was greatly increased.

Nevertheless, his position was in other respects unhappy. The economic measures taken by his government had, by its own admission, been ill-conceived. A modish passion for industrialization led to the construction of factories for the manufacture in Cuba of articles which could be imported from abroad at less cost than the cost of the raw materials for their manufacture. In the countryside peasants displayed the worldwide dislike of their kind for co-operatives, the nationalization of land, and the enforced cultivation of crops destined for sale at fixed low prices. The middle class, which had been a more active ingredient in the revolution than the peasantry or the urban working class, became antagonized when nationalization was extended from foreign to domestic enterprises, and when the new regime took to the bad old ways of its predecessors in putting political opponents away in noisome jails. By 1962 there was an economic crisis, a general refusal to work by the peasants, food rationing and widespread disillusion, discontent and poverty.

At the end of 1961 Castro declared himself a Marxist. The Cuban Communist Party was a distinct entity which had at the outset little or nothing to do with Castro's 'July 26' movement. It was not a party with mass support and in the Batista period it had preferred backstage political manoeuvres which secured it a humble position on the periphery of the ruling constellation. Before the Castroist victory in 1959 there were in both the Castroist and the communist camps some who encouraged a rapprochement or even a fusion and others who opposed it. During 1961 the former prevailed and the parties effected a considerable degree of integration. Cuba became a part of the communist world in terms of international politics, but Castro did not become either an orthodox communist (he seemed to care little about communist teaching) or a captive of a communist machine. As independent in his way – and within the limits imposed by Cuba's need for foreign friends – as Mao or Tito, he also remained domestically the leader of a government and a movement which were only partly communist. Leaders of the Cuban Communist Party were promoted to office and influence but in 1962 the most eminent of them, Aníbal Escalante, was dismissed and fled to Czechoslovakia shortly before Castro set out for an extended visit to the USSR. The two parties had fallen out, the Castroists prevailed and Moscow backed the winners.

Moscow's support for Castro became an economic burden with exciting political and strategic possibilities. Keeping Castro afloat economically was probably costing the USSR more than it had bargained for in financial terms; keeping Castro afloat politically in the face of the US determination to destroy him could be an even more costly and risky policy, but it was also an exceptionally tempting one since an effective alliance between the USSR and Cuba would give the Russians a foothold in Latin America with all its unpredictable revolutionary possibilities, and a base within 160 km of the United States to offset the bases with which the USSR was ringed by its antagonists. According to Cuban – and Chinese – sources, the idea of sending to Cuba the missiles and jet aircraft which were first observed by United States reconnaissance in October 1962 was Khrushchev's. However that may be, Cuba, which Castro had made an economic and political ward of the USSR, was converted by Khrushchev into an armed pawn. Whereas Castro had wanted to equip Cuba to defend itself against a second attack like that in the Bay of Pigs, Khrushchev despatched weapons of an altogether different significance. The upshot has already been discussed (see pp. 27–30). In the narrower Latin American context the results were that the OAS (which had expelled Cuba from its ranks at the beginning of the year) approved the deployment of force by the United States against the approaching Russian ships; that a number of Latin American states contributed to the blockade of Cuba instituted by the United States; that Cuba was left out of the reckoning as Kennedy and Khrushchev moved to resolve the crisis; but that Castro was given an outstandingly splendid reception when he revisited Moscow in 1963 and won assurances of continuing Russian favour and support.

The missile crisis of 1962 involved for Castro a threat of extinction inasmuch as the rebuff to the USSR might carry with it an implicit freedom for the United States to work its will in Cuba and remove a government which had connived at an attempt to alter the balance of power in the American hemisphere more radically than at any time since the eighteenth century. But time seemed to show that Kennedy's triumph over Khrushchev was not to be so interpreted. Castro himself felt secure enough against renewed intervention by the United States to engage, towards the end of 1963, in a plot against the government of Venezuela (for which the OAS declared him an aggressor and recommended the severance of diplomatic and commercial connections, a step which only Mexico then refused to take). Castroism was also one of the ingredients in a rising in Andean Peru in 1965 in which desperate underdogs tried, with the help of Castroist and communist supplies and moral support over the radio, to force their plight upon the attention of their government. But the ostracism of Castro in 1964 was a reminder that he was still there to be ostracized, and if he was still there part of the reason was that his state was under the protection of a major power.

The Russians had been physically beaten out of the Caribbean but they retained a protective or intrusive capacity of another order. The assertion of the Monroe Doctrine had revealed its limitations. There were to be no foreign bases in the American continent but the American hemisphere's politics could no longer be sealed off from wider international politics. The United States had been harping for some time on the dangers of international communism in Latin America, but this ideological approach had missed the main point, which was the opening of Latin America to the processes of non-ideological international politics, in much the same way as the Middle East and the rest of Asia and then Africa had become international magnetic fields as soon as both the superpowers decided to exercise there the powers which nobody could prevent them from exercising. In the first postwar decades it had been assumed that two areas in the world were immune from this interplay: Latin America in the penumbra of the United States, and Moscow's satellite empire in Europe. The Cuban crisis showed that this assumption was at least an exaggeration. Khrushchev, with Castro as his eye-opener, scented that the time had come to question the unquestionable. This capacity was one of his strengths as a politician. Characteristically, however, he followed his instinct with more enthusiasm than caution and so exposed himself to a stinging defeat. The Cuban crisis demolished the theory that major powers have back gardens around which it suffices to put up notices against trespassers. Although interference in such areas remained preternaturally hazardous, the areas themselves were not enclosures but areas where the various winds of international politics blew with different force.

For Cuba itself the experience was bitter. During the period of United States dominance up to 1933 Cuba had been a quasi-colonial territory which was permitted to contract no foreign alliances and harbour no foreign bases. Castro reversed this situation to the extreme extent of making an alliance with the USSR and turning Cuba into a Russian base. He did so on a calculation of Cuban interests which turned out to be a miscalculation, since the USSR showed by retreating in the face of Washington's challenge that Cuba's interests played little part in Moscow's calculation of its own interests in the western hemisphere. Although the USSR had defied the Monroe Doctrine it had not done so in support of Cuban nationalism or ambitions. Castro, who had hoped to become the Latin American equivalent of Tito, Sukarno and Nasser, at once the personification of a new national dignity and the regional leader of revolution, found himself instead the ruler of an island which had become an international curiosity rather than an international fulcrum and which was beginning to look rather bedraggled as a consequence of economic and administrative muddle. For Guevara, the Argentinean pan-American for whom Cuba's revolution (not Mexico's or Bolivia's) was to have been the real beginning of Latin America's revolution, the reassessment necessitated by the Russian retreat was even bitterer than it was for Castro, and in the course of it the two men fell out and Guevara disappeared, taking with him much of the Cuban revolution's international flavour which he tried to inject into South America until he met his death in Bolivia in 1967.

Castro's adventures in Africa, which have been described in Chapter 26 of this book, increased and publicized his dependence on the USSR and coincided with the global inflation and recession of the late 1970s. In the first part of that decade the Cuban economy expanded at the rate of 10 per cent a year, but this rate fell to 4 per cent by 1980. Food, housing and transport became scarce and expensive; the price of fuel became prohibitive for large numbers of people; many workers were having to travel four hours a day to and from their work. Stricter regulations against small businesses created a large and economically stranded sub-proletariat. Nepotism, inequalities and stifling controls unaccompanied by commensurate benefits aggravated its plight. In 1979 a cyclone added its toll, the sugar crop failed and the tobacco crop was badly blighted. The weight of Washington's economic blockade was increasingly felt. In 1980 10,000 Cubans invaded the Peruvian embassy in Havana demanding to go to Peru and hoping to go to the United States. Some of them were common criminals or would-be political refugees, but the bulk were Cubans who had had enough of being in Cuba. Castro made the best of a bad job by allowing them to go, but they were a startlingly bad advertisement for his conduct of his country's affairs. His plight worsened a few years later when Gorbachev, who visited Cuba in 1989, cut Russian aid and trade to and from eastern Europe ceased altogether. Public services collapsed, industries closed for want of fuel as well as orders, wages and salaries went unpaid, emigration accelerated (over the whole Castro period Cuba lost about 15 per cent of its population). The ultimate symbol of Cuba's sorry state was Gorbachev's removal of 11,000 troops while US forces remained in Guantanamo.

But there was no revolt. Castro even contrived to turn the miseries of his people to his own advantage by permitting and even facilitating their exodus to the United States. The Clinton administration inherited a policy of admitting Cuban refugees with open arms but faced with a new wave of 50,000 it resolved to intercept them (or such of them as did not drown on the way) and transport them to the Guantanamo base. This, however, was already encumbered with 14,000 Haitian refugees and the cost of their indefinite upkeep. After an attack on civilian aircraft in Cuban airspace the United States imposed economic sanctions on foreign corporations trading with Cuba (or Iran or Libya), a move which excited much anger in Europe. Clinton, in a quandary, was forced into talks with a Cuban regime which showed no signs of collapse and whose single purpose was the removal of the sanctions which were his main weapon short of force.

In one sense Castro was a revolutionary leader who failed because his revolution was throttled by the United States but in a deeper sense the revolution failed because it turned optimism into pessimism or at best resignation. Before Castro, Cuba was a relatively prosperous but ill-governed Latin American state whose business was selling sugar to the United States. It was also a relatively new state, liberated from Spain towards the end of the nineteenth century but ruled by a narrow, inefficient and increasingly corrupt elite which purloined the fruits of development and failed to maximize them. Castro's revolution appeared to complement the revolution against Spain. It excited hopes. But its increasingly dogmatic elements fired few emotions and cut the ground from under the country's economic base; and when the revolution failed to fulfil hopes the revolution itself had failed. What the USSR supported until 1989 was no longer a revolution but a sadly disconsolate state which lost from that year Soviet aid equivalent to 10 per cent of its GPD and the markets for 90 per cent of its exports. In the next year Clinton relaxed the United States' strangulation but, given the political significance of the Cuban exiles in Florida, only modestly. From the same date Castro permitted 20,000 Cubans to emigrate annually. Almost all of them joined their fellows in Florida, who comprised one-tenth of the Cuban people. George W. Bush's denunciation of Cuba's democratic deficit re-froze Cuban–US relations. In 2008 Castro in ailing health transferred his positions and powers to his brother Raul.

The neighbouring island of *Hispaniola* was divided between Haiti and the Dominican Republic. Haiti had independence through a slave revolt against Revolutionary and Napoleonic France after being a French colony from 1697. French rulers set an example of atrocious behaviour which was not lost on their wards and successors. Until 1843 the island of Hispaniola comprised a single state but in that year it was divided into Haiti and the Dominican Republic. Haiti was occupied by the United States from 1915 to 1934. Society and politics revolved round a black majority and a mulatto elite which, after briefly combining to get rid of French rule, treated one another with savagery. Dictators were common but not always or entirely vicious. The main characteristics of the regime of Colonel Paul Magloire (1950–56) were extravagance, jollity and corruption. His place was taken by François Duvalier (Papa Doc) who had been in hiding in Magloire's time but emerged to win an election in 1957 and survived, first, by being a better plotter than his rivals and, secondly, by recruiting, clothing and equipping, mainly from the slums, a counter-army, the fearsome Tonton Macoute. He won the support of the army and the Church, extracting from the Vatican a concordat (1966) placing the appointment of bishops in his hands. He had support from the United States until Washington connived at a ludicrously incompetent invasion by his enemies in Florida. After this fiasco Washington switched back to Duvalier. His rule became rough, ruthless and crazed. He died in 1971 and was succeeded by his son, Jean-Claude (Baby Doc). Whereas Papa Doc had been the leader of a black middle-class coterie which hijacked the state and treated it as private property while at the same time extolling negritude, the national voodoo religion and the cruder ideas and practices of European fascism, Baby Doc found his friends among the rich mulattos. He was less intelligent than his father and perhaps less ruthless but he was evicted in 1986 after overstraining the indulgence of the Roman Catholic Church, the professional classes and the young (here, as in many countries, habitually referred to as students) The Duvalier regime was followed by instability, two elections in 1987 and 1990 marred by violence, and the eviction in 1990 of another strongman, Prosper Avril. A third post-Duvalier election gave Father Jean-Bertrand Aristide a convincing victory after a campaign in which he promised to make life better for oppressed and undernourished underdogs and the electorate allowed itself to hope that he might be allowed to do so. Aristide was a fearless left-wing priest who denounced his own ecclesiastical hierarchy as well as the Duvaliers. From the United States he got good marks and some aid as a reward for democracy but bad marks for being on the left. Within a year he was ousted, nearly killed and fled. Army and police chiefs took control – Generals Raoul Cédras and Philip Biamfy and Colonel Joseph François – and the Tonton Macoute reappeared under the name of *attachés*. By the Washington Accord of 1992 the United States undertook to reinstate Aristide if he would commend a military blockade, to which he reluctantly agreed. The OAS and UN also intervened, ineffectively. By the Governor's Island Accord in 1993 the new Clinton administration, broadly endorsing its predecessor's policies, tried to persuade the Haitian triumvirate to allow Aristide back without seriously curbing military rule. This manoeuvre failed but a swelling tide of refugees to the United States stiffened Clinton's resolve. He sent ex-President Carter, flanked by Senator Sam Nunn and General Colin Powell and closely followed by 20,000 troops, to negotiate Aristide's return in exchange for an amnesty for the triumvirs who, after some prevarication, left the country. Aristide was restored by American military force but with much misgiving in Washington, where it was hoped that when his term expired in 1995 he would be succeeded by a less radical figure. His successor René Préval was, however, more suspect. Haitians had few opportunities for economic activities except smuggling and when that failed they starved. The American forces were withdrawn in 1999 ahead of forthcoming elections.

Clinton's explicit aim in Haiti was to restore democracy. While laudable in itself and likely to stem inhuman atrocities, this attempt by one state to change by force the government of another was in breach of the UN Charter and was not rendered less so by Clinton's success in getting 20 other UN members to provide small token adjuncts for a US invasion. Even if inhumanity constituted grounds for international intervention that right was most questionable where the defence of human rights could be effected only by the overthrow of the government of a sovereign state. Clinton's Wilsonian purpose, placing democracy at the centre of his foreign policies, was a moral purpose not clearly supported by law.

In the other half of Hispaniola the *Dominican Republic*, ruled by Rafael Trujillo for more than 30 years until his assassination in 1961, was dominated for the next 30 by his political heir Joaquin Balaguer, a shrewd and comparatively unobtrusive politician who succeeded in the 1990s in mastering inflation and increasing overall production but not in reducing unemployment (which was running at about a quarter of the workforce) or in easing the lives of the poorer half of the population or redressing the country's balance of trade. Balaguer was persistently opposed by Juan Bosch, who won the first post-Trujillo election but was removed by the army after a few months. A bout of civil war was ended by US intervention and the beginning of the first of Balaguer's six presidencies. When these rivals were both in their eighties, a third man entered the political lists – José Francisco Gomez – who, in spite of the disadvantages of being black and born in Haiti, pushed Bosch into third place in elections in 1994 and defeated Balaguer too although those counting the votes ruled otherwise. The chief asset of the country was its sugar plantations, which were run by virtually slave labour.

The rest of the Caribbean was in 1945 colonial, mostly British ground from Jamaica, much the biggest of these islands, to the string of smaller islands tracing a line between the Caribbean Sea and the Atlantic. Decolonization was the main political topic in the first postwar decades. A federation of the British colonies, under discussion since the middle of the nineteenth century, was created in 1958 but came to grief in 1961. There have been divergent views about the causes of this failure. The delay in bringing it into being after the end of the Second World War allowed animosities to develop between the islands; the blame for this delay was laid upon the British government which, regarding West Indian leaders as much more left-wing than in fact they were, slowed down the pace towards independence and federation. On this view there was a genuine desire for federation, at the popular as well as the political level, despite the acknowledged difficulties – great disparities in the size and wealth of the different islands and the great distances between them. Alternatively, there was, except perhaps in the smaller islands, no popular interest in federation; the federation of 1958 rested on a narrow base of political and trade union leaders vulnerable to a popular revulsion; and such a revulsion was, in the event, stirred up by other leaders, who saw in it a way to take power. This view stresses the ways of thinking of the Caribbean peoples as islanders with a keen sense of belonging to their particular islands but little sense of community with others beyond the horizon (a habit accentuated by the fact that under colonial rule each colony had been treated by the British Colonial Office as a distinct object in a series of bilateral relationships with Britain).

Shortly after federation, the prime minister of Jamaica Norman Manley was challenged by his rival Alexander Bustamente to hold a referendum to see whether Jamaicans wished the federation to continue or not. The result was a narrow defeat for Manley and the federation, which Jamaica left in 1962. Trinidad–Tobago followed suit. Both became independent members of the Commonwealth and the OAS, as did Barbados in 1966. The smaller islands became associate members of the Commonwealth, self-governing except in relation to foreign and defence policies in which Britain retained a share of responsibility. There were six of these associates: Antigua with Barbuda, which progressed to independence and UN membership in 1981; Grenada, which became an international celebrity in 1983 (see p. 734); Dominica; St Lucia; St Vincent; and St Kitts–Nevis–Anguilla. The last proved unhappily assorted and Anguilla rebelled against the government on St Kitts. It achieved a *de facto* separation which Britain, despite some sympathy with Anguillan complaints, refused at first to endorse but accepted in 1980, when Anguilla became formally a separate state, Britain assuming responsibility for its defence, foreign affairs and internal security, with a say in its senior appointments. Grenada, Dominica, St Lucia and St Vincent formed a regional assembly to consider a federation of the Windward Islands. Four British colonies remained colonies: Montserrat, the British Virgin Islands, the Turks and Caicos Islands, and the Cayman Islands – some of them becoming favoured haunts of tax-evading bankers and their Third World associates in the drug business. On the mainland British Honduras, which changed its name to Belize in 1973, moved only slowly to independence under the shadow of Guatemala's claim to the whole territory. It became in 1981 an independent member of the Commonwealth, protected by a small British force, until in 1991, Guatemala formally renounced its claim and Britain terminated its commitment to its defence.

In 1968 a modest economic association, Carifta (Caribbean Free Trade Association), was formed by all Commonwealth states and territories except British Honduras and the Bahamas; the former joined three years later. The weaker members claimed that Carifta benefited the stronger members more than themselves. All were worried by

British accession to the EEC since they had, under the Commonwealth Sugar Agreement and similar schemes, an assured market and stable prices for their sugar, fruit, rum and other produce. With the exception of the solitary oil producer, Trinidad–Tobago, they were harder hit by rising oil prices in the 1970s which aggravated endemic unemployment and anti-government sentiment. In 1973 Jamaica, Trinidad–Tobago, Guyana and Barbados created a Caribbean Community (Caricom), membership of which was open to all Commonwealth countries which chose to join within a year. This new association had a small population but was nevertheless economically overpopulated: its two largest members, Jamaica and Trinidad, counted only half a million people between them but a quarter of the population of working age was unemployed and the average income was less than $500 a year. Caricom languished until resuscitated in the late 1980s.

Jamaica's politics gravitated around two parties: the People's National Party (PNP) of Norman Manley (in office 1957–62) and the Jamaica Labour Party (JLP) led by Alexander Bustamente and then by Donald Sangster, Hugh Shearer and Edward Seaga. The economic base was broadened from sugar and bananas to embrace tourism, bauxite and manufacture but the shift from agriculture to manufactures increased unemployment to 20–30 per cent of the working population at a time when the habitual escape – emigration to Britain – became all but barred. Hence conflict, notably in overcrowded Kingston, and discontent directed against the small oligarchy, foreign capital and Lebanese, Syrian and Chinese minorities. Discontent mounted to violence not far short of civil war and a helpless JLP government lost elections in 1972 to the PLP, now led by Manley's son Michael, a radical socialist who wanted to break away from Washington's economic stranglehold and, in rebellion against the terms on which the IMF did business with impecunious countries, to get aid from the USSR and eastern Europe. In 1980, in an election which claimed at least 500 lives, the comparatively right-wing JLP triumphed with a recovery programme based on conventional capitalist remedies with US approval. The new prime minister Edward Seaga made a quick tour of Washington and other western capitals and closed the Cuban embassy but he was unable to stem a slump in Jamaica's main exports or reduce foreign debts which were eating up half of Jamaica's export earnings. With the economic infrastructure collapsing and the poor getting poorer, Manley won elections in 1989. He secured fresh loans from the IMF but had to agree to cut subsidies, devalue the currency and keep inflation below 9 per cent a year. The soaring prices occasioned by the first part of this programme led to wage claims which endangered the undertaking on inflation and therefore the whole package. Economic decline, rising inflation and rising taxes weakened Manley, who was compelled by illness to resign in 1992. His successor P. J. Patterson won four elections in a row and all but eliminated the opposition.

For a generation after independence *Trinidad–Tobago*, besides being at the other end of the Caribbean, presented a contrast to Jamaica in its style and fortunes. Its two principal communities, of African and East Indian origin, coexisted without serious conflict. It pursued unselfish policies of lending to its neighbours and subscribing for World Bank loans. But after 1980 declining oil revenues and high interest rates dented its prosperity and stability. Meanwhile, it had lost its status as a developing country, while its attempts to diversify its economy and reduce its dependence on oil and sugar ran into protectionist obstacles from the United States and the European Community. As world prices for its exports collapsed, unemployment rose, a series of devaluations forced up prices, wages were frozen, crime and disorder increased, and the rule of the People's National Movement came to an end. In 1986 the National Alliance for Reconstruction, led by Robbie Robinson of Tobago (of African origin), won a convincing victory and the new government accepted the standard IMF remedies.

With the exception of Jamaica and Trinidad the new states of the Caribbean had electorates of eighteenth-century proportions to go with their constitutions of twentieth-century design. Consequently, elections were all too easily conducted with threats and promises – a promise to abolish taxes, for example. This circumstance did not make for good government. It also robbed electoral verdicts of much significance, so that generalizations about a leftward or rightward trend were misleading but there was in the 1970s a discernible rightward shift in *Antigua*, where Vere Bird's Labour Party recovered the power which it had lost to a more radical rival; in *Trinidad–Tobago* where the comparatively conservative Eric Williams won another term of the office which he had held since 1956; in *St Vincent* and *St Kitts–Nevis*; and in *Dominica*, where Patrick John was forced to resign over peculiar dealings with South Africa. Many of these small states were obliged to search for unorthodox sources of revenue, but Patrick John's scheme to lease a substantial part of his island to the South African government was too eccentric to pass muster. Barbados, by contrast, enjoyed fair economic winds and the Barbados Labour Party, to the right of its main rival, the more left-wing party of Errol Barrow, reaped electoral rewards in successive elections.

A contrary leftward trend, supported by Cuban aid and inspiration, won some success in *Grenada*, where Eric Gairy's United Labour Party, re-elected in 1976, failed to cope with the island's economic distress or maintain a semblance of honest government. It was removed by force by Maurice Bishop, an admirer of Castro. Other Caribbean parties sympathetic to Castroism remained in the wings, their fortunes still latent but their presence significant enough to induce Washington to quadruple its financial aid to the region between 1975 and 1980. A scare in 1980 over the supposed arrival in Cuba of a Russian brigade reinforced this beneficence and the feeling that the Caribbean was being drawn once more into world politics as it had been at the time of the Cuban missile crisis. The election of Reagan added a touch of gunboat diplomacy to the prevailing dollar diplomacy, its most notable exploit being the invasion of Grenada in 1983.

Bishop had begun his rule by making overtures to the United States but he was snubbed in Washington and found his development plans blocked by US votes in international financial institutions. He obtained nevertheless favourable mention from the World Bank in 1982 for his rural schemes and public services and he released in the same year some of the political prisoners whom he had put in jail upon coming to power. His party, the New Jewel Movement, was an amalgam of two roughly equal sections, the one led by himself and the other by Bernard and Janet Coard, who were regarded as closer in temperament and ideology to Castro (or even, in the eyes of their enemies, to Pol Pot). By 1983 these two groups were openly hostile and were murdering each other. Bishop was assailed from two sides – his more left-wing colleagues on the one hand and, on the other, the United States, which had decided to unseat him and began using blatantly exaggerated propaganda against him. The Coard faction murdered him. A US force landed and destroyed the Coards and their adherents, using a variety of excuses to cover a rehearsed operation: that the airport being built by British contractors was not, as alleged, intended to boost tourism but to serve the purposes of Castro and his allies; that the lives of a group of US nationals engaged in research in Grenada were at risk; and that a substantial Cuban military force was already on the island. The United States adventure was bungled; intelligence was poor; the invaders took ten days to conquer a small defenceless island and suffered over 100 casualties, inflicted mostly on themselves. There were no Cuban forces on Grenada and official statements were shown to be embarrassingly untrue. But the operation was far from unpopular. Washington secured endorsement of its action from neighbouring Caribbean governments, although most Commonwealth governments, including the British, were piqued by what they regarded as an illegal and politically unnecessary act. Washington got away with it because the operation was brief, welcome to the inhabitants of Grenada and in tune with prevailing anti-left-wing sentiments. A new political party was put together under Herbert Blaize and captured in 1984 all seats in the parliament except one. Blaize died in 1989 and in elections a few months later the ruling National Democratic Congress failed by one seat to secure a majority of the parliament's 15 members. Relics of Bishop's party won no seat and a mere 2 per cent of the vote. Nicholas Braithwaite became prime minister. He participated in desultory talks about a federation of the Windward Islands. His successor Keith Mitchell paid a friendly visit to Castro and in 1999 won every seat in the parliament.

At the northern edge of the Caribbean, north-east of Cuba and south-east of Florida, the Commonwealth of the *Bahamas*, an independent member of the Commonwealth from 1973, flourished as a principal ancillary of the seamier side of international finance and of the drugs trade. Sir Lynden Pindling, chief minister 1967–73 and prime minister 1973–92, rose to power as the champion of the black majority against the white merchant elite (the Bay Street Boys). His governments were periodically assailed by scandals but he survived until 1992 against the Free National Movement, which was accused of being equally corrupt and elitist to boot. He enjoyed the support, with diminishing enthusiasm, of the United States. The Bahamas was probably the only country in the world where over half the members of parliament were millionaires.

Note

Guyana and Surinam

Guyana, once British Guiana, is an almost equally divided bi-racial country in which the descendants of Indians imported by the British (after the abolition of slavery in 1838) slightly outnumber the Africans while a small Roman Catholic minority with European origins can in these circumstances be electorally important. The Indians have been predominantly rural, the Africans urban. The postwar leaders of these two groups were at first divided more by temperament than policy. The Indian leader Cheddi Jagan, a Rooseveltian liberal with a socialist American wife and founder in 1950 of the People's Progressive Party (PPP), won three-quarters of the seats in the legislative council in 1953 but was dismissed after a few months by the British governor. The PPP split on racial lines and the African element created the People's National Congress (PNC) led by James Burnham. Both leaders moved to the left but Jagan allowed himself to be pushed by conflict into the more extreme attitudes; his radicalness, and especially his plan to unionize labour, alarmed European planters while local American interests reported him to be a dangerous communist. This view of his impact on the colony was sharpened by riots necessitating the despatch of British troops and by Jagan's sympathies with Castro's Cuba, an inclination partly temperamental but partly also economic: Cuba was one of British Guiana's principal markets for its rice.

With independence in the offing the United States and the British were anxious to ensure a victory for Burnham over Jagan. Burnham cultivated the small Roman Catholic party and the British conveniently altered the constitution by introducing proportional representation for elections in 1964 in which the PPP won the greater number of seats but not a majority. The PPP was out of office for nearly 30 years. After independence in 1966 British Guiana became Guyana and joined the UN but not, owing to a border dispute with Venezuela, the OAS. Burnham moved to the left, impelled chiefly by the needs of the urban unemployed Africans and by anti-American and anti-planter imperatives. The PPP suffered a series of defeats too overwhelming to be credible and the alternative opposition, the Working People's Alliance, retired from the elections of 1980 after its leader was assassinated. Burnham died suddenly in 1985. His successor Desmond Hoyte maintained the PNC's dominance, subject, however, to increasingly trenchant accusations of electoral malpractices and a steep decline in the economy. Revenues from sugar and bauxite flagged, the currency was devalued, food and electric power became scarce, wages were cut. Hoyte was obliged to postpone elections more than once because it was impossible to guarantee proper procedures. The PPP returned to power with Jagan and, after his death, Sam Hinds as president. Mrs Jagan became the latter's prime minister and in 1997 president as, with the help of the IMF from 1991, the economy began to recover. The new century and a new generation brought an end to 50 years of feuding between Guyana's two main parties: Bharrat Jagdeo and Robin Corb, their new leader, declared it over.

East of Guyana, Surinam, independent of the Netherlands in 1975, was ruled directly or indirectly by Colonel Desi Butrese and the military for most of the period after 1980. It played an ancillary role in the cocaine business. French Guyana remained a department of France. A thousand miles west of Surinam, the Netherlands Antilles and Aruba had special status under the Dutch crown and were linked with one another for certain economic affairs.

Related reading: part seven

Grandin, Grey: *The Last Colonial Massacre – Latin America in the Cold War* (2004)
Jonas, Suzanne: *The Battle for Guatemala* (1999)
Lewis, Oscar: *The Children of Sanchez* (1961)
Reid, Michael: *Forgotten Continent* (2008)
Robb, Peter: *A Death in Brazil* (2004)

PART EIGHT

World order

CHAPTER 30

World order

Preventing wars

World order presents two principal aspects: wars and other armed conflicts and how to reduce their number; and slumps and other economic turmoils and how to manage them.

So long as the state remained the basic element in international society the prevention of wars could be secured only by states and co-operation among them. They had a choice of methods. Each major power might assume primary or exclusive responsibility in a given region; or all the major powers might together supervise and police the whole globe; or these same powers might equip and finance an association of states to do the job on their behalf. After the Second World War international organization and co-operation were theoretically based on the second of these methods after the first had been unsuccessfully advocated in some quarters; but the circumstances necessary for the success of the second method did not materialize, so that practice approximated rather to an adaptation of the third, imperfectly acknowledged and precariously pursued.

The forms of international organization were discussed during the war by the principal victors-to-be. Churchill and Roosevelt both inclined to a regional pattern, and Churchill elaborated a scheme for a number of local federations to be grouped in three regions under a supreme global council. Power would be concentrated in the three regions – European, American, Pacific – rather than above or below. This pattern did not appeal to Stalin, whose suspicions of Churchill, based on his mistrust of the British governing class and on disputes over the timing of the opening of a second front in western Europe, were sharpened by proposals which included the creation of Balkan and Danubian federations in an area of special concern to the USSR: Stalin wanted untrammelled sovereignty and, so far as the two were not incompatible, a continuing association with his allies in order to avoid a return of the USSR's prewar isolation. On the western side too there was opposition to regionalism, especially among professional politicians like Cordell Hull and Anthony Eden who feared that it would produce autarkic blocs, each dominated by a particular major power, and would revive American isolationism. At Moscow, in October 1943, the foreign ministers of the three allies adopted the principle of a global organization based on the sovereign equality of all states and laid the foundations for a new world organization which was to perpetuate the alliance of democracy and communism against fascism and keep the peace by the joint exercise of their allied power.

The United Nations was, in form, a revised version of the League of Nations. The principal organs of the two bodies were similar. The authors of the UN Charter aimed not to devise a new kind of organization, but to retain a familiar framework and insert into it more effective machinery for the prevention of war. The Covenant of the League had not proscribed war. It had bound its signatories to pause before resorting to war and attempt to resolve their differences by one of three recommended processes. If this interposition failed, there was no covenanted ban on the resort to war, and international sanctions were only applicable in the event of a resort to war in defiance of the preconditions laid down by the Covenant. In 1928 a more radical attempt to prevent war was made by the signatories of the Kellogg–Briand Pact, who engaged themselves to dispense with war altogether except for certain limited purposes, namely the defence of the Pact itself and of the Covenant and of existing treaties, and in the exercise of the right of self-defence (the justification for the exercise of this right being left to the state claiming it): the United States and Britain also attached conditions relating respectively to the Monroe Doctrine and the defence of the British empire. The UN Charter went far towards banning war except in defence of the Charter, or in pursuance of the obligations contained in it, or in self-defence but it did not totally proscribe war. It explicitly sanctioned not only the use of international force but also the use of national force, by one state or an alliance, in self-defence. The Charter vested considerable authority in the Security Council, which was empowered to determine whether a given situation contained a threat to international peace or a breach of the peace or an act of aggression and, if it so determined, to require all UN members to take action against the delinquent (except to use force, a sanction which remained voluntary to each member). On the other hand, this collective authority was offset by the procedural obstacles to reaching in the first place a collective decision in the Council, namely, a majority of the Council and the assent of all its five permanent members. In the absence of such a decision it was illicit for any UN member to reach an opposite decision or take measures of the kind envisaged in the Charter; whereas an affirmative decision of the Council automatically placed all members under obligation, a failure to reach a decision precluded all action under the Charter. Consequently, although the Council was in this field sovereign over the members, each of the permanent members was sovereign over the Council.

Like the League, the UN was designed as an association of sovereign states (notwithstanding that its ban on interference in the internal affairs of a member did not extend to measures for peace enforcement under chapter VII), and, like the League, it attempted to assert a degree of collective judgement and a field for collective action against its constituent sovereign members in a period when these members had been massively strengthened by the growth of modern technology and of modern ways of influencing people. The state had turned the industrial and the democratic revolutions of the nineteenth century to its own advantage by annexing modern armaments and popular chauvinism to its purposes. Neither the League nor the UN was able to steal the control of armaments from sovereign states nor to create in the peoples of the world an attachment to international organizations exceeding national patriotism. Besides these general handicaps the UN saw its peacekeeping machinery rendered inoperative early in its existence. The efficacy of this machinery depended upon the unanimity of the major powers in the Security Council and the provision by all members of forces adequate for the execution of the Council's decisions. The unanimity of the major powers faded in the first breath of peace, so that the veto became a common tactical instrument instead of a weapon of last resort and the Charter's prescription for raising international forces – a series of bilateral agreements between the Security Council and members – was never implemented because the body appointed to negotiate these agreements, the Military Staff Committee, never agreed even the general nature and size of the forces required.

The veto given to the permanent members of the Security Council was a special feature of the UN. In the Council of the League every member had a veto. The authors of the UN Charter had to decide how far to depart from this unanimity rule. They decided to introduce majority voting as a general practice but subject to limited exceptions: in the Security Council, but not in other organs, special power was accorded special privileges, with the result that major powers were able to prevent action against themselves or their friends, although they were not entitled to prevent discussion and criticism. No permanent member of the Council has ever objected to this principle, although particular permanent members have objected to the use of the privilege by other permanent members. During the late 1940s and 1950s the USSR, being in a semi-permanent minority in the Council, used the veto to such an extent that other members complained of a breach of the spirit, if not the provisions, of the Charter. Russians argued in return that the UN had become a tool of American policies and that these policies were basically anti-Russian – as evidenced by Truman's use of his nuclear monopoly for political purposes, by speeches of prominent western leaders beginning with Churchill at Fulton and Byrnes at Stuttgart in February and September 1946. The USSR, after an initial attempt to use the UN for its own political purposes by raising or supporting complaints about the Dutch in Indonesia, the British and French in Syria and Lebanon, the British in Egypt and Greece and western tolerance of Franco's fascism in Spain, fell back upon the veto and then in January 1950 ceased to attend meetings of the Security Council. This retreat from the UN was, however, reversed partly because it enabled the Security Council to initiate action in Korea in June 1950 and partly because the expansion of the UN – notably in 1955 and 1960, the years respectively of a package deal admitting an assortment of 16 blocked candidates and of the major African afflux – altered the character of the organization and offered the USSR political opportunities outweighing its fundamentally minority position in the Security Council. (It was in this period that the USSR ceased to attack the leaders of new states as bourgeois stooges and began instead to make friends with them.)

American hostility to the frequent Russian use of the veto led to two attempts to circumvent it by transferring to the General Assembly some part of the Security Council's authority. In 1948 an ad hoc committee of the Assembly, popularly called the Little Assembly, was established as a means of keeping the Assembly in permanent session, but the Little Assembly's powers were circumscribed and it never became an organ of any importance. The Russians were not alone in regarding it as a contravention of the Charter and it faded away. More important was the adoption in 1950 of the Uniting for Peace resolution. This resolution was sponsored by the United States, which saw that the UN operations in Korea had been made possible only by the absence of the Russian member and his veto from the Security Council and which sought to ensure that their presence on a future occasion would not fatally obstruct similar action. The resolution, which was adopted by the Assembly by 50 votes to five with two abstentions, introduced machinery for calling an emergency session of the Assembly at short notice; asserted the right of the Assembly to pass judgement on threats to peace, breaches of the peace and acts of aggression when the Security Council was prevented from doing so; created a Peace Observation Committee of 14, available for missions of exploration and elucidation in trouble spots; also created a (stillborn) Collective Measures Committee of 14 to study international peacekeeping machinery; and asked members to earmark forces for service at short notice in UN peacekeeping operations. The Assembly twice stigmatized China as an aggressor in Korea under this procedure and again used it in 1956 to denounce the Anglo-Franco-Israeli attack on Egypt and raise an international force to supplant these aggressors. But the legality of the Uniting for Peace resolution was always in dispute. The USSR and other members attacked it and refused to pay for operations set in motion by the Assembly within its terms of reference. In 1962 the International Court was asked to advise on this issue and declared by nine votes to five that the Security Council's responsibility for peacekeeping was primary but not exclusive.

Thus disputes of a legal nature, reflecting fundamental political disagreements, threatened to thwart the hopes of those who sought in 1945 to produce a document and an organization which would secure peace and order. Disharmony among the permanent members made a mockery of the Security Council's name and turned the Council itself into an arena for the public display of wrangling and propaganda. Open diplomacy became as discredited as secret diplomacy had once been suspect. Likewise, the General Assembly became noted for the marshalling of block votes and the trading of unattached ones, especially after the afflux of new members had increased the number of those who were likely to have no direct interest in a particular issue and who would therefore vote either for ulterior reasons or not at all. Recourse to the UN became in consequence something of a gamble owing to the unpredictability of the attitudes of many members.

Disappointment with the functioning of the central organs of the UN led to a recrudescence of interest in regionalism. Although the authors of the Charter had come down on the side of centralism as opposed to regionalism, they had not totally excluded the latter from their design. The Charter recognized (article 51) the right of collective as well as individual self-defence and (chapter VIII) sanctioned regional alliances such as NATO, whose primary purpose was not the maintenance of peace and order within their area but the defence of it from outside threats, and regional organizations intended to police the region and resolve disputes within it. The Organization of American States was, however, the only organization of this kind to achieve any significant claim to effectiveness in the first 50 years of the UN's existence, with the result that regionalism did not in this period offer any substantial alternative to the UN's central organs as a means of keeping the peace within a region.

But although the Security Council failed to function as anticipated by its authors the UN became continuously active in security operations, developed a variety of experimental techniques and even engaged – in the Congo – in a major operation in which it deployed a total of nearly 100,000 men over four years. UN intervention in dangerous situations ranged from comparatively modest missions to establish facts, lower tension and gain time, through more complex mediatory operations involving military units but not the use of military force, to military expeditions prepared not only to defend themselves but also to attack others. The line between one type of operation and another cannot be precisely drawn. Thus UN intervention in Kashmir, Palestine and the Suez War could be classified as mediatory and in Korea and the Congo as military, whereas intervention in Cyprus could arguably be placed in either category, or in one category to begin with and in another at a later stage. But classification is no index of activity and the UN's activity in peacekeeping is not to be denied. Where the League had been criticized for passivity, the UN came to be criticized for doing too much.

In the first or pre-Korean phase of this activity the Security Council was faced with situations arising out of the Second World War: the lingering of the Russians in Iran beyond the term set by wartime agreements, and the slowness of British and French troops to leave Syria and Lebanon. These matters were debated in the Council and resolved outside it without further ado. Precedents of recourse to the Council were quickly set. The Council declined to act on a Russian complaint of British interference in Greek affairs through British troops in Greece, but it later investigated Greek complaints of foreign aid to Greek rebels by Yugoslavia, Bulgaria and Albania. It despatched teams of observers who, after being denied access to the non-Greek sides of the frontiers in question, issued a report condemning Greece's enemies. The Council did not put an end to the fighting in progress (which was only stopped when American aid had re-equipped the Greek army and restored its morale and when Yugoslavia, after the breach with the USSR and its communist neighbours in 1948, stopped helping the rebels), but the UN had set a precedent for on-the-spot investigations and could claim that it had contributed to elucidating and holding a potentially dangerous situation until it was eliminated by other means. This function was further exemplified in Indonesia and Kashmir. In Indonesia the Council succeeded in establishing a ceasefire which temporarily halted the first Dutch police action against the Indonesian nationalists and secured a temporary agreement between the two sides through a conciliation committee. Although these achievements were at first transitory, the eventual transfer of sovereignty from the Netherlands to the Indonesian republic at the end of 1949 was mediated by international intervention. In Kashmir too the UN negotiated a ceasefire and succeeded in putting a stop to fighting, even though it failed to secure a withdrawal of Pakistani or Indian troops or to resolve the underlying political dispute between Pakistan and India. Kashmir was the first clear example of a paradox which was later to become explicit and teasing: the fact that a ceasefire and the immobilization of hostilities could obstruct the solution of basic disputes by relieving the contestants of the urgency to come to terms in order to save lives and money. UN observers, sent to Kashmir in 1949, were still there half a century later.

In Palestine, the final pre-Korean illustration of UN security operations, UN emissaries negotiated a ceasefire, repaired it when it was broken and helped to secure armistice agreements. The Arabs and Israel did not, however, make peace and a UN Truce Supervisory Organization found itself established in the Middle East for more years than its originators had contemplated, subjecting both sides to the hazards of having their infractions of the truce exposed by an impartial body of observers – a sanction which unhappily they got used to.

The Korean War which, like other events referred to in this summary of UN activities, is described in more detail elsewhere in this book, was a test of a different kind since it arose out of an act of aggression to which there could be no effective response except the use of force. Chapter VII of the Charter was invoked and the Security Council, in the absence of the USSR, in effect endorsed American action and commissioned the United States, which had forces available in Japan and the surrounding waters, to meet force with force. The Korean War became therefore a war conducted by an American general responsible to the American president acting as the agent of the UN. Fifteen other states, mostly allied with the United States for other reasons, sent units to the battlefield but half the ground forces engaged, 93 per cent of air forces and 86 per cent of naval forces were American, and when the Chinese invaded Korea and the war gradually evolved into a trial of strength between the United States and China many UN members began to feel that the UN's motives in going to war had been lost sight of and that no future UN operation ought to be conducted in the same way. After the Korean War there was for a time a general rule that major powers should not be invited to make a fighting contribution to UN operations – an axiom only attenuated in Cyprus by the obvious advantage of using the British forces already present in the island. Korea became therefore an exception, although it reinforced the image of the UN as a body prepared to take action.

The next important operation – the UN intervention at Suez in 1956 – was a combined operation by medium powers set in motion by the General Assembly and placed under the executive control of the secretary-general. The force, which was recruited and despatched with astonishing speed, was equipped for self-defence but not for attack: ten nations contributed troops. Its arrival and deployment were secured in advance by agreement with Egypt (necessary, since the operation fell within chapter VI of the Charter on peaceful settlement of disputes and was not an enforcement action under chapter VII) and by the knowledge that the British and French governments would not use the power which they had to oppose it. The Anglo-French attack on Egypt having been halted by the United States, the UN was used to lever the Anglo-French forces out, to patrol the troubled areas along the Suez Canal and, incidentally, to clear the canal, which the Egyptians had blocked when they were attacked. Peace was restored through the agency of the UN after the United States had displayed a determination, which neither Britain, France nor Israel could gainsay, to stop the fighting. The role of the UN in this crisis was performed within the framework of collective security but was in fact something different. The proponents of collective security, whether in the League or the UN, envisaged the mustering, under pre-existing commitments, of overwhelming force to deter or stop a transgressor. At Suez in 1956 the transgressors were not stopped by such a collective show of force but by the United States. The collective force sent to the area could not have fought the Anglo-French or Israeli aggressors, nor was it meant to. It was intended not to push the intruders out but to keep the major powers out. Hammarskjöld's aim was to forestall by a UN presence the incursion into the conflict zone of the Americans and Russians, and his experiences at Suez fashioned his policy in the Congo four years later. Some of the limitations on action of this kind were demonstrated when, in 1967, the UN force was removed on Egypt's abrupt demand. Others were demonstrated simultaneously with the war of 1956 when the USSR refused to allow even a personal visit to Budapest by Hammarskjöld.

Between Suez and the Congo, a period of less than four years, the UN was again invoked in the Middle East and was required to use its techniques as observer and mediator. In 1958 the Lebanese government complained of interference in its internal affairs by the United Arab Republic and called in American troops. The UN despatched a few groups of mobile observers to check and report on what was happening along Lebanon's borders and subsequently enlarged this mission to enable it to replace the American units, whose presence had become an embarrassment to all concerned, including the Americans. The UN thereby shed light on a confused situation, deflated it and finally smoothed the way for a return to normality. This was an adaptation of previous experiences. It was followed, more or less, in Laos in 1959; in West Irian in 1962–63, when a UN presence eased the transfer from the Netherlands to Indonesia;

in North Borneo and Sarawak in 1963, when UN investigators reported that the inhabitants of these territories were not, as Indonesia alleged, opposed to the creation of Malaysia; in Yemen in 1963–64, when a situation as obscure as it was contentious was to some extent clarified by UN observers; and in discovering the wishes of the inhabitants of the trust territories of Togoland and the Cameroons when the administering powers were about to withdraw between 1956 and 1960.

The involvement of the UN in the Congo was a consequence of the precipitate Belgian withdrawal and the mutiny a few days later of the Congolese army, upon which the Belgians returned to protect their nationals, Katanga purported to secede and the Congolese government turned to the UN for help in keeping order, securing essential services, getting foreign forces out and holding the new state together. This involvement had therefore from the start a mixture of international and internal aspects. It was international in so far as it aimed at removing the Belgians and pre-empting the Americans and the Russians but it was also internal in so far as the UN forces were filling the gap created by the mutiny or inadequacy of the Congolese government's own forces and, besides securing law and order, became involved in maintaining the integrity of the new state by preventing the secession of part of it. Hammarskjöld used his right under article 99 of the Charter to bring the matter to the attention of the Security Council. In the four years in which the UN then operated in the Congo, a force which reached a strength of 20,000 and averaged 15,000 was used (at a total cost of over $400 million, of which 42 per cent was paid by the United States and none by the USSR) to keep order, prevent civil war and, more contentiously, to force Katanga to acknowledge the authority of the Congolese state. Its operations were based on chapter VI of the Charter. Chapter VII was never explicitly invoked, although shifting circumstances produced a situation very like enforcement action under chapter VII. These operations were initiated by the Security Council, but they were conducted by the secretary-general and medium powers.

Once again only medium states were asked to supply combat units and the secretary-general was given executive control. He created an ad hoc advisory committee of representatives of the states with troops engaged, in order to help him to interpret the general directives given by the Security Council and apply them to the circumstances of the moment. Acting in this way, the UN became the prime factor in preserving the unity and integrity of the new state and in preventing foreign intervention and perhaps a clash between major powers; it also alleviated human distress by containing civil war, minimizing bloodshed, helping refugees and providing a range of basic medical, administrative and other services; but in the short run it strained itself by incurring the hostility of major powers who distrusted the growth of the secretary-general's authority, sometimes disapproved of his objects and actions, and jibbed at the price which they were asked to pay towards keeping the peace. But if the major powers were not to allow and enable the UN to act in defence of international security, they would have to assume the role of policemen themselves, whether jointly or severally – or permit degrees of disorder in the world beyond the bounds of prudence. They were in a dilemma, afraid on the one hand to tolerate too much international disorder and reluctant on the other to sanction the growth of an international peacekeeping authority with an independent competence of its own; and the only escape from this dilemma was to use the machinery of the UN, which they had themselves constructed in the first place and which enabled them to act vicariously instead of directly and to keep a curb on any particular operation. The solution to their dilemma was to have a UN capable of acting reasonably effectively, but not too effectively, in keeping the peace; to have a competent but subordinate police force whose wish to become more competent would not be gratified if it entailed a serious move away from subordination.

The limitations were strikingly demonstrated in 1982 when two states, Argentina and Britain, went to war to assert their irreconcilable sovereign claims to islands of minimal value to either of them (see Chapter 27). Argentina's action was certainly, Britain's arguably, a breach of the Charter. Although only one among some 150 wars with which the world has been plagued since 1945, the Falklands War had a special standing as the only war deliberately waged by aggressive action by two members of the UN. It was also the first war waged by a European state other than the USSR since France abandoned its imperial pretensions in Algeria a generation earlier. The Argentinean seizure of the Falklands was a blatant breach of the obligations accepted by every member of the UN. Britain claimed that this act of aggression brought into play article 51 of the Charter which – by way of exception to article 2 – sanctions an act of war by a member state in self-defence. This claim is not without blemish. Neither in the Charter nor anywhere else is self-defence defined, so that there exists a grey area between self-defence and retaliation. The British government declared promptly its intention to recover the islands, if necessary by force, and wasted no time in assembling the means to do so. On the other hand, if self-defence is to be strictly interpreted, it could be held to mean no more than hitting back at the time of attack with the forces available at the point of attack. The question is a moot one, less clear than statements from the British side chose to portray it. But whatever the true legal judgment on this matter, it can more confidently be asserted that political considerations were uppermost and that, whatever the advice of any number of competent lawyers might have been (if sought), the British government would not have acted otherwise than it did.

The war for the Falklands was a setback for the UN as an organization and for those aspirations to world order which it embodied. For this setback the initial aggressors were overwhelmingly to blame, but the British government did not wholly escape the embarrassment of demonstrating that in a crisis a powerful state will not welcome UN diplomacy and will subordinate the rule of law and its treaty obligations under the Charter to its own assessment of national advantage and prestige. This was in 1982 no great surprise but it was not what the generation of 1945 had hoped for.

A more serious blow to the rule of law in international affairs followed when, in 1986, the United States delivered a heavy naval and air attack on Libya. The occasion for the attack was the explosion ten days earlier of a bomb in a night club in West Berlin. Two persons were killed. The perpetrators were Palestinians. Messages sent by the Libyan People's Bureau (embassy) in East Germany were intercepted and deciphered and disclosed official Libyan involvement. The precise nature of this involvement was uncertain since published English versions of these messages appeared to be not so much translations as paraphrases. Nevertheless, Libyan support for Palestinian groups prepared to use violence was uncontestable. The American administration sought agreement for the use of aircraft based in Britain and the right for them to fly over France: the first was granted, the second not. The attack was at first described as reprisal or retaliation but later as self-defence within article 51 of the UN Charter. It was an act of war in clear violation of the treaty obligations accepted by all signatories of the Charter (the appeal to article 51 was so vapid as merely to add hypocrisy to illegality) and also in contravention of the laws of war which, for 1,000 years before the Charter, had prescribed that the force used in a punitive venture must not be disproportionate to the offence which gave rise to it. The action was widely applauded by the American people who, like their president, felt outraged and frustrated by such crimes as the Berlin bombing, the hijacking of the *Achille Lauro* (see p. 365) and more. Unable to get at the small gangs responsible for these crimes, the US administration decided to label certain states (Libya, Syria) as 'terrorist' organizations and so claim the right to attack them. The attack was a political act undertaken in defiance of international rules and obligations but in the belief, or hope, that its political expediency would muffle its illegality. This it was not well calculated to do. It had no logical or obvious effect on those small but fervent groups which, needing few arms and little money, could remain in business whether Libyan cities were bombed or not. Qaddafi himself was neither killed nor overthrown and did not appear to be intimidated; domestic rivals who had been encouraged to intrigue against him by Libya's economic problems dropped their opposition at least for a time. Other Arab leaders, including those who disliked Qaddafi as an upstart and a nuisance, rallied to him; an American attempt to enlist President Mubarak in the raid seriously weakened his position; Arab public opinion gave Qaddafi some sympathy as a victim of brute force. Washington's European allies, with the notable exception of the British prime minister and some of her colleagues, were aghast at what they regarded as political folly, but muted in their public criticism of Reagan because of their own feebleness in response to Qaddafi's lethal meddlings; they were reluctant to apply (alternative and legitimate) economic measures since economic sanctions against Libya would undermine their refusal to use such sanctions against South Africa. In Britain the prime minister's willingness to allow the use of British bases provoked questions about the secret Anglo-American agreement governing their use, particularly for operations which were in nobody's mind when the agreement was made and which had nothing to do with NATO. Although, like many acts of violence, the American attack changed little, it accentuated some trends of which the more important were, first, the declining ability of the United States to solve rather than aggravate the turmoils of the Middle East and, secondly, the declining ability of Britain to stave off a choice between a junior – even humiliating and now unpopular – role in an Anglo-American partnership and a more wholehearted partnership with the European Community. In the last resort the American action was a massive political miscalculation. On the one hand was a widespread hankering, to which the American administration responded, to find a way to police international and cross-national affairs – even some readiness to put order before law. But in assuming the police role Reagan flew in the face of the fact that, not only was the communist bloc not prepared to entrust this role to the United States, but neither was the Arab world nor Asia nor Africa nor – most strikingly – western Europe. After the attack they were the less willing. So the action lacked not only legitimacy but also post hoc endorsement and defenders. American action in Nicaragua and Panama (see Chapter 28) underlined the difficulty of finding a policeman willing to undertake rough work and at the same time stay within the law.

The revolution in the USSR effected by Gorbachev changed this situation by smothering the Cold War, inducing the superpowers to co-operate in international affairs instead of opposing one another as a matter of principle, and by introducing therefore for the first time since 1945 the prospect of making the Charter work as it had been intended to work in the business of keeping the peace and upholding the law. The first test came with Iraq's invasion and annexation of Kuwait in 1990. This was a blatant act of aggression and it raised the question which had been raised on a number of earlier occasions, including Argentina's occupation of the Falkland Islands and Iraq's own attack on Iran ten years earlier: whether counter-action would be taken through or outside the UN. President Bush decided to do both. He despatched large armed forces to Saudi Arabia and he resorted to the UN to impose sanctions against Iraq. Both these undertakings were international in the sense that numerous states participated in both, but only the latter was action by the United Nations. The former was action initiated and led by the United States independently of the Charter. It did not conflict with the terms of the Charter but would do so if these forces were used to make war otherwise than in support of UN resolutions, at UN request and under a system of command established by the UN.

The Security Council took action under chapter VII of the Charter. This chapter comes into operation when the Council itself determines the existence of a threat to peace, a breach of the peace or an act of aggression. If the Council does so, it may prescribe action of two kinds: measures not involving the use of armed force (article 41) and action by air, sea or land forces (article 42 – blockade being specified under this article). In the case of measures under article 41 the Council may call on members of the UN to apply these measures and (by article 25) they are obliged to comply. There is no such compulsion in the case of measures under article 42.

In a series of resolutions adopted during August the Security Council, unanimously, demanded Iraq's immediate withdrawal from Kuwait and a negotiated settlement;

imposed, by 13 votes to two, a commercial, financial and military embargo (medical supplies specifically excepted and rules permitting the supply of food on humanitarian grounds to be worked out by a committee of the Council); declared, unanimously, that the annexation of Kuwait was null and void; demanded, unanimously, that Iraq allow and facilitate the immediate departure from Kuwait and Iraq of all nationals of third states; and authorized, by 13 votes to two, the use of force to make the embargo effective by, if necessary, stopping and inspecting merchant ships. These first resolutions established sanctions against Iraq and the use of force to monitor them, but not the use of force for any other purpose. Further resolutions defined and regulated UN actions, culminating in a twelfth resolution on 29 November which, by authorizing the use after 15 January 1991 of all measures necessary to achieve the aims set out in the earlier resolutions, sanctioned recourse to war.

The governments of the United States and Britain maintained that, these resolutions apart, they were entitled under article 51 of the Charter to use military force against Iraq but this contention was almost certainly false. Article 51 is one of the least satisfactory articles of the Charter. It expressly safeguards the state's inherent right to defend itself but it makes no attempt to define the line between self-defence and retaliation and, by using the phrase 'individual and collective self-defence', it perpetuates an ambiguity. There are two distinct issues to be met before article 51 may legitimately be invoked: first, the question whether the action proposed or undertaken is defence or retaliation (which was the question posed in the Falklands case) and, secondly, the meaning and scope of the term 'collective' in article 51. Collective self-defence, besides being a contradiction in terms, implies that an attack on one UN member may be resisted by forces other than those of the state attacked. They are presumably the forces of allies, but it is open to question whether the alliance needs to be in existence at the time of the attack or may be concluded after it. In considering this conundrum it is necessary to revert to the circumstances in which article 51 was drafted and adopted at San Francisco in 1945. It was a late addition to the draft Charter and was designed to meet the worries of members of existing regional alliances (the Organization of American States and the Arab League) who feared that by signing the Charter they would invalidate the arrangements in their regions for mutual help against aggression. It is evident that an attack on a UN member may be opposed by the victim's regional partners in accordance with the provisions of the regional alliance, but it is not evident – nor is it easy to argue – that states outside the relevant regional partnership at that time may intervene by force. The broader interpretation would permit any state to throw itself into a dispute simply by declaring itself an ally of the victim of aggression, with the result that every threat to or breach of the peace would become an invitation to military action by self-appointed white knights – or red knights or black knights – on the single condition that the victim of aggression was prepared to welcome that action.

In terms of world order and the usefulness of the UN Iraq's attack on Kuwait served to reanimate the mechanisms of the UN, testing its strengths and exposing its weaknesses.

The use of the Charter by the United States was made possible by broad accord between the permanent members of the Security Council and particularly between the United States and the USSR, but few in Washington believed that action under chapter VII would by itself restore the independence of Kuwait or forestall further possible aggression by Iraq – against, for example, Saudi Arabia. The United States therefore established in Saudi Arabia a powerful force which, while it might by its presence in the area reinforce the coercion applied by the UN, was evidently capable of attacking Iraq and not unlikely to be used in order to overthrow the Iraqi regime as well as to restore the Kuwaiti. This display of American purpose and power was a unilateral act which was given international support by securing the participation of the host country and of numerous other states in and beyond the Middle East. It was also an expression of no confidence in the efficacy of the mechanisms and procedures of the UN.

The attempt made in 1945 by the United Nations to shift the making of war from the unsafe hands of the nation state to the safer hands of the community of nations had been obstructed by two things: the Cold War and the developing nature of war. The Cold War undermined the existence of a global community of nations and negated the Charter's provisions for assembling and using international force. The development of nuclear, chemical and other new weapons superposed on the question of who should be authorized to use armed force the question of whether the use of such force was acceptable or justifiable or even efficient in relation to specific political or military purposes. The crisis over Kuwait was prolonged in a way barely imaginable in the previous century by perplexity over the uses of armed force and a rising under-current of opinion against the resort to what war had become. There were, as there ever had been, three main ways of overcoming an enemy: starve him, scare him or beat him. Chapter VII of the Charter is the modern version of the siege, using deprivation to secure surrender but keeping in reserve, as did besiegers, direct force to back it and clinch it. But an embargo in accordance with chapter VII is, like siege warfare, likely to be slow and even ultimately ineffective: besiegers sometimes marched away. The American host assembled in Saudi Arabia was an alternative, a second string. It was intended to scare Saddam Hussein or, if he were not scared, to beat him. It represented the view that if measures under chapter VII failed or did not work quickly enough, the United States and those of like mind would resort to force rather than accept rebuff.

As the crisis developed month by month so did the dilemma between the two aims of chastising the law-breaker and resolving the crisis: between recourse to war and recourse to diplomacy. Saddam Hussein's violation of the Charter created the crisis. The first of the Security Council's resolutions required him to purge his offence by retreating from Kuwait. It required also discussion of matters in dispute between Iraq and Kuwait. It said nothing about the relative timing of these two requirements. Saddam Hussein proclaimed repeatedly that he would not budge from Kuwait, although he expressed willingness to participate in a general conference on Middle Eastern affairs with an agenda from which Kuwait would not be excluded. The United States and some of its associates refused to consider any matters before a total and unconditional Iraqi withdrawal. This was tantamount to the rejection of diplomacy in parallel with retreat. It was a high-risk policy which gave to surrender an absolute priority over negotiation, risking a war which – although caused in a primary sense by Iraq's aggression – would be caused in a second sense by the equal obduracy of the protagonists. In such a contest Bush suffered a double disadvantage. As chief in a democracy and chief of an ad hoc alliance he was constrained to a far greater extent than his autocratic adversary, who could take much less heed, or none at all, of popular opinion or the misgivings of associates. The overwhelming power of the United States rendered the use of that power obnoxious to much public opinion and barely reconcilable with the well-established rule of law which, for well over 1,000 years, had decreed that the use of force must be proportional to the object to be achieved. The tilt towards war was accentuated by the American tactics of reinforcing a policy of sanctions with a deployment of vast armed forces whose cost was unsustainable over a long run and which could not be brought back home without a commensurately unequivocal victory: Bush adopted measures which were economically and politically unsustainable.

That the United States should play the leading part in the UN's undertakings was proper and desirable. But Bush did both more and less. He conducted simultaneously an American operation which overshadowed the UN undertaking almost to the point of obliterating it; and in the American operation he relied on force and the threat of force to the exclusion of diplomacy, even insisting that the direct bilateral talks in Washington and Baghdad which he proposed in December must stop short of anything that might be labelled negotiation. He arrived therefore at a position in which he was demanding unconditional observance of UN resolutions which themselves demanded no such thing. During the Cold War the UN's role in keeping world order and upholding international law had been effaced, but the Cold War had provided the UN with an alibi for its ineffectiveness. The Kuwait crisis, the first serious crisis after the end of the Cold War, reanimated the UN – the United States was among the first to hail this change – but it showed also that the UN's new freedom to perform its central role in world affairs might still be cramped by its more powerful members and would have to be performed without benefit of the excuses for failure provided by the Cold War. Freedom of manoeuvre for the UN could turn out to be useless or – worse – catastrophic if it were to mean freedom only to demand unconditional surrender. By pressing UN resolutions beyond the objectives explicitly envisaged in them, and by conducting supposedly UN operations without reference to the UN, the United States abused the UN and weakened it while nevertheless fulfilling some of its aims. American aims – the overthrow of a barbarous regime which had, among other things, violated the Charter and the laws of nations – were widely approved, but the methods used demonstrated something different: the power and will of a single national government in the context of a threat to its national interests or its own perception of what the international situation required.

There was a dilemma between acting strictly in accordance with, and thereby strengthening, the rule of law in international affairs or, alternatively, taking the action which seemed to be dictated by the circumstances of a particular case. This dilemma was accentuated by events in Iraq after the end of the war in 1991 (see Chapter 14) and by the break-up of Yugoslavia leading to war over the partition of Bosnia and civil war in the Kosovo province of Serbia (see Chapter 7). Iraq's persistent obstruction of UNSCOM and the United States' determination to overthrow Saddam Hussein led through a series of crises to the resumption of war on Iraq by the United States and Britain alone and without the explicit authority of the Security Council – ostensibly on the grounds that implicit authority had already been given, but in reality because, had it been sought, it would not have been granted. In the case of Kosovo the same two states were prepared to remove Serbian rule from Kosovo by air warfare, a clearer breach of the UN Charter. A crucial element in the duel between the United States and Serbia was Slobodan Milosevic's knowledge that the United States had resorted to war against Iraq regardless of the rules of international law and regardless too of what most of its European allies wanted or approved. That American forces were vastly superior to Serbia's was obvious. That the United States would use that force was not obvious but, in the view of Iraq, at least possible. But the Iraqi example cut two ways. Beyond demonstrating American determination the bombing of Iraq achieved nothing and Milosevic could see that the European members of the Contact Group (Britain again excepted) were at least lukewarm about air attacks on Serbia, not because of any squeamishness about breaking the law but because they judged that bombing Belgrade would not achieve its purpose. In both Iraq and Kosovo the United States acted to impose its will and a kind of order for at least a short time. It showed that it could, and in circumstances of its own choosing would, pursue immediate aims by any means which it regarded as sensible or imperative: that law is not the whole of politics or at times the main ingredient.

The Gulf War had a second and no less far-reaching consequence. By Resolution 688 of 1991 the Security Council asserted that the situation in Iraq was a threat to international peace and demanded access for humanitarian organizations to parts of Iraq where minorities were being abused. It also demanded the right to patrol and monitor these areas. Since the war was at this point over in the sense that Iraq had been defeated, the Council was implicitly raising a semi-concealed issue – the conflict between the UN's obligations to standards of behaviour and the prohibition in article 2(7) against intervention in the essentially domestic matters of a state except in the circumstances defined in chapter VII of the Charter. In pursuance of Resolution 688 an international force provided by the United States, Britain and France maintained the pressure on Iraq, defining Kurdish and Shi'ite areas in northern and southern Iraq respectively as no-fly areas for Iraqi aircraft and using Turkish air bases for their operations in the north. (The Turks were anxious to prevent Kurdish refugees from entering Turkey and Kurdish armed groups from reinforcing Kurds in Turkey. Turkey even invaded northern Iraq on the plea that it was in chaos and a threat to stability in south-eastern Turkey.) Resolution 688 had a more contentious passage in the Security Council than earlier resolutions for waging war against Iraq's invasion of Kuwait. Three members of the Council opposed it and two abstained. Nevertheless, it raised an issue which would not have been formally ventilated during the Cold War and was made precise only by the Gulf War.

The relevant circumstances included three factors beyond the facts of any particular case: the development of international law and its interpretation; the volume of simultaneous demands on the UN; and the practices of the UN in relation to intervention to keep the peace, supply humanitarian aid and enforce humanitarian standards. The law relating to armed conflict was reviewed and recodified after the Second World War by the four Geneva Conventions of 1949 and the two Geneva Protocols of 1972. The term 'armed conflict' itself implied an extension of the law beyond a state of war. These conventions and protocols updated the law in detail and prescribed penal sanctions for 'gross breaches' but failed to establish effective mechanisms for enforcement. Of the two protocols, on international and internal armed conflict respectively, the second was fiercely mutilated before being adopted and ratification of both by the world's more powerful states was patchy. Most states approved their provisions but feared their application to themselves or their friends in an uncertain future.

Demands on the UN had increased dramatically from the late 1980s. In the five years from 1988 the UN's peacekeeping and supervisory operations quadrupled in volume and their cost soared. At the peak of UN involvement in the conflicts in Yugoslavia, where 32 states were contributing 25,000 troops, the forces deployed by the UN throughout the world reached more than 50,000 in place of 10,000 on average in previous decades, and their cost was about $3 billion. The UN was hard-pressed to recruit the numbers required and its members unwilling to shoulder their prescribed share of the cost. This increase in the demand for world order was occasioned not only by the opportune cessation of the Cold War but also by the redefinition of what sort of order ought to be secured and how the UN should set about the task. World order no longer meant no more than stopping wars between states. It also meant responsibility for domestic order at some undefined level where disorder either threatened international peace or grossly offended against humanitarian norms established by international law and conventions.

In the aftermath of the Gulf War the plight of the Kurds in northern Iraq and of Shi'ites in the south cried out for international intervention partly because of Saddam Hussein's atrocious record against them and partly also because they had been encouraged by the United States to rebel unsuccessfully against their government: 2 million Kurds were in flight in harsh terrain and dreadful weather and were being refused asylum over the Iraqi–Turkish frontiers. This situation raised the question of the right of the UN to intervene by force in a member state for humanitarian purposes and did so at a time when other disasters, notably in Somalia and Yugoslavia, were demanding attention from the UN and its new secretary-general Boutros Boutros-Ghali.

The Security Council's Resolution 688, taken without invoking chapter VII of the Charter and so without ostensibly side-stepping article 2(7), to use air power and (in the north) ground troops to protect threatened minorities within Iraq was a breach of article 2(7) unless either the situation fell within chapter VII – in which case article 2(7) did not by its own formulation apply – or the circumstances giving rise to the intervention could be classed as falling outside Iraq's 'essentially domestic jurisdiction'. For the latter proposition a series of arguments, all forceful but inconclusive, could be adduced. The first was that article 2(7) was at variance with other provisions of the Charter – for example articles 1(3) and 55 – which imposed on the UN a commitment to uphold humanitarian principles. The second was that the word 'domestic' was to be interpreted by the import rather than the location of the enormities to be remedied: that, for example, acts verging on genocide might not properly be termed domestic. A third was that acts in direct contravention of international conventions signed by the peccant state created a right of international intervention.

International intervention in Iraq was a reaction to circumstances, opportunity and emotions (including compassion and shame). It was not clearly legitimate. The protection of the Kurds and Shi'ites seemed relatively easy since the UN was already at war with and had defeated Iraq, and the costs were not impossibly incalculable. Whether the Kurdish venture might come to be accepted as part of the law of the Charter could be determined only with time. On the one hand the International Red Cross reported at this juncture that nine in ten of war victims throughout the world were civilians and refugees, that refugees had reached 17 million, of whom 7 million were children, and that half the severe casualties of wars were under 18 years old. On the other hand any readiness for more intervention was countered by failures in Somalia and Yugoslavia.

In Somalia there was anarchy following the overthrow of Siad Barre, no government with which to negotiate the usual preliminaries to the despatch of a peace-keeping mission and a conflict between humanitarian and political aims – the relief of famine as distinct from stopping the fighting and restoring the integrity of the country. The former required not only the provision of food and medicines but also a force to protect those supplying them; the latter required negotiation with warring factions and their disarming. The United States endorsed and took part in UN operations but also despatched forces of its own and pursued ends of its own: it was not easy to tell whether these were UN or US operations or a bit of both. In Yugoslavia the confusion was worse. Although the disintegration of that state began with conflicts between Serbs and Croats, the crux internationally was the attempt of Serbs to annex parts of Bosnia. International concern was twofold: to prevent the fighting from spreading throughout Yugoslavia and beyond, and to succour civilian victims and refugees from the usual consequences of wars and the unusually horrible atrocities of this one. These aims were in conflict in so far as humanitarian intervention required some measure of compliance from the combatants, who simultaneously resented external attempts to stop them from carrying on their warfare.

UN missions could be divided into two broad categories which shaded into one another: observer missions, whose main purpose was to prepare, invigilate and report on elections; and peace-keeping missions sent to a scene of violence which had been halted by a truce with the purposes of maintaining the truce and aiding victims of the violence. The latter were normally empowered to defend themselves but not otherwise to use force and they presupposed a cessation of violence. In Yugoslavia, however, the despatch of UN missions preceded any effective or believable truce. Secondly, the UN became directly involved (from September 1991) in the wake of EC intervention, partly because President Bush encouraged EC leadership in place of UN action which would inevitably and perhaps deeply involve the United States, and partly because some European leaders saw an opportunity for the EC to play a significant role. The UN's first measure was an embargo on the delivery of arms to all the warring parties, a measure which favoured the Serbs, who were better armed than others. The UN also nominated Cyrus Vance, formerly US secretary of state, to co-operate with the EC in its diplomatic attempts to stop the fighting by negotiation. In 1992 the UN raised and despatched a Protection Force (UNPROFOR) to succour victims of the fighting and protect aid workers, first in Croatia, later in Bosnia–Herzegovina, later still to establish a UN presence in Macedonia. The UN imposed economic sanctions which were for a time evaded (with the help of Greece and Cyprus) but did considerable damage to the Serbian economy and inflamed popular emotions and irredentist nationalist rhetoric. The UN also assembled a committee of experts to collect evidence on breaches of the Geneva Convention and Protocols. The Security Council resolved in 1993, under chapter VII of the Charter, to create an ad hoc tribunal to hear charges of serious violations of international humanitarian law in Yugoslavia from 1991.

The UN was hampered by genuine differences of opinion among its leading members. Clinton, who succeeded Bush in mid-crisis, was anxious to keep his distance or – if that were to prove impolitic – to intervene only through air power. He was revolted by the enormities perpetrated by (although not exclusively) Serbs against Muslims, uneasy about repercussions in the Muslim world and attracted by the calculation that air strikes could be used to compel a ceasefire and a negotiated peace without costing American lives and without irreversible entanglement. Europeans, on the other hand, were opposed to the use of air power on the grounds that it must abort their diplomacy, could not be an effective substitute for ground operations in a bitter war in wooded mountainous country and would abruptly end all relief work. All parties were reluctant to face the fact that a negotiated peace could not be a just peace, that justice for the Muslims and perhaps the Croats too could not be achieved without escalating the war against the Serbs, who had won it. Hence the proffering of a sequence of partition plans which not everybody wanted to accept, and threats of military action which not everybody wanted to carry out.

Boutros-Ghali, presenting in 1992 an *Agenda for Peace*, laid bare the conclusion that, whatever its rules or restraints or practices, no international organization could live up to the expectations embodied in the UN Charter if it were half-heartedly supported by its members, underfunded, sparsely equipped, belatedly informed of likely troubles ahead and uncertain of its capacities and purposes. At the time when he was writing this report the UN was running 17 separate missions of widely different cost but the total annual cost to the UN's nearly 200 members was no more than 1 per cent of the defence expenditure of the United States, 10 per cent of the British. This was the negative side of the picture. The positive side was the simple fact that wars are impossible without arms but that arms were being manufactured and traded in plenty. Most of the arms trade was conducted by governments anxious to reduce their heavy military expenditure by selling to other states, and in competition with one another, a surplus on current production or an obsolescent overstock. There was also a black market in arms estimated to be worth billions of dollars a year. In 1991 the UN resolved to establish a register of arms transfers but progress was obstructed by disputes over what arms to include and then brought to a halt when China, in protest against American and French sales of arms to Taiwan, boycotted the proceedings.

There was a further conundrum. That the UN was an organization for keeping the peace between states was not in doubt. That it was also an organization for keeping the peace within states, or intervening in civil wars, or ensuring certain standards of behaviour within states, was much doubted – except in so far as any given situation could be clearly classified as a threat to international peace. Yet civil wars and domestic anarchy or tyranny were by the 1990s no longer off the international agenda as matters for concern and possibly action in their own right. Parts of the UN Charter at least implied that the UN was committed to the protection of human rights and it had created or sponsored a formal framework through a series of (mainly declaratory) instruments of three kinds: general, regional and specific. The first category included the Universal Declaration of Human Rights (1948) and the Covenants on Civil and Political Rights and on Economic, Social and Cultural Rights (1966). Regional bodies had adopted similar instruments – for example, the European Convention on Human Rights (1953), the OAU's Banjul Charter (1981). In the third category were conventions on specific derelictions such as the Genocide Convention of 1948. To this framework non-official bodies – Amnesty International, the International Commission of Jurists, the Quakers – had contributed pressures, ideas and drafts, but implementation lagged far behind. In 1992 the UN created the office of High Commissioner for Human Rights, an acknowledgement of the *Zeitgeist* and of the growing impact of inhumane activities on international affairs and the international agenda. Yet international action in the cause of justice did not necessarily add to world order, for, as in national affairs, the claims of justice were not coterminous with the pursuit of stability.

There was yet another source of confusion. In so far as American foreign policies rested on a general principle, that principle was not so much the assertion of international law and order but the promotion, by force if practicable, of democracy, a Wilsonian crusade which could run foul of the law of the UN Charter (see for example the case of Haiti in Chapter 29), besides fostering democracy at the expense of stability.

In the judicial sphere ad hoc tribunals were established to try persons accused of war crimes and crimes against humanity in Bosnia and Rwanda. They worked under considerable disadvantages, some of them inherent in circumstances of appalling confusion and some due to the reluctance of forces on the spot to make arrests. A conference in Rome in 1998, convoked by the UN, debated the creation of a permanent court on the basis that it might impose no death penalty, conduct no trials *in absentia* and be limited in its jurisdiction to war crimes, crimes against humanity and genocide (crimes of universal jurisdiction) – thus ruling out, among other charges, international terrorism and drug trafficking. The debates were protracted, mainly on account of strenuous efforts to meet objections of the United States, which wanted a court with severely restricted powers, particularly over American citizens. These efforts failed to secure American adherence to the final outcome which, however, was substantially watered down in the process. By 120 votes to seven (United States, China, Iran, Iraq, Sudan, Libya, Algeria) the conference agreed on the creation of an International Criminal Court (ICC) to come into existence at The Hague upon ratification by 60 states. The ICC was to have jurisdiction over individuals accused of the crimes enumerated in the UN's proposals. It would have 18 judges and a prosecutor appointed by a majority of participating states. A prosecution might be initiated by the Security Council, by a state which had ratified the treaty or by the prosecutor, subject, however, to the right of a special panel of three judges to stay proceedings. A prosecution might also be barred by the Security Council acting by a majority without the imposition of a veto. In cases of war crimes a state might claim the right for seven years after its ratification to exclude its own citizens from prosecution. The treaty expressly denied immunity from prosecution for heads of state.

The notion of crimes of universal jurisdiction received judicial (and public) attention when General Augusto Pinochet Ugarte, former dictator in Chile (see p. 694), was arrested in Britain in 1998 on a warrant for his extradition to Spain to face charges of murder and torture. Pinochet had been granted immunity from prosecution in Chile but the House of Lords, overruling a decision of a lower court, ruled that by English law (with particular reference to the adoption in 1998 of the International Convention on Torture) and by customary international law, English courts were empowered to entertain proceedings relating to certain crimes irrespective of where they were committed or of the nationality of the victims. The House rejected a plea by Pinochet for immunity as a former head of state: this judgment did, however, affect the immunity normally extended to heads and other dignitaries of state while executing their official functions. At this point confusion set in. The decision of the House of Lords was set aside by the House on the grounds that one of the Lords of Appeal who had voted in the 3–2 majority against Pinochet had a connection with Amnesty International, which had argued in favour of his extradition. A fresh hearing by seven other Lords of

Appeal produced seven different and incompatible judgments but on the central issue the House declared by 6–1 that Pinochet had no immunity. This finding, however, was limited to charges relating to events occurring before 1988 and the House added a rider to the effect that, since most of the charges related to such events, the Home Secretary should reconsider his decision not to impose a ban on the Spanish application. Having done so, he decided not to prevent the case from proceeding on the remaining counts. In Chile opinion polls suggested that Chileans were equally divided over whether Pinochet should face trial outside his country or not. A significant item in the final decision of the House of Lords was its ruling that the immunity granted by Chile to Pinochet as part of the restoration of democracy in Chile had no force in judicial proceedings outside Chile even when that democratic regime requested that it should. This would appear to establish that political factors could in international law have no part in judicial decisions. Meanwhile, Pinochet remained in England for more than a year. When his fitness to stand trial was questioned on medical grounds the Home Secretary sought the advice of a panel of doctors, who reported that he was not fit, and the Home Secretary directed his release for return to Chile. (These conflicts between law and political expediency/imperative aggravated by the United States' determination to use force to overthrow the regime in Iraq without adequate attention to either are more fully considered in Chapter 14.)

Preventing economic disasters

A strong economy is the prime element in political power and in the public mood. Economic weakness and inequality promote disorders. The Second World War was an economic and psychological calamity which wrought death and destruction farther, wider and deeper than any other in history. But recovery was no less extraordinary, primed by the United States and fuelled also by western Europe and Japan: all the more remarkable since the postwar mood demanded of the economy not only the repair of the sinews of power but also full employment and social welfare on a scale never before achieved or attempted and, as these aspirations began to be realized, sustained growth at levels sufficient to entrench and enlarge these social aims. Social objectives rose to the top of the political agenda. For two decades the fortunes of the so-called developed world were advanced by the basic strength and wartime invulnerability of the American economy and the postwar extraversion of American policies; by western Europe's reserves of skills and untapped labour; by the consequent stimulation of consumer demand; by the emergence of global markets, particularly after the decolonization of Asia and Africa which quickly followed the end of the war; and by the development of new technologies, many of which had been generously funded during the war. These were, however, unfavourable factors. The globalization of what had been a geographically limited international economy enlarged markets but also multiplied opportunities for economic blunders and recklessness. Growth and stability encouraged lax monetary policies, deficit financing (borrowing too much) and intractable wage demands; the familiar traps of inflation and commercial cycles were not eliminated; by the mid-1960s stagnation and recession loomed and in the early 1970s the international monetary system devised at Bretton Woods in 1944 disintegrated.

Before the war ended, the United States, Britain and their western allies confronted at a conference at Bretton Woods the problems of international economic management. They established certain principles and organizations. The principles were free trade, non-discrimination and stable exchange rates (fixed within bands set in relation to the dollar); the organizations were the International Bank for Reconstruction and Development (the World Bank), the International Monetary Fund (the IMF) and the General Agreement on Tariffs and Trade (GATT). These organizations were subordinate to the states which created and dominated them and the system itself depended crucially on the strength and discipline of the US dollar.

The World Bank was founded to assist in the postwar reconstruction of Europe. When this task was largely taken over by the Marshall Plan the Bank gradually turned its attention to development and to the rest of the world. Like the IMF, with which the Bank was allied by their common location in Washington and by the requirement that the Bank must be a member of the Fund, the Bank was governed by a professional board where the larger contributors to its capital funds carried commensurate weight. Besides these funds the Bank raised money by floating its own bonds on international stock exchanges. It made loans to creditworthy states at commercial rates of interest, for limited periods (at the end of which the funds could be lent again elsewhere) and principally for economic infrastructure. Its strictly conservative policies were necessary in order to enable it to borrow in money markets at the best available rates but these policies restricted its initial activities to enhancing the rich rather than aiding the poor. For the latter purpose it established the International Finance Corporation, which was designed to help the poorer states to get finance from the private banking sector and, in 1960, the International Development Association which made 50-year interest-free loans to poorer states. These IDA loans were financed mainly by western governments, were used mainly for economic infrastructure and were expected to produce a reasonable, if belated, return. In development therefore the Bank's principal function was that of mediator or procurer. Until the 1970s its activities were restrained but in that decade the scale of its operations was magnified by a factor of ten or more and this expansion was accompanied by a new doctrine which, in order to justify lending to less conventionally creditworthy recipients, emphasized the potential economic value of poor societies, once they were developed or developing. Nevertheless, and in spite of this expansion, the Bank's material contribution to development was small. By the last years of the century less than 1 per cent of the sums borrowed by developing countries from beyond their borders came directly from the World Bank and the Bank was constrained to lend only (or not much more than) what it could itself borrow for fear of being accused of plundering taxpayers in rich countries in order to help the distant poor.

The parallel functions of the IMF were to stabilize national currencies in terms of one another and, as a consequence, to promote commerce by ensuring predictable rates of exchange and so avoid the financial anarchy of the 1930s when competitive devaluations engendered worldwide recession by halting trade. The British, more ambitious than the Americans, argued – in vain – for an international currency, variable volumes of credit geared to the expansion of trade and much larger initial reserves than the $25 billion with which the Fund started. The drawing rights of the members of the Fund and their voting weight in its counsels were regulated by their respective contributions to its capital. In its early years it was mostly engaged in making short-term loans, principally to cushion balance of payments difficulties and principally to developed states, and it provided a monitoring and forecasting service on national and international economic affairs. Its basis was called in question by the almost simultaneous abrogation in 1971 of the dollar's convertibility into gold and the pegging of other currencies to the dollar. The context in which it operated was then transformed by the drastic oil price rises of 1973 and 1979, which created massive imbalances (particularly for states which were oil importers and relatively underdeveloped), while the consequent flood of petrodollars made floating currencies float more wildly. The Fund was all but swamped, lost prestige and influence, and was forced to reconsider its ambit and its methods. Ostensibly worldwide in its purposes, the Fund – like the Bank – had operated as an adjunct of an economic system created by and largely for the developed capitalist world, but from the 1970s it was impelled to take a wider view as the developing (and now independent) Third World clamoured to be treated as part of the world's economic problems and the richer countries began to realize the extent of their economic involvement with the poorer. The IMF became something of a financial physician, even surgeon, called upon to advise and succour national economies which had got into trouble or desperation through poverty or profligacy or bad management. Its standard remedies included balanced budgets, higher and more efficiently collected taxes, higher interest rates and – in later years – better government. These remedies fitted some situations better than others and unfailingly exacted a harsh price in lower employment or wages or profits, so that the IMF became unpopular with governments and governed, the more so where its help was most needed. Its attempts to strengthen good government became identified in the eyes of lenders with democracy which, however desirable, was not always or everywhere reinforced by the imposition of multiparty politics from the outside.

Beginning with the Mexican crisis of 1994 (see Chapter 28) and intensifying with the crises in ASEAN, South Korea and Brazil (Chapters 18, 4 and 27) two new dilemmas presented themselves. In order to prevent collapse in these national economies with unpredictable damage beyond their national borders, the IMF assembled very large salvage packages stretching over a number of years. These programmes stretched the IMF's resources to the point where each crisis threatened to become a crisis too far and called in question the propriety of providing for countries in trouble large sums which were used to rescue banks in the developed world whose incautious lending had aggravated the crises. The IMF risked becoming a guarantor of rich lenders instead of a helping hand for stricken countries in temporary trouble. This was neither the IMF's proscribed role nor one likely to appeal to taxpayers in rich countries who were the ultimate source of its funds.

Both the IMF and World Bank had extended their scope at a time when national governments and legislatures, particularly those of the United States, were becoming unwilling to countenance such changes or contribute more than a minimal proportion of their own GDP to them. The IMF was directing its efforts and funds to the relief of poverty in addition to its prime purpose of currency stabilization while the Bank was lending beyond its original purpose of supporting developments incapable of attracting private commercial backing.

As the third arm of its system the Bretton Woods conference considered but rejected an international trading organization. What emerged was the GATT – a process rather than an organization – which pursued the freeing of trade through a series of meshed quinquennial bargainings to reduce tariffs, abolish quotas, rule out new or extended preferences and assure to all every preference available to any – beginning with the reduction of obstacles to trade in manufactured goods. The average industrial tariff when the GATT came into force was over 40 per cent, but by 1980 this average had been reduced to not much more than 4 per cent and the volume of world trade had quintupled in 25 years. It was in the nature of the GATT process that each round of negotiations would be more difficult to conclude than the last and the Uruguay Round inaugurated in 1986 – the eighth in a sequence begun in Geneva in 1947 – did not reach agreement for seven years. Besides the ever-increasing number of participants, negotiations were complicated by the shift from manufactured to agricultural products, financial services, so-called intellectual properties (patents, royalties) and the larger export earners of richer countries (civil aircraft, film, cassette and television products). Most intractable for political as well as economic reasons were agricultural subsidies on which agreement was reached only at the cost of abandoning parts of the Round's ambitious programme.

The principal contestants were the European Community acting as a single unit (subject however to the approval of the Council of Ministers and its individual members) and the United States with the support of 15 other major food exporters collectively denominated the Cairns Group. The United States began by demanding, as a condition for subscribing any of the Round's voluminous packet of provisions, that the Community reduce its export subsidies to cereals by 90 per cent of current rates over ten years. The Community offered cuts of 30 per cent from levels prevailing in 1986. Attempts to close the considerable gap created by the unrealistic opening stance of each side were complicated by the impact of the GATT's debate on the Community's Common Agricultural Policy (CAP – see pp. 194–6) which the members of the Community were painfully and slowly unravelling in the face of strong opposition from their farmers.

The Community had reached agreement on reductions in subsidies which, they claimed, would have to be renegotiated – a horrifying prospect – if American demands in the GATT process were accepted. The United States had little sympathy with this argument, particularly in the approach to the presidential election of 1992. They responded with threats to impose tariffs up to 200 per cent (in effect total proscription) on selected European commodities, beginning with French wines.

A further source of mutual exasperation was a quarrel, outside the GATT Round, over the volume of exports and the production of oilseeds, although this issue was narrowed to a sticking point of half a million tons of Community oilseeds valued at a mere $100 million. A bargain was struck between the EC and the United States by the Blair House agreement of 1992 under which EC subsidies for cereal exports were to be cut by 21 per cent over six years. But European farmers remained unreconciled and French farmers in particular put pressure on their government to reject the deal and therewith the entire Round (notwithstanding that these farmers were not on the whole cereal growers, a sector which had been largely taken over by agribusinesses). A contest in obduracy was kept up until the eve of the date fixed by the US Congress for allowing the president to approve the Round's Final Act without Congressional endorsement of its details: Congress might approve or reject but not move amendments to anything accepted by the president before the date. The final stages of the Round were dramatized as a conflict between the United States and the EC – predominantly France with varying degrees of sympathy from other EC members. France's principal aims were to protect a corner of French agriculture, to ward off American attacks on export subsidies and to try to win protection for European against American filmmakers (a booming industry) and aircraft manufacturers. These aims were largely secured either by concessions or postponement to a later Round.

When in 1994 the Final Act of the Round was adopted (subject to necessary ratifications) much had been achieved, even if at some cost in postponing the more intractable issues. The agreement gave promise of massive gains in commerce and employment. Measured in money the benefits worldwide were, very speculatively, put at $5,000 billion after ten years but with relatively little immediate impact and more for rich than poor countries. The Uruguay Round marked a shift away from tariffs and quotas to financial and other services and rights in intellectual properties. There was some attempt, notably by the United States and France, to import social and environmental criteria into the world's commercial and economic order – a thrust which was unexceptionable so long as it was restricted to such issues as prison or child labour but was suspect in developing countries, which feared that the richer, by enforcing standards unacceptable to low-wage countries, might introduce a new kind of protectionism under the cloak of social justice. The conclusion of the Round after seven strenuous years was a relief but also an omen, for it owed much to political pressures in the closing stages: there was more fear of disagreement than readiness to agree.

The American position on the Uruguay Round was softened only after Clinton had won Congressional approval for the addition of Mexico to a regional North American Free Trade Area (NAFTA – see Chapter 28) and had made a personal appearance at a conference at Seattle to applaud the Asian Pacific Economic Co-operation Forum (APEC) created in 1989 on Australian initiative to foster a large regional bloc comprising the South Pacific, South-east Asia, North Asia and North America. Bruised and wearied by the complexities and rebuffs of the Uruguay Round, the United States had concluded a commercial treaty with Canada whose main aims were to counter Japanese penetration of the United States market through Canada and to cut Canada's subsidizing of its exports (e.g. timber) into the United States. The extension of this agreement to Mexico created a free trade area with a population of 370 million. But Congressional and public opinion in the United States was uneasy about NAFTA (and its possible extension to other parts of South America) on the grounds that it would encourage United States industries to move south and Mexican job-seekers to pour north. Bush postponed action as elections approached and Clinton secured Congressional ratification only with difficulty. Nevertheless, in 1993 the Clinton administration floated the idea of a Free Trade Area of the Americas (FTAA) and pursued it through two conferences of 34 presidents (Cuba was left out) in 1994 and 1998.

Japan had similar visions for a Japanese sphere of economic influence in the three continents which formed the Pacific rim. At a second APEC meeting in Japan in 1994 17 of the 18 states which attended agreed to abolish all barriers to imports from their associates by 2010 in the case of the five major states and by 2020 in the case of the rest: only Malaysia refused to accept either date. Although Clinton once more appeared in person there were unspoken doubts whether the United States was a natural member of the Asian–Australasian group or an eager intruder into an organization whose members might account for half of all international trade by 2010.

With the end of the Uruguay Round the GATT was transformed into the World Trade Organization (WTO – 1995) which was given wider powers to adjudicate disputes and pursue breaches of its rules but set to work in a harsher climate. Its greater authority was unwelcome to those who detected in it a trend away from a mere forum and towards a political federation and to those who were edging away from free trade and towards protectionism. It tackled in its first years hundreds of particular disputes but could do little to mitigate the hardening hostility between the major trading blocs – the United States, the EU and Japan. Its general conference in Seattle in 1999 was disrupted by a concurrence of protest demonstrations of varying substance and it ended without agreement on any of the main subjects on its agenda: an EU proposal, apparently backed by the United States and Japan, to exempt from customs duties all (or many) products of developing countries; a possible conclusion to the long dispute over domestic and export subsidies for farm produce between the EU and the United States/Cairns Group of exporters; linkage between trade and labour conditions which were common in developing countries but widely repugnant on humane grounds; and a United States proposal to secure international rules governing trade in biotechno-logically modified products (e.g. genetically modified seeds and hormonally reared cattle) which the EU wished to ban as unsafe to health but the United States regarded as objectionable only because Europeans were scientifically uneducated. Behind these specific issues lay the important facts that the WTO's international governing body had failed to produce a workmanlike agenda and, secondly, that the United States arrived at the conference undecided over how or in what directions it proposed to exercise its acknowledged dominance of world trade.

Certain features of world economic affairs in the second half of the century were dis-mal. They illustrated the uncertainty and fragility of the economic system inaugurated at Bretton Woods and its incapacity to act in emergencies. In 1944 worldwide free trade had the status of unchallengeable virtue. Yet the American commitment to it was less than total. Through much of the period presidents and their cabinets were more markedly attached to free trade than the Congress, whose members represented par-ticular domestic areas and interests, resented the protectionist practices of other states (notably Japan and other Asian countries), suspected the EC of nursing similar selfish ambitions and so repeatedly enacted legislation to restrain the president's powers in international economic negotiations. There was a reaction against both the ideal of free trade and the global approach to international economic relations. Regional or zonal associations seemed more manageable, more likely to work, more in accord with the interests of countries which knew one another; they gave states the feeling, valid or not, that they were still running their own affairs. Third World states openly challenged the principle of free trade on the grounds that it created a system tailored to the needs of rich developing countries. From its rejection of the Marshall Plan the USSR deliberately absented itself and its satellites from a world system, and when the USSR collapsed, attempts to associate Russia with the international economy were hardly more than perfunctory: the cost was frighteningly high and the political will at best uncertain. In the monetary field the failure of the Bretton Woods plans was even more blatant than in the commercial. American foreign policies in the first phases of the Cold War precipitated an outflow of dollars from the United States and, particularly in Europe, a dollar glut in which the IMF drowned. In 1971 Nixon cancelled the convert-ibility of the dollar into gold and in effect devalued the dollar. All major currencies were decoupled from the dollar or floated in 1972–73 and the Bretton Woods exchange rate regime ceased to exist. All attempts to devise a replacement failed. There was nei-ther a world economic order nor efficient mechanisms for the prevention of disorder.

World order is commonly measured by the sum of international and civil wars but financial turmoil, if seemingly less calamitous, may jeopardize world order no less than armed conflict. And just as the international political system was proving too weak to cope with the swelling range of armed conflict, the international economic order – both as provider and as regulator – was lagging behind the pace of change. In 1944 international economic order meant the co-ordination of national economies for certain limited purposes, but 50 years later a worldwide economy had come into being, divorced from, rather than co-ordinated by, states. The revolution in communications technology had created financial markets which were capable of handling vast numbers of transactions and which never closed: at no hour of the day or night was it impossible to find somewhere to buy or sell currencies or commodities or speculate in futures. A significant part of this business was done by operators using borrowed money or phantom money. Attempts by powerful central banks to impose checks and regulations were too easily countered by the intervention in the markets not of governments but of speculators, whose interests were diametrically opposed, since they thrived on instability rather than the stability which governments, industry and the world of commerce wished for.

In the same years the volume of capital which nourished speculation and made its movement dangerous had also become a necessity for rich and poor countries alike. All faced irresistible needs which could, if not met, produce disasters – whether a collapse of investment in research and production and so in employment, or a collapse in support for the (multiplying) poor. Rich countries, whose standards of living depended on exports, found that trade among themselves was growing more slowly than their trade with poor countries. But the ability of the latter to go on buying the products or services of the former was manifestly limited. They were not themselves creating the domestic capital, the savings or the financial institutions necessary to attract foreign capital to underpin their own development and so in turn sustain the growth of the richer parts of the world.

The magnitude of the problem was illustrated by the cost to Germany alone of rescuing and rehabilitating its eastern Länder after reunification: $100 billion a year for a comparatively small territory with a population of less than 20 million. Rescue plans for the remaining Soviet satellites, let alone for Russia itself and Ukraine, were grievously understated and then unmet; and Europe was only a small part of a world where India, China, South Africa and many others were embarking on ambitiously costly expansion without the necessary capital or likely ways of attracting it. If at the end of the century there was a need to reconsider and redefine the UN's role in keeping the peace, there was a no less urgent need to review and reinforce the operations of the World Bank and the IMF. World order was an empty phrase without the capital to sustain it, the conditions for that capital to fructify, and the regulation to keep a global economic system under the control of responsible national or international government rather than predators stirring up trouble.

By the close of the twentieth century world order was not an alternative to several and separable regional orders: the alternative was world disorder. But the role of worldwide organizations was a limited one. The Cold War against the Soviet Union had marginalized the UN as the resurgence of Germany in the 1930s and the failure of the

European powers to deal with it had marginalized the League of Nations. The UN Charter presupposed a cultural congruence which was grounded more in hope than observation. Although the second half of the century witnessed the collapse of intransigent communist ideologies it witnessed also an intensification of intolerant religious fundamentalism in the Islamic Middle East, among Christians in the United States, in Judaism and in Hinduism; and it witnessed internationalism flourishing most vigorously in the form of commerce which was illegal and even criminal.

The defeat of Soviet communism – *pace* what might happen to Chinese communism – was a triumph for parliamentary democracy and for capitalism. Yet it was a triumph with reservations. The formal advances of democracy during the century and in all continents had less than heartfelt public acclaim. Politicians as a class did not command great respect; they seemed to devote too much effort to scoring silly points against one another in a world of their own. Democracy defeated rival ideologies but without gaining credit either in new states or in older strongholds. Capitalism had shown that communism provided no alternative economic system but capitalism had itself failed to cope with inflation or unemployment, than which few matters were more important to most people. Democratic governments had found no way to restrain inflationary wage demands and were careless about the inflation generated by wars which forced up prices of raw materials and were financed by printing or borrowing money.

Neutralism and realignment

One of the biggest changes that can occur in a world divided into sovereign states is the multiplication of these states. This happened in Europe with the dissolution of the Ottoman and Habsburg empires. A generation later it happened worldwide upon the dissolution of European empires outside Europe. This process was protracted but the greater part of it was consummated during the 25 years after the Second World War. This period was dominated by the Cold War and that conflict gave the new states one of their initial basic characteristics.

Both the protagonists in the Cold War were uninhibited in their hostility to European colonialism, but as the Cold War created the Euro-American alliance embodied in NATO, American hostility to the British, French and other European presences in Asia and Africa was transformed. While commercially it was frequently intensified by competition in areas hitherto dominated by the colonialists, governmentally it became muted by the American need for European allies and bases.

The phrase 'Third World' was first proposed by Dag Hammarskjöld to designate the poor countries of Asia and Latin America. It was a Third World because it rejected the notion of a world divided into two, a world in which only the United States and the USSR counted and everybody else had to declare for the one or the other. It feared the power of the superpowers, exemplified and magnified by nuclear weapons. It distrusted their intentions, envied (particularly in the American case) their superior wealth and rejected their insistence that, in the one case in democratic capitalism and in the other in communism, they had discovered a way of life which others need do no more than copy. Nationalist leaders, although anti-European in the nature of things, had at least one characteristic in common with their retreating masters: their temper was pragmatic. Moscow's rigid communist dogmatism, and Washington's increasingly rigid anti-communism, offended them. Above all, they felt beholden neither to the United States nor to the USSR for their independence from European rule, which they attained with unexpected speed and ease.

The decision of the new states of Asia and Africa, with few exceptions, to throw in their lot with neither superpower was much influenced by one man, Jawaharlal Nehru. Nehru was a world figure before becoming in 1947 prime minister of the most populous of the new states, and he held that office uninterruptedly for 17 years. He was a pragmatic and eclectic patrician who had imbibed western liberal and democratic values and was also attracted by the USSR's record in auto-industrialization. He was repelled by Stalin's tyranny and police rule, but also by the crudities of McCarthyism in the United States and by the arrogant and moralistic division of the world into communists and anti-communists. (Parenthetically, and with hindsight, it is worth emphasizing the worldwide impact of McCarthyism, a domestic upheaval in the United States which seemed to betoken a sharp swing to the right in American politics, coupled with a myopically oversimplified view of world politics. McCarthy's indiscriminate charges of treason and conspiracy flourished on the shocks of the Korean War. In the United States the mood and the methods induced by these shocks were mastered when the peak of the war passed but the damage to the American image abroad persisted much longer.)

Nehru was the principal creator of the post-imperial Commonwealth as an association of monarchies and republics of all races whose links were not ideological but historical and accidental. When he decided that India should remain in the British Commonwealth (as it was still called at this date) he did so upon the conditions that India should become a republic and that it should have the right to conduct without cavil a foreign policy distinct from, conceivably even at odds with, the foreign policies of Britain and its other Commonwealth associates. Thus he stressed the political independence which all new states needed to assert, while retaining links which had economic, cultural and sentimental value. His example was widely followed. Although Burma severed these links with Britain in 1948, no other British possession did so and at the end of the century the Commonwealth had 53 members, including Pakistan, which had resigned in 1973, rejoined in 1989 and was suspended – barred from meetings but not from membership – in 1999. It had members in every part of the world. (Its French counterpart *La Francophonie*, created in the 1990s, had 49 members.)

Nehru's insistence that each member of the Commonwealth should be free to pursue its own foreign policy meant that neither the Commonwealth as a whole nor its several members need follow Britain's example in taking the American side in the Cold War. This was the beginning of the Third World's neutralism or non-alignment, to which France's former colonies also adhered in the 1960s. In western Europe there had been at the close of the Second World War a hankering after a similarly independent – and mediatory – stance between the United States and the USSR (a so-called Third Force, championed for example by Georges Bidault), but it shrivelled under the impact of heavy-handed Russian measures such as the Prague coup of 1948. Europe became the seat of the Cold War. The rest of the world liked to think that it lay apart.

Its attitudes passed through a number of phases. They were rooted in the concept of neutrality. Neutrality was a general declaration of intent to remain out of any war which might occur, but it had not proved very useful to its various adherents during the Second World War and in any case the new states were not thinking of a shooting war and how to keep out of it, but of the Cold War and how to behave in regard to it. Neutralism and non-alignment, therefore, as distinct from neutrality, were the expression of an attitude towards a particular and present conflict: they entailed, first, equivalent relations with both sides and, secondly – in the phase called positive neutralism – attempts to mediate and abate the dangerous quarrels of the great. In its more negative phase non-alignment involved a reprobation of the Cold War, an assertion that there were more important matters in the world, an acknowledgement of the powerlessness of new states, and a refusal to judge between the two giant powers.

The positive phase of neutralism represented the desires of new states to evade the Cold War but not to be left out of world politics. If at first sight the postwar bipolar world seemed to leave as little scope for small powers as in the days of the great struggles between the Roman and Persian empires, on second thoughts it seemed that the neutralists might nevertheless play a gratifyingly honourable and sensible part. When Africa as well as Asia became independent the number of neutralists and the space they occupied around the globe became considerable. They might at the very least prevent the Cold War from spreading to these areas; by merely setting limits to bipolar commitment they could reduce the occasions and areas of conflict. They could too, by virtue of their combined importance, cause the great powers to woo them, thus becoming a kind of lightning conductor in world politics. More positively still, they might exert influence by the time-honoured method of holding conferences to publicize their views or by the newer method of arguing and voting in the General Assembly of the United Nations. In this last respect the Indian voice was again decisive. The new states hesitated at first in their attitudes towards the UN, not knowing whether it might turn out to be dominated by its European members, as the League of Nations had been, or by the west or by the great powers. They feared that the new organization might be used to buttress colonialism or to subserve the purposes of the Cold War, in either of which events they would have had little use for it, but after a little experience they decided otherwise. India in particular became prominent in its discussions and its field commissions and supplied for emergency operations units without which those operations could hardly have been contemplated (especially after Hammarskjöld developed the principle that major powers must not contribute fighting units to UN forces).

The effects of anti-colonialism, the Cold War and neutralism upon one another cannot be precisely calculated, but it is evident that the neutralists had some effect on states outside their ranks. In the first years after the Second World War American attitudes to Asians were affected by the need to rescue western Europe and the call to fight an aggressor in Korea. The European Recovery Programme engendered by the Marshall Plan absorbed a great deal of American talent and attention as well as American money and made Americans less critical of the European colonialism which they had in the past so unequivocally decried. To Asians the American voice seemed to become muted by the need to find sure and strong allies against a Russian communist threat: in other words, the Cold War was perverting the American attitude on colonialism and even carrying the United States, spiritually and physically, into the imperialist camp. To the Americans the war in Korea was a major event in the conflict between communism and anti-communism, in which too few people gave too little help (no more than 10 per cent of the combat effort) and some, notably Asians, indulged in ill-timed carping. The American attitude to Asian neutralism was one of righteous indignation. Thus the events of these years made Asians dub Americans imperialists and Americans dub Asians traitors or at least hypocrites.

As professed anti-imperialists, the Russians had been equivocal, supporting some communist movements but doubtful about others. What struck them about the leaders of new states was their bourgeois character, and they attacked them accordingly as western stooges. Men like Nehru and Nasser seemed at first no better than any western European politician who joined NATO. But the arrival of such leaders at the UN in increasing numbers converted the Russians to the idea that they constituted, and must therefore be treated as, a separate group midway between the communist bloc and the USSR's enemies.

To be effective, non-alignment, negative or positive, presupposed solidarity among the non-aligned. The new states were weak and aware of their weakness, which – no less than their repudiation of the Cold War – was their hallmark. Their weakness made them wary of too close an association with a single major power and so obliged them to seek strength by unity among themselves. Many of them were far from being nations, and such political unity as they possessed had been a function of xenophobia. Their governments were metamorphosed liberation movements which had to create the broadest possible consensus in order to prevent the new state from disintegrating or becoming ungovernable. In so far as this problem impinged on external policies it suggested the advisability of the broadest range of contacts and friendships among foreign states and the need to eschew any precise and discriminatory alignment. Economic needs pointed the same way: no new state was so important to the world's rich powers as to be able to command from one rich power all the aid it needed;

better therefore not to contract an alliance with one power which would rule out the possibility of getting aid from others. (This argument was not conclusive. Many of the small states which emerged from French rule in Africa were so weak that they had no choice but to take what they could get from France.) Similarly, in the field of defence, while there was a superficial argument in favour of attachment to a particular strong protector, it was also observable that major powers wanted to keep out of the sort of local disputes in which new states wanted help – as opposed to local aspects of global conflict, in which new states did not want to get involved.

The search for solidarity preceded independence among both Asians and Africans. The first notable postwar Asian conference – the Asian Relations Conference held in New Delhi in March 1947 – assembled 28 delegations of which only eight came from sovereign states. Its motive force was a desire to ensure that the United Nations should not become an organization dominated by European or white states and viewpoints, but the tone of the discussions was not markedly anti-colonial. The conference was a gathering of Asians to discuss Asian problems including land reform, industrialization, Asian socialism and the application of non-violence in international affairs. The conference established a permanent organization which existed for eight years but did not do much else. Soon afterwards India, Pakistan, Burma and Ceylon became independent. They did so in a world which had expected peace but not got it. There were guerrilla wars and insurrections in Burma, Malaya and the Philippines, and open fighting in Indonesia, Indo-China and Palestine. In domestic politics violence claimed notable victims in Burma in June 1947 with the assassination of Aung San and six colleagues, and an even more notable victim in January 1948 when Mahatma Gandhi was killed.

In January 1949 another Asian conference assembled in New Delhi. The Soviet Asian republics, which had attended the 1947 meeting, were not this time asked, and Turkey refused an invitation. Otherwise Asia, including the Middle East, was fully represented and Australia and New Zealand sent observers. The immediate occasion for the conference was Indonesia, where an Asian liberation movement was being threatened with extinction by the Dutch, and where, to Asian eyes, the UN seemed bent on facilitating the reimposition of white colonial rule. In the previous December the Dutch had resorted to their second police action and had captured and imprisoned a number of Indonesian leaders. The conference demanded their release and the establishment of an interim government and independence for Indonesia by 1950. Like its predecessor, this conference created a permanent organization which proved ineffective, partly because a number of Asian states were becoming jealous of India's predominance and did not wish to see it institutionalized. The Indonesian issue gave the conference a clear anti-colonial note, but it was divided between friends of the west and neutralists. This division was accentuated in the following months when Asian leaders took up different attitudes towards the two outstanding Asian events of the year, the victory of Mao Zedong and communism in China and the war in Korea. Asian solidarity was proving difficult to achieve, even on an anti-colonialist programme; the

British and French campaigns in Malaya and Indo-China did not evoke the same united protest as the Dutch proceedings in Indonesia, partly because of the communist flavour in the Malayan and Vietnamese anti-colonialist movements.

In the 1950s Asian solidarity and neutralism waxed and then wore thin. Some Asian states, putting their economic and strategic needs before their neutralism, signed commercial and even defence treaties with the United States or the USSR. India, by its treaty of 1954 with China embodying the Panch Shila, maintained its principles, but in the same year Pakistan, Thailand and the Philippines concluded military agreements with the United States, while Afghanistan became the first non-communist country to receive Russian aid, and the USSR, which already had a trade agreement with India and was about to conclude another with Burma, intensified the diplomatic and economic wooing of Indonesia which was to lead Sukarno to visit Moscow in 1956. The great powers were taking a gratifying interest in Asian affairs but one consequence was to make it more difficult for Asians to maintain a common attitude towards the great powers or to keep their distance as pure neutralism required.

Another conference, originally suggested by Ceylon and taken up by Sukarno and Nehru, assembled at Bandung in April 1955. The background comprised the treaty between the United States and Taiwan, the Manila Pact creating SEATO, and the Baghdad Pact. The USSR and China welcomed what looked at first like an anti-western conference, while Washington's friends – Thailand and the Philippines – were half-inclined not to go. Israel was excluded on account of Arab opinion. The 29 participants included six from Africa (Egypt, Libya, Sudan, Ethiopia, Liberia, Ghana), so that Bandung became the prototype of Afro-Asian as opposed to purely Asian solidarity. It was an assembly of the needy and the indignant, not a concentration of power. Its members were divided among themselves even on the issue of non-alignment, but the timing was propitious. The Cold War in Europe had, since the Berlin blockade of 1948–49 and the growth of Russian nuclear power to match the American, lapsed into stalemate but not into a thaw. Both sides were looking elsewhere and competing for the allegiance of states in other continents with the vague intention of building up a new preponderance by additional alliances, or of turning the enemy's flank by carrying influence and bases into new terrain. The Russians and the Chinese hoped to advance communism by exploiting anti-western nationalisms, while the Americans hoped to exploit fears of communism and of China and so create new, and if necessary heavily subsidized, military groups: American policy, freshly illustrated by the signing of the Manila Pact, ran counter to the spirit of Bandung. Zhou Enlai, on the other hand, who put in a personal appearance at Bandung, went some way towards showing that Chinese communism was reconcilable with other Asian nationalisms and that at least one Chinese leader was more sensible and amenable than some current pictures of the new China suggested. The Russians had already, by accident or astuteness, taken a number of steps which brought them into closer accord with the Asian mood. The proposal to neutralize Austria was welcome to Asian neutralists, and gestures like the return of Port Arthur to China and of Porkkala to Finland heartened those who hoped that Stalin's death had changed the face of world politics. In 1955 Bulganin and Khrushchev visited Asia with tremendous acclaim (Khrushchev paid a second visit early in 1960) and the Russian campaign to win over the neutralists was so well launched that even the suppression of the Hungarian revolt of 1956 only dented it (the Anglo-French attack on Suez being invaluable to the Russians in saving their new reputation at this juncture).

For the neutralists themselves the principal achievements of the Bandung conference were that they had met and got to know one another (most of them were new to international politics); that they had laid the foundations for joint action at the UN and, through solidarity, increased their security, their status and their diplomatic weight in the world; that they had attracted new men like Nasser to the group and made it bigger; that they were making the giant powers take them seriously and treat their policies as respectable (a trend which was fortified by the admission of 16 new members to the UN by the package deal of 1955 and still further by the big increase in African membership in 1960); and finally that they had seen one of the leaders of the new, formidable China, had found him not at all frightening and had perhaps inducted China into their pacific circle. In the summer of 1956 Nehru and Nasser visited Tito at Brioni in Yugoslavia. With an Asian, an African and a European leading them, the neutralists became more ambitious in international affairs and hoped to be able to bring pressure to bear on the giant powers in Cold War matters, but this association was already passing the peak of its influence, partly because of the activities of those who wanted to turn it into an alliance of communists and black men against non-communist whites by emphasizing anti-colonialism in place of neutralism. Non-alignment became in practice anti-western non-alignment, particularly with the Afro-Asian People's Solidarity Movement, which sponsored a variety of conferences in the late 1950s.

In September 1961 a conference of the unaligned was held in Belgrade. Whereas Bandung had been an exploratory conference, Belgrade had about it an atmosphere of crisis. The background included French nuclear tests in the Sahara and the resumption of Russian tests, the Bay of Pigs and the Berlin wall, the Franco-Tunisian clash over Bizerta and the grinding crisis in the Congo. A new conflict between India and China seemed to be emerging, a conflict between the USSR and China certainly was. Bandung's 29 participants had been overwhelmingly Asian and not overwhelmingly anti-western. The only serious conflict over admissibility had been the Arab veto on Israel. At Belgrade the African representation reflected the division of African states between radicals and moderates, Latin American participants were selected with an anti-western bias and the Europeans included Yugoslavia and Cyprus but not the traditional neutrals, Sweden and Switzerland. An attempt by Nehru to concentrate on peace rather than anti-colonialism and sponsor Russo-American talks met with little success, and a number of delegations displayed a partisan indifference to the nuclear explosion which the Russians set off on the eve of the conference. A proposal to fix a terminal date for colonial rule throughout the world at two to six years was enlarged during the debates to a demand for its immediate and total abolition.

After a pause, plans for another conference led to a meeting in Cairo, more African than Asian, in October 1964 and to a project for a conference in Algiers in 1965. This plan was vitiated by the fall of Ben Bella a few days before a preliminary meeting in June and by increasing embarrassment among the likely participants at the prospect of a Sino-Soviet conflict. The Chinese wished to exclude the USSR and assume the leadership of the underprivileged but at a second preliminary meeting in October the invitation to the USSR was approved, whereupon the Chinese threatened to stay away. In these circumstances a majority thought it better to have no conference at all. The movement seemed to be wilting but it was reanimated during 1967 by visits by Tito to Asian and African countries and in 1969 a conference in Belgrade gave it fresh impetus. At Havana ten years later 92 full members attended. Whereas the original members had been non-aligned in their policies and their sympathies, the much wider flock of the 1970s contained a number of states which, although non-aligned by policy, had definite pro-western or pro-communist sympathies.

African solidarity and non-alignment, which began to join forces with the Asian current at Bandung in 1955, had its own remoter origins. Pan-Africanism began as an assertion of the distinctiveness and value of an explicitly African or (by extension to those lands to which the slaves had been consigned) black culture. As such it was primarily Caribbean and West African, but it became also part of the wider movement for colonial emancipation in which nationalists from all parts of Africa could consort with and seek strength from one another. Thirdly, there were those (Nkrumah, for example) who saw that political freedom was not the whole of freedom, that economic dependence would persist after the winning of sovereign statehood, and that Africa might stand on its own feet economically only by developing its continental resources in common. This third aspect of pan-Africanism pointed logically to a political union or at least a federation and it was therefore in conflict with the creation of new sovereign states committed to the preservation of their integrity as well as their independence.

Six pan-African conferences had been held between 1900 and 1945. The first of them and the four which followed in the 1920s were predominantly Caribbean and North American, but the last was dominated by African leaders from Africa itself. All of them were meetings of personalities. With the beginnings of independence came meetings of African parties and African governments. The former created an All African People's Organization which, at conferences in Accra in 1958, Tunis in 1960 and Cairo in 1961, discussed schemes for African unity or an African commonwealth on the basis that co-operation between governments was not enough. But the third meeting was the last. As the tally of independent states grew, the states' system took hold. Nkrumah continued to beat the drum for a union government until his fall in 1966 but this theme, although a standard item at conferences of the Organization for

African Unity for some years, attracted declining support, both because it was regarded as unpractical and because it became increasingly identified with a left-wing radical minority.

At the date of the first meeting of independent African states, held in Accra in 1958, there were nine independent states in the continent. One of them, South Africa, declined the invitation to Accra. The others were Ethiopia, Liberia, Egypt, Morocco, Tunisia, Libya, Ghana and Guinea. They were chiefly concerned with anti-colonialism, the racial and nationalist struggles in South Africa and Algeria, and the problem of achieving some sort of African unity while at the same time respecting the independence and integrity of African states. This conference was followed in 1959 by the Declaration of Conakry whereby Ghana and Guinea formed a union which was declared to be the starting point of a wider African union. This step was an unpremeditated retort to the ostracizing of Guinea by France, a practical demonstration of Nkrumah's pan-African principles and a lifeline for Guinea. It was followed in the same year by the Declaration of Saniquellie which, primarily on Liberian insistence, emphasized the independence and integrity of existing states.

By 1960, when the second conference of independent African states assembled in Addis Ababa, their number had almost doubled and their unity was about to be tested by the special strains of the Congo as well as by inherited border disputes. Fifteen states were represented. Active border disputes involved Ethiopia and Somalia, Ghana and Togo, Guinea and the Cameroons. The first of these led to fighting but the others did not. More serious for the prospects of African unity was a contest between Ghana and Nigeria in which Ghana urged the case for immediate steps to unity and Nigeria argued in favour of a slow approach to some kind of looser federation. This dispute was spiced with some bitterness since the Nigerians resented Nkrumah's assumption of leadership and distrusted his aims, while Nkrumah feared that Nigeria intended to throw the influence of its vast size on to the side of conservatism versus socialism and of Nigerian nationalism versus pan-Africanism. In the Congo the independent African states tried, both at the UN and in a conference at Leopoldville in August 1960, to present a united front and play a constructive pacificatory role, but they were not successful.

From this point the independent African states began to form separate groups, which were later reassembled in one organization by the founding of the Organization for African Unity. The largest of these was the Brazzaville group, consisting of all the former French colonies except Guinea, with the addition of Mauritania (whose claim to be independent and not a part of Morocco was accepted by the group). The Brazzaville group began as an ad hoc meeting at Abidjan in October 1960, when the principal topic for discussion was Algeria, but at Brazzaville in December and at further meetings during 1961 at Dakar, Yaoundé and Tananarive it developed into a permanent association, discussed ways of perpetuating the co-operation and common services which had existed in the colonial period, set up an organization for economic co-operation, and considered joint institutions and defence arrangements. This group was neither pan-African nor regional, but an expression of common needs and a common outlook.

A second group took shape at a conference at Casablanca in 1961. It consisted of six independent African states plus the Algerian revolutionaries and Ceylon. The six African states were Morocco, Egypt and Libya (which soon afterwards transferred to the Brazzaville group) and Ghana, Guinea and Mali (which had joined the Ghana–Guinea union in the previous year). The Casablanca group opposed the independence of Mauritania and was pro-Lumumbist in the Congo, although at its second conference in May in Cairo Nkrumah successfully opposed proposals to withdraw troops from the UN force and switch them to Lumumba's political heir, Antoine Gizenga. This group too established permanent political, economic and cultural committees, a supreme command, and a headquarters at Bamako in Mali.

Later in the same year 20 states assembled in conference at Monrovia. They included the whole of the Brazzaville group, Libya and a majority of former British territories. The Monrovia group thus subsumed the Brazzaville group and, owing to the prominence of Nigeria, acquired a specifically anti-Ghanaian and anti-Nkrumah flavour. The movement for African unity seemed to have been blocked by current problems (the Congo and, to a lesser extent, Mauritania) and by personalities. Nevertheless, the idea remained alive. Even if Nkrumah's vision of a union extending into every part of the continent was unacceptable or impracticable, lesser unions might be attempted. The Ghana–Guinea union, with or without Mali, had proved of little practical consequence, but it had been a political demonstration. In the north-west Morocco, Tunisia and Algeria had espoused federation at a meeting in Tangier in 1958. In east and central Africa there was talk of a federation between Kenya, Uganda, Tanganyika, Zanzibar, Malawi, Zambia and Rhodesia – with possible extensions in some barely visible future to Rwanda, Burundi, Mozambique and even South Africa. A Pan-African Freedom Movement of East and Central Africa (Pafmeca) came into existence in 1958, was enlarged four years later by adding 's' for South as its penultimate letter and was dissolved in 1963; these were associations for self-help in the struggle for liberation.

The French connection was at the base of a number of inter-state organizations: the Entente Council (Ivory Coast, Niger, Upper Volta, Togo and Dahomey; see Chapter 22); the Senegal River Association (Senegal, Mali, Guinea, Mauritania; Chapter 22); a West African and a Central African Customs Union. More important was the African and Malagasy Economic Union (UAMCE) founded in 1965 by 13 formerly French and Belgian territories and converted into the African and Malagasy Common Organization (OCAM) whose charter, signed at Tananarive in 1966, declared it to be open to all African states – provided all existing members accepted each newcomer. OCAM created a number of useful agencies, which were sometimes more effective than those of the OAU, but politically its members were often divided. In the 1960s it was seen as a weapon for Houphouët-Boigny of the Ivory Coast against Nkrumah and in support of Tshombe; in the Nigerian civil war, in which it tried in vain to mediate,

Ivory Coast and Gabon recognized Biafra while the remainder were anti-separatist; some members had diplomatic relations with China, others with Taiwan. As the colonial period receded, the common French inheritance became a weaker link. There were a number of absentees from the eighth congress held at Lomé in 1972 and Zaïre, feeling that it was not getting enough out of membership, resigned from the organization.

Although the Congo had demonstrated the difficulty of preserving unity among independent African states, it had no less demonstrated the advantages of doing so and a conference at Lagos in 1962 produced a draft charter for an organization of African states. At a further conference in Addis Ababa in 1963 the Organization for African Unity was born with an initial membership of 32. The OAU was not a collective security organization as envisaged by article 51 of the charter of the UN but an organization for the promotion of African unity and collaboration and for the eradication of colonialism. It consisted of an annual assembly of heads of state, a council of ministers and a secretariat. A projected commission of mediation, conciliation and arbitration did not materialize, although these functions were in fact performed: in border disputes between Morocco and Algeria, Somalia and Ethiopia, Somalia and Kenya, Ghana and Upper Volta. In the last case, which rose out of the construction by Ghana of a school on territory claimed by Upper Volta, Ghana conceded the claim at a meeting of the OAU's council of ministers. In the other cases the OAU provided mediators and commissions of inquiry which helped to appease the disputes.

The establishment of this organization epitomized two processes which had been going on for a generation or more and had gathered force in the 20 years after the end of the Second World War. Africans ceased to be cut off from each other and they ceased to be cut off from world affairs. Their emancipation had a great variety of causes: the essential liberalism (reinforced by weariness) of the principal colonial powers, the growth of the movement for human rights, American and Russian attacks on colonialism, the Gandhian example, the development of roads and of international airways. While this process was taking place a new class of African, the politician, the lawyer, the intellectual, the *évolué*, was taking the place of the chief (in so far as chiefs did not join the new class) and was at the same time rejecting the models prepared for his country by the French and the British. The French had assumed that their colonies would grow into worthy pieces of France, but they had hardly noticed that their doctrine worked neither in terms of government, which was paternalistic and white, nor in terms of society, where low wages and even forced labour were too long tolerated and the favoured few tended not to become leaders in their society but to be extracted from it. The British, who had based themselves originally on paternalism and chiefs, realized the limitations of this model but planned to substitute for it an inapplicable British parliamentary system to be worked by an elite. Consequently, the new states – albeit that many of their first leaders, themselves a western-educated and relatively affluent elite, had originally insisted on western democratic institutions as the best available and had expected them to work without essential modification – found that they had to innovate in theory as well as in practice. They had to find administrators, public servants, economists, teachers, doctors, accountants and trade union leaders and at the same time construct institutions and develop conventions which would reconcile the Africans' traditions with their thirst for modernity and enable them to enjoy the fruits of efficiency, liberty and justice. They looked at the outside world with a mixture of admiration and suspicion, ready to take the best of what could be learned but convinced that however much they adopted they would evolve a distinct African way of doing things. This community of aim gave the new states of Africa points of contact with one another but the OAU was an association of sovereign states in a continent which, in the wake of decolonization, was becoming more fragmented than it had been under foreign rule.

The creation of the OAU represented not only a negation of federal ideas but also an emphasis on specifically African issues. The Charter of the OAU and its founding conference stressed the sacrosanctity of existing frontiers and the role of the new organization in the peaceful settlement of disputes between African states. To some extent, therefore, it derogated from the concept of Afro-Asian solidarity. The two continents were becoming increasingly concerned each with its own affairs; some of their common concerns faded as the anti-colonial struggle passed into history. Even within each continent solidarity came under strain. In Asia China's attack on India (pp. 433–6) destroyed what was left of the Panch Shila, while India's unpreparedness compelled it to approach the giant powers from which, as leaders of the non-aligned, it had tried to keep at arm's length. India lost a degree of its detachment. After the Chinese invasion in 1962 Ceylon, Burma, Cambodia and Indonesia, in company with Egypt and Ghana, tried to use their good offices to effect a Sino–Indian reconciliation but their efforts were of little effect and were welcomed neither in New Delhi nor Beijing.

Poverty

Yet there remained a powerful bond – poverty, and the realization that political independence and sovereignty did not remove economic dependence. In the same year as the Chinese invasion of India, and midway through the Congo crisis, which threatened to split African opinion, the first UN Conference on Trade and Development (UNCTAD) was held in Geneva. This was not an Afro-Asian affair but something larger. It was a point of junction between the Afro-Asians on the one hand and a posse of other states, mostly Latin American, which were not only poor in comparison with the developed industrial world but also found themselves obliged to live in an economic system devised by the rich.

The trading system designed at Bretton Woods presupposed a community of interests between all trading nations and it also supposed that tariffs and quotas were the principal barriers to commerce between states. But neither assumption was true of the economically weaker states. Although they needed to enter the international economy, they needed also to be protected in it; freedom worked against them. Further, their main problems were not tariffs or quotas but the instability of world prices for their products and the difficulty of getting into foreign markets to sell them. They were for the most part not only very poor – with an average annual income per head around one-tenth of the average in NATO countries, even with Greece and Turkey included – but also ill-equipped for international economic competition. Many had inelastic one-crop economies. Their products were primary products, for which the demand (except in the case of oil) was rising less quickly than world income. Their customers were making synthetic or substitute products and, especially in the case of agriculture, were susceptible to domestic protectionist lobbies anxious to close the market to imports. Although the Korean and Vietnam wars produced booms in commodity prices from which a number of these countries benefited, they did so only temporarily. Another palliative was aid, that is to say, cash, credits, goods or skills given free or transmitted at less than the ruling market price. Considerable benefits were transferred in this way and the donors, totting up the yearly sacrifices, congratulated themselves on their generosity.

The recipients, however, thought otherwise. They came to the conclusion that aid was the wrong answer to their problems. Apart from the fact that there was too little of it, and apart too from the realization that most of it was given for political purposes in the Cold War, aid was condemned for a variety of reasons: because the burden of interest payments and capital repayments became a sizeable charge on export earnings; because aid was frequently tied so that the recipient, instead of using it to buy what he wanted where it could be had most cheaply, was obliged to accept schemes not at the top of his list of priorities or buy goods from the donor instead of more cheaply else-where; because aid perpetuated an economic pattern created in colonial times, when colonies were kept to the business of producing raw materials for their owners' needs; because aid impeded the essential business of diversifying the post-colonial economy and making a start with industrialization in order to enable the new state to create capital. For all these reasons the weaker countries quickly found that aid was no sub-stitute for what they really wanted – a change in the rules governing the international economy and particularly guaranteed prices for their products and ease of access to the world's more affluent markets where, if at all, these products must be sold. The UN, which first set aside special funds for developing Third World countries (United Nations Fund for Economic Development [SUNFED]) in 1960, asked the richer coun-tries to contribute 0.7 per cent of their GNP to help the poor to grow at the rate of 5 per cent a year and convened a special conference, planned in 1962 and held in Geneva in 1964. This conference spawned a permanent institution whose main thrust was for higher and more stable commodity prices. In 1967 the poorer states of Asia, Africa and Latin America established the Group of 77 which chose Raul Prebisch of Argentina as its director and transformed the international scene by demanding for economic relations between states as much attention as their political relations. The

Group of 77 stressed the unfairness of an economic order dominated by purchasers and consumers of raw materials and by the volatility of world prices and argued in favour of commercial preferences (as opposed to the GATT's rules of equal treatment for the economically weak and strong), for transfers of technology at bargain prices and for cheap borrowing. But although the Group of 77 changed the way in which people thought about international affairs it had much less success in altering the way they behaved. It became divided between so-called moderates and radicals and was further divided when the oil price rises of the 1970s served the Group's oil producers well but impoverished its oil importers. The emergence of OPEC (Organization of Petroleum-Exporting Countries) as a distinct group illustrated this cleavage. OPEC maintained a general Third World stance while at the same time gravitating into the western economic order as an operator rather than a rebel. When in 1974 the UN proclaimed the need for a New International Economic Order the declaration testified to the number of votes commanded by the Third World in the General Assembly but the sequel testified to the limited effectiveness of national votes in economic affairs. With its overwhelming economic power the west was able to fend off the complaints and campaigns of the Third World and keep western economic relief at levels of charity to be set by the west itself.

The European Community took note of those problems with benevolent but measured intent. When the Treaty of Rome was being negotiated France insisted on the creation of an associate status. It had in mind its African territories, then all still colonies. Part IV of the treaty therefore empowered the Community to accord to non-European states tariff reductions and quota extensions and permit them to impose tariffs of their own to protect infant industries (provided that these tariffs did not discriminate between members of the Community). The Community established a Development Fund which disbursed $581 million in a first quinquennium and $730 million in a second. In 1964, by the first Convention of Yaoundé, 18 former French colonies took advantage of these provisions and in 1969 three former British territories – Kenya, Uganda, Tanzania – were granted the same privileges for one year (until, that is, a revised Yaoundé Convention should come into operation in 1971). Nigeria too negotiated an agreement with the Community. Although at first suspicious of these arrangements as a form of neo-colonialism, Nigeria could not afford to see its neighbours trading on better terms than itself with the Community, to which two-thirds of its exports were despatched. In 1974 a new five-year convention was signed at Lomé between the EC and 46 African, Caribbean and Pacific (ACP) states. It made provision for non-reciprocal tariff reductions, created an aid fund of $1.6 billion and a scheme for stabilizing export prices, and promised Commonwealth sugar producers access to the EEC for all their sugar at the prices assured by the Commonwealth Sugar Agreement. By Lomé II (1979) the EC undertook to take exports from the ACP countries to the value of $15 billion a year and to provide annually aid rising from an initial base of $850 million, most of it designed for roads, education, hospitals, water and electricity. Lomé III and IV followed at quinquennial intervals but by 1990 aid flowing from the conventions, while helpful, was equivalent to no more than half of the aggregate given by members of the Community separately and bilaterally. Recipients were irked by the concomitant dependence and also by the costs and bureaucratic formalities of operating the conventions. In 1995, when Lomé V was concluded after protracted negotiations, beneficiaries numbered 70. The Conventions did little to redress inequalities between or within states or to foster democracy or to make money a modern substitute for gunboats in the relations between strong and weak states. Lomé V was overshadowed by the increasingly heavy foreign debts of the recipients and the declining ability of the EU to satisfy their expectations as its own expanding membership made inroads on its available funds. (See also SADC, p. 636.)

While money and other benefits flowed to the poorer countries from a variety of sources the cost of borrowing grew and debt service became a principal charge on government budgeting. Debtor states sought to reschedule their debts by postponing interest payments and the repayment of capital. At UNCTAD IV in Nairobi in 1976 the Third World presented a comprehensive plan for the rescheduling of debts, technical aid, the promotion of manufacturing industries and the diversification of one-crop economies. The plan was severely mangled by the richer countries who – particularly former colonial powers – were irked by being told that they were not so much commercial creditors as moral debtors. Largely in vain they pointed to the fact that the expansion in the 1950s and 1960s of the world market had been halted and reversed. The effects of world recession on the attitudes and capabilities of the rich were even more in evidence at UNCTAD's fifth conference in Manila in 1979. The desperate poverty, in some areas famine, in the Third World; the prognosis of a world population doubled by the end of the century, with cities under siege and the outbreak of wars for raw materials; a Third World external debt of $300 billion or more; and western aid in decline and western protectionism rising – all these pointers produced a sense of despair which the conference could find no way of alleviating. By this date the concept of a Third World was obsolete. A new group of countries had come into being whose wealth distinguished them dramatically from the world's poor and whose solidarity enabled them to play a forceful role in international affairs. This was the Fourth World of OPEC whose members owed their wealth to oil and their political and economic clout to the fact that, although very different in geographical extent and population, they were few enough and united enough to subordinate their differences to common action. In the 1970s they raised the price of oil so steeply as to make all their customers, rich and poor, tremble. They were able to do this because oil had been gravely underpriced in relation to demand and because its ownership – and therewith the power to fix prices in a sellers' market – had shifted from western companies to producer governments. The OPEC countries were peculiar because, in a world accustomed to regard all developing countries as poor, they were developing countries which were rich. But they

30.1 The world's major oil producers (Source: Data from *CIA World Factbook 2007*)

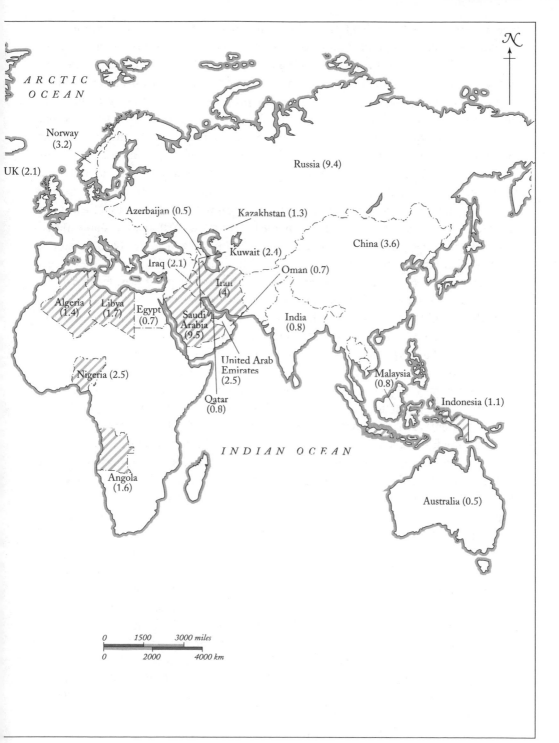

*ARCTIC
OCEAN*

Norway
(3.2)

UK (2.1)

Russia (9.4)

Azerbaijan (0.5)   Kazakhstan (1.3)

China (3.6)

Kuwait (2.4)

Iraq (2.1)   Oman (0.7)

Iran
(4)

Algeria   Libya   Egypt   India
(1.4)   (1.7)   (0.7)   (0.8)

Saudi
Arabia
(9.5)

United Arab
Emirates
(2.5)

Nigeria (2.5)

Malaysia
(0.8)

Indonesia (1.1)

Qatar
(0.8)

INDIAN OCEAN

Angola
(1.6)

Australia (0.5)

0   1500   3000 miles

0   2000   4000 km

were rich in a special way, rich from selling a finite resource, not rich from the infinitely repeatable process of manufacture and agriculture. They foresaw a fixed term to their years of affluence. Their motives in forcing up the price of their commodity were economic (to coin money for development, affluence and ostentation); strategic (to amass armaments); and political (to put anti-Israeli pressure on customers, a majority of OPEC's 13 members being Arab). These price rises were the more disturbing because they coincided with other unsettling economic factors: a decline in the value of the dollar (already under strain from excessive overseas spending, culminating in the Vietnam War), the collapse of the Bretton Woods system, and international inflation. Many OPEC members made more money than they knew what to do with in their relatively underdeveloped and underpopulated countries. By investing their huge surpluses (over $100,000 million a year by the end of the 1970s) in an unstable industrialized world they found themselves acquiring property which, partly as a result of their own actions, was being steadily devalued, while their price increases were squeezing their customers to the point where these must cut their purchases. Furthermore, the massive transfer of capital from countries which could use it productively to countries which could not – from the industrial world to members of OPEC – mothballed resources and so caused a shrinkage of the world economy.

The Third World was doubly hit. It could no longer pay for an essential commodity and it could no longer expect the financial assistance which it had been getting from the governments and private banks of the industrialized countries. The oil-importing developing countries had incurred foreign debts totalling $300 billion; the combined deficit on their balance of payments was edging up to $100 billion a year and increasing by $25 billion a year on account of oil alone. At this rate not only they themselves but their creditors too were facing bankruptcy. Their exports were in decline because of the squeeze on their own production and because their principal markets (the developed countries) were also being squeezed. The OPEC countries accepted some responsibility for alleviating these burdens. They did so by the established practice of giving aid to the poor. In the late 1970s this aid was flowing at rates between 1 and 3 per cent of their GNP and three OPEC members touched 10 per cent. Such rates compared favourably with an OECD target of 0.7 per cent (achieved in practice by no OECD member except Norway, Sweden, Denmark and the Netherlands). On the other hand the OPEC total was achieved partly by diverting OPEC contributions from the World Bank (on political grounds) and much the greater part of it was given to the more impecunious Arab countries in the Middle East and northern Africa.

From the point of view of the Third World OPEC's munificence had its limitations. In terms of a proportion of GNP, OPEC aid was generous. But OPEC's GNP was much smaller than the OECD's (by a factor of about 16), so that the volume of OECD aid remained much larger than OPEC's. Furthermore, OPEC's aid programme was no more than one more palliative; and alms-giving on whatever scale was no substitute for the reform of a fundamentally unbalanced world economic system which was itself contracting. Givers and receivers – OPEC, the EEC or the OECD on the one hand, the UNCTAD majority on the other – assumed a tussle, an adjustment of conflicting interests and divergent fortunes. Theorists had been talking for decades about the interdependence and mutual interests of rich and poor without getting much of a hearing but in 1980 an unofficial group of public personalities under the chairmanship of Willy Brandt produced a report which attempted to restate the problems and persuade its readers that the north–south conflict between rich and poor was as dangerous for the whole world as the east–west conflict between the armed camps of the superpowers. Given the catastrophic properties of nuclear weapons, this was a difficult point to make. It was common knowledge that millions of poor people were dying because of the world's extreme economic imbalance (some 800 million were living below the harshest poverty line) but it was not evident that this constituted a danger as well as a disgrace. The Brandt Report set out to scare, to shame and to argue that the common interests of rich and poor were more potent than what divided them. It abandoned UNCTAD's essentially adversarial stance. It did not speak for the poor against the rich but for everybody, on the assumption that everybody was on the same slippery slope.

The report set out a comprehensive programme of reforms: let OPEC's plutocrats lend their surpluses to the poor; let these and other funds be used to end famine in the Third World and develop its agriculture and industry; help the Third World, rescued from stagnation, buy the manufacture of the industrial world; let the rich expand their business with the Third World (the source of much of its profits in colonial days) and so find the money to pay OPEC for its oil. At the core of these proposals was a massive transfer of resources to the poorer countries by the new rich and the old rich of the order of $50 billion a year by 1985 (at 1980 prices) – an increase in official aid of $8 billion a year, so that this aid would be equivalent to 0.7 per cent of the GNP of the contributing countries by 1985 and 1 per cent by the end of the century. There were two major obstacles to the acceptance of this statistically modest recipe. In so far as it maintained that it would pay the rich to help the poor it seemed to affront common sense. Secondly, it presupposed something like world government, of which there was not the faintest sign, for it was virtually inconceivable that a programme of this nature could be initiated and pursued by a conference of representatives of sovereign states lacking the executive authority to take decisions, to decree action or to tax. The Brandt Report required a politically fragmented world to tackle universal economic problems, for which it did not have the requisite institutions. It was an exercise in persuasion, unbacked by authority or power.

The problem nevertheless persisted much in the terms of the analysis made in the Brandt Report and every improvement in the world's economy enticed the poor into more hopeless positions. Thus a short boom in the rich world in the early 1970s stimulated, as had the Korean War, demand for primary products, but when the demand petered out with the boom the producers of these products found that they had been seduced into putting more eggs into leaky baskets. The oil price rises of the 1970s, which aggravated the collapse of the boom, forced the poor to borrow, not for invest-ment, but simply to keep afloat. The rich lent money openhandedly as banks, flush with money from oil producers and encouraged to lend and so foster the private cap-italist sector, searched for borrowers – to whom they might lend at rates higher than they were paying to their own depositors. So long as this pattern persisted rich banks and other financial institutions got richer still on paper but by the 1980s the debts of the poor to the rich had become so obviously unpayable that one or two statesmen said so openly: President Nyerere in so many words and President Garcia of Peru by uni-laterally limiting repayment of Peruvian debt to a fixed percentage of national income. The rescheduling of debts became a pretence, obscuring the fact that these were bad debts of such magnitude that the risk of insolvency was threatening creditors as well as debtors.

Insolvency – particularly the insolvency of states halfway between poverty and riches, heavily indebted and gambling on being able to finance their debts out of oil revenues at the mercy of oil prices – enforced new measures. In 1982 Mexico defaulted on its interest payments. Such a default threatened disaster for many major banks. The IMF took the lead in co-ordinating a relief operation with funds contributed by the threatened banks, and it went on to deal with dozens of other indebted states, funnelling fresh funds to them from commercial banks in return for the adoption of rigorous economic reforms. The IMF thereby tided over a crisis. Besides lending sums of its own it extracted five or six times as much money from banks. But the debtors, who discovered that even states forced to beg cannot choose, were obliged to impose domestic economic programmes which, by raising prices and restricting social ser-vices, bore heavily on their poorer citizens and purchased respite rather than lasting relief. During the 1980s African debt (excluding South Africa and the northern fringe) increased by more than $7 billion a year and passed $200 billion; in a number of years payments to the IMF exceeded receipts. A plan to convert debt into long-term IOUs found favour with creditors who despaired of ever getting their money back and pre-ferred to postpone payment rather than write the debts out of their balance sheets. Latin American debt was twice as large as African debt, with Brazil and Mexico each owing (in round figures) $100 billion and Argentina $70 billion. The Third World as a whole, in spite of receiving $50 billion (net) a year from the World Bank, was piling up $30 billion of new debt every year: the total exceeded $1,300 billion. Economies were growing by 1 per cent and populations by 2 per cent.

In 1985 the Secretary of the US Treasury, James Baker, proposed that creditor banks should advance a further $20 billion and that international institutions should make similar new loans – that is to say, lend money to enable debtors to meet the interest on old loans. This idea was elaborated by his successor, Nicholas Brady, who devised a scheme whereby creditor banks might choose between three ways of relieving their debtors: by exchanging existing bonds for new ones at 65 per cent of their face value, redeemable after 30 years and paying the original rate of interest; exchanging existing bonds for new 30-year bonds with the face value unchanged but interest reduced and fixed at 6.25 per cent throughout the 30 years; and fresh loans payable in annual instalments over three years. A prototype agreement under the Brady plan was signed with Mexico in 1990. This and similar measures in Latin America were devised principally to rescue banks in rich countries with debts in poor countries but the problem of international indebtedness was broader both geographically and in the range of creditors who included, besides banks, governments and international institutions. The measures of the 1980s did more to rescue creditors than debtors and many of the poorest countries in the world continued to remit to the rich in interest more than they received in loans. In 1996 a new category of Highly Indebted Poor Countries, whose debts were acknowledged to be unrecoverable, was recognized but the conditions defining them were too rigorous to afford radical relief and they remained not only incapable of repaying debt but also of improving their economic infrastructure, their education or other social services. At the end of the century the United States and Canada set an example of cancelling the government to government debts of the most impoverished states and in 1999 Britain declared its intention to cancel (by stages) the entirety of the debt of all 41 of the world's most highly indebted countries in return for guarantees that the money saved would be used only for the relief of poverty and associated social services.

It is commonly said that the League of Nations was a failure and many would say the same of the UN. The League failed to prevent Japan's attacks on Manchuria and China and Italy's conquest of Ethiopia, and the UN failed to prevent wars in Vietnam, the Falklands and Iraq and countless atrocities in various parts of the world. But the charges are too glib. First, neither organization may act or refrain from acting in such matters except as determined by its members. The members, if anybody, are the culprits. Secondly, the League, and – much more so – the UN have, often routinely, done valuable things. But the tally of pluses and minuses is not to be judged by a count of things done or left undone. The UN has changed the world by its very existence. In a world comprising nearly 200 independent sovereign states, most of them with modest or negligible military or economic power, the UN brings into world politics countless people who were politically invisible a century ago. Through their representatives' daily presence at UN HQ in New York and their attendance at the annual jamboree there of the General Assembly they discover how the world works and how in greater or lesser degree it may be made to work for their advantage. This may lead to some horse-trading of votes and other unlovely practices but such wheeling and dealing is a commonplace of life internationally, nationally and in the world of business and is an acceptable price to pay for what amounts to a democratization of world politics – not democracy in terms of counting individual heads but democracy at the level of corporate associations and a reminder that at any level democracy is, in a famous phrase, the least bad form of government.

This aspect of the UN has been developed by something almost certainly unforeseen by its founders: the appearance and proliferation of NGOs (non-governmental organizations), which cluster round the UN, have rights of audience there, discover and publicize information which would otherwise remain arcane, and so add hitherto unconsidered voices to public debate. Some of these organizations have a venerable history (the Anti-Slavery Society, for example) but most are new and do as much as any other component in world affairs to affect not only the content of such affairs but also how they are handled. They are by now far too numerous, and often too sensible, to be ignored. The UN is their carapace. From it they bring into focus matters hitherto unknown or blurred, insist that these things matter and so make a difference.

Notes

A. Canada

Canada, the world's second or third largest country, has played a benign and, mainly through its membership of international bodies such as NATO and the G7, prominent part in international affairs. It fought in two world wars not for itself but for others. It was unusually secluded in geographical and political terms with, to all intents and purposes, only one neighbour and no serious external disputes. It had considerable resources and a relatively small population. It had been, after Britain, the senior member of the old British Commonwealth and became in the postwar multiracial Commonwealth the most attentive of the older (white) members to the needs and susceptibilities of the newer. To Canada's historical, political and sentimental attachment to Britain was juxtaposed its economic, strategic and geographical attachment to the United States. The shift in importance from the former to the latter was accelerated by the Second World War and the Cold War and recognized by the Ogdensburg Declaration of joint Canadian–United States responsibility for the security of North America, by the wider commitments entailed by membership of NATO, by participation in the Early Warning System for nullifying surprise Soviet missile attacks on North America and by the creation in 1958 of North American Defence Command (NORAD). By sending troops to the Korean War, Canada associated itself with the view that the paramount issue in world affairs was the fight against the Soviet Union and international communism. Yet it did so with reservations. Many Canadians resisted the simplistic demonology of the Cold War. Some Canadian leaders toyed with non-alignment and queried the usefulness of Canadian troops in Europe: at one point the government unilaterally halved their number (after observing the total withdrawal of French forces from NATO commands). The conduct of the war in Vietnam by the United States was widely condemned and Canadians were quick to feel hurt when the

United States overlooked – as, for example, in the Cuban missile crisis – the need to tell its continental allies what was going on.

Canada was a prominent supporter of the abortive provisions in the UN Charter for an international force and a military staffs committee and Canada's was the main voice in insisting that NATO be committed by article 2 of the North Atlantic Treaty to economic as well as military purposes. More effectively, Canada worked to mollify the asperities created by the British assault on Egypt in 1956 and the tensions caused by apartheid in South Africa (when these proved irresolvable Canada aligned itself with those members who judged that the Commonwealth would be better off without South Africa).

If, as was supposed, President William H. Taft had coined in 1911 the expression 'special relationship' to describe US–Canadian relations he was not far wrong, particularly in economic terms. Economic links grew throughout the century as the Canadian economy expanded in old ways and new: in grain, lumbering and established mineral (chiefly nickel) undertakings, and, additionally, in electronic and chemical industry, petroleum research and extraction, and the exploitation of radium deposits which enhanced a nuclear programme initiated during the war. These activities were on such a scale that Canadian capital did not suffice for them and was supplemented by money from the United States to the point where control of half Canada's manufacturing, mining and carbon fuel industries passed into US hands. For the United States Canada was a neighbour of vast space and unmeasured, untapped resources, which might replace United States resources in food and raw materials that were threatening to become inadequate through natural exhaustion and population increase. The United States might the more easily concentrate its economic efforts in the manufacturing sector if it were assured of supplies of Canadian primary products. For Canadians, on the other hand, the flow of US capital was unwelcome as well as welcome. Economically, it was not only welcome but essential. Yet it was also a source of resentment and apprehension for those Canadians who complained of a loss of control over their own assets and even scented a loss of national identity. This imbalance began to be reduced in the 1970s and 1980s when Canada became the fourth largest investor in the United States – behind Japan, Britain and the Netherlands. Each of the two countries was the other's biggest trading partner and the two together constituted the world's biggest bilateral trading partnership. A free-trade agreement which came into force at the beginning of 1989 provided for the elimination of all tariffs and other obstacles to trade over the next ten years. Nevertheless, this commingling did not remove all the acerbities. Nixon's surprise decoupling of the US dollar from its fixed gold price in 1971, accompanied by a 10 per cent surcharge on US import duties, hurt Canadian businesses and angered Canadian politicians. This shock was quickly followed by the sharp rises in the price of imported oil caused by a war in the Middle East in which Canada had no part but the United States, by promising to rearm Israel after its initial setbacks, had. Canada's eastern provinces, being importers of oil, were badly hit and although the oil-bearing western provinces benefited from higher prices, they were embroiled in disputes over the transport of Alaskan oil to the United States by sea or through pipelines through Canada. In this segment of economic affairs nationalist considerations tended on both sides to prevail over the prospective value and virtue of internationalism.

Canadian politics of the first postwar decades were dominated by two Liberal leaders: Lester Pearson as minister of external affairs and then prime minister for 20 years (1948–68) and Pierre Trudeau as prime minister with one short break for 16 (1968–84). Both were pronounced champions of an international as distinct from an American regional role for Canada. Both were notable and more effective for what they said than for what they achieved: Canada's resources were in a worldwide context modest but these leaders made Canada's voice significant. Pearson, who spent a lifetime in the public service, conformed the more easily with the Cold War consensus and with Washington's priorities in the era of Truman, Eisenhower, Kennedy and Johnson. Trudeau, almost a newcomer to high office when he first became prime minister, was faced with lesser presidents and was by nature more cynical or disdainful. He had travelled widely in four continents. In 1970, soon after succeeding Pearson, he recognized the communist government of China and led the way for other states to do so too. Trudeau's hold on power was less secure than Pearson's. He nearly lost the election of 1972, recovered his majority in 1974, lost office in 1979, and regained it in 1980 but as the choice of the eastern provinces only – the Liberals won few seats in the west. He was also uncomfortably placed in Canada's great domestic drama, the status of Quebec, for he was a determined federalist as well as himself a Québecois.

The rapid increase in Canadian prosperity posed a special problem in Quebec, the seat of Canada's French heritage and culture. Four-fifths of the inhabitants of the province were French-speakers, most of them rural conservatives. In spite of their numbers they owned, however, only one-fifth of its productive economy and their average income was substantially below that of English-speakers. From 1944 to 1959 the province was dominated by Maurice Duplessis (prime minister also in 1936–39), who presented himself as a traditional Québecois while associating also, and not always openly, with English-speaking Canadian and US capitalists who were contributing to Quebec's economic transformation. He was succeeded in office by the Liberal Jean Lesage, who espoused the modernization of Quebec with a more determined policy of securing the benefits for the French-speaking majority, but in 1966 the Liberals were unexpectedly defeated, losing working-class voters who had come to the conclusion that modernization was benefiting the middle classes only. A visit by de Gaulle in 1967 enthused separatists. It is unlikely that de Gaulle wanted to disrupt Canada. What he did want was to recruit Quebec to the international, mostly African, francophone community and by ending a public speech in Montreal with the old and emotive slogan 'Vive le Québec libre' he both dramatized Canada's rumbling domestic discords and forced his affronted hosts in Ottawa to issue a deprecating rejoinder. He went

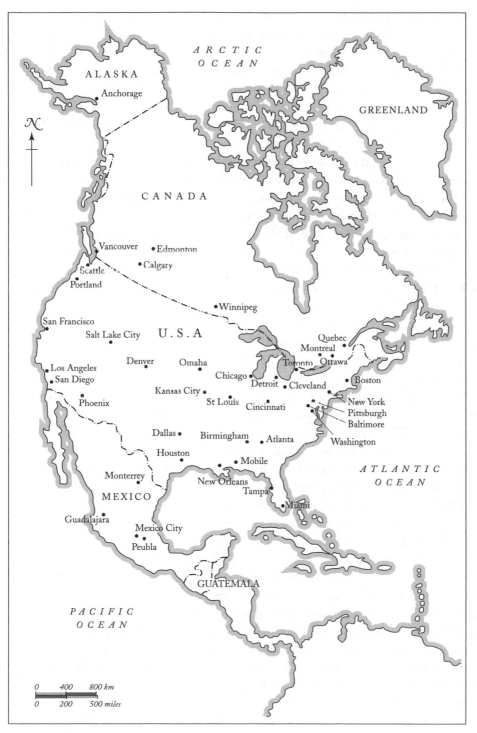

30.2 North America

home without visiting Ottawa. Much ill will was generated over the next few years over whether the province of Quebec or the government of Canada should be invited to francophone meetings in Africa.

In 1968 – the year when Trudeau became prime minister – a new party, the Parti Québecois (PQ), was formed to campaign for independence for Quebec. More extreme than the PQ, the Front de Libération de Québec (FLQ) advocated and practised violence in order to win the independence which the PQ aimed to win peacefully. The FLQ consisted of a tiny handful of men and women who, invoking Che Guevara and Mao Zedong, committed a number of bank robberies and other acts of violence without attracting widespread support or, until 1970, much attention. In elections in that year the PQ won a quarter of the votes cast but only seven seats out of 108: the winners were the Liberals under Robert Bourassa. The FLQ resorted to more serious violence, kidnapping the British Trade Commissioner James Cross and the province's minister of labour Pierre Laporte, whom they strangled. The central government applied the War Measures Act and outlawed the FLQ but gave the kidnappers a safe exit to Cuba in return for the release of Cross after two months' confinement. The security forces, whose ineffective intelligence had allowed the FLQ a surprisingly long lease of life, succeeded in extinguishing it by 1972. The separatists' cause became limited to the non-violent route which, however, got them nowhere.

The problem reverted to constitutional debate. A conference in 1971 between the federal government and Canada's ten provinces produced the Victoria Charter, a compromise which was rejected by Quebec, and in 1976 the PQ won elections in the province. Its leader, René Lévesque, became provincial prime minister, visited France and introduced a series of measures giving the French language a special status (the federation as a whole had been declared officially bilingual by statute in 1969). But the separatist cause was set back when a referendum in Quebec proposing negotiations for 'sovereign-association' was defeated in 1980.

Quebec's nationalism impinged on federal positions when Trudeau's Conservative successor Brian Mulroney tried to woo Liberal voters in Quebec in 1984 by supporting constitutional changes (the Meech Lake Amendment) designed to increase the influence of provincial governments in senior judicial and senatorial appointments, immigration and financial affairs. In provinces other than Quebec the amendment was not popular and it failed in 1990 to win the necessary endorsement of a majority of the provinces. This rebuff to the Québecois produced for the first time a poll showing a majority in the province in favour of sovereign independence. Mulroney's next attempt to solve the problem by giving Quebec a special status in the federation, although backed by all ten provincial prime ministers (the Charlottestown Accord), was rejected in plebiscites in five provinces as well as Quebec. These constitutional setbacks, combined with economic recession, higher taxes and unemployment and an air of inconsequence at the centre, destroyed Mulroney's standing to the point where he was compelled to resign.

Mulroney was succeeded in 1993 by Canada's first female prime minister Kim Campbell, who led her party to a defeat verging on extermination. Her party won two seats and the Liberals returned to power with Jean Chrétien as prime minister and the familiar problems of relations with the United States (in the guise of NAFTA – see Chapter 28); balancing the public accounts, particularly financing generous social services from a relatively narrow tax base; and, still, Quebec where, however, the PQ won in 1994 provincial elections with so small a margin of the popular vote that its promise to proceed to a referendum on independence appeared rash – the more so when the Inuit and other indigenous peoples began to suggest that the right of the province to secede from the federation implied a similar right for them to secede from the province. A referendum in 1995 gave the federalists victory by 1 per cent, an inconclusive result. Acrimony festered. In 1998 unilateral secession was declared by the Supreme Court to be unconstitutional and provincial elections in Quebec gave the PQ the most seats but only second place in the popular vote.

Canada's last constitutional link with Britain, derived from the British North America Act of 1867, was demolished in 1982, when at Canada's request the British parliament enacted an entrenched charter of rights and simultaneously extinguished its own remaining powers to legislate for Canada. This measure had been anachronistically delayed by disputes within Canada over the allocation between the centre and the provinces of the rights to be relinquished by Britain; by differing judicial decisions on whether the central government might petition the British parliament without the consent of all the provinces (which Trudeau failed to get at two constitutional conferences); and by Trudeau's determination to secure the enactment in Britain of what amounted to a Canadian Bill of Rights. In Quebec, Lévesque objected to the enactment of such rights by either the British or the Canadian parliament and they remained ineffective in Quebec except in so far as they were already or in future might be enacted by the provincial legislature.

In 1949 Newfoundland became part of Canada after a referendum in which a narrow majority chose confederation with Canada in preference to penurious self-government. More significantly, Canada was becoming a split country. In elections in 1997 the Liberals retained an overall parliamentary majority but their nearest rivals – the Bloc Québecois and the Reform Party – were strictly regional. The latter overtook the former in the federal parliament but failed to attract meaningful support outside British Columbia and Alberta. The Conservatives were the fifth of the five parties in parliament.

B. Very small states

At the end of the twentieth century the world had over 40 independent states with a population below 2 million and another 30 territories of similar dimensions which were geographically distinct but not fully independent. Virtually all the latter were islands or groups of islands. So were most of the former, which included nine states in the Caribbean and eight in Oceania. The states and self-governing territories differed widely in extent, population and wealth, but with few exceptions they were too weak to defend themselves against predators attracted by their strategic value or by some exploitable asset – the beauty that appeals to tour operators or the remoteness that appeals to crooks. They can be to all intents and purposes bought by foreign mafias in league with local politicians, since a little money suffices to buy the few votes needed to win elections. Against bigger states they have no defence, as the invasion of Grenada by the United States in 1983 showed. In the 1960s proposals were canvassed for the invention of a new status for very small territories about to be released from colonial empires into a nominal independence which they lacked the resources, human and material, to defend; but these discussions came to nothing, largely from fear of giving offence to nascent nations. Association with a great power, or regional associations, offered some protection and hope of betterment. A number of islands, most of them in the Pacific, made association agreements with the United States or France (as Overseas Territories); others became associates of the Commonwealth. The South Pacific Forum, created in 1971, embraced by 1990 11 independent states and non-independent but self-governing territories; established links with other international associations such as ASEAN and the EC and with the Specialized Agencies of the UN; and combined with larger states in the much older (1947) South Pacific Commission which included the United States, Australia, New Zealand, Britain and France. By a treaty of 1985 ten Pacific island states, with Australia, New Zealand and Papua New Guinea, proclaimed a South Pacific Nuclear-Free Zone; ancillary protocols were signed by the USSR and China, rejected by France and 'not accepted' by the United States and Britain. The treaty imposed a ban on the manufacture, testing and deployment of nuclear weapons in the zone; called on the five principal nuclear powers not to test or locate nuclear weapons in it; but refrained from attempting to prevent warships or aircraft from using international waters or airspace.

The principal island states which achieved independence in the South Pacific were: Western Samoa, independent in 1962 after German and then New Zealand rule; Tonga or the Friendly Islands, a nineteenth-century monarchy which became fully independent in 1970 (and did not sign the 1985 treaty); Fiji, independent in 1970 (see below); the Gilbert and Ellice Islands which were separated in 1975 and became independent in 1979 and 1978 as Kiribati and Tuvalu; Solomon Islands, independent in 1978; and the Anglo-French condominium of New Hebrides, independent in 1980 as Vanuatu after internal dissension and fighting. Vanuatu pushed the concepts of state and nation to the limits: it contained 150,000 people speaking 100 different languages in what was a geographical, but neither a political nor cultural entity. In New Caledonia, the world's third-largest supplier of nickel and a French Overseas Territory from 1958, conflict between indigenous kanaks and white immigrants who had become the majority was at least temporarily resolved by the Matignon agreement of 1988, which provided for direct French rule for one year, the division of the territory into three regions (two of them with a kanak majority), considerable economic aid from France and a referendum on independence in 1998. For accepting these arrangements the kanak leader Jean-Marie Tjibaou was assassinated by his more militant compatriots. In 1998 all parties agreed to postpone the referendum for another 15 years.

Fiji had a similar racial problem. Fiji – an extent of land the size of Wales divided into over 600 islands embracing 160,000 sq. km of water and a population of 750,000 – had made unsuccessful approaches in the nineteenth century to Germany and the United States for protection before finally yielding itself in 1874 to Britain. Under British rule Indians were encouraged to migrate to Fiji where they became the main-stay of the sugar industry and, by the time of independence in 1970, a majority of the population. Tensions between the races were supplemented by tensions between the western and eastern islands and between the generations. In elections in 1987 the ruling Fiji party, which rested upon chiefly paternalism, was defeated by a coalition under Sir Timothy Bavadra who assembled a cabinet with a bare Indian majority. With a considerable part of its small army away in the Middle East in UN service, Colonel Sitiveni Rabuka, a leader of the anti-Indian Tsakei movement for Fiji-for-the-Fijians, was able to stage a coup with a handful of men who invaded the parliament and seized the new prime minister. Fiji became a republic and left the Commonwealth. Bavadra appealed unsuccessfully to the British government and crown but Rabuka had covert support from the CIA, which looked askance at Bavadra as a neutralist: he died in 1989. Rabuka progressively lost ground, particularly in the eastern islands, and Indian emigration exposed the dangers of scaring Indians away from the sugar industry which was Fiji's principal economic resource. Nevertheless, elections in 1994 confirmed him in power and three years later he sought readmission to the Commonwealth. Fiji was a member of the South Pacific Forum.

The Bismarck archipelago, annexed by Germany in 1874 and administered by Australia first under mandate from the League of Nations and, after 1947, as part of the UN Trust Territory of New Guinea, became in 1975 part of the new state of Papua New Guinea.

Further north, in equatorial waters, the Caroline, Marshall and Mariana groups of islands, acquired by Germany in the nineteenth century, occupied by Japan in the First World War and retained under mandate after that war, were occupied by the United States in the Second World War and then brigaded together as the UN Trust Territory of the Pacific Islands from 1947 to 1986. The Marshalls, including Bikini and Enewetok atolls which were used for nuclear tests until 1958, became the Republic of the Marshall Islands with a treaty or 'compact' of Free Association with the United States (1982). The Carolines became the Federated States of Micronesia with a similar treaty. The purpose of these 'compacts' was to allow the United States to acquire special rights after the end of the period of trusteeship. This device caused trouble in the westernmost district of Micronesia – the Pelau archipelago. In 1979 the Pelauans voted overwhelmingly

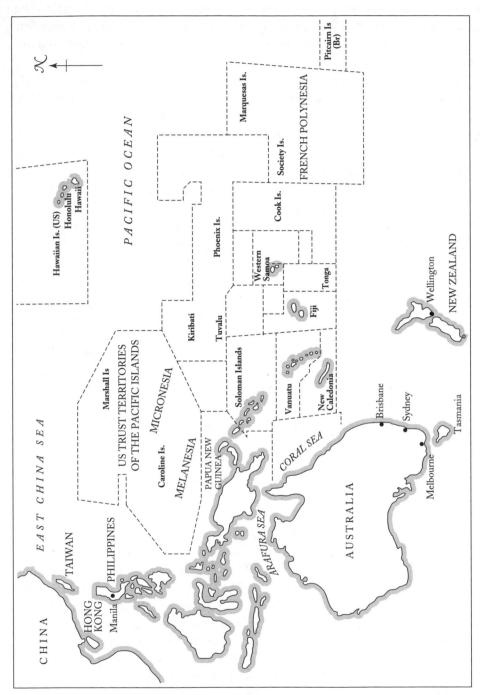

30.3 The South Pacific

THE LAW OF THE SEA

to ban nuclear weapons from their islands. When attempts to reverse this decision (which included attempts to change the constitution) failed, the United States propounded a 'compact' whereby a third of the Pelau archipelago would become available to the United States for military exercises and experiments. The compact was repeatedly rejected by the Pelauans in campaigns which included bribery and murders. Finally, the Marianas – originally and opprobriously called by Magellan the Ladrones – comprised Guam and the Northern Marianas. Guam was taken by the United States from Spain in 1898 and has remained part of the United States. The Northern Marianas became in 1986 a commonwealth within the United States.

C. The Poles

The Antarctic continent is rich in fish and minerals, including oil. Modern technology has given it possible military significance and has drawn attention to the damage which may be done there to the global environment. Seven states have overlapping territorial claims. Encouraged by co-operation during the International Geophysical Year of 1957–58, 12 states signed in 1959 an Antarctic Treaty whose aims were peace and co-operation and freedom for scientific research. The Treaty created a standing organization which expanded to 39 full or associate members. The parties bound themselves not to seek expansion of their sovereign rights in the region. A pioneering, if modest, Convention on Marine Living Resources was concluded in 1980 and a Convention on the Regulation of Mining Activities (for 50 years) was drafted in 1988, but the latter was controversial. Australia and France led opposition to it from the conservationist point of view against the Americans, British and others who wanted only a moratorium (a voluntary moratorium had been in force since 1972), to be followed by internationally approved and supervised mining activities. The Convention came into force in 1998 upon ratification by its 26 signatories. In 2007 Great Britain laid claim to a considerable extension of its share of Antarctica, prompted by serious doubts about the supply of oil and gas and by the hope that evolving technology would find a way to extract these and other minerals from under the ice and the exceptionally deep seas.

The Arctic, frozen ocean rather than *terra firma*, was transformed by climate change. The North West Passage, sought in vain for centuries, became a navigable waterway for at least part of the year and its legal status therefore subject to the law of the sea. Canada was quick to stake a claim as nature presented opportunities for traffic and revenues not seen since human engineers had done likewise at Suez and Panama.

D. The law of the sea

The sea entered into international politics, economics and strategies in the twentieth century by reason of technical invention. Besides the invention of military weapons with ranges beyond the traditional sovereign limit of three miles, the century saw the arrival of the submarine, the capacity to extract oil and other minerals from the seabed

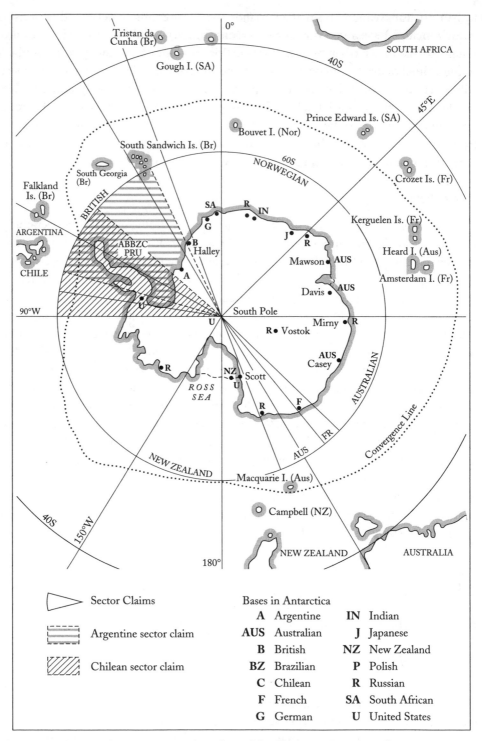

30.4 Antarctica (Source: *An Atlas of World Affairs*, Andrew Boyd)

and overfishing which was destroying the fish. Attempts to create an international authority with generally accepted rules were obstructed by many things, including a division between states with and states without the technology and the money to exploit the riches and opportunities of the seas. The former wanted the freedom to do what they could do, while the rest wanted wider controls and a share in the profits. Years of negotiations produced in 1982 a Convention which by 1994 had been signed by the number of states (60) required to bring it into force. Ratification was, however, refused by the all-important United States, where the Senate voted against it in 1999. The principal items in the Convention were: the extension of sovereignty to 12 miles subject only to a right of innocent passage for shipping; further sovereign rights up to 200 miles for fishing and other economic activities subject to freedom of passage for shipping and aircraft in and over this zone; the recognition of a continental shelf extending for at least 200 miles from the shore and subject to sovereign rights of exploration and exploitation; a right for the international community to share in revenues derived from the continental shelf beyond 200 miles; the creation of an International Seabed Authority and an International Tribunal for the Law of the Sea.

Early in the next century a new Convention was under discussion to provide for a yet wider extension (perhaps to 250 miles) of the continental shelf, to be ready for enactment in 2009.

Related reading: part eight

Babbitt, Philip: *The Shield of Achilles – War, Peace and the Course of History* (2002)
Best, Geoffrey: *War and Law since 1945* (1994)
Milward, A. S.: *War, Economics and Society 1939–1943* (1977)
Pearton, Maurice: *The Knowledgeable State – Diplomacy, War and Technology since 1830* (1982)
Price, Don K.: *The Scientific Estate* (1963)
Reynolds, David: *Summits – Six Meetings that Shaped the Twentieth Century* (2008)
Taylor, Telford: *Nuremberg and Vietnam – An American Tragedy* (1970)
Wight, Martin: *Power Politics*, 2nd edition, revised Brian Porter (1986)

The sovereign state

The international political system is largely the European states system writ large. In that system all states have sovereignty: that is to say, all states have in regard to one another the right to do what they want to do subject only (a) to engagements entered into by treaty or otherwise to which they are themselves party and (b) international law. Few states have the power to exercise their sovereignty against the wishes of more powerful states. Nevertheless the state is the basic unit in the world's political system. It is essentially a European construct which, perhaps surprisingly, has been endorsed by the rest of the world.

For the ancient Greeks the world was divided into city states. Greeks and Romans both knew of the existence of worlds beyond theirs and even explored them but neither had nor needed a political theory to accommodate a global world.

When the Roman world fell into two parts both the eastern and the western halves remained in theory a political entity. Each, however, had to face a new political question in the relation in its world between the secular and the spiritual (Christian) authority. The Byzantine empire solved this problem by giving the emperor a spiritual status which placed him above the Patriarch of Constantinople. The western empire, however, adopted a different solution: a duopoly in which emperor and pope were to be equal partners – the doctrine of the Two Swords. This concept did service for about 1,000 years (say, AD 330–1250) The western European world was already sub-divided in that it consisted of the western half of the old Roman empire together with lands east of the Rhine which had never or merely passingly been part of it. When in the fourth century AD Rome (in the person of the emperor Constantine) joined forces with Christendom (largely through the impact of Saint Augustine) this union contained seeds of dissolution. The emperor who eventually succeeded his Roman predecessors lived north of the Alps, the pope south of them. The emperor came to be called the Holy Roman Emperor but his title in German did not include the word Roman and did include the term German Nation: *Heilges Reich der deutschen Nation.* What developed between the coronation of Charlemagne by one pope (AD 800) and the destruction of the Hohenstauffen dynasty by another (AD 1250) proved to be an unserviceable fiction whose failure destroyed the notion that Christendom could constitute a political entity. (Today some Muslims claim that Islam should be what some Christians failed to make of Christendom.) From this disenchantment emerged the secular state, pioneered by France and England whose growing identity as states was fostered by their distance from the Italo-German core of the Two Swords experiment and by their own mutual hostility (notably in the Hundred Years War) The doctrine of state sovereignty developed to support and justify the claim of the secular state to be the prime component in a multi-states system and to give it a legal framework.

This phase became the seedbed for much thinking and writing (but little practical action) from lawyers and statesmen such as Hugo Grotius and the Duc de Sully, through philosophers such as Immanuel Kant, to the progenitors of the League of Nations and the UN whose main endeavours have been and still are to find a way by which a state and its rights may co-exist with international bodies and therefore to formulate acceptable restrictions on state rights – particularly in the making of war and their conduct in war and, more recently, the definition and enforcement of human rights and the regulation of competitive commercial and financial interests. These endeavours, extending beyond the UN itself to its Special Agencies and regional counterparts, amount to a search for a new universalism such as the European Middle Ages failed to contrive but without the autocratic implications of the words emperor and pope. The main impulses have come from the defects and disasters of the states system and from the new and inescapable fact that the globe has become a singularity.

This is a balancing act. But as Macchiavelli insisted at the end of the Middle Ages balance is the essence of politics. At the end of the Second World War the German historian Ludwig Dehio wrote of the attempts by one European state after another to dominate Europe.* All these attempts were defeated and Hitler's was almost certainly the last. But the issue has not gone away. It has been moved to a wider stage with states only reluctantly ceding authority to international, particularly global, bodies.

The modern sovereign state is in one important respect weaker than its ancestors or at any rate markedly different. The sovereign was originally a visible and tangible reality – a monarch. When Louis XIV said "L'etat, c'est moi" he was stating a truism. But the modern state is a concept, sometimes little more than a fiction; you cannot put a state on a plinth. Its defining features – territorial, historical, national – are mutable and disputable even when seemingly fundamental. So statecraft has become dauntingly intricate. The state has moreover lost its moral moorings. Plato believed that statesmen had a moral function and the medieval Christian churches held similar beliefs which however they too often betrayed. Neither established morality as a dominant ingredient of statecraft leaving it to the atheist Thomas Hobbes to strive after a new rationale to fit the modern world. Morality continues to enter into debates over international affairs but is more evident in rhetorical indignation than practical action, not an imperative but at least an itch.

---

* *Gleichgewicht oder Hegemonie.* English translation: *The Precarious Balance, The Politics of Power in Europe 1494–1945.*

In this context this book may conclude with a few tentative reflections upon the not-too-distant future as seen from the present and recent past. World politics is an historical sequence, part of it still undisclosed, its future course partially susceptible to human intervention. Some speculation, grounded in the story so far, is therefore a proper coda.

Seven leading questions

One. The evolution of permanent associations of states in different parts of the world.

Two. The rule of law in a globalizing world of sovereign territorial states.

Three. The clash between domestic sovereignty and the right/obligation to intervene in defence of human rights anywhere.

Four. Democracy vs. stability.

Five. How to stop the growing gap between rich and poor which was produced in Europe by the Industrial Revolution from spreading to the rest of the world.

Six. If the globalizing world subordinates the state to economic forces/entities what will be the role of the state:

(a) none – Hayek, Friedman, free marketers;

(b) passive beneficiary of vigorous but high-risk capitalism leading to disasters – Schumpeter;

(c) socially corrective marginal player, public–private partnership – Keynes.

Seven. Except for being 200 years out in his timing, was Malthus right in arguing that the population of the earth was outgrowing its vital resources?

Index